MONTGOMERY'S
AUDITING

TENTH EDITION

Revised College Version

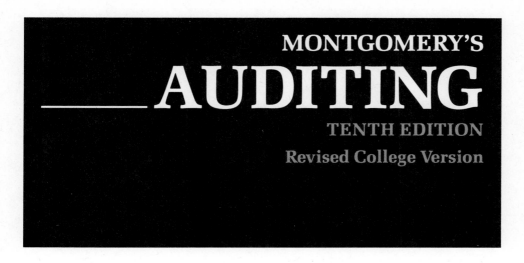

MONTGOMERY'S
AUDITING
TENTH EDITION
Revised College Version

Philip L. Defliese, C.P.A.

Professor, Graduate School of Business, Columbia University
Retired Chairman, Coopers & Lybrand
Past Chairman, American Institute of Certified Public Accountants
Member, Governmental Accounting Standards Board

Henry R. Jaenicke, Ph.D., C.P.A.

C. D. Clarkson Professor of Accounting, College of Business
and Administration, Drexel University

Jerry D. Sullivan, C.P.A.

Director of Audit Policy, Coopers & Lybrand
Chairman, Auditing Standards Board of the American Institute of
Certified Public Accountants

Richard A. Gnospelius, C.P.A.

Managing Partner, Central Region, Coopers & Lybrand
Former National Director of Auditing, Coopers & Lybrand

John Wiley & Sons

New York   Chichester   Brisbane   Toronto   Singapore

Library of Congress Cataloging-in-Publication Data

Montgomery, Robert Hiester, 1872–1953.
  Montgomery's Auditing.

  Bibliography: p.
  Includes index.
  1. Auditing.   I. Defliese, Philip L.   II. Title.
III. Title: Auditing.

HF5667.M7   1987   657′.45   86-28938
ISBN 0-471-85423-9

Printed in the United States of America

10 9 8 7 6 5 4 3 2 1

Historical Perspective

Robert H. Montgomery (1872–1953) together with William M. Lybrand (1867–1960), Adam Ross (1869–1929), and T. Edward Ross (1867–1963) founded the firm of Lybrand, Ross Bros. & Montgomery (now Coopers & Lybrand) in 1898, two years after the first CPA law was passed. The four had for some time previously practiced public accounting in Philadelphia.

Montgomery was a prolific writer and leader of his profession. He wrote many books, including a series on federal income taxes, and he was instrumental in the organization and served as president of what is now the American Institute of Certified Public Accountants. Earlier, he also taught at Columbia University, New York University, and the University of Pennsylvania.[1] He saw the need for a practical book on auditing and in 1905 and 1909 published American editions of Dicksee's *Auditing*, a British work. Noting the radical departure of American practice from Dicksee's work, however, he wrote the first American book on the subject, *Auditing: Theory and Practice*, in 1912. Eight subsequent editions followed from 1916 through 1975. For the seventh edition, coauthors Alvin R. Jennings and Norman J. Lenhart joined him and the book was renamed *Montgomery's Auditing*. The eighth edition, published after his death, was coauthored by Norman J. Lenhart and Philip L. Defliese. The ninth edition, published in 1975, was coauthored by Philip L. Defliese, Kenneth P. Johnson, and Roderick K. Macleod. Comparisons of the various editions reveal the development of accounting in the United States.

In 1956, Cooper Bros. & Co. in the United Kingdom and other countries (founded in 1854) and MacDonald Currie & Co. in Canada (founded in 1910) joined Lybrand, Ross Bros. & Montgomery to form the multinational firm of Coopers & Lybrand in recognition of the growing needs of international practice. Dropping the Montgomery name from a firm that had so long celebrated his contributions was not easy. The continued association of the Montgomery name, however, with his major contribution to the literature of the profession is a proper tribute to his memory.

---

[1]For a full account of Montgomery's contributions, see his autobiography, *Fifty Years of Accountancy* (New York: The Ronald Press Co., 1939).

v

Preface

In the concluding paragraphs of the preface to the ninth edition, the authors stated—after recounting the turmoil in which the accounting profession then found itself—"Of the future we can be sure of only one thing—change!" Yet, as we examine more closely the developments of the intervening years, it seems that the profession more aptly reflects that overdone cliché: "The more things change, the more they stay the same."

Broad, fundamental auditing standards and the concepts underlying them have not changed: We still seek the best way to assure readers of financial statements that the statements present a "true and fair" view (to borrow the expression of our British counterparts) of a company's financial position and results of operations, recognizing that because of limitations inherent in the audit process, the assurance can never be insurance. Terminology may change as the result of standard-setters reaching agreement on uniform terms for particular concepts, and technology may change as computers inject themselves into both recording and auditing, but the objectives remain the same.

Some quotes from Montgomery's second edition (1916) are still relevant:

Ordinarily, what is known as a "test and scrutiny" audit is sufficient, but in every case there must be a careful survey . . . in order that the auditor may satisfy himself that the assets and the income are accounted for, and that the liabilities and expenses are properly supported. The auditor need not verify every item, but he must not omit any part of an audit which the custom of the profession decrees should be covered. (p. 7)

Opportunities for wrong-doing [defalcations] vary, as a rule, with the size of the undertaking. In a small business the details are apt to be supervised by one or all of the proprietors, while in a large business much of the detail is necessarily left to subordinates. The auditor must be governed by the circumstances surrounding each engagement and then determine the amount of detail to be covered. (p. 13)

The auditor must have all these purposes [management fraud] constantly in mind when determining his course of action. If he does not consider all the elements involved before commencing a given engagement, he may find at the end of a detailed audit that a balance sheet audit would have enabled him to secure satisfactory results in much less time. (p. 14)

Errors of principle. This is the most important class of errors and is one which the auditor must never overlook. . . . Errors of principle are most easily detected by making an intelligent analysis of the accounts in connection with the preparation of the [statements]. (p. 16)

Shades of sampling, audit risk, audit strategy, and analytical review—these are not newly discovered concepts. However, with standard terminology, we can now, at last, understand each other when we discuss the conceptual underpinnings of our procedures.

One change that has taken place—whether for better or worse is uncertain—is the increased competition within the profession. With the removal from our ethical codes of restrictions on advertising, bidding, and direct solicitation—at the insistence of the antitrust government lawyers—has come what the Commission on Auditors' Responsibilities referred to as excessive and potentially destructive competition. That competition has resulted in a combination of lower fees and greater auditor attention to the economical use of auditing resources. The emphasis is now on the "efficient" audit, and this book reflects that emphasis. Fortunately, computerization and all of its ramifications have come at an opportune time, helping to increase audit efficiency.

The report of the Commission on Auditors' Responsibilities in 1978 warned of the effect of competitive pressures on audit quality. Aided by peer review, both internal and external, accounting firms have recognized the need to strengthen their procedures to prevent audit failures. The AICPA Division for CPA Firms, with its requirements designed to protect the public from substandard audits, has done much to avoid the problems such pressures can bring.

Nevertheless, audit failures continue to occur, and to demonstrate that there is no such thing as a foolproof audit. Nor will there ever be a foolproof audit. For the most part, an analysis of recent audit failures does not indicate a weakness in standards or procedures—the sampling process is rarely at fault—suggesting that we may be overemphasizing the technical side of auditing. Instead, the failures are usually the result of clever management deceits or of poor audit judgments involving clients' liberal applications or misuse, deliberate or otherwise, of accounting principles. For this there is only one cure—eternal vigilance and objective, independent auditing—as has always been the case. Thus, the cliché cited earlier about things staying the same becomes all the more appropriate.

We are optimistic about the future of the profession. The profession as a whole has always considered its public responsibility as paramount. We are tempted to quote from Montgomery's third edition in 1921:

> It is a cause for congratulation that accounting is living up to the best traditions of a learned profession and is discarding obsolete theories and substituting new ones as rapidly as conditions warrant. . . . It is imperative that financial statements should reflect full and true financial conditions.

It is to that end and to enhancing the ability of auditors to meet it that we dedicate the tenth edition of *Montgomery's Auditing*.

Preface
to the College Version

Except for two short-lived college versions published in 1915 and 1923, when Montgomery was teaching at Columbia University, and a privately distributed prototype of a student supplement to the eighth edition, a college text based on the professional reference book known as *Montgomery's Auditing* has not been available. Early editions of the book frequently were used as college texts but were eventually replaced by new texts better suited to classroom use.

This, then, is an adaptation of the tenth edition tailored to the needs of college courses in auditing. It may also be used in professional development courses conducted by accounting firms and others for training auditors. Like its predecessor editions, it emphasizes the development of judgment by the auditor and provides aids for enhancing decision-making skills. The book covers and explains all current authoritative pronouncements relevant to the audit process. It expounds an approach to auditing based on what the authors believe is the best of practice, but it also incorporates alternative viewpoints. While the authors are or have been associated with Coopers & Lybrand, the text is not limited to that firm's policies and practices. The intent was to cover all viewpoints objectively.

Many readers will use this book in studying for the CPA examination and as a reference work after they embark on their professional careers. Accordingly, the authoritative auditing literature is heavily referenced and cited, and the problem material presented at the end of each chapter includes an ample selection of CPA examination questions.

The problem material is divided into four categories, as follows:

• *Review Questions* (numbered 1 through 29): These are designed to assist students in reviewing and testing their comprehension of the chapter. They serve as a form of refresher to determine whether the student has grasped the salient points made.

• *Discussion Questions* (numbered 30 through 39): These are designed to provide topics for class discussion. They assist in applying the principles or practices described in the text, and thus often introduce business practices or situations not explicitly covered in the chapter.

• *AICPA Multiple Choice Questions* (numbered 40 through 59): These are taken from the Auditing part of Uniform CPA Examinations and provide a test of the ability to discriminate, from several choices, among practical applications of the concepts covered in the chapter.

• *Problems and Cases* (numbered starting with 60): These are longer problems involving, in many instances, the preparation of audit working papers and analytical treatment of case material. They vary in length and complexity and may be assigned as time permits depending on the length and level of the course. A case study (Quinn Hardware) is begun in Chapter 6 and continued in Chapters 8, 12, and 18, providing students with a comprehensive, integrated view of the audit process. The case is lengthy, as its purpose is to provide a realistic setting in which audit decisions are made. If the case is assigned, an additional audit case or "practice set" might prove redundant. (The Quinn Hardware case in Chapter 8 requires students to complete a systems flowchart and an internal control questionnaire for part of a buying cycle. The instructor may assign that case as part of the coverage of Chapter 8 or, alternatively, as part of the coverage of Chapter 13, "Auditing the Buying Cycle.") The Acme case (8–61) in Chapter 8 includes illustrations of certain forms related to the buying cycle—purchase order, receiving report, invoice, voucher, and perpetual inventory record—that will be helpful to students who would otherwise be unfamiliar with such forms.

The numbering system for the problem material was devised to enable students and instructors to identify the type of problem by its number. For example, any problem with a number between 40 and 59 is an AICPA multiple choice question. Of course, not all numbers are used in each chapter.

In addition to the multiple choice questions, questions from Uniform CPA Examinations have been used as discussion questions and problems, and are labeled "AICPA adapted." That designation indicates that the authors have not felt constrained in taking considerable liberties with the questions, including but not limited to updating them to reflect revised terminology (except as explained in Chapter 10), dividing questions among two or more chapters, and deleting parts of questions.

Organization of the Text

This book has been organized into four parts, with the chapters for the most part arranged to follow the sequence in a typical audit. The four parts are:

Part 1: The Audit Environment. The four chapters in Part 1 provide an overview of auditing (Chapter 1), the professional structure and organization into which auditing has evolved (Chapter 2), and the standards and responsibilities to which auditors are held (Chapters 3 and 4). These provide an understanding of the environment in which the auditor operates.

Part 2: Theory and Concepts. These seven chapters provide the conceptual basis for an understanding of the way in which audits are planned and conducted. Chapter 5 presents an overview of the audit process, including the types of evidence and tests that constitute that process. Chapter 6 considers how audit risk, materiality, and other factors enter into engagement strategy. Internal controls are described in depth in Chapter 7; assessing inherent and control risks and evaluating controls, including compliance testing, are covered in Chapter 8. Chapter 9 discusses substantive testing, including analytical review procedures. Audit sampling, both statistical and nonstatistical, is covered in Chapter 10. Finally, auditing in an EDP environment is the topic of Chapter 11. Throughout Part 2, the topics are covered at the conceptual level rather than in the context of specific systems cycles or account balances, although numerous realistic illustrations of the application of those concepts are provided.

Part 3: Auditing Specific Cycles and Accounts. These chapters apply the concepts from Part 2 to the audit of specific transaction cycles and account balances that form the body of the financial statements examined in an audit. The five chapters in Part 3 cover all the areas required to be examined by the auditor. Three segments of the audit are presented using the cycle or systems approach, and six, covered in two chapters, using the account balance or balance sheet approach.

The text stresses the need for audit efficiency as well as audit effectiveness, and the reader is constantly reminded of the need to inject efficiency considerations into strategy decisions for each particular audit. Efficiency considerations and the resultant strategy will determine whether, in auditing a particular cycle or group of accounts for a particular client, the auditor is in a "compliance test mode," in which partial reliance will be placed on specific internal accounting controls, or in a "substantive test mode," in which total reliance will be placed on the results of substantive tests, including analytical reviews. On many engagements, the most likely segments of the audit for which a compliance test mode produces the desired level of audit satisfaction in the most efficient manner are the revenue cycle, the buying cycle, and the production cycle, and those cycles are the subject matter of Chapters 12, 13, and 14, respectively. On the other hand, the auditor will more often than not find that the most efficient audit of other accounts in the financial statements can be accomplished by relying solely on analytical reviews and substantive tests of the details of transactions and balances. Chapters 15 and 16 cover the audit of those accounts: cash, property, investments, prepayments and accruals, income taxes, and debt and equity. In Chapters 12, 13, and 14, the text describes typical transactions and controls, audit objectives, the strategy considerations that enter into audit planning, and typical compliance and substantive tests. Chapters 15 and 16 describe substantive tests that are performed to meet the audit objectives of specific accounts. In all of the chapters in Part 3, the selection of tests is linked to the audit strategy; the tests associated with specific accounts are linked to the audit of other, related accounts. Thus, for example, in Chapter 16, consideration is given to income statement classification of expenses that are related to prepaid expenses and accrued liabilities on the balance sheet.

Part 4: Completing the Work and Reporting the Results. The auditor's work culminates in drafting the report—the only manifestation of the audit that the user sees. Completing the audit, which entails evaluating the overall findings, is a prerequisite to the report and is covered in Chapter 17. Chapter 18 deals with the auditor's standard report on a set of financial statements. Special reporting situations, including an extensive discussion of the CPA's involvement with prospective financial information, are covered in Chapter 19.

The sequence of some of the chapters can be rearranged to some extent without affecting continuity. Chapter 18 on the auditor's report, for example, could be assigned early in the course. Although the material in Chapters 3 and 4 on professional ethics and legal liability, respectively, could be moved to the end of the course, as is frequently done, it would probably be best to assign the first parts of each of those chapters—on auditing standards and on responsibility for detecting errors and irregularities, respectively—early in the course. The chapters in Part 3 could be assigned in virtually any order without causing problems in continuity. Even though the Revised College Version has been condensed from the professional version of *Montgomery's Auditing*, many opportunities still exist for deleting or covering lightly chapters that cannot be covered in depth because of time constraints. Among those are one or two of the cycle chapters and one or more sections of the account balance chapters in Part 3 and Chapter 19 on special reporting situations. Some instructors may want to supplement the text with other materials, for example, Statements on Auditing Standards or other AICPA materials such as industry audit guides or auditing procedure studies, a series begun in 1984.

Major Changes to the Revised Edition

A principal feature of the Revised College Version is the condensing of the text, largely in response to the suggestions of those who adopted the book. The authors believe that this has been done carefully and judiciously and with the least possible damage to the comprehensiveness of the previous edition—an aspect of the book that many users stated was also important to them and their students. Users should be aware, moreover, that the professional version of the book contains discussions of the topics deleted in the condensing process. Adopters of the Revised College Version may reproduce and distribute, for classroom use only, pages from Chapters 1 to 27 of the professional version that cover topics not included in the present version.

Other major changes to the Revised College Version include the following:

- Chapters 8 and 9 on assessing inherent and control risks and controlling detection risk have replaced the chapters on systems review and documentation and on audit tests and audit objectives. The material has been restructured and updated to focus more directly on the auditor's responsibilities with respect to audit risk. The risk model of SAS No. 47, *Audit Risk and Materiality in Conducting an Audit*, has greatly influenced the way that auditors conceptualize the work they do and the way that auditing standard-setters articulate and justify new authoritative auditing pronouncements, and this revision reflects that model.

- Largely at the suggestion of our constituents, the material on computer systems that previously was dispersed over five chapters has now been assembled into Chapter 11, "Auditing in an EDP Environment." While auditors do not overlay an EDP environment on a manual one when they plan and conduct their audits, students should be better able to grasp (or recall) EDP concepts once they understand the manual counterpart, admittedly a feat more easily accomplished.

- The two separate chapters on statistical and nonstatistical sampling have been reorganized and integrated into one chapter on the extent of testing and audit sampling. In that process, statistical sampling concepts have been given greater prominence, and much of the earlier repetitive discussion has been deleted.

- Several significant legal cases have occurred since the previous edition that affect the common law relationship between the auditor and third parties. Chapter 4 tracks these recent developments and their impact on the profession.

- Chapter 2, in addition to being substantially reorganized, discusses the *Attestation Standards* issued by the AICPA in 1986 and compares them with the 10 GAAS. At a time when nonaudit, attest services are expanding, those standards are conceptually significant in setting boundaries around the attest function.

- Since the publication of the first College Version of the Tenth Edition, the AICPA has issued an authoritative statement on *Financial Forecasts and Projections* and *A Guide for Prospective Financial Statements*. Chapter 19 updates the discussion of reporting on prospective financial information to include the guidance provided in those two documents.

Acknowledgments

We acknowledge with thanks the permission granted to us by the American Institute of Certified Public Accountants and the Financial Accounting Standards Board to quote or paraphrase passages from their publications. Copies of the complete documents can be obtained from those organizations.

This book represents the efforts and ideas of many people. The following individuals, presently or formerly associated with Coopers & Lybrand, contributed to various portions of the book: Murray S. Akresh, James B. Alfano, R. Michael Allen, Nigel Ampherlaw, A. James Anderson, Robert L. Anthony IV, Beth H. Bacon, Alan M. Bangser, Marvin L. Baris, Thomas A. Basilo, John L. Binkly, Timothy J. Botts, David A. Cace, Frank T. Caveney, Robert Chakrin, Myra D. Cleary, Donald L. Clement, Jr., Kirk S. Die, L. Frederick

Eberbach, Jr., John J. Fox, Richard M. Gargano, Richard E. Gilbert, Lynford E. Graham, Jr., Robert S. Haas, Edward R. Hansen, Robert B. Hetler, Ellen Downey Hylas, Keith E. Johnson, Jack Keeney, Arthur L. Knight, Chester L. Latin, A.J. Lorie, Salvatore Luiso, Florence M. Mazzella, Robert J. McDonald, David L. McLean, Frank C. Munn, James E. Newman, P. Jarlath O'Neil-Dunne, Xenia Ley Parker, Derinda S. Pell, Bent Petersen, Felix Pomeranz, Dennis D. Powell, Leonard J. Proscia, Marta B. Reese, Walter G. Ricciardi, Lawrence Salva, Darryl C. Spurlock, Catherine E. Stafford, Richard M. Steinberg, Richard G. Stevens, James R. Taucher, Gary Thomas, William W. Warrick, and Delmar G. Wilsey.

We also wish to thank the following individuals for their valuable comments and suggestions: Paul R. Brown, New York University; Robert E. Hamilton, Miami University of Ohio; Samuel K. Kniffen, University of South Dakota; Philip T. May, Wichita State University; Frederick L. Neumann, University of Illinois; James T. Robey, Old Dominion University; Harry F. Sieber, Franklin and Marshall College; and George W. Ulseth, Rensselaer Polytechnic Institute.

We owe a special acknowledgment to the following Coopers & Lybrand partners: Murray B. Hirsch, National Director of Auditing, for his ongoing support of this endeavor; Stanley D. Halper, for his assistance with Chapter 11, "Auditing in an EDP Environment"; and Garrett L. Stauffer, for his participation in a team-teaching experiment at Drexel University using this text. Particular thanks are due to Myra D. Cleary, whose editorial skills and administrative abilities contributed significantly to this project. To all those individuals, and any who were inadvertently omitted, go not only our thanks, but also the usual absolution from blame for errors and omissions.

P.L.D.
H.R.J.
J.D.S.
R.A.G.

Contents

_____ **Part 1**

The Audit Environment 1

1. An Overview of Auditing 3
Definition of Auditing 3
Origins and Early History of Auditing 7
Historical Development of External Auditing in the United States 8
The Role of Independent Audits 10
Audit Reports 15
An Overview of an Audit of Financial Statements 20

2. The Organization and Structure of the Auditing Profession 30
Types of Audits and Auditors 30
The Organization of an Accounting Firm 34
The Organization of the Auditing Profession 38
Professional Certification and Licensing 41
Professional Standards and Standard-Setting Bodies 43

3. Auditing Standards and Professional Ethics 53
Auditing as a Profession 53
Generally Accepted Auditing Standards 55
    General Standards
    Standards of Field Work
    Standards of Reporting
The AICPA Code of Ethics 60
    Concepts of Professional Ethics
    Independence, Integrity, and Objectivity
    General and Technical Standards
    Responsibilities to Clients
    Responsibilities to Colleagues
    Other Responsibilities and Practices
Incentives for Maintaining Audit Quality 74
    Introduction
    Quality Controls
    Disciplinary System
Enhancing the Independence of Auditors 81
    Protecting the Auditor from Management Influence
    Policies and Procedures of Accounting Firms and Their Effect on
        Independence
    Other Proposals to Enhance Independence

4. Professional Responsibility and Legal Liability　100

Responsibility for Detecting Misstatements　101
AICPA Professional Requirements
Client Deterrents to Irregularities
Illegal Acts by Clients
Responsibilities on Discovering a Possible Irregularity or Illegal Act
Engagement Letter
Auditors' Legal Liability　108
The Litigation Explosion
Liability to Clients
Civil Liability to Third Parties Under Common Law
Civil Liability to Third Parties Under the Federal Securities Acts
Criminal Liability
Other SEC Sanctions
The Profession's Responses to the Litigious Environment

_____ Part 2

Theory and Concepts　147

5. The Audit Process　149

Audit Assertions, Objectives, and Procedures　149
Audit Evidence and Audit Tests　152
Types of Evidence
Competence of Evidential Matter
Sufficiency of Evidential Matter
Types of Audit Tests or Procedures
Audit Evidence Decisions
The Steps in an Audit　161
Obtaining and Documenting Information About the Client
Planning and Documenting the Audit Strategy
Performing Tests and Other Procedures
Formulating the Auditor's Report and Communicating Control
　Weaknesses
Working Papers　169
Form and Content of Working Papers
Working Paper Organization
Typical Working Papers
Common Working Paper Deficiencies

6. Audit Risk, Materiality, and Engagement Strategy　186

Audit Risk　186
Overall Audit Risk

Audit Risk Related to Account Balances and Audit Objectives
The Components of Audit Risk
Summary of the Risk Model
Materiality 193
Audit Strategy 196
Planning and Controlling the Audit 197
Implementation Planning
Using the Work of Internal Auditors
Using the Work of a Specialist
Rotating Audit Emphasis
Using the Work of Other Auditors
Using a Report on Internal Control at a Service Organization
Controlling the Engagement

7. Internal Control Systems 217
Definitions and Objectives of Internal Control 218
Internal Accounting Control
Administrative Control
Transaction Cycles 225
Elements of Internal Control Systems 227
Control Environment
Accounting Systems
Internal Accounting Controls
Management's Responsibility for Internal Accounting Control Under the Foreign Corrupt Practices Act 238
Illegal Payments
Internal Accounting Control

8. Assessing Inherent Risk and Control Risk 251
Obtaining Information to Assess Inherent Risk 252
Obtaining Knowledge of the Client's Business and Industry
Analyzing Recent Financial Information
Reviewing Prior Years' Audit Results
Obtaining Knowledge of Applicable Accounting, Auditing, and
Regulatory Standards
Related Party Transactions
Assessing Control Risk: Minimum Requirements 256
Developing an Understanding of the Control Environment and
Accounting Systems
Assessing the Control Environment
Documenting Accounting Systems
Deciding Whether to Perform Compliance Tests 264
Compliance Testing to Rely on Specific Controls 265
Types of Compliance Tests

Continuous Operation of Controls
Dual-Purpose Samples and Tests
Evaluating the Results of Compliance Tests
Documenting Controls and Compliance Tests   270
Documenting Controls
Documenting Compliance Tests
Documenting Control Weaknesses
Communicating Control Weaknesses   278
Management Letters
Required Communication of Material Weaknesses in Internal Accounting
   Control
Reports on Internal Accounting Control

9. Controlling Detection Risk: Substantive Tests   329

Review: Audit Objectives, Risk Assessment, and Strategy   329
Audit Objectives
Risk Assessment
Audit Strategy
Substantive Test Considerations   332
Audit Objectives
Types of Accounts
Substantive Tests of Details   336
Types of Tests and Audit Objectives
Timing of Tests of Details
Exceptions
Other Auditing Procedures
Analytical Review Procedures   341
Timing and Objectives of Analytical Reviews
Types of Analytical Review Procedures
Assessing Assurance from Analytical Review Procedures
Audit Programs   349
Summary: Flowchart of an Audit   350

10. The Extent of Testing: Audit Sampling   364

Procedures Not Involving Sampling   365
Audit Risk and Sampling   367
Nonsampling Risk
Sampling Risk
Determinants of Sample Size   370
Sampling Risk
Tolerable Deviation Rate or Error Amount
Expected Deviation Rate or Error Amount
Other Planning Considerations
Choosing Statistical or Nonstatistical Methods   374

Statistical Compliance Testing 375
Basic Concepts of Attributes Sampling
Determining Statistical Compliance Test Sample Sizes
Selecting the Sample
Evaluating Statistical Compliance Test Sample Results
Discovery Sampling
Sequential Sampling
Statistical Substantive Testing 384
Applying Variables Sampling
Monetary Unit Sampling (MUS)
Mean-Per-Unit Estimation
Difference and Ratio Estimation
Nonstatistical Sampling 400
Determining Sample Size
Selecting Representative Samples
Evaluating Sample Results
Documenting Audit Sampling 407

11. Auditing in an EDP Environment 423
An Overview of Computer Auditing 423
Auditing Computer-Generated Data Around, Through, and with the
Computer
Differences Between Manual and Computerized Systems
Features of Computer Environments 425
Computer Operations
Organization of the EDP Department
General Controls: Objectives and Techniques 430
Overview of General Controls
Implementation Controls
Program Security Controls
Computer Operations Controls
Data File Security Controls
System Software Controls
Application Controls: Objectives and Techniques 437
Completeness of Input
Accuracy of Input
Completeness and Accuracy of Updating
Validity of Transactions
Maintenance of Data on Files
Asset Protection
Computer Fraud and Abuse 442
Auditing Computer-Generated Financial Information 444
Audit Strategy
Compliance Testing EDP Controls

Substantive Tests Using Computer Software
Substantive Tests of Programmed Accounting Procedures
Statistical Sampling Software
Audit Documentation Software
Analytical Review Software
Audit Management 454

_____ **Part 3**

Auditing Specific Cycles and Accounts 473

12. Auditing the Revenue Cycle 475

Definitions and Accounts Related to the Revenue Cycle 475
Typical Transactions and Internal Control 477
Sales of Goods and Services
Payments Received for Goods and Services
Goods Returned by and Claims Received from Customers
Planning the Audit Strategy 486
Audit Objectives
Audit Strategy
Compliance Tests 489
Sales of Goods and Services
Payments Received for Goods and Services
Goods Returned by and Claims Received from Customers
Substantive Tests 502
Accounts Receivable
Confirmation Procedures
Lapping
Procedures in Lieu of Confirmation
Other Substantive Tests
Tests for Collectibility
Analytical Reviews
**Auditing Procedures: Special Considerations for Particular Types of
Revenues** 517
Cash Sales
Consignment Sales
Rents, Interest, and Similar Fixed Payments for the Use of
Property
Royalties, Production Payments, and Similar Variable Revenues
Gifts and Donations
Deferred Income or Unearned Revenue
Revenues from Long-Term Contracts

13. Auditing the Buying Cycle 539

Accounts Related to the Buying Cycle 540
Typical Transactions and Internal Control 541
    Acquisition of Goods and Services
    Payment for Goods and Services
    Returning Goods to Suppliers
    Payrolls
    Payroll Processing
    Payment of Wages
Planning the Audit Strategy 554
    Audit Objectives
    Audit Strategy
Compliance Tests 556
    Acquisition of Goods and Services
    Payment for Goods and Services
    Returning Goods to Suppliers
    Payroll Processing
    Payment of Wages
Substantive Tests 575
    Accounts Payable
    Salaries, Wages, and Payroll Taxes
    Costs and Expenses
    Other Audit Procedures

14. Auditing the Production Cycle and Inventory Balances 592
Accounts Related to the Production Cycle 593
Typical Transactions and Internal Control 594
    Storing Raw Materials and Component Parts
    Producing Goods for Sale
    Storing Finished Goods
Planning the Audit Strategy 604
    Audit Objectives
    Audit Strategy
Compliance Tests 607
    Storing Raw Materials and Component Parts
    Producing Goods for Sale
    Storing Finished Goods
Substantive Tests 612
    Observation of Physical Inventories
    Ownership of Inventories
    Inventory Costing and Summarization
    Auditing Cost of Sales
    Purchase Commitments
    Analytical Reviews
    Management Representation Letter

15. Auditing Cash Balances and Property, Plant, and Equipment   644

Introduction   644
Cash Balances   645
  Audit Objectives
  Substantive Tests of Cash Balances
Property, Plant, and Equipment   657
  Audit Objectives
  Substantive Tests of Balances

16. Auditing Investments, Prepayments and Accruals, Taxes, and Debt and Equity Accounts   677

Investments and Related Income   677
  Audit Objectives
  Substantive Tests of Balances
Prepaid Expenses, Estimated and Accrued Liabilities, and Related Expenses   684
  Audit Objectives
  Substantive Tests of Balances
Income Taxes   691
  Audit Objectives
  Substantive Tests of Balances
Debt and Equity; Interest and Dividends   697
  Audit Objectives
  Substantive Tests of Balances

_____ Part 4
Completing the Work and Reporting the Results   715

17. Completing the Audit   717

Tests for Contingent Liabilities   718
  Accounting Overview
  Auditing Procedures
Lawyers' Letters   720
  Auditing Procedures
  Inquiry of a Client's Lawyer
  Evaluating Lawyers' Responses
  Need for Clarification of Sources of Information on Legal
    Matters
Client Representations   727
  Written Representations
  Representations in Other Than Audit Engagements
Researching Auditing Problems   732

Summarizing and Evaluating the Audit Findings 733
Categories of Errors to Be Evaluated
Preparing and Using the Score Sheet
Aggregating and Netting
Quantitative Aspects of Materiality Judgments
Qualitative Considerations in Assessing Materiality
Treatment of Prior-Year Waived Adjustments
Resolving Material Differences
Working Paper Review 742
Levels of Reviews
Key Engagement Matters
Review by a Second Partner
Aids for the Reviewer
Timing of the Review Process
Documentation of Significant Review Findings
Review of Financial Statements for Appropriate Disclosure 746
Responsibilities for Subsequent Events 747
Dating the Report
Subsequent Events
Auditing Procedures in the Subsequent Period
The Securities Act of 1933
Administrative Wrap-Up 753

18. The Auditor's Report 762

Standard Reports 763
History of the Standard Report
The Meaning of Fair Presentation in Conformity with GAAP
Routine Variations in the Standard Report
Modifications in Wording of the Standard Report 768
Opinion Based in Part on Report of Another Auditor
Departures from a Promulgated Accounting Principle with Which an
Auditor Agrees
Predecessor Auditor's Report Not Presented
Audited and Unaudited Financial Statements Presented in
Comparative Form
Report on a Balance Sheet Only
Emphasis of a Matter
Material Inconsistency Between Financial Statements and Other
Information Reported by Management
Departures from Unqualified Opinions 775
Qualified Opinions
Adverse Opinions
Disclaimers of Opinion
Piecemeal Opinions
Adverse Opinions Versus Disclaimers

The Effect of Materiality on Auditors' Reports
Responsibilities After the Report Date   800
Discovery of Information After the Report Date
Consideration of Omitted Procedures After the Report Date

19. Special Reporting Situations   823

Nonaudits, Compilations, and Reviews   825
Association with Financial Data
Services Other Than a Compilation or Review of Financial Statements
Compilations of Financial Statements
Reviews of Financial Statements
Reporting When the Accountant Is Not Independent
Negative Assurance
Interim Reviews   831
Objective of Reviews of Interim Financial Information
Nature of Reviews
Timing of Reviews
Extent of Reviews
Reporting Standards
Special Reports   835
Non-GAAP Financial Statements
Reports on Parts of a Financial Statement
Reports on Compliance
Reports on Prescribed Forms
**Reporting on Information Accompanying Basic Financial
Statements**   843
Additional Details or Commentary in Auditor-Submitted Documents
Supplementary Information Required by FASB Pronouncements
**Reporting on Prospective Financial Statements and Pro Forma
Statements**   846
Prospective Financial Statements
The Accountant's Role in the Prospective Presentation Process
Types of Prospective Financial Information
Scope of Services
Reporting
Pro Forma Statements
Reports on Internal Control   851
Types of Engagements
Study and Evaluation
Forms of Reporting
Material Weaknesses
Reports on Internal Control at Service Organizations
Opinions on Accounting Principles   855
Preferability Letters
Pooling Letters

Reports on the Application of Accounting Principles   857
Opinions on Tax Consequences, Proposed Systems, and Other
Matters   858
Letters for Underwriters   859

Appendix A
Tables for Determining Sample Size: Attributes Sampling   867

Appendix B
Tables for Evaluating Sample Results: Attributes Sampling   870

Appendix C
**Tables for Two-Stage Sequential Sampling Plans: Attributes
Sampling**   875

Index   877

Abbreviations and References

Abbreviations

References in this book to names of organizations, committees, and publications are often abbreviated, as follows:

AAA	American Accounting Association
AcSEC	Accounting Standards Executive Committee
AICPA	American Institute of Certified Public Accountants
ALI	American Law Institute
APB	Accounting Principles Board
ARB	Accounting Research Bulletin
ASB	Auditing Standards Board
ASR	Accounting Series Release
AudSEC	Auditing Standards Executive Committee
FASB	Financial Accounting Standards Board
GAO	General Accounting Office
GASB	Governmental Accounting Standards Board
IAPC	International Auditing Practices Committee
IFAC	International Federation of Accountants
IIA	Institute of Internal Auditors
IRS	Internal Revenue Service
SAP	Statement on Auditing Procedure
SAS	Statement on Auditing Standards
SEC	Securities and Exchange Commission
SFAS	Statement of Financial Accounting Standards
SOP	Statement of Position
SSARS	Statement on Standards for Accounting and Review Services

References

In addition to citations to original AICPA or FASB pronouncements (or later codifications, where applicable), second references are provided wherever possible. For pronouncements contained in *AICPA Professional Standards*, second references are to the appropriate section in that publication. Second references for accounting pronouncements are to the General Standards volume of the *Current Text* of FASB Accounting Standards; however, all quotations from the accounting literature are taken from the original pronouncements.

Part 1
The Audit Environment

Chapter 1
An Overview of Auditing

This book covers auditing—what auditors do and should do when they perform an audit—and the auditing profession—the institutional framework within which the practice of auditing takes place. Understanding what an audit is and how it is performed is necessary to understanding the social function of an audit and the professional responsibilities that auditors assume in filling that function. Understanding the environment and institutions within which an audit occurs is necessary to understanding the background and logic that support the degree of care and the methods and techniques that auditors use in conducting an audit. Knowing what constitutes an audit performed with due professional care and why particular audit procedures are followed permits the auditor to adapt to changing circumstances in order to meet social, legal, and professional responsibilities.

Definition of Auditing

Different types of audits and the purposes of audits have evolved over many years, and this evolution is still taking place. Accordingly, auditing should be defined broadly enough to encompass the various types and purposes of audits. The definition of auditing that appeared in *A Statement of Basic Auditing Concepts*, published in 1973 by the American Accounting Association (AAA) Committee on Basic Auditing Concepts, meets that objective by embracing both the process and purposes of auditing:

> Auditing is a systematic process of objectively obtaining and evaluating evidence regarding assertions about economic actions and events to ascertain the degree of correspondence between those assertions and established criteria and communicating the results to interested users. (p. 2)

The AAA Committee noted that its definition was intentionally quite broad and encompassed "the many different purposes for which an audit might be conducted and the variety of subject matter that might be focused on in a specific audit engagement" (p. 2). The following discussion of each of the key phrases in the definition is in the context of an audit of the financial statements of a business organization, usually referred to as a financial audit, since the reader is assumed to be familiar with such statements. Chapter 2 discusses compliance audits and operational audits as well as financial audits.

Assertions About Economic Actions and Events. The assertions of enterprise management that are embodied in a set of financial statements are the subject matter of an audit of those statements. For example, the item "inventories. . . . . $5,426,000" in a balance sheet of a manufacturing company embodies the following assertions, among others: The inventories physically exist; they are held for sale or use in operations; they include all products and materials owned and on hand or stored elsewhere, and only those products and materials; $5,426,000 is the lower of their cost or market value (as both terms are defined under generally accepted accounting principles); they are properly classified on the balance sheet; and appropriate disclosures related to inventories have been made, such as their major categories and amounts pledged or assigned. Comparable assertions are embodied in all the other specific items and amounts in financial statements.

These assertions are made by the preparer of the financial statements—the enterprise management—and communicated to the readers of the statements; they are not assertions by the auditor. The auditor's assertions are contained in the auditor's communication to the readers in the form of the auditor's report. Similar assertions are also the subject matter of compliance and operational audits.

The fact that the subject matter of auditing is information about economic actions and events suggests that the assertions must be quantifiable to be auditable. Building costs are quantifiable, as is the number of stock options outstanding; the morale of employees is not. Information that is quantifiable is also generally verifiable; information that is not verifiable is by definition not auditable. Information is verifiable if it "provides results that would be substantially duplicated by independent measures using the same measurement methods" (Accounting Principles Board Statement No. 4, para. 90).

Degree of Correspondence Between Assertions and Established Criteria.
Everything that takes place during an audit has one primary objective: the for-

mation of an opinion by the auditor on the assertions about economic actions and events that have been audited. The auditor's opinion will specify the extent to which those assertions (for example, that the inventories on the balance sheet exist and are owned by the enterprise) conform to established criteria or standards; for inventories, those criteria are accounting principles that generally require that inventories must exist and be owned by the enterprise before they can be included among its assets. If the inventories exist and are owned by the reporting enterprise, and if the other assertions implicit in the item "inventories. . . . . $5,426,000" also conform to generally accepted accounting principles (GAAP), the auditor will come to the conclusion that there is complete correspondence between those assertions and established criteria.

In the case of financial audits, generally accepted accounting principles are the established criteria against which the assertions are measured. Although alternative accounting principles often exist, those criteria are, for the most part, explicit and precisely defined. The same may be true in the case of many compliance audits. For example, the established criteria against which the assertions on a tax return are measured are the tax laws, regulations, and rulings that pertain to the particular tax return. In other instances, such as an operational audit of an enterprise's capital budgeting system, the criteria are far less precise and are generally ill defined. In those situations, the auditor and the client will have to agree on the criteria to be used, and those criteria should be explicitly stated in the auditor's report.

Objectively Obtaining and Evaluating Evidence. Obtaining and evaluating evidence constitute the essence of auditing. "The types of evidence obtained and the criteria employed to evaluate evidence may vary from audit to audit, but all audits center on the process of obtaining and evaluating evidence" (*A Statement of Basic Auditing Concepts*, p. 2). In a financial audit, for example, evidence about the degree of correspondence between assertions in the financial statements and generally accepted accounting principles consists of underlying accounting data (such as journals and ledgers) and corroborating information (such as invoices, checks, and information obtained by inquiry, observation, physical examination of assets, and correspondence with customers). To continue with the inventory example, the auditor may examine purchase contracts or paid invoices to ascertain that the enterprise owns the inventory, observe an inventory count to determine that it exists, and retotal the perpetual inventory ledger to ascertain the mathematical accuracy of the dollar amount of inventory reported on the balance sheet.

The evidence obtained must also be interpreted and evaluated in order for the auditor to make the accounting judgments that are usually necessary before reaching the conclusion that the assertions conform to objective criteria. Those judgments are often extremely difficult and require significant analytical and interpretive skills. For example, an assertion that inventories are properly valued at the lower of cost or market requires the auditor to understand and evaluate the enterprise's methods of applying accounting principles for determining cost, which may be particularly difficult if sophisticated last-in, first-out costing methods are used or if a standard cost system is employed, to cite just two examples. That same assertion also requires the exercise of judgment in evaluating management's determination of replacement cost, estimated selling price, and normal profit margins in the course of ascertaining ''market'' value. Finally, the assertion also requires the auditor to evaluate the adequacy of any provisions for obsolete and slow-moving items, and conclusive evidence is rarely available to support those judgments. The types of judgments discussed in this paragraph are crucial to an audit of financial statements and usually require the auditor to be able to evaluate evidence that may be inconclusive and subject to varying interpretations.

The definition of auditing specifies that the process of obtaining and evaluating evidence must be carried out objectively. Objectivity in the process of obtaining and evaluating evidence must be distinguished from the objectivity of the evidence itself. Objectivity of evidence is one of several factors related to the usefulness of the evidence in achieving the purposes for which it was gathered. Objectivity of the process refers to the auditor's ability to maintain an impartial attitude in selecting and evaluating evidence. That impartial attitude is part of the concept of auditor independence. The very definition of auditing offered above suggests that an audit must be performed by an independent person.

Systematic Process. The word ''systematic'' implies several things—that planning the audit and formulating an audit strategy are important parts of the audit process, that the audit plan and strategy should relate the selection and evaluation of evidence to specific audit objectives, that many of the specific audit objectives and the evidence to achieve those objectives are interrelated, and that those interrelationships require the auditor to make many decisions in the course of planning and performing an audit.

A Statement of Basic Auditing Concepts notes that the phrase ''systematic process'' suggests that ''auditing is based, in part at least, on the discipline and philosophy of scientific method'' (p. 2). Most auditors, however, do not think of themselves as applying the scientific method, probably because the term implies a more highly structured method of inquiry than is possible or even desirable in most audits. Certainly an audit should be the result of a carefully conceived and implemented audit strategy, but that strategy is subject to extensive modification during an audit as the auditor obtains and evaluates evidence relating to the specific assertions about the various, often interrelated components of financial statements, or of whatever is the subject of the audit.

Communicating the Results to Interested Users. The end and aim of all audits is a report that informs the reader about the degree to which the assertions made by the auditor's client correspond to the criteria that have been agreed to as the basis of the evaluation. In the case of an audit of a set of financial statements, the communication, called an auditor's report, states the conclusions reached on whether or not the financial statements conform to generally accepted accounting principles. (The report that follows the conclusion of an audit of financial statements is discussed briefly later in this chapter and at length in Chapter 18.) Other types of audits similarly require that the auditor report the findings to interested parties. Thus, the definition of auditing includes the reporting phase of an audit, in which the auditor communicates an opinion or evaluation to interested parties, as well as the investigative phase, in which the auditor gathers and evaluates evidence to form that opinion or evaluation.

Relationship Between Accounting and Auditing. It should be clear from the definition of auditing and the references to various types of possible audits that there *need not* be any relationship between auditing and accounting. Virtually any information that is quantifiable and verifiable can be audited, as long as the auditor and the auditee agree on the criteria to be used as the basis for determining the degree of correspondence. For example, an auditor for the United States General Accounting Office may be requested to audit the effectiveness of a particular airplane. The criteria for measuring effectiveness, which will have to be agreed to before the audit takes place, will most likely be concerned with speed, acceleration, cruising altitude, number and type of armaments, and so on. None of these criteria involve accounting data.

The subject matter of most audits, and all financial audits, is usually accounting data that are contained in the books, records, and financial statements of the audited entity. Much of the evidence that an auditor gathers and evaluates consists of data drawn from the accounting system. The assertions about economic actions and events that the auditor is concerned with are often assertions about accounting transactions and other events of accounting significance and account balances that are the result of those transactions and events. Lastly, the established criteria that accounting assertions ordinarily must correspond with are generally accepted accounting principles. Thus, while an accountant need not be knowledgeable about auditing, an auditor must be knowledgeable about accounting. Accounting creates financial statements and other useful information; auditing generally does not create accounting data or other information. Rather, auditing enhances the value of the information created by the accounting process by critically evaluating that information and by communicating the results of that critical evaluation.

Origins and Early History of Auditing[1]

Historians believe that record keeping originated about 4000 B.C., when ancient civilizations in the Near East began to establish organized governments and businesses. From the beginning, governments were concerned with accounting for receipts and disbursements and collecting taxes. An integral part of this concern was establishing controls, including audits, to reduce errors and fraud on the part of incompetent or dishonest officials.

[1]Much of the material in this section is based on Richard Brown, *A History of Accounting and Accountants* (Edinburgh: T. C. & E. C. Jack, 1905); and Michael Chatfield, *A History of Accounting Thought,* rev. ed. (Huntington, N.Y.: Robert E. Krieger Publishing Company, 1977).

The oldest surviving accounting records and references to audits, in the modern sense of the word, of English-speaking countries are those of the Exchequers of England and Scotland, which date back to 1130. The early audits in Great Britain were of two types. Audits of cities and towns were held publicly before the governing officials and citizens and consisted of the auditors' hearing the accounts[2] read by the treasurer; similarly, audits of guilds were heard before the membership. By the middle of the sixteenth century, auditors of cities often annotated the accounts with phrases such as "heard by the auditors undersigned." The second type of audit involved a detailed examination of the accounts maintained by the financial officers of large manors, followed by a "declaration of audit," that is, an oral report before the lord of the manor and the council. Typically, the auditor was a member of the manorial council, and thus was the precursor of the modern internal auditor.

Both types of audits performed in Great Britain prior to the seventeenth century were directed primarily at examining the accountability for funds entrusted to public or private officials. Those audits were not designed to test the quality of the accounts, except insofar as inaccuracies might point to the existence of fraud. The economic changes of the following 200 years introduced new accounting concerns that focused on the ownership of property and the calculation of profits and losses in a business sense. Auditing also began to evolve from an auditory process to a close examination of written records and the testing of supporting evidence. At the end of the seventeenth century, the first law was enacted (in Scotland) prohibiting certain officials from serving as auditors of a town, thus introducing the modern notion of auditor independence to the Western world.

Despite these advances in auditing practices, it was not until well into the nineteenth century—which brought the construction of railways and the growth of insurance companies, banks, and other joint-stock companies—that the professional auditor became an important part of the business scene. The railroad industry in the United States was among the first employers of internal auditors. By the latter part of the nineteenth century, so-called "traveling auditors" visited widely dispersed ticket agencies to evaluate management's accountability for assets and its reporting systems.

Historical Development of External Auditing in the United States[3]

Independent audits in the United States up to the turn of the twentieth century were modeled on British practices. The audit work consisted of detailed scruti-

---

[2]The practice of "hearing the accounts," which originated in the days when few people were literate, continued until the seventeenth century. The word "audit," in fact, derives from the Latin word for a hearing.

[3]A more comprehensive history of American auditing appears in C. A. Moyer, "Early Developments in American Auditing," *The Accounting Review* (January 1951), pp. 3–8.

nies of clerical data relating to the balance sheet. Robert H. Montgomery, in the first edition of this book, called the early American audits "bookkeeper audits," and he estimated that three-quarters of the audit time was spent on footings and postings. Since there were no statutory requirements for audits in America, and since most audits were performed by auditors from Britain who were sent by British investors in U.S. companies, the profession grew slowly at first. Only a small amount of auditing literature was published in the United States prior to the 1900s. In 1905 and again in 1909, Montgomery published American editions of *Auditing: A Practical Manual for Auditors*, written by Lawrence R. Dicksee in England, and in 1912, recognizing the departures of U.S. practice from the British, he wrote the first American auditing book, *Auditing: Theory and Practice,* subsequently to be retitled *Montgomery's Auditing.*

Gradually, American audits evolved into "test audits" as procedures were adapted to rapidly expanding American businesses, which considered the British-type detailed checking of footings and postings too time consuming and expensive. In addition to the increased use of testing methods, auditors began to secure evidence from outside clients' records as a means of examining transactions and, because of investors' concerns, to pay closer attention to the valuations of assets and liabilities. These developments point to a broadening of audit objectives beyond checking clerical accuracy and detecting fraud.

Financial statement users in the early years of this century focused on the balance sheet as the primary indicator of a company's health, and, for the most part, auditors emphasized the balance sheet in their work. The first U.S. authoritative auditing pronouncement, prepared by the American Institute of Accountants (now the American Institute of Certified Public Accountants [AICPA]) at the request of the Federal Trade Commission, was published in 1917 and referred to "balance-sheet audits." A revised pamphlet was published in 1929, under the title "Verification of Financial Statements." Although the pronouncement still emphasized the balance sheet audit, it discussed income statement accounts in detail, thus reflecting the growing interest in results of operations. The 1929 pamphlet also covered reporting practices and stressed reliance on internal controls. The 1936 edition of the pamphlet was entitled "Examination of Financial Statements by Independent Public Accountants" and was influenced by a number of significant events of the previous few years, most notably the AICPA's collaboration with the New York Stock Exchange in an effort to improve reporting standards and the enactment of the Securities Act of 1933 and the Securities Exchange Act of 1934, which required listed companies to file audited financial statements.

The modern era of audit standard-setting began in 1939, when the AICPA created the Committee on Auditing Procedure and that committee issued the first Statement on Auditing Procedure (SAP). Fifty-four SAPs were issued through 1972, at which time the name of the committee was changed to the Auditing Standards Executive Committee (later renamed the Auditing Standards Board), which codified all the SAPs in Statement on Auditing Standards (SAS) No. 1; that series of statements continues to the present.

The Role of Independent Audits

The social purpose that independent audits serve today has been concisely stated by the Financial Accounting Standards Board in Statement of Financial Accounting Concepts No. 1, *Objectives of Financial Reporting by Business Enterprises,* as follows:

> The effectiveness of individuals, enterprises, markets, and government in allocating scarce resources among competing uses is enhanced if those who make economic decisions have information that reflects the relative standing and performance of business enterprises to assist them in evaluating alternative courses of action and the expected returns, costs, and risks of each. . . . Independent auditors commonly examine or review financial statements and perhaps other information, and both those who provide and those who use that information often view an independent auditor's opinion as enhancing the reliability or credibility of the information. (para. 16)

By enhancing the confidence that users have in the reliability or credibility of financial information, an audit reduces the "information risk" to users of that information. "Information risk" is the risk that information, in this case information contained in financial reports, is incorrect. Information risk is distinguishable from business risk, which is the risk that, even with correct information, the return on an investment will be less than anticipated because of some unforeseen circumstance or event. Investors and lenders demand, and the "market" pays, a return for the assumption of risk. Reducing the information risk in financial information reduces the risk premium that must be paid by enterprises and lowers the audited enterprise's cost of capital, thereby promoting the efficient allocation of scarce economic resources among competing uses.

Considerable research has taken place in recent years on the value of annual financial statements to investment and credit decision makers. That research, with its focus on the "efficient market hypothesis," seems to suggest that annual financial statements have little effect on security prices because information available to investors in the financial press and from investment analysts is acted on before the annual financial statements are published. There is widespread agreement, however, that *audited* financial statements do have "information content," that is, they contain *new* information merely by virtue of their having been audited. The Commission on Auditors' Responsibilities, also known as the Cohen Commission, after its chairman, Manuel C. Cohen, concluded that "*audited* financial statements provide a means of confirming or correcting the information received earlier by the market. In effect, the audited statements help to assure the efficiency of the market by limiting the life of inaccurate information or by deterring its dissemination."[4]

The AAA Committee on Basic Auditing Concepts considered the control dimension as another aspect, in addition to the credibility dimension, of the value added to financial information by the audit function.

[4]*Report, Conclusions, and Recommendations*, 1978, p. 6.

The addition of the audit function serves as a *control* over the quality of information because:

1. It provides an independent check on the accounting information against established criteria presumably reflecting the user's needs and desires.

2. It motivates the preparer of the information to carry out the accounting process under his control in a way that conforms to the user's criteria since he (the preparer) knows his efforts will be subjected to independent, expert review.[5]

The motivational aspect of an audit has long been recognized: Knowing that an audit will be performed is a strong deterrent to the potential dissemination of erroneous information.

Objectives of Audits of Financial Statements. In contrast to the social role filled by an audit of financial statements, the AICPA has stated, in SAS No. 1, *Codification of Auditing Standards and Procedures*, the immediate objective of an audit, as follows:

> The objective of the ordinary examination of financial statements by the independent auditor is the expression of an opinion on the fairness with which they present financial position, results of operations, and changes in financial position in conformity with generally accepted accounting principles. (para. 110.01)

Thus, the immediate objective of an audit can be thought of as meeting the specific needs of people and organizations that require an entity to present audited financial statements. Several groups or organizations have the power or authority to require that specific entities by audited. (The authors are not suggesting that without those specific requirements audits would not occur.) Those groups include creditors and potential creditors, the SEC and the various stock exchanges acting on behalf of actual and potential investors, and governmental agencies that require nonbusiness organizations to file audited financial statements.

Lending institutions, such as banks and insurance companies, frequently want audited financial statements of borrowers and prospective borrowers. Other creditors, such as vendors, may request audited financial statements to assist their credit and lending decisions. All of those organizations may want audited financial statements throughout the life of the credit or loan agreement. To a great extent, audits are performed because lenders and creditors demand them. In addition, the Securities Act of 1933 and the Securities Exchange Act of 1934 require that companies (with several exceptions) that issue securities to the public or seek to have their securities publicly traded on the various securities exchanges and in the securities market must file audited financial statements with the SEC. Since 1933, the New York Stock Exchange

[5]*A Statement of Basic Auditing Concepts*, 1973, p. 13.

has required independently audited financial statements to be filed with listing applications and to be published annually after a security has been listed for trading.

Finally, auditors are required to inform their client's management about material weaknesses in internal accounting control that come to their attention in the course of an audit. In practice, auditors often extend that communication to encompass weaknesses that do not meet the carefully defined materiality standard in the professional literature and weaknesses in internal administrative as well as internal accounting controls; suggestions for improving internal control are also usually included. The communication is ordinarily in writing, although it is customary to review its contents with the organization's management before the document, known as either a "management letter" or an "internal control letter," is finalized. The management letter is provided to the client as a service and is an important by-product or secondary objective of an audit. Performing an audit also gives the auditor substantial knowledge of the client's business and financial operations; that knowledge frequently enables the auditor to provide other, nonaudit but accounting-related services such as tax planning advice and recommendations on the effects of alternative acceptable accounting principles on financial statements.

Concerns of Users of Financial Information. While few of the direct beneficiaries of audited financial information are likely to be very expressive about why they want the financial information they rely on to be audited, the reason is basically their desire for increased assurance about the quality of that information in order to reduce the information risk discussed earlier. Information risk manifests itself in two broad ways, both of which are concerns of users of financial information. First, financial statements or other financial information may be misstated because of unintentional errors in processing or recording the transactions that are summarized in the financial statements, because of deliberate financial statement misrepresentations by the management of the reporting entity, or because assets have been stolen or otherwise misappropriated. Examples of each of these types of errors include, respectively, the unintentional failure to record a valid sale that actually took place, the deliberate recording of sales that never occurred, and the undiscovered theft of customers' remittances.

Second, financial statements may be misstated because the preparers of those statements may have unintentionally made incorrect judgments in interpreting facts or in presenting those facts in conformity with generally accepted accounting principles, either in terms of how financial statement items are measured or in terms of the disclosures that should be made. For example, enterprise management may truly believe that a particular lease is an operating lease when in fact the terms of the lease agreement are such that under generally accepted accounting principles it should be classified as a capital lease, which would change the appropriate accounting measurements and disclosures.

User concerns about both types of misinformation arise from an awareness of the inherent potential conflict of interests between preparers and users of financial statements. This is not to say that there is or must be a conflict of interests; nor does it suggest that managements are dishonest. It merely suggests that preparers may have certain biases in preparing financial information, as do those who use the information. Audits have a restraining influence in that auditors serve as independent third-party intermediaries between preparers and users of financial information.

Addressing User Concerns. In performing audits that meet the concerns of users of financial statements, independent auditors perform two functions, which are distinguished by the type of assertions for which evidence is gathered. One broad group of assertions about components of financial statements is concerned with the completeness, genuineness, and arithmetical accuracy of the information presented. For example, the item ''accounts receivable—trade'' shown in a balance sheet implies that the accounts receivable exist, that the enterprise owns them, that all trade accounts receivable that exist and are owned are included in the total, that the computations behind the amount shown are mechanically accurate—that is, the arithmetic involved in preparing customer invoices, posting the invoice amounts to individual customer accounts, and summarizing the individual accounts was done correctly—and that the effects of transactions with enterprise officers and other related parties have been excluded. An auditor will obtain and evaluate evidence to ascertain that those assertions are reliable, and this will typically be a major part of an audit, at least as measured by the time involved. In this function, the auditor serves as an expert gatherer and evaluator of evidence.

The other group of assertions is concerned with proper disclosure and valuation according to generally accepted accounting principles. For example, certain disclosures about the accounts receivable may be necessary to make the financial statements useful to interested readers or, at a minimum, to ensure that the statements are not misleading. Also, generally accepted accounting principles require that accounts receivable be valued net of appropriate allowances, such as for bad debts and returns or allowances. Presenting the appropriate disclosures and estimating the necessary allowances require the preparer of the financial statements to exercise considerable judgment. An integral part of the auditor's function is to interpret the facts supporting the preparer's judgments and to evaluate the judgments made. To serve as an interpreter of facts and evaluator of accounting judgments, the auditor must have a thorough understanding of the client's business and of generally accepted accounting principles.

Over the years, and particularly in the last two decades, the relative importance of the evidence-gathering function has decreased and that of the interpreting/evaluating function has increased. This is not to suggest either that the former function is unimportant or that it is not extremely time consuming, but merely that the latter has taken on greater significance. In part, this has resulted from the increased attention enterprises are paying to internal control systems designed to ensure the correctness of accounting information from a mechanical point of view. Auditors frequently find it more efficient to test the client's internal control system and then rely on that system to prevent or detect errors in the processing and accumulating of data than to test directly the output of the system. Another reason underlying this change is the prevalence of complex and innovative transactions and the attendant increase in the number and complexity of accounting principles created to deal with those transactions in a way that reflects their economic substance rather than their legal form. Both the transactions themselves and the related accounting principles require the auditor to expend increased amounts of time and effort to obtain the facts and evaluate the judgments made in accounting for the underlying substance of the transactions.

The Limitations of Auditing.   No audit provides complete assurance that the financial statements are free from material error arising from either incorrect processing of accounting data or incorrect judgments on the selection and application of accounting principles. As the Commission on Auditors' Responsibilities (Cohen Commission) noted,

> Audited financial statements cannot be perfectly accurate, in part because of the ambiguity of the accounting concepts they reflect. . . . [Also,] accounting results—the financial statements—cannot be more accurate and reliable than the underlying accounting measurement methods permit. For example, no one, including accountants, can foresee the results of many uncertain future events. To the extent that the accuracy of an accounting presentation is dependent on an unpredictable future event, the accounting presentation will be inaccurate. The *audited* accounting presentation can be no more accurate, for the auditor cannot add certainty where it does not exist.[6]

Moreover, accounting measurement principles frequently provide more than one alternative to account for a given transaction or event. For example, there are several ways of accounting for the flow of inventory costs through an enterprise and for the depreciation of tangible assets. Neither the authoritative accounting literature nor logic supports the selection of one alternative over another. This flexibility of generally accepted accounting principles permits preparers of financial information to influence the information presented and thereby affect the reliability of that information. Also, accounting principles often require interpretation and the application of judgment before they can be applied to specific transactions and other events and circumstances, and reasonable preparers of financial statements and auditors can disagree about those interpretations and judgments. In effect, the "established criteria" of generally accepted accounting principles against which financial statement assertions are evaluated are sometimes less than completely "established."

[6]*Report, Conclusions, and Recommendations, op. cit.*, p. 7.

In addition to the limitations imposed on the audit process by the constraint of the existing accounting framework, there are limitations imposed by the audit process itself and by auditing technology. Ideally, an auditor would like to have firsthand evidence to support every assertion that is implicit in a set of financial statements, but that is sometimes either impracticable or impossible. For one thing, even if that goal could be achieved, it is unlikely that it would be worth the cost to either the preparer or the user of financial statements. Standards widely accepted by auditors recognize this by requiring that sufficient evidence be obtained to provide a *reasonable* basis for the auditor's opinion regarding the financial statements being audited. As a result of cost constraints imposed on the auditor by both the client and society, the auditor, in evaluating some characteristic of an account balance or class of transactions, will frequently examine less than 100 percent of the items in the balance or class. Moreover, to the extent that the entity fails to record events and transactions, the auditor cannot audit their results. In particular, if controls over the completeness of processing and recording data are nonexistent or ineffective, it may be impossible to audit aspects of the financial statements or even the statements as a whole.

Audit Reports

The final phase of any audit is communicating the auditor's findings to interested users in what is known as the auditor's report. Standardized language has been developed for the auditor's report on the results of a financial audit conducted for the purpose of ascertaining the degree to which financial statements conform to generally accepted accounting principles. Reports following audits of financial statements are discussed briefly in this section; they are considered in greater detail in Chapter 18. The discussion here is restricted to the level of detail needed to understand the document that is the primary end and aim of an audit of financial statements.

The auditor's report that appears in Figure 1.1 is an example of the standard, so-called "short form" report. The following paragraphs explain the language used in the report and its organization.

Title. The report in Figure 1.1 is titled "Report of Independent Certified Public Accountants." The title "Auditor's Opinion" is often used, but is slightly less precise because the opinion is only one of several elements in the communication. A term that is decidedly less precise and is subject to misinterpretation by readers but that is still occasionally used is "Auditor's Certificate." The term "certificate" conveys a degree of factuality or exactness that is not present and should not be implied. The auditor's conclusions are expressed in the form of an opinion, not a fact. If the financial statements are audited by a CPA or a CPA firm, the auditor or auditors, not the statements, are "certi-

Figure 1.1   Auditor's Standard Report

Report of Independent Certified Public Accountants

To the Board of Directors and
Stockholders of American Brands, Inc.:

We have examined the consolidated balance sheet of American Brands, Inc.
and Subsidiaries as of December 31, 1985 and 1984, and the related
consolidated statements of income and retained earnings and changes in
financial position for the years ended December 31, 1985, 1984 and 1983. Our
examinations were made in accordance with generally accepted auditing
standards and, accordingly, included such tests of the accounting records and
such other auditing procedures as we considered necessary in the
circumstances.

   In our opinion, the aforementioned financial statements present fairly the
consolidated financial position of American Brands, Inc. and Subsidiaries at
December 31, 1985 and 1984, and the consolidated results of their operations
and changes in their financial position for the years ended December 31, 1985,
1984 and 1983, in conformity with generally accepted accounting principles
applied on a consistent basis.

Coopers & Lybrand

1251 Avenue of the Americas
New York, New York 10020
February 3, 1986

fied.'' Even to refer to certified financial statements suggests a degree of accuracy and precision that neither the preparer nor the auditor should want to
convey.

Scope Paragraph.   The first paragraph of the auditor's report, the scope paragraph, relates what was done and the manner in which it was done. The standard scope paragraph conveys the message that an audit was performed (although the word ''audit'' is not used) and that it was performed in accordance
with generally accepted auditing standards—guidelines promulgated by the
profession for performing professionally responsible audits—using such tests
and procedures as the auditor considered necessary.

   The scope paragraph names the statements examined and the dates of and
periods covered by those statements. It is important that the reader of the document in which the financial statements appear know precisely what is covered

by the auditor's report and, by inference, what is not. Since an annual report or prospectus contains much more than the financial statements, the reader must be told specifically what has been audited (the financial statements and the related notes that are, as stated on each page of the body of the financial statements, an ''integral part of the financial statements'') and what, by implication, has not been audited (the letter from the president and chairman of the board, supplementary information such as financial ratios and stock prices, and all other communications about the enterprise). Publicly traded companies are now required to publish comparative financial statements that include balance sheets for the two most recent year-ends and income statements and statements of changes in financial position covering the three latest years. The auditor should state that the financial statements as of those dates and for those periods have been audited if that is in fact the case.

Opinion Paragraph. The opinion paragraph of the auditor's report, usually the second, and final, paragraph, states the auditor's conclusions reached from the work performed. It is because of the importance of the auditor's conclusions to the users of financial statements that the entire auditor's report is sometimes called the auditor's opinion. As noted earlier, the auditor's opinion, in the narrower sense of the word, represents a judgment made after evidence about the assertions implicit in the financial statements has been evaluated; the phrase ''in our opinion'' is intended to convey this element of judgment, as opposed to a statement of fact. (As discussed later, in some cases the auditor may be unable to form an opinion.)

The conclusion that the auditor reaches in most audits of financial statements, and in the example presented, is that the financial statements ''present fairly . . . in conformity with generally accepted accounting principles applied on a consistent basis.''[7] The opinion illustrated is technically called an unqualified opinion—that is, it is not qualified by any exceptions or uncertainties. A less technical term for an unqualified opinion is a ''clean'' opinion. Although authoritative AICPA literature describes other types of opinions (discussed briefly later and in detail in Chapter 18), such as qualified opinions, adverse opinions, and disclaimers of opinion, the usual expectation of every audit is that the auditor will be able to render the positive, unqualified opinion illustrated in the figure. Anything less is usually undesirable, and often unacceptable either to the client or to regulatory bodies. Users of financial statements are best served if the client's financial statements do ''present fairly . . . in conformity with generally accepted accounting principles.'' Thus, an auditor has a responsibility to both the public and the client to seek to improve financial reporting practices in general and those of the client in particular.

---

[7]Note that the illustrative opinion is about the financial statements, not about individual account balances. The auditor may express an opinion about specific accounts, rather than about the financial statements taken as a whole, in a ''special report,'' which is discussed in Chapter 19.

The words "present fairly" should not be interpreted separately from "in conformity with generally accepted accounting principles"; "fairness" has meaning in the auditor's standard report only in the context of generally accepted accounting principles. The auditor's positive opinion about fair presentation in conformity with generally accepted accounting principles implies a belief that the financial statements have the following qualities:

1. The accounting principles selected and applied have general acceptance;
2. The accounting principles are appropriate in the circumstances;
3. The financial statements, including the related notes, are informative of matters that may affect their use, understanding, and interpretation;
4. The information presented in the financial statements is classified and summarized in a reasonable manner, that is, neither too detailed nor too condensed; and
5. The financial statements reflect the underlying events and transactions in a manner that presents financial position, results of operations, and changes in financial position stated within a range of acceptable limits, that is, limits that are reasonable and practicable to attain in financial statements. (SAS No. 5 [AU Section 411.04])

Lastly, the reference to consistency is required by generally accepted auditing standards. When the independent auditor reports only on the current period, the reference to consistency should be expressed as "on a basis consistent with that of the preceding year." When the audit report covers two or more years, as in Figure 1.1, the auditor should report on the consistency of the application of accounting principles throughout those years (SAS No. 1, paras. 20 and 21).

Departures from the Standard, Unqualified Report. An independent auditor will issue a standard, unqualified, two-paragraph report if:

1. The audit was conducted with due professional care by independent persons with adequate training and proficiency.
2. Sufficient evidence was obtained and evaluated to enable the auditor to conclude that the financial statements are presented fairly in conformity with GAAP applied on a consistent basis.

If those circumstances are not present, a standard, unqualified report will not be issued. Other types of auditor's reports disclaim the ability to form an opinion, state that the financial statements are not presented fairly in conformity with GAAP applied on a consistent basis, or contain qualifying language. Such reports express disclaimers of opinion, adverse opinions, and qualified opinions, respectively.

Disclaimers of opinion state that the auditor does not express an opinion on the financial statements or any part of them. This form of report is used when one or more of the following circumstances are present:

1. The auditor is not independent.
2. The auditor was unable to obtain sufficient evidence to form an opinion on the financial statements, either because of restrictions imposed by the client or because of circumstances beyond either the client's or the auditor's control.
3. There is an uncertainty whose resolution could have a material, pervasive effect on the financial statements.

A disclaimer of opinion indicates that the auditor lacks the knowledge necessary to form *any* opinion on the financial statements, and that can occur only in the three situations mentioned. Any other opinion (unqualified, adverse, or qualified) indicates that the auditor has sufficient knowledge, based on the evidence gathered and evaluated, to form an opinion of one kind or another. A disclaimer of opinion adds nothing to the credibility of the financial statements and has the same effect as if an audit had not been performed at all.

Adverse opinions state that the financial statements are not presented fairly in conformity with GAAP. Such an opinion is used when the auditor believes that inappropriate accounting principles have been applied or the disclosures in the notes to the financial statements are inadequate or otherwise misleading and that the effect on the statements is so pervasive that, taken as a whole, they are misleading. Unlike a disclaimer of opinion, an adverse opinion is given only when the auditor has knowledge, after sufficient evidence has been evaluated, that the financial statements are not presented fairly in conformity with GAAP. Disclaimers and adverse opinions are not interchangeable; the former are based on a lack of knowledge whereas the latter are based on knowledge. It is rare for an enterprise to be willing to accept the practical consequences of preparing and publishing financial statements that as a whole are believed by the auditor to be false and misleading; therefore, adverse opinions are very rarely found in practice.

Qualified opinions state that "except for" or "subject to" the effect of a specified matter, the financial statements are presented fairly in conformity with GAAP. A qualified opinion would be used in the following circumstances, provided that the auditor believed that the financial statements taken as a whole were otherwise presented fairly in conformity with GAAP:

1. There is a lack of sufficient competent evidence or there are restrictions on the scope of the examination that preclude expressing an unqualified opinion. (Example: In accordance with the terms of the engagement, the auditor did not examine records supporting the client's investment in a foreign company or its equity in that company's earnings.)
2. Significant uncertainties that affect the financial statements but are not susceptible of reasonable estimation have not been resolved as of the date of the auditor's report. (Example: A lawsuit against the enterprise is unresolved and the likelihood of an adverse resolution is greater than remote.)

3. The financial statements contain a departure from GAAP, the effect of which is material. (Examples: The enterprise excluded from its balance sheet lease obligations that, to conform with GAAP, should have been classified as capital leases and capitalized; the enterprise declined to disclose the basis of valuing inventories or of depreciating plant and equipment.)

4. There was a material change in an accounting principle or in the method of applying it between periods. (Example: During the current year, the client changed from the last-in, first-out method to the first-in, first-out method for determining the cost of its inventories.)

In the second circumstance listed, the auditor's qualification should use the words "subject to." In the other three cases, the expression "except for" or its equivalent should appear. The auditor's decision on whether to issue a qualified opinion on the one hand or a disclaimer of opinion or an adverse opinion on the other is grounded in materiality considerations that are discussed in Chapter 18.

In all reports that do not contain an unqualified opinion (other than a qualified opinion occasioned by a change in accounting principle), the auditor should disclose the reason for the qualification, disclaimer, or adverse opinion in a separate explanatory paragraph of the report and should refer to that separate paragraph in the opinion paragraph. If a qualified opinion or disclaimer of opinion results from a scope limitation or from the insufficiency of audit evidence, the situation should be referred to in the scope paragraph as well as in the opinion and explanatory paragraphs.

Summary. Figure 1.2 summarizes this section of the chapter on the auditor's report. Note that only one type of qualification is possible for each condition described; similarly, each condition leads to either a disclaimer or an adverse opinion, but not both, if the circumstance giving rise to the qualification is sufficiently material. The only exception occurs when the auditor is not independent. In that circumstance, an audit in accordance with generally accepted auditing standards was not performed and a disclaimer of opinion is the only appropriate response.

An Overview of an Audit of Financial Statements

An audit is based on a single premise: The auditor's objective is to understand the subject matter under examination in sufficient detail and depth to express an informed opinion on it. Every step in the audit process should enhance that understanding. The process of performing a financial statement audit is expanded on throughout this book. The steps in that process are described briefly in this section and summarized in Figure 1.3.

Figure 1.2 Summary of Departures from Unqualified Reports

Conditions Requiring a Departure	Materiality Dimension		
	Immaterial	Material, but Overall Statements Are "Presented Fairly"	So Material That Overall "Fairness" of Statements Is in Doubt
Auditing Related			
Scope limitation (imposed by client or by other circumstances)	Unqualified report	Qualified scope ("except as") Explanatory paragraph Qualified opinion ("except for")	Qualified scope ("except as") Explanatory paragraph Disclaimer of opinion
Uncertainties not susceptible of reasonable estimation	Unqualified report	Explanatory paragraph Qualified opinion ("subject to")	Explanatory paragraph Qualified opinion ("subject to") (Disclaimer of opinion permissible but not required)
Auditor not independent	Auditor disclaims opinion whenever not independent.		
Accounting Related			
Departure from GAAP	Unqualified report	Explanatory paragraph Qualified opinion ("except for")	Explanatory paragraph Adverse opinion
Change in accounting principle	Unqualified report	Explanatory paragraph Qualified opinion ("except for")	Not applicable

Figure 1.3 Summary of the Audit Process for Audits of Financial Statements

---

1. Information-Gathering Phase:
- Obtain (or update) and document information about the client and related risk factors.
- Understand and document principal features of the internal control system.

---

2. Planning Phase:
- Make preliminary materiality judgments and assess the risk that various management assertions may be materially misstated.
- Select and document the appropriate audit strategy for each account balance or group of account balances.

---

3. Performance Phase:
- Obtain, evaluate, and document evidence to corroborate whether the management assertions embodied in account balances and financial statement disclosures are reasonable.
- Revise audit strategy as appropriate.

---

4. Reporting Phase:
- Prepare auditor's report on financial statements.
- Prepare letter to management on internal controls.

---

1. Obtain (or, for a continuing client, update) and document information about the client and consider how that information may affect the audit strategy.

This step consists, among other things, of learning about the client's business and matters affecting the business or the industry in which it operates and about the client's accounting systems; internal accounting controls; accounting policies, practices, and methods; operations; organization; management policies and practices; business and control environments; and legal constraints. The auditor obtains that information through review of prior-year working papers and research in business and professional publications and publications of the client enterprise, such as annual reports and news releases; through interviews of knowledgeable client, audit firm, and other personnel; by plant and office tours; by reviewing the client's procedures and policy manuals; by reading the minutes of meetings of the board of directors and the stockholders; and by studying and comparing relationships among various financial and operational data gathered for audit planning purposes. The information obtained (or updated) by the auditor is used to make preliminary judgments about materiality, assess the risk that certain management assertions may be materially misstated, and anticipate where reliance on the client's internal controls may be both desirable and feasible.

2. Plan and document an effective and efficient audit strategy.

An effective audit provides the auditor with the reasonable level of assurance required under generally accepted auditing standards for the purpose of expressing an opinion on financial statements. That level of assurance should limit to an appropriately low level the risk that the auditor may unknowingly issue an unqualified opinion when the financial statements are materially misstated. The audit should also be designed to provide the auditor with the desired level of assurance most efficiently, that is, at the lowest practicable cost. Planning the audit to achieve those ends requires the auditor to assess the risk of material misstatement associated with each of management's assertions and then choose an audit strategy that is effective in light of those risks and, among equally effective alternatives, the most efficient. Audit planning is not confined solely to the early stages of an audit, but is an ongoing process that may result in changes to the audit strategy as additional knowledge that warrants a reassessment of various risks is obtained in the course of the audit.

The audit strategy specifies the nature, timing, and extent of audit procedures to be carried out in assessing risks and in obtaining and evaluating the audit evidence that forms the basis for expressing an opinion on financial statements. The nature of audit procedures refers to the kinds of work the auditor performs to assess risks or to obtain and evaluate evidence—such as confirming balances due from customers; timing refers to when in the audit the risks are assessed or the evidence is examined—either before the end of the client's accounting year or after year-end; the extent of audit procedures refers to how much of any kind of work—for example, the number of customers' accounts to be confirmed—the auditor performs for the purpose of formulating a judgment about each management assertion embodied in the financial statements.

3. Obtain, evaluate, and document sufficient competent evidence to corroborate whether the management assertions embodied in individual account balances and in the financial statements as a whole, including the disclosures, are reasonable.

That evidence consists of information derived from the auditor's risk assessments, including the study and evaluation of the client's system of internal control, and information underlying the auditor's conclusions about the reasonableness of management's assertions embodied in specific account balances. The extent to which the auditor seeks to rely on the client's internal controls as a basis for restricting direct tests of account balances is determined, and specified in the audit strategy, based on the auditor's risk assessments and professional judgment as to an effective and efficient way of obtaining the desired level of assurance about the financial statements as a whole.

In the course of studying and evaluating the client's system of internal control and obtaining and evaluating evidence regarding account balances, the auditor may find that the audit strategy needs to be revised. Audit procedures are interrelated; the study and evaluation of the client's internal controls provides a basis for assessing the risk that account balances may be materially misstated, and obtaining and evaluating evidence for assurance about account balances may reveal inadequacies in the client's system of internal control. It is only after all of the steps in the audit have been completed that the auditor can reach a conclusion regarding the opinion that should be expressed on the financial statements as a whole. Therefore, tentative conclusions reached during the earlier stages of an audit may have to be revised, and the audit strategy initially contemplated or preliminary judgments about materiality may have to be changed, based on the results of subsequent audit procedures.

4. Formulate and prepare the auditor's report and communicate weaknesses and breakdowns in the system of internal control to the client.

This is the reporting phase of an audit, and it results in two reports: the auditor's report on the financial statements discussed earlier and the "management letter" on suggested improvements in the system of internal control. Although the auditor's report is the primary objective of an audit, the management letter provides a useful and relatively inexpensive client service, which auditors are particularly well qualified to perform after developing an understanding of the business and studying and evaluating the system of internal control for audit purposes.

The auditor must apply significant judgment throughout the audit process just described. How the interrelationships among auditing procedures require the auditor to make certain decisions has already been explained. The need for other decisions arises at every stage of the audit. All of these decisions require the exercise of judgment; they cannot be made by rote or by formula. Merely saying that every decision about the type of audit procedure to perform, when to perform it, and how extensively to apply it requires judgment severely understates the number of judgments necessary on even the smallest audits. Decisions about audit strategy are based on the auditor's risk assessments, considering knowledge obtained about the client's business and its system of internal controls; the audit strategy in turn determines the nature, timing, and extent of audit procedures. Judgment is needed in planning and performing those assessments and tests and in evaluating the results. The assessments made and the evidence obtained enable the auditor to exercise judgment in making the ultimate audit decision—the type of opinion to render on the financial statements.

Review Questions[8]

1-1. The terms accounting, auditing, and financial reporting are often mistakenly used interchangeably. Define and contrast these three terms.

1-2. Compare and contrast the responsibilities of enterprise management and of the auditor regarding financial statements.

1-3. What are some examples of established criteria against which assertions can be measured in various types of audits?

1-4. How do auditors communicate their results to interested users in financial audits? Give examples of interested users.

1-5. What are some of the limitations of a financial audit?

1-6. Why is the term ''auditor's certificate'' imprecise?

1-7. What are the four major types of reports that can be given under generally accepted auditing standards? Explain how they differ.

1-8. Nature, timing, and extent of audit tests and procedures are specified in the audit strategy. What objectives does an audit strategy seek to accomplish?

1-9. Obtaining and evaluating evidence is the essence of auditing. What does audit evidence consist of in a financial audit? What are some of the difficulties encountered in evaluating audit evidence?

1-10. In recent years the relative importance of the two aspects of auditing has shifted from the gathering of audit evidence to interpreting facts and evaluating accounting judgments. Why has this shift occurred?

1-11. What is a management letter (internal control letter) and what purpose does it serve?

1-12. What are the steps involved in every financial statement audit?

Discussion Questions

1-30. Many people believe that auditing is an exact science, using standard procedures that are applied by rote. Do you agree or disagree? State why.

1-31. Feiler, the sole owner of a small hardware business, has been told that the business should have financial statements reported on by an independent CPA. Feiler, having some bookkeeping experience, has personally prepared the company's financial statements and does not understand why such statements should be examined by a CPA. Feiler discussed the matter with Farber, a CPA, and asked Farber to explain why an audit is considered important.

  Required:
  a. Describe the objectives of an independent audit.
  b. Identify the ways in which an independent audit may be beneficial to Feiler.

  (AICPA adapted)

[8]See *Preface to College Version* for an explanation of the numbering system used for end-of-chapter questions and problems.

1-32. A CPA's report on financial statements includes an opinion on whether the statements are presented in conformity with generally accepted accounting principles. In evaluating the general acceptability of an accounting principle, the CPA must determine whether the principle has substantial authoritative support.

Required:

  a. Describe the procedure that the CPA should follow in forming an opinion on whether to accept an accounting principle proposed by a client for use in preparing the current year's financial statements. Assume that the principle has been consistently applied.
  b. Cite primary sources and authorities that the CPA might consult in determining whether an accounting principle has substantial authoritative support. (A source is primary if it is sufficient evidence by itself to constitute substantial authoritative support.)
  c. Cite secondary sources and authorities that the CPA might consult in determining whether an accounting principle has substantial authoritative support. (A source is secondary if it must be combined with one or more other secondary sources to constitute substantial authoritative support.)

(AICPA adapted)

1-33. The following two statements are representative of attitudes and opinions sometimes encountered by CPAs in their professional practice:

  1. Today's audit consists of test checking. This is a dangerous practice because test checking depends on the auditor's judgment, which may be defective. An audit can be relied on only if every transaction is verified.
  2. Audits by CPAs are essentially negative and contribute to neither the gross national product nor the general well-being of society. Auditors do not create; they merely check what someone else has done.

Required:
Evaluate each of the above statements and indicate

  a. Areas of agreement with the statement, if any.
  b. Areas of misconception, incompleteness, or fallacious reasoning included in the statement, if any.

Complete your discussion of each statement (both parts a and b) before going on to the next statement.

(AICPA adapted)

1-34. On completion of the examination of a client's financial statements, the CPA must either express an opinion or disclaim an opinion on the statements taken as a whole. The opinion may be unqualified, qualified, or adverse.

Required:

  a. Under what general conditions may a CPA express an unqualified opinion on a set of financial statements?
  b. Define and distinguish among (1) a qualified opinion, (2) an adverse opinion, and (3) a disclaimer of opinion on the statements taken as a whole.

(AICPA adapted)

AICPA Multiple Choice Questions

These questions are taken from the Auditing part of Uniform CPA Examinations. Choose the single most appropriate answer.

1-40. The essence of the attest function is to

    a. Detect fraud.

    b. Examine individual transactions so that the auditor may certify as to their validity.

    c. Determine whether the client's financial statements are fairly stated.

    d. Assure the consistent application of correct accounting procedures.

1-41. Which of the following is responsible for the fairness of the representations made in financial statements?

    a. Client's management.

    b. Independent auditor.

    c. Audit committee.

    d. AICPA.

1-42. The first standard of reporting requires that "the report shall state whether the financial statements are presented in accordance with generally accepted accounting principles." This should be construed to require

    a. A statement of fact by the auditor.

    b. An opinion by the auditor.

    c. An implied measure of fairness.

    d. An objective measure of compliance.

Problems and Cases

1-60. On completion of all field work on September 23, 1987, the following "short-form" report was rendered by Timothy Ross to the directors of The Rancho Corporation.

To the Directors of The Rancho Corporation:

We have examined the balance sheet and the related statement of income and retained earnings of The Rancho Corporation as of July 31, 1987. In accordance with your instructions, a complete audit was conducted.

In many respects, this was an unusual year for The Rancho Corporation. The weakening of the economy in the early part of the year and the strike of plant employees in the summer of 1987 led to a decline in sales and net income. After making several tests of sales records, nothing came to our attention that would indicate that sales have not been properly recorded.

In our opinion, with the explanation given above, and with the exception of some minor errors that are considered immaterial, the aforementioned financial statements present fairly the financial position of The Rancho Corporation at July 31, 1987, and the results of its operations for the year then ended, in conformity with pronouncements of the Accounting Principles Board and the Financial Accounting Standards Board applied consistently throughout the period.

Timothy Ross, CPA
September 23, 1987

Required:

List and explain deficiencies and omissions in the auditor's report. The type of opinion (unqualified, qualified, adverse, or disclaimer) is of no consequence and need not be discussed.

Organize your answer by paragraph (scope, explanatory, and opinion) of the auditor's report.

(AICPA adapted)

1-61. Roscoe, CPA, has completed the examination of the financial statements of Excelsior Corporation as of and for the year ended December 31, 1986. Roscoe also examined and reported on the Excelsior financial statements for the prior year. Roscoe drafted the following report for 1986:

March 16, 1987

We have examined the balance sheet and statements of income and retained earnings of Excelsior Corporation as of December 31, 1986. Our examination was made in accordance with generally accepted accounting standards and accordingly included such tests of the accounting records as we considered necessary in the circumstances.

In our opinion, the financial statements mentioned above are accurately prepared and fairly presented in accordance with generally accepted accounting principles in effect at December 31, 1986.

Roscoe, CPA
(Signed)

Other Information:

- Excelsior is presenting comparative financial statements.
- Excelsior does not wish to present a statement of changes in financial position for either year.
- During 1986, Excelsior changed its method of accounting for long-term construction contracts and properly reflected the effect of the change in the current year's financial statements and restated the prior year's statements. Roscoe is satisfied with Excelsior's justification for making the change. The change is discussed in footnote 12.
- Roscoe was unable to perform normal accounts receivable confirmation procedures but alternate procedures were used to satisfy Roscoe about the validity of the receivables.

- Excelsior Corporation is the defendant in a litigation, the outcome of which is highly uncertain. If the case is settled in favor of the plaintiff, Excelsior will be required to pay a substantial amount of cash, which might require the sale of certain fixed assets. The litigation and the possible effects have been properly disclosed in footnote 11.
- Excelsior issued debentures on January 31, 1985, in the amount of $10,000,000. The funds obtained from the issuance were used to finance the expansion of plant facilities. The debenture agreement restricts the payment of future cash dividends to earnings after December 31, 1991. Excelsior declined to disclose these essential data in the notes to the financial statements.

Required:

a. Identify and explain any items included in "Other Information" that need not be part of the auditor's report.
b. Explain the deficiencies in Roscoe's report as drafted. (Do not rewrite the report.)

(AICPA adapted)

Chapter 2
The Organization and Structure of the Auditing Profession

Although the focus of this book is on financial audits, the definition of auditing is sufficiently broad to encompass other types of audits that serve other purposes. This chapter discusses compliance and operational audits as well as financial audits, and relates them to the various groups of auditors who perform them. It also describes the typical organization of a firm of CPAs and outlines the major organizations of the auditing profession, the certification and licensing systems in effect, and the auditing pronouncements issued by the various standard-setting bodies.

Types of Audits and Auditors

Financial Audits. In a financial audit, the assertions about which the auditor seeks evidence relate to financial and, occasionally, operating information. The key concepts in a financial audit are that the assertions are financial in nature and that the established criteria against which they are measured are generally accepted accounting principles or some other specified basis of accounting (such as might be stipulated in a rental agreement). Generally, the information will be used by parties other than the management of the entity that prepares it. Sometimes, however, the information is intended to be used primarily by management for internal decision-making purposes; in that event, it may include operating as well as financial data. While financial audits are generally associated with independent auditors whose work results in an opinion on financial statements, both internal auditors and government auditors also perform financial audits, often in conjunction with compliance or operational audits.

Compliance Audits. Compliance audits are intended to determine whether an entity has complied with specified policies, procedures, laws, regulations, or contracts that affect operations or reports. Examples of compliance audits include the audit of a tax return by an Internal Revenue Service agent, the audit of components of financial statements to determine compliance with a bond indenture, the audit of the expenditures of a researcher performing under a government grant to determine compliance with the terms of the grant, and the audit of an entity's hiring policies to determine the extent of compliance with the Equal Employment Opportunity Act. As with all audits, a compliance audit requires the existence of established criteria against which the relevant assertions can be measured. Compliance audits are performed by independent auditors (generally as part of an audit of financial statements) and by internal and government auditors (often as part of an operational audit).

If a policy, contract, law, or regulation has an effect on an entity's financial statements, determining the extent of compliance with the policy, contract, law, or regulation will usually be an integral part of an audit of the financial statements. For example, an auditor reviews an enterprise's conformity with the restrictive covenants in a long-term bond indenture to ascertain that a violation of the covenant has not made the entire bond issue due and payable at the lender's option, which might require that the debt be reclassified as a current liability. Independent auditors do not, however, as part of an ordinary examination of financial statements, evaluate an enterprise's compliance with policies, contracts, laws, and regulations unless there is a potential effect on the financial statements.

Operational Audits.   An operational audit may encompass evaluating some or all of the following:

1. Internal controls, including those that safeguard assets;
2. Compliance with laws, regulations, and company policies;
3. The reliability and integrity of financial and operating information;
4. The economical and efficient use of resources; and
5. The achievement of established objectives and goals for operations or programs.[1]

The first three elements listed are usually considered aspects of financial and compliance audits, and are not discussed further in this section. The last

[1]Adapted from *Standards for the Professional Practice of Internal Auditing.* The Institute of Internal Auditors, Inc., 1978.

two, which are unique to operational audits, are further elaborated on here.

The economical use of resources refers to the ability to achieve a specified level of output or performance at the lowest possible cost. An enterprise that met or exceeded the specified level at the lowest cost would be using its resources most economically. The efficient use of resources relates to the attainment of the highest possible level of output or performance at a certain cost. The ability to increase output or performance without incurring additional costs implies that a more efficient use of resources is possible. The achievement of established objectives and goals refers to the extent to which the desired benefits or *results* of an operation or program are accomplished. Results that are consistent with established objectives and goals indicate that the operation or program is being carried out effectively.

Objectives and goals may be established by federal or state legislatures or granting agencies or they may be set by management of an enterprise. As noted in Chapter 1, to be auditable the objectives and goals must be quantifiable. They may not always relate to economic actions and events, however, which raises the question of whether their evaluation falls within the definition of auditing. For example, in an ''audit'' of the effectiveness of program results in a state's prison system, program objectives and goals will almost surely not be stated in terms of economic actions or events; instead, they are likely to be stated in terms of the number of prisoners rehabilitated and released, the number of repeat offenders, or the percentage of prison capacity utilized. While operational audits of program results may at times stretch the definition of auditing, they are widely performed, particularly by government auditors, and are almost always referred to as audits.

Audits of economy and efficiency involve determining whether

1. Operating standards have been established for measuring economy and efficiency.
2. Established operating standards are understood and are being met.
3. Deviations from operating standards are identified, analyzed, and communicated to those responsible for corrective action.
4. Corrective action has been taken.[2]

Audits of the accomplishment of established objectives and goals for operations or programs involve ascertaining whether such ''objectives and goals conform with those of the organization and whether they are being met.''[3] These kinds of audits focus on controls instituted for managerial decision making.

Types of Auditors. A popular classification of auditors uses three categories: independent, internal, and government. Independent auditors are also referred to as external auditors, and frequently as ''CPAs,'' public accountants, or ''outside'' auditors. Independent auditors practice as sole practitioners or

[2]*Ibid.*, Standard No. 340.
[3]*Ibid.*, Standard No. 350.

are employees or partners in accounting firms. Implicit in the concept of independence is that independent auditors are never owners or employees of the organization that retains them to perform an audit (their client), although they receive a fee from the client for their audit services. Independent auditors perform audits of financial statements to meet the needs of investors and creditors and the requirements of regulatory bodies such as the Securities and Exchange Commission (SEC), which result in an opinion on the degree to which the financial statements conform to generally accepted accounting principles. Occasionally, they perform compliance audits that are not part of an audit of financial statements and, to a lesser extent, operational audits.

Internal auditors are employed by the enterprise whose activities they audit. The Institute of Internal Auditors has defined internal auditing as "an independent appraisal function established within an organization to examine and evaluate its activities as a service to the organization. The objective of internal auditing is to assist members of the organization in the effective discharge of their responsibilities. . . . The internal auditing department is an integral part of the organization and functions under the policies established by management and the board [of directors]."[4] The primary function of internal auditors is examining and evaluating the adequacy and effectiveness of their organization's system of internal control. In performing that function, internal auditors often conduct primarily operational audits that are broadly designed to accomplish financial and compliance audit objectives as well as the specific operational audit objectives of evaluating economy, efficiency, and program results, discussed earlier.

The independence of internal auditors is different from that of independent, external auditors. The independence of internal auditors comes from their organizational status—essentially, the level of management to whom they report—and their objectivity. For external auditors, independence derives from the absence of any obligation to or financial interest in their client, its management, or its owners.

Government auditors are employed by agencies of federal, state, and local governments. When the audit is of the government agency or department that employs them, they function as internal auditors; when they audit recipients of government funds (including other government agencies), they act as external auditors. For example, auditors employed by the U.S. Department of Agriculture may audit the internal operations of that department; they may also audit the economy, efficiency, and program results of research funded by the Department of Agriculture but performed by others, such as colleges and universities. Government auditors perform primarily operational audits of economy, efficiency, and program results, although their work may also involve compliance audits. Some audits performed, such as those by the Internal Revenue Service, are almost exclusively for compliance purposes.

There are many different groups of government auditors; virtually every

[4]*Ibid.*, p. 1.

level of government and every government agency has its own auditors. One group in particular warrants further discussion—the General Accounting Office (GAO). A nonpolitical agency headed by the Comptroller General of the United States, it was created by and reports directly to Congress. The GAO has the authority to audit virtually every federal agency and expenditure. The GAO formulated the notion of and standards for audits of economy, efficiency, and program results, which account for the major part of its activities.

As suggested by the foregoing discussion, the work performed by "independent," "internal," and "government" auditors is not mutually exclusive. There is considerable overlap in the types of audits they perform, and characterizing the three groups is difficult. All possess varying degrees of independence. This book uses the terms *independent*, *internal*, and *government auditors* to refer to the three groups, acknowledging that those words do not do full justice to the three branches of the auditing profession.

The Organization of an Accounting Firm

Accounting firms range in size from an individual CPA in business as a sole practitioner to large international firms with hundreds of offices worldwide and thousands of partners and employees. In between these two extremes are countless small and medium-sized firms employing varying numbers of professional accountants. In general, the larger firms offer a broader scope of services to clients than do the smaller ones. The majority of medium-sized and large accounting firms are multicapability firms, meaning that they serve clients in several major practice areas—among them, accounting and auditing, taxation, management consulting, and actuarial, benefits, and compensation consulting. Although the structure of the firms varies with their size and the areas in which they practice, some generalizations can be made about the services typically offered by the majority of small, medium-sized, and large accounting firms.

Auditing Services. The largest and most basic practice area of a CPA firm is accounting and auditing and consists primarily of performing independent audits of companies' financial statements, leading to the expression of an opinion on their conformity with generally accepted accounting principles. Chapter 1 discussed the objectives of audits of financial statements; the remainder of this book explores the theory of auditing, sets up a framework for viewing the entire audit process, and describes how an audit is performed.

A number of audit-related services are generally offered to clients, either in conjunction with an audit or as separate engagements. One of these services is the issuance of a management letter containing recommendations for improvements in internal control and other matters of concern to the client, such as comments on operating efficiencies and profitability. As additional examples of audit-related services, accounting firms often perform acquisition audits of other entities for clients that are contemplating acquiring those entities, and they also issue debt compliance letters on a client's compliance with the covenants of debt instruments.

As part of their audit and audit-related services to clients, most firms provide specialized knowledge in certain areas, most notably EDP auditing. They do this by employing professionals who have a combination of auditing knowledge gained from formal education and on-the-job training and specialized skills and capabilities. In the area of EDP auditing, for example, a firm may establish a separate group composed of auditors who have specialized data processing skills and experience. These computer professionals are assigned to audit teams (described subsequently) to enhance the team's ability to audit clients' computerized systems effectively and efficiently. Many accounting firms also offer expertise in various specialized industries and types of business, such as emerging and privately held businesses, which have special characteristics and needs.

Compilation and Review Services. CPAs also perform compilation and review services. A compilation consists of presenting information in the form of financial statements without expressing any opinion on the statements. A review consists of applying certain limited procedures to financial statements to enable the reviewer to express limited assurance that there are no material modifications that should be made to them. Compilation and review services for nonpublic entities were defined by the American Institute of Certified Public Accountants (AICPA) in 1978 in the first of a series of Statements on Standards for Accounting and Review Services (SSARSs). Those statements resulted from the AICPA's recognition of the need for professional services that are less than an audit, but that provide some assurance about the reliability of a nonpublic entity's financial statements. The SSARSs establish guidelines for performing and reporting on compilation and review engagements. Compilations and reviews are discussed further in Chapter 19.

Other Services. A major service provided by accounting firms is in the area of taxation—tax and business planning and compliance services offered to corporations, other businesses, and individuals. Tax services offered to businesses by accounting firms cover a broad spectrum, encompassing preparing consolidated tax returns, planning merger or acquisition approaches, minimizing state and local taxes, reviewing tax returns for compliance with applicable laws and regulations, structuring operations to take advantage of tax opportunities, and advising on international tax matters and other aspects of taxation. Services to individuals include tax, financial, and estate planning.

A firm's tax practice often embraces one or more special service groups that address complex issues related to taxation. For instance, some accounting firms maintain support groups composed of senior tax professionals who monitor new tax laws, regulations, rulings, cases, and other related developments and communicate this specialized knowledge to the rest of the firm. Many firms employ lawyers and engineers to advise clients on tax aspects of various transactions. Other groups may be established to provide tax services relating to state and local tax matters; mergers, acquisitions, divestitures, sales of businesses, and related financing transactions; specialized industries that are affected by legislative, regulatory, and judicial proceedings; and international tax developments that concern multinational clients.

Management consulting services (MCS), sometimes called management advisory services, are offered in several diversified areas, such as planning, finance, inventory and supply, transportation, computers, and manpower. For example, professionals working in the MCS practice area of an accounting firm may undertake work and make recommendations to client management in one or more of the following areas:

- Designing and implementing management information systems in both the public and private sectors.
- Establishing long-range strategic planning programs.
- Improving materials controls, from consumer goods sales forecasting to manufacturing planning and control.
- Developing data processing strategy, including long-range planning, equipment and software evaluation and selection, telecommunication network and security evaluation, and planning.
- Analyzing and improving administration—organization, methods, procedures, productivity, and controls.

Actuarial, benefits, and compensation consulting services professionals employed by accounting firms function as advisors to clients in endeavors such as the following:

- Planning executive compensation arrangements, conducting salary surveys, and devising wage programs.
- Designing pension and profit-sharing plans, performing annual actuarial valuations, and implementing medical, life, and disability insurance programs.
- Communicating benefits and compensation policies to employees.
- Developing benefits and compensation administration systems.
- Determining compliance with government reporting requirements.

Those consultants may also provide technical support to audit engagement teams.

Firm Structure. It is difficult to generalize about the organization of accounting firms because each one has its own structure and no two are exactly alike. Some multioffice firms are organized by groups or regions, with one partner designated overall responsibility for the practice offices in each group or region. The group or regional partners may report to a number of vice chairmen or other designated partners. Each practice office is headed by a partner, often called the managing partner or partner in charge of the office, who is responsible for day-to-day operations. Within each practice office, there may be separate units for auditing, tax, MCS, and perhaps one or more specialized practice areas. In addition to professional personnel, each practice office may have an administrative staff to meet such needs as personnel management, including recruiting, and to support the office's accounting and reporting function.

In addition to their practice offices, many accounting firms have a number of specialized departments, usually organized as part of a national office, established to provide support to the practice on a firmwide basis. Examples of such resource groups are industry specialization, marketing and planning, professional education, and accounting and auditing policy setting, research, and consulting. Firms that practice in different countries are further organized under an international structure usually governed by a committee of representatives from the various member firms.

The Audit Engagement Team. Each audit is staffed by a team headed by an engagement partner who signs the audit report and is ultimately responsible for the audit and its results. Especially on large or complex engagements, there may be more than one partner or the partner may delegate many functions to one or more managers; however, the engagement partner retains responsibility for the quality of the audit and thus should be actively involved in planning the audit and evaluating the results, as documented and summarized by the members of the engagement team. The team usually includes a manager (or more than one on a large engagement), one or more in-charge accountants (sometimes called supervisors), and anywhere from a few to a large number of staff accountants. Although the exact titles vary among firms, all firms have established staff classifications through which employees progress. Firms also have policies that set forth the responsibilities of audit personnel on each staff level. While these also vary from one firm to another, it is possible to describe generally the typical functions and duties of each audit staff classification.

Manager. Under the direction of a partner, a manager is responsible for administering all aspects of an engagement, including planning and coordinating activities with client personnel, delegating duties to team members, coaching them, supervising and reviewing their work, controlling engagement time and expenses, and overseeing billings and collections. A manager is expected to have attained a degree of technical competence in accounting and auditing sufficient to ensure that an audit complies with all applicable professional and firm standards. Specifically, a manager is responsible for, among other things, reviewing the management letter, reviewing the financial statements first in draft form and then in final form, reviewing the documentation of the engagement, reviewing proposed changes in the audit program, and keeping the engagement partner informed of all significant developments throughout the audit.

In-Charge Accountant. An in-charge accountant (sometimes called an ''in-charge'') is responsible, under the manager's direction, for the overall quality, timeliness, and efficiency of the field work in an audit. This involves assisting the manager in audit administration matters during the planning phase of the engagement as well as during and after the field work. During the field work, the in-charge is responsible for understanding the client's business, industry, and systems, evaluating internal controls, reviewing working papers prepared by other staff members, drafting the management letter and the proposed audit report, and preparing a summary of audit findings for submission to the engagement partner.

Staff Accountant. A staff accountant (sometimes there is more than one level of staff accountant, determined by a person's audit experience) is responsible for completing assigned tasks on an engagement, under the supervision of the in-charge. Staff assignments, which vary with the size and complexity of the engagement, generally include preparing documentation of the understanding of the client and its accounting systems and internal controls, performing various types of audit tests and documenting the results, and keeping the in-charge informed of all findings.

The Audit Staffing Pyramid. The numbers of engagement team members at the various staff levels are commonly viewed as forming a pyramid. This ''staffing pyramid'' expresses the concept that there are generally more staff accountants than any other classification on an engagement team, with proportionately fewer people at each succeeding level of responsibility and one partner, with ultimate responsibility for the conduct of the audit, at the top. The shape of the staffing pyramid varies both by the size and organization of the accounting firm and by the circumstances of the client's business and industry. For example, on multilocation, technically complex engagements, there may be several in-charge accountants with differing amounts of experience; the less experienced individuals will be assigned responsibility for specific aspects of the field work, under the supervision of a more experienced in-charge who will direct the overall field work. The specific needs of the engagement, as determined by the client's operations and industry, also affect the shape of the staffing pyramid. For instance, if the audit work includes extensive detailed testing, such as counting securities or confirming customers' accounts receivable, a larger number of staff accountants may be necessary than on an engagement in which detailed testing is limited.

The Organization of the Auditing Profession

The auditing profession has formed numerous groups with various purposes, among them the AICPA, state societies or institutes of CPAs, and The Institute of Internal Auditors, all of which have broadly based memberships. In addition, there are more specialized organizations of government auditors, computer auditors, teachers of auditing, and internal auditors with particular industry interests.

American Institute of CPAs. More than half of the AICPA's approximately 240,000 members, who are required to be CPAs, are in public practice either with CPA firms or as sole practitioners. The AICPA provides a broad range of services to members, including continuing professional education, technical accounting and auditing assistance, auditing standards, and self-regulation of the profession.

Ultimate authority over the AICPA is vested in its Council. Its resources are administered and policy is set by its 21-member Board of Directors, which includes three non-Institute members who represent the public. Pronouncements in the form of technical and ethical standards are issued by senior technical committees composed of Institute members in public practice and, to some extent, in industry, government, and academe. The Institute's bylaws authorize six senior technical committees to make public statements, in some cases in the form of authoritative pronouncements, on matters related to their areas of practice, without clearance by Council or the Board of Directors. Those six senior technical committees and the public statements they issue are shown in Figure 2.1.

In addition, the AICPA has four voluntary membership divisions. Three of them are for individual members with a special interest in tax, management advisory services, or personal financial planning. The fourth is the Division for CPA Firms.

Through its Continuing Professional Education Division, the AICPA provides programs that cover a wide range of technical and professional subjects of interest to members in public practice, business, teaching, and government. The Institute also publishes the *Journal of Accountancy* and *The Tax Adviser* monthly, which are available to nonmembers as well as members; several newsletters of interest to practicing members; and numerous pamphlets, reports, and studies. The Institute's Board of Examiners prepares, administers, and grades the semiannual CPA examinations. Through its Professional Ethics Division, the AICPA issues interpretations of the Rules of Conduct of the Code of Professional Ethics, investigates complaints against members regarding unethical practices, and assists in the investigation and presentation of ethics cases referred to the AICPA Trial Board. The examination and disciplinary processes are intertwined with those of the state societies, state boards of accountancy, and the Institute's Division for CPA Firms.

State Societies of CPAs. In addition to belonging to the AICPA, most CPAs belong to a state society of CPAs. The purpose of the state societies is to improve the profession and help their members better serve the public interest. To accomplish this, the state societies offer their members continuing professional education courses, provide consultation services, maintain liaison with members of state legislatures and relevant administrative agencies of state governments, publish professional journals, clarify and enforce professional technical and ethical standards, and provide other services to members, such as various types of group insurance. Members of a state society are automatically

Figure 2.1 AICPA Senior Technical Committees and Their Public Statements

Senior Technical Committee	*Titles of Public Statements Issued*
Accounting and Review Services Committee	Statements on Standards for Accounting and Review Services[a]
	Accounting and Review Services Interpretations
	Statements on Standards for Attestation Engagements[a]
Accounting Standards Executive Committee	Statements of Position
	Issues Papers
	Practice Bulletins
Auditing Standards Board	Statements on Auditing Standards[a]
	Auditing Interpretations
	Statements on Standards for Attestation Engagements[a]
	Statements on Standards for Accountants' Services on Prospective Financial Information[a]
	Notices to Practitioners
Federal Taxation Executive Committee	Statements on Responsibilities in Tax Practice[b]
Management Advisory Services Executive Committee	Statements on Standards for Management Advisory Services[a]
Professional Ethics Executive Committee	Interpretations of Rules of Conduct[a]
	Ethics Rulings

[a]The Rules of Conduct of the AICPA Code of Professional Ethics and implementing resolutions of Council require that AICPA members must comply with standards contained in these pronouncements; departures therefrom must be justified by those members who do not follow them.
[b]As discussed on page 48, these statements have been withdrawn by the AICPA.

members of a specific chapter located within the state, which holds meetings on a regular basis and coordinates its activities with those of the state society.

The Institute of Internal Auditors. The Institute of Internal Auditors (IIA) was formed in 1941 to promote the professionalism and education of internal auditors. The organization now has more than 29,000 members in over 150 chapters throughout the world. The Institute actively sponsors training seminars, conferences, research, and books and other publications, including a monthly professional journal entitled *The Internal Auditor*. A professional staff of 75 provides management continuity for the Institute and services the needs of members. Individual members set Institute policy and promote leadership at the chapter level and through membership on the Institute's International Board of Directors and other committees. The IIA offers a certification program leading to the professional designation of Certified Internal Auditor (CIA). IIA achievements include codification of ethics, development of professional standards, and identification of a conceptual common body of practitioner knowledge.

Other Organizations. Auditors with specialized interests have formed various organizations, usually with more precisely defined objectives than the broadly based AICPA and IIA. Among those groups are computer, insurance company, government, and bank auditors. Members of the American Accounting Association who are interested in auditing research and teaching have established an Auditing Section of the Association, which publishes *Auditing: A Journal of Theory and Practice*. Membership in some of these organizations is limited to auditors practicing in a specific field or industry.

Professional Certification and Licensing

The main professional designations relating to the practice of auditing are "Certified Public Accountant," "Certified Internal Auditor," and "Certified Information Systems Auditor."

Certified Public Accountant (CPA). The semiannual, two and one-half day CPA examination is prepared by the Board of Examiners of the American Institute of Certified Public Accountants (AICPA) and is given uniformly throughout the United States in May and November. Only individuals who pass the written examination and meet the educational and experience requirements of their state governmental authorities are granted a license to practice by the state and are entitled to use the designation "Certified Public Accountant" or "CPA." The CPA certificate is granted to qualified candidates to ensure the professional competence of those who offer their services to the public as professional accountants.

The examination in all states consists of at least the following four parts:

- Accounting Theory—designed to test conceptual knowledge of accounting.
- Business Law—designed to test knowledge of legal problems inherent in business transactions and accounting and auditing implications of those problems, including auditors' legal liability.
- Auditing—designed to test knowledge of professional responsibilities, auditing standards and procedures, and standards relating to nonauditing services provided by CPAs.
- Accounting Practice—designed to test a candidate's ability, judgment, and knowledge in applying accounting concepts, authoritative accounting pronouncements, cost accounting concepts, and federal tax accounting principles and procedures.

Some states may require candidates to take additional tests in other subjects that are not part of the uniform examination.

The Uniform CPA Examination and Advisory Grading Service of the AICPA are used by all state boards of accountancy. Even though the papers are graded by the AICPA, the state boards are responsible for the quality, composition, and grading of the examination and for licensing individuals, and thus may review the Institute's grading. Educational and experience requirements differ from state to state, even though all states use the same examination. Although in some states individuals receive a CPA certificate on passing the examination, most states require a period of experience before they issue a license to practice.

Additional information concerning a state's regulations and requirements can be obtained from the following sources:

- The appropriate state education department or state board of accountancy.
- National Association of State Boards of Accountancy, 545 Fifth Avenue, New York, New York 10017.
- American Institute of Certified Public Accountants, 1211 Avenue of the Americas, New York, New York 10036.
- The appropriate state society of certified public accountants.

Publications that may be of assistance concerning the CPA examination and state accountancy laws include

- *Information for CPA Candidates*, published by the American Institute of Certified Public Accountants.
- *Digest of State Accountancy Laws and State Board Regulations*, published by the National Association of State Boards of Accountancy and the AICPA.
- *Accountancy Law Reporter*, published by Commerce Clearing House.
- Listing of the State Boards of Accountancy, published by the National Association of State Boards of Accountancy.

Certified Internal Auditor (CIA). The Certified Internal Auditor examination measures the technical competence of individuals as it relates to the practice of internal auditing. The test is administered by the Board of Regents of The Institute of Internal Auditors (IIA). The IIA's Director of Certification is responsible for preparing, administering, and grading the examination within the guidelines established by IIA's Board of Regents and Board of Directors. The Certified Internal Auditor Program is open to internal auditors and others who have the required professional qualifications. The certificate provides professional recognition to the holder, but it does not include a license to practice. States do not license CIAs, as they do not offer their services to the public.

Additional information relating to the work experience and educational requirements for the CIA examination can be obtained by writing to The Institute of Internal Auditors, Inc., 249 Maitland Avenue, P.O. Box 1119, Altamonte Springs, Florida 32701.

Certified Information Systems Auditor (CISA). In 1979, the EDP Auditors Foundation engaged Educational Testing Service to develop a certification examination for Certified Information Systems Auditor (CISA) to test the individual's knowledge and skills in the various fields of EDP auditing. The EDP Auditors Foundation appointed a Certification Board to supervise and control the program and the content of the test. The CISA program is also one of professional recognition rather than state licensure.

Additional information about the work experience and educational requirements for the CISA examination can be obtained by writing to the EDP Auditors Foundation, Inc., 373 South Schmale Road, Carol Stream, Illinois 60188.

Professional Standards and Standard-Setting Bodies

Auditing standards, in the broadest sense, are guidelines for performing professionally responsible audits. The AICPA, IIA, and General Accounting Office have all formulated auditing standards to guide their members.

Generally Accepted Auditing Standards. The membership of the AICPA has approved and adopted 10 broad statements collectively entitled "generally accepted auditing standards," often abbreviated as "GAAS." Nine of them were originally adopted in 1948 and have not changed basically since (although our understanding of several of them has changed significantly over the years). The tenth was adopted some years later, but the basic principle had existed before. Three of the standards are concerned with personal qualities that the auditor should possess (general standards), three with how an audit should be conducted (field work standards), and four with the form and content of the auditor's report (reporting standards). The 10 GAAS are discussed in detail in Chapter 3; they are listed in Figure 2.2 on pages 46 and 47 (where they are compared with the AICPA's attestation standards).

The authority to amplify and interpret the 10 original generally accepted auditing standards resides in a senior technical committee of the AICPA. From 1939 to 1972, that committee was called the Committee on Auditing Procedure and issued 54 pronouncements called Statements on Auditing Procedure. The Committee on Auditing Procedure was replaced in 1972 by the Auditing Standards Executive Committee, and in 1978 the Auditing Standards Board was formed to succeed the Executive Committee and is now responsible for the promulgation of auditing standards and procedures to be observed by AICPA members in accordance with the Institute's Rules of Conduct. The pronouncements of the Auditing Standards Executive Committee and the Auditing Standards Board are called Statements on Auditing Standards (SASs) and are intended to define the nature and extent of auditors' responsibilities and provide guidance to auditors in carrying out their duties. From 1972 to July 31, 1986, the two committees issued 51 Statements on Auditing Standards. While statements issued by the three committees are technically amplifications and interpretations of the 10 original GAAS, they and the 10 GAAS are frequently referred to collectively as generally accepted auditing standards.

In addition to issuing SASs, the Auditing Standards Board approves for publication Auditing Interpretations of the SASs; the Interpretations are prepared by the staff of the Auditing Standards Division of the AICPA. As they are issued, Statements on Auditing Standards, Auditing Interpretations, and other AICPA professional standards are incorporated in the AICPA's looseleaf service, *Professional Standards*, which results in a continuous codification of those pronouncements. Once a year, a bound version of the latest *Professional Standards* is published for Institute members by the AICPA and for non-Institute members by Commerce Clearing House.

In an effort to promote international uniformity in auditing, the International Auditing Practices Committee (IAPC) of the International Federation of Accountants (IFAC) issues guidelines on generally accepted auditing practices and audit reports. The guidelines are not authoritative in the way AICPA professional standards are in the United States, but IAPC members have agreed to work toward implementation of the provisions of the guidelines to the extent practicable. Twenty-three international guidelines have been issued through July 1986; for the most part, their provisions conform with comparable U.S. GAAS. Thus, if a guideline is issued that deviates significantly from GAAS, the Auditing Standards Board considers ways of resolving the differences.

The Role of the SEC and the Courts in Setting Auditing Standards. The various federal acts that the Securities and Exchange Commission (SEC) administers give it broad powers. Those powers probably include promulgating auditing standards and may extend even to prescribing specific steps to be followed by auditors of financial statements filed with the Commission. The Commission has, however, adopted the general policy of relying on the public accounting profession to establish auditing standards, largely in response to the profession's willingness to address issues that the SEC deems significant. The policy stated by the Commission in 1940 in Accounting Series Release No. 19 continues to be effective:

> Until experience should prove the contrary, we feel that this program is preferable to its alternative—the detailed prescription of the scope of and procedures to be followed in the audit for the various types of issuers of securities who file statements with us—and will allow for further consideration of varying audit procedures and for the development of different treatment for specific types of issuers.

This is not to suggest that the SEC has not or will not influence the development of auditing standards. Indeed, it has done so on several occasions and is likely to continue doing so. That influence takes essentially two forms: stimulating the Auditing Standards Board to issue a pronouncement when the Commission believes one is needed (as occurred with SAS No. 36, *Review of Interim*

Financial Information [AU Section 722]) and informing the Auditing Standards Board of its views during the standard-setting process. The Auditing Standards Board must continually acknowledge the presence of the SEC throughout its deliberations, but must not sacrifice the independence and objectivity that are essential to its standard-setting function.

Despite numerous opportunities to interpret auditing standards when auditors have been the subject of litigation, only rarely have the courts failed to apply the auditing standards of the profession. In cases in which the courts have applied lay standards, they have done so primarily in areas involving reporting standards. Conformity with promulgated professional auditing standards generally has been an effective defense for auditors.

Standards for an Expanded Attest Function. In March 1986, the AICPA's Auditing Standards Board and its Accounting and Review Services Committee jointly issued Statement on Standards for Attestation Engagements, *Attestation Standards*, the first in a new series of statements. The Statement defines an attestation (often referred to as an attest) engagement as "one in which a practitioner is engaged to issue or does issue a written communication that expresses a conclusion about the reliability of a written assertion that is the responsibility of another party." The attestation standards provide guidance and establish a broad framework for performing and reporting on attest services generally. While the standards do not supersede any existing SASs or other authoritative standards, they are a natural extension of the 10 GAAS. Because of their breadth, the attestation standards can serve as a basis for establishing interpretive standards that would apply to a wide range of services in the future, while at the same time setting reasonable boundaries around the attest function. The 11 attestation standards are listed and compared with the 10 GAAS in Figure 2.2.

Attest services traditionally were limited to expressing an opinion about historical financial statements on the basis of an audit conducted in accordance with GAAS. Increasingly, however, CPAs are expressing opinions about many other kinds of representations, such as those about internal control systems, prospective financial information, historical occupancy data for hospitals, and the characteristics of particular computer software. In giving opinions on those and a myriad of other representations, CPAs were at times able to look for guidance either to SASs or to other authoritative pronouncements, such as SSARSs, that addressed standards for nonaudit engagements or to apply the concepts underlying GAAS. As the range of attest services grew, however, it became increasingly difficult to look for guidance to the existing 10 GAAS and the SASs that interpret them.

The Statement specifies several conditions that must be present for an attest service to be performed. The *practitioner* must be independent, have adequate knowledge of the subject matter, and have adequate training and proficiency in the attest function. The *assertions* being attested to must be capable of being evaluated against reasonable measurement and disclosure criteria and of

Figure 2.2 Attestation Standards Compared with Generally Accepted Auditing Standards

---

Attestation Standards	*Generally Accepted Auditing Standards*
General Standards	
1. The engagement shall be performed by a practitioner or practitioners having adequate technical training and proficiency in the attest function.	1. The examination is to be performed by a person or persons having adequate technical training and proficiency as an auditor.
2. The engagement shall be performed by a practitioner or practitioners having adequate knowledge in the subject matter of the assertion.	
3. The practitioner shall perform an engagement only if he or she has reason to believe that the following two conditions exist: • The assertion is capable of evaluation against reasonable criteria that either have been established by a recognized body or are stated in the presentation of the assertion in a sufficiently clear and comprehensive manner for a knowledgeable reader to be able to understand them. • The assertion is capable of reasonably consistent estimation or measurement using such criteria.	
4. In all matters relating to the engagement, an independence in mental attitude shall be maintained by the practitioner or practitioners.	2. In all matters relating to the assignment, an independence in mental attitude is to be maintained by the auditor or auditors.
5. Due professional care shall be exercised in the performance of the engagement.	3. Due professional care is to be exercised in the performance of the examination and the preparation of the report.
Standards of Fieldwork	
1. The work shall be adequately planned and assistants, if any, shall be properly supervised.	1. The work is to be adequately planned and assistants, if any, are to be properly supervised.
	2. There is to be a proper study and evaluation of the existing internal control as a basis for reliance thereon and for the determination of the resultant extent of the tests to which auditing procedures are to be restricted.

Figure 2.2 *Continued*

2. Sufficient evidence shall be obtained to provide a reasonable basis for the conclusion that is expressed in the report.

3. Sufficient competent evidential matter is to be obtained through inspection, observation, inquiries, and confirmations to afford a reasonable basis for an opinion regarding the financial statements under examination.

Standards of Reporting

1. The report shall identify the assertion being reported on and state the character of the engagement.

2. The report shall state the practitioner's conclusion about whether the assertion is presented in conformity with the established or stated criteria against which it was measured.

1. The report shall state whether the financial statements are presented in accordance with generally accepted accounting principles.

2. The report shall state whether such principles have been consistently observed in the current period in relation to the preceding period.

3. Informative disclosures in the financial statements are to be regarded as reasonably adequate unless otherwise stated in the report.

3. The report shall state all of the practitioner's significant reservations about the engagement and the presentation of the assertion.

4. The report on an engagement to evaluate an assertion that has been prepared in conformity with agreed-upon criteria or on an engagement to apply agreed-upon procedures should contain a statement limiting its use to the parties who have agreed upon such criteria or procedures.

4. The report shall either contain an expression of opinion regarding the financial statements, taken as a whole, or an assertion to the effect that an opinion cannot be expressed. When an overall opinion cannot be expressed, the reasons therefor should be stated. In all cases where an auditor's name is associated with financial statements, the report should contain a clear-cut indication of the character of the auditor's examination, if any, and the degree of responsibility he is taking.

Source: Statement on Standards for Attestation Engagements, *Attestation Standards*, AICPA, March 1986.

being reasonably and consistently estimated or measured using those criteria. The Statement permits two levels of assurance that can be reported for public distribution when an attest service is performed—positive assurance on the basis of an examination and negative assurance on the basis of a review. When expressing a positive opinion, the practitioner states a conclusion about whether the assertions are presented in conformity with established or stated criteria. In providing negative assurance, the practitioner states only whether information has come to his or her attention that indicates that the assertions are not presented in conformity with those criteria. The Statement also provides for attest services based on agreed-upon procedures or agreed-upon criteria, but the report must be restricted to the parties that agreed to the procedures or criteria.

Standards for Tax Practice. The AICPA's Tax Division had issued Statements on Responsibilities in Tax Practice, which provided guidance on tax practice and accountants' responsibilities in this area. They were not as authoritative as SASs since they were not enforceable under the Rules of Conduct of the AICPA Code of Professional Ethics. Those standards have been withdrawn by the AICPA; at the time of this writing, the Institute's Federal Taxation Executive Committee is considering a new set of statements in this series.

Standards for MAS Practice. In 1981, the AICPA's Management Advisory Services Executive Committee issued Statement on Standards for Management Advisory Services (SSMAS) No. 1, which defines two types of management advisory services—MAS engagements and MAS consultations—and sets forth a number of general and technical standards for MAS practice. Two subsequent statements provide guidance on the application of the standards in SSMAS No. 1 and establish additional standards. Compliance with the MAS standards is required under the Code of Ethics. The MAS general and technical standards, adapted from *AICPA Professional Standards* MS Sections 11.05, 11.06, and 31.11, are summarized in Figure 2.3.

Standards of Internal Auditing. The Institute of Internal Auditors in 1978 adopted a series of *Standards for the Professional Practice of Internal Auditing.* Those standards address the independence of internal auditors, their professional proficiency, the scope and performance of their work, and the management of internal auditing departments. The IIA standards differ somewhat in their philosophy from the AICPA standards for external auditors in that the former represent the practice of internal auditing as it *should be*, whereas to a large extent Statements on Auditing Standards represent the Auditing Standards Board's view of the consensus among practitioners—what is "generally accepted." That difference should not be exaggerated, however; the IIA Standards are also a consensus, but of the best of practice rather than of what is minimally acceptable. The IIA also periodically issues Statements on Internal Auditing Standards to provide guidance on issues of interest to internal auditors.

Standards of Government Auditing. The General Accounting Office, the largest employer of government auditors in the United States, has issued a set of *Standards for Audit of Governmental Organizations, Programs, Activities, and Functions*, popularly referred to as the "Yellow Book." The standards were first published in 1972 and have been revised twice since then, most recently in 1981. At the time of this writing, the GAO is considering again revising the Yellow Book, principally to clarify the existing standards. Adherence to the

Figure 2.3 Standards for MAS Practice

General Standards:

Professional competence. A member shall undertake only those engagements which he or his firm can reasonably expect to complete with professional competence.

Due professional care. A member shall exercise due professional care in the performance of an engagement.

Planning and supervision. A member shall adequately plan and supervise an engagement.

Sufficient relevant data. A member shall obtain sufficient relevant data to afford a reasonable basis for conclusions or recommendations in relation to an engagement.

Forecasts. A member shall not permit his name to be used in conjunction with any forecast of future transactions in a manner that may lead to the belief that the member vouches for the achievability of the forecast.

Technical Standards:

Role of MAS practitioner. In performing an MAS engagement (consultation), an MAS practitioner should not assume the role of management or take any positions that might impair the MAS practitioner's objectivity.

Understanding with client. An oral or written understanding should be reached with the client concerning the nature, scope, and limitations of the MAS engagement (consultation) to be performed.

Client benefit. Since the potential benefits to be derived by the client are a major consideration in MAS engagements (consultations), such potential benefits should be viewed objectively and the client should be notified of reservations regarding them. In offering and providing MAS engagements (consultations), results should not be explicitly or implicitly guaranteed. When estimates of quantifiable results are presented, they should be clearly identified as estimates and the support for such estimates should be disclosed.

Communication of results. Significant information pertinent to the results of an MAS engagement (consultation), together with any limitations, qualifications, or reservations needed to assist the client in making its decision, should be communicated to the client orally or in writing.

---

standards is required for audits of federal organizations, programs, activities, functions, and funds received by contractors, nonprofit organizations, and other external entities. The GAO recommends that the standards be followed for state and local government audits performed by government auditors or CPAs, and several state and local audit agencies have adopted them. The GAO standards incorporate the AICPA's auditing standards and are compatible with the standards issued by the IIA. Since government audits are usually concerned with economy, efficiency, and program results, the GAO standards cover these activities as well as financial and compliance audits. In 1977, the AICPA's Management Advisory Services Executive Committee published guidelines for independent auditors' participation in government audit engagements, which acknowledged that audits performed in accordance with GAO standards have a broader scope than audits performed in accordance with GAAS.

. The GAO standards define three elements of the scope of audit work: financial, compliance, and economy, efficiency, and program results. In addition, the standards encompass general standards, including independence and due professional care, and field work and reporting standards for the three elements of audits identified. The introduction to the standards notes that an audit of a government entity may include all three elements or only one or two of them, and that the scope of a specific audit should be tailored to the needs of users of the results.

Review Questions

2-1. Audits can generally be classified into three types. How do they differ in their objectives?

2-2. Auditors can generally be classified into three types. What are they?

2-3. How does an internal auditor's independence differ from an external auditor's independence?

2-4. Describe several audit-related services that may be offered to clients.

2-5. Describe several nonaudit services that may be offered to clients.

2-6. What is an acquisition audit?

2-7. What is the major responsibility of the engagement partner and how is that responsibility met?

2-8. What are the responsibilities of an audit manager?

2-9. What are the responsibilities of an in-charge accountant?

2-10. What is the major responsibility of a staff accountant?

2-11. What is meant by the audit pyramid?

2-12. What types of services does the AICPA provide to its members?

2-13. Name the four parts of the CPA examination and describe what they are designed to test.

2-14. What is the responsibility of the Auditing Standards Board?

2-15. What are the 10 generally accepted auditing standards? Compare the 10 GAAS with the 11 attestation standards.

2-16. What is the SEC? Briefly describe its jurisdiction.

2-17. What is the purpose of state societies of CPAs and how do they accomplish their purpose?

2-18. What is the Institute of Internal Auditors and what do its standards address?

2-19. Who is responsible for administering the CIA examination?

2-20. What is the General Accounting Office? Describe its Yellow Book.

Discussion Questions

2-30. You are meeting with executives of Cooper Cosmetics Corporation to arrange your firm's engagement to examine the corporation's financial statements for the year ended December 31, 1986. One executive suggested that the audit work be divided among three audit staff members so that one person would examine asset accounts, the second would examine liability accounts, and the third would examine income and expense accounts to minimize audit time, avoid duplication of staff effort, and curtail interference with company operations.

   Required:

   a. To what extent should a CPA follow a client's suggestions for the conduct of an audit? Discuss.
   b. List and discuss the reasons why audit work should not be assigned solely according to asset, liability, and income and expense categories.

   (AICPA adapted)

2–31. Medium-sized and large accounting firms generally categorize their staffs as audit, tax, and management consulting services (including EDP). Some accounting firms also have an actuarial, benefits, and compensation consulting group.

   Required:

   a. Briefly describe the types of service each group would provide clients.
   b. Most audit engagements require that people from each of the firm's practice areas join the engagement team to assist in the audit. Describe the roles each of those groups could play (interacting with the auditors) in fulfilling the requirements of an audit.

2–32. In the early 1970s, the responsibility for setting *accounting* standards was transferred from the AICPA to the FASB. Furthermore, the SEC has often intervened directly in the accounting standard-setting process, particularly with respect to disclosure standards. The responsibility for setting *auditing* standards continues to rest with the AICPA, and although the SEC has the authority to do so, it has only rarely intervened directly in the auditing standard-setting process.

   Required:

   a. Discuss the pros and cons of transferring responsibility for setting auditing standards to an organization other than the AICPA.
   b. Why do you think the SEC has only rarely intervened directly in the auditing standard-setting process?

AICPA Multiple Choice Questions

These questions are taken from the Auditing part of Uniform CPA Examinations. Choose the single most appropriate answer.

2–40. A CPA certificate is evidence of

   a. Recognition of independence.
   b. Basic competence at the time the certificate is granted.
   c. Culmination of the educational process.
   d. Membership in the AICPA.

2–41. An individual just entering upon an auditing career must obtain professional experience primarily in order to achieve a

   a. Positive quality control review.
   b. Seasoned judgment.

       c. Favorable peer review.

       d. Specialty designation by the AICPA.

2-42. Governmental auditing often extends beyond examinations leading to the expression of opinions on the fairness of financial presentation and includes audits of efficiency, effectiveness, and

       a. Internal control.

       b. Evaluation.

       c. Accuracy.

       d. Compliance.

2-43. Operational audits generally have been conducted by internal auditors and governmental audit agencies but may be performed by certified public accountants. A primary purpose of an operational audit is to provide

       a. A means of assurance that internal accounting controls are functioning as planned.

       b. Aid to the independent auditor, who is conducting the examination of the financial statements.

       c. The results of internal examinations of financial and accounting matters to a company's top-level management.

       d. A measure of management performance in meeting organizational goals.

Chapter 3
Auditing Standards and Professional Ethics

All professions have technical and ethical standards to guide their members in carrying out their duties and in their relationships with the various groups with which they come in contact. Also, all professions have means for enforcing those standards. This chapter presents and elaborates on the auditing profession's—or, more specifically, the public accounting profession's—technical standards relating to the conduct of an audit (generally accepted auditing standards) and the ethical principles that guide members of professional auditing organizations in their working relationships with clients, colleagues, and the public. Compliance with the profession's technical standards and ethical principles is enforced through various mechanisms created by the AICPA and by state societies of CPAs, state boards of accountancy, the SEC, the courts, and accounting firms themselves, all of which are discussed below. The chapter concludes with a discussion of ways of enhancing auditor independence.

Auditing as a Profession

While various writers and organizations have different criteria for defining an activity as a profession, there seems to be widespread agreement that the following characteristics must be present:

1. Formal recognition of professional status by means of a license issued by a governmental body after admission standards have been met.
2. A body of specialized knowledge, usually acquired through formal education.
3. A code of ethics to provide standards of conduct, and a means of enforcing compliance with the ethical code.
4. Informal recognition and acceptance of professional status by the public and public interest in the work performed.
5. Recognition by the professionals of a social obligation beyond the service performed for a particular client.

There can be little doubt that auditing has the attributes necessary to qualify as a profession. In a majority of jurisdictions, the privilege of practicing as a public accountant is limited by the statutes of the various states and territories to those who have been granted the designation of Certified Public Accountant by a particular state or territory. The certification is granted only to those who have passed the CPA examination and, in many jurisdictions, who have also met specified educational and experience requirements. At least in part because the CPA examination is uniform throughout all licensing jurisdictions and because it has a well-deserved reputation of being difficult, the public has come to expect a high level of expertise in accounting and auditing from a person who is a CPA.

The specialized knowledge of accounting and auditing that an auditor must have is usually acquired through an academic program at the undergraduate level, the graduate level, or both. It is also acquired through on-the-job training and attendance at continuing education courses, sometimes to meet licensing or membership requirements of various bodies. For example, many states require an average of 40 hours of annual attendance at approved continuing education courses for CPAs to keep their license to practice; the membership requirements of the AICPA's Division for Firms also stipulate that member firms provide a similar level of professional education for their professional personnel.

As discussed later in this chapter, membership in the AICPA requires adherence to the Institute's Code of Professional Ethics. The Institute of Internal Auditors also has such a code, adherence to which is required of those internal auditors who have qualified as Certified Internal Auditors by virtue of having met examination, educational, and experience requirements. The AICPA's Code of Professional Ethics and its enforcement are designed to ensure that CPAs who are members of the AICPA accept and achieve a high level of responsibility to the public, clients, and colleagues.

It is apparent that the public considers public accountancy a profession. Universities have established schools and programs of professional accountancy, and a mechanism is in place for separate accreditation of those programs by the American Assembly of Collegiate Schools of Business (AACSB). There is a high level of public interest in the work performed by CPAs, particularly with regard to auditing services. Rarely is someone other than a CPA asked to attest to information of a financial nature or to other information that can be quantified.

Lastly, it is clear that the profession has long recognized an obligation to the public at large that extends well beyond the services performed for a particular client. While auditors realize that they have an obligation or responsibility to the client that has retained them, they are also aware that their audience is much larger; audited financial statements are read, used, and relied on by many other groups—present and potential investors and creditors, suppliers, employees, customers, and governmental agencies. Testimony before legislative bodies at all levels of government and other less formal recommendations regarding the tax laws, securities acts, and other relevant legislation have indicated a concern for the public interest that extends far beyond the parochial interests of auditors whose livelihood could be enhanced or diminished as a result of the proposed legislation. Often, the positions taken publicly on such matters conflict with the specific interests of one or more clients, but professionals should place the interests of the public ahead of their own or those of a particular client. Above all, however, CPAs have an awareness of a professional's responsibilities to the public at large, an awareness that is continually enhanced by the courts, the SEC, the AICPA, and other organizations, such as the Commission on Auditors' Responsibilities.

Generally Accepted Auditing Standards

Professions set technical standards to ensure a specified minimum quality of performance, primarily because those who hire professionals or benefit from their work are usually unable to judge the work for themselves—and this is undoubtedly true for the auditing profession. It is neither possible nor desirable to relieve auditors of their professional responsibility by establishing detailed rules for performing an audit; to do so would undermine the professional responsibility that standards are designed to safeguard. Nevertheless, standards should be carefully defined and articulated to give practitioners the clearest possible guidance. Standards set the minimum level of quality that auditors are expected, by their clients and the public, to achieve. In contrast to auditing procedures—which are steps to be performed and vary depending on factors that are unique to each audit, such as client size, industry, accounting system, and other circumstances—standards are measures of the quality of performance. Auditing standards should be unvarying over a wide spectrum of audit engagements over long periods of time.

The balance between the exercise of professional responsibility and the establishment of specific rules to guide professional conduct pervades every aspect of accounting and auditing. The auditing profession has clearly rejected the two extremes: On the one hand, ''cookbook'' rules are not and never will be sufficient to cover every possible combination of circumstances and thereby allow auditors to shed their responsibility to exercise professional judgment; on the other hand, a framework exists to provide guidance for the exercise of that judgment in all significant aspects of audit practice. It is between the extremes that tensions and controversies arise: for example, the question of how much uniformity should be required in auditing practice versus how much flexibility should be permitted, or the question of to what extent standard sample sizes and auditing procedures should be spelled out versus the extent to which the exercise of pragmatic judgments should be required. Although the specific subject matter of debate changes from time to time, it is likely that the philosophical debate itself will never be concluded. It should be noted that this same issue of rules versus individual judgment pervades most professions.

In this light, the membership of the AICPA officially adopted the 10 generally accepted auditing standards in 1948. AICPA pronouncements—Statements on Auditing Procedure and Statements on Auditing Standards—have amplified and interpreted the 10 GAAS. Fifty-four Statements on Auditing Procedure (SAPs) were issued between 1939 and 1972; 51 Statements on Auditing Standards (SASs) have been issued since then, and others are in draft. Statement on Auditing Standards No. 1 codified the 54 SAPs; updated codifications of SAPs and SASs that are still effective are issued annually by the AICPA.

Practitioners and others who need to understand auditors' work and reports should be thoroughly familiar with the SASs, for they constitute the authoritative professional auditing literature. The 10 generally accepted auditing standards—the source of all subsequent SAPs and SASs—are found in SAS No. 1 (AU Section 150 of *AICPA Professional Standards*), as follows:

General Standards

1. The examination is to be performed by a person or persons having adequate technical training and proficiency as an auditor.
2. In all matters relating to the assignment, an independence in mental attitude is to be maintained by the auditor or auditors.
3. Due professional care is to be exercised in the performance of the examination and the preparation of the report.

Standards of Field Work

1. The work is to be adequately planned and assistants, if any, are to be properly supervised.
2. There is to be a proper study and evaluation of the existing internal control as a basis for reliance thereon and for the determination of the resultant extent of the tests to which auditing procedures are to be restricted.
3. Sufficient competent evidential matter is to be obtained through inspection, observation, inquiries, and confirmation to afford a reasonable basis for an opinion regarding the financial statements under examination.

Standards of Reporting

1. The report shall state whether the financial statements are presented in accordance with generally accepted accounting principles.

2. The report shall state whether such principles have been consistently observed in the current period in relation to the preceding period.
3. Informative disclosures in the financial statements are to be regarded as
reasonably adequate unless otherwise stated in the report.
4. The report shall either contain an expression of opinion regarding the financial statements, taken as a whole, or an assertion to the effect that an
opinion cannot be expressed. When an overall opinion cannot be expressed, the reasons therefor should be stated. In all cases where an auditor's name is associated with financial statements, the report should contain
a clear-cut indication of the character of the auditor's examination, if any,
and the degree of responsibility he is taking.

General Standards

The general standards relate to the qualifications of an auditor and the quality
of the audit work. They are personal in nature and are distinct from the standards governing the performance of field work and reporting.

Training and Proficiency. The first general standard suggests that the auditor must have proper education and experience in the field of auditing to meet
the requirements of the profession for adequate training and proficiency.
Training begins with formal education and continues with proper supervision
and review on the job, as well as formal continuing professional education.
Continuing education is a necessary part of this standard, especially as new developments in accounting, auditing, finance, data processing, taxes, and other
aspects of business management continue to force change on practitioners. The
need for formal continuing education, however, does not diminish the importance of on-the-job training, planned development of well-rounded experience,
and adequate supervision and review in maintaining proficiency.

Independence. The second general standard requires that the auditor not be
biased toward the client. Furthermore, to safeguard the confidence of the public and users of financial statements in the independence of auditors, auditors
must also be ''recognized'' as independent. SAS No. 1 (AU Section 220.03)
provides the following amplification of this:

> To *be* independent, the auditor must be intellectually honest; to be *recognized* as
> independent, he must be free from any obligation to or interest in the client,
> its management, or its owners. For example, an independent auditor auditing
> a company of which he was also a director might be intellectually honest, but it
> is unlikely that the public would accept him as independent since he would be
> in effect auditing decisions which he had a part in making. Likewise, an audi-
> tor with a substantial financial interest in a company might be unbiased in ex-
> pressing his opinion on the financial statements of the company, but the public
> would be reluctant to believe that he was unbiased. Independent auditors

should not only be independent in fact; they should avoid situations that may lead outsiders to doubt their independence.

The distinction drawn in this quotation is often referred to as that of "independence in fact" contrasted with "independence in appearance." The former—intellectual honesty—cannot be ensured by rules or prohibitions. The latter—avoiding potentially compromising situations—can be. To guard against any appearance or "presumption" of loss of independence, the AICPA has established specific rules on independence in its Code of Ethics, as discussed in the next section of this chapter. Likewise, the Securities and Exchange Commission has emphasized the importance of independence and has issued rules relating to it.

Due Care. SAS No. 1 (AU Section 230.04) notes that due care relates to what independent auditors do and how well they do it. Due care imposes a responsibility on each person in an auditing firm to exercise the skills he or she possesses with reasonable care and diligence; due care also requires critical review of the work done and of the judgments made. For example, due care is not exercised if the auditor fails to corroborate representations of client management that are significant to the financial statements, such as representations regarding the collectibility of old accounts receivable.

Standards of Field Work

The standards of field work cover planning and supervising the audit, evaluating internal control, and obtaining audit evidence.

Adequate Planning and Supervision. Planning an audit engagement encompasses both technical and administrative considerations. The technical aspect of planning entails formulating an overall audit strategy for the conduct and scope of the examination. Implementing the audit strategy encompasses numerous planning decisions of an administrative nature, such as decisions relating to scheduling the work, assigning personnel, and similar matters.

Audit planning is facilitated by early appointment of the independent auditor; a major advantage is the possibility of performing certain audit procedures during the year rather than at year-end. This increases both audit efficiency and the likelihood of identifying problems at an early date. In the initial planning stage, analytical reviews are often performed to aid in determining the nature, extent, and timing of other auditing procedures by identifying significant matters that should be addressed by the auditor.

SAS No. 22, *Planning and Supervision* (AU Section 311.09) states that supervision involves directing the work of assistants and determining whether the objectives of that work were accomplished. On many engagements, as much as one-fifth to one-fourth of the total audit time is spent on supervision. The time is usually considered well spent, because the total audit time is likely to be much greater without effective supervision.

Supervision starts with assigning tasks and ensuring that each task and its objectives are understood. It continues with frequent discussions between supervisor and assistants for the purpose of both keeping informed, especially about significant problems encountered, and providing ongoing advice and direction to assistants. That means discussions among the partner, manager, and staff members on an engagement; on large audits personal visits to many different groups and locations may be required. Supervision also entails dealing with differences of opinion among staff members concerning accounting and auditing issues. A final element of supervision is reviewing the completed work of assistants, discussing the review with them, and evaluating their performance.

Evaluating Internal Control. The importance of the second standard of field work has increased as internal control has become more sophisticated, as specialists have learned to construct computerized accounting systems that are highly reliable, and as auditors have become concerned with conducting efficient as well as effective audits. This standard requires the auditor to have a sufficient understanding of the client's system of internal control to adequately plan the tests of transactions and account balances to be performed; the standard does *not* require that the entire system of internal control, or even a part of it, be tested *unless* the auditor plans to rely on specific controls to restrict the testing of transactions and account balances. Subsequent chapters discuss the meaning of internal control, how it is studied and evaluated, and how that evaluation could affect the tests the auditor applies to the account balances and underlying transactions.

Obtaining Competent Evidence. A detailed understanding of the third standard of field work is important to all phases of auditing. The standard encompasses two main components, the "competence" of evidence and the "sufficiency" of evidence. The competence of evidence relates to its relevance and reliability; the sufficiency of evidence depends on the amount of assurance the auditor believes is needed to support an opinion that the financial statements are not materially misstated.

Standards of Reporting

Four standards of reporting govern this aspect of the audit effort.

Adherence to Generally Accepted Accounting Principles. The auditor is required first to be thoroughly familiar with generally accepted accounting principles, and second to determine whether the financial statements reported on "present fairly" the client's financial position, results of operations, and changes in financial position. Chapter 18, "The Auditor's Report," deals in depth with the auditor's reporting responsibilities relating to generally accepted accounting principles and fairness, and presents examples of appropriate auditors' reports in cases of departures from generally accepted accounting principles.

Consistent Application. The consistency standard requires the auditor to state explicitly in the audit report whether generally accepted accounting principles have been applied consistently from period to period; consistency within a period is presumed unless otherwise disclosed. The objective is to ensure either that changes in accounting principles do not materially affect comparability of financial statements between periods or that the effect is disclosed.

Adequate Disclosure. The intent of the third standard of reporting is that issuers of financial statements and auditors have a responsibility to ensure that disclosures are adequate, regardless of whether a specific authoritative pronouncement covers the matter. It is thus the auditor's responsibility to identify matters of potential interest to users of the financial statements and to form a conclusion about whether and how they should be disclosed. If the client does not make the necessary disclosures, the auditor must issue a qualified opinion.

Expression of Opinion. An auditor's report must be painstakingly precise in spelling out the opinion expressed. Leaving the meaning of an auditor's opinion open to readers' inferences is both inappropriate and dangerous. In some instances, an auditor's failure to state the reasons for disclaiming an opinion has permitted inferences that were either more or less favorable to a client than was warranted. In other instances, users of financial statements cited ambiguity in an auditor's report as grounds for claims against the auditor. From the time of its adoption, the fourth standard of reporting has been accompanied by detailed recommendations for reporting in all conceivable circumstances. This standard is the basis for those detailed prescriptions, which are intended to ensure that all auditors use precisely the same words in the same circumstances to prevent misinterpretation of their opinions and the responsibility they assume.

The AICPA Code of Ethics

The Code of Professional Ethics of the American Institute of Certified Public Accountants (AICPA) covers both the profession's responsibility to the public and the CPA's responsibility to clients and colleagues. While the AICPA Code is directly enforceable only against individual AICPA members, in reality its applicability is much more pervasive. Most of the significant portions of the Code have been adopted by the various state societies or institutes of CPAs and in many cases have also been incorporated into state statutes or the regulations of state boards of accountancy that license CPAs to practice before the public. In effect, all of these organizations enforce ethical behavior by CPAs.

Codes of ethical conduct are not unique to the practice of accounting. All professionals, including doctors, lawyers, and actuaries, to name a few, have deemed it essential to promulgate codes of ethics and to establish means for ensuring their observance. Such codes define the type of behavior that the public has a right to expect from the professionals, and thereby enhance the public's confidence in the quality of professional services rendered.

Most codes of ethics, including the AICPA's, contain general ethical principles that are aspirational in character and represent the objectives toward which every member of the profession should strive. The codes also usually contain a set of specific, mandatory rules that state the minimum level of conduct the professional must maintain to avoid being subject to disciplinary action. In the past, some sections of many codes of ethics have also had an ancillary effect of reducing competition, through prohibitions against advertising, solicitation of clients, and encroachment on the practice of a fellow professional. In recent years, however, the courts have deemed such prohibitions to be illegal. Accordingly, most professional associations, including the AICPA, have revised their codes to permit advertising and other forms of solicitation, so long as the professional does not seek to obtain clients by false, misleading, or deceptive advertising or other forms of solicitation.

The AICPA Code of Professional Ethics comprises four categories of ethical standards. The Introduction to the Code describes them as follows:

> The first, *Concepts of Professional Ethics*, is a philosophical essay approved by the professional ethics division. The essay suggests behavior which CPAs should strive for beyond the minimum level of acceptable conduct set forth in the Rules of Conduct and is not intended to establish enforceable standards.
>
> The second category, *Rules of Conduct*, consists of enforceable ethical standards and required the approval of the membership before the Rules became effective. The same is true of the Bylaws of the Institute.
>
> The third category, *Interpretations of Rules of Conduct*, consists of interpretations which have been adopted, after exposure to state societies and state boards, by the professional ethics division's executive committee to provide guidelines as to the scope and application of the Rules but are not intended to limit such scope or application. A member who departs from such guidelines shall have the burden of justifying such departure in any disciplinary hearing.
>
> The fourth category, *Ethics Rulings*, consists of formal rulings made by the professional ethics division's executive committee after exposure to state societies and state boards. These rulings summarize the application of Rules of Conduct and Interpretations to a particular set of factual circumstances. Members who depart from such rulings in similar circumstances will be requested to justify such departures.

Concepts of Professional Ethics

The Introduction to the Concepts of Professional Ethics emphasizes the professional's responsibility to the public, noting (in ET Section 51.01) that "a distinguishing mark of a professional is his acceptance of responsibility to the public." The Concepts of Professional Ethics also stress the CPA's responsibility to clients and colleagues. The Rules of Conduct set forth minimum levels of acceptable conduct, while the (higher) level of conduct for which CPAs should strive is embodied in the more philosophical Concepts of Professional Ethics. This philosophy is set forth in the Introduction (ET Section 51.06), as follows:

> It is in the best interests of the profession that CPAs strive for conduct beyond that indicated merely by prohibitions. . . . Rather [ethical conduct] requires unswerving commitment to honorable behavior, even at the sacrifice of personal advantage.

The five broad concepts, also called the "Ethical Principles," embodied in the Code are as follows (ET Section 51.07):

> *Independence, integrity and objectivity.* A certified public accountant should maintain his integrity and objectivity and, when engaged in the practice of public accounting, be independent of those he serves.
> *General and technical standards.* A certified public accountant should observe the profession's general and technical standards and strive continually to improve his competence and the quality of his services.
> *Responsibilities to clients.* A certified public accountant should be fair and candid with his clients and serve them to the best of his ability, with professional concern for their best interests, consistent with his responsibilities to the public.
> *Responsibilities to colleagues.* A certified public accountant should conduct himself in a manner which will promote cooperation and good relations among members of the profession.
> *Other responsibilities and practices.* A certified public accountant should conduct himself in a manner which will enhance the stature of the profession and its ability to serve the public.

A discussion of each of these concepts, along with the related Rules of Conduct, Interpretations, and Rulings, follows.

Independence, Integrity, and Objectivity

ET Section 52.01 states

> Independence has always been a concept fundamental to the accounting profession, the cornerstone of its philosophical structure. For no matter how competent any CPA may be, his opinion on financial statements will be of little value to those who rely on him—whether they be clients or any of his unseen audience of credit grantors, investors, governmental agencies and the like—unless he maintains his independence.

The significance of independence is indicated by the prevalence of the subject in the profession's authoritative literature. It is found not only in the Concepts of Professional Ethics and Rule 101 of the Rules of Conduct but also in the corresponding rules of professional conduct of the various state societies and state regulatory agencies; in SAS No. 1 (AU Section 220) (discussed in an earlier section of this chapter); in Statement on Quality Control Standards No. 1, *System of Quality Control for a CPA Firm* (QC Section 10); and in Rule 2-01 of Regulation S-X of the Securities and Exchange Commission.

The Concepts of Professional Ethics, ET Section 52.02, define independence as "the ability to act with integrity and objectivity." "Objectivity" is the ability to maintain an impartial attitude on all matters that come under the auditor's review. Rule 102—Integrity and objectivity (ET Section 102.01) of the Rules of Conduct states

> A member shall not knowingly misrepresent facts, and when engaged in the practice of public accounting, including the rendering of tax and management advisory services, shall not subordinate his judgment to others. In tax practice, a member may resolve doubt in favor of his client as long as there is reasonable support for his position.

Auditors, like practitioners in other professions, offer clients specialized technical skills and knowledge based on training and experience, but that is not all. Clients and others rely on auditors because they accept the auditors' professional integrity as an assurance that the auditors will do what is expected of them, using their skill and knowledge to the fullest and placing their clients' interest and the public interest ahead of their own. Professional integrity in any field ultimately depends on independence of mental attitude, that is, objectivity. In contrast to other professionals', auditors' independence and objectivity must be visible and explicit as well as underlying and implicit. Clearly, the published opinion of an auditor has little value unless it rests unquestionably on those qualities. They are personal, inward qualities not susceptible of objective determination or definition and are best maintained by the individual auditor's own conscience supported by the recognition that a professional's principal asset is a reputation for independence and integrity. It is also important to the public's confidence in an auditor's opinion that the individual's respect for those qualities be as apparent as possible.

The Code of Professional Ethics, as well as SAS No. 1, emphasizes *appearing* to be independent as well as *being* independent. The elusive and indefinable quality of independence has caused the accounting profession and the SEC to attempt to spell out detailed prohibitions, not only against those activities or relationships that might actually erode the mental attitude of independence but also against those that might even suggest or imply a possibility of lack of independence.

Parts of Rule 101 (ET Section 101.01) of the Rules of Conduct dealing with independence are quoted below.

Rule 101—Independence

A member or a firm of which he is a partner or shareholder shall not express an opinion on financial statements of an enterprise unless he and his firm are independent with respect to such enterprise. Independence will be considered to be impaired if, for example:

A. During the period of his professional engagement, or at the time of expressing his opinion, he or his firm
 1. (a) Had or was committed to acquire any direct or material indirect financial interest in the enterprise; or
    (b) Was a trustee of any trust or executor or administrator of any estate if such trust or estate had or was committed to acquire any direct or material indirect financial interest in the enterprise; or
 2. Had any joint closely held business investment with the enterprise or any officer, director, or principal stockholder thereof which was material in relation to his or his firm's net worth; or
 3. Had any loan to or from the enterprise or any officer, director, or principal stockholder thereof. This latter proscription does not apply to the following loans from a financial institution when made under normal lending procedures, terms, and requirements:
    (a) Loans obtained by a member or his firm which are not material in relation to the net worth of such borrower.
    (b) Home mortgages.
    (c) Other secured loans, except loans guaranteed by a member's firm which are otherwise unsecured.
B. During the period covered by the financial statements, during the period of the professional engagement, or at the time of expressing an opinion, he or his firm
 1. Was connected with the enterprise as a promoter, underwriter or voting trustee, a director or officer or in any capacity equivalent to that of a member of management or of an employee; or
 2. Was a trustee for any pension or profit-sharing trust of the enterprise.

Many of the foregoing prohibitions reach extremes that might appear ridiculous to a nonprofessional, but they reflect the profession's concern about the appearance of independence. For example, no partner in an auditing firm nor member of the partner's immediate family is permitted to own even one share of stock of a client or affiliated company or even to participate in an investment club that holds such shares, no matter what the individual's personal worth, the size of the company, or the partner's distance from the actual work of the audit. Some firms prohibit ownership of a client's stock by staff members as well, in some cases regardless of the office performing the audit. As another example, an auditing firm may not have its employees' pension fund managed by an investment counselor that also manages a mutual fund client; even though there is no actual financial relationship, there might be an appearance of lack of independence. In addition, the Interpretations and Ethics Rulings under Rule 101 outline specific prohibitions in this area.

Accounting Services. Interpretation 101-3 (ET Section 101.04) permits members to provide bookkeeping or data processing services to nonpublic audit clients only if the following requirements are met:

- There must be no relationship or conflict of interests between the CPA and the client that would impair the CPA's integrity and objectivity.
- The client's management must accept responsibility for the financial statements.

- The CPA must not assume the role of an employee or management of the client.
- In examining the financial statements, the CPA must comply with generally accepted auditing standards, i.e., must perform sufficient audit tests of statements prepared from records that the CPA has maintained or processed.

Family Relationships. Interpretation 101–4 (ET Section 101.05) addresses three categories of family relationships that may affect the independence of members. The first category comprises a member's spouse, dependent children, and any other relative living in the same household as or supported by the member. The financial interests and business relationships of such individuals are ascribed to the member and thus are governed by Rule 101 of the Rules of Conduct. The second category is close kin, defined as nondependent children, brothers and sisters, grandparents, parents, parents-in-law, and the spouses of any of those individuals. Close kin are not permitted to have a significant financial interest or investment in or business relationship with a client of a member, nor may they hold a responsible executive position, such as director or chief executive or financial officer, with a client. Finally, the financial interests and business relationships of remote kin, such as uncles, aunts, cousins, and so on, ordinarily are not ascribed to the member, unless other factors are present that indicate a closeness with the member.

Past-Due Fees. Ethics Ruling 52 (ET Sections 191.103–.104) addresses the effect of past-due fees on the independence of a member's firm. The Ruling states that independence may be impaired if more than one year's fees are unpaid when the member issues a report on the client's financial statements for the current year. (The reason for the ruling is that past-due fees may make it appear that the auditor is providing working capital for the client and that collecting the past-due fees may depend on the nature of the auditor's report on the financial statements.) The SEC rule on past-due fees is even more stringent; it provides that prior-year audit fees should be paid before the current-year engagement is begun.

General and Technical Standards

These rules of conduct require adherence to standards related to the conduct of the CPA's work.

General Standards. Rule 201 (ET Section 201.01) of the Rules of Conduct sets forth the following general standards:

> A member shall comply with the following general standards as interpreted by bodies designated by Council, and must justify any departures therefrom.
>
> A. Professional competence. A member shall undertake only those engagements which he or his firm can reasonably expect to complete with professional competence.

B. Due professional care. A member shall exercise due professional care in the performance of an engagement.

C. Planning and supervision. A member shall adequately plan and supervise an engagement.

D. Sufficient relevant data. A member shall obtain sufficient relevant data to afford a reasonable basis for conclusions or recommendations in relation to an engagement.

E. Forecasts. A member shall not permit his name to be used in conjunction with any forecast of future transactions in a manner which may lead to the belief that the member vouches for the achievability of the forecast.

Opinion Shopping. Interpretation 201-3 (ET Section 201.04) states that a member who is asked by another accountant's client for professional advice on an accounting or auditing technical matter should consult with the other accountant before providing such advice in order to be sure that the member is aware of all the available facts. The Interpretation also points out that the client and its accountant may have disagreed about the matter in question. When the client's purpose in seeking another professional opinion is to find an accountant willing to support a proposed accounting treatment that would favor a particular reporting objective but that is not necessarily in conformity with GAAP, the practice is commonly referred to as ''opinion shopping.'' The Auditing Standards Board has developed standards to be followed by an accountant who is asked to give an opinion on GAAP to another auditor's client (see discussion in Chapter 19). The SEC is also considering opinion-shopping situations and ways of improving public disclosure of them. The Commission has stated that an auditor's participation in opinion shopping impairs the auditor's appearance of independence.

Technical Standards. Rules 202 and 203 (ET Sections 202.01 and 203.01) are as follows:

Rule 202—Auditing Standards

A member shall not permit his name to be associated with financial statements in such a manner as to imply that he is acting as an independent public accountant unless he has complied with the applicable generally accepted auditing standards promulgated by the Institute. Statements on Auditing Standards issued by the Institute's Auditing Standards Executive Committee [succeeded in 1978 by the Auditing Standards Board] are, for purposes of this rule, considered to be interpretations of the generally accepted auditing standards, and departures from such statements must be justified by those who do not follow them.

Rule 203—Accounting Principles

A member shall not express an opinion that financial statements are presented in conformity with generally accepted accounting principles if such statements contain any departure from an accounting principle promulgated by the body designated by Council to establish such principles which has a material effect on the statements taken as a whole, unless the member can demonstrate that due to unusual circumstances the financial statements would otherwise have been misleading. In such cases his report must describe the departure, the approximate effects thereof, if practicable, and the reasons why compliance with the principle would result in a misleading statement.[1]

Rules 202 and 203 were adopted to require compliance with the profession's auditing standards and accounting principles. There is a strong presumption that adherence to such official rules would result in financial statements that are not misleading.

Rule 203 and Interpretation 203-1 (ET Sections 203.01 and .02) also recognize that occasionally there may be unusual circumstances in which the literal application of pronouncements on accounting principles would have the effect of rendering financial statements misleading. In such unusual cases, the proper accounting treatment is one that will render the financial statements not misleading. Chapter 18 discusses the appropriate wording of the auditor's report in these circumstances.

Responsibilities to Clients

The Concepts of Professional Ethics note that a CPA has responsibilities to clients as well as to the public. CPAs should serve their clients with competence and with regard for the clients' interests. They must also, however, maintain their obligation to the public as evidenced by their independence, integrity, and objectivity.

A fundamental responsibility of the CPA concerns confidentiality and conflict of interests. Rule 301 (ET Section 301.01) states that a member ". . . shall not disclose any confidential information obtained in the course of a professional engagement except with the consent of the client."

Need for Confidentiality. Both common sense and the independence concept dictate that the auditor and not the client should decide what information the auditor needs to conduct an effective audit. That decision should not be influenced by a client's belief that certain information is confidential. An efficient and effective audit requires that the client have the necessary trust in the auditor to be extremely candid in supplying information. Therefore, the client must be assured of confidentiality. and that, except for disclosures required by law, custom, and generally accepted accounting principles, information shared with the auditor will go no further without explicit permission.

[1]In 1973, Council of the AICPA designated the Financial Accounting Standards Board as the body to establish accounting principles. Accounting Research Bulletins and Opinions of the Accounting Principles Board that have not been superseded by the FASB also are covered by Rule 203; in 1986, standards promulgated by the Governmental Accounting Standards Board were added to the list of accounting principles covered by Rule 203.

Maintaining Confidentiality. At one time, auditors emphasized the need for confidentiality by imposing formal restrictions on their staffs. For example, staff members were not even supposed to tell their spouses where or for which clients they were working. The need to preserve confidentiality is now as great as ever, but this is usually achieved by constantly emphasizing to the staff the need for and ethics of maintaining a client's confidence. Auditors can usually gain access to otherwise restricted data by promising to keep the working papers in a separate, confidential file.

Despite the profession's emphasis on confidentiality, executives of some companies are concerned about losing control of sensitive material through an auditor's staff. They may believe that certain material is so sensitive that they cannot be comfortable with an auditor's general assurances about the character and training of the audit staff. If access to the material is necessary to the auditor's opinion, the client's executives have no alternative but to grant access; if they wish to limit that access to the auditor in charge, that condition should be respected. Although awareness of clients' sensibilities is important, the authors have observed that clients' fears generally tend to subside as the working relationship is strengthened and mutual confidence grows.

Confidentiality Versus Privilege. Except as noted earlier, communications between the client and the auditor are confidential; that is, the auditor should not reveal the information contained in the communication without the client's permission. Ordinarily, however, that information is not "privileged." Information is privileged if the client can prevent a court or government agency from gaining access to it through a summons or subpoena. Information given to an auditor by a client is generally not privileged; it is subject to summons or subpoena in most jurisdictions. (In those states where an auditor–client privilege does exist, its purpose is to enhance full and honest disclosure between client and auditor.) Auditors and their professional organizations generally support clients' legal resistance to summonses and subpoenas to produce documents or other communications given to or received from their auditors when it appears that there are legitimate reasons for maintaining confidentiality.

One particularly sensitive area involves the auditor's review of the client's analysis of the provision for income taxes. As a result of Internal Revenue Service subpoenas of auditors' tax provision working papers, and several lawsuits resulting from CPA firms' refusal to comply, many clients are reluctant to provide the auditor with such tax analyses. Regardless of a client's fears, however, the auditor must review sufficient evidential matter to reach the conclusion that the tax provision is adequate. Fortunately for the public as well as for the profession, the courts have placed significant limitations on the extent to which these working papers may be subpoenaed.

Insider Information. Auditors and their staffs have the same responsibilities as management for handling insider information: not to turn it to personal profit or to disclose it to others who may do so. Those responsibilities are clearly encompassed in the general injunctions of the Code of Professional Ethics: Independence forbids personal profit, and confidentiality forbids aiding others in that pursuit. The ways in which insider information may be used, even inadvertently, are many and subtle; society's heightened standards of accountability have focused attention on the responsibility of all insiders to use insider information only for the benefit of the enterprise.

Conflict of Interests.   Some clients' fears that secrets will be passed on to competitors are so great that they refuse to engage an auditor whose clients include a competitor; others are satisfied with assurances that the staff on their engagement has no contact with a competitor's personnel. The price paid by a client for so high a degree of confidentiality is the loss of industry expertise that can be provided by auditors who are familiar with more than one company in an industry. Experience suggests that the risk of leakage of information having competitive value is extremely slight.

A more difficult and quite common conflict of interests results if two of an auditor's clients do business with each other. For example, an auditor of a commercial bank is likely also to have clients among the bank's depositors and borrowers. Suppose the auditor observes the September 30th physical inventory of a company that is also a borrower at the client bank, and finds a substantial shortage. Under the terms of the company's loan agreement with the bank, audited financial statements are not due at the bank until the next March 31. The client understandably wants time to determine the cause of the shortage. What does the auditor do? This is a practical conflict of interests quite apart from problems of potential formal legal liability or expression of an opinion on either set of financial statements. On the one hand, the auditor must not use insider information from one client to profit by improving his or her relationship with the other client. On the other hand, it is absurd for the auditor to pretend not to know something that he or she does know. One party will be unhappy if the auditor does nothing; the other party will be upset if the auditor does anything.

The way out of the dilemma is clear in principle, though following it in practice may be difficult. Court cases have clarified the client's responsibility: As soon as a significant event—good or bad—happens, it should be disclosed to all concerned. Neither the client bank nor the client borrower has priority, and the incidental fact of their parallel relationship with the auditor should not affect the handling of the matter. The auditor's duty is to persuade the client borrower to make the necessary prompt disclosures—to the other party if it affects only the two, and publicly if it affects the public.

If the client's management refuses, the auditor must treat the incident as if it were a significant problem in the financial statements: The auditor must decide whether it is possible to continue to serve the client. Usually the auditor will consider going to the board of directors, and in some cases to the SEC and the stock exchanges, and to anyone else known to be affected. Those are very serious steps, and whether to take them is as weighty a decision as an auditor can ever be called on to make. But the auditor would risk even more serious problems by favoring a client over other concerned parties. The courts have made clear, as indicated by the *Fund of Funds*[2] case, discussed in Chapter 4, that an auditor who has reason to believe, from whatever source, that a client's financial statements are inaccurate cannot issue an unqualified opinion.

Another problem of confidentiality and conflict of interests may result if a client company that is considering the possibility of acquiring another company engages its own auditor to examine that company. What happens to the auditor's findings and to whom is the duty of confidentiality owed? Common practice in those circumstances is to obtain written confirmation from the chief executives of both companies regarding the extent and limitations of the auditor's responsibilities to each. Usually that confirmation approves delivering the findings to the acquiring company, but only after discussing them with the company to be acquired.

Contingent Fees. Rule 302 (ET Section 302.01) states that

> Professional services shall not be offered or rendered under an arrangement whereby no fee will be charged unless a specified finding or result is attained, or where the fee is otherwise contingent upon the findings or results of such services. However, a member's fees may vary depending, for example, on the complexity of the service rendered.

A professional relationship between an auditor and a client requires the auditor to charge a fee for services rendered. There is a presumption that the services will be performed in a competent manner and that the fee will not depend on audit findings or other contingencies. For example, specific Ethics Rulings prohibit fees as a percentage of a bond issue (ET Sections 391.015–.016), finder's fees based on a percentage of the acquisition price (ET Sections 391.017–.018), and fees as expert witness based on the amount awarded the plaintiff (ET Sections 391.019–.020).

Fees are not regarded as being contingent if fixed by courts or other public authorities or, in tax matters, if determined based on the results of judicial proceedings or the resolution of a controversy with governmental agencies. Although Rule 302 is explicit that in tax matters fees set as a result of judicial proceedings are not considered contingent, an Ethics Ruling (ET Sections 391.023–.024) states that basing a fee for tax services on the amount of tax savings to the client would violate Rule 302.

A proposal to change the contingent fee rule was considered and then rejected by Council of the AICPA on two separate occasions in 1984. Broadly, the proposal would have permitted contingent fees only from clients for whom no services were performed that required the CPA to be independent. Some

[2]*Fund of Funds, Ltd.* v. *Arthur Andersen & Co.*, 545 F. Supp. 1314 (S.D.N.Y. 1982).

opponents of the proposal maintained that it was too permissive and could impair the perception of the profession as independent and objective. Proponents, on the other hand, pointed to, among other reasons for supporting the change, AICPA counsel's opinion that the present rule is subject to legal challenge.

Responsibilities to Colleagues

While there are currently no specific Rules of Conduct governing a CPA's responsibility to colleagues, the Concepts of Professional Ethics set forth the fundamental principle of cooperation and good relations among members of the profession. ET Section 55.01 states that a CPA should "deal with fellow practitioners in a manner which will not detract from their reputation and well-being." Furthermore, in developing a practice, a CPA should not seek to displace another accountant in any way that reflects negatively on fellow practitioners. Thus, while competition among auditors is strong, an auditor's actions should nevertheless be governed by proper professional courtesy to colleagues.

Other Responsibilities and Practices

The final section of the Rules of Conduct addresses the ethical principle in the Code (ET Section 56) that states that the CPA should behave "in a manner which will enhance the stature of the profession and its ability to serve the public."

Acts Discreditable to the Profession. Rule 501 (ET Section 501.01) states: "A member shall not commit an act discreditable to the profession." Ethical Interpretations under Rule 501 provide examples of specific acts that would be discreditable to the profession:

1. Retention of client records after a demand is made for them;
2. Discrimination based on race, color, religion, sex, age, or national origin in hiring, promotion, or salary practices;
3. Failure to follow government audit standards, guides, procedures, statutes, rules, and regulations (in addition to generally accepted auditing standards) that may be specified in an audit of government grants, government units, or other recipients of government monies if an engagement has been accepted under those conditions; and
4. Negligence in the preparation of financial statements or records (thus explicitly including CPAs who are not in public practice and who serve as preparers rather than auditors of financial statements).

In addition to sanctions under Rule 501, the AICPA's bylaws provide for automatic termination of membership if a member is convicted of (1) a crime punishable by imprisonment for more than one year, (2) the willful failure to file any income tax return that he or she is required to file as an individual tax-payer, (3) filing a false or fraudulent income tax return on the member's own or a client's behalf, or (4) the willful aiding in the preparation and presentation of a false and fraudulent income tax return of a client.

Advertising and Solicitation. In response to a U.S. Supreme Court ruling (*Bates* v. *State Bar of Arizona*) that held that the Arizona Bar Association's restrictions on advertising were unconstitutional in that they violated the right of free speech guaranteed by the First Amendment to the U.S. Constitution, the AICPA in 1978 lifted the ban on advertising by accountants. One year later, the AICPA removed its prohibition against the direct solicitation of clients when it abolished Rule 401—"Encroachment." That Rule stated that "a member shall not endeavor to provide a person or entity with a professional service which is currently provided by another public accountant. . . ." In 1983, Rule 502 was amended to include the sentence, "Solicitation by the use of coercion, overreaching or harassing conduct is prohibited."

The present Rule 502 (ET Section 502.01) on advertising and solicitation is as follows: "A member shall not seek to obtain clients by advertising or other forms of solicitation in a manner that is false, misleading, or deceptive." Under Rule 502, all proper forms of advertising and promotion are permitted; there are no restrictions on the type of advertising media or frequency of placement. At the time the present rule was adopted, many expected the change to result in a flood of media advertising. Although some CPAs and CPA firms have sought to obtain clients by advertising their services in both local and national publications, the profession as a whole has been slow to make use of advertising, and solicitation of another CPA's client is usually done subtly.

Fees. The Concepts of Professional Ethics summarize the profession's attitudes toward adequate compensation. ET Sections 56.06 and .07 state

> In determining fees, a CPA may assess the degree of responsibility assumed by undertaking an engagement as well as the time, manpower and skills required to perform the service in conformity with the standards of the profession. He may also take into account the value of the service to the client, the customary charges of professional colleagues and other considerations. No single factor is necessarily controlling.
>
> Clients have a right to know in advance what rates will be charged and approximately how much an engagement will cost. However, when professional judgments are involved, it is usually not possible to set a fair charge until an engagement has been completed. For this reason CPAs should state their fees for proposed engagements in the form of estimates which may be subject to change as the work progresses.

Some auditors prefer to include in the "engagement letter" to management, information related to the estimated amount of the audit fee and when it is expected to be paid, as well as projected dates for delivering the audit report and other arrangements. Other auditors prefer to cover those matters in separate communications with the client.

Commissions. Rule 503 (ET Section 503.01) states

> A member shall not pay a commission to obtain a client, nor shall he accept a commission for a referral to a client of products or services of others. This rule shall not prohibit payments for the purchase of an accounting practice or retirement payments to individuals formerly engaged in the practice of public accounting or payments to their heirs or estates.

Interpretation 503-1 (ET Section 503.02) notes that Rule 503 was adopted to avoid a client's having to pay fees for which commensurate services were not received.

Incompatible Occupations. Rule 504 (ET Section 504.01) states: ''A member who is engaged in the practice of public accounting shall not concurrently engage in any business or occupation which would create a conflict of interest in rendering professional services.''

While certain occupations are clearly incompatible, the profession has never listed them since in most cases the individual circumstances indicate whether there is a problem. For example, it would be incompatible for a CPA to serve on a tax assessment board since the individual would be open to accusations of favoring clients, whether this was done or not (ET Section 56.09).

Form of Practice and Name. Rule 505 (ET Section 505.01) states

> A member may practice public accounting, whether as an owner or employee, only in the form of a proprietorship, a partnership or a professional corporation whose characteristics conform to resolutions of Council.
>
> A member shall not practice under a firm name which includes any fictitious name, indicates specialization or is misleading as to the type of organization (proprietorship, partnership or corporation). However, names of one or more past partners or shareholders may be included in the firm name of a successor partnership or corporation. Also, a partner surviving the death or withdrawal of all other partners may continue to practice under the partnership name for up to two years after becoming a sole practitioner.
>
> A firm may not designate itself as ''Members of the American Institute of Certified Public Accountants'' unless all of its partners or shareholders are members of the Institute.

Appendix C to the Code contains a resolution of AICPA Council that specifies the characteristics that a professional corporation must have to comply with Rule 505. In essence, such corporations must take on the characteristics of partnerships—including the unlimited liability of the stockholders unless specified amounts of liability insurance or minimum capitalization requirements are maintained—in order to protect the public.

Incentives for Maintaining Audit Quality

Introduction

Audit quality embraces the concepts of professional competence and the meeting or exceeding of professional standards (both technical and ethical) in expressing an opinion on audited financial statements, being associated with unaudited financial statements, and providing other types of accounting services. Aside from the natural desire of most professionals to achieve a reputation for professional excellence, incentives for maintaining audit quality are provided through regulatory mechanisms and other means.

The regulatory mechanisms include both the self-regulatory system of the profession and the disciplinary systems provided by government agencies such as the SEC and state boards of accountancy. The self-regulatory system of the profession provides a disciplinary system that imposes penalties for performance or conduct that departs from professional standards. In addition to the disciplinary system, the profession has developed recommendations for quality control systems to provide reasonable assurance that CPA firms conform with professional standards in the conduct of their accounting and auditing practices.

Changes in the past decade in the self-regulatory and disciplinary systems, including the creation of the AICPA Division for CPA Firms and the peer reviews that are a requirement for membership in the Division, can be traced at least in part to criticisms of the accounting profession by governmental bodies. In the late 1970s, two congressional committees held hearings and issued recommendations about how accounting and auditing standards should be created and applied, how audits should be conducted, and how auditors should be regulated and overseen. While no legislation resulted from those reports, the criticism and the threat of legislation clearly were motivating forces behind the birth of the Division for CPA Firms and other developments in the self-regulatory and disciplinary systems. All professions, notably law and medicine, have been subjected to criticism from external groups, and auditing is no exception. Even if, as many believe, the criticisms were unwarranted, they have brought about structural changes within the profession that greatly increase the penalties for substandard audit work.

Other incentives for maintaining audit quality, beyond the regulatory mechanisms, also exist. For one thing, firms are increasingly exposed to litigation in the conduct of their audit practices and to sanctions by the SEC. In addition, clients, and particularly audit committees, are putting increasing pressure on firms to maintain an image of high audit quality. This image is also a significant factor in a firm's ability to attract new clients and to recruit high-caliber personnel. Furthermore, through the efforts of financial writers and other news media, there is increasing public awareness of a firm's image and of the events that shape it.

The remainder of this section describes the profession's quality control system and the disciplinary systems of the profession and the state boards of accountancy.

Quality Controls

The objectives of quality control policies and procedures are to improve individual and firm performance and to ensure compliance with technical and ethical standards. Although professional standards do not explicitly require a CPA firm to adhere to quality control standards established by the AICPA Quality Control Standards Committee, adherence to those standards is a membership requirement of the Division for CPA Firms, as discussed later.

Quality Control Standards. Statement on Quality Control Standards (SQCS) No. 1, *System of Quality Control for a CPA Firm* (QC Section 10), requires CPA firms to have a system of quality control. Issued in November 1979 by the AICPA Quality Control Standards Committee—the senior technical committee of the Institute then designated to issue pronouncements on quality control standards—SQCS No. 1 superseded Statement on Auditing Standards No. 4, *Quality Control Considerations for a Firm of Independent Auditors*, which first gave formal recognition to a CPA firm's need for quality control policies and procedures.

The relationship of generally accepted auditing standards to quality control standards is discussed in SAS No. 25, *The Relationship of Generally Accepted Auditing Standards to Quality Control Standards* (AU Section 161):

> Generally accepted auditing standards relate to the conduct of individual audit engagements; quality control standards relate to the conduct of a firm's audit practice as a whole. Thus, generally accepted auditing standards and quality control standards are related, and the quality control policies and procedures that a firm adopts may affect both the conduct of individual audit engagements and the conduct of a firm's audit practice as a whole.

SQCS No. 1 describes nine elements of quality control and requires that a firm consider each of them, to the extent applicable to its practice, in establishing its quality control policies and procedures. The nine elements of quality control, as listed below, are interrelated (for example, a firm's hiring practices affect its policies relating to training).

1. *Acceptance and Continuance of Clients.* Policies and procedures should be established for deciding whether to accept or continue a client in order to minimize the likelihood of association with a client whose management lacks integrity.
2. *Assigning Personnel to Engagements.* Policies and procedures for assigning personnel to engagements should be established to provide the firm with reasonable assurance that work will be performed by persons having the degree of technical training and proficiency required in the circumstances.
3. *Supervision.* Policies and procedures for the conduct and supervision of work at all organizational levels should be established to provide the firm with reasonable assurance that the work performed meets the firm's standards of quality.

4. *Hiring*. Policies and procedures for hiring should be established to provide the firm with reasonable assurance that those employed possess the appropriate characteristics to enable them to perform competently.

5. *Professional Development*. Policies and procedures for professional development should be established to provide the firm with reasonable assurance that personnel will have the knowledge required to enable them to fulfill responsibilities assigned.

6. *Advancement*. Policies and procedures for advancing personnel should be established to provide the firm with reasonable assurance that those selected for advancement will have the qualifications necessary for fulfillment of the responsibilities they will be called on to assume.

7. *Consultation*. Policies and procedures for consultation should be established to provide the firm with reasonable assurance that personnel will seek assistance, to the extent required, from persons having appropriate levels of knowledge, competence, judgment, and authority.

8. *Independence*. Policies and procedures should be established to provide the firm with reasonable assurance that persons at all organizational levels maintain independence to the extent required by the rules of conduct of the AICPA.

9. *Inspection*. Policies and procedures for inspection should be established to provide the firm with reasonable assurance that the procedures relating to the other elements of quality control are being effectively applied.

The element relating to accepting clients formalizes a long-standing practice of auditors of seeking to ascertain the reputation and business integrity of potential clients as a means of protecting their own reputation and avoiding inadvertently accepting an audit of high or unknown risk. The extent of the inquiry varies with the circumstances. It will be informal and brief, for example, if the potential client is well-known in the community or can be easily investigated through mutual business associates. In other instances, more extreme and more formal inquiries are called for, as often happens with companies having new management or diverse private ownership or with companies in industries or areas with which the auditor is relatively unfamiliar.

The inspection element is performed internally by individuals acting on behalf of the firm's management, as contrasted with peer reviews, discussed later, which are conducted by individuals not associated with the firm being reviewed. SQCS No. 1 also requires a monitoring function, of which inspection is one aspect. In monitoring the effectiveness of its system of quality control, the firm should make timely modification of its policies and procedures to address not only findings from its inspection program but also changed circumstances in its practice and new authoritative pronouncements.

AICPA Division for CPA Firms. The AICPA Division for CPA Firms comprises two sections, one for SEC practice and the other for private company practice. Participation in both sections is strictly voluntary and is open to all CPA firms. The AICPA publishes an annual directory of member firms.

The principal objective of each section is to improve the quality of CPA firms' practice by establishing requirements for member firms and an effective system of self-regulation. Requirements that have the most direct effect on audit quality are

Requirements common to both sections:

- Adhere to quality control standards established by the AICPA Quality Control Standards Committee.

- Submit to peer reviews of the firm's accounting and audit practice every three years or at such additional times as designated by the section's executive committee. The reviews will be conducted in accordance with review standards established by the section's peer review committee.

- Ensure that all professionals in the firm achieve at least the minimum hours of continuing professional education prescribed by the section.

Additional SEC practice section requirements for all SEC engagements:[3]

- Periodically rotate partners.

- Have a partner other than the audit partner in charge review and concur with the audit report on the financial statements before it is issued.

- Refrain from performing certain proscribed management advisory services. These proscribed services include psychological testing, public opinion polls, merger and acquisition assistance for a finder's fee, executive recruitment, and, in certain situations, actuarial services to insurance companies.

- Report to the audit committee or board of directors the total fees received from the client for management advisory services during the year under audit and describe the types of such services rendered. (See the discussion later in this chapter of issues related to nonaudit services and auditor independence.)

- Report to the audit committee or board of directors the nature of disagreements with the management of the client on financial accounting and reporting matters and auditing procedures that, if not satisfactorily resolved, would have caused the issuance of a qualified opinion on the client's financial statements.

There are no significant additional requirements for membership in the private company practice section.

Each section is governed by an executive committee composed of representatives from member firms that establishes the section's general policies and oversees its activities. Each section also has a peer review committee that administers its peer review program. The executive committee of the SEC practice section has in addition organized a special investigations committee to look into alleged audit failures involving member firms. The activities of the SEC practice section are also subject to review by an independent public oversight

---

[3]The section's definition of an SEC engagement includes audits of certain banks and other lending institutions and certain sponsors or managers of investment funds, even though they are not registered with the SEC.

board that issues publicly available reports. The board consists of five members drawn from prominent individuals of high integrity and reputation, including, but not limited to, former public officials, lawyers, bankers, securities industry executives, educators, economists, and business executives.

Peer Review.   Peer reviews must be conducted in conformity with the confidentiality requirements in the AICPA Code of Professional Ethics. (Rule 301 contains an exception that allows a peer review of a member's practice.) Information obtained concerning a reviewed firm or any of its clients is confidential and should not be disclosed by review team members to anyone not "associated with the review." (The executive and peer review committees and the public oversight board are encompassed by the phrase "associated with the review.") While the AICPA Code of Professional Ethics does not deal specifically with independence in relationships between reviewers, reviewed firms, and clients of reviewed firms, the concepts of independence expressed in the Code should be considered in regard to these relationships. The firm under review has the option of either having the peer review committee appoint the review team or engaging another member firm to conduct the review; however, reciprocal reviews are not permitted.

The review team evaluates whether the reviewed firm's quality control system is appropriate, whether policies and procedures are adequately documented and communicated to its personnel, whether they are being complied with to provide reasonable assurance of conforming with professional standards, and whether the firm is in compliance with the membership requirements of the section. Some tests made by the review team are performed at practice offices, others on a firmwide basis, and still others on an individual engagement basis. The review is of the firm's accounting and auditing practice, but other segments, such as tax, are covered to the extent that personnel from those segments assist on accounting and auditing engagements.[4] The review also covers compliance with membership requirements.

At the completion of the peer review, the review team furnishes the reviewed firm with a formal peer review report and, if applicable, a letter of comments on matters that may require action by the firm. The report is available to the public, as is the letter of comments for firms in the SEC practice section.

With respect to member firms with SEC clients, a procedure has been established to enable the SEC to make its own evaluation of the adequacy of the peer review process and the public oversight board's oversight of that process. The procedure permits the SEC access, during a limited period following the issuance of the peer review report, to defined areas of the peer review working

---

[4]At this writing, the peer review committee of the SEC practice section has defined a firm's accounting and auditing practice as being "limited to all auditing, and all accounting, review, and compilation services covered by generally accepted auditing standards, standards for accounting and review services, standards for accountants' services on prospective financial information, and standards for financial and compliance audits contained in the *Standards for Audit of Governmental Organizations, Programs, Activities, and Functions* issued by the U.S. General Accounting Office."

papers, with appropriate safeguards to prevent the SEC from identifying the clients whose audit working papers were reviewed. After their review of the working papers on a specific peer review, the SEC representatives discuss with representatives of the public oversight board and the peer review committee any matters that they believe the committee should consider.

The following circumstances ordinarily would require a modified report:

- The scope of the review is limited by conditions that preclude the application of one or more review procedures considered necessary.
- The system of quality control as designed results in one or more applicable objectives of quality control standards established by the AICPA not being accomplished and as a result a condition was created in which the firm did not have reasonable assurance of conforming with professional standards.
- The degree of noncompliance with the reviewed firm's quality control policies and procedures was such that the reviewed firm did not have reasonable assurance of conforming with professional standards.
- The reviewed firm did not comply with the membership requirements of the section in all material respects.

The objective of the letter of comments is to report to the reviewed firm matters that resulted in a modified report or that the review team believes resulted in the creation of a condition in which there is more than a remote (i.e., slight) possibility that the firm would not conform with professional standards on accounting and auditing engagements. The letter should include appropriate comments regarding the design of the reviewed firm's system of quality control, its compliance with that system (including professional standards), and its compliance with the membership requirements of the section. The review team may also communicate orally to senior management of the reviewed firm comments that were not deemed sufficiently significant to be included in the letter of comments.

Disciplinary System

The profession, state boards of accountancy, the courts, and the SEC all impose sanctions on individuals and firms for performance or conduct that violates professional standards or civil or criminal laws. The paragraphs that follow discuss disciplinary actions of the profession and state boards of accountancy.

Disciplinary System Within the Profession for Individuals. The profession's self-disciplinary mechanism for individuals consists of the AICPA's Professional Ethics Division and Joint Trial Board Division, which comprises regional trial boards and a National Review Board.

The Professional Ethics Division is responsible for interpreting the Code of Professional Ethics and proposing amendments to it. The Division is also responsible for investigating violations of the Code for possible disciplinary action, including hearings before joint trial boards. The Division may initiate an investigation on the basis of complaints from individuals, state societies of CPAs, or government agencies, or on the basis of information from news media, the SEC *Docket*, or the IRS Bulletin.

The Division can take the following types of disciplinary actions against individual members:

- *Letter of minor violation*, which is used if the Division concludes that a violation is of insufficient gravity to warrant an administrative reprimand or trial board hearing. There is no publication of this finding. The member has the right to reject the letter of minor violation, which may result in a hearing panel of the trial board.
- *Administrative reprimand*, which is used if the Division concludes that a prima facie violation of the Code of Professional Ethics or bylaws is not of sufficient gravity to warrant further formal action. The Division may issue an administrative reprimand and may direct the member or members concerned to complete specified continuing professional education courses, provided, however, that there will be no publication of such administrative reprimand in the Institute's principal membership periodical (*The CPA Letter*). The member has the right to reject the reprimand, which may result in a hearing panel of the trial board.
- *Presentation of a prima facie case to a joint trial board*, which is used for serious or repeated violations that may require suspension or expulsion from membership or public censure.

The bylaws of the Institute provide for automatic suspension or expulsion of a member without a hearing if the member is convicted for (1) committing a crime punishable by imprisonment for more than one year, (2) willfully failing to file a required income tax return, (3) filing a false or fraudulent income tax return on one's own or a client's behalf, or (4) willfully aiding in the preparation and presentation of a false or fraudulent income tax return of a client, or if the member loses the right to practice through suspension or revocation of the member's certificate or license or permit by a governmental authority. Automatic suspension or expulsion does not preclude the Division from summoning a member to appear before a joint trial board.

The Joint Trial Board Division was organized in 1975 and is designed to integrate the enforcement activities of the Institute's Professional Ethics Division and the participating state societies. Twelve regional trial boards have been established to hear complaints made under the ethics codes of the Institute and participating state societies. A National Review Board is the final appellate authority in matters heard and determined by the regional trial boards; it also exercises some original jurisdiction. Both the National Review Board and the regional trial boards act through panels of members appointed to hear specific cases.

Disciplinary System Within the Profession for Firms. The executive committee of each section of the AICPA Division for CPA Firms has the authority to impose sanctions on member firms, either at its own initiative or on the basis of recommendations from that section's peer review committee. The following types of sanctions may be imposed on member firms for failure to maintain compliance with the requirements for membership:

- Corrective measures by the firm, including consideration by the firm of appropriate actions with respect to individual firm personnel.
- Additional requirements for continuing professional education.
- Accelerated or special peer reviews.
- Admonishments, censures, or reprimands.
- Monetary fines.
- Suspension from membership.
- Expulsion from membership.

State Boards of Accountancy. A state board of accountancy is charged with enforcing laws that regulate the practice of public accounting in that state. Generally, a board has the power to revoke or suspend the certificates of certified public accountants; to revoke, suspend, or refuse to renew permits to practice; and to censure the holders of permits to practice.[5] Those penalties can be assessed for a wide variety of acts or omissions specified in accountancy laws. Several states also require the registration of firms, issue permits for firms to practice in the state, and have the power to revoke or suspend those permits.

Enhancing the Independence of Auditors

Generally accepted auditing standards, the AICPA Code of Ethics, the Securities and Exchange Commission, and individual accounting firms require auditors to maintain an attitude of independence and prohibit certain relationships with clients. Nevertheless, some people believe that there are potential threats to auditor independence because the client selects the auditor and pays the fee and because the auditor may undertake nonaudit services for the client.

Since auditors are often selected and paid, retained, or replaced at the sole discretion of the management on whose representations they are expected to report, many people believe that total professional independence is impossible. While "total" independence may be impossible, auditors are highly conscious that their independence is vital and that they must preserve the standards of the profession for the sake of their own reputation. At the same time, their relationship with financial management involves subtle pressures in matters re-

---

[5]It should be noted that the AICPA has no such powers, since it does not issue certificates or permits to practice. AICPA disciplinary actions are related only to membership in the Institute.

quiring judgment, and they are often caught between an articulate, persuasive client and the silent, impersonal public.

The profession, the SEC, and responsible leaders of the financial community have recognized this alleged threat and have taken steps to deal with it. Some companies require that the selection and retention of auditors be ratified by the stockholders. In the case of companies whose securities are publicly traded, the SEC requires public notice of the termination of auditors, disclosure of any accounting or auditing disputes within two years between the client and the former auditor, and a letter from the former auditor concurring in such disclosure. Those are worthwhile steps, but they mitigate rather than eliminate the threat to auditor independence.

Another alleged threat to auditor independence arises from the various types of nonaudit services provided by public accounting firms. Such services include tax services (such as tax return preparation, tax planning advice, and representation before the IRS); management services, some that are related to accounting and auditing (such as advice on systems, controls, data processing, and cost accounting) and some that are not (for instance, market studies, executive recruiting, and studies of factory layout); and other accounting services (such as bookkeeping, compilations and reviews for nonpublic companies, special investigations of accounting information, and advice on selection and application of accounting principles and the accounting implications of proposed management decisions). Neither the SEC nor the AICPA prohibits the performance of nonauditing services for audit clients generally; the SEC has at times in the past monitored such relationships and required their disclosure, and the AICPA Division for CPA Firms prohibits members of its SEC practice section from providing certain specific services.

Many proposals have been made to strengthen auditor independence. They fall into three general categories:

- Protecting the auditor from management influence, through the use of audit committees, scrutiny of auditor changes, prohibitions against ''opinion shopping,'' and rotation of auditors.
- Ensuring that public accounting firms are managed in a manner that provides the necessary internal support for the independence of individual partners and staff, such as various ways of reducing time and deadline pressures.
- Other proposals to increase auditor independence, including transfer of the audit function to the public sector, auditor selection of generally accepted accounting principles for clients, and the prohibition of the performance of nonaudit services for audit clients.

The Cohen Commission considered and evaluated those proposals in its 1978 report. The remainder of this chapter discusses those proposals, along with the Commission's conclusions and recommendations and the profession's response.

Protecting the Auditor from Management Influence

Neither audit effectiveness nor audit efficiency would be strengthened if the auditor were isolated from client management. An auditor must work with management because management's active and positive cooperation is required in the conduct of an audit, and that in turn requires the auditor and management to have a high degree of confidence in one another. Yet auditor independence must be maintained despite the need for cooperation. Another difficulty auditors face in maintaining their independence is that they are members of a profit-making firm that depends on fees over which client management may exert considerable control. Several proposals to increase the auditor's ability to resist pressure from management are discussed next.

Audit Committees. Over the years, several professional and regulatory bodies have suggested requiring companies to have audit committees of boards of directors as a means of reinforcing auditors' independence from management. As a direct result of the McKesson & Robbins scandal, audit committees were proposed in 1939 by the New York Stock Exchange and in 1940 by the Securities and Exchange Commission. The Securities and Exchange Commission endorsed the establishment of audit committees composed of outside directors in 1972 (ASR No. 123) and subsequently adopted nonbinding rules underscoring this commitment. The AICPA recommended in 1967 that audit committees be established for all publicly held companies. In 1978, the New York Stock Exchange mandated that domestic companies with listed securities establish audit committees made up entirely of outside directors; in 1979, the American Stock Exchange strongly recommended similar action. A special House subcommittee in 1976 also noted the desirability of audit committees. The Cohen Commission strongly endorsed the use of audit committees to recommend to shareholders the appointment of independent auditors and to evaluate the relationship between auditor and management. The Institute of Internal Auditors also endorses the establishment of audit committees consisting of outside directors by both public companies and other organizations, such as not-for-profit and governmental bodies.

Today, although not universally required, audit committees are an important part of our corporate structure. They oversee a company's accounting and financial reporting policies and practices, help the board of directors fulfill its fiduciary and corporate accountability responsibilities, and help maintain a direct line of communication between the board and the company's external and internal auditors. Although occasionally the entire board may turn to the independent auditors for assistance in reviewing the financial statements or other data, contact between the board and the auditors is generally through the audit committee.

Over the years, the AICPA and the New York Stock Exchange have issued general guidelines for audit committees but have not mandated specific duties, responsibilities, or activities. Since specific functions have not been prescribed for audit committees, their activities vary from one company to the next. Effective committees, however, generally perform certain common tasks, including

- Reviewing the independent auditors' proposed audit scope and approach.
- Communicating with and reviewing the activities and effectiveness of the internal auditors.
- Reviewing the financial statements and the results of the independent audit.
- Considering the selection of accounting policies.
- Reviewing recommendations of both the internal auditors and the independent auditors about improvements in internal controls.
- Considering management's recommendation on the appointment of independent auditors.
- Overseeing or conducting special investigations or other functions on behalf of the board of directors.

In the authors' opinion, the trend toward establishing audit committees of outside directors has been beneficial to management, directors, stockholders, and the auditing profession. Auditors and outside directors have common interests that are vastly strengthened by interaction between the two groups. A properly active and involved audit committee serves to protect corporate interests by overseeing the activities of the auditor and, at least to some extent, of company management. This takes both a theoretical and a practical form. Theoretically, the existence of an audit committee of outside directors demonstrates that all parties are diligently carrying out their duties to the stockholders concerning financial reporting and disclosure. An audit committee reinforces the auditor's independence, while the auditor provides an independent source of information to the directors; management's support of the relationship demonstrates a sense of accountability. Practically, an audit committee brings a number of specific benefits to the auditor-client relationship.

The Cohen Commission recommended that the audit committee take a sufficiently active role in the total arrangements for the audit, including matters of fees and timing, to ensure that management makes cost-versus-quality decisions in a manner that does not sacrifice audit quality.[6] The authors agree with the Commission that auditor independence will be enhanced if fiscal decisions regarding audit arrangements are made by the board of directors or the audit committee and are not delegated to corporate officers.

Scrutiny of Auditor Changes. In the past, management has sometimes threatened to dismiss the auditor when there is a disagreement on accounting principles. Management would then "shop around" for a more compliant auditor. Ratification of auditor changes by an audit committee is one way of decreasing pressure on the auditor from management. Outside scrutiny of the dismissal of an auditor will also inhibit the tendency to apply such pressure. The scrutiny of auditor changes has been enhanced by two professional developments.

[6]*Report, Conclusions, and Recommendations*, 1978, pp. 106-7.

Communicating with Predecessor Auditors. SAS No. 7, *Communications Between Predecessor and Successor Auditors*, issued in 1975, requires a successor auditor to attempt to communicate with the predecessor as part of the process of determining whether to accept an engagement. The SAS outlines, in paragraph 6 (AU Section 315.06), the procedures to be followed by a successor auditor:

> The successor auditor should make specific and reasonable inquiries of the predecessor regarding matters that the successor believes will assist him in determining whether to accept the engagement. His inquiries should include specific questions regarding, among other things, facts that might bear on the integrity of management; on disagreements with management as to accounting principles, auditing procedures, or other similarly significant matters; and on the predecessor's understanding as to the reasons for the change of auditors.

AU Section 315 indicates that the predecessor auditor is obligated to "respond promptly and fully" to any "reasonable" question, but it also recognizes that, in unusual situations such as when litigation is or may be involved, the predecessor may need to advise the successor that the response is limited. In that event, the successor auditor should consider whether the information obtained from all sources is adequate to support acceptance of the client. If the client refuses to allow the successor auditor to talk to the predecessor auditor, the successor auditor should also consider whether to accept the engagement.

After a successor auditor has been appointed, there are two occasions when communications between the predecessor and the successor auditors are appropriate. One reflects the successor's need to review the prior auditor's working papers and the other arises if the successor believes that there is an error in the financial statements on which the predecessor auditor expressed an opinion.

Working papers are the property of the auditor who prepared them, and that individual is under no compulsion to share them with a successor auditor. In the absence of unusual circumstances, however, such as litigation between the client and the predecessor auditor or amounts owed to the predecessor auditor by the client, predecessor auditors customarily allow successor auditors access to at least certain working papers.

Disagreements with Clients. The second development affects outside scrutiny of auditor changes by publicly held companies. In 1971, the Securities and Exchange Commission required specific disclosure in a timely Form 8-K filing of a change in auditor made by the registrant, including disclosure of any disagreements between the registrant and the auditor in the 18 months prior to the change that could have required or did require mention in the auditor's report. This was designed to strengthen auditors' independence by discouraging the practice of changing auditors in order to obtain more favorable accounting treatment.

In 1974, the SEC issued ASR No. 165, which increased the level of disclosure regarding relationships between independent auditors and their clients. A predecessor auditor is now required to provide a letter, which is generally filed by the company with its Form 8-K, either stating agreement with the company's reporting or setting forth any disagreements within the preceding two years. To clarify that it intended only for serious matters to be so reported, the SEC stated in ASR No. 165, "Disagreements contemplated by this rule are those which occur at the decision-making level, i.e., between personnel of the registrant responsible for presentation of its financial statements and personnel of the accounting firm responsible for rendering its report." The letter gives the auditor an opportunity to explain disagreements, whether resolved or unresolved, relating to accounting measurement and disclosure principles or audit scope or procedures. In addition, if the predecessor auditor objected to an accounting method or disclosure that had a material effect on the financial statements and the successor auditor agrees to it, Item 304 of Regulation S-K requires the registrant to disclose the disagreement and the effect on the financial statements that would have resulted if the method advocated by the former auditor had been followed. The Cohen Commission praised these pronouncements and suggested that the accounting profession require that they apply to all audited financial statements.[7] At the date of this writing, the AICPA has not adopted this suggestion, although independent auditors who are members of the SEC practice section of the AICPA Division for CPA Firms must report any disagreements (as defined before) to the audit committee or board of directors of each SEC-engagement client, even though there is no change in auditors. Also, at the time of this writing, the SEC was considering increasing the required disclosures in this area by extending them to include changes in accountants and reportable disagreements with former accountants that occurred before a registrant became subject to the SEC's reporting requirements.

Opinion Shopping. An apparent increase in the incidence of opinion shopping has resulted in proposals by the SEC for more direct disclosure of this practice. At the time of this writing, the SEC was considering a number of approaches, including requiring disclosure of issues concerning which the opinion of another accountant was sought, either in connection with a change of auditors or otherwise, and requiring a preferability letter and disclosure of all accountants consulted when a change in accounting principle is made. As noted earlier, the ASB has established performance and reporting standards for engagements in which an accountant is asked to provide advice on the application of accounting principles or auditing standards for nonaudit clients. Those performance and reporting standards, which are discussed in Chapter 19, may reduce the SEC's concern in this area.

Rotation of Auditors. To decrease the auditor's incentive for yielding to pressure from management, some people have proposed mandatory rotation of auditors, with a new auditor to be appointed every three to five years. Also, some argue that a new auditor would bring a fresh viewpoint to the engagement. Rotation would considerably increase audit costs, however, because of the start-up and learning time necessary on a new engagement. In addition, the Cohen

[7]*Ibid.*, pp. 107–8.

Commission, noting that most cases of substandard performance by auditors were first- or second-year audits, stated, "Once an auditor becomes well acquainted with the operations of a client, audit risks are reduced" (p. 109).

Because of this, the Cohen Commission concluded that rotation of audit firms should not be required. The Commission also pointed out that the primary advantage of rotation—the fresh viewpoint—can be achieved if the personnel assigned to an engagement are systematically rotated.[8] This recommendation was adopted by the AICPA Division for CPA Firms in the requirement for membership in its SEC practice section that certain personnel on audits of publicly held companies be periodically rotated.

Policies and Procedures of Accounting Firms and Their Effect on Independence

The Cohen Commission concluded that the management policies and procedures of public accounting firms have an important effect on the independence of auditors.[9] The Commission noted the excessive price competition among accounting firms, and that the resulting desire to cut fees often results in time and budget pressures on the audit staff that may cause substandard auditing. (The Commission concluded that "excessive time pressure is one of the most pervasive factors leading to audit failures."[10]) While many audit failures resulted from poor planning and inadequate supervision, the reason for the poor planning and inadequate supervision was often time pressure. A closely related factor is client demands for early earnings releases, preliminary issuance of financial statements, and quick filing of registration statements. If such client demands are unreasonable, agreeing to them would compromise the auditor's independence.

Independence is also impaired if the auditor eliminates or reduces audit procedures or fails to corroborate management representations in order to stay within the budget. A Cohen Commission survey indicated that some staff auditors had "signed off" for completing audit steps when they had not performed the work.[11] The desire not to exceed the budget thus detracts from the auditor's independence.

While the Commission blamed time and budget pressures for many auditing problems, it failed to provide specific solutions. The authors believe that accounting firms must adopt strict quality-control practices, tailored to meet the particular circumstances of various types of accounting and auditing engagements. Public accounting firms cannot abandon time budgets, but the budgets must be realistic so that audit quality is not eroded. While there will always be time pressures in auditing, sufficient audit tests must be done to comply with professional standards.

[8]*Ibid.*, pp. 108–9.
[9]*Ibid.*, pp. 109–21.
[10]*Ibid.*, p. xxx.
[11]*Ibid.*, p. 116.

Other Proposals to Enhance Independence

Over the years, there have been many other proposals to enhance auditor independence, several of which would require a sweeping change in the relationship between auditor and client. They have not been supported, however, by the AICPA, SEC, Cohen Commission, or the authors of this book. Three of the more frequently presented of those proposals are discussed next.

Transfer to the Public Sector. In order to sever the ties between auditor and management, proposals have been made to have independent auditors approved, assigned, or compensated by a government agency or by the stock exchanges or to have audits conducted by a group of government auditors. The Cohen Commission concluded that having auditors approved, assigned, or compensated by the government is not warranted either by the magnitude of deficiencies in present practice or by the promise of potential improvements. It also noted that independence would not necessarily be enhanced by such proposals because of government involvement in using accounting data to accomplish its own objectives.[12]

Auditor Selection of GAAP for Clients. Traditionally, management has had the direct responsibility for the financial statements, including selection of the accounting principles utilized and the disclosures made. Proposals have been made to require the auditor to assume those responsibilities. The authors believe that the present division of responsibility is sound and should not be changed. Management, with firsthand knowledge of what has occurred, should be responsible for ensuring that events and transactions are properly reported. Furthermore, management is in the best position to make the judgments and estimates necessary to prepare the financial statements, and the auditor is in the best position to challenge and evaluate those judgments and estimates.

Occasionally, an issue involving reporting standards or the application of generally accepted accounting principles becomes a ''disagreement'' between management and the auditor. Such disagreements are frequently resolved by the auditor's convincing management of the propriety of an accounting principle or the necessity and justification for a particular disclosure. If, however, the auditor is not successful, a qualification results. Probably the most effective way of avoiding this is for the client to seek the auditor's early involvement and consultation in the formative stages of nonroutine transactions. In that way, neither party is faced with an unavoidable accounting or auditing outcome that is unsatisfactory to the client.

The linkage between the selection of accounting principles and the accumulation and classification of accounting data is very close. If auditors were responsible for the selection of accounting principles and disclosures, they would lose the independent evaluation function that they perform today. Rather, auditors should use their expertise to advise and counsel management in the

[12]*Ibid.*, p. 105.

preparation of financial statements, with management retaining the ultimate responsibility for the presentation.

Prohibition of Nonaudit Services. Proposals have been made to prevent public accounting firms from performing all or some nonaudit services on the grounds that they may be incompatible with auditing and could pose a threat to the auditor's independence. Proponents of this view say, for example, that an auditor who provides management services to a client may not maintain an independent viewpoint. The Commission on Auditors' Responsibilities analyzed this alleged threat in detail and concluded:

> There is little question that the provision of some other services to audit clients poses an obvious *potential* threat to the auditor's independence. This potential threat, at least theoretically, is entirely credible.
>
> Except for [one] case, the Commission's research has not found instances in which an auditor's independence has been compromised by providing other services. Indeed, some of our research indicates that performing consulting services may improve the audit function and benefit users. If the empirical evidence were the only consideration, the Commission's conclusion would be clear: The evidence does not support the theory. No prohibition of management services is warranted.
>
> Nevertheless, consideration must be given to the belief of a significant minority that some other services do impair the auditor's independence. The auditor's effectiveness, and ultimately his livelihood, depend on the *belief* of users in his integrity. Despite the lack of evidence to support the belief that other services compromise independence, the belief persists and, therefore, represents a continuing threat to the credibility of the independent auditor.[13]

The authors do not endorse requiring CPA firms to discontinue their other services merely because of the mistaken beliefs of a minority; there are other, more effective ways to enhance the independence of auditors.

Review Questions

3-1. What attributes of auditing qualify it as a profession?

3-2. What requirements generally must be met for certification as a CPA?

3-3. What are auditing standards? How do they differ from auditing procedures?

3-4. Name the 10 generally accepted auditing standards and classify them into 3 basic categories.

3-5. What is the auditor's responsibility for evaluating internal control?

3-6. What is the objective of the consistency standard of reporting?

3-7. Why must an auditor's report be painstakingly precise in spelling out the opinion expressed?

[13]*Ibid.*, p. 102.

3-8. What are the five broad concepts or Ethical Principles embodied in the AICPA Code of Professional Ethics?

3-9. What forms of advertising, promotion, or solicitation are permitted under the AICPA Code of Professional Ethics?

3-10. Distinguish between the appearance of independence and the fact of independence. Give examples of how an auditor could be independent in fact but not in appearance, and vice versa. Do professional standards require the auditor to possess independence in both appearance and fact? Why?

3-11. What are some examples of activities that will result in an auditor's independence being considered impaired?

3-12. How does the existence of past-due fees affect an auditor's independence and how does the auditor resolve the issue?

3-13. What should be done if an auditor does not possess the competence to perform the services needed by the client?

3-14. What should the auditor do when the literal application of a pronouncement on accounting principles would have the effect of rendering the financial statements misleading?

3-15. What is the difference between confidential information and privileged information?

3-16. What are a CPA's responsibilities regarding confidential information? Insider information?

3-17. What is the AICPA's stand with respect to contingent fees and commissions? Which are specifically prohibited and in what circumstances?

3-18. Describe the past and present position of the AICPA regarding advertising and solicitation.

3-19. What specific acts are considered discreditable to the profession? Which acts provide for automatic termination of membership under the AICPA bylaws? Who can revoke a CPA's certificate?

3-20. What is the prohibition against incompatible occupations as it affects the CPA? Why does the prohibition exist?

3-21. What are the elements of quality control described by SQCS No. 1?

3-22. What is a peer review and how is it accomplished?

3-23. What types of sanctions may be imposed on member firms for failure to comply with the membership requirements of the AICPA Division for CPA Firms?

3-24. What is the role of the audit committee of the board of directors? How does an audit committee act as a check on the auditor?

3-25. What developments have increased the scrutiny of auditor changes?

Discussion Questions

3-30. Discuss CPAs' responsibilities to their clients and to the public at large.

3-31. Give some examples of due professional care not being exercised in the course of an ordinary examination.

3-32. Discuss the pros and cons of proposals to enhance auditor independence by transferring the audit function to the public sector or by making auditors responsible for selecting accounting principles for their clients.

3-33. In your examination of Client A you discover information that, if known, would have an adverse effect on the financial statements of Client B. Explain how you would proceed in this situation, considering the auditor's responsibility concerning confidentiality.

3-34. Rotation of auditors has frequently been recommended by critics of the profession. Discuss the profession's attitude toward rotation, including the conclusion of the Commission on Auditors' Responsibilities on this subject.

3-35. Some critics of the profession feel that auditors should not render management consulting services to clients being audited by them. Discuss the profession's position on this subject, including the conclusion of the Commission on Auditors' Responsibilities on this subject.

3-36. Fred Browning, CPA, has examined the financial statements of Grimm Company for several years. Grimm's president has now asked Browning to install an inventory control system for the company.

> *Required:*
> Discuss the factors that Mr. Browning should consider in determining whether to accept this engagement.

(AICPA adapted)

AICPA Multiple Choice Questions

These questions are taken from the Auditing part of Uniform CPA Examinations. Choose the single most appropriate answer.

3-40. Which of the following *best* describes what is meant by generally accepted auditing standards?

    a. Acts to be performed by the auditor.
    b. Measures of the quality of the auditor's performance.
    c. Procedures to be used to gather evidence to support financial statements.
    d. Audit objectives generally determined on audit engagements.

3-41. The third general standard states that due care is to be exercised in the performance of the examination. This standard means that a CPA who undertakes an engagement assumes a duty to perform each audit

    a. As a professional possessing the degree of skill commonly possessed by others in the field.
    b. In conformity with generally accepted accounting principles.
    c. With reasonable diligence and without fault or error.
    d. To the satisfaction of governmental agencies and investors who rely upon the audit.

3-42. The fourth reporting standard requires the auditor's report to contain either an expression of opinion regarding the financial statements, taken as a whole, or an assertion to the effect that an opinion cannot be expressed. The objective of the fourth standard is to prevent

a. The CPA from reporting on one basic financial statement and *not* the others.
b. Misinterpretations regarding the degree of responsibility the auditor is assuming.
c. The CPA from expressing different opinions on each of the basic financial statements.
d. Management from reducing its final responsibility for the basic financial statements.

3-43. A CPA, while performing an audit, strives to achieve independence in appearance in order to

a. Reduce risk and liability.
b. Become independent in fact.
c. Maintain public confidence in the profession.
d. Comply with the generally accepted standards of field work.

3-44. An independent auditor must be without bias with respect to the financial statements of a client in order to

a. Comply with the laws established by governmental agencies.
b. Maintain the appearance of separate interests on the part of the auditor and the client.
c. Protect against criticism and possible litigation from stockholders and creditors.
d. Ensure the impartiality necessary for an expression of the auditor's opinion.

3-45. Mavis, CPA, has audited the financial statements of South Bay Sales Incorporated for several years and had always been paid promptly for services rendered. Last year's audit invoices have not been paid because South Bay is experiencing cash flow difficulties, and the current year's audit is scheduled to commence in one week. With respect to the past-due audit fees Mavis should

a. Perform the scheduled audit and allow South Bay to pay when the cash flow difficulties are alleviated.
b. Perform the scheduled audit only after arranging a definite payment schedule and securing notes signed by South Bay.
c. Inform South Bay's management that the past-due audit fees are considered an impairment of auditor independence.
d. Inform South Bay's management that the past-due audit fees may be considered a loan on which interest must be imputed for financial statement purposes.

3-46. Prior to the acceptance of an audit engagement with a client who has terminated the services of the predecessor auditor, the CPA should

a. Contact the predecessor auditor without advising the prospective client and request a complete report of the circumstance leading to the termination with the understanding that all information disclosed will be kept confidential.
b. Accept the engagement without contacting the predecessor auditor since the CPA can include audit procedures to verify the reason given by the client for the termination.
c. Not communicate with the predecessor auditor because this would in effect be asking the auditor to violate the confidential relationship between auditor and client.

    d. Advise the client of the intention to contact the predecessor auditor and request permission for the contact.

3-47. Smith, CPA, issued an "except for" opinion on the financial statements of Wald Company for the year ended December 31, 1986. Wald has engaged another firm of CPAs to make a second audit. The local bank has knowledge of Smith's audit and has asked Smith to explain why the financial statements and his opinion have *not* been made available.

    a. Smith *cannot* provide the bank with information about Wald under any circumstances.

    b. If Wald consents, Smith may provide the bank with information concerning Wald.

    c. If the other firm of CPAs consents, Smith may provide the bank with information concerning Wald.

    d. The only way the bank can obtain information concerning Smith's audit is to obtain it by subpoena.

3-48. Richard, CPA, performs accounting services for Norton Corporation. Norton wishes to offer its shares to the public and asks Richard to audit the financial statements prepared for registration purposes. Richard refers Norton to Cruz, CPA, who is more competent in the area of registration statements. Cruz performs the audit of Norton's financial statements and subsequently thanks Richard for the referral by giving Richard a portion of the audit fee collected. Richard accepts the fee. Who, if anyone, has violated professional ethics?

    a. Only Richard.

    b. Both Richard and Cruz.

    c. Only Cruz.

    d. Neither Richard nor Cruz.

3-49. In which of the following circumstances would a CPA who audits XM Corporation lack independence?

    a. The CPA and XM's president are both on the board of directors of COD Corporation.

    b. The CPA and XM's president each owns 25 percent of FOB Corporation, a closely held company.

    c. The CPA has a home mortgage from XM, which is a savings and loan organization.

    d. The CPA reduced XM's usual audit fee by 40 percent because XM's financial condition was unfavorable.

3-50. Working papers prepared by a CPA in connection with an audit engagement are owned by the CPA, subject to certain limitations. The rationale for this rule is to

    a. Protect the working papers from being subpoenaed.

    b. Provide the basis for excluding admission of the working papers as evidence because of the privileged communication rule.

    c. Provide the CPA with evidence and documentation that may be helpful in the event of a lawsuit.

    d. Establish a continuity of relationship with the client whereby indiscriminate replacement of CPAs is discouraged.

3-51. In pursuing its quality-control objectives with respect to assigning personnel to engagements, a firm of independent auditors may use policies and procedures such as

    a. Designating senior qualified personnel to provide advice on accounting or auditing questions throughout the engagement.

    b. Requiring timely identification of the staffing requirements of specific engagements so that enough qualified personnel can be made available.

    c. Establishing at entry levels a policy for recruiting that includes minimum standards of academic preparation and accomplishment.

    d. Requiring auditing personnel to have current accounting and auditing literature available for research and reference purposes throughout the engagement.

3-52. Williams & Co., a large international CPA firm, is to have an ''external peer review.'' The peer review will most likely be performed by

    a. Employees and partners of Williams & Co. who are *not* associated with the particular audits being reviewed.

    b. Audit review staff of the Securities and Exchange Commission.

    c. Audit review staff of the American Institute of Certified Public Accountants.

    d. Employees and partners of another CPA firm.

3-53. The SEC has strengthened auditor independence by requiring that management

    a. Engage auditors to report in accordance with the Foreign Corrupt Practices Act.

    b. Report the nature of disagreements with former auditors.

    c. Select auditors through audit committees.

    d. Acknowledge their responsibility for the fairness of the financial statements.

3-54. The CPA firm of Knox & Knox has been subpoenaed to testify and produce its correspondence and workpapers in connection with a lawsuit brought by a third party against one of their clients. Knox considers the subpoenaed documents to be privileged communication and therefore seeks to avoid admission of such evidence in the lawsuit. Which of the following is correct?

    a. Federal law recognizes such a privilege if the accountant is a Certified Public Accountant.

    b. The privilege is available regarding the working papers since the CPA is deemed to own them.

    c. The privileged communication rule as it applies to the CPA–client relationship is the same as that of attorney–client.

    d. In the absence of a specific statutory provision, the law does *not* recognize the existence of the privileged communication rule between a CPA and his client.

Problems and Cases

3-60. Lester Savage, CPA, has been requested by an audit client to perform a nonrecurring engagement involving the implementation of an EDP information and control system. The client requests that in setting up the new system and during the period prior to conversion to the new system Savage

- Counsel on potential expansion of business activity plans.
- Search for and interview new personnel.
- Hire new personnel.
- Train personnel.

In addition, the client requests that during the three months after the conversion Savage

- Supervise the operation of the new system.
- Monitor client-prepared source documents and make changes in basic EDP-generated data as he may deem necessary without concurrence of the client.

Savage responds that he may perform some of the services requested, but not all of them.

Required:
a. Which of these services may Savage perform and which of these services may he not perform?
b. Before undertaking this engagement, Savage should inform the client of all significant matters related to the engagement. What are these significant matters?
c. If Savage adds to his staff an individual who specializes in developing computer systems, what degree of knowledge must Savage possess in order to supervise the specialist's activities?

(AICPA adapted)

3–61. The auditor should obtain a level of knowledge of the entity's business, including events, transactions, and practices, that will enable the planning and performance of an examination in accordance with generally accepted auditing standards. Adhering to these standards enables the auditor's report to lend credibility to financial statements by providing the public with certain assurances.

Required:
a. How does knowledge of the entity's business help the auditor in planning and performing an examination in accordance with generally accepted auditing standards?
b. What assurances are provided to the public when the auditor states that the financial statements "present fairly . . . in conformity with generally accepted accounting principles applied on a consistent basis"?

(AICPA adapted)

3–62. For many years the financial and accounting community has recognized the importance of the use of audit committees and has endorsed their formation.

At this time, the use of audit committees has become widespread. Independent auditors have become increasingly involved with audit committees and consequently have become familiar with their nature and function.

Required:
a. Describe what an audit committee is.
b. Identify the reasons why audit committees have been formed and are currently in operation.
c. What are the functions of an audit committee?

(AICPA adapted)

3–63. Your client, Nuedel Corporation, requested that you conduct a feasibility study to advise management of the best way the corporation can utilize electronic data processing equipment and which computer, if any, best meets the corporation's requirements. You are technically competent in this area and accept the engagement. On completion of your study, the corporation accepts your suggestions and installs the computer and related equipment that you recommended.

> ### Required:
>
> a. Discuss the effect the acceptance of this management services engagement would have on your independence in expressing an opinion on the financial statements of the Nuedel Corporation.
> b. Instead of accepting the engagement, assume that you recommend Liz Mackey, of the CPA firm of Campbell and Mackey, who is qualified in specialized services. On completion of the engagement, your client requests that Mackey's partner, Jim Campbell, perform services in other areas. Should Campbell accept the engagement? Discuss.
> c. A local printer of data processing forms customarily offers a commission for being recommended as a supplier. The client is aware of the commission offer and suggests that Mackey accept it. Would it be proper for Mackey to accept the commission with the client's approval? Discuss.
>
> (AICPA adapted)

3–64. Gilbert and Bradley formed a corporation called Financial Services, Inc., each person taking 50 percent of the authorized common stock. Gilbert is a CPA and a member of the American Institute of CPAs. Bradley is a CPCU (Chartered Property Casualty Underwriter). The corporation performs auditing and tax services under Gilbert's direction and insurance services under Bradley's supervision. The opening of the corporation's office was announced by an ad in the local newspaper.

One of the corporation's first audit clients was the Grandtime Company. Grandtime has total assets of $600,000 and total liabilities of $270,000. In the course of the examination, Gilbert found that Grandtime's building with a book value of $240,000 was pledged as security for a 10-year-term note in the amount of $200,000. The client's statements did not mention that the building was pledged as security for the 10-year-term note. However, as the failure to disclose the lien did not affect either the value of the assets or the amount of the liabilities and the examination was satisfactory in all other respects, Gilbert rendered an unqualified opinion on Grandtime's financial statements. About two months after the date of the opinion, Gilbert learned that an insurance company was planning to lend Grandtime $150,000 in the form of a first-mortgage note on the building. Realizing that the insurance company was unaware of the existing lien on the building, Gilbert had Bradley notify the insurance company of the fact that Grandtime's building was pledged as security for the term note.

Shortly after the events described above, Gilbert was charged with a violation of professional ethics.

> ### Required:
>
> Identify and discuss the ethical implications of those acts by Gilbert that were in violation of the AICPA Code of Professional Ethics.
>
> (AICPA adapted)

3–65. For each of the following unrelated cases, state whether there has been a violation of the AICPA's Code of Professional Ethics, and, if so, explain why the rule is necessary.

a. Jones, CPA, has retired and sold his audit practice to Smith, CPA, who has taken over Jones' office and files and begun routine work on the practice. Jones, fearful of the loss of clients because of the change, has not advised his clients, but intends to introduce Smith as his successor as each engagement commences.

b. Smith, CPA, specializes in taxes and includes on his letterhead and business card the designation "Tax Expert."

c. Riley, a real estate broker and insurance agent, regularly refers his clients to Smith, CPA, for tax return preparation. Pursuant to their arrangement, Smith pays Riley 5 percent of all fees collected from Riley's clients.

d. Smith, CPA, has installed a medium-sized computer in his office, which he uses to service audit and nonaudit clients not large enough to support computers of their own. In many instances, the data processing provided includes maintenance of the general ledger and the preparation of financial statements, on which Smith (after auditing) expresses unqualified opinions.

e. Smith, CPA, has obtained licenses as a real estate broker and insurance agent, and combines his practices in one office. In many instances, his audit clients are also his insurance and real estate clients.

f. Smith, CPA, and Jones, CPA, have combined their practices and have incorporated to practice public accounting. They are the only shareholders.

g. Quinn, CPA, an SEC specialist, has written an article for publication. The publisher insists on including among her credits the fact that Quinn is the SEC specialist for her firm.

h. Smith, CPA, having recently been granted his certificate, has begun practice and is advertising in the local paper as "Accountant and Auditor." He is sending fliers to the heads of all local businesses indicating his availability for services.

i. Smith, CPA, and Jones, CPA, were fellow panelists at a seminar conducted by the local chapter of their state society of CPAs. Impressed by Jones' expertise, Smith offered Jones a position with his firm at a salary greater than that which she was receiving as a staff member of another firm.

3-66. Ray, the owner of a small company, asked Holmes, CPA, to conduct an audit of the company's records. Ray told Holmes that the audit was to be completed in time to submit audited financial statements to a bank as part of a loan application. Holmes immediately accepted the engagement and agreed to provide an auditor's report within three weeks. Ray agreed to pay Holmes a fixed fee plus a bonus if the loan was granted.

Holmes hired two accounting students to conduct the audit and spent several hours telling them exactly what to do. Holmes told the students not to spend time reviewing the controls, but instead to concentrate on proving the mathematical accuracy of the ledger accounts and summarizing the data in the accounting records that support Ray's financial statements. The students followed Holmes' instructions and after two weeks gave Holmes the financial statements, which did not include footnotes. Holmes reviewed the statements and prepared an unqualified auditor's report. The report, however, did not refer to generally accepted accounting principles nor to the year-to-year application of such principles.

Required:
Briefly describe each of the generally accepted auditing standards and indicate how Holmes' action(s) resulted in a failure to comply with each standard.

Organize your answer as follows:

Brief Description of Generally Accepted Auditing Standards	Holmes' Actions Resulting in Failure to Comply with Generally Accepted Auditing Standards

(AICPA adapted)

3-67. a. Mio & Mio, CPAs, were engaged for several years by Famous Carpet Company, manufacturers of woolen carpet, to conduct an annual audit. Excellent Carpet Company, a competitor of Famous, now seeks to engage the Mio firm to install a more advanced accounting system and to conduct an annual audit. The officers of Excellent approached Mio & Mio because of its outstanding reputation in the community and its acknowledged expertise in the carpet industry.

Required:
May Mio & Mio accept the Excellent Carpet Company as a client? Explain.

b. (Continuing the facts in *a*) Subsequently, one of the officers of Excellent offered to pay Mio & Mio a substantial bonus if they would disclose confidential information about Famous' operations to permit the officer to make a comparative study of the operating performance of the two carpet companies.

Required:
May Mio & Mio accept this offer? Explain.

(AICPA adapted)

3-68. Parker Products, Inc., is suing Flagstone Specialties, Inc., your client, in the state court system, alleging a breach of contract. The contract provided for Flagstone to construct a piece of highly technical equipment at Flagstone's cost plus a fixed fee. Specifically, Parker alleges that Flagstone has calculated costs incorrectly, loading the contract billings with inappropriate costs. Parker seeks to recover the excess costs.

Charles Lake, your CPA firm's partner in charge of the Flagstone account, has been subpoenaed by Parker to testify. Neither Lake nor the firm wishes to become involved in the litigation. Furthermore, if Lake testifies, some of the facts he would reveal might be prejudicial to the client.

Required:
a. Must Lake testify? Explain.
b. If the cause of the action had been such that the suit would have been brought in a federal court, would Lake have had to testify? Explain.

(AICPA adapted)

3-69. Ralph Sharp, CPA, has audited the Fargo Corporation for the last 10 years. It was recently discovered that Fargo's top management has been engaged in some questionable financial activities since the last audited financial statements were issued.

Subsequently, Fargo was sued in state court by its major competitor, Nuggett, Inc. In addition, the SEC commenced an investigation against Fargo for possible violations of the federal securities laws.

Both Nuggett and the SEC have subpoenaed all of Sharp's working papers relating to his audits of Fargo for the last 10 years. There is no evidence either that Sharp did anything improper or that any questionable financial activities by Fargo occurred prior to this year.

Sharp estimates that the cost for his duplicate photocopying of all of the working papers would be $25,000 (approximately one year's audit fee). Fargo has instructed Sharp not to turn over the working papers to anyone.

Required:

Answer the following, setting forth reasons for any conclusions stated.

a. If Sharp practices in a state that has a statutory accountant–client privilege, may the state's accountant–client privilege be successfully asserted to avoid turning over the working papers to the SEC?

b. Assuming Sharp, with Fargo's permission, turns over to Nuggett working papers for the last two audit years, may the state's accountant–client privilege be successfully asserted to avoid producing the working papers for the first eight years?

c. Other than asserting an accountant–client privilege, what major defenses might Sharp raise against the SEC and Nuggett in order to resist turning over the subpoenaed working papers?

(AICPA adapted)

Chapter 4
Professional Responsibility and Legal Liability

The terms *auditors' responsibility* and *auditors' legal liability* often confuse nonauditors. The distinction is subtle, yet it must be drawn in order for auditors and nonauditors to communicate with each other. This entire book, with the exception of the second section of this chapter, "Auditors' Legal Liability," is concerned with auditors' responsibilities; auditors' legal liabilities are discussed in that section of this chapter.

An appropriate way of viewing the relationship between responsibility and liability is to think of "responsibilities" as synonymous with "professional duties," and "legal liabilities" as relating to society's means of enforcing adherence to those professional duties, that is, compliance with professional standards, and providing compensation to victims of wrongful conduct. The concept of auditor responsibility usually arises in two related contexts: responsibility for what, and to whom? Answers to both questions are found primarily in the technical and ethical standards of the public accounting profession; they are occasionally specified in state and federal statutes and in court decisions. All of these sources provide guidance to auditors on how to conduct audits with due professional care and thus meet their professional responsibilities, and on the duties that auditors owe to their clients and third parties.

Chapter 3 described the various mechanisms that auditing firms, the AICPA, and state boards of accountancy have for maintaining the quality of audit practice. The legal process is another such mechanism that helps to ensure that auditors meet their responsibilities. Litigation and threats of litigation serve as enforcers of duties; they also help to define auditors' responsibilities and on rare occasions create what some perceive to be new responsibilities. The Commission on Auditors' Responsibilities noted that ''court decisions are particularly useful [in defining auditors' responsibilities] because they involve consideration of competing theories of responsibility. However, they must be considered carefully because a decision is usually closely related to the facts of a particular case. Consequently, the language used in a particular decision may not be the best expression of the technical issues involved.''[1] The outcome of a specific legal case also may not be a reliable indicator of auditors' responsibilities because it is often impossible to discern the rationale of a jury verdict, and appellate decisions are often clouded by procedural rules, such as the requirement that factual determinations not be disturbed.

To a great degree, auditors' responsibilities reflect the expectations of users of audited financial statements. Users expect an auditor to evaluate the measurements and disclosures made by management and to determine whether the financial statements contain material errors or misstatements, either unintentional or not. Auditors have long accepted the responsibility to design their examinations to detect material unintentional errors in financial statements; after all, if that is not a purpose of an audit, what is? The auditor's responsibility for designing audits to detect deliberate misstatements in financial statements has been less clear over the years, primarily because of the difficulty, or even impossibility, of detecting skillfully contrived employee or management[2] fraud, particularly if any form of collusion is present. Accordingly, the first section of this chapter discusses auditors' responsibilities with regard to financial statement misstatements, with an emphasis on management fraud.[3] Responsibilities for detecting and reporting illegal acts by clients are also covered. The second section deals with the legal liabilities that auditors have to various parties when they fail to detect either unintentional errors or deliberate misstatements.

Responsibility for Detecting Misstatements

The authoritative auditing literature has long reflected the view that auditors are not responsible for detecting deliberate financial statement misstatements unless the application of generally accepted auditing standards would result in such detection. Many users of financial statements, however, have asserted that one of the primary purposes of an audit is the detection of management

---

[1]*Report, Conclusions, and Recommendations*, 1978, p. 2.

[2]''Management'' as used in this chapter includes both top management and all lower levels of management that may have reasons to deceive top management.

[3]Although management fraud is only one of several categories of misstatements affecting financial statements, it has probably received more attention from the public and been alleged in more instances of litigation involving auditors than has any other category.

fraud or other intentional misstatements in all circumstances. Indeed, the Commission on Auditors' Responsibilities, charged by the AICPA with delineating the appropriate responsibilities of independent auditors, stated: "Significant percentages of those who use and rely on the auditor's work rank the detection of fraud among the most important objectives of an audit" (p. 31).

In June 1985, a National Commission on Management Fraud was established under the sponsorship of the AICPA, the American Accounting Association, the Financial Executives Institute, and the Institute of Internal Auditors. The Commission's objectives are "to develop initiatives for the prevention and detection of fraud and, in particular, to determine the role of the independent auditor in detecting management fraud." It expects to complete its work and issue a final report to the sponsoring organizations during 1987. In addition, the AICPA has formed a task force charged with determining whether the authoritative auditing literature appropriately describes the auditor's responsibility for detecting and reporting errors, irregularities, and illegal acts.

The Securities and Exchange Commission (SEC) has long taken the position that an audit can be expected to detect certain kinds of fraud, stating in Accounting Series Release (ASR) No. 19, "In the Matter of McKesson & Robbins, Inc.," issued in 1940, that

> Moreover, we believe that, even in balance sheet examinations for corporations whose securities are held by the public, accountants can be expected to detect gross overstatements of assets and profits whether resulting from collusive fraud or otherwise. We believe that alertness on the part of the entire [audit] staff, coupled with intelligent analysis by experienced accountants of the manner of doing business, should detect overstatements in the accounts, regardless of their cause, long before they assume the magnitude reached in this case. Furthermore, an examination of this kind should not, in our opinion, exclude the highest officers of the corporation from its appraisal of the manner in which the business under review is conducted. Without underestimating the important service rendered by independent public accountants in their review of the accounting principles employed in the preparation of financial statements filed with us and issued to stockholders, we feel that the discovery of gross overstatements in the accounts is a major purpose of such an audit even though it be conceded that it might not disclose every minor defalcation.

This position was reiterated in 1974 in exactly the same terms in ASR No. 153. In ASR No. 292, issued in 1981, the SEC expressed its view that extended audit procedures are sometimes necessary when there are signs of fraud.

AICPA Professional Requirements

Official pronouncements on the subject of auditors' responsibilities for many years were broad, vague, and sometimes overly defensive and self-serving. The latest AICPA pronouncement on the auditor's responsibility to detect financial statement misstatements, however, SAS No. 16, *The Independent Auditor's Responsibility for the Detection of Errors or Irregularities* (AU Section 327), issued in 1977, states:

> Under generally accepted auditing standards the independent auditor has the responsibility, within the inherent limitations of the auditing process . . ., to plan his examination to search for errors or irregularities that would have a material effect on the financial statements, and to exercise due skill and care in the conduct of that examination. The auditor's search for material errors or irregularities ordinarily is accomplished by the performance of those auditing procedures that in his judgment are appropriate in the circumstances to form an opinion on the financial statements; extended auditing procedures are required if the auditor's examination indicates that material errors or irregularities may exist. . . . An independent auditor's standard report implicitly indicates his belief that the financial statements taken as a whole are not materially misstated as a result of errors or irregularities.

One point that has been clear throughout all of the AICPA's pronouncements is the statement in paragraph 13 of SAS No. 16 that "the auditor is not an insurer or guarantor; if his examination was made in accordance with generally accepted auditing standards, he has fulfilled his professional responsibility."

As used in SAS No. 16, the terms *errors* and *irregularities* are precisely defined:

> The term *errors* refers to unintentional mistakes in financial statements and includes mathematical or clerical mistakes in the underlying records and accounting data from which the financial statements were prepared, mistakes in the application of accounting principles, and oversight or misinterpretation of facts that existed at the time the financial statements were prepared.
>
> The term *irregularities* refers to intentional distortions of financial statements, such as deliberate misrepresentations by management, sometimes referred to as management fraud, or misappropriations of assets, sometimes referred to as defalcations. Irregularities in financial statements may result from the misrepresentation or omission of the effects of events or transactions; manipulation, falsification, or alteration of records or documents; omission of significant information from records or documents; recording of transactions without substance; intentional misapplication of accounting principles; or misappropriation of assets for the benefit of management, employees, or third parties. Such acts may be accompanied by the use of false or misleading records or documents and may involve one or more individuals among management, employees, or third parties.

Management fraud usually involves the deliberate misapplication of accounting principles, such as failure to provide for uncollectible accounts receivable or the deliberate overstatement of inventory. This type of irregularity is called "management fraud" because it is perpetrated by management and because its objective is often the furtherance of a management goal, such as higher reported earnings, rather than direct personal enrichment. Such irregularities are likely to have a significant effect on financial statements. Management fraud sometimes includes defalcations or misappropriation of assets or services. Those types of management fraud are difficult to detect, because they involve management override of controls.

Employee defalcations are generally less significant than management fraud. Clever concealment of defalcations can result in overstatements of assets (paid receivables reported as still due) or understatements of liabilities (payments misappropriated and reported as paid). In many instances where defalcations have occurred, however, the financial statements are theoretically accurate, because the asset that has been misappropriated is no longer included in the balance sheet and total expenses on the income statement are correct, although amounts related to the misappropriation are misclassified. (For example, inventory that was stolen may have been properly removed from the balance sheet, but charged to cost of sales rather than to a loss account.)

As cited above, SAS No. 16 states that the auditor's responsibility under generally accepted auditing standards is "to plan his examination to search for errors or irregularities that would have a material effect on the financial statements, and to exercise due skill and care in the conduct of that examination." Thus, the auditor should plan the audit with the possibility of irregularities in mind. Neither SAS No. 16 nor any other auditing standards, however, set forth specific procedures that are required in this area, nor do they mandate that procedures be specifically designed for this purpose. Instead, the emphasis is placed on an awareness of how circumstances that arise during an audit, as well as the client's particular situation, affect the likelihood of different types of irregularities. For example, management that places undue stress on increased earnings may be disinclined to acknowledge the need to provide for uncollectible accounts receivable or unsalable inventory. Similarly, pressure on divisional executives to meet unrealistic budgets may lead to the recording of sales in advance of shipment or other means of inflating income artificially. The existence of management that is oriented toward a favorable earnings trend, however, or tight budgets imposed on divisions, does not necessarily mean that there is a likelihood of management fraud. Also, while a perceived reluctance on the part of management to segregate responsibilities appropriately among employees, or the existence of an accounting function that is distinctly weaker than one would expect in a particular organization, may increase the possibility of both management fraud and defalcations, it does not necessarily imply that such irregularities are probable. Unless evidence to the contrary comes to light, the auditor may reasonably assume that management has not made material misrepresentations or overridden internal controls.

How, then, does the auditor fulfill the professional responsibility with respect to significant irregularities? Simply put, with respect to defalcations the auditor is responsible for designing and performing audit procedures that professional responsibility would ordinarily dictate in a particular set of client circumstances, such as designing audit procedures with respect to cash that reflect the strengths and weaknesses of the client's internal accounting controls over cash. The question is more difficult to answer with regard to management fraud, because the result of such an irregularity is a significant misapplication of accounting principles, which the audit as a whole is designed to detect. The auditor should perform the audit with an awareness of the possibility of willful manipulation, keeping in mind the particular circumstances of the engagement and maintaining an attitude of professional skepticism. Because of the characteristics of certain irregularities, particularly those involving forgery and collusion, a properly designed and executed audit may not detect a deliberate scheme to falsify financial statements, no matter how much work is done. For example, an auditor is neither required nor trained to authenticate documents; also, audit procedures that are effective for detecting an unintentional misstatement may be ineffective when the same misstatement is intentional and concealed through collusion.

Client Deterrents to Irregularities

There are various provisions that a company can make—some of them also necessary to manage the business effectively—that serve as deterrents with respect to irregularities.

Internal Control and Internal Audit. A comprehensive system of internal control prescribes that transactions should be recorded based on adequate documentation and requires appropriate review and authorization of those transactions. A system of internal controls also provides for reconciliation of subsidiary ledgers (for example, accounts receivable and inventory) to control accounts and to the extent practicable appropriately segregates duties among various employees. If different people initiate and approve the recording of transactions, and if access to cash or other assets is possible only through the action of more than one employee, there is a lesser possibility of irregularities.

An internal audit department—reporting either to the board of directors or audit committee or to a senior executive removed from the accounting function—that performs comprehensive examinations in key areas of a company's operations is also likely to detect both defalcations and management fraud in areas that it examines; it may also have a deterrent effect on individuals who might otherwise be tempted to steal or to manipulate the financial statements.

Insurance. Fidelity bond insurance indemnifies a company against losses that are discovered and that are the result of employee defalcations. A secondary benefit of employee bonding is the investigation of an employee's background that the insurance company often makes prior to issuing a bond. As an aside, it should be noted that some insurance companies, after settling claims with insured companies, have in turn asserted claims under their rights of subrogation against auditors, charging that the auditors' negligence permitted the loss to go undetected longer than necessary. More than 40 years ago, a committee of the AICPA explored this matter with representatives of a large number of insurance companies. As a result, in exchange for a promise by the AICPA to encourage its members to recommend fidelity bond coverage to their clients, many such companies signed a letter stating that they would not assert claims under their rights of subrogation against auditors if affirmatively dishonest or criminal acts or gross negligence on the part of the auditors was not involved.

The letter further stated that such claims would not be asserted unless an impartial committee of three nonaccountants concluded, after a hearing, that the circumstances warranted that action. Although some insurance companies have withdrawn from the agreement, it remains in force with respect to many others, and its continuing validity has been recognized by several courts in recent years.

Illegal Acts by Clients

In the 1970s, various governmental bodies, particularly the SEC, focused attention on illegal or questionable corporate acts, such as bribes, political payoffs, and kickbacks—usually made at least ostensibly for the benefit of the enterprise. One consequence of this scrutiny was the Foreign Corrupt Practices Act, which is discussed in Chapter 7. At the same time, the SEC, members of Congress, the Commission on Auditors' Responsibilities, and others in the profession proposed that independent auditors assume more responsibility for the detection and disclosure of illegal or questionable acts by clients. As a result, the AICPA issued SAS No. 17, *Illegal Acts by Clients* (AU Section 328), in 1977, covering the auditor's responsibility with respect to possible illegal acts committed by management. Those acts involve violations of laws or governmental regulations other than irregularities.

SAS No. 17 recognizes that an audit made in accordance with generally accepted auditing standards cannot be expected to ensure that illegal acts by client management will be uncovered. The consequences of illegal acts, however, could have a significant effect on a client's financial statements and on the auditor's assessment of management's integrity. Therefore, auditors are expected to be aware of the possibility of illegal acts when performing their normal work. In addition, auditors are required to inquire about a client's procedures relating to the prevention of illegal acts, such as the issuance of communications to, and the receipt of representations from, various levels of management. Those representations often include statements signed annually by all levels of management that they have not violated company policy— which is usually defined to cover all of the actions proscribed by the Foreign Corrupt Practices Act and also conflicts of interests—and that they are not aware of any such violations. Finally, through the performance of procedures to determine the existence of loss contingencies, including communication with attorneys, and by virtue of a working (although imprecise) familiarity with laws governing income taxes and securities, it is possible that violations of laws may be uncovered during the course of normal audit work.

Responsibilities on Discovering a Possible Irregularity or Illegal Act

An auditor who becomes aware of a possible irregularity or illegal act should attempt to determine the potential effect on the financial statements under examination. In addition, the auditor should bring the matter to the attention of management at a level that is sufficiently high to be able to deal appropriately with the matter, including further investigation, if considered necessary. If matters are considered to be important enough, the auditor should inform the board of directors or the audit committee. In addition to the need to quantify the possible effect of irregularities and illegal acts and to report to the appropriate level of management, the auditor must consider whether the resulting assessment of management's integrity will permit him or her to continue to serve the client. The need to inform the appropriate regulatory authority must also be considered if the auditor perceives that management is not reacting appropriately to a possible illegal act. Auditors would be well advised to consult their legal counsel with respect to this decision.

AU Section 327.14 notes that in some cases the auditor may not be able to determine the extent of a possible irregularity, and presents the following guidance:

> When the auditor's examination indicates the presence of errors or possible irregularities, and the auditor remains uncertain about whether these errors or possible irregularities may materially affect the financial statements, he should qualify his opinion or disclaim an opinion on the financial statements and, depending on the circumstances, consider withdrawing from the engagement, indicating his reasons and findings in writing to the board of directors. In such circumstances, the auditor may wish to consult with his legal counsel.

AU Section 328.16 contains similar guidance with respect to an illegal act whose financial statement effect cannot be reasonably estimated. AU Section 328.14 notes that in some circumstances an auditor may not be able to determine whether an act is in fact illegal and states that this might constitute a scope limitation, which would lead to a qualified opinion or a disclaimer of opinion.

Engagement Letter

Most auditors recognize the necessity of a written communication to the client that specifies the responsibilities of both the client and auditor. That communication, called an ''engagement letter,'' is not required by generally accepted auditing standards, but is widely employed to avoid misunderstandings about the auditor's responsibility for discovering errors, irregularities, and illegal acts, and to remind clients of the inherent limitations of an audit. (Some auditors also include fee terms and other arrangements.) A typical engagement letter is shown in Figure 4.1. Some auditors request clients to sign and return a copy of the engagement letter to indicate their acceptance of and agreement with the contents of the letter.

Figure 4.1 Typical Engagement Letter

To the Board of Directors
X Corporation

This letter confirms the nature and scope of our engagement to examine the financial statements of X Corporation.

Our examination of your financial statements will be made in accordance with generally accepted auditing standards and will include such tests of the accounting records and such other auditing procedures as we consider necessary in the circumstances. The objective of such an examination is the expression of our opinion on whether the statements present fairly the financial position, results of operations, and changes in financial position in conformity with generally accepted accounting principles applied on a consistent basis.

As a part of our examination, we will make a study and evaluation of the Company's system of internal accounting control to the extent we consider necessary to evaluate the system as required by generally accepted auditing standards. Under these standards, the purpose of such evaluation is to establish a basis for reliance on the system of internal accounting control in determining the nature, timing, and extent of other auditing procedures that are necessary for expressing an opinion on the financial statements and to assist the auditor in planning and performing the examination of the financial statements.

Auditors' Legal Liability

Beyond the disciplinary system of the profession discussed in the previous chapter, auditors,[4] in common with other professionals, are subject to legal and other sanctions as a consequence of deficiencies, that is, failures to meet professional responsibilities, in the performance of their work. Unlike many other professionals, however, whose liability often is limited to their clients and patients, independent auditors are also liable to growing numbers of nonclient third parties, primarily investors and creditors, who rely on audited financial statements in making decisions that expose them to substantial potential losses. As a result, auditors' exposure to possible loss is great, and the amount of potential loss is usually indeterminate at the time the audit is performed. This section of the chapter examines auditors' civil liabilities to clients and to third parties, as well as criminal liability and civil regulatory remedies.

[4]In this section of the chapter, the words *auditor* and *auditors* apply to both individuals, whether sole practitioners or employees of CPA firms, and auditing firms, unless otherwise specified or indicated by context.

Figure 4.1 *Continued*

Such examinations include procedures designed to detect errors and irregularities that would have a material effect on the financial statements. However, as you are aware, there are inherent limitations in the auditing process; for example, such examinations are based on the concept of selective testing of the data being examined and are, therefore, subject to the inherent limitation that such matters, if they exist, may not be detected.

Likewise, in making our examination we will be aware of the possibility that illegal acts may have occurred. However, it should be recognized that such an examination cannot be expected to provide assurance that illegal acts will be detected.

You recognize that the establishment and maintenance of a system of internal accounting control is an important responsibility of management. Appropriate supervisory review procedures are necessary to provide reasonable assurance that adopted policies and prescribed procedures are adhered to and to identify errors and irregularities or illegal acts. As part of our aforementioned review of the Company's system of internal control, we will inform you of weaknesses that we believe should be corrected and our recommendations in this respect.

Very truly yours

(Firm name, manually signed)

The Litigation Explosion

Auditors' liability derives from both common and statutory law. Common law evolves from judicial rulings on matters of law in specific cases. Statutory law may codify or change common law. Judicial interpretation of statutory law, in turn, leads to the development of case law precedents. This interaction permits the courts continually to redefine the auditor's role and duties.

The increase in the number of lawsuits filed against auditors since the mid-1960s has been so tremendous that it has been described as a "litigation explosion." In large part, it has resulted from both social changes and changes in the ways in which the courts have interpreted both common law and the federal securities laws to extend auditors' liability beyond clients to a number of different classes of third parties.

The Extent of Litigation Against Auditors. Prior to 1965, lawsuits brought against accountants by third parties claiming damages as a result of a negligent audit were generally unsuccessful. Several decisions in the late 1960s signaled dramatic changes in the attitude of the courts and the expectations of the public concerning auditors' responsibilities and their consequent legal liabilities to third parties. The June 15, 1968, issue of *Fortune* reported that "there have been as many suits filed against auditors in the past twelve months as in the previous twelve years."[5] By the mid-1980s, literally hundreds of lawsuits were pending against auditors, most based on alleged federal securities law violations. There are also indications of an increase in suits being brought by clients and former clients for an auditor's failure to detect management fraud and for negligent performance of nonauditing services, such as those involving tax practice and management advisory services.

In addition, auditing firms, in common with other financial institutions, have recently been sued under the Racketeering Influenced and Corrupt Organizations (RICO) provisions of the Organized Crime Control Act of 1970. That law, which provides for triple damages and the awarding of attorneys' fees, was intended to be used against organized crime; however, it was written so broadly that during the 1980s large numbers of legitimate businesses as well have been charged with violating it by doing business through a "pattern of racketeering," which is defined as two illegal acts (such as mail fraud). The civil sanctions of the law have been invoked against auditing firms charged with being associated with financial statements known to be materially misstated. At the time of this writing, no cases brought against auditing firms under this law have been adjudicated on other than procedural issues.

In July 1985, in *Sedima, S.P.R.L.* v. *Imrex Co., Inc.,*[6] the Supreme Court noted that three-quarters of the cases brought to date under RICO involved allegations of securities fraud or common-law fraud on the part of legitimate businesses. The Court held that although such lawsuits may not reflect Congress's intent when RICO was enacted, the language of the law clearly permits it to be used in civil actions against enterprises that have no connection with organized crime or other criminal activity. A House subcommittee has held hearings on a bill that would limit civil actions under RICO to instances in which a business or an individual was previously convicted of racketeering activity or of a criminal violation. At the time of this writing, it is not known what revisions Congress might eventually make to the law. (The existing law cuts both ways, however. In August 1985, a federal appellate court upheld an accounting firm's right to sue one of its clients under RICO for loss of reputation and other injuries resulting from the client's fraudulent activities involving its financial statements.[7])

The annual malpractice insurance premiums being paid by the 17 largest public accounting firms are conservatively estimated at more than $100 million; uninsured losses, loss deductibles paid by the firms, and the in-house costs of developing information for the defense of lawsuits probably account for at least $30 to $40 million. In addition, the size of the internal legal staffs of the

[5]Arthur M. Louis, "The Accountants Are Changing the Rules," *Fortune*, June 15, 1968, p. 177, as cited in Denzil Y. Causey, Jr., *Duties and Liabilities of Public Accountants*, rev. ed. (Homewood, Ill.: Dow Jones–Irwin, 1982), p. 2.

[6]105 S. Ct. 3275 (1985).

[7]*Alexander Grant & Co.* v. *Tiffany Industries*, 770 F.2d 717 (8th Cir. 1985).

major accounting firms provides an indication of the significance of the actual and potential legal exposure of auditors. In 1986, for example, 11 of the large national accounting firms employed approximately 55 lawyers who worked solely on the legal affairs of those firms. There is no expectation that this number will decrease; the greater likelihood is that the size of legal staffs will increase, and that firms that do not already have internal lawyers will hire them. The first such internal lawyer was employed by a major accounting firm in 1968.

Major Influences on the Legal Environment. A number of factors have contributed to the increase in litigation against auditors since the 1960s, including technical legal developments that made legal remedies available to third parties (discussed in a later section) and social changes that influenced the public's expectations of auditors. Most notable of these social changes are the growth of consumerism and the perception of auditors as "insurers" of the accuracy of a company's financial statements.

Consumerism. It was inevitable with the passage of the federal securities laws in the early 1930s and the growth of the securities markets that investors and creditors would make increased use of audited financial statements. Paralleling this development has been the growth of an attitude that just as consumers of the products and services of American business are entitled to expect more from their purchases than they did in the past, so too are investors and creditors as consumers of financial information. This attitude has been buttressed by the access that disappointed consumers of financial information have to new and far-reaching remedies, perhaps the most significant of which from the auditor's point of view is the class action lawsuit (discussed later in this chapter). The result of these developments has been a heightening of the public's expectations of auditors and their work, and a far greater willingness on the part of investors and creditors who relied on that work to seek recovery from auditors for losses suffered. Rightly or wrongly, many people believe that auditors can act to prevent investor and creditor losses and are thus a logical choice to bear those losses.

Auditors as "Insurers." A second important influence on the legal environment is the public's perception of auditors as "guarantors" of the accuracy of a company's financial statements. The public, perhaps because of the apparent precision of financial statements and the prominence of the auditor's report accompanying them, often does not recognize that a company's management has primary responsibility for its financial statements and that the auditor's role in examining them inherently involves numerous necessarily imprecise judgments.

Thus, when the "guarantor" is viewed as a large, successful organization with substantial resources (including professional liability insurance), and frequently in troubled situations is also the only financially viable entity available to sue, it should not be surprising that auditors are looked to for their "deep pockets" and are sued by injured persons primarily because of their ability to pay, regardless of their culpability. The fact that an auditor's fees for an engagement rarely bear any reasonable relationship to the auditor's potential liability, and that the auditor derived no "equity" benefit from the operations of the entity, rarely elicits sympathy from disappointed investor-plaintiffs.

Substantial numbers of lawsuits against auditors alleging inadequacies in their professional services will probably continue to be a fact of life, at least for the foreseeable future. Efforts by the profession to articulate its objectives, assumed responsibilities, and the limitations of those responsibilities may have an effect on the public's expectations and perception of auditors. In the meantime, an auditor's best protection against liability (in addition to adequate malpractice insurance) is to do competent work and to keep in mind an understanding of how the courts perceive the professional's role and responsibilities, as expressed in judicial rulings on matters of law in specific cases (common law) and as codified in the securities laws.

Liability to Clients

An auditor's liability to clients is based on the direct contractual relationship between them, referred to as "privity," and on the law of torts, which relates to wrongful acts that injure another's person, property, or reputation. Almost all "wrongful acts" alleged against auditors fall into the category of misrepresentation. Under common law, a professional is liable to a client for breach of contract (for example, an auditor's issuing an unqualified opinion without conducting an examination in accordance with GAAS) and also, under tort law, for ordinary negligence. Obviously, if an auditor is liable to a client for ordinary negligence, gross negligence and fraud on the part of the auditor are also grounds for liability to a client.

Ordinary negligence is defined as the failure to exercise due professional care, that is, the level of care expected of a person of ordinary prudence, often referred to as the "prudent man concept." For auditors, due care essentially means adherence to generally accepted auditing standards. Gross negligence is the lack of even slight care; fraud involves deceit or intentional misrepresentation or omission of a material fact. Accordingly, an auditor owes a client the duty to use due professional care in performing an audit. The client has a cause for action against the auditor if the financial statements contain a misrepresentation of a material fact—that is, a material error or irregularity—that was not detected because of the auditor's failure to exercise due care and that injured the client.

Auditors should try to avoid misunderstandings with clients about their responsibility for the detection of errors or irregularities and illegal acts. Because this is a sensitive area, most auditors discuss these matters with their clients and follow up with a written communication spelling out a mutual understanding of functions, objectives, and responsibilities regarding the audit (see Figure 4.1). Such communications do not, however, relieve the auditor of legal liability for the failure to exercise due professional care.

Most of the claims that have been brought against auditors by clients have been based on negligent misrepresentation. Findings of negligence in suits brought by clients (or by a client's bonding company that made good the client's losses) often resulted from auditors' failures to detect defalcations. Although it is not the purpose of an audit to discover or provide specific protection against misappropriations, it is not unreasonable for a client to look for recompense from its auditor when the audit, if properly conducted, would have uncovered a misappropriation.

Contributory negligence by the client-plaintiff—negligence that is a substantial factor in causing the client's injury—is a defense available to the auditor and negates the basis for recovery if it has contributed to the client's loss. Moreover, if a fraudulent scheme is condoned by top management, the wrongdoing is attributed to the client and any claim against the auditor for failure to detect the scheme is barred.[8] Management, however, frequently ignores its own contributory culpability in failing to provide adequate internal controls, including proper supervision of employees. (In some states, the client's negligence must interfere with the audit before it will bar the client's claim.) A willingness to test the principle of contributory negligence by going to trial has recently shown signs of producing successful defenses for auditors, particularly when combined with auditors' willingness to seek restitution from culpable management that contributed to the client's loss. Several states, however, have adopted the concept of comparative negligence in which the burden of the client's loss is divided between the client and the auditor according to their relative fault, and this may weaken the effectiveness of the contributory negligence defense.

Potential liability also arises from the auditor's quasi-fiduciary relationship with a client. As discussed in Chapter 3, the auditor has a professional responsibility not to disclose confidential information obtained during an audit unless disclosure is required for the fair presentation by the client of financial information in conformity with generally accepted accounting principles. In *Fund of Funds, Ltd.* v. *Arthur Andersen & Co.*,[9] the auditors were found liable as a result of, among other things, failing to use information they obtained from another client to determine which of the two clients' financial statements accurately portrayed the facts of the same transaction. Thus, there may be a legal precedent for holding an auditor liable for not disclosing and using information obtained from services rendered to one client that is relevant to the audit of another client. The auditor's professional responsibility in this situation is discussed in Chapter 3.

Civil Liability to Third Parties Under Common Law[10]

Most civil suits brought by third parties against auditors under common law allege losses resulting from reliance on financial statements later found to be ma-

---

[8]*Cenco, Inc.* v. *Seidman & Seidman*, 686 F. 2d 449 (7th Cir.), *cert. denied*, 103 S. Ct. 177 (1982).

[9]545 F. Supp. 1314 (S.D.N.Y. 1982).

[10]Civil liability to third parties also exists under the federal securities acts, as discussed later in this chapter.

terially misleading. Suits of this type have increased as a result of a number of judicial decisions beginning in the 1960s that expanded the class to whom the auditor owed a duty of care and also raised the level of care owed to third parties. Today an auditor generally is liable for ordinary negligence to parties the auditor specifically knows may rely on an audit opinion (primary beneficiaries), as well as to any reasonably limited and reasonably definable class of persons the auditor might reasonably expect to rely on the opinion (foreseen third parties).[11] Liability for gross negligence and fraud extends to all third parties, including merely foreseeable third parties.

Privity of Contract Doctrine.   Unlike the auditor–client relationship, there is no privity of contract between the auditor and third parties. Traditionally, claims by third parties under common law were based not on contract law but on the law of torts, and only fraud, not ordinary negligence from failure to exercise due care, on the part of an auditor was considered a wrongful act. The first case to test the privity of contract doctrine involving auditors was *Ultramares Corp.* v. *Touche*[12] in 1931. The plaintiff, without the defendant's knowledge, had relied on financial statements audited by the defendant to make loans to a company that later became insolvent. The plaintiff alleged that the auditors were guilty of negligence and fraudulent misrepresentation in not detecting fictitious amounts included in accounts receivable and accounts payable. The court upheld the doctrine of privity of contract as a limitation on the auditors' liability to the unforeseen third party for ordinary negligence, based, at least in part, on Judge Cardozo's reasoning that auditors' liability for negligence should not be extended to third parties because doing so would have the potential effect of deterring people from entering the profession, which would be detrimental to society. Cardozo described the consequences of extending the auditor's duty to third parties as follows:

> If liability for negligence exists, a thoughtless slip or blunder, the failure to detect a theft or forgery beneath the cover of deceptive entries, may expose accountants to a liability in an indeterminate amount for an indeterminate time to an indeterminate class. The hazards of a business conducted on these terms are so extreme as to enkindle doubt whether a flaw may not exist in an implication of a duty that exposes to these consequences.

Primary Benefit Rule.   Subsequently, however, courts in some states have attempted to increase the auditor's liability to third parties for ordinary negligence by eviscerating the privity doctrine. The first crack in the privity rule occurred in the *Ultramares* case itself with the formulation of the "primary benefit rule," which held that an auditor would be liable to a third party for ordinary negligence if the auditor knew that the audit was being performed for the pri-

---

[11]As a result of several recent decisions, discussed later in this chapter, liability for ordinary negligence may be extended to reasonably foreseeable parties as well.

[12]255 N.Y. 170, 174 N.E. 441 (1931).

mary benefit of a specifically identified third party. Prior to the mid-1960s, however, most third-party plaintiffs bringing suit against auditors pursuant to the primary benefit rule were not successful, even in cases in which the auditor knew specific persons might rely on the opinion. For example, in *State St. Trust Co.* v. *Ernst*,[13] the auditor was found not liable to a lender for negligence, even though the auditor knew that the particular lender intended to rely on the audited financial statements.

Further weakening of the privity of contract doctrine in cases of professionals' liability did not occur until 1963, 32 years after *Ultramares*. It began with a series of cases that represented an attack on the primary benefit rule. The *Hedley Byrne* case[14] was decided by the highest court of England, the House of Lords, in 1963. The case involved, not auditors, but a negligently stated accommodation credit report by a bank on which a third person relied, to his damage. In their opinions, the justices stated that "where there is a relationship equivalent to contract but for the absence of consideration, there is a duty of care." The court's finding, however, was intended to have somewhat limited application in that it extended the duty of care to only a restricted class of third parties, as in *Ultramares*.

Foreseen and Foreseeable Third Parties. In 1965, the American Law Institute (ALI) issued its Second Restatement of the Law of Torts, an authoritative compendium of tort principles. Partly in reliance on *Hedley Byrne*, the ALI interpreted the law of negligent misrepresentations by professionals to third parties more broadly than it had been interpreted in the past, to apply to the (relatively small) group of persons whom a defendant expects and intends to influence (known as "foreseen persons"), in contrast to a "foreseeable class of persons," defined as an unlimited class of persons not identified by the auditor who may foreseeably be expected to rely on an audit report.

The distinction in the Restatement's interpretation of a professional's duty to third parties between *foreseen* and *foreseeable* persons is critical to an understanding of post-1965 legal decisions based on common law. In two significant cases, U.S. courts have accepted the foreseen class concept of the ALI's Second Restatement. In *Rusch Factors, Inc.* v. *Levin*,[15] the court ruled that the auditor could be liable to the third-party plaintiff, a lender of the client, for ordinary negligence. In this case, the audit was performed at the specific request of the plaintiff-lender, who was therefore a primary beneficiary; however, the court's decision extended liability for ordinary negligence to foreseen and limited classes of persons, such as lenders who receive a company's audit report, even if those persons are not specifically known to the auditor. In *Rhode Island Hospital Trust National Bank* v. *Swartz*,[16] the court found the auditors liable for ordi-

[13]278 N.Y. 104, 15 N.E. 2d 416 (1938).

[14]*Hedley Byrne & Co. Ltd.* v. *Heller & Partners, Ltd.*, 1964 A.C. 465 [1963] 2 *All E.R.* 575 (H.L. 1963).

[15]284 F. Supp. 85 (D.R.I. 1968).

[16]482 F. 2nd 1000 (4th Cir. 1973).

nary negligence under the foreseen class concept but not the primary benefit rule. In this case, the auditors knew that the plaintiff-bank required audited financial statements of the client, but did not know the specific identity of the plaintiff.

The Supreme Court of Canada, in a 1976 decision (*Haig* v. *Bamford*[17]), applied the foreseen class rule to invoke a duty of care that an auditor owed to third parties. The court held that "actual knowledge of the specific plaintiff who will use and rely on the statement" was too narrow a test, and instead applied a test of "actual knowledge of the limited class that will use and rely on the statement."

Until 1983, auditors' common law liability for negligence remained limited to foreseen third parties.[18] In that year, the New Jersey Supreme Court ruled in a motion for partial summary judgment that an auditor has a duty to reasonably foreseeable but unidentifiable third-party users who may rely on financial statements for appropriate business purposes.[19] The plaintiffs had alleged that they relied on financial statements audited by the defendants in making an investment that subsequently proved to be worthless, after the financial statements were found to be misstated. The plaintiffs were not members of an identifiable group of users to whom the financial statements were intended to be furnished. A few weeks later, the Wisconsin Supreme Court handed down a similar ruling.[20] Thus, the auditor's common law liability for negligence may be extended to reasonably foreseeable third parties.[21]

In a 1985 case, however, New York's highest court essentially reaffirmed the privity requirement. In *Credit Alliance Corp.* v. *Arthur Andersen & Co.*,[22] the court dismissed an $8.8 million judgment of a lower court against Arthur Andersen, finding that the allegations failed to set forth a relationship of contractual privity or its equivalent. The case involved a client's financial statements on which the plaintiff relied in making lending decisions; the client subsequently filed for reorganization under the bankruptcy laws. In dismissing the action, the court restated the standards it established in the *Ultramares* case 54 years earlier. In *Credit Alliance*, the court ruled that for accountants to be held liable for negligence to third parties, (1) the accountants must have been aware that the financial statements were to be used for a particular purpose; (2) a

[17][1977] 1 S.C.R. 466 (Can.).

[18]California has long had a negligent misrepresentation statute that provides broader protection to financial statement users.

[19]*H. Rosenblum, Inc.* v. *Adler*, 93 N.J. 324, 461 A. 2d 138 (1983).

[20]*Citizens State Bank* v. *Timm Schmidt & Co.*, 113 Wis. 2d 376, 335 N.W. 2d 361 (1983).

[21]In reaching its decision, the New Jersey Supreme Court raised issues that had not been explicitly addressed in any of the appeal briefs submitted in the case; the court also included citations supporting its findings that had not been cited by either party to the appeal. Many auditors, and doubtless many lawyers as well, might wish to contemplate whether major changes in legal precedents that have been adhered to for many years are best made by the courts or whether they are best wrought by legislative processes that include at least the potential for studying the social and economic consequences of the changes.

[22]66 N.Y. 2d 812, 489 N.E. 2d 249 (1985).

known party must have intended to rely on the statements in furtherance of that purpose; and (3) there must have been some conduct on the accountants' part linking them to that party and demonstrating that they understood that party's reliance.

In 1986, an Arkansas federal district court dismissed a claim of negligence on the part of an accountant because the plaintiffs were not in privity with the accountant.[23] In response to the plaintiffs' contention that new duties should be created to favor remote parties because of the ability to obtain insurance to cover the risk, the court stated:

> The standard of behavior ultimately being enforced in such a case is a "duty to buy insurance." Given the currently and widely expressed concerns among Arkansas legislators about the availability and cost of business insurance and their growing determination to act legislatively in this very area, either by limiting the kinds of claims that might be presented or by adjusting the premiums which might be charged, this court feels that it is most inappropriate for it to be creating "new torts" at this time.

However, also in 1986, an intermediate court of appeals in California held that "an independent auditor owes a duty of care to reasonably foreseeable plaintiffs who rely on negligently prepared and issued unqualified audited financial statements."[24] Thus, California became the third state to reject *Ultramares*, and the first to do so after its reaffirmation in New York.

The intermediate appellate court in North Carolina also abandoned the *Ultramares* doctrine in 1986. In *Raritan River Steel Co.* v. *Cherry, Bekaert & Holland*,[25] the court ruled that the plaintiff, a trade creditor of the defendant-auditor's client, may bring an action against the auditor for negligent misrepresentation concerning the issuance of an audit opinion on which the third party allegedly relied in extending credit. The court rejected the "reasonably foreseeable" test adopted in the New Jersey, Wisconsin, and California cases as too broad and the test contained in the Restatement as too narrow. Instead, the court adopted a six-factor balancing test that considers the extent to which the transaction was intended to affect the plaintiff, the foreseeability of harm to the plaintiff, the degree of certainty that the plaintiff suffered injury, the proximity between the defendant's conduct and the injury suffered, the moral blame attached to the defendant's conduct, and the policy of preventing future harm. After citing the allegation in the complaint that the auditor knew that the plaintiff would be relying on the information, the court held that the six-part test was satisfied.

Scienter Requirement. In addition to actions on the grounds of negligence, third parties may bring suits against auditors on the grounds of fraud or constructive fraud that is inferred from evidence of gross negligence. Constructive

[23]*Robertson* v. *White*, 633 F. Supp. 954 (W. D. Ark. 1986).
[24]*International Mortgage Co.* v. *John P. Butler Accountancy Co.*, No. 34-91-00 (Cal. App. 1986).
[25]339 S.E. 2d 62 (N.C. App. 1986).

fraud differs from actual fraud in that the former involves the lack of a reasonable basis for believing that a representation is true whereas the latter involves actual knowledge that a representation is false. Actions grounded in fraud (actual or constructive) require the plaintiff to be able to prove some form of knowledge on the auditor's part of the falsity (or its equivalent) of a representation. This knowledge is commonly referred to as *scienter* and the requirement of its proof as the *scienter* requirement. Essentially, it is a requirement to prove an intent to injure. In some jurisdictions, scienter may be established by proof of any one of the following three elements:

1. Actual knowledge of the falsity of the representation.
2. A lack of knowledge of the truth of the representation.
3. A reckless disregard for the truth or falsity of the representation.

The scienter requirement is closely related to the concept of privity, as can be illustrated by the *Ultramares* case. If the jury were to find that the defendant-auditors expressed an unqualified opinion on the financial statements when they had no knowledge of the facts, and if this would support an allegation of fraud in other respects,[26] then liability for the tort of deceit (fraud) could extend to third parties not in a contractual relationship (privity) with the auditor. Without scienter, the case would not involve fraud. As noted previously, in most jurisdictions the group of persons to whom the auditor is liable for less than fraudulent acts is limited to foreseen third-party users. Under common law, then, the distinction between negligence and fraud is significant and rests essentially on the requirement for scienter.

The question of the requirement for scienter and the elements that constitute scienter are further explored in the discussion, later in the chapter, of the auditor's liability for negligence under Section 10(b) of the Securities Exchange Act of 1934 and Rule 10b-5 thereunder.

Civil Liability to Third Parties Under the Federal Securities Acts

The principal provisions of the federal securities acts that have determined the auditor's civil liability are Section 11 of the Securities Act of 1933 and Section 10(b) of the Securities Exchange Act of 1934 and related Rule 10b-5. Class action suits against auditors under the federal securities laws became common after 1966, when the procedural rules governing them were liberalized. Class actions are litigations in which one or a relatively small number of plaintiffs sue on behalf of a very large number of allegedly injured persons. One of the prerequisites of a class action is that the number of potential claimants is so large that it would be impracticable for each of them to sue individually. The dollar amount of potential liability in class actions can run into the hundreds of millions of dollars, thereby making the class action technique a formidable weapon.

[26]Those ''other respects'' include proof of false representation that was relied on by and caused damages to the plaintiff.

The Securities Act of 1933. The Securities Act of 1933 regulates public offerings of securities and contains provisions intended to protect those who acquire securities by purchase or merger. Section 11(a) reads, in part, as follows:

> In case any part of the registration statement . . . contained an untrue statement of a material fact or omitted to state a material fact required to be stated therein or necessary to make the statements therein not misleading, any person acquiring such security . . . may . . . sue . . . every accountant . . . who has with his consent been named as having . . . certified any part of the registration statement . . . with respect to the statement in such registration statement . . . which purports to have been . . . certified by him.

Thus, Section 11 of the Securities Act of 1933 imposes civil liability on auditors for misrepresentations or omissions of material facts in a registration statement. The measure of damages under the civil provisions of the 1933 Act is based on the difference between the amount the plaintiff paid for the security and either the market price at the time of the suit or, if the security was sold, the selling price.

Section 11 expands the elements of an auditor's liability to third parties beyond that of common law in the following significant ways:

1. Privity with the plaintiff is not a necessary element; any purchaser of securities in a public offering may sue auditors.
2. Liability to third parties does not require proof of fraud or gross negligence; ordinary negligence is a basis for liability.
3. The burden of proof is shifted from the plaintiff to the defendant. The plaintiff has to prove only a material misstatement of fact.
4. The auditor is held to a standard of care described as the exercise of "due diligence"—a reasonable investigation leading to a belief that the financial statements are neither false nor misleading.
5. The plaintiff need not prove reliance on the financial statements or the auditor's report thereon, but the defendant-auditor will prevail if the plaintiff's knowledge of the "untruth or omission" is proved.

The first, and still the most significant, judicial interpretation of Section 11, *Escott* v. *BarChris Construction Corp.*,[27] did not appear until 1968. The *BarChris* case was a class action against a bowling alley construction corporation that had issued debentures and subsequently declared bankruptcy, and against its auditors. The suit was brought by the purchasers of the debentures for damages sustained as a result of false statements and material omissions in the prospectus contained in the registration statement. The court ruled that the auditors were liable on the grounds that they had not met the minimum standard of "due diligence" in their review for subsequent events occurring up to the effective date of the registration statement (required under the 1933 Act and known as an S-1 review) because the auditor performing the review failed to appropriately follow up management's answers to his inquiries.

[27] 283 F. Supp. 643 (S.D.N.Y. 1968).

A defense to a Section 11 action against auditors would require demonstrating that a reasonable investigation had been made and that the auditors had reasonable grounds for believing and did believe that the financial statements were true and not misleading. In the *BarChris* case, the court stated that "accountants should not be held to a higher standard than that recognized in their profession," but held that the individual accountant responsible for the S-1 review, who had little practical auditing experience, had not met even that standard. As a direct result of this case, professional standards governing auditing procedures in the subsequent period (described in Chapter 17) were made stricter, and auditing firms began to place more emphasis on staff members' knowledge of a client's business and industry. The influence of this case on professional standards is described in more detail later in the chapter.

A controversial aspect of the 1933 Act concerns the issues of reliance and causation. An auditor is liable to purchasers of securities who may not have relied on the financial statements or the auditor's opinion or who may not even have known of their existence. If the auditor can prove, however, that something other than the misleading financial statements caused the plaintiff's loss, the amount of loss related to those other factors is not recoverable. Section 11 thus provides a causation defense, but it clearly places the burden of proof on the defendant-auditor; it requires the defendant to prove that factors other than the misleading statements caused the loss (in whole or in part). The courts have rarely considered the causation defense in Section 11 cases against auditors because most cases are settled before trial, as happened in *BarChris*.

The Securities Exchange Act of 1934.   Many more suits alleging civil liability against auditors have been brought under Section 10(b) of the Securities Exchange Act of 1934 than under the 1933 Act. The 1934 Act, which requires all companies whose securities are traded to file annual audited financial statements and quarterly and other financial information, regulates trading of securities and thus has broad applicability. Auditors' liability under the 1934 Act, however, is not as extensive as under the 1933 Act in the following two significant respects:

1. As established by the *Hochfelder* case (described later) in 1976, ordinary negligence is not a basis for liability to third parties under Section 10(b) and Rule 10b-5. Thus, the auditor's liability to unforeseen third parties under the 1934 Act is essentially the same as it was under common law at the time of *Ultramares*.
2. The burden of proof of both reliance on the financial statements and causation (that is, that the loss was caused by reliance on the statements, known as "proximate cause") rests with the plaintiff, as it does under common law.

On the other hand, Section 10(b) of the 1934 Act is accessible to both buyers and sellers of securities; Section 11 of the 1933 Act applies only to purchasers.

Damages recoverable under the civil provisions of the 1934 Act are the plaintiff's "out-of-pocket" losses, determined by the difference between the contract price of the securities and their actual value on the date of the transaction. Actual value is ordinarily considered to be the market value on the date the misrepresentation or omission is discovered and rectified.

The majority of civil lawsuits against auditors have been based on Section 10(b) and Rule 10b-5. Their provisions apply to any purchase or sale of any security, and thus they can be used by a plaintiff with respect to both registered public offerings (also covered by the 1933 Act) and any other transactions in securities. Moreover, the statute of limitations in some states is quite long, and it is not uncommon to have a lawsuit four to five years after the event alleged to give rise to liability.[28] Rule 10b-5 states, in part, that

> It shall be unlawful for any person . . . (a) To employ any device, scheme, or artifice to defraud, (b) To make any untrue statement of a material fact or to omit to state a material fact necessary in order to make the statements made, in light of the circumstances under which they were made, not misleading, or (c) To engage in any act, practice, or course of business which operates or would operate as a fraud or deceit upon any person, in connection with the purchase or sale of any security.

Section 10(b) and Rule 10b-5 do not provide a good-faith defense; rather, the defendant must refute the specific charges brought by the plaintiff. On the other hand, in a Rule 10b-5 action, the burden of proof that the auditor acted fraudulently rests with the plaintiff; under Section 11 of the 1933 Act, the burden of proof that the auditor was not culpable rests with the defendant-auditor.

The SEC enacted Rule 10b-5 in 1942 as a disciplinary measure for its own use against fraudulent purchasers of securities. A series of judicial interpretations subsequently made the rule accessible to private claimants who were able to prove damages resulting from their reliance on financial statements containing misrepresentations or omissions. Unfortunately, Rule 10b-5 is not at all precise in defining standards for liability, and it does not include a due diligence defense. Between the time of its enactment and the *Hochfelder* ruling in 1976 (discussed later), the courts interpreted the rule in disparate ways. Thus, in some jurisdictions auditors were found liable to third parties for ordinary negligence (absence of due diligence) in rendering their opinions; in other jurisdictions the courts held that an element of knowledge of the wrongful act or an intent to commit fraud (scienter) was required. Much of the controversy was resolved by the Supreme Court in 1976 with its decision in *Ernst & Ernst* v. *Hochfelder*.[29]

---

[28]In civil litigation under Section 10(b), the courts apply the statute of limitations of the jurisdiction where the plaintiff is domiciled, and this varies from state to state. Under the 1933 Act, suit must be brought within one year of the discovery of the untrue statement or omission, or after such discovery should have been made by the exercise of reasonable diligence, and in any event within three years after the security was offered to the public. Suits brought under common law follow the statute of limitations of the state in which the suit is brought.

[29]425 U.S. 185, 96 S. Ct. 1375, 47 L. Ed. 2d 668 (1976).

The complaint in *Hochfelder* charged that the auditors had violated Rule 10b-5 by their failure to conduct proper audits and thereby aided and abetted a fraud perpetrated by the president of a securities firm. The plaintiff's case rested on a charge of negligence and did not allege fraud or intentional misconduct on the part of the auditors. The Supreme Court ruled that a private suit for damages under Section 10(b) and Rule 10b-5 required an allegation of scienter. The Court's opinion stated, in part,

> When a statute speaks so specifically in terms of manipulation and deception, and of implementing devices and contrivances—the commonly understood terminology of intentional wrongdoing—and when its history reflects no more expansive intent, we are quite unwilling to extend the scope of the statute to negligent conduct.

It is important to note that this decision deals solely with Section 10(b) and Rule 10b-5; it does not impose any general standard for civil liability under the federal securities laws. The negligence standard under those laws continues to be confined to those sections where Congress expressly intended it to apply or where the courts have determined that imposing liability without scienter in the implied liability sections of the law is compatible with the overall structure and philosophy of the statutes. For example, a negligence standard is still applicable to liability under Section 11 of the 1933 Act. Also, a negligence standard applied in a case involving the 1934 Act's proxy rules, *Gerstle* v. *Gamble-Skogmo*,[30] in which the appeals court held it was not necessary "to establish any evil motive or even reckless disregard of the facts."

The Supreme Court's definition of scienter is a strict one. More than knowledge of the alleged wrongful act is necessary to constitute scienter under Section 10; there must be actual intent to deceive, manipulate, or defraud. Still, the courts or juries must determine whether scienter is present in a particular case, and this could lead to a possible erosion of the Supreme Court's strict definition.

The Court noted in *Hochfelder* that "in certain areas of the law, recklessness is considered to be a form of intentional conduct for purposes of imposing liability for some act." Thus, although the Court declined to address the question of reckless behavior in that case, it did open the possibility that in some circumstances recklessness may be interpreted as constructive fraud under Rule 10b-5. Recklessness has been defined as highly unreasonable conduct that is an extreme departure from the standards of ordinary care. While the danger of misleading investors need not be known, it must be at least so obvious that any reasonable person would have known it.[31] The prevailing view of the appellate courts that have addressed the issue of reckless behavior is that recklessness is sufficient to constitute scienter under Section 10(b). Thus, auditors must be

[30]478 F. 2d 1281 (2d Cir. 1973).
[31]*Ohio Drill & Tool Co.* v. *Johnson*, 625 F. 2d 738 (6th Cir. 1979).

prepared to deal with such an allegation. The Supreme Court, however, has explicitly left the question open.[32]

Figure 4.2 summarizes the pertinent facts relating to each of the various sources of auditors' civil liability discussed in this chapter.

Criminal Liability

Violations of the securities acts that give rise to civil liability for association with misleading financial statements also subject auditors to criminal penalties (fines of up to $10,000 or imprisonment for not more than five years, or both) under Section 24 of the Securities Act of 1933 and Section 32 of the Securities Exchange Act of 1934 if the violations can be shown to be willful or intentional. Auditors are also exposed to criminal penalties under the federal mail fraud and conspiracy statutes.

Perhaps because of the availability of other legal remedies (including injunctions, administrative proceedings, and civil suits by third parties) and the absence of the element of personal gain, there have been few criminal actions against auditors. Four of the most widely publicized criminal prosecutions were *Continental Vending*, *Four Seasons*, *National Student Marketing*, and *Equity Funding*, which together produced the conviction of eight individuals. Those cases demonstrate that errors of judgment on the part of auditors in not insisting on appropriate accounting, including adequate disclosure, of certain matters known to them may result in criminal liability in certain circumstances, even though no motive can be proved and no personal gain can be shown to have resulted.

John C. Burton, former Chief Accountant of the SEC, stated the Commission's position on bringing criminal charges against auditors:

> While virtually all Commission cases are civil in character, on rare occasions it is concluded that a case is sufficiently serious that it should be referred to the Department of Justice for consideration of criminal prosecution. Referrals in regard to accountants have only been made when the Commission and the staff believed that the evidence indicated that a professional accountant certified financial statements that he knew to be false when he reported on them. The Commission does not make criminal references in cases that it believes are simply matters of professional judgment even if the judgments appear to be bad ones.[33]

The consequences of criminal prosecution to an auditor may go beyond the obvious ones of the costs of defense and the resultant fines and imprisonment. A successful criminal prosecution may help to establish civil liability and will generally preclude the individual from continuing to practice as an auditor.

[32]*MacLean* v. *Huddleston*, 459 U.S. 375 (1983).
[33]John C. Burton, "SEC Enforcement and Professional Accountants: Philosophy, Objectives and Approach," *Vanderbilt Law Review* 28 (January 1975), p. 28.

Figure 4.2 Auditor's Civil Liability

	Accessible to	Basis for Suit	Minimum Basis for Liability	Burden of Proof of				Defense
				Damage or Loss	Misleading Statements	Reliance ("Proximate Cause")	Defendant's Culpability	
Common Law	Clients	Breach of contract Tort	Ordinary negligence	P[a]	P	P	P	Refute charges Contributory negligence
	Foreseen third parties	Tort	Ordinary negligence	P	P	P	P	Refute charges
	Other (unforeseen) third parties[b]	Tort	Gross negligence or fraud	P	P	P	P	Refute charges
1933 Act Section 11	Purchasers of securities	Misrepresentation or omission of material fact	Ordinary negligence	P	P	Not required	D	Due diligence Causation
1934 Act Section 10	Purchasers and sellers of securities	Misrepresentation or omission of material fact	Gross negligence or fraud	P	P	P	P	Refute charges

[a] P = Plaintiff; D = Defendant.
[b] In some states, liability for ordinary negligence may be extended to reasonably foreseeable parties. See text, pages 116 and 117.

Other SEC Sanctions

Auditors are also subject under the federal securities acts to legal sanctions that do not involve criminal penalties or the payment of damages. The SEC, as the principal government regulatory agency charged with enforcement of financial reporting standards, has two civil remedies available to it: civil injunctive actions and disciplinary (administrative) proceedings under Rule 2(e) of its Rules of Practice. Either remedy may be sought against an individual auditor or an entire firm.

Injunctive Proceedings. The SEC has the authority under Section 20 of the 1933 Act and Section 21 of the 1934 Act to initiate injunctive actions in the courts to restrain future violations of the provisions of those acts (including Section 10[b] of the 1934 Act). Under currently prevailing standards, discussed subsequently, such injunctions are available only against those whom the SEC can persuade a court are likely to violate the federal securities laws again if not enjoined. In a case tried in 1980, *Aaron* v. *SEC*,[34] the Supreme Court held that injunctions under Section 10(b) of the 1934 Act (and one subsection of Section 17[a] of the 1933 Act) require scienter.[35]

The consequences of an injunction may extend far beyond an admonition to obey the law in the future. The injunction can be useful to plaintiffs in subsequent civil suits for damages, and the person enjoined is exposed to civil and criminal contempt proceedings. Moreover, an injunction resulting from a consent decree, pursuant to which guilt is neither admitted nor denied, may require the auditor or firm to adopt and comply with certain procedures to prevent future violations.

Requests for permanent injunctions are tried publicly before a judge without a jury. Thus, the injunctions are granted or denied largely at the discretion of the trial judge. The SEC must prove both that a violation of the securities laws has occurred and also that there is a reasonable likelihood that future violations will occur if an injunction is not imposed. For example, in *SEC* v. *Geotek*,[36] the court found that there was no evidence of a past violation. The issue of what constitutes a "reasonable likelihood" of future violations is unresolved. On the one hand, the courts tend to give great weight to the SEC's expert judgment of the immediate need for injunctive relief. On the other hand, however, in *SEC* v. *Bausch & Lomb, Inc.*[37] the court ruled against enjoining the auditors, on the grounds of insufficient evidence that they were likely to commit further violations.

---

[34]446 U.S. 680, 100 S. Ct. 1945, 64 L. Ed. 2d 611 (1980).

[35]The Supreme Court decided, however, that injunctions under two other subsections of Section 17(a) do not require scienter.

[36]426 F. Supp. 715 (N.D. Cal. 1976), *aff'd sub nom. SEC* v. *Arthur Young & Co.*, 590 F. 2d 785 (9th Cir. 1979).

[37]420 F. Supp. 1226 (S.D.N.Y. 1976), *aff'd*, 565 F. 2d 8 (2d Cir. 1977).

Administrative (Rule 2[e]) Proceedings. Rule 2(e) of the SEC's Rules of Practice states that the Commission

> May deny, temporarily or permanently, the privilege of appearing or practicing before it in any way to any person who is found . . . (i) not to possess the requisite qualifications to represent others, (ii) to be lacking in character or integrity or have engaged in unethical or improper professional conduct, or (iii) to have willfully violated or willfully aided and abetted the violation of any provision of the federal securities laws . . . or the rules and regulations thereunder.

Proceedings under Rule 2(e) are generally conducted in private hearings; however, the resulting Accounting and Auditing Enforcement Releases (previously Accounting Series Releases), in which the SEC's allegations and the terms of settlement are set forth, attract a great deal of publicity. Rule 2(e) gives the SEC the explicit authority to suspend from appearing or practicing before it auditors who have been permanently enjoined from violation of the securities laws or convicted of a felony or of a misdemeanor involving immoral conduct.

The SEC has devised imaginative, often sweeping sanctions against auditing firms under Rule 2(e), many of which involve agreements to institute new or improved control procedures and to subject those procedures to an independent compliance review. In the past, these sanctions were often announced in Accounting Series Releases (ASRs), and are now published in Accounting and Auditing Enforcement Releases. Among the sanctions that have been imposed are the following:

1. Requirement to conduct a study of the use of a specific accounting method and to establish guidelines for the firm's practice in this area. (ASR No. 173 [July 2, 1975].)
2. Employment of consultants to review and evaluate the firm's auditing procedures for publicly held companies. (ASR No. 176 [July 22, 1975].)
3. Participation in quality peer review and continuing professional education programs. (ASR No. 191 [March 30, 1976].)
4. Prohibition against merging or combining practices with another accounting firm. (ASR No. 196 [September 1, 1976].)
5. Examination of the firm's audit practice relating to SEC clients and agreement to take reasonable steps to implement recommendations resulting therefrom. (ASR No. 209 [February 16, 1977].)
6. Prohibition for 60 days against undertaking new engagements likely to result in filings with the SEC. (ASR No. 209 [February 16, 1977].)
7. Participation in the AICPA's voluntary quality control review program. (ASR No. 210 [February 25, 1977].)
8. Requirement to conduct or sponsor a research project relating to reliance on internal control systems and to incorporate, to the extent deemed appropriate, the results into the firm's audit practice. (ASR No. 241 [February 10, 1978].)

9. Censure of a firm, other than following a permanent injunction or criminal conviction. (ASR No. 248 [May 31, 1978].)

10. Requirement to name a new managing partner of one of a firm's offices. (ASR No. 288 [February 26, 1981].)

SEC sanctions such as those are generally publicly disclosed and can obviously have a significant impact on a CPA firm's practice. Almost all recent Rule 2(e) proceedings, however, have involved consent decrees, pursuant to which the auditing firm neither denied nor admitted guilt.

Some of the more innovative procedures consented to by CPA firms in recent Rule 2(e) proceedings raise questions of the SEC's intrusion into the area of creating specific professional standards. This intrusion may take two forms.

1. Language in a proceeding indicating auditing responsibilities not prescribed by the profession. An example is the view expressed in ASR No. 153 (1974) that successor auditors must review the work of predecessor auditors, and that a refusal by the client to permit the necessary communication should be grounds for rejecting the engagement. Professional literature at the time did not make predecessor-successor communications mandatory. Moreover, the present standards, while requiring such communication, leave room for the exercise of professional judgment on the effect of a prospective client's forbidding such communication.

2. Language in a consent decree requiring an auditing firm to develop specific audit procedures not addressed in the professional literature. An example is the auditing firm's consent in ASR No. 153 to develop and submit to the SEC procedures for the audit of related party transactions. An SAS on the subject did not exist at the time of ASR No. 153.

As discussed in Chapter 2, the SEC has traditionally left the specific implementation and interpretation of GAAS to the auditing profession. At the least, Rule 2(e) proceedings and the accompanying consent decrees provide a vehicle for selective departure from that policy.

The Profession's Responses to the Litigious Environment

The litigious environment has encouraged the public accounting profession as a whole and individual firms to reexamine and strengthen auditing standards and methods of encouraging compliance with them. Since the litigation explosion, the AICPA has issued a great many authoritative auditing pronouncements (36 SASs were promulgated between 1977 and mid-1986) and has revised its Code of Professional Ethics. The Institute has also devoted considerable attention to the design and implementation of quality control reviews of firms. Individual firms have devoted increasingly more resources to their own policies and procedures for maintaining and raising the quality of practice.

Authoritative Pronouncements. Many of the SAPs and SASs can be traced, either directly or indirectly, to audit failures that led to litigation. For example, the following pronouncements were related to the cases shown in parentheses:[38]

SAP No. 1 (October 1939): *Extensions of Auditing Procedure* (*McKesson & Robbins*)

SAP No. 27 (July 1957): *Long-form Reports* (*C.I.T. Financial*)

SAP No. 37 (September 1966): *Special Report: Public Warehouses—Controls and Auditing Procedures for Goods Held* (*Allied Crude Oil*)

SAP No. 41 (October 1969): *Subsequent Discovery of Facts Existing at the Date of the Auditor's Report* (*Yale Express*)

SAP No. 45 (July 1971): *Using the Work and Reports of Other Auditors* (*Atlantic Acceptance*)

SAP No. 47 (September 1971): *Subsequent Events* (*BarChris*)

SAP No. 48 (October 1971): *Letters for Underwriters* (*BarChris*)

SAS No. 6 (July 1975): *Related Party Transactions* (*Continental Vending* and *U.S. Financial*)

SAS No. 7 (October 1975): *Communications Between Predecessor and Successor Auditor* (*U.S. Financial*)

In addition, other auditing pronouncements originated from accounting pronouncements that in turn can be traced to alleged misconduct of one kind or another that led to litigation. For example, the origin of SAP No. 44 (April 1971), *Reports Following a Pooling of Interests*, was Accounting Principles Board Opinion No. 16, *Business Combinations* (August 1970). This in turn had its source in the deterioration of accounting principles, evidenced at least in part by litigation, such as the *Westec*[39] case, that raised questions of the propriety of the principles selected and applied to account for particular combinations.[40] Moreover, a number of auditing pronouncements further refined or clarified previous pronouncements that were traceable to litigation involving auditors. For example, several subsequent pronouncements further clarified the auditor's responsibilities set forth in SAP No. 1, *Extensions of Auditing Procedure*, which had its source in the *McKesson & Robbins* case.

The following paragraphs describe several cases that had a direct and significant influence on auditing and related authoritative pronouncements.

Fischer* v. *Kletz (Yale Express).[41] This case, brought under both the securi-

---

[38]Henry R. Jaenicke, *The Effect of Litigation on Independent Auditors.* Commission on Auditors' Responsibilities Research Study No. 1 (New York: American Institute of Certified Public Accountants, 1977), p. 79.

[39]*In re Westec Corp.*, 434 F. 2d 195 (5th Cir. 1970).

[40]The effect of litigation on authoritative accounting (as contrasted with auditing) pronouncements has not been as explicit. There has been an increased level of activity in the accounting as well as in the auditing area, and the profession has taken various procedural steps to enable authoritative accounting bodies to maintain or even increase that level of activity. The increased activity and improved procedures, however, are the result of numerous influences, and it is difficult, for the most part, to find specific evidence to link the level of activity of the Committee on Accounting Procedure, the Accounting Principles Board, and the Financial Accounting Standards Board, or the content of their pronouncements, to either specific litigation or the increased level of litigation.

[41]266 F. Supp. 180 (S.D.N.Y. 1967).

ties laws and common law, alleged that the auditors failed to disclose information acquired subsequent to the date of their audit report that caused the audit report to be misleading. The plaintiffs, investors of the company, alleged that the auditors discovered, after they had issued their report expressing an unqualified opinion and while conducting special studies of the company's past and current revenues and expenses, that the audited financial statements contained errors and were thus false and misleading. The plaintiffs contended that the auditors knew of the misstatements prior to the company's filing the audited statements in a Form 10-K; the auditors denied that the discovery had occurred prior to or at the time of the SEC filing. The common law case revolved around the issue of the auditors' liability to unforeseeable third parties for nondisclosure of material information—that is, whether nondisclosure constitutes negligence, for which the auditors would not have been liable to third parties, or intentional misrepresentation (fraud), which would have made the auditors liable. The court held that a duty to disclose subsequently discovered misstatements to those known to be relying on the original information does not require proof of the intent to deceive. The court deferred a decision on the liability issue, however, and the suit was subsequently settled out of court.

This case led to the promulgation, in 1969, of SAP No. 41, *Subsequent Discovery of Facts Existing at the Date of the Auditor's Report* (AU Section 561), which requires auditors to investigate information that they become aware of after the date of their report that might have existed at the date of the report and, if known to them, might have affected the report. If the information would have affected the report and people are relying on or are likely to rely on the statements, the auditor is further required to revise the audit report and to advise client management to disclose the information to people relying on the statements, the SEC, the stock exchanges, and appropriate regulatory agencies. If the client refuses to make the necessary disclosures, the auditor becomes responsible for notifying the SEC, the stock exchanges, and each person known to be relying on the financial statements and audit report. Auditors' responsibilities after the report date are discussed in more detail in Chapter 18.

Escott v. BarChris Construction Corp.[42] This case, the most significant to be tried under Section 11 of the 1933 Act, was discussed earlier in this chapter. One aspect of the suit concerned the S-1 review made by the auditors, as required in connection with the 1933 Act registration of the company's debentures, to determine whether, since the date of the audit report, any changes had occurred that should have been disclosed. The court held that a material adverse change requiring disclosure had taken place, and called the S-1 review ''useless'' because the auditors did not discover the change.

As a result of these findings, in 1971 the Committee on Auditing Procedure issued SAP No. 47, *Subsequent Events* (AU Section 560), which set forth specific procedures required to be performed in the subsequent period. SAP No. 47 provided much more detailed guidance than did professional standards (Chapter 11 of SAP No. 33) current at the time of the *BarChris* case.

---

[42]283 F. Supp. 643 (S.D.N.Y. 1968).

United States v. *Simon (Continental Vending).*[43] This case was a criminal action against the auditors of Continental Vending for having made a false and misleading statement under the 1934 Act by having inappropriately issued an unqualified opinion. A major issue was the wording of the disclosure, in a foot-note to the financial statements, of loan transactions involving the audited company, an affiliate, and an officer of the company. The government con-tended that the disclosure was inadequate because it did not state that amounts receivable from the affiliate were uncollectible at the balance sheet date nor did it specify the nature of the collateral, which was shares of the client's own stock. The auditors' defense was that the statements were in compliance with GAAP, which, they maintained, indicated that they had not intended to deceive. The judge instructed the jury, however, that the critical test was whether the finan-cial statements, as a whole, fairly presented the company's financial position and results of operations. Following those instructions, the jury found the de-fendants guilty. Minor fines were imposed because of the unusualness of the case.

The case was appealed to the second circuit, which refused to reverse the decision. The major issue in the appellate decision written by Judge Friendly was whether the auditors had acted in good faith in not disclosing information that they were aware of but that was not required by GAAP—essentially in the form of published authoritative pronouncements—to be disclosed. Friendly stated:

> We do not think the jury was . . . required to accept the accountants' evalua-tion whether a given fact was material to overall fair presentation, at least not when the accountants' testimony was not based on specific rules or prohibi-tions to which they could point, but only on the need for the auditor to make an honest judgment and their conclusion that nothing in the financial state-ments themselves negated the conclusion that an honest judgment had been made. Such evidence may be highly persuasive, but it is not conclusive, and so the trial judge correctly charged.

Thus, *Continental Vending* demonstrated—in a way that startled the profes-sion—that conformity to a formal set of authoritative accounting principles was insufficient if those pronouncements did not specify the appropriate accounting for the item at issue. When specific standards have not been established by for-mal pronouncements or when courts have deemed the standards incomplete or not definitive, compliance with authoritative pronouncements is not sufficient to excuse an auditor from liability. Thus, this case established the precedent that auditors must disclose misconduct of a client's management if it is known to them and if it may materially affect the financial statements. Although the court did not define "misconduct," it provided some guidelines, as follows:

> If certification does not at least imply that the corporation has not been looted by insiders so far as the accountants know . . . it would mean nothing, and the

[43]425 F. 2d 796 (2d Cir. 1969).

reliance placed on it by the public would be a snare and a delusion. Generally accepted accounting principles instruct an accountant what to do in the usual case where he has no reason to doubt that the affairs of the corporation are being honestly conducted. Once he has reason to believe that this basic assumption is false, an entirely different situation confronts him. Then . . . he must ''extend his procedures to determine whether or not such suspicions are justified.'' If as a result of such an extension or, as here, without it, he finds his suspicions to be confirmed, full disclosure must be the rule. . . .

The *Continental Vending* case, directly or indirectly, influenced the guidance provided by the profession for auditors in a number of areas in which this case demonstrated that standards were lacking. One significant area is related party transactions, the subject of SAS No. 6 (AU Section 335), issued in 1975, which provided guidelines for auditing and disclosing such transactions. Another is investigating the integrity of management of a prospective client; guidance on this subject is included in SAS No. 7 (AU Section 315), also issued in 1975, dealing with communications between predecessor and successor auditors. Still another SAS relating to this case is SAS No. 5 (AU Section 411) dealing with the meaning of ''present fairly'' as used in the audit report. This SAS was issued to explain what is meant by ''present fairly'' and concludes that the auditor's judgment about fair presentation should be made in the context of GAAP. A related change in Rule 203 of the Code of Professional Ethics, discussed in Chapter 18, permits auditors to express an unqualified opinion on financial statements that depart from GAAP if they can show that conforming with a principle would result in misleading statements.

Both *BarChris* and *Continental Vending* indicate the differences of opinion that exist among the AICPA, which has submitted *amicus curiae* briefs on behalf of auditor-defendants, the SEC, and the courts relating to a defense based on adherence to professional standards. The AICPA has stated that compliance with GAAP and GAAS or, in their absence, the views of experts, should constitute an effective defense. The SEC, on the other hand, has argued that an auditor's liability extends beyond professional standards to the disclosure of all known material information. The courts have only on rare occasions rejected adherence to GAAP and GAAS established by authoritative bodies as an effective defense. Earle[44] has stated that the courts ''have generally encouraged the auditor to adhere to these professional standards by shielding him from liability when he does.'' Although *Continental Vending* was not an exception to this general practice because authoritative pronouncements did not exist in the disputed areas, it did establish a precedent for viewing compliance with promulgated GAAP as persuasive but not conclusive in that situation.

Adams **v.** *Standard Knitting Mills, Inc.*[45] This case also involved auditors' failure to disclose in their audit report known information, in this instance, material weaknesses in internal control. A lower court found the auditors liable for

---

[44]Victor M. Earle, III, ''The Fairness Myth,'' *Vanderbilt Law Review* 28 (January 1975), p. 147.

[45]623 F. 2d 422 (6th Cir. 1980).

failing to follow and apply generally accepted accounting principles "by not disclosing or compelling management to disclose its gross EDP deficiencies," even though such disclosure was not then required by authoritative pronouncements. The decision was reversed on appeal, but the court indicated that, in certain circumstances, auditors could be held liable for not disclosing material internal control weaknesses.

In 1977, a year after this case was first heard, the Auditing Standards Executive Committee issued SAS No. 20, *Required Communication of Material Weaknesses in Internal Accounting Control* (AU Section 323), which requires auditors to communicate material weaknesses in internal accounting control to the client's management and board of directors or audit committee. SAS No. 20 does not, however, address the issue of public disclosure of material·control weaknesses. Reporting on internal control systems is the subject of SAS No. 30, *Reporting on Internal Accounting Control* (AU Section 642), promulgated in 1980. SAS No. 30 establishes standards for engagements to report specifically on internal accounting control systems. Communicating weaknesses in internal accounting control is discussed in Chapter 8 of this book, and special reports on internal control are covered in Chapters 8 and 19.

1136 Tenants' Corp. v. *Max Rothenberg & Co.*[46] This was the first important case in which accountants were held liable for negligence in a nonaudit accounting engagement. The defendants had been engaged to "write up" the books of a cooperative apartment house, that is, prepare unaudited financial statements, from data supplied by the cooperative's managing agent. The agent subsequently pleaded guilty to embezzlement charges, and the tenants of the cooperative sued the accountants for negligence and breach of contract. A lower court held the accountants liable for failing to detect the embezzlement and concluded that they had a duty to the tenants to investigate, to some extent, the financial information provided by the agent. An appellate court upheld the decision.

The case involved two separate issues. The first was the scope of the engagement, which was not documented in the contract with the accountants. The court decided—based at least in part on the defendants' admission that they had performed some auditing procedures, including the preparation of a worksheet entitled "missing invoices" that showed over $44,000 of invoices missing from the records—that an audit had taken place and thus the accountants were liable for breach of contract in not following up on the discovery that invoices were missing. The second, and more significant, issue was the standard of care owed by the accountants even if the engagement had not been found to be an audit. The court held that the accountants would still have had a duty to follow up on the exceptions discovered during the engagement.

Another case involving a nonaudit engagement, *Robert Wooler Co.* v. *Fidelity Bank*,[47] was heard by the Superior Court of Pennsylvania in 1984. The court held that the accounting firm, in not informing the client of deficiencies in its

---

[46]36 AD 2d 804, 319 N.Y.S. 2d 1007 (1971).
[47]330 Pa. Super. 523, 479 A. 2d 1027 (1984).

internal operating procedures that might allow employee defalcations to occur, might be liable for losses sustained because of such defalcations. In this case, the accounting firm had an engagement agreement for nonaudit services. The court ruled that the agreement, "in the absence of specific language relieving [the firm] from acts of negligence, did not relieve it from liability for ignoring suspicious circumstances which would have raised a 'red flag' for a reasonably skilled and knowledgeable accountant."

The profession's response to the court's position in *1136 Tenants* on engagements to prepare unaudited financial statements and render other nonaudit services took two directions. The AICPA strongly recommended that CPA firms issue detailed engagement letters on all engagements; such letters are now almost universally used and are discussed earlier in this chapter. The AICPA also issued, in 1979, SAS No. 26 (AU Section 504), dealing with *Association With Financial Statements*, which clarified accountants' "association" with financial statements in various types of engagements. In addition, the AICPA formed the Accounting and Review Services Committee to issue a separate series of pronouncements, Statements on Standards for Accounting and Review Services, covering unaudited financial statements and other unaudited financial information of nonpublic entities. Engagements to prepare unaudited financial statements and to perform compilations and reviews are discussed in Chapter 19.

Increased Attention to Quality Control. Both the profession and individual firms have recognized the need for more effective controls over the quality of audit practice. Statement on Quality Control Standards No. 1, *System of Quality Control for a CPA Firm* (QC Section 10), requires CPA firms to establish quality control policies and procedures. Efforts by the AICPA to improve and monitor the quality of audit practice, including the Division for CPA Firms, are described in Chapter 3. Both the profession and the state boards of accountancy have disciplinary systems through which sanctions are imposed on auditing firms and individual auditors for violations of the Code of Professional Ethics and state accountancy laws. These self-regulatory measures are also discussed in Chapter 3.

Measures to Protect Against Legal Liability. Individual firms have also designed and implemented programs for monitoring their audit practices. Evidence that supports expanded activity by CPA firms in this area includes, among other things,

- Increased resources devoted to continuing education.
- Institution of second-partner and interoffice reviews of working papers and reports.
- Practice bulletins directed at both accounting and auditing issues.
- Policy statements on internal quality-control programs.
- Engagement of other auditing firms to conduct independent quality reviews.

• Increased emphasis on research in auditing theory and applications, including the use of sophisticated technology such as microcomputers and statistical sampling, as a means of enhancing the quality of audit performance.

The practice, adopted by many auditing firms, of having a second-partner review of engagements has been traced directly to the *Continental Vending* case.[48] As discussed earlier, most auditors follow the practice of setting forth the scope and inherent limitations of an audit in an engagement letter to the client. Many of the points covered in a typical engagement letter are also addressed in the representation letter from management, which the auditor is required by SAS No. 19 (AU Section 333) to obtain. Management's representation letter provides written evidence of, among other matters, inquiries made by the auditor and management's responses to them. Chapter 17 contains a reproduction of the illustrative representation letter in Appendix A to SAS No. 19. Both the engagement letter and the management representation letter may constitute important evidence in the event of a lawsuit.

In very general terms, the best protection against legal liability for both CPA firms and individual practitioners is afforded by meticulous adherence to the technical and ethical standards of the profession and by establishing and implementing policies and procedures designed to ensure that all audits are systematically planned and performed, that the work is done by individuals who understand the client's business circumstances, that appropriate evidence is obtained and objectively evaluated, and that all work done is carefully documented.

Review Questions

4-1. During the course of an audit, what factors or circumstances may lead an auditor to believe that irregularities may exist?

4-2. Explain the difference between errors and irregularities. Give examples of each.

4-3. What client management policies should the auditor recognize as conducive to the possibility of irregularities?

4-4. How can the auditor's planning function be implemented to help detect fraudulent activities? Cite examples.

4-5. What should an auditor do on becoming aware of a possible irregularity or illegal act?

4-6. How should auditors convey their responsibilities for detecting errors, irregularities, and illegal acts to their clients? What information should be included?

4-7. What is ordinary negligence? To whom is the auditor liable for ordinary negligence under common law?

[48]A. A. Sommer, Jr., "Legal Liability of Accountants," *Financial Executive* 42 (March 1974), p. 24.

4-8. What is gross negligence? To whom is the auditor liable for gross negligence under common law?

4-9. What defense is available to the auditor for failure to detect management fraud? Explain.

4-10. What is the present position of the courts concerning an auditor's liability for ordinary negligence to foreseeable but unidentifiable third-party users who rely on financial statements?

4-11. Define the term "scienter." How is scienter established?

4-12. How does Section 11 of the Securities Act of 1933 expand the auditor's liability to third parties beyond that of common law?

4-13. What defenses does an auditor have against liability under the 1933 Act?

4-14. How does the 1934 Act differ from the 1933 Act in its impact on auditor liability?

4-15. What is a class action and how does it arise?

4-16. What impact on the auditing profession did the following cases have?

        a. *Fischer* v. *Kletz*
        b. *Hochfelder*
        c. *Continental Vending*
        d. *1136 Tenants' Corp.*

4-17. Name five or more sanctions imposed by the SEC on auditing firms to improve their quality control.

4-18. What measures have accounting firms undertaken to protect themselves against legal liability?

Discussion Questions

4-30. Briefly discuss the auditor's liability to third parties
        a. Under common law.
        b. Under the Securities Act of 1933.
        c. Under the Securities Exchange Act of 1934.

4-31. Paul Jackson was a junior staff member of an accounting firm. He began the audit of the Bosco Corporation, which manufactured and sold expensive watches. He quit in the middle of the audit. The accounting firm hired another person to continue the audit of Bosco. Due to the changeover and the time pressure to finish the audit, the firm violated certain generally accepted auditing standards when it did not follow adequate procedures with respect to the physical inventory. Had the proper procedures been used during the examination, it would have been discovered that watches worth more than $20,000 were missing. The employee who was stealing the watches was able to steal an additional $30,000 worth before the thefts were discovered six months after the completion of the audit.

    Required:
    Discuss the legal problems of the accounting firm as a result of these facts.

                                      (AICPA adapted)

4–32. Farr & Madison, CPAs, audited Glamour, Inc. Their audit was deficient in several respects:

- Farr & Madison failed to verify properly certain receivables that later proved to be fictitious.
- With respect to other receivables, although they made a cursory check, they did not detect many accounts that were long overdue and obviously uncollectible.
- No physical inventory was taken of the securities claimed to be in Glamour's possession, which in fact had been sold. Both the securities and cash received from the sales were listed on the balance sheet as assets.

There is no indication that Farr & Madison actually believed that the financial statements were false. Subsequent creditors, not known to Farr & Madison, are now suing based on the deficiencies in the audit. Farr & Madison moved to dismiss the lawsuit against them on the basis that the firm did not have actual knowledge of falsity and therefore did not commit fraud.

Required:
Answer the following, setting forth reasons for any conclusions stated.
May the creditors recover without demonstrating that Farr & Madison had actual knowledge of falsity?

(AICPA adapted)

4–33. Perfect Products Co. applied for a substantial bank loan from Capitol City Bank. In connection with its application, Perfect engaged William & Co., CPAs, to audit its financial statements. William completed the audit and rendered an unqualified opinion. On the basis of the financial statements and William's opinion, Capitol granted Perfect a loan of $500,000.

Within three months after the loan was granted, Perfect filed for bankruptcy. Capitol promptly brought suit against William for damages, claiming that it had relied to its detriment on misleading financial statements and the unqualified opinion of William.

William's audit workpapers reveal negligence and possible other misconduct in the performance of the audit. Nevertheless, William believes it can defend against liability to Capitol based on the privity defense.

Required:
Answer the following, setting forth reasons for any conclusions stated.
a. Explain the privity defense and evaluate its application to William.
b. What exceptions to the privity defense might Capitol argue?

(AICPA adapted)

4–34. Arthur & Doyle, CPAs, served as auditors for Dunbar Corp. and Wolfe Corp., publicly held corporations listed on the American Stock Exchange. Dunbar recently acquired Wolfe Corp. pursuant to a statutory merger by issuing its shares in exchange for shares of Wolfe. In connection with that merger, Arthur & Doyle rendered an unqualified opinion on the financial statements and participated in the preparation of the pro forma unaudited financial statements contained in the combined prospectus and proxy statement circulated to obtain shareholder approval of the merger and to register the shares to be issued in connection with the merger. Dunbar prepared a Form 8-K (the current report with unaudited financial statements) and Form 10-K (the annual report with audited financial statements) in connection with the merger. Shortly thereafter, financial disaster beset the merged company, resulting in large losses to the shareholders and creditors. A class action suit on behalf of the shareholders and creditors has been filed against Dunbar and its management. In addition, it names Arthur & Doyle as co-defendants, challenging the fairness, accuracy, and truthfulness of the financial statements.

Required:

Answer the following, setting forth reasons for any conclusions stated.

As a result of the CPAs having expressed an unqualified opinion on the audited financial statements of Dunbar and Wolfe and as a result of having participated in the preparation of the unaudited financial statements required in connection with the merger, indicate and briefly discuss the various bases of the CPAs' potential civil liability to the shareholders and creditors of Dunbar under

a. The federal securities acts.
b. State common law.

(AICPA adapted)

4-35. A CPA has been asked to audit the financial statements of a publicly held company for the first time. All preliminary verbal discussions and inquiries have been completed among the CPA, the company, the predecessor auditor, and all other necessary parties. The CPA is now preparing an engagement letter.

Required:

List the items that should be included in the typical engagement letter in these circumstances and describe the benefits derived from preparing an engagement letter.

(AICPA adapted)

AICPA Multiple Choice Questions ─────────────────────────────

These questions are taken from the Auditing and the Business Law parts of Uniform CPA Examinations. Choose the single most appropriate answer.

4-40. An auditor should recognize that the application of auditing procedures may produce evidential matter indicating the possibility of errors or irregularities and therefore should

a. Design audit tests to detect unrecorded transactions.
b. Extend the work to audit most recorded transactions and records of an entity.
c. Plan and perform the engagement with an attitude of professional skepticism.
d. *Not* depend on internal accounting control features that are designed to prevent or detect errors or irregularities.

4-41. An independent auditor has the responsibility to plan the audit examination to search for errors and irregularities that might have a material effect on the financial statements. Which of the following, if material, would be an *irregularity* as defined in Statements on Auditing Standards?

a. Misappropriation of an asset or groups of assets.
b. Clerical mistakes in the accounting data underlying the financial statements.

    c. Mistakes in the application of accounting principles.

    d. Misinterpretation of facts that existed when the financial statements were prepared.

4–42. Which of the following statements *best* describes the auditor's responsibility regarding the detection of fraud?

    a. The auditor is responsible for the failure to detect fraud only when such failure clearly results from nonperformance of audit procedures specifically described in the engagement letter.

    b. The auditor must extend auditing procedures to actively search for evidence of fraud in all situations.

    c. The auditor must extend auditing procedures to actively search for evidence of fraud where the examination indicates that fraud may exist.

    d. The auditor is responsible for the failure to detect fraud only when an unqualified opinion is issued.

4–43. If an independent auditor's examination leading to an opinion on financial statements causes the auditor to believe that material errors or irregularities exist the auditor should

    a. Consider the implications and discuss the matter with appropriate levels of management.

    b. Make the investigation necessary to determine whether the errors or irregularities have in fact occurred.

    c. Request that the management investigate to determine whether the errors or irregularities have in fact occurred.

    d. Consider whether the errors or irregularities were the result of a failure by employees to comply with existing internal control procedures.

4–44. Hall purchased Eon Corp. bonds in a public offering subject to the Securities Act of 1933. Kosson and Co., CPAs, rendered an unqualified opinion on Eon's financial statements, which were included in Eon's registration statement. Kosson is being sued by Hall based upon misstatements contained in the financial statements. In order to be successful, Hall must prove

	Damages	Materiality of the misstatement	Kosson's scienter
a.	Yes	Yes	Yes
b.	Yes	Yes	No
c.	Yes	No	No
d.	No	Yes	Yes

4–45. DMO Enterprises, Inc., engaged the accounting firm of Martin, Seals & Anderson to perform its annual audit. The firm performed the audit in a competent, nonnegligent manner and billed DMO for $16,000, the agreed fee. Shortly after delivery of the audited financial statements, Hightower, the assistant controller, disappeared, taking with him $28,000 of DMO's funds. It was then discovered that Hightower had been engaged in a highly sophisticated, novel defalcation scheme during the past year. He had previously embezzled $35,000 of DMO funds. DMO has refused to pay the accounting firm's fee and is seeking to recover the $63,000 that was stolen by Hightower. Which of the following is correct?

a. The accountants can *not* recover their fee and are liable for $63,000.

b. The accountants are entitled to collect their fee and are *not* liable for $63,000.

c. DMO is entitled to rescind the audit contract and thus is *not* liable for the $16,000 fee, but it can *not* recover damages.

d. DMO is entitled to recover the $28,000 defalcation, and is *not* liable for the $16,000 fee.

4–46. Walters & Whitlow, CPAs, failed to discover a fraudulent scheme used by Davis Corporation's head cashier to embezzle corporate funds during the past five years. Walters & Whitlow would have discovered the embezzlements promptly if they had *not* been negligent in their annual audits. Under the circumstances, Walters & Whitlow will normally *not* be liable for

a. Punitive damages.

b. The fees charged for the years in question.

c. Losses occurring after the time the fraudulent scheme should have been detected.

d. Losses occurring prior to the time the fraudulent scheme should have been detected and that could have been recovered had it been so detected.

4–47. Doe and Co., CPAs, issued an unqualified opinion on the 1985 financial statements of Marx Corp. These financial statements were included in Marx's annual report and Form 10-K filed with the SEC. Doe did not detect material misstatements in the financial statements as a result of negligence in the performance of the audit. Based upon the financial statements, Fitch purchased stock in Marx. Shortly thereafter, Marx became insolvent, causing the price of the stock to decline drastically. Fitch has commenced legal action against Doe for damages based upon Section 10(b) and Rule 10b-5 of the Securities Exchange Act of 1934. Doe's best defense to such an action would be that

a. Fitch lacks privity to sue.

b. The engagement letter specifically disclaimed all liability to third parties.

c. There is *no* proof of scienter.

d. There has been no subsequent sale for which a loss can be computed.

4–48. Lewis & Clark, CPAs, rendered an unqualified opinion on the financial statements of a company that sold common stock in a public offering subject to the Securities Act of 1933. Based on a false statement in the financial statements, Lewis & Clark are being sued by an investor who purchased shares of this public offering. Which of the following represents a viable defense?

a. The investor has *not* met the burden of proving fraud or negligence by Lewis & Clark.

b. The investor did *not* actually rely upon the false statement.

c. Detection of the false statement by Lewis & Clark occurred after their examination date.

d. The false statement is immaterial in the overall context of the financial statements.

4–49. Major, Major & Sharpe, CPAs, are the auditors of MacLain Industries. In connection with the public offering of $10 million of MacLain securities, Major expressed an unqualified opinion as to the financial statements. Subsequent to the offering, certain misstatements and omissions were revealed. Major has been sued by the purchasers of the stock offered pursuant to the registration statement, which included the financial statements audited by Major. In the ensuing lawsuit by the MacLain investors, Major will be able to avoid liability if

   a. The errors and omissions were caused primarily by MacLain.
   b. It can be shown that at least some of the investors did *not* actually read the audited financial statements.
   c. It can prove due diligence in the audit of the financial statements of MacLain.
   d. MacLain had expressly assumed any liability in connection with the public offering.

4-50. Donalds & Company, CPAs, audited the financial statements included in the annual report submitted by Markum Securities, Inc., to the Securities and Exchange Commission. The audit was improper in several respects. Markum is now insolvent and unable to satisfy the claims of its customers. The customers have instituted legal action against Donalds based upon Section 10(b) and Rule 10b-5 of the Securities Exchange Act of 1934. Which of the following is likely to be Donalds' best defense?

   a. They did *not* intentionally certify false financial statements.
   b. Section 10(b) does *not* apply to them.
   c. They were *not* in privity of contract with the creditors.
   d. Their engagement letter specifically disclaimed any liability to any party that resulted from Markum's fraudulent conduct.

4-51. An auditor's examination performed in accordance with generally accepted auditing standards generally should

   a. Be expected to provide assurance that illegal acts will be detected where internal control is effective.
   b. Be relied upon to disclose violations of truth-in-lending laws.
   c. Encompass a plan to actively search for illegalities that relate to operating aspects.
   d. *Not* be relied upon to provide assurance that illegal acts will be detected.

4-52. If as a result of auditing procedures an auditor believes that the client may have committed illegal acts, which of the following actions should be taken immediately by the auditor?

   a. Consult with the client's counsel and the auditor's counsel to determine how the suspected illegal acts will be communicated to the stockholders.
   b. Extend normal auditing procedures to ascertain whether the suspected illegal acts may have a material effect on the financial statements.
   c. Inquire of the client's management and consult with the client's legal counsel or other specialists, as necessary, to obtain an understanding of the nature of the acts and their possible effects on the financial statements.
   d. Notify each member of the audit committee of the board of directors of the nature of the acts and request that they give guidance with respect to the approach to be taken by the auditor.

4-53. An auditor who finds that the client has committed an illegal act would be most likely to withdraw from the engagement when the

   a. Illegal act affects the auditor's ability to rely on management representations.
   b. Illegal act has material financial statement implications.

c. Illegal act has received widespread publicity.

d. Auditor can *not* reasonably estimate the effect of the illegal act on the financial statements.

4–54. When management refuses to disclose illegal activities that were identified by the independent auditor, the independent auditor may be charged with violating the AICPA Code of Professional Ethics for

a. Withdrawing from the engagement.

b. Issuing a disclaimer of opinion.

c. Failure to uncover the illegal activities during prior audits.

d. Reporting these activities to the audit committee.

Problems and Cases

4–60. The CPA firm of Winston & Mall was engaged by the Fast Cargo Company, a retailer, to examine its financial statements for the year ended August 31, 1987. It followed generally accepted auditing standards and examined transactions on a test basis. A sample of 100 disbursements was used to test vouchers payable, cash disbursements, and receiving and purchasing procedures. An investigation of the sample disclosed several instances where purchases had been recorded and paid for without the required receiving report being included in the file of supporting documents. This was properly noted in the working papers by Martin, the junior who did the sampling. Bill Mall, the partner in charge, called these facts to the attention of Sam Harris, Fast Cargo's chief accountant, who told him not to worry about it, that he would make certain that these receiving reports were properly included in the voucher file. Mall accepted this and did nothing further to investigate or follow up on this situation.

Harris was engaged in a fraudulent scheme whereby he diverted the merchandise to a private warehouse where he leased space and sent the invoices to Fast Cargo for payment. The scheme was discovered later by a special investigation and a preliminary estimate indicates that the loss to Fast Cargo will be in excess of $20,000.

> *Required:*
> a. What is the liability, if any, of Winston & Mall in this situation? Discuss.
> b. What additional steps, if any, should have been taken by Mall? Explain.
>
> (AICPA adapted)

4–61. Meglow Corporation manufactured ladies' dresses and blouses. Because its cash position was deteriorating, Meglow sought a loan from Busch Factors. Busch had previously extended $25,000 credit to Meglow but refused to lend any additional money without obtaining copies of Meglow's audited financial statements.

Meglow contacted the CPA firm of Watkins, Winslow & Watkins to perform the audit. In arranging for the examination, Meglow clearly indicated that its purpose was to satisfy Busch Factors on the Corporation's sound financial condition and thus to obtain an additional loan of $50,000. Watkins, Winslow & Watkins accepted the engagement, performed the examination in a negligent manner, and rendered an unqualified auditor's opinion. If an adequate examination had been performed, the financial statements would have been found to be misleading.

Meglow submitted the audited financial statements to Busch Factors and obtained an additional loan of $35,000. Busch refused to lend more than that amount. After several other factors also refused, Meglow finally was able to persuade Maxwell Department Stores, one of its customers, to lend the additional $15,000. Maxwell relied on the financial statements examined by Watkins, Winslow & Watkins.

Meglow is now in bankruptcy and Busch seeks to collect from Watkins, Winslow & Watkins the $60,000 it lent Meglow. Maxwell seeks to recover from Watkins, Winslow & Watkins the $15,000 it lent Meglow.

Required:

a. Will Busch recover? Explain.
b. Will Maxwell recover? Explain.

(AICPA adapted)

4-62. The CPA firm of Martinson, Brinks & Sutherland, a partnership, was the auditor for Masco Corporation, a medium-sized wholesaler. Masco leased warehouse facilities and sought financing for leasehold improvements to these facilities. Masco assured its bank that the leasehold improvements would result in a more efficient and profitable operation. Based on these assurances, the bank granted Masco a line of credit.

The loan agreement required annual audited financial statements. Masco submitted to the bank its 1986 audited financial statements, which showed an operating profit of $75,000, leasehold improvements of $250,000, and net worth of $350,000. In reliance thereon, the bank lent Masco $200,000. The audit report that accompanied the financial statements disclaimed an opinion because the cost of the leasehold improvements could not be determined from the company's records. The part of the audit report dealing with leasehold improvements reads as follows:

Additions to fixed assets in 1986 were found to include principally warehouse improvements. Practically all of this work was done by company employees and the costs of materials and overhead were paid by Masco. Unfortunately, complete detailed cost records were not kept of these leasehold improvements and no exact determination could be made as to the actual cost of said improvements. The total amount of costs capitalized is set forth in note 4.

In late 1987 Masco went out of business, at which time it was learned that the claimed leasehold improvements were totally fictitious. The labor expenses charged as leasehold improvements proved to be operating expenses. No item of building material cost had been recorded. No independent investigation of the existence of the leasehold improvements was made by the auditors.

If the $250,000 had not been capitalized, the income statement would have reflected a substantial loss from operations and the net worth would have been correspondingly decreased.

The bank has sustained a loss on its loan to Masco of $200,000 and now seeks to recover damages from the CPA firm, alleging that the accountants negligently audited the financial statements.

Required:

Answer the following, setting forth reasons for any conclusions stated.

a. Will the disclaimer of opinion absolve the CPA firm from liability?
b. Are the individual partners of Martinson, Brinks & Sutherland who did not take part in the audit liable?

c. Briefly discuss the development of the common law regarding the liability of CPAs to third parties.

(AICPA adapted)

4-63. A CPA firm was engaged to examine the financial statements of Martin Manufacturing Corporation for the year ending December 31, 1986. The facts revealed that Martin was in need of cash to continue its operations and agreed to sell its common stock investment in a subsidiary through a private placement. The buyers insisted that the proceeds be placed in escrow because of the possibility of a major contingent tax liability that might result from a pending government claim. The payment in escrow was completed in late November 1986. The president of Martin told the audit partner that the proceeds from the sale of the subsidiary's common stock, held in escrow, should be shown on the balance sheet as an unrestricted current account receivable. The president was of the opinion that the government's claim was groundless and that Martin needed an "uncluttered" balance sheet and a "clean" auditor's opinion to obtain additional working capital from lenders. The audit partner agreed with the president and issued an unqualified opinion on the Martin financial statements, which did not refer to the contingent liability and did not properly describe the escrow arrangement.

The government's claim proved to be valid, and pursuant to the agreement with the buyers, the purchase price of the subsidiary was reduced by $450,000. This adverse development forced Martin into bankruptcy. The CPA firm is being sued for deceit (fraud) by several of Martin's unpaid creditors who extended credit in reliance on the CPA firm's unqualified opinion on Martin's financial statements.

Required:
Answer the following, setting forth reasons for any conclusions stated.
Based on these facts, can Martin's unpaid creditors recover from the CPA firm?

(AICPA adapted)

4-64. Smith, CPA, is the auditor for Juniper Manufacturing Corporation, a privately owned company that has a June 30 fiscal year-end. Juniper arranged for a substantial bank loan, which was dependent on the bank receiving, by September 30, audited financial statements that showed a current ratio of at least 2 to 1. On September 25, just before the audit report was to be issued, Smith received an anonymous letter on Juniper's stationery indicating that a five-year lease by Juniper, as lessee of a factory building that was accounted for in the financial statements as an operating lease, was in fact a capital lease. The letter stated that there was a secret written agreement with the lessor modifying the lease and creating a capital lease.

Smith confronted the president of Juniper, who admitted that a secret agreement existed but said it was necessary to treat the lease as an operating lease to meet the current ratio requirement of the pending loan and that nobody would ever discover the secret agreement with the lessor. The president said that if Smith did not issue the report by September 30, Juniper would sue Smith for substantial damages that would result from not getting the loan. Under this pressure and because the working papers contained a copy of the five-year lease agreement, which supported the operating lease treatment, Smith issued the report with an unqualified opinion on September 29.

In spite of the fact that the loan was received, Juniper went bankrupt within two years. The bank is suing Smith to recover its losses on the loan and the lessor is suing Smith to recover uncollected rents.

Required:

Answer the following, setting forth reasons for any conclusions stated.

a. Is Smith liable to the bank?

b. Is Smith liable to the lessor?

(AICPA adapted)

4-65. Whitlow & Company is a brokerage firm registered under the Securities Exchange Act of 1934. The Act requires such a brokerage firm to file audited financial statements with the SEC annually. Mitchell & Moss, Whitlow's CPAs, performed the annual audit for the year ended December 31, 1986, and rendered an unqualified opinion, which was filed with the SEC along with Whitlow's financial statements. During 1986, Charles, the president of Whitlow & Company, engaged in a huge embezzlement scheme that eventually bankrupted the firm. As a result, substantial losses were suffered by customers and shareholders of Whitlow & Company, including Jim Thaxton, who had recently purchased several shares of stock of Whitlow & Company after reviewing the company's 1986 audit report. Mitchell & Moss' audit was deficient; if they had complied with generally accepted auditing standards, the embezzlement would have been discovered. However, Mitchell & Moss had no knowledge of the embezzlement nor could their conduct be categorized as reckless.

Required:

Answer the following, setting forth reasons for any conclusions stated.

a. What liability to Thaxton, if any, does Mitchell & Moss have under the Securities Exchange Act of 1934?

b. What theory or theories of liability, if any, are available to Whitlow & Company's customers and shareholders under the common law?

(AICPA adapted)

4-66. The Chriswell Corporation decided to raise additional long-term capital by issuing $3,000,000 of 8 percent subordinated debentures to the public. May, Clark & Co., CPAs, the company's auditors, were engaged to examine the June 30, 1987, financial statements, which were included in the bond registration statement.

May, Clark & Co. completed its examination and submitted an unqualified auditor's report dated July 15, 1987. The registration statement was filed and became effective on September 1, 1987. Two weeks prior to the effective date, one of the partners of May, Clark & Co. called on Chriswell Corporation and had lunch with the financial vice president and the controller. The partner questioned both officials on the company's operations since June 30 and inquired whether there had been any material changes in the company's financial position since that date. Both officers assured the partner that everything had proceeded normally and that the financial condition of the company had not changed materially.

Unfortunately, the officers' representation was not true. On July 30, a substantial debtor of the company failed to pay the $400,000 due on its account receivable and indicated to Chriswell that it would probably be forced into bankruptcy. This receivable was shown as a collateralized loan on the June 30 financial statements. It was secured by stock of the debtor corporation, which had a value in excess of the loan at the time the financial statements were prepared but was virtually worthless at the effective date of the registration statement. This $400,000 account receivable was material to the financial condition of Chriswell Corporation, and the market price of the subordinated debentures decreased by nearly 50 percent after the foregoing facts were disclosed.

The debenture holders of Chriswell are seeking recovery of their loss against all parties connected with the debenture registration.

Required:

Is May, Clark & Co. liable to the Chriswell debenture holders? Explain.

(AICPA adapted)

4-67. Factory Discount Prices, Inc., is a chain store discount outlet that sells women's clothes. It has an excessively large inventory on hand and is in urgent need of additional cash. It is bordering on bankruptcy, especially if the inventory has to be liquidated by sale to other stores instead of the public. Furthermore, about 15 percent of the inventory is not resalable except at a drastic discount below cost. Faced with this financial crisis, Factory approached several of the manufacturers from whom it purchases. Dexter Apparel, Inc., one of the parties approached, indicated a willingness to lend Factory $300,000 under certain conditions. First, Factory was to submit audited financial statements for the express purpose of providing the correct financial condition of the company. The loan was to be predicated on these financial statements, and Factory's engagement letter with Dunn & Clark, its CPAs, expressly indicated this.

The second condition insisted on by Dexter was that it obtain a secured position in all unsecured inventory, accounts, and other related personal property. In due course, a security agreement was executed and a financing statement properly filed and recorded.

In preparing the financial statements, Factory valued the inventory at cost, which was approximately $100,000 over the current fair market value. Also, Factory failed to disclose two secured creditors to whom substantial amounts are owed and who take priority over Dexter's security interests.

Dunn & Clark issued an unqualified opinion on the financial statements of Factory, which they believed were fairly presented.

Six months later Factory filed a voluntary bankruptcy petition. Dexter received $125,000 as its share of the bankrupt's estate. It is suing Dunn & Clark for the loss of $175,000. Dunn & Clark deny liability based on lack of privity and lack of negligence.

Required:

Answer the following, setting forth reasons for any conclusions stated.

Is Dexter entitled to recover its loss from Dunn & Clark?

(AICPA adapted)

4-68. The CPA firm of Bigelow, Barton, and Brown was expanding very rapidly. Consequently, it hired several junior accountants, including a man named Small. The partners of the firm eventually became dissatisfied with Small's production and warned him that they would be forced to discharge him unless his output increased significantly.

At that time Small was engaged in audits of several clients. He decided that to avoid being fired, he would reduce or omit entirely some of the standard auditing procedures listed in audit programs prepared by the partners. One of the CPA firm's clients, Newell Corporation, was in serious financial difficulty and had adjusted several of the accounts being examined by Small so that they would appear to be financially sound. Small prepared fictitious working papers in his home at night to support purported completion of auditing procedures assigned to him, although he in fact did not examine the adjusting entries. The CPA firm rendered an unqualified opinion on Newell's financial statements, which were grossly misstated. Several creditors, relying on the audited financial statements, subsequently extended large sums of money to Newell Corporation.

Required:

Would the CPA firm be liable to the creditors who extended the money because of their reliance on the erroneous financial statements if Newell Corporation should fail to pay the debts? Explain.

(AICPA adapted)

Part 2
Theory and Concepts

Chapter 5
The Audit Process

Most of the auditor's work in forming an opinion on financial statements consists of obtaining and evaluating evidence about management's assertions that are embodied in those statements. To be able to express an opinion on financial statements, the auditor must establish specific audit objectives related to those assertions and then design and perform audit tests to obtain evidence that can be evaluated to determine whether the objectives have been met. Throughout the process the auditor must make decisions about whether the evidence obtained is sufficient, both qualitatively and quantitatively, to provide the necessary level of assurance for formulating an opinion.

The approach the auditor takes can be broken down into a series of systematic steps. The steps are usually the same in every audit, but the types of tests performed and the evidence obtained vary with each engagement. The auditor's working papers are the principal means of documenting the work performed, the evidence obtained, and the conclusions reached. This chapter explores the concepts of audit assertions, objectives, and evidence and presents an overall framework for viewing the steps in an audit.

Audit Assertions, Objectives, and Procedures

An entity's financial statements can be thought of as embodying a set of assertions by management. SAS No. 31, *Evidential Matter* (AU Section 326), groups financial statement assertions into the following broad categories:

- Existence or occurrence.
- Completeness.
- Rights and obligations.
- Valuation or allocation.
- Presentation and disclosure.

Many auditors find it helpful to consider explicitly two additional categories of assertions that are implicit in the SAS No. 31 list, namely

- Accuracy.
- Cutoff.

Assertions about existence relate to whether assets, liabilities, and ownership interests exist at a specific date. These assertions pertain to both physical items—such as inventory, plant and equipment, and cash—and accounts without physical substance—such as accounts receivable and accounts payable. Assertions about occurrence are concerned with whether recorded transactions, such as purchases and sales, represent economic events that actually occurred during a certain period. Assertions about existence and occurrence state that transactions and balances recorded in the accounts have real-world counterparts, for example, that there are real-world asset equivalents to the financial statement accounts representing the assets.

Assertions about completeness pertain to whether all transactions and other events and circumstances that occurred during a specific period and should have been recognized in that period have in fact been recorded. For example, *all* purchases of goods and services should be recorded and included in the financial statements. The completeness assertion also states that *all* recognizable financial statement items are in fact included in the financial statements. For example, management asserts that accounts payable reported on the balance sheet include all such obligations of the enterprise.

Assertions about rights and obligations relate to whether assets are the rights, and liabilities are the obligations, of the entity at a given date. For example, the reporting of capitalized leases in the balance sheet is an assertion that the amount capitalized is the unamortized cost of rights to leased property and that the amount of the lease liability is the unamortized obligation of the enterprise.

Assertions about valuation or allocation pertain to whether financial statement items are recorded at appropriate amounts in conformity with generally accepted accounting principles. For example, the financial statements represent that depreciation expense for the year and the carrying value of property, plant, and equipment are based on the systematic amortization of the historical cost of the assets, and that trade accounts receivable are stated at their net realizable value.

Assertions about presentation and disclosure relate to the proper classification, description, and disclosure of items in the financial statements; for example, that obligations classified as long-term liabilities will not require the use of assets classified as current, and that the accounting policy note to the financial statements includes the disclosures required by generally accepted accounting principles.

Assertions about accuracy relate to the mathematical correctness of recorded transactions that are reflected in the financial statements and the appropriateness of the way in which those transactions are summarized and posted to the general ledger. For example, the financial statements represent that accounts payable reflect purchases of goods and services that are based on correct prices and quantities and on invoices that have been accurately computed.

Assertions about cutoff relate to the recording of transactions in the proper accounting period. For example, a check to a vendor that is mailed on December 31 should be recorded in December and not, through either oversight or intent, in January.

SAS No. 31 is written in terms of audit assertions; auditors generally operationalize those assertions into audit objectives that they seek to achieve by performing audit procedures. For each assertion embodied in each item in the financial statements, the auditor develops a corresponding specific audit objective. Then the auditor designs procedures for obtaining sufficient competent evidential matter that will either corroborate or contradict each assertion and thereby achieve the related audit objective or reveal a deficiency in the financial statements.

Chapter 1 discussed two functions that auditors perform: first, gathering and evaluating evidence about verifiable "facts" and, second, interpreting those facts once they are known, which includes evaluating accounting judgments made by the client's management. In developing audit objectives and related audit procedures for certain categories of assertions—existence or occurrence, completeness, accuracy, cutoff, and rights and obligations—the auditor performs primarily the evidence-gathering function. The interpreting/evaluating function is exercised primarily in formulating audit objectives and designing audit procedures for testing the assertions relating to valuation or allocation and presentation and disclosure.

Figure 5.1 illustrates how auditors consider these seven broad categories of assertions in developing specific audit objectives and designing related audit procedures to obtain evidence that the information accumulated and presented by management in the financial statements is accurate, valid, complete, and recorded in the proper period (the evidence-gathering function) and to evaluate judgments by management (the interpreting/evaluating function). In Figure 5.1, a single audit procedure is linked to each stated audit objective. In an actual audit, a combination of auditing procedures will generally be necessary to achieve a single objective, and some auditing procedures will relate to more than one objective. For example, in addition to observing physical inventory counts by client personnel to obtain evidence that inventories included in the balance sheet physically exist, the auditor may also confirm the existence and amount of inventories stored in public warehouses or with other custodians at locations outside the entity's premises. Moreover, observing inventory counts also provides evidence that the inventory quantities include all products, materials, and supplies on hand (completeness objective); examining the documents used to transfer the inventory to an outside custodian may provide evidence indicating that a sale has taken place and that revenue should have been recognized (valuation or allocation objective). This suggests that, although the two functions of auditing are distinguishable by the type of assertion for which evidence is primarily gathered, in practice they are interrelated. Moreover, the auditor must evaluate all evidence that is obtained, regardless of why it was gathered. Hence, the function of interpreting/evaluating permeates all audit work.

Audit Evidence and Audit Tests

The third standard of field work states

> Sufficient competent evidential matter is to be obtained through inspection, observation, inquiries, and confirmations to afford a reasonable basis for an opinion regarding the financial statements under examination.

The evidence necessary to either corroborate or contradict the assertions in the financial statements and thus provide the auditor with a basis for an opinion is obtained by designing and performing auditing procedures or tests. This section of the chapter describes the various kinds of evidence that are available to the auditor and the types of tests that the auditor performs to obtain evidence.

Types of Evidence

SAS No. 31, *Evidential Matter* (AU Section 326), points out that evidential matter necessary to support the assertions in the financial statements consists of *underlying accounting data* and all *corroborating information* available to the auditor. Underlying evidence for the most part is available to the auditor from within the client company. It consists of the accounting data from which the financial statements are prepared, and includes journals and ledgers, accounting manuals, and memoranda and worksheets supporting such items as cost allocations, computations, and reconciliations.

Corroborating evidence is information that supports the underlying evidence, and generally is available to the auditor from both the client and outside sources. Client sources include documentary material closely related to accounting data, such as checks, invoices, contracts, minutes of meetings, correspondence, written representations by knowledgeable employees of the client, and information obtained by the auditor by inquiry of officers and employees and observation of employees at work. External sources of evidence include confirmations of amounts due or assets held by third parties (such as customers and custodians), correspondence with experts such as attorneys and engineers, and physical examination or inspection of assets such as marketable securities and inventories.

Figure 5.1 Examples of Audit Objectives and Procedures

Management Assertion	Primary Audit Function	Example of Audit Objective	Example of Audit Procedure
Existence or occurrence	Evidence gathering	Inventories in the balance sheet physically exist.	Observe physical inventory counts by client personnel.
Completeness	Evidence gathering	Sales revenues include all items shipped to customers.	Review the client's periodic accounting for the numerical sequence of shipping documents and invoices.
Accuracy	Evidence gathering	Accounts receivable reflect sales transactions that are based on correct prices and quantities and are accurately computed.	Compare prices on invoices with master price list and quantities with customer's sales order and client's shipping records; recalculate amounts on invoices.
Cutoff	Evidence gathering	Sales transactions are reported in the proper period.	Compare shipping dates with dates of journal entries for sales recorded in the last several days of the old year and the first several days of the new year.
Rights and obligations	Evidence gathering	Real estate in the balance sheet is owned by the entity.	Inspect deeds, purchase contracts, settlement papers, insurance policies, minutes, and related correspondence.
Valuation or allocation	Interpreting/ evaluating	Receivables are stated at net realizable value.	Review and evaluate client's aging of receivables to evaluate adequacy of allowance for doubtful accounts.
Presentation and disclosure	Interpreting/ evaluating	Loss contingencies not required to be recorded are appropriately disclosed.	Make inquiry of the client's lawyers concerning litigation, claims, and assessments.

Examination of underlying accounting data alone is not sufficient to meet the third standard of field work. The auditor must obtain satisfaction about the propriety and accuracy of the underlying evidence through corroborating evidence. For example, an auditor usually finds it necessary to confirm open accounts receivable to support receivable balances in the accounts receivable subsidiary ledger. To cite another example, the auditor should ordinarily corroborate lists of inventory items counted by client personnel by observing the client's physical inventory counting procedures and making some test counts.

Auditors use various methods—inspection, observation, inquiry, confirmation, and analytical tests—to obtain sufficient competent evidential matter. Each of those methods, as discussed subsequently, describes both the procedure employed to obtain the evidence and the type of evidence obtained by the procedure. Thus, "confirmation" is the procedure used to generate a specific piece of evidence known as a "confirmation." Auditors also use the word *test* as synonymous with *procedure*, so that confirming receivables can be described as an audit "test" or as an audit "procedure." (In the past, the word *test* has also been used to indicate that a procedure should be applied to a sample, but not the total population, of the items making up an account balance or class of transactions. Since it is important that auditors know when a procedure truly involves sampling, most auditors now restrict the word *sample* to those applications in which sampling theory is to be applied.)

In the discussion that follows, the reader should be aware that the classification of the various types of evidence is somewhat arbitrary. There are no authoritative definitions of the various types of evidence, and consequently auditors may disagree about the details of various classification schemes. For example, in the discussion to come, written representations from the client's management are presented as a form of response to the auditor's *inquiry*. Some auditors prefer to classify client representation letters as a form of *confirmation*. The way in which a particular type of evidence is classified is not very important; what is important is the auditor's ability to evaluate each kind of evidence in terms of its relevance and reliability, as discussed later in this chapter.

Inspection. The auditor may obtain evidence by inspecting assets or by inspecting documents and records.

Inspecting assets involves *counting* assets, such as petty cash or marketable securities on hand, to ascertain that the assets recorded in the accounts actually exist. The procedure of inspecting documents is often referred to as *examination of evidence*, and includes the activities of scanning, reading, scrutinizing, comparing, tracing, vouching, documenting, and reperforming. For example, the auditor may *scan* or *scrutinize* entries to an inventory control account for a period, looking for evidence of unusual amounts or unusual sources of input, which, if found, would be further investigated. The auditor may *read* the minutes of the board of directors' meetings for authorization of new financing. The auditor may *compare* purchase invoices with related receiving reports for evidence that merchandise has been received for bills rendered by creditors. The auditor may *trace* postings from customers' sales invoices to individual customer accounts. The auditor may *vouch* charges to a particular expense account by examining invoices, purchase orders, and receiving reports to ascertain that the charges are adequately supported. The auditor may *look for documentation* in the form of signatures or initials on a purchase invoice, indicating that the invoice has been compared, by appropriate client personnel, with the corresponding purchase order and receiving report, and that the footings and extensions on the invoice have been recalculated.

Reperforming involves repeating, either in whole or in part, the same procedures performed by the client's employees, particularly recalculations to ensure mathematical accuracy. Reperformance may also involve some of the other techniques previously mentioned, such as comparing or counting. For example, reperformance may involve comparing a vendor's invoice with the corresponding purchase order and receiving report where there is evidence in the form of initials on a document that the client's employees previously made that comparison. Reperformance may also involve recounting some of the client's physical inventory counts. Examples of tests of mathematical accuracy include recalculating the client's extensions and footings on sales invoices and inventory listings, repeating the client's calculations of depreciation expense, and reconstructing a client-prepared bank reconciliation.

Observation. Observation involves direct visual viewing of client employees in their work environment, and of other facts and events. It is a useful technique that can be employed in many phases of an audit. At the beginning of the audit, the auditor may tour the client's facilities to gain an understanding of the client's business. That tour may also provide possible indications of slow-moving or obsolete goods. Observation of the client's employees taking a physical inventory can provide firsthand knowledge to help the auditor assess the adequacy of the inventory taking. Watching employees whose functions have accounting significance perform their assigned tasks can help the auditor assess whether an internal accounting control is operating effectively.

Inquiry. Inquiry entails asking questions. The questions may be oral or written and may be directed to the client or to third parties. At the planning stage of the audit, the auditor needs to understand the client's business and accounting systems; one of the easiest ways to obtain this understanding is through inquiry. (Later in the audit, the understanding is either corroborated or contradicted by the results of the tests performed.) At various stages in the audit, the auditor may make specific inquiries of the client's employees to obtain answers to questions arising in the course of the audit work. Requesting a representation letter from client management as to the recording of all known liabilities, the existence of contingent liabilities, and the existence and carrying value of inventory is a form of inquiry. The auditor may also make specific inquiry of third parties, such as the client's outside legal counsel regarding legal matters or other specialists on matters outside the auditor's expertise.

Confirmation. Confirmation involves obtaining a representation of a fact or condition from a third party, preferably in writing. Examples are a confirmation from a bank of the amount on deposit or of a loan outstanding, or a confirmation from a customer of the existence of a receivable balance at a certain date. Auditors most often associate confirmations with cash (confirmation from a bank) and accounts receivable (confirmation from customers). Confirmation, however, has widespread applicability; depending on the circumstances, virtually any transaction, event, or account balance can be confirmed with a third party. For example, creditors can confirm accounts and notes payable; both customers and creditors can confirm specific transactions; insurance companies can confirm insurance premiums paid during the year and balances due at year-end, as well as borrowings on life insurance policies; transfer agents and registrars can confirm shares of stock outstanding; trustees can confirm balances due under long-term borrowings and payments required and made under bond sinking fund requirements. The list of items that can be confirmed is virtually endless.

Analytical Evidence. Analytical evidence involves ratio and trend analyses, which are frequently referred to as analytical review procedures or simply analytical reviews. Analytical review procedures are tests of accounting information made by studying and comparing relationships among data and trends in the data. The purpose of those procedures as they relate to gathering evidential matter is to corroborate the logical interrelationships that exist among accounts and to identify and obtain explanations for all significant changes or abnormalities. For example, a significant change in the gross profit rate from one period to another alerts the auditor to a possible error or irregularity; the unexpected change serves as a "red flag" that the auditor must be able to explain at the conclusion of the examination. Analytical reviews are employed at several stages of the audit, and are discussed at length in Chapter 9.

Competence of Evidential Matter

The third standard of field work requires the auditor to obtain evidential matter that is both competent and sufficient. In other words, the auditor must reach a decision, based on experience and judgment, on whether the evidence examined is "good" or "useful" evidence (competent evidential matter) and whether "enough" good evidence has been examined (sufficient evidential matter).

To be competent, evidence must be both relevant and reliable. The relevance of evidence relates to the degree to which it contributes to achieving stated audit objectives. To be relevant, the evidence must affect the auditor's ability to accept or reject a specific financial statement assertion. The auditor reaches a conclusion on the fair presentation of the financial statements taken as a whole through a series of evaluations made throughout the audit about specific financial statement assertions. Each piece of evidence obtained is evaluated in terms of its usefulness to the auditor for either corroborating or contradicting an assertion by management or the auditor's evaluation of evidence obtained at other stages of the audit. The relevance of evidence is measured by the extent to which it is useful for that purpose.

An example or two will illustrate the concept of relevance of evidence. Confirming accounts receivable by requesting the client's customers to inform the auditor about any differences between the customers' records of amounts owed to the client and the client's records of open balances is a common auditing procedure. A signed confirmation returned to the auditor indicating agreement with the open balance on the client's books can provide strong support for the implicit management assertion that the account receivable exists and that the balance in the account is not overstated. Confirmation is a relevant source of evidence for achieving the audit objectives related to management's assertions about existence/occurrence and valuation of individual account balances. Confirmations, however, do not provide evidence about collectibility, completeness, or rights and obligations. A confirmed account may not be collectible because the debtor does not intend or is unable to pay; receivables may exist that have not been recorded and therefore cannot possibly be selected for confirmation; or the client may have sold the receivables to another party and may be merely acting as a collection agent for that party. Similarly, physically inspecting and counting inventory gives the auditor evidence about its existence, but not about its valuation or about the client's title to it. Using irrelevant evidence to support an audit conclusion about a management assertion is a major source of "nonsampling error," as discussed in Chapter 10.

Evidence must also be reliable if it is to be useful to the auditor. The FASB's definition of reliability is also appropriate in the context of audit evidence. Reliability is "the quality of information that assures that information is reasonably free from error and bias and faithfully represents what it purports to represent."[1] Synonyms for reliability are "dependability" and "trustworthiness." The reliability of audit evidence is influenced by several factors.

• *Independence of the source.* Evidential matter obtained by the auditor from independent sources outside the entity under examination usually provides greater assurance of reliability than that secured solely within the entity. Examples of evidence from independent sources include a confirmation from a state agency of the number of shares of common stock authorized to be issued, and a confirmation from a bank of a cash balance, a loan balance, or securities held as collateral. (The high level of reliability that such evidence provides does not mean that errors in confirmations of this nature never occur.) In contrast, evidence arising from inquiries of the client or from inspecting documents provided by the client is usually considered less reliable from the auditor's viewpoint.

• *Qualifications of the source.* For audit evidence to be reliable, it must be obtained from people who are competent and have the qualifications to make the information free from error. (The independence-of-the-source criterion addresses the issue of possible deliberate errors in the evidence; the qualification-of-the-source criterion addresses the issue of possible unintentional errors in the evidence.) For instance, confirmations provided by business customers are usually more reliable than confirmations provided by individuals. Answers to inquiries about pending litigation from client counsel are usually more reliable

---

[1] Statement of Financial Accounting Concepts No. 2, "Glossary of Terms."

than answers to similar inquiries from persons not working in the legal department. The auditor should not necessarily assume that the higher up a person is in the client's organization, the more qualified that person is to provide evidence. The accounts payable clerk probably knows the "true" routine in the accounts payable section of the accounting department better than the corporate controller knows it. Furthermore, auditors should challenge their own qualifications when evaluating evidence that they have gathered. When inspecting or counting precious gems in a jeweler's inventory, for example, the auditor is probably not qualified to distinguish between diamonds and pieces of glass.

  • *System of internal control.* Underlying accounting data developed under satisfactory conditions of internal control are more reliable than similar data developed under less adequate conditions of internal control. The auditor does not accept the client's description of the system without corroboration. Instead, if the auditor plans to rely on controls, he or she observes the activities of company personnel and tests the controls to determine that they actually exist and are functioning as prescribed.

  • *Objectivity of the evidence.* Evidence is objective if it requires little judgment to evaluate its accuracy. Evidence obtained by an auditor's direct, personal knowledge through counting, observing, calculating, or inspecting is generally more objective than evidence based on the opinions of others, such as the opinion of an appraiser about the value of an asset acquired by the client in a nonmonetary transaction, the opinion of a lawyer about the outcome of pending litigation, or the opinion of the client's credit manager about the collectibility of outstanding receivables. Sometimes, however, more objective evidence is not attainable.

The auditor's twofold objective in performing an audit in accordance with generally accepted auditing standards is to achieve the necessary level of assurance to support the audit opinion and to perform the audit as efficiently as possible. Thus, in addition to considering the relevance and reliability of evidence, the auditor must also consider its availability, timeliness, and cost. Sometimes a desirable form of evidence is simply not available. For example, an auditor who is retained by the client after the company's accounting year-end cannot be present to observe and test-count the ending inventory. Time constraints may not permit an auditor to consider a particular source of evidence. For example, confirming a foreign account receivable might delay the completion of the audit by weeks or even months. Different types of evidence have different costs associated with them, and the auditor must consider cost–benefit trade-offs.

Fortunately, auditors usually have available more than one source of evidence or method of obtaining it for purposes of evaluating a specific financial statement assertion. If one source or method is not practicable to use, another can often be substituted. For example, a customer who may not be able to confirm an account receivable balance may be able to confirm specific sales transactions and cash remittances. Or a more costly source of evidence may be substituted for a less costly source that is not as reliable. For instance, a petroleum engineer who is independent of the client could be retained instead of the auditor's relying on engineers employed by the client for estimates of proven oil reserves. The auditor should choose the type or methods of evidence (corroborating evidence often is sought using more than one method) that provide the required level of assurance at the lowest cost.

The level of assurance that the auditor seeks to achieve through the process of gathering and evaluating audit evidence is that level needed to support an unqualified opinion on the financial statements. The auditor cannot be satisfied with anything less than that level of assurance and still express an unqualified opinion. The sources and methods of obtaining the necessary evidence, the amount of each type of evidence needed, and the timing of the procedures used to obtain the evidence, however, can all be varied to fit the circumstances of the individual engagement and thus enhance the efficiency with which the audit is performed.

Sufficiency of Evidential Matter

Determining the sufficiency of evidential matter is a question of deciding how much evidence is enough to achieve the needed level of assurance. The amount of evidence required depends in part on the thoroughness of the auditor's search for evidential matter, in part on the auditor's ability to evaluate it objectively, and in part on the level of assurance necessary to support the opinion in a particular audit. For some auditing procedures, the amount of evidence needed corresponds precisely with the decision to use a certain procedure at all: The auditor either performs the procedure or does not perform the procedure. For example, in the audit of a client with a single cash fund, a decision to count cash on hand is a decision to count *all* cash on hand. If the client had numerous cash funds, however, the two decisions would not be identical; the auditor could count cash on hand on a test or sample basis. In that case, the question of sufficiency becomes one of determining sample size, a topic that is discussed in Chapter 10.

Types of Audit Tests or Procedures

The types of evidence and the procedures for obtaining it described previously could also be classified according to the purpose for which the evidence is gathered. Viewed in terms of their purpose, all auditing procedures, often referred to as "tests," can be classified as one of two types: compliance tests and substantive tests. Although these two types of audit tests and their respective purposes are discussed at length in Chapters 8 and 9, they are described briefly here to set the stage for the overview of an audit that is presented later in this chapter.

Compliance tests are performed to determine how well specific internal accounting controls are functioning. The purpose of compliance tests is to provide the auditor with evidence that the controls are operating as prescribed by the system. If the auditor wishes to be able to rely on the operation of specific internal accounting controls to reduce the amount of evidence that would otherwise need to be obtained, the controls must be "compliance tested." To illustrate a compliance test, consider a client's system of internal accounting control that requires the accounts payable clerk to recalculate the extensions and footings on vendors' invoices as a means of determining that the vendors' calculations are mathematically accurate. As evidence that the control has been applied, the clerk initials the invoice after performing the calculations. To compliance test the operation of that control, the auditor should inspect the invoice for the presence of the clerk's initials and may reperform the calculations that the clerk was supposed to have made. If the initials are present and the extensions and footings are correct, the auditor would conclude that the control operated properly in that specific instance.

Substantive tests consist of tests of the details of transactions and account balances, analytical review procedures, and other auditing procedures. The purpose of substantive tests is to provide the auditor with direct evidence about management's assertions that are implicit in the financial statements or, conversely, to discover errors or irregularities in the financial statements. Analytical review procedures were mentioned earlier in this chapter and are discussed in detail in Chapter 9. An example of a test of the details of transactions is the vouching of purchases, sales, and retirements of property, plant, and equipment during the year as a means of forming an opinion about the assertions concerning existence, rights and obligations, and accuracy that are implicit in the balance reported for that account in the balance sheet. An example of a test of the details of an account balance is the confirming of accounts receivable in order to form an opinion about the existence of the receivables. Other substantive procedures include reading minutes of meetings of the board of directors and its important committees, obtaining letters from outside counsel regarding legal matters, and obtaining a letter of representation from management about the completeness of recorded liabilities.

Audit Evidence Decisions

The amount and kinds of evidence that the auditor decides are necessary to provide a reasonable basis for forming an opinion on the financial statements taken as a whole, and the timing of procedures used to obtain the evidence, are matters of professional judgment made after careful deliberation of the circumstances of a particular engagement and consideration of the various risks related to the audit. The goal in every audit should be to perform the examination in an effective and efficient manner.

Usually an auditor finds it necessary to rely on evidence that is persuasive rather than convincing. In deciding how much persuasive evidence is enough, by necessity the auditor must work within time constraints, considering the cost of obtaining evidence and evaluating the usefulness of the evidence obtained. In making these decisions, the auditor cannot ignore the risk of issuing an inappropriate opinion or justify omitting a particular test solely because it is difficult or expensive to perform. While an auditor is seldom convinced beyond all doubt with respect to all the assertions embodied in the financial statements, he or she must achieve the level of assurance necessary to support the opinion given.

An unqualified opinion requires that the auditor have no substantial doubt about any material item in the financial statements. Negative assurance—a statement that nothing came to the auditor's attention to cause a question about the fairness of the statements—is not adequate. The auditor must refrain from formulating an opinion until sufficient competent evidential matter has been obtained to remove all substantial doubt. For example, if the auditor attempts to communicate with a customer to confirm a material amount owed to the entity and if the customer fails to respond after repeated requests, the auditor should employ alternative procedures—such as examining evidence of subsequent cash receipts, cash remittance advices, the customer's purchase orders, and sales and shipping documents—to obtain satisfaction that the account receivable exists and that the balance is accurate.

In planning the examination and, as part of the overall audit strategy, deciding on the nature, timing, and extent of audit tests to be performed—what procedures to perform, when to perform them, and how much testing to do—the auditor has available a number of alternative strategies. For example, in one engagement the auditor might decide to rely on compliance tests designed to provide evidence of the consistent and proper operation of the accounting system from which the account balances are derived, in combination with limited substantive tests of the account balances themselves. In another engagement the auditor might decide to rely principally on substantive tests of account balances for assurance that they are properly stated. These decisions will be influenced by answers to questions such as: which approach provides a higher level of assurance; which approach is more efficient; are the accounting systems and the related internal controls satisfactory; what are the principal risks of the client's business; what are the significant account balances in the financial statements? These factors are not intended to be all-inclusive, but are indicative of the types of considerations and judgments the auditor must make. They are discussed throughout this book and particularly in Chapter 6.

The Steps in an Audit

Every audit comprises the following four major steps:

1. Obtaining (or updating) and documenting information about the client and considering how that information may affect the audit strategy.
2. Planning and documenting an effective and efficient audit strategy.
3. Performing tests and other audit procedures to obtain, evaluate, and document sufficient competent evidence to corroborate whether the

management assertions embodied in account balances and in the financial statements as a whole, including the disclosures, are reasonable and thus to determine whether the corresponding audit objectives have been met.

4. Formulating and preparing the auditor's report and communicating weaknesses and breakdowns in internal control.

The nature, timing, and extent of the work associated with each of the four steps varies from one audit client to another and may vary from year to year for a given client; moreover, they seldom appear as separate, isolated, specifically identifiable steps. Whether carried out sequentially or in various combinations, however, all four steps are found in one form or another in every engagement. These steps, which were first introduced in Chapter 1, are elaborated on in this section and graphically displayed in Figure 5.2.

Obtaining and Documenting Information About the Client

At an early stage in the audit, the auditor obtains (or updates) information about the client that is used to assess the risk that the financial statements are materially misstated and to plan the audit. Among other things, the auditor gathers information about

- The nature, size, and organization of the client's enterprise and its operations.
- Matters affecting the business and industry in which the client operates, such as

    The business environment and

    Legal constraints and requirements.
- The control environment and significant accounting and management policies, practices, and methods.
- Significant accounting systems and, depending on the audit strategy that is likely to be followed, specific internal accounting controls.
- Significant accounts or groups of accounts and the interrelationships among significant financial and operational data.
- Logistical matters relevant to the audit, such as

    Dates of the auditor's meetings with the audit committee of the board of directors

    Dates by which the client will have assembled the data, records, and documents required by the auditor

    Date or dates on which the client plans to physically count inventories or other assets

    Deadlines for issuing the report on the financial statements and any other audit-related reports.

The information is obtained in a number of different ways. The auditor may begin by consulting such materials as the client's recent annual reports

Figure 5.2 Summary of an Audit

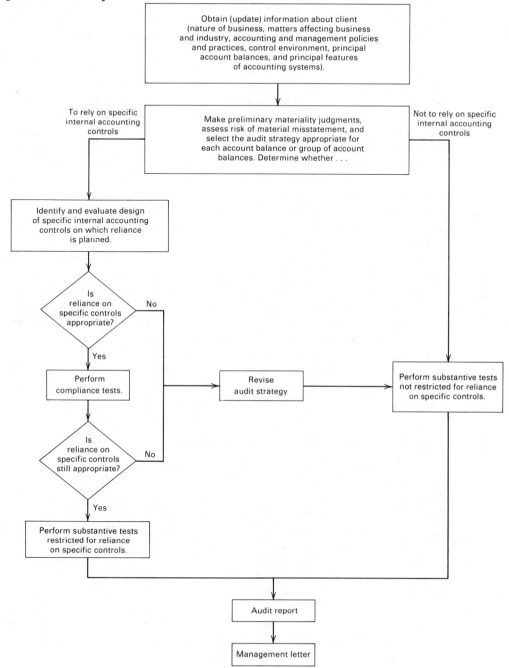

and interim earnings or other news releases; general business or industry publications; industry accounting and auditing guides developed by the AICPA, the auditor's firm, and others; and trade association materials. Unless the engagement is an initial examination, prior years' working papers and current correspondence files are also valuable sources of information. For an initial examination, the auditor makes inquiries and reviews preceding years' working papers of the predecessor auditor, if the client has been audited in the past. The auditor supplements this knowledge by interviewing officers and employees of the client and others knowledgeable about and experienced in the industry—particularly others within the auditor's firm, including personnel responsible for providing nonaudit services to the client. Additionally, the auditor typically reviews the company's policy and procedures manuals; tours its major plants and offices; reads the minutes of recent meetings of the board of directors, its important committees, and the stockholders; reads the client's significant contracts and other agreements; and compares the client's significant financial and operating data with those of its competitors, analyzing interrelationships and trends in the data.

A record of the information obtained by the auditor is needed for audit planning and control purposes and for documenting the auditor's compliance with generally accepted auditing standards. Some auditors prefer to document the information in narrative form; others prefer to use narratives for general information about the industry and company, and flowcharts or questionnaires supplemented by narratives to describe the accounting systems and controls. The extent of information necessary to design and carry out subsequent audit procedures is affected by whether there have been significant changes in matters affecting the client, its business, or its systems and controls since the preceding audit and by the audit strategy contemplated.

Planning and Documenting the Audit Strategy

The auditor uses the information about the client to determine the audit strategy and plan the engagement. The auditor makes preliminary materiality judgments and assesses the risk of material misstatement associated with the audit objectives relevant to each account or group of accounts. Those judgments and assessments form the basis for the auditor's determination of the nature, timing, and extent of audit procedures for each account or group of accounts that, in the auditor's judgment, will most efficiently limit to a low level the risk that the auditor may unknowingly fail to modify the opinion appropriately if the financial statements are materially misstated.

The basic audit strategy alternatives, which are equally applicable in manual and computerized environments, are to perform substantive tests without restriction for reliance on specific internal accounting controls or to compliance test and rely on specific internal accounting controls, with a corresponding restriction of the scope of substantive procedures. The auditor may adopt the same audit strategy for the entire audit or different strategies for different segments of the audit. Thus, it is possible to achieve one or more audit objectives for an account or group of accounts by relying on specific internal accounting controls and restricting substantive tests, while achieving other audit objectives by performing substantive procedures without restriction for reliance on specific internal accounting controls. This flexibility also applies to different client locations, subsidiaries, and components of business activities.

Regardless of the audit strategy selected, auditors have traditionally focused more on audit objectives related to balance sheet accounts than on their income statement counterparts, since that is frequently the most efficient way to conduct an audit. Emphasizing balance sheet accounts is also conceptually sound: Balance sheet accounts represent the enterprise's economic resources and claims to those resources at a point in time; as such, they represent the cumulative effects of transactions and other events and circumstances that have changed the enterprise's resources and claims to them through that point in time. Income statement accounts reflect the enterprise's performance during a period between two points in time, measuring the enterprise's revenues, expenses, gains, and losses that occurred during the period. Income statement accounts are logically and inextricably related to one or more balance sheet accounts. Audit objectives for income statement accounts, therefore, frequently can be achieved by achieving the corresponding audit objectives for related balance sheet accounts. For example, the audit objective relating to the occurrence of sales transactions during a period may be met by meeting the audit objective regarding the existence of trade accounts receivable at the beginning and end of the period. In some cases, however, it may be more efficient to achieve audit objectives for balance sheet accounts by achieving the corresponding audit objectives for related income statement accounts. For example, the audit objective relating to the completeness of trade accounts receivable at the end of a period may be met most efficiently by meeting the audit objective relating to the completeness of the sales account balance for the period.

The audit strategy selected for each audit segment and the significant reasons for selecting that strategy, which are based on the auditor's assessment of the risk of material misstatement occurring and the most efficient way of responding to that risk, should be documented. The documentation should also include the decisions made concerning certain other aspects of the audit plan, such as locations where work will be performed, analyses to be prepared by the client, the need to use the work of other auditing firms or specialists (such as actuaries), the effects of an internal audit function on the audit strategy, and the methods for documenting the accounting system and relevant internal accounting controls. The audit strategy as initially determined and documented should be reviewed and revised, if necessary, as the audit progresses and new information becomes available.

Performing Tests and Other Procedures

In the performance phase, the auditor obtains, evaluates, and documents evidence to corroborate management's assertions embodied in the accounts and other information in the financial statements and related notes and thus to determine whether the corresponding audit objectives have been achieved. That evidence is obtained in connection with the auditor's risk assessments, which, if controls are to be relied on, include the evaluation of the design of specific internal accounting controls and compliance tests of those controls, and from substantive procedures.

Study and Evaluation of Internal Control. Generally accepted auditing standards require the auditor to study and evaluate the client's internal control system, which comprises the control environment, accounting systems, administrative controls, and internal accounting controls. At a minimum, the study and evaluation must be sufficient to enable the auditor to understand the client's control environment and the flow of significant transactions through the accounting systems. That minimum study and evaluation, which is generally performed in connection with obtaining information about the client, is often adequate for developing an audit strategy that does not call for relying on and testing specific internal accounting controls, but not for one that does.

Based on the minimum study and evaluation of the client's internal control system, an auditor can identify the points in the accounting systems where significant errors and frauds could occur and can assess the risk that particular accounts or groups of accounts and the financial statements as a whole could be materially misstated as a result. Because the minimum study and evaluation does not cover the design and operation of specific internal accounting controls (i.e., the specific control procedures and methods being applied by the client), however, those risk assessments would not fully reflect the favorable effects of controls that may have been implemented by the client. An audit strategy developed on the basis of the minimum study and evaluation, therefore, may be effective, but may not be the most efficient audit strategy. Consequently, the auditor generally considers whether particular audit objectives for individual accounts or groups of accounts might be achieved most efficiently by extending the study and evaluation of internal control to encompass the design and operation of specific internal accounting controls.

In order for the auditor to enhance audit efficiency by relying on specific internal accounting controls, the reduction in audit time and effort realizable by restricting related substantive tests must exceed the audit time and effort required to evaluate the design and operation of those specific controls, which includes the time and effort required for compliance tests. Reliance on specific internal accounting controls is generally desirable, therefore, only when achieving the relevant audit objectives without such reliance would require substantial audit time and effort. Additionally, reliance on specific internal accounting controls is feasible only if (1) by design and (2) by effective and continuous operation those controls reasonably can be assessed by the auditor as limiting to a low level the risk that relevant account balances or the financial statements as a whole could be materially misstated by errors or frauds that the controls are supposed to prevent or detect.

The auditor's understanding of the client's business, including information about the control environment and accounting systems obtained through the minimum study and evaluation of internal control, forms the basis for the identification of audit segments that could benefit from reliance on specific internal accounting controls. The auditor uses that knowledge to identify the audit objectives for each account or group of accounts that may not be achieved most efficiently by a substantive audit strategy. In addition, that knowledge provides a basis for identifying the types of significant errors or frauds associated with those audit objectives and the points in the accounting systems where those errors and frauds could occur. With that in mind, the auditor documents the design of specific internal accounting controls over those critical points in the accounting systems and assesses whether those controls, assuming that they are applied properly and continuously, should effectively prevent or detect the relevant types of significant errors and frauds. That assessment relates only to the design of specific internal accounting controls. To meaningfully restrict substantive tests by relying on specific internal accounting controls, the auditor must also perform compliance tests of those controls.

The auditor obtains (or updates) knowledge of the client's specific internal accounting controls principally through inquiry and observation of client personnel, reference to relevant policy and procedures manuals, and inspection of books, records, forms, and reports. The auditor frequently uses flowcharts, internal control questionnaires, or other practice aids to assist in evaluating and documenting those controls. As a practical matter, the auditor often identifies many of those controls and may evaluate and document their design in the course of learning about the client's control environment and accounting systems. Additionally, the auditor generally does not "relearn" or redocument those controls in each year's engagement. Most audits are recurring engagements, for which the auditor carries forward the knowledge and documentation developed in prior years and updates them for significant changes since the preceding year's audit. Most (if not all) of those changes generally come to the auditor's attention through continuing contact with the client between the completion of one year's audit and the beginning of the next. If the auditor is concerned that the documented understanding of the client's accounting systems and specific internal accounting controls may be incorrect or incomplete, perhaps because of changes in the systems since the preceding audit, it may be efficient to trace a representative transaction through the systems (sometimes called a transaction review or a "walkthrough") before formalizing the audit strategy.

Performing Compliance Tests. Compliance tests are performed only on those specific internal accounting controls on which the auditor intends to rely as part of the audit strategy and that have therefore "passed" the auditor's evaluation of the effectiveness of their design. Compliance tests—which include making inquiries of client personnel who perform control procedures and of others in a position to be aware of control breakdowns, examining records and documents for evidence of performance, reperforming control procedures by duplicating the actions of the client's personnel, and observing how the controls are exercised—are designed to provide evidence as to whether the specific internal accounting controls that the auditor would like to rely on have operated effectively and continuously throughout the period of intended reliance.

The auditor should discuss with appropriate client personnel any significant weaknesses in the design of specific internal accounting controls and any significant breakdowns in compliance. The auditor should also consider the effects of such weaknesses and breakdowns on the assessment of the risk that relevant account balances or the financial statements as a whole could be materially misstated, and should plan the nature, timing, and extent of substantive procedures accordingly.

The auditor may formulate the audit strategy for each account or group of accounts, develop the audit program, and plan and schedule the work, particularly for recurring engagements, before completing the evaluation of the design of specific internal accounting controls and before compliance testing those controls. The auditor recognizes that the ultimate assessment of the design of the controls or the results of compliance tests may indicate that specific internal accounting controls may not have operated effectively and continuously throughout the period of intended reliance. This could require the auditor to reassess the risk that account balances or the financial statements as a whole could be materially misstated and to revise the audit strategy and engagement plan. In formulating the audit strategy and plan before completing compliance tests, the auditor assumes that the evaluation of the design and the compliance test results will be satisfactory. The basis for those assumptions on a new engagement generally is derived from the auditor's understanding of the control environment and from evidence, which may perhaps be limited in scope, obtained from inquiries, observations, and inspection of documents, records, and reports undertaken as part of developing an understanding of the accounting systems. On a recurring engagement, those assumptions are also supported by the prior year's audit experience, preliminary inquiries of knowledgeable client personnel, and the auditor's recognition that, except in rather extraordinary circumstances, a client's control environment and the effective operation of its accounting systems and internal accounting controls generally do not deteriorate markedly from one year to the next.

Performing Substantive Tests. Substantive procedures include tests of details of account balances and transactions, analytical comparisons and reviews, and other auditing procedures such as obtaining written representations from the client's management and attorneys. Substantive tests provide direct evidence about management's assertions and the corresponding audit objectives. The selection of substantive tests, when they are performed, and the extent to which they are performed depend on the auditor's materiality judgments and risk assessments. The major determinant is the basic strategy decision as to whether and to what extent internal accounting controls will be relied on to reduce the level of assurance that would otherwise be required from substantive tests. Furthermore, the assurance required from substantive tests may be obtained from tests of details, analytical review procedures, or some combination of both, with the assurance obtained from one reducing the assurance needed from the other.

Formulating the Auditor's Report and Communicating Control Weaknesses

After all of the previous steps in the audit have been performed, the auditor makes the final materiality judgments, evaluates the audit findings, reviews the financial statement presentation and disclosures for adequacy, and prepares the audit report. The auditor also generally prepares a management letter communicating internal control weaknesses noted during the course of the audit.

Working Papers

Statement on Auditing Standards No. 41, *Working Papers* (AU Section 339), specifies that the auditor should prepare and maintain working papers as a record of the work done and conclusions reached on significant matters. Although the auditor is not precluded from supplementing working papers by other means, the working papers are the principal support for the auditor's report. (The reference to generally accepted auditing standards in the auditor's report implies a representation regarding observance of the three standards of field work. Working papers provide documentation that those standards were observed.) Working papers also help the auditor in planning, conducting, and supervising the work.

More specifically, the working papers

- Record the understanding of the client's business and system of internal control.
- Document the audit strategy.
- Document the detailed systems evaluation, transaction reviews, and compliance tests (in situations in which controls are relied on).
- Document substantive test procedures applied to transactions, account balances, and other information presented in the financial statements.
- Document that the work of any assistants was supervised and reviewed.
- Document resolution of exceptions and unusual matters.
- Provide information for SEC reports, tax returns, and governmental agencies.
- Serve as a source of information for succeeding audits.
- Record recommendations for improving controls, as noted throughout the engagement.
- Support the auditor's opinion, including representations regarding compliance with generally accepted auditing standards and generally accepted accounting principles.
- Support amounts and footnote disclosures in the financial statements.

Working papers are the property of the auditor and not a substitute for the client's accounting records. (In some cases, as an accommodation to the client, working papers are transmitted to and accepted by the client as a substitute for a record that it would otherwise prepare.) The auditor should adopt reasonable procedures for the safekeeping and retention of working papers for a period sufficient to meet the needs of the firm's or individual's practice and to satisfy any pertinent legal requirements for records retention.

Form and Content of Working Papers

Working papers include audit programs, trial balances, schedules, analyses, memoranda, letters of confirmation, representative abstracts of company documents, flowcharts, and narratives. They may be handwritten, typewritten, or in the form of computer printouts or computer software. Often, portions of working papers are prepared by client personnel according to auditor-determined specifications; the auditor should, of course, test the accuracy of client-prepared working papers. The *content* of working papers generally cannot be standardized. Certain types of working papers, however, lend themselves to standardization, such as a summary of accounts receivable confirmation coverage and results. Working papers should be legible, complete, readily understandable, and designed to fit the circumstances and needs of the auditor for the particular engagement and subject matter under audit.

Unnecessary or irrelevant working papers that do not serve a useful purpose should not be prepared. If such working papers are inadvertently prepared, they should generally not be retained. Copies of client records usually fall into this category.

Although the content of working papers varies with the engagement, there are several advantages to adopting a standardized approach to their *format*. It facilitates the systematic organization of working papers for use during an engagement, enhances their ready access for reference or review, and aids in their orderly filing for future reference. Thus, every working paper should be headed, dated, and initialed by the preparer at the time the work is performed. (Figure 5.4 illustrates this.)

A *heading* identifies the client and the subject of the working paper.

Dating not only provides evidence of the time of preparation but also facilitates tracing the sequence in which steps were performed and helps to plan the timing of similar work in the next examination.

Initialing establishes responsibility for the work and also indicates to reviewers or subsequent users personnel who might be able to furnish additional information.

Every working paper should contain an explanation of the procedures followed (unless the information is included elsewhere in the working papers, such as in an audit program) and the results of those procedures. Sometimes the procedures are obvious from the computations or other data recorded; sometimes a narrative explanation is required. When an explanation is required, it is frequently placed at the end of the working paper and assigned a symbol or "tick mark," which is placed next to the appropriate item (generally a dollar amount) in the body of the working paper. For example, a working paper listing the details of notes receivable at a particular date may have the letter "E" after the details of each note, with the following explanation at the end of the working paper: "E = note examined," meaning that the auditor physically inspected the notes. Some auditors use a standardized group of symbols to document procedures.

Each working paper or set of working papers covering an audit objective should contain a clear record of all work performed. This record should include a narrative by the auditor who performed the work that sets forth the conclusion reached as a result of that work. For example, the working papers supporting the procedures applied in evaluating the allowance for uncollectible accounts should contain an overall conclusion on whether the auditor believes the allowance appears adequate or inadequate, based on the audit work performed. Language such as "are fairly stated" and "appear to be fairly stated" should be avoided, however, because the conclusion could be misinterpreted as having been reached in the context of the financial statements taken as a whole. That inference would be inappropriate and unsupportable since the conclusion is based on only a portion of the work done during the examination of the overall financial statements.

Working Paper Organization

There are no rigid guidelines for organizing a set of audit working papers. What follows should be viewed as general guidance that is subject to substantial modification by individual auditors and firms.

Detailed working papers are often summarized through the use of lead schedules for each financial statement caption. This technique enables the preparer, as well as reviewers, to "see the forest as well as the trees"; that is, it provides an overview of an entire audit area. In addition, a lead schedule enables a reviewer to look at as much or as little detail as is considered necessary in the circumstances.

Detailed support for lead schedules or other summary working papers is often filed behind the summary in order of relative significance or other meaningful sequence. There should always be an easy-to-follow trail between the detailed working papers and the amounts reflected in the financial statements. Each working paper should be able to stand on its own; that is, it should be complete and understandable in itself. Reference may be made to other working papers to document audit findings. Cross-referencing of working papers should be specific rather than general. The "to–from" technique is used to make the "direction" of referencing apparent; that is, it shows which number is the source and which is the summary. Figure 5.3 illustrates this suggestion.

Figure 5.3 Working Paper Organization

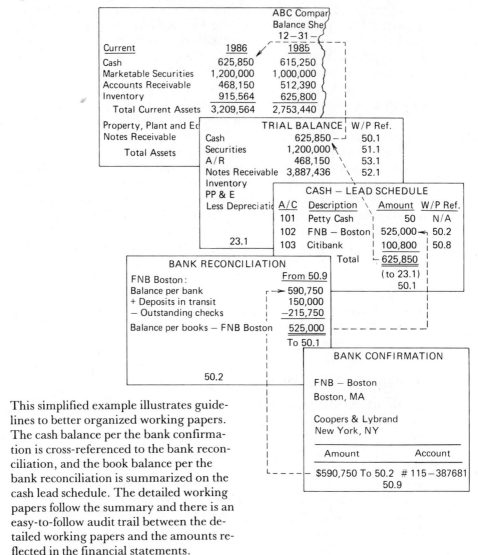

This simplified example illustrates guidelines to better organized working papers. The cash balance per the bank confirmation is cross-referenced to the bank reconciliation, and the book balance per the bank reconciliation is summarized on the cash lead schedule. The detailed working papers follow the summary and there is an easy-to-follow audit trail between the detailed working papers and the amounts reflected in the financial statements.

Typical Working Papers

As suggested earlier, the infinite variety of conditions encountered in practice generates an infinite variety of working papers. Nevertheless, some types of working papers have common characteristics, which are explained and illustrated in this section of the chapter.

The Trial Balance. The trial balance is the key working paper in many audits because it is the one on which data from all underlying working papers are inte-

Figure 5.4 Trial Balance (Partial)

COOPERS CABINET COMPANY
TRIAL BALANCE
12/31/86

ACCOUNT NUMBER	ACCOUNT DESCRIPTION	BALANCE 12/31/85 DR<CR>	BALANCE 12/31/86 DR<CR>	W/P REFERENCE	ADJUSTMENTS DR	ADJUSTMENTS CR	RECLASSIFICATIONS DR	RECLASSIFICATIONS CR	ADJUSTED BALANCE DR<CR>	PER FINANCIAL STATEMENTS DR<CR>
101	PETTY CASH	500.00	500.00							
103	CASH-COMMERCIAL ACCOUNT	20,438.00	26,675.00							
104	CASH-PAYROLL ACCOUNT	500.00	500.00							
110	ACCOUNTS RECEIVABLE	90,000.00	103,500.00							
111	ALLOWANCE FOR DOUBTFUL ACCOUNTS	<2,000.00>	<2,000.00>							
116	NOTES RECEIVABLE	15,000.00	17,500.00							
117	ACCRUED INTEREST RECEIVABLE	600.00	700.00							
120	MARKETABLE SECURITIES	55,000.00	43,000.00							
121	DIVIDENDS RECEIVABLE	1,650.00	925.00							
132	DEPOSITS	1,000.00	1,000.00							
134	PREPAID INSURANCE	7,848.00	10,953.00							
136	PREPAID TAXES	1,300.00	1,500.00							
138	PREPAID-OTHER	450.00	300.00							
140	INVENTORY	81,000.00	124,719.00							
150	LAND	81,950.00	99,700.00							
151	BUILDING	170,000.00	170,000.00							
152	MACHINERY AND EQUIPMENT	134,300.00	146,700.00							
153	VEHICLES	39,525.00	41,176.00							
155	ACCUMULATED DEPRECIATION	<94,061.00>	<104,010.00>							
123	SECURITIES VALUATION ALLOWANCE	-	<1,120.00>							
	TOTAL ASSETS	605,000.00 [P]	683,632.00 [G/L]							

P - Agreed to prior year's working papers
G/L - Agreed to the general ledger

Figure 5.5 Transaction Review—Buying Cycle—Flowchart Number 1, 19X2

Flowchart Operation Number	Documents Examined			
	Type I Raw Mat'l. Release	Type II Purchases Against P/Os	Type III Invoices Only	Type IV Check Requisition
1	Req. 204	Req. 223	N/A	N/A
2	R 1570	N/A	N/A	N/A
3	N/A	PO 10/3	N/A	N/A
4	R 1570 (Copy 5)	PO 10/3 (Copy 5)	N/A	N/A
5	"	N/A	N/A	N/A
6	Note 1	Note 1	N/A	N/A
7	N/A	N/A	VO 11-18	N/A
8	VO 11-389	VO 11-390	N/A	N/A
9	"	"	"	N/A
10	"	"	"	N/A
11	"	"	"	VO 11-1
12	"	"	"	"
13	"	"	"	"
14	"	"	"	"
15	"	"	"	Note 2
16	CK 11-1780	CK 11-3	CK 12-2	CK 11-340
17	"	M	M	M
18	"	M	M	M
19	"	M	M	M

Performed by: WS
Date: 10/11/X2

M = Commingled for processing purposes. (Only one tested through the rest of the system.)

Notes

1. Since the documents examined are no longer in the open files (flowchart operation number 6), we inquired into and observed procedures related to the open files and examined other documents on a test basis.

2. Type IV vouchers are approved by the accounting department supervisor, not by the chief accountant. Flowchart amended.

Identification of Transaction Types

Type I

This type involves raw materials. An annual buying contract is negotiated, requiring the company to purchase an aggregate tonnage, subject to periodic release.

The contract includes a specific price, certain price protection clauses in case of declining prices, and cancellation clauses.

Type II

This type involves production items other than raw materials. Specific purchase orders

Figure 5.5 *Continued*

are issued for each transaction; competitive bids are sought when aggregate cost is thought to exceed $1,000.

Type III

This type generally involves nonproduction items, such as office supplies, promotional materials, and the like. Department heads usually place orders with vendors by telephone. Materials are sent directly to the departments concerned; formal receiving reports are not used.

Type IV

This type involves check requisitions. A check requisition is used if there is no vendor invoice (e.g., tax payments, transfers between bank accounts).

---

grated, referenced, and summarized into the amounts appearing in the financial statements. There are a number of ways of preparing the trial balance, and each of them has its advantages. Often it is prepared in a form that compares the current figures with those of the previous period. It may be prepared in balance sheet and income statement order, and amounts may be grouped into subtotals to permit ready identification of trial balance amounts with those in the financial statements. Client adjustments made as a result of the audit and financial statement reclassification entries (made only on the trial balance) are shown in additional columns. The adjusted trial balance is usually cross-referenced to supporting working papers. Figure 5.4 is an example of a partial trial balance before adjustments and reclassifications have been posted.

Schedules and Analyses. Working papers recording *transaction reviews* should identify the specific transactions selected for review and each step in the transaction flow that was reviewed, together with a notation of the audit work performed at each point within the system. Figure 5.5 is an illustration of a working paper for a transaction review.

Compliance tests are often documented in narrative form by describing the tests performed and the controls tested. Sometimes a compliance test requires preparing a list of items to be extracted from the files or to be compared with data in another location. If so, the schedule or listing prepared can serve as the working paper. Figure 5.6 is an illustration of a working paper for a compliance test.

Substantive tests are most often evidenced by some kind of analysis; the form depends on the nature of the auditing procedures performed. For example, the working papers might include an analysis showing the composition of the ending balance in a particular account tested, or perhaps a summary of the account. They also might include an analysis of the activity in the particular account for the period, showing the beginning balance, a summary of the transactions during the period (logically classified so that relationships with related accounts are apparent), and the ending balance. The working papers

Figure 5.6 Payroll Compliance Test, 19X2

Change Notice #	Dept. Head Authorized	Per. Mgr. Authorized	Change Notice #	Dept. Head Authorized	Per. Mgr. Authorized
4142	A	B✔	4322	A	B✔
4172	A	B✔	4352	A	B✔
4202	A	B✔	4382	A	B✔
4232	A	B✔	4412	A	B✔
4262	A	B✔	4442	A	C✔
4292	A	B✔	4472	A	B✔

Legend

A—Examined payroll change notice for signature of appropriate department head, indicating proper authorization.

B—Examined payroll change notice for signature of personnel manager, indicating proper authorization and proper segregation of duties.

C—Payroll change notice not signed by personnel manager. Personnel manager indicated this was an oversight. See working paper XX.2 for evaluation of sample results.

✔—Agreed payroll change notice to payroll master file change report, indicating accounting supervisor had accurately performed a comparison of change notice with the master file change report.

should present both the account information and an indication of the evidence examined and other auditing procedures performed; sometimes the dollar amount or the percentage of the total tested is also shown. Figure 5.7 illustrates a working paper analyzing federal income taxes payable. Figure 5.8 indicates the variety of audit procedures performed on notes receivable and related interest accounts that can be documented on a single working paper.

Analytical tests involve a study and comparison of relationships among data; they are often evidenced by computations made by the auditor in the course of the review. The working paper evidence usually consists of a narrative description of the procedures, the results of the procedures, further investigation of matters identified as having a significant effect on the auditor's examination, and the effect on the scope of the auditor's examination of related accounts.

Memoranda. Questions, errors discovered by procedures performed, or unusual matters that arise during the audit should be documented. The steps taken to resolve them should be explained (such as additional auditing procedures, consultation with the client, the auditor's own research, and reasoning), people involved in the resolution identified, and the resulting conclusions explained. It is undesirable simply to check off a question or record a cryptic answer such as ''cleared.'' Explanations of material matters should be complete and conclusive.

Permanent Working Papers. Working papers for recurring engagements usually contain files that are carried forward from preceding years' audits; these are often referred to as permanent files. The file should include data hav-

Figure 5.7 XYZ Industries: Analysis of Federal Income Taxes Payable (A/C 3231)

Prepared _____

Reviewed _____

	Total	1987	1986	1985	Miscellaneous
Balance 1/1/87	36,000 T		18,500 T	8,100 T	9,400 T
Payment with automatic extension 3/15/87	(17,000) V		(17,000)		
Final payment with tax return	(2,700)		(1,500) TR, V		(1,200)
Estimated payments for 1987	(60,000) CR	(60,000) (2)			
Payment of additional assessment re: 1985	(6,300) RAR(1) W/P FF-1			(8,100)	1,800
1987 current provisions	193,200	193,200			
Balance 12/31/87	✓✓ 143,200 ✓✓	133,200 ✓✓	0 ✓✓	0	10,000 (A) ✓✓

Legend

T—Traced to prior year's working papers

V—Examined canceled check

TR—Agrees with tax return examined

✓✓—Checked calculations

CR—Traced 1st and 3rd quarter payments to check register

RAR—Agrees with revenue agent's report

W/P—Working paper source reference

(1) $2,300 interest on the assessment was separately charged to interest expense.
(2) No underpayment penalty because $60,000 exceeded last year's tax.
(A) Represents miscellaneous underaccruals and overaccruals not taken into income—not material.

Figure 5.8   Analysis of Notes Receivable and Related Interest Accounts

COOPERS CABINET COMPANY
NOTES RECEIVABLE
12/31/86

Prepared by: E.F.   Date: 3/10/87

DEBTOR	INTEREST RATE	NOTE DATE / DUE DATE	PRINCIPAL - A/C 116 — BALANCE 12/31/85	ADDITIONS	RECEIPTS	BALANCE 12/31/86	CURRENT PORTION	LONG-TERM PORTION	ACCRUED INTEREST - A/C 117 — BALANCE 12/31/85	INTEREST INCOME	RECEIPTS	BALANCE 12/31/86
④ WATTS ENGINEERING	c 15	4/30/85 DEMAND	φ 3,275.00			φ 3,275.00 c	c 3,275		245.62	491.26	491.26	245.62 c
④ MATCHOMATIC	c 16 φc	4/4/86 4/4/91 Payable #1570 annually, plus interest		7,850.00		7,850.00 c	c 1,570	6,280		1,016.58		1,016.58 c
④ POWER BELT CONVEYORS	c 12	3/1/85 3/1/83 Payable #2125 annually, plus interest	6,375.00			6,375.00 c	c 4,250	2,125	98.38	765.00	724.58	138.80 c
④ BORLAND PLUMBING	c 8	3/2/78 DEMAND	5,350.00		④ 5,350.00	— c	c		856.00	38.16	④ 894.16	c
			15,000.00	7,850.00	5,350.00	17,500.00	9,095	8,405	1,200.00	2,310.00	2,110.00	1,400.00
			✓	✓	✓	✓ T/B		✓	✓	✓	✓	✓ T/B

✓ = Footed   cf = cross footed
P — agreed to prior year w/p's
T/B — agreed to the trial balance
c — agreed to confirmation on w/p's 52.2 to 52.5
✓ Traced to approval in minutes of the Board of Directors meetings
④ Recomputed classification based on terms of the note
R — recomputed; appears reasonable
Ⓓ — agreed to copy of executed note in permanent file. Reviewed note for unusual terms, collateral arrangements and significant requirement restrictions or other covenants. None noted other than the note is collateralized by inventory (See confirmation on 52.3)
Ⓐ — agreed to customer remittance advice paid 2/3/86, totaling #6204.16 including interest
Traced to cash receipts journal and agreed to deposit slip on 2/3/86.

①—Agreed to remittance advice for collection of note installment and/or interest, date indicated next to Ⓣ∂mark.

④—Reviewed stated interest rate for reasonableness.

⑤—Note not collected at 3/10/87. Discussion with treasurer disclosed that demand for payment will be 6/11/87. D&B report of Watts Engineering indicates good credit rating. Balance appears collectible, no allowance deemed necessary.

Ⓐ—First installment due 3/1/86 was made on 2/3/87. Client indicated customer has experienced a cash flow problem in early 1986, which has now been remedied. Customer has indicated the second installment will be paid on time. D&B report of Power Belt indicates improved rating. Balance appears collectible; no allowance deemed necessary.

Ⓓ—Per review of the note and discussion with Treasurer, none of these are related parties as defined by SAS #6.

⑧—Reclassification entry for financial statement:

116	Notes receivable—short term		8405	
116	Notes receivable—long term			8405

QJE no. 47

Ⓓ—To footnote disclosure note collateralized by inventory. See confirmation 52.1

ing continuing use and not subject to frequent change. Examples of such data include copies or abstracts of the certificate of incorporation, bylaws, bond and note indentures, union agreements, important contracts having historical significance, organization charts, the client's accounting policies and procedures, key personnel, and location of plants. The file may also include activity schedules not maintained by the client, for example, schedules of future amortization or depreciation (sometimes referred to as "lapse schedules") and analyses and other working papers that have historical significance, such as analyses of various capital accounts. Audit programs, narrative descriptions of accounting and control systems, flowcharts, and internal control questionnaires also are frequently kept in the permanent files.

Common Working Paper Deficiencies

Deficiencies in working papers often result in confusion and wasted time in carrying out auditing procedures, in assisting new staff in the following year's au-

Figure 5.9 Common Working Paper Deficiencies

- Working paper not initialed and dated by preparer or reviewer.
- Working paper not properly "headed."
- Cross-referencing too general; reviewer unable to find referenced working papers.
- Reason for cross-referencing missing or not apparent.
- Tick marks appearing on the working paper without a descriptive legend.
- Purpose of working paper not apparent; no explanation given.
- Working papers sloppy or cluttered.
- Exceptions or unusual items not properly explained or evaluated.
- Working paper content illogical.
- Findings not evaluated; that is, no evidence that an account is properly stated or that audit objectives have been met.
- Amounts not in agreement with trial balance.
- Poor quality, illegible photocopy placed in the working papers.
- Detailed explanation given for insignificant items or differences, for which a simple notation, such as "Amounts insignificant; no audit work deemed necessary," would be sufficient.
- Arrangement of working papers not logical.
- Too much reliance placed on the prior year's working papers, which resulted in a lack of focus on unusual items or changes in significant account balances.
- Preparing a working paper because the client-prepared working paper was not in the exact format preferred by the staff accountant.
- Nature of audit procedures performed not described fully and clearly.
- Use of similar tick marks to denote different procedures.

dit, and in reconstructing work performed and judgments made, when the need to do so arises at a later date. Those deficiencies are generally discovered during the working paper review process, which is discussed in Chapter 17. Some of the more common working paper deficiencies are set forth in Figure 5.9.

Review Questions

5-1. For an opinion to be expressed, the auditor must determine the degree to which management's assertions embodied in the statements conform with GAAP. What are the categories into which these assertions are classified?

5-2. What do each of the above assertions relate to?

5-3. What does the third standard of field work require?

5-4. For which of the assertions does the auditor perform primarily the evidence-gathering function, as opposed to the interpreting/evaluating function?

5-5. What function does the auditor perform with respect to the assertions of valuation or allocation and presentation and disclosure?

5-6. How does underlying evidence differ from corroborating evidence?

5-7. Name and describe the basic methods used by auditors to obtain competent evidential matter.

5-8. What purposes are served in performing analytical review procedures?

5-9. Compare, contrast, and illustrate the two basic types of tests in auditing.

5-10. What are the four major steps in every opinion audit?

5-11. What is meant by audit strategy? What are the basic audit strategy alternatives?

5-12. Specify some of the considerations that should enter into the strategy decisions.

5-13. What documentation is necessary when the strategy adopted is to rely on specific controls?

5-14. What controls should be compliance tested?

5-15. How is the selection of substantive tests made?

5-16. What are the functions of working papers?

5-17. To whom do working papers belong and how long are they kept?

5-18. What types of working papers are there? What types of information should all working papers contain?

5-19. What is the key working paper in most audits and why is it important?

5-20. What are some common working paper deficiencies?

Discussion Questions

5-30. There is no necessary conflict of interests between the auditor and the management of an enterprise under audit. However, an auditor must maintain a certain professional skepticism in performing an audit. What is meant by professional skepticism? What are some of the things you can do as an auditor to maintain professional skepticism when communicating with a client?

5-31. The first major step in the performance of an audit is obtaining and documenting information about the client's business and accounting systems. When and how should an auditor obtain that information?

5-32. Auditors normally associate counting inventory with inspection. What other items might be subject to inspection?

5-33. How does an auditor know when enough evidence has been collected? How does an auditor determine whether documentation in the working papers is adequate?

5-34. Why is it necessary for working papers to be kept under the control of the auditor?

5-35. What are some techniques for improving the organization of working papers and keeping working paper preparation time to a minimum?

5-36. Auditors frequently refer to the terms ''standards'' and ''procedures.'' Standards deal with measures of the quality of the auditor's performance. Standards specifically refer to the 10 generally accepted auditing standards. Procedures relate to those acts that are performed by the auditor while trying to gather evidence. Procedures specifically refer to the methods or techniques used by the auditor in the conduct of the examination.

Required:
Describe several different types of procedures that an auditor would use during an examination of financial statements. For example, the observation of activities and conditions is a type of procedure that an auditor would frequently use. Do not discuss specific accounts.

(AICPA adapted)

5-37. Analytical review procedures are substantive tests that are extremely useful in the initial audit planning stage.

Required:
a. Explain why analytical review procedures are considered substantive tests.
b. Explain how analytical review procedures may be useful in the initial audit planning stage.
c. Give examples of the analytical review procedures that one might expect a CPA to use during an examination performed in accordance with generally accepted auditing standards.

(AICPA adapted)

AICPA Multiple Choice Questions ──────────

These questions are taken from the Auditing part of Uniform CPA Examinations. Choose the single most appropriate answer.

5-40. Most of the independent auditor's work in formulating an opinion on financial statements consists of

a. Studying and evaluating internal control.
b. Obtaining and examining evidential matter.

      c. Examining cash transactions.

      d. Comparing recorded accountability with assets.

5-41. Which of the following statements relating to the competence of evidential matter is always true?

      a. Evidential matter gathered by an auditor from outside an enterprise is reliable.

      b. Accounting data developed under satisfactory conditions of internal control are more relevant than data developed under unsatisfactory internal control conditions.

      c. Oral representations made by management are *not* valid evidence.

      d. Evidence gathered by auditors must be both valid and relevant to be considered competent.

5-42. During an audit engagement, pertinent data are compiled and included in the audit workpapers. The workpapers primarily are considered to be

      a. A client-owned record of conclusions reached by the auditors who performed the engagement.

      b. Evidence supporting financial statements.

      c. Support for the auditor's representations as to compliance with generally accepted auditing standards.

      d. A record to be used as a basis for the following year's engagement.

5-43. An auditor's working papers will generally be *least* likely to include documentation showing how the

      a. Client's schedules were prepared.

      b. Engagement had been planned.

      c. Client's system of internal control had been reviewed and evaluated.

      d. Unusual matters were resolved.

5-44. The permanent file section of the working papers that is kept for each audit client most likely contains

      a. Review notes pertaining to questions and comments regarding the audit work performed.

      b. A schedule of time spent on the engagement by each individual auditor.

      c. Correspondence with the client's legal counsel concerning pending litigation.

      d. Narrative descriptions of the client's accounting procedures and internal accounting controls.

Problems and Cases

5-60. In examining financial statements, auditors must judge the validity of the audit evidence they obtain.

    Required:

    Assume that an auditor has evaluated internal control and found it satisfactory.

      a. In the course of an examination, an auditor asks many questions of client officers and employees.

1. Describe the factors that the auditor should consider in evaluating oral evidence provided by client officers and employees.
2. Discuss the validity and limitations of oral evidence.

b. An auditor's examination may include computation of various balance sheet and operating ratios for comparison with prior years and industry averages. Discuss the validity and limitations of such analytical review procedures.

c. In connection with the examination of the financial statements of a manufacturing company, an auditor observes the physical inventory of finished goods, which consists of expensive, highly complex electronic equipment. Discuss the validity and limitations of the audit evidence provided by this procedure.

(AICPA adapted)

5–61. The third generally accepted auditing standard of field work requires that the auditor obtain sufficient competent evidential matter to afford a reasonable basis for an opinion regarding the financial statements under examination. In considering what constitutes sufficient competent evidential matter, a distinction should be made between underlying accounting data and all corroborating information available to the auditor.

Required:

a. Discuss the nature of evidential matter to be considered by the auditor in terms of the underlying accounting data, all corroborating information available to the auditor, and the methods by which the auditor tests or gathers competent evidential matter.

b. What presumptions can be made about the reliability of evidential matter in varying circumstances?

(AICPA adapted)

5–62. An important part of every examination of financial statements is the preparation of audit working papers.

Required:

a. Discuss the relationship of audit working papers to each of the standards of field work.

b. You are instructing an inexperienced staff person on how to examine an account on his or her first auditing assignment. An analysis of the account has been prepared by the client for inclusion in the audit working papers. Prepare a list of the comments, commentaries, and notations that the staff person should make or have made on the account analysis to provide an adequate working paper as evidence of the examination. (Do not include a description of auditing procedures applicable to the account.)

(AICPA adapted)

5–63. You are the auditor of the Star Manufacturing Company; you have obtained the following data:

a. A trial balance taken from the books of Star one month prior to year-end follows:

	Dr. (Cr.)
Cash in bank	$ 87,000
Trade accounts receivable	345,000
Notes receivable	125,000

	Dr. (Cr.)
Inventories	317,000
Land	66,000
Buildings, net	350,000
Furniture, fixtures, and equipment, net	325,000
Trade accounts payable	(235,000)
Mortgages payable	(400,000)
Capital stock	(300,000)
Retained earnings	(510,000)
Sales	(3,130,000)
Cost of sales	2,300,000
General and administrative expenses	622,000
Legal and professional fees	3,000
Interest expense	35,000

b. There are no inventories consigned either in or out.

c. All notes receivable are due from outsiders and held by Star.

Required:

Which accounts should be confirmed with outside sources? Briefly describe with whom they should be confirmed and the information that should be confirmed. Organize your answer in the following format:

Account Name	With Whom Confirmed	Information to Be Confirmed

(AICPA adapted)

5-64. During the current year, your client borrowed $800,000 from its bank to finance plant expansion. The long-term note agreement provided for the annual payment of principal and interest over five years. The existing plant was pledged as security for the loan. The borrowed funds were invested in securities until they were needed to pay for the construction work.

Required:

a. What are the audit objectives in the examination of long-term debt?

b. How could you audit the securities held by your client at year-end?

(AICPA adapted)

5-65. The preparation of working papers is an integral part of a CPA's examination of financial statements. On a recurring engagement, a CPA reviews the audit programs and working papers from the prior examination while planning the current examination to determine their usefulness for the current engagement.

Required:

a. What are the purposes or functions of audit working papers?

b. What records may be included in audit working papers?

c. What factors affect the CPA's judgment of the type and content of the working papers for a particular engagement?

(AICPA adapted)

5-66. In an examination of financial statements, the CPA is concerned with the examination and accumulation of accounting evidence.

Required:
a. What is the objective of the CPA's examination and accumulation of accounting evidence during the course of the audit?
b. The source of the accounting evidence is of primary importance in the CPA's evaluation of its quality. Accounting evidence may be classified according to source. For example, one class originates within the client's organization, passes through the hands of third parties, and returns to the client, where it may be examined by the auditor. List the classifications of accounting evidence according to source, briefly discussing the effect of the source on the reliability of the evidence.
c. In evaluating the quality of the accounting evidence, the CPA also considers factors other than the sources of the evidence. Briefly discuss these other factors.

(AICPA adapted)

5-67. The partnership of Smith, Frank, & Clark, a CPA firm, has been the auditor of Greenleaf, Inc., for many years. During the annual examination of the financial statements for the year ended December 31, 1987, a dispute developed over whether certain disclosures should be made in the financial statements. The dispute resulted in Smith, Frank, & Clark's being dismissed and Greenleaf's engaging another firm. Greenleaf demanded that Smith, Frank, & Clark turn over all working papers applicable to the Greenleaf audits or face a lawsuit. Smith, Frank, & Clark refused. Greenleaf has instituted a suit against Smith, Frank, & Clark to obtain the working papers.

Required:
a. Will Greenleaf succeed in its suit? Explain.
b. Discuss the rationale underlying the rule of law applicable to the ownership of working papers.

(AICPA adapted)

Chapter 6
Audit Risk, Materiality, and Engagement Strategy

The first standard of field work requires that the audit be adequately planned; good management practices require that the audit be controlled to ensure that it is performed efficiently and on a timely basis as well as in accordance with professional standards—that is, effectively. Planning and control are closely related aspects of engagement management. Engagement management is a continuous activity that involves determining the strategy to be used on an audit, planning the means of implementing that strategy, and exercising control over the performance of the audit in accordance with the audit plan.

Throughout the planning and performance phases of the audit, the auditor makes numerous decisions, ranging from overall strategy decisions to detailed decisions about specific audit procedures and their implementation. The most significant factor in all of those decisions is the auditor's assessment of the principal risks associated with the client's financial statements. The chapter begins with a discussion of the components of audit risk and of the concept of materiality, which is an integral part of the auditor's consideration of audit risk. Following that, audit strategy and planning considerations are described.

Audit Risk

Auditing standards, user expectations, and sound business practices require the auditor to design and execute audit procedures that will permit expressing an opinion on the financial statements with a low risk that the opinion will be inappropriate. The complement of that risk is an expression of the level of assurance the auditor has that the opinion issued is appropriate. An audit performed in accordance with generally accepted auditing standards can be described either as one in which the auditor has a low risk that the opinion expressed is inappropriate or as one in which the auditor has a high level of assurance that the financial statements are free from material misstatements. Obtaining audit assurance and reducing audit risk are alternative ways of looking at the same process.

Clearly, the auditor must accept some risk in order to perform a cost-effective audit. Determining how much risk is acceptable is a business decision constrained by the expectations of users that an audit opinion indicates that professional standards were adhered to and that sufficient evidence was accumulated and evaluated to support the opinion. The auditor should design the audit so that the risk of an inappropriate opinion is sufficiently low to meet those expectations.

The nature, timing, and extent of audit procedures are varied in response to the risk perceived by the auditor. Thus, when risk is perceived to be ''high,'' more reliable procedures, larger sample sizes, and procedures timed at or near the end of the period under examination are common. Risk analysis can also be used to balance the extent of compliance testing, substantive tests of details, and analytical review procedures in achieving an efficient audit.

Overall Audit Risk

The term *overall audit risk* is used to describe the risk that the auditor will conclude and report that the financial statements taken as a whole are fairly stated when they are not, and the risk that the auditor will conclude and report that the financial statements are not fairly stated when they are.[1] For practical reasons, auditors are particularly attuned to the risk of issuing a ''clean'' opinion on materially misstated financial statements. Issuing a qualified or an adverse opinion on fairly stated financial statements is considered unlikely, since client concern over the adverse consequences of such opinions normally leads to a protracted study and investigation by the auditor before issuing such an opinion. Nevertheless, both aspects of overall audit risk have cost implications for auditors.

Overall audit risk should not be confused with audit exposure. Audit exposure refers to the negative consequences for an auditor—such as economic losses, litigation, or an impaired reputation—that might result from issuing a technically inappropriate opinion or from being sued. Losses from litigation

[1]Statement on Auditing Standards No. 47, *Audit Risk and Materiality in Conducting an Audit* (AU Section 312), defines audit risk as ''the risk that the auditor may unknowingly fail to appropriately modify his opinion on financial statements that are materially misstated.'' Even though this definition does not include the risk that the auditor might erroneously conclude that the financial statements are materially misstated when they are not, the auditor should obtain sufficient evidence to give the proper opinion in all circumstances.

can occur whether a lawsuit is justified or not. In general, auditor attention should be focused on applying appropriate audit procedures to achieve a low level of overall audit risk as a means of meeting professional responsibilities, not on assessing the likelihood of litigation. In other words, even if the auditor believes the level of audit exposure is minimal, a strong sense of professionalism would suggest that the nature or extent of audit procedures that would otherwise be required in the circumstances should not be modified.

On the other hand, it would not be inconsistent with GAAS for an auditor to exercise extraordinary care and plan to reduce audit risk to an extraordinarily low level when faced with circumstances that are conducive to an extraordinarily high level of audit exposure. Examples of circumstances that might significantly increase the auditor's exposure to legal liability include a client whose financial condition may cause it to become bankrupt and a client that "goes public" for the first time, which would subject the auditor to the requirements of the Securities Act of 1933. In either circumstance, the risk of material losses to investors and creditors increases, and with it the risk that those who suffer losses will turn to those with "deep pockets," among whom will surely be the auditor.

Audit Risk Related to Account Balances and Audit Objectives

Overall audit risk is the combination of the various audit risks assessed for each account balance or group of account balances. Assessing overall audit risk in relation to the financial statements taken as a whole is usually impracticable. It ordinarily is practicable, however, to assess audit risk for particular audit objectives associated with particular account balances, groups of account balances, or related classes of transactions. This is because different accounts, groups of accounts, and types of transactions within an enterprise are likely to have different patterns of risk and the audit procedures applied to them are likely to have different relative costs. The primary objective in engagement management is limiting the audit risk in individual balances or classes of transactions so that, at the completion of the examination, overall audit risk is limited to a level sufficiently low—or conversely, that the level of assurance is sufficiently high—to permit the auditor to express an opinion on the financial statements taken as a whole. A secondary objective is to assess and control risks in such a way that the desired level of assurance is achieved as efficiently as possible.

While the auditor should always assess audit risk for each account or class of transactions, there is no requirement that audit risk or its components (discussed later) be quantified. In fact, it is not practicable to objectively quantify certain components of audit risk because of the large number of variables that affect those components and the subjective nature of many of those variables. Auditors generally do not attempt to assign specific values to risk factors. Stated differently, it is highly unlikely that two auditors would evaluate a particular set of facts and circumstances in the same way and conclude that the same level of audit risk existed.

The Components of Audit Risk

For the purpose of providing a frame of reference, it is convenient to think of audit risk—the risk that the auditor will unknowingly fail to appropriately modify his or her opinion on financial statements that are materially misstated—as having the following two major components at the account-balance or class-of-transactions level:

- The risk (consisting of inherent risk and control risk) that misstatements (from either error or fraud) that are material, either individually or in the aggregate, are contained within the financial statements. *Inherent risk* is the susceptibility of an account balance or class of transactions to material misstatements, without consideration of related internal accounting controls. *Control risk* is the risk that the client's system of internal controls will not prevent or detect material misstatements on a timely basis.
- The risk (called *detection risk*) that misstatements that are material, either individually or in the aggregate, and are contained within the financial statements will not be detected by the auditor's application of substantive tests (including analytical review procedures).

Inherent risk and control risk differ from detection risk in that they can only be assessed, but cannot be controlled, by the auditor. The auditor's assessment of inherent and control risks leads to a better understanding of those risks, but does not reduce or otherwise change them. The auditor can, however, control detection risk by varying the nature, timing, and extent of specific substantive tests.

Inherent Risk. Inherent risk is defined in the professional literature as the susceptibility of an account balance or class of transactions to misstatements that could be material, either individually or when aggregated with possible misstatements in other balances or classes, without consideration of the effects, if any, of related internal accounting controls. Financial statement misstatements may be caused by a condition (referred to in this book as an ''inherent risk condition'') that exists at the macroeconomic, industry, or company level or by a characteristic of an account balance or a class of transactions (referred to in this book as an ''inherent risk characteristic'').

Inherent Risk Conditions. Some aspects of inherent risk are not peculiar to a specific transaction or account and in some instances may relate to factors external to the entity. These aspects relate to *conditions* that are not subject to control by the enterprise and include changes in general business conditions, new governmental regulations, and other economic factors, such as a declining industry characterized by bankruptcies, other indications of financial distress, and companies with little financial flexibility, which might either affect the realization of assets and incurrence of liabilities or influence client management to deliberately misstate financial statements. The auditor's understanding of inherent risks that are related to conditions rather than to characteristics results from an understanding of the client's business and industry, from the performance of analytical review procedures, and from prior years' audits.

The audit objectives that are most likely to be affected by inherent risk conditions are those concerned with cutoff, valuation, rights and obligations, and presentation and disclosure. Certain inherent risk conditions might have a pervasive effect on the client's financial statements as a whole and accordingly would warrant special audit attention. For example, a severe recession might lead to questions about a company's ability to continue to operate as a going concern.

Inherent risk conditions are not normally addressed by systems of internal accounting control. However, special controls may be established or special year-end procedures may be performed by the client in response to inherent risk conditions. Examples of such procedures include special reviews of inventory obsolescence or of the provision for doubtful accounts receivable.

Inherent Risk Characteristics. Other aspects of inherent risk are peculiar to the specific type of transaction or account under consideration (i.e., they are *characteristics* of the transaction or account), in that the risk of errors or irregularities is greater for some types of transactions or accounts than for others. In general, transactions that require considerable accounting judgment are more likely to produce errors than are other transactions. Similarly, some assets are more susceptible to theft in the absence of strong custody controls than are others; cash is more prone to misappropriation than are steel beams. Account balances derived from accounting estimates are more likely to be misstated than are account balances composed of more factual data. The characteristics of accounts with generic titles differ from one company to another and even within a company. For example, all inventories are not the same. Consequently, in assessing risk, the auditor considers the characteristics of the specific items underlying the particular account. In some instances, the auditor is mainly concerned with the inventory's existence, while in other situations, the auditor might be more concerned with inventory valuation. The auditor's understanding of inherent risks that are related to the characteristics of specific types of transactions and accounts results from a knowledge of the business and an understanding of the transactions, their flow through the system, and the accounts they generate.

Inherent risk characteristics are often addressed by internal accounting controls. If an inherent risk characteristic has been addressed by a control and if the auditor intends to test that control and rely on it because it is efficient to do so, then the auditor's assessment of that inherent risk becomes inextricably intertwined with the evaluation of control risk, and only a joint assessment of the two is useful. For example, the auditor may determine in the planning phase of the audit that an asset (such as cash) with characteristics (liquidity and transferability) that make it extremely prone to theft (that is, it gives rise to a high inherent risk of misappropriation) is subject to extremely strong internal accounting controls. In effect, the enterprise has designed specific internal accounting controls in light of the asset's characteristics, and has thereby created an environment in which the auditor may be able to rely on those controls after appropriately testing them (if that is the most efficient audit strategy). The auditor may then be able to assess the risk of misappropriation, and thus the risk of a financial statement misstatement, as extremely low.

Control Risk. There are likely to be errors in the accounting process that are not detected because of weaknesses or breakdowns in the client's existing internal control system. No affordable system of internal control can be so effective that it completely eliminates the risk that misstatements will be reflected in the financial statements. Therefore, some risk is normally associated with every internal control system; effective systems carry a relatively lower risk, less effective systems, a relatively higher risk.

If controls over transactions and balances exist and if the auditor intends to rely on those controls, they will be compliance tested. If those compliance tests reveal that deviations from prescribed procedures have not occurred, the auditor will be able to draw conclusions about the risk of misstatement occurring, but will not be able to draw conclusions about the levels of inherent risk and control risk separately. That is because the auditor usually cannot or does not determine whether the absence of misstatements was the result of correct transactions entering the system or whether it was the result of errors entering the system and being detected and corrected by the proper operation of accounting controls.

Moreover, some transactions and balances are not addressed—either intentionally or otherwise—by the client's control system and procedures. For example, there may not be controls over special management incentives and unusual transactions; in addition, management override of controls is always possible. For those transactions and accounts that are not addressed by internal accounting controls or that are addressed by controls on which the auditor does not plan to rely, the inherent risk and the risk of error occurring are the same from the auditor's perspective for the purpose of designing audit procedures to control detection risk.

Detection Risk. Detection risk is the combination of the possibilities that neither analytical review procedures nor substantive tests of details of transactions or account balances will reduce undetected misstatements to a cumulatively immaterial amount. Since analytical review procedures and substantive tests of details complement each other, the assurance derived from one reduces proportionately the assurance required from the other to limit detection risk to the level desired by the auditor. In other words, the risks associated with them are multiplicative, as the following example illustrates. As a conceptual exercise—recalling that it is not practicable to attempt to assign specific values to the various risk factors—suppose an auditor performs no substantive tests of details or analytical review procedures. If there is an error in the financial statements, there is a 100 percent chance that it will not be detected (detection risk is 100 percent). On the other hand, if substantive tests of details and analytical review procedures are performed and there is a 40 percent risk that analytical review procedures will not detect cumulatively material misstatements and a 20 percent risk that substantive tests of details will not detect them, the chance that neither procedure will detect the error is the product of 40 percent and 20 percent—8 percent. For a misstatement in the financial statements to go undetected by the auditor, both substantive tests of details and analytical review procedures must fail to detect it.

Summary of the Risk Model

The basic components of overall audit risk and of audit risk associated with specific accounts are summarized in Figure 6.1. The model suggests that for a given desired level of audit risk, the level of acceptable detection risk varies inversely with the auditor's assessment of the risk of material misstatement ocurring. That is, the higher the perceived risk of material fraud or error, the greater the assurance the auditor needs from substantive tests (i.e., the lower the acceptable level of detection risk) to achieve a specified (presumably low) level of audit risk, and vice versa. Similarly, given the desired amount of assurance from substantive tests as a result of the auditor's assessment of the risk of material misstatement occurring, the assurance derived from substantive tests of details varies inversely with the assurance desired from analytical review procedures, and vice versa.

Various combinations of audit effort devoted to risk assessment activities, analytical review procedures, and substantive tests of details can produce the same level of audit assurance (i.e., reduce audit risk to the same low level), but some combinations are more efficient (i.e., less costly to perform in the aggregate) than others. The auditor recognizes this by formulating an audit strategy, based on his or her initial expectations about the level of inherent and control risks, that will, at the lowest possible cost, provide sufficient competent evidence to (1) confirm those initial expectations about inherent and control risks, and (2) drive detection risk to a level compatible with a low level of audit risk.

Before issuing an unqualified opinion, the auditor should be satisfied that the *overall* audit risk is sufficiently low. Although the individual audit risks should be combined to assess overall audit risk, to date no single, simple, generally agreed-on mathematical approach to combining these risks has been developed. Nor has the profession been able to agree on what a sufficiently low level of overall risk is. While the auditor may at times think in quantitative terms when considering alternative audit strategies and evaluating risks, risk management ultimately requires seasoned judgment based on experience, training, and business sense. The way the audit results of each component of the financial statements should be combined is a function of the way the auditor approaches the materiality apportionment and risk combination question. The various means by which materiality can be apportioned and audit risks combined is a subject of current research whose fruition may come only in the distant future.

Figure 6.1 Basic Audit Risk Components

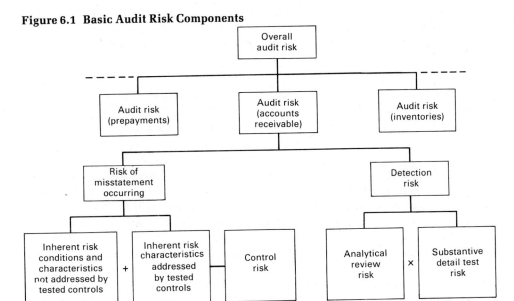

Materiality

A concept of materiality is a practical necessity in both auditing and accounting. Allowing immaterial items to complicate and clutter up the auditing process or financial statements is uneconomical and diverts users' attention from significant matters in the financial statements. Materiality judgments influence audit planning and, in the evaluation of audit results, are critical to determining whether the financial statements are fairly presented. Inherent in the rendering of an audit opinion is the recognition that the financial statements cannot ''precisely'' or ''exactly'' present financial position and results of operations. Such precision is not attainable because of limitations in the accounting measurement process and constraints imposed by the audit process and auditing technology, as discussed in Chapter 1.

Materiality is ''the magnitude of an omission or misstatement of accounting information that, in the light of surrounding circumstances, makes it probable that the judgment of a reasonable person relying on the information would have been changed or influenced by the omission or misstatement'' (FASB Statement of Financial Concepts No. 2, *Qualitative Characteristics of Accounting Information*). Ultimately, the user of financial statements determines what is material. There are many users, however, including enterprise management, shareholders, creditors, audit committees, financial analysts, investors, and labor unions, and each user may have a different view of what is important. Investors may rely on information about cash flows and income; short-term creditors may focus more on issues of asset liquidity.

SEC Regulation S-X (Rule 1-02) defines ''materiality'' as follows:

> The term "material," when used to qualify a requirement for the furnishing of information as to any subject, limits the information required to those matters about which an average prudent investor ought reasonably to be informed.

This definition has been reinforced by court decisions such as the *BarChris* case,[2] in which the judge clearly indicated that the materiality issue involved amounts that he believed would motivate the "average prudent investor," not the average banker or security analyst. In developing a standard of materiality for a particular situation, other court cases refer to the "reasonable shareholder";[3] FASB Concepts Statement No. 2, to the "reasonable person"; and an American Accounting Association publication,[4] to the "informed investor." Thus, the consensus seems to be that materiality is determined by the user, who may be informed, but is not necessarily sophisticated, about financial statements.

Materiality has both qualitative and quantitative aspects. A financial statement misstatement may be quantitatively immaterial, but the nature of the misstatement may warrant disclosure in the financial statements. SAS No. 47, *Audit Risk and Materiality in Conducting an Audit* (AU Section 312), cites as an example "an illegal payment of an otherwise immaterial amount [that] could be material if there is a reasonable possibility that it could lead to a material contingent liability or a material loss of revenue" (AU Section 312.07). Moreover, such matters may have broad implications regarding the integrity of management, and thus may warrant further investigation to assess the possible pervasiveness of the problem, a reassessment of internal control effectiveness, and reporting of the findings to appropriate company officials. Similarly, qualitatively innocuous mistakes in the form of small unintentional errors can aggregate to quantitatively material dollar misstatements, causing the auditor to qualify the opinion if corrections are not made to the accounts. Materiality judgments also influence items that are or should be disclosed without directly affecting the financial statement amounts. Because of the dual influence of qualitative and quantitative factors in determining materiality, the concept is difficult to operationalize, and trying to establish an agreed-on single quantitative standard is an exercise in futility.

The assessment of materiality takes place throughout an audit, particularly during planning and when evaluating the results of audit procedures. SAS No. 47 (AU Section 312.10) requires the auditor, in planning an engagement, to consider a "preliminary judgment about materiality levels for audit purposes." That preliminary judgment may include assessments of what constitutes materiality for significant captions in the balance sheet and income statement individually, and for the financial statements taken as a whole. One

---

[2]*Escott* v. *BarChris Construction Corp.*, 283 F. Supp. 643 (S.D.N.Y. 1968).

[3]For example, *TSC Industries* v. *Northway, Inc.*, 44 U.S.L.W. 4852 (1976).

[4]*Accounting and Reporting Standards for Corporate Financial Statements* (Evanston, Ill.: American Accounting Association, 1957).

purpose of such a preliminary materiality judgment is to focus the auditor's attention on the more significant financial statement items during the process of determining the audit strategy. As a practical matter, however, SAS No. 47 indicates that the preliminary judgment about materiality for the financial statements taken as a whole is generally the smallest aggregate level of errors that could be considered material to any one of the financial statements (AU Section 312.12).

The materiality of an item should influence the nature, timing, and extent of audit procedures applied in the course of the engagement. For example, an auditor may establish for planning purposes that misstatements aggregating less than $100,000 are not material to net income, and may establish a different (often higher) materiality level for misstatements that affect only the balance sheet (such as misclassifications) since the relative magnitude of the balance sheet components may, depending on the circumstances, cause the $100,000 amount to be immaterial to the balance sheet. Similarly, when planning procedures at the line item level (such as receivables or inventories), the auditor must consider that immaterial misstatements in separate line items may aggregate to a material amount. Thus, audit procedures in one area—for example, receivables—may have to be designed to detect income statement misstatements of much less than $100,000, because some misstatements may come to the auditor's attention as a result of performing procedures in other areas of the audit (e.g., inventories or fixed assets).

To perform an effective and efficient audit, the auditor must continually assess the results of the tests and procedures as the audit progresses, and must also repeatedly reevaluate whether the scope of planned procedures in the various accounts is adequate, or possibly excessive, based on the results of tests and procedures already completed. For example, individually immaterial misstatements of certain expenses may aggregate to a material amount. As audit work progresses, the auditor may find that the individually immaterial misstatements are not offsetting, but are causing income to be overstated. In these circumstances, the auditor may need to adjust the scope of planned procedures for the expenses remaining to be examined to gain assurance that a material aggregate misstatement will be detected if it exists. It may also be necessary to apply additional procedures to audit areas that have already been examined.

New facts and circumstances may also change the amount the auditor considers material to individual financial statement line items or to the financial statements taken as a whole. For example, if adjustments and corrections are made to the accounts during the course of the audit, the parameters used by the auditor in determining materiality in the planning stage (e.g., amounts for net income, revenues, and shareholders' equity) may change. Thus, by the end of the audit, "materiality" may be different than at the planning stage. An auditor who does not continually reassess materiality and audit scope as the engagement progresses will be likely to perform an inefficient or ineffective audit if changes that affect the materiality judgments established in the planning stage occur. Materiality and audit planning should be viewed as dynamic rather than static auditing concepts.

To keep track of the results of various tests and procedures performed during an audit and to help in drawing conclusions about the effect of errors discovered, the auditor often maintains a "score sheet." This practice tool summarizes the unadjusted errors present in the financial statements that were identified during the audit. It assists the auditor in accumulating known errors found through audit tests, errors based on projections developed from representative samples, and errors relating to client accounting estimates that the auditor believes are unreasonable. Sometimes the score sheet points out client adjustments that the auditor believes are necessary for an unqualified opinion to be given. It also assists in evaluating whether misstatements, if uncorrected, would affect only the balance sheet, only the income statement, or both. The score sheet is discussed in further detail in the section on "Summarizing and Evaluating the Audit Findings" in Chapter 17.

Audit Strategy

Formulating an audit strategy is the process of selecting an appropriate plan for performing an audit in accordance with generally accepted auditing standards. The most significant decision the auditor generally makes in planning the audit of each account balance or class of transactions in the financial statements concerns the degree of reliance that can be placed on the client's internal controls and the level of assurance that the auditor needs from substantive tests. Audit strategy also encompasses detailed decisions about the nature, timing, and extent of specific audit procedures to be applied in auditing each account or group of accounts. In addition, decisions must be made about whether to use the work of the client's internal auditors and of specialists. In audits of large clients with numerous locations or components, strategy decisions may also be needed about whether and how to rotate audit emphasis by varying the locations or components visited each year, and about using the work of other independent auditors who have audited one or more of the client's affiliates.

Several factors influence the choice of an efficient and effective audit strategy. The auditor's assessment of inherent and control risk in the context of materiality is of primary importance. Other matters relevant to determining the overall strategy include

• *The quality of the client's internal controls that are believed to exist as a result of the auditor's understanding of the system.* If internal controls are not in place or if they are not likely to be found effective, the auditor's strategy options are considerably reduced.

• *The cost of the procedures necessary to establish the reliability of controls versus the cost of performing substantive procedures.* "Cost" includes more than simply the number of hours of auditor time; it includes consideration of optimal staff utilization, on-the-job training, and similar factors that influence the choice of the combination and timing of audit procedures. Cost determinations are also affected by the availability of computer resources. The auditor may employ a variety of computer-assisted audit techniques instead of performing tests manually since such techniques are often more cost effective.

• *Prior decisions about the nature, timing, and extent of specific procedures.* For example, the client might request the audit report shortly after year-end. A decision to perform substantive tests of details before year-end and rely on controls and analytical reviews to obtain satisfaction about account balances at year-end requires consideration, at the planning stage, of the nature, timing, and extent of other procedures that will give the auditor the requisite assurance that the financial statements are not materially misstated. As another example, the decision to use negative rather than positive confirmations may lead the auditor to perform additional procedures such as analytical reviews or more extensive confirmation procedures, because negative confirmations that are not returned are less conclusive evidence than positive confirmations.

• *Client expectations about auditor review of controls.* In setting the audit strategy, the auditor should consider whether additional responsibilities arise from requests of the client (e.g., a request for a review of internal accounting controls beyond that required for the audit function), or because the company is subject to special regulatory or other requirements.

Determining the audit strategy is normally delegated to experienced staff members under the direction of the engagement partner because it requires a high degree of professional judgment. Approval of the final strategy should rest with the engagement partner. Audit strategy and other planning documentation varies in form and substance among auditing firms. Such documentation normally includes the auditor's understanding of the client's business, the control environment, and significant accounting systems; assessments of audit risk and judgments about materiality; and the audit strategy adopted for major account balances and classes of transactions in the financial statements. Many auditors incorporate other materials in the planning section of the working papers, for example, detailed time budgets, the audit timetable, and certain audit-related correspondence such as communications with internal auditors.

Planning and Controlling the Audit

Once the audit strategy has been determined, documented, and approved, the detailed planning necessary to implement the selected strategy can be carried out. The order of the planning steps may vary from engagement to engagement, and there is often some overlap between steps.

Implementation Planning

The auditor should first establish a timetable for completing the principal segments of the engagement; the timetable sets forth the planned audit work and provides a basis for exercising control over the engagement. The client's scheduling requirements should be considered in establishing the timetable.

An audit program should then be prepared, listing the detailed procedures to be undertaken on the engagement. Those procedures vary from engagement to engagement according to the strategy decisions about their nature, timing, and extent.

The audit program is the basis for the time and expense budgets. These budgets facilitate the completion of the work within the client's and the auditor's time requirements and provide a basis for establishing the fee for the audit. The budgets should include data for the different tasks and levels of personnel to be employed on the engagement, and they should be sufficiently detailed to enable staff members to complete tasks in relatively short periods and thereby manage their time efficiently. The complexity of multilocation audits and audits of multinational companies makes detailed time and expense budgets critical to the timely and efficient conduct of those examinations. Both during and at the end of the audit, it is desirable to evaluate such matters as time or expense overruns because the circumstances that caused them are likely to be repeated and thus may affect the budget for the following year. The evaluation helps ensure that the next year's budget will be realistic, and it also promotes more efficient staff utilization. Evaluating overruns during the audit may also help the engagement team identify tasks that can be completed more quickly than budgeted, thereby offsetting the negative impact of the overruns.

Personnel for the engagement must be identified and assigned. In assigning personnel to a particular engagement, the engagement manager and partner generally consider: the technical complexity of the engagement and whether industry expertise is necessary, engagement continuity, personnel career development, and commitments of staff to other engagements. The availability of staff and cost considerations sometimes lead to adjustments in the timing of certain procedures and other strategy decisions.

If computer processing is used in significant accounting applications, specialized audit skills may be needed. SAS No. 48, *The Effects of Computer Processing on the Examination of Financial Statements* (AU Section 1030), specifies that even if a computer specialist is used, the auditor must have sufficient computer-related knowledge to communicate audit objectives to the specialist, to evaluate whether the procedures applied by the specialist meet the auditor's objectives, and to determine how the results of those procedures affect the nature, timing, and extent of other planned audit procedures. A computer audit specialist requires the same supervision and review as does any other member of the audit team.

Personnel to whom work is delegated should be informed of their responsibilities, the objectives of the procedures they are to perform, and the completion dates for their work within the context of the overall audit timetable. They should also be informed about matters that may affect the nature, timing, and extent of audit procedures, such as the nature of the client's business and potential accounting and auditing problems. The audit plan should be communicated to the audit team, including other offices that are involved in the engagement. A communication link between the principal auditor and other independent auditors involved in the engagement should be established; timetables, procedures to be performed, and the type of report needed by the principal auditor should be communicated early in the audit.

The auditor may also find it helpful at times to discuss the general audit strategy with the client's management. For example, the auditor may wish to inform management that testing of and reliance on the system of internal control is not planned as a result of weaknesses noted in prior years' audits. Management may alert the auditor to changes in the control system that might permit such reliance in the current year; if reliance on controls would be cost effective, the auditor may consider a strategy change. Some administrative elements of the planning process (e.g., determining the timing of inventory observation procedures, the schedules and analyses to be prepared by the client's staff, and other ways client personnel can assist the auditor) will almost inevitably need to be discussed and agreed on before implementation of the audit strategy.

The following sections cover five topics—using the work of internal auditors, using the work of a specialist, rotating audit emphasis, using the work of other auditors, and using a report on internal control at a service organization—that may require consideration in the planning stage.

Using the Work of Internal Auditors

Historically, the responsibilities of internal audit departments have varied widely among companies, with respect to both the scope of work and the organizational standing of the individual to whom the department reports. In some companies the internal audit department operates with few or no restrictions and reports to the board of directors or audit committee on a wide range of matters. In other companies the department may be restricted in its duties and may not enjoy organizational independence. Internal audit departments may operate in a variety of ways, including

- Functioning as a part of the internal control system, focusing heavily on matters such as surprise cash and inventory counts.
- Functioning essentially parallel with the external audit function as described in this book, focusing on the evaluation of systems and substantiation of account balances.
- Having broad responsibility for evaluating compliance with company policies and practices.
- Performing operational audits, which are described in Chapter 2.
- Serving as management training grounds for rising executives.
- Working on special projects or being responsible for specific parts of the system, such as bank reconciliations or voucher approval.

The external auditor should gain a comprehensive understanding of the internal audit function to reach a decision about the extent to which the work of the internal auditors can be used. That extent may range from ''coordination'' of the efforts of the two groups of auditors, if the external auditor is satisfied as to the effectiveness of the internal audit department, to use of the work performed by the internal auditors to reduce the time the external auditor spends on the engagement—a relationship characterized as ''reliance'' rather than coordination. Coordination of efforts involves the participation of both the external and internal auditors in coverage of the total ''audit universe.'' The extent to which such coordination is possible depends largely on the responsibilities and organizational independence of the internal audit department.

If the internal auditors and external auditor coordinate their efforts on an engagement, the internal auditors' work affects the external auditor's strategy and procedures. SAS No. 9, *The Effect of an Internal Audit Function on the Scope of the Independent Auditor's Examination* (AU Section 322), notes, however, that the work of internal auditors cannot substitute for the work of the independent auditor, and it prescribes procedures that the external auditor should follow in considering the internal auditors' work in determining the nature, timing, and extent of independent audit procedures. SAS No. 9 requires the external auditor to

- Review the competence and objectivity of the internal auditors.
- Consider the appropriateness and adequacy of the work performed.
- Perform duplicative or parallel tests of the audit work performed.
- Reach independent judgments.

There are different ways of dividing the audit work between the external auditor and the internal auditors. In a decentralized or diversified company, the internal auditors may examine some divisions and departments and the external auditor may examine others, rotating their assignments from examination to examination and exchanging and making use of each other's working papers. Alternatively, the internal auditors may examine certain cycles and accounts at a particular location, while the external auditor examines the others. In participating in planning the divisions, departments, cycles, or accounts to be covered by the internal auditors, the external auditor should consider the risk, exposure, and sensitivity of the areas, as well as the competence and degree of independence of the internal audit staff.

Using the Work of a Specialist

Client management always has the responsibility to make the appropriate valuations and other assertions that are necessary to the fair presentation of the financial statements in conformity with generally accepted accounting principles, and to provide evidence to support those assertions. The auditor has the responsibility to obtain and evaluate sufficient competent evidence to evaluate the assertions that management has made. On occasion, an auditor may encounter a matter that is outside the realm of his or her general business knowledge and requires special expertise. The auditor cannot be expected to have or develop the expertise of a person qualified to engage in the practice of a related profession or occupation. As a result, the auditor may decide to arrange for the assistance of a specialist to obtain competent evidential matter. The need to do so should be established in the planning stage of the audit, so that the appropriate arrangements can be made on a timely basis.

Specialists may be used on a recurring basis or for special matters that arise during an audit. An actuary will ordinarily be engaged to perform certain actuarial calculations in order to arrive at the annual costs related to pension plans. In determining the carrying value of real estate owned by a bank, an appraiser may be used to establish fair market value. Lawyers may be used as specialists in connection with matters other than litigation, claims, or assessments. Petroleum engineers may be used to estimate oil reserves, and gemologists may be used to appraise precious gems.

The auditor should be satisfied with the competence, reputation, and standing of the specialist in the particular field. The specialist's competence may be demonstrated by professional certification, license, or other formal recognition. The specialist's peers or others familiar with the individual's work may be able to vouch for the specialist's reputation and standing.

As indicated in paragraph 6 of SAS No. 11, *Using the Work of a Specialist* (AU Section 336.06), the ''work of a specialist unrelated to the client will usually provide the auditor with greater assurance of reliability because of the absence of a relationship that might impair objectivity.'' The auditor should take steps to ascertain the nature of any relationship the specialist may have with the client. Specialists are not required to be ''independent'' in the same sense as auditors are; however, the materiality of any relationship must be evaluated. If the auditor determines that the specialist has a relationship with the client that might impair the specialist's objectivity, consideration should be given to performing additional procedures with respect to some or all of the specialist's assumptions, methods, or findings to determine that the findings are not unreasonable.

The work of a specialist may be used as an audit procedure to obtain competent evidential matter, but it is not sufficient in itself. Additional audit procedures must be performed to meet the requirements of particular circumstances. The procedures should not duplicate any of the work performed by the specialist, but are generally needed to corroborate the accounting data provided by the client to the specialist. The specialist is responsible for the propriety, reasonableness, and application of any methods or assumptions used. The auditor must understand the methods or assumptions used, however, to determine whether the specialist's findings are suitable for corroborating the related information in the financial statements. The auditor is not required to conclude that the specialist's findings are reasonable, but is required to conclude only that they are not unreasonable. For example, an appraisal of real estate owned may indicate a 25 percent increase in fair market value over the prior year. This finding would appear to be unreasonable if current market conditions generally indicated a decline in values of comparable real estate during the same period. The auditor should perform additional procedures, including inquiry of the specialist, if it is believed that the specialist's findings are unreasonable.

If the auditor is not able to resolve a matter after performing additional procedures, consideration should be given to obtaining the opinion of another specialist. An unresolved matter will result in a qualified opinion or a disclaimer of opinion because the inability to obtain sufficient competent evidential matter constitutes a scope limitation (paragraphs 10 and 11 of SAS No. 2, *Reports on Audited Financial Statements* [AU Sections 509.10 and .11]). The auditor should not mention the work or findings of a specialist when expressing an unqualified opinion on financial statements.

Rotating Audit Emphasis

A practical strategy that may enhance audit efficiency and lessen the financial burden of a complex engagement (such as a multilocation audit) is rotating the audit emphasis within the enterprise from year to year. The manner in which this is accomplished varies with the circumstances of the engagement; however, the auditor must ensure that each year's audit work is adequate to support a conclusion on the fairness of the financial statements for that year. Subject to audit risk considerations, auditors may vary both the locations visited and the strategies employed at various locations. In a large multilocation engagement, often only a few, if any, locations are individually material to a specific account balance or class of transactions. For example, a retail chain store operation might consist of 300 separate stores of varying size, none of which is individually material to the enterprise in terms of its sales volume or inventory.

Using the Work of Other Auditors

In reporting on the financial statements of a company or group of companies, an auditor may utilize the work and report of other auditors who have examined one or more components (subsidiaries or divisions) of the entity. Other auditors may be utilized to carry out part of an engagement on grounds of efficiency; problems associated with physical distance among components of an entity and language barriers may also be overcome most economically through these arrangements. When more than one auditor is involved in the examination, one usually serves as principal auditor. Determining whether an auditor can serve as the principal auditor involves consideration of the extent of work performed relative to the entire engagement as well as the auditor's overall knowledge of the engagement.

Even though each auditor has individual responsibility for the work performed and the opinion rendered, the principal auditor should apply certain procedures in order to be able to use another auditor's report and express an opinion on the overall financial statements. SAS No. 1 (AU Section 543) contains guidelines about what procedures should be employed. They include: inquiring about the other auditor's professional reputation and ascertaining that the other auditor is independent; is aware of the intended use of the financial statements and report; is familiar with GAAP, GAAS, and other (e.g., SEC) reporting requirements; and has been informed about matters affecting the elimination of intercompany transactions and the uniformity of accounting principles among the components. In some circumstances, the principal auditor may review the other auditor's audit programs or working papers, read summaries of the work performed and conclusions reached by the other auditor, or attend key meetings between the other auditor and management. Visiting the other auditor's premises or obtaining written representations about various matters may also be deemed necessary. The need for such steps should be considered early in the planning process and continually reviewed during the engagement. When another auditor's work is utilized, reference in the opinion may, but need not always, be made to the other auditor's involvement. That issue is discussed in Chapter 18, "The Auditor's Report."

Using a Report on Internal Control at a Service Organization

A client may use a service organization to record certain transactions, process data, or even execute transactions and maintain the related accounting records. In those circumstances, transactions may flow through an accounting system that is, in whole or in part, separate from the client's organization, and the auditor may find it necessary or efficient to consider the accounting procedures performed by and the controls exercised over those procedures at the service organization. The auditor may further determine that the most efficient strategy is to obtain a report on the service organization's procedures and controls that has been prepared by the service organization's auditor.

SAS No. 44, *Special-Purpose Reports on Internal Accounting Control at Service Organizations* (AU Section 324), provides guidance on the auditor's use of a special-purpose report of another independent auditor on internal accounting control at a service organization. The SAS provides that, depending on the nature and location of control procedures on which the auditor intends to rely, he or she should obtain either a report on the design of the system or a report that covers both the design and compliance tests of those controls over a satisfactory period. If the service organization's auditor's report discloses weaknesses in either design or compliance, the auditor of the client that uses the service organization should assess the effect of such weaknesses on the nature, timing, and extent of substantive tests. If the service organization executes transactions for the client user, it may be necessary to perform either compliance or substantive tests at the service organization. The service organization's auditor may be requested to perform the tests or the auditor of the client user may perform the tests.

The decision to use the report on internal control, along with appropriate inquiries and other steps necessary to implement the decision, should be made during the planning phase of the audit. As explained in the SAS, reference in the auditor's report to the service organization's auditor is not appropriate. The SAS also provides guidance on the responsibilities of the auditor who issues the report on internal control.

Controlling the Engagement

Supervision and review are essential parts of managing an engagement, since ultimate responsibility for forming and expressing an opinion on the financial statements remains with the engagement partner and cannot be delegated. Supervision is usually the responsibility of the engagement manager or other experienced staff and includes monitoring the work done to ensure that it is in accordance with the audit strategy and detailed audit plan. Supervision also entails comparing the completed work with established timetables and budgets, training and coaching staff, and identifying differences in professional judgment among personnel and referring them to the appropriate level for resolution, as well as directly reviewing the work performed. The work done by each member of the audit team is supervised, reviewed, and approved by another, more senior auditor. Queries raised during the review process should be followed up and resolved prior to completing the engagement and issuing the audit opinion.

Review Questions

6-1. What are the key aspects of engagement management?

6-2. What is meant by audit strategy formulation?

6-3. What is the most significant decision made in planning an audit?

6-4. What is meant by overall audit risk?

6-5. Aside from audit risk, what other factors are considered in determining audit strategy?

6-6. As used in auditing, what is materiality?

6-7. What is the relationship between materiality and audit risk?

6-8. What is an audit program and what is its purpose?

6-9. Why are audit budgets prepared? Why should actual hours be summarized and reviewed at the end of the audit?

6-10. What does supervision of the audit entail and whose responsibility is it?

6-11. Why is it necessary for an auditor to understand the client's internal audit function?

6-12. Explain how internal and external auditors may interact in the course of an engagement.

6-13. What procedures should the external auditor follow in considering the effect of the internal auditors' work in determining the nature, timing, and extent of audit procedures?

6-14. When would a principal auditor use the work of another auditor?

6-15. What are the major components of audit risk? Describe them.

6-16. What is the difference between audit risk and audit exposure?

6-17. In what circumstances does an auditor employ compliance testing procedures?

6-18. Why may audit risks be perceived differently after some or all of the audit work has been completed?

6-19. When in the audit should the auditor's assessment of materiality take place?

6-20. Is obtaining the work of a specialist sufficient to preclude audit procedures in that area?

Discussion Questions

6-30. Although dollar amount is the first consideration in determining whether an item is material, what other factors should be considered?

6-31. What are some of the things an auditor should do to ensure that the audit team fulfills the responsibility to exercise due care in the conduct of the examination?

6-32. Briefly list the circumstances or types of activity that might indicate possible errors or irregularities in the following accounts:

- Accounts receivable
- Inventory

6-33. Why are time budgets important in all phases of an audit?

6-34. The increasing use of internal auditors by clients has had an effect on the approach external auditors take toward the formulation of their strategies and programs. Discuss how internal and external auditors interact on an engagement, giving recognition to the following:

a. The degree of independence exhibited by internal auditors.
b. The background, training, and competence of internal auditors.
c. The effect of internal audit activities on the nature, timing, and extent of tests and procedures performed by external auditors.

6-35. The CPA firm of May & Marty has audited the consolidated financial statements of BGI Corporation. May & Marty performed the examination of the parent company and all subsidiaries except for BGI-Western Corporation, which was audited by the CPA firm of Dey & Dee. BGI-Western constituted approximately 10 percent of the consolidated assets and 6 percent of the consolidated revenue.

Dey & Dee issued an unqualified opinion on the financial statements of BGI-Western. May & Marty will be issuing an unqualified opinion on the consolidated financial statements of BGI.

Required:

a. What procedures should May & Marty consider performing with respect to Dey & Dee's examination of BGI-Western's financial statements that will be appropriate whether or not reference is to be made to other auditors?
b. Describe the various circumstances under which May & Marty could take responsibility for the work of Dey & Dee and make no reference to Dey & Dee's

examination of BGI-Western in May & Marty's auditor's report on the consolidated financial statements of BGI.

(AICPA adapted)

6-36. During the course of an audit engagement, an independent auditor gives serious consideration to the concept of materiality. This concept of materiality is inherent in the work of the independent auditor and is important for planning, preparing, and modifying audit programs. The concept of materiality underlies the application of all the generally accepted auditing standards, particularly the standards of field work and reporting.

Required:

a. Briefly describe what is meant by the independent auditor's concept of materiality.
b. What are some common relationships and other considerations used by the auditor in judging materiality?
c. Identify how the planning and execution of an audit program might be affected by the independent auditor's concept of materiality.

(AICPA adapted)

6-37. You have examined Hagren Appliance Corporation's financial statements for several years and have always rendered an unqualified opinion. To reduce its current auditing cost, Hagren limited the scope of your examination of its financial statements for the year just ended to exclude accounts receivable and commissions payable. Hagren's officers stated that the type of auditor's opinion you would render was not important because your report would be used for internal management purposes only and would not be distributed externally. The materiality of the accounts not examined required you to disclaim an opinion on the fairness of the financial statements as a whole.

Required:

a. Why does a CPA prefer that the scope of the auditing engagement not be limited? Discuss.
b. How would a client's assurance to a CPA that the auditor's report will be used only for internal purposes affect the scope of the CPA's examination and the kind of opinion rendered? Discuss.

(AICPA adapted)

AICPA Multiple Choice Questions

These questions are taken from the Auditing part of Uniform CPA Examinations. Choose the single most appropriate answer.

6-40. Which of the following *best* describes how the detailed audit program of the CPA who is engaged to audit the financial statements of a large publicly held company compares with the audit client's comprehensive internal audit program?

a. The comprehensive internal audit program is more detailed and covers areas that would normally *not* be reviewed by the CPA.
b. The comprehensive internal audit program is more detailed, although it covers fewer areas than would normally be covered by the CPA.

   c. The comprehensive internal audit program is substantially identical to the audit program used by the CPA because both review substantially identical areas.

   d. The comprehensive internal audit program is less detailed and covers fewer areas than would normally be reviewed by the CPA.

6-41. Early appointment of the independent auditor will enable

   a. A more thorough examination to be performed.

   b. A proper study and evaluation of internal control to be performed.

   c. Sufficient competent evidential matter to be obtained.

   d. A more efficient examination to be planned.

6-42. Which of the following is an effective audit planning and control procedure that helps prevent misunderstandings and inefficient use of audit personnel?

   a. Arrange to make copies, for inclusion in the working papers, of those client supporting documents examined by the auditor.

   b. Arrange to provide the client with copies of the audit programs to be used during the audit.

   c. Arrange a preliminary conference with the client to discuss audit objectives, fees, timing, and other information.

   d. Arrange to have the auditor prepare and post any necessary adjusting or reclassification entries prior to final closing.

6-43. If the independent auditors decide that the work performed by the internal auditor may have a bearing on their own procedures, they should consider the internal auditor's

   a. Competence and objectivity.

   b. Efficiency and experience.

   c. Independence and review skills.

   d. Training and supervisory skills.

6-44. Rogers & Co., CPAs, policies require that all members of the audit staff submit weekly time reports to the audit manager, who then prepares a weekly summary work report regarding variance from budget for Rogers' review. This provides written evidence of Rogers & Co.'s professional concern regarding compliance with which of the following generally accepted auditing standards?

   a. Quality control.

   b. Due professional care.

   c. Adequate review.

   d. Adequate planning.

6-45. In the audit of a medium-sized manufacturing concern, which one of the following areas would be expected to require the *least* amount of audit time?

   a. Owners' equity.

   b. Revenue.

   c. Assets.

   d. Liabilities.

6-46. In using the work of a specialist, an understanding should exist among the auditor, the client, and the specialist as to the nature of the work to be performed by the specialist. Preferably, the understanding should be documented and would include all of the following *except*

    a. The objectives and scope of the specialist's work.

    b. The specialist's representations as to his relationship, if any, to the client.

    c. The specialist's understanding of the auditor's corroborative use of the specialist's findings in relation to the representations in the financial statements.

    d. A statement that the methods or assumptions to be used are *not* inconsistent with those used by the client.

Problems and Cases

6–60. In late spring of 1986 you are advised of a new assignment as in-charge accountant of your CPA firm's recurring annual audit of a major client. You are given the engagement letter for the audit covering the calendar year ending December 31, 1986, and a list of personnel assigned to this engagement. It is your responsibility to plan and supervise the field work for the engagement.

    Required:

    Discuss the necessary preparation and planning for the annual audit *prior to* beginning field work at the client's office. In your discussion include the sources you should consult, the type of information you should seek, the preliminary plans and preparation you should make for the field work, and any actions you should take relative to the staff assigned to the engagement. *Do not write an audit program.*

                                            (AICPA adapted)

6–61. You have been assigned to the Quinn Hardware audit engagement. Review the client background information and interim financial statements that follow and answer the following questions.

    a. Identify the risk factors that should be considered by the engagement team in determining an effective and efficient engagement strategy for the audit of Quinn Hardware for the year ended May 31, 1986. Support your responses with information obtained from your review of the client background information and your analytical review of the financial information. Identify which audit objectives these risk factors affect and the impact of the risk factors on the audit strategy and audit procedures. In your solution, classify the risk factors according to whether they are the result of an inherent risk condition, an inherent risk characteristic, or a control risk.

    b. Identify other considerations that should enter into the audit strategy.

    c. What specific additional information not contained in the client background information would you need to assist you in determining the audit strategy?

QUINN HARDWARE
DESCRIPTION OF THE BUSINESS

Company History

    The Company was founded in 1947 by the present chairman, Harvey Quinn. The business began in Chicago as a wholesale distributor of building materials and of heavy mining and industrial equipment to large industrial companies in the Chicago area. The wholesale business has grown rapidly since its founding in 1947 and the Company now distributes a very wide range of hardware products all across the United States.

In 1959, the Company opened its first retail hardware outlet under the name of "Quinn's Hardware Store." The retail hardware business has grown quickly and the Company now operates six company-owned retail hardware stores and a hardware dealers' franchise system with over 200 franchised dealerships. Negotiations are currently in progress for a term loan to expand the franchise system. In 1967, a wholly owned subsidiary company, Quinn Hardware Stores, Inc., was established to carry on the retail business and to provide managerial and marketing expertise to the franchised dealerships in what is now a very competitive industry. A significant portion of Quinn's wholesale business is with Company-franchised dealerships, which have credit terms similar to those with other customers. Quinn also supplies several U.S. Government agencies with various products and services, including industrial tests, mining equipment, and building supplies. Discussions with Quinn's management, coupled with analytical review procedures, disclosed that during the past year the Company lost six franchised dealerships because of bankruptcy; it was the first time the Company lost any of its franchises.

Organization

The Company employs 318 people, all of whom participate in the Company's defined contribution pension plan, as follows:

Head Office:

Executive Staff	15	
Purchasing Department	35	
Finance and Accounting	12	
Data Processing	29	
Internal Audit	3	
Other	2	
		96

Marketing:

Eastern region	20	
Great Lakes region	22	
Central region	10	
Western region	10	
		62

Branch Operations:

New York	23	
Pittsburgh	10	
Chicago	46	
Detroit	16	
Houston	13	
Los Angeles	21	
		129

Retail Stores		31
Total Employees		318

An organization chart is shown on page 210.

Quinn Hardware Organization Chart

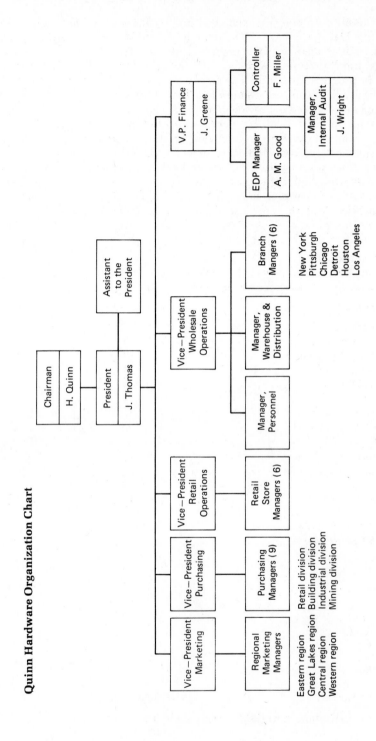

Litigation

The Company is currently being sued by three vendors for nonpayment on certain contractual obligations. Quinn has stated that there are counterclaims and offsets in excess of amounts claimed by these vendors and that its cash flow problems are not an issue here. The Company and its counsel are unable to determine the outcome or the range of potential loss, if any, that may result from this litigation; however, they believe that the cases are without merit and intend to defend them vigorously. No trial dates have been set at this time.

Products

In addition to heavy mining, building materials, and industrial equipment, the Company buys and sells over 35,000 different hardware products on a wholesale basis. These products are purchased from more than 2500 different vendors in the United States and Canada. Hardware products may be generally categorized as follows:

1. Housewares (new line started as of December 1984)
2. Sporting goods
3. Hand tools
4. Machine tools
5. Building materials
6. Architectural hardware
7. Paint
8. Plumbing materials
9. Garden supplies

The Company has been made aware of new government safety regulations relating to mining and industrial equipment. Quinn is conducting an evaluation of the inventory affected by these regulations to determine what modifications, if any, can be made.

Purchasing

All purchasing is done centrally by the purchasing department in Chicago. The purchasing department employs approximately 20 buyers, each of whom is responsible for purchases from certain vendors of hardware merchandise.

The purchasing function, which is considered critical to the successful overall operation of the Company, is highly complex because of the large number of different inventory products, the different types of customers, and varying product mixes at the various warehouse locations. For these reasons, the Company has implemented a computer-based Purchasing and Inventory Management System (PIMS), which assists purchasing, warehousing, marketing, and financial personnel in the administration of purchases and inventory.

Information about the volume of purchase and cash disbursement transactions is as follows:

Transaction	Annual Volumes
Purchase orders/receiving memos	100,000
Check disbursements	100,000
Inventory count requests	150,000

Standing data amendments

• Price	100,000
• Product	20,000
• Vendor	2,000

Revenue

The revenue system was updated in August 1985. Despite the addition of several automated features, the Company has not fully developed the new system to eliminate certain control weaknesses. The Company anticipates that it will take approximately six months before the revenue system is fully functional.

Line of Credit

The Company is required to maintain a gross profit percentage of at least 19 percent and to limit its other costs and expenses to 15 percent of its net sales in order to maintain its current line of credit of $1,000,000. These provisions stipulate that if the operating criteria are not met, the Company will be required to maintain a separate cash account equal to two months' interest expense.

Warehousing/Distribution

The Company maintains a warehouse at the location of each of the six branch operations. Three are company owned and three are leased from H. Quinn under operating leases. Two of the warehouse managers were terminated during the year because they were unable to maintain operating schedules.

The Controller informed your audit manager that idle buildings and improvements being offered for sale are included in the property, plant, and equipment item on the balance sheet. The net book value approximates $3,000,000.

Inventory mix varies considerably from warehouse to warehouse. For example, the Chicago and Detroit warehouses handle primarily heavy industrial hardware and equipment, whereas the warehouses in other metropolitan centers handle mainly small hardware items and building materials.

There is a Vice-President of Wholesale Operations whose department is responsible for inventory control and for the physical inventories, which are taken each year at the end of March when inventory is historically at the lowest level. This also allows the auditors to issue the audit report by July 15.

The Company has its own fleet of delivery trucks for local deliveries at each warehouse location. All deliveries to points further than 100 miles from distribution points are made via commercial carriers.

Auditors

Your firm has been the auditor of the Company since it was founded and has been retained by Quinn to examine its financial statements for the year ended May 31, 1986. Quinn requested that it receive the audit report no later than July 15, 1986 in order to meet proposed closing schedules for a new term loan. Quinn also requested that you comment on any weaknesses found in its system of internal accounting control.

Financial Personnel

Mr. Greene is the third Vice-President of Finance that the Company has employed within the last six years; his predecessors were terminated because of poor earnings. Mr. Miller, Controller, has been with the Company for two years; Mr. Wright, Manager, Internal Auditing, for four years; and Mr. Good, EDP Manager, for three years.

Marketing

The Company employs a sales force of over 60 salespeople, operating from 11 sales offices in 4 marketing regions.

Annual sales by major customer category are approximately as follows:

	No. of Customers	Sales ($000's)	%
Retail division			
Hardware chain stores	2,000	$16,000	25
Independents	800	6,400	10
Department stores	15	9,000	14
	2,815	31,400	49
Industrial division	1,200	14,100	22
Mining division	130	9,600	15
Building division	60	8,900	14
	4,205	$64,000	100

Credit sales are made on a 1/10 net 30 day basis. Cash sales represent 10 percent of the hardware chain stores' volume.

Operating Results

Operating results of the Company for the last four years and the nine months ended February 28, 1986 (in $000's) are as follows:

	Year Ended May 31				Nine Months Ended Feb. 28, 1986	
	1982 ($)	1983 ($)	1984 ($)	1985 ($)	($)	%
Sales	41,900	48,200	53,100	58,800	48,518[a]	100.0
Cost of sales	37,000	38,600	45,000	47,600	39,027	80.4
Gross margin	4,900	9,600	8,100	11,200	9,491	19.6
Percent	12	20	15	19		
Other costs and expenses	5,600	7,200	8,600	8,600	7,131	14.7
Income (loss) before taxes	(700)	2,400	(500)	2,600	2,360	4.9

[a]1986 sales includes sales of $3,950,000 to DAP Mining Company in which J. Thomas, Quinn Hardware's President, is a significant stockholder.

EDP Processing

The Company used manual accounting systems during its early years. In the late 1960s, the auditors recommended that Quinn change to a batch mode computer system. During fiscal year 1985, they recommended that Quinn upgrade its computer hardware and convert its purchasing/payments system to include remote data entry and on-line processing functions. The new system has been in place throughout fiscal year 1986.

General audit practice and the EDP audit staff performed an implementation review of the new system to determine that it has been suitably designed, adequately tested, correctly implemented, and properly documented.

The computer system consists of an IBM 4381 computer with 8 megabytes of real main storage installed at its head office in Chicago. The computer configuration includes:

Quantity	Description
20	3270 Terminals
4	3211 2000 line/minute printers
1	3504 1200 card/minute card punch reader
1	3036 Operator console
8	3350 IBM disk drives (635 megabytes each)
6	3420 IBM tape drives (6250 b.p.i.)
1	3830 IBM control unit for disk drives
1	3803 IBM control unit for tape drives

The computer configuration is depicted on page 215.

Present computerized applications include:

Invoicing and accounts receivable system
Purchasing, accounts payable, and inventory management system
Payroll system
General ledger system
Marketing analysis
Truck routing system

The data processing department employs 29 people as follows (see "Quinn Hardware Organization Chart"):

Manager	1	
Secretary	1	
		2
Systems Development		
Manager	1	
Systems analysts	4	
Programmers	8	
		13
Data Control		
Supervisor	1	
Clerical	5	
		6
Operations		
Manager	1	
Operators	6	
Librarian	1	
		8
Total Employees		29

Quinn Hardware
Computer Hardware Configuration

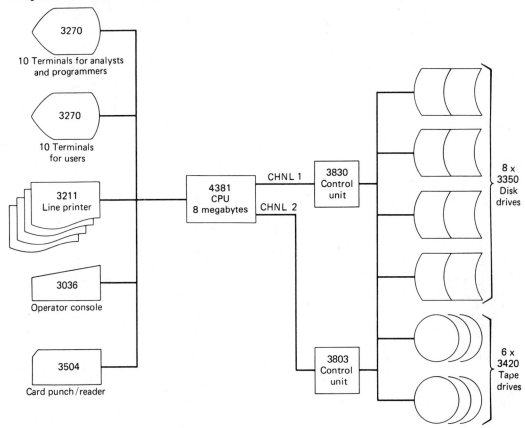

Comparative consolidated balance sheets appear on page 216.

QUINN HARDWARE
CONSOLIDATED BALANCE SHEETS
FEBRUARY 28, 1986 (UNAUDITED) AND MAY 31, 1985

ASSETS	*1986*	*1985*
Current Assets:		
Cash	$ 21,000	$ 12,000
Marketable securities	100,000	100,000
Accounts receivable	9,000,000	8,548,000
Merchandise inventory at lower of FIFO cost or market	13,500,000	11,862,000
Prepaid expenses and other assets	430,000	392,000
	23,051,000	20,914,000
Property, Plant, and Equipment, at Cost:		
Buildings and improvements	9,325,000	9,157,000
Furniture and fixtures	3,072,000	2,989,000
Automotive equipment	320,000	226,000
	12,717,000	12,372,000
Less: Accumulated depreciation	4,190,000	3,720,000
	8,527,000	8,652,000
Land	2,000,000	1,800,000
	10,527,000	10,452,000
	$33,578,000	$31,366,000

LIABILITIES AND STOCKHOLDERS' EQUITY	*1986*	*1985*
Current Liabilities:		
Accounts payable and accrued liabilities	$ 6,258,000	$ 5,921,000
Income taxes payable	1,200,000	662,000
Dividends payable		130,000
	7,458,000	6,713,000
Deferred Income Taxes	860,000	690,000
Bond Debenture, bearing interest at 10% per annum	10,000,000	10,000,000
Stockholders' Equity:		
Preferred stock, $1.00 par value, nonparticipating, 9% cumulative preference, 1,000,000 shares authorized, 500,000 shares issued and outstanding	500,000	500,000
Common stock, no par value, 1,000,000 shares authorized, issued, and outstanding	2,000,000	2,000,000
	2,500,000	2,500,000
Retained earnings	12,760,000	11,463,000
	15,260,000	13,963,000
	$33,578,000	$31,366,000

Chapter 7
Internal Control Systems

An enterprise's internal control system comprises several elements, including the control environment, accounting systems, and internal accounting and administrative controls. These elements, which consist of policies, procedures, and the means of monitoring compliance with them, are designed by enterprise management to safeguard its assets, to generate reliable accounting records, to promote operational efficiency, and to encourage adherence to prescribed managerial policies. Collectively, the various elements of an internal control system operate within an enterprise to reduce its unintended exposure to business, financial, and accounting risks.

The auditor's responsibility with regard to a client's system of internal control is formalized in the second standard of field work, stated in Section 320 of Statement on Auditing Standards No. 1, as follows:

> There is to be a proper study and evaluation of the existing internal control as a basis for reliance thereon and for the determination of the resultant extent of the tests to which auditing procedures are to be restricted.

As specified by this standard, the extent to which audit procedures must be performed to test transactions and account balances is directly related to the degree of reliance the auditor is able to or intends to place on the client's system of internal control. The auditor determines a basis for reliance on the internal control system first by evaluating the control environment to determine whether it appears to be conducive to the maintenance of a reliable internal control system; next, the auditor obtains and records an understanding of the system and the controls encompassed by it; finally, the auditor tests those controls on which reliance is planned to ensure their proper and continued operation. If these "compliance" tests of controls support the reliability of the accounting system and controls, the auditor can thereby limit the direct (or "substantive") tests applied to the related account balances. In other words, if the underlying evidence from the accounting system and controls is highly reliable, the auditor needs less corroborating evidence; as the reliability of the underlying evidence decreases, the extent of corroborating evidence required increases. For example, if the auditor is satisfied, based on the results of compliance testing, that the internal controls over sales transactions are adequate to ensure that all authorized shipments of products, and only authorized shipments, are accurately billed and recorded, the auditor can then significantly reduce substantive tests of the sales and accounts receivable accounts that would otherwise be performed.

Definitions and Objectives of Internal Control

The formal definition of internal control, originally published by the accounting profession in 1949 and repeated in subsequent publications, including paragraph 320.09 of SAS No. 1 (AU Section 320.09), states:

> Internal control comprises the plan of organization and all of the coordinate methods and measures adopted within a business to safeguard its assets, check the accuracy and reliability of its accounting data, promote operational efficiency, and encourage adherence to prescribed managerial policies. This definition . . . recognizes that a "system" of internal control extends beyond those matters which relate directly to the functions of the accounting and financial departments.

Thus, two different aspects of internal control are included in this broad definition: internal accounting controls and administrative controls. (Administrative controls are sometimes referred to as operational controls because they deal with the operations of the enterprise rather than with the accounting for those operations.)

Internal Accounting Control

In gaining an understanding of internal accounting control, it is helpful to distinguish between accounting controls and accounting procedures. Examples of accounting procedures include the recording of the shipment and receipt of goods, the posting of transactions to subsidiary ledgers, and the recording of summarized transactions in the general ledger. Internal accounting controls, on the other hand, are procedures designed to ensure the reliability of accounting data and to safeguard assets. For example, the recording of cash receipts and disbursements in the cash receipts and disbursements journals and the posting of monthly totals to the general ledger are typical accounting procedures. The monthly reconciliation of the general ledger cash balance to the related balance reported by the bank on the bank statement is an internal accounting control designed to ensure that cash transactions have been properly recorded.

Internal accounting control is defined in SAS No. 1 (AU Section 320.28) as

The plan of organization and the procedures and records that are concerned with the safeguarding of assets and the reliability of financial records and consequently are designed to provide reasonable assurance that:

a. Transactions are executed in accordance with management's general or specific authorization.

b. Transactions are recorded as necessary (1) to permit preparation of financial statements in conformity with generally accepted accounting principles or any other criteria applicable to such statements and (2) to maintain accountability for assets.

c. Access to assets is permitted only in accordance with management's authorization.

d. The recorded accountability for assets is compared with the existing assets at reasonable intervals and appropriate action is taken with respect to any differences.

SAS No. 1 elaborates on each of these "basic concepts," as follows:

Execution of Transactions
Obtaining reasonable assurance that transactions are executed as authorized requires independent evidence that authorizations are issued by persons acting within the scope of their authority and that transactions conform with the terms of the authorizations. (AU Section 320.37)

Recording of Transactions
The objective of accounting control with respect to the recording of transactions requires that they be recorded at the amounts and in the accounting periods in which they were executed and be classified in appropriate accounts. (AU Section 320.38)

Access to Assets
The objective of safeguarding assets requires that access to assets be limited to authorized personnel. In this context, access to assets includes both direct physical access and indirect access through the preparation or processing of documents that authorize the use or disposition of assets. . . . The number and caliber of personnel to whom access is authorized should be influenced by the nature of the assets and the related susceptibility to loss through errors and irregularities. (AU Section 320.42)

Comparison of Recorded Accountability With Assets

The purpose of comparing recorded accountability with assets is to determine whether the actual assets agree with the recorded accountability, and consequently, it is closely related to the foregoing discussion concerning the recording of transactions. Typical examples of this comparison include cash and securities counts, bank reconciliations, and physical inventories. (AU Section 320.43)

These basic concepts provide the framework for what this book will designate as the five *general* objectives of internal accounting control, which are to ensure:

1. *Completeness*—that all transactions that occurred are recorded in the accounting records.
2. *Validity*—that all recorded transactions represent economic events that actually occurred and were properly authorized.
3. *Accuracy*—that transactions are recorded at the correct amount, in the right account, and on a timely basis at each stage of their processing.
4. *Maintenance*—that the accounting records, after the entry of recurring and authorized transactions in them, continue to reflect the operations and financial position of the business.
5. *Physical Security*—that access to assets and the documents that control their movement is suitably restricted to authorized personnel.

These general objectives are consistent with the objectives of internal accounting control expressed in SAS No. 1. The major difference is that this book divides the objective relating to the recording of transactions into two distinct objectives, completeness and accuracy. This division is advantageous because separate control techniques are normally incorporated into accounting systems to achieve the completeness and accuracy objectives. The general objectives provide a practical basis for the design of internal accounting control systems and for the auditor's evaluation of those systems.

Relationship of Control Objectives to Audit Objectives. The general control objectives of completeness, validity, and accuracy that were just described are closely related to the audit objectives of completeness, existence, and accuracy, as discussed in Chapter 5. For example, controls over accuracy that are designed to prevent or detect errors in the processing of sales transactions that could arise because wrong prices were used, invoices were improperly computed, or shipments were billed to the wrong customer reduce the risk that the sales account in the income statement and accounts receivable in the balance sheet are not accurate. Clearly, if there are controls over the accuracy of recorded transactions and the auditor has tested the controls and found them to be effective, that reduces the level of assurance the auditor must obtain to meet the audit objective of accuracy.

While the control objectives of completeness and validity are related to the audit objectives of completeness and existence, the relationship is more complex than it is with the accuracy objective, primarily because of the double-entry system, which records two aspects of every transaction. Consider sales transactions: If a sale is made and goods are shipped but the transaction is not recorded, failure to achieve the control objective of completeness of transaction processing has resulted in both sales in the income statement and accounts receivable in the balance sheet being incomplete. If, however, control weaknesses permit the incomplete recording of cash receipts from charge customers, but the receipts have been properly deposited, then the cash account per the books is not complete and accounts receivable now contain nonexistent receivables. In this instance, weaknesses in a completeness control have generated an error with respect to existence.

The same type of analysis for the validity objective leads to the conclusion that while control weaknesses that permit invalid transactions to be recorded generally lead to the recording of nonexistent assets (for example, a fictitious sale that generates a nonexistent account receivable), in some circumstances those weaknesses may result in assets or liabilities being omitted from the balance sheet (for example, the removal of a receivable due from an employee by recording a fictitious sales return). In practice, auditors relate the control objectives of completeness and validity to the audit objectives of completeness and existence by determining what could go wrong in the processing of specific transactions (control weaknesses) and then determining how that could affect specific accounts in the financial statements (audit objectives). Attempting to delineate how the relationship between those control objectives and audit objectives would apply to specific transactions and accounts is not practicable, because of the immense number of possible combinations of transactions and errors that could occur.

The maintenance objective deals with the completeness, validity, and accuracy of entries to an account other than those that result from the processing of recurring transactions. Accordingly, an entity's failure to achieve the maintenance objective could lead to account balances that are incomplete, nonexistent, or inaccurate.

Finally, inadequate controls over the physical security of assets and the documents that control their movement permit unauthorized access to those assets and could result in unrecorded loss of assets. In that situation, assets that did not exist would continue to be recorded.

It is important to understand how a client's ability to meet its control objectives can affect the risk that errors of various types could be present in the unaudited financial statements. The audit objectives that the auditor must achieve for each material account balance in the financial statements are that the balances are complete and accurate and that they represent real-world counterparts that exist. The auditor's assessment of how well the client's control system contributes to those objectives determines in large part the strategy selected to achieve the necessary low level of audit risk with respect to each account and each audit objective.

Figure 7.1 Relationship of Objectives of Internal Accounting Control to Audit Objectives

		Objectives of Internal Accounting Control				
		Completeness	Validity	Accuracy	Maintenance	Physical Security
Audit Objectives	Completeness	X	X		X	
	Existence	X	X		X	X
	Accuracy			X	X	

The relationships between control objectives and audit objectives discussed in the preceding paragraphs are summarized in Figure 7.1. Several of the audit objectives discussed in Chapter 5—namely, cutoff, valuation, rights and obligations, and presentation and disclosure—are not included in that figure. That is because those objectives are rarely addressed specifically by an entity's internal accounting controls (although controls may address data that form the basis for certain of management's assertions, such as data about the age of open receivable balances that are used to determine the adequacy of the allowance for bad debts).

Limitations on the Effectiveness of Internal Accounting Control. While internal accounting control aims at ensuring the completeness, accuracy, validity, and maintenance of recorded accounting data, as well as the security of assets, absolute prevention and detection of errors cannot be guaranteed. SAS No. 1 discusses the inherent limitations on the effectiveness of any system of internal control, in paragraph 34 of Section 320 (AU Section 320.34). That paragraph notes the following factors that may reduce or eliminate the effectiveness of internal accounting control procedures:

- Misunderstanding of instructions, mistakes of judgment, personal carelessness, distraction, or fatigue on the part of the person responsible for performing the control procedure.
- Collusion between responsible individuals, circumventing control procedures whose effectiveness depends on segregation of duties.
- Errors or irregularities perpetrated by management with respect to transactions or to the estimates and judgments required in the preparation of financial statements.

The Concept of "Reasonable Assurance." Professional auditing literature (SAS No. 1 [AU Section 320.32]), the Foreign Corrupt Practices Act of 1977 (the Act), and sound financial management all recognize that a system of internal accounting control comprehends reasonable, but not absolute, assurance that its objectives will be accomplished. While internal accounting control aims to prevent and detect errors, absolute prevention or 100 percent detection is costly and probably impossible. Since controls have a cost in both time and money, management must always make economic judgments on whether a further degree of risk reduction is worth the cost of providing it.

The judgments that must be made are similar to most other judgments by management. The manner in which they are made reflects the ability to identify and measure risks; it also reflects management's broad philosophy or style of managing, for example, a policy of maintaining a "lean" organization in which administrative overhead is kept at a minimum. Fortunately, management needs only reasonable, not absolute, assurance that errors will be prevented or will be detected if and when they occur. SAS No. 1 (AU Section 320.32) expresses this idea in words that have been in the auditing literature for many years but are equally relevant today in discussing management's decisions on internal control.

> The concept of reasonable assurance recognizes that the cost of internal control should not exceed the benefits expected to be derived. The benefits consist of reductions in the risk of failing to achieve the objectives implicit in the definition of accounting control. Although the cost-benefit relationship is the primary conceptual criterion that should be considered in designing a system of accounting control, precise measurement of costs and benefits usually is not possible; accordingly, any evaluation of the cost-benefit relationship requires estimates and judgments by management.

Determining the level of risk that should "reasonably" be accepted is a subjective process. The costs of particular controls are not always measurable, and the benefits are even less so. As a result, applying the concept of reasonable assurance requires reliance on subjective determinants. Cost-benefit analysis, while important to the decision process, is presently not developed to the point where it alone should be used. As the AICPA Special Advisory Committee on Internal Accounting Control noted, "Subjective knowledge, experience, specific industry and business conditions, management style, cost-benefit judgments, among other factors, affect the selection of appropriate control procedures and techniques. . . ."[1]

Administrative Control

Administrative control is described in SAS No. 1 (AU Section 320.27) as including, but not limited to,

> The plan of organization and the procedures and records that are concerned with the decision processes leading to management's authorization of transactions. Such authorization is a management function directly associated with the responsibility for achieving the objectives of the organization and is the starting point for establishing accounting control of transactions.

Broadly, the prime responsibility of management is to operate an enterprise at a profit, or within the available resources if it is a not-for-profit organization. In both types of enterprise, management must produce goods or services at acceptable cost; it must develop markets in which the goods or services can be sold at competitive prices; and because of the pressure of competition, changes in customer demand, and other factors that cause obsolescence, it must develop new or improved goods or services.

To accomplish those goals, management must develop policies and procedures to promote efficiency in every area of activity; implement them through proper personnel selection, training, and compensation; communicate the means of effecting them; and monitor performance through adequate supervision. In this book, the "plan of organization and all of the coordinate methods and measures adopted within a business to . . . promote operational efficiency and encourage adherence to prescribed managerial policies" (AU Section 320.09) are referred to as administrative controls.

Administrative controls are distinguished from internal accounting controls by their primary purpose. The definitions of administrative control and internal accounting control are, however, not mutually exclusive. Some of the methods and procedures comprehended in administrative control may also be involved in internal accounting control. For example, sales and cost records classified by products may be used both for accounting control purposes and for making management decisions about product pricing. Other administrative controls may be based on or integrated with accounting data, or more than one purpose may be served by the same controls. For example, certain administrative controls may be based on data or information furnished by accounting or financial departments, such as investigating and acting on the underlying causes of variances found in variance reports. On the other hand, some administrative controls may also help to satisfy internal accounting control objectives.

[1]*Report of the Special Advisory Committee on Internal Accounting Control* (New York: American Institute of Certified Public Accountants, 1979), p. 27.

The distinction between administrative controls and accounting controls is important to independent auditors because of their relatively narrowly defined responsibilities for the study and evaluation of internal accounting control under generally accepted auditing standards. The AICPA's Committee on Auditing Procedure clarified the scope of the auditor's study, contemplated under generally accepted auditing standards, in its Statement on Auditing Procedure No. 33, issued in 1963, and presented the following conclusion, now incorporated in AU Section 320.11:

> The independent auditor is primarily concerned with the accounting controls. Accounting controls . . . generally bear directly and importantly on the reliability of financial records and require evaluation by the auditor. Administrative controls . . . ordinarily relate only indirectly to the financial records and thus would not require evaluation. If the independent auditor believes, however, that certain administrative controls may have an important bearing on the reliability of the financial records, he should consider the need for evaluating such controls. For example, statistical records maintained by production, sales, or other operating departments may require evaluation in a particular instance.

Hence, the auditor has a responsibility under generally accepted auditing standards to evaluate administrative controls only if they have a significant bearing on the reliability of the financial statements.

The distinction between administrative and accounting controls is also important to management because of the specific requirements of the Foreign Corrupt Practices Act relating to the maintenance of an adequate system of internal accounting control, as discussed in more detail later in this chapter.

Transaction Cycles

The auditor's approach to the evaluation of internal accounting control described in this book requires that transaction flows be viewed in terms of "cycles" into which they can be conveniently grouped and for which specific internal control objectives and control procedures for achieving those objectives can be identified.[2] Three major transaction cycles are identified in this book and are discussed in detail in Chapters 12 through 14. They are the revenue, buying, and production cycles.[3] Each cycle comprises several transaction types that

[2] The FASB defines "transaction" as "an external event involving transfer of something of value . . . between two (or more) entities" (Statement of Financial Accounting Concepts No. 3, para. 77). The term is used more broadly in this book to include all events and circumstances that require accounting recognition. In the context of computer systems, the term is used even more broadly to encompass any change to the computerized records.

[3] Other transaction cycles—for example, determining, recording, and paying income taxes—may be identified if the client has created one or more specific controls unique to a group of transactions. These additional cycles will have audit significance only if the auditor plans to rely on the controls and has compliance tested them.

vary with the operations of a particular business. For example, sales of goods and services, cash receipts, and customer returns may be three distinct transaction types making up the revenue cycle. Furthermore, each transaction type may have two or more subtypes; for example, sales of goods and services may be subdivided into cash sales and credit sales, or into foreign sales and domestic sales. Transaction types and subtypes are distinguished from each other primarily by differences in accounting control procedures applied to each. The importance of the cycle concept is its focus on whether there is appropriate control over each type of transaction as the transaction flows through the processing system. The auditor studies each transaction type and subtype to determine whether adequate internal controls have been designed and are operating properly and consistently to achieve the objectives of internal accounting control.

As mentioned earlier, most business activities can be grouped into three major transaction cycles:

Revenue Cycle—Transaction flows relating to revenue generating and collection functions and related controls over such activities as sales orders, shipping, and cash collection.

Buying Cycle—Transaction flows relating to purchases and payments and related controls over (among other activities) ordering and receipt of purchases, accounts payable, payroll functions, and cash disbursements.

Production Cycle—Transaction flows relating to production of goods or services and related controls over such activities as maintenance of inventory balances, inventory transfers, and charges to production for labor and overhead.

The auditor's evaluation of internal accounting control must also consider other activities, not strictly related to transaction flows. These activities include events caused by the passage of time, such as interest accruals and the amortization of prepayments; controls that are applied only periodically, such as procedures to verify the physical existence of inventories, fixed assets, and investment securities; and the financial reporting process.

In computer environments, it may be necessary to identify another type of controls that do not fit into any of the transaction cycles, but that may have a significant impact on some or all of them. These controls, commonly referred to as general controls, operate over the implementation, maintenance, security, and use of computer programs, and the security of data files. A more descriptive term for these controls (and one whose use appears to be growing) is information technology controls. They are discussed in detail in Chapter 11.

The five general objectives of internal accounting control identified earlier apply to each of the major transaction cycles. When evaluating the controls over various transaction types within the transaction cycles, the auditor should translate the general control objectives into specific control objectives applicable to each transaction type. For example, Figure 7.2 identifies the specific control objectives related to the general control objectives for credit sales transactions in the revenue cycle.

Figure 7.2 Control Objectives for Credit Sales Transactions

General Control Objective	Specific Control Objective
Completeness	All valid credit sales transactions are recorded and processed.
Validity	All recorded sales transactions represent actual shipments of goods or rendering of services to nonfictitious customers, as authorized by responsible personnel.
Accuracy	Sales are correctly recorded as to amounts, quantities, dates, and customers in the proper period in books of original entry and detail subsidiary records, and are correctly summarized in the general ledger.
Maintenance	Both individual accounts receivable in the subsidiary ledger and the general ledger control account reflect all authorized transactions and only those transactions.
Physical security	(This objective is not directly applicable to this transaction type, except that physical controls over finished-goods shipments are necessary to attain the completeness objective.)

The control objectives fit every enterprise, since they remain essentially the same no matter how the processing is performed. For example, it does not matter whether procedures are performed manually or by computer. The focus on specific control objectives for each type of transaction allows the auditor to identify the principal control procedures designed and implemented by management to attain the objectives.

Elements of Internal Control Systems

As noted earlier, a system of internal control comprises a number of interrelated elements, namely, the control environment, the accounting systems, internal accounting controls, and internal administrative controls. Internal accounting controls encompass basic controls, division of duties, and supervisory controls. Internal administrative controls were discussed earlier. Each of the other elements of internal control is discussed in the following sections.

Control Environment

An enterprise's management can foster an environment that is conducive to the functioning of internal controls. Such a control environment can have "a significant impact on the selection and effectiveness of a company's accounting control procedures and techniques"[4] and, as stated in SAS No. 30 (AU Section

[4]*Report of the Special Advisory Committee on Internal Accounting Control* (New York: American Institute of Certified Public Accountants 1979), p. 12.

642), is a factor to be considered in planning the scope of an audit engagement. Broadly, the control environment encompasses the attitudes, abilities, perceptions, and actions of an enterprise's personnel, particularly its management.

The control environment concept is useful because it addresses the interrelationships among the elements of internal control and thereby provides a framework within which specific control procedures can be evaluated. The AICPA Special Advisory Committee on Internal Accounting Control concluded that it is possible to make an overall evaluation of a company's internal accounting control environment, and that such an evaluation is a "necessary prelude to the evaluation of control procedures and techniques." The Committee further stated: "A poor control environment would make some accounting controls inoperative for all intents and purposes because, for example, individuals would hesitate to challenge a management override of a specific control procedure. On the other hand, a strong control environment, one with tight budgetary controls and an effective internal audit function, can significantly complement specific accounting control procedures and techniques."[5]

Evaluating the control environment provides the auditor with a basis for determining whether it appears to be conducive to the maintenance of a reliable system of internal control and the extent to which it reduces the incentives and opportunities for deliberate distortions of the financial statements by management. Additionally, the evaluation provides the auditor with other information, such as significant reports and procedures that management uses to control the business, that can be useful in developing the audit strategy. The factors that affect an enterprise's control environment are typically reflected in

1. The composition and activities of its board of directors, audit committee, and internal audit function, if any.
2. Its organizational structure.
3. The competence and integrity of its personnel, especially those in key management positions.
4. Methods of communicating responsibilities and authority.
5. The management information system.
6. Methods of supervision.
7. Codes of conduct and policies.
8. Physical conditions (e.g., workplaces and equipment).
9. Plans and budgets.
10. Methods of developing accounting estimates.

An important aspect of the control environment is management's review of and responses to various internal reports prepared in the process of managing the business. Such reviews include the analysis of reports of periodic operating results and comparisons of current data with benchmarks such as budgets or historical performance. Those reviews may help the client achieve one or more

[5]*Ibid.*

objectives of internal accounting control, and thereby provide evidence to the auditor about the reliability of the underlying transaction processing and the related account balances.

Another aspect of the control environment is the presence of an internal auditing function, which, among other objectives, may ensure operational efficiency and monitor compliance with company policies and procedures. In evaluating an internal auditing function, the auditor should consider

- Whether the nature and scope of internal audit operations have been reviewed and approved by top management and the audit committee or board of directors.
- To whom the internal audit group reports (e.g., it would be more desirable from the auditor's standpoint for the internal auditing manager to report to a person or group that is not responsible for accounting and financial reporting).

Subject to review and evaluation by the independent auditor, effective internal auditing performed under the direction of appropriate management often allows the independent auditor to significantly reduce the audit scope in affected areas.

After considering the factors that contribute to the control environment, the auditor should be able to reach an overall conclusion about the extent to which the environment is conducive to the maintenance of reliable internal controls and reduces the likelihood of intentional distortion of the financial statements by management. If the auditor concludes that the control environment is favorable, there is a lower risk that the system of controls will be overridden or neglected and that misstatements may occur. That in turn assists the auditor in determining the nature, timing, and extent of other audit procedures.

Accounting Systems

All enterprises have some form of accounting systems for processing transactions. AU Section 320 distinguishes between accounting systems and internal accounting control systems, as defined earlier. "An accounting system comprises the coordinate functions by which exchanges of assets or services with parties outside the business entity and transfers or use of assets or services within it are recognized, and data representing such exchanges, transfers, and uses are assembled, processed, analyzed, and reported." Management designs accounting systems in response to the nature of the business, its size and organizational structure, the types and volumes of transactions, and whether it is subject to regulatory requirements. The accounting systems encompass procedures, which may be manual, computerized, or a combination of both, for identifying, assembling, classifying, analyzing, and recording transactions, as well as the documents produced by the systems. Those procedures and documents assist in the effective operation of the business and permit the proper preparation of financial statements.

The documents produced by the accounting systems provide third parties, management, and employees with information about the processing and recording of transactions. These documents, for example, checks, bills of lading, and accounts receivable aging schedules, are often subject to review and scrutiny by those users, who may detect errors in the information resulting from the failure of accounting procedures or related internal controls to operate effectively and continuously. In determining the reliability of the accounting systems, the auditor should consider the likelihood that users would detect and report potential errors in data underlying the financial statements.

Two principal types of data are processed through the accounting systems, *standing data* and *transaction data*. Standing data are data of a permanent or semi-permanent nature that are used repeatedly during processing. Examples are rates of pay used for calculating salaries and customer credit limits used in deciding whether to accept customer orders. Transaction data relate to individual transactions, for example, the number of hours worked by an individual employee in a particular week, which is used to calculate that employee's salary. Errors in standing data are likely to be of greater significance than errors in transaction data, because errors in standing data will affect many transactions until they are corrected. This is particularly true of computerized systems in which standing data used in processing are usually reviewed only when originally set up on files and not each time they are used.

Internal Accounting Controls

The techniques or procedures through which control is exercised may be classified as basic controls, division of duties, and supervisory controls. Basic controls are those controls necessary to meet the general objectives of control over processing and recording transactions, maintaining accounting records, and restricting access to assets and records to authorized personnel. Basic controls are applied directly to data, records, and assets and related documents. Division of duties consists of arrangements that limit the activities of an individual so that that person's ability to misappropriate assets or conceal fraud or errors is restricted. It can be accomplished, for example, by separating responsibility for the custody of assets from the related record keeping. Supervisory controls consist of routines for overseeing or reviewing the performance of basic controls. Examples are the review and approval of a monthly reconciliation of a control account with supporting detailed records, or the review and approval of the testing carried out on a new computer program. The importance of distinguishing among these types of controls arises because the auditor's assessment of each can have different effects on the audit strategy.

In noncomputerized accounting systems, all internal accounting controls are, of course, performed manually. In computerized systems, accounting controls may include computerized operations, known as programmed control procedures, that generate data that are then subject to a manual operation. For example, before a vendor's invoice is paid on its due date, a computer program may match all open invoices due on that date with the file of open receiving reports. If there is a match, the computer removes both the invoice and the receiving report from their respective files, puts them into a paid invoice file, and prints out the vendor's check. If there is no match, either because there is no receiving report or because the data on the receiving report differ from the data on the invoice, the computer does not print out the check but instead prints out an "exception report" of invoices due for which no receiving report exists. An accounting supervisor reviews and "clears" the exception report by determining that, in fact, the goods have not been received, no receiving report should have been created, and the vendor should not be paid. The computerized matching and the generation of the exception report are programmed control procedures; the review and clearing of the exception report is a manual control procedure. Both operations are necessary for the control objective to be achieved—in this example, that all payments to vendors are valid.

Basic Controls. Basic controls are procedures designed to ensure that all valid transactions, and only those transactions, are recorded completely and accurately, that errors in execution or recording are detected as soon as possible—regardless of whether the error is the processing of an unauthorized transaction, the failure to process an authorized one, the failure to process it accurately, or the failure to maintain the accounting records accurately after the initial recording of transactions—and that access to assets is restricted, that is, that the control objectives of completeness, validity, accuracy, maintenance, and physical security are achieved and reliable financial records thereby generated. The following paragraphs discuss different ways of achieving those objectives.

Completeness. Controls for ensuring that all transactions that occur are entered on a control document (e.g., a receiving report or shipping advice) and included in the accounting records are an important part of internal accounting control. Without adequate completeness controls, there is a possibility that control documents may be lost or misplaced, and this could result in a failure to record valid transactions. In computer systems, controls are necessary not only to ensure that all transactions are input to and accepted by the computer but also to ensure that all appropriate master files include data input to and accepted by the computer. Examples of control procedures designed to ensure completeness are:

• *Numbering all transactions as soon as they originate (or, preferably, prenumbering them) and then accounting for all the transactions after they have been processed.* Numbering documents is an accounting procedure; the basic control procedure is the act of reviewing to see that all numbered documents complete the expected processing. In a computer-based system, a technique known as a computer sequence check can be used to have the computer ascertain that the sequence of serially numbered documents is maintained and report missing or duplicate numbers for manual investigation. The possibility of purposeful or accidental errors in the numbering process is reduced if the numerical sequence is printed in advance on the forms to be used for documenting transactions. If the risk of error or misuse is not considered significant, the numbering is often originated simultaneously with the document. For example, a computer preparing checks in the course of an accounts payable processing run can be programmed to number the checks sequentially.

- *Determining that all data are processed by using "control totals."* This can be done by totaling the critical numbers for a batch of transactions before and after processing; the assumption is that the processing is correct if the two totals agree. There is, of course, a possibility of one error exactly offsetting another error or omission, but the possibility is slight. Control totals do not provide control in themselves; they provide information by means of which control is exercised. The actual basic control procedure is the comparison of two totals and the searching out and correction of errors giving rise to differences. Control totals appear in many forms. The double-entry system provides control totals in the sense that the totals of the debits must always equal the totals of the credits, both in individual entries and in the accounts as a whole.

- *Matching data from different sources.* For example, unmatched documents (such as receiving reports or vendors' invoices) can be reviewed periodically, possibly by computer, and long-outstanding items investigated to ascertain that a document has not been lost in the processing.

- *Determining that all transactions are entered in a register.* For example, all chargeable service hours may be recorded in a service register that is reconciled to the hours for which payment is made.

Completeness controls are also needed to ensure proper summarization of information and proper preparation of financial reports for both internal and external purposes. Such controls are particularly important if general ledger entries are generated from sources other than summarized totals taken from books of original entry. For example, it is relatively easy for both client personnel and the auditor to test the completeness of postings to the general ledger for sales transactions if the postings are made directly from the summarized totals in the sales journal. A simple review to ensure that there are 12 monthly postings in the general ledger may suffice. If, however, general ledger entries arise from other sources as well, additional controls may be needed to ensure that all transactions are summarized and posted. The use of standard journal entry numbers may facilitate achieving the control. Reviews performed to determine that all appropriate standard journal entries were used and posted to the general ledger each month would help ensure that all related postings have been recorded.

Basic controls over completeness may have a particularly significant effect on the conduct of an audit. Auditors often find it particularly difficult to obtain sufficient evidence to support client assertions about the completeness of recording of all transactions in the books and records. Sufficient assurance about the validity, accuracy, and maintenance of account balances can usually be achieved, even if basic controls are inadequate, by directly testing those balances or the transactions giving rise to them, for example, examining supporting documentation and reperforming accounting procedures. Since the objectives of validity, accuracy, and maintenance are concerned primarily with *recorded* transactions and balances, supporting evidence is normally available to test whether those objectives have been achieved.

When evaluating the completeness of transaction processing and the resultant accounting records, however, the auditor is concerned with the possibility of *unrecorded* transactions, for which there is usually no evidence. For example, if prenumbered documents are used to record transactions, the auditor can, by accounting for the numerical sequence of the documents, obtain evidence that all transactions for which a prenumbered document has been prepared have been recorded in books of original entry. Accounting for the numerical sequence of existing documents, however, is not effective for detecting unrecorded transactions if documents have not been prepared for all transactions. The auditor should therefore pay particular attention to those basic controls designed to ensure that all transactions are recorded on a document, for example, a requirement that a shipping document be prepared before a storeroom clerk releases merchandise for shipment.

Authoritative auditing literature notes that "in the great majority of cases, the auditor finds it necessary to rely on evidence that is persuasive rather than convincing" (SAS No. 31, *Evidential Matter* [AU Section 326.19]). This is particularly true with regard to evidence supporting the completeness of recording of transactions that have occurred. In most instances, persuasive evidence about completeness can be obtained, but in extreme circumstances, if completeness controls are found to be absent or particularly weak, the auditor should question the auditability of the accounting records. Not all transaction types of a particular enterprise may be auditable; at the extreme, the significance of unauditable transaction types may be so great that it makes the enterprise as a whole unauditable.

Validity. Recorded transactions can be reviewed in various ways to ensure that they represent economic events that actually occurred. The most elementary control procedure to ensure validity consists of the examination of documentation by someone who understands the accounting system for evidence that a recorded transaction actually took place, that it took place in accordance with prescribed procedures, and that the transaction was authorized by responsible personnel. In more sophisticated systems, control procedures to ensure validity are built into the system itself so that transactions are tested against predetermined expectations.

Procedures to accomplish the validity objective involve establishing controls to:

• *Ensure that only valid transactions are recorded, that is, entered on a document or into a computer file that can later be compared with accounting records, reports, or other documents.* For example, accounting procedures are normally established to record goods received on receiving reports and goods shipped on shipping reports. Control procedures designed to ensure the validity of these transactions include inspecting the related goods to determine that their description, condition, and quantities are correct and comparing that information with data on sales and vendors' invoices. Any significant discrepancies noted must also be investigated and resolved if the foregoing control procedures are to be effective. As another example, canceling the voucher and related documents supporting a purchase transaction at the time of payment prevents their reuse to support a duplicate payment or a payment for a nonexistent purchase.

• *Ensure that transactions are authorized by responsible personnel in accordance with established guidelines.* One of the primary controls over individual transactions is the act of authorizing them. This is the principal means for ensuring that only valid transactions are processed and that all other transactions are rejected. Authorization can be general or specific. A general authorization may take the form of giving a department or function permission to enter into transactions against some budgeted amount. The approval of the budget for a capital expenditure, for example, in effect serves as an authorization to commit the enterprise for expenditures up to the budgeted amount. Another example, from the retail industry, is the "open to buy" concept in which a buyer is authorized to buy merchandise up to a specified amount. A specific authorization, on the other hand, would grant permission to a person to enter into a specific transaction, for example, to buy a specific amount of a raw material needed for the production of a made-to-order item.

Controls over authorization of transactions are increasingly being automated by specifying in advance the conditions under which a transaction will be automatically authorized and executed. For example, a production order can be automatically authorized when the on-hand amount of an inventory item falls to a predetermined point requiring replenishment. Even in nonautomated systems, general authorizations can be used to accomplish the same objective. Note that, for control to exist, some form of authorization must be carried out before, after, or during the initiation and execution of a transaction.

There is potential confusion in another common use of the term "authorization." The control procedure of authorizing individual transactions must be distinguished from that aspect of the accounting system that spells out which member of an organization is authorized to do what. The basic control procedure of authorizing individual transactions is frequently referred to as "approval." For example, a designated person approves a transaction or the validity of a document. For a transaction to be properly authorized, not only must it be approved; it must be approved by a person having the right and competence to do so under conditions specified by the system.

Accuracy. Controls are necessary to ensure that each transaction is recorded at the correct amount, in the right account, and on a timely basis. The accuracy of amount and account is most frequently achieved by establishing control procedures to review calculations, extensions, additions, and account classifications. Such reviews might be performed and evidenced by insertion of the performer's initials on sales invoices, credit memoranda, or payroll summaries. Occasionally an additional "double check" is made by another individual who repeats the calculations, extensions, and additions, and reviews the account classifications.

Controls to ensure that transactions are recorded on a timely basis are also essential to achieve the accuracy objective. This requires procedures to establish the dates on which transactions took place. (Those procedures also help to ensure a proper "cutoff," that is, that transactions are recorded and reported in the proper accounting period.) As an example, goods received are inspected and recorded at the time of their receipt. Usually the receiving records are matched with related vendors' invoices as part of a further control on the timely recording of transactions.

Various procedures by which transactions are processed through the accounting systems may generate "exception reports" that are used by management for operational purposes; these reports may also provide evidence about the absence of certain types of errors. For example, before cash receipts from customers are credited to their accounts, they may be matched to specific sales charged to the customers' accounts and an exception report of unmatched receipts generated. The purpose of the match and the exception report is to ensure that the full amount of specific invoices is collected. The matching of receipts to sales and the follow-up of the exception report, however, also provide evidence of the accuracy and genuineness of the sales transactions.

Maintenance. The maintenance objective seeks to ensure that after recurring transactions (which for each transaction cycle have been subjected to controls over completeness, validity, and accuracy) have been properly recorded, the accounting records continue to be correct. In a manual accounting system, the maintenance objective requires controls to ensure that all other valid transactions that should be recorded (and only valid transactions) are accurately recorded. In a computer environment, the maintenance objective also requires that procedures be designed to ensure that transactions are processed using only the most recently updated computer files and that the current files can be recovered in the event of a computer failure.

In a manual accounting system, controls over maintenance center around the use of subsidiary ledgers and control accounts. Since individual transactions are the source of the balances used in financial statements and other financial data, subsidiary ledgers and control accounts must be maintained to permit proper summarization of recorded transactions. Controls are necessary to ensure that the accounting records have been maintained properly subsequent to the entry of transactions in them. Although completeness, validity, and accuracy controls may ensure that raw material purchases are properly recorded, for example, they do not necessarily ensure that the related raw material inventory balance is correct. Assume, for instance, that during the year a company disposes of some spoiled raw materials. The quantities disposed of are removed from the detailed perpetual inventory records, but adjustment of the control account is inadvertently omitted. In this situation, adequate completeness, validity, and accuracy controls may not be enough to prevent misstatement of the inventory balance. Maintenance controls, such as reconciling the perpetual inventory records to the control account and investigating differences disclosed, are also necessary to ensure that the accounts accurately reflect all operations of the business. If, in the foregoing example, the materials disposed of were not removed from either the detailed perpetual inventory records or the control account, neither the detailed records nor the control account would properly reflect the existing assets. Physically counting the inventory, reconciling the count to the accounting records, and investigating differences would be the appropriate maintenance control procedures. Physical counts, reconciliations, and investigations of differences are the principal procedures to achieve the maintenance objective. Controls to meet the maintenance objective in computerized systems are described in Chapter 11.

Physical Security. Physical security controls, often called custody controls, are designed to restrict access to assets to authorized personnel. As indicated earlier, effective protection of assets depends on adequate division of duties. If unauthorized transactions are to be prevented, whether they constitute theft or simply well-intentioned activity not consistent with the system, it is also necessary to restrict access to all items that could be used to initiate or process a transaction. Custody controls are most commonly thought of in connection with the security of negotiable assets—cash, securities, and sometimes inventory and other items that are easily convertible to cash or personal use. The concept of limited access applies equally to access to the books and records and the means of altering them, such as unused forms, unissued checks, check signature plates, files, and ledgers. Controls over the security of computer programs and stored data are particularly relevant in computerized systems where there may be potentially wide access to programs and data through terminals. Such control is normally achieved by general controls over program and data file security, as discussed further in Chapter 11.

Not all custody controls are accounting controls. If the absence of a custody control cannot cause accounting errors, the control is administrative rather than accounting in nature. For example, management may consciously accept a degree of risk of pilferage of small tools in preference to installing tool-room procedures. As long as any losses are properly accounted for, the books and financial statements will reflect accurately what has taken place. As noted earlier, it may be advisable for the auditor to include administrative controls in the evaluation of internal controls, even though it is not required by generally accepted auditing standards.

In its simplest form, custody control is evidenced by such things as a safe, a vault, a locked door, a storeroom with a custodian, or a guarded fence. Physical safeguards are useless, however, without a control that prevents unauthorized persons from entering. That control can be automated to some degree. For example, issuing a key to only one person is an elementary form of "automated" authorization to enter a locked area. Custody controls should also protect assets and records from physical harm such as accidental destruction, deterioration, or simply being mislaid.

The absence of adequate custody controls affects primarily the timing and extent of audit procedures. For example, the absence of adequate controls over the physical access to inventories that are susceptible of theft may mean that a complete inventory count must be performed at the balance sheet date, even if other controls over the inventory records are adequate. If adequate custody controls do exist, the auditor may be able to place some degree of reliance on cycle counts of portions of the inventory performed by the client during the year, or may be satisfied to observe a physical inventory count at an interim date and then roll forward inventory balances to the balance sheet date based on recorded activity.

Segregation of Duties. By dividing the custody of assets, performance of accounting procedures, and related accounting control procedures among several individuals, segregation of duties restricts the ability of employees to misappropriate assets or conceal fraud or error. Aside from the objectives of accounting control, it is usually more efficient to specialize tasks and people, provided that the volume of activity is sufficient. The control features of segregation of duties are so important, however, that this control often exists regardless of whether it leads to operating efficiencies. The potential risk of errors and fraudulent asset conversion may justify the segregation of duties even if it is otherwise inefficient. For example, in a store that sells items for cash, control considerations may justify having one person obtain the totals from a cash register for accounting purposes and another clear the machine for the next salesclerk.

If two accounting procedures related to a single transaction are handled by different people, each serves as a control on the other; a control over those procedures should be performed by a third person. For example, one bookkeeper can process a day's cash receipts received through the mail and another can post the receipts to the accounts receivable records. A third person's comparison of the total of the postings with the total receipts is a basic control that provides evidence that each operation was accurately performed. If the comparison of the postings total with the total receipts is not performed by a third person, there is an increased risk of misstatement in the accounting records resulting from impairment of the basic control. This may cause the auditor to extensively reperform the basic control, which is generally not efficient, or to not rely on the control, but to proceed to substantive tests.

Segregation of duties also serves as a deterrent to fraud or concealment of error because of the need to recruit another individual's cooperation (collusion) to conceal it. For example, the separation of responsibility for the physical security of assets and the related record keeping is a significant control over the fraudulent conversion of the assets. Similarly, the treasurer who signs checks should not be able to hide an unauthorized disbursement through the ability to make a false entry in the disbursements records. Control is even further enhanced if neither the treasurer nor the bookkeeper is responsible for periodically comparing cash on hand and in the bank with the cash records and taking appropriate action if there are any differences.

Supervision. The presence of supervisory controls affords reasonable assurance that the accounting and basic control procedures are functioning as designed at all times, not just in those instances selected by the auditor for formal review. Supervisory controls also help ensure that when errors do occur they are detected on a timely basis. Supervising the system and those who operate it has an obvious effect on the reliability of the accounting records. Effective supervision of personnel performing accounting and basic control procedures will lead to necessary modifications of the system when new types of transactions occur, corrective action when errors are revealed, and follow-up when weaknesses in the system become evident.

Many supervisory controls consist of specific, observable routines for regularly ensuring supervisors that the required basic controls are operating. The performance of these administrative routines must be documented; means of accomplishing this include checklists; exception reports; initials evidencing review of batch controls, bank reconciliations, vouchers, and the like; log books for review routines; and written reports. The documentation can then be tested by the auditor to obtain evidence of the quality and continuity of the supervisory controls.

The presence of adequate supervisory controls within an internal control system greatly affects the scope of work the auditor needs to perform to obtain a sufficient basis for reliance on any portion of the system. In the absence of supervisory controls, the auditor has no assurance that identified basic controls have operated properly and consistently throughout the period under review. Thus, the auditor must design procedures to obtain this assurance if a basis for reliance is to be formed. The auditor may accomplish this by directly testing the operation of the related basic control throughout the period. By ''spreading'' tests of the basic control throughout the period, the auditor can obtain evidence about its continued and consistent operation. On the other hand, if adequate supervisory controls exist and are tested, it is unnecessary for the auditor to spread the testing of the basic control since the supervisory controls can be relied on to ensure its proper and consistent operation.

Management's Responsibility for Internal Accounting Control Under the Foreign Corrupt Practices Act

Changes in the business and legal environment over the past decade, and in particular the Foreign Corrupt Practices Act of 1977 (the Act), have magnified the importance of internal control to management. The Act, which amended the Securities Exchange Act of 1934, has two parts: One deals with specific acts and penalties associated with certain corrupt practices; the second, with standards relating to internal accounting controls.

Illegal Payments

The Act prohibits any domestic company—or its officers, directors, employees, agents, or stockholders—from paying or offering to pay a foreign official to act on its behalf. Specifically, the law prohibits payments to foreign officials, political parties, and candidates for the purpose of obtaining or retaining business by influencing any act or decision of foreign parties in their official capacity, or by inducing such foreign parties to use their influence with a foreign government to sway any act or decision of such government. This section of the Act applies to virtually all U.S. businesses, and noncompliance with its provisions can result in fines of up to $1 million for corporations and up to $10,000 for individuals. Individuals may also be subject to imprisonment for up to five years for violations.

Internal Accounting Control

The section of the Act addressing internal accounting control imposed many legal obligations on publicly held companies. Although the penalties just described do not apply to these provisions of the Act, failure by publicly held companies to maintain appropriate books and records and systems of internal control violates the Securities Exchange Act of 1934. Specifically, the legislation established a legal requirement that every SEC registrant do the following:

A. Keep books and records that, in reasonable detail, accurately and fairly reflect transactions.
B. Maintain a system of internal accounting control sufficient to provide reasonable assurances that

> Transactions are executed in accordance with management's general or specific authorization.

> Transactions are recorded as necessary to permit preparation of financial statements in conformity with generally accepted accounting principles or any other criteria applicable to such statements, and to maintain accountability for assets.

> Access to assets is permitted only in accordance with management's general or specific authorization.

> The recorded accountability for assets is compared with the existing assets at reasonable intervals and appropriate action is taken with respect to any differences.

The requirements in B are identical to the objectives of internal accounting control as defined in SAS No. 1 (AU Section 320.28), cited earlier in this chapter.

It is clear from the legislative history of the Act that Congress' primary intent was to prevent corrupt payments to foreign officials and that the requirements for accurate books and systems of internal accounting control are intended to help accomplish that objective. The Act's provisions dealing with accurate books and records and internal accounting control are, however, considerably more far reaching in that those requirements cover *all* transactions, not only those related to illegal foreign payments. In fact, court proceedings instituted by the SEC for failure to comply with the Act's record-keeping and internal control provisions have shown that the SEC intends to enforce these provisions of the law not only in connection with illegal foreign payments, but in connection with domestic improprieties as well.

While the passage of the Act increased the need for more direct management involvement in the design and maintenance of internal accounting control systems, the auditor's responsibility for evaluating those systems remained unchanged from that prescribed by the second standard of field work in SAS No. 1. This was explicitly articulated by the AICPA in an Interpretation of SAS No. 17 (AU Section 9328) dealing with illegal acts by clients. This Interpretation stated that although auditors should be aware that some client acts coming to their attention during an audit might be illegal, SAS No. 17 ''does not require the auditor to plan his examination specifically to search for illegal acts. Furthermore, there is nothing in the [Foreign Corrupt Practices] Act or the related legislative history that purports to alter the auditor's duty to his client or the purpose of his study and evaluation of internal accounting control. The Act creates express new duties only for companies subject to the Securities Exchange Act of 1934, not for auditors'' (AU Section 9328.02).

Review Questions

7-1. What is the purpose of the required ''proper study and evaluation of the existing internal control'' according to the second standard of field work?

7-2. What is the difference between accounting controls and accounting procedures? Give an example of each.

7-3. What is the difference between internal accounting controls and administrative controls? Give an example of each.

7-4. When does the independent auditor have a responsibility to evaluate an administrative control?

7-5. Name the five general objectives of internal accounting control as specified in this book. How do they differ from the four objectives specified in SAS No. 1?

7-6. Give three reasons why a system of internal accounting control, no matter how well designed and monitored, cannot be relied on to provide complete assurance that errors and irregularities will be prevented or detected.

7-7. What is meant by the concept of reasonable assurance with respect to internal accounting control?

7-8. Name the three major transaction cycles into which most business activities can be grouped. What other cycles may exist?

7-9. Illustrate how each of the following control objectives can be achieved: completeness, validity, accuracy, maintenance.

7-10. What *two* major purposes are served by segregation of duties?

7-11. What steps should an independent auditor take when physical security is absent?

7-12. Name the two basic requirements of the Foreign Corrupt Practices Act (FCPA) of 1977. What companies are affected by the FCPA?

7-13. What effect does the FCPA have on the independent auditor's responsibilities?

Discussion Questions

7-30. Mary Baker is the bookkeeper for the Davis Plumbing and Heating Co. and is the sole office employee. She handles all billing, cash, and payroll activities, as well as the general ledger, financial statements, and tax returns. The proprietor, John Davis, knows little about accounting and trusts Ms. Baker implicitly because she is meticulous in her clerical operations, has been functioning in her capacity for 10 years, and appears well systemized (e.g., prenumbered bills, checks, etc.). Because he is quite active in the supervision of the business, Mr. Davis always signs a substantial number of regular and payroll checks in advance so that timely disbursements can be made. Mr. Davis intends to expand his business and his bank requires an audit as a condition for a loan.

> *Required:*
> a. Discuss the independent auditor's approach to the evaluation of internal accounting control in these circumstances and give some indication of how to proceed with the examination.
> b. What simple changes in procedures could you suggest to provide better internal accounting control?

7-31. The Foreign Corrupt Practices Act (FCPA) has had an impact on the attitudes of managements toward internal controls and the control environment. In this context, discuss the following:

> a. The meaning of control environment.
> b. Steps a management can take to strengthen the control environment.
> c. Requirements of the FCPA and the steps a management can take to prevent violations of the FCPA.
> d. Impact of management's FCPA compliance procedures on the audit.

7-32. Jerome Paper Company engaged you to review its internal control system. Jerome does not prelist cash receipts before they are recorded and has other weaknesses in processing collections of trade receivables, the company's largest asset. In discussing the matter with the controller, Tom Kolby, you find he is chiefly interested in economy when he assigns duties to the 15 office personnel. He feels the main considerations are that the work should be done by people who are most familiar with it, capable of doing it, and available when it has to be done.

The controller says he has excellent control over trade receivables because receivables are pledged as security for a continually renewable bank loan and the bank sends out positive confirmation requests occasionally, based on a list of pledged receivables furnished by the company each week. You learn that the bank's internal auditor is satisfied with an acceptable response on 70 percent of the requests.

Required:

a. Explain how prelisting of cash receipts strengthens internal control over cash.

b. Assume that an employee handles cash receipts from trade customers before they are recorded. List the duties that that employee should not do so as not to have the opportunity to conceal embezzlement of cash receipts.

(AICPA adapted)

AICPA Multiple Choice Questions

These questions are taken from the Auditing part of Uniform CPA Examinations. Choose the single most appropriate answer.

7–40. Internal accounting control comprises the plan of organization and the procedures and records that are concerned with the safeguarding of assets and the

    a. Decision process of management.
    b. Reliability of financial records.
    c. Authorization of transactions.
    d. Achievement of administrative objectives.

7–41. In the evaluation of internal accounting control, the auditor is basically concerned that the system provide reasonable assurance that

    a. Controls have *not* been circumvented by collusion.
    b. Errors have been prevented or detected.
    c. Operational efficiency has been achieved in accordance with management plans.
    d. Management can *not* override the system.

7–42. The basic concept of internal accounting control that recognizes that the cost of internal control should *not* exceed the benefits expected to be derived is known as

    a. Management by exception.
    b. Management responsibility.
    c. Limited liability.
    d. Reasonable assurance.

7–43. What is the independent auditor's principal purpose for conducting a study and evaluation of the existing system of internal control?

    a. To comply with generally accepted accounting principles.
    b. To obtain a measure of assurance of management's efficiency.
    c. To maintain a state of independence in mental attitude in all matters relating to the audit.
    d. To determine the nature, timing, and extent of subsequent audit work.

7–44. Which of the following would be *least* likely to suggest to an auditor that the client's management may have overridden the internal control system?

    a. Differences are always disclosed on a computer exception report.

b. Management does *not* correct internal control weaknesses that it knows about.

c. There have been two new controllers this year.

d. There are numerous delays in preparing timely internal financial reports.

7–45. The auditor would be *least* likely to be concerned about internal control as it relates to

a. Land and buildings.

b. Common stock.

c. Shareholder meetings.

d. Minutes of board of directors meetings.

7–46. Which of the following is an internal control weakness for a company whose inventory of supplies consists of a large number of individual items?

a. Supplies of relatively little value are expensed when purchased.

b. The cycle basis is used for physical counts.

c. The storekeeper is responsible for maintenance of perpetual inventory records.

d. Perpetual inventory records are maintained only for items of significant value.

7–47. For internal control purposes, which of the following individuals should preferably be responsible for the distribution of payroll checks?

a. Bookkeeper.

b. Payroll clerk.

c. Cashier.

d. Receptionist.

7–48. Which of the following is an effective internal accounting control over cash payments?

a. Signed checks should be mailed under the supervision of the check signer.

b. Spoiled checks that have been voided should be disposed of immediately.

c. Checks should be prepared only by persons responsible for cash receipts and cash disbursements.

d. A check-signing machine with two signatures should be utilized.

7–49. Which of the following represents the greatest point of contrast in comparing the work of the CPA and the internal auditor?

a. Attention given to system of internal control.

b. Gathering of evidence.

c. Emphasis on administrative controls.

d. Use of tests and samples.

7–50. The Foreign Corrupt Practices Act requires that

a. Auditors engaged to examine the financial statements of publicly held companies report all illegal payments to the SEC.

b. Publicly held companies establish independent audit committees to monitor the effectiveness of their system of internal control.

c. U.S. firms doing business abroad report sizable payments to non-U.S. citizens to the Justice Department.

d. Publicly held companies devise and maintain an adequate system of internal accounting control.

7–51. Of the following statements about an internal accounting control system, which one is correct?

a. The maintenance of the system of internal accounting control is an important responsibility of the internal auditor.
b. Administrative controls relate directly to the safeguarding of assets and the systems of authorization and approval.
c. Because of the cost-benefit relationship, internal accounting control procedures may be applied on a test basis in some circumstances.
d. Internal accounting control procedures reasonably ensure that collusion among employees can *not* occur.

Problems and Cases

7-60. For each of the following situations, indicate whether there are weaknesses in internal accounting control and, if so, indicate the errors or irregularities that could occur (consider each independently):

a. Sales are authorized by the sales order department without reference to the credit department.
b. Sales invoices are not reexamined for correct prices and extensions.
c. Accounts receivable write-offs are authorized by the credit department.
d. Complete purchase orders are furnished to receiving department personnel who count incoming shipments and prepare receiving reports.
e. Incoming mail is opened by the cashier, who lists checks received, makes deposits, and records cash receipts.
f. Reconciliation between the accounts receivable subsidiary ledger and the control account is performed monthly by the general ledger bookkeeper, who also posts cash receipts.
g. Monthly statements to customers are prepared and mailed by the cashier.
h. A payroll clerk prepares payroll checks, has them signed by the Comptroller, and distributes them to the foremen of each department.
i. Disbursement checks to vendors are prepared by the cashier and signed by the Comptroller, who returns them to the cashier for mailing.
j. Supporting documents (purchase order, receiving report, invoice) are not canceled at the time of disbursement.
k. Monthly bank statements are reconciled to the cash book and general ledger by the Comptroller.

7-61. The Y Company, a client of your firm, has come to you with the following problem: It has three clerical employees who must perform the following functions:

1. Maintain general ledger.
2. Maintain accounts payable ledger.
3. Maintain accounts receivable ledger.
4. Prepare checks for signature.
5. Maintain disbursements journal.
6. Issue credits on returns and allowances.
7. Reconcile the bank account.
8. Handle and deposit cash receipts.

Assuming that there is no problem regarding the ability of any of the employees, the company requests that you assign these functions to the three employees in such a manner that the highest degree of internal accounting control is achieved. It may be assumed that these employees will perform no other accounting functions than the ones listed and that any accounting functions not listed will be performed by persons other than these three employees.

Required:
a. State how you would distribute these functions among the three employees. Assume that with the exception of the simple jobs of the bank reconciliation and the issuance of credits on returns and allowances, all functions require an equal amount of time.
b. List four unsatisfactory combinations of the functions.

(AICPA adapted)

7-62. Dunbar Camera Manufacturing, Inc., is a manufacturer of high-priced precision motion picture cameras in which the specifications of component parts are vital to the manufacturing process. Dunbar buys valuable camera lenses and large quantities of sheet metal and screws. Screws and lenses are ordered by Dunbar and are billed by the vendors on the basis of weight. The receiving clerk is responsible for documenting the quality and quantity of merchandise received.

A preliminary review of the system of internal control indicates that the following procedures are being followed:

Receiving Report:
1. Properly approved purchase orders, which are prenumbered, are filed numerically. The copy sent to the receiving clerk is an exact duplicate of the copy sent to the vendor. Receipts of merchandise are recorded on the duplicate copy by the receiving clerk.

Sheet Metal:
2. The company receives sheet metal by railroad. The railroad independently weighs the sheet metal and reports the weight and date of receipt on a bill of lading (waybill), which accompanies all deliveries. The receiving clerk only checks the weight on the waybill to the purchase order.

Screws:
3. The receiving clerk opens cartons containing screws, then inspects and weighs the contents. The weight is converted to number of units by means of conversion charts. The receiving clerk then checks the computed quantity to the purchase order.

Camera Lenses:
4. Each camera lens is delivered in a separate corrugated carton. Cartons are counted as they are received by the receiving clerk and the number of cartons is checked to purchase orders.

Required:
a. Explain why the internal control procedures—as they apply individually to receiving reports and the receipt of sheet metal, screws, and camera lenses—are adequate or inadequate. *Do not discuss recommendations for improvements.*.

b. What financial statement distortions may arise because of the inadequacies in Dunbar's system of internal control, and how may they occur?

(AICPA adapted)

7-63. The division of the following duties is meant to provide the best possible controls for the Meridian Paint Company, a small wholesale store.

a. Assemble supporting documents for disbursements and prepare checks for signature.
b. Sign general disbursement checks.
c. Record checks written in the cash disbursements and payroll journals.
d. Cancel supporting documents to prevent their reuse and mail disbursement checks to suppliers.
e. Approve credit for customers.
f. Bill customers and record the invoices in the sales journal and subsidiary ledger.
g. Open the mail and prepare a prelisting of cash receipts.
h. Record cash receipts in the cash journal and subsidiary ledger.
i. Prepare daily cash deposits.
j. Deliver daily cash deposits to the bank.
k. Assemble the payroll time cards and prepare the payroll checks.
l. Sign payroll checks.
m. Post the journals to the general ledger.
n. Reconcile the accounts receivable subsidiary account with the control account.
o. Prepare monthly statements for customers by copying the subsidiary ledger account.
p. Reconcile the monthly statements from vendors with the subsidiary accounts payable account.
q. Reconcile the bank account.

Required:

You are to divide the accounting-related duties a through q among Robert Smith, Jane Cooper, and Bill Miller. All of the responsibilities are assumed to take about the same amount of time and must be divided equally between the two employees, Smith and Cooper. Both employees are equally competent. Miller, who is president of the Company, is willing to perform a maximum of three of the functions, provided that no great amount of detail is involved. He prefers not to sign checks.

(AICPA adapted)

7-64. In 1986, XY Company purchased over $10 million of office equipment under its "special" ordering system, with individual orders ranging from $5000 to $30,000. "Special" orders entail low-volume items that have been included in an authorized user's budget. Department heads include in their annual budget requests the types of equipment and their estimated cost. The budget, which limits the types and dollar amounts of office equipment a department head can requisition, is approved at the beginning of the year by the board of directors. Department heads prepare a purchase requisition form for equipment and forward the requisition to the purchasing department. XY's "special" ordering system functions as follows:

Purchasing:

Upon receiving a purchase requisition, one of five buyers verifies that the person requesting the equipment is a department head. The buyer then selects the appropriate vendor by searching the various vendor catalogs on file. The buyer then phones the vendor, requesting a price quotation, and gives the vendor a verbal order. A prenumbered purchase order is then processed, with the original sent to the vendor, a copy to the department head, a copy to receiving, a copy to accounts payable, and a copy filed in the open requisition file. When the buyer is orally informed by the receiving department that the item has been received, the buyer transfers the purchase order from the unfilled file to the filled file. Once a month the buyer reviews the unfilled file to follow up and expedite open orders.

Receiving:

The receiving department receives a copy of the purchase order. When equipment is received, the receiving clerk stamps the purchase order with the date received, and, if applicable, in red pen prints any differences between quantity on the purchase order and quantity received. The receiving clerk forwards the stamped purchase order and equipment to the requisitioning department head and notifies the purchasing department orally.

Accounts Payable:

Upon receipt of a purchase order, the accounts payable clerk files the purchase order in the open purchase order file. When a vendor invoice is received, the invoice is matched with the applicable purchase order, and a payable is set up by debiting the equipment account of the department requesting the items. Unpaid invoices are filed by due date and, at due date, a check is prepared. The invoice and purchase order are filed by purchase order number in a paid invoice file, and then the check is forwarded to the treasurer for signature.

Treasurer:

Checks received daily from the accounts payable department are sorted into two groups: those over $10,000 and those $10,000 and less. Checks for $10,000 and less are machine-signed. The cashier maintains the key and signature plate to the check-signing machine, and maintains a record of usage of the check-signing machine. All checks over $10,000 are signed by the treasurer or the controller.

Required:

Describe the internal accounting control weaknesses relating to purchases and payments of ''special'' orders of XY Company for each of the following functions:

    a. Purchasing.
    b. Receiving.
    c. Accounts payable.
    d. Treasurer.

(AICPA adapted)

7-65. Identify control weaknesses in the following case and suggest ways of correcting those weaknesses.

The Vacation Paradise Company, Ltd., is engaged in selling convention vacation packages throughout North America. Salespeople are paid on a commission basis, selling the trips based on standard prices established by the marketing department.

Salespeople may negotiate special cut rates; however, these are subject to approval by the marketing manager, Mr. East. Special commitments obtained by the salespeople are submitted to Mr. East, who signs them to indicate his approval and then returns them to the salespeople. Specially priced commitments and regularly priced commitments are then forwarded by the salespeople to the data input department where a clerk reviews the special commitments for the presence of Mr. East's signature and batches the input, totaling trips sold. Batching procedures and computer input controls are to be considered adequate.

The computer processes each commitment by extending the number of trips by the standard price stored on the pricing file, or in specially negotiated situations, by the price on the input document. The sales file, accounts receivable file, and reservation file are updated and invoices produced. An exception report of special prices is produced by data processing and sent to the salespeople to ensure that the specially negotiated commitments were processed correctly.

7–66. The Witt Company is engaged in manufacturing. Certain features of its operating methods are described in the following list.

You are to consider the procedure for each of the activities as described and point out the existing deficiencies, if any, in internal control, including an explanation of the errors or irregularities that might occur in view of each weakness and your recommendations as to changes in procedures that could be made to correct the weakness.

1. When materials are ordered, a duplicate of the purchase order is sent to the receiving department. When the materials are received, the receiving clerk records the receipt on the copy of the order, which is then sent to the accounting department to support the entry to accounts payable and material purchases. The materials are then taken to stores where the quantity is entered on bin records.

2. Time cards of employees are sent to a tabulating machine department, which prepares punched cards for use in the preparation of payrolls, payroll checks, and labor cost distribution records. The payroll checks are compared with the payrolls and signed by an official of the company, who returns them to the supervisor of the tabulating department for distribution to employees.

3. The company has an employee bond subscription plan under which employees subscribe to bonds and pay in installments by deductions from their salaries. The cashier keeps the supply of unissued bonds in a safe, together with the records showing each employee's subscription and payments to date. The amounts of unissued bonds in the hands of the cashier and the balances due from employees are controlled on the general ledger, kept in another department. However, the employees may, if they desire, pay any remaining balance to the cashier and receive their bonds.

   When an employee makes a payment, the cashier notes the amount in the records, delivers the bond, and receives a receipt from the employee for the amount of the bond. The cashier deposits bond cash received in an employee bond bank account and submits a report showing the transaction to the general ledger department; this report is used as a basis for the necessary adjustments of the control accounts. Periodic surprise counts of bonds on hand are made by independent employees, who compare the amounts of unissued bonds and employees' unpaid balances with the control accounts.

   During the cashier's lunch hour or at other times when the cashier is required to be absent, another employee, with keys to the safe in which unissued bonds and employee bond payment records are kept, comes in and carries out the same procedures as enumerated above.

4. A sales branch of the company has an office force consisting of the manager and one assistant. The branch has a local bank account that is used to pay branch

expenses. This is in the name of "The Witt Company, Special Account." Checks drawn on the account require the manager's signature or the signature of the treasurer of the company. Bank statements and canceled checks are returned by the bank to the manager, who retains them in the files after making the reconciliation. Reports of disbursements are prepared by the manager and submitted to the home office on scheduled dates.

(AICPA adapted)

7-67. The town of Commuter Park operates a private parking lot near the railroad station for the benefit of town residents. The guard on duty issues annual prenumbered parking stickers to residents who submit an application form and show evidence of residency. The sticker is affixed to the auto and allows the resident to park anywhere in the lot for 12 hours if four quarters are placed in the parking meter. Applications are maintained in the guard office at the lot. The guard checks to see that only residents are using the lot and that no resident has parked without paying the required meter fee.

Once a week the guard on duty, who has a master key for all meters, takes the coins from the meters and places them in a locked steel box. The guard delivers the box to the town storage building where it is opened, and the coins are manually counted by a storage department clerk, who records the total cash counted on a "Weekly Cash Report." This report is sent to the town accounting department. The storage department clerk puts the cash in a safe and on the following day the cash is picked up by the town's treasurer, who manually recounts the cash, prepares the bank deposit slip, and delivers the deposit to the bank. The deposit slip, authenticated by the bank teller, is sent to the accounting department where it is filed with the "Weekly Cash Report."

Required:

Describe weaknesses in the existing system and recommend one or more improvements for each of the weaknesses to strengthen the internal control over the parking lot cash receipts.

Organize your answer as follows:

Weakness	Recommended Improvement(s)

(AICPA adapted)

7-68. Western Meat Processing Company buys and processes livestock for sale to supermarkets. In connection with your examination of the company's financial statements, you have prepared the following notes based on your review of procedures:

1. Each livestock buyer submits a daily report of purchases to the plant superintendent. This report shows the dates of purchase and expected delivery, the vendor, and the number, weights, and type of livestock purchased. As shipments are received, any available plant employee counts the number of each type received and places a check mark beside this quantity on the buyer's report. When all shipments listed on the report have been received, the report is returned to the buyer.

2. Vendors' invoices, after a clerical check, are sent to the buyer for approval and returned to the accounting department. A disbursement voucher and a check for the approved amount are prepared in the accounting department. Checks are forwarded to the treasurer for signature. The treasurer's office sends signed checks directly to the buyer for delivery to the vendor.

3. Livestock carcasses are processed by lots. Each lot is assigned a number. At the end of each day a tally sheet reporting the lots processed, the number and type of animals in each lot, and the carcass weight is sent to the accounting department, where a perpetual inventory record of processed carcasses and their weights is maintained.

4. Processed carcasses are stored in a refrigerated cooler located in a small building adjacent to the employee parking lot. The cooler is locked when the plant is not open, and a company guard is on duty when the employees report for work and leave at the end of their shifts. Supermarket truck drivers wishing to pick up their orders have been instructed to contact someone in the plant if no one is in the cooler.

5. Substantial quantities of by-products are produced and stored, either in the cooler or elsewhere in the plant. By-products are initially accounted for as they are sold. At this time the sales manager prepares a two-part form; one copy serves as authorization to transfer the goods to the customer and the other becomes the basis for billing the customer.

Required:

For each of the numbered notes 1 to 5, state:

a. What the specific internal control objective(s) should be at the stage of the operating cycle described by the note.

b. The control weaknesses in the present procedures, if any, and suggestions for improvement, if any.

(AICPA adapted)

7–69. The United Charities organization in your town has engaged you to examine its statement of receipts and disbursements. United Charities solicits contributions from local donors and then apportions the contributions among local charitable organizations.

The officers and directors are local bankers, professionals, and other leaders of the community. A cashier and a clerk are the only full-time salaried employees. The only records maintained by the organization are a cashbook and a checkbook. The directors prefer not to have a system of pledges.

Contributions are solicited by a number of volunteer workers. The workers are not restricted as to the area of their solicitation and may work among their friends, neighbors, coworkers, and the like, as convenient for them. To ensure blanket coverage of the town, new volunteer workers are welcomed.

Contributions are in the form of cash or checks. They are received by United Charities from the solicitors, who personally deliver the contributions they have collected, or directly from the donors by mail or by personal delivery.

The solicitors complete official receipts, which they give to the donors when contributions are received. These official receipts have attached stubs that the solicitors fill in with the names of the donors and the amounts of the contributions. The solicitors turn in the stubs with the contributions to the cashier. No control is maintained over the number of blank receipts given to the solicitors or the number of receipt stubs turned in with the contributions.

Required:

Discuss the control procedures you would recommend for greater assurance that all contributions received by the solicitors are turned over to the organization. (Do not discuss the control of the funds in the organization's office.)

(AICPA adapted)

Chapter 8
Assessing Inherent Risk and Control Risk

The two major components of audit risk were discussed in Chapter 6 in connection with planning and controlling an engagement. The first component, the risk that the financial statements contain material misstatements, is beyond the auditor's ability to control or change; however, the auditor can and does assess that risk as a basis for determining the nature, timing, and extent of audit procedures. This chapter discusses the ways auditors assess risk, including the performance of compliance tests, under different audit strategies. It also describes and illustrates different means of documenting the risk assessment procedures performed and their results. The following chapter deals with the second component of audit risk—detection risk—and the substantive tests the auditor performs to reduce it to an acceptably low level.

Risk assessment is the process of arriving at an informed judgment of the risk of cumulatively material misstatements reaching the financial statements. That risk has two aspects, inherent risk and control risk. The auditor assesses those risks, within the context of materiality, during the planning stage of an engagement as a basis for determining the level of assurance required from substantive tests. Inherent and control risks should be assessed at the account balance level, and the assessment should address individual audit objectives.

Risk assessment aids the auditor in identifying

• Inherent risk conditions that create a high risk of material misstatement and thus require emphasis on particular audit objectives and accounts.

- Accounts that can be subjected to limited audit procedures because the risk of material misstatement is low.
- Internal accounting and, in some situations, administrative controls that reduce the risk of material misstatement and may enable the auditor to restrict substantive tests for particular audit objectives and accounts.

Obtaining Information to Assess Inherent Risk

The basis for the auditor's assessment of both inherent and control risks is information about various aspects of the client and its business. For a continuing client, much of the relevant information is available from prior years' working papers and needs to be updated, not gathered all over again. Both client personnel and the auditor need to be aware, however, of a dangerous tendency to treat changed circumstances perfunctorily. A client's personnel can easily forget changes that took place during the year because they have become routine by the time the auditor makes inquiries; the auditor can easily treat significant changes as trivial and fail to think through their implications. An auditor approaching a recurring engagement must remember that gradually changing conditions can easily make last year's risk assessments obsolete and a misleading guide to the nature and extent of procedures required. Accordingly, the auditor should exercise special care in planning a recurring engagement. Audit tests based on the previous year's assessments should not be started before reviewing changed circumstances.

The information needed for assessing inherent and control risks is obtained from many sources and is documented in a number of places in the audit working papers. Most of the information-gathering procedures are performed during the planning stage of the audit; however, the auditor is likely to obtain additional information about the client throughout the engagement and should consider that information as well in determining the nature, timing, and extent of audit procedures.

As discussed in Chapter 6, the inherent risks in an entity result from both *conditions* that are not under the entity's control and *characteristics* of the transactions it enters into and related account balances. Because inherent risk conditions relate to changes in general business conditions, new governmental regulations, and other economic factors, they are generally not addressed by the entity's internal control system. Inherent risk characteristics, in contrast, often are addressed by internal controls. For that reason, it is for the most part not practicable to assess inherent risk characteristics independently from control risk.

Information about the client's business and industry, recent financial information, prior-year audit results, and a knowledge of applicable accounting, auditing, and regulatory standards are useful primarily for identifying inherent risk conditions. Those sources of information may also be useful to the auditor in identifying inherent risk characteristics and the controls that the client may have created in response to those characteristics. The paragraphs that follow describe how the auditor gathers or updates information used for assessing inherent risk conditions. Later sections of this chapter describe how the auditor makes the *combined* assessment of inherent risk characteristics and control risk.

Obtaining Knowledge of the Client's Business and Industry

Relevant information about the client's business includes its product lines, sources and methods of supply, marketing and distribution methods, sources of financing, and production methods. The auditor should also obtain information about the locations and relative size of the client's operating plants, divisions, and subsidiaries, and the extent to which management is decentralized. Concerning the client's industry, the auditor needs to know such matters as industry characteristics and the client's position in the industry. Industry conditions that can affect a client include its market share and relative size, industry practices (for example, with regard to quantity discounts and consignment sales), and competition from other industries. If the client operates in more than one industry, the auditor should obtain information about each industry in which the client has significant activities. A variety of sources of information about the client's business and industry are available to the auditor, including government statistics; economic, financial, industry, and trade journals; client publications and brochures; where applicable, internal audit reports; and reports prepared on the entity, its competitors, or its industry by underwriters, merchant bankers, and securities dealers.

The auditor should also learn about economic conditions that affect the client's business and industry. Economic conditions affect an entity's continuing ability to generate and collect revenues, operate profitably, and provide a return to investors. Unfavorable economic conditions may raise questions about the recoverability of the entity's assets, the measurement of its liabilities, and, ultimately, its ability to remain in business. Unfavorable economic conditions may also increase the likelihood of intentional financial statement misrepresentations.

Analyzing Recent Financial Information

The auditor reviews recent financial statements and other available financial information and performance indicators to identify which account balances and classes of transactions are material and which are immaterial and to identify relationships among accounts. In addition, comparing recent financial information with prior-year financial data and with budgets for the current period may alert the auditor to favorable or unfavorable operating trends, significant deviations from expected results, recent financing or investment activities, and other changes in the entity's business. Analytical review of recent financial information thus serves as an early warning of unexpected changes. The nature and extent of the review vary with the size and complexity of the client's business and the availability of appropriate financial information.

Reviewing Prior Years' Audit Results

The knowledge obtained from reviewing prior years' audit results assists the auditor in determining the likelihood of material misstatements in account balances in the current year, thereby affecting the current year's assessment of inherent and control risks and the level of assurance required from substantive tests. For example, when there have been no changes in the system of internal control and low error rates were found in prior years, this knowledge should be considered in planning substantive tests.

Prior-year working papers that are ordinarily reviewed include financial information, the documented understanding of the client's business and industry, and the documented risk assessment. The auditor should also refer to the prior year's documentation of errors found in the course of the audit and of the matters brought to the attention of the engagement partner, particularly as they relate to significant accounting and auditing matters such as the nature, cause, and amounts of prior-year errors found by the auditor—both those that resulted in adjustment of the financial statements and those that did not because they were immaterial.

Obtaining Knowledge of Applicable Accounting, Auditing, and Regulatory Standards

The auditor's understanding of the business also includes knowledge of the accounting policies and practices employed by the client. The auditor should evaluate the appropriateness of those policies and practices in the light of both the terms and methods by which the client conducts its business and generally accepted accounting principles. If the client has changed any accounting policies or practices during the current year, the auditor should determine whether those changes were made in response to changes in its methods of doing business or changes in accounting or regulatory standards, and should consider their possible effects on the audit.

The auditor should identify any accounting and auditing standards that warrant special attention by the client or the auditor in the current year, such as standards that have become applicable or have taken on increased significance because of changes in the client's business or because of significant, unusual, or nonrecurring transactions. The client may not be aware that such standards apply to its financial statements or may not fully understand how to apply the standards. New or changed regulatory standards may have a similar impact on the client's financial statements. The auditor should consider discussing such standards with management at the earliest possible date so that it can take action to address them properly and on a timely basis.

Related Party Transactions

One specific aspect of the auditor's responsibility to understand the client's business pertains to knowledge of the client's relationships and transactions with related parties. Statement of Financial Accounting Standards (SFAS) No. 57, *Related Party Disclosures* (Accounting Standards Section R36), sets forth disclosure requirements with regard to related parties and contains (in Section R36.406) the following definition of related parties:

> Affiliates of the enterprise; entities for which investments are accounted for by the equity method by the enterprise; trusts for the benefit of employees, such as pension and profit-sharing trusts that are managed by or under the trusteeship of management; principal owners of the enterprise; its management; members of the immediate families of principal owners of the enterprise and its management; and other parties with which the enterprise may deal if one party controls or can significantly influence the management or operating policies of the other to an extent that one of the transacting parties might be prevented from fully pursuing its own separate interests. Another party also is a related party if it can significantly influence the management or operating policies of the transacting parties or if it has an ownership interest in one of the transacting parties and can significantly influence the other to an extent that one or more of the transacting parties might be prevented from fully pursuing its own separate interests.

The terms "affiliates," "control," "immediate family," "management," and "principal owners" are further defined in SFAS No. 57.

Under SAS No. 45 (AU Section 334), the auditor has the responsibility to understand the client's business activities well enough to evaluate the appropriateness of the client's disclosures regarding related parties, including the propriety of any client representations about related party transactions having taken place at terms equivalent to arm's-length transactions. AU Section 334 sets forth specific audit procedures that the auditor should consider in determining the existence of related parties, procedures intended to provide guidance for identifying material transactions with related parties, and procedures that should be considered in examining identified related party transactions.

The client has the ultimate responsibility for identifying, recording, and disclosing related party transactions, and the auditor should obtain specific representation from client management that management is aware of, and has fulfilled, that responsibility. The auditor's procedures, however, should extend beyond inquiry of, and obtaining such representations from, management. The auditor should also review other potential sources of information, such as proxy material, stockholder listings, and minutes of meetings of the board of directors and executive or operating committees. To the extent possible, related parties should be identified at the beginning of the audit and the names distributed to all members of the audit team, including those responsible for examining other divisions or subsidiaries of the enterprise, to aid them in identifying related party transactions in the course of the audit work. The internal controls that the client uses to identify related parties and transactions should be reviewed and evaluated to determine the nature and scope of audit tests necessary to identify related party transactions.

The auditor should also consider any business conditions that might give rise to related party transactions. For example, a significant portion of management compensation may be in the form of bonuses, the amount of which is dependent on the company's earnings performance and stock price. In a year of declining sales, members of management may arrange to have companies owned or controlled by the client make significant purchases, in order to support its earnings and stock price. Even though these transactions may have been effected on the same terms as nonrelated party transactions, disclosure in the financial statements is necessary for a proper understanding of the results of operations for the year. In addition, the auditor should consider other implications of these transactions, such as the effect of the sales on the assessment of the adequacy of any provisions for sales returns and allowances.

Assessing Control Risk: Minimum Requirements

The information gathered or updated about the client also contributes to the auditor's identification of the principal inherent risk characteristics associated with each account balance or class of transactions. As noted earlier, those characteristics are typically addressed by the enterprise's system of accounting procedures and controls. To the extent that there are controls that address the inherent risk characteristics of accounts, those risks are assessed as part of the assessment of control risk. This section of the chapter describes the minimum amount of work the auditor must do in assessing control risk and how the knowledge obtained as a result of that work is documented.

The authoritative literature, in the second standard of field work (AU Section 320.01), requires the auditor to study and evaluate the client's internal control system in determining the nature, timing, and extent of audit procedures. The extent of the study needed depends on the audit strategy that will be followed in the particular engagement. If the audit strategy calls for reliance on specific internal controls, the auditor evaluates and documents the design of those controls and performs and documents compliance tests of them. On the other hand, if no reliance on specific controls is planned, the control risk assessment can be limited to consideration of the control environment and understanding the flow of transactions through the accounting systems. (AU Section 320.53 refers to these two activities as the *preliminary phase* of the review of internal control. That term is not used in this book because in many audits the "preliminary phase" is the only phase of the review that is performed.)

SAS No. 47, *Audit Risk and Materiality in Conducting an Audit* (AU Section 312), requires the auditor to assess and consider control risk; Section 320 of SAS No. 1 requires the auditor to study and evaluate internal control. The two requirements are identical; they are both met by performing the audit procedures described in this chapter. The extent of the study and evaluation of internal control—which is essentially the issue of whether compliance tests of specific controls are to be performed—can vary. The more extensive the study and evaluation, the more likely it is that control risk will be assessed as being low. While the linkage between the risk model set forth in SAS No. 47 and the second standard of field work is not explicit, at the time of this writing a task force of the ASB is considering revising the language of Section 320 to conform it to the language of SAS No. 47. In any event, there is no difference conceptually between assessing control risk and studying and evaluating internal control.

Developing an Understanding of the Control Environment and Accounting Systems

The auditor obtains information about the control environment to determine whether it appears to be conducive to the maintenance of reliable systems of accounting and control procedures and to determine the extent to which it reduces the incentives and opportunities for deliberate distortions of the financial statements by management. An understanding of the flow of transactions through the accounting systems provides the auditor with a general knowledge of the various classes of transactions, their volume and typical dollar values, and the procedures by which each is authorized, executed, initially recorded, and subsequently processed, including the methods of data processing.

The auditor is also generally interested in the apparent presence or absence of controls over completeness, validity, accuracy, and maintenance of accounting records and of controls over access to assets; that information helps the auditor to identify the possible misstatements that could occur and to design and carry out substantive tests to detect those misstatements. Furthermore, controls over the completeness of recorded transactions usually cannot be ignored regardless of the audit strategy adopted.

The auditor's understanding of both the control environment and the flow of transactions ordinarily is obtained by a combination of previous experience with the entity, reference to prior-year working papers, inquiry, observation, and reference to client-prepared descriptions of the systems or other appropriate documentation. Those sources also provide information about specific internal controls that the auditor may be interested in for the purpose of designing appropriate substantive tests or for performing compliance tests.

Prior Year's Working Papers. In a recurring examination, much of the information about the control environment and the flow of transactions is already available in the prior year's working papers. This information should be used to the fullest extent possible; however, it should be thoroughly reviewed and updated each year.

If a client changes auditors, professional courtesy calls for the predecessor auditor to make certain information in the working papers available to the new auditor. The predecessor auditor's working papers can be a convenient source of information about the accounting systems, internal controls, and accounting principles used by the client, as well as the composition of beginning balances of individual accounts, although most of this information can also be obtained from the client.

Interviews and Client Manuals. Interviewing is one of the most effective ways to gain an initial understanding of the client's accounting systems and related controls. Interviews with client personnel who are knowledgeable about the accounting systems and controls can provide the auditor with an understanding of how the company's accounting, internal control, and related activities are carried out. In those interviews, questions and answers can be highly detailed, specific, and directed because the auditor and knowledgeable client personnel know the types of information the auditor needs. Deciding how many interviews are required is a matter of judgment, and avoiding omissions or duplications may be difficult in a large and complex operation. Some auditors like to interview both those who perform accounting functions and their supervisors early in the audit; others defer interviews with nonsupervisory personnel until later, usually during the testing phase. Interviews are sometimes accompanied by observation of the accounting personnel performing their tasks; client personnel may prefer to explain what they do by showing the auditor specific examples of their work.

Interviewing personnel who are immediately responsible for performing procedures and operating controls enables the auditor to learn about the main features of the accounting and control systems and about potential problem areas with implications for internal control or the financial statements. Auditors are sometimes reluctant to take up the time of operating managers, but a skilled interviewer can learn all that is needed from a supervisor or middle manager in a short time. Potential interviewees are usually willing to oblige after proper introduction, and the time spent is a good investment in more intelligent planning of the audit and evaluation of the results.

Many companies, particularly large and complex ones, maintain extensive manuals of policies and procedures. The auditor should obtain a complete set of procedures manuals covering accounting and internal control activities; familiarity with those manuals will help the auditor conduct more insightful interviews with client accounting personnel. The extent to which it is useful to obtain manuals of activities peripherally related to accounting, such as purchasing and personnel policies, depends on the client's systems. Although those procedures manuals can often help to clarify an auditor's understanding of a particular phase of a client's system, they are often too detailed and extensive to contribute effectively to the initial effort to understand the client's accounting and control systems. Instead, they often serve as major reference sources as the audit progresses.

Computerized Systems. If the client's accounting systems are computerized, the auditor also needs a general understanding of the principles of computers and computer processing and how those principles are applied in the client's systems. The auditor should become familiar with the hardware and software used to process financially significant applications. This information serves as a basis for identifying the client's significant computer applications, identifying purchased accounting software, ascertaining the likely scope of general controls, and determining whether audit software may be usable in the audit. The auditor generally obtains the relevant information by inquiry of data processing management. The auditor should also consider whether specialized skills are needed to assess the effect of EDP on the audit, to understand the flow of transactions, or to design and perform audit procedures.

Assessing the Control Environment

In assessing the control environment, the auditor considers factors that contribute to its quality and forms an overall conclusion about the environment. The factors that affect an enterprise's control environment were outlined in Chapter 7. Some of those factors affect the entity's ability to maintain a reliable system of internal accounting controls. Other factors affect management's ability to make the informed judgments that are necessary to prepare financial statements. Still other factors affect the entity's ability to restrict the opportunity for management fraud. All of those factors are interrelated. The auditor should consider them both individually and collectively in assessing the extent to which they contribute to the control environment.

Management's review of various operating reports is an aspect of the control environment that the auditor frequently considers important because it may provide evidence about the entity's accounting and control systems. In assessing the usefulness of such reviews, the auditor should consider:

- The competence of the individuals reviewing the reports. They should have an adequate level of business acumen and technical expertise and a general knowledge of the company's operations.
- The ability of the individuals performing the reviews to take corrective action. They should be adequately positioned within the organization to act effectively.
- The independence of the individuals performing the reviews. The individuals should be independent of those who perform the work to which the control is applied, both functionally (that is, there should be adequate segregation of duties) and motivationally (for example, intense review by a vice president might be of less value from the auditor's standpoint if the vice president's compensation is based on operating results that the individual can manipulate).

The independence of the manager who reviews operating reports is a particularly important consideration in audits of small businesses that are dominated by owner-managers or others who have the authority to establish policies and make decisions regarding how business objectives are to be pursued. Determining the extent to which their reviews enhance the control environment often presents a dilemma for the auditor. On the one hand, owner-manager reviews may compensate for an otherwise weak internal control system by demonstrating the importance of control procedures to other employees and by providing an additional level of segregation of duties in the accounting function. On the other hand, an increased potential for management override of lower-level controls exists in entities dominated by owner-managers. Since there is normally no level of review above that of management, this may limit the contribution of management reviews to the control environment, particularly if management's objectives regarding the financial statements do not coincide with those of the auditor—as would be the case if management's primary concern were maximizing reported earnings rather than fair presentation in conformity with GAAP. Auditing standards at present provide little guidance on how the auditor should consider the effect of management reviews on the control environment or on the auditor's assessment of control risk.

After considering all of the factors that contribute to the control environment, the auditor reaches an overall conclusion as to the extent to which the environment is conducive to the maintenance of reliable internal controls and reduces the likelihood of intentional distortion of the financial statements by management. If the auditor concludes that the control environment is favorable, there is a lower risk that the system of controls will be overridden or bypassed and that misstatements may occur. That, in turn, assists the auditor in determining the nature, timing, and extent of other audit procedures, including both compliance tests and substantive tests.

Documenting Accounting Systems

The auditor's documentation of the understanding of the internal control system may be limited to a record of the reasons for deciding not to rely on specific controls. The authoritative literature does not require that the understanding of the internal control system be documented if the auditor does not plan to rely on specific controls to restrict substantive tests. Many CPA firms exceed professional standards, however, and require documentation of at least the accounting systems. That documentation usually includes a record of the significant transaction types and principal accounting procedures, files, ledgers, and reports.

The accounting systems may be documented in the form of narratives or flowcharts. Flowcharts are symbolic diagrams that express procedures in graphic form and thus facilitate comprehension and communication of information. While the degree of detail required in a flowchart varies, basically there are two different types of flowcharts, each with different objectives. *Overview flowcharts*, described subsequently, are particularly useful for recording the understanding of the accounting systems when no compliance tests are planned. *Systems flowcharts*, described in a later section, are used primarily to document the design of specific internal controls when compliance tests are planned.

Flowcharts are appropriate for all engagements, regardless of size or complexity. On many recurring engagements, flowcharts will already have been prepared; they should be reviewed and updated annually and used as long as they continue to be relevant. A complete redrawing of flowcharts annually is usually unnecessary unless the underlying procedures have changed or the clarity of the flowcharts has become impaired as a result of previous amendments. Supporting documentation—such as copies of (or extracts from) accounting records, procedures manuals, and filled-in specimen forms or documents—should be filed with the flowcharts to aid the auditor in understanding the system.

It is often necessary to prepare more than one flowchart to cover an entire transaction cycle. For example, within the buying cycle, separate flowcharts may be necessary for the purchase of goods or services and for the payment of wages. The decision to prepare separate flowcharts depends on the significance of the transactions and whether the accounting procedures and reports generated are different for different types of transactions.

The flowcharting symbols described and explained in Figure 8.1 should be used for both types of flowcharts. Flowcharts should flow from left to right and should be clear and simple. Only procedures, controls, documents (or copies of documents), and reports that have audit significance need be shown. As a rule, the degree of detail documented in the flowcharts should be the minimum needed to carry out the audit strategy.

An overview flowchart displays, normally on one page, a complete transaction processing cycle in summary form. It provides the auditor with information about the accounting systems within that cycle and the nature and estimated volume of transactions that flow through the systems. An overview flowchart should depict the principal features of the accounting systems, including the following:

1. The nature, source, and estimated volume of transactions.
2. The means of processing.
3. Files or records used for editing and reference purposes.
4. Updating of ledgers and master files.
5. For computerized systems, significant programmed accounting procedures.
6. Reports of accounting significance produced, their frequency, and their distribution.

Since an overview flowchart is in summary form, it does not show the path of a transaction from its inception to the update of the general ledger and it does not show internal accounting controls. Therefore, an overview flowchart does not provide sufficient information for designing compliance tests. Since an overview flowchart should contain sufficient information for designing substantive tests, reports of accounting significance that are used to update the general ledger should be noted briefly on the flowchart. An example of an overview flowchart for a computerized revenue cycle is shown in Figure 8.2.

Figure 8.1 Flowcharting Symbols

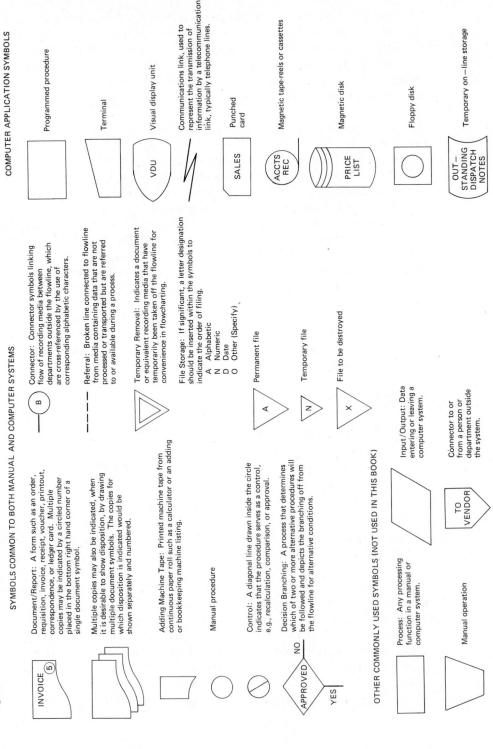

Figure 8.2 Overview Flowchart

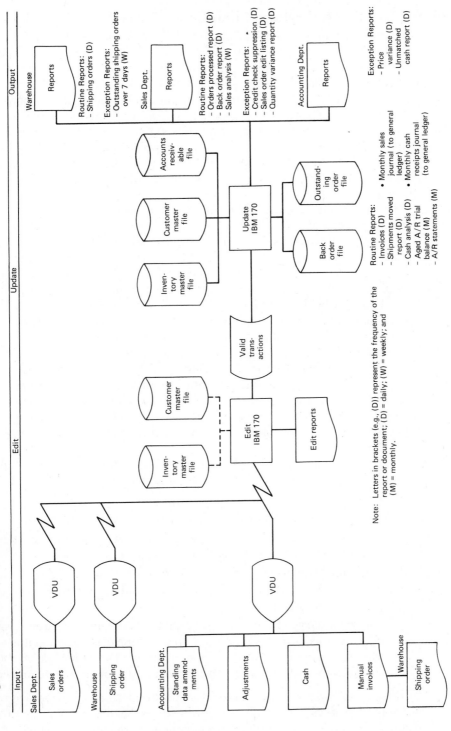

Deciding Whether to Perform Compliance Tests

After considering the client's control environment and accounting systems, the auditor makes a decision about whether to continue the risk assessment by evaluating the design of specific internal controls relevant to specific audit objectives and account balances and performing compliance tests of those controls. That decision is based primarily on the auditor's judgment about the relative efficiency of testing controls as a basis for further reducing the assessment of control risk and thereby restricting substantive tests of the accounts in a particular transaction cycle, as compared with proceeding directly to substantive testing. Often, different strategies may be equally effective, but may differ in efficiency. The strategy decision is usually documented in a planning memorandum.

In some situations, the auditor may be concerned that the documented understanding of the accounting system and internal controls in one or more transaction cycles may be incorrect or incomplete and thus not be an adequate basis for determining the most efficient audit strategy. In that event, the auditor may decide to trace a transaction of each type through the system in each transaction cycle in which the auditor is considering relying on specific controls. This may be done by inspecting or reviewing transactions, records, documents, or reports, in what is sometimes referred to as a "transaction review" or "walkthrough." Even if the auditor does not intend to rely on specific controls in a particular transaction cycle, a transaction review may be helpful in identifying the types of errors that could occur because of absent controls, and may thereby assist in designing substantive tests to detect those errors. The decision to perform transaction reviews entails weighing the risk that the auditor's understanding of the client's system of internal control at this stage of the audit is incorrect or incomplete against the cost of performing the transaction reviews.

The auditor commonly decides that it would not be efficient to perform compliance tests when one or more of the following circumstances are present:

1. The prior year's audit or other information about the client indicates that there are weaknesses in the internal control system.
2. Volumes of transactions are low or inherent risk characteristics make substantive tests relatively easy to apply.
3. The control environment appears to be unfavorable.
4. The client has a manual system or its computer systems are neither complex nor pervasive.
5. The necessary compliance tests entail reperforming a large number of control procedures, as might be the case, for example, when it is not possible to rely on relevant general controls in a computer system to ensure the continued and proper operation of programmed control procedures.

In these circumstances, the auditor designs and performs substantive tests for all audit objectives and for all account balances, taking into consideration the results of the materiality and risk assessment activities already carried out.

In circumstances other than those enumerated in the foregoing list, the auditor generally considers it efficient to perform compliance tests of controls in transaction cycles. In most instances, this strategy will enable the auditor to reduce the amount of assurance needed from substantive tests with respect to the audit objectives of accuracy, completeness, and existence (and, in some cases, cutoff) for accounts that are derived from transaction cycles.

For large clients with pervasive, complex, and integrated computer systems, it may be readily apparent that compliance testing of all types of controls in all transaction cycles is an efficient strategy. For such clients, the auditor usually expects to be able to reduce significantly the assurance needed from substantive tests of accounts derived from transaction cycles, although some specific weaknesses in internal accounting controls may have to be taken into consideration.

Some enterprises, however, have relatively complex, computerized accounting systems, but the number and expertise of computer personnel are limited. There may be extensive internal accounting controls, but some general controls may be informal and not well documented. There are typically some weaknesses in controls over program and data file security; certain of these weaknesses may be mitigated by the use of purchased accounting packages for which the source code is not readily available (i.e., the client's personnel are effectively unable to amend the programs). These clients require the auditor to exercise the most judgment in deciding whether to perform compliance tests. The auditor can often achieve worthwhile reductions in the assurance needed from substantive tests about accounts derived from transaction cycles by testing and relying on controls, particularly if it is possible to obtain indirect evidence about the ongoing proper operation of controls from such factors as management reviews of accounting reports and the absence of recurring problems in the use of data produced by the system.

The auditor's decision about whether to test some or all internal accounting controls, together with the other factors discussed in Chapter 6 that determine the audit strategy, provides a basis for drafting the audit program. An audit program is a list, generally in detail, of steps to be performed in the course of an audit. It specifies the nature and extent of the examination, aids in scheduling and assigning the work, guards against possible omissions and duplications, and provides part of the documentation of the work done. An audit program is necessary for adequate planning and supervision of an engagement under the first standard of field work and is required by SAS No. 22, *Planning and Supervision* (AU Section 311). The audit program should be viewed as a tentative working document, to be revised as new information is gathered during subsequent stages of the audit. Audit programs are discussed further in Chapter 9.

Compliance Testing to Rely on Specific Controls

If the audit strategy is to rely on specific controls in a particular transaction cycle, the auditor first determines whether the system, as designed, appears to include adequate controls to prevent or detect misstatements related to specific audit objectives. In making that determination, which in AU Section 320.60 is referred to as the "preliminary evaluation," the auditor considers the inherent risk characteristics associated with the related account balance or class of transactions. The auditor may need to make further inquiries of client personnel, examine documentation, and observe the processing of transactions and the handling of assets.

The understanding of the client's accounting systems and related controls should be reviewed each year, and the documentation of the system should be updated as required. As a practical matter, the auditor often identifies specific controls and may evaluate and document their design as part of the earlier risk assessment activities. Auditors commonly document their understanding of the system and their conclusions about its design in the form of answers to an internal control questionnaire, systems flowcharts, narratives, or control matrices, as discussed later in this chapter.

The auditor then determines whether specific internal accounting controls whose design has been found to be appropriate have operated effectively and continuously throughout the period during which reliance on them is intended. That determination is made by compliance testing the controls. The auditor's purpose in performing compliance tests is to obtain evidence about whether internal accounting controls necessary to achieve specific control objectives are being applied continuously and as prescribed. That purpose dictates that all controls that the auditor intends to rely on should be tested. Conversely, only those controls should be tested for audit purposes. A client's control system is likely to include many controls that an auditor can ignore because they are redundant or because they do not directly affect the financial statements; other controls can be ignored because it is more cost-effective to perform substantive tests than to rely on the controls; and still others can be ignored because the related account balances are not material to the financial statements. As a practical matter, compliance tests are normally restricted to accounts derived from transaction cycles because the other accounts typically are not addressed by controls or usually reflect relatively low volumes of transactions.

The key to determining the appropriate controls to compliance test is to identify the specific internal accounting controls designed to achieve the control objectives of completeness, validity, accuracy, maintenance, and physical security applicable to a particular transaction cycle. The auditor identifies the controls implemented by the client for a particular cycle that, if they operated effectively, would satisfy specific control objectives. The auditor then designs and performs the appropriate compliance tests.

Figure 12.2 on page 490 to 494 provides an example of an auditor's specific audit objectives applicable to a client's sales of goods and services, illustrates the relationship between the general and specific audit objectives, and notes the financial statement errors that could occur if controls are not present or are not operating as designed. It also provides examples of compliance tests the audi-

---

[1]Figures 12.3, 13.2, 13.3, 13.4, and 14.1 illustrate the same principles for other types of transactions.

tor may perform, given the internal accounting controls identified. As the figure indicates, one or more specific controls should be identified for each internal accounting control objective, and a compliance test should be designed for each control that the auditor intends to rely on to be able to restrict the scope of substantive tests.

Types of Compliance Tests

The techniques that are used in compliance testing are observation, inquiry of client personnel, examination of evidence, and, in some cases, reperformance of control procedures. Observation involves direct visual viewing of client employees in their work environment. Inquiry entails asking specific questions of the client's employees, which may be done informally or in formal interviews. Examination of evidence entails the inspection of records, documents, reconciliations, and reports for evidence that a control has been properly applied. Reperformance is the repeating of a procedure performed by the client.

During the inquiry process, the auditor should, wherever possible, corroborate the explanations received by inspecting procedures manuals and reports or other documents used in or generated by the performance of the control procedures. The auditor also may make corroborative inquiries of individuals other than those performing the control procedures. For elements of a control that are manually performed (such as the follow-up of items contained in computer-generated exception reports), the auditor should examine evidence of the performance of the relevant control procedures when it may reasonably be expected to exist (for example, there may be written explanations, check marks, or other indications of performance on a copy of a report or document used in performing the control).

Provided that they are sufficiently comprehensive, tests based on observation, inquiry, and examination of evidence often provide sufficient evidence about the effective operation of a control. In some situations, it is not necessary to reperform a control procedure to obtain sufficient evidence that it is operating effectively. There may be instances, however, in which the auditor believes that a control is so significant that further evidence of its effective operation is considered necessary; then it may be appropriate to reperform the control procedure. For example, the effective operation of a client control designed to ensure the completeness and accuracy of the update of a standing data file of interest rates in a bank may be so significant to the accuracy of interest charged to loan customers that the auditor may wish to reperform the updating procedure a few times to gain additional evidence that the control is operating as prescribed. In those infrequent cases when the auditor believes that reperformance of a programmed or manual accounting or control procedure is appropriate, it will ordinarily be sufficient to reperform the control only once or a few times. (See Chapter 10 for a discussion of the extent of testing and audit sampling.) If extensive reperformance of control procedures is needed, the auditor should consider whether it is still efficient to perform compliance tests in order to restrict the scope of substantive testing.

Continuous Operation of Controls

When assessing the ability of internal accounting controls to reduce control risk to a sufficiently low level to permit restricting the scope of substantive tests, the auditor needs to determine that the controls have operated continuously during the period. Spreading compliance tests throughout the period is not always necessary to obtain evidence about the continuous operation of controls. For example, if a control in the form of an exception report is cumulative, transactions or circumstances meeting specified criteria continue to be reported as long as the criteria are met (examples would be reports of "outstanding packing slips" or "goods received not invoiced"). For such controls, compliance tests that provide evidence that the control operated effectively at a point in time will also provide evidence about the proper operation of the underlying accounting procedures throughout the period up to that point in time.

Manually performed control procedures are prone to random failures. An auditor assessing manually performed procedures should obtain evidence of their performance, and if necessary reperform them, for control events occurring at different times during the period of assessment. These tests need not necessarily be extensive. Supervisory procedures that the auditor can test may provide evidence of the continuous operation of the underlying manually performed control procedures.

In contrast, the operation of programmed accounting and control procedures in computer systems is not subject to random failures or deterioration over time, provided that the relevant general computer controls, including program maintenance controls, are operating effectively. If general controls appear to be operating appropriately and effectively, the auditor could choose to test them as a basis for determining that the programmed accounting and control procedures operated continuously throughout the period.

Dual-Purpose Samples and Tests

Compliance tests of internal accounting controls normally precede substantive tests, since the results of compliance tests affect the auditor's decision about the appropriate nature, timing, and extent of substantive tests. Sometimes, however, to achieve greater audit efficiency, compliance and substantive tests may be performed simultaneously using the same document or record. For example, the same sample of accounts receivable balances selected for confirmation (a substantive test) may be used to determine that the customers' files contain documents indicating that the sales orders were appropriately approved (a compliance test). The auditing literature refers to this process as one that involves a "dual-purpose sample."

In addition, some compliance and substantive tests are "dual-purpose tests." For example, a compliance test, as a by-product of the auditor's reperformance of calculations or procedures, may provide evidence about dollar errors in the accounts. Also, a substantive test may provide evidence about the proper or improper functioning of accounting controls if no errors were found as a result of the substantive test or if errors that were found were investigated and determined to be the result of a control weakness. Audit tests are not considered dual-purpose tests unless they accomplish the purposes of both types of tests concurrently.

Evaluating the Results of Compliance Tests

After completing a program of compliance tests, the auditor should review the results and consider whether the planned level of reliance on internal accounting controls is still justified. The need to reassess the planned level of reliance on controls will depend on two factors: the original planned level of reliance (and, implicitly, the deviation rate in the operation of the controls that would be acceptable to the auditor, given the planned level of reliance) and the deviation rate that was actually found to exist as a result of performing the compliance tests. The deviation rate found to exist might cause the auditor to revise the audit strategy to rely less or more on substantive tests than was originally planned, depending on whether the actual deviation rate was greater or less than that anticipated when the planned level of reliance was originally determined. In the extreme situation, the actual deviation rate might be so high that no reliance could be placed on a particular control.[2] On the other hand, and depending on the nature of the control, if a departure or breakdown is corrected long enough before year-end, and this is confirmed by appropriate tests, no amendment to other audit tests will normally be necessary.

In addition to assessing the implications of the rate at which client procedures departed from prescribed policies, the auditor should consider the cause of the deviations and document the conclusions reached. If the deviation rate is unacceptably high, the auditor will have to amend the planned substantive tests. The specific amendments will depend in part on the reasons for the deviations. For example, the appropriate audit response to breakdowns in the application of controls should be different if the cause was a poorly trained clerk who substituted for a highly trained clerk during the latter's three-week vacation than if the cause was incompetent work or weak supervision throughout the year. In some instances, it may be possible to ascertain the reason for a control breakdown by inquiry and examination of the circumstances; in other cases, it may be necessary to extend the testing. In the latter event, the auditor should ensure that extending the testing will be helpful in determining the cause and extent of the breakdown.

Departures from and breakdowns in internal controls revealed by tests should be considered for reporting to the client, as discussed later. Also, the documentation of the accounting systems and internal controls should be amended as required.

---

[2]As noted earlier, it would not ordinarily be efficient for the auditor to perform compliance tests unless the expected deviation rate (and the corresponding assessment of control risk) was low.

Documenting Controls and Compliance Tests

If the control risk assessment extends beyond developing an understanding of the control environment and the flow of transactions through the accounting systems, professional standards require that the auditor "document his understanding of the system and the basis for his conclusion that the internal accounting control procedures on which he intends to rely are suitably designed to provide reasonable assurance that those procedures will prevent or detect particular types of errors or irregularities concerning particular classes of transactions or balances" (SAS No. 43, paragraph 2 [AU Section 320.61]). The degree of detail and the means of documentation will vary according to the complexity and circumstances of the engagement. This section presents several alternative documentation formats, provides examples, and explains when each could be used. Individual auditors and firms often express a preference for one type of documentation by means of their internal policy pronouncements and the practice aids (for example, forms, checklists, and questionnaires) that they provide, which may be either required or optional.

Documenting Controls

Internal accounting controls on which the auditor intends to rely are typically documented by narratives, systems flowcharts, control matrices, or internal control questionnaires.

Narratives. While many auditors prefer flowcharting as the means of documenting the design of the system of internal control, narratives are often useful and, depending on the circumstances, may be more cost effective (usually for unsophisticated systems). When narratives are used, however, the auditor should ensure that they contain the same information as flowcharts would have contained.

Systems Flowcharts. A systems flowchart depicts, for each significant type of transaction, the path of the transaction from its inception (that is, the point where the transaction first enters the system) to the update of the general ledger. It provides, in a convenient form, a description of the system necessary for the auditor to design compliance tests. A systems flowchart typically contains, for each significant type of transaction:

1. The details of significant procedures and controls, including division of duties and supervision.
2. The job titles of the people performing the controls.
3. The frequency of the operation of the controls.

The information is usually organized by area of responsibility within a system. Depending on the responsibilities involved, an organizational unit may vary from a large department (such as a sales department) to one individual (the credit manager). The names of the organizational units through which transactions flow should be shown at the top of the flowchart. The flow of transactions usually is from top left to bottom right. Controls should be distinctly marked on the flowchart by a diagonal line inside a procedure symbol and may include a narrative supplement noting the type of control being exercised (e.g., "approval").

Systems flowcharts need not be excessively detailed, as only significant procedures should be depicted. One or more procedures and related controls may be depicted by one symbol, with a narrative explanation of each significant procedure provided separately on the flowchart. This normally makes it possible to show each transaction cycle on one or two pages. A sample of a systems flowchart for the sales order and billing portions of a computerized revenue cycle is provided in Figure 8.3.

Control Matrices. Some auditors capture information about the principal basic controls and any apparent weaknesses in those controls (such as omitted controls) through the use of a control matrix, an illustration of which is presented in Figure 8.4. (Although the control matrix illustrated is for a computerized revenue cycle, the general format would be equally suitable for a manual system.) It describes the principal control procedures that have been designed by the client to meet the objectives of internal accounting control and serves as an aid in understanding the system. It may even serve as a substitute for an internal control questionnaire (described later).

An explanation of the columns in the illustrated control matrix follows.

- The *transaction/document column* describes each transaction type (e.g., adjusting entries) or document (e.g., sales order, shipping order) with audit significance. Transaction types should be grouped together if the method of control is identical. If different control considerations apply to different types of information (e.g., customer number, quantity, and price) on the same document, that information should be separately identified. Significant transaction data generated by computer (e.g., shipping documents or interest charges) should be identified as transaction types and included in the matrix. Amendments to standing data (e.g., prices, pay rates, and interest rates) should be similarly treated.
- The *completeness column* identifies the principal control procedures used to ensure that all transactions are recorded and processed.
- The *accuracy column* identifies the principal control procedures used to ensure that relevant data (e.g., value, quantity, account numbers, price, and date) are accurately recorded.
- The *validity/authorization column* identifies the principal control procedures that prevent processing of invalid or unauthorized transactions. The following should be considered:

  How the transaction is authorized or how its validity is ensured.

Figure 8.3 Systems Flowchart—Revenue Cycle, Shipping and Billing

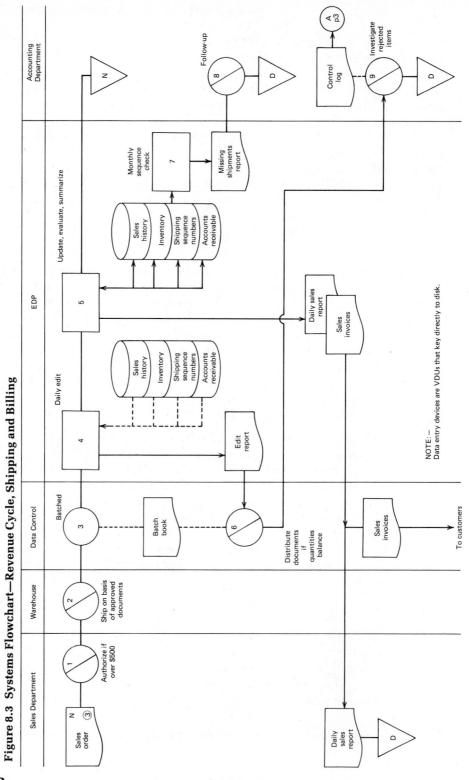

The stage in processing when the transaction is authorized or its validity ensured (e.g., before or after completeness and accuracy controls have been applied).

- The *master file update and ledger posting column* identifies the principal control procedures used to ensure that computer master files are completely and accurately updated for all transactions, including those generated by computer. In many cases, more than one master file will be involved; for example, sales transactions may be posted in different forms to an accounts receivable master file and an inventory master file. In some cases, postings to the general ledger may be more conveniently dealt with on a separate general ledger control matrix.
- The *ledger/master file maintenance column* identifies the principal control procedures used to ensure that data posted to various master files and ledgers remain complete and accurate.

The control matrix illustrated does not identify controls over the physical custody of assets, controls that address segregation of duties and supervision, or general controls in computerized systems. Control matrices could, of course, be designed to address these aspects of a system of internal control.

Internal Control Questionnaires. Since control objectives and the means of achieving them are much the same from one system to another, most auditors find that both efficiency and effectiveness are greatly enhanced by designing an internal control questionnaire (ICQ) that identifies and lists expected controls, and then using the questionnaire to document the control system on all or most engagements.

The questionnaire is usually divided into transaction cycles that cover the main transaction flows in a typical manufacturing company. The ICQ may be classified by the control objectives that should be achieved by the client's control procedures at each stage of transaction processing. The questions relating to each control objective are sometimes further subdivided between:

1. Those that seek information concerning *accounting procedures* within the system that are not in themselves internal accounting controls, but that form the basis for the exercise of internal accounting controls.
2. Those that seek to determine whether or not internal accounting *controls* are present.

A portion of this type of questionnaire is illustrated in Figure 8.5. Questions in an ICQ also frequently indicate the type of control being addressed: basic, segregation of duties, supervisory, physical, or general computer. While it is not necessary to have this degree of subdivision for an ICQ to be effective, it allows for a better understanding of the system of internal control and is helpful in designing both compliance and substantive tests.

Figure 8.4 Control Matrix—Revenue Cycle, Shipping, Billing, and Collection

Control Matrix
Computer System

Application ___ Revenue Cycle ___ Date _____

Client ___ Alpha Corporation ___ Prepared By _____

Transaction/ Document	Completeness	Accuracy	Validity/ Authorization	Master File Update and Ledger Posting	Ledger/ Master File Maintenance
Shipping Copy of Order and Invoices (a) Customer # (b) Product # (c) Quantity (d) Price	• Sequence check (4, 5, 7) (c) • Batching (3, 6) (c)	• Match (4, 5) (a), (b) • Batching (3, 6) (c)	• Orders over $500 (1) • No shipments without order (2)	**Inventory File** **Sales History File** **A/R File** Completeness— • Sequence check (4, 5, 7) (c) Accuracy— • Match (4, 5) and batching (3, 6) (a), (b), (c)	**Inventory File** See separate flowchart **Sales History File** **A/R File** Control book and G/L (22)

Customer and Sales Price Changes (a) Customer #, name, and address (b) Product # (c) Price	Manual sequence check and 100% item comparison (13) (a), (b), (c)	Manual sequence check and 100% item comparison (13) (a), (b), (c)	V.P. Finance (9a) (c)	Manual sequence check and 100% item comparison (13) (a), (b), (c)	*Inventory Sale Price* — Manual check; *Customer Standing Data* — Manual check
Cash Remittances (a) Customer # (b) Invoice # (c) Amount	Immediate banking (14) (c); • Remittance advice reconciled to cash edit report (16) or (19) (c)	• Match (17) (a), (b); • Remittance advice reconciled to cash edit report (16) or (19) (c)	N/A	*A/R File*; *Paid History File* Accuracy • Match (17) • Remittance advice reconciled to cash edit report (16) or (19)	*Paid History File*; Not known; *A/R File* — Control book and G/L (22)

Figure 8.5 Internal Control Questionnaire

Controls over Goods Shipped and Services Performed	Flowchart Reference	Yes	No
Validity/Accuracy			
Accounting Procedures—Basis for Control			
1. Are the following recorded for accounting control purposes at the time the goods are shipped or the services performed? (a) Quantities and description of all goods shipped. (b) All services performed for customers.			
Controls			
2. Are shipments of goods or the performance of services authorized?			
3. Are goods physically counted at the time of shipment?			
4. Is the count in question 3 carried out or checked by persons other than those who: (a) Have custody of or access to inventories? (b) Authorize or make shipments?			
Completeness			
Accounting Procedures—Basis for Control			
5. Are the records referred to in question 1 maintained in such a way that it can subsequently be			

The ICQ is also a convenient way of documenting the specific internal accounting controls that the auditor intends to compliance test. If systems flowcharts have been prepared, the information contained in them should be used, as much as possible, in answering the ICQ questions. The questions in the ICQ are usually phrased so that they may be answered "Yes" or "No" to indicate, respectively, the presence or absence of a control procedure. If a question does not apply to a specific client or location, the appropriate response is "Not Applicable."

The ICQ is often completed as part of the evaluation of the design of the system, which is in part the basis for the auditor's decision to test specific controls. The auditor should reconsider the answers to the ICQ questions during subsequent stages of the audit, particularly after performing compliance tests of controls and substantive tests. Departures from or weaknesses in prescribed controls may be revealed by compliance tests, and errors or deviations from procedures may be disclosed by substantive tests. In that event, the ICQ should be amended to reflect the new information.

Figure 8.5 Continued

Controls over Goods Shipped and Services Performed	Flowchart Reference	Yes	No
established whether all the related transactions have been accounted for (e.g., by sequentially prenumbering delivery slips) in respect of: (a) Goods? (b) Services?			
6. Are records maintained of goods shipped and services performed that have not been matched with the related sales invoices in respect of: (a) Goods? (b) Services?			
Controls			
7. If sequentially prenumbered forms are used, are all numbers accounted for as part of the procedure for ascertaining unmatched items in respect of: (a) Goods? (b) Services?			
8. Are unmatched records of goods shipped and services performed reviewed on a regular basis (e.g., monthly) to determine the reasons for any such items that have not been matched within a reasonable period of time in respect of: (a) Goods? (b) Services?			
9. Are the results of the procedure in question 8 reviewed and approved by a responsible official?			

Documenting Compliance Tests

When compliance tests are performed, they must be documented, and auditors use many different means of doing so. The choice, once again, depends on such factors as the complexity of the compliance test (for example, observing that a control is operating versus reperforming the control procedure) and the policies of the particular CPA firm. Some compliance tests can conveniently be recorded directly on the control matrices or internal control questionnaires, in which case the matrices and ICQs, with minor adaptations, document both the controls identified and the tests performed on those controls to ensure that they are operating as designed. (Conceptually, compliance tests can also be documented as part of a narrative description of the system of controls or on a systems flowchart, but those methods of documentation make it difficult for a reviewer to evaluate the tests performed.) Alternatively, separate working papers could be used to document the tests performed; this method is particularly useful when a test consists of examining evidence of the operation of a control (such as authorization of payroll changes by department heads and personnel managers) or reperformance of a control procedure (such as reperforming, at year-end, the client's monthly follow-up of all unmatched cash receipts included in a suspense account, for evidence that the receipts were credited to the proper account). An example of a compliance test working paper for a payroll test was presented in Figure 5.6 on page 176.

Documenting Control Weaknesses

To assist the auditor in responding to weaknesses found in internal accounting controls on which reliance was planned, a document that summarizes control weaknesses is often prepared at the same time as the ICQ. The purpose of documenting control weaknesses is to permit the auditor to consider their effect on planned audit procedures. Control weaknesses identified during later stages of the audit should also be documented to facilitate preparation of the management letter (discussed later). The documentation should be amended whenever new information that affects control weaknesses is found. The working paper documentation should include a description of the nature of the weakness and its possible effect on the financial statements, a decision on whether the weakness could give rise to material misstatement in the financial statements and the justification for this decision, and an explanation of the audit response to the weakness, including any amendment to the nature, timing, or extent of substantive audit procedures.

Communicating Control Weaknesses

Management Letters

Management is usually interested in an auditor's observations about possible weaknesses in internal accounting controls and suggestions for remedying them. Discussion of apparent weaknesses and problems that is cooperative and constructive and aims to explore possible courses of action is by far the best way to communicate findings to clients. Often those discussions are confirmed in a formal letter to a representative of the client—the so-called management letter or internal control letter. Some companies request such a letter, or the audit committee or board of directors may require it.

It is good practice for the auditor to "clear" all comments on internal control with the client before drafting the management letter. If the auditor's understanding of controls was mistaken in some respect, discussing the comments will clarify the misunderstanding and save the auditor the embarrassment of discovering it later. In many instances, management's responses to the auditor's suggestions are included in the management letter.

The best time to discuss weaknesses in controls and related problems and to write a management letter is at the conclusion of compliance tests. That point ideally occurs when both auditor and management have time to consider the auditor's findings. It should preferably take place sufficiently before year-end to permit corrective action that can affect the scope of the auditor's remaining work. Often, however, the pressure of other demands on both the client and the auditor causes formal delivery of the management letter to be deferred until after year-end, although certain findings may be of such importance that they should be brought to the attention of management as soon as they are identified. If the management letter is prepared before year-end, and if further weaknesses or problems are identified as a result of substantive tests performed after year-end (as is likely), a second management letter may be appropriate. Figure 8.6 provides an example of a management letter, including specific comments.

Many auditors believe that all recommendations for improvements in controls that are communicated to any level of management should be brought to the attention of the client's audit committee and board of directors; a passive audit committee or board of directors does not alleviate this need. If the suggestion is significant enough to be brought to the attention of management, it is also significant enough for the audit committee and the board. Of course, the higher the level of corporate governance, the fewer the details required.

On a recurring engagement, some comments made in the prior year may not have been acted on. Whether those comments should be repeated in the current year generally depends on their continued significance and on consideration of the client's reasons for not taking corrective action. Significant accounting control weaknesses that remain uncorrected should be discussed with management. If the auditor finds management's explanations unreasonable or unsatisfactory, the comments should be presented again in subsequent communications. For example, the auditor may have previously communicated a significant finding to management, which management believed was not practicable to correct. If the auditor disagrees, the later communication should repeat the comment and make it clear that management—not the auditor—believes that corrective action is not practicable. Care should be taken, however, to ensure that such disagreements are handled diplomatically and constructively.

Required Communication of Material Weaknesses in Internal Accounting Control

SAS No. 20, *Required Communication of Material Weaknesses in Internal Accounting Control*, as amended (AU Section 323), requires the auditor to communicate to senior management and the board of directors or its audit committee material weaknesses in internal accounting control that are revealed during an audit. That SAS (as amended) defines a material weakness in internal accounting control as ''a condition in which the specific control procedures or the degree of compliance with them do not reduce to a relatively low level the risk that errors

Figure 8.6 Management Letter

JONES & SMITH, CPAs
New York, N.Y.

Board of Directors
XYZ Corporation
New York, N.Y.

As an integral part of our audit examination of the consolidated financial statements of XYZ Corporation, we reviewed certain accounting and operating procedures, systems, and controls to the extent we considered necessary for expressing an opinion on the company's financial statements. As a result of such reviews, and in an effort to be of assistance to management, we are submitting for your consideration, as attachments hereto, a number of comments and recommendations. All of our comments have been discussed with the key personnel of the respective departments. Additional comments may be forthcoming on completion of our audit.

It should be understood that our comments deal exclusively with operational, accounting, and record-keeping systems, procedures, and controls, and should not be regarded as reflecting on the integrity or capabilities of anyone in your organization. It should be further recognized that our comments have been restricted to suggested improvements, and are not intended as a commentary on the various favorable aspects of the company's procedures and controls.

In the event you have any questions or require additional information with respect to any of the matters discussed in the accompanying report, please do not hesitate to contact us.

Very truly yours,

Jones & Smith, CPAs

---

or irregularities in amounts that would be material in relation to the financial statements being audited may occur and not be detected within a timely period by employees in the normal course of performing their assigned functions'' (AU Section 323.01). In discharging this responsibility to report material weaknesses, the auditor is not required to evaluate each control or identify every material weakness. Instead, the auditor is required to report only those material weaknesses discovered in the course of implementing the audit program for the examination of the financial statements. (In practice, if a management letter is prepared in which weaknesses are described and some indication of their relative importance is provided, a separate letter on material weaknesses rarely is written.)

Figure 8.6 Continued

Comments and Recommendations

Employee Additions Sometimes Lack Approval

   After a new employee's application for employment has been approved, a payroll addition form is prepared. This form contains the name, address, and starting rate of pay of the new employee. The form and the approved application constitute authorization for the addition of an employee to the payroll. Our review indicated that applications are not always signed as approved and that the data processing payroll addition forms do not always evidence approval.

   We recommend that all new employee applications and payroll addition forms be approved in writing prior to data processing. The personnel department has informed us that this procedure will be followed in the future.

Access Controls to Data by Terminals Can Be Bypassed

   At the present time, there is a critical "file protect" system that prohibits the access of production data by remote terminal users. Our review disclosed a method (special coding of a control card) by which this system can be bypassed and remote terminal users can access and/or alter disk resident financial data. Unauthorized access to disk resident production data files can result in inaccurate financial data being reported by the systems or confidential data being available to unauthorized personnel. Management is currently implementing a procedure to rectify this situation.

Incompatible Duties Exist in Purchasing and Accounts Payable

   Under the current system, the buyer in the department is responsible for the preparation of purchase orders. Price, quantity, description, and terms are entered on the purchase order. The same person is also responsible for comparing that information to the purchase order as part of the invoice checking process.

   We recommend that the invoice checking function be performed by persons not involved in the purchasing function.

Reports on Internal Accounting Control

An auditor may be engaged specifically to report on an entity's system of internal accounting control. A report on internal accounting control expresses the auditor's opinion on the adequacy of the system of internal control to prevent or detect material misstatements in relation to the financial statements taken as a whole. While that report should not give assurance of compliance with the Foreign Corrupt Practices Act (discussed in Chapter 7), it usually provides considerable information to management and directors about whether appropriate steps have or have not been taken to comply with the Act. A management letter, on the other hand, discusses weaknesses individually, contains suggestions and other comments on specific aspects of controls, but does not express an opinion on the system itself.

Review Questions _____

8-1. Define inherent risk conditions an give some illustrations.

8-2. Define control risk and give some examples of high-control-risk situations.

8-3. How does risk assessment affect audit strategy?

8-4. How does an auditor obtain the information to assess inherent risk conditions?

8-5. What are related parties and what are the auditor's responsibilities with respect to related party transactions?

8-6. What governs the extent to which control risk is assessed?

8-7. How does the auditor obtain an understanding of the control environment and the accounting systems?

8-8. What factors should the auditor consider in assessing the usefulness of management's review of operating reports?

8-9. When is an auditor not required to document in detail an understanding of the client's internal control system?

8-10. Describe the different ways in which the auditor may document an understanding of the internal control system.

8-11. What are the principal features of an accounting system that an overview flowchart should depict?

8-12. What factors help decide whether certain controls should be compliance tested?

8-13. Distinguish between a transaction review and a compliance test.

8-14. Name the techniques used in compliance testing.

8-15. Describe and illustrate a "dual-purpose test."

8-16. How does a control matrix differ from a systems flowchart?

8-17. How does using an ICQ enhance audit efficiency and effectiveness?

8-18. What are the auditor's responsibilities regarding weaknesses in internal control?

Discussion Questions _____

8-30. After completing your preliminary work in a recurring audit, including evaluation of internal accounting control and compliance tests, you are about to prepare a draft of the management letter. You find that certain of the recommendations you made last year have not been adopted by management. They can be categorized as follows:

   a. Management believes that certain recommendations are impracticable.

   b. Management believes that certain recommendations are not cost effective considering the exposures involved.

   c. Management disagrees with certain facts alleged in last year's letter.

   Required:
   What approach should you take in each instance in drafting this year's letter?

8-31. Internal control comprises the plan of organization and all of the coordinate methods and measures adopted within a business to safeguard its assets, check the accuracy and reliability of its accounting data, promote operational efficiency, and encourage adherence to prescribed managerial policies.

> *Required:*
> a. What is the purpose of the auditor's study and evaluation of internal control?
> b. What are the minimum requirements for the evaluation of internal control?
> c. How is the auditor's understanding of specific internal controls documented?
> d. What is the purpose of tests of compliance?

(AICPA adapted)

8-32. Adherence to generally accepted auditing standards requires, among other things, a proper study and evaluation of the existing internal control. The most common approaches to reviewing the system of internal control include the use of a questionnaire, preparation of a memorandum, preparation of a flowchart, preparation of a control matrix, and combinations of these methods.

> *Required:*
> Discuss the advantages to a CPA of reviewing internal control by using:
>
> a. An internal control questionnaire.
> b. The memorandum (or narrative) approach.
> c. A flowchart.
> d. A control matrix.

(AICPA adapted)

8-33. Distinguish between an overview flowchart and a systems flowchart. Explain their uses in connection with the evaluation of internal accounting control.

8-34. Internal control weaknesses and suggested improvements are usually communicated by the auditor to management by means of a management letter. Explain the usual procedures followed by auditors in preparing a management letter.

AICPA Multiple Choice Questions

These questions are taken from the Auditing part of Uniform CPA Examinations. Choose the single most appropriate answer.

8-40. Which of the following would be *inappropriate* during a preliminary evaluation of the system of internal control?

> a. Completion of an internal control questionnaire.
> b. Use of attributes sampling.
> c. Oral inquiries.
> d. Review of an accounting manual prepared by the client.

8–41. The auditor who becomes aware of a material weakness in internal control is required to communicate this to the

    a. Audit committee and client's legal counsel.
    b. Board of directors and internal auditors.
    c. Senior management and board of directors.
    d. Internal auditors and senior management.

8–42. When erroneous data are detected by computer program controls, such data may be excluded from processing and printed on an error report. The error report should most probably be reviewed and followed up by the

    a. User department control group.
    b. System analyst.
    c. Supervisor of computer operations.
    d. Computer programmer.

8–43. Which of the following is *not* a medium that can normally be used by an auditor to record information concerning a client's system of internal accounting control?

    a. Narrative memorandum.
    b. Procedures manual.
    c. Flowchart.
    d. Decision table.

8–44. The preliminary phase of the auditor's review of internal control is designed to provide information on several matters. Which of the following is *not* a purpose of the preliminary phase of the review?

    a. Determine the extent to which EDP is used in significant accounting applications.
    b. Understand the flow of transactions in the system.
    c. Comprehend the basic structure of accounting control.
    d. Identify the controls on which reliance is planned.

8–45. Which of the following statements regarding auditor documentation of the client's system of internal control is correct?

    a. Documentation must include flowcharts.
    b. Documentation must include procedural write-ups.
    c. No documentation is necessary, although it is desirable.
    d. No one particular form of documentation is necessary, and the extent of documentation may vary.

8–46. Which of the following symbolic representations indicates that a sales invoice has been filed?

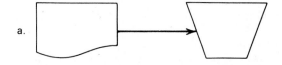

a.

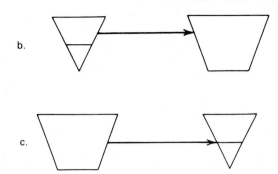

b.

c.

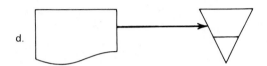

d.

8-47. After performing a study and evaluation of the client's system of internal control, an auditor has concluded that the system is well designed and functioning as anticipated. Under these circumstances the auditor would most likely

    a. Cease to perform further substantive tests.
    b. Not increase the extent of predetermined tests.
    c. Increase the extent of anticipated analytical review procedures.
    d. Perform all compliance tests to the extent outlined in the preplanned audit program.

8-48. Compliance testing is performed in order to determine whether or not

    a. Controls are functioning as designed.
    b. Necessary controls are absent.
    c. Incompatible functions exist.
    d. Material dollar errors exist.

8-49. The program flowcharting symbol representing a decision is a

    a. Triangle.
    b. Circle.
    c. Rectangle.
    d. Diamond.

8-50. Which of the following would be *least* likely to be included in an auditor's test of compliance?

    a. Inspection.
    b. Observation.

c. Inquiry.

d. Confirmation.

Problems and Cases

8-60. The figure on the following page illustrates a manual system for executing purchases and cash disbursements transactions.

Required:

Indicate what each of the letters "A" through "L" represents. Do not discuss adequacies or inadequacies in the system of internal control.

(AICPA adapted)

8-61. As a result of your preliminary evaluation of the system of internal control of the ACME Manufacturing Co. Inc., you have gathered the five documents shown on pages 288 to 292 as examples of the flow of transactions through the accounting system.

Required:

a. What significant information concerning ACME Manufacturing can be obtained from the purchase order, receiving report, invoice, and perpetual inventory record?

b. What is the purpose of the voucher?

c. What documents might a voucher package contain?

d. What is the significance of the purchase order and receiving report from an accounting control perspective? (Discuss each document separately.)

8-62. You have been approached by a young entrepreneur, Mr. Kent, who is starting a new business called Sooperman, Inc. The business will purchase television sets and radios from Krypto, Inc., at a favorable price for resale to small retailers throughout the United States. Mr. Kent is confident of success as the products are competitively priced.

To carry out this business, Mr. Kent will use the warehouse and offices that he uses for his existing business. However, the areas will be strictly segregated for the new operations. Mr. Kent needs advice in setting up an accounting system and procedures to ensure that he can control the new business. He realizes that he has no idea where to start, and has approached you for general advice about an accounting system.

Required:

Outlined on pages 288 and 289 is a general description of how Mr. Kent intends to operate the business of buying and selling the equipment. Using this information:

a. List the books, documents, and other records that will be required to record transactions for purchases and payments.

b. List the books, documents, and other records that will be required to record sales transactions and collections.

c. Write out in narrative form a basic accounting system for the buying and revenue cycles of Sooperman, Inc. The accounting system should focus on the

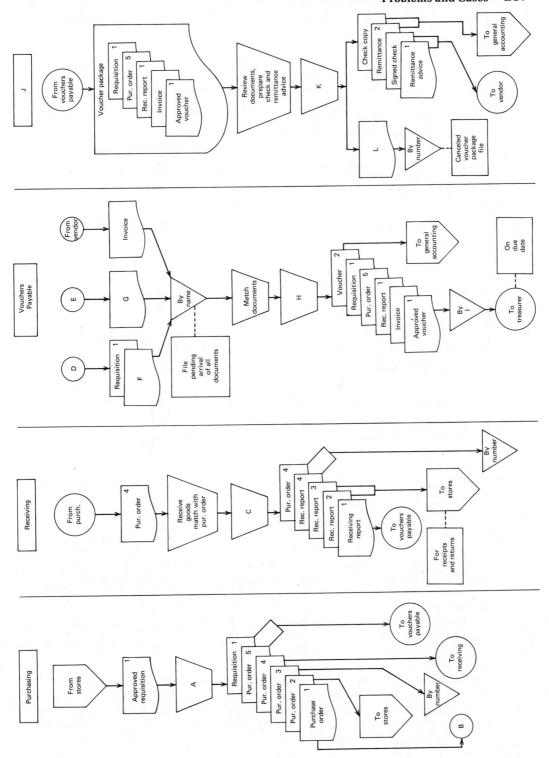

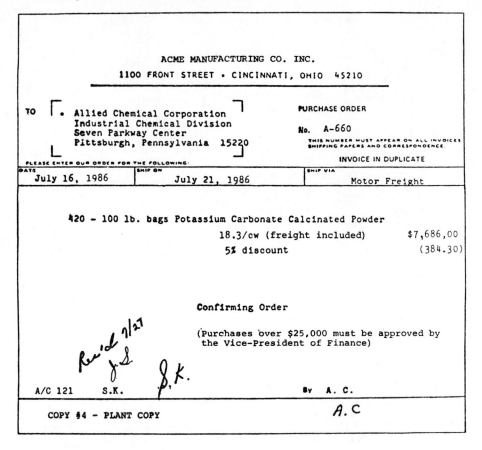

books, documents, and other records identified in Parts a and b. (Do not consider controls in your narrative.)

Buying Cycle

TVs and radios will be received bimonthly from Krypto, Inc., and invoiced at that time for payment 30 days later. At the end of each quarter, a bulk discount will be granted based on the number of units purchased during the quarter.

The discount will be calculated by Krypto, Inc., and remitted by check 10 days after the end of each quarter.

Orders must be sent to Krypto in writing and delivery will be made within two weeks.

All deliveries will be made to Sooperman's warehouse, and never directly to its customers.

Mr. Kent wishes to pay all his suppliers at the same time. Although Krypto will be his sole supplier for goods for resale, he knows that there will be expenses for stationery, utilities, fixtures, traveling, and entertaining. Mr. Kent will have two warehouse employees and a sales manager, in addition to a bookkeeper and six other administrative and secretarial personnel.

```
┌─────────────────────────────────────────────────────────────────┐
│                    ACME MANUFACTURING CO. INC.                    │
│                                                                   │
│                       RECEIVING REPORT                            │
│                                                                   │
│  FROM: Allied Chemical Corp.          Receiving Report            │
│        Industrial Chemical Division      No. R-660                │
│        Seven Parkway Center           (Identify damaged           │
│        Pittsburgh, Penn. 15220         stock specifically)        │
│ ─────────────────────────────────────────────────────────────────│
│  Purchase        July 16, 1986 │Requested          │Requested Shipping:│
│  Order Date:                   │Ship Date: July 21, 1986 │ Motor  Freight │
│ ─────────────────────────────────────────────────────────────────│
│                                                                   │
│  Goods ordered:                                                   │
│                                                                   │
│      420- 100 lb bags  Potassium Carbonate Calcinated             │
│             Powder                                                │
│               18.3/CW <freight included>      $7,686.00           │
│               5% Discount                      <384.30>           │
│  Goods received:                                                  │
│                                                                   │
│      400- 100 lb bags <18.3/CW> received in good                  │
│      condition. Stock stored at Public Warehouse Co.              │
│      <9th and Main St.>                                           │
│                                                                   │
│ ─────────────────────────────────────────────────────────────────│
│  Damaged Goods     │ Received by       │ Date Received            │
│  - 20 bags sent back│  Jim Smith       │  July 27, 1986          │
└─────────────────────────────────────────────────────────────────┘
```

Revenue Cycle

Mr. Kent intends to sell the sets via sales agents in nine major cities. The agents will communicate the orders they receive to the company, and shipments will be made to the customers.

At present, Mr. Kent has a list of interested customers, but he is leaving the development of new customers to the agents and the sales manager. Agents will be paid a base salary and a commission on each sale in the month in which the goods are delivered.

Mr. Kent also appreciates that cash flow will be very important in the early days of the new business, so he intends to bill customers on delivery with 30-day payment terms, offering a 2 percent cash discount to customers who pay within 10 days.

All sets are guaranteed by the manufacturer, and warranty claims will be made directly to Krypto, Inc., by customers.

8-63. Charting, Inc., a new audit client of yours, processes its sales and cash receipts documents in the following manner:

1. *Payment on account.* The mail is opened each morning by a mail clerk in the sales department. The mail clerk prepares a remittance advice (showing customer and amount paid) if one is not received. The checks and remittance advices are then for-

		Customer P.O. #	Invoice #	Invoice Date
Allied Chemical		A-660	01693	7/29/86

Ship to: Acme Manufacturing Co., Inc.
          1100 Front Street
          Cincinnati, Ohio 45210

8/19

Bill to: Acme Manufacturing Co., Inc.   Remit to: Allied Chemical Corp.
          1100 Front Street   P.O. Box 360142M
          Cincinnati, Ohio 45210   Mellon Square
                                                 Pittsburgh, Pa 15230

Terms: Net Cash 30 Days

Description	Code	Price	Quantity	Amount
Pot. Carb. Calc.	097-6130-84017	18.30/cw	420-100 1b bags	$7,686.00
Less	097-6130-84017	.05%		384.30
Plus Pallets	0-51837	1.05 Ea.		21.00

RECEIVED
July 27 86
ACME MANUFACTURING

DATE	CHECK NO.	QUAN. & PRICE
7/31	6253	*T.A.*
ACCOUNT CHARGE 121		AUDITOR *J.B.*

Packed By	# of Pkgs.	Date Shipped	Shipped Via		Total Amount
J.Y.	20	7/25/86	Motor Freight		$7,322.70

warded to the sales department supervisor, who reviews each check and forwards the checks and remittance advices to the accounting department supervisor.

The accounting department supervisor, who also functions as credit manager in approving new credit and all credit limits, reviews all checks for payments on past-due accounts and then forwards the checks and remittance advices to the accounts receivable clerk, who arranges the advices in alphabetical order. The remittance advices are posted directly to the accounts receivable ledger cards. The checks are endorsed by stamp and totaled. The total is posted to the cash receipts journal. The remittance advices are filed chronologically.

After receiving the cash from the previous day's cash sales, the accounts receivable clerk prepares the daily deposit slip in triplicate. The third copy of the deposit slip is filed by date and the second copy and the original accompany the bank deposit.

2. *Sales*. Sales clerks prepare sales invoices in triplicate. The original and second copy are presented to the cashier. The third copy is retained by the sales clerk in the sales book. When the sale is for cash, the customer pays the sales clerk, who presents the money to the cashier with the invoice copies.

A credit sale is approved by the cashier from an approved credit list after the sales clerk prepares the three-part invoice. After receiving the cash or approving the invoice, the cashier validates the original copy of the sales invoice and gives it to the customer. At the end of each day the cashier recaps the sales and cash received and forwards the cash and the second copy of all sales invoices to the accounts receivable clerk.

```
                  ACME MANUFACTURING CO. INC.

          1100 FRONT STREET      CINCINNATI, OHIO  45210

                              DATE      Check No.
                              8/19/86     6253
                                                              AMOUNT
     PAY   Allied Chemical Corporation
     TO    P.O. Box 360142M                                 $7,322.70
    THE
   ORDER   Mellon Square
     OF    Pittsburgh, Pa  15230                        VOID 90 DAYS AFTER DATE


                                                        NOT NEGOTIABLE

       THE FIRST NATIONAL BANK
          CINCINNATI, OHIO
        ELMWOOD PLACE OFFICE
                                                        AUTHORIZED SIGNATURE


            DETACH THIS REMITTANCE ADVICE BEFORE DEPOSITING CHECK
```

ENTRY DATE	REFERENCE	AMOUNT	DISCOUNT	PREVIOUS	BALANCE	A/C DIST.	DESCRIPTION
7/31/86	01693	$7,707.00	$384.30	-0-	$7,322.70	121	Pot. Powder
				H. M.			
COPY 2 - ACCOUNTING							6253

The accounts receivable clerk balances the cash received with cash sales invoices and prepares a daily sales summary. The credit sales invoices are posted to the accounts receivable ledger and then all invoices are sent to the inventory control clerk in the sales department for posting to the inventory control cards. After posting, the inventory control clerk files all invoices numerically. The accounts receivable clerk posts the daily sales summary to the cash receipts journal and sales journal and files the sales summaries by date.

The cash from cash sales is combined with the cash received on account, and this constitutes the daily bank deposit.

3. *Bank deposits.* The bank validates the deposit slip and returns the second copy to the accounting department where it is filed by date by the accounts receivable clerk.

Monthly bank statements are reconciled promptly by the accounting department supervisor and filed by date.

Required:
Flowchart the sales and cash receipts functions of Charting, Inc.

(AICPA adapted)

8–64. Anthony, CPA, prepared the flowchart on page 293, which portrays the raw materials purchasing function of one of Anthony's clients, a medium-sized manufacturing company, from the preparation of initial documents through the vouching of invoices for

INVENTORY RECORD

Item Description _POTASSIUM CARBONATE CALCINATED POWDER_

Unit Size _100 LB. BAGS_

ORDER				GOODS ON HAND			
Date	P.O.#	Quantity	Estimated Receipt Date	Date	Material Requisition Number	Quantity	Cumulative Balance
				6/3		520	520
				6/30	8623	⟨500⟩	20
7/16	A-660	420	7/21	7/21	–	400	420

payment in accounts payable. The flowchart was a portion of the work performed on the audit engagement to evaluate internal control.

Required:

Identify and explain the systems and control weaknesses evident from the flowchart. Include the internal control weaknesses resulting from activities performed or not performed. All documents are prenumbered.

(AICPA adapted)

8-65. You are reviewing audit workpapers containing a narrative description of the Tenney Corporation's factory payroll system. A portion of that narrative is as follows:

Factory employees punch time clock cards each day when entering or leaving the shop. At the end of each week the timekeeping department collects the time cards and prepares duplicate batch-control slips by department showing total hours and number of employees. The time cards and original batch-control slips are sent to the payroll accounting section. The second copies of the batch-control slips are filed by date.

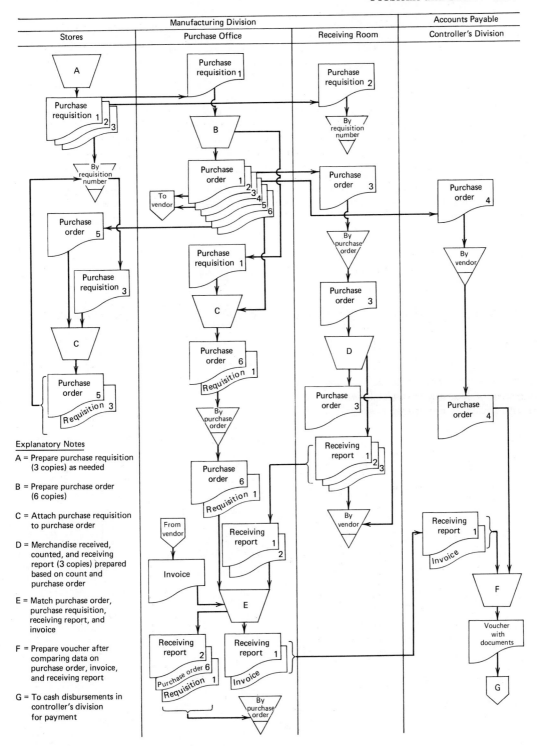

Explanatory Notes

A = Prepare purchase requisition
    (3 copies) as needed

B = Prepare purchase order
    (6 copies)

C = Attach purchase requisition
    to purchase order

D = Merchandise received,
    counted, and receiving
    report (3 copies) prepared
    based on count and
    purchase order

E = Match purchase order,
    purchase requisition,
    receiving report, and
    invoice

F = Prepare voucher after
    comparing data on
    purchase order, invoice,
    and receiving report

G = To cash disbursements in
    controller's division
    for payment

In the payroll accounting section payroll transaction cards are keypunched from the information on the time cards, and a batch total card for each batch is keypunched from the batch-control slip. The time cards and batch-control slips are then filed by batch for possible reference. The payroll transaction cards and batch total card are sent to data processing, where they are sorted by employee number within batch. Each batch is edited by a computer program that checks the validity of employee number against a master employee tape file and the total hours and number of employees against the batch total card. A detailed printout by batch and employee number is produced that indicates batches that do not balance and invalid employee numbers. This printout is returned to payroll accounting to resolve all differences.

In searching for documentation you found a flowchart of the payroll system that included all appropriate symbols (American National Standards Institute, Inc.) but was only partially labeled. The portion of this flowchart described by the foregoing narrative appears below.

Required:

a. Number your answer 1 through 17. Next to the corresponding number of your

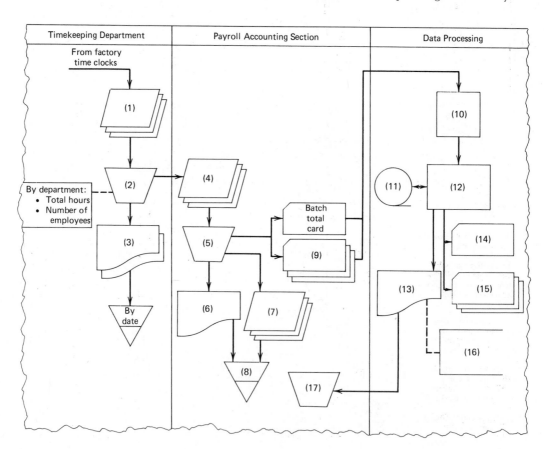

answer, supply the appropriate labeling (document name, process description, or file order) applicable to each numbered symbol on the flowchart.

b. Flowcharts are one of the aids an auditor may use to document and evaluate a client's internal control system. List advantages of using flowcharts in this context.

(AICPA adapted)

8–66. While auditing the Top Manufacturing Corporation, the auditor prepared the flowchart of credit sales activities on page 296. (In this flowchart Code Letter ''A'' represents CUSTOMER.)

Required:
Indicate what each of the code letters ''B'' through ''P'' represents. Do *not* discuss adequacies or inadequacies in the system of internal control.

(AICPA adapted)

8–67. The following internal accounting control procedures are employed by the Cooper Company:

1. Shipments of goods are authorized by the sales manager, who initials the sales order prepared by the sales personnel after approving terms and credit.
2. Sequentially prenumbered sales order forms are accounted for; sales order forms are matched with copies of invoices and shipping documents (bills of lading) on a monthly basis, and unmatched records are reviewed.
3. The accounts receivable subsidiary ledger is reconciled monthly with the control account in the general ledger.
4. Checks received through the mail are restrictively endorsed immediately on receipt.
5. Customers in the company cafeteria are given a receipt printed out by the cash register when they pay for their food; if the receipt has a star imprinted on it (as is the case 2 percent of the time), the meal is free.
6. All purchases of raw materials are made using purchase orders prepared by a purchasing agent; purchase orders over $2000 are reviewed and initialed by the vice-president—purchasing.
7. Goods received are inspected and counted or weighed by the receiving department and recorded on a receiving report.
8. Prenumbered receiving reports are matched with purchase orders and invoices; unmatched receiving reports are periodically investigated.
9. Supporting documents are canceled by the controller when she signs checks made out to vendors.
10. The numbers of sequentially prenumbered checks are periodically accounted for.

Required:
For each of the controls described

a. State the specific control objective that the procedure is designed to achieve.
b. Describe an error or irregularity that could occur if the control were absent or ineffective.
c. Describe a compliance test that the auditor could use to determine whether the control is operating effectively.

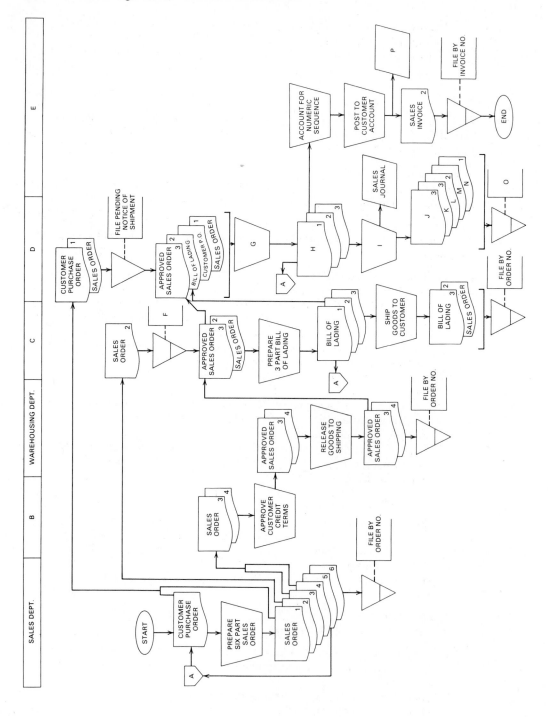

8-68. *Quinn Hardware* (Comprehensive Case on Documenting and Evaluating Internal Control)

Notes:

1. Before proceeding with this case, review the client background information for Quinn Hardware in Problem 6–61 in Chapter 6.
2. It will also be necessary to read the reference material that follows the case requirements. That material includes a narrative summary of the auditor's preliminary understanding, systems flowcharts for parts of Quinn's buying cycle, and selected sections (nos. 1, 2, 3, and 4) of an internal control questionnaire (Sections 1, 3, and 4 have been completed). Assume that the general computer controls have been evaluated and tested and can be relied on.

Required:

Part I: Complete a systems flowchart of the *ordering and receiving* segment of the Quinn Hardware buying cycle (steps 1 through 15 in the narrative). Cross-reference the numbered paragraphs in the narrative to the manual or computer procedure symbols in your flowchart.

Part II: A. List the significant programmed procedures in the *ordering and receiving* segment (steps 1 through 15) of Quinn Hardware's buying cycle. (Use the systems flowchart to assist you.)

B. Identify and describe the purpose of any reports generated from the programmed procedures identified in Part II (A).

Part III: Complete Internal Control Questionnaire Section 2 (furnished at the end of the case) on controls over receipt of goods and services for Quinn Hardware. (Use the systems flowcharts to assist you.) Cross-reference your responses on the questionnaire to the numbered paragraphs in the narrative. (The entire narrative and all flowcharts may be relevant to Section 2 of the ICQ.)

Note: Sections 1, 3, and 4 have already been completed.

Part IV: A. Identify and describe control weaknesses noted in Sections 2, 3, and 4 of the internal control questionnaire for the buying cycle. Cross-reference the weaknesses to the numbered questions on the questionnaire.

B. Determine whether the weaknesses identified in Part IV (A) could give rise to material errors in the financial statements and explain why.

C. Determine the effect of the weaknesses on the nature, timing, and extent of audit tests in the examination of Quinn Hardware's buying cycle.

REFERENCE MATERIAL
Summary of Auditor's Preliminary Understanding (Narrative)
(Note: Paragraph numbers correspond to
numbers indicated on the systems flowcharts.)

Ordering and Receiving

1. Purchase orders are prepared by either of the following methods:
   a. Quinn's computer generates a stock requirement report (SRR) weekly based on economic order quantity (EOQ) criteria.

    b. A purchase order requisition (POR) is prepared by a purchasing clerk, as required, and processed with other items not covered on the SRR.

2. The SRR is reviewed by the purchasing clerk, who can change quantities. The clerk also confirms prices and estimated receiving dates for items on the SRR and POR with suppliers and notes those details on the documents.

3. The purchasing clerk then uses a terminal in the purchasing section to perform the following functions:

    a. Amend quantity details, as necessary, on SRR-generated information.

    b. Input POR information.

    c. Record estimated delivery dates for SRR and PORs.

4. The system then generates a five-part prenumbered purchase order (PO) and a Purchase Order Listing. PO sequence numbers are allocated by the computer on the basis of last PO on file plus one. The Purchase Order Listing contains details of all POs generated and indicates whether the PO was generated from the SRR or POR.

POs contain the following details:

- Quantities ordered.
- Prices agreed with supplier.
- Any other charges or discounts.

At the same time as POs and the Purchase Order Listing are generated, the following computerized functions take place:

- Matching of product number to the Product Number Table to ensure that the product number exists.
- Matching of vendor number to the Vendor Master File to ensure that the vendor number exists.
- Updating of the "Outstanding Purchase Order File" with details of all POs.
- Earmarking stock items on the Inventory Master File to show that the item has been ordered.

Invalid matches of product numbers or vendor numbers are rejected on the screen for the purchasing clerk to correct.

5. Both POs and the Purchase Order Listing are reviewed by the purchasing supervisor and initialed to indicate approval. The Purchase Order Listing and SRR are permanently filed by date and the five-part POs are handled as follows:

    1. To vendor.

    2. To warehouse receiving department and temporarily filed by vendor number (see next paragraph).

    3. To central accounts payable department and temporarily filed alphabetically.

    4. Permanently filed alphabetically.

    5. Permanently filed numerically.

6. When goods are received at the warehouse receiving department, the second part of the PO is matched with the packing slip. The goods are inspected and counted by the receiver. The packing slip and PO are attached and are now

called a receiving memo (R/M). The date received is entered on the R/M and the R/M is initialed and dated by the receiver.

If goods are refused, they are sent back to the vendor with the packing slip. If only partial shipment is received, the quantity received is entered on the PO, which is returned to the temporary file. A partial shipment form is completed and treated in the same manner as a normal receipt. There is a separate numerical sequence for partial receipt forms. The original PO is submitted when the final shipment is made. Partial shipment forms must be approved by the supervisor. (Partial shipments represent an immaterial transaction volume; therefore, you need not include them on your flowchart.)

7. A clerk in the warehouse uses a terminal (located in the warehouse) to input R/M details.
8. The following edit checks are performed by the computer as each R/M is input:
   a. The PO number is matched to the Outstanding Purchase Order File to ensure that it is a valid PO number.
   b. For each line item on the R/M, the product number is matched to a Product Number Table to ensure that the product number exists.
   c. For each line item on the R/M, the quantity is matched to the Outstanding Purchase Order File. If the quantities differ, the system requests the clerk to confirm the quantity input.
   d. The date received is matched to calendar date.
   e. The vendor number is matched to the Vendor Master File to ensure that it is a valid vendor number.

If any of the above edit checks fail, the transaction is rejected on the terminal. It is the responsibility of the warehouse clerk to determine the reason for the rejection. Errors are corrected and re-input in the same fashion as new input.

9. On accepting the R/Ms, the computer updates the following files:
   - Inventory Master File.
   - Receipts History File (at standard costs per the Inventory Master File).
   - Outstanding Receipts File (at standard cost per the Inventory Master File).

   Accepted receiving memos are written directly to the Outstanding Receipts File and Receipts History File, priced at the standard cost recorded on the Inventory Master File.

   At the same time as the Inventory Master File is referred to for the extraction of standard cost, the "quantity on hand" and the "date of last receipt" fields are updated. (The SRR is generated based on EOQ criteria after the quantity on hand has been updated.)

   The Outstanding Purchase Order File is updated to reflect filled purchase orders (PO deleted). Partial deliveries do not delete the related PO but earmark them as such.

   The computer also generates the following *daily* output:
   a. Daily Edit Report, containing the following information:
      - Duplicate R/M numbers. (*Note:* For processing efficiency, duplicate R/Ms are accepted and reported for subsequent follow-up.)
      - Differences in quantities recorded on PO and input from R/Ms.

- Details and totals at standard cost of R/Ms accepted and R/Ms deleted as a result of purchase invoices being matched against R/Ms.

b. Daily transaction tape of R/Ms, which is filed in the library for three generations.

c. Inventory Summary Report (opening and closing totals of inventory at standard cost).

d. Receipts Update Report showing (at standard cost):

- Opening balance of the Outstanding Receipts File.

- Updates to the Outstanding Receipts File arising from the matching of R/Ms to the Outstanding Purchase Order File and deletions of R/Ms as a result of purchase invoices being processed.

- The theoretical balance of the Outstanding Receipts File, which is determined by adding/subtracting updates to/from the opening balance.

- The actual closing balance of the Outstanding Receipts File, which is determined by accumulating the value of all outstanding R/Ms on file.

- The difference, if any, between the theoretical and actual closing balances of the Outstanding Receipts File.

The system also produces the following general ledger entry on the basis of items written to the Outstanding Receipts File:

Inventory	Recorded at Standard Cost
Accrued Liabilities	Recorded at Standard Cost

The system interfaces with the general ledger system. Posting to the General Ledger Master File is done daily, and the foregoing information is shown on the General Ledger Posting Summary. This report is sent to the controller's department (use and follow-up of this report are not part of the buying cycle of Quinn Hardware).

10. At the conclusion of overnight processing, the edit reports are transmitted to the warehouses. The edit reports containing the duplicate R/Ms and differences in quantities are investigated by the warehouse clerk. The clerk identifies the reason for the discrepancy by reference to the original documents. The edit report is stamped "corrected" and the corrections are reentered along with the regular transactions for the day.

11. Daily, the warehouse clerk performs the following functions:

Receipts Update Report:

a. Agrees the opening balance to the closing balance on the prior day's report.

b. Agrees the "updates" figure on the Receipts Update Report to the "accepted" totals on the Daily Edit Report.

c. Follows up any differences between the theoretical and actual closing balances by reference to the Daily Edit Report.

Inventory Summary Report:

d. Reconciles the movements on the Inventory Summary Report to the Receipts Update Report. (*Note:* For the purposes of this case, assume that the reconciliation includes inventory issuances and adjustments.)

12. The warehouse supervisor reviews the reconciliation of the Inventory Summary Report to the Receipts Update Report and the reconciliation of the Receipts Update Report to the Daily Edit Report and initials the reports and

reconciliations as evidence. The Inventory Summary Report, Receipts Update Report, and reconciliations are filed daily. The Daily Edit Report is reviewed, and initialed as evidence, to ensure that rejections have been followed up. This report is filed daily.

13. Weekly, the computer department generates a listing of all outstanding POs (i.e., not flagged as received). This report is sent to the purchasing department.

14. An expediter in the purchasing department investigates the listing of outstanding POs. The reported items are agreed to the POs, overdue orders are investigated, and corrections are entered and each item on the listing is marked.

15. A supervisor reviews the report on a monthly basis and initials it to evidence the review. It is then filed by date.

Processing Invoices Received

16. When vendor invoices are received in the accounts payable department, a function stamp is stamped on the invoice. The PO number (which is also called the R/M number), vendor number, and a product number are recorded, if missing. The invoices are batched for control purposes, and a batch header is prepared by a control clerk who computes and logs the value batch total and document count. A batch number is also assigned and logged. A clerk in the accounting department inputs the invoice details using a terminal. Due dates for invoices are also input.

17. The invoices in a batch are totaled and agreed to header details by the computer. If the totals disagree, the entire batch is rejected.

The following programmed edit checks are performed by matching the invoices to the Vendor Master File and Product Number Table:

- Syntax of all fields.
- Existence of vendor and product numbers.
- Additions and extensions of invoice.

If an invoice fails one of those edits, only that invoice is rejected. Rejected invoices are written to an Error Suspense File and remain there until corrected.

After invoices pass the initial edit and batch total checks, the computer matches invoices to the Outstanding Receipts File (keys are PO number and vendor number). The match of the invoice to the Outstanding Receipts File includes price and quantity data, which are matched on line items.

Invoices are rejected when any of the following conclusions are encountered:
a. No R/M in the Outstanding Receipts File. (This includes duplicate invoices.)
b. Like item quantities differ.
c. Prices (actual versus standard) differ by the lesser of $10 or 1 percent per line item.

Rejected invoices are written to the Error Suspense File and remain there until corrected. As valid matches occur, the R/M is deleted from the Outstanding Receipts File.

18. Accepted invoices are written to a transaction tape, which is filed in the library and retained for three generations.

The following daily reports are generated:

- Totals (documents and dollars) of accepted transactions.
- Complete details and totals of rejected batches.
- An edit report containing complete details and totals of rejected transactions (with error code):

    Invalid syntax fields.
    Invalid vendor and product number.
    Incorrect additions and extensions of invoice.
    Missing R/M.
    Quantity differences.
    Price differences.

Note: Where the price differences are smaller than the lesser of $10 or 1 percent per line item, the invoices are accepted. However, these items are still reported for investigation, although they are *not* included in the totals of rejected transactions.

19. The accepted invoices are written to the Vendor Master File.

    Daily, an A/P Update Report is generated that reflects opening and closing balances in the Vendor Master File.

20. The edit reports and the A/P Update Report are sent to the A/P department, where a control clerk totals the rejected batches and transactions from the edit report and records them in the log. The total of the accepted transactions is reconciled to the adjusted input total. The closing log total is calculated and reconciled to the A/P Update Report.

21. The log is initialed by an A/P supervisor to evidence review of the reconciliation.

22. The clerk traces rejected batches to the original document and verifies each transaction. The batch header is corrected and the batch resubmitted and recorded in the control log. The clerk also traces the rejected invoices to the original supplier's invoice and determines and corrects the error. A corrected batch header is prepared for the batch of corrected invoices and entered in the log and the batch is resubmitted. The edit and A/P Update Reports are filed by date.

23. An A/P supervisor reviews the edit report to ensure that the above procedures are being properly performed and that the rejected and resubmitted invoice totals are in balance. The edit report is initialed as evidence of the review. The edit and A/P Update Reports are filed by date.

    Note: As all rejections are written to the Error Suspense File, they continue to be reported on the edit reports until cleared. Corrections are processed in the same way as usual transactions, with the exception that they are identified as corrections so that they may be deleted from the Error Suspense File.

24. Weekly, the following reports are generated:
    - Missing invoices.
    - Cash Requirements Report (listing invoices scheduled for payment in the next payment run and a summary of projected payments for the next six weeks).
    - General Ledger Weekly Posting Totals (including purchase price variances, reversals of accruals, and A/P control account). (*Note:* This report can be ignored for the purposes of this case since it is not part of the buying cycle.)

The Missing Invoice Report is sent to the A/P department; the Cash Requirements Report is sent to the budget clerk.

25. The A/P clerk follows up on the Missing Invoice Report.
26. The A/P department supervisor reviews the Missing Invoice Report weekly to ensure that proper action has been taken. The supervisor initials the reports to evidence the review. The Missing Invoice Report is filed by date in the A/P department.

Cash Disbursements

27. The budget clerk in the controller's department reviews the Cash Requirements Report and alters payment dates, as appropriate. The clerk prepares the bank transfer advice.
28. The controller examines the Cash Requirements Report and signs the bank transfer advice.
29. The payment date changes are input by the budget clerk using a terminal.
30. Weekly, the computer department updates the Vendor and Outstanding Check Master Files for check disbursements.

    The following check run output is generated:
    - Payments Control Report (total of checks produced and number of invoices paid).
    - Check Register.
    - Payment Summary (listing of checks over $10,000 and total value of all checks produced).
    - Checks.

31. The Payments Control Report is sent to the accounts payable department and the total value of disbursements is entered into a control log by the control clerk. The Payments Control Report is filed by date.
32. The controller reviews the Payment Summary and agrees the transfer advice total to the Payment Summary total. Both documents are initialed by the controller and filed by date for later use in the bank reconciliation.
33. The controller's secretary signs the checks by machine and enters the total in a log; she obtains that total by referring to the Check Register. She has custody of the keys and is a bonded employee.
34. The controller examines the machine counter and initials the Check Register and log. The checks are sent directly to the mail room to be forwarded to vendors.
35. The Check Register and transfer advices are summarized monthly by an accounting clerk who prepares a journal entry (J/E).
36. The chief accountant approves and initials the J/E. The J/E is sent to EDP.
37. The computer department updates the Outstanding Check Master File by using a paid check computer tape received from the bank (keys are vendor number, check number, and amount) and generates an Outstanding Check Listing.
38. The Outstanding Check Listing, along with the Payment Summary and transfer advice, is used by the chief accountant to prepare the monthly bank reconciliations.
39. The controller examines and initials the reconciliations.

Quinn Hardware Buying Cycle: Systems Flowchart No. 2—Quinn Hardware Processing Invoices Received

Accounts Payable

EDP

From purchasing

A

Purchase order

From vendor

Invoice

A

16

Invoices stamped

Batch header
Invoice order
Purchase order

Control log

Terminal

Error suspense file
O/S receipts file

Vendor master file
Product number table

Edit and match 17

Vendor master file

Update 19

O/S receipts file
G/L file

Vendor master file

Report generation 24

Accepted transaction totals 18
Rejected batches
Edit report

To tape library and retained for 3 generations

Trans. tape

A/P update report

Cash requirements report
G/L totals
Missing invoices

To budget clerk

B

Control log reconciled to A/P update report

Rejections corrected and re-input

20

21 Reviewed by supervisor

22

23 Reviewed by supervisor

Batch header
Invoice
PO

Reports

25 Missing invoices followed up

26 Reviewed by supervisor

D

D

N

Daily

Weekly

Quinn Hardware Buying Cycle: Systems Flowchart No. 3—Quinn Hardware Cash Disbursements

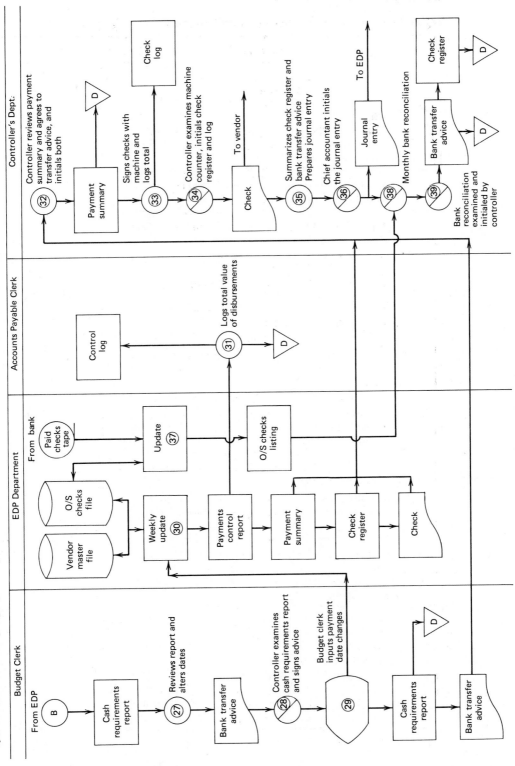

Quinn Hardware Internal Control Questionnaire for Buying Cycle

Section 1: Controls over Purchase Orders Issued			
Questionnaire	*Flowchart Reference*	*Yes*	*No*
Purchase Authorization			
1.1 Are all significant purchase commitments and changes thereto initiated only on the basis of appropriate written authorizations?	5	X	
1.2 Are all purchase commitments referred to in 1.1 recorded in written form?	4	X	
1.3 Do the commitment records state, insofar as practicable:			
(a) quantities;	4	X	
(b) prices;	4	X	
(c) other relevant terms (e.g., discounts, freight terms)?	4	X	
Completeness of Input and Updating			
Specify below the principal control that ensures that all details of purchase commitments and changes thereto are input to the computer and updated. If the principal control is:			
(a) computer sequence check of serially numbered input documents, answer questions 1.4 to 1.9;		X	
(b) agreement of manually established batch totals, specify totals used and answer questions 1.10 to 1.14.	N/A		
Computer Sequence Check			
1.4 Are there adequate controls to ensure that all transactions are recorded on a serially numbered document?	4	X	
1.5 Is the method used in the program for reviewing numerical sequence appropriate (i.e., does it permit changes in sequence and more than one sequence running at a time)?	4	X	
1.6 Is a printout of missing documents produced at regular intervals (e.g., weekly)?	13	X	
1.7 Is a total of accepted items accumulated by the computer during the sequence check run agreed to the total of items written to the purchase commitment file or, alternatively, are such totals carried through intermediate processing (including summarization			

	of totals or changes in the totals used) so that it is established that all accepted input items are updated to the purchase commitment file?			X
1.8	Is the reconciliation of totals in 1.7 carried out manually or, alternatively, is the reconciliation carried out by the computer with adequate evidence of this check being printed out?			X
1.9	Are there adequate procedures for: (a) investigation of missing documents (1.6); (b) investigation and correction of differences disclosed by the update reconciliations (1.8)?	14	X	X
Batch Totals 1.10	Are there adequate controls to ensure that: (a) a document is created for all purchase commitments; (b) all documents are included in a batch; (c) all batches are submitted for processing?	N/A		
1.11	Are the totals of individual items accepted by the computer compared manually with predetermined control totals or, alternatively, is such a comparison made by the computer with adequate evidence of the check being printed out?	N/A		
1.12	Are the totals in 1.11 agreed to the total of items written to the purchase commitment file or, alternatively, are such totals carried through intermediate processing (including summarization of totals or changes in the totals used) so that it is established that all accepted input items are updated to the purchase commitment file?	N/A		
1.13	Is the reconciliation of totals in 1.12 carried out manually or, alternatively, is the reconciliation carried out by the computer with adequate evidence of this check being printed out?	N/A		
1.14	Are there adequate procedures for: (a) investigation and correction of differences disclosed by the input reconciliations (1.11); (b) resubmission of all rejections; (c) investigation and correction of differences disclosed by the update reconciliations (1.13)?	N/A		

Continued

Questionnaire	Flowchart Reference	Yes	No
Disciplines over Basic Input Completeness and Updating Controls			
1.15 Are the following procedures either performed or checked by persons other than those involved in computer operations:			
(a) investigation of missing documents (1.9(a)); (D)	14	X	
(b) manual agreement of input totals (1.11); (D)	N/A		
(c) investigation and correction of differences disclosed by the input reconciliations (1.14(a)); (D)	N/A		
(d) resubmission of all rejections (1.14(b)); (D)	N/A		
(e) manual agreement of update totals (1.8, 1.13); (D)			X
(f) investigation and correction of differences disclosed by the update reconciliations (1.9(b), 1.14(c))? (D)			X
Note: (D) = disciplinary control—segregation of duties			
1.16 Are the results of the following procedures reviewed and approved by a responsible official:			
(a) investigation of missing documents (1.9(a)); (S)	15	X	
(b) manual agreement of input totals (1.11); (S)	N/A		
(c) investigation and correction of differences disclosed by the input reconciliations (1.14(a)); (S)	N/A		
(d) resubmission of all rejections (1.14(b)); (S)	N/A		
(e) manual agreement of update totals (1.8, 1.13); (S)			X
(f) investigation and correction of differences disclosed by the update reconciliations (1.9(b), 1.14(c))? (S)			X
Note: (S) = disciplinary control—supervision			
Accuracy of Input and Updating			
1.17 Are there adequate controls to ensure that the following fields are accurately input and updated (e.g., batch totals, edit checks in program, reporting of nonmatched items):			
Input			
(a) quantity—unchanged SRR items;	1	X	
—changed SRR items and POR;			X
(b) inventory and vendor reference fields?	4	X	
Update			
(a) quantity;			X
(b) inventory and vendor reference fields?			X

1.18 Are there adequate procedures for: *Input*				
(a) agreement of totals, where applicable;	N/A			
(b) investigation and correction of differences or exceptions?	4	X		
Update				
(a) agreement of totals, where applicable;	N/A			
(b) investigation and correction of differences or exceptions?				X
1.19 Are the following procedures either performed or checked by persons other than those involved in computer operations: *Input*				
(a) agreement of totals, where applicable (1.18(a)); (D)	N/A			
(b) investigation and correction of differences or exceptions (1.18(b))? (D)	4	X		
Update				
(a) agreement of totals, where applicable (1.18(a)); (D)	N/A			
(b) investigation and correction of differences or exceptions (1.18(b))? (D)				X
1.20 Are the results of the following procedures reviewed and approved by a responsible official: *Input*				
(a) agreement of totals, where applicable (1.18(a)); (S)	N/A			
(b) investigation and correction of differences or exceptions (1.18(b))? (S)	5	X		
Update				
(a) agreement of totals, where applicable (1.18(a)); (S)	N/A			
(b) investigation and correction of differences or exceptions (1.18(b))? (S)				X
Computer-Generated Orders **1.21** Are the methods used in the program to generate the commitments appropriate?	1,9	X		
1.22 Is there an adequate check over the accuracy of the commitments generated (e.g., reasonableness check, manual review of generated commitments)?	2	X		
1.23 Are the results of the check (1.22) reviewed and approved by a responsible official? (S)	5	X		
1.24 Is a total (specify total used) of generated items accumulated by the computer and agreed manually to a				

Continued

Questionnaire	Flowchart Reference	Yes	No
total of items written to the purchase commitment file or, alternatively, are the totals agreed by the computer with adequate evidence of this check being printed out?			X
1.25 Are there adequate procedures for investigation and correction of differences disclosed by the update reconciliation (1.24)?			X
1.26 Are the following procedures either performed or reviewed by persons other than those involved in computer operations: (a) manual agreement of update totals (1.24); (D) (b) investigation and correction of differences disclosed by the update reconciliation (1.25)? (D)			X X
1.27 Are the results of the following procedures reviewed and approved by a responsible official: (a) manual agreement of update totals (1.24); (S) (b) investigation and correction of differences disclosed by the update reconciliation (1.25)? (S)			X X
Authorization 1.28 If data are authorized prior to the establishment of the controls for completeness and accuracy of input (e.g., prior to establishment of batch control totals or recording on a sequentially numbered document), are there adequate controls (e.g., reviewing authorization after batch control totals have been established or sequentially numbered documents have been created) to ensure that: (a) no unauthorized alterations are made to authorized data during subsequent processing; (b) unauthorized data are not added; (c) all authorized items are included in subsequent processing?	 N/A N/A N/A		
Record of Unfulfilled Commitments 1.29 If the computer evaluates unfulfilled purchase commitments, are there adequate controls over: (a) where applicable, file creation; (b) the authorization of amendments; (c) the completeness of writing amendments to the file; (d) the accuracy of writing amendments to the file; (e) the maintenance of the data on file?	N/A		

		Flowchart Reference	Yes	No
1.30	Is the method used in the program for the calculation of value appropriate?	N/A		
1.31	Are there adequate controls over the file holding details of outstanding purchase commitments to ensure that details of purchase commitments and changes thereto are completely and accurately maintained (e.g., manual control account)?			X
1.32	Is the method used in the program to match goods and, where applicable, services received to purchase commitments on file appropriate (e.g., does it flag or delete matched items)?	8	X	
1.33	Is a printout of items outstanding for an unreasonable length of time (e.g., over one month) produced at regular intervals?	13	X	
1.34	Are unmatched commitments (1.33) reviewed on a regular basis (e.g., monthly) to determine the reason for any that have not been matched?	14	X	
1.35	Are the following procedures either performed or reviewed by persons other than those involved in computer operations: (a) maintenance of the outstanding purchase commitments file (1.31); (D) (b) review of unmatched commitments (1.34)? (D)	14	X	X
1.36	Are the results of the following procedures reviewed and approved by a responsible official: (a) maintenance of the outstanding purchase commitments file (1.31); (S) (b) review of unmatched commitments (1.34)? (S)	15	X	X

Section 2: Controls over Receipt of Goods and Services

	Questionnaire	*Flowchart Reference*	*Yes*	*No*
Initial Recording of Receipt of Goods and Services				
2.1	Are the following ascertained by suitable methods (such as by counting or weighing and inspecting goods received) and the results recorded at the time of their receipt for subsequent comparison with the related invoices: (a) nature, quantity, and condition of goods received (including property, plant, and equipment and major supplies); (b) major services received (to the extent practicable)? (not in case)			

Continued

Questionnaire	Flowchart Reference	Yes	No

Completeness of Input and Updating
    Specify below the principal control that ensures that all details of goods and, where applicable, services received are input to the computer and updated. If the principal control is:
    (a) computer matching with a file of purchase commitments placed, answer questions 2.2 to 2.5;
    (b) computer sequence check of serially numbered input documents, answer questions 2.6 to 2.11;
    (c) agreement of manually established batch totals, specify totals used and answer questions 2.12 to 2.16.			

Computer Matching 2.2 Are the matching procedures adequate to ensure that details of goods and, where applicable, services received are input completely? (*Note*: Your answer to this question should be based on answers in Section 1 of the questionnaire.)			
2.3 Is a total of accepted items accumulated by the computer during the matching run agreed to the total of items written to the receipts file or, alternatively, are such totals carried through intermediate processing (including summarization of totals or changes in the totals used) so that it is established that all accepted input items are updated to the receipts file?			
2.4 Is the reconciliation of totals in 2.3 carried out manually or, alternatively, is the reconciliation carried out by the computer with adequate evidence of this control being printed out? (manually)			

2.5   Are there adequate procedures for:
    (a) investigation and correction of differences disclosed by the matching process (2.2);
    (b) investigation and correction of differences disclosed by the update reconciliation (2.4)?			

Computer Sequence Check 2.6 Are there adequate controls to ensure that all transactions are recorded on a serially numbered document?			

2.7	Is the method used in the program for reviewing numerical sequence appropriate (i.e., does it recognize changes in sequence and more than one sequence running at a time)?			
2.8	Is a printout of missing documents produced at regular intervals (e.g., weekly)?			
2.9	Is a total of accepted items accumulated by the computer during the sequence check run agreed to the total of items written to the receipts file or, alternatively, are such totals carried through intermediate processing (including summarization of totals or changes in the totals used) so that it is established that all accepted input items are updated to the receipts file?			
2.10	Is the reconciliation of totals in 2.9 carried out manually or, alternatively, is the reconciliation carried out by the computer with adequate evidence of this control being printed out?			
2.11	Are there adequate procedures for: (a) investigation of missing documents (2.8); (b) investigation and correction of differences disclosed by the update reconciliations (2.10)?			
Batch Totals 2.12	Are there adequate controls to ensure that: (a) a document is prepared for all goods and services received; (b) all documents are included in a batch; (c) all batches are submitted for processing?			
2.13	Are the totals of individual items accepted by the computer compared manually with predetermined control totals or, alternatively, is such a comparison made by the computer with adequate evidence of the control being printed out?			
2.14	Are the totals in 2.13 agreed to the total of items written to the receipts file or, alternatively, are such totals carried through intermediate processing (including summarization of totals or changes in the totals used) so that it is established that all accepted input items are updated to the receipts file?			
2.15	Is the reconciliation of totals in 2.14 carried out manually or, alternatively, is the reconciliation carried out by the computer with adequate evidence of this control being printed out?			

Continued

Questionnaire	Flowchart Reference	Yes	No
2.16 Are there adequate procedures for: (a) investigation and correction of differences disclosed by the input reconciliations (2.13); (b) resubmission of all rejections; (c) investigation and correction of differences disclosed by the update reconciliations (2.15)?			
Disciplines over Basic Input Completeness and Updating Controls 2.17 Are the following procedures either performed or reviewed by persons other than those involved in computer operations: (a) investigation and correction of differences disclosed by the matching process (2.5(a)); (b) investigation of missing documents (2.11(a)); (c) manual agreement of input totals (2.13); (d) investigation and correction of differences disclosed by the input reconciliations (2.16(a)); (e) resubmission of all rejections (2.16(b)); (f) manual agreement of update totals (2.4, 2.10, 2.15); (g) investigation and correction of differences disclosed by the update reconciliations (2.5(b), 2.11(b), 2.16(c))?			
2.18 Are the results of the following procedures reviewed and approved by a responsible official: (a) investigation and correction of differences disclosed by the matching process (2.5(a)); (b) investigation of missing documents (2.11(a)); (c) manual agreement of input totals (2.13); (d) investigation and correction of differences disclosed by the input reconciliations (2.16(a)); (e) resubmission of all rejections (2.16(b)); (f) manual agreement of update totals (2.4, 2.10, 2.15); (g) investigation and correction of differences disclosed by the update reconciliations (2.5(b), 2.11(b), 2.16(c))?			

Accuracy of Input and Updating			
2.19 Are there adequate controls to ensure that the following fields are accurately input and updated (e.g., batch totals, edit checks in programs, reporting of nonmatched items):			
Input			
(a) quantity;			
(b) inventory/vendor reference fields?			
Update			
(a) quantity;			
(b) inventory/vendor reference fields?			
2.20 Are there adequate procedures for:			
Input			
(a) the agreement of totals, where applicable;			
(b) investigation and correction of differences or exceptions?			
Update			
(a) the agreement of totals, where applicable;			
(b) investigation and correction of differences or exceptions?			
2.21 Are the following procedures either performed or reviewed by persons other than those involved in computer operations:			
Input			
(a) agreement of totals, where applicable (2.20(a));			
(b) investigation and correction of differences or exceptions (2.20(b))?			
Update			
(a) agreement of totals, where applicable (2.20(a));			
(b) investigation and correction of differences or exceptions (2.20(b))?			
2.22 Are the results of the following procedures reviewed and approved by a responsible official:			
Input			
(a) agreement of totals, where applicable (2.20(a));			
(b) investigation and correction of differences or exceptions (2.20(b))?			
Update			
(a) agreement of totals, where applicable (2.20(a));			
(b) investigation and correction of differences or exceptions (2.20(b))?			

Continued

Questionnaire	Flowchart Reference	Yes	No
Liability for Unprocessed Invoices 2.23 If the computer evaluates details of goods and services received, are there adequate controls over: (a) where applicable, file creation; (b) the authorization of amendments; (c) the completeness of writing amendments to the file; (d) the accuracy of writing amendments to the file; (e) the maintenance of the data on file? (not in case)			
2.24 Is the method used in the program for the calculation of value appropriate? (Value is a generic term for price, quantity, or other measurements.)			
2.25 Are there adequate controls over the file holding details of outstanding goods and, where applicable, services received, so that such details are completely and accurately maintained and subject only to authorized adjustments (e.g., manual control account)?			
2.26 Is the method used in the program to match invoices to goods and, where applicable, services received appropriate (i.e., does it flag or delete matched items)?			
2.27 Is a printout of items outstanding for an unreasonable length of time (e.g., over one month) produced at regular intervals?			
2.28 Are unmatched records of goods and, where applicable, services (2.27) reviewed on a regular basis (e.g., monthly) to determine the reasons for any such receipts that have not been matched within a reasonable period of time?			
2.29 Are there systematic procedures for determining on a regular basis the liabilities for major services received and payments to be made other than any covered by the procedures in 2.25 to 2.28 (e.g., telephone services, municipal taxes or rates, liabilities under leases, royalties, commissions)? (not in case)			

2.30	Are the following procedures either performed or reviewed by persons other than those involved in computer operations: (a) maintenance of and control over the outstanding goods and services received file (2.25); (b) review of unmatched records of goods and, where applicable, services received (2.28); (c) determination of liability for services not covered in 2.25 to 2.28 (2.29)?			
2.31	Are the results of the following procedures reviewed and approved by a responsible official: (a) maintenance of and control over the outstanding goods and services received file (2.25); (b) review of unmatched records of goods and, where applicable, services received (2.28); (c) determination of liability for services not covered in 2.25 to 2.28 (2.29)?			

Entries in Inventory Records

2.32	Where required, are the records of goods received (2.1) used to post quantities to detailed inventory records?			

Section 3: Controls over Accuracy and Validity of Invoices Received

Questionnaire	*Flowchart Reference*	*Yes*	*No*
Specify below whether invoices for goods and, where applicable, services rendered are compared manually or by the computer with receiving reports and purchase orders with regard to: (a) quantities and condition of goods and services received; (b) nature and quantities of goods ordered; (c) prices and other terms	3,16 3,16 3,16	computer computer computer	
As to (a) above, if the comparison is done by the computer, answer question 3.1 or, if the comparison is done manually, answer questions 3.7 and 3.8.			
As to (b) above, if the comparison is done by the computer, answer question 3.2 or, if the comparison is done manually, answer question 3.9.			
As to (c) above, if the comparison is done by the computer, answer questions 3.3 to 3.6 or, if the comparison is done manually, answer question 3.10.			

Continued

Questionnaire	Flowchart Reference	Yes	No
Computer Comparisons			
3.1 Review the answers to Section 2:			
(a) are there adequate controls to ensure that:			
(i) quantities of goods and services received have been accurately recorded and maintained on the file (2.2 to 2.31);	11,12	X	
(ii) unauthorized records are not added (2.25);	11,12	X	
(b) is the method used in the program to match quantities on invoices with goods and services received records appropriate (2.26);	17	X	
(c) are differences disclosed by the matching process adequately investigated and suitable action taken (2.28)?	25	X	
3.2 Is the method used in the program to match goods and services received to purchase commitments appropriate?	8	X	
3.3 If purchase invoices are compared by computer with a record of goods and services ordered and/or received for prices and other terms, review the answers to questions 2.25 to 2.31:			
(a) is the method used in the program to match invoices and goods and services received to purchase orders appropriate;	8,17	X	
(b) are there adequate controls to ensure that unauthorized records are not added to the relevant files?	11,12	X	
3.4 If invoice/credit memoranda prices are compared by computer with a standard price file:			
(a) are there adequate controls over:			
(i) where applicable, file creation;			
(ii) the authorization of amendments;			
(iii) the completeness of writing amendments to the file;	N/A to case study		
(iv) the accuracy of writing amendments to the file;			
(v) the maintenance of the data on the file; (not in case)			
(b) is the method used in the program for matching appropriate;	17	X	
(c) is suitable action taken on variances (such as reporting and investigating items exceeding a predetermined tolerance)?	22	X	

3.5	Are the procedures in 3.4(c) performed or reviewed by persons other than those involved in computer operations?	22	X	
3.6	Are the results of the procedures in 3.4(c) reviewed and approved by a responsible official?	23	X	
Manual Comparisons				
3.7	Are invoices for goods and services received compared with receiving records as to quantities and condition of goods and services received?	N/A		
3.8	Are invoices for services received, other than those covered in 3.1 and 3.6, compared with the underlying documentation (e.g., completion reports, leases, records of meter readings) or, if such documentation is not available, approved by a responsible official?	N/A		
3.9	Are invoices for goods and, where applicable, services received compared with purchase orders as to nature and quantity of goods or services ordered?	N/A		
3.10	Are invoices for goods and, where applicable, services received compared with purchase orders or vendors' price lists as to prices and other terms?	N/A		
Recalculating Extensions and Additions				
	Specify below the method used for recalculating extensions and additions of invoices and credit memoranda. If the recalculating is done: (a) by the computer, answer questions 3.11 to 3.14; (b) manually, answer questions 3.15 and 3.16.	N/A	X	
Computer Recalculations				
3.11	Is the method used in the program to recalculate extensions and additions of invoices and credit memoranda appropriate?	17	X	
3.12	Is suitable action taken on differences disclosed by the recalculations in 3.11?	22	X	
3.13	Are the procedures in 3.12 performed or reviewed by persons other than those involved in computer operations?	22	X	
3.14	Are the results of the procedures in 3.12 reviewed and approved by a responsible official?	23	X	

Continued

Questionnaire	Flowchart Reference	Yes	No
Manual Recalculations			
3.15 Are the extensions and additions of invoices and credit (or debit) memoranda recalculated to an adequate extent?	N/A		
3.16 Do the invoices and credit (or debit) memoranda bear adequate evidence that the manual recalculating (3.7 to 3.10, 3.15) has been carried out?	N/A		
Other Comparisons			
3.17 Are credit (or debit) memoranda reviewed to confirm that: (a) they agree with the original records of goods returned or claims made; (b) where applicable, the prices agree with the original invoice? (not in case)	N/A to case study		
3.18 Are the following functions performed by separate individuals: (a) preparation of purchase commitments; (b) preparation of receiving records; (c) comparing and recalculating of invoices (3.7 to 3.10, 3.15); (d) computer operations? (not in case)	1 6 N/A N/A to case study	X X	
3.19 If invoices and credit (or debit) memoranda are reviewed manually, are they subject to final written approval by a responsible official prior to entry as accounts payable?	N/A		
Adjustments to Suppliers' Accounts			
3.20 Are adjustments to suppliers' accounts properly documented? (not in case)	N/A to case study		
3.21 Are the adjustments and related documentation (3.20) reviewed and approved by a responsible official prior to entry in the accounts payable records? (not in case)	N/A to case study		

Section 4: Controls over Recording Accounts Payable			
Questionnaire	*Flowchart Reference*	*Yes*	*No*
Accounting for and Control over Processing of All Transactions Specify which of the following are input to update the accounts payable file: (a) purchase invoices; (b) credit (or debit) memoranda; (c) adjustments to vendors' accounts; (d) details of cash payments; (e) other (specify). (not in case)	19 N/A to case study	X	
Completeness of Input and Updating Specify, for each type of input, the principal control that ensures that all documents in (a) to (e) above are input to the computer and updated. If the principal control is: (a) computer matching with a file of goods received, answer questions 4.1 to 4.4; (b) agreement of manually established batch totals (specify totals used), answer questions 4.5 to 4.9; (c) computer sequence check of serially numbered input documents, answer questions 4.10 to 4.15; (d) review of printouts of items written to the accounts payable file, answer questions 4.16 to 4.19.	17 N/A N/A N/A	X	
Computer Matching 4.1 Review the answers to Section 2. Are the matching procedures adequate to ensure that invoices are input completely? (Outstanding Receipts File to which invoices are matched is controlled.)		X	
4.2 Is a total of accepted items accumulated by the computer during the matching run agreed to the total of items written to the accounts payable file or, alternatively, are such totals carried through intermediate processing (including summarization of totals or changes in the totals used) so that it is established that all accepted input items are updated to the accounts payable file?	20	X	
4.3 Is the reconciliation of totals in 4.2 carried out manually or, alternatively, is the reconciliation carried out by the computer with adequate evidence of this control being printed out?	20	X	

Continued

Questionnaire	Flowchart Reference	Yes	No
4.4 Are there adequate procedures for: (a) investigation and correction of differences disclosed by the matching process (4.1); (b) investigation and correction of differences disclosed by the update reconciliations (4.3)?	22 22	X X	
Batch Totals 4.5 Are there adequate controls to ensure that: (a) a document is created for each transaction; (b) all documents are included in a batch; (c) all batches are submitted for processing? (4.5–4.9 not applicable because reliance is placed on the matching process.)	} N/A		
4.6 Are the totals of individual items accepted by the computer compared manually with predetermined control totals or, alternatively, is such a comparison made by the computer with adequate evidence of the control being printed out?	N/A		
4.7 Are the totals in 4.6 agreed to the total of items written to the accounts payable file or, alternatively, are such totals carried through intermediate processing (including summarization of totals or changes in the totals used) so that it is established that all accepted input items are updated to the accounts payable file?	N/A		
4.8 Is the reconciliation of totals in 4.7 carried out manually or, alternatively, is the reconciliation carried out by the computer with adequate evidence of this control being printed out?	N/A		
4.9 Are there adequate procedures for: (a) investigation and correction of differences disclosed by the input reconciliations (4.6); (b) resubmission of all rejections; (c) investigation and correction of differences disclosed by the update reconciliations (4.8)?	} N/A		
Computer Sequence Check 4.10 Are there adequate controls to ensure that all transactions are recorded on a serially numbered document?	N/A		

4.11	Is the method used in the program for reviewing numerical sequence appropriate (i.e., does it recognize changes in sequence and more than one sequence running at a time)?	N/A		
4.12	Is a printout of missing documents produced at regular intervals (e.g., weekly)?	N/A		
4.13	Is the total of accepted items accumulated by the computer during the sequence run agreed to the total of items written to the accounts payable file or, alternatively, are such totals carried through intermediate processing (including summarization of totals or changes in the totals used) so that it is established that all accepted input items are updated to the accounts payable file?	N/A		
4.14	Is the reconciliation of totals in 4.13 carried out manually or, alternatively, is the reconciliation carried out by the computer with adequate evidence of this control being printed out?	N/A		
4.15	Are there adequate procedures for: (a) investigation of missing documents (4.12); (b) investigation and correction of differences disclosed by the update reconciliations (4.14)?	N/A		
Reviewing of Printouts 4.16	Are there adequate controls to ensure that all documents are submitted for processing (e.g., by comparing with retained copy, by manual sequence check)?	N/A		
4.17	Is there a regular (e.g., monthly) review of source documents for unprocessed items?	N/A		
4.18	Is the method used in the program for the production of the printout appropriate (e.g., does it contain details of items that have been written to the accounts payable file)?	N/A		
4.19	Are there adequate procedures for investigation and correction of differences disclosed by the comparison?	N/A		

Continued

Questionnaire	Flowchart Reference	Yes	No
Disciplines over Basic Input Completeness and Updating Controls			
4.20 Are the following procedures either performed or reviewed by persons other than those involved in computer operations or in maintaining a manual accounts payable control account:			
(a) investigation and correction of differences disclosed by the matching process (4.4(a));	23	X	
(b) manual agreement of input totals (4.6);	N/A		
(c) investigation and correction of differences disclosed by the input reconciliations (4.9(a));	N/A		
(d) resubmission of all rejections (4.9(b));	N/A		
(e) investigation of missing documents (4.15(a));	N/A		
(f) regular (e.g., monthly) review of source documents for unprocessed items (4.17);	N/A		
(g) investigation and correction of differences disclosed by the review of printouts (4.19);	N/A		
(h) manual agreement of update totals (4.3, 4.8, 4.14);	21,23	X	
(i) investigation and correction of differences disclosed by the update reconciliations (4.4(b), 4.9(c), 4.15(b))?	21,23	X	
4.21 Are the results of the following procedures reviewed and approved by a responsible official:			
(a) investigation and correction of differences disclosed by the matching process (4.4(a));	23	X	
(b) manual agreement of input totals (4.6);	N/A		
(c) investigation and correction of differences disclosed by the input reconciliations (4.9(a));	N/A		
(d) resubmission of all rejections (4.9(b));	N/A		
(e) investigation of missing documents (4.15(a));	N/A		
(f) regular (e.g., monthly) review of source documents for unprocessed items (4.17);	N/A		
(g) investigation and correction of differences disclosed by the review of printouts (4.19);	N/A		
(h) manual agreement of update totals (4.3, 4.8, 4.14);	21,23	X	
(i) investigation and correction of differences disclosed by the update reconciliations (4.4(b), 4.9(c), 4.15(b))?	21,23	X	

Accuracy of Input and Updating			
4.22 Are there adequate controls to ensure that the following fields are accurately input and updated (e.g., batch totals, edit checks in program, reporting of nonmatched items):			
Input			
(a) value;	17	X	
(b) vendor reference?	17	X	
Update			
(a) value;	20	X	
(b) vendor reference?			X
4.23 Are there adequate procedures for:			
Input			
(a) agreement of totals, where applicable;	17	X	
(b) investigation and correction of differences or exceptions?	22	X	
Update			
(a) agreement of totals, where applicable;	20	X	
(b) investigation and correction of differences or exceptions?	22	X	
4.24 Is the method used in the program for updating of individual accounts appropriate?	19	X	
4.25 Are the following procedures either performed or reviewed by persons other than those involved in computer operations or in maintaining a manual accounts payable control account:			
Input			
(a) agreement of totals, where applicable (4.23(a));	21,23	X	
(b) investigation and correction of differences or exceptions (4.23(b))?	21,23	X	
Update			
(a) the agreement of totals, where applicable (4.23(a));	21,23	X	
(b) investigation and correction of differences or exceptions (4.23(b))?	21,23	X	
4.26 Are the results of the following procedures reviewed and approved by a responsible official:			
Input			
(a) agreement of totals, where applicable (4.23(a));	21,23	X	
(b) investigation and correction of differences or exceptions (4.23(b))?	21,23	X	

Continued

Questionnaire	Flowchart Reference	Yes	No
Update			
(a) the agreement of totals, where applicable (4.23(a));	21,23	X	
(b) investigation and correction of differences or exceptions (4.23(b))?	21,23	X	
Authorization			
4.27 If data are authorized prior to the establishment of the controls for completeness and accuracy of input (e.g., prior to establishment of batch control totals or recording on a sequentially numbered document), are there adequate controls (e.g., reviewing authorization after batch control totals have been established or sequentially numbered documents have been created) to ensure that:			
(a) no unauthorized alterations are made to authorized data during subsequent processing;	N/A		
(b) unauthorized data are not added;	N/A		
(c) all authorized items are included in subsequent processing?	N/A		
Computer-Generated Data—Payment Details			
4.28 Where the computer is programmed to generate checks on the basis of information held on file, are there adequate controls to ensure that only valid items are selected for payment and that the amount is accurately calculated (e.g., calculation of discount)? (not in case)	N/A to case study		
4.29 Is a total (specify total used) of generated items accumulated by the computer and agreed manually to a total of items removed from the accounts payable file or, alternatively, are totals agreed by the computer with adequate evidence of this control being printed out? (not in case)	N/A to case study		
4.30 Are there adequate procedures for the investigation and correction of differences disclosed by the update reconciliation? (not in case)	N/A to case study		
4.31 Are the following procedures either performed or reviewed by persons other than those involved in computer operations or in maintaining a manual accounts payable control account:			

	(a) manual agreement of update totals (4.29); (b) investigation and correction of differences disclosed by the update reconciliations (4.30)? (not in case)	} N/A to case study		
4.32	Are the results of the following procedures reviewed and approved by a responsible official: (a) manual agreement of update totals (4.29); (b) investigation and correction of differences disclosed by the update reconciliations (4.30)? (not in case)	} N/A to case study		

Maintenance of the Accounts Payable File

4.33	Is an accumulation of the items on file regularly reconciled with a manual control account maintained by a user department or, alternatively, reconciled with a control record on file with adequate evidence of the reconciliation being printed out?			X
4.34	Where the reconciliation is carried out by the computer, is the brought forward total verified or, alternatively, are there adequate controls over access to data files?			X
4.35	Are there adequate procedures for investigating differences disclosed by the reconciliations (4.33, 4.34) before any adjustments are made?			X
4.36	Are the following procedures either performed or reviewed by persons other than those involved in computer operations or in maintaining a manual accounts payable control account: (a) manual agreement of totals (4.33); (b) verifying of brought forward total (4.34); (c) investigation and correction of differences disclosed by the reconciliations (4.35)?			X X X
4.37	Are the results of the following procedures reviewed and approved by a responsible official: (a) manual agreement of totals (4.33); (b) verifying of brought forward total (4.34); (c) investigation and correction of differences disclosed by the reconciliations (4.35)?			X X X

Agreement with Vendors' Records

4.38	Are the accounts payable subsidiary records periodically reconciled to vendors' records (e.g., by comparison with vendors' statements)?			X

Continued

Questionnaire	Flowchart Reference	Yes	No
4.39 Is the procedure in 4.38 either performed or reviewed by persons other than those who are involved in: (a) maintenance of a manual accounts payable control account; (b) computer operations?			 X X
4.40 Are the results of the reconciliation in 4.38 reviewed and approved by a responsible official?			X

Chapter 9
Controlling Detection Risk: Substantive Tests

As stated in earlier chapters of this book, the primary purpose of an audit is the expression of an opinion on whether the entity's financial statements are presented fairly in conformity with generally accepted accounting principles. The auditor needs a high level of assurance that the opinion is appropriate; that is, audit risk must be limited to a low level. Audit risk was defined in Chapter 6 as consisting of the risk of material misstatement occurring, comprising inherent and control risks, which the auditor assesses as part of developing the audit strategy, and the risk, known as detection risk, of not detecting material misstatement that is contained in the financial statements. The auditor controls detection risk by performing substantive tests to gain the necessary assurance that the various assertions embodied in the financial statements are valid. This chapter covers the substantive testing phase of the audit. To fit that phase into the perspective of the overall audit process, some of the underlying concepts and earlier steps in the process, which were discussed in detail in previous chapters, are first reviewed and summarized.

Review: Audit Objectives, Risk Assessment, and Strategy

Audit Objectives

Each audit procedure performed on an engagement should be designed to meet one or more specific audit objectives that, in turn, correspond with specific assertions embodied in the financial statements. Seven categories of management assertions and corresponding general audit objectives were identified in Chapter 5: existence or occurrence, completeness, accuracy, cutoff, rights and obligations, valuation or allocation, and presentation and disclosure. The audit objectives are the same for all engagements; the emphasis given to particular objectives for specific account balances and classes of transactions varies according to the auditor's materiality judgments and risk assessments. Accordingly, the nature, timing, and extent of audit procedures performed to achieve the audit objectives also vary.

Risk Assessment

The process by which inherent and control risks are assessed was described in Chapter 8. The results of those assessments have an inverse relationship to the level of acceptable detection risk. That is, the lower the risk of a material misstatement occurring, the higher the level of detection risk the auditor can accept in planning substantive tests to gain the assurance needed to limit audit risk to a sufficiently low level. Conversely, the greater the risk of a material misstatement occurring, the lower the acceptable level of detection risk.

Each of the auditor's risk assessment activities—considering inherent risk conditions, assessing the control environment, understanding the flow of transactions through the accounting systems, and evaluating the design of and compliance testing specific internal accounting controls—can result in a reduction in the perceived level of risk that a material misstatement has occurred, which in turn reduces the amount of assurance that the auditor needs from substantive tests. It would be rare for the auditor to be unable, as a result of the first three risk assessment activities noted above, to reduce to some degree the assurance needed from substantive tests. Beyond that, as discussed in Chapter 7, it is often possible to correlate the audit objectives of completeness, existence, and accuracy with control objectives that may be specifically addressed by an entity's internal accounting controls. For those audit objectives, and for accounts that are derived from transaction cycles, the auditor may, by evaluating the design of specific internal accounting controls and performing compliance tests of those controls, be able to assess control risk as sufficiently low to reduce even further the level of assurance that would otherwise be required from substantive tests. The key factor in the decision to adopt an audit strategy that includes compliance testing is the relative efficiency of relying on specific internal accounting controls to restrict the amount of substantive testing, compared with performing substantive tests without restriction for reliance on those controls.

The client's system of internal control and the auditor's substantive procedures can be viewed as a series of checkpoints—or screens—designed to prevent misstatements from reaching the financial statements or to detect them during the audit. Figure 9.1 illustrates this using the analogy of a hailstorm that represents potential misstatements. If the screens are effective, the risk of the hailstones reaching the financial statements is reduced. Depending on the intensity of the downpour or the size of an individual hailstone, it is conceivable that any one of the screens could prevent the hailstones—or cumulatively material misstatements—from reaching the financial statements. In the figure, the financial statement misstatements are screened by both client controls and audit procedures. If the screens are collectively effective, a material misstatement will rarely reach the audited financial statements.

Audit Strategy

Generally accepted auditing standards require that, on all engagements, the auditor understand the control environment and the flow of transactions

Figure 9.1 Hailstorm Audit Risk Analogy

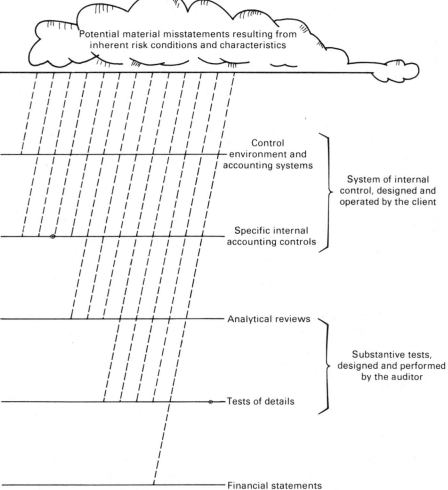

through the accounting systems. Beyond that, as the hailstorm analogy suggests, there are two ways of achieving specific audit objectives related to specific accounts: indirectly, by relying on specific internal accounting controls to prevent misstatements from reaching the financial statements, and directly, by testing the account balances themselves to corroborate the management assertions underlying them. This is expressed in the professional literature (AU Section 326.12) as follows: ''The combination of the auditor's reliance on internal accounting control and on selected substantive tests should provide a reasonable basis for his opinion.''

To cite an example of how both compliance tests and substantive tests contribute to an auditor's ability to express an opinion, a set of financial statements includes management's assertion that accounts receivable that are included in the financial statements exist and are the result of sales of goods and services to customers. The auditor seeks evidence to support this assertion, which corresponds with the audit objective of existence/occurrence. This audit objective may be achieved directly, perhaps in part by confirming accounts receivable (a substantive test), or it may, at least in part, be achieved indirectly, by testing the specific internal accounting controls that the client has devised to ensure that only valid sales of goods and services and all cash collections are properly processed and recorded (a compliance test).

The audit strategy will depend on both the auditor's judgment about the design and effectiveness of the relevant controls and the relative efficiency of testing how well client personnel comply with the prescribed controls versus directly testing the account balances. The auditor *may* choose to rely entirely on direct, substantive tests of account balances, but *may not* choose to rely entirely on the operation of internal controls to reduce audit risk to an appropriately low level; some substantive testing must always be done. The evidence obtained from performing substantive tests will either confirm or contradict the auditor's conclusions reached as a result of the assessments of inherent and control risks. If the auditor learns that the level of those risks is higher than was previously thought, the decision about the level of assurance needed from substantive tests should be reconsidered. Chapter 8 described the risk assessment activities, including the evaluation of the design of specific internal accounting controls and compliance tests of those controls, undertaken by the auditor if the strategy is to rely on those controls. This chapter covers substantive tests performed to provide direct evidence about financial statement assertions.

Substantive Test Considerations

Substantive tests consist of analytical review procedures, tests of details of account balances and related transactions, and other auditing procedures. The nature, timing, and extent of the substantive tests to be performed with respect to the specific audit objectives associated with each account balance and class of transactions are determined by the results of the auditor's risk assessment activities. Assessing the level of assurance that can be attained from a particular substantive procedure is a matter of professional judgment and cannot be specified without knowledge of the full context in which the procedure is to be performed. A large number of substantive audit procedures are described in this chapter. Auditors rarely perform all, or even a majority, of these procedures on an engagement; instead, they select the specific procedures, for each audit objective relevant to each financial statement account and disclosure, that will provide the evidence needed in the particular circumstances, after considering the evidence obtained from compliance testing and other risk assessment activities. This section of the chapter describes the major considerations that determine the substantive tests that should be performed in varying circumstances.

Audit Objectives

The key to selecting appropriate substantive tests is the auditor's understanding of management's assertions and of the corresponding general and specific audit objectives. Keeping in mind the general audit objectives, the auditor develops specific audit objectives for each account balance under examination and designs audit procedures to provide the necessary assurance that those objectives have been achieved. Figure 9.2 provides examples of specific audit objectives that may be applicable to an entity's trade accounts receivable and sales and illustrates the relationship between the general and specific audit objectives. It also provides examples (which are not intended to be exhaustive) of substantive tests the auditor may perform to satisfy the objectives illustrated.

Types of Accounts

The nature, timing, and extent of substantive tests appropriate for a particular audit objective and account vary with the type of account. Accounts may be classified as three types:

1. Accounts that are derived from a transaction cycle typically involving large volumes of transactions. These accounts are commonly subjected to internal accounting controls that address the control objectives of completeness, validity, and accuracy. Examples are cash, accounts receivable, inventory, accounts payable, purchases, and sales. Decisions about whether the audit strategy should include compliance tests of specific internal accounting controls are generally related only to the most efficient way to achieve the completeness, existence, and accuracy objectives for these transaction cycle accounts.

2. Accounts that reflect internal allocations of revenues or expenses over time through the accrual, deferral, amortization, or valuation of assets or liabilities. These accounts often require the exercise of judgment by management in determining the period or method of allocation and also in selecting and applying accounting measurement and recognition principles. While the transactions that form the basis for these accounts are sometimes subjected to internal accounting controls, it is usually more efficient not to compliance test those

Figure 9.2 General and Specific Audit Objectives, Trade Accounts Receivable and Sales

General Audit Objectives of Substantive Tests	Specific Audit Objectives Illustrated for Trade Accounts Receivable and Sales	Illustrative Substantive Tests
Existence or occurrence	Trade accounts receivable exist at the balance sheet date and sales transactions recorded during the period have occurred.	Select customers' accounts for confirmation and the method of confirmation (positive, negative, or a combination), investigate any discrepancies reported or questions raised, and determine whether any adjustments are necessary.
Completeness	All material amounts due to the company at the balance sheet date have been recorded and all valid sales transactions have been processed and recorded.	Determine that all goods shipped and services performed have been billed and recorded by: (a) If practicable and if shipping documents are prenumbered, accounting for the numerical sequence of shipping documents issued to the shipping department. (b) From the records of goods shipped and services performed, examining the related sales invoices and entries in the sales journal.
Accuracy	Recorded sales transactions and trade accounts receivable are mathematically accurate, are based on correct amounts, have been classified in the proper accounts, and have been accurately summarized and posted to the general ledger.	Examine invoices supporting sales transactions during the year and/or accounts receivable at year-end: (a) Trace prices to approved price lists. (b) Recalculate extensions and footings. (c) Compare data on invoices with data on shipping documents. (d) Review propriety of account classification. (e) Ascertain proper posting to the subsidiary and general ledgers.
Cutoff	Sales and sales returns are recorded in the proper period.	Perform cutoff tests: (a) Determine that sales invoices are recorded as sales in the proper period by comparing the related records of goods shipped and services performed with the entries in the sales journal for several days before and after year-end.

Figure 9.2 Continued

General Audit Objectives of Substantive Tests	Specific Audit Objectives Illustrated for Trade Accounts Receivable and Sales	Illustrative Substantive Tests
		(b) Determine that credit memoranda are recorded in the proper period by examining the related records of returns and claims from customers for several days before and after year-end. (*Note*: Improper cutoff of cash receipts is generally a low risk, since only the composition of current assets could be in error.)
Rights and obligations	Trade accounts receivable are owned by the company at the balance sheet date.	Make inquiries and read agreements relating to the possible sale of receivables that the client continues to service.
Valuation or allocation	Trade accounts receivable are carried at net collectible amounts.	Determine whether the allowance for doubtful accounts is adequate by reviewing the aged trial balance and identifying significant old receivables and receivables in dispute based on confirmation replies or other factors and: (a) Review cash collections after the balance sheet date and examine related remittance advices or other supporting documentation to ascertain that payments relate to the balance that was due at the balance sheet date. (b) Determine the adequacy of collateral, if any. (c) Review relevant credit file information, such as customer financial data and correspondence. (d) Discuss all significant potentially doubtful accounts with management.
Presentation and disclosure	Trade accounts receivable pledged as collateral are properly identified and disclosed.	Identify liens, security interests, and assets pledged as loan collateral by reviewing debt and lease agreements, confirmation replies, and minutes of directors' meetings, by inspecting public records, and by inquiring of management. Consider confirming these items with the appropriate public filing offices.

controls as a basis for relying on them. Examples of such accounts include accrued receivables and payables, deferred charges and credits, and asset valuation and estimated liability accounts.

3. Accounts that typically reflect a relatively small number of material transactions in an accounting period. These accounts are carried forward from one year to the next, unless transactions affecting them take place. Examples of these accounts include bonds payable, property and equipment, and contributed capital accounts. Because transactions affecting these accounts occur infrequently, specific internal accounting controls are not usually designed to ensure their completeness, validity, and accuracy. Even when the transactions affecting these accounts are subject to specific internal accounting controls, it is usually not efficient to compliance test the controls as a basis for reliance.

For accounts derived from transaction cycles, client management may have designed specific internal accounting controls to achieve the objectives of completeness, existence, and accuracy. If so, the auditor will face a strategy decision with respect to those objectives for those accounts. For other accounts, the risks associated with completeness, existence, and accuracy, and for all accounts, the risks associated with the audit objectives of valuation, rights and obligations, and presentation and disclosure are generally not addressed in the auditor's assessment of control risk; therefore, the auditor requires a higher level of assurance from substantive tests directed at those objectives. An enterprise may design controls to ensure a proper cutoff of purchases, sales, cash receipts, and cash disbursements, but the auditor generally finds it more efficient not to test and rely on those controls and instead to obtain the necessary high level of assurance with respect to proper cutoffs directly from substantive tests.

Substantive Tests of Details

Of the three categories of substantive tests, the one probably most commonly thought of in connection with providing assurance about audit objectives is tests of details of account balances and transactions. This section discusses the different types of tests of details and the question of when in the audit they can be performed. Chapter 10 discusses the extent of testing—how many items to test.

Types of Tests and Audit Objectives

Substantive tests that involve tests of the details of transactions and account balances or of other information in the financial statements normally consist of confirmation, inspecting assets, observation, reperformance, vouching, and evaluating the selection and application of accounting principles. The following paragraphs describe each of these and suggest how they relate to the audit objectives.

Confirmation consists of obtaining a representation of a fact or condition from a third party, preferably in writing. Although many facts can be confirmed, this procedure is generally applied to items making up an account balance and often serves as the principal test of details related to that balance. Confirmations obtained from parties that are independent of the client provide strong support for the existence of the relevant fact or account balance and often provide some evidence with respect to the accuracy objective. For example, a customer's acknowledgment that $1500 is owed to the client is strong evidence that the debt exists and that it is not overstated. Confirmations also provide some evidence that the transactions underlying the account balances were recorded in the proper period. Confirmation provides little or no evidence, however, with respect to completeness, valuation, rights and obligations, or presentation and disclosure of receivables.

Inspecting assets involves counting or examining physical items represented by accounts in the financial statements. This procedure is generally performed by client personnel, with the auditor participating or observing, although on occasion the auditor actually performs the function. A typical example of *observation* and inspection is the physical count of inventory by the client while the auditor observes and tests the counting procedures, in part by recounting some of the client's counts. Other items subject to inspection (which may be counted or examined directly by the auditor) include cash, marketable securities, and property, plant, and equipment. Inspecting assets is a principal source of assurance about the existence of assets and may provide some assurance that all items counted were recorded (completeness).

In many instances an account balance may represent the result of a computation or an accumulation of computations. The substantiation of the accuracy of such an account balance often includes *reperforming* some or all of the detailed computations or otherwise making an overall evaluation of the balance. If judgment is the basis of a computation, such as would be necessary in achieving the valuation objective with respect to accounts receivable, reperformance of the computation should also include evaluating the reasoning process supporting the judgment, in order to determine its propriety. For example, if the client's determination of the provision for doubtful accounts, giving appropriate consideration to past experience, is based on a formula related to the age of the receivables, the auditor should evaluate the reasonableness of the formula as well as reperform the mathematical calculations. (The auditor would also perform other procedures regarding the collectibility of accounts receivable in reviewing the adequacy of the provision for doubtful accounts.)

Vouching involves the examination of evidence supporting a transaction or item in the financial statements and reperforming the client's related procedures in order to determine that the transaction was accounted for accurately. In addition, vouching often provides assurance that transactions are authorized and valid and thus that related assets or liabilities exist or are complete. The cutoff objective is often achieved by vouching transactions that were recorded shortly before and shortly after the client's year-end. Vouching normally includes examining evidence that the client has performed all of the required procedures on the various supporting documents, reperforming those procedures (on a test basis if appropriate), and determining whether any aspects of the transaction appear unreasonable (such as a supplier's invoice not addressed to the client). That evidence may have been generated wholly or in part by entities outside the client (such as suppliers' invoices, customers' orders, signed contracts) or by the client itself (such as purchase orders, receiving reports, marketing plans). If external evidence is available, it would usually be considered more reliable than internal evidence.

The auditor should *evaluate the selection and application of accounting principles* to address the risk of the intentional or unintentional misuse of generally accepted accounting principles relating to accounting recognition and measurement and to financial statement presentation and disclosure—a pervasive aspect of audit risk that the auditor should keep in mind throughout the examination. The auditor's responsibility entails more than achieving specific audit objectives related to specific transactions and more than merely substantiating facts about those transactions and other events and circumstances. The auditor also has the responsibility to evaluate how the client has translated those facts into appropriate accounting presentations. The way in which that responsibility affects the audit strategy is subtle and depends on the industry involved, the client environment, economic conditions, and numerous other intangible considerations. Meeting that responsibility requires an extensive knowledge of accounting principles and of the ways in which they should be applied to produce financial statements that reflect, in all material respects, the substance of the client's transactions and present a picture of the enterprise that is not misleading. Many audit failures in the past have resulted from the auditor's failure to evaluate whether GAAP were properly applied, even when all of the relevant facts were available. The audit objectives of valuation, rights and obligations, and presentation and disclosure are pervasive; accordingly, the auditor should keep them in mind throughout the audit, not only when performing specific substantive tests relating to those objectives.

Many tests of the details of transactions and account balances involve procedures, such as examination of evidence or reperforming calculations, that are the same as procedures used in performing compliance tests. This is not surprising; whether a particular procedure is a compliance test or a substantive test depends not on the procedure itself, but on the purpose for which it is performed. For example, footing and extending a purchase invoice could be part of a compliance test of an accounting control over the accuracy of recorded purchase transactions; it could also be a substantive test of the accuracy of recorded machinery and equipment. Similarly, reperforming the client's bank reconciliation could be a compliance test of the internal accounting control over maintenance of the cash account that calls for periodic reconciliation; if done by the auditor at year-end, the reconciliation would be a substantive test of the existence and valuation of the cash balance. As a general rule, if the auditor performs compliance tests of specific internal accounting controls as part of the risk assessment, tests of details of transactions that pass through those controls will be compliance tests; tests of details of ending balances of balance sheet accounts will be substantive tests. Of course, if the auditor does not perform compliance tests, all tests of transactions and balances will be substantive tests. Regardless of the purpose (compliance or substantive) for which a particular test is performed, however, many tests provide evidence that serves the other purpose as well. For example, testing the extensions and footings on an invoice for substantive test purposes may provide some evidence about the effectiveness of controls over the accuracy of recorded purchases.

Timing of Tests of Details

It is often desirable to perform tests of details before year-end (early substantive testing), particularly if the client wants the audit to be completed shortly after year-end. This may be done in appropriate circumstances without impairing the effectiveness of the audit, although before doing so the auditor should assess the difficulty of controlling the incremental audit risk (SAS No. 45, *Omnibus Statement on Auditing Standards—1983* [AU Section 313]).

If early substantive testing is done, the auditor will have to obtain satisfaction about the accounting for transactions affecting the balances subject to the early testing during the intervening period between the early testing date and year-end. The auditor should link the balances subject to early substantive testing to year-end balances by reviewing entries in the relevant general ledger accounts (including control accounts) to determine that no expected entries have been omitted and to see whether the entries appear to be reasonable in relation to the normal level of activity. The auditor should also perform analytical review procedures and investigate any unexpected fluctuations in the accounts and any unusual entries since the time of the early substantive tests.

If the auditor needs additional evidence about the transactions occurring during the intervening period, it may be obtained in one of the following ways:

• Examining evidence of the operation of specific internal accounting controls during the intervening period. This could include reviewing reconciliations of individual ledger balances with control accounts and investigating any unusual items in the reconciliations. However, if physical controls are necessary to safeguard assets (such as inventories) but are ineffective, early substantive testing (such as observing early physical inventory counts) is normally not appropriate, because the auditor will be unable to rely on controls over the custody of those assets in the intervening period to provide evidence about their existence at year-end.

• Examining evidence of the operation of special procedures established by the client for the intervening period. (As an example, a management review of sales transactions recorded around year-end to ensure a proper cutoff would provide some evidence about the validity and accuracy of sales recorded after an early accounts receivable confirmation.)

The approach taken will depend on the client's procedures and the auditor's judgment as to the most efficient way of gaining the necessary satisfaction about the intervening period.

It is usually efficient to perform substantive tests on related accounts as of a common date. Therefore, when considering early substantive testing of a specific account balance, the auditor should consider the relationship of that account to others in the financial statements and the extent to which a single substantive test may apply to more than one account. For example, a cutoff test of shipments relates to sales, accounts receivable, cost of sales, and inventory accounts.

Significant changes in the client's circumstances after the date of early substantive testing may require the performance of additional procedures. The auditor should be mindful of the possibility of such changes when determining the audit strategy. SAS No. 45 contains the authoritative guidance on performing substantive tests before the balance sheet date.

Exceptions

When exceptions (that is, errors and deviations from prescribed procedures) are found as a result of substantive tests, the auditor should ascertain the reason for them and consider their implications. If the nature or frequency of exceptions indicates the possibility of material misstatements in the account balance or related account balances, the auditor should consider whether to increase the levels of substantive tests or to change their nature or timing. The auditor should also consider the implications of the exceptions with respect to the functioning of the client's accounting systems. If exceptions disclose a weakness not previously identified in evaluating internal accounting controls, the relevant documentation should be amended.

Other Auditing Procedures

Substantive tests (other than analytical review procedures) that do not involve direct tests of the details of transactions and account balances or of other information in the financial statements are referred to as ''other auditing procedures.'' Examples include reading minutes of meetings of the board of directors and its important committees and obtaining letters from lawyers regarding legal matters and letters of representation from management. Those three procedures are summarized here and are discussed again in Chapter 17.

• *Minutes of meetings.* Reading the minutes of meetings of the board of directors and its important committees enables the auditor to examine the board's approval of the significant actions for which such approval is required and to determine whether significant decisions that affect the basic financial statements or require disclosure in the notes have been dealt with properly. The auditor should be satisfied that copies of minutes of all meetings held during the period have been provided, including meetings held after year-end but before the date of the audit report.

• *Letters from lawyers.* Obtaining letters from the client's lawyers regarding legal matters provides additional assurance that all active, pending, or expected litigation has been brought to the auditor's attention. Letters of inquiry should be sent to all lawyers who have performed significant legal services for the client during the period being examined.

• *Letters of representation.* Although obtaining letters of representation from a client's management normally does not relieve the auditor of the responsibility to perform sufficient audit tests in the relevant areas, such letters are useful because they focus management's attention on the matters being reported and help to ensure that no information is inadvertently withheld from the auditor. The auditor should obtain letters of representation regarding such matters as the recording of all known liabilities, the existence of contingent liabilities, events occurring subsequent to year-end, and the existence and valuation of inventory.

Analytical Review Procedures

Analytical review procedures are an integral part of obtaining audit assurance. They are defined in SAS No. 23, *Analytical Review Procedures* (AU Section 318.02), as "substantive tests of financial information made by a study and comparison of relationships among data." That definition, however, fails to suggest the wide variety of purposes for which auditors use analytical reviews throughout the audit. Those purposes include gathering and updating information about the client, determining the audit strategy, performing substantive tests, performing overall reviews of financial statements near the completion of field work, and reviewing subsequent events. (Analytical reviews are also used in complying with professional standards in connection with various reports on unaudited financial information, as discussed in Chapter 19.)

A major decision that the auditor makes in designing substantive tests is the relative amounts of reliance to place on analytical review procedures as opposed to tests of details. That decision is based on both the level of assurance required and the efficiency with which the evidence can be obtained. Analytical review procedures commonly provide an efficient means of obtaining assurance with respect to one or more audit objectives for a particular account balance or class of transactions. By contrast, tests of details, although less efficient, commonly provide a higher level of assurance with respect to an audit objective. In designing and performing both analytical reviews and substantive tests of details, the auditor should consider the relationship among accounts and the likelihood that evidence obtained about one or more audit objectives with respect to a particular account balance or class of transactions may also provide assurance about other account balances or classes of transactions.

Many auditors believe that if specific internal accounting controls have been compliance tested as a basis for the auditor's assessment that there is a low risk of material misstatement occurring with respect to a certain account and audit objective (such as the accuracy of recorded purchases and accounts payable), and given the assurance obtained about that objective from tests directed primarily to other accounts or objectives (for example, cutoff tests of purchases may provide some evidence of accuracy if the auditor looks at the reasonableness of the extensions and footings on the vendors' invoices), then all of the assurance required for that objective can be obtained solely from the performance of analytical review procedures. No substantive tests involving reperformance of invoice calculations would be necessary in those circumstances. Like other auditing procedures, analytical review procedures that are directed specifically to one or more audit objectives for a particular account balance or class of transactions may also simultaneously address other accounts or objectives as well; the auditor should take this into consideration when deciding how to obtain the necessary level of assurance for a particular account or objective.

Before performing analytical review procedures, the auditor should develop expectations about the results of those procedures, against which the actual results will be compared. The basic premise underlying analytical review procedures is that relationships among data may reasonably be expected to exist and continue in the absence of known conditions to the contrary. It is the presence of those relationships, together with compliance tests and substantive tests of details of transactions and balances that the auditor performs, that provides the evidential matter required by the third standard of field work.

Unexpected relationships or other items that appear to be unusual should be investigated if the auditor believes that they provide indications of matters that may have a significant effect on the examination. In investigating unusual items, the auditor generally considers them in the light of the information obtained about the client and its business, and seeks additional evidence to corroborate management's replies to inquiries triggered by the results of analytical reviews. Analytical review procedures are effective only if the auditor exercises skepticism in evaluating management's explanations of unexpected results and seeks relevant and reliable evidence to support those explanations.

Timing and Objectives of Analytical Reviews

The discussion that follows relates the objectives of analytical review procedures to the stage of the audit at which they are performed.

Gathering or Updating Information. When used in gathering or updating information about the client, analytical review procedures can assist in directing the auditor toward such business factors as changes in product mix, marketing methods, or profitability. Additionally, if information about the client's industry and competitors is available, the auditor may be able to become more knowledgeable about such important general business factors as changes in the client's position in the marketplace. For example, information that the client has a decreasing share of a decreasing market assists the auditor in evaluating the general condition of the business and focuses attention on certain accounts, such as the allowance for obsolete inventory. Models or formulas that are used as bankruptcy indicators may also be helpful in assessing the client's overall business risk. Information about a company's business and the risks associated with it is particularly helpful in screening potential clients.

Determining the Audit Strategy. During the planning stage, analytical review procedures help the auditor determine the audit strategy by identifying, among other things, significant matters that require consideration during the examination, such as material accounts, increases or decreases in account balances, and changes in relationships among accounts. In effect, applying analytical review procedures at this stage of the audit directs the auditor's attention toward accounts or groups of accounts with high inherent risk. An unexpected increase in sales, for example, should alert the auditor to consider carefully the extent of cutoff tests that should be performed. Analytical reviews may also provide indications of changes in the efficiency of the client's operations and in its financial flexibility—factors that could have a bearing on the enterprise's ability to continue as a going concern.

The Testing Phase. The auditor may choose to use analytical review procedures during the testing phase to assist in determining sample size, to stratify a population, or to assist in the design of other substantive tests. In determining the sample size necessary for audit procedures related to inventory obsolescence, for example, the auditor may examine the change in inventory turnover rates for various components of inventory to assess which inventory items should be given more attention. As substantive tests, analytical review procedures provide corroborative evidence about the accounting treatment of transactions and balances. Analytical review procedures can also be good detectors of changes in accounting principles, but of course they will not alert the auditor to a misstatement if an inappropriate accounting principle remains unchanged.

Analytical review procedures may be the primary procedures applied to a specific account balance as the means of meeting the third standard of field work. For example, if the auditor has performed compliance tests of specific controls in the client's buying cycle, analytical review procedures may be the only substantive tests applied to certain expense accounts. Or the reasonableness of interest received from short-term investments may be tested by an overall calculation of the average interest rates applied to the average investment balance, after the auditor has obtained and evaluated evidence about the existence, completeness, and accuracy of that balance. Analytical reviews may be particularly useful in helping the auditor identify transactions that have not been recorded and may also be used to test the remaining portion of an account balance after the auditor has examined several large items that constitute a significant portion of the balance. Similarly, if the auditor performs substantive tests of details before year-end, analytical review procedures can often be employed to provide evidence about the proper recording of transactions in the period between early testing and year-end.

The results of analytical review procedures may possibly lead the auditor to extend testing. For example, if controls in the revenue cycle are effective and no exceptions resulted from compliance testing, the auditor might ordinarily decide to confirm fewer customer accounts receivable or confirm such accounts at a date prior to year-end. If the auditor also observed, however, that the number of days' sales outstanding had increased significantly and was not satisfied with the explanation provided for that trend, the decision might be made to confirm more accounts at the end of the year to ensure that fictitious receivables had not been created, and to expand tests for collectibility to ensure that the allowance for doubtful accounts was adequate.

Reviewing Financial Statements. The auditor relies heavily on analytical review procedures in performing an overall review of financial statement presentation near the completion of field work. At this stage of the examination, the auditor can integrate the results of all the audit work to assess the overall reasonableness of components of the financial statements as well as of the statements as a whole. By analyzing changes in ratios and other aspects of the financial statements, the auditor can determine on an overall basis that changes in account balances are in agreement with explanations obtained during other audit procedures. For example, the auditor may have assessed inventory obsolescence to be an insignificant risk. Examining inventory turnover ratios in relationship to sales trends should enable the auditor to reassess the reasonableness of that conclusion. In short, an overall analytical review of the financial statements gives the auditor added assurance that there is a low risk that the statements are materially misstated because of errors or irregularities that remain undetected.

Analytical review procedures may also provide a basis for making recommendations to management about improvements in administrative controls. Through analyzing the client's accounts receivable turnover by major product group and comparing the client's ratio with industrywide data, for instance, the auditor could postulate that the client may be losing sales because its higher turnover ratio has been accomplished by too strict a credit screening policy.

Reviewing Subsequent Events. The auditor is required to perform certain procedures for the period after the balance sheet date up to the date of the auditor's report. During that period, known as the "subsequent events period," interim financial statements or other financial information may become available. Analytical review procedures as part of the "subsequent period" review include comparing the latest available interim financial statements with the financial statements being reported on, as well as other comparisons considered appropriate in the circumstances.

Types of Analytical Review Procedures

Paragraph 6 of SAS No. 23, *Analytical Review Procedures* (AU Section 318.06), states that analytical review procedures include the following five general types of comparisons or studies:

- Comparison of the financial information with information for comparable prior period(s).
- Comparison of the financial information with anticipated results (for example, budgets and forecasts).
- Study of the relationships of elements of financial information that would be expected to conform to a predictable pattern based on the entity's experience.
- Comparison of the financial information with similar information regarding the industry in which the entity operates.
- Study of relationships of the financial information with relevant nonfinancial information.

Those procedures may be performed using monetary amounts, physical quantities, ratios, or percentages; they may be applied to overall financial information of the entity, to financial information of components such as subsidiaries or divisions, and to individual elements of financial information. Some auditors have developed specialized software programs to extract appropriate client data from computer files and perform standardized procedures. Other software packages require the auditor to input client data to a computer (often a microcomputer) that processes those data and generates analytical review reports.

Comparison of Financial Information with Information for Comparable Prior Periods. The auditor may compare the client's current-period "key indicators" with the corresponding historical data to determine whether significant changes have occurred. As an example, the auditor may be concerned with evaluating the reasonableness of revenue because it generally provides the single most meaningful indication of the level of an enterprise's business activity. Monthly, quarterly, and annual revenue patterns reflect many variables such as seasonality, product introductions and mix, plant shutdowns, sales campaigns, and major acquisitions. Revenue is also most directly and significantly affected by outside influences and is therefore especially well suited to trend analysis and projections. Understanding the client's revenue patterns is an effective way to obtain insights into the nature of its business that are essential to interpreting other financial information about operations and liquidity. Therefore, many analytical ratios use revenue as a component, and analysis that assesses the reasonableness of reported revenue is the cornerstone of the analytical review of business operations.

The following are among the possible objectives of analyzing current-year and past revenue activity:

- Assessing the reasonableness of reported activity.
- Identifying potential cutoff problems.
- Sounding an early warning that the client's forecasts may need to be revised.
- Identifying potential going-concern or liquidity implications.

- Assessing the effectiveness of the client's budgeting and planning process.
- Evaluating inventory and receivable levels, production scheduling, and cash requirements.
- Understanding seasonal and other revenue patterns to gain insights into the nature of the business and its behavior in the marketplace.

Revenue analysis often focuses on identifying trends and seasonality patterns. In comparing current-year annual revenue with the prior-year amount, the auditor assesses whether the current-year amount appears reasonable when compared with prior amounts and trends. The auditor also looks for new trends or continuations of existing trends that may have audit implications in the current year. For example, recent rapid growth in sales may lead the auditor to investigate the reasons for this growth. If a reason is a lowering of credit standards, the auditor may want to extend the testing of uncollectible accounts and the allowance for doubtful accounts. The objective of comparing current-year monthly or quarterly revenue with equivalent prior-year amounts is similar. In making these comparisons, however, the auditor assesses whether activity within the year appears reasonable when compared with prior years. For example, assume that a company historically has had relatively low sales in the last month of its fiscal year. In the current year, the final month's sales are very high. If no explanation can be given for this, the auditor might consider increasing the scope of the test of the sales cutoff.

Another effective comparison frequently made is one that often results in minimizing other substantive testing of expense accounts. Month-to-month comparisons with prior-year amounts for overhead, administrative, and other expenses can highlight unusual variations for investigation. For example, abnormal maintenance costs not in line with the trend or seasonal patterns can point to either internal control breakdowns that need further investigation or capital additions that were improperly expensed instead of capitalized.

Comparison of Financial Information with Anticipated or Predicted Results. Financial information may also be compared with anticipated or predicted results. The auditor must judge whether variance or lack of variance warrants further attention, either by revising the audit strategy, if the comparison is done in the planning stage, or by corroborating management's explanations, if the information is obtained later in the audit. One widely used analytical review procedure is to compare actual financial data with budgets for comparable periods. The auditor should, in those comparisons, consider both the reliability and the relevance of the budget data available. The auditor's experience with a particular client could indicate that budgets are prepared with inadequate care or that they are intended to serve as goals rather than expected results.[1]

Regression analysis and time-series analysis are other examples of tech-

---

[1]International Federation of Accountants, International Auditing Guideline No. 12, *Analytical Review*, para. 11 (AU Section 8012.11).

niques that may be applied. Regression analysis is used to describe a relationship among several variables—a dependent variable and one or more independent variables—and is a first step in comparing actual financial information with anticipated results. A typical application is testing the reasonableness of an account balance by predicting its value and then comparing the recorded value with the predicted value. For example, when testing the reasonableness of the sales commission expense account, the auditor would expect sales commission expense to vary, although not necessarily proportionately, with sales for the period. Based on the mathematical equation that the auditor uses to describe the relationship between these two variables, given a known value for sales (the independent variable), the auditor can predict the sales commission expense (the dependent variable) and compare this predicted value with the recorded value. There are various methods—such as the least squares method—for determining the mathematical formula that describes the relationship between the dependent and independent variables and for measuring the strength of that relationship. Descriptions of those methods are found in most statistics books.

Another technique that auditors sometimes use to compare financial information with predicted results is time-series analysis. A time series is a set of observations taken at specified times, usually at equal intervals. The results are often depicted on graphs or charts on which the horizontal axis represents time and the vertical axis measures values of a particular account or activity. The data are analyzed to identify components of time-series behavior such as long-term trend, seasonal variation, cyclical movements, and random variation. Once these components have been identified, a variety of methods can be employed to make projections to the future; those methods are described in most statistics books.

Study of the Relationships of Elements of Financial Information. The financial statements are an integrated presentation of financial elements, and various accounts and changes in accounts are related to one another. For example, changes in sales affect cost of goods sold, inventory, and receivables. The auditor should be aware of how a change in one account influences other accounts. Ratios are one means of describing the relationship between two variables; however, ratios describe the relationship between variables at only one level of activity. If the activity level changes, the ratio typically changes. In fact, the only time a ratio remains constant at all levels of activity is when, in a graphic depiction, it forms a straight line passing through the point of origin. All other ratios change with activity levels, even if the underlying relationship between the two components behaves predictably.

Comparison of Financial Information with Similar Industry Information. Although clients vary in size and business activities, comparison of a client's financial results with its industry group may be a useful way to determine whether the client's performance is consistent with that of other similar entities. Use of information compiled by services such as Dun & Bradstreet, Robert Morris Associates, or Standard & Poor's can give the auditor standard "benchmarks" against which to monitor performance or judge performance change over time. Auditors are increasingly using microcomputers (or computer terminals) to access such information from public data bases.

Economic variables may affect various companies' performance differently or may affect an entire industry in the same way. One way to address this issue is to compare the client's financial information with that of the leading performer in its industry over time. Data made available by various financial services, such as Robert Morris Associates, may assist in this comparison. Also, the company's industry may have a trade organization that collects information and publishes composite data that will allow the auditor to view the client relative to its competitors. Those data, while useful, can also be potentially misleading, for the following reasons:

1. The financial statements made available to the financial service or trade organization are probably not selected by a random or statistically reliable method.

2. Many companies have varied product lines, making it difficult to categorize them by their primary product.

3. An "extreme" set of financial statements can be present in a sample, causing a disproportionate influence on the industry composite. This is particularly true in a relatively small sample.

4. Companies in the same industry may differ in their method of operations, which in turn can directly influence their financial statements.

5. Variations in financial data among different companies engaged in the same general line of business may be caused by geographical location, accounting methods used, sources and methods of financing, and other factors.[2]

Study of the Relationships of Financial Information to Relevant Nonfinancial Information. Studying relationships between financial and nonfinancial data may be useful, particularly for audits of enterprises in industries in which an "average" rate has meaning. Figure 9.3 provides examples of such relationships that may be significant in assessing the overall reasonableness of revenue in various industries.

Assessing Assurance from Analytical Review Procedures

In general terms, the level of assurance that can be derived from an analytical procedure is a function of several factors:

• The correlation of analytical results (quantitative and qualitative) with past experience and results of other current-year procedures (including other analytical procedures). If past experience and the results of current-year procedures indicate that material misstatement is not present, the auditor has attained a higher level of assurance than if each test result was considered separately or if some test results appeared contradictory.

---

[2]Adapted from "Interpretation of Statement Studies Figures," *'85 Annual Statement Studies* (Philadelphia: Robert Morris Associates, 1985), p. 2.

Figure 9.3   Overall Reasonableness Tests of Revenue

Industry	Item Being Tested	Overall Reasonableness Test for Item Being Tested
Baking	Sales	Projected revenue based on volume of ingredients used
Banking	Interest earned	Average loans outstanding × average days outstanding × average interest rates
Colleges and universities	Tuition revenue	Enrollment statistics × average tuition
Hospitals	Patient bed revenue	Hospital beds × occupancy rate × average room rate
Hotels	Room revenue	Rooms × occupancy rate × average room rate
Laundromats	Washing machine revenue	Projected revenue based on water usage
Municipalities	Tax revenue	Assessed values × tax rates
Professional services	Fees billed	Employees × utilization rate × hours in a year × average billing rates
Real estate	Rental revenue	Rental units × occupancy rate × average rent

Source: Adapted from "Appendix C: Overall Verification Procedures" in D. G. Smith, *Analytical Review* (Toronto: Canadian Institute of Chartered Accountants, 1983), p. 65.

- The reliability of the underlying data. Analytical results based on data generated from a well-controlled environment provide greater assurance than those based on data generated from an environment with limited or inconsistent controls.
- Level of information analyzed. The potential for detecting misstatements increases when data used for comparisons are disaggregated. Analytical procedures performed at lower levels (e.g., by product line, inventory location, plant, or subsidiary) are more effective than procedures performed at an overall level, such as the consolidated financial statement line-item level.
- Frequency of measurement. In many instances, the more frequently a relationship is measured, the more predictable it becomes. Relationships analyzed on a daily, weekly, or monthly basis generally provide greater assurance that one-time material misstatements will be "flagged" than if relationships are analyzed on an annual basis. For example, performing a detailed monthly or quarterly trend analysis of sales may be more effective than a simple comparison of year-end sales with the prior-year balance.

Audit Programs

As noted in Chapter 8, auditing procedures are compiled into a document referred to as an audit program. The audit program should be organized in a manner that will provide for the efficient performance of the procedures listed. More specifically, the program should be organized so that when a particular document is examined, as many audit procedures as possible are performed on it. For example, assume that one audit procedure calls for examining vendor invoices for initials indicating that the invoice was reviewed for mathematical accuracy and matched to a purchase order and receiving document, and that another audit procedure calls for examining vendor invoices for evidence of authorization for payment. Combining these audit procedures into one audit program step will enhance audit efficiency. Since the authors believe that audit programs should be tailored to the specific circumstances of individual clients, a "complete" audit program as such is not presented in this book, although specific compliance and substantive tests are presented and discussed in Part 3 in the context of auditing the various transaction cycles and account balances.

Auditors differ among themselves over the degree of detail that should be included in an audit program. Some auditors believe that an audit program should be as general as possible and that someone seeking to know what detailed audit steps were performed can find that information by looking at the working papers that report the results of the audit tests. At the extreme, such an audit program might, for example, include the step: "Perform compliance tests of controls over shipments." Other auditors believe that the audit program should be as detailed and specific as possible. The advantage of such specificity is that two people reading the audit program would perform exactly the same audit tests on the same number of transactions or balances. An audit program that reflected this attitude to the extreme might contain the step: "Examine 75 shipping documents for signature of individual authorized to release merchandise from warehouse." The disadvantage of this approach is that it eliminates much judgment from the audit process and makes that process somewhat mechanical. Either approach may be consistent with an efficient and effective audit as long as the planning and supervising of the work are carefully correlated with the particular type of audit program, and the education and training of the auditor performing the procedures are adequate to enable the individual to make the necessary judgments.

Summary: Flowchart of an Audit

In the summary of the audit process that follows, numbers in parentheses refer to steps on the flowchart in Figure 9.4 on pages 351 and 352.

To conduct an effective and efficient audit, the auditor gathers, or on a recurring engagement updates, and documents information about the client's business and industry (1). (The need for working papers that appropriately document the information gathered, the auditing procedures performed, and the judgments made throughout the audit is taken for granted and is not explicitly referred to in this summary on every occasion when such documentation would be appropriate.) The auditor also obtains, or updates, and documents information about the client's control environment and the flow of significant transactions through the accounting systems, on a cycle-by-cycle basis (2).

Figure 9.4 Flowchart of the Audit Process

Description	*Step No.*	
Information-Gathering Phase		
Gather or update necessary information about the client.	1	
Obtain or update information about the client's control environment and accounting systems.	2	
Planning Phase		
Make preliminary materiality judgments and assess the risk of material misstatement occurring.	3	
Determine an effective and efficient audit strategy (may be selected by audit objectives for individual accounts or by cycle, location, subsidiary, or component of business activity) and prepare the audit program in accordance with the planned strategy and other engagement objectives.	4	
Complete the other planning aspects of the engagement in a manner consistent with the strategy (e.g., prepare time budgets, select appropriate staff for engagement, and prepare interoffice instructions).	5	
Note: The above steps should be performed prior to the start of field work.		
Performance Phase		
Study and evaluate the design of specific internal accounting controls.	6	
Perform transaction reviews (if necessary).	7	
Based on knowledge obtained in Steps 6 and 7, determine if the planned audit strategy (i.e., reliance on specific internal accounting controls) is still effective and efficient. If not, go back to Step 4 and revise the audit strategy and program.	8	
Design and perform compliance tests in accordance with the audit strategy and program.	9	

Flowchart labels: Not to rely on controls; To rely on some or all controls; No; Yes; A

(*Continued*)

Figure 9.3   Continued

Description	Step No.	
Based on the results of compliance tests, determine if controls are operating as designed and can actually be relied on. If not, revise documentation of controls, go back to Step 4, and revise the audit strategy and program. Indicate revised approach in the planning documentation.	10	
Perform restricted substantive tests and other audit procedures. (If the substantive tests indicate internal control weaknesses not previously known, revise documentation of specific controls, go back to Step 4, and revise the audit strategy and program.)	11	
Perform substantive tests, not restricted for reliance on specific controls, and other audit procedures.		
Evaluate results of all compliance and substantive tests; consider need to plan and perform additional substantive tests to further reduce detection risk.	12	
Reporting Phase		
Issue audit report.	13	
Communicate weaknesses in and suggestions for improving internal control. (This may be done earlier in the audit.)	14	

The information obtained thus far enables the auditor to make preliminary materiality judgments and assess the risk of material misstatement occurring (3). The auditor then decides whether, for each transaction cycle, continuing the risk assessment by evaluating the design of specific internal accounting controls and testing compliance with them is likely to be efficient, or whether the audit objectives related to accounts or groups of accounts can be achieved more efficiently by not pursuing further the internal control system (4). The strategy decision for each account or group of accounts is documented in a planning memorandum and an audit program of compliance tests (if appropriate) and of substantive tests. Other planning aspects of the engagement are then completed in a manner consistent with the strategy selected (5).

If the auditor decides that continuing the risk assessment for particular audit objectives and accounts or groups of accounts may enhance audit efficiency, the auditor studies and evaluates specific internal accounting controls in the transaction cycle for those audit objectives (6). This entails identifying the specific control procedures and methods implemented by the client and assessing whether their design is suitable for limiting control risk to a low level, assuming that they are applied effectively and continuously throughout the auditor's intended period of reliance. In connection with this step, some auditors perform a transaction review—that is, trace one or two of each type of transaction through the accounting systems and specific internal accounting controls—to resolve any doubts about their understanding of those systems and controls before continuing the risk assessment (7). Such doubts may exist when the audit is a new engagement or the auditor suspects that a recurring client has significantly changed the accounting systems or internal accounting controls since the preceding audit.

If the auditor's evaluation is that weaknesses in the design of specific controls cause them to be unsuitable for assessing control risk as low, the auditor will reassess the risk of material misstatement of the related audit objective(s) in light of those weaknesses and revise the audit strategy and program so that sufficient assurance will be obtained from substantive audit procedures to achieve the objective(s) (8). If the auditor's evaluation is that the design of specific controls is suitable for assessing control risk as low, the auditor can continue to plan to rely on them. The auditor's understanding of the system and conclusions about the design of specific controls are documented, either in narrative form or using a systems flowchart, internal control questionnaire, or other practice aid.

If the strategy for particular audit objectives continues to call for reliance on specific controls, the auditor designs, performs, and documents compliance tests of those controls to determine whether they have operated in reality as they were designed to operate and can thus be relied on (9). Based on the results of the compliance tests, the decision to rely on specific controls is reevaluated once again. Where specific controls have not operated effectively and continuously, the auditor, unable to assess control risk as low, reassesses the risk of material misstatement for the related audit objective(s) and revises the audit strategy and program accordingly (10). Once the audit strategy has been finalized, appropriate substantive tests, restricted for reliance on specific controls where appropriate, are performed and documented (11).

Substantive tests may reveal weaknesses or breakdowns in specific internal accounting controls not previously perceived by the auditor. If those controls are being relied on, the auditor revises the documentation of the controls and reconsiders the risk of material misstatement, the audit strategy, and the audit program. After substantive tests, including analytical review procedures, have been performed in a way that provides the auditor with a reasonable basis for concluding that the risk of an undetected material misstatement is low (12), the auditor is in a position to issue an audit report (13). A management letter may be prepared at this time, or earlier if possible, informing the client about weaknesses or breakdowns in the system of internal control and providing suggestions for remedying them (14).

Review Questions _____

9–1. How do inherent risk and control risk differ from detection risk?

9–2. In what two ways may an auditor achieve the specific audit objectives related to specific accounts?

9–3. Can substantive tests be relied on to the exclusion of compliance tests? Can compliance tests be performed to the exclusion of substantive tests?

9–4. Name the three major categories of substantive tests.

9–5. What determines the nature, timing, and extent of substantive tests?

9–6. Name the three types of accounts that require different approaches to substantive tests.

9–7. Name the techniques generally used for substantive tests of details. What audit objectives is each of these techniques designed to achieve?

9–8. When is early substantive testing feasible?

9–9. When early substantive testing is followed, what additional procedures are necessary?

9–10. When are analytical review procedures performed?

9–11. What are the various types of analytical review procedures?

9–12. What are the various techniques by which financial information can be compared with anticipated or predicted results?

9–13. What caveats should the auditor consider in using industry information?

9–14. How does an audit program aid in performing an effective and efficient audit?

Discussion Questions _____

9–30. How do the inherent risk characteristics of an account affect the extent of substantive test procedures? What balance sheet (and related income statement) accounts are usually audited by relying principally on substantive testing procedures?

9–31. If an auditor decides to rely on compliance tests of internal accounting controls and on interim substantive procedures to reduce the year-end substantive procedures, and those tests and procedures at the interim date prove satisfactory, what additional tests of controls are likely to be performed at year-end?

9–32. At an interim date an auditor was satisfied, as a result of compliance testing, with the adequacy of internal control over certain accounts. The auditor planned to rely on those controls and perform limited substantive tests at year-end. What modifications to the auditor's strategy might be necessary if the results of year-end substantive tests indicated a breakdown in segregation of duties or in supervisory controls after the interim work was done?

9–33. Assume that a comparison between last year's and the current year's number of days' sales in accounts receivable outstanding shows a significant increase. Sales terms did not change during the year. What effect would this have on an audit strategy that calls for relying on internal control?

9–34. What would be the effect on audit strategy of discovery of an unexpected change in the gross margin ratio determined by analytical review procedures?

9-35. When performing an analytical review, should an auditor be satisfied with explanations that appear to account for observed trends? Explain.

9-36. In performing an analytical review of fluctuations in payroll and payroll-related accounts, what might be the effect on audit strategy if all amounts are comparable with those of the prior year?

9-37. The first generally accepted standard of field work requires, in part, that "the work is to be adequately planned." An effective tool that aids the auditor in adequately planning the work is an audit program.

> *Required:*
> What is an audit program, and what purpose does it serve?
>
> (AICPA adapted)

AICPA Multiple Choice Questions ————————————

These questions are taken from the Auditing part of Uniform CPA Examinations. Choose the single most appropriate answer.

9-40. The sequence of steps in gathering evidence as the basis of the auditor's opinion is:

a. Substantive tests, internal control review, and compliance tests.
b. Internal control review, substantive tests, and compliance tests.
c. Internal control review, compliance tests, and substantive tests.
d. Compliance tests, internal control review, and substantive tests.

9-41. Failure to detect material dollar errors in the financial statements is a risk that the auditor primarily mitigates by

a. Performing substantive tests.
b. Performing compliance tests.
c. Evaluating internal control.
d. Obtaining a client representation letter.

9-42. The reliance placed on substantive tests in relation to the reliance placed on internal control varies in a relationship that is ordinarily

a. Parallel.
b. Inverse.
c. Direct.
d. Equal.

9-43. Each of the following might, in itself, form a valid basis for an auditor to decide to omit a test *except* the

a. Relative risk involved.
b. Relationship between the cost of obtaining evidence and its usefulness.
c. Difficulty and expense involved in testing a particular item.
d. Degree of reliance on the relevant internal controls.

9-44. As a result of analytical review procedures, the independent auditor determines that the gross profit percentage has declined from 30 percent in the preceding year to 20 percent in the current year. The auditor should

  a. Express an opinion that is qualified due to inability of the client company to continue as a going concern.
  b. Evaluate management's performance in causing this decline.
  c. Require footnote disclosure.
  d. Consider the possibility of an error in the financial statements.

9-45. Which of the following ratios would be the *least* useful in reviewing the overall profitability of a manufacturing company?

  a. Net income to net worth.
  b. Net income to total assets.
  c. Net income to sales.
  d. Net income to working capital.

9-46. An auditor compares 1986 revenues and expenses with those of the prior year and investigates all changes exceeding 10 percent. By this procedure the auditor would be most likely to learn that

  a. An increase in property tax rates has *not* been recognized in the client's accrual.
  b. The 1986 provision for uncollectible accounts is inadequate, because of worsening economic conditions.
  c. Fourth-quarter payroll taxes were *not* paid.
  d. The client changed its capitalization policy for small tools in 1986.

9-47. Which of the following is *not* a typical analytical review procedure?

  a. Study of relationships of the financial information with relevant nonfinancial information.
  b. Comparison of the financial information with similar information regarding the industry in which the entity operates.
  c. Comparison of recorded amounts of major disbursements with appropriate invoices.
  d. Comparison of the financial information with budgeted amounts.

9-48. An inventory turnover analysis is useful to the auditor because it may detect

  a. Inadequacies in inventory pricing.
  b. Methods of avoiding cyclical holding costs.
  c. The optimum automatic reorder points.
  d. The existence of obsolete merchandise.

9-49. The controller of Excello Manufacturing Inc. wants to use ratio analysis to identify the possible existence of idle equipment or the possibility that equipment has been disposed of without having been written off. Which of the following ratios would best accomplish this objective?

  a. Depreciation expense/book value of manufacturing equipment.
  b. Accumulated depreciation/book value of manufacturing equipment.
  c. Repairs and maintenance cost/direct labor costs.
  d. Gross manufacturing equipment cost/units produced.

9-50. If accounts receivable turned over 7.1 times in 1987 as compared to only 5.6 times in 1988, it is possible that there were

  a. Unrecorded credit sales in 1988.
  b. Unrecorded cash receipts in 1987.

    c. More thorough credit investigations made by the company late in 1987.

    d. Fictitious sales in 1988.

9-51. After the study and evaluation of a client's system of internal accounting control has been completed, an auditor might decide to

    a. Increase the extent of compliance and substantive testing in areas where the system of internal accounting control is strong.

    b. Reduce the extent of compliance testing in areas where the system of internal accounting control is strong.

    c. Reduce the extent of both substantive and compliance testing in areas where the system of internal accounting control is strong.

    d. Increase the extent of substantive testing in areas where the system of internal accounting control is weak.

9-52. Analytical review procedures are

    a. Substantive tests designed to evaluate a system of internal control.

    b. Compliance tests designed to evaluate the validity of management's representation letter.

    c. Substantive tests designed to evaluate the reasonableness of financial information.

    d. Compliance tests designed to evaluate the reasonableness of financial information.

9-53. Which of the following would be *least* likely to be comparable between similar corporations in the same industry line of business?

    a. Earnings per share.

    b. Return on total assets before interest and taxes.

    c. Accounts receivable turnover.

    d. Operating cycle.

9-54. To test for unsupported entries in the ledger, the direction of audit testing should be from the

    a. Journal entries.

    b. Ledger entries.

    c. Original source documents.

    d. Externally generated documents.

Problems and Cases

9-60. The auditing procedures listed herein are procedures that an auditor might employ in an audit of a client's revenue cycle.

    1. For selected sales, compare the date that sales invoices are recorded with the date that goods were shipped, as found on shipping documents.

    2. Divide sales commissions by gross sales and compare the result to the client's stated commission rate.

    3. Mail itemized statements to customers along with a request that they indicate whether the balances due are correct or incorrect.

4. For selected sales, compare customers' sales orders, invoices, and shipping documents for consistency of quantities, prices, customers' names, and other data.

5. Examine supervisor's initials indicating review of sales orders, invoices, and shipping documents for consistency before the invoices are mailed and recorded.

6. Examine shipping documents, copies of sales invoices, and customers' sales orders for evidence supporting unpaid balances in accounts receivable.

7. Review the aged trial balance of accounts receivable, identify old receivables, and evaluate their collectibility.

8. Calculate "days' sales outstanding" (average accounts receivable divided by average daily sales) and compare it with comparable figures for the past three years.

9. Examine reports indicating review of shipping documents for which no invoice has been prepared.

10. Examine documentation supporting credit memos issued after the balance sheet date and determine when the sales took place.

11. For a sample of invoices, recalculate extensions and footings.

12. Observe that a record of goods shipped is maintained.

Required:

a. For each of the foregoing auditing procedures:
1. State whether it is a compliance test or a substantive test, or whether it could be either, depending on its purpose.
2. Classify it according to whether it involves confirmation, observation, inspecting assets, reperformance, examining evidence (inspecting documents), or inquiry. (An auditing procedure may involve more than one type of evidence.)

b. If the procedure is a compliance test:
1. State the internal accounting control objective that is being met and on which the auditor will rely if the test indicates that the control is being operated effectively.
2. State the error that could result if the control is absent or ineffective.
3. State a substantive test that the auditor could use that would provide evidence of the dollar amount of error.

c. If the procedure is a substantive test, state the audit objective that the procedure is designed to meet.

9-61. In auditing the financial statements of a manufacturing company that were prepared from data processed by electronic data processing equipment, the CPA has found that the traditional "audit trail" has been obscured. As a result the CPA may place increased emphasis on overall tests of the data under audit. These overall tests, which are also applied in auditing visibly posted accounting records, include the computation of ratios, which are compared with prior-year ratios or with industrywide norms. Examples of such overall tests or ratios are the computation of the rate of inventory turnover and the computation of the number of days' sales in receivables.

Required:

a. Discuss the advantages to the CPA of the use of ratios as overall tests in an audit.

b. In addition to the computations mentioned, list the ratios that a CPA could compute during an audit as overall tests of balance sheet and related income statement accounts. For each ratio listed, name the two (or more) accounts used in its computation.

c. On discovering that there has been a significant change in a ratio when compared with the prior year's ratio, the CPA considers the possible reasons for the change. Give the possible reasons for the following significant changes in ratios:

1. The rate of inventory turnover (ratio of cost of sales and average inventory) has decreased from the prior year's rate.

2. The number of days' sales in receivables (ratio of average daily accounts receivable and sales) has increased over the prior year.

(AICPA adapted)

9-62. The inspection of the minutes of meetings is an integral part of a CPA's examination of a corporation's financial statements.

Required:

a. A CPA should determine if there is any disagreement between transactions recorded in the corporate records and actions approved by the corporation's board of directors. Why is this so and how is it accomplished?

b. Discuss the effect each of the following situations would have on specific audit steps in a CPA's examination and on the auditor's opinion.

1. The minute book does not show approval for the sale of an important manufacturing division, which was consummated during the year.

2. Some details of a contract negotiated during the year with the labor union are different from the outline of the contract included in the minutes of a meeting of the board of directors.

3. The minutes of a meeting of directors held after the balance sheet date have not yet been written, but the corporation's secretary shows the CPA notes from which the minutes are to be prepared when the secretary has time.

c. What corporate actions should be approved by stockholders and recorded in the minutes of the stockholders' meetings?

(AICPA adapted)

9-63. What are the general objectives or purposes of the CPA's observation of the taking of a physical inventory? (Do not discuss the procedures or techniques involved in making the observation.)

(AICPA adapted)

9-64. A CPA accumulates various kinds of evidence on which the auditor's opinion on the fairness of financial statements examined will be based. Among this evidence are confirmations from third parties and written representations from the client.

Required:

a. 1. What is an audit confirmation?

2. What characteristics should an audit confirmation possess if a CPA is to consider it as valid evidence?

b. 1. What is a written representation?

2. What information should a written representation contain?

3. What effect does a written representation have on a CPA's examination of a client's financial statements?

c. 1. Distinguish between a positive confirmation and a negative confirmation in the auditor's examination of accounts receivable.

2. In confirming an audit client's accounts receivable, what characteristics should be present in the accounts if the CPA is to use negative confirmations?

(AICPA adapted)

9–65. The following errors and irregularities were found by the auditor as a result of performing substantive tests:

1. Goods shipped were not billed because the shipping document (bill of lading) was lost.
2. A cash payment from a customer was stolen by a clerk in the mailroom before any record was made of it.
3. Equipment repairs were unintentionally recorded as an equipment purchase.
4. A vendor's invoice was paid twice; the second payment was stolen by the accounts payable clerk after the treasurer had signed the checks. No entries were made for the second payment.
5. A check for $4321 was recorded as $1234.
6. The plant supervisor submitted a time card for a fictitious employee, received the check, endorsed it with the fictitious name, and deposited it in her bank account.

Required:
For each of those errors or irregularities:

a. State the financial statement assertion that is relevant to the error or irregularity. Be specific.
b. State the substantive test that the auditor probably used to detect the error or irregularity.
c. State the internal control objective that is not being met. Be specific.
d. Specify one or more controls that the client could install that would prevent or detect the error or irregularity.
e. Specify compliance tests that could be used to test the effectiveness of the controls specified in d.

9–66. Identify the accounts and other factors that, singly or in combination, might help to explain a fluctuation in each of the accruals listed below. Your answer should include an explanation of the possible effect of each account or factor on the accrual.

- Accrued hourly and salaried payroll
- Accrued royalties payable
- Accrued vacation pay
- Income and social security taxes withheld and accrued
- Accrued general and automobile insurance
- Accrued real and personal property taxes
- Accrued utilities (electricity and gas)
- Accrued rent
- Accrued bonus payable
- Accrued interest payable

- Accrued pension liability
- Accrued royalties payable

9–67. Your client, XYZ Corp., fabricates electronic components for the automotive industry. Based on your knowledge of this client's operations, its competitors, the economy, and current activity in the automotive industry, you expected the gross margin for a particular product line, a climate control system, to remain relatively flat or increase only slightly from the prior year.

   Just before performing substantive tests of details, you analyze the gross margin for this particular product line and identify an increase of 20 percent over the previous year. You discuss this with both the company controller and the individual responsible for this product line and learn that the purchase of several new machines resulting in significant labor efficiencies was responsible for the increase in the gross margin.

   Required:
   a. How would you follow up and corroborate management's explanation for the increase in the gross margin of this particular product line?
   b. Would the fact that new equipment is included on the schedule of fixed assets, in itself, corroborate management's explanation of the increase in the gross margin of this particular product line? Why or why not?

9–68.   *Part a.*

   Between the time trade accounts receivable confirmations were sent and year-end (a two-month period), the chief executive officer of a client implemented a new sales policy that resulted in an immediate, marked increase in reported sales. The chief executive called customers to obtain their consent to accept shipments of the company's product "on approval." Under the terms offered by the chief executive, the company would ship goods without customers' orders and bill those shipments as though they were sales. However, customers were not obligated to pay for the goods they received unless and until they decided to purchase them. The chief executive assured customers that they had an unconditional right to return any goods accepted "on approval" at any time. The company recorded those "on approval" shipments as sales without waiting for customers to decide which of the goods so shipped, if any, they would purchase. The new policy improved not only the company's sales, but also the chief executive's sales-dependent bonus.

   Required:
   What analytical review procedures could you perform that have the potential to identify the irregularity described?

   Part b.

   Assume you performed the analytical review procedures in your answer to Part a and discovered the unusual sales activity during the last two months of the year. You discussed this with management and learned that the sales increase near year-end is common in the industry. You questioned this response because, while you agree that the trend is consistent with the industry, you noted the *absence* of similar activity in the prior year.

   Required:
   What additional analytical procedures could you design to specifically address the irregularity in the sales and accounts receivable accounts?

9-69. Comparative balance sheets and statements of income and retained earnings (deficit) for Ace Battery Company at June 30, 1986 and 1985 and for the two years then ended are presented below and on page 363. Prior years' financial statements include the following information relative to the year ended June 30, 1984:

> Accounts receivable, net, totaled $5,001,000
> Inventories totaled $5,003,000

Required:

Compute the following for 1986 and 1985, based on the Ace Battery Company's financial data. (Use end-of-year data if necessary.)

- Current ratio
- Accounts receivable turnover
- Inventory turnover
- Return on common stock equity
- Return on total assets
- Gross profit percentage
- Net income to sales
- Long-term debt to equity ratio

What does your analysis of Ace Battery's financial statements indicate?

Ace Battery Company
Statement of Income and Retained Earnings (Deficit)
For the Years Ended June 30, 1986 and 1985
(Client prepared)

	1986	1985
Net sales	$40,000,000	$45,000,000
Cost of sales	31,000,000	32,000,000
Gross profit	9,000,000	13,000,000
Selling, general, and administrative expenses	8,505,000	8,700,000
Income from operations	495,000	4,300,000
Other income (expense)		
Interest	(4,000,000)	(1,000,000)
Loss on sale of machinery and equipment	—	(100,000)
Gain on sale of marketable securities	300,000	100,000
	(3,700,000)	(1,000,000)
Income (loss) before provision for income taxes	(3,205,000)	3,300,000
Recovery of (provision for) income taxes	1,500,000	(1,500,000)
Net income (loss)	(1,705,000)	1,800,000
Retained earnings at beginning of the year	850,000	1,050,000
Dividends[a]	—	(2,000,000)
Retained earnings (deficit) at end of the year	$ (855,000)	$ 850,000

[a]No preferred stock dividends were declared in 1986.

Ace Battery Company
Balance Sheet
June 30, 1986 and 1985

(Client prepared)

Assets	1986	1985
Current assets:		
Cash	$ 10,000	$ 100,000
Marketable securities	40,000	500,000
Accounts receivable, net of allowance for doubtful accounts of $409,000 in 1986 and $286,000 in 1985	6,000,000	5,000,000
Inventories	10,000,000	5,000,000
Prepaid expenses	50,000	200,000
Total current assets	16,100,000	10,800,000
Property, plant, and equipment, net of accumulated depreciation of $9,000,000 in 1986 and $6,000,000 in 1985	37,000,000	17,000,000
Other assets, net of accumulated amortization of $20,000 in 1986 and $15,000 in 1985	45,000	50,000
Total assets	$53,145,000	$27,850,000

Liabilities	1986	1985
Current liabilities:		
Bank loans	$ 2,500,000	$ 4,000,000
Accounts payable	9,000,000	1,000,000
Accrued liabilities	3,000,000	
Notes payable, current portion	3,000,000	1,000,000
Income taxes payable		1,500,000
Dividends payable		2,000,000
Total current liabilities	17,500,000	9,500,000
Notes payable, net of current portion	30,000,000	11,000,000
Deferred income taxes	500,000	500,000
Stockholders' Equity		
Preferred stock, 5% noncumulative, 100,000 shares authorized, issued, and outstanding	1,000,000	1,000,000
Common stock, 500,000 shares authorized, issued, and outstanding	5,000,000	5,000,000
Retained earnings (deficit)	(855,000)	850,000
Total stockholders' equity	5,145,000	6,850,000
Total liabilities and stockholders' equity	$53,145,000	$27,850,000

Chapter 10
The Extent of Testing: Audit Sampling

This book has noted on several occasions that the auditor has several decisions to make in gathering evidence about each assertion implicit in the individual measurements and disclosures in a set of financial statements. Those decisions include how much evidence to acquire, that is, decisions about the extent of audit tests. This chapter addresses that decision. Audit sampling is defined, and procedures that do not involve sampling are discussed; then audit risk is described in the context of sampling, and the determinants of sample size are outlined. Those discussions provide background for guidance on applying statistical and nonstatistical sampling techniques in both compliance and substantive testing.

In the first edition of this book, published in 1912, Montgomery recognized as an "obvious conclusion" the notion that "no audit can or should embrace a complete verification of all the transactions of the period under review."[1] If for every procedure selected by the auditor for gathering evidence, or even if for a few of those procedures, the auditor were to examine every item that could possibly be selected for examination, it would be virtually impossible to complete an audit on a timely basis, not to mention at a reasonable cost. Neither the client nor the public expects the auditor to examine every transaction. Consequently, the auditor is continually faced with the question: How much testing is enough?

[1] R. H. Montgomery, *Auditing Theory and Practice* (New York: Ronald Press, 1912), p. 81.

In some instances, that question is answered by deciding not to perform a specific procedure at all. For example, if controls over payroll disbursements are compliance tested and found to be strong, the auditor may decide neither to prepare a reconciliation of the payroll bank account at year-end nor even to review the client's year-end reconciliation. (In that situation, the decisions about what kind of evidence and how much evidence to acquire are identical.) In other instances, the question is answered by deciding to perform some procedure, but not to apply it to all the items in an account or to all transactions of a specific type. For example, the auditor may decide to confirm accounts receivable, but to limit the procedure to only a portion of receivables under $10,000. Examining (testing) less than the entire population or class of items that could be examined or tested (e.g., all of the client's accounts receivable under $10,000) is referred to as sampling.

SAS No. 39, *Audit Sampling* (AU Section 350.01), provides a formal definition of audit sampling: ''Audit sampling is the application of an audit procedure to less than 100 percent of the items within an account balance or class of transactions for the purpose of evaluating some characteristic of the balance or class.''

Based on the results of applying an audit procedure to a representative sample of items, the auditor can make an inference (by projecting or extrapolating the sample results) about the entire population from which the sample was selected. In fact, SAS No. 39 requires that the items be selected in such a way that the sample can be expected to be representative of the population. After performing the necessary audit procedures, the auditor is required to project the sample results to the population and to use that projection in considering whether the audit objective has been met. When evaluating whether the financial statements as a whole may be materially misstated, the auditor should aggregate all projected errors (discussed later) determined from sampling applications and other likely errors[2] determined from nonsampling procedures.

Audit sampling is used by auditors in both compliance and substantive testing. It is especially useful when the auditor's selection of items to be tested is drawn from a large population and the auditor has no specific knowledge about the characteristics of the items being tested, such as whether an account may be overstated or understated as a result of various types of errors. For example, accounts receivable, inventory, and accounts payable balances could be overstated or understated as a result of the use of incorrect quantities or prices or because of errors in arithmetic extensions and footings.

Procedures Not Involving Sampling

SAS No. 39 promulgated professional standards for all uses of audit sampling. Although in the past the term *sampling* was used to describe virtually all forms

---

[2]In addition to projected error, likely error includes known errors specifically identified by the auditor in nonsampling procedures and differences between unreasonable estimates in the financial statements and the auditor's closest reasonable estimate of those amounts.

of detailed audit testing in which not every item was examined, the definition of sampling in SAS No. 39, cited earlier, excludes several types of tests frequently performed in an audit. To clarify the circumstances in which an auditor's examination of less than 100 percent of the items in a class of transactions or an account balance would not be considered audit sampling, in January 1985 the ASB issued an Auditing Interpretation of SAS No. 39 (AU Sections 9350.01 and .02).

The auditor's purpose in applying a procedure is the governing factor in determining whether the procedure constitutes sampling. Sampling is not involved if the auditor does not intend to extend the conclusion reached by performing the procedure to the remainder of the items in the class or account balance. For example, the auditor might trace one or two transactions through the client's accounting system only for the purpose of gaining or updating an understanding of the flow of transactions through the system, and not for assessing the effectiveness of specific controls. Similarly, auditors sometimes reperform calculations or trace journal entries into ledger accounts on a test basis for the purpose of obtaining additional evidential matter relating to a financial statement assertion. SAS No. 39 does not apply in those situations because the auditor's intent is not to evaluate a characteristic of all transactions passing through the system or all balances in the account. Substantive tests other than tests of details of transactions and balances (for example, reading the minutes of meetings of the board of directors) also do not involve sampling.

Furthermore, sampling is not involved when the auditor divides a class of transactions or an account balance into two groups and then examines 100 percent of the items in one of the groups and tests the other group by other means or does not test it at all because it is immaterial. For example, in what is known as the "high dollar coverage" approach, the auditor might divide the accounts receivable balance into two groups: (1) several large items that constitute a significant portion of the balance, and (2) the remaining (smaller) items. All the accounts in the first group may be confirmed, while those in the second group, which may be material in the aggregate, may be tested through analytical review, reliance on internal controls, or procedures performed on related accounts. The auditor would be using sampling only if an auditing procedure were applied to individual items that constituted less than 100 percent of the population in the second group for the purpose of drawing a conclusion about all of the items in that group.

An auditor's compliance tests of controls that are not documented do not involve sampling. Those tests often consist of inquiry and observation. An example is an auditor's observation of a client's physical inventory count procedures, such as controls over inventory movement and counting procedures. (Audit sampling may be involved in certain compliance tests or detailed substantive tests of inventory, such as tracing selected test counts into inventory records.)

A testing method in which less than 100 percent of an account balance is examined and that is similar to, but is not, sampling is referred to as "accept-reject'' testing. It is used when projecting an error amount (discussed later) is not practical, for example, test counts made as part of a physical inventory observation and tests of reconciling items. As another example, analytical procedures may be applied to prepaid insurance balances as the primary source of audit assurance about the accuracy of that account; the auditor may then subject one or two insurance policies to detailed tests for added assurance about the accuracy of expense allocations. In those circumstances, the auditor either ''accepts'' that the test supports its objective (that is, no or few errors are found) or ''rejects'' the test (more than negligible errors are found) and performs other procedures or additional tests to achieve the objective. However, the auditor still must consider the extent of testing (that is, assurance levels and materiality) in planning to use ''accept–reject'' testing.

Other examples of audit procedures that usually do not involve sampling are cutoff tests in which the auditor examines all significant transactions around the cutoff date and analytical review procedures. Also, sampling may not always be necessary in compliance testing controls that operate repeatedly throughout the period. Sometimes, if such a control operates cumulatively, the auditor can achieve the audit objective by examining a single item. For example, a review of the year-end bank reconciliation may be sufficient to achieve the auditor's objective with respect to controls over bank reconciliations generally. Similarly, examination of other year-end cumulative reconciliations (such as a reconciliation of the accounts receivable subsidiary ledger to the control account) may be sufficient to achieve the relevant audit objectives.

Generally accepted auditing standards do not require auditors to use sampling; they do require that auditors plan their audit strategy to ensure that significant components of all material account balances receive some audit attention, whether through sampling or nonsampling procedures, and that auditors document their sources of audit assurance, regardless of whether sampling is employed.

Audit Risk and Sampling

Having decided that a particular auditing procedure will be applied to a sample of an audit population, the auditor must then determine the minimum sample size that is needed to control the risk of material error in the financial statements. That risk—referred to as audit risk—is the risk that an improper conclusion may be reached about the client's financial statements. Audit risk was discussed in Chapter 6 in the context of formulating the audit strategy on an overall basis. How that discussion relates to sampling is explained here.

Nonsampling Risk

Nonsampling risk encompasses all risks that are not specifically the result of sampling. Nonsampling risk is the risk that any factor other than the size of the sample selected will cause the auditor to draw an incorrect conclusion about an account balance or about the effectiveness of an accounting control. Examples of nonsampling risk are:

- Omitting necessary audit procedures (e.g., failing to review management or board minutes).
- Applying audit procedures improperly (e.g., giving confirmation requests to the client for mailing).
- Applying audit procedures to an inappropriate or incomplete population (e.g., excluding an entire class of purchases from the process of selecting a sample for substantive tests of transactions and then concluding that all purchase transactions are appropriate).
- Failing to detect the improper selection or application of accounting recognition, measurement, or disclosure principles.
- Failing to take action either in response to audit findings or because factors requiring attention have been overlooked.

Sample size is not a consideration in assessing nonsampling risk. Analyses of past alleged audit failures indicate that such nonsampling risk factors as failure to understand business situations or risks, errors in interpreting accounting principles, mistakes in interpreting and applying standards, and misstatements caused by client fraud are among the most significant audit risk factors and sources of auditor liability. Since sample size is irrelevant if the auditor fails to apply appropriate audit procedures or examines an inappropriate population, adequate control over nonsampling risk is a prerequisite to controlling sampling risk.

Most auditors deal with nonsampling risk, in part, by carefully planning the audit strategy and maintaining high standards of audit quality. Quality standards address matters such as independence and professional development of staff, independent review of working papers, and supervision of the performance of procedures by senior and managerial personnel. These are covered in detail in Chapter 3.

Sampling Risk

Sampling risk is the risk that, when an audit test is restricted to a sample, the conclusion reached from the test will differ from the conclusion that would have been reached if the same test had been applied to all items in the population rather than to just a sample. It is the chance that the test will indicate that a control is reliable or an account is not materially misstated when the opposite is true, or that the control is not reliable or an account is materially misstated when the opposite is true. Sampling risk can also be viewed as the complement of the desired level of assurance specified for a particular sample. Thus, if the auditor seeks a high level of assurance from a test, a low sampling risk should be specified. (The auditor usually specifies a low sampling risk, e.g., in testing critical internal controls on which significant reliance is planned.) Sampling risk is inversely related to sample size (i.e., with all other factors remaining the same, the larger the sample, the lower the sampling risk).

Sampling risk has the following aspects:

1. In the context of compliance tests of internal accounting controls
   (a) The *risk of overreliance* on internal accounting controls is the risk that the auditor will conclude, based on a sample, that the compliance rate justifies the planned level of reliance on a control when examination of every item in the population would reveal that the true compliance rate does not justify such reliance.[3]
   (b) The *risk of underreliance* on internal accounting controls is the risk that the auditor will conclude, based on a sample, that the compliance rate does not justify the planned level of reliance on a control when examination of every item in the population would reveal that the true compliance rate justifies such reliance.[4]

2. In the context of substantive tests of account balances
   (a) The *risk of incorrect acceptance* is the risk that the auditor will conclude, based on a sample, that the recorded account balance is not materially misstated when examination of every item in the population would reveal that it is materially misstated.[5]
   (b) The *risk of incorrect rejection* is the risk that the auditor will conclude, based on a sample, that the recorded account balance is materially misstated when examination of every item in the population would reveal that it is not materially misstated.[6]

The risks of underreliance and of incorrect rejection relate primarily to audit efficiency. For example, if the auditor initially concludes, based on an evaluation of an audit sample, that an account balance is materially misstated when it is not, the performance of additional audit procedures and consideration of other audit evidence would ordinarily lead the auditor to the correct audit conclusion. Similarly, if the auditor's evaluation of a sample leads to reducing the planned reliance on an internal accounting control when in fact that is not necessary, substantive tests are likely to be increased to compensate for the perceived inability to rely on the control. Although the audit might be less efficient in those circumstances, it would nevertheless be effective.

The risks of incorrect acceptance and of overreliance are of greater concern to the auditor, since they relate directly to the effectiveness of an audit in detecting material misstatements. It is thus necessary to ensure that the extent of testing (sample size) and method of sample selection are adequate to keep those risks from exceeding acceptable levels. The complement of the risks of overreliance and of incorrect acceptance is the desired level of assurance, which is sometimes referred to by the terms ''reliability'' or ''confidence level.'' For example, an auditor's willingness to accept a 5 percent risk of overreliance on an

---

[3]This risk is sometimes referred to in statistical literature as the *beta* risk.
[4]This risk is sometimes referred to in statistical literature as the *alpha* risk.
[5]This risk is sometimes referred to in statistical literature as the *beta* risk.
[6]This risk is sometimes referred to in statistical literature as the *alpha* risk.

internal accounting control in a compliance test could also be expressed as a requirement for a desired reliability level of 95 percent.

Determinants of Sample Size

In planning a sampling application, an auditor must consider three factors: the level of risk that can be accepted that the sample results will be misleading (sampling risk), how much error can be accepted (tolerable error), and how much error there might be in the population (expected error). The auditor then determines an appropriate sample size, either by applying statistical sampling techniques, described later in this chapter, that incorporate those factors, or on a nonstatistical[7] basis by applying professional judgment in considering the relative impact of each of the three factors on sample size. The population size is sometimes important to the statistical computations, but when the population is large (e.g., over 2000 items), the effect on the computations is often minimal. For small samples taken from large populations, the population size has the least influence of all the relevant factors on sample size. This increased emphasis on the planning aspects of sampling applications means that the auditor must thoroughly develop the sampling strategy before the testing begins.

Sampling Risk

As noted previously, sampling risk is inversely related to sample size. The auditor determines the acceptable level of sampling risk after considering the effectiveness of other procedures performed on the account or control under review. Thus, a higher level of sampling risk may be accepted for detailed substantive tests when significant reliance is placed on controls over the transactions that enter into the account balance being tested.

The following example will illustrate these relationships. If an auditor is relying significantly on internal controls and is performing extensive analytical review procedures, then a high sampling risk (small sample size) is acceptable for the substantive tests of details (or perhaps it may not even be necessary to perform any detailed tests). On the other hand, if the auditor is not relying on internal controls and is not performing extensive analytical reviews, then a low sampling risk (large sample size) is required. Very low levels of sampling risk are normally attainable only with very large sample sizes (i.e., several hundred items).

Tolerable Deviation Rate or Error Amount

The *tolerable deviation rate* (usually shortened to ''tolerable rate'') is the rate of deviation from prescribed procedures that may be found, as a result of com-

---

[7]The term ''nonstatistical sampling'' is used in SAS No. 39 to describe what many auditors previously referred to as ''judgmental sampling.'' Statistical sampling procedures involve the exercise of substantial amounts of audit judgment, as, of course, does nonstatistical sampling.

pliance testing, without causing the auditor to either revise the planned reliance on a control procedure or modify the substantive tests.[8] The *tolerable error amount* (usually shortened to "tolerable error") is the amount of dollar errors in an account balance that may be discovered as a result of performing a substantive test and not require other audit procedures or affect the auditor's opinion on the financial statements. For substantive test samples, the tolerable error cannot be larger than the smaller of the materiality amount for the individual item or for the financial statements taken as a whole (which is the smaller of balance sheet or income statement materiality). For example, if balance sheet materiality is $200,000 and income statement materiality is $100,000, the tolerable error should be no larger than $100,000 or the materiality amount for the individual item, if smaller. Determining materiality levels is discussed in Chapter 6.

Even if financial statement materiality is smaller than materiality for a specific account, the auditor may establish a tolerable error that is less than financial statement materiality because of the possibility that other accounts may also contain errors. The chance of the true error in every sampling application equaling tolerable error is remote, however, so that auditors normally plan audit procedures so that the sum of the individual tolerable errors exceeds the amount considered "tolerable" (material) for the financial statements as a whole. In other words, tolerable error for an account balance is usually set somewhere between overall materiality and a proportional allocation of overall tolerable error to that account.

As the tolerable rate or error increases, the sample size required to achieve the auditor's objective at a given level of sampling risk (or of its complement, reliability) decreases. (This conclusion is derived from the sample size table for statistical samples, Table 10.1, on page 379; the same concept applies to nonstatistical samples.) Thus, with all other factors remaining the same, sample size can be almost halved if the tolerable rate or error is doubled (e.g., from 5 percent to 10 percent) at a reliability level of 95 percent with an expected deviation rate (discussed later) of one-half of 1 percent. For compliance tests using statistical sampling, SAS No. 39 suggests a range of possible tolerable deviation rates between 5 percent and 10 percent. No such guidelines can be given for substantive tests, however, since tolerable error for a specific account must be determined judgmentally based on a number of factors—overall materiality, account balance materiality, and type and amount of individual items within an account balance—that are not precisely definable. For example, if inventory and accounts receivable have the same total account balance but inventory is more complex and prone to error because it comprises numerous products in various stages of completion, then inventory may be allocated a larger tolerable error than accounts receivable.

---

[8]Some auditors use the term "tolerable error rate" instead of "tolerable deviation rate." The word "error" implies financial statement misstatements; an inoperative accounting control *may* cause financial statement errors, but it need not. To avoid confusion, the word "deviation" is used in this book in referring to a departure from a prescribed control.

The auditor should be aware that designing a sample with a high tolerable rate or error may lead to procedures that are too imprecise to support a conclusion at a low risk level that the account and the financial statements taken as a whole are not materially misstated. Also, a large sample can generally detect both frequent and infrequent errors that aggregate to a material amount, but a small sample can be relied on to detect only frequent errors. At the extreme, some items in an account may individually be so material or may have such a high likelihood of error that the auditor should be unwilling to accept any sampling risk; those items should not be sampled but should be examined 100 percent.

Expected Deviation Rate or Error Amount

Expected deviation rate or error amount also has an impact on sample size. As the expected rate or amount increases, the sample size necessary to meet the auditor's specified sampling risk at a given tolerable deviation rate or error amount increases as well. The auditor's specification of the expected deviation rate or error amount in the population to be sampled is the best estimate of the true deviation rate or error amount in that population. Auditors commonly use the results of prior years' compliance tests to estimate the expected deviation rate; if those results are not available, a small preliminary sample from the current year's population can be used for that purpose, or the auditor's "best guess" can be used. The estimate need not be exact, since it affects only the determination of sample size and not the auditor's evaluation of sample results.

In a statistical sampling context, the relationship between the increase in expected deviation rate or error amount and the increase in sample size is not proportionate. For example, if the auditor estimates the expected deviation rate at 2 percent for a particular compliance test and specifies a tolerable deviation rate of 5 percent at a 95 percent reliability level, the appropriate minimum statistical sample size is 190. If, given the same circumstances, the expected rate were estimated at 3 percent, the sample size would be 370. (This can be seen by referring to Table 10.1 on page 379.) When the expected deviation rate is close to the tolerable deviation rate, very large sample sizes are often necessary. On the other hand, if the auditor sets an expected deviation rate that is below the true deviation rate, the sample is likely not to be large enough to support a conclusion at the desired level of reliability that the true deviation rate does not exceed the tolerable rate.

Figures 10.1 and 10.2 summarize the effect of the factors discussed previously on sample size.

Other Planning Considerations

SAS No. 39 (AU Section 350.17) requires the auditor to "determine that the population from which he draws the sample is appropriate for the specific audit objective. For example, an auditor would not be able to detect understatements of an account due to omitted items by sampling the recorded items. An appro-

Figure 10.1 Factors Influencing Sample Size in a Compliance Test of an Internal Accounting Control

	Conditions Leading to	
	Smaller Sample Size	Larger Sample Size
Extent to which the auditor wishes to reduce substantive tests by relying on the control	Lesser	Greater
Expected deviation rate	Lower	Higher
Tolerable deviation rate	Higher	Lower
Number of items in population	Virtually no effect on sample size unless population is very small (fewer than 2000 items)	

priate sampling plan for detecting such understatements would involve selecting from a source in which the omitted items are included.'' In general, audit sampling (or any testing) directed at a recorded balance will not provide assurance as to the completeness of the balance. To test the completeness of an account balance (e.g., accounts receivable), it is often necessary to test some other source in which the potentially omitted items are included (e.g., the shipping log).

Figure 10.2 Factors Influencing Sample Size in a Substantive Test of Details

	Conditions Leading to	
	Smaller Sample Size	Larger Sample Size
Planned reliance on internal accounting control based on results of compliance tests	Greater	Lesser
Stratification[a]	Greater	Lesser
Expected error:		
Size of expected individual errors	Smaller	Larger
Frequency and aggregate amount of expected errors	Lower	Higher[b]
Tolerable error	Higher	Lower
Reliance on other substantive tests (e.g., analytical reviews)	Significant	Little or none
Number of items in population	Virtually no effect on sample size unless population is very small (fewer than 2000 items)	

[a]Stratification is the separation of population items into groups or strata on the basis of some characteristic related to the specific audit objective.

[b]If the auditor's assessment of the amount of expected errors exceeds an acceptable level of materiality, it may be inadvisable to perform the test on a sample basis.

Choosing Statistical or Nonstatistical Methods

SAS No. 39 explicitly recognizes that both statistical and nonstatistical approaches to audit sampling, when properly applied, can provide sufficient evidential matter. Moreover, the guidance in SAS No. 39 applies equally to both approaches. Both approaches have advantages and disadvantages, and the auditor should choose between them after considering those advantages and disadvantages.

The major advantages of statistical sampling are the opportunity to determine the minimum sample size needed to meet the objectives of audit tests and the opportunity to express the results quantitatively. In statistical sampling, sampling risk can be measured in quantitative terms and objectively evaluated and controlled. This is because the process of determining the appropriate sample size entails specifying a level of reliability[9] and a desired degree of precision.[10]

There are also disadvantages to using statistical sampling, however, and they can result in practical problems that might make the use of statistical techniques less efficient than nonstatistical sampling procedures. For example, the statistical sampler *must* use random sample selection techniques, which can be more time consuming than the unsystematic (haphazard) techniques available to the nonstatistical sampler. In selecting a random sample, the auditor may have practical problems establishing a correlation between a table or computer printout of random numbers and the population under audit. For example, an auditor who plans to use random number selection of unpaid invoices in the audit of accounts receivable may face a population that is made up of invoices from three client locations, with the invoice numbers assigned at each location without regard to the numbers assigned at the other locations. Not only will problems be caused by missing numbers in the population as a result of paid invoices, but duplicate numbers could also exist because of the lack of coordination among locations in assigning invoice numbers. Thus, the auditor might have to renumber the population in order to use random number selection.

The use of specialized audit software to extract a sample from a population stored in machine-readable form may greatly reduce the costs of selecting a sta-

---

[9]As noted on page 369, reliability may be thought of as the auditor's level of assurance or confidence—expressed as a percentage—that the statistical results provide correct information about the true population value. A 95 percent reliability level is considered a high level of audit assurance for substantive tests of details. If additional assurance is obtained from reliance on internal controls or other substantive tests and procedures, such as analytical reviews, the auditor often designs the sample at a level below 95 percent.

[10]Precision may be defined as the difference between the rates or amounts specified for tolerable error and expected error (both of which were explained on pages 370-372) in planning a sample. For example, if tolerable error is set at 5 percent and expected error is set at 1 percent, the desired precision of the test is 4 percent. In some types of sampling, such as attributes sampling used in compliance testing, precision is stated in terms of a rate of occurrence (e.g., 5 percent). In other types, such as variables sampling used in substantive tests of details, it is expressed as a dollar amount (e.g., $25,000). SAS No. 39 (AU Section 350) uses the concepts of "tolerable error" and an "allowance for sampling risk" instead of precision.

tistical sample. When appropriate audit software is used, statistical samples may not be more costly than nonstatistical samples. As a result, the availability of computerized sample selection and evaluation programs is often a deciding factor in determining whether it is efficient to use statistical sampling techniques. Before deciding whether to use a statistical sampling procedure in a particular circumstance, the auditor should make a cost-benefit analysis, weighing the additional costs of determining sample size, extracting the sample, and evaluating the results using appropriate formulas against the benefits of knowing the reliability and precision associated with the sample results.

Statistical Compliance Testing

A statistical technique called *attributes sampling* that deals with proportions and rates is commonly used for compliance tests of internal controls. Attributes sampling techniques are used to estimate the true proportion (not dollar value) of an attribute in a population. The auditor must carefully define the attribute being measured—such as proper approval of an invoice for payment—because the person who examines each sample item must have criteria for determining whether the sample item possesses that attribute or not. The sample results are then projected to the population and statistical computations made to measure the precision and reliability associated with the sample results.

In compliance testing, departures from prescribed procedures (i.e., deviations) are generally measured in rates of incidence. For example, in a sample of 50 disbursement checks, the absence of evidence of proper authorization of 1 check is generally expressed as a 2 percent sample deviation rate (1/50). Since the control either operates or not, percentages are a convenient way to express compliance test sample results.

The true deviation rate in the population is likely to be higher or lower than the rate found in a sample. The statistical sampler can make a statement about how high the true deviation rate could be, at a given level of reliability. For example, an auditor, having evaluated a statistical sample, could state

> One deviation was found in a random sample of 50 items (a 2 percent deviation rate); thus, there is a 90 percent level of reliability (10 percent sampling risk) that the true deviation rate in the population is less than 8 percent.

Auditor judgment must then be used to determine whether, and to what extent, reliance can be placed on the tested control.

Basic Concepts of Attributes Sampling

If the true deviation rate in a population were known, the exact (discrete) probability of obtaining a specific sample result (such as 1 error in a sample of 50 items) could be computed. The auditor does not, however, know the true deviation rate and thus can only infer what it could be, based on sample results. Because the auditor samples from a finite population and removes each item from the population as it is sampled (i.e., sampled items are not replaced), the auditor must use the appropriate statistical formulas to compute the reliability and precision of the sample results.

To illustrate the sampling technique typically used by auditors in compliance testing, consider a simple example in which the true population deviation rate is known. The example is later varied to resemble more closely a realistic audit situation. Assume the following:

Population	= 1000 invoices
Properly approved invoices	= 950 items
Improperly approved invoices	= 50 items

The attribute being measured by the auditor is the approval of invoices for payment. In determining whether the approval control could be relied on to limit the extent of substantive procedures, the auditor might use the following decision rule: If no deviations were found in a sample of five items, the control would be relied on, but if one or more deviations were found in the sample (a 20 percent or more sample deviation rate), the control would not be relied on. (Small sample sizes are used to illustrate the concepts and computations and are not indicative of suggested sample sizes.) What is the chance the auditor would find no deviations in a random sample of five items from this population?

If a sample of five invoices is taken from the population, one item at a time, there will be 950 chances out of the total population of 1000 of drawing a properly approved invoice as the first sample item. If the first invoice was properly approved and is not placed back into the population, there will be 949 properly approved invoices out of the total of 999 items in the population available for the second draw. The probability of a sample of five invoices from this population containing no deviations is

$$\frac{950}{1000} \times \frac{949}{999} \times \frac{948}{998} \times \frac{947}{997} \times \frac{946}{996} = .7734\text{[11]}$$

That is, there is a 77 percent chance of finding no deviations in a sample of five items when the true deviation rate in the population is 5 percent (50/1000).

Ordinarily, the auditor would not know the true deviation rate in the population. Assume that the auditor would not rely on the internal accounting control if he or she believed that the true deviation rate exceeded 5 percent. In other words, a 5 percent deviation rate is "tolerable," but a greater deviation

---

[11]The proper general formula for computing probabilities in this situation is the hypergeometric formula, which can be found in most introductory statistics books. In certain circumstances, calculations using the binomial and Poisson probability distributions can yield approximations close to the exact hypergeometric probabilities. Normal distribution theory, however, is often inappropriate for attributes sampling in auditing because it approximates the hypergeometric probabilities only when deviation rates are between 30 and 70 percent. Generally, much lower deviation rates are found in audit populations. The mean-per-unit estimation technique, discussed later in this chapter, is an appropriate application of normal distribution theory.

rate is not. In this case, having drawn a sample of five invoices, all of which were found to be properly approved, the auditor would be accepting a 77 percent sampling risk (the risk of overreliance, as defined in SAS No. 39) that the true deviation rate might not be acceptable, even if no deviations were found in the sample of five items. The complement of the sampling risk (100% – 77% = 23%) is the reliability level of the test. Stated another way, the auditor obtained from the sample of five items a 23 percent level of reliability that the true deviation rate does not exceed 5 percent.

Increasing the sample size will reduce the sampling risk and thus increase the reliability of the test. For example, if one more item were added to the sample, the sampling risk would be reduced from 77 percent to 73 percent (.7734 × 945/995 = .7345). To achieve a 90 percent reliability level (10 percent sampling risk) for the conclusion that the true deviation rate does not exceed 5 percent, a sample of approximately 45 items would be required, with no exceptions noted. Thus, by setting a tolerable deviation rate (5 percent) and a reliability level (90 percent) in the planning stage of the sampling application, the auditor could estimate, using statistical formulas, the minimum required sample size (45) to satisfy a stated audit objective.

The relationship among reliability, tolerable deviation rate, and sample size is particularly significant. For a given sample size (e.g., 60) and a tolerable deviation rate (e.g., 5 percent), only a certain level of reliability (in this case, 95 percent) can be obtained. To obtain a higher level of reliability or to be able to set a lower tolerable deviation rate (or both), the sample size must be increased. That is the price that must be paid by the auditor to reduce the risk of overrelying on an internal accounting control (the *beta* risk).

The auditor may also buy "insurance" that the sample will not contain so many deviations that reliance on the control will have to be reconsidered even though the true deviation rate in the population is in fact less than the tolerable deviation rate—the risk of underreliance (the *alpha* risk). This insurance is also bought at the cost of a larger sample size. To control this risk of underreliance (i.e., the risk that the sample will indicate that the deviation rate in the population may be unacceptable when, in reality, it is acceptable), a larger sample must be taken. By specifying a conservative (higher) expected deviation rate, the auditor protects somewhat against unnecessarily reducing reliance on controls when some deviations are found in the sample. Another way to control this risk is for the auditor to specify an acceptable deviation rate, lower than the tolerable deviation rate, at which the risk of underreliance is to be controlled, and a reliability level commensurate with the specified risk of underreliance. For example, the auditor may wish to be able to conclude at a 90 percent reliability level (10 percent risk) that the true deviation rate does not exceed the tolerable deviation rate of 5 percent, and may also wish to be assured at an 80 percent reliability level that, if the population deviation rate is actually 2 percent (the lower acceptable deviation rate), the sample results will not include so many deviations that they will lead to the conclusion that the population may contain an unacceptable deviation rate. The closer the lower acceptable rate is set to the tolerable rate, and the higher the associated reliability level is set, the larger will be the sample size necessary to protect against the risk of underreliance. In practice, controlling the risk of underreliance at a meaningful level is often inefficient, given the significant flexibility available to the auditor in designing additional substantive procedures when sample results may indicate that less reliance should be placed on controls than was planned. Controlling this risk is covered in more advanced statistical sampling discussions.

Determining Statistical Compliance Test Sample Sizes

When designing a statistical test, the auditor should decide if it is necessary to estimate the range within which the true deviation rate lies (i.e., whether upper and lower deviation limits are relevant) or if it is sufficient to test whether the true deviation rate either exceeds or falls below a certain tolerable level. (For example, the auditor may need to know only if the true deviation rate exceeds the tolerable rate.) That decision affects the size of the sample that is appropriate for performing the statistical test. A sample in which the auditor is concerned with both the upper and lower limits is evaluated on a two-sided basis; if only one limit is of interest, the sample is evaluated on a one-sided basis. A possible conclusion for a two-sided estimate is

- The auditor can be 95 percent assured that the true deviation rate is between 2 percent and 8 percent.

A possible conclusion for a one-sided test is

- The auditor can be 95 percent assured that the true deviation rate is not greater than 8 percent.

Usually the auditor needs assurance only that the true deviation rate does not exceed the tolerable rate. Knowing the lower limit of the true rate would not add to the audit usefulness of the information from a sample. Sometimes, however, the client asks the auditor to estimate the range within which the true deviation rate may lie. Internal auditors may appropriately design two-sided estimates for internal reporting purposes to aid in making the cost-benefit determinations associated with improving control systems.

If the auditor needs only a one-sided evaluation, the sample should be designed accordingly. One-sided testing is efficient because it is generally possible to use a smaller sample size to meet the same reliability level and tolerable deviation rate for one-sided tests than for two-sided estimates. Most standard attributes tables and some computer programs designed for audit use assume a one-sided testing plan. If a two-sided plan is desired, the documentation for the one-sided computer program or table usually explains how to make the conversion.

Table 10.1 is an abbreviated table for sample sizes at the 95 percent reliability level. To use the table, the auditor specifies a tolerable deviation rate and an expected population deviation rate, and locates the column for the tolerable

Table 10.1 Determination of Sample Size (Reliability = 95%)

Expected Deviation Rate (Percent)	Tolerable Deviation Rate (Percent)											
	1	*2*	*3*	*4*	*5*	*6*	*7*	*8*	*9*	*10*	*12*	*14*
0.00	300	150	100	75	60	50	45	40	35	30	25	20
0.50		320	160	120	95	80	70	60	55	50	40	35
1.0			260	160	95	80	70	60	55	50	40	35
2.0				300	190	130	90	80	70	50	40	35
3.0					370	200	130	95	85	65	55	35
4.0						430	230	150	100	90	65	45
5.0							480	240	160	120	75	55
6.0									270	180	100	65
7.0										300	130	85
8.0											200	100

rate along the top of the table and the row for the expected rate along the left-hand side of the table. The intersection of the row and column indicates the minimum necessary sample size. For example, if the tolerable rate is 6 percent and the expected rate is 1 percent, the minimum sample size is 80 items.

Reliability levels for tests of controls are generally set high (e.g., as high as 90 percent or 95 percent) if the compliance test is the auditor's primary source of evidence concerning the operation of the control. If additional evidence about the effectiveness of the control is obtained through extensive observation and inquiries, tests of related controls, and examination of the control aspects of sample items selected for substantive tests, lower reliability levels, such as 80 percent or 85 percent, may be warranted. Tolerable deviation rates of between 5 percent and 10 percent are common; the more critical the control and the more likely that a deviation will cause a financial statement misstatement, the lower the tolerable deviation rate should be set. Appendix A contains tables for determining sample size in attributes sampling at reliability levels of 80, 85, 90, and 95 percent. Because of rounding in those and other tables, however, the auditor should consider using computer software to determine the most efficient sample size. Computer programs may be particularly helpful in determining sample sizes in situations not covered by tables or where the population size is small, requiring more precise computations than are possible using tables.

Selecting the Sample

A statistical sample must be selected randomly, regardless of whether it is expensive, inconvenient, or time consuming to do so. (A nonstatistical sample does not have to be selected randomly; however, knowing how to select a true random sample may help an auditor using nonstatistical sampling to select a representative sample.) Random sample selection is any method of selection in which every item (element) in the population has the same probability of being included in the sample. The two most common methods of achieving a random sample are random number selection and systematic selection.

For random number selection, the auditor needs a source of random numbers such as random number tables or a computer program for random number generation and a scheme establishing a one-to-one correspondence between each random number selected and a particular population item. The correspondence scheme is simple if the documents are numbered and can be retrieved based on the numbers. If documents are unnumbered or are filed other than numerically, the auditor may have to assign sequential numbers to them. If correspondence cannot be easily made, or the auditor cannot determine the size of the population, it may be difficult to conclude that the population is complete.

In systematic sample selection, the auditor calculates a sampling interval (n) by dividing population size by sample size, randomly identifies a starting point between 1 and n, and then methodically selects every nth item in the entire population to be sampled. Alternatively, the auditor may use multiple random starts to overcome any possible nonrandomness in the population arrangement and to avoid potential criticism about the randomness of a sampling population. The use of computer programs to generate random numbers or of batch programs to select items randomly is often an efficient way of selecting specific items for examination.

Often the auditor finds it efficient to perform more than one compliance test using the same sample. For example, the auditor may wish to reperform the basic control over the mathematical accuracy of cash disbursement vouchers at a reliability level of 95 percent, an expected deviation rate of 1 percent, and a tolerable deviation rate of 8 percent. By reference to Table 10.1, it can be determined that the appropriate sample size is 60, or three-quarters of the sample size necessary in the preceding sample for proper approval. After selecting the sample of 80 disbursements, the auditor could randomly (or systematically) select 60 items from the initial 80 items for purposes of testing the basic control over mathematical accuracy. Otherwise, both tests may be performed using 80 items (the larger of the two sample sizes) when it is not too costly to do so.

Evaluating Statistical Compliance Test Sample Results

After the auditor has performed the audit procedures, the results must be evaluated, using mathematical formulas, tables, or computer programs, to determine the upper (and, if desired, lower) deviation rate limits for a specified reliability level, based on the sample results. To determine the upper limit on the deviation rate, the auditor must have four pieces of information:

- The reliability level (which is selected judgmentally).
- The sample size.

- The number of observed deviations in the sample.
- The population size.

Table 10.2 is an abbreviated table for evaluating sample results at a desired reliability level of 95 percent. The sample size used is located along the left-hand column and the number of deviations found in the sample is located along the sample size row. The achieved upper deviation rate limit is read from the top of the column. This is compared to the tolerable deviation rate to determine whether the objective of the test has been met. Alternatively, some auditors may seek to know the achieved reliability of the test for a fixed tolerable deviation rate; this would require the use of several tables for varying reliability levels. Appendix B contains tables for evaluating sample results in attributes sampling at reliability levels of 80, 85, 90, and 95 percent.

Continuing with the earlier example, suppose in the test of 80 disbursement checks for proper authorization, 1 deviation was found. By using Table 10.2, the auditor determines an upper deviation rate limit of 6 percent. If the tolerable rate is 6 percent, the objective of the test has been met, and reliance on the control to the extent planned is warranted. If, however, 2 deviations were found in the test of disbursement vouchers for mathematical accuracy, from a sample of 60 items, the upper deviation rate limit would be 12 percent, which would be in excess of the specified tolerable deviation rate of 8 percent. In this instance, the auditor does not have the assurance sought from the test, and a reduction in the planned reliance on the control is called for.

Table 10.2 Evaluation of Results Based on Number of Observed Deviations (Reliability = 95%)

Sample Size	*Achieved Upper Deviation Rate Limit (Percent)*											
	1	*2*	*3*	*4*	*5*	*6*	*7*	*8*	*9*	*10*	*12*	*14*
30										0		
35									0			1
40								0			1	
45							0				1	2
50						0				1		2
55						0			1		2	3
60				0				1			2	3
65				0				1		2	3	4
70				0			1		2		3	4
75				0			1		2		4	5
80				0		1		2		3	4	5
85				0		1		2	3		5	6
90				0		1	2		3	4	5	6
95				0	1		2	3		4	5	7
100			0		1		2	3	4		6	8

Discovery Sampling

Discovery sampling is a special application of attributes sampling and is used when the attribute being tested is of such critical importance that a single exception in the sample may have audit significance. This single instance is a "red flag" that indicates the existence of a problem or a need for further investigation. Some examples of such significant attributes are

- Inaccuracies in an inventory of securities held in trust.
- Fraudulent transactions.
- Illegal payments.
- Circumvented controls.
- Fictitious employees.

When setting a discovery sample size, the auditor determines how many items to examine to gain assurance at a high level of reliability (e.g., 95 percent) that, if the true deviation rate in the population is at some low level (e.g., 1 percent), one or more instances will be found in the sample. Since the attribute being examined is a critical one, auditors often use high reliability levels (95 percent or above) and low "tolerable" deviation rates (less than 5 percent). The procedure for determining sample size is the same for discovery sampling as for attributes sampling in general, except that since no deviations are expected, the expected deviation rate is assumed to be zero.

To find an appropriate sample size, the auditor may use tables or computer programs. For example, in a population of over 10,000 items, the auditor would require a sample of about 300 items to be assured at a 95 percent reliability level that if the population incidence were 1 percent or more, 1 instance would appear in the sample (see Table 10.1).

Evaluating discovery sampling results is straightforward: If no instances of the critical attribute appear in the sample, the auditor has the assurance specified when the sample was designed. No evaluation tables or computer programs are necessary.

Although discovery sampling has been described in terms of compliance testing, the auditor may use any random sample of items—whether selected for compliance or for substantive testing—to gain assurance that a deviation from a defined critical attribute would have appeared in the sample under certain conditions. For example, in a random sample of 300 accounts receivable selected for confirmation from a population of 2000 or more, the auditor may use computer programs or standard tables to determine that, at a 95 percent level of reliability, the sample would have contained at least 1 instance of a fictitious receivable if 1 percent of the items in the population were fictitious.

Sequential Sampling

In the previous discussion of attributes sampling, the sample was designed using a fixed-size sampling plan. Another form of attributes sampling is sequential sampling, in which the auditor selects the sample in several stages, using computer programs or tables specifically designed for sequential sampling to determine the sample size for each stage. Depending on the results of the first-stage sample, the auditor either meets the criteria for reliability and tolerable deviation rate, discontinues sampling because the criteria were not met, or examines a second sample to determine whether the established criteria are met or not. The process continues until a decision is ultimately reached. Sequential plans may be designed to include any number of stages. The risk of underreliance may or may not be specifically controlled and the sample sizes at each stage may be varied; for example, some plans have larger initial sample sizes and smaller second-stage sample sizes and others have smaller initial sample sizes and larger second-stage sample sizes. Regardless of the plan adopted, the auditor must follow the rules established for the plan to obtain the desired level of assurance.

An excerpt of a two-stage sequential sampling plan is presented in Table 10.3. The sampling plan was designed for a 95 percent level of reliability. By following the decision rules, the auditor will be able to determine whether the specified criteria have been met or not. In the illustration, the auditor stops testing after the first-stage sample if no deviations or if two or more deviations are found, but goes on to the second stage if one deviation is found. Separate sample evaluation tables are unnecessary, because the decision rules are an integral part of the sampling plan. Appendix C contains tables for two-stage sequential sampling plans at reliability levels of 80, 85, 90, and 95 percent.

A sequential plan allows the auditor to examine additional sample items if an unexpected deviation is found in the sample (thus controlling the risk of un-

Table 10.3 Two-Stage Sequential Sampling Plan (Reliability = 95%)

Tolerable Deviation Rate (Percent)	Initial Sample Size	Second-Stage Sample Size
10	31	23
9	34	29
8	39	30
7	45	33
6	53	38
5	65	42

Decision Rules

	No Deviations	One Deviation	Two or More Deviations
Initial sample	Stop—achieved goal	Go to next stage	Stop—failed
Second stage	Stop—achieved goal	Stop—failed	Stop—failed

derreliance), or to stop the work after examining a small number of items if no deviations are found in the first sample. Thus, it may be efficient for the auditor to use a sequential sampling plan if a zero or very low deviation rate is expected or if it is difficult to estimate an expected deviation rate. In a fixed sample plan, if unfavorable results were obtained from the first sample, the auditor would be precluded from simply extending the sample and evaluating the combined results using a fixed sample table as though they were a single sample. To evaluate the results of a sequential plan properly, the exact plan and all the decision rules must be specified before the sample sizes are determined.

Statistical Substantive Testing

A group of statistical techniques called *variables sampling* can be used in substantive testing. Variables sampling techniques are used to estimate the true dollar value of a population or the total error amount in the population and thereby permit the auditor to conclude that a recorded balance is not materially misstated. Since variables techniques deal with dollar values, their use in substantive testing is common. Although a variety of variables techniques may be used, two—monetary unit sampling and stratified mean-per-unit sampling— are particularly effective in auditing and are widely used. A third—difference and ratio estimation technique—is also effective in certain circumstances. All three are discussed herein.

From a statistical variables sampling test, the following type of conclusion can usually be drawn:

> The amount of population error projected from the sample is $20,000. It can be stated with a 95 percent level of reliability, however, that the true amount of error in the population is between $10,000 and $30,000.

This means that the direct projection, or point estimate, of the error in this account or class of transactions is $20,000, but the true error amount at a 95 percent level of reliability may be anywhere between $10,000 and $30,000. The auditor must decide whether a $30,000 misstatement would be material to the account or class of transactions being examined. If it is not material, the auditor may conclude, exclusive of any reliance on other tests, that there is a 95 percent reliability level that no material error exists in the population. If an amount less than $30,000 but greater than $20,000 could be material, the auditor may be assured only at less than a 95 percent level of reliability that a material error does not exist. After considering the results of all the other tests and procedures performed, if the auditor still cannot be assured at a reasonable level of reliability that the account or class is fairly stated, additional audit procedures may need to be performed.

Some variables techniques project sample results in terms of audited amounts; others project sample results in terms of the amount of error—or difference (recorded amount minus audited amount)—as in the foregoing example. If the results are in terms of the error amount, it must be added to or subtracted from the total recorded amount to produce an estimate of the total audited amount.

Applying Variables Sampling

An auditor using variables sampling relies on statistical theory (including the auditor judgments that must be made) to draw conclusions about whether material error is present in the population sampled. Statement on Auditing Standards No. 39, *Audit Sampling* (AU Section 350), requires that before sampling, the auditor remove from the population for 100 percent examination those items that, based on auditor judgment, are either so large in dollar amount or so error prone that they should not have a chance of not appearing in the sample. Those items are not considered as sample items. In some circumstances, the auditor may be able to achieve high dollar coverage of the population by examining a relatively small number of items, and by doing so may reduce the risk of an undetected material error to an acceptably low level. Examining items to achieve a specified level of dollar coverage is not sampling according to the definition in SAS No. 39. If risk is reduced to an acceptably low level by nonsampling procedures, sampling the remaining items may not be necessary.

In general, variables sampling may be an efficient sampling approach in any of the following situations:

- The population consists of a large number of items.
- High dollar coverage cannot be achieved by examining an economical number of items.
- The auditor is unable to select the specific items in the population whose examination will meet the audit objectives.
- The auditor desires a quantitative evaluation of sampling risk from the audit test, as might be appropriate when an unusually high-risk situation is present.

As in attributes sampling, the auditor can buy "insurance" against erroneously concluding that the population may be materially misstated when examining all items in the population would reveal that the population was not materially misstated—the *alpha* risk. Controlling this risk requires the auditor to increase the sample size, which is determined by setting an acceptable amount of error, less than materiality, and an associated reliability level.

Monetary Unit Sampling (MUS)

In this relatively new statistical technique, the individual monetary unit in the population (i.e., the dollar) is the sampling unit. Thus, the sample is composed of random dollars, not random items, in the population. When a particular dollar is identified for examination, the auditor examines the entire item or transaction of which the identified dollar is a part and determines an audited value for the entire transaction. The ratio of the error amount, if any, found in the transaction to the recorded amount is used to "taint" the sample dollar. For example, a recorded transaction value of $200 with an audited value of $150 yields a 25 percent tainting of the identified dollar. This tainted dollar information is used to project a point estimate of the error and create an upper (and, if desired, a lower) error limit at a specified reliability level.

Since the sample in monetary unit sampling is randomly selected from a population of dollars, large value transactions have more chances of being selected and are more likely to enter the sample than are small value transactions. Consequently, a transaction containing an understatement would have relatively fewer chances of being selected than would a properly stated transaction or a transaction containing an overstatement. MUS is a form of variables sampling referred to as probability-proportional-to-size (PPS) sampling. Since large value transactions may be of greater concern to auditors than small value transactions, this selection method often has audit appeal.[12] Common applications where MUS may be an effective audit tool include

- Selecting accounts for confirmation of receivables.
- Testing the pricing of inventory.
- Determining the existence of recorded amounts of fixed assets.
- Selecting employees for payroll tests.

There are both advantages and disadvantages to MUS. Some of its advantages are

- The sample sizes used with MUS are generally efficient.
- It is usually easy to apply.
- It is an effective statistical technique for substantiating that an expected low error population is not materially misstated.

The disadvantages of MUS are

- It requires that the population be cumulatively totaled so that random dollars can be identified.
- Since it is less likely to detect understated balances than overstated ones, there may be circumstances in which another statistical technique is more appropriate.
- It cannot select zero-value items for examination.
- Either credit balance items must be sampled as a separate population or the selection of sample items must be based on the absolute recorded value of the population items.

[12]Stratification can be used with an item-based sample selection method to accomplish a similar objective. Stratification is discussed later in this chapter in connection with mean-per-unit estimation.

Determining Sample Size. Determining sample size for an MUS sampling application is similar to the method used for attributes sampling applications in compliance testing, as discussed previously. The auditor must specify the dollar value of the population, a level of reliability, a maximum tolerable error rate expressed as a percentage of the dollar value of the population, and an expected error rate expressed as a percentage of the dollar value of the population. The auditor may use the same tables or computer programs as are used for attributes sampling to determine sample size.

For example, assume that accounts receivable has a balance of $1,000,000 as of the confirmation date and the auditor has specified a reliability level of 95 percent. If the maximum tolerable error amount is $50,000, the maximum tolerable error rate is 5 percent $\left(\dfrac{\$50,000}{\$1,000,000}\right)$. If the expected error amount is $10,000, the expected error rate is 1 percent $\left(\dfrac{\$10,000}{\$1,000,000}\right)$. Using Table 10.1 on page 379, the sample size is determined to be 95. Before determining sample size, the auditor should consider whether any population items exceed the maximum tolerable error amount—in this case, $50,000. Any items in excess of the maximum tolerable error amount should be segregated from the population for 100 percent examination, and their value should be subtracted from the total population value.

Selecting the Sample. To determine which items in the population contain the selected dollar units, the population is cumulatively totaled by item. If the records are computerized, those totals should be easy to obtain; however, if the records are manual, this process may be time consuming. MUS sample selection can then be made using random or systematic selection to identify unique dollars in the cumulatively subtotaled population, resulting in a random selection of dollar units from the population since each item has a chance of selection proportional to its dollar value.

The most common method of MUS sample selection is systematic selection with at least one random starting point between $1 and the sampling interval (the population value divided by sample size—in the illustration, $1,000,000 divided by 95, or $10,526). When using systematic selection, the auditor is assured that all items in the population greater in value than the sampling interval will be selected; those items should be treated as items selected for 100 percent examination, because there is no chance that they will not be selected. Alternatively, the auditor may remove these large value items from the population before selecting the sample items, reducing the population by the dollar value of the items removed.

Evaluating MUS Results. After selecting the sample, the auditor applies the planned audit procedures to the sample items, determines an audited value for each item examined, and evaluates the results. The first step in the evaluation is to calculate the "tainting" of the errors found in the sample. The tainting is determined by computing the ratio of each error amount found in the sample

Figure 10.3 Calculation of Error Tainting Amounts

	Amount			
Error	*Recorded*	*Audited*	*Difference*	*Tainting*
1	$100	$ 60	$40	.40
2	200	180	20	.10
3	80	76	4	.05

items to the recorded amount.[13] To continue with the earlier illustration, the three errors in Figure 10.3 are assumed to have been found in a population of $1,000,000 from which a sample of 95 items had been chosen.

The next step is to calculate the projected error for the population. This is done by dividing the sum of the individual tainting factors by the sample size, in this case (.40 + .10 + .05) ÷ 95, or .0058, and multiplying the result by the population amount ($1,000,000), yielding the point estimate of the error amount, in this case $5800. (Had all three errors been 100 percent tainted— that is, had the audited amounts been zero in each case—the point estimate of the error amount for the population would have been $31,579, derived as follows: [(1.00 + 1.00 + 1.00) ÷ 95] × $1,000,000.)

The last step is to compute an upper error dollar limit. This requires two calculations. First, the table for evaluating the results of an attributes sample[14] is used to calculate an upper error rate limit for three errors in a sample of 95 items at a 95 percent reliability level. Since the errors were not 100 percent taintings, a more precise upper error rate limit can be obtained by using a "building block" approach, that is, by multiplying the increment in the upper error rate limit for each error by the individual tainting factors and adding the products to calculate the upper error rate limit, as illustrated in Figure 10.4.

For conservatism, the errors are arranged in descending order according to the size of the tainting. Also, an allowance for possible, but unfound, errors is labeled "0" and is conservatively assigned a tainting of 1.00. (This is done to consider the possibility that errors existed in the population, even if no errors had been found in the sample.)

Next, the auditor converts the upper error rate limit to a dollar amount by multiplying it by the total population amount, in this case $1,000,000 ×

---

[13]Error amounts found in sample items are those differences between recorded values and audited values that the auditor determines are in fact errors after applying audit procedures to the sample items. For example, a response to a confirmation request might indicate that the recorded balance of an account receivable is incorrect because the balance had been paid before the confirmation was received. The auditor should determine whether a payment for that amount was in fact received within several days of the mailing of the confirmation. If it was, the audited value of the customer's balance and the recorded value would be in agreement as of the date of the confirmation and no error would exist.

[14]More precise results may be obtained by using other tables or computer programs that are less subject to rounding errors than the attributes evaluation tables. Another method of computing the upper error dollar limit that uses a different set of tables is illustrated in the AICPA Audit and Accounting Guide, *Audit Sampling* (New York: AICPA, March 1983).

Figure 10.4 Calculation of Upper Error Rate Limit

Number of Errors	Upper Error Rate Limit[a]	Increment	Tainting	Product
0	.04	.04	1.00	.0400
1	.05	.01	.40	.0040
2	.07	.02	.10	.0020
3	.08	.01	.05	.0005
			Upper error rate limit	.0465

[a]Determined by reference to Table 10.2, "Evaluation of Results Based on Number of Observed Deviations (Reliability = 95%)," on p. 381.

.0465, or $46,500. (Had all three errors been 100 percent tainted errors, the auditor would have used the attributes evaluation table [Table 10.2] to determine an upper error rate limit of 8 percent, which would have been converted directly to dollars by multiplying it by the population dollar amount [$1,000,000 × 8%, or $80,000].)

In the foregoing example, the auditor may conclude that, at a 95 percent level of reliability, the true amount of error in the population is less than $46,500.[15] This upper error dollar limit of $46,500 is then compared with the tolerable error amount used in determining the sample size, $50,000. If at the specified reliability level the tolerable error is greater than the upper error dollar limit, the results support acceptance of the recorded amount as not being materially misstated. If at the specified reliability level the tolerable error is less than the upper error dollar limit, the true population error amount could exceed the tolerable error.[16] When the tolerable error is initially significantly below the upper error dollar limit (i.e., there is a higher than desired sampling risk that the true error amount may exceed the tolerable error), the auditor should recalculate the upper error dollar limit at successively lower reliability levels until the tolerable error and upper error dollar limit are approximately equal, to determine the additional risk implied by the test results. This may help the auditor choose among several possible courses of action, among them to (1) reconsider additional assurance obtained or obtainable from other substantive tests, such as analytical reviews; (2) extend or modify planned substantive audit procedures; (3) select highly suspect elements in the population for more work by the client; and (4) request the client to correct the errors found or considered likely in the population.

In any event, errors found in the sample should always be considered for adjustment. Any additional amount relating to projected errors proposed as an adjustment is a matter of auditor judgment. Knowledge of the upper error dol-

[15]Other ways to state this conclusion are as follows:
  1. The auditor is 95 percent confident that the true amount of the population is at least $1,000,000 − $46,500, or $953,500.
  2. The auditor is 95 percent confident that the true amount of error in the population is not more than $5800 + $40,700.

[16]If at the specified reliability level the tolerable error is also less than the point estimate, there is a high risk (greater than 50 percent) of misstatement.

lar limit and point estimate may be helpful to the auditor in determining the appropriate amount of any proposed adjustment.

Considering Other Techniques. Although it would be cost effective to be able to use one variables technique in all audit situations, the auditor should be knowledgeable about several techniques to be able to choose the technique that will yield the most precise and relevant statistical results in a particular sampling application. For example, some audit tests, such as those involving samples from accounts payable, have as their specific objective the detection and evaluation of understated amounts within the population of recorded accounts. In other cases, such as some inventory pricing tests, a number of understatements may be expected, even if the primary audit objective is to detect and evaluate overstatements. Because MUS is more likely to detect overstatements, its use in situations in which understatements are suspected may not be desirable. Furthermore, MUS methods of evaluating understatements found in the sample and those methods that suggest netting them with overstatements in the sample remain an area of controversy and require further research. Additionally, MUS may sometimes be less efficient than other statistical techniques in situations in which expected error rates are high.

The following techniques are based on normal distribution theory. Although their use in auditing has diminished as a result of advancements in MUS technology, they remain important and effective techniques in those circumstances in which MUS is ineffective or inefficient.

Mean-Per-Unit Estimation

In the mean-per-unit (MPU) technique, the auditor selects a random sample of accounts or items from the population, and, using the audited values of the sample items or balances, projects the average (or mean) value of the audited sample values to the population to create a population point estimate. For example, if the auditor selected a sample of 50 items from a population of 10,000 items and found their average audited value to be $20.25, the point estimate of the population amount would be $202,500 ($20.25 × 10,000). The auditor would have very little confidence, however, that the point estimate of $202,500 was the true population amount. Confidence can be expressed only in terms of the upper and lower precision limits that are determined in a statistical test. If upper and lower precision[17] limits have been calculated, the auditor can make the following type of statement:

> I am 95 percent confident that the true amount of the population falls within the interval of $202,500 plus or minus 10 percent (or, plus or minus $20,250).

One advantage of MPU is that it can be used on populations that do not have detailed recorded amounts. For example, it may be used to estimate the audited value of an inventory where only quantity information is recorded. Al-

[17]Recall that SAS No. 39, *Audit Sampling*, uses the term ''allowance for sampling risk'' rather than ''precision.''

though MPU can be an effective technique in a wide variety of audit situations (e.g., those in which expected error rates may be low or high and those in which understatement is as likely as overstatement), the large sample sizes necessary to achieve the precision that is commonly sought in many audit tests may not always make it the most efficient statistical technique to use, unless stratification (explained later in this chapter) is employed.

A key factor in determining how close the point estimate of the population value will be to the true population value is the degree of variability (also referred to as dispersion) in the population. For example, if the average audited value of $20.25 in the foregoing example was developed from 50 invoices that were each valued at exactly $20.25, the auditor would intuitively be more comfortable with the point estimate than if the sample revealed 20 zero-value items, 20 items valued at $1, and 10 items valued at $99.25. Statistical computations of the upper and lower precision limits for the population (or error) amount at a given level of reliability take into consideration the observed variability in the sample data. The more variable the sample data, the wider the range between the upper and lower precision limits will be (i.e., precision deteriorates as variability increases).

Because of the key role that sample values and their variability play in determining the point estimate and upper and lower precision limits, the sample should be as representative of the population as possible. Very small samples cannot be relied on to provide representative sample values, since the selection of one or several unusually large or small items in the sample would significantly affect the point estimate.

Basic MPU Concepts. SAS No. 39 requires the auditor to project sample results to the population as a basis for considering whether material error exists in the population. In meeting this requirement, the auditor uses the information obtained from a sample to estimate the extent of error in the population or the true value of the population.

To make statistical inferences about dollar values or errors in a population from a sample, the auditor must compute the sample mean and the sample standard deviation. For example, an auditor, not knowing the audited values of the population of 10,000 accounts receivable, might take a random sample of 100 items totaling $3318.73. The sample mean is computed by dividing $3318.73 by 100, to get $33.19, which is multiplied by the number of items in the population ($33.19 × 10,000) to compute an estimate, or projection, of the total value of the population ($331,900).

It is extremely unusual for any one sample mean to be exactly the same as the true mean in the population. Each different random sample of items from the population would most likely yield a different sample mean. For audit purposes, it is desirable for the sample mean to be close to the true mean. This is accomplished by both taking a representative sample from the population and choosing an adequate sample size.

A second measure that must be computed for the mean-per-unit technique is the sample standard deviation, which is a measure of the variability of particular item values around the mean value of the sample and serves as an estimate of the population standard deviation. In a sample whose values are very close to each other, and thus to the mean, the standard deviation will be very small. If there are both very large and very small values in the sample, however, the standard deviation will be larger. The sample standard deviation is computed using the following formula:

$$\text{Sample standard deviation} = \sqrt{\frac{\text{Sum of squared differences between sample audited values and mean value}}{\text{Sample size} - 1}}$$

Applying the Concepts. The calculation of a sample standard deviation is illustrated in Figure 10.5. The example assumes that a sample of 100 items drawn from a population of 10,000 items produced a sample mean of $33.19.

The individual sample audited values are listed in Column (1). In Column (2), the average or mean value of the sample items is shown, and in Column (3), the differences between the individual audited sample values and the mean value are computed. In Column (4), the differences are squared and totaled. [The differences are squared to keep them from netting out to zero, as they do in Column (3).] The total of the squared differences is divided by the sample size minus one, and the square root of the result is taken, giving the standard deviation of the sample, in this case $27.729.

The calculations involved in computing the standard deviation can be confusing, but it is important that the auditor grasp the mathematical relationships involved. The standard deviation decreases as the variability of the sample values around the mean value decreases (holding sample size constant), and it also decreases as the sample size increases (holding the variability constant). (As mentioned earlier, very small sample sizes do not generally give reliable information about the total population, because small samples sometimes contain one or more items that are unrepresentative of the population and that can significantly distort the point estimate of the population value and the calculations of the variability among items.)

The standard deviation (a sample statistic) is used to compute the standard error (a statistic related to the population value), which determines the upper and lower precision limits of the point estimate of the population value, which in this example is $331,900 (mean value of $33.19 × population size of 10,000 items). The standard error of the estimate is the population size multiplied by the sample standard deviation divided by the square root of the sample size,[18] as follows:

$$\text{Standard error} = \frac{10,000 \times \$27.729}{\sqrt{100}} = \$27,729$$

[18]The sample standard deviation should also be multiplied by a finite population correction factor $\left(\sqrt{1 - \frac{\text{size of sample}}{\text{size of population}}} \right)$ when computing the standard error. When the sample size is small relative to the population (less than 10 percent), however, the factor has little influ-

Figure 10.5 Calculation of a Sample Standard Deviation

Sample Observation	(1) *Audit* *Value*	(2) *Mean* *Value*	(3) *Difference*	(4) *Difference* *Squared*
1	$ 80.29	$33.19	$47.10	$ 2,218.41
2	6.97	33.19	– 26.22	687.49
.	.	.	.	.
.	.	.	.	.
.	.	.	.	.
100	10.30	33.19	– 22.89	523.95
Totals	$3,318.73			$76,120.85

$$\sqrt{\frac{\$76,120.85}{100 - 1}} = \$27.729$$

The upper and lower precision limits can then be computed by multiplying the standard error ($27,729) by a reliability factor (discussed later) appropriate for the desired level of reliability (e.g., the factor for 95 percent reliability is 1.96; for 90 percent reliability, 1.64), and calculating an interval on either side (plus or minus) of the projected population value (in this example, $331,900 ± [1.96 × $27,729]). The conclusion, at a 95 percent reliability level, is that the lower precision limit is $277,551 and the upper precision limit is $386,249.

The statistical sampling results can be summarized by the statement that the total population amount is between $277,551 and $386,249 with 95 percent reliability. Thus, there is only a 5 percent risk (the complement of reliability) that the true value falls outside this range. SAS No. 39 refers to this risk for substantive test sampling applications as the risk of incorrect acceptance. If the true value of the population can be in the interval between $277,551 and $386,249 without causing the auditor to conclude that material error exists in the population, then the auditor can say with 95 percent confidence that no material error exists in this population. The limits are of primary importance when MPU sampling is employed. Point estimates are of lesser importance; they are used to compute the interval, or limits, on the population value. A reliability percentage can be associated only with computed upper and lower precision limits. No statistical statement or reliability level can be associated with point estimates.

In the preceding calculations, a 95 percent reliability level has been used. Sampling results, especially in the audit environment, do not always require a 95 percent level of reliability. Auditors often have information in addition to their sample results that they can rely on in reaching audit conclusions, and thus a reliability level of less than 95 percent frequently is appropriate for audit applications. The Appendix to SAS No. 39 contains an illustration leading to a substantive test sampling application with a desired reliability level of less than

ence on the computations. For many audit sampling applications this factor will not be significant and therefore is not illustrated in this chapter.

50 percent. For practical purposes, if sampling is such a minor element in the auditor's strategy or if the sampling effort is minimal, it is rarely economical to perform a statistical procedure to be able to measure precisely the reliability of the sample.

Reliability Factors. The concept of reliability factors, as illustrated earlier, is derived from statistical theory based on the known mathematical properties of the normal, or bell-shape, distribution. The theory is that if repeated large samples from the population are taken and the frequency distribution of the point estimates of the population value from each sample is plotted (with the values along the horizontal axis and the frequency along the vertical axis), the distribution of the point estimates would create the distribution commonly referred to as the normal distribution. The normal, or bell-shape, distribution is illustrated in Figure 10.6.

The properties of the normal distribution that are used in the MPU technique have the following effect: If repeated samples were taken from the population and a point estimate of the population value from each sample was computed, 68 percent of the point estimates would lie at less than 1 standard error on either side of the true population value and 95 percent of the point estimates would lie at less than 1.96 standard errors on either side of the true population value. That result is adapted to fit the audit situation (i.e., the auditor takes a single sample and makes inferences about the true population value from that sample). Thus, the auditor can determine, at a particular reliability level, upper and lower precision limits between which the true population value is expected to lie.

Reliability factors associated with different reliability levels are shown in Figure 10.7. Thus, if the auditor wanted to evaluate sample results at a 90 percent level of reliability and if a two-sided evaluation was appropriate (see subsequent discussion), the standard error would be multiplied by 1.645 to measure the allowance for sampling risk, or precision. Similarly, for a 99 percent reliability level, the auditor would multiply the standard error by 2.576 to measure the allowance for sampling risk.

When designing a statistical test, the auditor should consider whether a two-sided estimate is needed, or whether it is sufficient to use a one-sided test to determine whether the true value either exceeds or falls below a certain tolerable level. By designing a one-sided evaluation, the auditor may be able to

Figure 10.6 Normal Distribution

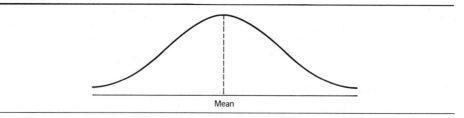

Mean

Figure 10.7 Factors for Different Reliability Levels

Two-Sided Evaluation

Reliability	Factor
80%	1.282
85%	1.440
90%	1.645
95%	1.960
99%	2.576

One-Sided Evaluation

Reliability	Factor
80%	.842
85%	1.037
90%	1.282
95%	1.645
99%	2.326

draw the desired conclusion using a smaller sample size than that necessary for a two-sided evaluation. Alternatively, for the same sample size and reliability level, a one-sided evaluation yields greater precision (a smaller allowance for sampling risk). For example, the auditor may use statistical techniques in lieu of determining exact amounts for inventory values. In that event, the auditor may desire a two-sided estimate, using the "plus and minus" as a benchmark for evaluating the accuracy of the sample result. However, when the auditor assesses the principal risk as either overstatement or understatement, such as in evaluating accounts receivable (in which the principal risk is generally overstatement), a one-sided test may be sufficient for audit purposes. Other procedures may be applied (e.g., analytical procedures) to assess the risk of understatement.

Stratified Mean-Per-Unit Estimation. One method of improving the accuracy of the mean-per-unit technique without increasing the required sample size is to stratify the population and sample each stratum independently. In stratification, the auditor segments the population into groups of items that are likely to be close to each other in audited value. After the mean and standard error in each stratum have been calculated, the results for the individual strata can be combined to create an overall estimate. The first several strata dramatically reduce the required sample size (or reduce the allowance for sampling risk for the same sample size). Although increasing the number of strata generally improves the accuracy of the estimate (or reduces the required sample size necessary to achieve a specific precision), diminishing returns and other factors often lead the auditor to use between three and ten strata in most audit circumstances.

Research has shown the stratified mean-per-unit technique to be a very effective audit tool. It can be used in suspected low-error and high-error situations and, with the use of a sufficient number of strata, can often result in relatively efficient sample sizes. Since, unlike MUS, the technique requires a random selection of items, zero (recorded) value items have a chance for selection. The technique can be equally effective for evaluating overstatements and understatements of recorded values and net error amounts.

Despite the advantages of stratified MPU, however, there are a number of significant constraints on its efficiency. Stratifying the population often requires reorganizing the underlying data, which, unless there is extensive computer assistance in data manipulation and sample selection, can be expensive. To compute the sample size required to meet the auditor's objectives, estimates of the variability among audited values need to be developed. Since accurate estimates are somewhat difficult to obtain, auditors often use the recorded values to estimate the necessary sample size and then include a safety factor (add extra sample items to the computed sample size). If the auditor performed a statistical application in the prior year, past experience is often a useful guide in estimating variability.

The steps required to apply stratified mean-per-unit estimation are summarized in the following paragraphs. Some of the steps in the evaluation process require the use of computations discussed earlier in the chapter. The steps are as follows:

1. Determine the number of strata to be used.
2. Determine stratum boundaries (the high and low population values for each stratum).
3. Determine an appropriate overall sample size.
4. Allocate the overall sample size to the individual strata.
5. Randomly select the sample items from each stratum.
6. Perform audit procedures to determine an audited value for each sample item.
7. Compute an overall point estimate (projection) of the population value.
8. Compute the overall upper and lower precision limits at the desired reliability level.

As previously indicated, between three and ten strata are generally sufficient to meet audit objectives efficiently. A number of formulas (or judgment) can be used to satisfy steps 2, 3, and 4. One formula option for steps 2 and 4 determines stratum boundaries so that each stratum contains approximately an equal proportion of population dollars, and allocates sample size so that each stratum is allocated approximately the same sample size. Another option attempts to minimize the overall sample size by determining stratum boundaries and allocating sample size in such a way that the overall standard error is minimized.[19] As a rule of thumb, the auditor should plan for at least 20 to 25 items in each stratum so that representative results for each stratum are more likely.

[19] For more details, see Donald M. Roberts, *Statistical Auditing* (New York: AICPA, 1978).

The computations in steps 3 and 4 are often based on recorded values or small preliminary samples from the population. (As noted, to the extent that these figures may not be exactly representative of the final sample audited values, the auditor may want to add a "cushion" [10 percent is common] to the computed stratum sample sizes to ensure that the desired precision of the sample will be achieved.) Computer software can be designed to accomplish steps 2 through 5, 7, and 8 with a minimum of effort on the part of the auditor, except for supplying the key judgments or information (such as reliability, precision, population size, and other options). Computer software can efficiently analyze a population, stratify it, determine sample sizes, allocate them to different strata, select a valid random sample from each stratum, and evaluate sample results. In this as well as other statistical sampling applications, manual computations of the formulas are often unnecessary and inefficient, given the current availability of timesharing and microcomputer software.

To evaluate the results of a stratified sample, the auditor calculates a sample mean, sample standard deviation, point estimate, and standard error for each stratum; finally, the auditor combines the results from the individual strata (steps 7 and 8). The combined (overall) point estimate is simply the sum of the individual point estimates. The combined standard error is computed as the square root of the sum of the squared individual standard errors.

To illustrate, assume the following facts:

	Stratum 1	Stratum 2
Population	4,000	1,200
Sample size	50	50
Sample mean	$343.19	$989.91
Standard deviation	$21.98	$85.42
Point estimate	$1,372,760	$1,187,892
Standard error	$12,434	$14,496

Based on these facts, the results of the two strata can be combined as follows:

1. Combining of sample results
   (a) Point estimate = $1,372,760 + $1,187,892 = $2,560,652
   (b) (Standard error)^2 = $154,604,356 + $210,134,016 = $364,738,372
       Standard error = $\sqrt{\$364,738,372}$ = $19,098
2. Calculation of two-sided precision limits and total audited amount, 95% reliability
$$\$2,560,652 \pm 1.96\,(\$19,098)$$
$$\$2,560,652 \pm \$37,432$$
3. Summary of error limits

Recorded value	$2,787,200	$2,787,200
Lower precision limit	2,523,220	
Upper precision limit		2,598,084
Error limits	$ 263,980	$ 189,116

Although the recorded value lies outside the computed precision limits of $2,523,220 and $2,598,084, the auditor may be able to accept it if the difference between the recorded value ($2,787,200) and the farthest limit ($2,523,220) is not material. Another way to arrive at the same conclusion is to compare the computed upper error limit ($263,980) with the tolerable error used in planning the sample. Even if the sample supports acceptance of the recorded amount, the auditor is likely to propose for adjustment errors found in the sample as well as errors identified as a result of other procedures performed on the account.

Difference and Ratio Estimation

Difference and ratio estimation techniques are other variables sampling techniques, also based on random item selection. These techniques have many features in common with mean-per-unit sampling and can be used in stratified or unstratified populations, but are most effective when stratification is employed. These techniques have long been used in statistical sampling audit tests because of their apparent ability to generate precise results with relatively small sample sizes. Recent research has demonstrated, however, that they may not be dependable (i.e., the auditor may believe the sample yielded a 95 percent level of reliability when it actually yielded a lower reliability) in low error rate populations or when used in unstratified form with small sample sizes.[20] For this reason, their use today is recommended only when high error rates are expected, such as in some inventory pricing situations (even if the error rates are high, the amounts may still be small and offsetting) or for conversions of inventory bases (such as FIFO to LIFO conversions in which each item can be expected to show a "difference"). Either technique can be used in tests for both overstatements and understatements. The superiority of one technique over the other in terms of the preciseness of the resulting estimate depends on the characteristics of the errors found in the sample.

The computations used in these techniques are based on the differences between the recorded and audited amounts of the sample items. The techniques require estimating a standard deviation and, if stratification is used, employ similar formulas for obtaining stratum limits and combining them to obtain overall limits.

In the difference estimation approach, the auditor calculates the point estimate of the population error amount (or difference) by computing the average sample error and multiplying it by the number of items in the population. In the ratio approach, the point estimate of the population value is based on the ratio of the audited amount to the recorded amount of the sample items. In both approaches, the auditor should ascertain that the sample contains differences that are representative of those in the population. Unlike mean-per-unit sampling, difference and ratio estimation techniques require that each population item have a recorded amount.

[20]See John Neter and James K. Loebbecke, *Behavior of Major Statistical Estimators in Sampling Accounting Populations*, Auditing Research Monograph No. 2 (New York: AICPA, 1975).

These techniques are most effective if many small differences are expected between the recorded and audited amounts of the sample items. As a rule of thumb, between 20 and 50 differences are considered a sufficient number of differences. If no differences are found in the sample, these techniques cannot be used, and the auditor should consider evaluating the sample as a mean-per-unit sample.

An example of how an auditor might evaluate a sample using difference estimation at a 95 percent reliability level and with two-sided limits is summarized here:

1. Assumed facts
    (a) Population
        Size   100,000
        Amount $1,700,000
    (b) Sample
        Size   100
        Audited amount $1,500
        Recorded amount $1,600
        Difference amount   − $100
        Mean difference   − $1
        Standard deviation of sample differences[21] $2

2. Calculations
    (a) Point estimate of difference
        Population size × mean difference
        $100,000 \times -\$1 = -\$100,000$
    (b) Standard error

        $$\frac{\text{Population size} \times \text{standard deviation of sample differences}}{\text{Square root of sample size}}$$

        $$\frac{100,000 \times \$2}{\sqrt{100}} = \$20,000$$

    (c) Upper and lower error limits
        Point estimate ± standard error × reliability factor
        $\$100,000 \pm \$20,000 \times 1.96$
        $\$100,000 \pm \$39,200$

Thus, the true amount of error is indicated as falling between $60,800 and $139,200 at a 95 percent reliability level. Provided that these possible error amounts do not exceed the tolerable error for the account, the auditor may be able to conclude at the desired reliability level that the balance is not materially misstated.

An example of a ratio estimation computation is not presented, but the calculations would be similar to those presented for difference estimation. The ra-

---

[21]The standard deviation of sample differences is a measure of variability of *differences* between recorded values and audit values around the mean of those *differences*. In the earlier discussion of MPU estimation, the sample standard deviation was a measure of variability of audited *values* around the mean of those *values*.

tio technique point estimate is based on a ratio of the audited sample values to the recorded sample values (using the foregoing example, $1500/$1600 × $1,700,000 = $1,593,750; $1,700,000 − $1,593,750 = $106,250 projected error amount), and the precision is calculated by measuring the variability of the sample ratios, using a computational formula.[22]

The difference estimation technique is often more precise when all the differences found in the sample are of a similar amount and are not related to the recorded values of the items containing the errors. The ratio estimation technique may be more precise when the differences in the sample are roughly proportional to the recorded values of the items containing the errors (i.e., when large items contain the large differences and small items contain the small differences).

Nonstatistical Sampling

The auditor is faced with the same decisions in applying both nonstatistical and statistical sampling, namely, determining an appropriate sample size, selecting the sample, performing the tests, and evaluating the results. This section provides guidance to the auditor in applying nonstatistical sampling techniques. Much of that guidance is, of course, based on statistical sampling principles and techniques.

Determining Sample Size

If the sampling application involves nonstatistical sampling, only the most general guidance can be given regarding the appropriate sample size in different circumstances. No rule of thumb is appropriate for all applications. Many auditors, in an effort to provide some uniformity among nonstatistical sampling applications throughout their practice, have developed more specific guidance for nonstatistical sampling applications, in some cases based on sample sizes used in similar circumstances on other engagements, and in other cases based on statistical sampling concepts and technology.

The guidance that follows represents the authors' views on appropriate sample sizes in nonstatistical applications, also based in part on experience and in part on conclusions reached in statistical sampling applications. This discussion, however, is clearly only one approach to providing guidance for the auditor's judgment process.

---

[22]One such computational formula to measure the variability of the sample ratios (i.e., the standard deviation [SD_R] for an unstratified ratio estimator) is:

$$SD_R = \sqrt{\frac{\Sigma x_i^2 + \hat{R}^2 \Sigma y_i^2 - 2\hat{R}\Sigma x_i y_i}{n - 1}}$$

where
- x_i = individual sample audited values
- y_i = individual sample recorded values
- $\hat{R}$ = the computed overall sample ratio $\left(\frac{\Sigma x_i}{\Sigma y_i}\right)$
- n = sample size
- Σ = summation.

Many auditors establish a minimum sample size (e.g., 20 items) for compliance tests because they believe that, while there may be degrees of reliance on internal controls, there is some amount of testing below which reliance on the control is so limited that the test has little value. No minimum sample size should be established for substantive tests of details since the extent of these tests varies inversely with the extent of the auditor's planned reliance on internal controls and on the extent of other substantive test procedures and analytical reviews. Therefore, a very small sample size (under 20) may be appropriate if a low level of assurance from the sample is acceptable.

A sample size of 260 for both compliance tests and substantive tests of details is a practical ceiling above which diminishing returns limit the audit assurance available from a few additional sample items. An auditor contemplating selecting more than 260 items for a nonstatistical sample should either consider using statistical sampling to increase the efficiency and effectiveness of the sampling application or ascertain that the cost–benefit trade-off of sampling versus other auditing procedures has been fully assessed. Experience has demonstrated that in many audit situations statistical samples of fewer than 260 items will achieve the audit objectives.

Selecting Representative Samples

Whenever sampling is used in an audit, SAS No. 39 requires that sample items be selected in such a way that they can be expected to be representative of the population from which they are drawn. The dictionary defines "representative" as "typical of a group or class." If each item in a population or subpopulation has a chance (not necessarily an equal chance) of being selected, the resulting sample is potentially representative of the characteristics contained in that population or subpopulation. For example, a sample cannot be relied on to be representative if it is made up of one or a few blocks of items in sequence (such as all items in a particular time period, on a particular page, or in a particular alphabetical section of a ledger) or if it is not drawn from the whole population. As another example, sample items that will be used to evaluate the reasonableness of a client's entire accounts receivable balance should be selected from the details of that entire balance, so that each item in the population has a chance of being selected. Conversely, sample items that will be used exclusively to evaluate balances outstanding for more than 90 days should be potentially representative of that group of balances, but may not necessarily be representative of the entire accounts receivable balance. Other procedures or a separate sample may be necessary to draw conclusions about the remainder of the receivables.

The auditor may achieve representative samples through either unsystematic, systematic, or dollar-weighted selection techniques. In the first two methods, the population may be stratified or unstratified. Unsystematic sample selection (sometimes referred to as haphazard sample selection) attempts to avoid personal bias in selecting items for testing. It is called haphazard selection because auditors intend it to approximate random sample selection; the term does not imply any element of carelessness. It is still susceptible of personal bias toward selecting certain items, however, such as a subconscious tendency to favor items in a particular location on each page or never to pick the first or last items in a listing. In its purest hypothetical form, unsystematic selection would involve blindfolded selection from a thoroughly mixed pile of all the records. More commonly, an auditor will choose a number of items from throughout the ledger or file drawers, after gaining satisfaction about the completeness of the population from which the sample is selected.

The only difference between the nonstatistical and statistical sampler's use of systematic sample selection is that the nonstatistical sampler often does not specifically identify a random starting point. Systematic selection is presently a commonly used nonstatistical sample selection method and in all likelihood it will continue to be, because it is usually a cost-effective approach to extracting a potentially representative sample.

For substantive tests of details, sampling risk can be reduced without increasing sample size by stratifying the population by size or nature in order to permit different intensities of sampling for different strata. This technique may be efficiently used to help ensure representative samples in either statistical or nonstatistical sampling applications. Often the auditor can use strata already inherent in the client data (e.g., location or product line). The sample sizes would be varied in accordance with the auditor's assessment of the risk of material misstatement associated with each stratum; that is, a larger number of sample items should be apportioned to those strata in which the auditor has assessed a high risk of material misstatement. Either systematic or unsystematic selection methods can be used with a stratified population.

Dollar-weighted selection techniques can lead to sample sizes that are nearly as efficient as those used with stratified techniques. Dollar-weighted selection is similar to the unsystematic method except that the auditor judgmentally "weights" the selection of sample items based on their recorded amount, giving more weight to items with large recorded values. (This should not be confused with 100 percent examination of items above a specified dollar level and a sample of other items or with a formal stratification plan.)[23]

Evaluating Sample Results

Regardless of whether statistical or nonstatistical techniques are applied, the auditor should extrapolate (project) the sample results to the whole population. Because conclusions based on sample results apply only to the population from which the sample items were drawn, it is important that the auditor carefully define the population (i.e., the aggregate of items about which information is desired) and keep it in mind when evaluating the sample results. For example, conclusions about the entire accounts receivable balance cannot be supported on the basis of a sample selected only from accounts outstanding for more than 90 days.

---

[23]For a discussion of dollar-weighted sample selection, see page 387.

Compliance Tests. Sample results for compliance tests are appropriately stated as deviation rates, which are determined by dividing the number of sample deviations by the sample size. The deviation rate in the sample is the best estimate of the deviation rate in the population from which the sample was selected.

The auditor should follow up on identified control deviations to determine if they are "isolated incidents," such as a clerk's being on vacation, or indications of a possible control breakdown. Isolated incidents should always be included as sample deviations and projected to the population; their impact on the auditor's decision to rely on the control procedure should be carefully evaluated. If the projected deviation rate exceeds the tolerable deviation rate, the auditor should consider revising the planned reliance on the control. The aggregate impact of control deviations (from whatever source, whether "isolated" or not) can sometimes be sufficient to cause the auditor to reduce or eliminate reliance on a control. Similarly, a single instance of a control breakdown (i.e., circumvention of a control) may be sufficient to eliminate reliance on a control.

Substantive Tests. There are several acceptable methods of projecting the impact of dollar errors in a substantive test sample to the population. In the *ratio approach*, for example, the projected population error is determined by multiplying the total dollar amount of the population by an error rate obtained by dividing the total dollar amount of sample errors by the total dollar amount of the sample, as follows:

$$\frac{\$1,000,000}{\text{(population amount)}} \times \frac{\$100\,\text{(sample errors)}}{\$1000\,\text{(sample amount)}} = \frac{\$100,000\,\text{(projected}}{\text{population error)}}$$

In the *average-difference approach*, the total number of items in the population is multiplied by the average error amount obtained by dividing the total dollar amount of sample errors by the number of sample items, as follows:

$$\frac{15,000}{\text{(population items)}} \times \frac{\$1000\,\text{(sample errors)}}{140\,\text{(sample items)}} = \frac{\$107,143\,\text{(projected}}{\text{population error)}}$$

The ratio approach is generally the most appropriate technique when the error amounts are roughly proportional to the recorded values of the sample items (i.e., the larger dollar errors are from the larger sample items). The average-difference approach is more appropriate when the error amounts are disproportionate to the recorded values of the sample items (e.g., large items have small dollar errors and small items have large dollar errors, or the dollar errors are all about the same size regardless of recorded amount).

Another acceptable (but infrequently used) method is the *projection of average audit values*. This approach is used, for example, in constructing a balance sheet value for inventory if recorded values are not available and only quantity (not price) information can be obtained from the client.[24] This approach may also be most appropriate if there are recorded amounts but the general ledger control account does not agree with the sum of the individual recorded amounts. In the average-audit-value approach, the total number of items in the population is multiplied by the quotient obtained by dividing the total "audited" dollar amount of the sample items by the number of sample items, as follows:

$$\begin{matrix} 150,000 \\ \text{(population items)} \end{matrix} \times \frac{\$900 \text{ (total sample audited value)}}{150 \text{ (sample items)}} = \begin{matrix} \$900,000 \\ \text{(projected} \\ \text{population} \\ \text{amount)} \end{matrix}$$

In this technique, the error projection is the difference between the recorded and projected population dollar amounts.

Other methods of projection may also be appropriate. It is important to remember that different projection techniques often result in different projected error amounts. Auditors may find the ratio approach useful for a wide variety of situations, but no one method of projecting the error is necessarily "better" than the others in all circumstances.

To ascertain the total projected error for the account balance being examined, the projected error from the sample results should be added to any known errors discovered as a result of nonsampling procedures performed, such as errors identified in 100 percent examinations of selected items or from high dollar coverage tests. Since, by definition, the dollar amount of the projection of sample results already includes the sample errors found, those errors should not be separately added to the projected error. Similarly, errors affecting the account balance that were found in related compliance tests should also not be separately added to the projected error.

An auditor using stratification in the sampling plan should project the results for each stratum separately and then add the strata projections to determine the projected error for the account or class of transactions being examined.

The auditor should compare the projected error obtained from sampling procedures and other likely errors with the tolerable error. (If the tolerable error was not quantified for purposes of determining sample size, the auditor may find it useful to use overall financial statement materiality or some smaller amount for this comparison.) Even if the projected error from sampling procedures plus other likely errors are less than tolerable error—the error the auditor can accept before modifying the opinion—the auditor should post the projected error to the "score sheet" (a working paper that summarizes errors and potential adjustments, discussed in Chapter 17) maintained to determine whether all likely errors discovered during the audit equal or exceed the auditor's determination of materiality. The auditor should also evaluate the nature of the errors and discuss them with the client. In some circumstances it may be practicable

---

[24]In developing estimated amounts for financial reporting or tax reporting purposes, statistical samples are generally employed.

for client personnel to review the remaining population for items having characteristics similar to those in the sample that were found to contain errors. When adjustments are made to the recorded balance, the related projected error should be reduced by the amount of the adjustments. For example, if the auditor calculated a projected overstatement error of $20,000 in an inventory balance based on errors found in the sample, but by investigating a few instances of a particular problem was able to identify $11,000 of overstatement that the client agreed to record as an adjustment to the recorded inventory balance, the projected error would be reduced to $9000.

If the projected error from sampling combined with other likely errors is greater than the tolerable error (or financial statement materiality), the auditor must consider the implications for the audit opinion and planned audit strategy and take appropriate action. Possible auditor actions include

- Asking the client to adjust for all or some of the known and projected errors.
- Asking the client to perform additional work either to identify the sources of errors in the account balance and correct the account balance or to justify the balance.
- Extending the planned audit procedures to identify and correct the errors or to demonstrate that the account balance is not materially misstated. Since extended sampling of the same population is usually not cost effective, this would likely involve designing other audit procedures. For example, additional samples may "target" high-error segments of the original test population.
- Concluding that the financial statements are materially misstated and modifying the audit report accordingly.

Allowance for Sampling Risk. Even if the projected error amount or deviation rate is less than the tolerable error or deviation rate, the auditor still must consider the risk that the true error in the population exceeds the tolerable error amount or deviation rate. Thus, an allowance for sampling risk, defined as a margin for inaccuracy or imprecision in the sample result, must be determined. (The concept is similar to "precision," a term defined earlier in connection with statistical sampling applications.) When statistical sampling is applied, the allowance for sampling risk is computed. However, the nonstatistical sampler must rely on rules of thumb and judgment to consider the allowance for sampling risk. For example, assume that the tolerable error in an account balance of $2,000,000 is $80,000 and that the total projected error based on an appropriately sized sample is $20,000. A statistical test might result in a computed precision of plus or minus $40,000 for a specified level of reliability, such as 95 percent. Since the projected error (i.e., $20,000) plus the allowance for sampling risk (i.e., $40,000) does not exceed the tolerable error, the auditor may conclude that there is an acceptably low sampling risk (i.e., 5 percent, the complement of the 95 percent reliability level) that the true population error does not exceed the tolerable error. In part because of the difference between the $20,000 projected error and the $80,000 tolerable error, the nonstatistical sampler, not knowing the exact precision, would make a judgment that he or she may be reasonably assured that there is an acceptably low sampling risk that the true monetary error in the population exceeds the tolerable error. On the other hand, if the total projected error approaches or exceeds the tolerable error, the auditor may conclude that there is a high sampling risk that the true monetary error in the population exceeds the tolerable error.

A possible rule of thumb for the nonstatistical sampler when considering an allowance for sampling risk is: If the deviation rate or number or amount of errors actually identified in the sample does not exceed the expected deviation rate or error amount used in determining the sample size, the auditor can generally conclude that the risk that the true deviation rate or error amount exceeds the tolerable deviation rate or error amount is consistent with the risk considered acceptable when the sample was initially planned. For example, if an auditor performing a compliance test of an accounting control had established expected and tolerable deviation rates of 1 percent and 5 percent, respectively, a deviation rate approximating 1 percent would be a satisfactory result consistent with the risk considered acceptable when the sample was planned. Conversely, if the number or amount of errors identified in the sample exceeds the expected error used in determining the sample size, the auditor should generally conclude that there is a higher-than-planned sampling risk that the true error exceeds the tolerable error.

If, based on this rule of thumb, the auditor concludes that there is an unacceptably high risk that the true deviation rate or error amount in the population exceeds the tolerable deviation rate or error amount (or financial statement materiality), appropriate action is necessary. For compliance tests, the auditor should consider revising the planned reliance on the control. For substantive tests, the auditor's possible actions are the same as those, discussed in the preceding section, appropriate when projected error exceeds tolerable error. In using this rule of thumb for substantive tests, the auditor may encounter situations in which the acceptability of the achieved sampling risk for a particular account balance or class of transactions is not clear—for example, if the sampling risk indicated by the sample only slightly exceeds the level the auditor originally desired from the test, and other auditing procedures have not yet been applied to the account or related accounts. In these cases, the auditor should consider deferring further action until the aggregation and evaluation of errors for the remaining areas in the financial statements have been completed.

Aggregating Errors. The auditor should consider the aggregate of all projected error results from all sampling applications and all other likely errors from nonsampling applications and other relevant auditing procedures in evaluating whether the financial statements taken as a whole may be materially misstated. The aggregation and the disposition of the errors entering into it should be documented in the working papers. The score sheet discussed in Chapters 6 and 17 is an effective way of doing the aggregation.

After the projected errors have been aggregated, the auditor must determine an appropriate overall dollar allowance for sampling risk to compensate for the fact that sample results may indicate the absence of material misstatements even though the true misstatements in the populations exceed the tolerable amount (financial statement materiality). This overall allowance is not the sum of the allowances for individual samples, because it is very unlikely that the true amount of error in each sample is the extreme high or low of the range of possible values and because errors may be offsetting. Practically, the auditor must decide if the dollar difference between the aggregation of projected errors plus other likely errors and the amount deemed material to the financial statements is large enough to provide an adequate overall allowance for sampling risk.

For nonstatistical applications, the allowance should be based on the number of individual sampling applications and the size of the samples. For example, if the amount of misstatement material to the financial statements as a whole is $1,000,000 and there are net projected errors of $800,000 from sampling procedures and other likely errors of $20,000 from nonsampling procedures, the auditor must judge whether $180,000 ($1,000,000 − $820,000) is an adequate allowance for sampling risk. If a total of 1000 to 1200 items were examined in numerous (e.g., eight to ten) sampling applications, $180,000 may be adequate, because those sample sizes would be likely to yield quite precise results. Alternatively, if the auditor examined 100 to 200 items in the same number of sampling applications, $180,000 might not be adequate, because the smaller sample sizes would produce less precise results. The deciding factor in determining the allowance for sampling risk in nonstatistical sampling is the probable accuracy of the results of individual samples, which is generally related to sample size.

If the auditor judges the allowance for sampling risk to be adequate, the decision should be documented in the working papers and the auditor would conclude that the financial statements as a whole are not materially misstated. Conversely, if the allowance for sampling risk is considered inadequate, the auditor's actions may include

- Requesting the client to perform additional work in those areas that were subject to large error projections and to adjust for all or some of the errors.
- Extending the tests in those areas that were subject to large error projections.

Documenting Audit Sampling

Documentation of the sampling applications used on an audit engagement must satisfy the professional standards for working papers promulgated in Statement on Auditing Standards No. 41, *Working Papers* (AU Section 339). Working paper documentation of audit procedures is discussed in Chapter 5 of

Figure 10.8 Summary of Audit Sampling Documentation

	Documentation Needed	
Type of Information	*Related to Planning the Sample*	*Related to Performing and Evaluating the Results of the Sample*
Objective and description of test	X	
Definition of errors (deviations)	X	
Population:		
1. Definition	X	
2. Description of how completeness was ensured	X	
3. Identification of items for 100 percent examination, if any	X	
Sample size determination factors:		
1. Degree of assurance/sampling risk	X	
2. Tolerable error	X	
3. Expected error	X	
4. Other factors, if any	X	
Sample size, including how determined	X	
Description of sample selection methods, including stratification	X	
Evaluation of sample results:		
1. Projection of errors		X
2. Aggregation with items examined 100 percent		X
3. Investigation of error sources (causes)		X
4. Consideration of allowance for sampling risk		X
5. Conclusion on test		X
Aggregation with other test results and consideration of overall allowance for sampling risk		X

this book. The documentation should relate to planning the sampling application and performing it and evaluating the results. Figure 10.8 identifies and categorizes information that should be documented.

Review Questions

10-1. What is meant by the concept of audit sampling?

10-2. Describe some audit procedures that do not involve sampling.

10-3. Describe compliance tests that do not lend themselves to sampling.

10-4. Define "accept–reject" testing.

10-5. Define nonsampling risk.

10-6. How can an auditor evaluate and control nonsampling risk on an engagement?

10-7. What is sampling risk? How is sampling risk related to sample size?

10-8. Distinguish between sampling and nonsampling risk.

10-9. What factors must an auditor consider in planning a sampling application?

10-10. Define the statistical term precision as it relates to determining sample size.

10-11. Define the statistical term reliability as it relates to determining sample size.

10-12. How do auditors estimate the expected deviation rate in attributes sampling?

10-13. What is the relationship between sample size and reliability? Between sample size and tolerable deviation rate? How do these relationships affect the auditor's approach to statistical sampling?

10-14. What are the similarities and dissimilarities between statistical sampling and nonstatistical sampling?

10-15. What are the major advantages and disadvantages of using statistical sampling?

10-16. What methods of sample selection are appropriate in statistical sampling applications?

10-17. Distinguish between evaluating a compliance test statistical sample on a one-sided basis and evaluating a sample on a two-sided basis. Give an example of a possible audit conclusion for each.

10-18. What information must the auditor have to determine the upper limit on the deviation rate for attributes sampling?

10-19. What is sequential sampling and how does it work?

10-20. What is discovery sampling and how does it work?

10-21. What is variables sampling and when is it used?

10-22. What is monetary unit sampling and when is it an effective audit tool?

10-23. How are monetary unit sampling results evaluated?

10-24. How is the mean-per-unit estimation technique used?

10-25. Define standard deviation and give the formula for sample standard deviation.

10-26. How is the standard deviation used in statistical sampling?

10-27. Define stratification and explain its usefulness to the auditor.

10-28. What are the steps required to apply stratified mean-per-unit estimation?

Discussion Questions

10-30. Describe the SAS No. 39 requirements that the auditor should address when planning to use either statistical or nonstatistical audit sampling on an engagement.

10-31. When an auditor performs 100 percent tests of major parts of an account balance (e.g., vouching a significant portion of accounts payable), why is this *not* considered a form of audit sampling?

10-32. Describe and illustrate the acceptable methods for projecting the sample results to the population from which the sample was drawn.

10-33. Why is a precise definition of an attribute deviation important to the auditor?

10-34. Explain the action the auditor should take if the aggregate of projected error from sampling procedures plus other likely errors from nonsampling procedures is greater than tolerable error.

10-35. Explain how an auditor should go about determining tolerable error for a sampling application designed to test additions to property, plant, and equipment.

10-36. The following is a list of substantive test procedures that might be performed during an audit. Identify those that could involve sampling and thus be covered by SAS No. 39.

   a. Performing an analytical review of inventory statistics.
   b. Reviewing all accounts receivable over 90 days old for collectibility.
   c. Performing sales cutoff tests.
   d. Observing physical inventory procedures.
   e. Performing a reasonableness test of depreciation expense.
   f. Confirming all accounts receivable over $100,000.
   g. Reviewing minutes of board of directors' meetings.
   h. Examining all disbursements over $50,000 after the balance sheet date for payment of unrecorded liabilities.
   i. Recomputing commissions paid to salespeople.
   j. Comparing market prices of selected marketable securities with an independent source.

10-37. Explain how the auditor may be able to test a variety of attributes from a sample of disbursement voucher packages. Explain how the auditor would approach the evaluation of results from this procedure.

10-38. The use of statistical sampling techniques in an examination of financial statements does not eliminate judgmental decisions.

   Required:
   a. Identify and explain four areas where a CPA may exercise judgment in planning a statistical sampling test.
   b. Assume that a CPA's sample shows an unacceptable error rate. Describe the various actions that the CPA may take based on this finding.
   c. A nonstratified sample of 80 accounts payable vouchers is to be selected from a population of 3200. The vouchers are numbered consecutively from 1 to 3200 and are listed, 40 to a page, in the voucher register. Describe four different techniques for selecting a random sample of vouchers for review.

(AICPA adapted)

10-39. Jiblum, CPA, is planning to use attributes sampling in order to determine the degree of reliance to be placed on an audit client's system of internal accounting control over sales. Jiblum has begun to develop an outline of the main steps in the sampling plan:

   1. State the objective(s) of the audit test (e.g., to test the reliability of internal accounting controls over sales).
   2. Define the population (define the period covered by the test, the sampling unit, and the completeness of the population).
   3. Define the sampling unit (e.g., client copies of sales invoices).

Required:

a. What are the remaining steps in the outline that Jiblum should include in the statistical test of sales invoices? *Do not present a detailed analysis of tasks that must be performed to carry out the objectives of each step. Parenthetical examples need not be provided.*

b. How does statistical methodology help the auditor to develop a satisfactory sampling plan?

(AICPA adapted)

AICPA Multiple Choice Questions

These questions are taken from the Auditing part of Uniform CPA Examinations. Choose the single most appropriate answer.

Note: As indicated in the chapter, SAS No. 39 introduced new terminology into the auditing literature. The multiple choice questions presented here have not been revised from their original use, which in many cases predated SAS No. 39.

10–40. At times a sample may indicate that the auditor's planned degree of reliance on a given control is reasonable when, in fact, the true compliance rate does not justify such reliance. This situation illustrates the risk of

   a. Overreliance.
   b. Underreliance.
   c. Incorrect precision.
   d. Incorrect rejection.

10–41. An accounts receivable aging schedule was prepared on 300 pages with each page containing the aging data for 50 accounts. The pages were numbered from 1 to 300 and the accounts listed on each were numbered from 1 to 50.

Godla, an auditor, selected accounts receivable for confirmation using a table of numbers as illustrated:

Procedures performed by Godla

Select column from table of numbers	Separate 5 digits: First 3 digits Last 2 digits	
02011	020–11	x
85393	853–93	*
97265	972–65	*
61680	616–80	*
16656	166–56	*
42751	427–51	*
69994	699–94	*
07942	079–42	y
10231	102–31	z
53988	539–88	*

x Mailed confirmation to account 11 listed on page 20
y Mailed confirmation to account 42 listed on page 79
z Mailed confirmation to account 31 listed on page 102
* Rejected

This is an example of which of the following sampling methods?

a. Acceptance sampling.
b. Systemic sampling.
c. Sequential sampling.
d. Random sampling.

10-42. Which of the following best illustrates the concept of sampling risk?

a. A randomly chosen sample may *not* be representative of the population as a whole on the characteristic of interest.
b. An auditor may select audit procedures that are *not* appropriate to achieve the specific objective.
c. An auditor may fail to recognize errors in the documents examined for the chosen sample.
d. The documents related to the chosen sample may *not* be available for inspection.

10-43. An underlying feature of random-based selection of items is that each

a. Stratum of the accounting population be given equal representation in the sample.
b. Item in the accounting population be randomly ordered.
c. Item in the accounting population should have an opportunity to be selected.
d. Item must be systematically selected using replacement.

10-44. In which of the following cases would the auditor be most likely to conclude that all of the items in an account under consideration should be examined rather than tested on a sample basis?

	The measure of tolerable error is	Error frequency is expected to be
a.	Large	Low
b.	Small	High
c.	Large	High
d.	Small	Low

10-45. Using statistical sampling to assist in verifying the year-end accounts payable balance, an auditor has accumulated the following data:

	Number of accounts	Book balance	Balance determined by the auditor
Population	4100	$5,000,000	?
Sample	200	$ 250,000	$300,000

Using the ratio estimation technique, the auditor's estimate of the year-end accounts payable balance would be

a. $6,150,000
b. $6,000,000

        c. $5,125,000
        d. $5,050,000

10-46. If the size of the sample to be used in a particular test of attributes has *not* been determined by utilizing statistical concepts, but the sample has been chosen in accordance with random selection procedures

    a. No inferences can be drawn from the sample.
    b. The auditor has committed a nonsampling error.
    c. The auditor may or may *not* achieve desired precision at the desired level of confidence.
    d. The auditor will have to evaluate the results by reference to the principles of discovery sampling.

10-47. An example of sampling for attributes would be estimating the

    a. Quantity of specific inventory items.
    b. Probability of losing a patent infringement case.
    c. Percentage of overdue accounts receivable.
    d. Dollar value of accounts receivable.

10-48. The tolerable rate of deviations for a compliance test is generally

    a. Lower than the expected rate of errors in the related accounting records.
    b. Higher than the expected rate of errors in the related accounting records.
    c. Identical to the expected rate of errors in the related accounting records.
    d. Unrelated to the expected rate of errors in the related accounting records.

10-49. An advantage of using statistical sampling techniques is that such techniques

    a. Mathematically measure risk.
    b. Eliminate the need for judgmental decisions.
    c. Define the values of precision and reliability required to provide audit satisfaction.
    d. Have been established in the courts to be superior to judgmental sampling.

10-50. In attribute sampling, a 10 percent change in which of the following factors normally will have the *least* effect on the size of a statistical sample?

    a. Population size.
    b. Precision (confidence interval).
    c. Reliability (confidence level).
    d. Standard deviation.

10-51. If all other factors specified in an attribute sampling plan remain constant, changing the specified precision from 6 percent to 10 percent, and changing the specified reliability from 97 percent to 93 percent, would cause the required sample size to

    a. Increase.
    b. Remain the same.
    c. Decrease.
    d. Change by 4 percent.

10-52. Approximately 5 percent of the 10,000 homogeneous items included in Barletta's finished-goods inventory are believed to be defective. The CPA examining Barletta's financial statements decides to test this estimated 5 percent defective rate. He learns that by sampling without replacement a sample of 284 items from the inventory will permit specified reliability (confidence level) of 95 percent and specified precision (confidence interval) of $\pm$ .025. If specified precision is changed to $\pm$ .05, and specified reliability remains 95 percent, the required sample size is

a. 72.   [This question should be answered without reference to tables.]
b. 335.
c. 436.
d. 1543.

10–53. When using statistical sampling for tests of compliance, an auditor's evaluation of compliance would include a statistical conclusion concerning whether

a. Procedural deviations in the population were within an acceptable range.
b. Monetary precision is in excess of a certain predetermined amount.
c. The population total is not in error by more than a fixed amount.
d. Population characteristics occur at least once in the population.

10–54. An auditor selects a preliminary sample of 100 items out of a population of 1000 items. The sample statistics generate an arithmetic mean of $120, a standard deviation of $12, and a standard error of $1200. If the sample was adequate for the auditor's purposes and the auditor's desired precision was plus or minus $2000, the *minimum* acceptable dollar value of the population would be

a. $122,000.
b. $120,000.
c. $118,000.
d. $117,600.

10–55. In an examination of financial statements a CPA generally will find stratified sampling techniques to be most applicable to

a. Recomputing net wage and salary payments to employees.
b. Tracing hours worked from the payroll summary back to the individual time cards.
c. Confirming accounts receivable for residential customers at a large electric utility.
d. Reviewing supporting documentation for additions to plant and equipment.

Problems and Cases

10–60. A staff accountant, whom you are supervising, has come to you for approval of a plan for confirming accounts receivable. The staff accountant has identified three primary objectives for requesting confirmations. Those objectives are to ensure the

- Accuracy of individual recorded balances.
- Completeness of the recorded balance.
- Validity of individual recorded balances.

The following characteristics have been identified using a printout of the accounts receivable subsidiary ledger:

- There are approximately 900 individual accounts.
- Most of the individual account balances are relatively small and of similar size, but there are approximately 40 large accounts that constitute 60 percent of the total dollars.
- There are very few credit balances.

Based on this information, the staff accountant has concluded that limiting the sample to the 40 largest accounts will satisfy the audit objectives.

Required:
Evaluate the staff accountant's plan.

10–61. A nonstatistical sample of 200 accounts receivable from a total of 5000 accounts was drawn for confirmation at December 31, 1986. The accounts ranged in size from $1000 to $2500. "Positive" confirmations were mailed. All responses indicated agreement with the balances reported by the client, with a few exceptions. The exceptions, and the results of the auditor's investigation, are reported here.

1. "The balance indicated includes your invoice No. 8769 dated December 30, 1986, for $1725; we did not receive the merchandise until January 5, 1987." (The auditor's investigation showed that shipment was made on December 31, 1986; the terms were F.O.B. shipping point.)
2. "Your balance is overstated by $2375; our records show that payment of that amount was sent to you on December 27, 1986." (The auditor's investigation showed that payment was received and recorded on January 2, 1987.)
3. "Your balance includes $500 of merchandise received on December 15, 1986, on invoice No. 8524, which was returned to you because of an error in part number; a credit memo has not been received." (The auditor's investigation showed that the returned merchandise was received on December 22, 1986, and a credit memo issued on January 5, 1987; in the meantime the credit was held in a suspense account pending determination of whose error it was.)
4. "Your balance includes $1500 for invoice No. 8463 dated December 5, 1986. We have never received these goods." (The auditor's investigation showed that shipment was made on December 4, 1986, as evidenced by receipted bill of lading. A tracer was sent.)
5. "Your balance is overstated by $1100. Apparently you failed to consider your credit memo for that amount dated October 10, 1986, for damaged merchandise." (The auditor's investigation showed that the customer's assertion was correct.)
6. "Your balance includes an $800 overcharge on invoice No. 8623 dated December 18, 1986, because of incorrect pricing; you were notified immediately." (The auditor's investigation showed that the prices used were correct, but the customer had not been notified of price increases.)
7. "We regret we cannot confirm your receivable balance. We use an accounts payable voucher system." (The auditor's investigation substantiated shipment of the merchandise.)
8. "The balance indicated, $2365, is not owing. Per your request we advanced $3000 to cover our purchase." (The auditor's investigation showed that the $3000 had been credited to a liability account, "Customers' Advances.")
9. "Your balance of $2450 is correct. However, these goods were sent on consignment and have not been sold." (The auditor's investigation showed the customer's assertion to be correct.)

Required:

For each exception, indicate

a. Whether you would treat the exception noted as an error to be used in projecting the population error. (Give reasons for your answers.)
b. The error amount you would assign for the projection.

10–62. The following population and sample data are available to the auditor:

Number of items in the population	12,000
Number of items sampled	150
Total population amount	$1,500,000
Total sample amount	$18,500
Total errors found in the sample	$200
Total sample audited value	$18,700

Required:

a. From the data provided, compute the projected population dollar error using the (1) ratio approach, (2) average-difference approach, and (3) projection-of-average-audit-values approach.
b. In what circumstances is each of the three approaches the most appropriate one?

10–63. In determining a sample size for a nonstatistical sample, a tolerable error of $100,000 was considered along with an expected error of $20,000 in arriving at a sample size of 50 items. The results of the test were that 10 errors were found that totaled to an overstatement of $400 of the total sample value of $10,000.

Required:

a. What is the direct projection of the error in the population book value of $1,000,000 if the ratio approach is used?
b. What is the allowance for sampling risk?
c. Is the allowance adequate?

10–64. You are confirming accounts receivable using nonstatistical sampling. The population of accounts receivable is as follows:

Number of accounts	8900
Total recorded book value	$23,689,423

The sample was designed to include the 50 largest accounts, which total $6,843,902, and a random selection of 160 of the remaining accounts.

The sample, when audited, contained 24 errors totaling an $8717 overstatement, none of which are in the 50 largest accounts.

Required:

Calculate the projected population error amount using the average-difference estimation technique.

10–65. During the course of an audit engagement, a CPA attempts to obtain satisfaction that there are no material misstatements in a client's accounts receivable. Statistical sampling is a tool that the auditor uses to obtain representative evidence to achieve the desired satisfaction. On a particular engagement an auditor determined that a material misstatement in a population of accounts would be $35,000. To obtain satisfaction the auditor wanted to be 95 percent confident that the population of accounts was not in error by $35,000. The auditor decided to use unrestricted random sampling with replacement and took a preliminary random sample of 100 items (n) from a population of 1000 items (N). The sample produced the following data:

Arithmetic mean of sample items ($\bar{x}$)	$4000
Standard deviation of sample items (SD)	$ 200

The auditor also has available the following information:

Standard error of the mean (SE) = $SD \div \sqrt{n}$
Population precision (P) = $N \times R \times SE$

Partial List of Reliability Coefficients

If Reliability Coefficient (R) Is	Then Reliability Is
1.70	91.086%
1.75	91.988
1.80	92.814
1.85	93.568
1.90	94.256
1.95	94.882
1.96	95.000
2.00	95.450
2.05	95.964
2.10	96.428
2.15	96.844

Required:
a. Define the statistical terms reliability and precision as applied to auditing.
b. If all necessary audit work is performed on the preliminary sample items and no errors are detected:
   1. What can the auditor say about the total amount of accounts receivable at the 95 percent reliability level?
   2. At what confidence level can the auditor say that the population is not in error by $35,000?
c. Assume that the preliminary sample was sufficient.
   1. Compute the auditor's estimate of the population total.
   2. Indicate how the auditor should relate this estimate to the client's recorded amount.

(AICPA adapted)

10–66. The following data are available (assume a large population):

- Level of reliability   90 percent
- Sample size   100
- Deviations found   2

Required:
a. Use Appendix B to determine the upper deviation rate limit.
b. What evaluation statement can be made from this test?
c. What evaluation statement could you make if the sample had been obtained using nonstatistical sampling?

10–67. The following data are available (assume a large population):

- Level of reliability   90 percent
- Sample size   45
- Deviations found   2

Required:

a. Use Appendix B to determine the upper deviation rate limit.
b. What conclusions could be drawn from this result if nonstatistical sampling methods were used?
c. What can you conclude, assuming statistical attributes sampling methods were applied?
d. Assuming that a 12 percent deviation rate would not support the planned reliance on this control, what would you suggest?
e. Suppose your sample results indicate it is not desirable to rely on a control to the extent planned. Should you extend your sample so that acceptable conclusions from the combined sample results may be formed?

10–68. QRS, Inc., sells both wholesale and retail in the gourmet cookware industry. Its computerized accounts receivable system processes approximately 80,000 invoices related to 13,000 customer accounts annually. The year-end accounts receivable balance has historically been approximately 35 percent of total assets. Because the auditor's preliminary assessment is that QRS has an effective system of internal accounting control, the planned audit strategy for the revenue cycle is to place significant reliance on the operation of the controls with the objective of reducing substantive procedures.

You have been asked to select a representative sample of customer invoices for examination of certain attributes. The audit work to be performed on the sample items is to determine that

1. Each invoice is supported by a valid shipping document.
2. The invoice date is no more than three business days after the shipping date.
3. The invoice is clerically accurate.

In prior years, the deviation rates discovered by these compliance tests have been low (1 to 2 percent), with the exception of *invoice dating*, which has been as high as 3 percent.

Required:

a. Determine the sample size for each attribute to be tested. (*Note:* You will have to make certain judgments in solving this problem.) Use the format indicated below.

	Shipping Documents	*Invoice Dating*	*Clerical Accuracy*
Population:			
Tolerable deviation rate:			
Reliability:			
Estimated deviation rate:			
Risk:			
Sample size:			

b. Assuming that you will use one sample (i.e., use the same invoices) for all three attributes, determine the sample size and reliability level you would use.

10–69. ABC, Inc., has a computerized accounts receivable system that processes approximately 80,000 invoices related to 13,000 customer accounts annually. The year-end accounts receivable balance has historically been approximately 35 percent of total assets. The company has a comprehensive system of internal controls and the controls on which you plan to rely have been tested and found to be operating effectively. The accounts receivable are confirmed three months before year-end. At that time, the accounts receivable balance is $4,000,000, which is made up of approximately 9000 invoices. Credit balances are insignificant, and can be ignored for the confirmation. The ABC accounts receivable system is an open invoice system by customer. In previous years numerous confirmation requests were returned without verification because many customers have accounts payable voucher systems based on individual invoices and do not keep track of the total amount due a particular supplier.

You have decided to confirm all individual invoices that, if 100 percent overstated, would present a materiality problem. An overstatement of $160,000 would be material.

Since assurance has been obtained by testing the related internal controls, an 80 percent reliability level is appropriate for the confirmation. Because the internal controls were found to be operating properly, the estimated monetary amount of errors in the population is expected to be low (i.e., $40,000 or less).

Required:
a. Determine the sample size utilizing monetary unit sampling techniques.
b. Define the risk of incorrect rejection in the context of this sampling application. If it were specifically controlled, what would be the effect on the sample size? In what circumstances would you consider it necessary to control this aspect of sampling risk?
c. What would be the effect on sample size if the auditor had chosen to confirm accounts rather than invoices?
d. What are the pros and cons for selecting invoices as the sampling unit?

10–70. An auditor is designing a sample to evaluate whether a priced inventory of automobile parts may be materially overstated as a result of overstated inventory quantities. The inventory is physically located in a central warehouse, and price and quantity information for each part is available to the auditor. The auditor wants to test the physical counts. Based on prior experience, little or no deviation from the recorded quantities is expected to appear in the sample.

Required:
a. Evaluate the suitability of the following techniques in the circumstances described:
   • Attributes sampling
   • Monetary unit sampling
   • Mean-per-unit estimation
   • Difference or ratio estimation
b. How would your evaluation of the appropriate technique change if:
   1. Many differences between the recorded and audited quantities were anticipated?
   2. Understatements of quantities are likely to be found in the sample?

3. The inventory quantities are unpriced and the audit objective is to estimate the inventory value?

(Consider each situation separately.)

10-71. An auditor selected a sample of 150 receivable invoices from a $3,000,000 aged trial balance of accounts receivable for confirmation. Monetary unit sampling was contemplated in the sample design, a valid random sample of dollars from the recorded total value of the receivables was selected, and a confirmation was prepared for each invoice containing the selected random dollar. Based on direct confirmation responses and the performance of acceptable alternative procedures for unreturned confirmations, all but three invoices were determined to be "as recorded." The three exceptions and explanations are as follows:

Exception	Recorded	Audited	Explanation
1	$150	$125	Improperly added shipping charges to this customer's bill
2	200	100	Billed for entire order, but only in-stock items shipped
3	75	0	Shipment never arrived at customer location

Required:

a. Using monetary unit sampling, determine at a 90 percent level of reliability the upper error limit amount for the possible overstatement of the accounts receivable balance.

b. If a tolerable error of $150,000 had been established for the accounts receivable balance, what would your conclusion be regarding whether this test alone indicated a possible financial statement misstatement requiring auditor action?

c. Describe circumstances in which you would feel comfortable evaluating or accepting sample results at a level of reliability of less than 90 percent.

10-72. Assume the following facts in a substantive test of inventory pricing:

Number of inventory items	250,000
Recorded value of inventory items	$3,740,000
Size of sample	144 items
Recorded amount of sample	$2200
Audited amount of sample	$1912
Standard deviation of sample differences	$4

Required:

Using the difference estimation approach, calculate the upper and lower error limits at a 90 percent reliability level and with two-sided limits.

10-73. Assume the following facts in a substantive test of inventory pricing:

	Sample	
Item	Recorded Amount	Audited Amount
1	$10	$7
2	4	5
3	10	6

The population consists of 2000 items. Assume a two-sided 90 percent reliability level.

Required:

a. Compute the point estimate and the upper and lower precision limits using mean-per-unit estimation.
b. Compute the point estimate and the upper and lower error limits using the difference estimation approach.

Note: Sample size has been reduced to three items only for purposes of illustrating the required calculations.

10–74. Assume the same facts and assumptions as in Problem 10–73, and that the recorded amount of the population is $16,000.

Required:

Compute the point estimate of the error and the upper and lower error limits using the ratio estimation approach.

10–75. You are now conducting your third annual audit of the financial statements of Elite Corporation for the year ended December 31, 1987. You decide to employ unrestricted random number statistical sampling techniques in testing the effectiveness of the company's internal control procedures relating to sales invoices, which are all serially numbered. In prior years, after selecting one representative two-week period during the year, you tested all invoices issued during that period and resolved to your satisfaction all of the errors that were found.

Required:

a. Explain the statistical procedures you would use to determine the size of the sample of sales invoices to be examined.
b. Once the sample size has been determined, how would you select the individual invoices to be included in the sample? Explain.
c. Would the use of statistical sampling procedures improve the examination of sales invoices as compared with the selection procedure used in prior years? Discuss.
d. Assume that the company issued 50,000 sales invoices during the year and the auditor specified a confidence level of 95 percent with a precision range of plus or minus 2 percent.
   1. Does this mean that the auditor would be willing to accept the reliability of the sales invoice data if errors are found on no more than 4 sales invoices out of every 95 invoices examined? Discuss.
   2. If the auditor specified a precision range of plus or minus 1 percent, would the confidence level be higher or lower than 95 percent, assuming that the size of the sample remains constant? Why?

(AICPA adapted)

10–76. Items 1 through 5 apply to an examination, by Robert Lambert, CPA, of the financial statements of Rainbow Manufacturing Corporation for the year ended December 31, 1987. Rainbow manufactures two products: Product A and Product B. Product A requires raw materials that have a very low per-item cost, and Product B requires raw materials that have a very high per-item cost. Raw materials for both products are stored in a single warehouse. In 1986 Rainbow established the total value of raw materials stored in the warehouse by physically inventorying an unrestricted random sample of items selected without replacement.

Mr. Lambert is evaluating the statistical validity of alternative sampling plans Rainbow is considering for 1987. Lambert knows the size of the 1986 sample and that Rainbow did *not* use stratified sampling in 1986. Assumptions about the population, variability, tolerable error rate, and specified reliability (confidence level) for a possible 1987 sample are given in each of the following five items.

Required:

In each case, indicate the effect on the size of the 1987 sample compared with the 1986 sample. Each of the five cases is independent of the other four and is to be considered separately. Your answer choice for each item 1 through 5 should be selected from the following responses:

   a. Larger than the 1986 sample size.
   b. Equal to the 1986 sample size.
   c. Smaller than the 1986 sample size.
   d. Of a size that is indeterminate based on the information given.

1. Rainbow wants to use stratified sampling in 1987 (the total population will be divided into two strata, one each for the raw materials for Product A and Product B). Compared with 1986, the population size of the raw materials inventory is approximately the same, and the variability of the items in the inventory is approximately the same. The specified tolerable error rate and specified reliability are to remain the same.

Under these assumptions, what should be the required sample size for 1987?

2. Rainbow wants to use stratified sampling in 1987. Compared with 1986, the population size of the raw materials inventory is approximately the same, and the variability of the items in the inventory is approximately the same. Rainbow specified the same tolerable error rate but wishes to change the specified reliability from 90 percent to 95 percent.

Under these assumptions, what should be the required sample size for 1987?

3. Rainbow wants to use unrestricted random sampling without replacement in 1987. Compared with 1986, the population size of the raw materials inventory is approximately the same, and the variability of the items in the inventory is approximately the same. Rainbow specifies the same tolerable error rate but wishes to change the specified reliability from 90 percent to 95 percent.

Under these assumptions, what should be the required sample size for 1987?

4. Rainbow wants to use unrestricted random sampling without replacement in 1987. Compared with 1986, the population size of the raw materials inventory has increased, and the variability of the items in the inventory has increased. The specified tolerable error rate and specified reliability are to remain the same.

Under these assumptions, what should be the required sample size for 1987?

5. Rainbow wants to use unrestricted random sampling without replacement in 1987. Compared with 1986, the population size of the raw materials inventory has increased, but the variability of the items in the inventory has decreased. The specified tolerable error rate and specified reliability are to remain the same.

Under these assumptions, what should be the required sample size for 1987?

(AICPA adapted)

Chapter 11
Auditing in an EDP Environment

Through the 1970s, computers used for processing financial data were often treated by users and auditors alike as huge adding machines with a somewhat greater ability to manipulate data. Most auditors believed that it was possible to perform the usual audit tests the way they always had. As computer memory, storage capacity, and software sophistication increased, however, and data base management systems, on-line, real-time systems, and telecommunications networks were introduced, the role of computers in business quickly shifted from that of useful tool to functional necessity. Today, computers are so critical to many businesses, such as banking and financial services, that they literally could not survive without computers.

This chapter discusses different types of computer systems, controls that are part of those systems, compliance tests of those controls, substantive tests performed using computerized techniques, and ways that auditors can be assisted by computers in managing audit engagements. The chapter begins with a brief overview of computer auditing.

An Overview of Computer Auditing

Changes in computer technology have been accompanied by changes in auditing standards. When the AICPA issued SAS No. 3, *The Effects of EDP on the Auditor's Study and Evaluation of Internal Control,* in December 1974, it was still possible to consider the impact of computers on an audit in relative isolation. With the issuance of SAS No. 48, *The Effects of Computer Processing on the Examination of Financial Statements*, in July 1984, the profession formally acknowledged that computers had so permeated organizations that they must be considered throughout the audit. SAS No. 48 integrated guidance on the effects of EDP on financial statement audits with other SASs, ''because auditors consider the methods of data processing, including the use of computers, in essentially the same way, and at the same time, they consider other factors that may affect their examination.''

Auditing Computer-Generated Data Around, Through, and with the Computer

In early computer systems that printed out all results of processing, the auditor's assurance about the accuracy of computer-generated data was frequently attained by obtaining detailed printouts that included the calculations performed, data used, and all exceptions and rejections, and then reperforming the computerized procedures. Since this in essence bypassed the computer, it was called ''auditing around the computer.'' Today, auditing this way is often difficult, and sometimes impossible, since modern systems generally do not print out processing steps in detail, and many paperless systems have no hard-copy source documents. (A common exception is microcomputer applications in small organizations, which in some cases still may print processing details.)

Using the computer itself in the audit, by testing general controls over computer processing or using computer software to test directly the computerized procedures that carry out accounting and control activities, is today the usual method of conducting an audit. Originally called ''auditing through the computer,'' this technique has become all but essential in modern processing systems. The distinction between auditing ''around'' and auditing ''through'' the computer is no longer meaningful in the current environment, since it implies a choice that usually does not exist. The terms also make it seem as if auditors should make different kinds of audit strategy decisions when computers are involved, which, except in extremely sophisticated computer environments, is not so. In every audit in an EDP environment, the auditor must make decisions about the relative extent of reliance on specific internal accounting controls (based on the results of compliance tests) and substantive tests of computer-generated data. Moreover, virtually all audit strategies in a computer environment present opportunities to increase audit efficiency by ''auditing with the computer'': Whether using the client's or the auditor's computer, the auditor can use computer software to perform many tests that would be too time consuming and perhaps not even possible to do manually.

Differences Between Manual and Computerized Systems

When computer systems are appropriately designed, they process data far more consistently than do manual systems. Processing is done by computer application programs, which are precise instructions to the computer to perform specific steps, referred to as *programmed procedures*, to achieve a particular task. Programmed procedures can be divided into two types:

- *Programmed accounting procedures* that replace manually performed accounting operations, for example, the calculation and production of sales invoices, the updating of master files, and the generation of data within the computer.
- *Programmed control procedures* that replace manually performed control operations that ensure the completeness, accuracy, and validity of the data being processed and maintained. Normally, manual procedures, called user controls, such as the follow-up of exception reports produced by the system, are necessary for control over completeness, validity, and accuracy to be effective.

The consistency of both programmed accounting procedures and programmed control procedures is one of the benefits of computer use and is made possible in part by general computer controls over the design, security, and use of programs and data files. If the design and implementation of programmed accounting and control procedures are subject to adequate general controls, those procedures should not vary in their application; random errors, as might occur in a manual accounting system, should not occur in a computerized accounting system.

Features of Computer Environments

As discussed in Chapter 8, in assessing control risk, the auditor considers the control environment, the accounting systems, and, if appropriate, specific internal accounting controls. Computerized accounting systems that process financial data, and the controls over them, have a potential impact on all three of those elements of internal control systems. Computer systems and configurations vary widely from one computer environment to another. Even when the same mainframe from the same vendor is used, there is an almost infinite variety of combinations of types of peripheral devices, software options, telecommunications networks, and applications software.

Computer Operations

To provide some background about different computer environments, an overview of computer processing concepts and terminology is presented herein. Detailed discussion is beyond the scope of this book and is available in works dealing specifically with EDP.

Hardware: Microcomputers, Minicomputers, and Mainframes. When computers were first used in business, only mainframes existed. Because their memory and storage capacity were quite small by today's standards, they were limited in their ability to do complex tasks. Punched cards were the input for both data and programs. The evolution in memory capacity and type of storage allowed increasing versatility, and the introduction of "virtual memory" allowed complex programs to be kept separately and called into use as needed in processing; additional memory allowed the use of more intricate procedures. Next came the smaller, fairly powerful minicomputers. Originally developed for scientific applications and control processes, they were quickly adopted by the business community. Advances in technology led to the introduction of microcomputers in the late 1970s. At present, departmental minicomputers, end users' microcomputers, and large mainframes frequently coexist in the same organization. These machines often communicate with each other and share data and programs via telecommunications and area networks.

Regardless of their capacity, computers basically consist of a central processing unit, internal storage (memory) and external storage, input/output devices, and other peripheral equipment. External storage can be on magnetic tape, disk, or both, depending on the system. Input/output devices consist mainly of terminals with screens and keyboards and printers for hardcopy output. Other peripheral equipment includes telecommunications devices such as modems, which translate digital computer signals into analog form for transmission over phone lines and retranslate them at the other end, as well as devices like multiplexors and controllers, which handle complex communications message requirements, directing the information to the appropriate part of the system or computer.

Types of Processing Systems. Originally, business data processing systems were batch systems, in which jobs were assembled and processed in groups of transactions, called batches. Since the earliest computers could handle only one program at a time, it was most efficient to apply that program to all the appropriate transactions at the same time. This required careful scheduling and resulted in slow turnaround time. Work could be entered only at the computer.

The development of multitasking, multiprogramming computers made it possible for multiple users to use many programs in one machine at the same time. To enter jobs for processing from different locations, remote job entry was created, in which terminals in other locations could be used to submit jobs to the central computer. All processing was still done at the central location.

Continuing developments led to on-line systems, which allowed users to query the computer for information. In on-line systems, a copy of the file is often used for update during the day (called a memo update) to provide users access to the most current information. Then, overnight or at set intervals, jobs are processed in batches, entering the accumulated transactions into the actual files; the results can be compared with the memo update created during the day. In contrast, in on-line, real-time systems, transactions immediately update the files.

To provide more local processing capability, small mainframes or minicomputers can be installed in various locations, a practice described as dispersed or distributed data processing. These computers can do processing themselves as well as provide entry of jobs to the main, sometimes called the host, computer.

Data base management systems (DBMS) eliminate much of the redundancy of data that exists when each program requires its own file structure. In a standard file structure, each program has data available to it in files specifically designed for that program. (A file consists of records, which in turn contain data fields or elements.) For example, in a payroll system, the payroll program would use an employee master file containing, for each employee, data fields for employee name, number, social security number, address, and pay rate. The personnel department would typically have another program, with its own file that duplicated much of the information held in the payroll system. In a DBMS, on the other hand, all data elements are held in a central data base and are called on as required by the particular application program. In the foregoing example, a "human resources data base" would contain elements used by the payroll, personnel, and other applicable departments.

Types of Input and Output. Computer systems can accept input from a variety of sources. In the older batch systems, transactions on source documents were grouped for processing and transcribed onto machine-readable input media, such as punch cards. Today, information is often entered directly into on-line, real-time systems. These systems, known as paperless systems, require sophisticated programmed "edit checks" to help ensure that the data are entered completely and accurately, as well as methods to provide audit trails of transactions.

Forms of output consist mainly of terminal screen responses and printed reports produced by the system. The distribution of output to appropriate parties is a major internal control concern; unauthorized users should be prevented from receiving output or browsing through screens of other users' information.

Software. With the expansion of computer power came a similar expansion of more useful and more versatile software. The programs that run the system and direct its operations are called the *system software*. System software includes the *operating system*, which directs internal operations and makes it possible for specific *applications software* to be run. Among other components of system software in a modern system are *utilities,* which are normally used for system and program development and enhancement, and include report generators and powerful editors used to write or change programs; *telecommunications software*; *file and program access software*; and *data base management system software.*

Originally, software had to be created specifically for each application program, such as accounts receivable or payroll, to accomplish particular tasks. These were developed in-house by EDP department staffs of systems analysts and programmers, following a standard system development methodology intended to ensure that applications developed were appropriate, were adequately controlled, and met management's and users' needs. Many organizations still develop custom-designed applications in-house; auditors of those organizations may want to compliance test specific controls over the design and implementation of in-house software.

Because the system development process is obviously expensive and time consuming, the marketplace began to develop standard applications, referred to as purchased systems or packaged software. Purchased systems are normally sold with a maintenance agreement that provides program "fixes" as required to correct programming errors. Depending on the vendor, purchased systems may be available with or without source code. (Source code is the series of instructions within a computer program that governs its operation.) If the source code is not available to users, they cannot make changes to the programs easily. (Users can, however, change some program functions through other methods, such as "user exits," which allow the insertion of user programs, or selecting different options provided by the program.)

Extensive in-house changes to software, which are sometimes required to meet user needs, can make vendor maintenance impractical or even impossible. To avoid these situations, vendors now build in numerous customizing features, called options, that allow users to make choices in how the software operates without having to rewrite it. In assessing these purchased systems, auditors may need to determine what options were implemented when the systems were installed and whether those options were subsequently changed.

Organization of the EDP Department

The organization of the EDP department depends largely on the extent of computer processing, the number of employees, and the control techniques used. The department can range from one or two employees responsible for running a self-standing minicomputer to a large organization consisting of hundreds of people responsible for developing, maintaining, and executing applications on a multimainframe operation linked to an extended data telecommunications network.

Regardless of the size and complexity of the organization, there are a number of specific duties that should be performed by individuals holding the following positions.

Manager. Develops long-range plans and directs application development and computer operations.

Systems analyst. Designs systems, prepares specifications for programmers, and serves as an intermediary between users and programmers.

Programmer. Develops logic, writes computer programs, and prepares supporting documentation.

Data base administrator (DBA). Designs, implements, and maintains the data base in a DBMS.

Computer operator. Operates the computer in accordance with manually supplied and computer-generated instructions.

Data entry operator. Converts data into machine-readable form primarily using terminals or cathode ray tube (CRT) devices.

Security administrator. Controls the security of the system, including the use of access controls and maintenance of user IDs and associated password files. (This position is normally found only in large installations.)

Librarian. Receives, maintains, and issues magnetic media files (data and programs) on tapes or disks; maintains systems libraries.

Control clerk. Maintains and exercises control over the completeness, accuracy, and distribution of input and output.

The organization of the EDP department is an important aspect of computer controls, because of its effect on segregation of duties within the department. To the extent possible, the aforementioned functions should be performed by different people, so that there is adequate separation of duties. For example, programmers should not have the ability to access programs actually in use. In general, the more sophisticated the system and the larger the department, the greater the opportunity to segregate incompatible functions. In small organizations, the same person may perform more than one function, which can present control problems with respect to incompatible duties, as, for example, when one person does almost all the work related to the operation of a departmental minicomputer.

Segregation of duties in computer environments, as in manual systems, also involves the separation of incompatible functions outside of the EDP department. It can be accomplished by permitting user department operators, normally via user IDs and passwords, to have access to only the functions required to perform their jobs. For example, if the payroll and personnel departments are among the users of a common data base, the payroll clerk should be able to access only the program that posts time sheets and enters paycheck-initiation transactions, while the appropriate personnel clerk should be able to access only the program that makes changes in pay status.

Supervisory controls in computer systems are similar to those in noncomputer systems. For example, in a user department, a responsible official should periodically determine that the investigation of data rejected by the computer is being carried out as prescribed. Similarly, in the EDP department, the adequacy of procedures for implementing and testing program changes should be reviewed and approved by a responsible manager. Supervisory controls can also be performed by the computer through its ability to match newly input information to preset tables or other files. Other supervisory tasks, such as checking the calculation of invoices, are performed by the system itself; once appropriate formulas have been set up in the programs, and assuming that the programs are adequately controlled, the computer will do the calculations the same way every time.

General Controls: Objectives and Techniques

General computer controls are procedures, principally over data processing as a whole, that ensure the reliable and consistent operation of programmed accounting and control procedures and the protection of stored data. Some auditors call general controls "computer integrity controls" or "information technology controls" because they believe that those terms better describe the purpose served by the controls. This section considers those controls in greater depth; a later section discusses methods of testing their continuing effectiveness as a basis for auditor reliance.

In early computer systems, general controls applied to all computer applications and data files at a location (which is why they were called general controls); however, this is not necessarily true today. Consequently, the auditor should distinguish those general controls that are common to all applications and data files from those that are specific to a particular application or data file.

Overview of General Controls

General controls can be divided into five basic categories:

- *Implementation controls* are designed to ensure that suitable programmed procedures exist and are included in computer programs, both when new systems are developed and when existing systems are amended.
- *Program security controls* are designed to ensure that changes to programmed procedures are accurately and properly made and that unauthorized changes cannot be made.
- *Computer operations controls* are designed to ensure that programmed procedures are correctly and appropriately executed.
- *Data file security controls* are designed to ensure that data files are completely and accurately maintained and that unauthorized changes cannot be made.
- *System software controls* are designed to ensure that appropriate system software is effectively implemented and protected against unauthorized changes.

The first three categories of controls are necessary for the effective operation of programmed procedures. The fourth category ensures that only properly approved transactions can change stored data. The fifth relates to system functions and, therefore, can affect both programmed procedures and data files. Controls over system software are particularly important because of their impact on the effectiveness of other general controls. For example, the password verification procedures that permit access to data files are usually incorporated into system software.

Implementation Controls

Every computer system has a system development life cycle that begins with its conceptual development, proceeds through an implementation process, and results in operational software. In some companies, this is a highly structured methodology that follows a clearly identifiable cycle, while in others it is more informal. The system development process typically includes the following activities: request for a new system, a feasibility study that includes a cost–benefit analysis, designing a general version of the system, preparing detailed specifications, writing the programs and testing the individual programs and then the system as a whole, converting data files to the new system, cataloguing the new programs and files, acceptance of the system by users and EDP personnel, and ongoing operations and maintenance. It is being increasingly recognized that successful implementation of a major EDP system requires that users, as well as EDP personnel and management, approve the system.

System Design and Program Preparation. Controls over system design and program preparation ensure that appropriate programmed procedures are designed and coded into computer language and that the appropriate application controls are created as part of the system. General design requirements should be converted into detailed system specifications. Programming should not proceed until detailed system specifications have been prepared and approved in both the user and computer departments. (This can be done in modules or for the system as a whole.) Once detailed specifications have been developed, the computer programs can be generated in a variety of ways, ranging from purchasing or customizing application software packages to writing programs inhouse. In any event, the programs should be documented in sufficient detail to facilitate subsequent testing, appropriate future modifications, and training of personnel.

Program and System Testing. Testing should normally be carried out in three distinct stages: program testing, system testing, and parallel running.

Program testing consists of verifying the logic of individual programs, usually through *desk checking* and machine processing of *test data*. Desk checking involves determining visually that the program coding is consistent with the program specifications; it should be done by a programmer other than the one who wrote the code. Desk checking is normally performed in conjunction with machine processing of hypothetical test data. Test data should be designed to cover all elements of data in all types of transactions that are likely to be encountered and for which input specifications have been written.

System testing consists of determining that the programs are logically compatible with each other and do not have an adverse impact on the system as a whole. Processing test data is the principal technique used in system testing; adjustments and reruns should be performed until all observed logic failures have been corrected. The user and system analysts are the principal parties involved in the system testing process; programmers primarily correct program errors.

Parallel running involves operating the system under conditions that approximate the anticipated "live" environment, while the old system (computer or manual) continues to operate. Results of operating the new system are compared with those of the old system, with appropriate follow-up of inconsistencies. Parallel running is a means of testing the logic, programming, and implementation of a complete system, including all user control procedures. One of its objectives is to confirm the system's ability to cope with actual conditions and volumes of transactions.

Conversion. This step involves converting the data from the old system into the format required by the new one. Because complete and accurate conversion of all data is so critical, auditors (either internal or external) are often involved in the conversion effort, even when they are not involved in the other phases of the development cycle.

Cataloguing. Cataloguing is the process of incorporating computer programs into various program libraries, which may contain programs in source code, object code, or load module form. *Source code* or language refers to the high-level computer languages that programmers use (such as COBOL); *object code*, also known as object modules, is the output of the compiler, in machine code or language (the Ø's and 1's a computer can understand). Ordinarily, a program is written in source language form, which is then incorporated into a test source library. The program is subsequently compiled by the computer into an object module and catalogued onto a test library. To be executable, the various object modules that make up a program are brought together in a process called link-editing. This process creates the *load module* that is actually used by the computer for program execution.

Program testing is performed using the program in a *test library*. After a program has been completely tested, the test source program should be transferred to the production source library. The program in the production source library should be used for cataloguing into the *production library*. This ensures that the production program is completely equivalent to the tested and approved source program.

It is important that cataloguing be controlled by effective manual and other control procedures. For example, programmers should have access to the test library only. Testing and documentation should be satisfactorily completed before programs are incorporated into production libraries. As part of the final acceptance procedures, operating and user instructions should be reviewed and approved by a responsible official. A formal manual procedure should transfer programs, at an appropriate cutoff point, from test to production status.

Program Changes. Program changes occur frequently in most data processing installations. They vary in complexity, ranging from relatively simple changes in editing procedures to major overhauls of large systems. Controls over program changes are similar to those for new systems. Requests for changes should be formalized and include sufficient details to enable the changes to be designed and approved. Testing of the changed programs should follow the same process as for new systems, and changes should be appropriately approved before implementation.

Users may inappropriately attempt to bypass formal change procedures by initiating program changes through direct contact with programmers. This can cause problems involving, for example, unauthorized changes, inappropriate installation dates, inadequate testing, and inconsistent application of accounting principles. In addition, EDP personnel may believe that there is no need to inform users of proposed program changes that are viewed as purely technical matters that users cannot comprehend and will not be affected by. Examples of such modifications are file reorganizations, changes from tape to disk, and optimizing restart procedures. All such changes should be appropriately approved by users; although they may defer in-depth technical review to data processing management, they should at least be aware that the system is being modified so as to have an opportunity to determine whether output data are affected.

Program Security Controls

Program security controls ensure that unauthorized changes are not made to production programs. Weaknesses in computer program security may allow unauthorized activity to occur in the form of fraudulently obtaining, using, or changing programs. There are several complementary methods of providing program security:

- Protecting the files containing the programs by access control software. This method entails the use of software that requires user IDs and associated passwords to gain access to programs. Its success depends on preventing unauthorized individuals from learning the passwords, and controlling the maintenance of the system of passwords (such as by disabling those of terminated employees or frequently changing passwords for sensitive applications).
- Physically securing the files containing the programs. When programs are held off-line, physical library controls should ensure that they are secure, issued only on appropriate authority, and promptly returned. On-line programs can be protected by access control software. Backup copies of programs and program documentation should be protected to prevent unauthorized personnel from obtaining knowledge of the contents of programs.
- Maintaining adequate separation of duties. With sufficient technical skill and detailed knowledge of the contents of production programs, operators and others can make changes. Appropriate segregation of duties helps prevent operators from obtaining such knowledge of the programs and restricts personnel responsible for developing and maintaining programs from gaining unsupervised access to the computer.
- Comparing production programs with independently controlled copies on a regular basis. These copies and the software used for the comparison are normally held either in a supervised physical library or at a remote location.

Computer Operations Controls

Computer operations controls ensure that programmed procedures are consistently applied, both when storing and when processing data. They include controls over processing of data and computer department operations.

Processing of Data. Computer programs require data to be input before useful information can be generated. A program will accept a newly submitted transaction and subject it to editing and other procedures. Another program may analyze data accumulated over an extended period, such as an open item accounts receivable file. In most situations, such as an inventory updating application, a program requires both transaction data and access to related files.

Controls should ensure that all data are input in the appropriate form. If the input was supplied in the form of source documents, they must be converted into magnetic media format. When data are input from a terminal or remote CRT, the accumulated input must be available and cutoff points must be appropriate. Similarly, if a job depends on the execution of a prior job, the results of the prior execution must be acceptable.

Operations Software and Computer Operating Procedures. As computer systems become more advanced, procedures are increasingly carried out by software, with manual functions limited to actions required or requested by the software. Regardless of the complexity of the operating environment and the degree to which software is used, effective controls should exist over operating instructions for system software, application procedures, procedures for restart and recovery after a disruption, file labeling, and disposition of tapes and disks. In addition, appropriate separation of duties should be maintained between operating and system functions.

Supervisory review of operator activity is usually based on computer-produced reports. Larger computers normally record on a file, known as a system log, details of all activity during processing. The information recorded on these logs can be printed out for review, but it is voluminous and technical in nature, making it difficult to review in detail. Audit software programs to edit the contents of the log and reduce the volume of data on the report are available or can be written.

Backup and Recovery Procedures. There should be backup arrangements so that, in the event of a computer failure, the recovery process for production programs, system software, and data files does not introduce errors into the system. The principal techniques that may be employed are

- A facility for restarting at an intermediate stage of processing. This is applicable to programs terminated before their normal ending.
- A system to copy or store master files and associated transactions, which makes it possible to restore files lost or damaged during disruption.
- Procedures to ensure that copies of operating instructions, run instructions, and other documentation are available if originals are lost.

- Formal instructions for the restoration of processing or its transfer to other locations, usually called a contingency plan.

Data File Security Controls

Data file security controls are designed to protect data from unauthorized accesses that could result in their modification, disclosure, or destruction or that could inappropriately move assets, such as cash or inventory. Data file security controls are particularly important with respect to master file, reference, and standing data, since such data of accounting significance are used repeatedly in processing transactions and may not be reviewed frequently enough to provide for timely identification of errors. Data file security controls are also significant from an operational viewpoint to protect files from accidental destruction or erasure.

Controls are required for both on-line and off-line data files. Similar to programs, on-line data files can be accessed by operators processing jobs or through terminals. On-line data files include tapes or disks that have been loaded for a specific processing run but are otherwise stored off-line, as in batch systems, and disks that are permanently loaded and available for inquiry or updating, as in on-line, real-time systems.

A variety of means and levels of security can be applied to data files, through physical security controls, file management software, and access controls. Absolute security is unattainable; even a high level of security can be expensive and cumbersome. (A comprehensive discussion of security is beyond the scope of this book.) It is usually most effective to apply stringent security measures on a selective basis to the more significant files than to apply a uniform level of protection to all files. If administratively burdensome procedures are applied to files needing only a low level of protection, users will often try to bypass security in general.

Physical Security Controls. Off-line files should be kept in a locked storage area, separate from the computer room, and preferably supervised by a full-time librarian responsible for their issue, receipt, and security. If there is no full-time librarian, a specific individual should be assigned such duties. Access to the library should be restricted to authorized staff.

Multiple generations of files, sometimes referred to as grandfather, father, and son files, with appropriate updating transactions, should be retained to permit file reconstruction in the event of accidental destruction. One generation of each file should be kept off-site to provide backup.

File Management Software. Data files contain internal labels with information such as file name, creation date, and authorized expiration date. This allows the computer program to determine that it is using the correct file and version and that it will not prematurely erase the file. Files can be assigned to a specific computer run or process, either manually or by software incorporated in the operating system.

Access Controls. Practically all computer system software to limit access to files uses some form of user ID or associated passwords to restrict access to data and programs. Password protection may be applied in various ways, singly or in combination. For example, a file may be accessed only from specific terminals or only by certain individuals; a user ID may be valid for ''reading'' purposes only; a transaction code may be required for certain types of transactions; a user ID may be valid only for selected programs or may be restricted to accessing only selected data within a record. Some access control systems provide reports of activities related to the terminals, including both attempted and rejected accesses. Those reports should be reviewed periodically to provide indications of potential abuses of the system.

In large installations, a security administrator is responsible for issuing and maintaining passwords. Every effort should be made to keep lists of assigned passwords confidential. Since it is practically impossible to keep all passwords confidential indefinitely, passwords should be changed periodically. User IDs should be canceled immediately on employees' termination.

In advanced systems, a data base management system lends an additional dimension to the need for control over access to information. Application programs written to access the data base should not be permitted unlimited use of all data elements. The elements accessible by a particular program should be specified by programmed procedures that are maintained within a software library. Changes in the ability of a program to access particular elements should be under the control of the data base administration function. From a control standpoint, people who maintain the definition of the elements in the data base and who maintain the related libraries of accessing procedures should not have responsibility for writing application programs or any other incompatible data processing duties.

System Software Controls

Computer programs that direct the computer and facilitate the operation and security of applications are known as system software. These programs are not specific to any particular application, but are essential to the effective processing and control of all applications.

System software controls ensure that the related software has been properly implemented and protected against unauthorized changes. These controls are of concern to the auditor because the system software can affect both the programs that process data and the data files, and consequently the auditor's ability to rely on other general computer controls. System software that may be significant to the auditor includes programs relating to cataloguing of application programs, job setup, reporting of jobs processed, file handling, data base management, password protection, telecommunications, reporting of operations, and library records.

The controls required for the successful implementation of system software are similar to those required for application programs. The principal differences concern the relatively limited involvement of personnel outside the data processing department in the development, modification, and testing of the various components of system software.

In most installations, controls over system software are less structured than those over application programs. Also, the people most directly involved in maintaining system software, the systems programmers, are usually among the most proficient in the data processing department. Consequently, their activities may not be subject to direct supervision and review. In some situations, systems programmers have direct access to computer hardware, as well as to the system as a whole. Because system software affects all programs executed and all records read or written, however, control over systems programmers as well as system software is critical.

Application Controls: Objectives and Techniques

Controls in a computer system that are related to a specific accounting system (such as cash collections from customers) are called *application controls*. Application controls consist of user controls and programmed control procedures designed to accomplish the same control objectives as in manual systems— namely, to ensure that valid transactions, and only valid transactions, are processed and recorded completely and accurately, that data in accounts and supporting files are properly maintained, and that assets are safeguarded from physical loss or theft. In considering controls in computer systems, it is helpful to distinguish between the stages of input of a transaction to the computer and the ultimate updating of a computer file, since in many cases different control techniques apply at the two stages. The control techniques that may be used are discussed briefly under each major objective and stage of processing.

For control to be effective, the programmed procedures typically generate reports (known as exception reports) of instances in which the computer, for one reason or another, is unable to complete the prescribed operation. For example, to ensure that only accurate data are entered into the system, the computer may be programmed to match cash receipts from customers with specific invoices that constitute the open accounts receivable file, to print out a report of cash receipts that cannot be matched with specific invoices, and to create a ''suspense'' file of unmatched cash receipts. For control to be effective, there should be manual procedures, known as user controls, for investigating and following up on those reports. For each technique described subsequently, the control accordingly consists of a combination of manual review and follow-up of computer-generated exception reports, and the programmed control procedures that generate the exception reports.

Completeness of Input

Completeness of input controls are designed to ensure that all transactions are initially recorded, input, and accepted for processing once and only once. The initial recording of transactions frequently involves manual procedures performed prior to their entry into the computer, although in many on-line systems, transactions are input at terminals as they occur and there is no prior manual recording. Techniques to ensure complete input to the computer include computer matching of transactions to other data within the system, a computer sequence check of document numbers, batching source documents and controlling batch totals, and one-for-one comparison of input with retained source documents.

- *Computer matching* is appropriate in batch, on-line, and real-time systems; it consists of the computer matching data on documents input with information held on files. Unmatched items are reported for manual investigation. For example, the computer might match time sheets with employee master files and identify and report missing and duplicate time sheets. The reports would then be investigated manually.

- *Computer sequence checks* are appropriate in batch, on-line, and real-time systems. The computer reports missing and duplicate numbers on documents input, which are investigated manually.

- *Batch totals* are commonly used in both batch and on-line systems. A total for the batch is established manually and compared, either manually or by computer, with a similar total accumulated by the computer. The use of batch totals is an effective completeness control technique only from the time the documents are batched. To be fully effective, the system must also include adequate controls to ensure that all documents are batched and all batches are presented for processing. These requirements are often met by reviewing, either manually or by computer, the sequence of numbered documents or batches. (Hash totals are a specific type of batch totals; a hash total is the *sum* of normally irrelevant [hence the term "hash"] numerical data, such as customer account numbers, which is determined before data are processed and is compared with the related computer total after processing to ensure that the proper accounts were posted.)

- *One-for-one checking* consists of comparing individual input or source documents with a detailed listing of items processed by computer to ensure that all documents are submitted for processing. This technique is implemented by having the originating department retain a copy of all documents sent for processing (the printout is then compared with the retained copy), by determining the sequence of input documents, or by using document counts. One-for-one comparison is time consuming and prone to error, and is normally used only for low-volume or high-value transactions.

Accuracy of Input

Accuracy of input controls are designed to ensure that key data elements are accurately recorded, converted into a form readable by the computer, and input to the computer. Not all data elements within a transaction are of equal importance, and different control techniques may be employed for different elements. The auditor is usually concerned principally with the key financial data fields that directly affect balances in the financial statements, although reference data such as customer number or invoice date may also be important.

Certain techniques employed to ensure completeness of input may also ensure accuracy of input. Examples are one-for-one checking, batching, and computer matching. Additional techniques to achieve accuracy usually include a wide range of edit checks, many of which can be carried out directly at terminals as transactions are input. These edit checks frequently depend on the operation of programmed control procedures. For example, the computer could be programmed to match a customer number input at a terminal with the customer master file and display the customer name on the screen for visual verification. The more common forms of edit checks are

- *Format checks*, which test the format of input and ensure that all expected data are present and contain the appropriate number or sequence of alphabetical or numerical characters.
- *Existence checks*, which compare input data codes with previously established lists of valid codes held on file, in tables, or in the program. They can be useful in ensuring that valid account numbers are input, for example.
- *Check digit verification*, a mathematical test carried out on reference numbers that enables the program to identify most incorrect numbers.
- *Reasonableness checks*, to test whether the data are reasonable in relation to a standard or to previous input. Examples are hours worked compared with standard hours, and prices of goods purchased compared with previous purchase prices.
- *Dependency checks*, to test whether the contents of two or more data fields on a transaction bear the correct logical relationship. For example, there should be a logical relationship among the amount of a loan, the interest rate, the number of installments, and the amount of each installment.

Completeness and Accuracy of Updating

Controls over completeness and accuracy of updating are designed to ensure that all transactions input and accepted for processing are accurately updated to the appropriate data file or element. In some cases, completeness of input controls can also ensure completeness of file updating. Examples are one-for-one checking carried out against a report produced after updating, and the application of a sequence check on an updated file if updating takes place using the same sequence as the input file. More commonly, some form of control total is used to ensure completeness of updating—for example, manual batch totals that are reconciled to updated file totals, or computer-generated exception reports indicating differences between computer-generated totals and control records. Accuracy of updating is often ensured by the same controls as those for completeness of updating. Unlike in manual systems, in which the possibility of random error in processing transactions is a concern and controls over the accuracy of data file updates frequently involve one person reviewing the work of another, accuracy of updating of data files in computer systems is often not specifically controlled. Instead, reliance is placed on programmed procedures which, in turn, are subject to the general computer controls discussed earlier.

Validity of Transactions

Controls over validity of transactions are designed to ensure that transactions are not fictitious and have been authorized. Typical control techniques include authorization by a responsible official, exception reporting (such as reporting employees working more than a given number of hours in a week, with a subsequent review by a responsible official), computer matching with authorized standing data (also called reference data) or transaction data (for example, matching customers' orders with stored authorized credit limits or matching goods received with authorized purchase orders), and security procedures that restrict access to data and programs to authorized users. Authorization by a responsible individual may be carried out on-line by the input of an appropriate password and authorization code at a terminal. With the exception of manual authorization, the foregoing techniques are likely to depend on the operation of programmed control procedures and on the security procedures over programs and files.

The authorization of computer-generated transactions depends on the controls over the data used to generate the transactions and the security of their storage on file. Examples of computer-generated transactions include the automatic posting of standard journal entries during month-end processing, the automatic reversal of monthly accrued or prepaid accounts in the subsequent month, and the automatic payment of recurring operating expenditures (such as rents and royalties). From a control perspective, the stored data that generate a transaction should be complete, accurate, and authorized, and the parameters, conditions, and programs used to initiate the transaction should be subject to appropriate general controls.

Maintenance of Data on Files

Control procedures should ensure that data stored on files, including account balances, remain correct between transaction updates. Clearly, not all files are of equal significance. The auditor is concerned primarily with files that support material balances in the financial statements. Within those files, certain data elements are of key importance, for example, the inventory balance, while others may be of less significance to the auditor, such as year-to-date sales by individual employees, which are prepared for operational or administrative reasons. Key data may be either standing or transaction data.

Periodically, the data on a file should be reviewed so that its correctness is confirmed and adjustments are made if necessary. The main types of maintenance controls in computer systems are

- *Periodic reconciliation* of items on a file with an independently maintained control account.

- *Periodic comparison* of data on a file with source data. Examples are the comparison of the file of physical assets with the assets themselves or with third-party evidence, such as counting inventory or comparing loans with loan certificates, and the cyclical comparisons of standing data with an authorized source, such as comparing prices with an authorized price list.

- *Management reviews* that are part of the control environment, such as the analysis of reports of periodic operating results. Such reviews may provide evidence regarding the correctness of both account balances and the underlying transaction processing. Other analyses, such as fluctuation analysis, are performed to point out unusual increases (or decreases) that should be investigated.

- *Matching techniques* that are carried out within the accounting system. If they involve matching evidence from third parties, such as cash received from customers to accounts receivable balances, they contribute toward ensuring the existence and accuracy of the related account balances. To be effective as a control, exception reports of mismatched items should be produced and followed up, and the programmed procedure performing the match must be effective and protected from unauthorized changes.

In computer systems there may be several versions of a file in existence; it is important that the correct data file be carried forward from one update process to the next update, that is, that the most current version be used for updating. In addition, failures in processing and recovery therefrom may introduce errors into the data. One of the most common techniques for ensuring the use of the appropriate file in a computer system is to keep control totals of the data on the file, often called run-to-run control totals. Alternatively, other controls over maintenance may also ensure use of the appropriate file, for example, counting inventory and comparing the results with the accounting records, and matching cash received to open accounts receivable balances. Those procedures would be likely to detect errors if for any reason continuity of processing was disrupted, although the errors might not be revealed on a timely basis. Finally, in the absence of other controls, evidence of use of the correct version of a file should be provided by computer operations controls within the EDP department. In particular, these would include procedures over recovery from processing failures and those, such as software label checking, that ensure that correct files are used. Computer operations controls were discussed in the section on general controls.

Asset Protection

It is important for the assets represented by the balances on files to be adequately protected. This is accomplished by a combination of

- Custody controls to make assets physically secure; and
- Controls over the security of computer programs and stored data to ensure that only authorized people have access to programs and files. These access controls are needed because assets can be moved by the manipulation of programmed procedures or data held on computer files (for example, transactions generating automatic check payments) and fraud or theft can be obscured by the processing of unauthorized transactions.

Custody controls are the same as in manual systems; computer program and data security controls were discussed in the section on general controls.

Computer Fraud and Abuse

As computers become more sophisticated and pervasive, the potential for an entity to be harmed by computer fraud and abuse increases. While the distinctions are not always clear, computer fraud (or computer crime) usually refers to use of a computer to commit a crime; in computer abuse, the computer and related software are the objects of the crime. Instances of computer fraud and abuse, when discovered, frequently make sensational headlines; often the auditor is criticized for failing to detect the fraud. Accordingly, auditors should be knowledgeable about controls to prevent computer fraud and abuse and about their responsibilities under GAAS to detect such acts.

Computer abuse encompasses the physical destruction and theft of computer hardware, software, or data and the unauthorized interception or alteration of software or data. Examples include sabotage of computers and software, unauthorized use of confidential records, unauthorized use of computer time for personal purposes, unauthorized alteration of data on file (such as student grades), the theft of portable computers, and the unauthorized copying of software.

Computer fraud involves using the computer to misappropriate assets (defalcation, or employee fraud) or to deliberately distort an enterprise's financial statements (management fraud). Both types of fraud can be perpetrated through the creation or alteration of computer programs and data on computer files or through the manipulation of transaction data (altering, omitting, or creating unauthorized transactions), or both. For example:

- At a bank, a program was written to round downward to the nearest penny interest credited to depositors' accounts, accumulate the amounts rounded off, and credit them to the programmer's account—a case of a defalcation via unauthorized transactions generated by an unauthorized program.

- An employee of an insurance company who had clearance to process customer claims made unauthorized payments to himself and his children and then deleted the transactions from the files—a case of a defalcation via entering unauthorized transactions.

- Top management created nonexistent receivables and revenues by entering fictitious transactions; they then wrote a program to suppress the fictitious receivables when the auditor selected a sample from the accounts receivable file for the purpose of confirming them—a case of management fraud via entering of fictitious transactions and creating a fraudulent program.

In most instances of computer fraud, it is clear that the fraud could have occurred in a manual system as well—particularly when the fraud was perpetrated by the inappropriate entry of transactions. Even many of the frauds involving the unauthorized creation or alteration of computer programs would be possible in manual systems; for example, crediting fractional cents of interest to an unauthorized account could have been done in a manual system. In most instances, however, an enterprise uses a computer because of large transaction volumes. It is the combination of the existence of the computer and the large volumes of transactions that makes it possible for a person (or collusive group of people) to employ the computer to assist in stealing assets or to intentionally distort the financial statements, and then to conceal those actions.

The incidence of employee computer fraud can be reduced, at a price, through the design and effective operation of application controls over transactions and general controls over computer program and data security. (As with any type of fraud, computer fraud can never be completely eliminated; even if it could, the cost of doing so would usually be far greater than the benefits derived.) Management fraud, however, whether perpetrated in a manual or a computer environment, is less susceptible to prevention or detection by means of internal accounting controls because of management's ability to override those controls.

The auditor's responsibility for detecting computer fraud is the same as the responsibility for detecting other types of fraud. Employee fraud rarely results in material financial statement misstatements; management fraud, which typically is material to the financial statements, is often difficult to detect because its perpetration ordinarily involves control override and collusion. As discussed in Chapter 4, auditors have the responsibility to plan their audits to search for material fraud and to exercise due skill and care in performing them. They also have the responsibility under SAS No. 20, *Required Communication of Material Weaknesses in Internal Accounting Control* (AU Section 323), to inform the client of material weaknesses in internal accounting controls—whether computer-related or otherwise—that come to their attention in the course of the audit.

Auditing Computer-Generated Financial Information

To plan an effective and efficient audit, the auditor of an enterprise with computerized accounting systems needs to have and document the same kinds of information about the client's control environment and significant accounting systems as does the auditor of an entity whose systems do not involve the use of EDP. Knowledge of the accounting systems provides the auditor with an overview of the flow of significant transactions through both the manually operated and the computerized elements of such systems. That overview enables the auditor to identify the significant EDP accounting applications and understand such matters as the mode in which they operate (such as batch or on-line, real-time), what accounting functions they perform (that is, the principal programmed accounting procedures), who operates them (including the relationships among users, operators, and programmers), how significant data used in processing those applications originate (for example, whether they are input through remote terminals or extracted from previously generated data files), the significant data files generated or updated by the processing, and information about important reports produced—when and how they are produced, when and to whom they are distributed, and how they are used.

Additionally, the accounting systems overview generally enables the auditor to identify specific application controls that may later prove useful in maximizing audit efficiency. The required information about the client's control environment extends to the EDP department and, among other things, provides the auditor with an overview of the client's general controls.

Depending on the auditor's level of expertise about computer systems, assistance from computer audit specialists may be necessary for understanding the flow of transactions through computerized accounting systems and for assessing the control environment. Computer specialists are more likely to be needed to perform compliance and substantive tests that use some of the more sophisticated types of audit software or manual procedures that are discussed later.

Audit Strategy

Audit objectives and the basis for audit strategy decisions do not change because significant applications within accounting systems are computerized. As with manual systems, the auditor is still concerned with whether particular audit objectives for individual accounts or groups of accounts can be achieved most efficiently by restricting substantive procedures through reliance on specific controls or by performing substantive procedures without reliance on specific controls. What does change when accounting systems are computerized are the points within the systems where errors and frauds relating to the audit objectives can occur, the ways in which they can occur, and the ways in which they can be prevented or detected. Also, in a computerized environment the auditor may be able to use the computer to efficiently perform audit procedures that would otherwise be impractical.

Audit strategy decisions in a computerized environment typically focus first on the reliability of general controls, because of their importance in ensuring the propriety, integrity, and appropriate operation of programmed accounting and control procedures, and then on application controls. The control environment in computerized systems typically leads to one of the following audit strategies:

- All categories of general controls over programmed accounting and control procedures can be and are relied on after they have been tested.
- Certain categories of general controls, such as those over program or data security, cannot be or are not relied on. In those cases, the auditor should assess the risk of material misstatement of the financial statements by considering such factors as the susceptibility of relevant assets to theft, the sensitivity of the stored data, and the adequacy and interrelationship of other relevant elements of the internal control system, including the control environment, the accounting systems, and application controls. If the auditor cannot conclude that the risk of material misstatement is low, substantive procedures should be designed to provide the required assurance that related audit objectives are achieved.
- The client lacks reliable general controls, in which case the auditor develops a substantive audit strategy (provided the client's financial statements are deemed auditable).

Application controls that are dependent on programmed control procedures are typically not relied on unless the related general controls are relied on. This is because it would be necessary to compliance test the programmed control procedures if the auditor wanted to rely on them and could not obtain the necessary evidence about their effective and continuous operation from general controls. Testing those programmed procedures, however, may not be cost effective when there are many such procedures. In these circumstances, the auditor would obtain the necessary assurance from substantive tests. Similarly, an audit strategy that is based on no reliance on specific internal accounting controls will probably require testing the client's programmed accounting procedures; those tests will also be costly because of the sheer volume of such procedures in a typical accounting system.

Compliance Testing EDP Controls

The auditor's purpose in performing compliance tests of both general and application controls in EDP systems is the same as for controls in manual systems, namely, to test the effective and continuous operation of specific controls that will be relied on in determining the nature, timing, and extent of substantive tests. Compliance tests of EDP controls involve the same types of auditing procedures as do tests of manual controls, that is, inquiry, observation, examination of evidence, and, if appropriate, reperformance. In computerized environments, however, the auditor may be able to use software to assist in performing the tests.

Testing General Controls. As noted earlier, the current trend away from centralized operations and toward data entry from user department terminals and via telecommunications networks has resulted in a dispersion of the overall EDP function. Furthermore, the variety of data processing methods within a computer facility has tended to increase. Accordingly, general controls are typically classified into two categories: those that are common to all applications and those that are application specific. The auditor can test common general controls without prior consideration of the applications involved and arrive at a conclusion regarding the effectiveness of the controls. General controls that are application specific, on the other hand, must be tested and evaluated with reference to the related applications; the results are not necessarily relevant to other applications.

In drafting the compliance test audit program, it is often most convenient to consider the common general computer controls first. EDP functions that are typically addressed by common general controls include computer operations in the EDP department, centrally controlled data files and program libraries, standards for developing and maintaining programs, and centralized software support operations. Once the overall audit scope with regard to common general controls has been established, the auditor should identify the general control areas that have not been covered by common controls and relate those areas to specific applications. Examples include scheduling and operating functions performed in user departments, data files and programs maintained in decentralized areas, computers at remote sites that process data and communicate with a central computer, application development and maintenance functions under user control, and system software not resident at or under the control of the centralized software support group. In designing tests of application-specific general controls, the auditor should give primary emphasis to applications containing programmed procedures on which audit reliance is planned.

Computer software can provide information to assist the auditor in testing the client's general controls. For example, the auditor can use software to generate reports that identify who can access sensitive programs and utilities and when such access was made, or to identify the data base structure and programmed physical and logical relationships within it.

Testing Application Controls. As noted on several occasions, application controls consist of programmed control procedures that direct the computer to perform certain activities, such as matching one file of cash receipts against another file and producing a report of unmatched exceptions, and manual operations, known as user controls, such as the follow-up of a computer-generated exception report. If the auditor intends to rely on specific application controls to be able to restrict substantive testing, evidence from compliance tests is needed that both the relevant programmed control procedures and the user controls operated effectively and continuously.

Compliance tests of user controls are no different from compliance tests of controls in manual systems. Evidence about the effective and continuous operation of programmed control procedures can be obtained either from compliance testing the general controls that operate over the programmed procedures or from compliance testing the programmed procedures themselves. The first approach was discussed earlier. The second approach involves the same techniques as are used in substantive tests of programmed accounting procedures and is discussed in the following section.

As an alternative, particularly in computerized systems in which general controls may be less pervasive or sophisticated or programmed accounting and control procedures are limited in number, the auditor may be able to obtain indirect evidence as to the continuous operation of application controls. Material misstatements that should have been prevented or detected by controls over the client's principal activities (such as sales, purchases, and receipt and disbursement of cash) may also be detected through management's use of the related data in managing the business. For example, material failures to bill for goods shipped or services rendered would generally come to management's attention through the adverse effect on profitability. Other misstatements affect relations with employees, customers, suppliers, or others. For instance, overbillings for goods shipped or services rendered would generally provoke unfavorable reactions from customers, including nonpayment of excess billings. The auditor may obtain evidence as to whether such circumstances have arisen during the period by inquiring of client personnel, performing analytical review procedures, or examining various management reports. The absence of such occurrences provides some evidence as to the continuous and effective operation of controls.

Finally, the auditor should consider whether a significant risk of material misstatement exists as a result of the failure of programmed accounting and control procedures to operate continuously and effectively. If, considering this risk and all relevant sources of evidence, the auditor determines that additional evidence is needed, tests of specific programmed procedures may be necessary. Before undertaking such tests, however, the auditor should consider whether it would be more efficient to perform additional substantive tests directed to the audit objective in question.

Substantive Tests Using Computer Software

The objectives of substantive tests and the relationship between the system of internal control and substantive tests remain the same for a computerized system as for a noncomputerized system. Many of those tests, however, can be most efficiently performed using audit software on either the client's or the auditor's computer. Auditing "with" the computer can increase audit efficiency by mechanizing audit procedures and enabling the auditor to test large numbers of transactions. Software is available or can be developed by the auditor to test transactions, master file and reference data, historical data, programs, activity logs—in fact, almost anything that is stored in a computer system. The auditor can also perform various audit procedures with the assistance of audit software designed specifically for that purpose. Auditors can use a microcomputer, a terminal connected to a large computer, or a micro–mainframe link in many phases of the audit—planning, engagement management, performing audit tests (including analytical reviews), and documenting the audit work.

The same software tools may be used in more than one testing technique; in certain circumstances these tools could also be used in compliance testing controls. Sometimes a combination of different types of software is required to meet a single audit objective. Audit software can assist in calculating, summarizing, selecting, sorting, and comparing data, and producing reports to the auditor's specifications. Sometimes, such as when generalized audit software packages (discussed later) are used, data can be accessed and processed by the same software tools. For example, the auditor can use software to examine all data on a file in a consistent and accurate manner, to quantify precisely data meeting a particular condition (e.g., a total of debtors' balances that exceed their credit limits), and to print out selected data, such as the results of tests or items selected for investigation. Figure 11.1 lists typical functions used by auditors in processing data.

Software tools that the auditor may use to access and process data include generalized audit software packages, application audit software packages, customized audit software, inquiry programs, and systems utility software and service aids. These techniques are discussed in the next sections.

Generalized Audit Software Packages. The most widely used computer-assisted audit techniques employ generalized software packages specifically designed for audit purposes. Audit tasks performed on client files include adding a file, identifying exceptions, selecting items for manual review, and formating reports. Generalized audit software packages assist the auditor in carrying out those tasks on a variety of files at different installations. Their use allows the auditor to avoid much of the work involved in writing individual computer programs to accomplish those functions.

To use audit software, the auditor defines the computer configuration on which the program is to be run and the files to be used. The logic of the program is controlled by simplified procedural statements or parameters. The packages normally have special functions to facilitate programming, such as report formating (page numbering, page breaking, column placement, and headings), totaling and subtotaling data, automatic production of processing statistics (number of records read and processed, and number of positive, negative, and zero value records), and sorting and summarizing data.

Figure 11.1 Common Audit Processing Functions

Function	Example
Total	Add invoice amounts on the accounts receivable open item file and agree to the control total.
Compute	Multiply inventory quantities by unit costs.
Sort Summarize	Sort the file into customer number sequence and summarize to obtain customers' outstanding balances.
Analyze	Produce a frequency distribution.
Create	Produce a file for later comparison with another file.
Select	Produce a list of customers whose balances outstanding over 90 days are greater than $10,000.
Sample	Statistically sample the file for customer accounts to be confirmed.
Compare	Compare the file created at the confirmation date with the file at the balance sheet date and print out accounts with large percentage changes.
Format Reports	Print confirmation letters and working papers.

Generalized audit software packages permit programs for specific applications to be developed in a relatively short time by people with somewhat limited programming skills. The use of generalized packages also reduces the auditor's reliance on the client's EDP staff, though client assistance is usually required to install the package and develop instructions to operate it. The main disadvantage of generalized packages is that there are usually limitations on the number and structure of files that can be accessed. Frequently the auditor can overcome those limitations by using a generalized audit software package in combination with customized software or utilities.

Application Audit Software Packages. Certain auditing procedures and requirements are so similar from one audit to another that the same programs can be applied with only minor changes, even though the data files vary. Some auditing firms have developed application audit software packages to achieve common audit objectives in several areas, such as accounts receivable, accounts payable, and payroll. For example, application audit software can be used to analyze the accounts receivable ledger by age, select items for audit testing, produce confirmation letters, and match subsequent collections received. To run the software, the auditor converts the data files into a compatible format, determines the appropriate parameters, and executes the software. Some audit tests are unique to certain industries and to applications within those industries; some firms have also developed packages for these specialized areas.

Customized Audit Software. Although generalized and application software packages are useful in many applications, the auditor normally requires the ability to develop software for special needs beyond the capabilities of packaged software. For example, software packages may not be available for the client's computer, the output required may be very specialized, or the computations and data handling may be particularly intricate. In those circumstances, the auditor may use the computer languages available on the client's system to develop customized audit software. In addition, many generalized audit software packages allow additional routines written in computer languages to be integrated into the package, allowing increased flexibility and wider applicability. If no compatible language is available, or if for other reasons it is impractical to integrate additional routines, an EDP audit specialist or a computer programmer can write programs to order.

Inquiry Programs. When available, standard data inquiry (or interrogation) programs can be an economical audit tool. Relatively easy-to-use interrogation methods exist for many smaller computers, and are often built into larger data base management systems. A disadvantage of using inquiry programs is that they are often unique to a particular computer or data base, which means that the auditor may have to read manuals and learn the particular program.

Systems Utility Software and Service Aids. Systems utilities and service aids are provided by computer manufacturers and software vendors to perform limited predefined tasks. Utilities and service aids are normally used to enhance system functioning or for programming. The auditor may use them to examine processing activity, interrogate data, and test programs and operational procedures. For example, one utility can copy and rearrange sequential files; another can extract particular records from one file and create a subset file for audit testing.

The auditor often needs utilities to set up and execute computerized audit procedures. Some utilities may substitute for procedures that would otherwise be performed by generalized audit software or specially written programs. Most utilities come with a user manual that describes their functions. In smaller systems, utilities may allow the auditor access to many powerful, easy-to-use techniques. In larger systems, they may be much more difficult to use. Utilities are usually specific to a particular computer and operating system, so that the auditor must learn how to use each one for the different computers and systems that are audited.

Substantive Tests of Programmed Accounting Procedures

If the auditor intends to rely on the client's programmed accounting procedures, it is necessary to obtain evidence of the continued and proper operation of those programs. One way of accomplishing this is to test the programmed procedures directly throughout the period, generally using various types of audit software, although in certain circumstances manual techniques may be appropriate. While these tests are discussed as substantive tests, they can also be used as compliance tests if the strategy calls for reliance on specific programmed control procedures. As noted earlier, however, testing specific programmed procedures is costly and the auditor usually applies an alternative audit strategy. Therefore, only a brief description of some of the techniques used for testing client programs is presented here.

Flowcharting Programs. This software assists the auditor in understanding the programmed procedures by producing flowcharts and other documentation of the program being analyzed. The voluminous flowcharts produced, however, may contain more detail than is needed for that understanding. Lists of commands and data names in the program are also generated and are often helpful in program code analysis (described subsequently).

Program Tracing and Mapping. These techniques involve processing test data through application programs and are used primarily by programmers when developing and testing programs. Program tracing identifies the actual steps executed; program mapping identifies any unexecuted program instructions. These techniques are only occasionally used by auditors because of the technical skills needed to analyze the results.

Program Code Analysis. This technique involves analyzing computer programs. Its main purpose is to confirm the existence of programmed procedures in a program or series of programs. Program code analysis consists of

- Identifying the program to be examined, by reference to the company's documentation.
- Selecting the form of code to be examined, which is normally the source code. The auditor must know the programming language and ensure that the source version examined is equivalent to the production program in use.
- Analyzing the selected coding. It is usually difficult to follow another person's coding, but adherence to standard programming methods may make this task a little easier. Software aids, such as flowcharting programs, can produce additional documentation. In subsequent periods, comparison programs can be used to indicate changes.

Test Data and Integrated Test Facility (ITF). The test data method tests processing and controls in application systems. Application audit software tests actual client data; in the test data method, client programs are used to process test data. The output of the processing is then compared with predetermined results.

There are two methods of running test data:

- Test data can be processed using the company's operational programs, but separately from the company's data, and using either copies of master files or dummy files set up for testing purposes.

- Test data can be included in the company's regular data processing, with approval from a responsible official.

The latter method is referred to as an Integrated Test Facility (ITF). If specific records on the master files are reserved or created for this purpose and consistently processed during testing at regularly established intervals, an ITF is also referred to as a "Base Case System Evaluation."

Manual Testing. Techniques for testing programmed procedures manually can be used if adequate visible evidence is available. Data that must be tested to test the programmed procedures can be voluminous, however, making manual testing techniques impractical and inefficient. Although some visible evidence of the operation of programmed procedures is usually available, the results of processing are rarely printed out in detail (except in some microcomputer systems). Instead, totals and analyses are printed out without supporting details, thus rendering it impossible for the auditor to determine the correctness of a total or an analysis. Exception reports and rejection listings that are produced do not provide evidence that all items that should have been reported or rejected were properly treated. In those instances, the auditor may request and sometimes obtain reports generated specifically to meet audit needs.

Sometimes visible evidence not readily provided by the system can be re-created. Methods to achieve this are known collectively as "manual simulation techniques" and include

- Reassembling processed data into the same condition that existed when the programmed procedure was applied (e.g., reassembling batches of sales invoices to test the batch totals posted to the sales ledger control account).
- Using current data before processing by computer (e.g., testing the additions of batches before they are sent for processing, to determine that accurate batch totals are established to control subsequent processing).
- Selecting a small number of items from those submitted for processing and processing them in a separate run (e.g., splitting a batch into two batches, one large and one small, processing the small batch separately, and agreeing the resulting computer-produced total to manually pre-calculated results).
- Simulating a condition that will produce a report if the programmed procedure is working properly (e.g., altering a batch total to an incorrect figure so that the batch should be rejected, or withholding a document to see whether it is reported as missing); this approach requires careful planning and coordination with user departments.
- Requesting a special printout of items processed (e.g., a listing of sales invoices included in a sales total produced by the computer).

Manual tests cannot be performed if visible evidence of the operation of a programmed procedure neither exists nor can be produced, and the appropriate condition cannot be simulated. This often occurs in paperless systems, where transactions are entered directly through terminals without source documents.

Statistical Sampling Software

Statistical sampling applications, in both compliance and substantive testing, are particularly well suited to assistance from audit software. Using software reduces the need to make calculations manually and relieves the auditor of the need to understand fully some of the mathematical methods and concepts involved in sampling. In fact, many statistical sampling applications would be impractical without computer power.

A number of statistical sampling software packages are available to the auditor, some of which require almost no understanding of statistics. Most such packages support a limited number of statistical methodologies—usually those most frequently used by the accounting firm that developed the software. Other packages provide a wider selection of statistical methods, permitting the auditor to select the method best suited to the objective under consideration. Many of these packages can be used on microcomputers.

Two types of statistical sampling programs are generally available:

- Programs designed to develop strata boundaries, determine sample sizes, perform sample selection, and evaluate sampling results for variables sampling applications.
- Programs to calculate sample sizes and evaluate sampling results for attributes samples.

Audit Documentation Software

Software packages are available that automate some of the labor-intensive tasks associated with the preparation of financial statements, including footing the trial balance and financial statements, ensuring the arithmetical accuracy and consistency of account groupings, and listing relevant financial statement ratios for subsequent analysis. Documentation programs can also be used to prepare opening and closing trial balances, lead schedules showing both current and prior-period information, financial statements, and other working papers. Software can be used to produce and format reports so that they can be used as audit working papers. Auditors can use documentation software packages, instead of preparing working papers, to document the use of other audit software. The audit software packages—both for audit documentation and for the other purposes described in this chapter—are often designed to be used on the auditor's microcomputer at the client's office, a practice that is becoming increasingly common.

Analytical Review Software

Software can be used to calculate absolute dollar and percentage changes, ratios, and trends and to highlight significant changes, enabling the auditor to concentrate on evaluating the differences and obtaining explanations for them. This software is available on microcomputers, or by using utilities or software packages on minicomputers and mainframes. Auditors are increasingly using computers to compare client data with industry data using public data bases and microcomputer software. Virtually all of the analytical review techniques discussed in Chapter 9 can be performed using software.

Audit Management

Computers can contribute to efficient engagement management, particularly in planning, budgeting, and scheduling. Extremely time consuming when performed manually, these tasks can be expedited considerably by software such as calculation worksheets, or "spread sheets." Once a spread sheet is set up, the user can input and change data, conditions, and formulas, and the results are recalculated automatically. Software can facilitate the effective use of, and control over, audit resources by determining the cost of assigned staff and evaluating alternatives, allocating staff and available chargeable hours to assignments, and scheduling staff by client, tasks to be performed, expected utilization, and available hours.

Accounting firms also use computers in a number of other ways to enhance the efficiency of their practices. Some of these computer applications are

- *Word processing.* Many standard letters and documents can be maintained in word processing libraries, including engagement and representation letters, financial reports, audit programs, and audit reports. Many management letters contain similar comments, which can be stored in a library to assist in the preparation of these letters.
- *Audit statistics.* In performing analytical reviews of clients' financial results, comparisons are often made with industry results. The collection and maintenance of industry statistics and key business ratios can be stored on computer files.
- *Electronic mail.* Electronic mail has the benefits of speed and ease of response. It can be sent by telecommunications to and from geographically dispersed locations, thereby improving communications within a firm.
- *Audit department accounting and management.* Many accounting firms have management information systems to record budgets and time charges, assist in prompt billing and revenue collection, and produce management and exception reports, such as staff utilization rates and overdue accounts. In some firms this processing is done on a centralized basis. In the future, accounting firms will probably follow the trend in the business community toward decentralizing systems using mini- or microcomputers at the local level that process local data and then input results to, and retrieve reports from, the central processing site(s).

Review Questions

11-1. Distinguish between programmed accounting procedures and programmed control procedures found in an EDP environment.

11-2. Explain how computers can perform some supervisory controls.

11-3. Describe the organization of a typical EDP department.

11-4. Describe how purchased software affects the risk of error occurring.

11-5. Briefly describe the five basic categories of general computer controls.

11-6. What is program testing and how is it performed?

11-7. What is parallel running and what is its primary purpose?

11-8. What is the process of cataloguing and how should it be controlled?

11-9. How are program changes controlled and why is controlling them important?

11-10. Describe the various ways in which computer input can be controlled for completeness and accuracy.

11-11. What are the objectives of application controls and how do they differ from general controls?

11-12. Why are backup arrangements important and what techniques are used?

11-13. Explain how general controls and application controls affect audit strategy.

11-14. Explain how computer software can be used in compliance testing general controls.

11-15. Illustrate how evidence obtained from other auditing procedures can assist in compliance testing application controls.

11-16. Explain the similarities and differences between compliance testing and substantive testing in an EDP installation as compared with a manual environment.

11-17. Explain how the computer can be used to assist and expedite the auditing process.

11-18. What software tools are available to the auditor in using the computer in performing substantive tests of programmed procedures?

11-19. Explain the two methods of running test data to evaluate a programmed procedure.

11-20. Explain how the computer can assist in the use of statistical sampling techniques.

11-21. Explain how the auditor can use the computer in engagement administration.

Discussion Questions

11-30. An auditor wishes to restrict computer audit procedures to an evaluation of, and reliance on, general controls. Discuss whether this is possible and, if so, how it is possible.

11-31. If considerable reliance is to be placed on the system by testing general controls, should some programmed procedures also be tested? Explain.

11-32. Since programmed procedures can be tested directly, why should general controls be tested?

11-33. What may happen in the event of weaknesses in computer program security? Describe various ways of achieving program security.

11-34. An auditor must have a basic knowledge of computer terminology and procedures in order to audit properly a client with a computer system.

> *Required:*
>
> a. From an audit viewpoint, which is more important—a transaction file or a master file?
> b. What does update mean and why is it important?
> c. What is an edit report and why is it important?
> d. What are some of the techniques commonly used to assist in controlling the accuracy of input?
> e. Why doesn't sequence checking ensure both completeness and accuracy of input?
> f. Why don't batch totals control the accuracy of all aspects of input?

11-35. The Lakesedge Utility District is installing an electronic data processing system. The CPA who conducts the annual examination of the Utility District's financial statements has been asked to recommend controls for the new system.

> *Required:*
> Discuss recommended controls over
>
> a. Program documentation.
> b. Program testing.
> c. EDP hardware.
> d. Tape files and software.

(AICPA adapted)

11-36. The following five topics are part of the relevant body of knowledge for CPAs having field work or immediate supervisory responsibility in audits involving a computer:

> 1. Electronic data processing (EDP) equipment and its capabilities.
> 2. Organization and management of the data processing function.
> 3. Characteristics of computer-based systems.
> 4. Fundamentals of computer programming.
> 5. Computer center operations.

CPAs who are responsible for computer audits should possess certain general knowledge with respect to each of these five topics. For example, on the subject of EDP equipment and its capabilities, the auditor should have a general understanding of computer equipment and should be familiar with the uses and capabilities of the central processor and the peripheral equipment.

> *Required:*
> For each of the topics numbered 2 through 5 above, describe the general knowledge that should be possessed by those CPAs who are responsible for computer audits.

(AICPA adapted)

11-37. When auditing an electronic data processing (EDP) accounting system, the independent auditor should have a general familiarity with the effects of the use of EDP on the various characteristics of accounting control and on the auditor's study and evaluation of such control. The independent auditor must be aware of those control procedures that are commonly referred to as "general" controls and those that are commonly referred to as "application" controls. General controls relate to all EDP activities and application controls relate to specific accounting tasks.

Required:

a. What are the general controls that should exist in EDP-based accounting systems?

b. What are the purposes of each of the following categories of application controls?

1. Input controls.
2. Processing controls.
3. Output controls.

(AICPA adapted)

11-38. In the past, the records to be evaluated in an audit have been printed reports, listings, documents, and written papers, all of which are visible output. However, in fully computerized systems that employ daily updating of transaction files, output and files are frequently in machine-readable form such as cards, tapes, or disks. Thus, they often present the auditor with an opportunity to use the computer in performing an audit.

Required:

Discuss how the computer can be used to aid the auditor in examining accounts receivable in such a fully computerized system.

(AICPA adapted)

11-39. Talbert Corporation hired an independent computer programmer to develop a simplified payroll application for its newly purchased computer. The programmer developed an on-line, data-based microcomputer system that minimized the level of knowledge required by the operator. It was based on typing answers to input cues that appeared on the terminal's viewing screen, examples of which follow:

A. Access routine:

1. Operator access number to payroll file?
2. Are there new employees?

B. New employees routine:

1. Employee name?
2. Employee number?
3. Social security number?
4. Rate per hour?
5. Single or married?
6. Number of dependents?
7. Account distribution?

C. Current payroll routine:

1. Employee number?
2. Regular hours worked?
3. Overtime hours worked?
4. Total employees this payroll period?

The independent auditor is attempting to verify that certain input validation (edit) checks exist to ensure that errors resulting from omissions, invalid entries, or other inaccuracies will be detected during the typing of answers to the input cues.

Required:

Identify the various types of input validation (edit) checks the independent auditor would expect to find in the EDP system. Describe the assurances provided by each identified validation check. Do not discuss the review and evaluation of these controls.

(AICPA adapted)

AICPA Multiple Choice Questions

These questions are taken from the Auditing part of Uniform CPA Examinations. Choose the single most appropriate answer.

11-40. The initial debugging of a computer program should normally be performed by the

    a. Control group.
    b. Programmer.
    c. Machine operator.
    d. Internal auditor.

11-41. Which of the following would *lessen* internal control in an electronic data processing system?

    a. The computer librarian maintains custody of computer program instructions and detailed program listings.
    b. Computer operators have access to operator instructions and detailed program listings.
    c. The control group maintains sole custody of all computer output.
    d. Computer programmers write and debug programs that perform routines designed by the systems analyst.

11-42. A customer inadvertently ordered part number 12368 rather than part number 12638. In processing this order, the error would be detected by the vendor with which of the following controls?

    a. Batch total.
    b. Key verifying.
    c. Self-checking digit.
    d. An internal consistency check.

11-43. When an on-line, real-time (OLRT) electronic data processing system is in use, internal control can be strengthened by

    a. Providing for the separation of duties between keypunching and error listing operations.
    b. Attaching plastic file protection rings to reels of magnetic tape before new data can be entered on the file.
    c. Preparing batch totals to provide assurance that file updates are made for the entire input.
    d. Making a validity check of an identification number before a user can obtain access to the computer files.

11-44. A batch of cards was next to the computer waiting for processing. The personnel manager, showing some visitors through the installation, pulled a card from the batch to show the visitors what it looked like. He absent-mindedly put the card into his pocket rather than back into the batch. The missing card was not detected when the batch was processed. The best control procedure would be a

   a. Trailer label.
   b. Transmittal control log.
   c. Control total.
   d. Missing data check.

11-45. After a preliminary review of a client's EDP control, an auditor may decide not to perform compliance tests related to the control procedures within the EDP portion of the client's internal control system. Which of the following would *not* be a valid reason for choosing to omit compliance tests?

   a. The controls duplicate operative controls existing elsewhere in the system.
   b. There appear to be major weaknesses that would preclude reliance on the stated procedure.
   c. The time and dollar costs of testing exceed the time and dollar savings in substantive testing if the compliance tests show the controls to be operative.
   d. The controls appear adequate enough to be relied upon.

11-46. Which of the following is *not* a characteristic of a batch processed computer system?

   a. The collection of like transactions that are sorted and processed sequentially against a master file.
   b. Keypunching of transactions, followed by machine processing.
   c. The production of numerous printouts.
   d. The posting of a transaction, as it occurs, to several files, without intermediate printouts.

11-47. An auditor will use the EDP test data method in order to gain certain assurances with respect to the

   a. Input data.
   b. Machine capacity.
   c. Procedures contained within the program.
   d. Degree of keypunching accuracy.

11-48. If a control total were to be computed on each of the following data items, which would best be identified as a hash total for a payroll EDP application?

   a. Net pay.
   b. Department numbers.
   c. Hours worked.
   d. Total debits and total credits.

11-49. Which of the following is necessary to audit balances in an on-line EDP system in an environment of destructive updating?

   a. Periodic dumping of transaction files.
   b. Year-end utilization of audit hooks.
   c. An integrated test facility.
   d. A well documented audit trail.

11-50. The primary purpose of a generalized computer audit program is to allow the auditor to

a. Use the client's employees to perform routine audit checks of the electronic data processing records that otherwise would be done by the auditor's staff accountants.
b. Test the logic of computer programs used in the client's electronic data processing systems.
c. Select larger samples from the client's electronic data processing records than would otherwise be selected without the generalized program.
d. Independently process client electronic data processing records.

11-51. Which of the following is likely to be of *least* importance to an auditor in reviewing the internal control in a company with automated data processing?

a. The segregation of duties within the EDP center.
b. The control over source documents.
c. The documentation maintained for accounting applications.
d. The cost–benefit ratio of data processing operations.

11-52. In the weekly computer run to prepare payroll checks, a check was printed for an employee who had been terminated the previous week. Which of the following controls, if properly utilized, would have been most effective in preventing the error or ensuring its prompt detection?

a. A control total for hours worked, prepared from time cards collected by the timekeeping department.
b. Requiring the treasurer's office to account for the numbers of the prenumbered checks issued to the EDP department for the processing of the payroll.
c. Use of a check digit for employee numbers.
d. Use of a header label for the payroll input sheet.

Problems and Cases

11-60. Roger Peters, CPA, has examined the financial statements of the Solt Manufacturing Company for several years and is making preliminary plans for the audit for the year ended June 30, 1987. During this examination Mr. Peters plans to use a set of generalized computer audit programs. Solt's EDP manager has agreed to prepare special tapes of data from company records for the CPA's use with the generalized programs.

The following information is applicable to Mr. Peters' examination of Solt's accounts payable and related procedures:

1. The formats of pertinent tapes are on page 461.
2. The following monthly runs are prepared:
   a. Cash disbursements by check number.
   b. Outstanding payables.
   c. Purchase journals arranged (1) by account charged and (2) by vendor.
3. Vouchers and supporting invoices, receiving reports, and purchase order copies are filed by vendor code. Purchase orders and checks are filed numerically.
4. Company records are maintained on magnetic tapes. All tapes are stored in a restricted area within the computer room. A grandfather–father–son policy is followed for retaining and safeguarding tape files.

Master File — Vendor Name

| Vendor code | Recd type | Space | Blank | Vendor name | Blank | Card code 100 |

Master File — Vendor Address

| Vendor code | Recd type | Space | Blank | Address — line 1 | Address — line 2 | Address — line 3 | Blank | Card code 120 |

Transaction File — Expense Detail

| Vendor code | Recd type | Voucher number | Blank | Batch | Voucher number | Voucher date | Vendor code | Invoice date | Due date | Invoice number | Purchase order number | Debit account | Prd type | Product code | Blank | Amount | Quantity | Card code 150 |

Transaction File — Payment Detail

| Vendor code | Recd type | Voucher number | Blank | Batch | Voucher number | Voucher date | Vendor code | Invoice date | Due date | Invoice number | Purchase order number | Check number | Check date | Blank | Amount | Blank | Card code 170 |

Required:

a. Explain the grandfather–father–son policy. Describe how files could be reconstructed when this policy is used.
b. Discuss whether company policies for retaining and safeguarding the tape files provide adequate protection against losses of data.
c. Describe the controls that the CPA should maintain over
   1. Preparing the special tape.
   2. Processing the special tape with the generalized computer audit programs.
d. Prepare a schedule for the EDP manager outlining the data that should be included on the special tape for the CPA's examination of accounts payable and related procedures. This schedule should show the
   1. Client tape from which the item should be extracted.
   2. Name of the item of data.

(AICPA adapted)

11–61. A client has established a data processing department for processing its financial applications. The department is relatively small, with personnel consisting of a supervisor, a programmer, a computer operator, and two data entry operators. The following observations were made during the initial stages of the audit:

- The supervisor develops the applications, which includes consulting with the users.
- In some cases the programs are written by the programmer and in other situations programs are purchased from software vendors and customized to accommodate the client's requirements.
- Programs may be defined, developed, or modified on the basis of written specifications or oral communication, depending on the complexity and urgency of the requirements.
- The supervisor determines the nature and extent of testing.
- The programmer is responsible for maintaining the operating system software and may operate the computer when the operator is absent.
- The operator is aware of all of the computer programs in production status and determines when it is necessary to initiate the production runs.
- The data entry operators convert transactions into machine-readable form through key-driven devices maintained in the data processing department.
- All magnetic disk files are maintained in the computer room where they are directly available to the operator for use on production runs.

Management has stated that since the business is relatively stable, major changes are not likely to occur in either the composition of personnel or the equipment configuration during the next two or three years. Management is content with the organization of the department and feels that the personnel assignments provide a good level of flexibility at a reasonable cost. It also feels that deemphasizing formality, both within and outside the department, results in a significant reduction of administrative cost.

Required:

a. What are some general observations that might be made concerning potential control weaknesses within the computer environment?
b. What is the probable level of reliance that the auditor will place on the existing level of general computer controls?

c. What are some practical considerations that the auditor must take into account with respect to communicating observations and recommendations to management?

11–62. A client uses a computer-generated report as the basis for writing the following monthly journal entry:

	Debit	*Credit*
Work in Process	$XXXX	
Raw Materials Inventory		$XXXX

(To record monthly issues of raw materials on a FIFO basis.)

A review of the journal entry as written for the more recent months disclosed that the computer had erroneously priced the detail transactions supporting the entry on a moving average rather than a FIFO basis. A review of earlier journal entries indicated that the supporting transactions had been correctly priced on a FIFO basis.

The auditor received the following comments from members of the Data Processing and Accounting Departments.

Programmer—In order to improve processing efficiency, a number of computer files were restructured and the affected software was modified accordingly. In the case of the cost accounting system, the files were converted from magnetic tape to disk. It was also determined that the FIFO pricing procedure, requiring specific lot identity, resulted in a more extensive master file than would be required for a system using only cumulative totals for pricing, that is, a moving average basis. Consequently, the new files were redesigned to eliminate the individual lot data and the pricing programs were modified to cost the issued raw material on a moving average basis. Since the printed report format had not changed, it was felt that the system had not changed from the user's perspective. Therefore, it was considered unnecessary to involve the Cost Accounting Department in the modification process. In fact, the moving average method appeared to present a more equitable method of distributing inventory costs.

Data Processing Manager—Company policy requires that changes directly affecting users be approved by the users. Changes affecting only internal activities of the Data Processing Department are considered to be purely technical items outside the responsibility and the expertise of users, and therefore do not require their approval. The file reorganization effort was inadvertently considered by Data Processing Management to be such a project. Unfortunately, since the general appearance of the report had not changed, it was considered unnecessary to inform the Cost Accounting Department of the program modification effort. The programmer assigned to the modification task was the person most familiar within the department with respect to the cost accounting application. It was felt that minimum supervision was required in the circumstances.

Cost Accounting Manager—Since the Company's financial statements were prepared on a FIFO basis, it was inappropriate to incorporate moving average pricing into the computer program. Because the report contained only one line of dollarized totals for each product, it was impossible for the recipient of the report to readily determine that the supporting details had been correctly priced on an individual basis. The programmed procedures for the FIFO calculation were extensively checked by the Cost Accounting Department at the time the system was originally implemented. Consequently, there was no reason for the Cost Accounting Department to believe that the calculations would not be performed correctly on a continuing basis.

Required:

Identify the control weaknesses that contributed to the foregoing situation and discuss how such problems could be avoided.

11–63. All user department requests for program modifications at Ideal Controls, Inc., are submitted to data processing on a program change request form. These forms are logged on receipt by data processing and assigned a sequential control number. Before the request form is sent to data processing by the user department, the manager of the user department approves the modification request. Data processing will not accept or log a modification request without a user department manager's signature.

The data processing clerk receiving and logging the modification requests distributes them to the responsible programmer. The programmer then obtains the production program documentation binder and a copy of the source version of the program from the production library, makes the coding changes, and tests the modified program. Test results are reviewed with the requesting user and a formal approval of the test results is obtained from the user.

The programmer uses the formal approval of the test results as authorization to have the modified program put into production. Placing the program into production is the responsibility of a production library control clerk. This clerk receives a copy of the user approval of the test results and the source version of the modified program from the programmer. As part of the control procedures for placing modified programs into production, this clerk recompiles the modified version of the source program and places the resulting object program on the production library. A form is sent to the user department notifying it when the modified program will begin to be used as part of normal production. A copy of this form is returned to the clerk who originally logged the request and that clerk notes the request as completed.

Required:

a. What control weaknesses, if any, may be present in this situation?
b. What are the ramifications of any weaknesses noted?
c. To what degree may the auditor place reliance on the program modification procedure?

11–64. A CPA's client, Boos & Baumkirchner, Inc., is a medium-sized manufacturer of products for the leisure time activities market (camping equipment, scuba gear, bows and arrows, etc.). During the past year, a computer system was installed, and inventory records of finished goods and parts were converted to computer processing. The inventory master file is maintained on a disk. Each record of the file contains the following information:

Item or part number
Description
Size
Unit of measure code
Quantity on hand
Cost per unit
Total value of inventory on hand at cost

Date of last sale or usage
Quantity used or sold this year
Economic order quantity
Code number of major vendor
Code number of secondary vendor

In preparation for year-end inventory, the client has two identical sets of pre-printed inventory count cards. One set is for the client's inventory counts and the other is for the CPA's use to make audit test counts. The following information has been key-punched into the cards and interpreted on their face:

- Item or part number
- Description
- Size
- Unit of measure code

In taking the year-end inventory, the client's personnel will write the actual counted quantity on the face of each card. When all counts are complete, the counted quantity will be keypunched into the cards. The cards will be processed against the disk file, and quantity-on-hand figures will be adjusted to reflect the actual count. A computer listing will be prepared to show any missing inventory count cards and all quantity adjustments of more than $100 in value. These items will be investigated by client personnel, and all required adjustments will be made. When adjustments have been completed, the final year-end balances will be computed and posted to the general ledger.

The CPA has available a general-purpose computer audit software package that will run on the client's computer and can process both card and disk files.

Required:

a. In general and without regard to the foregoing facts, discuss the nature of general-purpose computer audit software packages and list the various types and uses of such packages.

b. List and describe at least five ways a general-purpose computer audit software package can be used to assist in all aspects of the audit of the inventory of Boos & Baumkirchner, Inc. (For example, the package can be used to read the disk inventory master file and list items and parts with a high unit cost or total value. Such items can be included in the test counts to increase the dollar coverage of the audit verification.)

(AICPA adapted)

11-65. You are the auditor of a medium-sized wholesaler whose major financial asset is inventory. For the past four years you have run your generalized audit software package as part of the substantive testing of inventories.

During the current fiscal year, the company changed hardware and is currently in the process of converting all files and programs.

During discussions with the EDP manager you discover that

1. Your generalized audit software package is not compatible with the new hardware.

2. The company has purchased, and is using, an "easy-to-use" report-generator package, which is suitable only for that type of hardware.

3. A COBOL compiler is available. The two audit staff members who will work on the assignment have experience in COBOL programming.
4. The EDP manager is unhappy with the performance of the new hardware and software, and hints that a further change is a definite possibility within the next two to three years.

The audit software application involves reading multiple files and producing complex, specially formated reports. In the past, both of these tasks were handled easily and efficiently using the built-in features of the generalized audit software package, and could be easily handled by the report-generator package. The audit team is unfamiliar with the report-generator package, however. On the other hand, if customized audit programs were written using COBOL, all procedures would have to be coded by the audit staff.

Required:

Of the two possible alternatives (using the report-generator package or preparing customized audit programs), which would you choose and why? Your answer should include a discussion of the advantages and disadvantages of each alternative, given the *particular circumstances* of the audit.

11–66. The ABC Company is a medium-sized manufacturer that has approximately 1500 customers. Each month the EDP department produces a detailed listing of customers, an aged list of individual accounts, and monthly statements.

Twice each year, the auditor confirms the accounts receivable. This involves one audit assistant for two days to

- Add the listing.
- Tie the information on the listing into the balance in the control account.
- Test the individual balances to source documents.
- Select accounts for confirmation.
- Prepare audit working papers.
- Draft confirmation letters.
- Coordinate the typing, proofing, and mailing of the letters.

The engagement partner has requested that you investigate the feasibility of computerizing some of these audit procedures, all of which are now performed manually. Your generalized audit software package is already loaded on the system.

Required:

a. What information do you need to make a preliminary judgment on the feasibility of using the generalized audit software package? What further information, if any, would you need to prepare the software?
b. Would it be efficient to computerize any or all of these procedures? Why or why not? You should consider the cost and time involved, the usefulness of the technique in performing the procedures, and any possible extra benefits.

11–67. You are the auditor of a large insurance company. Each month the company calculates its earned and unearned income. This calculation is extremely complex, involving a large number of variables. Your audit objective is to ensure that the correct amount of income is recognized.

The company has a large amount of long-term debt outstanding. Interest on the debt is paid every six months. The calculation for the interest payment is extremely simple. Your audit objective is to ensure that the interest payment to individual bond-holders is correctly calculated.

Both of these objectives are to be achieved by ensuring the continued and proper operation of the programmed procedures that perform the calculations.

After discussion and investigation, you determine that there are two possible testing techniques:

1. Using test data.
2. Using generalized audit software to simulate processing.

Required:

a. What particular problems are associated with each of the techniques? What additional steps must be performed when they are used?
b. Which technique(s) would you recommend given the particular circumstances and why?

11-68. Identify control weaknesses in the following case and suggest ways of correcting those weaknesses.

Mary Jones is responsible for batching shipping documents and submitting them to EDP where the computer updates the inventory and the accounts receivable files, produces the invoices, and produces sales summaries for posting to the general ledger. Jones receives the shipping documents and batches them in groups of 20 to 50.

The number of units shipped is totaled on an adding machine tape that accompanies the batch. Periodically during the day a clerk picks up the completed batches as part of the regular interoffice mail procedures and delivers them to EDP.

The supervisor of data processing distributes the batches to clerks for input to the computer. After processing, the batches of source documents are returned to Jones in the shipping department, where they are filed by batch date. The following day, after the evening processing run, Jones receives the "Input Validation Batch Report" (an example of the report is shown below) from EDP, which indicates the adding machine total, the computer total of the batch, and a caption "accept" or "reject." If a batch has been rejected, a detail list of the batch contents is produced.

Jones reviews this report to ensure the batch units per the adding machine tape agree to the batch units accumulated by the computer and that the status is "accept." When she encounters a "reject" batch, she pulls the batch and makes the necessary corrections, reprocessing the batch at some later date through the regular processing stream.

Internal Controls
Input Validation Batch Report—Date May 10, 1987

Batch Units Adding Machine Tape	*Batch Units Accumulated by Computer*	*Status*
1,000	1,000	Accept
1,036	1,036	Accept
5,897	5,897	Accept
5,091	5,126	Reject

11-69. Read the background material for the Vader Motor Company given on the following pages. For each purpose of internal control—(a) completeness and accuracy of input,

(b) completeness and accuracy of update, (c) validity and maintenance of data—do the following:

a. Identify and explain the weaknesses, if any, in controls of the automated sales/accounts receivable system.
b. For each weakness indicate the techniques that provided control in the manual system.
c. Identify the programmed or manual procedure that should be instituted to eliminate the weakness.
d. Discuss the risk of error caused by the weaknesses that you have identified.

Vader Motor Company (VMC) is a manufacturer of small fuel-efficient, pollution-free, and extremely safe automobiles. Sales consist principally of automobiles and related parts sold to independent dealers. Once a delivery is made, the sale is final and there is no right of return. VMC has prided itself on the quality of service that it provides to its independent dealers and to consumers. No VMC automobiles have ever been recalled or had a significant mechanical breakdown.

VMC has recently introduced an automated sales/accounts receivable system to replace the old manual system that had been in place since the company was founded in 1971. The manual system had worked effectively for years with no significant problems. As the company grew, however, management decided that an automated system would be less costly and more effective. The following narrative describes the manual system and the replacement system.

VMC—Manual Sales/Accounts Receivable System

Under the old VMC manual sales/accounts receivable system, a three-part shipping document (shipper) is prepared when a truckload of automobiles leaves the plant. The shipper is filled out manually from a supply of prenumbered forms controlled by the loading dock supervisor based on information contained on the sales order obtained from the sales department. The loading dock supervisor issues shippers only on proper authorization from the sales department. The following data are entered on the shipper by loading dock personnel, who inspect the vehicles and verify the vehicle description to the invoice:

- Customer name and address.
- Vehicle registration numbers.
- Price of each vehicle or group of vehicles (from a printed manual maintained by the marketing department).
- Total sales price.
- Date of shipment.

Copies 1 and 3 are sent with the driver. Copy 1 is given to the customer and serves as the invoice. Copy 3 must be signed by the customer as evidence of receipt. Copy 2 is held in an open file by the traffic manager until the driver returns copy 3 as proof of delivery.

At the end of each day, the traffic manager routes the matched copies 2 and 3 to the accounts receivable (A/R) clerk. Corrections that are numerically controlled are also sent to the A/R clerk. The A/R clerk compares the price to the pricing manual (printed manual maintained by marketing) and posts the sale to the A/R subledger, which is kept in alphabetical order by customer name. Also, the A/R clerk reviews corrections for proper approval and posts corrections to the A/R subledger. All postings are coded by their source (that is, shipping order number and date of correction). Copy 2 is filed alphabetically by customer name and copy 3 and the corrections are filed numerically. All filing is done after the A/R subledger has been reviewed by the A/R supervisor.

Cash receipts are received and summarized daily by the mail clerk. Checks and remittance advices are then photocopied and forwarded to the collections clerk (the cash receipts and the related summary are sent to the Treasury Department for preparation of the deposit). The collection clerk matches each receipt to the appropriate invoice entry in the A/R subledger and then records the receipt as a credit next to the related debit. If any question arises regarding the appropriate application, the collection clerk will telephone the customer. The cash receipt documents are then filed in the related customer's file after the day's activity and A/R subledger have been reviewed by the A/R supervisor.

At the end of each day, the A/R supervisor foots all cash applications and agrees the total to the cash deposit validated by the bank. At the end of each month, the A/R clerk prepares an aged statement for each customer (detailing all outstanding invoices) on a two-part form. Each statement is reviewed by the A/R supervisor. Copy 1 is sent to the customer and copy 2 is filed in the customer's file. The A/R supervisor foots the month's additions to the numerical file of sales invoices and corrections and posts the totals to the general ledger (the A/R control account and sales). The completeness of the numerical file is also verified. The accounting manager then reconciles the subledger to the general ledger.

VMC—Automated Sales/Accounts Receivable System

A three-part shipper/invoice is manually prepared when a truckload of automobiles leaves the plant. All procedures at the loading dock are identical to those for the old manual system except that

1. Sales orders are input via a CRT terminal on receipt in the sales department and maintained for future reference on the sales file.
2. At the end of each day, all the number 2 copies of the shipper/invoice are batched and sent to the data processing department for data entry.
3. The number 3 copies of the shipper/invoice, when returned by the driver, are sent to accounting and filed by customer.
4. The sales price and customer address are obtained from the computer via a CRT terminal.

Changes to the master file can be executed from any of the company's 10 terminals so that updated information may be input promptly.

Data processing enters the customer name, vehicle registration number, date of shipment, and vehicle price via the terminal. Each day the computer performs the following programmed procedures:

- Foots the individual sales amount on each invoice and compares the total with the total shown on the invoice.
- Posts the total amount to the A/R subledger computer file by matching the customer name to names existing on the file. (If no match is obtained, a new customer account is created.)
- Creates an entry in the sales file maintained by the computer.

At month-end, the total from the sales file is posted automatically to Accounts Receivable and Sales in the general ledger and a Sales Register is printed.

Cash receipts are received by the mail clerk. The mail clerk prepares a prenumbered "cash remittance input form" for each receipt, an "input control form," and a bank deposit ticket. (The "cash remittance input form" includes customer names submitted and numerical sequence of forms used.) The mail clerk compares the deposit ticket to the "input control form" for agreement of amount and enters the numerical sequence of "cash remittance input forms" used into a log book for future completeness checks. The documents are then distributed as follows:

- To the Treasury Department for daily deposits into the bank:
  Checks and deposit ticket
- To Accounting for input via the terminal:
  Cash remittance input forms
  Input control form

The following programmed procedures are performed by the computer:

- Reviews the numerical sequence and foots the amounts of "cash remittance input forms," and agrees the information to the "input control form." (If the information is not in agreement, an edit report is printed.)
- For accepted batches, compares the remittance to the A/R subledger computer file by matching the customer name, invoice number, and vehicle identification number. (If the information does not match, the computer prints an edit report indicating discrepancies and showing the total amount accepted and an unapplied cash report.)
- Posts the accepted remittances by matching customer name, invoice number, and vehicle identification number to the A/R subledger file and totals the amounts posted. (A daily report is generated showing total cash receipts posted.)
- Creates an entry in a computer file of cash receipts for all accepted transactions. (The cash file is automatically posted monthly to accounts receivable and cash in the general ledger; additionally, a daily report is generated showing the change in the cash receipts file, and at month-end a Cash Receipts Journal is printed by the computer.)

On a daily basis, the accounting clerk resolves the errors noted on the edit reports and enters the corrected information via the terminal. Corrected information is approved by the accounting manager.

In addition, the clerk compares the amount accepted on the edit report with the amounts posted to the A/R subledger and cash receipts file. The clerk investigates any differences and makes corrections, again approved by the accounting manager.

Each day, edit routines reject a number of invoice/shippers because they are mathematically incorrect. This occurs because of errors in the invoices or errors in entering the data on the invoices. The rejected items are printed out each morning and sent to the appropriate clerk for correction and resubmission during the clerk's spare time. Resubmitted items are processed exactly like the original documents.

At the end of each month, the computer generates a statement (detailing all outstanding invoices) for each customer with an outstanding balance on the A/R subledger file, and a report listing the customer's account balance (A/R subledger). The statements are delivered to the mail room for prompt issuance.

When a complaint is received from a customer regarding a billing error, a corrections clerk in the A/R department will prepare a "correction request" form and file it in an open bin to await investigation. If subsequent investigation discloses that a correction is in order, the investigation clerk will prepare a two-part prenumbered correction input form. Copy 1 is sent to the A/R clerk, who summarizes all such forms for the month and prepares a "net" entry to the general ledger. Copy 2 is sent to the accounting manager for approval. The accounting manager signs the form as evidence of approval and then returns it to the corrections clerk, who sends it to EDP, where it is input and updated to the A/R subledger file.

The accounts receivable software operates on an "overlay" system whereby when a correction is processed, the item being corrected is erased from the file and the new information is put in its place.

At month-end, the A/R manager reconciles the computer-printed A/R subledger to the general ledger and prepares a list of reconciling items. Additionally, at month-end an accounting clerk independent of cash receipts or receivables reconciles cash per the general ledger to the bank statements.

In order to ensure efficient processing and development of modifications to the software, VMC has a computer specialist who is responsible for both programming and operating the computer. Requests for program modifications are sent to him for implementation when time permits.

Much to the dismay of VMC management, problems began to surface almost as soon as the automated sales/accounts receivable system was introduced. The first month after the new system was installed, the A/R subledger could not be reconciled to the general ledger control account. The accounting manager who always performs this reconciliation was unable to explain what had gone wrong. Shortly after the first computer-printed statements were sent to VMC's customers, complaints began to pour in, claiming that paid invoices were included on the statements.

Part 3
Auditing Specific Cycles and Accounts

Chapter 12
Auditing the Revenue Cycle

Revenue transactions that are completed within a relatively short period of time—when sale, delivery, and collection occur within a few weeks or months of each other—are the most common revenue transactions and are the subject of this chapter. Accounts encompassed by the revenue cycle are defined and described. Typical revenue transactions and internal controls over them are then presented in detail, followed by a discussion of the audit objectives and audit strategy for the revenue cycle. Subsequent sections of the chapter present specific compliance and substantive tests that may be used in auditing revenue transactions and related account balances, including auditing procedures for specialized types of revenues.

Definitions and Accounts Related to the Revenue Cycle

Revenues are generally given descriptive labels in financial statements. For example, a manufacturing or retail enterprise calls its revenue transactions "sales." Revenues in a service organization may be referred to as fees or commissions, rents or royalties, or tuition or dues, or even more generally as "revenues" or "service revenues." In a governmental service organization, revenues may be referred to as grants or appropriations. Accounts related to ancillary revenue transactions include dividends and interest (including lessor income), gains from the sale of nonproduct assets, such as property, and by-product sales.

Most companies have one or more major sources of revenues and several less significant types of miscellaneous revenues, commonly referred to as "other income." The term used for a given type of revenue depends on the principal business activities of an enterprise. For example, sales of transformers by an electrical supply company would be "sales," whereas such transactions would be "other income" to an electric utility. Conversely, interest and dividends from investments would be "other income" to almost all enterprises except investment companies, for which interest and dividends are a primary source of revenues.

If sales of products are the primary source of revenues, certain marketing and collection techniques are often used to increase sales and speed up the collection period. For example, guarantees and warranties are often given; returns are allowed if the customer is not completely satisfied or an allowance may be given if the goods were damaged; discounts may be available to customers who pay promptly. Management monitors such policies by establishing accounts for sales discounts, returns, and allowances.

Numerous balance sheet and income statement accounts are affected by transactions in the revenue cycle. The most significant of these is accounts receivable. Accounts receivable are generally short-term assets, often outstanding for little more than the amount of time needed for sellers and buyers to process transactions—shipping, billing, receiving, processing the invoice for payment, and processing and recording the cash receipt. Accounts receivable also generally include claims arising from transactions not related to sales to customers in the ordinary course of business, such as sales of plant and equipment or investments, or loans to employees and other non-customers.

Valid accounts receivable, properly recorded and maintained, provide no assurance, however, of collectibility. Accordingly, the allowance for doubtful accounts and related bad debt expense accounts are additional accounts in the revenue cycle. The balance of accounts receivable, net of the allowance for doubtful accounts, provides an estimate of the net realizable value of the receivables, while the bad debt expense account indicates the effect of evaluating the allowance at the end of the current period.

The unearned revenue and deferred income accounts reflect various kinds of advance receipts for goods and services not yet delivered, such as prepayments from customers for goods to be delivered in the future, advance payments on transportation or entertainment ticket sales, and magazine subscriptions.

T-accounts are presented in Figure 12.1 to illustrate the transactions and accounts encompassed by a typical revenue cycle.

Figure 12.1 Revenue Cycle Accounts

Balance Sheet Accounts		*Income Statement Accounts*	
Cash		**Sales**	
Beginning balance			Cash sales
Cash sales			Sales on account
Collections from customers			Sales previously paid for
Advances by customers		**Sales Discounts**	
Accounts Receivable		Discounts allowed for prompt payment	
Beginning balance	Payments by customers		
Sales on account	Return of merchandise	**Sales Returns and Allowances**	
Ending balance	Write-off of uncollectible accounts	Return of merchandise	
		Bad Debt Expense	
Allowance for Doubtful Accounts		Estimated bad debt expense for year	
Write-off of uncollectible accounts	Beginning balance		
	Estimated bad debt expense for year		
	Ending balance		
Unearned Revenue			
Delivery of goods previously paid for	Beginning balance		
	Advances by customers		
	Ending balance		

Note: Inventory and cost of sales accounts are covered in Chapter 14. Figure 12.1 assumes that the periodic inventory system is used.

Typical Transactions and Internal Control

The revenue cycle in most contemporary businesses can be classified into three typical transaction types:

- Sales of goods and services.
- Payments received for goods and services.
- Goods returned by and claims received from customers.

Sales of Goods and Services

The process of selling goods and services generally includes the following steps:

- Receiving customers' orders.
- Authorizing credit terms and discounts and accepting orders.
- Preparing order forms.
- Preparing execution instructions.
- Executing orders: withdrawing goods from stock, packing and shipping goods, or dispatching services.
- Preparing invoices.
- Billing customers.

The objective of accounting controls over these steps is to ensure that all valid sales transactions are processed accurately after they have been authorized; administrative controls, on the other hand, are concerned with processing customers' sales orders from the time they are received until they are authorized. An unauthorized shipment is likely to result in financial statement misstatements of the sales and accounts receivable accounts. A valid sales order that was not processed at all does not result in financial statement errors, but does result in lost revenues. Accordingly, the authorization of credit terms should be viewed as an administrative control with accounting and auditing significance rather than as an accounting control; lack of a policy that requires approval of credit leads to potential bad debts, but does not have a direct impact on the completeness, validity, and accuracy of revenue transactions. The client should have a control procedure to ensure that appropriate adjustments for bad debts are made at the end of the period; the auditor should undertake procedures to obtain the necessary assurance that the allowance for doubtful accounts and related bad debt expense accounts are fairly stated.

Receiving Customers' Orders. A customer usually prepares a purchase order, which provides authorization for an outside vendor to provide a product or service. A purchase order initiates two independent processes. For the buying enterprise, a purchase order begins the "buying cycle," which is discussed in depth in Chapter 13. For the selling enterprise, a customer's purchase order starts the "revenue cycle." When received, the customer's purchase order may go directly to the credit department for approval or may be logged in a sales order book, usually by the sales department, for subsequent use in following up on unprocessed customer orders. Customer orders may also be verbal and may be received by salespeople. A log of such orders is also usually maintained for follow-up. The log acts primarily as an administrative control to ensure that orders from credit-worthy customers are filled as promptly as possible. If orders are received by sales personnel, the sales usually involve a sales commission. Since it is in the salesperson's best interest to follow up on unprocessed customer orders, valid sales orders received by salespeople are rarely unprocessed. In any event, communication between the initial sales contact and the next step in the selling process, usually the credit department, is essential to prevent valid sales orders from not being processed.

Authorizing Credit Terms and Discounts and Accepting Orders. Procedures for authorizing credit vary among companies but certain practices are similar in most credit departments. Orders from repeat customers with a good record of payment, unless in excess of historical order amounts, are usually routinely processed. The credit department should determine, by referring to published sources or by requesting audited financial statements, whether a customer's financial condition has deteriorated. The same means are used to ascertain a new customer's credit worthiness. Many companies establish minimum sales order amounts before a credit check is performed and credit extended. In any event, credit approval should be evidenced in writing by the credit manager or other designated individual.

Accounting control over sales begins when all necessary approvals have been obtained, the order has been accepted, and the shipment of goods or the rendering of services is authorized. The sequence in which these steps occur varies from enterprise to enterprise, and it may or may not include the administrative control of credit approval, as explained. Acceptance of the sales order and authorization to ship are basic controls that should be subject to supervision and review by responsible personnel. Acceptance of the order and authorization to ship (and supervisory review of those functions) may be noted on the customer's purchase order, on the sales order form discussed next, or on a separate form called a shipping order.

Preparing Order Forms. No two customer purchase orders received will be in exactly the same format. Thus, to facilitate processing, customer orders (both written and verbal) are usually transcribed onto a uniform internal sales order form. This step may be done earlier in the system, possibly as soon as the order is received. If the order form is prepared early in the process, it can be used to facilitate control over sales orders. The order form can be compared with the customer's purchase order for accuracy and completeness, and all subsequent authorizations and approvals can be evidenced on the form. Effective control over the completeness of processing of sales orders can be achieved with the aid of many alternative procedures, such as by numerical sequencing of the sales order forms, using prenumbered forms; a holding file, for example, a backlog listing of open customers' orders; or an open file of control copies of order forms from which fully processed orders are deleted periodically. In each case, the control consists of periodic review of the sequencing or the file by a responsible person.

Preparing Execution Instructions. The steps in executing an order are usually requisitioning, packing, shipping, and invoicing, all of which should be preceded by an authorization to ship. A customer's order may be requisitioned from stored finished goods inventory, from the factory by means of a production order, or from suppliers by means of a purchase order. A packing slip is needed to instruct the proper department to gather and prepare the order for shipment. Formal authorization is needed for the shipping department to prepare routing, to schedule necessary transportation, and to authorize release of the goods. Each department needs sufficient copies of the instructions to enable it to advise related departments of its action and also to retain in its own files evidence of performance.

Control over execution should be through numerical sequencing, a holding file, or both. If execution involves a number of steps, a holding file is preferable because it affords ready access to information on uncompleted transactions. In many systems, it is useful to prepare and partially complete the invoice (described later) as part of preparing the execution instructions; the invoice can then serve as a holding file for control over the other execution steps. Sometimes invoices are not prepared until requisitioning, packing, and shipping have been completed; then a copy of the order form serves as a holding file. Either way, the control operation consists of matching the control file with notices of performance by each of the executing departments and examining the file periodically to discover and investigate incomplete transactions.

Executing Orders: Withdrawing Goods from Stock, Packing and Shipping Goods, or Dispatching Services. Control within the executing departments is most often operational in nature and consists of a procedure similar to that described in the previous step: reviewing a holding file of execution instructions, which are canceled by notice of performance, and investigating long outstanding items.

Control outside the executing departments is likewise maintained by comparing documents received from the executing departments evidencing performance (such as shipping documents or completed execution instructions noting shipment) with the holding file of original execution instructions, by accounting for the numerical sequence of documents, or both. This control should be performed frequently, and unmatched documents or documents that are unaccounted for should be investigated to ensure that all shipments result in timely preparation of an invoice and billing, and recording of sales and accounts receivable.

Preparing Invoices and Billing Customers. These steps generally initiate the formal recording of revenue transactions for accounting purposes. Control over originating invoices is established by authorization to bill, which in turn is based on proper supporting documents: customer's order, sales order form, shipping order, and so on. Billing authorization is often ''automated'' by originating an invoice automatically when the supporting documents are accumulated. Controls over the accuracy and validity of invoice data should be provided. For example, in a manual system:

- Quantities should be based on actual records of goods shipped or services performed and should be reviewed by a person other than the person who records shipments.
- Prices should be based on approved sales orders or price lists and should be reviewed by persons independent of the sales function.

- Extensions and additions should be recomputed by someone independent of invoice preparation.
- Customers' names should be compared with the master customers' list or customer orders.

Many of these procedures are performed by the computer in EDP systems. Programmed control procedures remove the need for manual recomputations and reviews to ensure accuracy.

Since invoices are the basis for recording sales and accounts receivable, accountability over them is imperative. Numerical sequencing is generally used for accountability over individual invoices, and control totals are used for posting to the accounts receivable control account and subsidiary ledger. A typical control technique used to ensure the completeness of recorded sales transactions is periodic accounting for prenumbered shipping documents and sales invoices, with investigation of unmatched items by a person independent of the shipping and billing functions. Many automated systems produce "missing items" reports that are used for follow-up. Whether manual or automated, the investigation and resolution process should be documented and periodically reviewed by supervisory personnel.

A common technique for controlling the maintenance of the accounts receivable control account and subsidiary ledger is periodic comparison of the subsidiary ledger with the general ledger control account by a person independent of the billing and cash receipts functions and supervisory review of the comparison procedure.

Absent or ineffective controls in the invoice and billing step can result in critical errors. For example:

- Goods shipped or services performed but not invoiced could cause an understatement of revenues and accounts receivable, with a potential overstatement of inventory.
- Fictitious or invalid transactions could be recorded, causing an overstatement of revenues and receivables.
- Errors on invoices or shipping documents could go undetected, causing an under- or overstatement of revenues, receivables, or inventory.
- Errors in recording transactions in the subsidiary and control accounts could result in the misstatement of related balances. (Errors or delays in posting could also affect the collectibility of receivables.)

Management Reviews. Because management is often particularly concerned about sales of goods and services, top management may review sales and budgetary reports. For example, reviews typically encountered in the revenue cycle include, but are not limited to, the following:

- Comparison of actual sales with budgets or forecasts.
- Comparison of actual gross margins with budgets.
- Comparison of actual write-offs, credit memoranda, and other noncash reductions of receivables with budgets and historical information.

- Review of the aging of accounts receivable.
- Periodic review of unfilled sales commitments.

The revenue portion of the budget often receives the most critical review by top management. Actual sales, in both dollars and volume, are usually compared with budget, with explanations provided for fluctuations. These reports are generally broken down by salesperson or account executive and are related to sales force productivity reports. Top management often requests personal meetings with salespeople and account executives to discuss sales trends and delinquent accounts, and to encourage the penetration of new sales areas. Expense accounts are often reviewed to determine whether entertainment and other expenses are resulting in increased revenues.

Payments Received for Goods and Services

Payments received for goods and services generally include the following steps:

- Receiving cash and depositing it in the bank.
- Comparing amounts remitted with invoice amounts.
- Authorizing discounts and allowances.
- Posting accounts receivable.
- Preparing debit memoranda.

Receiving the Cash and Depositing It in the Bank. Cash received by mail is usually in the form of checks; cash received over the counter, by collectors, or by salespeople may be in the form of either currency or checks. Since cash and checks are easily transferred, the primary control objectives in the receipt stage are completeness of recording and safeguarding of all receipts. The first step in establishing control over cash receipts is to list them. Collections by mail should be listed showing names and amounts (the customer's bill stub is commonly used for that purpose); receipts over the counter may be listed on cash register tapes or counter sales slips prepared in the presence of customers; cash received from collectors or salespeople and not accompanied by listings should also be listed on receipt. Counter sales slips, cashiers' receipts, and collectors' receipts should be prenumbered, and the numerical sequence should be accounted for.

If more than one list or batch is prepared in a day, they should be identified for accountability, for example, by batch number. Lists of receipts should be totaled, usually at least daily, and the totals should be compared with the corresponding totals of cash and checks received, cash book totals, deposit slip totals, and totals of credits to accounts receivable or sales control accounts.

Since cash received should be deposited promptly in a bank account, items that are not suitable for immediate deposit, such as postdated checks or checks containing errors in amounts, should be separately listed and the two lists later reconciled with the deposit.

Receipts should be recorded promptly and those at branch offices should be reported immediately to the main office. If receipts flow from a number of sources, such as collection departments, cash registers, vending machines, and ticket sellers, procedures should be adopted to ensure the inclusion of receipts from all locations daily. For example, a control form or checklist can be used to highlight missing entries.

Good internal accounting control over cash receipts requires that persons who record amounts in cash receipts books or prepare bank deposits should be independent of those who post the related credits to accounts receivable records and general ledger accounts. Similarly, persons independent of other cash functions should prepare the initial detail listings of cash receipts and should obtain authenticated duplicate deposit slips from banks and compare them in total with cash book entries, listings of cash receipts, receivable control account totals, and credits on bank statements.

Checks should be endorsed as soon as they are received, using an endorsement stamp including the notation ''For Deposit Only.'' Each day's cash receipts should be deposited intact and without delay; authorized exclusions, as separately listed, should be reconciled with original listings and delivered to a responsible independent employee for review and disposition.

Deposit or collection items charged back by a bank as uncollectible should be delivered to an employee other than those who make deposits or record accounts receivable credits. Items charged back by a bank should be investigated by someone who has no responsibility for either cash operations or entries in cash books. Banks should be instructed not to cash checks or money orders drawn to the order of the company or to accept them for deposit in payroll or other special accounts. Cash receipts of branch offices should be deposited in a bank account subject to withdrawal only by the main office.

Use of a ''lock box'' system—a service offered by many banks to reduce cash transit time, thus increasing the funds available to a company—also improves accounting control over cash receipts. Company personnel do not have access to cash receipts because customers send their remittances to a post office box under control of the bank. The bank records deposits and furnishes the company with remittance advices and statement stubs or other correspondence from customers that serve to identify the receipts. Thus, both separation of functions and custodial control of cash are enhanced.

The total cash received is generally entered by source (such as cash sale or payment from customer) in a cash receipts journal or other book of original entry that serves as the basis for posting to the general ledger control accounts. The detail lists, on the other hand, are often used as the source documents for updating the detail subsidiary ledgers. Later in the control process, independent supervisory personnel should compare the total of cash received per the numerically controlled listings, the bank deposits, and the postings to the cash receipts journal and general ledger control accounts. This comparison may be performed by the person who does the bank reconciliations.

Comparing Amounts Remitted with Invoice Amounts. This procedure is generally performed by the person responsible for maintaining the accounts receivable subsidiary ledger. The comparison is important to ascertain if credits for sales returns or allowances were taken and, if so, whether they were authorized. The comparison also discloses whether discounts taken by customers were within the discount period, whether the receipt was applied to the correct customer's account, and whether there are any potential disputes regarding amounts due. Discrepancies should be investigated and documentation of the resolution should be reviewed by supervisory personnel.

Authorizing Discounts and Allowances. Discounts and allowances represent noncash reductions of the recorded invoice and receivable amount. Discounts taken by customers should be reviewed to ascertain their validity (that they are within stated terms) and proper amount. In some companies, discounts are routine and the approval and recording function is well systematized. Allowances, on the other hand, are less frequent, more difficult to ascertain, and often based on evaluations of customer complaints. Allowances should be controlled by policies specifying who may authorize them and under what conditions. Forms and reporting procedures should be adopted to establish prompt authorization, approval, and documentation of allowances. Investigation of uncollected receivables may reveal unrecorded allowances.

Nonroutine discounts and allowances taken by customers should be approved by supervisory personnel independent of persons who receive cash or checks and maintain the accounts receivable detail ledger. Documentation of approval is ordinarily noted on prenumbered credit memoranda, which should be accounted for by reviewing the numerical sequence for missing numbers.

Posting Accounts Receivable. Accounts receivable should be posted based on receipt of cash, authorized discounts and allowances, write-offs of uncollectible accounts, and goods returned for credit. Credits to receivables should be based on valid transactions that have been approved, and must be complete and accurate to generate reliable control account and detail subsidiary ledger records. Posting to the accounts receivable subsidiary ledger should be performed by persons independent of cash functions; the general ledger control account is generally posted by someone other than the person who relieves the accounts receivable subsidiary ledger. This segregation serves as a control over both validity and accuracy; its effectiveness is typically ensured by periodic reconciliation of the control account and subsidiary ledger (either performed or reviewed by someone independent of the account maintenance function). Validity and accuracy are also enhanced by periodic mailing of customer statements and review of the aging of receivables by the credit department and financial management.

The control account is typically credited periodically based on posting of receipts from the cash receipts journal, approved journal entries for discounts and allowances, returned merchandise, and write-offs of uncollectible accounts. In some cases, the credit is based on the listings of cash received and various credit memoranda. The subsidiary ledger is credited based on the detail listings (such as receipts, discounts and allowances, and journal vouchers) that support the total used in crediting the control account. Typically, a person independent of the posting procedure prepares or reviews a reconciliation of credits to the subsidiary ledger and credits to the control accounts.

Preparing Debit Memoranda. Chargebacks for unauthorized discounts and allowances often result from the foregoing steps. Debit memoranda should be prepared for all disputes resolved in favor of the company; they should be authorized by a responsible company official and controlled as a basis for supporting the restoration of receivable balances. Since debit memoranda often indicate some form of dispute between the company and customer, they should be closely monitored by a key person in financial management and by the credit department. Typically, debit memoranda are numerically controlled and accounted for much in the same way as credit memoranda and invoices, with periodic reconciliations of outstanding items in a holding file to the detail receivables subsidiary ledger.

Goods Returned by and Claims Received from Customers

The third transaction type in the revenue cycle provides for authorization and execution of returns and claims. These transactions are often less well controlled than sales or receipt transactions: Returns and claims are likely to be sporadic, problematic, and lacking in common characteristics. Accordingly, it is important to establish control over returns and claims as early as possible. Since returned goods represent an asset to the company and result in relief of receivables, many of the same procedures and controls described earlier for receipt transactions are relevant.

Typically, goods returned by customers and the processing of claims are handled in the following steps:

- Receiving and accepting goods or claims.
- Preparing receiving reports.
- Reviewing claims.
- Authorizing credits.
- Preparing and mailing credit memoranda.

Receiving and Accepting Goods or Claims. Receipt of goods returned for credit is handled by the receiving department. Returned goods may go through the same receiving routine as other receipts of goods or may be processed through a separate receiving area, inspection procedure, and paperwork system. The critical function in this step is counting, inspecting, and noting quantities and condition as a basis for later determining the credit to be given the customer and whether the goods need repair or can be placed back in stock.

Preparing Receiving Reports. Receiving reports are essential means of documenting and establishing control over goods returned. Generally, they are completed when goods are received. They should be prepared on prenumbered reports by persons independent of the shipping function and subsequently accounted for by persons independent of the shipping and receiving functions. All pertinent data should be recorded, such as customer name, date, description of items returned or nature of claim, original invoice number and price (if appropriate), quantities, and description of the general condition and reason for return. If appropriate, reports are preferably completed in the presence of the customer to ensure that all customer complaints are recognized.

Reviewing Claims. After goods have been received and accounted for by the receiving department, the related claims are reviewed by a customer service department that is independent of the receiving function. This procedure establishes the validity of claims for goods returned and determines the amount of credit, if any, to be granted. Sometimes the customer service department prepares credit memoranda for approval by the credit, sales, and accounting departments. In other organizations, the results of the inspection and review are noted directly on the receiving reports and forwarded to the three departments for final authorization.

Authorizing Credits. Final authorization of credits should be determined by the sales department. This approval should be made only on the basis of receiving reports and after careful independent and documented inspection of goods. The approval should be evidenced on the receiving and inspection reports. To avoid conflicts of interests, there should also be operating policies for an independent review of any credit memoranda initiated solely by the sales department.

Preparing and Mailing Credit Memoranda. Credit memoranda should be prepared only on the basis of authorized and approved receiving and inspection reports, by individuals, preferably in the sales department, other than those who receive cash and record accounts receivable. Credit memoranda should be numerically controlled, and quantities, terms, prices, and extensions should be reviewed for accuracy before mailing, by someone other than the preparer. Listings of credit memoranda issued, containing all pertinent data, should be prepared to support the appropriate journal entry and for posting the accounts receivable subsidiary ledger.

Returns and claims should be recorded in the accounts as promptly as possible, to correct the balances of revenues and accounts receivable. There is a natural inclination to delay the processing of returns; periodic review of the open file of receiving reports is a preferred control technique for identifying valid but unprocessed claims.

Planning the Audit Strategy

Audit Objectives

The objectives of auditing procedures for the revenue cycle are to provide evidential matter that is sufficient and competent to give the auditor reasonable assurance that

- Revenue and related expense accounts such as bad debt expense and warranty expense include all transactions applicable to the period.
- Accounts receivable are authentic and represent amounts that are probable of collection and to which the entity is legally entitled.
- Judgments on which valuation allowances are based represent a reasonable evaluation of known facts.
- Descriptions, classifications, and related disclosures are adequate and not misleading.

Audit Strategy

As discussed in Chapter 8, developing an audit strategy requires developing an understanding of the control environment and the flow of transactions through the client's systems. The methods used to develop this understanding involve a review of prior-year working papers, if available, and interviews of knowledgeable client personnel. These procedures normally reveal information about all significant cycles and account balances.

In addition to the general information obtained regarding management's philosophy and style, the control environment, and the predominant means of processing transactions (manually or by computer) and the level of its sophistication, the auditor should obtain the following specific information related to the revenue cycle:

- The predominant means of generating revenues.
- The volume and dollar amount of sales and the number of customers to whom the company sells.
- The historical trend of the volume of sales.
- The historical trend of the accounts receivable aging and receivable turnover ratios.
- The usual credit and discount terms.

The information enables the auditor to make an initial evaluation for each type of transaction about whether it is likely to be effective and efficient to rely on specific controls to reduce the level of substantive tests. If the control system appears to be adequate, in light of the risks involved, the auditor identifies controls over sales orders, shipping documents, invoices, and cash collections, and the extent to which duties are segregated, and evaluates the design of those controls, with the ultimate goal of performing compliance tests to determine whether those controls can in fact be relied on. Alternatively, even if controls appear to be strong, the auditor may decide that it would be more efficient to perform extensive substantive tests, as would normally be the case if the client has low volume or predominantly high dollar value transactions.

The use of substantive tests of accounts that are integral to the revenue cycle must be considered in developing the audit strategy. For example, if controls over the shipping, billing, and collection process are deemed adequate and there is a large number of customers, the auditor is likely to perform a combination of compliance tests and limited substantive tests of accounts receivable balances. If controls are deemed inadequate or there are a few large customers, the auditor may decide that extensive substantive testing is appropriate.

Analytical reviews of revenue, accounts receivable, and related accounts are often a particularly useful tool in the planning phase of the audit. As discussed in Chapter 9, analytical review procedures can, for example, indicate trends in sales, returns, and collection of receivables that may assist the auditor in assessing potential audit risks. For example:

- An unexplained unusual variation in month-to-month sales may indicate a breakdown in internal controls that may result in the auditor concluding that substantive tests should be directed at revenue account balances, with emphasis on revenue transaction cutoffs at year-end.

- A substantial deterioration in the aged receivables may indicate the need for extended substantive tests of the validity and collectibility of account balances.

- An unexplained unusual variation in gross margins between periods may indicate a breakdown in controls in either the revenue or production cycle, necessitating extended substantive tests.

Analytical procedures frequently highlight relationships between accounts and risks not otherwise apparent from other planning techniques; their use often results in more informed decisions in selecting the audit strategy. Discussing the results of analytical procedures with company personnel may also give the auditor insight into the quality of the control environment. Analytical reviews as substantive tests are discussed later in this chapter.

Professional judgment is required in selecting an effective and efficient strategy. The following examples demonstrate the thought process and documentation the auditor should use in developing the appropriate audit strategy for the revenue cycle in two different situations.

- Revenue is generated from the manufacture and sale of golf clubs. Sales to retailers are somewhat seasonal, with 75 percent occurring in the spring and summer months, and orders are usually for large numbers of items of low dollar value. The system of controls over sales transactions appears adequate for audit reliance. Therefore, the controls are evaluated and compliance tests designed and carried out in October after the peak season. The compliance tests focus primarily on the operation of controls during the peak sales season. At year-end, the compliance tests will be updated and limited substantive tests, primarily analytical reviews of fluctuations in sales and gross margins during the intervening period, will be performed.

- Sales are generally on account to established customers with good credit histories. Terms are ''net 30'' with few collection problems, and because of the seasonal nature of sales and receivables, receivable balances at year-end are minimal (historically, 5 percent of total assets). Therefore, substantive testing of year-end balances is considered the most efficient audit approach and consists primarily of confirming selected accounts and testing subsequent receipts.

Ancillary revenues from interest on temporary investments or savings accounts, income from investments, gains from the sale of noninventory assets, and rental income from leasing idle equipment are generally subjected to substantive tests rather than compliance tests. Ancillary revenues are less likely to be subject to sophisticated systems of control than are revenues from operations, are generally not significant, and are usually more efficiently audited as part of the audit of the balance sheet accounts to which they relate. There are exceptions, of course, for which the auditor designs compliance tests necessary to meet specific control objectives.

Compliance Tests

The key to determining the appropriate compliance tests is to identify the specific control objectives applicable to a particular transaction type. Once these control objectives have been identified, professional judgment is required in selecting for compliance testing those controls that the auditor plans to rely on to limit the extent of substantive testing.

Sales of Goods and Services

Compliance tests applicable to sales of goods and services are discussed from the perspective of the steps involved in selling goods and services. The tests are also summarized in Figure 12.2 according to the objectives of internal accounting control—completeness, validity, accuracy, maintenance, and physical security—to which those tests are related.

Sales Order Control. The sales order control function generally includes the first four steps in a typical revenue cycle: receiving customers' orders, authorizing credit terms and discounts and accepting orders (including authorization to ship goods or perform services), preparing order forms, and confirming orders. The most important of those steps from the auditor's point of view is that of accepting customers' orders. The auditor is also usually concerned with controls over authorizing credit terms because of the risk of uncollectible receivables if controls over authorizing credit are ineffective. Accordingly, when compliance tests are performed, the auditor invariably examines evidence of credit department approval of a sample of invoices and determines that they were approved in compliance with company policy.

The results of that test assist the auditor in evaluating the client's allowance for doubtful accounts. For example, amounts due from sales made to potentially high credit-risk customers close to year-end would be classified as current in the accounts receivable aged trial balance, which normally would not indicate a potential collection problem. In the absence of controls over granting

Figure 12.2 Sales of Goods and Services: Control Objectives, Potential Errors, Accounting Controls, and Compliance Tests

	General Objectives of Internal Accounting Control				
	Completeness	Validity	Accuracy	Maintenance	Physical Security
Specific objectives of internal accounting control	All valid sales transactions are processed and recorded.	All recorded sales transactions represent actual shipments of goods or rendering of services to nonfictitious customers as authorized by responsible personnel.	Sales are accurately recorded as to amounts, quantities, dates, and customers in the proper period in books of original entry and detail subsidiary records, and are accurately summarized in the general ledger.	The accounts receivable subsidiary ledger and general ledger control account are in agreement, do not contain any posting errors, and reflect all authorized transactions and only those transactions.	*Note:* The physical security control objective relates principally to the proper control and release of items from inventory and is not directly applicable to this transaction type. However, adequate physical controls over finished goods shipments are necessary to ensure that all valid shipments are recorded (see principal control techniques for achieving the completeness objective). Physical controls over inventories are discussed further in conjunction with the production cycle in Chapter 14.

Potential errors in account balances from absent or ineffective controls	Goods may be shipped or services performed but not recorded, causing an understatement of revenues, receivables, and cost of sales, and an overstatement of inventory and income.	Fictitious or otherwise invalid transactions may be recorded, resulting in an overstatement of revenues, receivables, and income.	Errors on sales invoices or shipping documents may go undetected, causing an understatement or overstatement of revenues, receivables, or inventory. Transactions may be misclassified in the accounts; sales and/or cost of sales may be recorded in the wrong period.	Revenues and accounts receivable may be either understated or overstated because the control account balance is not in agreement with the subsidiary ledger. Even if these records are in agreement, the subsidiary ledger may contain mispostings of correct amounts to the wrong customer account.	Not directly applicable to this transaction type.
Principal control techniques Legend: B = Basic control (other than physical control) D = Division of duties S = Supervisory control P = Physical control	Physical controls over finished goods inventories requiring appropriate documentation, and physical inspection of all shipments prior to their leaving the storage area (P). Periodic accounting for prenumbered shipping documents and sales invoices, including investigation and resolu-	Authorization for shipment of goods or performance of services, prices, and terms (B). Review of shipping documents and sales invoices for evidence of authorization, particularly for transactions subject to special terms or specified amounts, by responsible supervisory personnel indepen-	Examination of shipping documents and sales invoices for quantities shipped, prices, dates, customers, terms, extensions, and footings by personnel independent of the shipping, billing, and inventory control functions (B). Review and approval of invoices over specified	Periodic reconciliations of the accounts receivable subsidiary ledger to the general ledger control account by personnel independent of the billing and cash receipts functions (B). Review of reconciliation procedures and results by responsible supervisory personnel (S).	

(Continued)

Figure 12.2 Continued

	General Objectives of Internal Accounting Control				
	Completeness	Validity	Accuracy	Maintenance	Physical Security
	tion of unmatched items, by persons independent of the shipping and billing functions (B). Periodic review and approval of results of above procedure by responsible supervisory personnel (S).	dent of the shipping and inventory control functions (D,S).	amounts by responsible supervisory personnel independent of the shipping, billing, and inventory control functions (D,S). Procedures for reviewing summarization of transactions and related account classifications, and posting to the general ledger (B). Review and approval of monthly summarizing entries by responsible supervisory personnel (S). Periodic mailing of customer statements, with procedures for investigating disputes or queries (B). Review of responses to cus-	Monitoring and follow-up of customer billing complaints by personnel independent of the billing and cash receipts functions (B). Review and approval of disposition of customer complaints by responsible supervisory personnel (S). Review by responsible supervisory personnel of the aged accounts receivable summary for unusual items (S).	

(Continued)

Typical compliance tests

Legend:

1 = Examination of evidence and/or reperformance of the related basic controls described above. If supervisory controls are believed to be effective, reperformance can normally be restricted to part of one period, with testing of the related supervisory controls spread throughout the period of intended reliance.

2 = Examination of evidence that the related supervisory control described above

Inquire about and observe physical controls over finished goods inventories designed to ensure that all shipments are appropriately documented (3). Examine evidence of periodic accounting for the numerical sequence of shipping documents and invoices (1). Examine reports of unmatched documents for evidence of independent review and approval of investigation and resolution of unmatched items (2).

For a sample of transactions selected from the sales journal, examine supporting sales orders, invoices, and shipping documents for consistency among documents of prices, descriptions, customers, quantities, dates, and terms, and for evidence of appropriate authorization (1). Examine above documents for evidence of review by responsible personnel (2).

tomer statements by supervisory personnel (S).

For a sample of invoices selected from the sales journal and related shipping documents (1):

- Trace prices to approved price lists.
- Recalculate extensions and footings.
- Compare quantities, descriptions, dates shipped and recorded, and other details on documents.
- Review propriety of account classification.
- Ascertain proper posting to subsidiary records, including date of transaction.

Examine invoices over specified amounts for evidence of supervisory review and

Review reconciliation of accounts receivable subsidiary ledger to control account, establishing mathematical accuracy and reasonableness of documentation and explanations for reconciling items (1).

Examine above reconciliation for evidence of supervisory review and approval (2).

Trace balances in aged accounts receivable summary to the subsidiary ledger and test accuracy of aging (1).

Review customer correspondence files for adequacy of follow-up procedures on customer complaints (1).

Examine customer complaint file for

Figure 12.2 Continued

	General Objectives of Internal Accounting Control				
	Completeness	Validity	Accuracy	Maintenance	Physical Security
			approval (2). Test arithmetical accuracy of sales journal and compare totals to general ledger postings (1). Examine monthly summarizing entries of sales transactions for evidence of review and approval (2). Review shipping and billing cutoff procedures (3).	evidence of supervisory review and approval of disposition of complaints (2). Examine aged accounts receivable summary for evidence of supervisory review and approval (2).	

is present to ensure the continued operation of the related basic controls. These tests should be spread throughout the period of intended reliance.

3 = Observation of the operation of a control; may be performed one or more times during the year, as appropriate.

credit, however, the auditor may deem it necessary to test the collectibility of current receivables by reviewing collections in the post–balance sheet period to a greater extent than might otherwise be considered necessary.

Although procedures for establishing control over customers' orders are operationally important to an enterprise, those procedures are usually not significant to the auditor. Lost or overlooked sales orders obviously represent a potential loss of revenues, but customers' orders do not become sales until the goods or services are shipped to or accepted by the customer. Sometimes, however, control over orders received may be a key link in the series of controls that provide reasonable assurance that all shipments are billed and all bills are for bona fide shipments. Also, if the client does not confirm sales orders with customers, the auditor may be concerned about the potential effect on accounts receivable that remain unpaid because of disputes with customers concerning goods not meeting the specifications of the sales order. In either situation, the audit program might call for a compliance test such as the following: From the customer order backlog report (or the file of order forms), select a sample of customer orders and trace recorded data to the original orders and related documents; note indication of supervisory follow-up of unprocessed orders.

Executing Orders and Shipping Goods. While proper execution of a sales order is important to achieving customer satisfaction, the auditor's primary concern is the client's shipping procedures and controls, including timely shipment of goods.

The completeness objective of internal accounting control in the revenue cycle is important to the auditor because goods shipped but not billed result in potentially unrecorded revenues. If discovery of unbilled revenues relating to goods shipped but not invoiced results in accrued revenues, the enterprise (and the auditor) will have to evaluate the collectibility of such receivables. The longer a receivable has been outstanding, the greater the likelihood that it will not be paid. To satisfy the audit objective of completeness, the following compliance test should be performed: From the shipping log or file of completed shipments, select a sample of shipments and determine that invoices were prepared; compare the dates of invoices with shipment dates and dates requested by customers.

Invoice Control. The control of sales invoices encompasses the last two steps in a typical revenue cycle: completing the invoice and billing the customer. Control over completing invoices and billing customers is essential because it serves as the basis for an accounting entry. The following compliance tests are often performed:

> For a sample of invoices, compare supporting customer orders, shipping documents, and invoice data.
>
> Inspect open file of unmatched orders and shipping reports. Obtain and evaluate explanations for delays in shipping and billing. Examine evidence of supervisory review over the file.

For a sample of invoices, compare prices with price lists; compare payment terms, discounts, and allowances with authorized lists; test arithmetical accuracy; review account coding; and examine evidence of supervisory approval.

For a sample of invoices, trace to sales journal and to accounts receivable subsidiary ledger.

Test arithmetical accuracy of sales journal; compare sales journal total with total of accounts receivable control account.

Examine evidence of supervisory review of the reconciliation of the accounts receivable control account to the accounts receivable subsidiary ledger.

In practice, all of the foregoing tests, including those in the earlier examples, could be combined and applied to the same sample of invoices. In doing so the auditor must be careful not to confuse the separate audit objectives of each test.

In manufacturing companies, compliance tests of controls over the revenue cycle and those over finished goods inventory are related. Compliance tests relating to the revenue cycle and finished goods inventory can be originated from either finished goods inventory data or revenue data. In the latter case, the compliance test program might call for tracing items sold per the sales invoices tested in the invoice control function to their removal from perpetual finished goods inventory records.

Payments Received for Goods and Services

The objectives of internal accounting control over payments received for goods and services are to ensure that all receipts are promptly deposited in the bank, that they are accurately and completely recorded in the proper period, and that those functions are not performed by the same employees. Figure 12.3 summarizes the control objectives, potential errors, principal control techniques, and typical compliance tests of controls over payments received for goods and services.

Goods Returned by and Claims Received from Customers

The third transaction type in the revenue cycle is usually less significant than shipping and receiving payment for goods sold or services rendered. Accordingly, compliance tests would be performed only if the transaction type was significant and the audit strategy called for reliance on the related controls. Those tests might include the following:

Inquire about and observe physical controls designed to ensure that all goods returned by customers are appropriately documented.

Review accounting for the numerical sequence of documents supporting goods returned by customers, claims made, and credit memoranda.

Figure 12.3 Payments Received for Goods and Services: Control Objectives, Potential Errors, Accounting Controls, and Compliance Tests

	General Objectives of Internal Accounting Control				
	Completeness	Validity	Accuracy	Maintenance	Physical Security
Specific objectives of internal accounting control	All receipts of currency and checks are processed and recorded.	All recorded receipts represent actual collections of cash from sales of goods and services or collections of receivables.	Receipts are accurately recorded as to amounts, dates, and customer names in the proper period in the books of original entry and detail subsidiary records, and are accurately summarized in the general ledger.	The cash receipts journal, accounts receivable subsidiary ledger, and general ledger control account reflect all authorized transactions and only those transactions.	Access to receipts is suitably restricted to authorized personnel and receipts are promptly deposited in the company's bank account.
Potential errors in account balances from absent or ineffective controls	Unprocessed or unrecorded receipts may result in an understatement of cash and an overstatement of receivables or an understatement of revenues (if sales are for cash) or an understatement of unearned revenue (for deposits and advance payments).	Cash received from sources other than payments for goods and services and applied erroneously to related accounts in the revenue cycle may result in: • Overstatement of revenues. • Understatement of receivables. • Overstatement of other assets. • Understatement of liabilities or	Errors in recording receipts may result in misstatement of revenues and receivables; errors may go undetected, causing an under- or overstatement of cash, accounts receivable, revenues, and assets; and update to detail subsidiary ledgers may be inaccurate, resulting in misstatement of individual customer account	Cash, accounts receivable, revenue, and other asset or liability accounts may be understated or overstated because transactions are not recorded in both the cash and accounts receivable control accounts. Even if those accounts are in agreement, the detail subsidiary ledger may contain mispostings of	Misappropriations of cash and related overstatements of receivables or understatements of revenues may occur.

(Continued)

Figure 12.3 Continued

	General Objectives of Internal Accounting Control			
Completeness	Validity	Accuracy	Maintenance	Physical Security
	unearned revenue. • Understatement of equity accounts.	balances and aging.	correct amounts to the wrong customer accounts.	
Opening of mail and prelisting of receipts supervised by a responsible official (B). Accounting for numerical (or daily) sequence of prelistings of receipts (B). Validated deposit slips compared with totals of receipts per prelistings by a person independent of the receipt function (B). Review and approval of comparison of cash received per the numerically controlled prelistings, deposit slips, and	Remittance advices or other documentation evidencing the source and purpose of receipts examined for applicability to revenues or reduction of accounts receivable (B). Periodic review of the above procedure by responsible supervisory personnel (S).	Procedures for comparing currency and checks, either individually or in the aggregate, with the receipts records used for posting the accounts receivable subsidiary records and cash book as to amounts, dates, and payees by persons other than those who maintain the accounts receivable subsidiary records or control account (B). Periodic review and approval of above procedures by responsible	Periodic reconciliations of accounts receivable subsidiary ledger to accounts receivable control accounts and of the bank statement to the general ledger cash account by personnel independent of the cash receipts and receivable posting functions (B). Review of reconciliation procedures and results by responsible supervisory personnel (S).	Checks received are restrictively endorsed on receipt (P). Receipts are deposited intact daily (P). Persons involved in the receipt and deposit function are not authorized check signers (D).

Principal control techniques
Legend:
B = Basic control (other than physical control)
D = Division of duties
S = Supervisory control
P = Physical control

supervisory personnel (S).

Procedures for reviewing summarization of transactions and related account classifications, and posting to the general ledger (B).

Review and approval of monthly summarizing entries by responsible supervisory personnel (S).

Periodic mailing of customer statements, with procedures for investigating disputes or queries (B).

Review of responses to customer statements by supervisory personnel (S).

For a sample of transactions selected from the cash receipts journal, examine remittance advices and other documents supporting

For a sample of transactions selected from the files of remittance advices, compare amounts, dates, invoice numbers, and names to the

Review client's reconciliations of accounts receivable subsidiary ledger to accounts receivable control accounts and of bank statement to

Inquire about and observe that:
• Authorized check signers do not handle receipts or post receivable details (3).

(Continued)

posting of control totals with the cash receipts journal and general ledger by independent supervisory personnel (D,S).

Typical compliance tests
Legend:
1 = Examination of evidence and/or reperformance of the related basic

Observe procedures for opening mail and preparation of prelistings (3).

Examine evidence of accounting for numerical (or

Figure 12.3 Continued

	General Objectives of Internal Accounting Control			
Completeness	Validity	Accuracy	Maintenance	Physical Security
daily) sequence of prelistings (1). Compare totals per prelistings to entries in the cash receipts journal and deposits on bank statement (1). Compare summarized totals per cash receipts journal to postings in the general ledger (1). Examine evidence of supervisory review and approval of reconciliations of receipts per prelistings, deposit slips, cash receipts journal, and general ledger control accounts (2).	receipts for applicability to receipts for goods and services (1). Examine above documents for evidence of review by responsible personnel (2).	prelisting and in total to the cash receipts journal (1). Inquire about and observe review and approval of above comparison by responsible personnel (2). Test arithmetical accuracy of cash receipts journal and compare totals to general ledger postings (1). Examine monthly summarizing entries of cash receipts for evidence of supervisory review and approval (2). Review and/or inquire about results of customer	general ledger cash account, ascertaining arithmetical accuracy and reasonableness of documentation and of explanations for reconciling items (1). Examine above reconciliations for evidence of supervisory review and approval (2).	• Procedures for restrictively endorsing checks are performed (3).

controls described above. If supervisory controls are believed to be effective, reperformance can normally be restricted to part of one period, with testing of the related supervisory controls spread throughout the period of intended reliance.

2 = Examination of evidence that the related supervisory control described above is present to ensure the

statement mailings and examine evidence of resolution of disputed amounts (1). Examine customer files for evidence of supervisory review and approval of disposition of customer complaints (2).

continued operation of the related basic controls. These tests should be spread throughout the period of intended reliance.

3 = Observation of the operation of a control; may be performed one or more times during the year, as appropriate.

For a sample of transactions selected from the accounts receivable subsidiary ledger and related records of goods returned and claims made, customer correspondence or complaint file, and credit memoranda:

- Examine supporting receiving documents.
- Trace prices to original sales invoices.
- Recalculate footings and extensions.
- Ascertain consistency between documents of quantities, descriptions, dates returned and recorded, and other information.
- Review propriety of account classifications.
- Determine proper posting to subsidiary records, including dates of transactions.

Substantive Tests

Before implementing the planned program of substantive tests, the auditor should evaluate the results of compliance tests performed, if any, to determine whether the planned substantive tests are still appropriate.

Also, as discussed in the "Audit Strategy" section earlier, answers to questions resulting from analytical review procedures related to accounts in the revenue cycle have an impact on the nature, timing, and extent of substantive tests. For example, updating the interim comparison of current-year revenues (prices and volume) with budgeted or prior-year amounts provides additional information that either confirms earlier impressions and judgments or raises further questions and issues that must be resolved to the auditor's satisfaction. Also, an increase in sales and receivables activity in light of a known depressed market may indicate control weaknesses or breakdowns and possibly raise questions concerning potential client errors or irregularities.

The balance of this chapter discusses substantive test procedures that are likely to be performed on accounts related to the revenue cycle under various conditions.

Accounts Receivable

Before performing substantive tests of the validity and accuracy of the accounts receivable trial balance, the auditor should be reasonably assured that it contains all sales transactions that remain uncollected at year-end. If results of compliance tests of completeness controls provide that reasonable assurance, substantive tests of the completeness of accounts receivable at year-end will consist primarily of various cutoff tests.

Cutoff Tests of Shipments and Collections. Cutoff tests are intended to ascertain that all significant transactions applicable to the period under examination have been recorded and no transactions applicable to the succeeding period have been recorded. In the absence of strong completeness controls, the sooner accounts are closed after year-end, the greater the likelihood that there will be unrecorded sales invoices. Thus, examining files of unmatched shipping reports and unprocessed invoices, the sales journal, the cash receipts book, and other relevant records for a period after year-end to review the accuracy of the client's cutoff is a virtually universal auditing procedure. The extent of the search is based on the results of compliance tests and on errors found in performing other substantive tests.

If the basic transaction documents are in numerical sequence, the auditor can note the number of the last shipping report and the last sales invoice recorded and can also compare the date of the last entry in the cash receipts journal with the date those receipts were deposited in the bank. The auditor can examine perpetual inventory records, the sales journal, and the listing of unmatched shipping reports for evidence that goods sold before year-end have been removed from inventory. The auditor should apply the same procedures to obtain assurance that sales, shipments, and cash receipts applicable to the following year were not recorded in the year under examination. If the basic transaction documents are not prenumbered, it may be necessary to examine a sample of documents, with emphasis on transaction dates and large amounts, selected from the sales journal, cash receipts journal, perpetual inventory records, and shipping reports both before and after the cutoff date to obtain sufficient evidence that the cutoff was properly made.

Cutoff tests of shipments are usually coordinated with the auditor's observation of the client's physical inventory count. When physical inventories are taken at a date other than year-end, it is important that shipment cutoff tests be made at that time. Cutoff errors are compounded when perpetual inventory records and the general ledger inventory account are adjusted for differences between book and physical amounts (see Chapter 14, "Auditing the Production Cycle and Inventory Balances").

Confirming Accounts Receivable. One of the most widely used substantive tests for determining the existence and accuracy of accounts receivable is direct communication by the auditor with customers, commonly referred to as "confirmation." Confirmation by the auditor of individual sales transactions or accounts receivable balances by direct communication with customers is one of only a few procedures that are designated as "generally accepted auditing procedures." Paragraphs 331.01 and .03 of SAS No. 1 state

> Confirmation of receivables and observation of inventories are generally accepted auditing procedures. The independent auditor who issues an opinion when he has not employed them must bear in mind that he has the burden of justifying the opinion expressed.
>
> Confirmation of receivables requires direct communication with debtors either during or after the period under audit; the confirmation date, the method of requesting confirmations, and the number to be requested are determined by the independent auditor. Such matters as the effectiveness of in-

ternal control, the apparent possibility of disputes, inaccuracies or irregularities in the accounts, the probability that requests will receive consideration or that the debtor will be able to confirm the information requested, and the materiality of the amounts involved are factors to be considered by the auditor in selecting the information to be requested and the form of confirmation, as well as the extent and timing of his confirmation procedures.

Confirmation of receivables has been required by the profession since 1939 when Statement on Auditing Procedure No. 1 was adopted by the AICPA as a direct result of the McKesson & Robbins fraud. In the intervening years, confirmation has been the subject of extensive authoritative and other professional pronouncements. That emphasis has been unfortunate because the disproportionate attention given to the confirmation procedure tends to distort the cumulative, corroborative, interrelated nature of audit tests within which all auditing procedures must be viewed. Confirmation is one substantive procedure among several, just as substantive tests produce one kind of audit evidence among several. If the auditor determines in a particular situation that confirmation is not an effective procedure or that there are more effective and efficient means of substantiating the validity and accuracy of receivables, confirmation need not be used at all.

The reliability of confirmation as a source of evidence depends on the care with which debtors respond to confirmation requests. Auditors should not blindly accept confirmation replies; they should be aware that many traditional audit procedures, including confirming receivables, do not in all circumstances produce the assurances they were intended to provide. In its *Report, Conclusions, and Recommendations*, the Commission on Auditors' Responsibilities pointed out that ''. . . in several cases, outsiders either ignored incorrect information that was clearly shown in confirmations or actively cooperated with management in giving incorrect confirmation'' (p. 40).

Moreover, confirmation produces evidence about the existence and (to some extent) the accuracy of accounts receivable; other procedures are needed to establish their collectibility. The most direct evidence regarding collectibility of receivables is subsequent customer payments. Those payments also provide more reliable evidence about existence and accuracy than does confirmation because it is highly unlikely that a customer will pay an invalid or overstated balance. Only the accuracy of the date the sale took place is not substantiated by a subsequent customer payment. Confirmation may, however, reveal the improper application of customer payments to older, disputed invoices, perhaps to conceal an unfavorable aging schedule.

In obtaining evidence about the existence and accuracy of accounts receivable, the decision regarding the type of substantive tests to perform should not be thought of as one between confirming or examining subsequent customer payments. The auditor's best judgment should always be the deciding factor in selecting an effective and efficient combination of tests to employ; if the auditor believes that the existence and accuracy of receivables can be effectively and efficiently substantiated without confirmation, then the requirement of justification as expressed in SAS No. 1 has been satisfied. In practice, a combination of confirmation, examination of subsequent customer payments, and other procedures is often used to test the existence and accuracy of accounts receivable.

When it is effective and efficient to use confirmation, a decision must be made regarding the confirmation date. If there were no deadline for the client's issuance of financial statements, confirming at year-end would be most effective. In today's business environment, however, there is usually a deadline, and accordingly the auditor often confirms receivables (and performs many other audit procedures as well) at an earlier date, particularly if internal controls are strong. In this situation, the auditor performs early substantive tests and obtains evidence that internal accounting controls have remained strong during the intervening period between the confirmation date and the client's year-end, or relies on other substantive procedures. During this intervening period, the auditor usually performs analytical reviews aimed at detecting exceptions to known trends. In addition to the types of analytical reviews that will be discussed later in this chapter, the auditor looks at the level of sales and cash collections during the intervening period and the level of credit memoranda issued or other adjustments made to accounts receivable. When early confirmation is used, the intervening period review is commonly referred to as a "roll-forward."

Substantive tests may, of course, provide evidence about accounting controls if the source of errors found as a result of those tests is investigated and found to be the result of a control weakness. Specifically, confirmation procedures may provide evidence of the effectiveness of controls in the revenue cycle. Accordingly, many auditors consider receivable confirmations as a source of evidence about the effective functioning of accounting controls as well as a source of evidence about financial statement assertions.

Confirmation Procedures

Before selecting accounts for confirmation, the auditor should ascertain that the accounts receivable trial balance ties in with the related control accounts. The client should routinely compare general ledger control account balances with the totals of individual accounts receivable, investigate discrepancies between the two, and make appropriate adjustments. The auditor should compare the accounts receivable trial balance prepared by the client with the individual subsidiary ledger accounts in detail or, if internal control is strong, on a test basis, and should review the arithmetical accuracy of the trial balance. Reasons for recurring discrepancies between the control account and subsidiary ledger should be investigated.

The paragraphs that follow describe the procedures involved in confirming receivables.

Selection of Accounts for Confirmation. Depending on the audit strategy and the results of any compliance tests performed, the auditor should decide whether all or only part of the accounts should be confirmed and, if the latter, the basis for selecting the accounts to be confirmed. As a general rule, accounts receivable selected for confirmation should include a representative portion of both the dollar amount and the number of accounts. Chapter 10 discusses various methods of sample selection. The selection should exclude debtors from whom replies to requests for confirmation cannot reasonably be expected, such as certain governmental agencies, foreign concerns, and some large industrial and commercial enterprises that use a voucher or computerized system that makes confirmation impracticable.

An experienced auditor usually confirms accounts that appear unusual. Accounts with zero or credit balances should also be considered for confirmation. A credit balance suggests the possibility of an incorrect entry, especially if internal control is weak. Occasionally a client requests that accounts in addition to those selected by the auditor be included among the accounts to be confirmed, usually in the hope that the confirmation request may speed up collection; the auditor may properly accede to those requests.

To preserve the integrity of the confirmation process, the plan for selecting accounts and the accounts selected for confirmation should not be revealed in advance to the client. If the client does not wish statements or confirmation requests to be sent to certain debtors, the auditor should be satisfied that there is an adequate reason before acceding to the request. If such accounts are material, the auditor should employ alternative procedures to obtain satisfaction that the accounts are valid and accurate. If the results of the alternative procedures are satisfactory, such a client request would not be considered a scope limitation.

Replies to confirmation requests are sometimes difficult to obtain if a debtor's accounts payable processing is decentralized, uses a voucher system, or is performed mechanically, which is increasingly the case in a number of governmental departments and agencies as well as in many large industrial and commercial enterprises. In many instances, however, those difficulties can be overcome with care and ingenuity; for example, an auditor may supply details of the balance to be confirmed, such as invoice dates, numbers (including customer purchase order numbers), and amounts, or may confirm specific transactions rather than an account balance.

Processing Confirmation Requests. After selecting the accounts for confirmation, the auditor should observe the following procedures in processing the requests. They are applicable to both negative and positive confirmations (which are described and compared in later sections of this chapter).

- Names, addresses, and amounts shown on statements of accounts selected for confirmation or on the confirmation letters should be compared with the debtors' accounts. The auditor should maintain control over confirmations until they are mailed; this does not preclude assistance from appropriate client personnel, under the auditor's supervision.
- Requests for confirmation, together with postage-paid return envelopes addressed to the auditor, should be mailed in envelopes showing the au-

ditor's address as the return address. If the client objects to using the auditor's address, returns may be addressed to the client at a post office box controlled by the auditor; the post office should be directed to forward mail to the auditor after the box is surrendered.

- All requests should be mailed by the auditor; the client's mail room may be used for mechanical processing under the control of the auditor, who should deposit the completed requests at the post office.
- Undelivered requests returned by the post office should be investigated, corrected addresses obtained, and the requests remailed by the auditor.

The purpose of those procedures is not so much to protect against possible fraud on the part of the client (although that possibility is clearly implied) as to preserve the integrity of the confirmation procedure. The audit evidence obtained from confirmation is less reliable if there is the possibility of accidental or purposeful interference with direct communication with debtors; the auditor should take all reasonable steps to minimize that possibility.

Negative Confirmations. A negative confirmation is a request that a debtor communicate directly with the auditor only if the statement balance is considered in any way incorrect. It is the most frequently used form of confirmation. Since debtors are asked to reply only if they wish to report differences, the auditor may conclude, in the absence of any reason to believe the contrary, that no reply signifies a debtor's acceptance of the balance.

It is important to impress on debtors the necessity for communicating directly with the auditor when discrepancies exist. If the auditor has reason to believe that the negative form of confirmation request will not receive consideration, sending out that form of confirmation request does not constitute compliance with generally accepted auditing standards. In that respect, SAS No. 1 (AU Section 331.05) states, in part

> The negative form is useful particularly when internal control surrounding accounts receivable is considered to be effective, when a large number of small balances are involved, and when the auditor has no reason to believe the persons receiving the requests are unlikely to give them consideration. If the negative rather than the positive form of confirmation is used, the number of requests sent or the extent of the other auditing procedures applied to the receivable balance should normally be greater in order for the independent auditor to obtain the same degree of satisfaction with respect to the accounts receivable balance.

If statements of account are not mailed at the time confirmations are requested, or if statements are not to be sent to debtors, a letter form of request may be sent. With appropriate changes of language to express the negative form, the form of positive confirmation letter shown in Figure 12.4 may be employed.

If statements are sent to debtors, they may be inscribed by means of a rubber stamp or have a sticker affixed reading somewhat as follows:

PLEASE EXAMINE THIS STATEMENT CAREFULLY.

If it is not correct, please write promptly, using the enclosed envelope and giving details of all differences, to our auditors,

[Name and Address of Auditors]

who are now making their periodic examination of our accounts.

Unless you promptly report a difference to our auditors, they will assume that you consider the statement to be correct.

Remittances should not be sent to the auditors.

It should be noted that the request is worded as coming from the client. Even though the auditor drafts the request, prepares it, and selects the accounts, all confirmation requests should be made in the client's name because the relationship exists between client and customer (or client and creditor, when liabilities are being confirmed) and information about it should not be given out to a third party without authorization.

The value of negative confirmation requests has been the subject of much discussion. Although the incidence of debtors who simply ignore and discard requests is unknown and unmeasurable, the results can nonetheless be relied on to an appropriate degree for two reasons.

- Since the objective of confirmation is to provide reasonable assurance of the existence and accuracy of the aggregate accounts receivable, not of any single account, a discrepancy is significant only if it is evidence of a condition that affects a great many accounts (unless that is true, use of negative confirmations is not appropriate). There is a very high probability, amounting to "reasonable assurance," that some debtors receiving negative confirmation requests will be either responsible enough or incensed enough to report differences. Extrapolating any discrepancies found then becomes another procedure for the client and auditor.

- Confirmation of accounts receivable is only one procedure that provides evidential matter. Audit evidence is cumulative, and one procedure tends to corroborate another. Therefore, some audit detection risk can be tolerated in a single procedure because that procedure does not serve as the sole basis for a conclusion.

Figure 12.4 Positive Confirmation Letter

[Name and Address of Debtor]

Dear Sirs:

In accordance with the request of our auditors [name and address of auditors], we ask that you kindly confirm to them your indebtedness to us at [date] which, according to our records, amounted to [amount].

If the amount shown is in agreement with your records, please so indicate by signing in the space provided below and return this letter directly to our auditors in the enclosed envelope. Your prompt compliance will facilitate the examination of our accounts.

If the amount is not in agreement with your records, please inform our auditors directly of the amount shown by your records, with full details of differences.

Remittances should not be sent to the auditors.

Very truly yours,

[Name of the Client]

The above stated amount is correct as of [date].

_____
[Debtor of Client]

_____
[Title or Position]

Depending on the circumstances of an engagement, negative confirmation requests may be supplemented by requests for positive confirmations, particularly of larger balances.

Positive Confirmations. A positive confirmation is a request that a debtor reply directly to the auditor stating whether the account balance is correct. Positive confirmations may be used for all accounts or for selected accounts, such as those with larger balances, those representing unusual or isolated transactions, or others for which an auditor needs greater specific assurance of validity and accuracy. The positive form of confirmation is called for if there are indications that a substantial number of accounts may be in dispute or inaccurate or if the individual receivable balances are unusually large or arise from sales to a few major customers. The request may be conveyed by a letter or directly on the statement by means of a rubber stamp or sticker. To facilitate replies, a postage-paid envelope addressed to the auditor should be enclosed.

Because the form of the request specifically asks for a reply, an auditor may not assume that failure to reply indicates that the debtor agrees with the stated balance. Second requests should be sent, and sometimes third requests by registered mail. Replies to "positive" requests may be facilitated if the auditor furnishes the details of the individual items included in the balances, usually by providing a copy of the client's detailed customer statement. That may be particularly helpful if the debtor's system of accounting does not readily permit identification of account balances. If the auditor fails to receive positive confirmation, alternative auditing procedures should be employed, as described later in the chapter.

It is impracticable for an auditor to determine the genuineness or authenticity of signatures on replies to confirmation requests. Accordingly, if the account being confirmed is material or the auditor has determined that inherent risk is high, the auditor should ask the client to request an officer of the debtor to sign the confirmation reply. The auditor may then wish to communicate with that officer by telephone or other means to corroborate the validity of the confirmation.

Experience has shown that a form of positive request, whether made by letter or by a sticker affixed to the statement, that requires a minimum of effort on the part of the recipient produces more responses. The letter form, illustrated in Figure 12.4, is designed for use if statements of account are not to be mailed to debtors or if the confirmation requests are sent separately from the statements. It is designed so that, when the amount shown is in agreement with the debtor's records, the individual need only sign in the space provided and return the letter in the envelope enclosed with the request. Auditors often employ various techniques to improve the response rate, such as "personalizing" the request by using postage stamps rather than a postage meter.[1]

If statements of account prepared by the client are to be used for positive confirmation requests, they may be sent in duplicate, with an appropriately worded request (often imprinted on the statement) that the debtor acknowledge the correctness of the statement by returning the duplicate, duly signed, directly to the auditor. A variation is the form of monthly statement in which the balance and the name of the debtor appear in two places, one of which is separated from the main body of the statement by perforations. That part may be torn off, signed by the debtor, and returned directly to the auditor.

[1]An empirical study of ways to increase confirmation response rates is described in Robert H. Ashton and Robert E. Hylas, "Increasing Confirmation Response Rates," *Auditing: A Journal of Practice and Theory*, Summer 1981, pp. 12–22.

Exceptions to Confirmation Requests. Debtors may not agree with the information on an accounts receivable confirmation request because of differences that do not have audit significance. Those differences are generally the result of either payments in transit at the confirmation date or delays in recording goods received by the debtor. The auditor should corroborate debtor assertions involving those kinds of differences by examining the cash receipts journal and remittance advices for debtor payments received after the confirmation date to determine that the payments were for receivables existing at the confirmation date, and by examining bills of lading or other evidence of shipment. (Differences that are appropriately reconciled in this manner are not errors.) Those procedures are normally performed on a test basis. Other reported exceptions, usually involving small amounts, may result from disputes over allowances, discounts, shipping charges, or returned merchandise. These exceptions are usually neither material in amount nor indicative of serious weaknesses in the accounting or control systems. After the auditor has made a copy or other record for control purposes, investigation of replies may properly be turned over to a responsible client employee whose regular responsibilities do not involve cash, receivables, or credit functions. The auditor should review the employee's findings and, if considered necessary, employ additional procedures to obtain satisfaction that the balance is accurate.

Exceptions other than those described previously warrant close scrutiny by the auditor. The client should respond to each such exception; adjustments to reduce revenues and accounts receivable are usually necessary. The auditor should evaluate all exceptions and decide whether they represent isolated situations (such as a customer's not receiving goods or the client's not receiving a payment) or indicate a pattern of disputed sales or payments involving more than one customer. A pattern of disputed sales should be investigated; it could lead to the discovery of errors or irregularities and possibly result in a departure from an unqualified opinion or withdrawal from the engagement. Debtors' responses indicating that payments were sent but were not received by the client usually indicate collectibility problems; payments received but not recorded may result from misappropriations of cash and "lapping" of receivables (discussed next). In the latter instance, receivables should be reduced (since the client received the payment) and a loss recorded in the amount of the misappropriation.

Lapping

Lapping is a means of concealing a cash shortage by manipulating credits to the accounts receivable subsidiary ledger. To accomplish lapping, an employee must have access to incoming cash receipts, the cash receipts journal, and the detailed accounts receivable records. Accordingly, if there is not appropriate segregation of duties, the auditor's normal degree of skepticism should be increased because of the possibility of lapping and other irregularities.

Lapping is perpetrated in the following manner: An employee receives a customer's payment on an account receivable and misappropriates the cash, recording neither the cash receipt nor the reduction of the customer's account. Subsequent cash collections from another customer are later credited to the customer from whom the original collection was misappropriated, to prevent that customer's paid account from appearing as outstanding for more than a short time. Lapping is made easier when customers make periodic payments on their accounts, particularly in round amounts, rather than pay for specific invoices. Even if customers designate that remittances apply to specific invoices, the difference in amount between the second customer's remittance and the amount misappropriated from the first customer's remittance can be concealed by depositing additional cash if the subsequent payment is smaller or by making an additional credit to the first account, or even another account, if the subsequent payment is larger. Obviously, the lapping must continue indefinitely or until the cash shortage is replenished. Accordingly, the auditor should inquire about employees who are rarely absent from work or who do not take vacations that would require someone else to perform their work.

Internal accounting controls that should prevent or detect lapping include proper segregation of duties, required vacations for personnel responsible for handling cash and posting credits to customer accounts, mailing monthly statements to customers that show all activity in the accounts by dates, and reviewing entries to customers' accounts for unusual amounts.

The confirmation process, including careful attention to client explanations for delays in posting remittances when a customer states that the amount to be confirmed is not due because it was paid before the confirmation date, should reveal lapping if it is present. If lapping is strongly suspected, the auditor may want to perform additional procedures. For example, comparing customer remittance advices to credits in the accounts receivable subsidiary ledger, individual amounts on deposit slips to individual amounts in the cash receipts journal, and individual amounts in the cash receipts journal to credits to individual customer accounts (in each case, scrutinizing the dates of the entry or posting) may also uncover lapping. The auditor should be aware, however, of the possibility of altered bank deposit slips and may wish to confirm the accuracy of individual deposit slips with banks.

Procedures in Lieu of Confirmation

If replies to confirmation requests cannot reasonably be expected or if the number and character of replies to positive confirmation requests are not satisfactory, the auditor should attempt to obtain satisfaction about the existence and accuracy of receivable balances by alternative procedures.

Receivable balances due from governmental agencies frequently cannot be confirmed; in such cases, the auditor can examine relevant contracts, shipping documents, and evidence that the agency has acknowledged receipt of shipment. In other cases, in addition to the procedures suggested in the next section, "Other Substantive Tests," the auditor may wish to examine transactions for a period around the confirmation date. Procedures that might be employed include tracing individual sales invoices and collections to their source; testing the arithmetical accuracy of underlying records and reviewing daily postings to control accounts; reviewing the accuracy of cash discounts and other discounts allowed; reviewing returns and trade discounts; and accounting for the numerical sequence of sales invoices and cash receipts reports. The auditor may substantiate sales and related accounts receivable by examining orders, sales contracts, and shipping documents; collection of receivables may be tested by examining subsequent cash receipts, cash remittance advices, and other records. The auditor sometimes assumes physical control of cash receipts for a certain period and subsequently compares the record of receipts with daily accounts receivable postings.

Other Substantive Tests

In some circumstances, even though receivable balances have been confirmed, the auditor may consider it advisable to compare, on a test basis, billings, shipping documents, and other data with recorded transactions in accounts receivable for some period. Those comparisons should be made for a period immediately preceding and immediately following the fiscal year-end and may be performed at the same time as the compliance testing of internal accounting controls. The comparison should also help to determine that a proper sales cutoff was made. Improper cutoffs may result from errors or from intentional recording of sales in an improper period because of bonus arrangements, sales quotas, royalty agreements, income tax considerations, or other reasons.

Substantive tests to provide assurance about the completeness of invoicing and recording goods shipped may consist primarily of the analytical review procedures discussed later in this chapter and an analysis of the size and direction of adjustments to recorded inventory quantities as a result of the client's physical inventory count. If there are few instances where book inventory quantities must be reduced as a result of the physical count, the risk of unbilled or unrecorded receivables is reduced. When combined with analytical review procedures, the auditor's review of physical inventory findings may provide most of the assurance needed about the completeness of recorded revenues and receivables.

The auditor should usually examine credit memoranda issued during a period after the close of the fiscal year to determine that reported sales were not inflated by recording invalid sales in one year and issuing credit memoranda to eliminate them in the next year, and that proper provision has been made in the year under audit for any such credit memoranda and for applicable discounts, returns, and allowances. The auditor should be alert for sales under terms permitting customers to return merchandise that they are unable to sell.

The auditor should read sales contracts with selling agents and other agreements affecting receivables to become aware of matters such as title to accounts receivable, time of billings, method or time of payments, commissions, and special discounts or rebates.

The auditor should examine receivables other than trade accounts—such as debit balances in accounts payable, claims, and advances—by reviewing the transactions as recorded in the accounts and noting supporting evidence. The precise nature of those accounts should be determined for purposes of the scope of audit testing, evaluation of their collectibility, and their classification in the balance sheet. Confirmations should be obtained by direct communication with debtors to the extent considered reasonable and practicable. Although those receivables may not be significant in amount, if they are not subject to adequate internal accounting controls, audit risk considerations may require that they be subjected to relatively more extensive substantive testing than are trade receivables.

Tests for Collectibility

The collectibility of receivable balances should be reviewed to determine that the client's estimate of the allowance necessary to state the receivables at their net realizable value as of the balance sheet date is adequate. Before making the review, the auditor should determine if the client's method of determining the allowance for doubtful accounts is consistent with prior years, and, if so, whether any current business or economic conditions might indicate that the method used is not appropriate in the current year. For example, if the client estimates an allowance for doubtful accounts based on the historical relationship of write-offs to total sales (percent of sales method), a significant economic downturn may require a revision of the historical percentage. That same circumstance may also make it inappropriate to develop an allowance for doubtful accounts by applying historical percentages to groupings of an aged trial balance. For example, accounts receivable less than 30 days old do not usually enter into the calculation of the allowance for doubtful accounts; however, the allowance may have to take those balances into consideration if the customer mix has changed in a time of economic distress.

Reviewing the Aged Trial Balance. The usual starting point for an auditor's review of collectibility is an aged trial balance. The client should prepare periodic aging analyses as a routine accounting procedure; if that is not done, the auditor should request that one be prepared. In either event, the auditor should establish the accuracy of the analysis by testing the aging of some of the accounts; the arithmetical accuracy of the analysis should also be tested and the total compared with the total receivables in the ledger.

Often computers are, or can be, programmed to produce an aging analysis as a by-product of the reconciliation of detail accounts to control accounts. Alternatively, the auditor may be able to provide the client with a general-purpose computer program that can age accounts. In some cases, it may be desirable to employ statistical sampling and extrapolate the results of aging a representative selection of accounts to conclusions about the total.

In reviewing an aging analysis, the most obvious characteristic to evaluate is the number and dollar amount of overdue accounts. The auditor should probe more deeply than that, however, and scrutinize a number of accounts closely for evidence of special situations (such as "dated" invoices) that might indicate collectibility problems. The auditor's purpose in inquiring into those matters is not to judge the collectibility of each individual account examined, but to gather evidence supporting judgments, first, on the adequacy of the client's investigation and evaluation of individual accounts (a management function usually performed by the credit manager) and, second, on the overall reasonableness of the allowance for doubtful accounts.

Past-due receivable balances and other unusual balances should be reviewed with the credit manager to obtain information on which to base an opinion regarding their collectibility. Files of correspondence with collection agents and debtors should be examined. Past experience in collecting overdue accounts should be related to current balances as a guide to probable current collectibility. Changes in the number and size of overdue accounts and possible changes in business conditions affecting collectibility should be discussed with the credit manager. As a result of those reviews and discussions, the auditor should understand the basis for the client's estimate of the allowance for doubtful accounts and should be able to judge whether the allowance is reasonable.

Other Procedures. The auditor should also scan revenue and receivable transactions after the balance sheet date, including sales, cash receipts, discounts allowed, rebates, returns, and write-offs; those transactions—or their absence or an unusual increase or decrease in them—may reveal abnormal conditions affecting collectibility at the balance sheet date. Events after the close of the fiscal period are often the best proof of whether the receivable balances at the balance sheet date are actually what they purport to be. Approvals for notes and accounts receivable written off during the year should be examined.

Notes receivable, whether past due or current, may themselves be indicative of doubtful collectibility if they were received for overdue accounts receivable. The origin of notes should be determined because current notes may sometimes represent renewals of matured notes. If usual trade practice is to obtain notes from debtors of high credit standing, the collectibility of the notes should be considered in the same way as that of other receivables.

The collectibility of notes against which collateral has been pledged may depend on the value of the collateral. If the collectibility of significant collateralized notes in the ordinary manner is in question, the auditor may find it desirable to have an independent appraiser value the collateral.

Receivables collectible over a long period are subject to the same auditing procedures as other receivables, but the evaluation of collectibility takes on added importance. In addition, a client's policy and procedures for computing imputed interest, where that factor is present, must be reviewed.

The auditor should be particularly attentive to revenue transactions that the client has entered into that include contingent sales agreements, customer rights of return, repurchase agreements, or other "special" terms that call into question the collectibility of the receivable and even the validity of the revenue transaction itself. The possibility of misapplication of GAAP increases when those revenue transactions are with related parties. Many audit failures were caused by the auditor's not sufficiently understanding the nature of the client's business and the substance of transactions the enterprise entered into. Detecting transactions of the type described in this paragraph is particularly difficult if management consciously withholds information from the auditor. Understanding transactions the client enters into and the industry in which the client operates is an essential first step in determining the proper accounting for and reporting of "unusual" and often complex revenue transactions. The auditor should pay particular attention to large or unusual transactions recorded at or near year-end, and should perform the analytical review procedures discussed in Chapter 9 and scrutinize the appropriate journals for unusual entries. The auditor should also inquire of management about the existence of transactions such as those described earlier, and additional management representations beyond the matters usually covered (see Chapter 17) should be included in the client representation letter if the client is in an industry in which those and other similar practices are common or if for other reasons the auditor is concerned that a high level of risk continues to exist.

Receivables from affiliates, directors, officers, and employees should be reviewed to determine that they have been properly authorized and are actually what they purport to be. If loans have been made over a long period of time, past experience often provides evidence of the intentions of the debtors. It is good practice to review those receivable accounts even though they appear to have been settled before the balance sheet date, especially to see whether the underlying debt was renewed after the balance sheet date. Those that in fact represent advances or loans should be segregated and so described. Disclosure on the balance sheet of receivables from affiliates, directors, officers, and employees does not reflect on the integrity of those debtors.

Analytical Reviews

Relationships among revenue accounts and between revenue and other accounts should be reviewed and compared with those of prior periods and those anticipated in budgets. The most common relationships between accounts are the ratios of accounts receivable to sales, various allowance accounts to sales, and cost of goods sold to sales. It may also be useful to relate sales of certain product lines to one another. The ratios and the balances in the accounts themselves should be compared from month to month and with the corresponding period of the prior year. Trends and fluctuations should be noted and explanations sought for unusual patterns. Sometimes sales can be related to units sold or produced and the trend of an "average unit price" examined.

Analytical review procedures are helpful in providing assurance that sales and accounts receivable are neither understated nor overstated. Particularly if the auditor is not relying on controls over completeness of invoicing of goods shipped and recording of goods invoiced, tests of the reasonableness of recorded sales and analytical comparisons of accounts and relationships may provide much of the assurance the auditor needs and receives about completeness of sales and receivables.

Analytical reviews are particularly helpful in substantiating certain types of revenues. For example, the auditor can usually substantiate dues, tuition, and similar revenues rather easily by comparing receipts with membership or registration records. Sometimes the substantiation can be done on an overall basis: numbers of members or students multiplied by annual dues or tuition. At other times it is necessary to compare (usually on a sample basis) individual items from the accounting records with the membership or registration rolls. Auditing revenues from services provides another example. Often there are independently generated statistical data, such as numbers of rooms cleaned, beds made, meals served, and the like, which can be used to corroborate revenues.

Auditing Procedures: Special Considerations for Particular Types of Revenues

For the most part, the auditing procedures described in previous sections are adaptable to the great variety of circumstances encountered in practice. One auditing procedure may take on greater significance than another, or certain procedures may be used more extensively, but on the whole auditing procedures for many accounts in the revenue cycle are basically similar. Some of the more common variations that require emphasis on particular procedures are the following:

Cash sales.
Consignment sales.
Interest, rents, and similar fixed payments for the use of property.
Royalties, production payments, and similar variable revenues.
Gifts and donations.
Deferred income or unearned revenue.
Revenues from long-term contracts.

Chapter 16 discusses auditing procedures for income from marketable securities and investments.

Cash Sales

If sales for cash are significant, internal control is especially important. Cash sales are characteristic of relatively small unit value goods, which often are easily converted to cash and at the same time are difficult to keep under strict physical and accounting control. And, of course, cash itself is easy to lose or misappropriate. Therefore, management is likely to be deeply concerned with the control environment and the presence of regular and systematic accountability routines, segregation of duties between handlers of merchandise and handlers of cash, limited access to cash and merchandise, and close supervision. The auditor's examination of revenues from cash sales should focus more heavily on those controls than on cash and inventory counts because, however important the existence of the cash on a particular date may be, the ongoing control over cash and the recording of sales is more significant to both client and auditor.

Consignment Sales

Receiving confirmation from a consignee of sales for the account of a client and of inventory on hand is sufficient in most cases. There are important exceptions, however, for which more rigorous and specific procedures are required. Chapter 14 also discusses consignment inventories.

Rents, Interest, and Similar Fixed Payments for the Use of Property

Revenues from fixed payments can usually be substantiated fairly easily by an overall computation of amounts due and a comparison with amounts recorded. Usually, the client prepares a list of the properties, loans, and so on, and the related income; the auditor should test the list by examining leases, loan agreements, and similar contractual bases for revenues, noting and evaluating all special terms having financial statement implications. The auditor may also evaluate controls over the receipt and recording of revenues, including measures for controlling and accounting for the vacancy rate in rental properties, and should note and evaluate delinquencies and arrearages and their implications for the realizability of the related assets. Some or all significant loans receivable should be confirmed; the auditor may also wish to confirm leases and similar contractual obligations.

There are various methods of recognizing revenues from the use of property, particularly leased property. The auditor must evaluate not only the method employed but also the alternative methods in order to have a positive basis for concluding which most clearly reflects the economic facts of the client's business.

Royalties, Production Payments, and Similar Variable Revenues

Many kinds of revenues are based on a stipulated variable, such as production or sales. Usually, the buyer of a right subject to variable payments for its use is required to report to the seller from time to time the amount of the variable and the computation of the resulting payment. If the amount of revenue is not significant, most companies simply accept the payer's statement after a superficial scrutiny for reasonableness. In that event, the auditor can do much the same, by examining the agreement on which the payment is based, comparing receipts with those of the prior year, and possibly requesting confirmation that all amounts due have been reported and paid. If amounts are significant, contracts usually provide for an independent audit of the accounting for the variable, either by the seller's auditor or by an independent auditor acceptable to the seller. Satisfactory audit reports on the payments ordinarily provide reasonable assurance that the related revenues are fairly stated.

Gifts and Donations

Accountability for donations can be a problem because they are rarely covered by contract and they lack a delivery of goods or services to provide evidence that the revenue is due. If gifts are received centrally—as in development offices of colleges, hospitals, museums, and similar institutions—reasonably effective control procedures can be established: properly supervised opening of mail and recording of receipts, segregation of duties between handling and recording, early accountability through means such as issuing prenumbered receipt forms, and so forth. The auditor can test and evaluate those procedures in the same manner as controls over conventional sales are tested.

If donations are received by numerous volunteers—as in many agencies financed by ''annual drives''—control is likely to be poor because management may feel that it is impolitic or impossible to ask volunteers to submit to control procedures. In those cases, the auditor may have to make it clear in the audit report that responsibility for an opinion that all donations were recorded cannot be assumed and that the report covers only ''recorded receipts.''

It is possible, however, to establish adequate control over volunteer solicitations, as the systems in use in many United Way drives have proven. Solicitation forms are prepared in advance, and their issuance to volunteers, processing, and return are controlled. The possibility of abuse is thus minimized though not eliminated. In those cases, the auditor can test and evaluate the systems and controls and usually obtain reasonable assurance that gift revenue is fairly stated.

Deferred Income or Unearned Revenue

Sometimes accounting systems provide trial balances of detailed items supporting deferred income or unearned revenue balances, for example, students' advance payments of tuition. In those cases, the auditor can obtain the necessary assurance by reviewing the trial balance and comparing it with the control account, and examining individual items.

More often, transactions flowing through unearned revenue accounts are not controlled in detail. The input to the account may be on one basis—for example, ticket sales or subscription receipts—and the relief of the account may be on a different basis—a statistical measure of service delivered such as revenue per passenger mile or per issue delivered. In those cases, the client makes a periodic analysis or "inventory" of the account balance. That inventory consists of a detailed scrutiny of underlying data, for example, of subscription records or of transportation tickets subsequently "lifted." It can often be an extremely arduous and time-consuming effort, comparable in many ways to physically counting inventories. For that reason, the date selected is usually based on practicality and convenience, and seldom coincides with the fiscal year-end.

The auditor's observation and participation in the analysis should be similar to the observation and testing of physical inventory procedures. The auditor should observe and test the client's procedures and evaluate the results. If controls appear adequate and the resulting adjustment of the account balance is small enough to indicate that the method of relieving the account is reasonably accurate, the auditor can be satisfied with analytical reviews of activity and balances between the testing date and year-end.

Revenues from Long-Term Contracts

Audit evidence for revenues from long-term contracts is obtained from confirmations and the various means management uses to monitor and control fulfillment of contract terms and the allocation of revenues to fiscal periods. The client should provide the auditor with an analysis of each contract and the change orders that act as amendments. In many instances, an analysis prepared for management purposes will suffice, but in others an analysis will have to be prepared especially for audit purposes. Depending on the size and significance of the contracts, the auditor can compare the analysis to underlying data, including the contract itself, and can review the accounting for costs incurred to date, the estimates of cost to complete each contract, and the amounts of revenue recorded in the period under audit.

Revenues from long-term contracts are usually accounted for by the percentage-of-completion method. Under that method, revenues and receivables are recognized in proportion to the degree of completion of a contract. Accordingly, the auditor's primary objective is to obtain evidence about the reasonableness of the client's estimate of the degree of completion of the project. The client's estimate may be made by relating costs incurred to date to the estimated total cost to complete the contract (the cost-to-cost method), by obtaining an architect's or engineer's estimate of the stage of completion, or by physical measurement (usually accompanied by the auditor's observation) of the stage of completion, such as the number of production units completed.

After reviewing the client's documentation supporting the estimated total cost to complete a project, the auditor should compare the estimate with the contract price. If the estimated total cost to satisfy contract requirements exceeds the total contract price, a loss should be recognized in most circumstances. The auditor should also review the client's financial statement presentation, including disclosures, for conformity with the recommendations for long-term contracts found in the AICPA Audit and Accounting Guide, *Construction Contractors* (1981).

Review Questions

12-1. Specify the transaction types that make up the revenue cycle.

12-2. What are the objectives of internal accounting controls and administrative controls over sales of goods and services? Be specific.

12-3. With respect to invoice data, what controls should exist to ensure accuracy, validity, and completeness?

12-4. What are some typical errors that could occur in the absence of effective controls over the invoicing and billing procedures in the revenue cycle?

12-5. What types of management reviews may be encountered in the revenue cycle?

12-6. How is good internal accounting control achieved over cash receipts?

12-7. Explain the use and advantage of a lock box system.

12-8. On what basis, and by whom, should credit memoranda be issued?

12-9. What are the audit objectives for the revenue cycle? Be specific.

12-10. In developing an audit strategy for the revenue cycle, what information should the auditor obtain?

12-11. What are the objectives of internal accounting control over payments received for goods and services?

12-12. Give three examples each of typical compliance tests and substantive tests for the revenue cycle.

12-13. Distinguish between negative confirmations and positive confirmations of accounts receivable and indicate when each would be used.

12-14. When are confirmations particularly useful? What procedures should the auditor observe when processing confirmation requests?

12-15. What alternative procedures can be used when confirmation is not possible?

12-16. What are typical follow-up procedures for confirmation differences?

12-17. What procedures should be followed for the period between the interim date and year-end when confirmations were sent at the interim date?

12-18. What is lapping? How is it perpetrated? How can it be detected?

12-19. What would an auditor's approach be if the accounts receivable confirmation replies produced a sample error that, when projected to the population, exceeded the established tolerable error amount?

12-20. What procedures would you initiate if a second request for positive confirmation produces no response?

12-21. In performing an analytical review of the collectibility of receivables, what steps should be considered?

12-22. What would you do if the analytical review procedures revealed that the number of days' sales in the receivable balance is increasing?

12-23. If executive compensation is based on earnings, what additional concerns would an auditor have regarding receivables?

12-24. How would an auditor determine that all trade accounts receivable pledged as collateral are identified and disclosed?

12-25. What control procedures can be employed for gifts received by institutions?

Discussion Questions

12-30. Dodge, CPA, is examining the financial statements of a manufacturing company with a significant amount of trade accounts receivable. Dodge is satisfied that the accounts are properly summarized and classified and that allocations, reclassifications, and valuations are made in accordance with generally accepted accounting principles. Dodge is planning to use accounts receivable confirmation requests to satisfy the third standard of field work regarding trade accounts receivable.

> *Required:*
> a. Identify and describe the two forms of accounts receivable confirmation requests and indicate what factors Dodge will consider in determining when to use each.
> b. Assume Dodge has received a satisfactory response to the confirmation requests. Describe how Dodge could evaluate collectibility of the trade accounts receivable.

> (AICPA adapted)

12-31. Items 1 through 4 are based on the following information:

The following sales procedures were encountered during the annual audit of Marvel Wholesale Distributing Company.

Customer orders are received by the sales order department. A clerk computes the dollar amount of the order and sends it to the credit department for approval. Credit approval is stamped on the order and returned to the sales order department. An invoice is prepared in duplicate and the order is filed in the "customer order" file.

The "customer copy" of the invoice is sent to the billing department and held in the "pending" file awaiting notification that the order was shipped.

The "shipping copy" of the invoice is routed through the warehouse and the shipping department as authorization for the respective departments to release and ship the merchandise. Shipping department personnel pack the order and prepare a three-copy bill of lading: The original copy is mailed to the customer, the second copy is sent with the shipment, and the third copy is filed in sequence in the "bill of lading" file. The invoice "shipping copy" is sent to the billing department.

The billing clerk matches the received "shipping copy" with the customer copy from the "pending" file. Both copies of the invoice are priced, extended, and footed. The customer copy is then mailed directly to the customer, and the "shipping copy" is sent to the accounts receivable clerk.

The accounts receivable clerk enters the invoice data in a sales and accounts receivable journal, posts the customer's account in the "subsidiary customers' accounts ledger," and files the "shipping copy" in the "sales invoice" file. The invoices are numbered and filed in sequence.

> 1. In order to gather audit evidence concerning the proper credit approval of sales, the auditor would select a sample of transaction documents from the population represented by the
>   a. "Customer order" file.
>   b. "Bill of lading" file.
>   c. "Subsidiary customers' accounts ledger."
>   d. "Sales invoice" file.
> 2. In order to determine whether the system of internal control operated effectively to minimize errors of failure to post invoices to the customers' accounts

ledger, the auditor would select a sample of transactions from the population represented by the
    a. "Customer order" file.
    b. "Bill of lading" file.
    c. "Subsidiary customers' accounts ledger."
    d. "Sales invoice" file.

3. In order to determine whether the system of internal control operated effectively to minimize errors of failure to invoice a shipment, the auditor would select a sample of transactions from the population represented by the
    a. "Customer order" file.
    b. "Bill of lading" file.
    c. "Subsidiary customers' accounts ledger."
    d. "Sales invoice" file.

4. In order to gather audit evidence that uncollected items in customers' accounts represented valid trade receivables, the auditor would select a sample of items from the population represented by the
    a. "Customer order" file.
    b. "Bill of lading" file.
    c. "Subsidiary customers' accounts ledger."
    d. "Sales invoice" file.

(AICPA adapted)

12-32. In a small corporation that publishes fiction and other nontechnical books, four salespeople sell to about 1000 retail bookstores. Because of his knowledge of the bookstores, Dick Tolman, the sales manager, is required to approve each order before shipment is made. In the case of delinquent accounts the sales manager decides whether to extend further credit or to grant approval for any write-offs. One bookkeeper and two billing clerks handle the accounting records. The other personnel consist of three editors and their secretaries, and one production person who contracts with printers for the manufacture of the books. Shipments are made from the printers' warehouses directly to the bookstores.

Required:
Evaluate the controls over granting credit and writing off delinquent accounts.

12-33. The High Rise Condominium Association utilizes the services of the Jones Management Co. to oversee the operation of its clubhouse and recreation facilities, maintain and repair the property's common areas, and collect the monthly tenant assessments for membership. Membership is not mandatory and some tenants are not members. Tenants are instructed to make payments directly to a lock box account maintained at a local bank. The bank records the deposits and provides the management company with a monthly statement of receipts. Money is transferred periodically from the lock box account to an operating checking account at the request of the management company. The management company follows up delinquent assessments by telephone and requests the tenant to bring the delinquent payment directly to its clubhouse office. The management company's contract is renewed once a year at the annual meeting of the board of directors of the Condominium Association. The directors have no other involvement in the operations during the year.

Required:
a. Discuss the strengths and weaknesses of internal control over collection of tenant assessments.

b. What audit procedures would you use to test the cash receipts function of the High Rise Condominium Association?

12-34. The ABC Appliance Company, a manufacturer of small electrical appliances, deals exclusively with 20 distributors located throughout the country. On December 31, the balance sheet date, receivables from those distributors aggregated $875,000. Total current assets were $1,300,000.

With respect to receivables, the auditor followed the procedures outlined in the following list in the course of the annual examination of the financial statements.

1. Reviewed and tested system of internal accounting control; it was found to be exceptionally good and specific controls were relied on.
2. Tied in detail with control account at year-end.
3. Aged accounts; none were overdue.
4. Examined detailed sales and collection transactions for the months of February, July, and November.
5. Received positive confirmations of year-end balances.

Required:
Evaluate the adequacy and efficiency of this program. Give reasons for your recommendations concerning the proposed addition or omission of any procedures.

12-35. Briefly describe audit procedures that would be uniquely applicable in the examination of

1. Tuition income of private schools.
2. Rental income of office buildings.
3. Annual dues of golf clubs.
4. Donations to charity organizations.

12-36. In connection with an examination of the financial statements of Houston Wholesalers, Inc., for the year ended June 30, 1987, a CPA performs several cutoff tests.

Required:
a. 1. What is a cutoff test?
   2. Why must cutoff tests be performed for both the beginning and the end of the audit period on initial engagements?
b. The CPA wishes to test Houston's sales cutoff at June 30, 1987. Describe the steps that should be included in this test.

(AICPA adapted)

12-37. Generally accepted auditing standards call for confirmation of receivables by direct correspondence with the debtors, when practicable and reasonable. However, the usefulness to the auditor of receivable confirmations varies from client to client.

Required:
a. What are the purposes for which the auditor confirms receivables?
b. Briefly indicate why the usefulness of the replies might vary.
c. What should the auditor consider in arriving at a decision on whether to confirm all receivables or to confirm on a sample basis? What should the auditor consider in determining the extent of the sample?
d. Under what conditions would the auditor consider it impracticable to confirm receivables?

e. If accounts receivable are material, but the client refuses to permit the auditor to confirm them, what alternative procedures should the auditor perform? Are there other steps in addition to the alternative procedures that the auditor should take?

12-38. Harris, CPA, has been engaged to audit the financial statements of the Spartan Drug Store, Inc. Spartan is a medium-sized retail outlet that sells a wide variety of consumer goods. All sales are for cash or check. Cashiers utilize cash registers to process these transactions. There are no receipts by mail and there are no credit card or charge sales.

Required:
Construct the "Processing Cash Collections" segment of the internal accounting control questionnaire on "Cash Receipts" to be used in the evaluation of the system of internal accounting control for the Spartan Drug Store, Inc. Each question should elicit either a yes or no response. Do *not* discuss the internal accounting controls over cash sales.

(AICPA adapted)

12-39. The Micro Programming Company specializes in the sale of standardized software programs, principally to the accounting and legal professions. Its operation is located on the East Coast but it solicits sales through a network of independent commissioned salespeople throughout the country. On receiving an order, a salesperson notifies the sales department, which processes all orders from the East Coast location. Micro also offers a "trouble-shooter" service whereby customers can call a toll-free number and get expert answers to questions and problems concerning their software systems. This service is billed to customers based on the length of the phone conversation at a standard rate per minute.

Required:
What procedures should be followed to ensure that all time incurred for the "trouble-shooter" service is properly billed and recorded?

AICPA Multiple Choice Questions

These questions are taken from the Auditing part of Uniform CPA Examinations. Choose the single most appropriate answer.

12-40. Which of the following is not a primary objective of the auditor in the examination of accounts receivable?

  a. Determine the approximate realizable value.
  b. Determine the adequacy of internal controls.
  c. Establish validity of the receivables.
  d. Determine the approximate time of collectibility of the receivables.

12-41. For effective internal control, the billing function should be performed by the

  a. Accounting department.
  b. Sales department.
  c. Shipping department.
  d. Credit and collection department.

12-42. Which of the following internal control procedures will *most* likely prevent the concealment of a cash shortage resulting from the improper write-off of a trade account receivable?

    a. Write-offs must be approved by a responsible officer after review of credit de-
partment recommendations and supporting evidence.

    b. Write-offs must be supported by an aging schedule showing that only receiv-
ables overdue several months have been written off.

    c. Write-offs must be approved by the cashier who is in a position to know if the
receivables have, in fact, been collected.

    d. Write-offs must be authorized by company field sales employees who are in a
position to determine the financial standing of the customers.

12-43. At which point in an ordinary sales transaction of a wholesaling business would a lack
of specific authorization be of *least* concern to the auditor in the conduct of an audit?

    a. Granting of credit.
    b. Shipment of goods.
    c. Determination of discounts.
    d. Selling of goods for cash.

12-44. When a customer fails to include a remittance advice with a payment, it is a common
practice for the person opening the mail to prepare one. Consequently, mail should be
opened by which of the following four employees?

    a. Credit manager.
    b. Receptionist.
    c. Sales manager.
    d. Accounts receivable clerk.

12-45. An auditor confirms a representative number of open accounts receivable as of December 31, 1986, and investigates respondents' exceptions and comments. By this procedure the auditor would be most likely to learn of which of the following?

    a. One of the cashiers has been covering a personal embezzlement by lapping.

    b. One of the sales clerks has *not* been preparing charge slips for credit sales to fam-
ily and friends.

    c. One of the EDP control clerks has been removing all sales invoices applicable to
his account from the data file.

    d. The credit manager has misappropriated remittances from customers whose ac-
counts have been written off.

12-46. During the process of confirming receivables as of December 31, 1986, a positive confirmation was returned indicating the ''balance owed as of December 31 was paid on
January 9, 1987.'' The auditor would most likely

    a. Determine whether there were any changes in the account between January 1
and January 9, 1987.

    b. Determine whether a customary trade discount was taken by the customer.

    c. Reconfirm the zero balance as of January 10, 1987.

    d. Verify that the amount was received.

12-47. If the auditor obtains satisfaction with respect to the accounts receivable balance by alternative procedures because it is impracticable to confirm accounts receivable, the auditor's report should be unqualified and could be expected to

a. Disclose that alternative procedures were used due to a client-imposed scope limitation.

b. Disclose that confirmation of accounts receivable was impracticable in the opinion paragraph.

c. Not mention the alternative procedures.

d. Refer to a footnote that discloses the alternative procedures.

12-48. The use of the positive (as opposed to the negative) form of receivables confirmation is indicated when

a. Internal control surrounding accounts receivable is considered to be effective.

b. There is reason to believe that a substantial number of accounts may be in dispute.

c. A large number of small balances are involved.

d. There is reason to believe a significant portion of the requests will be answered.

12-49. When scheduling the audit work to be performed on an engagement, the auditor should consider confirming accounts receivable balances at an interim date if

a. Subsequent collections are to be reviewed.

b. Internal control over receivables is good.

c. Negative confirmations are to be used.

d. There is a simultaneous examination of cash and accounts receivable.

12-50. Which of the following procedures would ordinarily be expected to best reveal unrecorded sales at the balance sheet date?

a. Compare shipping documents with sales records.

b. Apply gross profit rates to inventory disposed of during the period.

c. Trace payments received subsequent to the balance sheet date.

d. Send accounts receivable confirmation requests.

12-51. To conceal defalcations involving receivables, the auditor would expect an experienced bookkeeper to charge which of the following accounts?

a. Miscellaneous income.

b. Petty cash.

c. Miscellaneous expense.

d. Sales returns.

12-52. Customers having substantial year-end past-due balances fail to reply after second request forms have been mailed directly to them. Which of the following is the most appropriate audit procedure?

a. Examine shipping documents.

b. Review collections during the year being examined.

c. Intensify the study of the client's system of internal control with respect to receivables.

d. Increase the balance in the accounts receivable allowance (contra) account.

12-53. The audit working papers often include a client-prepared, aged trial balance of accounts receivable as of the balance sheet date. This aging is *best* used by the auditor to

a. Evaluate internal control over credit sales.

b. Test the accuracy of recorded charge sales.

    c. Estimate credit losses.

    d. Verify the validity of the recorded receivables.

12–54. Smith is engaged in the audit of a cable TV firm that services a rural community. All receivable balances are small, customers are billed monthly, and internal control is effective. To determine the validity of the accounts receivable balances at the balance sheet date, Smith would most likely

    a. Send positive confirmation requests.

    b. Send negative confirmation requests.

    c. Examine evidence of subsequent cash receipts instead of sending confirmation requests.

    d. Use statistical sampling instead of sending confirmation requests.

Problems and Cases

12–60. The Sodium Drug Co. has recently been notified by the Food and Drug Administration (FDA) that its product, "Lull-A-Bye Tablets," an aid for insomnia, contains an excessive amount of salt and is a danger to people with high blood pressure. The FDA has instructed Sodium Drug Co. to recall all of the Lull-A-Bye tablets sold during the past year. As a result of the national publicity the case has received, returns of Lull-A-Bye tablets have started to pour in from around the country. The returns are from stores and individuals in the form of both unopened cases and boxes and half-empty individual bottles. Customers are demanding credit against existing accounts receivable or refunds. Mr. Gilbert, president of Sodium Drug Co., has requested your help in setting up procedures to handle this situation in an economical and efficient manner.

    Required:

    a. List the procedures you would recommend to handle the recall of Lull-A-Bye tablets from receipt of the returns to the granting of credit or refunds.

    b. Assuming that you are also the auditor for Sodium Drug Co. and the recall occurred in the middle of the fiscal year, what potential audit problems would you face for the year-end audit and what audit procedures would you perform?

12–61. During the year, Strang Corporation began to encounter cash flow difficulties, and a cursory review by management revealed receivable collection problems. Strang's management engaged Stanley, CPA, to perform a special investigation. Stanley studied the billing and collection cycle and noted the following:

The accounting department employs one bookkeeper, who receives and opens all incoming mail. This bookkeeper is also responsible for depositing receipts, filing remittance advices on a daily basis, recording receipts in the cash receipts journal, and posting receipts in the individual customer accounts and the general ledger accounts. There are no cash sales. The bookkeeper prepares and controls the mailing of monthly statements to customers.

The concentration of functions and the receivable collection problems caused Stanley to suspect that a systematic defalcation of customers' payments through a delayed posting of remittances (lapping of accounts receivable) is present. Stanley was surprised to find that no customers complained about receiving erroneous monthly statements.

Required:

Identify the procedures Stanley should perform to determine whether lapping exists. *Do not discuss deficiencies in the system of internal control.*

(AICPA adapted)

12-62. After determining that computer controls are valid, Hastings is reviewing the sales system of Rosco Corporation in order to determine how a computerized audit program may be used to assist in performing tests of Rosco's sales records.

Rosco sells crude oil from one central location. All orders are received by mail and indicate the preassigned customer identification number, desired quantity, proposed delivery date, method of payment, and shipping terms. Since price fluctuates daily, orders do not indicate a price. Price sheets are printed daily and details are stored in a permanent disk file. The details of orders are also maintained in a permanent disk file.

Each morning the shipping clerk receives a computer printout that indicates details of customers' orders to be shipped that day. After the orders have been shipped, the shipping details are input in the computer, which simultaneously updates the sales journal, perpetual inventory records, accounts receivable, and sales accounts.

The details of all transactions, as well as daily updates, are maintained on disks that are available for use by Hastings in the performance of the audit.

Required:

a. How may a computerized audit program be used by Hastings to perform substantive tests of Rosco's sales records in machine-readable form? *Do not discuss accounts receivable and inventory.*

b. After having performed these tests with the assistance of the computer, what other auditing procedures should Hastings perform in order to complete the examination of Rosco's sales records?

(AICPA adapted)

12-63. The flowchart on page 530 depicts the activities relating to the shipping, billing, and collecting processes used by Smallco Lumber, Inc.

Required:

Identify weaknesses in the system of internal accounting control relating to the activities of (a) warehouse clerk, (b) bookkeeper #1, (c) bookkeeper #2, and (d) collection clerk.

(AICPA adapted)

12-64. In connection with the audit of the financial statements of ABC Corporation for the year ended December 31, 1987, you have been requested to confirm accounts receivable, age the accounts, and adjust the related allowance accounts.

The general ledger accounts receivable control account showed a balance of $36,547.75. The accounts receivable subsidiary ledger contained the following data:

Account	*Invoice Dates* *1987*	*Amount*
Albany and Randolph Co.	12/15	$1,692.37
Asaph and Sons	10/20	2,750.00
Black Hardware Co.	9/13	550.00
	8/23	3,275.80
Collins & Jackson	12/21	1,125.50
Columbia Hardware Co.	10/14	1,302.20

SMALLCO LUMBER, INC.
Flowchart—Shipping, Billing, and Collecting

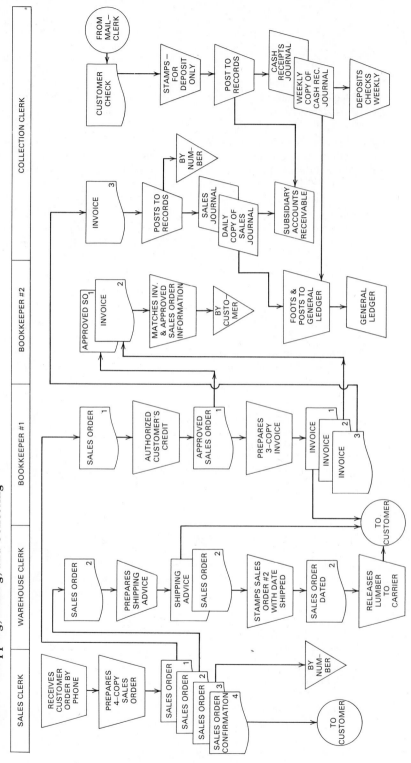

Account	Invoice Dates 1987	Amount
Daisy & Williams	11/15	$1,527.39
Davis, Edward J.	12/15	2,232.71
	12/24	200.00
Esterly Merchandise Co.	12/5	10,735.10
Grace Exporters, Inc.	12/10	(365.00)
Hanson, John E.	12/20	2,000.00
Hurdman & Jones	9/27	305.72
Lyons and Carnahan	12/7	(75.00)
McCavanaugh & Co.	12/10	320.00
Olson Hardware Co.	12/15/85	165.00
	8/10/85	932.20
Pacific Traders, Inc.	12/5	3,675.00
Simmonds Outlet Co., Inc.	11/25	1,249.80
Thompson & Co.	11/8	2,495.00
Wilson, David	12/10	250.00
Zoro and Son	8/17	203.96

(   ) = Credit balances.

Positive confirmations were mailed to customers with balances over $2500, and negative confirmations were sent to all others. Since the account of the Olson Hardware Co. was in the hands of the company's attorney, no request for confirmation was sent.

Replies acknowledging the correctness of the accounts were received from Albany and Randolph Co., Asaph and Sons, Esterly Merchandise Co., Hurdman & Jones, and Simmonds Outlet Co., Inc. Second requests were sent and received (affirmatively) from Black Hardware Co. and Pacific Traders, Inc.

Replies disputing the balance shown on the statements were received, as follows:

- Columbia Hardware Co. claimed an allowance of $250 for defective goods. This had been investigated and denied.

- McCavanaugh & Co. claimed a payment of $320 was made on December 31. This was received by the mail department on January 2 of the following year and credited on that date.

- John E. Hanson is a vice-president of the ABC Corporation and received an advance of $2000, which is to be repaid in monthly salary deductions of $200 each. This was authorized by the Board of Directors at the meeting of December 15.

- David Wilson is an employee of the ABC Corporation and received an advance of $250 to be repaid in monthly salary deductions of $50 each. This was approved by the treasurer.

- The Esterly Merchandise Co. is a wholly owned subsidiary. The balance in this account represents cash advanced for normal operations.

The credit balance in the account of Grace Exporters, Inc., represents an allowance made because of a mistake in pricing a quantity sale. The credit balance in the account of Lyons and Carnahan represents an overpayment resulting from a failure to take a cash discount.

Credit terms to all customers are 2/10, n/30. The policy of the company (which had always proven adequate) was to provide an allowance (on an individual account basis, after all adjustments, collections, etc.) of 10 percent on balances overdue 1 to 30 days, 25 percent on balances overdue 31 to 60 days, 50 percent on balances overdue more than 60 days or in dispute, and 100 percent on accounts in the hands of the company's attorney. The allowance for doubtful accounts showed a credit balance of $210 on December 31, 1987.

Required:

Prepare the necessary working papers for your analysis of the accounts receivable account and the allowance for doubtful accounts. Your working papers should clearly indicate all auditing procedures performed. (Solve this problem without regard to materiality considerations in order to illustrate all steps required.)

12–65. You are engaged in auditing the financial statements of the Darwood Company for the year ended December 31, 1988. In connection with your review of the adequacy of the allowance for doubtful accounts, the balance of which on December 31, 1987, was $45,000 (no amount has been provided for doubtful accounts for 1988), the following data are submitted to you:

	Net Sales		Uncollectible Accounts
Year Ended	For Credit	For Cash	Charged Off
December 31, 1985	$ 718,500	$52,200	$26,100
December 31, 1986	774,000	68,000	28,400
December 31, 1987	967,000	83,000	35,900
December 31, 1988	1,345,000	94,000	43,000

The aging schedule at December 31, 1988, shows $75,000 as being past due. However, this is considered by management to be a temporary seasonal situation and in line with previous years.

Required:

a. What audit procedures would you perform to determine the adequacy of the allowance for doubtful accounts?

b. What provision for doubtful accounts do you believe necessary (before considering the results of your audit work) to ensure the adequacy of the allowance for doubtful accounts?

12–66. You are auditing the Alaska branch of Far Distributing Co. This branch has substantial annual sales, which are billed and collected locally. As a part of your audit, you find that the procedures for handling cash receipts are as follows:

Cash collections on over-the-counter sales and C.O.D. sales are received from the customer or delivery service by the cashier. On receipt of cash, the cashier stamps the sales ticket "paid" and files a copy for future reference. The only record of C.O.D. sales is a copy of the sales ticket that is given to the cashier to hold until the cash is received from the delivery service.

Mail is opened by the secretary to the credit manager, and remittances are given to the credit manager for review. The credit manager then places the remittances in a tray on the cashier's desk. At the daily deposit cutoff time, the cashier delivers the checks and cash on hand to the assistant credit manager, who prepares remittance lists, makes up the bank deposit, and takes it to the bank. The assistant credit manager also posts remittances to the accounts receivable ledger cards and verifies the cash discount allowable.

You also ascertain that the credit manager obtains approval from the executive office of Far Distributing Co., located in Chicago, to write off uncollectible accounts, and that some remittances that were received on various days during the last month are in the custody of the credit manager as of the end of the fiscal year.

Required:
  a. Describe the irregularities that might occur under the procedures now in effect for handling cash collections and remittances.
  b. Give procedures that you would recommend to strengthen internal control over cash collections and remittances.

(AICPA adapted)

12–67. Your client is the Quaker Valley Shopping Center, Inc., a shopping center with 30 store tenants. All leases with the store tenants provide for a fixed rent plus a percentage of sales, net of sales taxes, in excess of a fixed dollar amount computed on an annual basis. Each lease also provides that the landlord may engage a CPA to audit all records of the tenant for assurance that sales are being properly reported to the landlord.

You have been requested by your client to audit the records of the Bali Pearl Restaurant to determine that the sales totaling $390,000 for the year ended December 31, 1986 have been properly reported to the landlord. The restaurant and the shopping center entered into a five-year lease on January 1, 1986. The Bali Pearl Restaurant offers only table service. No liquor is served. During mealtimes, there are four or five waitresses in attendance who prepare handwritten prenumbered restaurant checks for the customers. Payment is made at a cash register, manned by the proprietor, as the customer leaves. All sales are for cash. The proprietor also is the bookkeeper. Complete files are kept of restaurant checks and cash register tapes. A daily sales book and general ledger are also maintained.

Required:
List the auditing procedures that you would employ to substantiate the total annual sales of the Bali Pearl Restaurant. (Disregard vending machine sales and counter sales of chewing gum, candy, etc.)

(AICPA adapted)

12–68. This problem is a continuation of the Quinn Hardware case developed in Chapters 6 and 8. As the in-charge accountant, you are now considering the revenue cycle.

A revenue cycle narrative and accounts receivable data are provided in subsequent paragraphs. The following factors should also be considered:

  1. Discussion with the controller during a preliminary interview indicated that he was very confident of the adequacy of the year-end balance of the allowance for doubtful accounts and that any variances from prior years were "strictly temporary."
  2. A decision to perform substantive testing procedures for accounts receivable was made by the engagement manager and partner.
  3. Quinn's revenues are evenly distributed between its wholesale business (heavy mining and industrial equipment and building materials) and the retail hardware business in which it has six company-owned stores and over 200 franchised dealers.

4. As a result of your review of prior-year working papers and discussions with the engagement manager, you determined that in previous years computer software applications for accounts receivable were confined to various confirmation programs. Procedures for evaluating cutoff data, aging of outstanding balances, subsequent payment tests, and so on, were performed without the use of software. Apparently, there are no reasons or explanations given for not having used other available software applications.

QUINN HARDWARE
REVENUE CYCLE—NARRATIVE
(prepared by client)

Sales orders are received from customers over the telephone and through the mail. On receipt of the order, a sales clerk inputs order details from a terminal located in the sales department, determines the customer number from a listing of valid customers, and inputs the order details from a terminal located in the sales department. The sales clerk compares the customer data, which are shown on the screen, with the sales order and makes corrections, if necessary.

On input to the computer, the following computerized functions are performed:

a. Credit limit check—to ensure that the balance of the customer's account plus amount of the current order does not exceed the credit limit.

b. Availability of stock—if sufficient stock is not available, the order is processed as a back order.

Orders larger than $1000 and those that fail the credit limit check are forwarded to a supervisor for disposal/approval.

Shipping documents are generated and printed on a printer located in the warehouse. Stock is assembled and shipped based on the shipping documents.

Shipping document details are input via a terminal at the warehouse to produce sales invoices. Accepted shipping documents are priced against the Inventory Master File to determine cost of sales. The computer produces a weekly listing of unprocessed shippers, which is followed up by a warehouse clerk. The listings are retained for six months.

Inventory and accounts receivable master files are updated for stock movement; a general ledger transaction tape is produced daily to update the general ledger control.

The accounts receivable manager reviews sales analyses, accepted shipping documents, and inventory reports for reasonableness; periodically a reconciliation of data from the reports is completed although not documented.

Detailed customer statements, aged accounts receivable listings, and inventory summaries are produced monthly.

The current aged accounts receivable listing is reconciled to the previous month's total using current-month transaction data. The reconciliations are not reviewed by anyone other than the preparer.

QUINN HARDWARE
SELECTED DATA FOR FIVE YEARS:
(000's Omitted)

	1982	1983	1984	1985	1986
Sales	$41,900	$48,200	$53,100	$58,800	$64,200
Accounts receivable	7,770	8,950	9,159	9,448	10,068
Allowance for doubtful accounts	(650)	(700)	(800)	(900)	(900)
Net	$ 7,120	$ 8,250	$ 8,359	$ 8,548	$ 9,168
Bad debt expense	$ 625	$ 1,080	$ 950	$ 735	$ 775

COMPOSITION OF YEAR-END BALANCES (AGING)[a]

	1982	1983	1984	1985	1986
Current	$ 4,540	$ 5,100	$ 5,250	$ 4,868	$ 4,948
30–59 days	1,445	1,290	1,200	1,600	1,620
60–89 days	1,100	1,645	1,689	1,810	2,175
Over 90 days	685	915	1,020	1,170	1,325
	$ 7,770	$ 8,950	$ 9,159	$ 9,448	$10,068

[a]Tested and found reliable.

Required:

Determine a *strategy* (do not develop an audit program) to analyze the adequacy of Quinn Hardware's allowance for doubtful accounts at May 31, 1986.

In developing your strategy, recognize that the following additional information is available, on request, from the client:

1. Detailed listing of aged accounts receivable by customer for each year.
2. Summary of written-off balances for each year.

You should focus your attention on general factors and on the additional information you would expect to obtain in completing the analysis.

12–69. The aged trade accounts receivable trial balance on page 537 was prepared by the controller of Gold Importing Company for use by the independent auditors during their examination of Gold's financial statements as of and for the year ended December 31, 1986. All procedures performed by the audit assistant on the aged trial balance were noted on the working paper and explained in the "Legend and Comments" section.

The "customer confirmation responses" listed on page 536 represent information received directly by the audit assistant. The working paper entitled "Customer Confirmation Responses: Audit Procedures Performed" on page 538 indicates the procedures applied by the audit assistant to the confirmation responses and the conclusions reached. Both working papers were properly initialed, dated, and indexed and then submitted to the in-charge auditor for review. The risk of material misstatement of accounts receivable was assessed as being less than "high," but compliance tests of specific internal accounting controls over sales and cash receipts were not performed.

As the in-charge auditor, you have the following information that was not known to the audit assistant:

1. Company M is also a supplier. The $16,000 balance results from a netting of accounts receivable and accounts payable.
2. The working papers prepared during the physical inventory observation on December 31, 1986, indicated that merchandise for customer H was segregated and not included in inventory because the customer was expected to pick up the merchandise within a few days.

Required:

a. For each of the customer confirmation responses, indicate whether you agree or disagree with the audit procedures performed and conclusions reached by the audit assistant. If you disagree, specify what procedures should have been applied or conclusions reached.
b. What essential audit procedures were not noted as having been performed by the audit assistant?

Customer	Customer Confirmation Responses
A	"A check for $5000 was given to your salesman on November 15, 1986."
C	"Returned by post office, marked 'address incorrect, addressee unknown'."
F	"No balance is due since merchandise was shipped on consignment and goods have not been sold."
G	"Agree."
H	"The $10,000 represents an advance payment against a future purchase."
I	"Cannot confirm—accounts payable utilizes the voucher system."
J	"We cannot identify invoice for $7000—please send duplicate."
M	"Our records indicate a balance due of $39,000."
O	"A credit is due for $5000 for merchandise returned on January 12, 1987, for incorrect size."

Gold Sporting Company
Aged Trade Accounts Receivable Trial Balance
December 31, 1986

Customer	Total	Current Under 30 days	31-60 Days	Past Due 61-90 Days	Over 90 Days	Customer Confirmation Response
A	$ 25000	$ 20000	5000			"A check for $5,000 was given to your salesman on November 15, 1986."
B	15000	7000	5000	3000		"Returned by post office, marked 'address incorrect, address unknown.'"
C	7500				7500	
D	12000	2500		5000	4500	"No balance is due since merchandise was shipped on consignment and goods have not been sold."
E	(11000) S1				(11000)	
F	30000	15000		7500	7500	"Agree."
G	45000	45000				"The $10,000 represents an advance payment against a future purchase."
H	5000	(10000)	15000			"Cannot confirm - accounts payable utilizes the voucher system."
I	75000	50000	10000	10000	5000	"We cannot identify invoice for $7,000 - please send duplicate."
J	22000	15000		7000		
K	14000			14000		
L	8100	2700	2700	2700		
M	16000	21000	18000	(23000)		"Our records indicate a balance due of $39,000."
N	17000		17000			
O	27000	22000			5000	"A credit is due for $5,000 for merchandise returned on January 12, 1987, for incorrect size."
TOTALS	$307,600	$ 140,200	$ 72,700	$ 26,200	$ 18,500	
	W T Z	W	W	W	W	

Legend and Comments:

S1 = Selected for positive confirmation; however, the client indicated that this credit balance was due to a duplicate payment and requested that a confirmation not be sent. Auditor concurs but will perform alternative audit procedures.

S = Selected for positive confirmation; confirmation includes specific invoice numbers and amounts.

T = Agreed to general ledger.

W = Totals footed.

Z = Totals crossfooted.

GOLD IMPORTING COMPANY
Trade Accounts Receivable
December 31, 1986

Customer Confirmation Responses: Audit Procedures Performed

Customer	*Audit Procedures Performed*
A	Determined that the $5000 payment was given to the salesman and subsequently deposited into the company's cash account on January 7, 1986; no exception.
C	Reviewed shipping documentation to ensure that receivable is valid. No exception.
E	Examined cash receipts journal and noted that $11,000 in payments were received on August 7 and September 21; no exception.
F	Examined invoices, shipping documentation, and consignment listing and determined that customer was correct. Determined that the consigned merchandise was included in the year-end inventory; no exception.
G	No additional audit procedures necessary since account was confirmed as correct; no exception.
H	Determined that customer response was correct by examining cash receipts journal in December and an invoice dated January 31, 1987. The January invoice was offset against the advance payment; no exception.
I	Examined invoices and subsequent cash receipts of $25,000 in January; no exception.
J	The $7000 invoice was found to have been charged to customer J in error. The shipping records indicated that customer G received the merchandise and was never billed for it. Client will send bill and correct their records. Since the sale was recorded, there is no misstatement of the books and records and therefore this is not considered an error.
M	Determined that the $23,000 was related to the purchase of merchandise by examination of the related invoice, purchase order, and receiving documentation; no exception.
O	Examined receiving report and client approval for merchandise received in January. This requires an adjustment to reduce sales and accounts receivable by $5000; exception.

Chapter 13
Auditing the Buying Cycle

This chapter covers the "buying cycle" common to every business: the acquisition of goods and services in exchange for cash or promises to pay cash. Accounts encompassed by the buying cycle are defined and described. Typical buying transactions and internal controls over them are then presented in detail, including those for payrolls, followed by a discussion of the audit objectives and audit strategy for the buying cycle. Subsequent sections of the chapter present specific compliance and substantive tests that may be used in auditing buying cycle transactions and related account balances.

The buying cycle is part of the larger "expenditure cycle," in which some goods and services acquired are accounted for as assets until they are used and others are accounted for as expenses in the period of acquisition. The expenditure cycle comprises all transactions in which assets are produced or acquired, expenses are incurred, and payments are made to discharge liabilities incurred. Since the expenditure cycle is too broad to be covered in a single chapter and because it is usually more efficient to divide the cycle into more manageable segments when performing an audit, the expenditure cycle is discussed in several chapters. The discussion in this chapter is limited to auditing transactions involving purchases of and payments for goods and services generally, including human resources, and accounts related to those transactions.

As discussed in earlier chapters, the auditor's strategy and audit procedures vary depending on a number of factors, including materiality considerations, audit risk associated with different types of transactions and account balances, and audit efficiency considerations. For example, in determining the audit strategy for travel and entertainment costs, the auditor may conclude that the inherent risks associated with such costs in a particular enterprise or organization are relatively high and that internal control over certain aspects of the related transactions is not effective. This may prompt the auditor to rely heavily on substantive tests of travel and entertainment costs rather than to rely principally on compliance tests of controls. Conversely, if controls over payroll costs are effective and there is no significant inherent risk, the auditor may find it more efficient to rely principally on compliance tests and limit substantive procedures. Audit strategy decisions relating to the buying cycle are discussed in further detail later in this chapter.

Accounts Related to the Buying Cycle

Transactions that are part of the buying cycle affect numerous balance sheet and income statement accounts. This section discusses the accounts that are likely to be affected by transactions in the buying cycle. Subsequent chapters deal with accounts in the more broadly defined expenditure cycle, such as pension costs; rent expense; interest expense; prepayments and accruals; income taxes; property, plant, and equipment; inventories; and cost of goods sold.

The term *accounts payable* is used to describe specific amounts owed by an entity, usually arising from purchases of goods or services. In a narrow sense, it represents amounts due on open account to suppliers of merchandise, materials, or supplies, and evidenced by vendors' invoices. The term is also sometimes used broadly to encompass a wide variety of other amounts owed, such as accrued expenses or accrued liabilities, credit balances in customers' accounts, and refundable deposits received from customers. Buying activities that generate accounts payable involve purchases of merchandise or raw materials and the incurring of selling, general, administrative, and other expenses.

Depending on their purpose, expenditures for payroll may be recorded as assets, expenses, or both. Amounts withheld from employees' gross pay for such items as federal and state income taxes and miscellaneous authorized deductions are recorded as *agency obligations* (amounts held in trust for third parties) until such time as the liabilities are paid. Other agency obligations arise from payroll taxes and fringe benefits paid by employers. At the end of an accounting period, salaries and wages earned but not yet paid are recorded as an accrued payroll liability. Other related accruals must be recorded for certain compensated absences and rights to severance pay. Agency obligations and accrued liabilities are discussed in Chapter 16.

Selling expenses include expenditures for sales personnel salaries, commissions, and expenses, and other costs of selling goods and services, such as advertising, delivery, and overhead of the sales department. Also classified as selling expenses are warehousing costs for inventory pending sale, estimated losses from uncollectible accounts, and credit and collection expenses.

General and administrative expenses include salaries and expenses of corporate executives and of an enterprise's general offices and departments, such as accounting and credit, corporate expenses such as business licenses and fees, costs of reports to stockholders, and legal and auditing fees. Charges related to the occupancy of buildings, such as rent, depreciation, utilities, maintenance, taxes, and insurance, are usually allocated among manufacturing, selling, general, and administrative activities.

Other expense accounts affected by transactions in the buying cycle include research and development, maintenance and repairs, and travel and entertainment, which may also be allocated.

T-accounts are presented in Figure 13.1 to show the various transactions and accounts in a typical buying cycle.

Typical Transactions and Internal Control

The normal and repetitive procedures involved in buying goods and services in most contemporary businesses can be classified into three typical transaction types:

- Acquisition of goods and services.
- Payment for goods and services.
- Returning goods to suppliers.

Conceptually, payrolls are part of the buying cycle, but controls and procedures over payroll are somewhat unique to payroll processing. Accordingly, two additional transaction types relating to payrolls are often identified:

- Payroll processing.
- Payment of wages.

Acquisition of Goods and Services

The process of acquiring goods and services includes the following steps:

- Determining needs.
- Ordering.
- Receiving, inspecting, and accepting.
- Storing or using.
- Recording.

Determining Needs.   The buying cycle starts when someone identifies a need, which may occur in several different ways. For example:

Raw material inventory replenishment needs may be determined by a person or automatically when stock on hand reaches a reorder point or when a bill of materials for a job order is prepared. Sometimes sophisticated

Figure 13.1 Buying Cycle Accounts

Balance Sheet Accounts		*Income Statement Accounts*	
Cash		**Purchases of Raw Materials (Net)**	
Beginning balance	Cash purchases Payments to suppliers Payments to employees Payments of agency obligations	Cash purchases Purchases on account	Discounts granted for prompt payment Goods returned to suppliers
Accounts Payable		**Selling, General, and Administrative and Other Expenses**	
Payments to suppliers Goods returned to suppliers	Beginning balance Purchases on account Various expenses incurred on account Ending balance	Various expenses incurred on account	
Salaries and Wages Payable		**Compensation Expense**	
Payments to employees	Net salaries and wages payable	Salaries and wages Payroll taxes and fringe benefits	
Agency Obligation Accounts			
Payments of agency obligations	Payroll taxes and fringe benefits Amounts withheld for taxes and other deductions		

computer programs identify needs by reference to records of quantities on hand or production orders and simultaneously execute some of the steps in the buying process, for example, selecting vendors and preparing purchase orders.

Needs for occasional goods and services are identified and described by the user, usually on a requisition form that must be approved by the person (who may be the same as the user) responsible for authorizing the transaction.

The need for some services that are provided on a recurring basis by the same vendor, such as utilities, telephone, periodicals, or janitorial services, is usually determined initially and thereafter provided continuously or not redetermined until the end of the contract period.

Determining the need for specialized services, such as insurance, advertising, and legal and auditing services, is ordinarily the responsibility of designated individuals.

Needs for fixed assets are usually identified by a capital budgeting process.

The purpose of controlling requisitions is more closely related to operations than to accounting; the controls provide a means of collecting and documenting information needed to process requisitions efficiently. Requisitions are usually approved by a supervisor who has responsibility for a specific type of purchase. They may be prenumbered to aid in controlling the completeness of their processing.

Controls over requisitions can also have accounting significance if, for instance, overstocking results in the holding of assets that become obsolete. Control is often exercised by determining the optimum inventory level or purchase quantities. Examples of controls over overstocking are establishing economic order quantities and stock reorder points for inventory purchases and cost justification procedures for other expenditure requests.

Ordering. For most enterprises of significant size, administrative control is enhanced if trained purchasing agents rather than personnel from user departments determine sources, negotiate terms, and place orders. A separate purchasing function increases the efficiency and effectiveness of a modern business and is considered essential.

When the purchasing department receives a requisition, it first determines that the amount of the requisition is within the approved limit of the requisition, and then establishes administrative control over the requisition. The handling of requisitions before placing purchase orders requires specialized skills and experience for grouping items most efficiently, concentrating orders to obtain volume discounts while also maintaining multiple sources of supply, soliciting bids effectively, negotiating schedules for vendor production and storage prior to delivery, and generally getting the best possible prices and services. Weaknesses in administrative controls over ordering are often difficult to quantify because the cost of inefficient purchasing is generally not measurable; however, those weaknesses probably result in an increase in the cost of items acquired.

The purchase order authorizes a vendor to deliver goods or services and bill on specified terms. It should be complete and specific regarding time and method of delivery, specifications for materials, and quantity and price. The purchase order should also serve to authorize the receiving department to accept the goods described. Since the purchase orders authorize execution of transactions, control over their issuance is important and serves both accounting and administrative control purposes. For example, absent or ineffective completeness controls over purchase orders could result in failure to record provisions for losses on purchase commitments; they could also result in operational inefficiencies.

Accounting controls over purchase orders generally consist of procedures to

Ensure completeness by, for example, prenumbering purchase orders and subsequently accounting for all numbers.

Ensure validity by, for example, reviewing purchase orders for evidence of required authorization before mailing to vendors.

Ensure accuracy by, for example, reviewing purchase order preparation, including data transcribed from requisitions and master files of data on vendors, prices, quantities, and other data; extensions and footings; and account distribution. That review may be automated in part; prices may be compared with standards or averages based on past experience. Purchase orders with small dollar amounts or routine characteristics may be subjected to less detailed review.

Segregate the functions of purchasing, accounting, and receiving. Control is also enhanced if requisitioners receive copies of the purchase orders and review them for conformity with expectations.

Some specialized goods and services cannot be handled by a purchasing department because the technical and performance requirements are too esoteric or in some cases cannot be specified in advance. For example, the purchase of property and casualty insurance generally requires that an insurance risk analysis be performed. This analysis and the subsequent negotiations with an independent insurance agent or broker require special skill and training. Such types of specialized purchases must be negotiated directly between representatives of the responsible department and the vendor. Bypassing the purchasing department is likely to be a persistent and sometimes highly sensitive problem for most companies because of the conflict between the need for administrative and accounting control, which calls for a centralized purchasing function, and the desires of individual users, almost all of whom are likely to believe that they can get better quality and service by dealing directly with vendors. Deciding where to draw the line between operating autonomy and centralized purchasing varies from company to company, but even in companies with highly centralized purchasing systems some specialized services are allowed to bypass the purchasing function. In those cases, adequate accounting control is provided by controls that require agreements to be in writing, goods to be approved on receipt, and the user to approve the invoices.

Receiving, Inspecting, and Accepting. Most enterprises need written evidence that goods ordered and shipped by vendors were received, and must therefore have an organized means for securing it, even if it consists only of informal instructions to the people who accept deliveries. The receiving function should be organized to serve control purposes as well, as described later. In many enterprises the volume of receiving is so large that the receiving function is carried out in a specially organized department separate from the requisitioning, purchasing, and accounting departments.

The receiving function should inspect goods for conformity with specifications on purchase orders. Quantities should be verified by counting, weighing, or measuring. To improve the likelihood that receiving personnel will independently determine quantities, some systems provide for omitting quantities from the copy of the purchase order sent to the receiving department. The receivers should also determine the quality of goods to the extent possible, including lack of shipping damage. Laboratory or technical analysis of goods may be necessary in some cases to determine that their quality meets specifications. This requires specialized technical skills and is usually assigned to an appropriately staffed inspection department.

Receipt and acceptance of a shipment should be reported to the purchasing and accounting departments, usually by forwarding copies of a receiving report identifying the vendor, date received, quantity of goods received and their condition, and sometimes the carrier. Failure to report receipt of goods on a timely basis may result in understatement of payables and assets or expenses. Therefore, receipts should be controlled by prenumbering receiving reports and subsequently accounting for their use or by entering receipts in a register.

Services and some goods do not arrive through the receiving department but are received directly by users. While formal procedures may be prescribed for users to originate receiving reports, more often the vendor's invoice for the service or goods is forwarded to the user for approval and acknowledgment of receipt.

Storing or Using. Goods received through the receiving department should be forwarded to the appropriate location for storage or use. Controls over storage and issuance of purchased goods are covered in Chapter 14, "Auditing the Production Cycle and Inventory Balances."

Recording. An asset or expense and the related liability are most often recorded by people independent of the ordering and receiving functions on the basis of a vendor's invoice for goods or services and its agreement to an approved purchase order, and evidence of receipt or performance. Sometimes perpetual inventory records are posted from the receiving report after it is forwarded to the accounting department, while the control accounts are posted only after the invoice has been received and matched with the related purchase order and receiving report. Receiving reports not matched with invoices at the end of a period should generate an entry to record a liability for goods received but not billed.

Failure to establish control over vendors' invoices as soon as they are received is a common control weakness, particularly if many invoices must be routed for approval to operating personnel whose main interests are directed elsewhere. The resulting delay in recording the invoice can cause the misstatement of accounts payable and the related asset or expense accounts. Unless the movement of invoices is otherwise controlled, it is advisable to establish a record of and numerical control over them by some means such as immediate entry in an invoice or ''prevoucher'' register listing the vendor's name, amount of the invoice, voucher number assigned, and department to which it is forwarded.

Authorization for recording may be systematized: A clerk can be authorized to record invoices that have been properly approved by a supervisor in the requisitioning department (in the case of services) or invoices that match related purchase orders and receiving reports as to quantities, prices, and other terms (in the case of goods).

Once invoices have been authorized for recording, the transactions are recorded in a voucher register or purchases journal and are then summarized and posted. Before recording transactions, a clerk should recompute the calculations on the invoices and compare them with amounts on the purchase orders to determine that they are correct. This matching process should be evidenced in writing; usually a cover sheet is prepared and attached to the supporting documents. This cover sheet is commonly referred to as a ''voucher,'' and all of the supporting documents as the ''voucher package.'' The account distribution should be reviewed and entered (sometimes an initial account distribution is noted on the purchase order) to prevent transactions from being misclassified. Procedures should be established to ensure that invoices are recorded in the proper period.

Supervision over the clerical processes of authorizing invoices for recording and actually recording them is exercised by review and approval of those procedures by a responsible, knowledgeable individual. Alternatively, invoices could be approved by supervisors when checks for payment are prepared or when they are signed. Supervisory review and approval are sometimes performed on only a representative sample of vendors' invoices or on specific types of vendors' invoices, most commonly if there are a large volume of low dollar value transactions and strong basic controls. Occasionally, basic control procedures for processing invoices are also performed on a sample basis; however, those procedures are usually limited to recomputing amounts and extensions on vendors' invoices.

Recording, summarizing, and posting may consist of entering invoice data in a voucher register from which totals are posted to ledgers either manually or using electronic data processing equipment. In either event, control over the completeness of processing and posting is provided by control (batch) totals that arithmetically prove that the ending result is equal to the sum of the beginning balance (in this case, of accounts payable) and the total of processed transactions (including payments). This arithmetically proved ending result should also be reviewed for postings of correct amounts to incorrect vendor accounts. Numbering the invoices early in the recording process, subsequently accounting for the numerical sequence, and periodically reviewing open files of invoices, receiving reports, and purchase orders awaiting the arrival of missing documents also serve as completeness controls over the recording of acquisitions of goods and services.

Control over the summarizing and posting process is provided primarily by supervision over reconciliations of accounts payable subsidiary ledgers to control accounts or, if companies do not maintain accounts payable subsidiary ledgers, as is the case with some voucher systems, by supervisory review of the reconciliation of total open (unpaid) vouchers to the accounts payable control account. The resolution of errors detected by the reconciliation and review processes should also be adequately supervised. Segregating the duties of those who prepare vouchers, approve them, post the detailed inventory and accounts payable records, maintain control accounts, perform the reconciliations and reviews, and resolve errors also enhances the effectiveness of the basic controls.

Payment for Goods and Services

Because of the liquid nature of cash, accounting controls over the cash disbursements process—the second transaction type in the buying cycle—are organized to provide all practicable and reasonable assurance that no unauthorized payments are made, that accurate records are made of each payment, and that unclaimed checks are adequately identified, controlled, and ultimately voided. Administrative controls should be designed to ensure that all liabilities are paid on a basis that meets cash flow and vendor relationship objectives, including taking all available discounts for timely payment.

Basic controls to prevent unauthorized payments include requiring valid support for all requests for payment and cancellation of invoices and receiving documents after checks are signed, to prevent those documents from being processed again. People who prepare checks should not have conflicting duties, such as originating requests for payment. The check signer should have evidence at the time the check is signed that the payment has been authorized. Physical security controls should provide that signed checks are mailed by the signer or handled in a way that makes them inaccessible to the people who authorize or process payments; unissued checks should be safeguarded and spoiled checks should be mutilated or otherwise controlled.

If the number of employees is limited and the same person performs duties that are incompatible from a strict internal control viewpoint, some measure of control can be achieved by involving the supervisor in the processing. For example, sometimes the same person records payments to vendors and draws the checks. In this situation, the supervisor who signs the checks should require that all supporting evidence accompany the checks presented for signature and should assign someone other than the processor to cancel the supporting documents and mail the checks directly to the vendors.

Administrative controls are required to ensure that all acknowledged liabilities are paid in time to take advantage of cash discounts, promote good relations with suppliers, and maintain the enterprise's credit rating. Control over timely payment is provided by periodic reviews of files of unmatched receiving reports and invoices and the aging of open accounts payable.

In addition, control over cash disbursements may be enhanced by management reviews of budgetary or financial reports. For example, management may receive detailed cash flow projections by month and type of expenditure, accompanied by explanations of unusual trends or significant deviations from projections. If management reviews the analyses in detail and obtains explanations for unusual or unexpected items, the risk of a significant unauthorized payment not being detected should be reduced.

A detailed listing of disbursements by check, showing payees and amounts, should be prepared and totaled daily or at other regular intervals. The list may be in the form of entries in a cash disbursements journal, a written tabulation of requests for checks to be issued, a computer printout, or an adding machine tape, perhaps supported by copies of checks issued. Totals on the list should be compared with credits to the cash control account in the general ledger and with debits to accounts payable or other control accounts. Transfers of funds between banks should be controlled to ensure that both sides of a transaction are recorded in the same accounting period.

If checks are prenumbered, all numbers should be accounted for. If they are numbered as they are processed, the numbering device should permit the client to be sure that the numbering is in fact sequential. When checks are signed, the signer should have written evidence in the form of approved vouchers that the payments are for valid enterprise obligations and that the data on each check have been compared with the details on the related vouchers. The check signer should cancel the vouchers and supporting documents by appropriate means to prevent their reuse to support accidental or intentional duplicate payments. Signed checks should be kept in the custody of the signer until mailed. The signer should be independent of all functions pertaining to cash receipts or payments, preparation of vouchers, preparation or distribution of payrolls, custody of cash funds, and general ledger posting.

Blank checks should be kept in a safe place with access restricted to those authorized to prepare checks. The numerical sequence of prenumbered checks should be accounted for as the blank checks are released for use. Checks should be protected against alteration, by use of both special paper and a protective writing device.

Individuals authorized to sign checks, either manually or in facsimile using a mechanical check signer, should not have duties that include preparing or approving vouchers, preparing checks, recording and accounting for the sequence of check numbers, or custody of blank checks. This separation of duties helps to ensure that checks are issued only to pay approved liabilities and that all checks issued are recorded in the cash disbursements journal. If a mechanical check signer is used, the signature plate should be in the sole custody of the person authorized to use it, who should also be responsible for ascertaining that only authorized checks are signed.

Checks should be drawn specifically to the order of the creditors being paid or to custodians of imprest funds being reimbursed. Checks should never be drawn payable to ''cash'' or to ''bearer.'' Drawing checks to the order of a specific entity or individual limits their negotiability and provides an acknowledgment of receipt through payees' endorsements. Machine processing makes it impracticable for banks to examine endorsements on all checks, but a bank that honors an improperly endorsed check that is made out to a specific payee is liable for the payment.

Signing or countersigning checks in advance should be prohibited. The dangers of signing checks in advance are obvious, and are easily avoided. Countersignatures are effective as an internal control procedure only if each signer makes an independent examination of checks and supporting documents. Although a countersignature affixed with proper understanding and discharge of assigned responsibility affords good internal control, signature by a single employee after careful examination of supporting documents offers greater protection than superficial countersignatures, which create an illusion of security and possible reliance by one person on functions not performed by another.

Disbursements made in currency are normally for advances, freight bills, and other minor expenditures and sometimes for wage and salary payments. Accounting control over currency disbursements is best maintained by keeping the fund (or funds) from which disbursements are made on an imprest system. In an imprest system, the fund is maintained at a fixed amount as determined by the requirements of the particular circumstances. Disbursements from the fund are supported by vouchers signed by the recipients and by appropriate documents; sometimes advance approval of disbursements may be required. The sum of unexpended cash in the fund and the vouchers for disbursements should always equal the fixed amount of the imprest fund. At regular intervals, or when the cash in the fund is low, the vouchers, with supporting documents attached, are presented for reimbursement of the imprest fund from general cash. When the fund is reimbursed, the vouchers should be canceled in an appropriate manner to prevent their reuse to support duplicate reimbursements. Cash balances in imprest funds should be reconciled periodically to balances in general ledger control accounts; the vouchers supporting reimbursement should be reviewed by a responsible person whenever reimbursement is sought.

Payments of payrolls in currency should ideally be made from a specially designated cash fund, usually provided by a withdrawal from general cash of the exact net amount of each payroll. The cash should be inserted in envelopes provided by the payroll office showing payee and amount payable. After the envelopes have been prepared, the information on them should be compared with an approved payroll list. Signed receipts should be obtained from employees when they receive their envelopes.

Unclaimed envelopes of employees who are absent on payday should remain in the custody of the paymaster (whose duties should not include payroll preparation, cash receipts, or petty cash) for distribution to the employees when they return to work or for a specified period, whichever occurs first. After the specified period, the unclaimed envelopes should be listed and at regular intervals the currency in them should be deposited in the general bank account and a liability for unclaimed wages recorded, to be handled as required by state law.

Returning Goods to Suppliers

Every credit due an enterprise because goods were returned or an allowance was negotiated is an asset equivalent to a receivable, although its recording is usually different, as discussed later. It is important, therefore, that these claims be adequately controlled. Such claims are likely to be nonroutine and infrequent, which makes their recording somewhat difficult to systematize and thus difficult to control. Some well-controlled companies, however, have policies for processing their own internally generated vendor debit memoranda.

Returns for credit must be prepared for shipment to the vendor, and the shipping department should have procedures for notifying the accounts payable and purchasing departments at the time items are returned. Control can be exercised through procedures similar to those used for controlling sales, for example, through a subsystem that requires all shipping documents and supporting materials to be accompanied by a numerically controlled debit memorandum, usually prepared by the purchasing department, which is recorded in a debit memorandum journal by the accounting department. Control of freight claims can usually be achieved in a similar manner.

When a credit memorandum is received from a vendor, it should be matched with the related debit memorandum, if any, shipping documents, and other relevant internally generated documents. Quantities returned, prices, dates, vendor's name, extensions, and footings should be compared by personnel independent of the purchasing, shipping, and inventory control functions. The transactions should be approved by responsible personnel on review of the documents for evidence that appropriate comparisons and reviews have been made. If companies have formal debit memorandum procedures, credits and claims are often deducted immediately from the next vendor payment without waiting for a vendor credit memorandum.

Claims for allowances, adjustments, and occasional returns that are not subject to the foregoing procedures should be subject to a procedure for notifying the accounting and purchasing departments of a dispute or claim due.

Since there are no positive means for controlling compliance with that type of procedure, periodic inquiry of all knowledgeable people throughout the company should be made regarding the existence of outstanding claims or allowances, which should be compared with the related records.

Even though they represent a valid asset, vendor credit memoranda or internally generated debit memoranda are usually not recorded as receivables, but rather as reductions of the payable to the vendor, because a legal right of offset ordinarily exists in such instances. If this offsetting results in a debit balance in a vendor payable account, the debit balance may be recorded as a receivable. Vendor debit balances are usually not reclassified unless the total amount of such accounts is material. If reclassification is necessary, appropriate allowances for collectibility should be considered because the debit balances often arise from deposits with vendors who no longer do business with the company.

Payrolls

Payroll processing is the one function that is most likely to have similar characteristics from one organization to another. This similarity has made payroll processing the service most commonly offered by data processing service bureaus. Over the years, payroll systems have become increasingly organized and generally well controlled. The payroll transaction system, while conceptually similar to the broad buying cycle, is usually subject to different procedures and controls. Additionally, a feature of the typical payroll transaction that distinguishes it from the typical buying transaction is the withholding of amounts to cover various types of employee obligations, for example, taxes and insurance premiums, and the payment of those accumulated amounts.

Payroll Processing

Payroll processing includes authorizing employment, recording time worked or output produced, and calculating gross pay and deductions.

Authorizing Employment. Documents authorizing employment should be prepared independently of the prospective employee's immediate supervisor and those responsible for preparing the payroll. Preferred practice is to lodge that responsibility in the personnel department, which, in the formal hiring process, creates records authorizing employment, the rate of pay, and payroll deductions. The personnel department should also be responsible for formally preparing pay rate changes and employee termination notices.

The employment records contain data of a permanent or semipermanent nature, sometimes referred to as standing data. Standing data such as employee name, social security number, rate of pay, and tax exemptions are used for calculating gross pay and deductions each time a payroll is processed. Consequently, errors in standing data usually lead to more material errors than do errors in data unique to each pay period, such as hours worked. Changes to standing data are relatively infrequent. The completeness, accuracy, validity, and maintenance of the standing data should be controlled by using and accounting for prenumbered input forms for new hires and terminations, and by personnel department review of recorded payroll standing data and changes thereto, which are frequently computer generated in the form of "exception" reports. This type of review is sometimes supplemented by using "hash" totals. A hash total is the sum of any numerical data. For example, hash totals could be calculated for any standing data used in processing a payroll, such as rates of pay or even employee social security numbers. If the total of these data after processing does not agree to a predetermined hash total, one or more transactions were not processed properly (e.g., an employee was listed more than once or not at all, or the wrong social security number was used).

Recording Time Worked or Output Produced. Evidence of performance of services (including overtime) should be produced in the form of time reports or clock cards, which should be controlled by supervisory review and approval. If pay is based on production rather than time, as with piece work or commissions, the quantity basis should be similarly approved and reconciled to available production or sales data that are under accounting control. Control is also facilitated by comparison of payroll costs with standards or budgets or by reconciliation to production cost or job order records.

The records created in this step contain data that are unique to each transaction and thus are sometimes referred to as transaction data. This information is used in only one payroll processing and is more likely to change each time a payroll is processed than are the standing data used in the calculation of gross pay and deductions.

Calculating Gross Pay and Deductions. Calculating gross pay and deductions involves matching the transaction data and standing data for each employee. The computation of pay may be simple or exceedingly complex; it may be done manually or by computer. In any event, basic control consists of reviewing the resulting payroll journal and recalculating the gross pay (including the rates used) if the payroll, or a section of the payroll, is calculated on an hourly rather than a straight salary basis, or using control totals derived from a separate calculation of the aggregate payroll amount. In either event, the payroll should be approved by a responsible official based on evidence that the basic control was applied effectively. The self-interest of employees and their ready access to the personnel department also act to limit the risk of underpayment. Normally the risk of overpayment is reduced by limit controls, for example, specifying the maximum amount of a payroll check, or by establishing payroll grade levels with maximum salaries for each level.

Accounting distribution for financial statement purposes is ordinarily not difficult to control because the wages of most employees are usually charged to the same account from one period to another. Accounting distribution for detailed cost accounting systems may call for allocation of pay among cost centers; in those cases, control is usually exercised by the use of control totals. The accuracy of the allocation is controlled by the investigation of differences revealed by variance analysis.

The computation of payroll deductions is governed either by statute (in the case of payroll taxes) or contract (union agreement, group insurance contract, or agency agreements with charitable organizations or credit unions). The authorization to make deductions from an individual's pay is given by the employee in writing and is ordinarily obtained and maintained by the personnel department. Cumulative records of deductions are required for each employee, and the posting to the cumulative records acts as a control total for comparison with the amounts withheld from each payroll. Control over payments of withheld amounts is similar to control over payments of recorded accounts payable.

Once the standing data have been appropriately updated and information regarding the current pay period has been ascertained, many companies contract with a data processing service bureau for the actual calculating of gross pay and deductions. If this is done, the output from the service bureau should be reviewed in the same manner as discussed earlier. The fact that the payroll processing is done by someone else does not eliminate the necessity of maintaining good control over output.

Payment of Wages

Payment of the net pay amount is usually accomplished by check, most often prepared as an integral part of the payroll calculation. Therefore, approval of payroll checks usually includes comparing the total of all checks with the total of the payroll summary. Segregation of duties related to payroll disbursements made by check should be the same as that related to other cash disbursements. It is especially important to segregate duties if the checks are distributed rather than mailed. For example, employees' checks should be distributed by persons who do not have responsibility for preparing or approving the payroll.[1]

Cash payrolls, once common, are becoming a rarity, primarily because of the additional costs entailed in maintaining control over currency and the increasing availability of personal banking. As with noncash payrolls, the handling of cash payrolls can be turned over to specialized contracting agencies. If a cash payroll is handled internally, each payroll should be accounted for on an imprest basis. The required denominations of currency and coin should be pretallied; preparation of pay envelopes should consume all the currency drawn for that purpose, and the pay envelopes should be totaled after preparation for reconciling to the imprest total. Pay envelopes should be controlled until turned over to employees in exchange for signed receipts. The pay should be distributed by a person without conflicting duties. The signed receipts and un-

---

[1]Internal auditors may observe a payroll distribution to provide assurance that payments are not made to nonexistent personnel. At one time, it was not uncommon for external auditors to perform the same test, but, except for special "fraud audits," this is rarely done at present.

claimed pay envelopes should be promptly reconciled when the distribution is complete.

Unclaimed wages (checks or currency) should be listed at once, kept under control, investigated with the personnel department to determine the existence of the employees, and returned to cash if unclaimed within a short time.

In most organizations, the recognized advantages of segregation of duties are not difficult to achieve. In the accounts payable system, the duties of purchasing, receiving, recording, and paying are segregated as a matter of operational logic and efficiency as well as good accounting control. Similarly, in the case of payroll, the duties of the personnel and accounting departments are separated, and the person who approves time records is independent of both departments. The handling of payroll checks or cash should be separate from all three.

Planning the Audit Strategy

Audit Objectives

The objectives of auditing procedures for the buying cycle are to provide an auditor with sufficient and competent evidence that

- Accounts payable are properly authorized, represent the correct amount of currently payable items, and reflect all outstanding obligations.
- Accrued payroll accounts accurately reflect amounts earned but not yet paid.
- Expense accounts include all costs, expenses, and losses applicable to the period, including unrealized losses on unfavorable purchase commitments.
- Account descriptions, classifications, and related disclosures are adequate and not misleading.

Liabilities are more likely to be understated or omitted from the accounts than overstated because the account balances consist of items that have been scrutinized and acknowledged before being recorded, and any inclination to improve financial statement presentation only adds to that likelihood. Therefore, auditing procedures in the buying cycle concentrate heavily on seeking evidence of omitted or understated liabilities, although the possibility of overstatement is not ignored.

Audit Strategy

As discussed in Chapter 8, the process of determining an effective and efficient audit strategy begins with the auditor's developing and documenting an understanding of the control environment and the flow of transactions through the client's systems. Based on this understanding, appropriately documented, the auditor makes an initial evaluation of whether it would be efficient to rely on controls. Even if controls exist, the auditor may conclude that the reduction in the amount of substantive testing that could be achieved through reliance on controls would not be sufficient to justify the amount of compliance testing that would have to be performed or that it would simply be more practicable to perform substantive testing, as would normally be the case with a client that has low volume or predominantly high dollar value transactions. If, in light of the risks involved, the control system appears to be adequate, and the auditor believes that it is likely to be effective and efficient to rely on specific controls to reduce the level of substantive tests, the auditor will identify those controls, evaluate their design, and perform compliance tests to determine whether they can in fact be relied on.

Analytical review procedures, discussed in Chapter 9, frequently highlight account relationships and inherent risks not otherwise apparent from other planning techniques; their use often results in more informed decisions in selecting the audit strategy. Discussing the results of analytical procedures with company personnel may also give the auditor insight into the quality of the control environment. For example, logical and meaningful answers to questions about differences between current-year expenses and budgeted amounts as of an interim date or corresponding prior-year amounts would indicate, in the absence of evidence to the contrary, that the company's management is in ''control'' and the internal accounting and administrative controls appear to be functioning as intended. Those procedures, however, also may indicate trends, even in well-controlled companies, that may force the auditor to extend substantive tests. For example, a combination of high inventory levels, depressed sales, and normal levels of profit and cash in poor economic conditions may cause the auditor to extend substantive tests in searching for unrecorded liabilities. Examples of analytical review procedures performed as substantive tests are discussed later in this chapter under the heading ''Substantive Tests.''

If the auditor's risk assessment indicates that the client is in a good cash and working capital position; has an effective budgeting system; has strong general controls in its electronic data processing department and strong application controls over processing of vendors' invoices; has no overlapping of duties in the purchasing, receiving, and accounting departments; exercises numerical control and periodic follow-up over purchase orders and receiving reports; records all vendors' invoices immediately in a voucher register or other book of original entry on agreement of the invoice to the purchase order and receiving report; and has supervisory review over this matching process and the subsequent vendor invoice recording process, the client would be a strong candidate for an audit strategy geared toward performance of compliance testing to reduce significantly the amount of substantive testing. It would be rare, however, for the auditor to rely solely on the control system in searching for unrecorded liabilities.

On the other hand, the audit strategy should emphasize substantive testing if the client has a weak cash and working capital position and other potential motives for not recording liabilities; a nonexistent or an ineffective budgeting system, which could result in employees purchasing unnecessary goods and incurring unwarranted expenses; weak general and application controls, which create the possibility of purchases not being recorded or being recorded in incorrect amounts; or lack of numerical control over purchase orders and receiving reports and lack of supervisory review over the processing of invoices, which also could result in unrecorded or incorrectly recorded amounts. In that type of client environment, there obviously would be very few, if any, controls to compliance test and, accordingly, the amount of substantive testing could not be reduced. Such a situation may on rare occasions raise an auditor's doubts about whether the enterprise is auditable, as the potential for unrecorded liabilities could be so great that a disclaimer of opinion might be unavoidable.

The previous two paragraphs describe extreme situations to highlight the effect of client controls in the buying cycle on the determination of the audit strategy. In practice, many companies are not either that well or that poorly controlled. Professional judgment is required to select an effective and efficient audit strategy, that is, the appropriate combination of compliance and substantive testing, when a client's controls are somewhere between the two extremes just described. If the client's system contains at least minimal controls over the buying cycle, the auditor usually need not perform extensive detailed testing aimed specifically at supporting the existence of recorded liabilities, since the risk associated with overstated liabilities is relatively low and because many of the compliance and substantive tests discussed in this chapter that support assertions about accuracy and valuation of payables provide assurance about their existence as well.

Compliance Tests

Acquisition of Goods and Services

Acquiring goods and services, as described earlier in this chapter, includes the following steps:

- Determining needs.
- Ordering.
- Receiving, inspecting, and accepting.
- Storing or using.
- Recording.

Compliance tests applicable to acquisition of goods and services are discussed from the perspective of the steps involved in acquiring goods and services. The tests are also summarized in Figure 13.2 according to the objectives of internal accounting control—completeness, validity, accuracy, maintenance, and physical security—to which those tests are related.

Figure 13.2 Acquisition of Goods and Services: Control Objectives, Potential Errors, Accounting Controls, and Compliance Tests

	General Objectives of Internal Accounting Control				
	Completeness	Validity	Accuracy	Maintenance	Physical Security
Specific objectives of internal accounting control	All valid purchase transactions are recorded and processed.	All recorded purchase transactions represent actual receipts of goods and services as authorized by responsible personnel.	Purchases are accurately recorded as to amounts, quantities, dates, and vendors in the proper period in books of original entry and detail subsidiary records, and are accurately summarized in the general ledger.	The unpaid items in a voucher register or accounts payable subsidiary ledger and the general ledger control account are in agreement, do not contain any posting errors, and reflect all authorized transactions and only those transactions.	*Note:* The physical security control objective relates principally to the proper control of tangible assets, such as inventory and plant and equipment. Adequate physical controls over those assets are necessary and are discussed further in conjunction with the production cycle in Chapter 14 and the audit of property, plant, and equipment in Chapter 15.
Potential errors in account balances from absent or ineffective controls	Goods and services may be received but not recorded, causing an understatement of inventory, expenses, and accounts payable, and thereby causing an over-	Invalid transactions may be recorded, resulting in an overstatement of expenses and accounts payable and inventory (if a physical inventory is not	Errors on receiving reports or vendors' invoices may go undetected, causing an understatement or overstatement of expenses, accounts payable, or inventory.	Purchases, expenses, and accounts payable may be either understated or overstated because the control account balance is not in agreement with the	

(*Continued*)

Figure 13.2 Continued

	General Objectives of Internal Accounting Control			
Completeness	Validity	Accuracy	Maintenance	Physical Security
statement of income by not recording expenses or understating cost of sales. Unrecorded commitments to purchase at prices higher than prevailing prices or in excess of current requirements may result in income being overstated and liabilities (provision for losses) being understated.	taken to adjust recorded amounts to amounts actually on hand), and an understatement of income by overstating operating expenses for goods or services paid for but not received.	Transactions may be misclassified in the accounts; inventory, accounts payable, or cost of sales may be recorded in the wrong period.	voucher register or subsidiary ledger. Even if the above records are in agreement, the detail subsidiary ledger may contain mispostings of correct amounts to the wrong vendor account.	Not directly applicable to this transaction type.

Principal control techniques
Legend:
B = Basic control
D = Division of duties
S = Supervisory control

Completeness	Validity	Accuracy	Maintenance
Forwarding by purchasing department of copies of valid purchase orders, and by receiving department of copies of valid receiving reports to accounting department for agreement to vendors' invoices (B). Periodic accounting for prenum-	Procedures for authorizing purchases of goods and services, including prices and terms (B). Procedures for comparing invoices for goods and services received to receiving reports or authorized purchase orders by person-	Counting or weighing and inspecting of goods received at the time of receipt by personnel independent of the purchasing and inventory control functions (B). Procedures for reviewing invoices as to quantities received, prices,	Periodic reconciliation of the accounts payable subsidiary ledger or unpaid items in a voucher register with the general ledger control account by personnel other than those who review and approve documents for validity, post the accounts

(Continued)

bered purchase orders, prenum-bered receiving reports, and ven-dors' invoices (e.g., through the use of an invoice or "prevoucher" register), including investigation and resolution of un-matched items by personnel other than those who maintain the ac-counts payable subsidiary records, unpaid items in a voucher register, or control ac-counts (B).

Periodic review and approval of results of above procedures by responsible super-visory person-nel (S).

nel independent of the purchasing and receiving func-tions (B).

Final approval of invoices by respon-sible supervisory personnel based on a review that the appropriate cleri-cal comparisons and agreements have been per-formed and rejec-tion of any docu-ments containing discrepancies (S).

dates, vendors, terms, extensions, and footings by personnel indepen-dent of the pur-chasing and receiv-ing functions (B).

Review and ap-proval of invoices (based on evidence that above proce-dures have been completed) by responsible super-visory personnel independent of the purchasing and receiving func-tions (D,S).

Procedures for reviewing summa-rization of transac-tions, related asset or expense classifi-cations, and their posting to the gen-eral ledger (B).

Review and ap-proval of monthly summarizing en-tries by responsible supervisory per-sonnel (S).

Review of receiv-ing and invoice

payable subsidiary ledger, maintain the control ac-count, or are in-volved in the cash disbursements function (B).

Review of reconcil-iation procedures and results by responsible super-visory person-nel (S).

Periodic reconcili-ation of accounts payable subsidiary ledger to vendor statements by personnel other than those who review and ap-prove documents for validity, post the accounts pay-able subsidiary ledger, or maintain the control account (B). (*Note.* Recon-ciliation of vendor statements to the detail of accounts payable in a voucher system is generally not per-formed because a voucher system

Figure 13.2 Continued

	General Objectives of Internal Accounting Control			
Completeness	Validity	Accuracy	Maintenance	Physical Security
		processing procedures at the end of a period by responsible personnel independent of the receiving and invoice processing functions to ensure that purchase transactions are recorded in the proper period (B).	identifies accounts payable by voucher number, not by vendor.) Review of reconciliation procedures and results by responsible supervisory personnel (S).	
Typical compliance tests Inquire about and observe controls designed to ensure that all receipts are appropriately documented (3). Review client's accounting for the numerical sequence of purchase orders, receiving reports, and vendors' invoices (by examination of the invoice or voucher register) (1). Examine reports of unmatched documents for reason-	For a sample of transactions selected from the voucher register, examine supporting purchase orders, receiving records, and vendors' invoices for consistency between documents of description, quantities, prices, terms, vendors, dates, and amounts, and for evidence of appropriate authorization of the purchase (1).	Inquire about and observe the receiving control function of counting and inspecting goods received at the time of receipt. Inquire about resolution of quantity differences between the receiving report and vendor's invoice (1). For a sample of transactions selected from the voucher register (1):	Review reconciliation of unpaid items in a voucher register or accounts payable subsidiary ledger to control account, determining mathematical accuracy and reasonableness of documentation and of explanations for reconciling items (1). Examine above reconciliation for evidence of supervisory review and approval (2).	

Legend:
1 = Examination of evidence and/or reperformance of the related basic controls described above. If supervisory controls are believed to be effective, reperformance can normally be restricted to part of one period, with

(Continued)

testing of the related supervisory controls spread throughout the period of intended reliance.

2 = Examination of evidence that the related supervisory control described above is present to ensure the continued operation of the related basic controls. These tests should be spread throughout the period of intended reliance.

3 = Observation of the operation of a control; may be performed one or more times during the year, as appropriate.

ableness of explanations and evidence of independent review and approval (2). Select a sample of completed receiving reports from throughout the year and determine that goods received were matched to the corresponding purchase order and vendor's invoice and recorded in the voucher register (1).

Examine above documents for evidence of review and final approval by responsible personnel, including available evidence of rejections or comparisons performed by the person before giving final approval (2).

- Trace prices to purchase order or vendor price list.
- Recalculate extensions and footings.
- Ascertain consistency between documents of quantities, descriptions, and dates received and recorded.
- Review propriety of account classification.
- Determine proper posting to subsidiary records, including date of transaction (not applicable to voucher systems).

Examine above documents for evidence that the above controls were applied by client (1).

Examine above documents for evidence of supervisory review and

Review reconciliations of accounts payable subsidiary ledger to suppliers' statements, determining reasonableness of explanations for and disposition of reconciling items (not applicable to voucher systems) (1).

Examine above reconciliation for evidence of supervisory review and approval (2).

Figure 13.2 Continued

	General Objectives of Internal Accounting Control			
Completeness	*Validity*	*Accuracy*	*Maintenance*	*Physical Security*
		final approval (2). Test arithmetical accuracy of voucher register and compare totals to general ledger postings (1). Examine monthly summarizing entries of purchase transactions for evidence of review and approval (2). Review receiving and invoice cutoff procedures (1).		

Determining Needs. Requisitioning, the first step in acquiring goods, does not have a direct effect on the accounts since a requisition does not give rise to an accounting entry, and the loss of control over requisitions, whatever operational problems it might create, does not necessarily create accounting problems. (One significant exception to that generalization is the encumbrance system of accounting used by units of government and related agencies, in which the requisition does give rise to an encumbrance entry.)

Therefore, an auditor may conclude that there is no audit purpose for compliance testing controls over requisitioning. On the other hand, an auditor may conclude that requisitioning establishes important initial conditions of documentation and accountability, which contribute to control over purchase orders and invoices, and, accordingly, that the results of compliance tests may contribute to the building of cumulative confidence in the system. In that event, the auditor would be interested in testing two control functions, control over creation and authorization of requisitions, and control over execution of authorized requisitions. Test data for the second function are generally found in the purchasing department; test data for the first function may be found in the files of the purchasing department or the requisitioning department, whichever is more convenient. The compliance test audit program might read as follows:

> Select x requisitions: Examine for completeness of descriptions, quantities, instructions as to delivery plans and dates; trace to underlying computations or control data; note evidence of authorization.
>
> Examine holding file of unfilled requisitions; note evidence of periodic review; inquire into old or otherwise unusual items.
>
> Examine file of completed requisitions; note evidence of accounting for numerical sequence; inquire into gaps in numerical sequence.

Ordering. Since the purchase order formally authorizes the execution of a purchase transaction, and is often used in its recording and payment, controls over preparation and processing of purchase orders are ordinarily of more interest to an auditor than are controls over requisitioning. The auditor is concerned that all valid purchase orders, and only valid purchase orders, are processed accurately and that there is evidence of supervisory review and approval. Since the auditor's interest in vendors' invoices is the same, compliance tests of controls over purchase orders are most often combined with compliance tests of controls over vendors' invoices. The compliance test program might read as follows:

> Select x paid invoices: Trace invoice data to comparable data on accompanying purchase order and receiving report.
>
> Examine purchase order for completeness: numbering, dating, description, quantity, price, delivery date, quality specifications, routing; examine evidence of approval.

> Examine vendors' invoices for evidence that extensions and additions have been reperformed and that data on the invoice have been compared with data on the purchase order and receiving document. Reperform those procedures (on a test basis if appropriate).
>
> Examine evidence of invoice approval.
>
> Examine open file of uncompleted purchase orders and inquire into reasons for old or unusual items; examine evidence of exception reports and other follow-up of old unfilled purchase orders.

Receiving, Inspecting, and Accepting. If goods are received in satisfactory condition and conform to the specifications on the purchase order, it is at this point that a liability has technically been created. The compliance test program under the ordering step includes determining that the vendor's invoice agrees with the receiving document. Additionally, the auditor may want to observe that the receiving department functions independently and produces adequate documentation to inform the accounting department and other interested parties about the receipt of goods ordered. The compliance test program might read as follows:

> Inquire about and observe the receiving department's checking of goods at the time of receipt.
>
> Review client's accounting for the numerical sequence of receiving reports and examine reports of unmatched documents for evidence of independent review and approval.
>
> Trace *x* receiving reports from the file of completed receipts and determine that purchases were recorded in a purchases journal or voucher register.

Storing or Using. Compliance tests of controls over storage and issuance of purchased goods are covered in Chapter 14, "Auditing the Production Cycle and Inventory Balances."

Recording. Once vendors' invoices have been tested for accuracy and validity (see the earlier discussion of "Ordering" in this section on "Compliance Tests"), the compliance test program for control over recording, summarizing, and posting of properly authorized, executed, and approved invoices might be as follows:

> For invoices examined in previous tests, trace to voucher register.
>
> Examine evidence of batch controls or other controls over the processing and posting and reperform the reconciliation of control totals, as appropriate.
>
> Test arithmetical accuracy of voucher register and trace postings from voucher register to control accounts.

Most accounting systems can be expected to include the control feature of reconciling the detail of accounts payable to the control account. The compliance test program might read as follows:

Examine reconciliation of unpaid items in a voucher register or accounts payable subsidiary ledger to control account, test the arithmetical accuracy of the open items in a voucher register or subsidiary ledger, and review significant reconciling items for propriety; examine reconciliation for evidence of supervisory review and approval.

In manufacturing companies, where most acquisitions are for raw materials, compliance testing controls over the buying cycle and those over raw material inventory can be closely related. A dual-purpose sample can be drawn from either raw material inventory data or purchasing data. In the latter case, the compliance test program might read as follows: For raw material purchase invoices included in the compliance tests under ordering, trace posting to perpetual inventory records.

Payment for Goods and Services

Payment for goods and services, whether accomplished by check or bank transfer, is usually well controlled. The objectives of internal accounting control related to the cash disbursements process are to ensure that all valid cash disbursements are accurately and completely recorded in the proper period and that the cash accounts are properly maintained subsequent to recording. Additionally, physical access to cash and unissued checks should be restricted to authorized personnel. Figure 13.3 summarizes the control objectives, potential errors, principal control techniques, and typical compliance tests of controls over the payment for goods and services.

Returning Goods to Suppliers

Returning goods to suppliers, the third transaction type in the buying cycle, is usually less significant than acquiring and paying for goods and services. Compliance tests would be performed only if the transaction type was significant and the audit strategy called for reliance on related specific controls. Those tests might include the following:

Inquire about and observe physical controls designed to ensure that all goods returned are appropriately documented.

Review client's accounting for the numerical sequence of documents supporting goods returned and claims made and debit memoranda.

For a sample of transactions selected from the voucher register or accounts payable subsidiary ledger and related records of goods returned/claims made and debit memoranda:

- Examine supporting shipping documents.
- Trace prices to original vendors' invoices.
- Recalculate footings and extensions.
- Ascertain consistency between documents of quantities, descriptions, dates returned and recorded, and other information.

Figure 13.3 Payment for Goods and Services: Control Objectives, Potential Errors, Accounting Controls, and Compliance Tests

	General Objectives of Internal Accounting Control				
	Completeness	Validity	Accuracy	Maintenance	Physical Security
Specific objectives of internal accounting control	All valid disbursements are recorded and processed.	All recorded cash disbursements are for actual receipt of goods and services as authorized by responsible personnel.	Cash disbursements are accurately recorded as to amounts, dates, and payees in the proper period in books of original entry and detail subsidiary records, and are accurately summarized in the general ledger.	The cash disbursements journal, unpaid items in a voucher register or accounts payable subsidiary ledger, and general ledger control account reflect all authorized transactions and only those transactions.	Access to cash and unissued checks is suitably restricted to authorized personnel.
Potential errors in account balances from absent or ineffective controls	Unrecorded cash disbursements may result in overstatements of cash and accounts payable and understatements of asset and expense accounts.	Erroneous or fraudulent payments may be made, resulting in: • Understatement of cash. • Overstatement of other assets. • Understatement of liabilities. • Misclassification of expenses.	Errors on checks or disbursements summaries may go undetected, causing understatements or overstatements of cash, accounts payable, assets, or expenses. Transactions may be misclassified in the accounts; changes in cash, accounts payable, and expenses may be recorded in the wrong period.	Cash, accounts payable, and assets or expenses may be understated or overstated because transactions are not recorded in both the cash and accounts payable control accounts. Even if the above accounts are in agreement, the detail subsidiary ledger may contain mispostings of correct amounts to the wrong vendor account.	Misappropriations of cash and related overstatements of income are possible because issuance of unauthorized checks may not be detected.

Principal control techniques
Legend:
B = Basic control (other than physical control)
D = Division of duties
S = Supervisory control
P = Physical control

Periodic accounting for prenumbered checks, both used and unused, and comparison to cash disbursements records, including adequate investigation of unaccounted-for items by personnel independent of any responsibility relating to accounts payable or cash disbursements (B).
Periodic review and approval of results of above procedures by responsible supervisory personnel (S).

Preparation of checks only on the basis of evidence that the validity of the transactions has been confirmed in accordance with the company's procedures by personnel other than those who initiate or approve documents that give rise to disbursements (B).
Signing of checks by officials independent of the invoice approval process (D).
Examination by the signatory, at the time of signing checks, of original supporting documents (e.g., invoices) that provide evidence of the transactions (B).
Cancellation of supporting documents by the signatory to prevent subsequent reuse (B).

Procedures for comparing checks, either individually or in the aggregate, with the disbursements records used for posting the accounts payable subsidiary records as to amounts, dates, and payees by persons other than those who maintain the accounts payable subsidiary records or control account (B).
Periodic review and approval of above procedures by responsible supervisory personnel (S).
Procedures for reviewing summarization of transactions and related account classifications, and their posting to the general ledger (B).
Review and approval of monthly summarizing en-

Periodic reconciliations of the unpaid items in a voucher register or accounts payable subsidiary ledger to the accounts payable control account, and of the bank statement to the general ledger cash account by personnel other than those who review and approve documents for validity, post the accounts payable subsidiary ledger, maintain the control account, or are involved in the cash disbursements function (B).
Review of reconciliation procedures and results by responsible supervisory personnel (S).

Proper safeguarding of supplies of unissued checks and control over their usage (P).
Voiding of and control over spoiled checks (P).
Adequate control over the custody and use of mechanical check signers and signature plates (P).
Forwarding of all checks, after signing, directly to payees (i.e., without being returned to originators) (P).

(Continued)

Figure 13.3 Continued

	General Objectives of Internal Accounting Control				
	Completeness	Validity	Accuracy	Maintenance	Physical Security
	Account for the numerical sequence of checks (1). Examine reports of unaccounted-for items for reasonableness of related basic controls described above.	For a sample of transactions selected from the disbursements records and paid checks, examine supporting documentation to determine that payment was approved in accordance with the company's procedures (1). Examine above documents to determine that checks were signed by an official independent of the invoice approval process (2). Examine above documents for evidence of review and final approval by the signatory, including available	tries by responsible supervisory personnel (S). For a sample of transactions selected from files of paid checks, compare amounts, dates, and payees to the cash disbursements journal and voucher register and examine evidence of the matching/comparison process by persons independent of the accounts payable processing function (1). Examine reports of discrepancies for evidence of independent review and approval (2). Test arithmetical accuracy of cash disbursements journal and com-	Review client's reconciliations of unpaid items in a voucher register or accounts payable subsidiary ledger to the accounts payable control account, and of the bank statement to the general ledger cash account, ascertaining arithmetical accuracy and reasonableness of documentation and of explanations for reconciling items (1). Examine above reconciliations for evidence of supervisory review and approval (2).	Inquire about and observe that: • Unissued checks are adequately safeguarded (3). • Spoiled checks are adequately voided and controlled (3). • Custody and use of check signers and signature plates are adequately controlled (3). • Checks are forwarded directly to payees after signing without being returned to originators (3).

Typical compliance tests

Legend:

1 = Examination of evidence and/or reperformance of the related basic controls described above. If supervisory controls are believed to be effective, reperformance can normally be restricted to part of one period, with testing of the related supervisory controls spread throughout the period of intended reliance.

pare totals to general ledger postings (1). Examine monthly summarizing entries of cash disbursements for evidence of review and approval (2).

evidence of rejections, performed by the person before signing (1). Determine that supporting documents are canceled by the signatory (2).

2 = Examination of evidence that the related supervisory control described above is present to ensure the continued operation of the related basic controls. These tests should be spread throughout the period of intended reliance.

3 = Observation of the operation of a control; may be performed one or more times during the year, as appropriate.

- Review propriety of account classifications.
- Determine proper posting to subsidiary records, including date of transaction.

Payroll Processing

In testing controls over payrolls, an auditor seeks reasonable assurance that the system accurately records all costs and expenses and related liabilities for valid salaries, wages, and related benefits. As indicated earlier in this chapter, payroll processing involves the use of both standing data and transaction data.

There are two main types of errors in payroll standing data that could have a direct effect on the calculation of gross pay: nonexistent employees or the exclusion of employees, and incorrect rates of pay. Management's (and the auditor's) primary concern is the potential overstatement of the gross payroll. For example, if employees are not paid because they were not included in the standing data, or were underpaid because of an incorrect rate of pay in the standing data, they will bring the situation to management's attention. On the other hand, employees are not necessarily inclined to acknowledge overpayments.

Since missing or ineffective controls over standing payroll data can affect payroll calculations each time a payroll is processed, the auditor may choose to design separate tests of compliance over client controls in this area. Compliance tests of controls over standing data may include the following:

> Review evidence of client's accounting for the numerical sequence of standing data change forms and examine reports of unaccounted-for documents for evidence of independent review and approval.
>
> Select a sample of employees listed in the payroll standing data file and:
> - Trace to authorization of employment, rate of pay, and deductions in the appropriate personnel records.
> - Note approval by appropriate responsible supervisory personnel.
> - Compare selected standing data change forms with standing data file and note evidence of comparison by personnel independent of payroll preparation.
> - If client uses hash totals as a standing data file control, review client's hash total reconciliations.

In addition to testing controls over payroll standing data, the auditor will also be interested in controls over transaction data (hours worked or output produced) and the matching of the two types of data in computing gross pay and deductions.

Figure 13.4 summarizes control objectives, potential errors, principal controls, and typical compliance tests of controls over payroll transactions. The maintenance objective is discussed in terms of payroll deductions only, because payroll deductions are the only aspect of payroll processing (other than changes to standing data) in which subsidiary records are created.

Figure 13.4 Calculating and Recording Payroll: Control Objectives, Potential Errors, Accounting Controls, and Compliance Tests

	General Objectives of Internal Accounting Control				
	Completeness	*Validity*	*Accuracy*	*Maintenance*	*Physical Security*
Specific objectives of internal accounting control	All valid payroll transactions are recorded and processed.	All recorded payroll transactions represent actual services rendered as authorized by responsible personnel.	Payroll is accurately recorded as to amounts, date, department or job, and employees in the proper period in books of original entry and in detail payroll records, and is accurately summarized in department or job summary records and the general ledger.	The payroll summary and general ledger control accounts for payroll deductions reflect all authorized transactions and only those transactions.	*Note:* The physical security control objective is not directly applicable to this transaction type.
Potential errors in account balances from absent or ineffective controls	Services may be provided but not recorded, causing an understatement of payroll expense, liabilities, inventory, or other assets.	Invalid transactions may be recorded, resulting in an overstatement of liabilities and payroll expense, inventory, other assets, or cost of sales.	Transactions may be misclassified in the accounts, resulting in a misstatement of inventory, other assets, cost of sales, or payroll expense.	The liability for amounts deducted may be misstated because errors in recording may not be detected.	
Principal control techniques Legend: B = Basic control S = Supervisory control	Procedures for summarizing total hours per time cards or time sheets and comparing these data to	Approval of time or output records by supervisory personnel, including approval of overtime for	Review of the calculation of gross pay and payroll deductions by agreeing totals with predeter-	Reconciliation of control accounts for payroll deductions to the related payrolls by persons other than those	

(Continued)

Figure 13.4 Continued

| | General Objectives of Internal Accounting Control | | | |
Completeness	Validity	Accuracy	Maintenance	Physical Security
total hours recorded in payroll register (B). Review and approval of results of above procedures by responsible supervisory personnel (S). Procedures for summarizing payroll totals and comparing them to predetermined control totals and resolving differences (B). Review and approval of results of above procedures by responsible supervisory personnel (S).	salaried employees (B).	mined control totals or by sufficient recalculation of individual amounts; recalculation of the extensions and additions of payroll summaries by persons other than those who prepare the payroll (B). Final written approval of payrolls by a responsible official based on evidence of the above procedures having been performed, before payroll checks are released to employees (S). Review of the summarization of transactions, related expense and asset classifications, and their posting to the general ledger (S).	who prepare the payrolls (B). Review and approval of results of above procedures by responsible supervisory personnel (S).	

(Continued)

Typical compliance tests

Legend:

1 = Examination of evidence and/or reperformance of the related basic control described above. If supervisory controls are believed to be effective, reperformance can normally be restricted to part of one period, with testing of the related supervisory controls spread throughout the period of intended reliance.

2 = Examination of evidence that the related supervisory control described above is present to ensure the continued operation of

---

Reperform the summarization of total hours per time cards or time sheets and the comparison of those hours with total hours recorded in payroll register (1). Examine evidence of supervisory review and approval of the procedure to test completeness of hours recorded (2).

Reperform the summarization of payroll totals and the comparison of those totals with predetermined control totals (1). Examine evidence of review and approval of results of above procedures by responsible supervisory personnel (2).

For a sample of transactions selected from the payroll register, examine time or output records used as a basis for the payroll calculation for evidence of proper approval (including overtime, if applicable) (1).

For a sample of transactions selected from the payroll register:

• Reperform the comparison/reconciliation of time or output records to records of time spent or production records, as appropriate (1).

• Reperform the comparison/reconciliation of sales commissions to sales records (1).

Examine above documents for supervisory review and approval by responsible personnel (2).

Reperform the calculation of gross pay and payroll deductions or the agreement to predetermined control totals; test arithmetical accuracy of the payroll and payroll summaries (1).

Review reconciliation of payroll deduction control accounts to the related payrolls, ascertaining mathematical accuracy and reasonableness of documentation and of explanations for reconciling items (1). Examine above reconciliation for evidence of supervisory review and approval (2).

Figure 13.4 Continued

	General Objectives of Internal Accounting Control				
	Completeness	Validity	Accuracy	Maintenance	Physical Security
	the related basic controls. These tests should be spread throughout the period of intended reliance.		Examine payroll for evidence of supervisory review and final approval prior to payment (2). Test arithmetical accuracy of payroll summaries and compare totals with general ledger postings; review propriety of account classifications (1). Examine monthly summarizing entries of payroll transactions for evidence of review and approval (2).		

Payment of Wages

The specific objectives of internal accounting control, potential errors in account balances, and principal control techniques are substantially the same for payment for goods and services and payment of wages. Consequently, the reader should refer to Figure 13.3, which summarizes the control objectives, potential errors, and accounting controls related to payment for goods and services.

The typical compliance tests described in Figure 13.3 under the completeness and physical security objectives are the same as those that the auditor would perform in connection with paying wages. Since payroll checks are usually prepared in conjunction with the calculation of the payroll, they are subjected to validity controls during that phase of processing. Therefore, the only compliance test that the auditor would perform beyond those discussed in Figure 13.3 under validity is to examine selected payroll checks to determine that they were signed by an appropriate official independent of the payroll preparation process. Like the validity objective, most of the controls to ensure the accuracy of payroll are built into the payroll calculation process. The only compliance test, in addition to those described in Figure 13.3 under accuracy, that the auditor performs involves comparing payroll checks with the payroll register and examining evidence that the comparison was performed by client personnel prior to release of the payroll checks. (If payroll checks are examined, double endorsements should be scrutinized; if the second endorsement is that of a person in a payroll or supervisory function, payroll "padding" may be a possibility.) The maintenance objective is not applicable to paying wages since subsidiary records are not created during this phase of processing.

Substantive Tests

As discussed earlier in this chapter, the auditor will have determined the nature, extent, and timing of substantive tests in the buying cycle on a preliminary basis when the audit strategy was selected. Before carrying out the planned program of substantive tests, the auditor must evaluate the results of the compliance tests performed, if any, to determine whether the planned substantive tests are still appropriate.

Also, as discussed in the "Audit Strategy" section earlier in this chapter, answers to questions resulting from analytical review procedures related to accounts in the buying cycle have an impact on the nature, extent, and timing of substantive tests. For example, updating the interim comparison of current-year expenses with budgeted or prior-year amounts provides additional information that either confirms earlier impressions and judgments, or raises further questions and issues that must be resolved to the auditor's satisfaction. As another example, a large amount, in relation to the total account balance, of trade accounts payable represented by unmatched receiving reports and invoices that have not been approved and recorded may indicate weaknesses, breakdowns, or delays in the procedures for processing and approving invoices, which, in turn, would increase the risk of misstatement of the total accounts payable balance. Also, no increase in the year-end accounts payable balance in light of known increased client purchasing activity may also indicate control weaknesses or breakdowns and possibly raise questions concerning potential client errors or irregularities.

The remainder of this chapter discusses audit objectives and substantive test procedures that are likely to be performed on accounts related to the buying cycle under various conditions.

Accounts Payable

Substantive tests of the completeness of accounts payable at year-end will consist primarily of various cutoff tests. Cutoff tests are intended to ascertain that all significant transactions applicable to the period under examination have been recorded and no transactions applicable to the succeeding period have been recorded. In the absence of strong completeness controls, the sooner the accounts are closed after the end of a period, the greater the likelihood that there will be unrecorded vendors' invoices. Thus, examining files of unmatched receiving reports and unprocessed invoices, the voucher register, the cash disbursements book, and other relevant records for a period after year-end to review the accuracy of the client's cutoff is a virtually universal auditing procedure. (Cutoff tests of the receipt of goods and recording of inventory are usually coordinated with the auditor's observation of the client's physical inventory count; those tests are discussed in Chapter 14.) The extent of the search is based on the results of compliance tests and on errors found in performing other substantive tests. (Controls may break down at year-end after having operated satisfactorily throughout the year.)

If the basic transaction documents are in numerical sequence, the auditor can note the number of the last receiving report, the last voucher recorded, and the last check issued (or other basic transaction documents) prior to year-end. The auditor can examine perpetual inventory records, the year-end accounts payable trial balance, and the listing of unmatched receiving reports for inclusion of goods received at or near year-end. The same procedure can be followed for the last voucher number, which should be traced to the voucher register and cash disbursements book. Similarly, the last check issued can be traced to the cash disbursements book and voucher register and the list of outstanding checks in the bank reconciliation. The auditor should apply the same procedures to obtain assurance that receipts and vouchers applicable to the following year were not recorded in the current year. If the basic transaction documents are not prenumbered, it may be necessary to examine a sample of documents, with emphasis on transaction dates and large amounts, selected from the various sources both before and after the cutoff date to obtain sufficient evidence that the cutoff was properly made.

Some companies that do not have a voucher system follow the practice of reconciling vendors' statements with the accounts payable subsidiary records.

In this situation, the auditor may gain additional assurance regarding the accuracy of the cutoff by examining evidence that the reconciliations have been performed. If the client's staff has not reconciled vendors' statements with the accounts payable subsidiary records, the auditor may do so for selected vendors. If the company does not normally receive or retain the suppliers' statements, consideration should be given to confirming balances directly with suppliers.

Confirmation of accounts payable balances does not have the widespread acceptance as a source of audit evidence that confirmation of accounts receivable has. Confirmation usually is a highly relevant form of evidence about financial statement assertions dealing with the existence/occurrence (validity), and to some extent the accuracy, of recorded transactions and balances, and existence is a major audit concern with regard to receivables. On the other hand, confirmation is a relevant form of evidence about assertions regarding the completeness of recorded transactions and balances only if vendors with zero balances are included in the test, and completeness is a major audit concern with regard to payables. Audit satisfaction about the completeness of receivables is usually obtained through reliance on controls, year-end cutoff procedures, review of subsequent collections, and analytical reviews. Satisfaction about the existence of payables is usually obtained through reliance on controls over ordering and receiving goods and over recording invoices, through analytical reviews, and through the substantive tests discussed later; only rarely is confirmation an effective or efficient means of obtaining the necessary satisfaction regarding the existence of payables.

Confirmation of payables usually should not be necessary to provide additional evidence about the completeness of processing and recording liabilities. If the buying cycle is adequately controlled, the proper functioning of controls over ordering, receiving, and recording provides reasonable assurance that liabilities have been properly authorized and recorded. Also, the normal review of vendor and disbursement activity subsequent to year-end, as previously described (commonly referred to as an unrecorded liability test), also satisfies the completeness objective of substantive tests. Confirmation may be called for in the absence of internal accounting controls or if the results of other substantive tests indicate that payables may be incomplete or otherwise misstated. If it is undertaken, the confirmation procedure is parallel to that described in Chapter 12 for the confirmation of accounts receivable, except that an additional step of circularizing known suppliers with zero balances may be included. In extreme situations, if the auditor still needs further assurance as to possible unrecorded liabilities, the client may be requested to deliver the mail, unopened, to the auditor daily, so that the auditor can search for vendors' invoices applicable to the year under audit.

Substantive tests to ensure that recorded accounts payable represent valid and accurate obligations and are properly recorded on a timely basis normally consist of vouching the accounts payable subsidiary ledger or trial balance, reviewing the reconciliation of the subsidiary ledger or trial balance to the general ledger, and looking for debit balances that should be reclassified. Vouching the accounts payable subsidiary ledger or trial balance normally involves tracing selected entries to subsequent cash disbursements or other supporting documents, such as vendors' invoices, examining evidence that the client has matched all invoices to purchase orders and receiving reports, and reperforming the matching procedure (on a test basis if appropriate) to determine that all aspects of the transaction appear reasonable (e.g., that suppliers' invoices are addressed to the client). Reviewing the client's reconciliation of the subsidiary ledger or trial balance to the general ledger control account consists of tracing totals and significant reconciling items to appropriate supporting documentation. The auditor should also test the arithmetical accuracy of the client's accounts payable subsidiary ledger or trial balance and reconciliation. In addition, the underlying causes of debit balances in accounts payable should be investigated. They may represent overpayments; if so, the auditor should consider whether they are collectible. Confirming debit balances may be desirable, as well as identifying the credit that a debit entry was apparently intended to pay or cancel. A reclassification entry may be appropriate in the circumstances.

Salaries, Wages, and Payroll Taxes

Substantive tests of the complete and accurate recording of accrued payroll and related liabilities consist primarily of examining the subsequent payment of the liability in the following year. The auditor should obtain an analysis of accrued salaries and wages and test its arithmetical accuracy; totals should be agreed to the payroll register. If the company has recorded an estimate (e.g., proration of the payroll for the overlapping period) rather than an exact computation, the appropriateness and consistency with prior years of the method of estimation should be ascertained. The general ledger accounts relating to payroll expense should also be reviewed. Analytical reviews can be helpful in this regard; for instance, the number of employees and the average salary per employee can be compared with the prior year. Any material unusual entries, any unusual fluctuations in normal recurring entries in the payroll summaries, and payroll amounts capitalized in fixed asset accounts should be investigated. Substantive tests of details are normally not performed on payroll expense account balances unless internal controls are extremely weak or the results of other procedures, primarily analytical review procedures, indicate the need to extend detail testing.

Unremitted payroll taxes and payroll withholdings, referred to as agency accounts, should be supported by a trial balance of the detail accounts. For many agency accounts, the balance at the end of a period is remitted to the principal shortly thereafter, so that examining the subsequent payment and supporting detail serves to substantiate the balance. Comparing current year-end balances with those of the prior year would indicate unusual items. Some accounts, such as unclaimed wages, are not currently remitted; for those accounts the auditor should examine and test a trial balance reconciling the details to a control account and should scrutinize the underlying details for unusual items. If old unclaimed wages have been written off, potential liability under state escheat or unclaimed property laws should be considered.

Accrued commissions should be substantiated by examining sales reports submitted by sales personnel, commission schedules, and contracts with sales personnel. If accrued commissions are significant, confirming amounts due and commissions earned during the year directly with sales personnel should be considered. The overall reasonableness of commission expense for the year may be tested by multiplying commission rates by sales.

The year-end liability for vacation pay, sick pay, and other compensated absences should be reviewed for compliance with FASB Statement No. 43. If vacation periods are based on length of service, a detailed computation of the accrued liability is normally prepared by the client. The auditor should review the method used and perform sufficient testing of the computation to determine that the amount accrued is appropriate.

A published statement of company policy may create liabilities for rights that accrue to employees even without formal labor contracts. Opinion of counsel may sometimes be necessary to determine whether there is a legal liability at the balance sheet date. Contracts and policies of that nature do not always clearly indicate whether employees' rights accrue ratably over a period or come into existence in their entirety at a specific date. An auditor must also be alert for possible liabilities arising from employee benefits so customary as to constitute an implied promise. Sick pay, severance pay, and some kinds of bonuses and pensions are examples.

Costs and Expenses

Auditor satisfaction with respect to the income statement is based primarily on auditing procedures applied to balance sheet accounts, correlation of amounts appearing on the income statement with balances appearing on the balance sheet, the performance of other auditing procedures such as the review of performance indicators, and, where applicable, the evaluation and testing of specific controls. If reliance is not placed on specific controls, procedures such as the correlation of income statement amounts with balances in the balance sheet assume greater importance. Many income statement items can be correlated with balance sheet accounts, such as interest with loan balances. In addition, the reasonableness of the amounts can be assessed, for example, by comparing the percentage of selling, general, and administrative expenses in relation to sales from period to period. In computer systems, this assessment may be made with the help of computer software.

When the procedures just outlined have been completed, there may still be income statement accounts about which the auditor believes further assurance is needed. Tests should be designed to provide such assurance, normally in one of the following forms:

• If further assurance is needed regarding the validity or accuracy of amounts appearing in specific expense accounts (such as travel expense or maintenance expense), the auditor should request or prepare an analysis of the account in question, or at least of the material items in it, and examine supporting documentation for enough items to gain assurance that there is no material misstatement. For example, an auditor may obtain a list of employees with expense accounts and make appropriate tests to determine whether all expenses have been reported and recorded in the accounts in the proper period, and may test related post–balance sheet entries to determine whether a proper cutoff was made.

• If the auditor is concerned about the possibility of misstatement associated with a particular type of transaction rather than with particular account balances (as might be the case when there are weaknesses in controls over certain types of payments), the areas in the expense accounts that might be affected should be isolated. For example, if certain payments are supported by receiving reports and other payments are not, the auditor need perform substantive tests only with respect to the payments that are not supported by receiving reports. In this situation, the auditor would select a sufficient number of accounts that might be misstated and examine them to the extent necessary to obtain assurance that no material misstatement had occurred.

Other Audit Procedures

In addition to the specific substantive tests described, the auditor is concerned with procedures designed to detect other unrecorded liabilities, such as uninsured claims and other loss contingencies, as well as with receiving a letter of representation from management and a letter from the company's counsel. Those topics are covered in detail in Chapter 17, ''Completing the Audit.'' The remainder of this section describes other procedures the auditor should perform to detect unrecorded liabilities.

The auditor should read minutes of meetings of stockholders, directors, and appropriate committees for the period under examination and up to the date of the audit report. Those minutes may reveal contracts, commitments, and other matters requiring investigation. The auditor should also examine contracts, loan agreements, leases, correspondence from taxing or other governmental agencies, and similar documents. The review of such documents may disclose unrecorded liabilities as of the balance sheet date.

One of the auditor's most difficult tasks is identifying liabilities for which no direct reference appears in the accounts. Clues to those obligations may be discovered in unexpected places, and the auditor should be constantly alert for indications of their existence. For example,

• The auditor should review responses to standard bank confirmation requests in addition to an analysis of interest expense to determine if there are any unrecorded bank loans.

• Responses to requests for confirmation of bank loans may list as collateral securities or other assets that do not appear in the records. They may be borrowed from affiliated companies or others.

- Manufacturers of machinery and equipment often sell their products at prices that include cost of installation. The auditor should determine that the estimated cost of completing the installation of equipment sold has been recorded in the same period as the sale of the equipment.

In a decentralized environment, the possibility of unrecorded liabilities may be more significant than in a centralized environment and may warrant a procedure for formal inquiry of department heads, supervisors, and other responsible officials regarding knowledge of unprocessed invoices, unrecorded commitments, or contingent liabilities. This procedure may apply in a loosely controlled centralized environment as well.

The auditor should take a broad look at the client's operations to determine whether all types of expenses and the related liabilities, if any, that are expected have been recorded in reasonable amounts. Familiarity with the client's operations should disclose whether such items as royalties, commissions, interest, consignments, and the myriad of taxes to which most businesses are subject have been properly accounted for.

The search for unrecorded liabilities cannot, of course, bring to light liabilities that have been deliberately withheld from the auditor's attention. The auditor's responsibility regarding irregularities and illegal acts is discussed in Chapter 4. The receipt of a client representation letter, as discussed in Chapter 17, does not relieve the auditor of professional responsibilities in this area.

Finally, transactions with affiliated entities often are not conducted on the same basis as transactions with outsiders; thus, they deserve special attention from the auditor. For example, charges for services rendered may not be billed on a timely basis. Whenever feasible, the auditor should review a reconciliation of the amount due to or from an affiliate by reference to both sets of books. If this cannot be done, the balance should be confirmed.

Review Questions

13-1. What types of activity are generally considered part of the buying cycle?

13-2. What are agency obligations and why are they important?

13-3. What is the financial statement significance of having good control over requisitions?

13-4. Why are the effects of weaknesses in administrative (operational) controls over ordering difficult to quantify?

13-5. What are the objectives of accounting controls over purchase orders and how are they implemented?

13-6. What are the responsibilities of a receiving department?

13-7. What are the accounting requirements at the end of an accounting period with respect to receiving reports not matched with invoices?

13-8. What is a voucher? What documents are normally included in a voucher package?

13-9. What controls can be used to help ensure that disbursements are completely and accurately recorded?

13-10. What measures should be taken to prevent duplicate payments?

13-11. What supervisory controls should be established over the summarizing and posting of purchases and disbursements?

13-12. What are standing data as related to payroll? Give examples of controls over standing data related to payroll.

13-13. What are the objectives of auditing the buying cycle?

13-14. What characteristics of a client's buying cycle would indicate that less substantive testing could be performed?

13-15. What types of compliance tests would the auditor perform for controls over the acquisition of goods and services?

13-16. What types of compliance tests would the auditor perform for controls over payment for goods and services?

13-17. What is the purpose of performing receiving cutoff tests? How are cutoff tests in the buying cycle performed?

13-18. When may it be desirable to confirm accounts payable?

13-19. What substantive tests are generally performed with respect to accrued liabilities?

13-20. What procedures can an auditor perform that may reveal unrecorded liabilities at year-end?

Discussion Questions _____

13-30. Mincin, CPA, is the auditor of the Raleigh Corporation. Mincin is considering the audit work to be performed in the accounts payable area for the current year's engagement.

   The prior year's working papers show that confirmation requests were mailed to 100 of Raleigh's 1000 suppliers. The selected suppliers were based on Mincin's sample that was designed to select accounts with large dollar balances. A substantial number of hours were spent by Raleigh and Mincin resolving relatively minor differences between the confirmation replies and Raleigh's accounting records. Alternative audit procedures were used for those suppliers who did not respond to the confirmation requests.

   Required:
   a. Identify the accounts payable audit objectives that Mincin must consider in determining the audit procedures to be followed.
   b. Identify situations in which Mincin should use accounts payable confirmations and discuss whether Mincin is required to use them.
   c. Discuss why the use of large dollar balances as the basis for selecting accounts payable for confirmation might not be the most effective approach and indicate what more effective procedures could be followed when selecting accounts payable for confirmation.

(AICPA adapted)

13-31. While examining vouchers, an auditor noticed that a vendor invoice called for 60 items whereas the receiving report showed only 40 had been received. Payment for 60 items had been made and charged to inventory. Discuss the effect of the discovery on audit strategy and audit procedures to be followed.

13-32. A company received, recorded, and paid the invoice for advertising brochures, but the receiving report was not attached to the voucher. The unmatched receiving report remained in the unpaid file and served as the basis for a year-end adjusting entry for supplies received, not billed. What journal entry will be needed at year-end to correct the error? What audit procedures might uncover the error?

13-33. A company received and paid for 100 items of part number 616, although the purchase order called for part number 661. It cannot use part number 616 and will be able to recover only 25 percent of the cost. Discuss the effect of the discovery on audit strategy and audit procedures.

13-34. Evaluate the effect on internal accounting control and state possible errors or irregularities that may result from each of the following unrelated situations:

1. The same person prepares purchase orders and receiving reports.
2. The same person prepares purchase orders and approves invoices for payment.
3. The same person prepares receiving reports and approves invoices for payment.
4. Amendments to payroll standing data are not authorized in writing.
5. The petty cash custodian is prohibited from making disbursements in excess of $100, cashing checks, or making advances in excess of one-half of an employee's weekly pay.

13-35. It is your client's policy to have invoices and supporting documents accompany all checks presented for signature. The signing officer insists that the invoices and documents be marked "paid" before she will review them and sign the checks. Her objective is to preclude resubmission of the same invoices and documents in support of another check. Do you believe this procedure is effective? Explain.

13-36. The audit of trade accounts payable requires a different audit strategy and different procedures than the audit of trade accounts receivable. Answer the following questions in the light of this statement:

1. Why are trade accounts payable auditing procedures heavily weighted toward unrecorded liabilities?
2. What typical audit procedures are applied to discover unrecorded liabilities?
3. How do the procedures applied to discover unrecorded liabilities assist the auditor in substantiating account balances for recorded liabilities?
4. In your review of the detailed trade accounts payable listing, you noted that there are several significant debit balances and long overdue payables. What transactions could have caused these situations? What audit procedures should be performed?
5. What representations should be obtained from management related to trade accounts payable? Why?
6. What accounts should be reviewed in connection with fluctuations in trade accounts payable balances from period to period?

13-37. Mention several different methods to which dishonest employees may resort in manipulating payrolls. (Do not give variations of the same method.)

AICPA Multiple Choice Questions

These questions are taken from the Auditing part of Uniform CPA Examinations. Choose the single most appropriate answer.

13–40. For control purposes the quantities of materials ordered may be omitted from the copy of the purchase order which is

   a. Forwarded to the accounting department.
   b. Retained in the purchasing department's files.
   c. Returned to the requisitioner.
   d. Forwarded to the receiving department.

13–41. Which of the following is an internal control procedure that would prevent a paid disbursement voucher from being presented for payment a second time?

   a. Vouchers should be prepared by individuals who are responsible for signing disbursement checks.
   b. Disbursement vouchers should be approved by at least two responsible management officials.
   c. The date on a disbursement voucher should be within a few days of the date the voucher is presented for payment.
   d. The official signing the check should compare the check with the voucher and should deface the voucher documents.

13–42. In order to efficiently establish the correctness of the accounts payable cutoff, an auditor will be *most* likely to

   a. Coordinate cutoff tests with physical inventory observation.
   b. Compare cutoff reports with purchase orders.
   c. Compare vendors' invoices with vendors' statements.
   d. Coordinate mailing of confirmations with cutoff tests.

13–43. Which of the following *best* explains why accounts payable confirmation procedures are *not* always used?

   a. Inclusion of accounts payable balances on the liability certificate completed by the client allows the auditor to refrain from using confirmation procedures.
   b. Accounts payable generally are insignificant and can be audited by utilizing analytic review procedures.
   c. The auditor may feel certain that the creditors will press for payment.
   d. Reliable externally generated evidence supporting accounts payable balances is generally available for audit inspection on the client's premises.

13–44. An examination of the accounts payable account is ordinarily *not* designed to

   a. Detect accounts payable that are substantially past due.
   b. Verify that accounts payable were properly authorized.
   c. Ascertain the reasonableness of recorded liabilities.
   d. Determine that all existing liabilities at the balance sheet date have been recorded.

13–45. When examining payroll transactions an auditor is primarily concerned with the possibility of

   a. Overpayments and unauthorized payments.
   b. Posting of gross payroll amounts to incorrect salary expense accounts.

    c. Misfootings of employee time records.

    d. Excess withholding of amounts required to be withheld.

13–46. A CPA reviews a client's payroll procedures. The CPA would consider internal control to be less than effective if a payroll department supervisor was assigned the responsibility for

    a. Reviewing and approving time reports for subordinate employees.

    b. Distributing payroll checks to employees.

    c. Hiring subordinate employees.

    d. Initiating requests for salary adjustments for subordinate employees.

13–47. To check the accuracy of hours worked, an auditor would ordinarily compare clock cards with

    a. Personnel records.

    b. Shop job time tickets.

    c. Labor variance reports.

    d. Time recorded in the payroll register.

13–48. In a properly designed accounts payable system, a voucher is prepared after the invoice, purchase order, requisition, and receiving report are verified. The next step in the system is to

    a. Cancel the supporting documents.

    b. Enter the check amount in the check register.

    c. Approve the voucher for payment.

    d. Post the voucher amount to the expense ledger.

13–49. For internal control purposes, which of the following individuals should preferably be responsible for the distribution of payroll checks?

    a. Bookkeeper.

    b. Payroll clerk.

    c. Cashier.

    d. Receptionist.

13–50. A common audit procedure in the audit of payroll transactions involves tracing selected items from the payroll journal to employee time cards that have been approved by supervisory personnel. This procedure is designed to provide evidence in support of the audit proposition that

    a. Only bona fide employees worked and their pay was properly computed.

    b. Jobs on which employees worked were charged with the appropriate labor cost.

    c. Internal controls relating to payroll disbursements are operating effectively.

    d. All employees worked the number of hours for which their pay was computed.

Problems and Cases

13–60. Long, CPA, has been engaged to examine and report on the financial statements of Maylou Corporation. In the course of assessing Maylou's system of internal accounting control over purchases, Long was given the document flowchart for purchases shown on the following page:

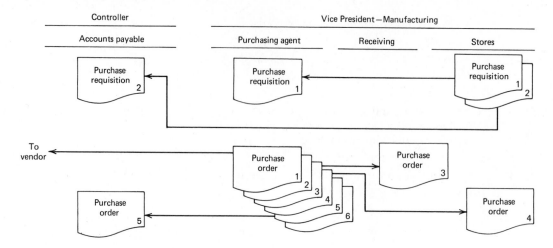

Required:

a. Identify the procedures, relating to purchase requisitions and purchase orders, that Long would expect to find if Maylou's system of internal accounting control over purchases is effective. For example, purchase orders are prepared only after giving proper consideration to the time to order and quantity to order. *Do not comment on the effectiveness of the flow of documents as presented in the flowchart or on separation of duties.*

b. What are the factors to consider in determining
  1. The time to order?
  2. The quantity to order?

(AICPA adapted)

13–61. A CPA's audit working papers contain a narrative description of *a segment* of the Croyden Inc. factory payroll system and an accompanying flowchart, as follows:

NARRATIVE

The internal control system with respect to the personnel department is well-functioning and is *not* included in the accompanying flowchart.

At the beginning of each work week, payroll clerk no. 1 reviews the payroll department files to determine the employment status of factory employees and then prepares time cards and distributes them as each individual arrives at work. This payroll clerk, who is also responsible for custody of the signature stamp machine, verifies the identity of each payee before delivering signed checks to the foreman.

At the end of each work week, the foreman distributes payroll checks for the preceding work week. Concurrent with this activity, the foreman reviews the current week's employee time cards, notes the regular and overtime hours worked on a summary form, and initials the aforementioned time cards. The foreman then delivers all time cards and unclaimed payroll checks to payroll clerk no. 2.

Required:

a. Based on the narrative and accompanying flowchart, what are the weaknesses in the system of internal control?

Croyden Inc.: Factory Payroll System

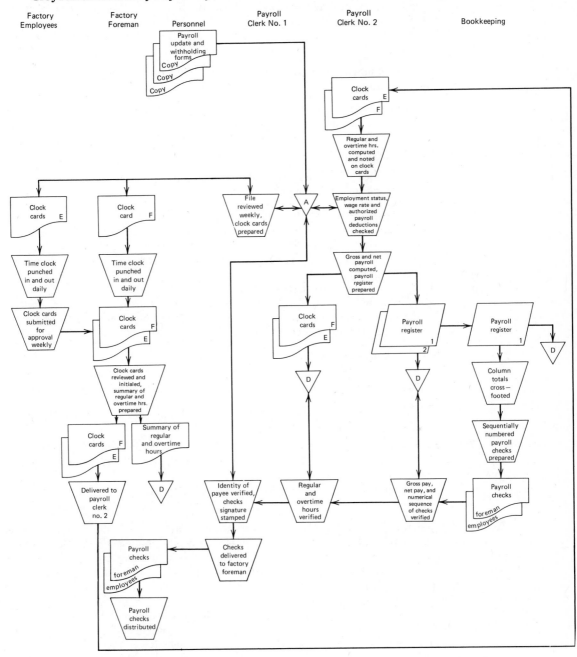

Factory Employees	Factory Foreman	Personnel	Payroll Clerk No. 1	Payroll Clerk No. 2	Bookkeeping

(Problem 13–61 continued overleaf)

b. Based on the narrative and accompanying flowchart, what inquiries should be made with respect to clarifying the existence of *possible additional weaknesses* in the system of internal control?

Note: Do not discuss the internal control system of the personnel department.

(AICPA adapted)

13-62. For each of the following audit procedures applied to the buying cycle (performed using sampling when appropriate), indicate

a. Whether the procedure is a compliance test or a substantive test.
b. The purpose of the procedure.
c. The possible errors or irregularities that the procedure may uncover.

In the Purchasing Area:

1. Account for the sequence of prenumbered purchase orders and review proper authorizations and supporting requisitions.

In the Receiving and Recording Area:

2. Account for the sequence of prenumbered receiving reports and trace receiving reports to vendors' invoices and voucher register.
3. Trace items on receiving log to receiving reports attached to related voucher disbursements.
4. Trace items on invoice register to voucher register.
5. Trace unmatched receiving reports at year-end to subsequent disbursements.
6. Perform purchasing cutoff procedures at time of physical inventory taking.
7. Foot and crossfoot voucher register. Trace totals to general ledger.

In the Disbursement Area:

8. Account for the sequence of prenumbered vouchers.
9. Account for the sequence of prenumbered checks; examine spoiled and canceled checks.
10. Examine vouchers for proper attachments: invoice, purchase order, receiving report, approval.
11. Examine vouchers for clerical accuracy, account distribution, recording in voucher register, cash disbursement recording, and cancellation of documents.
12. Foot and crossfoot cash books. Trace totals to general ledger.

13-63. The Generous Loan Company has 100 branch loan offices. Each office has a manager and four or five subordinates who are employed by the manager. Branch managers prepare the weekly payroll, including their own salaries, and pay employees from cash on hand. The employee signs the payroll sheet, signifying receipt of the salary. Hours worked by hourly personnel are inserted in the payroll sheet from time cards prepared by the employees and approved by the manager.

The weekly payroll sheets are sent to the home office, along with other accounting statements and reports. The home office compiles employee earnings records and prepares all federal and state salary reports from the weekly payroll sheets.

Salaries are established by home office job-evaluation schedules. Salary adjustments, promotions, and transfers of full-time employees are approved by a home office salary committee based on the recommendations of branch managers and area supervisors. Branch managers advise the salary committee of new full-time employees and terminations. Part-time and temporary employees are hired without referral to the salary committee.

Required:

a. Based on your review of the payroll system, how might funds for payroll be diverted?

b. Prepare a payroll audit program to be used in the home office to audit the branch office payrolls of the Generous Loan Company.

(AICPA adapted)

13-64. At the beginning of your annual audit of the Grover Manufacturing Company's financial statements, the company president confides in you that an employee, Bill Green, is living on a scale in excess of that which his salary would support.

Green has been a buyer in the purchasing department for six years and has charge of purchasing all general materials and supplies. He is authorized to sign purchase orders for amounts up to $200. Purchase orders in excess of $200 require the countersignature of the general purchasing agent.

The president understands that the usual examination of financial statements is not designed, and cannot be relied on, to disclose fraud or conflicts of interests, although their discovery may result. The president authorizes you, however, to expand your regular audit procedures and to apply additional audit procedures to determine whether there is any evidence that Green has been misappropriating company funds or has engaged in activities that were a conflict of interests.

Required:

a. List the audit procedures that you would apply to the company records and documents in an attempt to

1. Discover evidence within the purchasing department of defalcations being committed by Green. Give the purpose of each audit procedure.

2. Provide leads regarding possible collusion between Green and the suppliers. Give the purpose of each audit procedure.

b. Assume that your investigation disclosed that some suppliers have been charging Grover Manufacturing Company in excess of their usual prices and apparently have been making "kickbacks" to Green. The excess charges are material in amount. What effect, if any, would the defalcation have on (1) the financial statements that were prepared before the defalcation was uncovered, and (2) your auditor's report? Discuss.

(AICPA adapted)

13-65. The accounts payable schedule on page 590 was obtained from the accounting department of Taylor Processing Corp. by the independent auditors for the examination of the December 31, 1986, financial statements. An audit assistant has performed certain audit procedures that are noted on the schedule and has prepared the schedule of subsequent disbursements on page 591. The working papers were properly initialed, dated, and indexed and then submitted to the in-charge auditor for review. No reliance is being placed on specific internal accounting controls.

Required:

a. What essential audit procedures were not noted as having been performed on the accounts payable schedule?

b. What audit procedures performed on the January cash disbursements schedule were deficient?

Date Prepared	2/10/87
Prepared by: a) C & L	
b) Client and Examined by	BB
Reviewed by C & L SR/SUP	

Taylor Processing Corp.
Schedule of Account Payable
10/31/86

	Invoice Number	Invoice Date	Amount		
Dee Catering	—	10/31/86	1027 50		
Plasticar	09 22 22	9/15/86	56922 46		
Ace Construction	8 23	12/10/86	353173 00		
Rogers Moldings	601 11	12/15/86	120825 77		
" "			44803 15		
Brown Leasing	XY 10 25	12/8/86	122288 10		
Dean Packaging	7 91 26	12/30/86	15233 33		
Clavie Hardware	N/A	12/23/86	21880 0		
Chemcor	894 33	11/20/86	47826 10		
"	895 99	12/20/86	30222 00		
"	4 884 30	12/8/86	<3826 15>		
World Travel	N/A	12/16/86	21230 0		
American Distributors	88 - 122	12/1/86	124261 86		
" "	402318	12/2/86	<50114 60>		
" "	88 - 189	12/20/86	624800 00		
AK Trucking	L- 124	12/20/86	5000 00		
Pace Electronics	1925	12/14/86	27840 53		
" "	1983	12/21/86	108101 6		
Pacific Motors	188 03	12/1/86	123340 5		
Westfield Supplies	801	12/15/86	51861 0		
Industrial Suppliers	1103	6/10/86	57552 18		
Temp Service	N/A	12/15/86	51234 8		
Bell Telephone	N/A		187652		
City Chemicals	127 04	12/17/86	834115 0		
Excel	1886 53	12/20/86	61101 4		
Walter Landscaping	1400	12/15/86	25000 0		
H. L. Lee	N/A	12/31/86	5000 00		
Total			16094438 18	b	
Reconciling item			58160 00		
Balance per general ledger			15462781 8	a	
Accounts payable at 12/31/85			120464283		

a Agreed to the general ledger
b Footed

Date Prepared 2/11/87

Prepared by: BB
a) C & L and
b) Client and
Examined by ____

Reviewed by
C & L SR/SUP ____

Taylor Processing Corp.
January Cash Disbursements
12/31/86

	Check #	Check Date	Amount	Year of Acquisition or Expense ③
SK Chemicals	1022	1/3/87	4572645	1987 ⑤
Pacific Motors	1023	1/3/87	1233405	1986 ②
American Distributors	1024	1/3/87	12426186	1986 ②
" "	1025	1/3/87	62480000	1986 ②
Bell Telephone	1026	1/7/87	187652	1986 ④②
Rogers Moldings	1027	1/10/87	12082577	1986 ②
RL Corp.	1028	1/10/87	5872700	1987 ①⑤
Payroll	1029	1/15/87	6712640	1987 ⑤
Pace Electronics	1030	1/15/87	2784053	1987 ⑤
Chemcor	1031	1/15/87	4782610	1986 ②
First National Bank	1032	1/15/87	5000000	1987 ⑤
Excel	1033	1/20/87	611014	1986 ②
Dwersified Inc.	1034	1/20/87	3222375	1987 ⑤
Russell Stationers	1035	1/20/87	312650	1987 ⑤
World Travel Agency	1036	1/20/87	212300	1986 ②
Davis Metals	1037	1/27/87	182243	1987 ⑤
Ace Construction	1038	1/27/87	35317300	1986 ②
Chemcor	1039	1/31/87	320700	1987 ⑤
Payroll	1040	1/31/87	6841060	1987 ⑤
Wright Trucking	1041	1/31/87	168716	1987 ⑤

Note: Selected disbursements greater than $ 1000
from the January check register

① Inventory was shipped 12/30/86 with terms FOB
shipping point, and was received by the client
on 1/3/87.

② Agreed to 12/31/86 accounts payables listing.

③ Examined invoice, receiving reports and other
supporting documentation noting year expense
applies to

④ Examined invoice noting that phone bill is for the
period 11/3/86 – 12/2/86, thus properly included in
1986 accounts payable.

⑤ Noted that items were properly excluded from the 12/31/86
accounts payable schedule.

Chapter 14
Auditing the Production Cycle and Inventory Balances

The production cycle and inventories constitute one of the most significant and difficult areas in auditing and in business management generally. In spite of the trend from a manufacturing- to a service-based economy, many enterprises maintain significant amounts of goods awaiting or in process of production, or available for servicing customers. Difficulties arise in accounting for inventory and determining its appropriate valuation; in addition, management is concerned with attaining maximum production and distribution while minimizing costs, investment, and risk.

Since the production cycle is normally associated with manufacturing enterprises, this chapter is written primarily from that perspective. Much of the discussion in the chapter, however, applies to other enterprises as well, such as those that purchase and hold inventory for future sales without contributing to the production process, and those that consume inventory in the sale of services.

The chapter first defines and describes accounts encompassed by the production cycle. Typical production transactions and internal controls over them are described in detail, followed by a discussion of how the auditor assesses the risks associated with inventories and other accounts related to the production cycle, determines an effective and efficient audit strategy, and designs and performs audit procedures that provide evidence to support management's assertions with respect to those accounts.

The auditor's primary objective in this area is to gather evidence to support management's assertions about the existence, ownership, and valuation of inventory, and the accuracy of production costs. The audit risks associated with inventories vary based on the nature of an enterprise's inventory and its materiality to the financial statements. For example, there is a higher level of inherent risk associated with inventories such as precious metals or gems that can be easily converted to cash and have relatively high value. Accordingly, such inventories require a stronger system of accounting controls and procedures. Or, in estimating net realizable value, there is a higher level of risk associated with a product that must meet very strict technical standards or composition requirements than with a commodity that is generally acceptable to many potential users.

Accounts Related to the Production Cycle

The production cycle encompasses the production or purchase of tangible personal property for sale in the ordinary course of business. The term *inventory* is used to refer to tangible personal property held for sale, in process of production for sale, or consumed in the production of goods or services to be made available for sale. Inventory is usually characterized as either merchandise, raw materials, work in process, or finished goods. Merchandise refers to goods acquired for resale by dealers who incur little or no additional cost in preparation for resale. Raw materials are items or commodities that are consumed in the production process. Work in process represents products in intermediate stages of production. Finished goods represent the end products of the manufacturing process that are awaiting sale. Both finished goods and work in process normally have material, labor, and overhead components. Supplies may be classified as inventory or as prepaid expenses. Tools and spare parts ordinarily consumed in the production process within a year are also included in inventory. The classification of inventory depends on the entity holding it and the nature of its operations. For example, coil steel is a finished product to a steel mill, but a raw material to an appliance manufacturer.

Cost of sales (also called cost of goods sold) includes all costs incurred in purchasing and producing goods for sale, excluding those costs associated with inventory at the end of a period. Material costs assignable to inventory include merchandise, raw materials, and component parts used in the production process or purchased for resale, net of purchase returns, discounts, and other allowances. All direct costs incurred in the purchasing process, such as inbound transportation (freight in), duties and taxes, and warehousing are also included.

Other costs associated with production include *direct labor* and related costs, such as employee fringe benefits, and *allocated production* (manufacturing) *overhead*. The latter category comprises those costs that cannot be directly associated with specific units of production but are nonetheless directly associated with the production process. In this category are such items as indirect labor, supervision, occupancy costs, utilities, repairs and maintenance, and depreciation. Operating supplies and other materials that do not become parts of products, such as oils for lubricating machinery, normally are also included in overhead.

Cost of sales may include additional items such as losses from reducing cost of inventories to market value, royalties paid for the right to manufacture a product or use a patented process or equipment, and amortization of preproduction and tooling costs. Cost of sales is often reduced by sales of by-products and the disposal value of scrap. Estimated costs of warranties, guarantees, and other commitments for future expenditures are usually included in cost of sales, although sometimes they are included in other expense categories.

The term *operating expenses* is sometimes used to describe costs and expenses incurred in generating revenues from the sale of services.

T–accounts are presented in Figure 14.1 to show the transactions and accounts in a typical production cycle.

Typical Transactions and Internal Control

There are two major kinds of production systems—a job order system, in which goods are made in the quantities and to the specifications called for by a particular order, and a process system, in which goods are produced repetitively according to a schedule. The number of types of transactions in the production cycle of either system depends on the complexity of the production process. Among the specific transactions typically found in a production cycle are issuing raw materials for use in production, allocating labor and overhead costs, computing piecework and incentive pay, receiving materials directly into production, processing customers' materials, and transferring completed products to inventory. The production cycle also encompasses policies and procedures for storing raw materials, component parts, and finished goods.

There are virtually unlimited combinations and sequences that may occur in connection with producing goods for sale and storing raw materials and finished goods. The operating and accounting procedures and controls associated with production appear in many forms because of the technological diversity of modern manufacturing operations. The discussion in this chapter of typical transaction types and controls provides only a generalized suggestion of the kinds of conditions that may be encountered.

That discussion is organized under the following headings:

- Storing raw materials and component parts.
- Producing goods for sale.
- Storing finished goods.

Figure 14.1 Production Cycle Accounts

Balance Sheet Accounts

Income Statement Accounts

Inventory of Raw Materials

Beginning inventory Purchases Ending inventory	Raw materials used

Inventory of Work in Process

Beginning inventory
Raw materials used
Direct labor costs incurred
Manufacturing overhead
  costs incurred
Ending inventory
	Cost of goods finished
	  during the period

Inventory of Finished Goods

Beginning inventory Cost of goods finished dur- ing the period Ending inventory	Cost of goods sold

Various Asset and Liability Accounts

	Direct labor costs incurred Manufacturing overhead costs incurred

Cost of Sales

Cost of goods sold	

This sequence recognizes that administrative controls over raw materials often differ from those over finished goods; it also presents the production cycle in its chronological sequence. The accounting controls over inventories in which the auditor is primarily interested, namely, those concerned with the physical security of the inventory and the related accounting records, are, however, essentially the same for raw materials and finished goods. For that reason, storing raw materials and storing finished goods are sometimes treated as a single transaction type.

Storing Raw Materials and Component Parts

Raw materials and component parts must be accounted for and controlled from the time of receipt through utilization in the manufacturing process. Procedures for accomplishing this include safeguarding the inventory by restricting access to it to authorized personnel, issuing materials to production only on the basis of authorized bills of materials or materials requisitions, crediting the perpetual inventory records for issuances to production, and periodically counting materials on hand and agreeing the results to the perpetual inventory records. Physical counts are discussed later in the context of finished goods inventories. The procedures and controls noted there apply also to physical counts of raw materials. Procedures relating to receiving materials and updating perpetual inventory records are covered in Chapter 13, "Auditing the Buying Cycle."

The issue of materials to production from the materials storeroom may originate on the basis of a document such as an authorized bill of materials supporting an approved production order, an approved materials requisition, or a report of production orders scheduled to start, or materials may be released on the signature of the requisitioning foreman. In any event, an appropriately authorized document should be created to account for the movement of materials, both for production control and accounting purposes. Often these documents may serve as authorization to update the perpetual inventory records for issues of materials to production and should preferably be prenumbered or subject to some type of batch control so that it can subsequently be ascertained that all transactions have been processed and recorded.

Reviewing for slow-moving, obsolete, or damaged materials is necessary to avoid valuing inventories at amounts greater than their realizable value. A responsible employee should review and approve all nonroutine adjustments and entries to the inventory accounts. Periodically, provisions for safeguarding the entity's investment in materials, including both physical safeguards and decisions on the amount and kind of insurance coverage, should be reviewed.

Producing Goods for Sale

This transaction type comprises identifying production needs, planning and scheduling production, producing goods, and accounting for production costs and work in process throughout the manufacturing process. Controls over those procedures are important because errors in production data can result in wrong decisions. For example, inaccurate inventory records can result in poor purchasing or production planning decisions. Overstocking can lead to higher inventory carrying costs and a greater risk of obsolescence; understocking can lead to stock-outs, production downtime, and lost sales. Effective controls over inventory levels serve to reduce the probability of errors in accounting data and other data used by management in running the business, thereby contributing to more effective operations.

In many companies, control over inventory levels and production planning is initiated with the development of realistic sales forecasts. The forecasts are then translated into detailed production plans covering lead times for procuring necessary materials, parts, and supplies; machine scheduling; and personnel staffing. Careful monitoring of actual sales compared with forecasted sales enables management to adjust production plans to achieve the desired inventory levels.

Given the significance of inventory and the production cycle to many businesses, management is often particularly interested in the efficiency of manufacturing operations and the effectiveness of related accounting controls. As a result, management frequently reviews reports that evidence the operation of controls; such reviews often have accounting and auditing significance because of their impact on related financial statement balances. Examples are comparisons of actual production results and inventory levels with budgeted amounts and reviews of significant favorable and unfavorable production variances. If there is evidence of the operation of these reviews, the auditor should consider their potential impact on the audit strategy.

Identifying Production Needs. In a process system, in which production is for a finished goods inventory, identifying production needs may be an integral part of the system and may be accomplished by evaluating existing inventory levels in relation to sales projections. Needs may be signaled by a periodic scrutiny of inventory levels or by noting when stock on hand reaches a predetermined minimum. Stock replenishment systems may be systematized, and perpetual inventory records may be used instead of physical inspection to identify needs. Computerized inventory records offer the opportunity for highly sophisticated forecasting and modeling computations.

Planning and Scheduling Production. After a need has been identified, a production requisition is initiated, which, after review and approval, becomes the authorization to produce. Product specifications and time and cost estimates should be developed as part of the production planning and scheduling process. In particular, cost estimates permit informed scrutiny of actual costs and the exercise of managerial control. The result of planning and scheduling is a production order—the detailed execution instructions listing the operations and the desired results.

Planning and scheduling involve primarily administrative controls that have accounting significance and that are therefore of direct concern to the auditor. Poor product specifications and poor inspection procedures can cause rework, unsalable goods, or returned merchandise. Poor estimates can give rise to excess cost in inventory, especially overruns on contracts. Poor scheduling can likewise cause overruns and excess cost. An auditor who understands the role that planning and scheduling play in the production process will be able to more effectively evaluate the inherent and internal control risks associated with the related accounts.

Producing Goods. As mentioned earlier in this chapter, a document should be created and controlled to account for the movement of materials, both for production control and accounting purposes. The documents should preferably be numbered or batched under control totals. Issues of raw materials to production are often based on estimated quantities, and as a result actual usage may vary from the quantities drawn from storage. Management should institute controls to account for such excess materials and to ensure that they are appropriately returned to the raw materials inventory. Failure to do so may result in wasted materials and excessive production costs.

If material is ordered directly for production, the production order, sometimes supported by an accompanying purchase order, alerts those concerned to the expected delivery date. A receiving report notifies the production and accounting departments when the delivery is received.

Setup time for machines used in the production process may or may not be accounted for separately, depending on the informational needs of management, as incorporated in the cost accounting system. Tools and dies are sometimes charged as direct costs, particularly in job order production systems in which tools are likely to have been designed especially for a particular order and sometimes are paid for by the customer. Most often, though, tools and dies are capitalized because they can be reused on other work or production runs at other times. Usually, documents are prepared to record these processing steps: a time report or job ticket for the setup time and an issues slip or production order for the tool requirements. The documents should be reviewed and approved by the appropriate supervisory personnel.

Measuring production quantities is a problem in a great many operations. Both production managers and cost accountants want accurate production counts, but in many cases the large number of units, the inaccuracy of measuring devices, and the problems of distinguishing between acceptable and unacceptable units make it difficult or uneconomical to measure production precisely.

Production is often inspected at several stages and levels. Operators inspect for signs of problems as they complete their work; supervisors may inspect output on a test basis. There may be specialists in quality control, or it may be necessary to employ the special skills and equipment of a laboratory to test the quality of production.

Controls over the measurement and inspection of production output, while primarily administrative in nature, are of interest to the auditor since they provide evidence of the accuracy of inventory quantities on hand and the salability of the inventory.

Accounting for Production Costs. The accounting aspects of the production cycle are manifested in the entity's cost accounting system. The cost accounting systems employed by manufacturing concerns range from very simple systems, which account for ending inventory balances annually, to very well-developed standard cost systems, which continually account for all materials handling, production in process, and completed production, and generate analyses of related variances from predetermined standard costs. A well-developed cost system should provide the details of transfers between raw materials and work in process and between work in process and finished goods, and of the distribution and accumulation of material, labor, and overhead costs by cost centers, job orders, or production runs.

Depending on the structure of the cost accounting system, material costs may be charged to a job order or to a material usage account in a process system. If a standard cost system is employed, materials may be charged to production at standard quantities and prices, with resulting variances between standard and actual costs subsequently allocated to inventory and cost of sales.

Issues of raw materials may be recorded from a report of production orders scheduled to start, which should be controlled by comparison with production orders reported as actually started, or they may be recorded from raw materials storeroom issue slips, the numerical sequence of which should be accounted for. Occasionally, especially in computerized systems, raw materials usage may be measured by periodically—usually monthly—pricing the ending raw materials inventory and adjusting the account balance through a charge to production.

Production rejected as a result of inspection should be reported for managerial cost accounting purposes. Sometimes the time spent reworking faulty items to meet specifications is also reported separately. Controlling production to minimize the amount of scrap and rework is an important element of production control management; adequate identification and accounting are important elements of both production cost and managerial accounting information. Once scrap has been created, it should be subject to physical controls and recorded and accounted for to maximize cost recovery and thereby minimize production costs. Cost accounting is improved if scrap is identified with the operations or products creating it, but that is often impossible. In any event, controls over gathering, safeguarding, weighing, recording, storing, and disposing of scrap should be as effective as those over other assets.

The total cost of production payroll is accounted for through the buying cycle (covered in Chapter 13, "Auditing the Buying Cycle"). Payroll expense is distributed to detailed cost accounts from job tickets or production reports. When job tickets are used, the aggregate labor cost distributed to production or other expense accounts should be reconciled with a control total from the pay-roll records to ensure that all labor costs have been allocated. Production labor costs may be charged to job order or departmental expense accounts. The sys-tem may provide detailed accounts for idle time, waiting time, setup time, cleanup time, rework time, and so on. When a standard cost system is used, production labor is computed at standard rates and hours and, by comparison with actual costs, labor rate and efficiency variances are produced.

Many different kinds of cost enter into overhead, and they are accumu-lated in descriptive accounts as charges originate. The basis for charging over-head to job orders, departments, or work-in-process inventory is usually some measure of activity such as direct labor hours or dollars. There are likely to be different overhead rates for different departments, based on accounting or en-gineering studies.

In a standard cost system, overhead may be charged through several inter-mediate accounts to produce price, efficiency, and volume variances for mana-gerial information. Overabsorbed or underabsorbed overhead may be credited or charged in detail to job orders or departments, or it may be allocated to work-in-process and finished goods inventories on some overall basis. An ap-propriate fraction of overabsorbed overhead should always be removed from inventories to prevent stating them in excess of actual cost; the allocable por-tion of underabsorbed overhead should be allocated to inventories unless it arises from elements of cost that should be written off as incurred. Some com-panies establish and allocate separate overheads for materials handling (pur-chasing, receiving, inspecting, and storing) as distinguished from manufactur-ing overhead, when those costs are significant.

Entries to record overhead absorption may be originated as a separate ac-counting procedure, but most often they are integrated with entries for the data—payroll or material usage—on which the absorption rate is based.

Accounting for Work in Process. Physical inventory counts of work in proc-ess are often difficult because a great many items in many different stages of completion must be identified. Goods may be scattered or in hoppers, vats, or pipelines where access, observation, or measurement is difficult, or they may be in the hands of outside processors. Adequate production management, how-ever, requires that someone know the location and stage of completion of each item. The more difficult production control is, the more essential it is to have a means of ensuring that excess or "lost" costs do not build up in the work-in-process account. A physical inventory, properly summarized and priced, is the best practice, and most companies have found that, if adequately organized and timed, its cost and disruptive effect on the production process can be mini-mized. A later section of this chapter outlines the considerations in planning and executing a physical inventory.

In those instances where work in process is difficult to count because of the nature of the production process, arrangements can be made to count the end result of each production order in process as it is finished and "work back" to determine the account balance as of the physical inventory date.

Movement of production between departments during the production process must be reported for operational purposes, but often it is not recorded for accounting purposes. Sometimes production must be moved out of the plant for processing that the company is not equipped to do. Those moves should be documented and controlled. Simultaneous accounting control is highly desirable, but often accounting control is established only at the time of the physical inventory by accumulating documents related to the inventory movements and establishing the cost associated with that work in process. Periodic confirmation with outside processors of the quantities for which they are responsible is a preferred control procedure.

Work in process is credited and finished goods are charged on the basis of completed production orders, inspection reports, or finished goods receiving tickets. The documents must be properly authorized and approved, and most systems have rules for documenting evidence of inspection according to quality control standards. Accurate counts are necessary for the transfer to finished goods inventory.

Storing Finished Goods

After production has been completed and has passed final inspection, it goes either to finished goods inventory or to a storage area to await shipment to customers. The notice to production management may be a copy of the production order, signed off as completed, or it may be an inspection report or the receiving report of the finished goods storekeeper. The accounting document signifying an addition to finished goods may be any one of those documents; it may be either the same document used for managerial purposes or a different document. Control over the completeness of charges to finished goods is provided by accounting for the numerical sequence of receiving reports or by reconciling inventory additions to production reports.

Finished goods are credited on the basis of filled sales orders or the storekeeper's issue slips; the latter should be reconciled to the sales orders. The accounting document for withdrawal from finished goods is usually a copy of, or a document closely related to, the sales and shipping orders. Movements of finished goods should be accounted for by numerical or batch controls. Occasionally, the detailed perpetual inventory records (as adjusted periodically to agree with physical counts) are costed and aggregated, and the difference between that total and the controlling account balance is charged to cost of goods sold. Significant or recurring differences should be investigated to determine their causes, and corrective action should be taken as necessary.

While physical inventories are often considered an audit requirement, good internal control requires the taking of a physical inventory at least annually and sometimes more frequently, depending on the type of business and the nature of the inventory and related controls. The term *physical inventory* encompasses not only physically counting items but also translating the quantities into dollars, summarizing the dollars, and comparing the results with the accounts. A complete count of the inventory of a company, plant, or department may be made at one time while operations are suspended (referred to as a wall-to-wall inventory) or, if perpetual inventory records are maintained and other conditions are satisfactory, periodic counts of selected items may be made at various times during the year (known as a cycle count inventory). In the latter instance, all items in the inventory generally should be counted at least once each year. Sometimes both types of inventory taking are used. Since the two methods involve somewhat different techniques, they are discussed separately herein.

Inventories Taken at One Time. Taking a complete inventory at one time is a large task. It requires the cooperation of production, accounting, and store-keeping personnel since it often involves suspending or significantly reducing production, shipping, and receiving operations, and physically rearranging inventory to facilitate counting. It is essential that someone with authority assume overall responsibility for taking the inventory. Often an ''inventory committee'' is organized, consisting of management representatives of production departments, the controller's office, the general or cost accounting department, the shipping and receiving departments, the internal audit department, and the independent auditors. It is usually desirable for someone from production management to assume responsibility for rearranging the inventory and making available employees who are familiar with it to assist in the physical inventory procedures.

A physical inventory may be taken during the vacation period for factory employees, when production is stopped for some other reason, at a time when inventories are at a low level, at year-end, or at a convenient month-end prior to the balance sheet date. Inventory taking before the balance sheet date is advisable, however, only if there are adequate procedures to control and document inventory movements between the physical inventory and balance sheet dates.

The counts may be made by production, clerical, or accounting personnel, storekeepers, or internal auditors. Count teams often comprise one individual from a production department and one clerical employee. Such an arrangement provides an added degree of accounting control while utilizing the production department employee's familiarity with the inventory. However the initial counting is organized, the counts should be verified. Some companies have a complete recount by independent teams. Others assign production supervisors or internal auditors to make random test counts. These test counts should be documented to provide adequate evidence of their performance and to establish responsibility for them.

An almost invariable requirement for a good physical inventory is advance preparation of a written program. To be most effective, the program should include instructions pertaining to

1. Physical arrangement of the inventory as a means of simplifying the counts.

2. Proper identification and description of the inventory, including stage of completion and condition, when appropriate.

3. Segregation or proper identification of slow-moving, obsolete, or damaged goods.

4. Identification and listing of inventory belonging to others.

5. Numerical control of inventory tags or sheets.

6. Practices to be followed in the recording and verification of individual counts.

7. Practices to be followed in obtaining a proper cutoff of receipts and shipments and interdepartmental movements, and the related paperwork.

8. Practices to be followed in verifying goods in the hands of others.

9. Practices to be followed for correcting errors.

In addition to instructions for controlling and recording the inventory, the program should include instructions to the accounting department for summarizing quantities, costing (pricing), extending (multiplying quantity by price), and summarizing the priced inventory. Special procedures may be required for consignments in or out, goods in transit, and goods in public warehouses or at branches.

The inventory plan should provide for supervision adequate to ensure that procedures for arranging and counting the inventory, pricing, and summarizing the counts are properly followed and that the results are satisfactory.

The mechanics of counting vary. Seldom, if ever, can all individual items in an inventory be seen and counted; they are frequently in the packages or cartons in which they were purchased or are to be shipped, or they may be located in bins or stockpiles in large numbers that cannot be physically weighed or counted. The only rule that can be stated is that a reasonable number of items should be counted; some packages should be opened and some items inspected, particularly if there are any unusual circumstances.

Differences between physical and recorded inventories should be adequately investigated, and the possibility of leakage or pilferage should be considered. The records may be right and the count wrong; no significant adjustments should be made without a thorough investigation.

Inventories Taken Periodically Throughout the Year. Instead of a wall-to-wall inventory, periodic physical counts may be made throughout the year if adequate perpetual records are maintained and are up-to-date, controls over physical movement and cutoff are good, and the control environment is favorable. Generally, periodic counts should cover all items at least once during the year, but it is also good practice to count active items more often. Procedures used in making periodic counts differ from those for inventories taken at one time. Rather than having large numbers of production and other personnel rearrange and count all the stock in a plant, periodic counts are usually made by relatively small groups of employees who soon become expert at counting inventories and possibly spend a large part of their time doing so. When periodic counts are made and found to be reliable, the perpetual records may serve as the equivalent of a complete physical inventory and are priced, extended, and summarized for comparison with general ledger accounts at or near year-end.

A problem frequently encountered in practice is obtaining a good cutoff by arranging for perpetual records to be posted promptly and accurately; otherwise, the counts result in apparent differences that are actually delays in recording transactions. Employees making periodic counts usually should not know beforehand the amount shown in the perpetual records because they might then be less objective in their counts. If a particular item to be counted is stored at more than one location, however, the locations should be reported to the employees making the counts to minimize the possibility that quantities will be omitted and the inventory records erroneously adjusted.

Inventories in Public Warehouses. In addition to adequate insurance coverage on goods in custody of a public warehouse, the client's controls should generally include a preliminary investigation and continuing evaluation of the performance of the custodian. SAS No. 1, as amended by SAS No. 43 (AU Sections 901.26 and .27), suggests the following client control procedures:

> Consideration of the business reputation and financial standing of the warehouseman.
> Inspection of the physical facilities.
> Inquiries as to the warehouseman's control procedures and whether the warehouseman holds goods for his own account.
> Inquiries as to type and adequacy of the warehouseman's insurance.
> Inquiries as to government or other licensing and bonding requirements and the nature, extent, and results of any inspection by government or other agencies.
> Review of the warehouseman's financial statements and related reports of independent auditors.
> Review and update [of] the information developed from the investigation described above.
> Physical counts (or test counts) of the goods, wherever practicable and reasonable (counts may not be practicable in the case of fungible goods).
> Reconcilement of quantities shown on statements received from the warehouseman with the owner's records.

Planning the Audit Strategy

Audit Objectives

The objectives of auditing procedures for the production cycle and inventories are to provide evidential matter that is sufficient and competent to provide reasonable assurance that

- Inventories physically exist in salable condition and represent property held for sale in the ordinary course of business.
- Inventories are owned by the entity and all encumbrances are adequately disclosed.
- The accounts reflect all owned products, materials, and supplies on hand or in the hands of others and do not include the property of others or items billed to customers.
- Costs associated with inventories have been properly determined and accumulated.
- Inventories are not stated in excess of net realizable value.
- Cost of sales is properly stated in the income statement.
- Account descriptions, classifications, and related disclosures are adequate and not misleading.

The auditor can normally attain reasonable assurance about the physical existence and completeness of recorded inventory quantities if the client conducts adequate physical inventories. Assessments of management's assertions regarding inventory valuation can, however, be difficult because of the complexities associated with many cost accounting systems and methods.

Audit Strategy

As discussed in Chapter 8, the process of determining an effective and efficient audit strategy begins with the auditor's developing and documenting an understanding of the control environment and the flow of transactions through the client's systems. Based on this understanding, the auditor makes an initial evaluation of whether it would be efficient to rely on controls. Even if controls exist, the auditor may conclude that the reduction in the amount of substantive testing that could be achieved through reliance on controls would not be sufficient to justify the amount of compliance testing that would have to be performed or that it would simply be more practicable to perform substantive tests, as would normally be the case with a client that has low volume transactions, predominantly high dollar value transactions, or extremely low inventory levels at year-end. If, in light of the risks involved, the control system appears to be adequate, and the auditor believes that it is likely to be effective and efficient to rely on specific controls to reduce the level of substantive tests, the auditor will identify those controls, evaluate their design, and perform compliance tests to determine whether they can in fact be relied on.

Analytical review procedures, discussed in Chapter 9, frequently highlight relationships between accounts and risks not otherwise apparent from other planning techniques; their use often results in more informed decisions in selecting the audit strategy. Discussing the results of analytical procedures with company personnel may also give the auditor insight into the quality of the control environment. For example, logical and meaningful answers to questions about fluctuations in inventory turnover ratios from the prior year to the current year would provide some indication, in the absence of evidence to the contrary, that the company's management is "in control" and the internal accounting and administrative controls appear to be functioning as intended. Those procedures, however, also may indicate trends, even in well-controlled companies, that may force the auditor to extend substantive tests because, for example, the trends may raise questions about the realizability of recorded inventory values. Examples of analytical review procedures performed as substantive tests are discussed later in this chapter under the heading "Substantive Tests."

In addition to the general information obtained regarding management's overall philosophy and style, such as the predominant means of processing transactions (manually or by computer) and the level of its sophistication, its budgetary process, and working capital position, the auditor should obtain information such as the following, related specifically to the production cycle and related balances:

- Liquidity of the inventory, that is, the ease with which it can be converted into cash.
- The number of items in the inventory. It may be more difficult to test activity during the period between early substantive testing and year-end for a large number of small items than for a small number of large items.
- Extent to which judgments enter into the determination of the inventory value (e.g., judgments about inventory obsolescence).
- Susceptibility of major products to technical obsolescence, spoilage, or changes in demand.
- Availability of materials critical to the production process, number of vendors who are able to supply such materials, stability of prices of the materials, and ability of the client to pass along component price increases to its customers.
- Historical trends of applicable inventory turnover ratios, net realizable value, and inventory obsolescence problems.
- The accounting methods used to value inventory.
- Current-year production cost variances from standards or budgets.

If the auditor's risk assessment indicates that the client is in a good working capital position; has effective production planning, budgeting, and management information systems; has strong general controls in its electronic data processing department and strong application controls over significant production and inventory processing routines; has adequate segregation of duties between production and inventory storage functions and the accounting department, and between the inventory storage function and the receiving and shipping departments; exercises adequate physical security controls over all significant inventories; conducts adequate physical inventories designed to ensure the accuracy and salable condition of recorded inventory quantities; exercises adequate controls to ensure that all production costs are accumulated and properly allocated to inventory; and maintains adequate controls to ensure proper cutoffs in the receiving and shipping departments, the client would be a strong candidate for an audit strategy geared toward performance of compliance tests to reduce significantly the amount of substantive testing and perhaps to perform a significant portion of substantive testing before the balance sheet date. Performing substantive tests before the balance sheet date may be particularly efficient if the client desires the audit report relatively close to year-end, since the procedures necessary to achieve related audit objectives are often fairly extensive for inventory balances.

On the other hand, the audit strategy should emphasize substantive testing, most likely as of the balance sheet date, if the auditor's analysis of the client's inherent risk with regard to inventory accounts suggests that the client may have potential motives for overstating inventories; if there are nonexistent or ineffective forecasting, budgeting, or management information systems, which could result in overstocking of inventories and questions about their net realizable value; if there are weak general computer and application controls, which create the possibility of production costs being inaccurately accumulated and allocated between inventory and cost of sales; if there are inadequate physical security controls over and accounting for inventories; and if there are inadequate controls over shipping and receiving cutoffs. In such environments, there would be few, if any, controls to compliance test and, accordingly, the amount of substantive testing could not be reduced.

The degree of reliance that the auditor can place on controls, along with the length of time between early substantive testing and year-end and the results of those tests, will also affect the way in which the auditor obtains the necessary satisfaction as to the year-end inventory balance if the client takes its physical inventory before year-end. That satisfaction can be provided through an appropriate combination of reliance on basic controls, including physical security, and supervisory controls or on special control procedures implemented by the client for the intervening period; reviewing the client's method of calculating ending inventory and cost of sales if inventory activity is not recorded on a perpetual basis; performing analytical reviews of activity in the intervening period; reviewing production and sales reports generated for internal purposes; and performing substantive tests of purchase, sale, and production activity during the intervening period.

Compliance Tests

As discussed at length in Chapter 7, internal accounting control is important to an auditor primarily because reliance on it permits the amount of corroborative evidence needed from other tests to be limited. If the presence of controls will not influence other auditing procedures, an auditor has no need to perform compliance tests of controls. That principle is particularly applicable to inventories because the minimum testing necessary to achieve audit objectives is often extensive. The auditor must exercise professional judgment to identify those controls whose continued and proper operation would allow a large enough reduction in substantive testing to make the related compliance tests feasible from an audit efficiency standpoint.

Storing Raw Materials and Component Parts

Storing raw materials and component parts, as described earlier in this chapter, includes safeguarding the inventory, issuing materials to production, maintaining control over inventory quantities, and physically counting inventory on hand and reconciling perpetual inventory records to general ledger control accounts. Compliance tests applicable to this transaction type are discussed from the perspective of those steps.

Physical Security Controls. Physical security controls over inventory can normally be tested only by observation and inquiry. Observing that raw materials and component parts are stored in locked storage areas and that storeroom operations are under the control of a responsible custodian (whose records are verified by periodic independent counts) provides the auditor with a degree of assurance that inventories are not susceptible of misappropriation or misplacement. After gaining an understanding of the physical layout of storage areas, the auditor should normally inquire of the custodian about the procedures followed by company personnel when materials are received into the storage areas and when they are issued to production. Controls over receipts may have been evaluated in conjunction with the buying cycle; if not, they should be evaluated in conjunction with the production cycle. If the auditor is satisfied that inventories are adequately safeguarded, it may be possible to reduce the level of test counts to be performed during the physical inventory observation, as well as possibly performing physical inventory procedures prior to the balance sheet date (assuming that controls over inventory receipts and issues are effective).

Controls over Issuing Materials to Production. Controls over the physical security of raw materials and component parts are not effective unless they are accompanied by controls over the issuance of those materials to production. Such controls include procedures to ensure that materials are issued only on the basis of appropriate authorization and that issuances are sufficiently documented so that it can subsequently be established that related quantities have been completely and accurately charged to production and removed from raw materials. Compliance tests of controls over materials issued should include examining materials requisitions, production orders, or other documents that authorize inventory movement, and reperforming client controls designed to ensure the complete and accurate processing and recording of issuances. The compliance test audit program might read as follows:

Select requisitions for raw materials or component parts: Examine for completeness of descriptions, quantities, dates, and production order number; note evidence of authorization; trace to corresponding removal of quantities from raw materials perpetual inventory records and to summary document supporting entry to transfer related costs from the raw material account balance and entry charging materials to work in process.

Select entries for materials issued to production in the raw materials perpetual inventory records: Examine documentation supporting issuance, noting agreement of descriptions, quantities, dates, and so on; note evidence of authorization. (This test is similar to the preceding one except that the source for test items is the perpetual inventory records instead of the requisition file. The first test provides evidence that all requisitions were accurately processed; the second test provides evidence that all recorded materials issuances represent authorized requisitions.)

Test batches of raw materials requisitions for numerical sequence or batch control over processing of documents.

Maintaining Control over and Physically Counting Raw Material Quantities on Hand. The primary controls over raw material inventories exercised by most companies are physical counts of quantities on hand and periodic reconciliations of perpetual inventory records to general ledger balances. Audit tests of a client's physical inventory procedures are considered compliance tests to the extent that they involve observing the operation of client controls and reperforming client counts. The number of test counts performed by the auditor is typically a matter of judgment based on factors such as the degree of reliance the auditor wishes to place on the client's procedures.

Perpetual inventory records of varying degrees of sophistication are found in practice. Some companies maintain perpetual records that reflect both inventory quantities and costs; others keep perpetual records in quantities only; and still others with simple operations and relatively few inventory items do not maintain perpetual records at all. The relevance of perpetual records to the auditor's compliance tests depends on the assessment of their importance as a control technique. A typical compliance test program might read as follows:

Obtain the most recent reconciliation of the raw materials perpetual records to the related general ledger accounts; determine mathematical accuracy of reconciliation; review reconciliation for reasonableness and examine documentation for significant reconciling items; review reconciliation for evidence of supervisory review and approval.

Review the company's physical inventory instructions to ensure that all significant issues are adequately addressed; tour the storage area, noting that inventory appears to be arranged in a manner to facilitate an accurate count; observe client counting procedures, noting the independence of counters and the care with which counts are conducted and recorded, and that all items are counted or excluded, as appropriate; reperform counts recorded by the client on a test basis; inquire about client procedures for identifying obsolete, spoiled, or slow-moving items; review client procedures for inventory tag or count sheet control and reperform as necessary; review adjustments to recorded balances resulting from quantity differences for reasonableness, evidence of further investigation, and supervisory approval.

Producing Goods for Sale

As described earlier in this chapter, producing goods can be viewed as a single transaction type or as several separate transaction types such as issuing raw materials, distributing labor costs to production units, allocating overhead, accounting for scrap, and other events, depending on the complexity of the production process and the control environment in which production takes place. It is often necessary in practice to identify separate transaction subtypes for different cost components since, for example, the controls over direct labor distribution may vary significantly from those for overhead allocation.

To avoid unnecessary complexities, the production of goods is considered in this book as a single transaction type comprising identifying production needs, planning production, scheduling production runs, producing goods, and accounting for production costs and work in process. As discussed earlier in the chapter, identifying needs, planning and scheduling production, and actually producing goods are primarily of operational significance, except that they provide evidence of the control environment in which production takes place. These operations may provide some level of assurance to the auditor that goods produced are free from defects and are generally salable; however, direct tests of these controls are normally not performed. For this reason, the discussion of compliance tests for this transaction type is directed at controls over accounting for production costs and work in process.

For adequate inventory pricing, the minimum data required to be produced by the accounting system are properly classified cumulative totals of purchases, payrolls, and other expenses, and of units sold. Combining that information with units in opening and closing inventories, invoice prices of related materials purchases, and current labor rates permits an accurate allocation between cost of goods sold and cost of inventories.

The underlying data supporting inventory valuation are derived principally from the buying cycle. If compliance tests of controls over purchasing and payroll transactions produce evidence that related accounting data are reliable, they can be relied on for inventory valuation purposes as well, often with little additional compliance testing beyond that performed in conjunction with the buying cycle. This is particularly true if compliance tests of the buying cycle are planned and performed with production cycle audit objectives in mind. For example, compliance tests of payroll can easily be expanded to include the distribution of labor costs to specific production lots or units in the perpetual inventory records. This may allow the auditor to rely on unit costs reflected in the perpetual inventory records as a basis for pricing the inventory, with minimal additional compliance testing.

Highly developed cost systems often generate data that provide the details of

Transfers between raw materials and work in process (discussed earlier in conjunction with storing raw materials) and between work in process and finished goods.

Distribution of material, labor, and overhead expenses to cost centers, job orders, or production runs.

Stages of completion of work in process.

Variance accounts (in the case of standard cost systems) identifying differences between actual and standard.

Differences between actual and budgeted costs.

If the client applies the system effectively, the output usually includes analyses and explanations of standard cost variances or differences between actual and budgeted amounts.

Analyses of variances from standards or budgets are controls often given particular attention by management. Accordingly, those controls may render lower-level controls redundant for audit purposes and may allow audit procedures to be limited to testing the accuracy of the analyses and reviewing management's explanations for variances.

Audit judgment is particularly important in deciding how much compliance testing of controls in the cost accounting system is required. Certainly, compliance tests of controls in the cost accounting and quantity control systems provide an enhanced understanding of the client's operations and additional evidence of the functioning of the systems. Before conducting extensive tests, however, the auditor should measure each test against the audit objectives—reasonable assurance regarding existence, cost, and net realizable value of inventories—and evaluate whether the additional understanding and evidence add measurably to that assurance. In many cases, the assurance comes primarily from observing the physical inventory, testing its summarization and pricing, and compliance testing the variance analyses. In other cases, the sole purpose of compliance tests of controls over inventory movement is evidence of the continued and proper operation of controls between the interim physical inventory date and year-end, in which event tests are most appropriately made in that period.

Accordingly, a principal criterion in determining the scope of compliance tests is the extent to which an auditor's assurance depends on controls in the cost accounting and quantity control systems. That dependence is greater when the client's physical inventory, summarization, and pricing procedures are carried out at an interim date. The more effective the inventory accounting system, the longer the period the auditor may tolerate between the performance of substantive procedures and the balance sheet date.

Figure 14.2 illustrates typical compliance tests for this transaction type and how such tests relate to the general objectives of internal accounting control.

Storing Finished Goods

This transaction type involves the receipt of finished goods from production (or the receiving department in the case of nonmanufactured goods) and their safeguarding until they are shipped to customers. As discussed earlier in this chapter, controls over this transaction type, and hence related compliance tests, are similar to those for raw materials storage, except that finished goods are normally subject to more rigorous inspection procedures than are raw materials. Inspection, although typically viewed as an administrative control, is of interest to the auditor since it provides evidence of the quality and valuation of finished goods. Controls over inspection procedures are typically not directly tested by the auditor, however. Other differences between compliance tests for this transaction type and those for raw materials storage relate primarily to the documents used for controlling inventory movements. For example, raw materials issuances to production and receipts are typically controlled by numerical or batch controls over authorized materials requisitions and receiving reports, respectively. Movements into and out of finished goods are normally controlled by numerical or batch controls over completed production orders or inspection reports and shipping documents, respectively.

Substantive Tests

The planning for substantive tests of inventories and other accounts related to the production cycle is affected by various internal and external requirements and pressures. Inventory observation is required by generally accepted auditing standards. Client and outside reporting deadlines, tax considerations, economic conditions, the auditor's assessment of inherent risk and materiality, and the effectiveness of the client's system of internal accounting controls all influence the nature, extent, and timing of substantive tests.

Observation of Physical Inventories

Since the *McKesson & Robbins* case precipitated the issue in 1939, the observation of physical inventories has been a required auditing procedure and therefore the principal focus of substantive testing of inventories. For a long time after 1939, auditors were expected to make voluminous and extensive test counts, sometimes virtually taking the physical inventory side-by-side with client personnel. In recent years, the emphasis has shifted to observation and testing of the client's procedures for physical counts of inventories.

The official position of the profession is now stated in SAS No. 1 (AU Section 331.09), as follows:

Figure 14.2 Producing Goods for Sale: Control Objectives, Potential Errors, Accounting Controls, and Compliance Tests

	General Objectives of Internal Accounting Control				
	Completeness	*Validity*	*Accuracy*	*Maintenance*	*Physical Security*
Specific objectives of internal accounting control	All production costs (materials, labor, and overhead) and transfers to and from work in process are recorded and processed.	All recorded production costs (materials, labor, and overhead) and transfers of production within work in process and to finished goods and scrap represent valid activity as authorized by responsible personnel.	Charges to production for materials, labor, and overhead, and transfers within work in process and transfers of completed production to finished goods are recorded accurately as to quantities, descriptions, amounts, and dates in the general ledger control accounts and perpetual inventory records.	The perpetual inventory records and the general ledger control accounts reflect all authorized transactions and only those transactions.	Inventory is protected against access by unauthorized individuals.
Potential errors in account balances from absent or ineffective controls	Costs may be omitted from work in process or finished goods valuation, resulting in an understatement of inventory balances and income.	Unauthorized or nonexistent materials usage or labor and overhead costs may be charged to production, resulting in an overstatement of inventory balances and income.	Errors on documents supporting materials, labor, and overhead charges and transfers of completed production to finished goods may result in a misstatement of inventory balances and cost of sales. Transactions may	Entries to perpetual records may be omitted from the control accounts, and vice versa, resulting in a misstatement or misclassification of inventory balances.	Unauthorized issuances of inventories or pilferage may go undetected, resulting in a misstatement of inventory balances.

(Continued)

Figure 14.2 Continued

	General Objectives of Internal Accounting Control				
Principal control techniques	Completeness	Validity	Accuracy	Maintenance	Physical Security
Legend: B = Basic control (other than physical control) S = Supervisory control P = Physical control	Periodic accounting for requisitions of materials and component parts issued to and returned from production, including adequate investigation and resolution of unmatched items by persons independent of materials handling function (B). Periodic reconciliation of records of labor and overhead charges to payrolls and overhead cost incurred, including adequate investigation and resolution of differences (B). Periodic accounting for production reports or reconciliation of records	Procedures for authorizing materials, labor, and overhead charges to production and transfers within work in process and to finished goods and scrap (B). Review and approval of bills of materials, materials requisitions, and labor distribution by department and/or job number by supervisory personnel (S).	be misclassified in the accounts or recorded in the wrong period. Procedures for testing materials requisitions, production labor, and overhead charges, and transfers within work in process and transfers of completed production to finished goods as to quantities, descriptions, dates, extensions, footings, and account classifications by personnel independent of such functions (B). Review and approval of results of above procedures and summarizations of above transactions used for general ledger postings by appro-	Periodic reconciliation of the perpetual records with the general ledger control accounts by personnel other than those responsible for maintaining related perpetual records or for safeguarding inventories (B). Review and approval of the results of above reconciliations by supervisory personnel (S).	Adequate physical controls over materials inventories and completed production, including appropriate documentation (requisitions, production reports) and physical inspection of materials issued to production, transferred within production, and transferred out of production to the finished goods storage area (P). Inventory storage areas designed so as to prevent access by unauthorized individuals (P). Plant security personnel and lim-

ited plant access points (P).

Inquire about and observe physical controls over materials and finished production designed to ensure that all movements are appropriately

(Continued)

priate supervisory personnel (S).

Periodic verification of work-in-process records to inventories on hand (B).

Review of results of physical inventory by responsible supervisory personnel (S).

Review of period-end cutoff procedures by responsible personnel other than those who maintain related perpetual inventory records or accounting records or safeguard inventories (B).

Review and reperform reconciliations of the perpetual records to the general ledger control accounts, ascertaining mathematical accuracy

For a sample of charges to production for materials, labor, and/or overhead, and/or a sample of transfers of completed production to finished

of finished production and transfers within work in process and scrapped or spoiled work to quantities recorded, including adequate investigation and resolution of missing documents and differences (B).

Periodic review and approval of results of above procedures by responsible supervisory personnel (S).

Account for the numerical sequence or batch or other controls over materials requisitions and records of finished goods production and

For a sample of recorded materials issued to and returned from production, examine supporting bills of materials, materials requisitions,

Typical compliance tests
Legend:
1 = Examination of evidence and/or reperformance of the related basic

Figure 14.2 Continued

| | General Objectives of Internal Accounting Control | | | |
Completeness	Validity	Accuracy	Maintenance	Physical Security
transfers within work in process and to scrapped or spoiled work (1). Review and reperform reconciliation of labor and overhead charges to production to actual costs incurred (1). Examine reports of unmatched documents or reconciliations for reasonableness of explanations and evidence of supervisory review and approval (2).	and materials receipts for consistency of quantities and descriptions and for evidence of appropriate authorization (1). For a sample of labor charges to production, examine supporting timecards or summaries for agreement with payrolls and for evidence of appropriate authorization (1). For a sample of overhead charges to production, examine supporting documentation for overhead rates, for appropriate method of distribution, and for evidence of appropriate authorization. Review for reasonableness (1). For a sample of completed jobs or production runs	goods and supporting documentation: • Trace prices/rates to appropriate sources (perpetual inventory records, vendors' invoices, payrolls) (1). • Trace quantities to appropriate sources (materials requisitions, payrolls, cost records, production reports, shipping orders) (1). • Recalculate extensions and footings (1). • Ascertain consistency of dates, descriptions, and other data among appropriate documents (1). • Review propriety of account classifica-	and reasonableness of documentation and explanations of reconciling items (1). Examine above reconciliations for evidence of review and approval by supervisory personnel (2).	documented (3). Inquire about and observe plant security procedures designed to prevent unauthorized access to plant facilities (3).

controls described above. If supervisory controls are believed to be effective, reperformance can normally be restricted to part of one period, with testing of the related supervisory controls spread throughout the period of intended reliance.

2 = Examination of evidence that the related supervisory control described above is present to ensure the continued operation of the related basic controls. These tests should be

spread throughout the period of intended reliance.

3 = Observation of the operation of a control; may be performed one or more times during the year, as appropriate.

transferred to finished goods, examine supporting documentation for consistency with cost records and job reports, and for evidence of appropriate authorization (1).

Examine above documents for evidence of review and approval by supervisory personnel (2).

tions (1).

- Determine proper postings to appropriate work-in-process and finished goods records (1).

Review summarizations of above transactions used to prepare monthly entries for inclusion of documents tested (1).

Recalculate monthly summarizations and compare totals with general ledger postings (1).

Review summarizing entries for evidence of review and approval by supervisory personnel (2).

Observe client's physical inventory procedures, performing test counts as deemed necessary (1).

Review cutoff procedures (1).

It is ordinarily necessary for the independent auditor to be present at the time of count and, by suitable observation, tests, and inquiries, satisfy himself respecting the effectiveness of the methods of inventory-taking and the measure of reliance which may be placed upon the client's representations about the quantities and physical condition of the inventories.

AU Section 331.12 goes on to state

When the independent auditor has not satisfied himself as to inventories in the possession of the client through the procedures [of a physical count], tests of the accounting records alone will not be sufficient for him to become satisfied as to quantities; it will always be necessary for the auditor to make, or observe, some physical counts of the inventory and apply appropriate tests of intervening transactions.

Planning the Inventory Observation. The client has the primary responsibility for the conduct of the physical inventory and for making appropriate plans for its implementation. Because of the auditor's participation, however, the planning should be a joint effort. The client and auditor should agree on the timing of the inventory, taking into consideration the factors described earlier: The inventory should be counted at year-end if it is subject to significant volatility of movement or quantities, or if there are weaknesses in the controls over accounting for movement. If controls are adequate, the count can be taken prior to year-end or, if the client utilizes a system of cycle counts, on a staggered basis throughout the year; if the inventory is taken at one time, both client and auditor usually prefer a month in the last quarter of the fiscal year. Regardless of when the inventory of a particular product is taken, both work in process and finished goods inventory of that product should be counted at the same time to reduce the risk of errors in recording transfers from work in process to finished goods. The auditor should review and comment on the written instructions or memorandum of inventory plans. Often the client executive responsible for the inventory holds one or more instructional meetings with those who are to supervise the inventory taking. The auditor's presence at the meetings usually facilitates the plans for observing the inventory.

The need for a sufficient number of auditors to be present is naturally greater if a complete physical inventory is taken at one time than if cycle counts are taken. Audit staffing requirements must be determined based on the timing of inventories at various locations, the number of counting teams provided by the client, and the difficulty of the observations to be made. If the client's internal audit staff or outside inventory specialists participate in taking the physical inventory, the independent auditor's staffing requirements may be able to be reduced to some extent.

Observing the Physical Inventory. The auditor must keep in mind the objectives of observing a physical inventory: to ascertain that the inventory exists and to observe that the count and description of the inventory and its condition are accurate and properly recorded. An auditor is neither a taker of inventory nor an expert appraiser of inventory quality, quantities, or condition; nonetheless, an auditor cannot neglect the intelligent application of common sense. Well-arranged inventory is more likely to be accurately counted than is poorly arranged inventory. Signs of age and neglect are often obvious, for example, dust on cartons or rust and corrosion of containers, and they naturally raise questions about the inventory's usefulness and salability. The condition of the inventory is particularly important if the product must meet strict technical specifications. For example, in the aerospace industry, a metal part may have to possess specific size, weight, and shape characteristics, as well as conform to standards for a particular alloy mix. Failure to meet the specifications in the smallest way can mean that the part should be valued as scrap. Before observing the inventory, the auditor should know enough about the client's business to be able to recognize, at least in broad terms, the product under observation and the measures appropriate to determining its quality and condition. Thus, an auditor should spend some time examining the inventory being counted; however, the client, and everyone else concerned, should recognize that the auditor is not acting as an expert appraiser.

The auditor should spend most of the time observing the client's procedures in operation and the controls over them. The diligence of the counting teams should be noted: the care with which they count, weigh, and measure; their ability to identify and describe the inventory; the methods used to make sure that no items are omitted or duplicated. The auditor should also observe the presence of supervisory personnel, execution of planned recounting procedures, performance of cutoff procedures, control over inventory count documents, methods by which individual areas or departments are controlled and ''cleared,'' and adherence to instructions.

The auditor should make some test counts, both to confirm the accuracy of the client's counting and to record corroborative evidence of the existence of the inventory for later tracing into the inventory summarization. Recorded client counts should be selected and reperformed to test their accuracy; in addition, inventory items should be selected and independently counted and compared with quantities recorded by the client. This procedure provides evidence that all items on hand are accurately included in the client's recorded counts.

The auditor must use judgment in determining the number of test counts to perform. In the absence of specific reasons to do otherwise, the auditor usually performs a small number of test counts in relation to the total number of items in the inventory. The auditor should recognize, however, that such reasons are not uncommon. For example:

- The auditor's counts may disclose an unacceptable rate of errors in client-recorded counts. This would normally require the auditor to increase the number of test counts. In these circumstances, the client would ordinarily recount the inventory.
- The inventory may have some special characteristic, such as high value or volatility, that causes the auditor to expand the test counts.

- The client may lack enough responsible employees to reperform a sufficient number of recounts and may ask the auditor to perform that function.
- As an additional safeguard or for its ''psychological'' effect, the client may specifically request the auditor to expand the test counting activity.

The auditor should record the test counts for subsequent tracing into the inventory summarization.

Client inventory counts are commonly recorded at least in duplicate, with one copy retained at the scene of the count and another gathered for summarization. The client normally controls the summarization process and the auditor makes notations of tag or count sheet numbers or other control data on a test basis for later tracing to summarized records to provide corroborative evidence that the process was adequately controlled.

As part of the review of plans and observation of the physical inventory procedures, the auditor should note and evaluate the procedures followed in separately identifying and counting items moved from place to place (such as from department to department or from receiving area to storage area) and goods on hand belonging to others: consignments, bailments, goods on approval, property of customers returned for repair or held awaiting delivery instructions, and so on. All items belonging to others should be counted and recorded separately both because they should be as subject to control as the client's inventory and to preclude their mistaken or purposeful substitution for owned inventory items.

As noted earlier, adequately identifying work in process, particularly stage of completion, is likely to present particular difficulties. Production or operations personnel must be able to identify items in process and their condition or stage of completion in order to maintain control of the production process, and so they should be able to do so for physical count purposes as well. If they cannot, any number of practical compromises may be utilized to deal with the problems of work-in-process identification and valuation. Assumptions can be made that clearly, on the basis of experience and common sense, cannot be materially in error: Goods in a given department can be assumed to have passed through an average stage of completion; the variety of goods in a given department can be assumed to be of an average size, formula, or character; tote boxes, bales, or coils can be assumed to be of an average weight, and so forth.

Cycle Counts. All procedures applicable to wall-to-wall physical inventory observation can be readily adapted to cycle count observation. The auditor can review the cycle counting schedules, plans, and instructions, and can observe the physical arrangement and condition of the inventory, the diligence and proficiency of the inventory count teams in counting and identifying inventory, and provisions for identifying and segregating slow-moving, obsolete, or damaged goods, controlling records of test counts, and preventing omissions or duplications. Because the entire inventory is not being counted at one time, the auditor must take steps to ensure the proper identification of the items counted. The auditor can make a few test counts either with or independently of the count teams and can observe and, if desired, participate in the reconciliation of counts to perpetual records and investigation of differences.

As discussed earlier, effective cycle counting depends on a strong system of quantity control of inventory and timely recording throughout the production process. Having tested the effectiveness of the client's system for quantity control of inventory and related cycle counting, the auditor has no practical or theoretical reason not to observe and test physical inventory procedures at any time, including, if necessary, before or after the period under audit. Sometimes cycle counting is restricted to certain times of the month or year, in which case the auditor must plan to coincide with the client's schedule.

The auditor also needs evidence that the cycle counting procedures observed were functioning before and can be expected to function after they were observed and that they are applied to substantially all inventory items. A formal schedule of counts and specific assignments (covering both personnel to perform the counts and supervisory responsibility) is most persuasive, and some companies do have that degree of systemization and discipline. Many companies, however, operate under a loose policy of "counting all items at least once a year" and assign the counting to the stockkeepers to do as time allows. In those instances, the auditor can review worksheets, entries in the perpetual inventory records, and other evidence of the regularity of test counting, and can evaluate the results. The frequency of counting; absence of substantial differences between counts and records over a period of time; adequate cutoff of receipts, shipments, and transfers; quality of investigation of differences that occur (including segregation of duties between those performing initial counts and those investigating differences); and quality of storeroom housekeeping and inventory identification provide evidence of proper count procedures.

Difficult Inventories. Certain types of material—for example, logs in a river, piles of coal and scrap metal, vats of chemicals—by their nature may be difficult to count, and an auditor may have to use ingenuity to substantiate quantities on hand. Measurement of a pile of metals may be difficult for a number of reasons: The pile may have sunk into the ground to an unknown depth; the metals may be of varying weights, precluding the use of an average; or the pile may be of uneven density. The quality of chemicals and similar materials may be impossible to determine without specialized knowledge, and the auditor may find it necessary to draw samples from holding tanks and send them for independent analysis.

Clients sometimes use photographic surveys, engineering studies, and similar specialized techniques to take physical inventories, and an auditor can observe the care with which they are conducted. In such situations, the auditor should consider the need for the assistance of an expert or specialist in taking or evaluating the inventory. Guidance on the use of specialists is contained in Chapter 6.

In some circumstances, the auditor may be guided by the client's system of handling receipts and disbursements from the piles. For example, the client may use a pile rotation or exhaustion system, in which material received is placed in other piles until a pile is exhausted, at which time errors in the accounts are disclosed. If the pile rotation system functions satisfactorily, the auditor may be willing to rely to some extent on the accounting records.

In any event, both auditor and client should keep in mind that it is the client's responsibility to substantiate inventory quantities; the auditor's responsibility is to observe and evaluate the client's procedures and results.

Alternative Procedures If Observation of Physical Inventories Is Not Practicable. The auditor should consider carefully a decision that observation of inventories is impracticable or impossible. Experience has proven that observing inventories, while inconvenient perhaps, or expensive or difficult, is seldom impracticable. If the client does not or cannot take a physical inventory, however, or if the auditor cannot be present at the inventory taking, the auditor may be able to form an opinion regarding the reasonableness of inventory quantities by the application of alternative procedures. Those alternative procedures fall into the following two basic categories:

Examining other physical evidence that may be tantamount to observation of physical inventories.

Substantiating inventories through further examination of accounting evidence.

Procedures in the first category may be applied, for example, if the auditor is engaged to examine the financial statements after the physical inventory has been taken. Subsequent physical tests may be a satisfactory substitute for observation of the inventory taking. The auditor may also examine written instructions for the inventory taking, review the original tags or sheets, and make suitable tests of the summarization.

Governmental or production requirements may prohibit interruption of production for inventory purposes. If work-in-process inventory cannot be taken in the customary way for that or any other reason, the auditor may have to exercise ingenuity in finding a reasonable substitute. Quantity records maintained for labor bonus purposes may be priced and extended and the total compared with the control account; records of finished production may be examined after the inventory date to determine quantities produced. Those procedures, combined with overall observation of the work-in-process inventory and understanding of the production control system, may provide a satisfactory basis for an opinion.

In any event, the auditor must examine or observe some physical evidence of the existence of the inventory and make appropriate tests of intervening transactions or controls over them. If, on the basis of those procedures and tests of the accounts and internal controls, the auditor is satisfied that inventories are fairly stated, an unqualified opinion may be expressed. On the other hand, there may be no practicable substitute for observation of inventory taking, and an auditor may have to express a qualified opinion or disclaimer, depending on the materiality of the inventories and on whether the failure to observe was unavoidable or was due to management's decision to limit the scope of the audit.

Sometimes procedures for substantiating inventories must be based on examination of other accounting evidence. For example, an auditor making an initial examination of a client generally will not have observed the physical inventory at the previous year-end, which is a principal factor in the determination of cost of goods sold for the current year. If reputable independent accountants expressed an unqualified opinion on the prior-year statements, a successor auditor may accept that opinion and perhaps merely review the predecessor auditor's working papers supporting the prior-year balances. If no examination was made for the preceding year, the auditor may have no alternative but to substantially expand the tests of accounting evidence to attempt to establish the correctness of the beginning inventories in order to be able to express an opinion on the current year's results of operations.

Those expanded tests may include a detailed examination of physical inventory sheets and summaries, including review and testing of cutoff data, examination of perpetual inventory records and production records, and review of individual product and overall gross profit percentages. In connection with the latter procedures, cost accumulations for selected inventory items should be tested and significant changes in unit costs should be directly correlated to factors such as improvements in technology, mass buying economies and freight rate "breaks," changes in labor costs, and changes in overhead rates. Changes in gross profit percentages should be further related to changes in unit sales prices and changes in the profitability of the sales mix, if applicable.

An auditor who is unable to form an opinion on the opening inventory may wish to qualify the audit opinion or give no opinion with respect to results of operations for the year under examination.

Ownership of Inventories

Another audit objective for inventories is to establish that the client holds title to the inventories. In many cases, this is relatively straightforward. Theoretically, the accounting for purchases and sales in transit at year-end should be determined by the FOB terms (shipping point or destination), which determine title. Unless financial statements would otherwise be misleading, however, the legal test of title is often disregarded based on materiality considerations: Purchases are generally recorded when received and sales when shipped.

The primary focus for this objective is on proper control of receiving and shipping activities and cutoffs at year-end and, if different, at the physical inventory date. Control over sales cutoff at an early physical inventory date is particularly important because sales cutoff errors at that date—as compared with year-end—are compounded when perpetual inventory records and control account balances are adjusted for differences between book and physical inventory. Since cutoff errors correct themselves in the following period when the sales and cost of sales are recorded in the normal course of transaction processing, a reduction of inventory and increase in cost of sales, if goods were shipped before the physical count but not recorded until after the physical count, will be recorded twice. The effect in that situation is to misstate gross profit by the full cost of the inventory involved in the cutoff error. On the other hand, a sales cutoff error at year-end (when the physical inventory has been taken at an earlier date) will result in a misstatement of gross profit only to the extent of the gross profit on the sale.[1]

At the time of the inventory observation, the auditor should visit the receiving and shipping departments, record the last receiving and shipping document numbers, and ascertain that each department has been informed that no receipts after or shipments before the cutoff date should be included in inventory. The auditor should review the records of those departments after the inventory date and compare the last receiving and shipping numbers with accounting department records to ensure that a proper cutoff was achieved. Special care should be taken to control the movement of inventory when manufacturing operations are not suspended during the physical inventory.

If there are consignment inventories, inventories in public warehouses, or customer inventories, those procedures must be expanded. Inventory held by others should be substantiated by direct confirmation in writing with the custodians. If such inventory is material, the auditor should apply one or more of the following procedures, in accordance with SAS No. 1, as amended by SAS No. 43 (AU Section 331.14), to obtain reasonable assurance with respect to the existence of the inventory:

- Review and test the client's control procedures for investigating the warehouseman and evaluating the warehouseman's performance.
- Obtain an independent accountant's report on the warehouseman's system of internal accounting control relevant to custody of goods and, if applicable, pledging of receipts, or apply alternative procedures at the warehouse to gain reasonable assurance that information received from the warehouseman is reliable.
- Observe physical counts of the goods, if practicable and reasonable.
- If warehouse receipts have been pledged as collateral, confirm with lenders pertinent details of the pledged receipts (on a test basis, if appropriate).

Goods belonging to customers or others should be counted and, if significant in amount, should be confirmed with their owners. The auditor should be alert to the possibility of such goods and should make certain that the client has a system for controlling the goods and that they are properly identified and segregated.

---

[1]Cutoff errors involving receipt of goods at the physical inventory date also misstate gross profit by the full cost of the inventory; cutoff errors involving receipt of goods at year-end (when the physical inventory has been taken at an earlier date) have no effect on gross profit, except in the rare situation in which the merchandise was also sold.

The auditor should also be alert for liens and encumbrances against the inventories. These are normally evident from reading minutes and agreements, or as a result of confirmations with lenders relating to loans or loan agreements. It may be necessary to investigate whether additional liens and encumbrances have been filed with state or local governmental authorities.

Inventory Costing and Summarization

Inventory costing and summarization may be based on the physical inventory results or the perpetual inventory records (if those records have been determined to be reliable); in either case, the results are compared with the recorded book amounts. The procedures performed in testing the summarization of the physical inventory quantities are as follows:

1. Tests of the inventory tags to determine that all tags used for the physical counts and only those tags are included in the physical inventory summaries. The auditor should also obtain satisfaction that tags that were voided during the physical count have been properly accounted for. If count sheets were used for recording physical inventory results, the auditor should obtain satisfaction that unused spaces have not been filled in subsequent to the completion of the physical count.

2. Comparisons of the inventory summaries with the auditor's record of counts and with the client's count sheets or tags; tests of conversions and summarizations of units.

3. Comparison of quantities with perpetual records, if they exist, on a test basis, and review of differences and client dispositions; this is particularly important when inventories are taken prior to year-end and perpetual records will be the basis for year-end inventory valuation.

4. Tests of cutoff procedures.

5. Reviews and confirmation of customers' materials on hand and of client's inventories in the hands of others.

6. Tests of the costs to be applied to inventories to determine that they are reasonably computed in accordance with an acceptable and consistent accounting method.

7. Tests of the multiplication of prices and inventory quantities and the resulting footings and summarizations.

8. Reviews and tests of procedures for identifying obsolete or slow-moving items.

9. Reviews of the costing of damaged or obsolete items to determine that the assigned value is not in excess of net realizable value.

10. Reviews and tests of the determination of market prices to determine whether market is lower than cost.

The degree to which the auditor performs each of the foregoing procedures depends on the extent to which related internal controls can be relied on. This decision should be based on the auditor's observations during the physical inventory and knowledge of and experience with the client. Errors noted during the course of testing the summarization should be given particular consideration in assessing whether client procedures are effective and whether additional testing is necessary.

In testing the costing of merchandise inventories and inventories of simple manufacturing operations, the auditor can frequently relate costs directly to specific vendor invoices and labor summaries. For example, for merchandising operations in which goods are purchased for resale, the cost of inventory can be determined by reference to appropriate invoices supporting the purchase of the goods on hand. In simple manufacturing operations, the allocation of material costs, direct labor, and overhead to inventory may be straightforward. For such operations, it may be most efficient to place little reliance on controls and rely principally on substantive tests of the assigned costs.

In more complex manufacturing operations, the evaluation of material, labor, and overhead allocations may be more difficult. An example is the manufacturing operation of a steel mill in which the raw materials ore, coal, and limestone are converted into finished steel. The allocation of costs is less objective and requires an understanding of process costing and an in-depth knowledge of the manufacturing process. It may be difficult for the auditor to obtain satisfaction regarding the costing of inventory without some reliance on the client's procedures for product costing and tracking inventory through the various stages of completion.

The accounting method used to price inventory also affects the substantive tests to be performed. The differences in the procedures used under different valuation methods relate primarily to the sources of cost information and the mechanics of the pricing calculations. For example, pricing tests of inventory valued on a FIFO basis normally include a comparison of costs to most recent invoice prices for purchased merchandise and most recent unit production costs for manufactured goods. Pricing tests of LIFO inventories normally include procedures to test consistency of base-year prices between years, comparisons of base-year costs for new items with current-year costs, recalculation of indices used to value current-year LIFO increments, and an overall review of the accuracy of the LIFO application.

In reviewing for obsolete items in inventory, the auditor can compare quantities with those in previous inventories on a test basis to identify slow-moving items or abnormally large or small balances. Reviews of usage records can provide further indications of slow-moving items. If the client does not maintain perpetual records, the auditor may examine purchase orders or production orders to determine how recently certain items of inventory were acquired. Many companies have formulas or rules of thumb that translate overall judgments on obsolete inventory into serviceable detailed applications, such as all items over a year's supply, all items that have not moved within six months, or all items bearing certain identifying numbers with regard to date or class of product. The auditor must review whether the rules are realistic and sufficiently comprehensive as well as whether they are fully and accurately applied.

In addition to reviewing and testing the client's rules, the auditor must, based on knowledge of the client's business, evaluate whether, for each segment of the inventory, market conditions might raise questions about its realizability in the normal course of operations. The auditor may augment that knowledge by inquiring of sales and marketing executives about the salability of the inventories. Past experience can be the best guide to the net realizable value of items that must be disposed of at salvage prices. It is important to recognize that when certain finished goods are declared obsolete (or severe markdowns are required), related raw materials and work-in-process inventories may also need to be written down.

The lower of cost or market principle requires that inventories be carried in the balance sheet at the lower of historical cost or replacement cost, except that the carrying value should not exceed net realizable value (estimated selling price minus costs of completion and disposal) or be lower than net realizable value reduced by the normal profit margin. (Net realizable value is frequently referred to as the ''ceiling'' and net realizable value reduced by the normal profit margin is frequently referred to as the ''floor.'')

Testing the client's application of the lower of cost or market principle is one of the more difficult and subjective aspects of the audit. In most situations, the auditor's perception of the associated inherent risk determines the extent of substantive testing. For example, if the risk of defective production is high, the auditor may need to expand testing of the condition of inventories. Companies usually apply the lower of cost or market test on an exception basis when a problem is identified. Accordingly, the auditor has limited opportunity to rely on internal control. The greater audit risk is that all problems have not been identified, not that an identified problem may lead to an error in the financial statements.

The auditor should test the client's calculation of net realizable value of individual or major groups of products. Estimated selling prices may be compared with recent sales invoices—or preferably with the latest customer orders—and evaluated for possible trends in prices. Estimated costs of completion and disposal may be tested for reasonableness by overall computation. The auditor ordinarily need not determine the value of inventory at reproduction or replacement costs if there is acceptable evidence that, for individual or groups of products, the range between net realizable value and the market floor is not great. Replacement costs, however, may be tested by reference to cost records, current invoices, or purchase contracts. Reproduction costs may be tested in a similar manner, supplemented by discussions with production and accounting employees.

Auditing Cost of Sales

In planning the audit strategy, the auditor often views the income statement as the residual effect of changes in the balance sheet. The primary focus is on auditing balance sheet accounts at the beginning of the year and the end of the year. The audit opinion on results of operations, however, requires that the auditor perform audit procedures to obtain satisfaction that transactions are properly accounted for and classified in the income statement.

Substantive tests of cost of sales are usually limited for two reasons. First, the auditor is likely to have developed an audit strategy that contemplates reliance on specific controls in the production cycle. Second, if the auditor obtains satisfaction about the beginning and ending inventory balances from substantive tests, and about the completeness, validity, and accuracy of purchases of goods and services (including their proper classification) by testing and relying on controls that are part of the buying cycle, the auditor has in effect examined significant amounts of evidence about the "residual" cost of sales figure. Accordingly, substantive tests of cost of sales can normally be limited to analytical review procedures that test the proper classification of costs by focusing on expected or traditional relationships among various components of cost of sales and on obtaining explanations for fluctuations in expense account balances. Typical analytical review procedures are discussed later in this section.

If results of the foregoing procedures indicate that additional evidence is needed to support the cost of sales balance, or if the auditor has selected a substantive testing approach, the tests may include examination of selected invoices for material and overhead costs and tests of the allocation of payroll costs, together with tests of the summarization of detailed amounts in the account balances that enter into cost of sales. The scope of this testing would be that necessary for the auditor to be satisfied that the risk of a misstatement related to cost of sales was acceptably low. In assessing this risk, it is likely that the auditor would also use analytical review procedures.

Purchase Commitments

Losses from purchase commitments may arise in the case of commodity purchases, forward transactions, or purchase commitments in excess of short-term requirements. If material losses could arise from unfulfilled purchase commitments, the commitments should be identified and the potential need for a loss provision should be assessed. This may be accomplished by examining open purchase order records, inquiring of employees who make purchase commitments, or requesting major suppliers to provide details of any purchase commitments outstanding as of year-end. If there is doubt regarding whether all commitments have been identified, it may be appropriate to review suppliers' invoices and receiving reports for a period after year-end for evidence of purchases above prevailing prices or in quantities in excess of current requirements (by a review of perpetual inventory records for evidence of goods that are slow-moving or obsolete), which may indicate unfavorable purchase commitments at year-end. Also, since major purchase commitments generally require the approval of the board of directors, examination of minutes of board meetings may assist the auditor in discovering such purchase commitments. Chapter 17 contains a discussion of the statements about purchase commitments that should be included in the client's representation letter.

Analytical Reviews

Auditing inventories challenges an auditor's perception and analytical ability more than almost any other audit activity. The better the auditor understands the client's business, its operating problems, and the market and other economic conditions under which it operates, the greater the ability to determine that the inventory is fairly stated in conformity with generally accepted accounting principles. That understanding can be applied to specific inventory judgments in the design of analytical reviews.

Both internal and external data are abundantly available for designing and testing statistical, ratio, and other kinds of analyses. The auditor should make every effort to use analytical reviews unique to the client under examination, but only on the basis of the most careful and penetrating understanding. The following paragraphs describe only those analytical reviews that are likely to apply to most inventories.

If standard cost systems or budgetary systems produce variance reports, the system has, in effect, performed a large part of the analytical review for the auditor by identifying the variances. The auditor can then read the variance reports carefully and analyze reasons for variances. If variances are small, the auditor can infer that standards approximate actual costs and can significantly reduce price testing.

Balances of purchases, usage reports, and production costs should be compared from month to month. Fluctuations should be investigated and explained.

Significant ratios should be computed and compared from month to month and with the prior year. The ratios of cost of goods sold to inventory and to sales (or profit margin) are universally considered informative. They must be used with caution in a period of changing prices, however, as results under FIFO will differ, perhaps significantly, from those under LIFO. In a great many industries, the computation of the ratio of total units to total value—that is, average unit cost—is valid and informative, but if the "mix" of unit costs is likely to vary substantially, explaining fluctuations in average unit costs may not be cost effective. If they are valid, average unit costs can be computed for sales, purchases, and inventory account balances.

If available, sales forecasts and marketing plans can provide important information about salability and net realizable value of inventories. For example, the authors have experienced conditions in which marketing plans for a "new line" effectively rendered obsolete an inventory that otherwise appeared perfectly salable at normal profit margins. Sales forecasts and marketing plans, however, are often not well organized or in written form, and thus the auditor must take care not to waste time searching for material that is nonexistent or inconclusive. An auditor who has an adequate understanding of the client will know what to expect and of whom to inquire.

Analytical reviews must be particularly intensive and penetrating between an interim inventory date and year-end. Often the audit effort during this period is directed primarily toward compliance tests of controls, with minimal substantive testing of intervening activity or the year-end balance. Analytical reviews provide an excellent means of identifying changes in conditions that may require additional substantive tests or, in conjunction with the results of related compliance and other substantive tests, of providing the needed assurance regarding the year-end balances.

Management Representation Letter

It is standard practice for the auditor to require management to include certain matters relating to inventory in the representation letter. The focus of the letter is on judgments made by management in the financial accounting process; the letter includes representations relating to agreements to repurchase inventory or the absence thereof, net realizable value judgments, pledging of assets, and the nature of significant inventory purchase commitments. Management representation letters are discussed in Chapter 17.

Review Questions

14-1. What is meant by the production cycle?

14-2. What are the auditor's objectives in auditing the production cycle?

14-3. What audit risk factors are considered in determining the audit strategy for the production cycle?

14-4. What procedures should be in effect for the proper accounting for and control over raw materials and component parts from receipt to utilization?

14-5. Companies and their auditors must make reviews to discover slow-moving, obsolete, or damaged goods. Why?

14-6. Given the significance of inventory and the production cycle to many businesses, management reviews are often performed to ensure operational efficiency. Cite examples of management reviews related to inventory and production.

14-7. What are the audit objectives associated with variances generated by a standard cost system?

14-8. Why are physical inventory counts of work in process often difficult? What recommendations can an auditor make in this regard?

14-9. Distinguish between wall-to-wall and cycle count inventory taking. When is each appropriate?

14-10. What is an inventory committee and what are its functions?

14-11. Briefly outline the instructions a client's physical inventory program should contain.

14-12. Briefly outline the procedures an auditor's physical inventory program should contain.

14-13. What factors should the auditor consider in determining whether reliance should be placed on controls in the production cycle?

14–14. Under what conditions should the auditor employ the audit strategy of emphasizing substantive testing in lieu of compliance testing in auditing the production cycle?

14–15. What factors influence the nature, extent, and timing of substantive tests?

14–16. What types of compliance tests are generally used to test controls over storing and issuing of raw materials and component parts?

14–17. How are compliance tests in the buying cycle related to those in the production cycle?

14–18. Who has the primary responsibility for planning and conducting the physical inventory? What factors affect the timing of the physical inventory?

14–19. What should the auditor be doing when observing inventory taking?

14–20. Why does an auditor make test counts during the physical inventory?

14–21. What substantive tests should be performed with respect to consignment inventories, inventories in public warehouses, and inventory held for customers?

14–22. What analytical review procedures are applied in the audit of inventories? When should they be applied?

14–23. What matters relating to inventory should be included in the management representation letter?

Discussion Questions _____

14–30. ABC Co. determines its inventories by means of a complete physical inventory count at year-end. Actual costs are used for pricing. You attended the year-end physical count and observed that the count procedures were satisfactory. What additional steps should you take to satisfy yourself concerning the quantities and value of the inventories?

14–31. Outline the procedures you would follow in the observation of a physical inventory, indicating the purpose of each procedure. (Do not discuss the auditor's cutoff tests.) Assume that compliance tests have confirmed your evaluation of a very good system of internal control.

14–32. State what steps you would take to verify the book balance of the physical quantities of inventories in each of the following cases:

    a. A large, outdoor pile of coal.
    b. Grain in an elevator.
    c. A large quantity of nails, dumped in a bin, the book inventory being carried in pounds.

    The book balances are obtained as the result of a continuous record of receipts, withdrawals, and arithmetically computed balances.

(AICPA adapted)

14–33. State the procedures you would follow if a significant number of adjustments were necessary arising from differences between amounts shown on the perpetual inventory records and

  a. The client's cycle counts.
  b. The client's year-end counts.
  c. Your test counts.

Consider each case separately.

14-34. David Anderson, CPA, is engaged in the examination of the financial statements of Redondo Manufacturing Corporation for the year ended June 30, 1986. Redondo's inventories at year-end include merchandise on consignment with consignees and merchandise held in public warehouses. The merchandise held in public warehouses is pledged as collateral for outstanding debt.

Required:

Normal inventory and notes payable auditing procedures have been satisfactorily completed. Describe the specific additional auditing procedures that Anderson should undertake with respect to

  a. Consignments out.
  b. Merchandise in public warehouses pledged as collateral for outstanding debt.

(AICPA adapted)

14-35. Decker, CPA, is performing an examination of the financial statements of Allright Wholesale Sales, Inc., for the year ended December 31, 1987. Allright has been in business for many years and has never had its financial statements audited. Decker has gained satisfaction with respect to the ending inventory and is considering alternative audit procedures to gain satisfaction with respect to management's representations concerning the beginning inventory, which was not observed.

Allright sells only one product (bottled brand X beer), and maintains perpetual inventory records. In addition, Allright takes physical inventory counts monthly. Decker has already confirmed purchases with the manufacturer and has decided to concentrate on evaluating the reliability of perpetual inventory records and performing analytical review procedures to the extent that the prior year's unaudited records will enable such procedures to be performed.

Required:

What are the audit tests, including analytical review procedures, that Decker should apply in evaluating the reliability of perpetual inventory records and gaining satisfaction with respect to the January 1, 1987, inventory?

(AICPA adapted)

14-36. Often an important aspect of a CPA's examination of financial statements is the observation of the taking of the physical inventory.

Required:

  a. What are the general objectives or purposes of the CPA's observation of the taking of the physical inventory? (Do not discuss the procedures or techniques involved in making the observation.)
  b. For what purposes does the CPA make and record test counts of inventory quantities during the observation of the taking of the physical inventory? Discuss.

(AICPA adapted)

14-37. The client's cost system is often the focal point in the CPA's examination of the financial statements of a manufacturing company.

Required:

a. For what purposes does the CPA review the cost system?

b. The Summerfield Manufacturing Company employs standard costs in its cost accounting system. List the audit procedures that you would apply to satisfy yourself that Summerfield's cost standards and related variance amounts are acceptable and have not distorted the financial statements. (Confine your audit procedures to those applicable to materials.)

(AICPA adapted)

14-38. In an annual audit at December 31, 1986, you find the following transactions near the closing date:

1. Merchandise costing $1822 was received on January 3, 1987, and the related purchase invoice recorded January 5. The invoice showed the shipment was made on December 29, 1986, FOB destination.

2. Merchandise costing $625 was received on December 28, 1986, and the invoice was not recorded. You located it in the hands of the purchasing agent; it was marked "on consignment."

3. A packing case containing products costing $816 was standing in the shipping room when the physical inventory was taken. It was not included in the inventory because it was marked "Hold for shipping instructions." Your investigation revealed that the customer's order was dated December 18, 1986, but that the case was shipped and the customer billed on January 10, 1987. The product was a stock item of your client.

4. Merchandise received on January 6, 1987, costing $720 was entered in the purchase register on January 7, 1987. The invoice showed that the merchandise was shipped FOB supplier's warehouse on December 31, 1986. Since it was not on hand at December 31, it was not included in inventory.

5. A special machine, fabricated to order for a customer, was finished and in the shipping room on December 31, 1986. The customer was billed on that date and the machine excluded from inventory, although it was shipped on January 4, 1987.

Required:

a. State whether the merchandise should be included in the client's inventory.

b. Give the reason for your decision on each item in (a).

(AICPA adapted)

14-39. While reviewing purchase commitments, an auditor discovered that the purchase price in an unauthorized purchase commitment exceeded the current market price for that item at the time of the order. Discuss the effect of the discovery on audit strategy and audit procedures to be followed.

AICPA Multiple Choice Questions _____

These questions are taken from the Auditing part of Uniform CPA Examinations. Choose the single most appropriate answer.

14-40. When evaluating inventory controls with respect to segregation of duties, a CPA would be *least* likely to

    a. Inspect documents.
    b. Make inquiries.
    c. Observe procedures.
    d. Consider policy and procedure manuals.

14–41. Which of the following is an internal control weakness for a company whose inventory of supplies consists of a large number of individual items?

    a. Supplies of relatively little value are expensed when purchased.
    b. The cycle basis is used for physical counts.
    c. The storekeeper is responsible for maintenance of perpetual inventory records.
    d. Perpetual inventory records are maintained only for items of significant value.

14–42. In the audit of which of the following types of profit-oriented enterprises would the auditor be most likely to place special emphasis on testing the internal controls over proper classification of payroll transactions?

    a. A manufacturing organization.
    b. A retailing organization.
    c. A wholesaling organization.
    d. A service organization.

14–43. The primary objective of a CPA's observation of a client's physical inventory count is to

    a. Discover whether a client has counted a particular inventory item or group of items.
    b. Obtain direct knowledge that the inventory exists and has been properly counted.
    c. Provide an appraisal of the quality of the merchandise on hand on the day of the physical count.
    d. Allow the auditor to supervise the conduct of the count so as to obtain assurance that inventory quantities are reasonably accurate.

14–44. A client's physical count of inventories was lower than the inventory quantities shown in its perpetual records. This situation could be the result of the failure to record

    a. Sales.
    b. Sales returns.
    c. Purchases.
    d. Purchase discounts.

14–45. The physical count of inventory of a retailer was higher than shown by the perpetual records. Which of the following could explain the difference?

    a. Inventory items had been counted but the tags placed on the items had *not* been taken off the items and added to the inventory accumulation sheets.
    b. Credit memos for several items returned by customers had *not* been recorded.
    c. No journal entry had been made on the retailer's books for several items returned to its suppliers.
    d. An item purchased ''FOB shipping point'' had *not* arrived at the date of the inventory count and had *not* been reflected in the perpetual records.

14–46. During the first part of the current fiscal year, the client company began dealing with certain customers on a consignment basis. Which of the following audit procedures is *least* likely to bring this new fact to the auditor's attention?

a. Tracing of shipping documents to the sales journal.
b. Test of cash receipts transactions.
c. Confirmation of accounts receivable.
d. Observation of physical inventory.

14-47. When auditing a public warehouse, which of the following is the most important audit procedure with respect to disclosing unrecorded liabilities?

a. Confirmation of negotiable receipts with holders.
b. Review of outstanding receipts.
c. Inspection of receiving and issuing procedures.
d. Observation of inventory.

14-48. Which of the following is *not* one of the independent auditor's objectives regarding the examination of inventories?

a. Verifying that inventory counted is owned by the client.
b. Verifying that the client has used proper inventory pricing.
c. Ascertaining the physical quantities of inventory on hand.
d. Verifying that all inventory owned by the client is on hand at the time of the count.

14-49. A CPA is engaged in the annual audit of a client for the year ended December 31, 1987. The client took a complete physical inventory under the CPA's observation on December 15 and adjusted its inventory control account and detailed perpetual inventory records to agree with the physical inventory. The client considers a sale to be made in the period that goods are shipped. Listed below are four items taken from the CPA's sales-cutoff-test worksheet. Which item does *not* require an adjusting entry on the client's books?

	Date (Month/Day)		
	Shipped	Recorded as Sale	Credited to Inventory Control
a.	12/10	12/19	12/12
b.	12/14	12/16	12/16
c.	12/31	1/2	12/31
d.	1/2	12/31	12/31

14-50. When outside firms of nonaccountants specializing in the taking of physical inventories are used to count, list, price, and subsequently compute the total dollar amount of inventory on hand at the date of the physical count, the auditor will ordinarily

a. Consider the report of the outside inventory-taking firm to be an acceptable alternative procedure to the observation of physical inventories.
b. Make or observe some physical counts of the inventory, recompute certain inventory calculations, and test certain inventory transactions.
c. *Not* reduce the extent of work on the physical count of inventory.
d. Consider the reduced audit effort with respect to the physical count of inventory as a scope limitation.

14-51. A well-functioning system of internal control over the inventory/production functions would provide that finished goods are to be accepted for stock only after presentation of a completed production order and a (an)

      a. Shipping order.
      b. Material requisition.
      c. Bill of lading.
      d. Inspection report.

14-52. An auditor would be *most* likely to learn of slow-moving inventory through

      a. Inquiry of sales personnel.
      b. Inquiry of stores personnel.
      c. Physical observation of inventory.
      d. Review of perpetual inventory records.

Problems and Cases

14-60. Ace Corporation does not conduct a complete annual physical count of purchased parts and supplies in its principal warehouse but uses statistical sampling instead to estimate the year-end inventory. Ace maintains a perpetual inventory record of parts and supplies and believes that statistical sampling is both highly effective in determining inventory values and sufficiently reliable to make a physical count of each item of inventory unnecessary.

    Required:
      a. Identify the audit procedures that should be used by the independent auditor *that change or are in addition to* normal required audit procedures when a client utilizes statistical sampling to determine inventory value and does not conduct a 100 percent annual physical count of inventory items.
      b. List at least 10 normal audit procedures that should be performed *to verify physical quantities* whenever a client conducts a periodic physical count of all or part of its inventory.

                                      (AICPA adapted)

14-61. In connection with his examination of the financial statements of Knutson Products Co., an assembler of home appliances, for the year ended May 31, 1987, Ray Abel, CPA, is reviewing with Knutson's controller the plans for a physical inventory at the Company warehouse on May 31, 1987. *Note:* In answering the two parts of this question do not discuss procedures for the physical inventory of work in process, inventory pricing, or other audit steps not directly related to the physical inventory taking.

    Part a. Finished appliances, unassembled parts, and supplies are stored in the warehouse, which is attached to Knutson's assembly plant. The plant will operate during the count. On May 30, the warehouse will deliver to the plant the estimated quantities of unassembled parts and supplies required for May 31 production, but there may be emergency requisitions on May 31. During the count the warehouse will continue to receive parts and supplies and to ship finished appliances. However, appliances completed on May 31 will be held in the plant until after the physical inventory is taken.

    Required:
    What procedures should the Company establish to ensure that the inventory count includes all items that should be included and that nothing is counted twice?

Part b. Warehouse employees will join with accounting department employees in counting the inventory. The inventory takers will use a tag system.

Required:
What instructions should the Company give to the inventory takers?

(AICPA adapted)

14–62. An auditor is conducting an examination of the financial statements of a wholesale cosmetics distributor with an inventory consisting of thousands of individual items. The distributor keeps its inventory in its own distribution center and in two public warehouses. An inventory computer file is maintained on a computer disk and at the end of each business day the file is updated. Each record of the inventory file contains the following data:

- Item number
- Location of item
- Description of item
- Quantity on hand
- Cost per item
- Date of last purchase
- Date of last sale
- Quantity sold during year

The auditor is planning to observe the distributor's physical count of inventories as of a given date. The auditor will have available a computer tape of the data on the inventory file on the date of the physical count and a general-purpose computer software package.

Required:
The auditor is planning to perform basic inventory auditing procedures. Identify the basic inventory auditing procedures and describe how the use of the general-purpose software package and the tape of the inventory file data might be helpful to the auditor in performing such auditing procedures.

Organize your answer as follows:

Basic Inventory Auditing Procedure	*How General-purpose Computer Software Package and Tape of the Inventory File Data Might Be Helpful*
1. Observe the physical count, making and recording test counts where applicable.	Determining which items are to be test-counted by selecting a random sample of a representative number of items from the inventory file as of the date of the physical count.

(AICPA adapted)

14–63. Review the case study provided and answer the questions concerning inventory valuation.

RELIABLE PRESS COMPANY

The Reliable Press Company is engaged in the manufacture of large-sized presses under specific contracts and in accordance with the customers' specifications. Customers are required to advance 25 percent of the contract price. The company records sales on a shipment basis and accumulates costs by job orders. The normal profit margin over the past few years has been approximately 5 percent of sales, after providing for sales commissions of 10 percent that are paid at the time of delivery. Management values its inventory at the lower of cost or net realizable value.

Among the jobs you are reviewing in the course of your annual examination of the company's December 31 financial statements is Job 1468, calling for delivery of a three-color press at a firm contract price of $50,000. Costs accumulated for the job at year-end aggregated $30,250. The company's engineer estimated that the job was approximately 55 percent complete at that time. You have carried out the following procedures to date:

1. Examined all contracts, noting pertinent provisions.
2. Observed physical inventory of work in process and reconciled details to job order accounts.
3. Tested labor, material, and overhead charged to the various jobs to determine that such charges were authentic and had been posted correctly.
4. Confirmed customers' advances at year-end.
5. Balanced work-in-process job ledger with control account at year-end.

Required:
With respect to Job 1468:

a. State what additional audit procedures, if any, you would follow and explain the purposes of the procedures.
b. Indicate the value at which you would include Job 1468 on the balance sheet. You are to assume that no adjustment in the total selling price for this job is possible and that costs to completion will be incurred on the basis experienced to date.

14–64. Indicate the misstatements, if any, in financial position at July 31, and in operating results for the year ended July 31, arising from the following situation:

Assumptions: Physical inventory was taken June 30 and book inventory amount was adjusted to physical. Fiscal year ends July 31.

Case I

Item	Selling Price	Cost to Manufacture	Date Goods Shipped	Date Sale and Cost of Sale Recorded
A	$25,000	$15,000	6/25	6/29
B	30,000	18,000	6/29	7/5
C	40,000	25,000	7/3	6/29
D	50,000	32,000	6/15	7/1
E	60,000	40,000	7/27	8/2

Case II

Item	Cost of Raw Materials	Date Goods Received	Date Purchase Recorded
A	$25,000	6/26	7/3
B	10,000	7/2	6/29
C	30,000	7/29	8/1

14-65. Renken Company cans two food commodities that it stores at various warehouses. The company employs a perpetual inventory accounting system under which the finished goods inventory is charged with production and credited for sales at standard cost. The detail of the finished goods inventory is maintained on punched cards by the Tabulating Department in units and dollars for the various warehouses.

Company procedures call for the Accounting Department to receive copies of daily production reports and sales invoices. Units are then extended at standard cost and a summary of the day's activity is posted to the Finished Goods Inventory general ledger control account. Next, the sales invoices and production reports are sent to the Tabulating Department for processing. Every month the control and detailed tab records are reconciled and adjustments recorded. The last reconciliation and adjustments were made on November 30, 1986.

Your CPA firm observed the taking of the physical inventory at all locations on December 31, 1986. The inventory count began at 4:00 P.M. and was completed at 8:00 P.M. The company's figure for the physical inventory is $331,400. The general ledger control account balance at December 31 was $373,900, and the final "tab" run of the inventory punched cards showed a total of $392,300.

Unit cost data for the company's two products are as follows:

Product	Standard Cost
A	$2.00
B	3.00

A review of December transactions disclosed the following:

1. Sales invoice #1301, 12/2/86, was priced at standard cost for $11,700, but was listed on the Accounting Department's daily summary at $11,200.
2. A production report for $23,900, 12/15/86, was processed twice in error by the Tabulating Department.
3. Sales invoice #1423, 12/9/86, for 1200 units of Product A, was priced at a standard cost of $1.50 per unit by the Accounting Department. The Tabulating Department noticed and corrected the error but did not notify the Accounting Department of the error.
4. A shipment of 3400 units of Product A was invoiced by the Billing Department as 3000 units on sales invoice #1504, 12/27/86. The error was discovered by your review of transactions.
5. On December 27, the Memphis warehouse notified the Tabulating Department to remove 2200 unsalable units of Product A from the finished goods inventory, which it did without receiving a special invoice from the Accounting Department. The Accounting Department received a copy of the Memphis warehouse notification on December 29 and made up a special invoice, which was processed in the normal manner. The units were not included in the physical inventory.

6. A production report for the production on January 3 of 2500 units of Product B was processed for the Omaha plant as of December 31.

7. A shipment of 300 units of Product B was made from the Portland warehouse to Ken's Market, Inc., at 8:30 P.M. on December 31 as an emergency service. The sales invoice was processed as of December 31. The client prefers to treat the transaction as a sale in 1986.

8. The working papers of the auditor observing the physical count at the Chicago warehouse revealed that 700 units of Product B were omitted from the client's physical count. The client concurred that the units were omitted in error.

9. A sales invoice for 600 units of Product A shipped from the Newark warehouse was mislaid and was not processed until January 5. The units involved were shipped on December 30.

10. The physical inventory of the St. Louis warehouse excluded 350 units of Product A that were marked "reserved." On investigation, it was ascertained that this merchandise was being stored as a convenience for Steve's Markets, Inc., a customer. This merchandise, which has not been recorded as a sale, is billed as it is shipped.

11. A shipment of 10,000 units of Product B was made on December 27 from the Newark warehouse. The shipment arrived on January 6 but had been excluded from the physical inventories.

Required:

Prepare a worksheet to reconcile the balances for the physical inventory, Finished Goods Inventory general ledger control account, and Tabulating Department's detail of finished goods inventory ("Tab Run").

The following format is suggested for the worksheet:

	Physical Inventory	General Ledger Control Account	Tabulating Department's Detail of Inventory
Balance per client	$331,400	$373,900	$392,300

(AICPA adapted)

14-66. You have been assigned as the in-charge accountant of a new client, The Old Fashioned Ice Cream Co. Your firm obtained the client during the middle of the current year; thus you were unable to observe the opening inventory. The company has never had an audit before but has engaged your firm at the insistence of the company president's grandson, Mr. McCann, who has just joined the family business. You have arranged a meeting with Mr. McCann to familiarize yourself with the company's operation and discuss some of the potential problems Mr. McCann thought your firm could help with.

During the meeting, Mr. McCann stated that his principal concern is with the company's inventory. His grandfather, at age 89, is still active in the day-to-day operations of the company and has refused to modernize any of its production facilities or to develop any new products. As a result, the company has a reputation for making an excellent ice cream that is expensive, is high in calories, and comes in a limited number of flavors. A substantial share of the company's market has been lost to its chief competitor, which has developed a line of low-cost, low-calorie ice cream in 42 flavors.

No physical inventories have been taken in the past because no person could withstand the below-zero temperatures in the freezer warehouse long enough to count the inventory. The perpetual inventory records tend not to be very accurate because of the traditional afternoon "ice cream break" that all employees take daily.

In addition, Mr. McCann's grandfather is notorious for buying large quantities of raw materials and producing large quantities of product for stock whenever he gets a "bargain" on raw material prices. This creates problems because the product has only a six-month shelf life before it starts to have a stale taste.

Finally, the company's old delivery trucks constantly have problems with their refrigeration units and have on several occasions delivered shipments to customers in a rather "liquidated" condition.

Required:

Discuss the potential audit problems and the strategies and procedures to be followed for the audit of inventory for the current year.

14–67. The inventory detail schedule on page 642 was prepared by the controller of Friendly Phone Store Company for use by the independent auditors during their examination of Friendly's year-end financial statements. In addition, the audit assistant prepared a purchase cutoff schedule, shown below. All audit procedures performed and conclusions reached are listed below. Each schedule was properly initialed, dated, and indexed and then submitted to a senior member of the audit staff for review. Internal control was reviewed and is considered to be satisfactory. Friendly uses FIFO for determining cost. Perpetual records are kept for units only.

Required:

a. For each of the audit procedures performed, indicate whether the conclusions reached by the audit assistant are appropriate. If they are inappropriate, state why they are inappropriate.

b. What essential audit procedures were not noted as having been performed by the audit assistant?

Audit Procedures Performed and Conclusions Reached

1. Agreed quantities to counts taken at the physical inventory observation on 12/31/86. No exceptions noted.
2. Confirmed merchandise held at public warehouses. One exception noted on working paper; adjustment proposed.
3. Agreed unit cost with vendor invoices. No exceptions noted.
4. Footed inventory schedule. No exceptions noted.
5. Agreed total to general ledger. No exceptions noted.
6. Determined that a proper cutoff was achieved at year-end. No exceptions noted.
7. Determined that the average selling price of all inventory items exceeded the respective unit cost, therefore verifying that inventory valuation is at the lower of cost or market. No exceptions noted.

FRIENDLY PHONE STORE COMPANY
Inventory Detail Schedule
December 31, 1986

PRODUCT	PURCHASE DATE	QUANTITY ON HAND	UNIT COST	TOTAL COST	Y-T-D SALES	Y-T-D UNITS SOLD	AVERAGE SELLING PRICE
ROTARY	6/17/86	2500 T	$ 18.62	P 46,550	$ 26,551	978	$ 27.15
PUSH BUTTON	11/12/86	6000 } T	25.10	P 150,600	} 1,253,879	28,818	43.51
	12/18/86	4700	27.75	P 130,425			
CORDLESS	10/17/86	1200 } TW	93.19	P 111,828	} 613,040	4860	126.14
	11/25/86	1500	95.27	P 142,905			
SPEAKER	10/12/86	3200 T	47.19	P 151,008	627,968	7040	89.20
CLOCK RADIO PHONE	6/17/86	4200 T	22.98	S 96,516	1,132,994	38,511	29.42
ANSWERING MACHINES	8/10/86	800 C	112.30	P 89,840	} 1,245,143	6257	199.00
	12/30/86	1500 T	118.51	P 177,855			
CAR PHONES	6/15/86	250 T	672.20	P 168,050	189,840	120	1,582.00
				1,265,577	5,089,415		
				FG	F		

W = PERPETUAL INVENTORY RECORDS INDICATED THAT 3000 UNITS WERE IN INVENTORY AT YEAR-END. CONTROLLER COULD NOT RECONCILE DIFFERENCE.

S = PRODUCT IS IMPORTED AND COST EXCLUDES DUTY, FREIGHT AND INSURANCE COSTS OF $ 4 PER UNIT. DUTY AND INSURANCE IS CHARGED TO EXPENSE WHEN INCURRED.

P = UNIT COST AGREES WITH VENDOR INVOICE.

C = CONFIRMED WITH PUBLIC WAREHOUSE, WHICH INDICATED THAT 710 UNITS WERE ON HAND ON JANUARY 6, 1987. SALES CUTOFF SCHEDULE [NOT INCLUDED IN THIS PROBLEM] INDICATES THAT 90 UNITS WERE SHIPPED ON 1/4/87. JOURNAL ENTRY PROPOSED TO RECOGNIZE THE COST OF SALE AND REDUCE INVENTORY (AJE No. 13) AND TO RECOGNIZE THE RECEIVABLE AND THE SALE (AJE No. 14).

T = AGREES WITH PHYSICAL INVENTORY COUNTS

F = TOTALS FOOTED

G = TOTALS TRACED TO GENERAL LEDGER

Friendly Phone Store Company
Purchase Cutoff Test
December 31, 1986

VENDOR	INVOICE NUMBER	SHIPPING AND INVOICE DATE	PRODUCT	QUANTITY	TOTAL COST	DATE RECEIVED	DATE DEBITED TO INVENTORY CONTROL ACCOUNT
ACME	97852	12/16/86	PUSH BUTTON	4700	130 425	12/18/86	12/22/86
BARNES	57154	12/28/86	ANSWERING MACHINES	1500	177 855	12/28/86	12/30/86
KENDEL	86-852	12/30/86	CORDLESS	1200	115 824	12/30/86	1/4/87
MARTIN	16725	12/29/86	SPEAKER	1400	67 550	1/2/87	1/5/87
ACME	98102	12/31/86	PUSH BUTTON	1000	27 750	*	N/A
JONES	2669	1/3/87	CLOCK RADIO PHONE	800	25 048	1/5/87	1/7/87
ACME	98897	1/9/87	PUSH BUTTON	3000	83 250	1/12/87	1/15/87
KENDEL	87-122	1/15/87	CORDLESS	1100	105 182	1/15/87	1/17/87

- SHIPPING TERMS FROM ALL VENDORS ARE FOB SHIPPING POINT
- THE ABOVE SAMPLE WAS TAKEN FROM PURCHASE JOURNAL ENTRIES POSTED FROM 12/15/86 - 1/15/87
- * = SHIPMENT WAS DELIVERED DIRECTLY TO CUSTOMER. BILL OF LADING INDICATED SHIPMENT DATE WAS 12/31/86

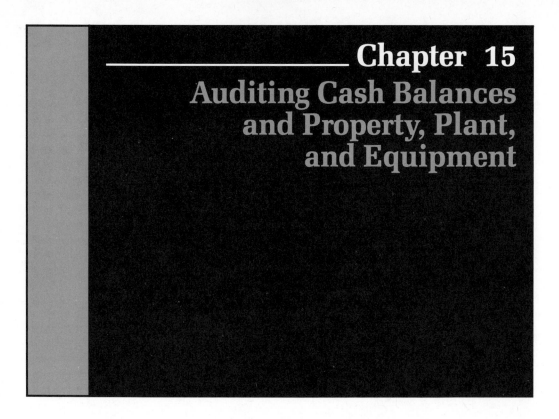

Chapter 15
Auditing Cash Balances and Property, Plant, and Equipment

Introduction

Most of an enterprise's transactions arise from buying, producing, and selling goods and services, and paying and collecting cash in connection with those activities. Those transactions are reflected in the revenue, expense, asset, and liability accounts that were discussed in the three preceding chapters on the revenue, buying, and production cycles.

Other financial statement accounts typically reflect a relatively small number of material transactions (such as financing and investing activities) and events (such as allocations of revenues and expenses between periods). For example, contributed capital may change because common stock was issued, a business may be purchased, or bonds may be retired. Similarly, plant and equipment depreciate, prepaid insurance expires, taxes accrue, and the realizable value of assets changes. Accounting principles require that these events be recognized, and if they are material, GAAS requires that the auditor gather and evaluate evidence to achieve the audit objectives relevant to the accounts that reflect them.

This chapter and the following chapter consider auditing procedures for financial statement accounts that in commercial and industrial enterprises are typically not derived from transaction cycles or that, even if they are derived from transaction cycles, for efficiency reasons are typically audited by performing substantive tests. The auditor's purpose for considering a class of transactions as a cycle is to increase audit efficiency by assessing and testing internal accounting controls and then restricting substantive tests from those that would otherwise be required. That strategy may be appropriate, even for the transactions and accounts considered in this and the following chapter, if in a particular enterprise the volume of transactions is large and controls over those transactions appear to be appropriately designed and operating effectively. That strategy is clearly not appropriate, however, when only a few transactions affect an account in a year, or if certain audit objectives can be achieved more efficiently by performing substantive tests.

This chapter considers two financial statement accounts, cash and property, plant, and equipment, for which the auditor is unlikely to adopt a strategy of performing compliance tests to meet audit objectives. The following chapter treats four other groups of accounts—investments, prepayments and accruals, taxes, and debt and equity accounts—that are usually audited by performing substantive tests. This is not to suggest that in auditing those accounts the auditor has necessarily assessed the risk of material misstatement occurring as high. Before performing substantive tests, the auditor will have gathered or updated sufficient information about the client to make preliminary materiality judgments and to assess inherent and control risks. Those assessments, which are based in part on an understanding of the control environment, the accounting procedures used to process transactions, and the reports generated by those procedures, are likely to permit the auditor to restrict substantive tests from those that would otherwise be required. The audit strategy discussed in this and the following chapter assumes that, principally because of the small number of transactions involved or because of the high level of risk of material misstatement occurring, the auditor has determined that it would not be efficient to compliance test controls in order to restrict substantive tests even further. But, as will be evident from the examples presented, that is far from suggesting that a 100 percent examination of all transactions or balances is appropriate or that none of the work can be performed before year-end.

Cash Balances

The volume of transactions involving cash is likely to be greater than for any other account. Those transactions and controls over them were discussed in Chapters 12 and 13. Questions of valuation or judgment rarely arise in connection with cash, and therefore the cash balance can be stated more precisely than can most other accounts. Because cash represents the highest form of liquidity and is easily transferable, it is more susceptible to misappropriation than are other assets. Consequently, the safeguarding of cash has historically been the focus of a large part of the audit effort.

An auditor's responsibility for the cash account on a balance sheet does not differ from the responsibility for other balance sheet accounts; the exercise of judgment in selecting and applying auditing procedures is required to enable the auditor to form an opinion about the fair presentation of cash in relation to the financial statements taken as a whole. In the past, many auditors spent an inordinate amount of time applying detailed auditing procedures to cash—for example, reviewing or reperforming bank reconciliations at one or more dates, performing one or more independent reconciliations, and examining every cash receipt and disbursement and supporting documents for one or more months. Those procedures have their place and, if controls over cash are weak, may be necessary to provide adequate audit evidence. On the other hand, the auditor is likely to be able to accumulate, from tests of the revenue and buying cycles, enough evidence about the completeness, accuracy, and validity of cash transactions to need very little additional assurance about those objectives from substantive tests of transactions. Accordingly, the auditor can concentrate on other audit objectives relevant to the balance in the cash account.

Audit Objectives

The objectives of auditing the cash balance are to provide reasonable assurance that

- Recorded cash on hand and in banks exists and is the unencumbered property of the client.
- All items properly included as part of cash are realizable in the amounts stated; for example, foreign currency on hand or on deposit in foreign countries is properly valued.
- Cash restricted as to availability or use is properly identified and disclosed.

Of these, the existence and ownership objectives are primary, since they apply universally to all entities and cash is more likely to be overstated than understated. Objectives related to the completeness, accuracy, validity, and cutoff of cash transactions are addressed in Chapters 12 and 13.

Substantive Tests of Cash Balances

Four types of substantive tests are frequently performed in auditing cash balances to meet the audit objectives of cash:

- Confirming balances with banks.
- Preparing, reviewing, or testing bank reconciliations.
- Preparing bank transfer schedules.
- Cash counts.

Confirmation of Bank Balances

Bank Accounts—Client Procedures. All bank accounts should be formally authorized by designated officers: Often a vote of the board of directors is required. Discontinuance of accounts should also be formally approved. Authorization should include names of those who may sign checks. Lists of authorized check signers should be reviewed periodically by someone knowledgeable to determine that employees' duties have not changed in ways that make their signing of checks improper or inconsistent with segregation of duties.

It is particularly important that the names of those authorized to sign checks be changed immediately on retirement, death, or resignation if check signing machines are used. Instances have occurred in which signature plates with names of personnel no longer in the employ of the company were used long after their departure. Procedures should provide for immediate change when these events occur, even if the change has to be ratified by the board of directors at a later date.

Standard Bank Confirmation Form. An auditor ordinarily should confirm balances at year-end by direct correspondence with all banks with which the client has done business during the year, regardless of whether all year-end reconciliations are reviewed or tested. Since the confirmation form also seeks information about indebtedness to the bank and certain contingent liabilities, the usual practice is to confirm all bank accounts open at any time during the year under audit.

Requests to banks for confirmation should be made using the Standard Bank Confirmation Inquiry form, which appears as Figure 15.1. The original and duplicate of this form are mailed to each bank; one copy should be signed by the bank and returned to the auditor and the other retained by the bank. Because of increased mechanization of bank accounting, the confirmation procedure can be expedited if the bank receives the confirmation form before the confirmation date and at least two weeks before a reply is required. The exact name and number of the accounts to be confirmed should be prelisted in item 1 of the form.

The standard form has no space for reporting securities or other items held by the bank in safekeeping, as agent or trustee, or for collection for the account of the client, nor does it request a bank statement and related canceled checks for the cutoff period (usually a week or two after the balance sheet date if the testing is performed at year-end). Accordingly, the auditor should request the client to address a supplementary letter to the bank covering those items and any others on which information is desired. (On occasion, the auditor may also request names of authorized check drawers from the bank; those names should then be compared with the names of the people authorized by the board of directors to write checks.) The format of the letter is illustrated in Figure 15.2.

Compensating Balances. Banks may require borrowers to keep certain amounts on deposit—known as compensating balances—as a condition for a loan. The standard form does not provide for confirmation regarding compensating balance arrangements or other restrictions on availability or use. Because the confirmation of credit arrangements is not processed by the same personnel that handle the usual confirmation requests, a separate confirmation request should be sent, usually to the lending departments of banks that have extended credit.

Figure 15.1 Standard Bank Confirmation Form

STANDARD BANK CONFIRMATION INQUIRY
Approved 1966 by
AMERICAN INSTITUTE OF CERTIFIED PUBLIC ACCOUNTANTS
and
BANK ADMINISTRATION INSTITUTE (FORMERLY NABAC)

_____19_____

Your completion of the following report will be sincerely appreciated. IF THE ANSWER TO ANY ITEM IS "NONE," PLEASE SO STATE. Kindly mail it in the enclosed stamped, addressed envelope *direct* to the accountant named below.

Report from   Yours truly,

_____
(ACCOUNT NAME PER BANK RECORDS)

(Bank) _____   By _____
                                                            Authorized Signature

_____   Bank customer should check here if confirma-
                                                 tion of bank balances only (item 1) is desired.

_____   ☐

                                                 NOTE—If the space provided is inadequate,
                                                 please enter totals hereon and attach a state-
                                                 ment giving full details as called for by the
Accountant   Coopers & Lybrand   columnar headings below.
             2700 First National Bank Tower
             Portland, Oregon 97201

1. At the close of business on_____19_____our records showed the following balance(s) to the **credit** of the above named customer. In the event that we could readily ascertain whether there were any balances to the credit of the customer not designated in this request, the appropriate information is given below.

AMOUNT	ACCOUNT NAME	ACCOUNT NUMBER	Subject to With-drawal by Check?	Interest Bearing? Give Rate
$				

2. The customer was directly liable to us in respect of loans, acceptances, etc., at the close of business on that date in the total amount of $_____, as follows:

AMOUNT	DATE OF LOAN OR DISCOUNT	DUE DATE	INTEREST Rate	INTEREST Paid to	DESCRIPTION OF LIABILITY, COLLATERAL, SECURITY INTERESTS, LIENS, ENDORSERS, ETC.
$					

3. The customer was contingently liable as endorser of notes discounted and/or as guarantor at the close of business on that date in the total amount of $_____, as below:

AMOUNT	NAME OF MAKER	DATE OF NOTE	DUE DATE	REMARKS
$				

4. Other direct or contingent liabilities, open letters of credit, and relative collateral, were

_____

5. Security agreements under the Uniform Commercial Code or any other agreements providing for restrictions, not noted above, were as follows (if officially recorded, indicate date and office in which filed):

_____

Yours truly, (Bank) _____

Date_____19_____   By _____
                                            Authorized Signature

Additional copies of this form are available from the American Institute of CPAs, 1211 Avenue of the Americas, New York, N. Y. 10036

Figure 15.2 Supplementary Letter to Bank

(Name and Address of Bank)

Dear Sirs:

Will you kindly furnish directly to our auditors, (name and address of auditors), the following information relevant to their examination of our accounts as of the close of business December 31, 19____:

1. The information requested in the enclosed Standard Bank Confirmation Inquiry form;
2. Statement of all securities or other items you hold for our account as of December 31, 19____, for collection or safekeeping or as agent or trustee; and
3. Statement of our account and the related paid checks for the period from January 1 to January ____, 19____, inclusive.

Very truly yours,

(Name of Client)

(Signature and Title of Officer)

Confirmation of Other Balances. Commonly, confirmation of cash on hand is requested from other custodians of funds; often the request for confirmation of the fund balance is combined with a request for notification of any unrecorded expenses.

Bank Reconciliations. Periodic reconciliations of accounting records of cash in banks with amounts shown on bank statements are important basic controls over bank deposits and disbursements by check. For internal accounting control purposes, not only should the balance shown by the bank statement be reconciled to that shown by the accounts at the same date, but the detailed items listed on the bank statement should be reconciled to the detailed items recorded in the accounts during the period covered by the bank statement. The latter step ensures recognition of all items recorded in the accounts, including offsetting items within receipts or disbursements, and of all items recorded on the bank statement. The preferred reconciliation procedure is the "proof of cash," which is described in detail later in this chapter.

Effective segregation of duties requires that the person responsible for reconciling bank balances to account balances not be assigned functions relating to cash receipts, cash disbursements, or preparing or approving vouchers for payment; that the responsible person obtain the bank statements directly from the bank; and that specific comparisons be made as part of the bank reconciliation procedure, such as comparing paid checks and other debits and credits listed on the bank statement with entries in the accounts, examining checks for signatures and endorsements, and reconciling bank transfers.

There are two alternative audit approaches to bank reconciliations. If physical security and segregation of duties are sufficiently reliable, the auditor may *review the client's reconciliations and perform certain related tests*. If reliance cannot be placed on those controls, the auditor may *perform independent reconciliations*.

Review and Test of Client's Reconciliations. If the auditor has evaluated and tested physical security and segregation of duties relating to cash and concludes that they can be relied on, then reviewing and testing a client's reconciliations may be appropriate. Preferably, the client's reconciliation should reconcile not only the bank balances to the book balances but also bank activity to book activity, using the "proof of cash" form described later. The steps in reviewing and testing a client's bank reconciliation include

1. Comparing amounts on the reconciliation with amounts in the bank statements, cash journals, and general ledger.

2. Establishing the mathematical accuracy of the reconciliation.

3. Obtaining bank statements directly from the bank for the cutoff period; comparing paid checks dated before the end of the period with checks listed as outstanding; comparing deposits listed on the reconciliation as "in transit" with cutoff statements and investigating deposits that are recorded by the bank more than one or two days after the balance sheet date; tracing transfers of funds to account debits and credits, which should be recorded in the same accounting period (see the later discussion of bank transfer schedules); substantiating other reconciling items by reference to supporting documents; and considering further investigation of unusual outstanding checks and other reconciling items that have not cleared.

If supervisory controls are considered adequate to ensure the continuing operation of segregation of duties and physical controls, the foregoing procedures may be performed at an interim date and, if there are many bank accounts, may be limited to a representative sample. The following procedures would be performed at year-end if the reconciliations were reviewed and tested at an interim date:

1. Comparing the client's reconciliations of year-end balances with the bank confirmation.

2. Scanning reconciliations for evidence of proper preparation and supervisory approval.

3. Requesting the client to prepare a schedule of bank transfers before and after year-end, and comparing the schedule with the accounting records.

Independent Reconciliations. The following procedures should be considered on engagements in which the auditor determines that physical security and segregation of duties are not sufficient to warrant relying on them.

1. Perform steps 1 through 3 just listed as of year-end. Since the auditor is not relying on controls, the testing would generally be more extensive than when controls are relied on, and early substantiation of the cash balance would normally not be appropriate.
2. Perform "proof of cash" reconciliations of bank accounts (see below). If the proof of cash is performed at year-end, the procedures noted earlier, to the extent they are duplicative, are not required.

Proof of Cash. A proof of cash (also known as a "four-column reconciliation") is a form of reconciliation that summarizes and controls the examination of cash records for a selected period, regardless of length; it can be prepared by the client and reviewed or tested by the auditor, or prepared independently by the auditor. A proof of cash working paper is illustrated in Figure 15.3.

An advantage of the proof of cash is that it provides a reconciliation of balances at the beginning and end of the period and, with little additional effort, effects a reconciliation of transactions during the period as recorded in the accounts with those reflected on the bank statement. An auditor is thus able to "prove" the propriety of recorded transactions in the accounts to an independent source (the bank statement). Any other audit tests applied to the receipts, disbursements, or balances can be described on the form. The following tests are usually performed:

1. If the totals are not already shown on the bank statement, determine total receipts per the bank statement by footing deposits and determine total disbursements by subtracting the closing balance from the sum of the opening balance and deposits. (Checks returned with the statement need not be added to determine total bank disbursements unless the proof of cash does not reconcile.) Enter the totals on the "proof of cash" form.
2. Obtain the client's reconciliation as of the close of the preceding period and compare balances shown on that reconciliation with the corresponding amounts shown by the accounts and the bank statement; substantiate outstanding checks at the close of the preceding period by examining paid checks returned by the bank in the current period, investigating any still outstanding; and substantiate deposits in transit and other reconciling items at the close of the preceding period by reference to the current bank statement, bank notifications of charges and credits, and other supporting documents.
3. Compare daily totals of recorded cash receipts shown in the cash journal with daily deposits appearing on the bank statement. If there are time lags between the receipt, recording, and depositing of collections, investigate any that appear unreasonable in the light of the company's usual practices. (Delay in depositing receipts constitutes inefficient cash management and exposes cash items on hand to risk of loss or misuse, such as "lapping" collections of accounts receivable—a method of continuously concealing a defalcation by cred-

Figure 15.3 Proof of Cash

Date Prepared: 1/27/8—
Prepared by: PLD
a) C & L
b) Client and
Examined by:
Reviewed by: SAC
C & L SR/SUP.

XYZ Corporation
Proof of Cash–Month of December
12/31/8__

	Balance Beginning of period	Receipts	Disbursements	Balance End of period
Per bank statement	31268 A	42687 A	46560 A	27395 ✓ A C
Deposits in transit:				
Beginning	1000 T	(1000)		
End		2000		2000 T
Outstanding checks:				
Beginning	(3917)		(2817) φ	(1100) y
End			3460	(3460) φ
Unrecorded charges and credits:				
Collection from customer				
on note, credited by				
bank during period,				
entered on books after				
end of period		(2078)		(2078) CM
Per Books	28351	41609	47203	22757 w
	✓	✓	✓	✓
Audit adjusting entry #1:				
Collection of customer note				2078
Per books as adjusted				24835
				✓

Legend of audit procedures:

✓ = Footed & cross-footed; all mathematics proven

A = Agreed with amounts shown on bank statement/books

C = Balance confirmed with bank; see bank confirmation on W/P __

T = Traced to subsequent bank statement

φ = Checks cleared on subsequent bank statement

y = Check #895 dated 11/27/8 — for $ 1,100 is still outstanding.
Examined purchase order, receiving report and vendor
invoice. The purchase made and paid by this check appears
proper. No adjusting entry proposed

CM = Examined bank credit memo

iting later collections to accounts whose collections were not previously recorded.) Enter unmatched cash receipts items or deposit items on the "proof of cash" form.

4. Compare paid checks returned with the bank statement with the disbursements records for check number, date, payee, and amount. The comparison determines not only which checks have not cleared the bank during the period but also that dates, payees, and amounts of disbursements as shown by the paid checks agree with recorded disbursements. This comparison preferably should be made with a book of original entry (a disbursements journal, computer run, check register, check stub book, or file of duplicate checks) rather than a summary record. If a summary record must be used, the auditor should be satisfied that existing control procedures make the summary record reliable. List checks outstanding at the end of the period, foot the list, and enter the total on the "proof of cash" form.

5. Account for all checks issued in the sequence between the first and last checks drawn on the bank account during the period being examined.

6. Determine that the reconciliation foots and crossfoots and that all items appearing in it are proper. A subsequent entry in the accounts that apparently offsets an item in a reconciliation is not necessarily proof of its correctness; it may merely transfer an error to another account. Examine each material adjusting entry to determine its propriety. The propriety of reconciling items is not established merely by the fact that arithmetical reconciliation is effected by their inclusion.

7. If the end of the test period is also the balance sheet date, and a principal purpose of the reconciliation is to substantiate the cash account in the balance sheet, compare deposits in transit and outstanding checks revealed by the reconciliation with a subsequent bank statement and accompanying paid checks. This is usually done by means of the specially requested "cutoff bank statement" covering a period of a week or two and received directly from the bank. Substantiate by reference to properly approved vouchers or other available documents, checks outstanding at the date of the reconciliation that are not returned with the subsequent bank statement, if material in amount. If the end of the test period does not coincide with the balance sheet date, it is ordinarily not necessary to follow up reconciling items because the client's procedures in that area are tested in step 2.

Bank Transfer Schedule. To ensure that there has been a proper cutoff at year-end, the auditor should determine whether significant transfers of funds occurred among the client's various bank accounts near the balance sheet date. All transfers of funds within the organization should be considered—whether among branches, divisions, or affiliates—to make sure that cash is not "double counted" in two or more bank accounts and that "kiting" (explained later) has not occurred. The auditor should determine (1) that each transaction represented as a transfer is in fact an authorized transfer; (2) that debits and credits representing transfers of cash are recorded in the same period; and (3) that the funds are actually deposited in the receiving bank in the appropriate period.

Kiting is a way of concealing a cash shortage caused by a defalcation, such as misappropriating cash receipts; it involves the careful and deliberate use of the "float" (the time necessary for a check to clear the bank on which it was drawn). Kiting is effected by drawing a check on one bank, depositing it in another bank just before year-end, and not recording the transfer in the cash receipts or cash disbursements journals until after year-end. The float period will cause the check not to clear the bank on which it was drawn until after year-end, and the amount transferred is included in the balances of both bank accounts. Since the transfer is not recorded as a receipt or a disbursement until the following year, it will not appear as an outstanding check or a deposit in transit on the reconciliation of either bank account. The effect is to increase receipts per the bank statement; if the misappropriation of cash receipts and the kiting take place in the same period, receipts per the bank statement will agree with receipts per the cash receipts journal at the date of the bank reconciliation. (If the misappropriation of cash receipts takes place in the period before the kiting, a proof of cash for the current period may also reveal the kiting.) Kiting requires that the transfer process be repeated continually until the misappropriated funds have been restored.[1]

A bank transfer schedule is an efficient and effective tool that assists the auditor in determining that all transfers of funds among bank accounts near the balance sheet date are recorded in the books in the proper accounting period, that cash has not been double counted, and that kiting is not apparent. The schedule should indicate, for each transfer, the date on which the check that effected the transfer was recorded as a cash disbursement, the date it was recorded as a cash receipt, the date it cleared the bank on which it was drawn, and the date it cleared the bank in which it was deposited. The list of bank transfers should be compiled from both originating documents (paid checks or bank advices) returned with the cutoff bank statement and the client's cash receipts and disbursements records. A bank transfer schedule is illustrated in Figure 15.4.

The dates on the bank transfer schedule should be obtained from the cash records and the dates appearing on the check that indicate when it was received by the bank in which it was deposited and when it was canceled by the bank on which it was drawn. The date the check was recorded as a disbursement should be compared with the date it was recorded as a receipt; the dates should be the same. If they are not and the entries are in different fiscal years, an adjusting entry may be necessary to prevent double counting of cash, depending on the offsetting debit or credit to the entry that was made in the year being audited. Then, for each transfer, the bank dates (paid and cleared) should be compared with the corresponding dates on which the transaction was recorded in the

---

[1]Banks and other financial institutions use the term *kiting* to include the writing of checks against inadequate funds with the intent of depositing sufficient funds later, but before the checks clear the bank.

Figure 15.4 Bank Transfer Schedule

Check Number	Disbursement (Transfer Out)		Receipt (Transfer In)	
	Date Recorded in Books	Date Paid by Bank	Date Recorded in Books	Date Received by Bank
A	12/30/86	01/03/87	12/30/86	12/31/86
B	12/30/86	01/05/87	12/30/86	01/03/87
C	12/30/86	01/03/87	01/02/87	01/02/87
D	01/02/87	01/06/87	01/02/87	12/31/86
E	01/04/87	01/10/87	01/04/87	01/08/87

books (received and disbursed). If those dates are in different accounting periods, the transfer should appear on the bank reconciliation as a reconciling item—an outstanding check if the check cleared the disbursing bank in a later period than that in which it was recorded, and a deposit in transit if it cleared the receiving bank in a later period than that in which the receipt was recorded. Lastly, unusually long time lags between dates recorded and dates cleared should be investigated for possible holding of checks at year-end—a cutoff problem.

In Figure 15.4, there are no double-counting problems with the transfers involving checks A, B, and E because the transfer out of one bank account was recorded in the same period as the transfer into the other bank account. Transfers A and B should appear as outstanding checks on the reconciliation of the disbursing bank's account. Transfer B should also appear as a deposit in transit on the reconciliation of the receiving bank's account. Transfer E should not affect either the books or the reconciliations because it occurred in the following year and all dates are in the same accounting period.

The other transfers in the figure require further analysis. Transfer C should appear on the reconciliation of the disbursing bank's account as an outstanding check at December 31, 1986. If it does, the balance per the books will not be in error. If it does not, the total of outstanding checks will be understated and the balance per the books will be overstated, possibly covering up an unrecorded check drawn on that account that already cleared the bank.

Transfer D is an example of possible kiting. That transfer should appear as an outstanding check on the reconciliation of the disbursing bank's account; it should also appear as a recording error (an omitted disbursement) on the reconciliation. If kiting were taking place, it is unlikely that the preparer of the reconciliation would be aware that a check was outstanding that should be included on the outstanding check list; nor would the person doing the kiting call the "recording error" to anyone's attention. The funds transferred would thus be counted twice—once in the bank account that the check was drawn on and once in the account it was deposited in. Transfer D would result in a misstatement, though not from kiting, if the delay in recording was the result of an oversight or if it was done to conceal an overdraft at the bank.

Count of Cash and Negotiable Assets on Hand. Cash funds on hand, normally constituting one or more petty cash funds, are seldom significant in relation to the overall cash balance. Therefore, auditors generally do not perform substantive tests of the year-end balance of cash on hand. They may, nevertheless, wish to perform compliance tests of controls over the day-to-day operation of cash funds to obtain sufficient evidence that the activity in the funds is accurately recorded and valid. Inadequate procedures and controls could result in improperly classified expenses in the income statement.

Some circumstances require physical counting of currency and cash items on hand. If cash funds on hand and undeposited receipts are significant in relation to the overall cash balance, and if controls are weak, there may be no alternative to a year-end cash count. If an auditor concludes that a cash count is required, it should be coordinated with the examination or confirmation of other negotiable assets such as marketable securities, notes receivable, and collateral held as security for loans to others. If simultaneous physical examination of negotiable assets on hand is not practicable, the auditor should establish control over all such assets to avoid the possibility of a shortage in one group being covered up by other assets already examined. Less active negotiable assets·—such as notes receivable and marketable securities—may be counted in advance and placed under seal until completion of all counts. Occasionally it is necessary to permit movement of assets under seal; the auditor should control and record all such transactions. Totals of funds and other negotiable assets counted or confirmed should be reconciled to general ledger controlling accounts as of the date of the examination.

An auditor should not assume responsibility for custody of cash or negotiable assets in a physical count, but should insist on continuous attendance by a representative of the client while those assets are being examined. After the count has been completed, the client's representative should be asked to acknowledge its accuracy. Auditors should never count funds in the absence (even if temporary) of the custodian, and should always obtain a written acknowledgment of return of the funds intact from the client's representative. If the count discloses an overage or shortage in the fund, the auditor should ask for a recount and acknowledgment by the client's representative of the accuracy of the count.

Counting cash does not normally require counting the contents of coin packages or all packages of currency notes. Vouchers in the fund may be reviewed for validity, reasonableness, and approval. Checks or vouchers not of recent date should be investigated. It may at times be more efficient to avoid counting undeposited receipts by controlling those funds until deposited, obtaining an authenticated duplicate deposit slip, and determining from the subsequent bank statement whether any item deposited (and listed on the duplicate deposit slip) was subsequently charged back as missing or uncollectible.

Property, Plant, and Equipment

Most businesses use property, plant, and equipment in the process of generating revenues. The term *property, plant, and equipment* generally refers to noncurrent tangible assets, including those held under capital leases, used by a business to create and distribute its goods and services. The term *fixed assets* is also used (although its use is diminishing) to describe the property, plant, and equipment accounts. Related accounts that are audited in the same manner as property, plant, and equipment are *leasehold improvements* and *construction in progress*.

Accounting principles require that the cost of plant and equipment be allocated on a rational and systematic basis over the periods benefited. Various depreciation or amortization methods are utilized to allocate the net cost of an asset (acquisition cost less estimated recoverable salvage value) over the period of benefit.

Expenditures to maintain or improve property, plant, and equipment are normal following their acquisition. A major audit consideration is whether such expenditures should be accounted for as expenses of the current period or reflected on the balance sheet either as an addition to the cost of the asset or a reduction of the related accumulated depreciation. As a general rule, an expenditure should be capitalized if it benefits future periods by extending the useful or productive life of the asset. The distinction between the two categories of expenditures frequently is not clear-cut. Enterprises usually have stated policies defining which expenditures are to be capitalized, and the auditor must exercise judgment in determining whether the policies are appropriate and that they are being complied with.

Audit Objectives

The objectives of auditing property, plant, and equipment and related accounts parallel those for other asset accounts. The auditor should obtain sufficient competent evidence, consisting of both underlying accounting data and corroborating information, to provide reasonable assurance that

- Property, plant, and equipment recorded in the accounts exist and are owned or leased under capital leases by the company.
- Additions to and disposals of property, plant, and equipment are valid, have been properly authorized, and have been appropriately recorded.
- There are no material items charged to expense that should have been capitalized, or vice versa.
- The cost or other basis of recording property, plant, and equipment is appropriate.
- Appropriate methods of depreciation have been properly applied, on a basis consistent with that of the previous year, to all items of property, plant, and equipment that should be depreciated.

- Property, plant, and equipment pledged as collateral are identified and disclosed, along with other necessary disclosures.

Some of these objectives may be met through procedures performed in connection with other aspects of the audit or tests of other balance sheet accounts. For example, the pledging of property, plant, and equipment is generally discovered through reading and analyzing loan documents and minutes of meetings of the board of directors or other management groups. Property acquired under capital leases may be determined by reading minutes and analyzing lease or rental expense accounts. Similarly, the continued existence of property, plant, and equipment recorded in the accounts may be determined, though often not specifically or explicitly, as an auditor moves about the facilities in the course of observing physical inventories and performing other audit tasks. Auditors typically review charges to repair and maintenance accounts for items that should have been capitalized, and test the calculation and summarization of depreciation.

Determining the cost or other basis of recorded property, plant, and equipment usually presents few problems since most assets are acquired individually in cash transactions. The auditor must exercise judgment, however, as to the appropriate cost in situations involving business combinations, self-constructed assets, capitalized leases, and nonmonetary transactions. While they are not usually a major audit concern, the auditor must be alert for changes in laws or general business conditions that might make it impossible to recover the remaining costs of property through revenue generated or outright sale. Also, the auditor should be aware of conditions that might require reevaluation of the remaining depreciable lives of property, plant, and equipment.

Substantive Tests of Balances

As with other areas of the audit, the audit strategy should be based initially on an analysis of inherent risk factors relating to the nature of the property, plant, and equipment transactions and accounts and the company's accounting system and related internal controls. Efficiency considerations generally lead the auditor to rely principally on substantive tests, even if controls are strong. Many of the substantive tests described later can be traced to the "Summary of Property, Plant, & Equipment & Accumulated Depreciation," frequently referred to as a "lead schedule," which is shown in Figure 15.5.

Evaluating Risk. Most companies do not have a large volume of transactions in their property accounts, and most transactions are of high dollar value. Thus, the auditor can generally obtain evidence about the existence of particular assets from informal walkthroughs of client facilities or from observing and testing the client's fixed asset physical inventory counts. Because of the permanent nature of the assets, there is less likelihood of unrecorded transactions remaining undetected. For these reasons, it is generally easier to determine the

Figure 15.5

ACE Enterprises Inc.
Summary of Property, Plant, & Equipment & Accumulated Depreciation
12/31/8—

Classification	Balance at Beginning of period	Additions	Disposals	Other	Balance at End of period	
Cost	Ⓐ	Ⓑ Ⓒ	Ⓓ	Ⓔ	Ⓐ	TB
Buildings	10 745986 43	987 23 66	9161 31	(334783)	10 832200 95	
Machinery & Equipment	2088816 57	337937 01	19622 2 Ⓖ		2424791 36	TB
Furniture & Fixtures	58077 06	6684 91		334783	681098 0	TB
	12 8928800 6	4433455 8	111235 3	—0—	13325102 11 ⩗	
	√	√	√	√	√	
Accumulated Depreciation	Ⓐ	Ⓗ		Ⓔ	Ⓐ	
Buildings	3007975 34	2149292 7	9161 31 Ⓕ	(16735)	3213575 95	TB
Machinery & Equipment	743567 95	1045495 7	17584 6 Ⓖ		846359 06	TB
Furniture & Fixtures	185211 8	592733		16735	246158 6	TB
	3770064 47	3254061 7	1091977	—0—	4084550 87 ⩗	
	√	√	√	√	√	

Legend

ꝉ = Traced to prior year work papers

√ = Footed & cross-footed

TB = Agreed to trial balance

Ⓐ = Agreed to fixed asset subsidiary ledger

Ⓑ = Supported by detail listing of fixed asset additions. See
work papers —— to —— where additions were vouched

Ⓒ = See W/p —— For calculation of investment tax credit

Ⓓ = See W/p —— For calculation of investment tax credit recapture

Ⓔ = Reclassification for light fixtures erroneously classified as building

Ⓕ = Write off obsolete and scrapped items

Ⓖ = Sale of miscellaneous M & E - No further audit work deemed necessary

Ⓗ = See W/p's —— To —— where reasonableness of client's
calculation of depreciation was tested using the firm's
computer audit program for estimating depreciation

audit strategy for property, plant, and equipment than for other financial statement accounts.

Property, plant, and equipment are recorded and carried in the financial statements at amounts equal to the costs identified with specific assets; net realizable values of productive assets are not normally relevant to the values at which assets are carried. Subsequent to acquisition and recognition as an asset, the cost of property, plant, and equipment enters into the determination of periodic income through depreciation. A misstatement of income resulting from the property accounts would normally occur only through depreciation errors (including unrecognized premature obsolescence) or misclassification of expenditures between the asset account and the repairs and maintenance account.

For those reasons, property, plant, and equipment are usually audited by relying principally on the performance of substantive tests. Exceptions to this generalization occur in highly capital-intensive companies that have a large volume of property transactions. For example, utilities generally have a thorough and effective accounting system for processing and recording property transactions, most of which are for the acquisition or repair of utility properties. Selecting the audit strategy for property, plant, and equipment accounts in these companies depends on the auditor's evaluation of the internal controls and the extent to which they can be relied on to reduce the level of substantive tests.

Examination of Opening Balances and Prior Year's Transactions. If financial statements are being examined for the first time, the auditor must decide to what extent it is necessary to examine property accounts before the beginning of the year or years under examination. Since assets acquired in prior years and related accumulated depreciation are likely to be significant in the current balance sheet and income statement, the auditor must have a basis for believing that both are fairly stated in conformity with generally accepted accounting principles.

If financial statements for earlier years have been examined and reported on by independent auditors, reviewing the other auditors' working papers and the client's records should be sufficient to provide the necessary understanding of the accounting principles, policies, and methods employed. In some cases— for example, if no audit was made in earlier years or if the successor auditor does not choose to rely on the predecessor auditor's work—the successor auditor should perform a mix of analytical reviews and detailed substantive tests. Available property records should be reviewed in enough depth to give the auditor an understanding of the accounting procedures and principles used and the consistency with which they have been applied since the inception of the existing plant. The auditor may prepare or obtain analyses summarizing the annual changes in the asset and depreciation accounts and may examine evidence to support major additions and reductions. In particular, unusual items should be investigated to learn of revaluations or other major adjustments. The auditor should pay particular attention to property acquired by issuing common stock or exchanging other property. In an initial examination, numerous historical analyses—such as of long-term debt, capital stock, additional paid-in capital, retained earnings, and minutes of directors' meetings—are made. The auditor should be alert for matters in those analyses that affect the property accounts.

Existence and Ownership of Assets. An auditor making an initial examination should seek evidence that tangible assets exist and are, in fact, the property of the company. If a company's record keeping is adequate, deeds, purchase contracts, and other evidence of ownership will be on file and retrievable. Sometimes, however, those documents get mislaid over the years as successive generations of management come and go and files are moved, rearranged, or culled. If no other evidence can be found, the auditor can ask management to seek assurances from counsel concerning legal title to properties.

On subsequent audits, the examination of the existence and ownership of property, plant, and equipment normally comprises a review of the company's procedures for maintaining detailed records and for periodically comparing those records with the assets themselves, and performance of substantive tests of selected additions, disposals, and allocations during the year. If the company adequately tests the accuracy of its detailed records and if the auditor has evaluated and tested specific controls over the physical existence of and title to property, plant, and equipment and has found them to be satisfactory, substantive procedures can be limited to reviews of selected major additions and disposals and periodic allocations.

If the company periodically compares its detailed records with the actual assets but specific controls have not been evaluated and tested, the procedures set forth here should be carried out as of the date selected for testing.

- Review the company's procedures for conducting the physical inspection and comparison.
- Consider whether to observe those procedures.
- Review the actions taken to investigate discrepancies disclosed and to propose necessary adjustments to the records.

The auditor should determine that the company's comparison of assets with records is performed by a person who is independent of the custody of the assets and of maintaining the detailed property records. If the comparison is performed by a person who has custodial responsibility for or other access to the assets, the auditor should consider testing the client's comparison more extensively.

The comparison of the accounting records with the assets themselves should also be used to determine whether the carrying value of property, plant, and equipment requires adjustment because the assets are no longer in use or in good condition. The auditor should review the comparison to determine whether obsolete or damaged assets on hand have been included and whether these assets are carried at an amount in excess of their net realizable value.

If no comparison of assets with the accounting records is performed by the company, the auditor may consider performing a complete or partial comparison, depending on such factors as susceptibility to loss, theft, or destruction. If equipment is easily damaged, lost, stolen, or subject to personal use, such as in the case of small tools, the auditor should determine whether the depreciation rate used by the company considers those factors and, if not, should consider physically inspecting such assets, if material.

In many instances, the auditor may obtain evidence of the existence and condition of a major portion of the company's property, plant, and equipment through observation during physical inventory observations or routine plant tours. Other evidence may also be available regarding the existence of major property items; for example, continued sales of specific products provide evidence that the assets used to produce the products are still in existence and operating properly. Conversely, discontinuance of a product or product line should raise questions as to the carrying value of the related production facilities. Continued full occupancy of a hotel facility, for example, might also provide evidence regarding the existence and condition of the furniture and equipment used in the facility and might preclude the need for an annual physical inspection of those assets. Reliance on such observations, however, should be considered in relation to the risk of material errors arising in the property accounts if incorrect conclusions are drawn from the observations.

In selecting procedures for determining the existence and ownership of real property, if transactions are usually few and of high value, the auditor should consider inspecting documents of title (or confirming that such documents are held by proper custodians—normally banks or other lending institutions) for all or a substantial proportion of the properties, to ascertain that the company has valid title and that the assets have not been pledged. In addition to inspecting title documents, the auditor may examine title insurance policies, confirm with title insurance companies, or, in some cases, examine recorded deeds. Schedules of property covered by casualty insurance policies may be compared with recorded assets, as may schedules used for property tax records. Documentation and confirmations relating to notes payable and long-term debt should be reviewed for indications of assets that have been pledged as collateral. These procedures are normally performed at the balance sheet date.

Acquisition of Assets. If the auditor's compliance tests indicate that controls over acquisitions and additions to plant and equipment are strong, substantive tests of the property accounts may be limited to scanning the capital budget and the property accounts and reviewing documentation for some major additions not covered in the compliance tests. If, on the other hand, the auditor is not satisfied as to the reliability of controls, supporting data for additions should be examined for evidence of physical existence, approval and authorization, formal acceptance, and propriety of accounting classification. Substantially all additions may have to be examined, or a small number may constitute so large a percentage of the total that the remainder can be assumed to be insignificant; alternatively, additions may be so voluminous that a sample should be designed as a basis for inferring conclusions about the total.

Many clients must prepare, for SEC filings or tax purposes, schedules that summarize changes in asset and accumulated depreciation accounts. Even if they are not required, summary schedules serve as convenient worksheets for organizing substantive tests. For each major classification of property, plant, and equipment and the related allowance for depreciation, depletion, or amortization, the beginning balance is reconciled to the ending balance by identifying the total of each major type of addition, deduction, and transfer. Using a schedule of that type, an auditor can reconcile retirements to charges to the allowance accounts, and additions to the allowance accounts to depreciation, depletion, or amortization expense.

Substantive tests of property, plant, and equipment additions normally include the following (if specific controls are strong and are relied on, only major additions should be tested):

- Examining properly authorized and approved agreements, architects' certificates, deeds, invoices, and other documentary evidence. In the case of the purchase of land and buildings as a complete unit, the purchase price should be tested by comparing the data with the purchase agreement.
- Examining work orders and other supporting documentation for the company's own materials and labor. The percentage added for overhead should be reviewed to ensure that only factory overhead, as appropriate, has been allocated to the addition.
- Reviewing the minutes of meetings of the board of directors or other committees for appropriate authorizations for major additions.

Evaluating the appropriateness of approvals for additions should be based on the auditor's understanding of the authorization procedures and the level of the persons authorized to approve acquisitions. If written authorizations are not obtained, assets may be acquired that are not needed or portions of cost overruns that should be expensed may be capitalized. The approval process may not provide adequate control if authorizations do not include the reason for the expenditure, the estimated amount, the allocation between capital expenditures and charges to current operations, and procedures for comparing estimated amounts with actual. In that situation, the auditor should consider expanding the substantive tests, for example, by reviewing with senior company officials the usefulness of assets acquired during the year or reasons for budget overruns, to obtain satisfaction that the recorded additions are appropriate.

Disposition of Assets. Entries removing assets from the accounts should be tested by examining evidence of approval, comparing acquisition cost with underlying records, recomputing accumulated depreciation and resulting gain or loss, and evaluating the reasonableness of removal costs and recovery from scrap or salvage. If there is a properly controlled work order system or if numerous assets are disposed of at the same time, as in the case of a sale or an abandonment of a plant, the entries generally can be tested using a sample of the individual transactions.

As with acquisitions of assets, the auditor should also be familiar with the company's procedures for recording dispositions and with the levels of the people who approve them. If the company's procedures for recording new assets that replace existing assets do not identify the related retirement or disposal, the auditor may need to expand the testing of asset dispositions. The auditor should review additions for the year to determine whether they are replacements for other assets; if so, it is necessary to ascertain that the replaced asset has been correctly accounted for. Also, miscellaneous income accounts should be reviewed for evidence of sales or disposals of assets.

Classification of Expenditures. If compliance tests provide the auditor with evidence of the effectiveness of controls over procedures for classifying expenditures between capital expenditures and charges to current operations, testing of classifications may be limited to scanning the charges to repair and maintenance accounts for significant or unusual items, reviewing fluctuations, and other substantive tests of additions. Ordinarily, however, the auditor will perform additional substantive tests on at least a limited basis, even if specific controls are strong. Those tests may include

- Reviewing capitalizations, disposals, and repair and maintenance expense for reasonableness in relation to budgets and to the previous year, and obtaining explanations for any large or unusual fluctuations.
- Reviewing the propriety of the account distribution for all major additions and disposals during the year.
- Testing significant charges to repair and maintenance expense and reviewing the propriety of the account classification.

The extent to which these tests are performed should be increased significantly if the classification of expenditures is not approved by a designated official.

A company may routinely expense the cost of small dollar items, instead of capitalizing them, to reduce the clerical effort involved in maintaining detailed asset records. In reviewing charges to repair and maintenance accounts, the auditor should consider whether such items in the aggregate could have a material effect on the financial statements. Also, the auditor must recognize that determining whether an expenditure is capitalizable or should be charged to current operations may be subjective and highly judgmental. Even in a system with strong controls and review procedures, differences of judgment may arise over the nature and proper recording of a particular expenditure.

Carrying Values. Property, plant, and equipment is typically carried on the balance sheet at cost, which includes all expenditures necessary to make the asset ready for its intended use. The net realizable value of property, plant, and equipment ordinarily is not relevant to the value at which the assets are carried in the balance sheet, but may be relevant for supplemental disclosures. Accordingly, recoverable value of noncurrent assets is of concern to the auditor only in considering whether there has been a significant permanent diminution in value and in evaluating the supplemental disclosures. Determining whether the client has appropriately considered capitalizable costs requires the auditor to have extensive expertise in evaluating accounting principles selected and applied to asset acquisitions and carrying values.

That expertise should include an understanding of the criteria in FASB Statement of Financial Accounting Standards No. 13, *Accounting for Leases* (Accounting Standards Section L10), for classifying leases as operating leases or capital leases, as well as an understanding of lease measurement and disclosure principles. The auditor should ordinarily examine records of leased assets, lease agreements, and other data related to leases capitalized during the period, to determine that they were properly classified and valued. Documents supporting rentals classified as operating leases should also be reviewed to determine that they, too, were properly classified.

Depreciable assets are, in effect, "realized" in the normal course of business by charging depreciation to income, and thus provision for diminution in value may be necessary only if future income from an asset is unlikely to equal or exceed depreciation charges over the remaining life of the asset. This can normally be calculated only for a complete production unit or similar group of assets.

Depreciation and Salvage Values. Substantive testing of depreciation accounts should start with a review of the company's methods and policies. Policies preferably should be systematically documented, but if they are not they can be inferred from the computations and worksheets of prior and current years. Depreciation rates, salvage values, and useful lives may be compared with those in general use by similar enterprises. Computations of depreciation expense should be tested, which in many cases may be accomplished by making approximations on an overall basis.

The auditor should consider the reasonableness of useful lives and whether known factors require reducing or extending the lives of categories of plant assets. This can be accomplished by observing the pattern of gains and losses on disposition; consistent gains or consistent losses could suggest that lives are too long or too short or that salvage values used are inappropriate. For assets depreciated on the composite method, the auditor should review the relationship of the balances of allowance accounts to those of asset accounts. Ratios are, of course, affected by the pattern of additions, but after an auditor allows for unusually high or low additions in certain years, a significant upward or downward trend in the ratio of an allowance account to a related asset account should indicate whether useful lives are too short or too long. If either seems possible, an analysis of actual useful lives is called for.

The auditor should also be aware of changing business conditions that might suggest that the client should revise the estimated remaining lives of assets upward or downward for purposes of future depreciation charges. For example, leasehold improvements are depreciated over the estimated useful life of the improvements or over the original term of the lease, whichever is shorter, without regard to renewal options until those options are actually exercised or it becomes obvious they will be exercised. Significant expenditures for additional improvements with a life considerably longer than the remaining original lease might indicate management's intention to exercise a renewal option. Conversely, the auditor might learn that management intends to replace within the next two years computer equipment with a remaining depreciable life of four years. In these situations, the auditor must assess the likelihood of these events happening and consider proposing that the client review the estimated lives of the assets accordingly.

In practice, estimated lives, salvage values, and depreciation methods are not commonly reviewed, by either clients or auditors. Once established for particular assets, these items are usually left unchanged unless events or circumstances arise that call them into question. Auditors usually do not have the expertise to evaluate the remaining life of an asset and generally rely on other experts when necessary. Formal, in-depth reviews are usually made only for tax purposes, as part of acquisition reviews, or in industries in which depreciation has a significant effect on earnings, such as equipment leasing. In unusual circumstances, however, the auditor's risk assessment could suggest that such an evaluation is appropriate.

If the reasonableness of the depreciation charges cannot be determined by making approximations on an overall basis for each class of assets, the auditor should test the individual computations and the balances in the subsidiary ledgers, compare the totals with the control account, and investigate any differences at year-end.

Review Questions _____

Cash balances

15-1. List the types of substantive tests available for auditing cash balances.

15-2. Why are all bank balances usually confirmed regardless of their size?

15-3. State the alternative audit approaches to bank reconciliations.

15-4. What procedures should be performed at year-end if the review and test of bank reconciliations took place at an interim date?

15-5. What is a cutoff bank statement? What use does the auditor make of a cutoff bank statement?

15-6. What is a proof of cash and what is its purpose?

15-7. Define kiting and suggest ways in which an auditor may uncover it.

15-8. What is the objective of performing bank transfer tests?

Property, plant, and equipment

15-9. What are the objectives of auditing property, plant, and equipment? Give examples of how these objectives can be achieved through auditing other accounts.

15-10. Why are prior-year transactions involving fixed asset accounts of concern in an initial audit of financial statements?

15-11. What audit procedures are necessary to obtain assurance about the opening balances of fixed asset accounts?

15-12. How can an auditor obtain evidence of the existence and condition of property, plant, and equipment?

15-13. What substantive tests may be performed for the acquisition and disposition of assets if (a) internal control is considered strong? (b) internal control is not considered strong?

15-14. How does the auditor obtain assurance concerning correct classification of expenditures?

15-15. What tests are appropriate for depreciation?

Discussion Questions _____

Cash balances

15-30. Briefly discuss some of the circumstances or types of activity that might be indicative of irregularities involving cash.

15-31. Outline, in detail, what the auditor should do in performing substantive tests with respect to a client's bank reconciliation. Your answer should address the following areas:

  1. Bank account balance.
  2. Listing of outstanding checks.
  3. Checks that cleared in the subsequent bank statement.
  4. Deposits in transit.
  5. Bank statements for the reconciliation date and subsequent period.
  6. Other possible items on the reconciliation.

15-32. In relation to the audit of a client's bank reconciliation:

  1. What is a cutoff bank statement?
  2. Why would the auditor be interested in the dates of the outstanding checks that were returned with the cutoff statement?
  3. How might the auditor determine if any checks had been recorded but not issued at the reconciliation date?

Property, plant, and equipment

15-33. How would you determine that there are no significant items charged to expense that should have been capitalized, or vice versa?

15-34. What auditing procedures should be performed to ascertain that *all* disposals of property, plant, and equipment have been appropriately recorded?

15-35. The extent of audit work to determine the existence of property, plant, and equipment depends on whether physical inspection has been carried out by the client.

1. What audit procedures would you perform in the fiscal year in which the client makes a physical inspection?
2. What audit procedures would you perform when no inspection has ever been made?

15-36. The auditor should determine whether appropriate rates of depreciation have been properly applied to all items of property, plant, and equipment that should be depreciated, and that the method used is consistent with the previous year.

1. What are "appropriate" rates of depreciation?
2. What is "proper application"?
3. How would you determine that appropriate rates of depreciation have been properly applied?

15-37. How would you determine whether property, plant, and equipment have been pledged as collateral?

15-38. Discuss the effect each of the following items has in determining the audit strategy for property, plant, and equipment:

1. A large volume of small dollar transactions.
2. Property accounting records that are decentralized and maintained at various locations.
3. Prior-year compliance testing that indicates weaknesses in the system of internal control relating to property accounting systems.
4. Adoption by the client during the current year of a new computerized property accounting system.

15-39. Discuss events or situations in which the net realizable value of property, plant, and equipment may be of concern to the auditor.

AICPA Multiple Choice Questions

These questions are taken from the Auditing part of Uniform CPA Examinations. Choose the single most appropriate answer.

Cash balances

15-40. To gather evidence regarding the balance per bank in a bank reconciliation, an auditor would examine all of the following *except*

a. Cutoff bank statement.
b. Year-end bank statement.
c. Bank confirmation.
d. General ledger.

15-41. The auditor's count of the client's cash should be coordinated to coincide with the

a. Study of the system of internal controls with respect to cash.
b. Close of business on the balance sheet date.

    c. Count of marketable securities.
    d. Count of inventories.

15-42. An auditor who is engaged to examine the financial statements of a business enterprise will request a cutoff bank statement primarily in order to

    a. Verify the cash balance reported on the bank confirmation inquiry form.
    b. Verify reconciling items on the client's bank reconciliation.
    c. Detect lapping.
    d. Detect kiting.

15-43. Which of the following is one of the better auditing techniques that might be used by an auditor to detect kiting between intercompany banks?

    a. Review composition of authenticated deposit slips.
    b. Review subsequent bank statements received directly from the banks.
    c. Prepare a schedule of bank transfers.
    d. Prepare year-end bank reconciliations.

15-44. Wald, Inc. has a June 30 year-end. Its bank mails bank statements each Friday of every week and on the last business day of each month. For year-end, Saturday, June 30, 1984, the auditor should have the client ask the bank to mail directly to the auditor

    a. Only the June 29 bank statement.
    b. Only the July 13 bank statement.
    c. Both the June 29 and July 6 bank statements.
    d. Both the July 6 and 13 bank statements.

Property, plant, and equipment

15-45. In violation of Company policy, the Jefferson City Company erroneously capitalized the cost of painting its warehouse. The CPA examining Jefferson City's financial statements most likely would learn of this by

    a. Reviewing the listing of construction work orders for the year.
    b. Discussing capitalization policies with the Company controller.
    c. Observing, during his physical inventory observation, that the warehouse had been painted.
    d. Examining in detail a sample of construction work orders.

15-46. Which of the following is the *best* evidence of real estate ownership at the balance sheet date?

    a. Title insurance policy.
    b. Original deed held in the client's safe.
    c. Paid real estate tax bills.
    d. Closing statement.

15-47. Which of the following accounts should be reviewed by the auditor to gain reasonable assurance that additions to property, plant, and equipment are *not* understated?

    a. Depreciation.
    b. Accounts payable.
    c. Cash.
    d. Repairs.

15-48. The auditor may conclude that depreciation charges are insufficient by noting

     a. Insured values greatly in excess of book values.
     b. Large amounts of fully depreciated assets.
     c. Continuous trade-ins of relatively new assets.
     d. Excessive recurring losses on assets retired.

15–49. Which of the following *best* describes the independent auditor's approach to obtaining satisfaction concerning depreciation expense in the income statement?

     a. Verify the mathematical accuracy of the amounts charged to income as a result of depreciation expense.
     b. Determine the method for computing depreciation expense and ascertain that it is in accordance with generally accepted accounting principles.
     c. Reconcile the amount of depreciation expense to those amounts credited to accumulated depreciation accounts.
     d. Establish the basis for depreciable assets and verify the depreciation expense.

15–50. Which of the following audit procedures would be *least* likely to lead the auditor to find unrecorded fixed asset disposals?

     a. Examination of insurance policies.
     b. Review of repairs and maintenance expense.
     c. Review of property tax files.
     d. Scanning of invoices for fixed asset additions.

15–51. An auditor determines that a client has properly capitalized a leased asset (and corresponding lease liability) as representing, in substance, an installment purchase. As part of the auditor's procedures, the auditor should

     a. Substantiate the cost of the property to the lessor and determine that this is the cost recorded by the client.
     b. Evaluate the propriety of the interest rate used in discounting the future lease payments.
     c. Determine that the leased property is being amortized over the life of the lease.
     d. Evaluate whether the total amount of lease payments represents the fair market value of the property.

Problems and Cases

Cash balances

15–60. The E.F. Staley Corporation maintains two bank accounts. General ledger balances at year-end are as follows:

     Security Trust Co. $25,000
     First National Bank   (10,000) overdraft

The company's balance sheet presentation in the current assets section is as follows:

           Cash $15,000

Required:
State your position concerning the propriety of this presentation. In your discussion mention additional questions you may wish to raise and any auditing procedures you consider necessary.

15-61. In tracing checks to the cash disbursements book you find a series of 10 checks unentered in the last month of the year under review, none of which has been returned by the bank. Inquiry reveals that the checks in question were signed in blank by the treasurer and given to the vice president in charge of sales, who was making an extended business trip which ended two weeks after the close of the fiscal year. The vice president had requested the signed checks, which required only a countersignature, to avoid carrying a large amount of cash customarily expended on such trips for the usual traveling expenses and for entertaining customers and prospects.

Required:
a. What auditing procedures would you follow in view of this practice?
b. What recommendations would you make to your client to accommodate the vice president's desires?

15-62. Your client, who sells on credit, has several bank accounts. A reconciliation of one of these accounts as of the balance sheet date appears as follows:

Balance per bank, December 31	$5000
Add—Deposit in transit	1000
Total	6000
Less—Outstanding checks	50
Balance per books, December 31	$5950

Required:
As to the $1000 shown as a deposit in transit

a. Briefly describe the major possibilities of error or irregularity.
b. List the audit procedures that might be followed in an annual audit that would help to establish the validity and accuracy of the deposit in transit. Explain how each of those procedures would help to detect a possible error or irregularity.

15-63. In connection with your audit of the ABC Company at December 31, 1987, you were given the following bank reconciliation prepared by a company employee:

Balance per bank	$15,267
Deposits in transit	18,928
	34,195
Checks outstanding	21,378
Balance per books	$12,817

As part of your examination you obtained the bank statement and canceled checks from the bank on January 15, 1988. Checks issued from January 1 to January 15, 1988 per the books were $11,241. Checks returned by the bank on January 15 amounted to $29,219. Of the checks outstanding December 31, $4800 were not returned by the bank with the January 15 statement, and of those issued per the books in January 1988, $3600 were not returned.

Required:

a. Prepare a schedule showing these data in proper form.

b. Suggest four possible explanations for the condition existing here and state what your action would be in each case, including any necessary journal entries.

(AICPA adapted)

15-64. When you arrived at your client's office on January 11, 1987 to begin the December 31, 1986 audit, you discovered that the client had been drawing checks as creditors' invoices became due but not necessarily mailing them. Because of a working capital shortage, some checks have been held for two or three weeks.

The client informed you that unmailed checks totaling $27,600 were on hand at December 31, 1986. You were told these December-dated checks had been entered in the cash disbursements book and charged to the respective creditors' accounts in December because the checks were prenumbered. Heavy collections permitted the checks to be mailed before your arrival.

The client wants to adjust the cash balance and accounts payable at December 31 by $27,600 because the cash account had a credit balance. The client objects to submitting to the bank your audit report showing an overdraft of cash.

Required:

a. Prepare an audit program indicating the procedures you would use to satisfy yourself of the accuracy of the cash balance on the client's statements.

b. Discuss the acceptability of reversing the indicated amount of outstanding checks.

(AICPA adapted)

15-65. You are engaged in an audit of the financial statements of the ABC Corporation for the year ended December 31, 1987. In the course of your interim examination conducted early in the fall, you selected June as a test month for review of cash records and procedures.

Client's bank reconciliation—*May 31, 1987*

General ledger and cash book balance		$6388.50
Deduct:		
Bank service charges for May	$ 7.50	
Deposit of May 31, 1987 in transit	2175.00	2182.50
		4206.00
Add:		
Note of J. Smith collected by the bank May 30, 1987, $2000.00, less collection fee of $3.50 (debit and credit memos attached), recorded June 6, 1987		1996.50

Outstanding checks

#	Date	Amount	
25044	10/19/86	$ 27.50	
27918	2/03/87	1250.00	
28887	5/30/87	1345.70	
28888 (certified)	5/31/87	695.42	
28890	5/31/87	22.48	2645.68
Balance per bank statement			$8848.18

Client's bank reconciliation—*June 30, 1987*

General ledger and cash book balance			$9536.14
Deduct:			
Deposit of June 29, 1987 in transit		$1795.80	
Bank error: check #28890 cleared as			
$122.48 instead of $22.48		100.00	
Bank error: check of ABD Corp.			
incorrectly charged to our account		435.00	2330.80
			7205.34

Add:

Outstanding checks

#	Date	Amount	
25044	10/19/86	$ 27.50	
27918	2/03/87	1250.00	
28888 (certified)	5/31/87	695.42	
28902 (certified)	6/22/87	367.89	
28907	6/25/87	58.75	
28910	6/26/87	752.40	
28911	6/26/87	381.00	2469.65
Balance per bank statement			$9674.99

Other data available:

	Period
	June 1–30, 1987
Total credited by the bank	$6724.50
Cash receipts per books	8345.30
Cash disbursements per books	5197.66

A comparison of paid checks accompanying the June bank statement with the disbursements book and the May 31 reconciliation revealed that the following checks had cleared the bank: #28887, #28890 (cleared as $122.48), all of the checks drawn in June except #28902 $367.89 (certified June 2), #28907 $58.75, #28910 $752.40, #28911 $381.00. A check for $435.00 drawn on the ABD Corporation also cleared the account during this period. The deposit in transit at May 31 was credited by the bank on June 2; the June 29 deposit was credited on July 2. The bank was notified of its errors on July 15. Corrections were recorded on the July bank statement.

Required:
From the information given, prepare a proof of cash for the month of June. (*Note*: When banks certify checks, they charge the company's account immediately.) Indicate all auditing procedures applied.

Property, plant, and equipment

15–66. You have been assigned as a staff accountant for a new client, Hervis Rent-A-Car. The business involves primarily the rental and leasing of automobiles for personal and business use. The company continually purchases and disposes of automobiles throughout the year, with approximately 1500 acquisitions annually.

Required:
Discuss the risk factors and audit strategy for this client relative to the property ac-

counts. Include a discussion of procedures you would consider necessary to examine opening balances.

15-67. Rivers, CPA, is the auditor for a manufacturing company with a balance sheet that includes the caption "Property, Plant, and Equipment." Rivers has been asked by the company's management whether audit adjustments or reclassifications are required for the following material items that have been included or excluded from "Property, Plant, and Equipment."

1. A tract of land was acquired during the year. The land is the future site of the client's new headquarters, which will be constructed in the following year. Commissions were paid to the real estate agent used to acquire the land, and expenditures were made to relocate the previous owner's equipment. These commissions and expenditures were expensed and are excluded from "Property, Plant, and Equipment."
2. Clearing costs were incurred to make the land ready for construction. These costs were included in "Property, Plant, and Equipment."
3. During the land clearing process, timber and gravel were recovered and sold. The proceeds from the sale were recorded as other income and are excluded from "Property, Plant, and Equipment."
4. A group of machines was purchased under a royalty agreement that provides for royalty payments based on units of production from the machines. The cost of the machines, freight costs, unloading charges, and royalty payments were capitalized and are included in "Property, Plant, and Equipment."

Required:

a. Describe the general characteristics of assets, such as land, buildings, improvements, machinery, equipment, fixtures, and so on, that should normally be classified as "Property, Plant, and Equipment," and identify audit objectives in connection with the examination of "Property, Plant, and Equipment." *Do not discuss specific audit procedures.*

b. Indicate whether each of the foregoing items numbered 1 to 4 requires one or more audit adjustments or reclassifications, and explain why such adjustments or reclassifications are required or not required.

Organize your answer as follows:

Item Number	Is Audit Adjustment or Reclassification Required? ——————— Yes or No	Reasons Why Audit Adjustment or Reclassification Is Required or Not Required

(AICPA adapted)

15-68. In connection with a recurring examination of the financial statements of the Louis Manufacturing Company for the year ended December 31, 1987, you have been assigned the audit of the Manufacturing Equipment, Manufacturing Equipment—Accumulated Depreciation, and Repairs to Manufacturing Equipment accounts. Your review of Louis' policies and procedures has disclosed the following pertinent information:

1. The Manufacturing Equipment account includes the net invoice price plus related freight and installation costs for all of the equipment in Louis' manufacturing plant.
2. The Manufacturing Equipment and Accumulated Depreciation accounts are supported by a subsidiary ledger that shows the cost and accumulated depreciation for each piece of equipment.
3. An annual budget for capital expenditures of $1000 or more is prepared by the budget committee of the board of directors and approved by the full board of directors. Capital expenditures over $1000 that are not included in this budget must be approved by the board of directors and variations of 20 percent or more must be explained to the board. Approval by the supervisor of production is required for capital expenditures under $1000.
4. Company employees handle installation, removal, repair, and rebuilding of the machinery. Work orders are prepared for these activities and are subject to the same budgetary control as other expenditures. Work orders are not required for external expenditures.

Required:

a. Cite the major objectives of your audit of the Manufacturing Equipment, Manufacturing Equipment—Accumulated Depreciation, and Repairs to Manufacturing Equipment accounts. Do not include in this listing the auditing procedures designed to accomplish these objectives.
b. Prepare the portion of your audit program applicable to the review of 1987 additions to the Manufacturing Equipment account.

(AICPA adapted)

15–69. The decision to rely on internal controls to ensure the continued and proper operation of the accounting system for property, plant, and equipment has been made and the compliance tests indicate reliance on the system is appropriate. You can therefore limit your substantive tests and have decided to perform reasonableness tests and analytical review procedures on account balances. The client uses the straight-line method of depreciation for financial accounting purposes.

Required:
Describe an appropriate reasonableness test to be used to analyze the accuracy of the recorded amounts for depreciation expense.

15–70. While on a plant tour of ABC Company, it was brought to your attention that a specialized inventory order preparation machine, which had been put into service three years earlier, is now sitting idle. You inquired of the controller as to the company's intentions regarding the future use of this machine and she informed you of management's intentions to dismantle the machine and sell it for scrap.

Required:
Discuss the appropriate audit procedures you would employ in this situation.

15–71. While auditing an urban bus company in a city of 500,000 population, you encounter the following situation:

1. You have reviewed an authorization for the purchase of five engines to replace the engines in five buses.
2. The cost of the old engines was removed from property and that of the new engines properly capitalized. The work was done in the company garage.

3. You find no credits for salvage and none for the sale of any scrap metal at any time during the year. You have been in the garage and did not see the old engines.
4. The accountant is also treasurer and office manager. She is an authorized check signer and has access to all cash receipts. On inquiry, she says she does not recall the sale of the old engines or of any scrap metal.

Required:

Assuming that the engines were sold as scrap, outline all steps that this fact would cause you to take in connection with your audit. Give consideration to steps beyond those related directly to this one item.

(AICPA adapted)

Chapter 16
Auditing Investments, Prepayments and Accruals, Taxes, and Debt and Equity Accounts

This chapter continues the discussion of financial statement accounts that are typically audited by performing substantive tests. As noted in the introduction to Chapter 15, the choice of particular substantive tests and their timing and extent will be determined by the auditor's assessment of the level of risk of material misstatement occurring. Accordingly, not all of the procedures described in this chapter need be performed on a particular engagement, on 100 percent of the transactions and accounts under examination, or only after the client's accounting year has ended.

Investments and Related Income

Investments is a broad term used to describe nonoperating, income-producing assets of a commercial or industrial enterprise that are held either as a means of using excess cash or to accomplish some special purpose. Often, the description of investment assets in the financial statements gives further insight into the specific reasons they are held.

Short-term investments usually consist of marketable securities acquired for income-producing purposes by the temporary utilization of excess cash. In a classified balance sheet, short-term investments are classified as current, and ordinarily include futures contracts and forward contracts acquired for purposes other than to hedge inventory against the risk of changing commodity prices, in which case they should be accounted for as part of the cost of raw materials. The term *investments* without any modifier often identifies assets held for long-term yield and market appreciation and consequently classified as noncurrent assets.

The phrase *marketable securities* indicates a high degree of liquidity, that is, securities for which an organized and active market exists. Such securities may be held in either a current or long-term investment account and may consist of equity or other securities. It is important to identify marketable equity securities, since they are required by FASB Statement No. 12, *Accounting for Certain Marketable Securities* (Accounting Standards Section I89), to be carried in the financial statements at the lower of aggregate cost or market.

Long-term investments, investments in affiliates, or *investments* may also represent holdings of securities for purposes of control, affiliation, or financing of enterprises related to the operations of the investing company. Those investments, which are classified as noncurrent assets, may require use of the equity method of accounting. Sinking funds, building funds, and other funds accumulated for special purposes may consist of investments in securities and are classified as noncurrent assets.

Income statement accounts related to investments are generally *interest revenue* (including amortization of premium and discount, as appropriate), *dividend revenue, realized gain or loss on sale of securities, unrealized gain or loss from holding marketable equity securities,* and *earnings or losses from investments accounted for by the equity method.* The auditor should also be aware that market value adjustments made for long-term marketable equity securities are reflected in the equity section of the balance sheet and not on the income statement.

Particularly in recent years, investment bankers and securities underwriters have created an ever-growing array of new types of investments, sometimes referred to as ''new financial products'' or ''new financial instruments.'' Several notorious instances of significant investor losses suggest that many buyers of these rather exotic investments have little understanding of the nature and extent of the various risks they have undertaken. For example, in the mid-1980s several municipalities bought from a bond dealer securities that were either issued or guaranteed by the U.S. Treasury, and simultaneously entered into a contract to sell the securities back to the dealer the next day. These transactions, referred to as repurchase agreements (or ''repos,'' for short), were widely believed to be extremely safe because they were thought to be backed by the U.S. government. In several cases, the municipalities did not take possession of the securities because it was not practical to do so, and left them with the dealer for safekeeping. The bond dealer used the municipalities' bonds for fraudulent purposes and then went bankrupt. While the securities were guaranteed by the U.S. government, the contract with the bond dealer was not, and the municipalities found, often to their surprise, that their status was little more than that of unsecured creditors—the municipalities had in effect made unsecured loans to the bond dealer.

The auditor in this and similar situations needs to understand clearly the nature of the transaction that the client has entered into and the attendant risks. The auditor also needs to know how those risks affect management's assertions, particularly with regard to legal rights and asset valuations. The nature and extent of those risks may well affect the selection of accounting measurement and disclosure principles (e.g., the need to provide for possible losses and to disclose the substance of repo transactions as unsecured loans). The complexity of many of these new financial products makes the auditor's task particularly difficult.

Audit Objectives

The objectives of auditing the investment accounts are, in most respects, similar to those of other asset accounts. The auditor should design tests to provide reasonable assurance that

- The investments were authorized, exist, and are owned by the client at the balance sheet date. Establishing the physical existence and ownership of investments is paramount to the audit process, particularly because many securities are readily negotiable.
- All of the investments owned by the client are included in the balances of the investment accounts.
- The values at which investments are carried in the financial statements are appropriate and are adequately disclosed.
- Income from investments, including gains and losses on sales and adjustments in valuation allowances, are appropriately reflected in the financial statements.
- The investments are properly classified between their current and noncurrent components.
- Investments that are pledged as collateral or are otherwise restricted are appropriately identified and disclosed. Assets pledged as collateral or restricted in any other manner, as well as the purpose for which the assets are pledged, are generally required to be disclosed in the financial statements.

Substantive Tests of Balances

Many of the substantive tests of investments and related income are documented on a summary working paper similar to that shown for notes receivable and interest income in Figure 5.8 in Chapter 5.

Tests of Existence and Completeness. Substantiation of the physical existence and ownership of investments, as well as some assurance about the completeness of the investment accounts, is normally accomplished by confirmation or inspection. The auditor should agree the securities confirmed or inspected to the client's detail records. Whether these procedures are performed at year-end or at an interim date will be based on the auditor's evaluation of controls over physical custody and segregation of duties.

Physical safeguarding of securities is important because many marketable securities are negotiable; documents evidencing legal ownership also have value even if securities are not readily negotiable. Therefore, the physical control of restricted access and segregation of duties should receive careful attention. Securities should be kept in a vault, safe deposit box, or, at a minimum, fireproof safe. The custodian and other personnel who have access to the place of safekeeping should be independent of the functions of authorizing investment transactions, keeping investment records, handling cash, and maintaining the general ledger; preferably each of those employees should be independent of all the others.

Counts of Portfolios. If an investment portfolio is relatively large and active (as in banks, insurance companies, investment companies, and stock brokerages), the count of securities may be a major undertaking requiring extensive planning, precise execution, and a large staff of auditors. In contrast, most industrial and commercial companies do not own numerous securities, and physical inspection is not difficult. The auditor usually obtains a list of securities supporting the general ledger balance at the date of the count and arranges to visit the place where the securities are kept, accompanied by the custodian. The auditor examines the securities by comparing them with the list. This process normally affords the auditor an opportunity to observe evidence of internal accounting controls, for example, an accurate security list, proper endorsement or evidence of ownership on the securities, proper division of duties between custodian and record keeper, adequate physical safeguards (such as use of a bank's safe deposit vault), and requirements for dual access to the securities.

Generally, the auditor should count the securities at the balance sheet date; if it is done at another date, the vault or safe deposit box should be sealed during the intervening period. Banks ordinarily seal a safe deposit box on an auditor's request and subsequently confirm that no access to the box was granted during the specified period. Securities should be counted simultaneously with cash and other negotiable assets. A count is considered "simultaneous" if the securities are sealed or otherwise controlled until all negotiable assets have been examined.

The auditor should note that stock certificates and registered bonds are in the name of the client or an accredited nominee or, if they are not, that certificates are appropriately endorsed or accompanied by powers of attorney. Bonds with interest coupons should be examined on a test basis to determine that coupons not yet due have not been detached. If coupons presently coming due are not attached to the bonds, the auditor should inquire as to their location and either inspect them or confirm them with the holders. Likewise, explanations should be obtained and evaluated for any coupons past due that are attached and have not been presented for payment. Interest in default should be noted in the working papers for consideration in connection with the examination of accruals of income and carrying amounts of investments.

Reasons for differences between the count and the list of securities should be explored. Certain types of differences are normal and expected, for example, securities held by others and securities in transit. The holders of securities in other locations should be identified and requests for confirmation sent. In-transit items should be related to recent transactions; outgoing in-transit items should be confirmed with recipients. Securities received by the client through the mail for a few days subsequent to the date of the count should be examined to substantiate items in transit. Once the auditor is satisfied that all items on the security list have been counted or their location elsewhere has been confirmed and all differences have been reconciled, control over securities may be "released."

The auditor should not overlook the possibility of substitutions. If examinations are being made of one or more trust accounts handled by the same trustee, for example, securities in all accounts should be counted at the same time. Similarly, if different auditors are employed to examine several accounts, they should make their counts simultaneously. Otherwise, material shortages may be concealed by temporary transfers from accounts whose securities are not being counted. If a client is reluctant to permit an auditor to count securities of other accounts or is unwilling or unable to arrange for a simultaneous count by all auditors concerned, the auditor may identify securities owned by the client by accounting for certificate numbers of stocks and bonds; however, that procedure is difficult and time consuming for a large portfolio with numerous purchases and sales. Securities owned or held as collateral or for safekeeping should also be counted simultaneously with cash funds, undeposited receipts, notes receivable, and other negotiable assets if there is a possibility of substitution of one item for another.

Confirmation of Securities Not on Hand. Items on the list of securities owned at the count date but not counted should be confirmed with the holders. If a client's entire portfolio is held by a custodian, confirmation procedures usually take the place of the security count.

Items not on hand ordinarily include securities held by banks as collateral for loans or for safekeeping, securities with transfer agents, and, if the client is a stockbroker, items with other brokers on loan or awaiting delivery. The auditor should determine the location of those securities at the examination date, the appropriate responsible person acting as custodian, and the reasons they are held by the custodian. (If the securities are held by people or organizations unknown to the auditor, it may be considered necessary to inspect them physically rather than confirm them.) In examining the accounts of financial organizations, the auditor should also confirm contracts for the purchase or sale of securities on a "when issued" basis.

If the client's entire portfolio of securities is held in custody by a well-known, reliable financial institution independent of the client, the custodian should be requested to furnish directly to the auditor a list of securities held for the client at the examination date. The auditor should compare the list with the client's security records and account for differences noted. It is sometimes desirable to corroborate the custodian's confirmation by counting the securities.

The most common reasons are when the portfolio is large in relation to the custodian's assets or when assurance as to the adequacy of the custodian's procedures is considered desirable. A letter from the custodian's auditor evaluating internal controls can satisfy the latter purpose. Joint counts with other auditors having a similar interest are possible.

If securities are in the custody of an affiliate or are under the control of a person or group of people who take an active part in the management of the client, the auditor is not justified in relying solely on written confirmation from the custodian. Instead, the auditing procedures outlined earlier for counting securities under the control of the client should be followed.

Other Tests of Completeness. As noted before, some assurance about the completeness of investment accounts is obtained from confirmation and counting procedures. Other procedures relevant to the completeness objective include determining that specific transactions authorized in the minutes of the board of directors' meetings were in fact implemented and recorded, and obtaining a transcript of security transactions directly from the client's broker and determining that all purchases and sales reported on that transcript have been recorded.

Tests of Carrying Values. Cost of securities purchased and proceeds from securities sold are normally supported by brokers' advices. The auditor should examine these documents to substantiate the basis for recording those transactions. Additionally, the auditor should review the client's method of determining cost (FIFO, average, or specific identification) of securities sold and determine that it is consistent during the year and with prior years. Periodic valuation of investments is necessary for managerial control and decision making; it is also required so that market or fair value can be determined for financial statement purposes. If investments are few, relatively short term, and not significant to a company's operations, the valuation process may be performed informally by the officer responsible for investments. If investments are significant, the valuation should be formally executed and documented. The frequency of valuation depends on the amount of investment activity and the frequency of issuance of financial statements. (Some active investment portfolios are under virtually continual valuation.)

The auditor should test the client's identification of marketable equity securities that are required to be carried at the lower of aggregate cost or market and should determine that market values have been appropriately applied to those securities. Normally, this is accomplished by comparing values with published sources. Furthermore, the auditor should determine that any necessary valuation allowance adjustment is properly reflected in the financial statements.

If there are investments accounted for by the equity method and if the investee enterprise is audited by other auditors, the auditor will have to use the report of the investee's auditors to be able to report on the client investor's equity in the investee's underlying net assets and its share of the investee's earnings or losses and other transactions. This places the auditor in the position of a principal auditor who is using the work and reports of other auditors. The work and reports of other auditors may also serve as evidence with respect to investments carried on the cost basis or at the lower of cost or market, which would also place the auditor in a position analogous to that of a principal auditor. The procedures to be followed in those instances are discussed in Chapter 6; reporting aspects of using the work and reports of other auditors are discussed in Chapter 18.

The client's support for fair values of investments that are determined on a basis other than published values should be tested for propriety and consistency. The auditor should be alert to any indication that declines in market value below cost may be other than temporary.

Tests of Investment Income. Accounting for income from publicly held marketable securities is usually straightforward: Interest is accrued periodically and dividends are recorded as received (or when the shares first trade "ex-dividend"). Published records of interest, dividends, and other distributions should be compared with recorded income periodically to make sure that all income has been received on a timely basis. Often that task is left to the auditor and is performed as an extension of the tests of investment income. It is usually less expensive to have the comparison performed by a client employee; segregation of duties suggests the control should be exercised by a person other than the one responsible for the initial recording of investments. If an investment is accounted for on the equity method, copies of financial statements of the investee must be obtained for use in recording earnings or losses.

The auditor should determine that all income earned has been appropriately recorded and either collected or recognized as a receivable, and that all accrued income receivable has in fact been earned. The auditor usually obtains evidence about investment income and collection dates by reference to dates of purchase and disposal of investments, interest rates, and published dividend records. Analytical reviews such as comparisons with budgeted or prior-year data may be useful in testing revenue from investments.

Tests of Classification and Presentation. If the balance sheet is classified, the auditor should determine that the investments are properly classified between the current and noncurrent categories and that the financial statements contain all required disclosures regarding investment carrying values and realized and unrealized gains and losses. In addition, minutes, confirmation replies, loan agreements, bond indentures, and other appropriate documents should be reviewed to determine whether investments have been pledged as collateral or whether there is evidence of commitments to acquire or dispose of investments, both of which may require appropriate disclosures.

Financial statement classification of investments depends to a large extent on management's investment objectives and intentions. The auditor can ascertain management's objectives through inquiry and by reviewing minutes of meetings of the board of directors and the investment committee of the board. The inclusion of a statement of management's intent in the client representation letter (discussed in Chapter 17) may be desirable. To evaluate management's representations as to its intentions, the auditor should consider whether they are reasonable in light of the enterprise's financial position, working capital requirements, debt agreements, and other contractual obligations. For example, the client's needs may indicate a reasonable presumption that marketable securities will have to be sold to meet operating requirements and that therefore they should be classified as current assets.

Prepaid Expenses, Estimated and Accrued Liabilities, and Related Expenses

Prepaid expenses are assets, most often in the form of services (but sometimes for goods such as stationery and supplies), that have been acquired as part of the buying cycle but that apply to future periods or to the production of future revenues—for example, prepaid insurance, rent, and taxes. There is little conceptual difference between prepayments and assets such as inventories, plant and equipment, and intangibles: All are expected to be of benefit in future periods. Prepayments are often assumed to be less readily realizable than inventory or equipment, but there are significant exceptions; it may be easier to realize cash from the contractual right to cancel an insurance policy than on a custom-built, single-purpose structure.

The distinction between prepaid expenses and deferred charges is based primarily on whether the asset is appropriately classified as current or noncurrent. The precision with which that distinction is made is often modified by custom and materiality considerations. Prepaid insurance, for example, and many types of deposits do not expire and are not realized within one year or the enterprise's operating cycle, but are traditionally classified as current. The prepaid expense account is seldom material to the financial statements, and noncurrent items that are not material are included in prepaid expenses for convenience. If deferred costs (such as debt issuance costs) are material and will expire over several years, they are properly classified as noncurrent deferred charges.

Accrued liabilities, often referred to as accrued expenses, are items for which a service or benefit has been received and for which the related liability is acknowledged and reasonably determinable, but that are not yet payable (either because of the terms of the commitment or because the invoice has not been received). Most accrued liabilities accrue with the passage of time—for example, interest, rent, and property taxes—or with some service or activity— for example, payrolls, royalties, sales commissions, and payroll taxes. Deferred credits (such as unearned revenue and deferred income accounts) result from the receipt of revenues in advance of the related delivery of goods or services and were discussed in Chapter 12.

Agency obligations, such as payroll withholdings and deductions, are funds collected for others for which accountability must be maintained until the funds are turned over at the required time to the principal for whom they are held in trust. Those obligations result from transactions that are part of the buying and revenue cycles.

Many similarities exist among prepaid expenses, accrued liabilities, and agency obligations and among the underlying transactions that affect these accounts. All three categories of accounts are frequently subjected to similar types of internal controls and the general audit approach employed is also similar. The following examples of accounts in the three categories suggest the similarities of the underlying expenses or transactions reflected in the accounts:

Prepaid Expenses	*Accrued Liabilities*	*Agency Obligations*
Property taxes	Property taxes	Deposits
Rent	Rent	Payroll withholdings
Insurance	Insurance	Sales taxes
Compensation	Interest	Social security taxes
Commissions	Commissions	Insurance premiums
Pension costs	Pension costs	Union dues
Supplies inventory	Salaries and wages	Unclaimed payments
Unamortized debt issuance costs	Vacation and sick pay	
	Payroll taxes	
	Deferred compensation	
	Warranty costs	

Audit Objectives

As in auditing other assets and liabilities, the auditor should approach prepaid assets and accrued liabilities with the view that liabilities are more likely to be understated or omitted from the accounts than overstated and, conversely, assets are more likely to be overstated than understated. Therefore, audit objectives should focus on ascertaining that prepaid assets are not overstated and that accrued liabilities are not understated, but without ignoring the possibility that the opposite may occur.

In specifying audit objectives for prepaid expenses, the auditor should focus on seeking evidence that

- All amounts reported as assets were acquired in valid transactions and were properly recorded at the time of acquisition.
- The balance of the expenditure carried forward can be reasonably expected to be recovered from future income.
- The basis of amortization is reasonable and consistent with prior years and the related expenses are properly classified.

Principal audit objectives related to accrued expenses and other liabilities are to obtain audit evidence that

- All material accrued expenses, agency obligations, and other liabilities existing at the balance sheet date have been recorded and properly measured.
- The amounts recorded for accrued expenses, agency obligations, and other liabilities represent valid liabilities and are properly measured.
- Related expenses have been recognized and properly measured on a consistent basis.

Substantive Tests of Balances

Compliance tests in the buying cycle are often sufficiently comprehensive to encompass all purchases and expenses, including those that involve prepayments, deferred charges, or accruals. If those compliance tests have met their audit objectives, and if warranted by audit risk and materiality considerations, substantive tests of prepayments and accruals often are limited. In many cases, analytical reviews are the only type of substantive tests performed on prepayments and accruals. For that reason, they are discussed first in this section.

Analytical Reviews. Balances in prepaid and accrued accounts and the related expense accounts should be compared with the prior-year balance sheet and income statement amounts. The auditor may decide, based on general business knowledge and knowledge of the client's operations, that this comparative analysis is all the audit work necessary for certain prepaid and accrued accounts, such as prepaid insurance and accrued payroll and related tax accounts. The underlying causes of trends and fluctuations noted should be understood thoroughly and evaluated for their implications for other accounts. Unusual transactions should be vouched by examining underlying evidence.

If they exist, variance reports and analyses of actual costs and expenses compared with budgeted amounts should be examined. Explanations of variances should be critically evaluated both for their adequacy and for evidence they may provide concerning the accuracy and validity of the accounts.

In a stable business, predictable relationships often exist among certain accounts, and changes in those relationships may signal conditions requiring accounting recognition. Pertinent ratios should be computed and compared with corresponding ones for prior periods. For example, comparing selling expense with sales might prompt inquiries that could uncover sales commissions that should be but were not accrued. Unexplained changes in ratios involving revenue and expense accounts may indicate possible errors in related prepayments and accruals.

Substantive Tests of Specific Accounts. If the auditor does not place maximum reliance on internal controls over the acquisition of assets and incurrence of liabilities or if accounts are particularly sensitive or material, substantive testing beyond analytical review procedures should be performed. Often, the client is requested to prepare account analyses and assemble the underlying documentation to assist the auditor in analyzing the details of certain accounts. Additions to prepayments and accruals are typically vouched to determine their validity. Similarly, reductions in prepayments and accruals should be vouched or, if they represent amortization based on time, reviewed for accuracy. The balances remaining in asset accounts should be reviewed and a judgment formed as to their realizability. (If they are not realizable in future periods, no part of the balance should be allocated to those periods.) These are widely accepted audit procedures applicable to almost all prepaid and accrued accounts. Many of these procedures are discussed in Chapter 13, "Auditing the Buying Cycle." The following paragraphs focus on prepaid, accrued, and expense accounts that have particular characteristics worthy of note. The variety of conditions found in practice makes it impossible to be comprehensive: The comments can only illustrate the kinds of adaptations of basic tests, discussed earlier, that the auditor should consider, based on the audit strategy adopted.

Prepaid Insurance. Most well-controlled companies maintain an insurance register that indicates, for each policy, the insurance company, policy number, type and amount of coverage, policy dates, premium, prepayments, expense for the period, and any coinsurance provision.

From this register or from the insurance policies themselves, a schedule of prepaid insurance should be prepared, preferably by the client's staff. The auditor should test the data shown on the schedule. Insurance policies and vouchers supporting premiums should also be examined. In addition to these items, the auditor should note beneficiaries, special assessment clauses, and evidence of liens on the insured property.

If original insurance policies are not available for inspection, the auditor should determine the reason. Since lenders often retain insurance policies on property that collateralizes loans, the absence of policies may indicate the existence of liens on the property. The auditor should request the client to obtain the policies (or copies of them) and should examine them. In the absence of effective internal controls, the auditor may request confirmations from the insurance companies or brokers.

Prepaid liability and compensation insurance, if premiums are based on payrolls, may be compared with payrolls to determine that charges to expense appear proper. Premiums due may exceed advance payments so that at the end of a period there may be a liability rather than a prepayment. Total prepaid insurance per the insurance register or schedule of prepaid insurance should be compared with the general ledger.

An auditor is usually not an expert in determining insurable values and has no responsibility for management's decisions concerning insuring risks and coverage, but may render helpful service to the client by calling attention to differences among the amount of coverage, the insurable value (if available), and the recorded amount of insured property.

Prepaid and Accrued Property Taxes. The auditor should determine that the amount of prepaid taxes is actually an expense applicable to future periods. Reference should be made to local tax bills and laws because taxes are imposed by state and local authorities under statutes that vary widely in their proration provisions. The related expense account should be examined closely and compared with that of prior years. Since taxes are generally computed by multiplying a base by a rate, the two components can be analyzed and fluctuations explained.

Prepaid and Accrued Commissions. The propriety of amounts of prepaid or accrued commissions should be investigated. If commission expense is material, the auditor may wish to examine contracts with salespeople or obtain from management an authoritative statement of the terms of employment. Sales reports, commission records, or other evidence of commissions earned may be reviewed; entries in the salespeople's accounts may be traced from commission records and cash records. If there are many salespeople and internal control is effective, the examination may be limited to only a few accounts or to the entries for only a limited period. Transactions in the last month of the period may be reviewed to determine that commissions have been allocated to the proper period. The auditor should be satisfied that prepayments will be matched with revenues of future periods and are not current-period compensation. If amounts are significant, the auditor should consider confirming directly with salespeople amounts due and commissions earned during the year and should test the overall reasonableness of commission expense for the year, such as by applying commission rates against sales. If there is a subsidiary ledger for prepaid or accrued commission accounts, the balance of the general ledger account should be compared with the trial balance of the subsidiary ledger and differences investigated.

Travel and Entertainment Advances. Advances to employees for expenses may be tested by examining cash disbursements, expense reports, and cash receipts. If employees are advanced amounts as working funds on an imprest basis, the auditor may examine reimbursements in the month following the end of the period to determine whether material expenditures prior to the end of the period have been reimbursed. The auditor may review related entries after period-end to determine whether any should have been recorded in the period under examination. Advances may be confirmed by correspondence with employees. The general ledger account should be compared with the subsidiary ledger and differences investigated; the individual balances may be aged and long outstanding balances scrutinized. Unusual advances to officers should be identified and evidence of authorization examined

Accrued Professional Fees. The auditor should consider including in the audit inquiry letters to lawyers a request for the amounts of unpaid or unbilled charges, which can then be compared with the recorded liability.

Accrued Interest Payable. Many liabilities bear interest. For example, loan accounts of partners and corporate officers usually bear interest; judgments, overdue taxes, and other liens often bear interest at high rates; and occasionally accounts payable bear interest. If bond interest is in default and the indenture provides for interest to accrue thereon, the amount should be estimated and recorded. The computation of accrued interest at the balance sheet date normally can be easily reviewed by the auditor.

Royalties Payable. In evaluating the amount of royalties payable, the auditor should examine royalty and licensing contracts and extract important provisions for the permanent files. The auditor should attempt to determine from a royalty contract whether the payments are actually royalties or whether, in fact, they represent payments for the purchase of a patent or other asset covered by the agreement. If the contract is in reality a purchase agreement, the asset and liability should be recognized at the date of the contract and depreciation or amortization of the asset charged to expense. If provisions of a royalty contract are not clear, the auditor should request a legal interpretation of ambiguous provisions.

Many contracts provide for a minimum royalty payment regardless of whether a liability for royalties accrues on a unit basis. If royalty payments are based on sales, computations may be compared with recorded sales; statements of royalties due may be tested to substantiate recorded amounts. If royalty payments are based on the quantity or value of goods produced, rather than on sales, the auditor should review documents on file supporting amounts accrued and should test the underlying data. If accounting records are not kept in sufficient detail to furnish the required information, it may be necessary to analyze production records.

If data on which royalties are based are solely in the possession of lessors or vendors, statements of liability under royalty agreements may be secured from them. A request for confirmation may produce evidence of important differences in interpretation of contract provisions.

Suspense Debits and Credits. Every chart of accounts contains a place for debit and credit items for which the final accounting has not yet been determined. The person responsible may not have decided which expense account should be charged, the job order, cost center, or subaccount may not have been opened yet, or there may be some other unresolved question about the handling or propriety of the item. Although most suspense debit and credit accounts may be quite active during the year, all material issues should be resolved by year-end.

The auditor may wish to test balances at an interim date, however, and inquire into the disposition of items because doing so may contribute considerably to the understanding of the kinds of accounting problems that can occur and the implications for the system of internal control. In the rare instance of balances remaining at the end of the year, the auditor should inquire into the reasons why the proper distribution has not been determined. Particularly in the case of suspense debits, a client commonly and understandably often wishes to carry in the balance sheet items in dispute that someone in management "just doesn't want to give up on." If those debits are significant, the auditor needs evidence that they are likely to have a realizable value or to benefit future operations, and are therefore properly classified as assets.

Accrued Pension Costs. The auditor must understand the contractual and other arrangements giving rise to pension costs and must be aware of the requirements of the Employee Retirement Income Security Act of 1974 (ERISA), so as to ascertain that the liability for pension costs and the related expense have been determined in conformity with GAAP, as set forth in Statement of Financial Accounting Standards No. 87, *Employers' Accounting for Pensions* (Accounting Standards Section P16). The significance of pension costs to most companies, and the effect of a possible misstatement of those costs on the fairness of presentation of the financial statements, often calls for substantive testing. In determining the extent to which audit procedures should be applied to pension costs, however, the materiality of such costs in relation to the overall financial statements and the auditor's assessment of inherent risk should be considered.

Substantive tests of pension costs should be tailored to the specific circumstances of the client. The procedures should not duplicate work done by the actuary; rather, they should provide evidence of the appropriateness of the data given to the actuary by the client. Suggested audit procedures are set forth in the following list. They are not intended to be all-inclusive or to apply to all situations. The selection of audit procedures appropriate for a particular situation is a matter of judgment.

- Inquire into the existence of pension plans or a practice of paying pensions that may constitute a plan under FASB Statement No. 87.
- Compare the data relating to pension costs and information disclosed in the financial statements with prior year's data for changes affecting comparability.
- Obtain reasonable assurance that pension fund assets are properly valued.
- Determine whether employees ultimately entitled to participate in the plan have been excluded from the actuarial calculations and, if so; obtain some estimate of the maximum effect of the omission on the provision for pension costs.
- Read the actuary's report and determine whether the pertinent amounts agree with the financial statements.
- Ascertain whether any significant events occurred in the period from the date of the actuarial valuation to the company's year-end (and beyond, to the extent known) that would materially affect the computation of the provision for pension costs. If such events have occurred, consult with the actuary and obtain an estimate of the dollar effect on the provision for pension costs.
- Determine that the provision for pension costs is within the limits established by Statement No. 87 and that appropriate related disclosures have been made.

Provisions for Warranty Costs. Through inquiry and reading contracts and similar documents, the auditor should obtain an understanding of the client's warranty policies as a first step in evaluating the adequacy of the estimated liability for warranty claims. Audit procedures in this area commonly include examining documentation supporting open warranty claims, reviewing claims settled after the balance sheet date, and considering past activity in the account in the light of relevant changes (such as new products or changes in warranty periods)—all for the purpose of determining the adequacy of the estimated liability at the balance sheet date.

Income Taxes

Income tax differs from other costs and expenses because it is based on revenue received and costs and expenses incurred by an enterprise. It is largely a dependent variable. Management often has the ability to control the timing and amount of tax payments by controlling the related underlying transactions, particularly in closely held enterprises where minimizing taxes currently payable is often a significant management objective.

Problems in accounting for income taxes, in common with other costs and expenses, fall into two categories: how much tax is associated with a particular transaction and when the tax will become payable. Those two problems complicate presentation of the balance sheet liability and deferred tax accounts and the expense in the income statement. The actual liability is difficult to determine because of the complexities of the tax statutes and regulations. The accounting is further complicated by the number and variety of differences between generally accepted accounting principles (GAAP) and the treatment permitted or required by tax laws and related rulings and regulations.

Audit Objectives

The objectives in auditing income tax accounts are to obtain reasonable assurance that all valid tax liability (or refund receivable), tax expense, and deferred tax accounts are included in the financial statements; that they are properly measured, classified, and described; and that all necessary disclosures are made in the financial statements. The basic audit tasks are the same as for any other accrued liability: determining that the basis used in the tax calculations is appropriate and testing the accuracy of the computation of the year-end liability and of the charge to expense for the period. For income taxes, however, the amounts involved are more likely to be significant, and the issues affecting them to be many, complex, and often debatable. The analysis and evaluation of deferred tax debits and credits can be particularly complicated. The discussion that follows suggests some of the specific objectives that the auditor must meet in auditing income taxes.

In addition to obtaining reasonable assurance that the tax liability accounts accurately reflect the company's current tax obligations (including interest and penalty charges), the auditor must determine that probable contingencies that are reasonably estimable are provided for. Such contingencies may result from existing disagreements with taxing authorities or from the possibility that future disagreements may arise over positions taken by a company in its current tax return that may be interpreted differently by the Internal Revenue Service

(IRS). Guidance for dealing with contingencies of this nature is contained in Statement of Financial Accounting Standards (SFAS) No. 5, *Accounting for Contingencies* (Accounting Standards Section C59). Further, the auditor should obtain reasonable assurance that deferred tax debits and credits are fairly stated, properly classified (between current and noncurrent accounts), and aggregated (debits and credits appropriately netted), all in accordance with Accounting Principles Board (APB) Opinion No. 11, *Accounting for Income Taxes* (Accounting Standards Section I24).

The auditor should determine that the total tax provision in the income statement is properly classified between currently payable and deferred amounts. In addition, the auditor must ascertain that the tax effects of extraordinary items, discontinued operations, and changes in accounting principles have been considered separately and reflected in the income statement in accordance with provisions of APB Opinions No. 11 (Accounting Standards Section I24) and No. 30 (Sections I13 and I17).

Required disclosures relating to income taxes often contain information of particular interest to financial statement users. Those disclosures include the nature of and changes in the composition of deferred taxes, variations from statutory tax rates (including treatment of investment tax credits), operating loss and tax credit carryforwards, and information with respect to tax aspects of subsidiaries or investments. The auditor must also be satisfied that tax exposures not provided for in the financial statements but requiring disclosure under SFAS No. 5 are properly set forth in the notes to the financial statements. In addition, public companies are subject to specific disclosure requirements of the SEC.

The efficiency of the audit of income tax accounts can be enhanced by collecting tax data in the course of examining other accounts. Examples include collecting tax depreciation and investment tax credit (including recapture) data when auditing fixed asset accounts, and gathering officer compensation data when testing the payroll accounts. The auditor should be alert to tax planning and tax savings opportunities and should analyze significant nonrecurring transactions to determine their impact on the tax accrual. Equally important from a client service standpoint is the assistance that the professional accountant can provide in planning those transactions to result in the most favorable tax treatment.

Substantive Tests of Balances

Background Information. To achieve the fullest possible understanding of the client's tax system, the auditor should review the tax returns and related correspondence for all "open" years (for a recurring engagement this means reviewing the most recent year and updating the understanding of earlier years). Often the review can be combined with the auditor's participation in the preparation of the prior year's tax return or the technical review of the client's preparation. If a revenue agent's examination is in process, the auditor should request all related reports and memoranda and review and evaluate any issues set forth in them. Proposed adjustments discussed orally should be elicited from those involved in the examination. The auditor should determine whether the status of "open" tax years has been affected by extensions of the statute of limitations granted by the client.

An auditor is expected to have sufficient knowledge of the major taxing statutes to be able to evaluate the accrued liabilities for the various taxes to which a company is subject. Accordingly, for each examination, the auditor must review changes in the tax laws and regulations and court decisions since the preceding examination and consider their applicability to the company. Many auditors use reminder lists or checklists designed to make sure that all the factors commonly affecting the computation of tax liability have been considered and that the company has not overlooked additional tax saving opportunities not identified when the related transactions were in the planning stage.

An auditor does not have to be a specialist in income taxes to perform audit tests of tax accounts. It is extremely important, however, that the auditor have sufficient expertise in tax matters to resolve all questions that arise. The extent of involvement of a tax specialist in the audit process usually varies with the judgments required in the specific circumstances. In most cases, the audit of the tax accounts should at least be reviewed by an individual who is experienced in income taxes.

Summary Account Analysis. As the starting point in the examination of the tax accounts and to provide an orderly framework for testing, the auditor usually requests analyses of the tax accounts through the year-end date. The analyses may be prepared as of an interim date and later updated to year-end, and should show, for each kind of tax (including each type of deferred debit and credit) and for each year still "open," the beginning balance, accruals, payments, transfers or adjustments, and the ending balance. An example of an analysis of federal income taxes payable appears in Figure 5.7 in Chapter 5.

The auditor can then review the analyses, vouch transactions (to determine their existence or occurrence), determine that prior-year overpayments and underpayments are properly identified (completeness), that deferred debits and credits are properly identified and computed (completeness and valuation), and that amounts currently payable are identified and scheduled for payment on the due dates (completeness and presentation). The appropriateness of the tax and accounting principles employed and the mechanics of their application should also be ascertained (presentation and disclosure). Again, the level of detail that is examined by the auditor in support of account balances and the extent to which normal business transactions (generated from the other transaction cycles) are reviewed will depend on the strength of the company's internal control system and the materiality of the accounts in the financial statements.

Often the auditor obtains or prepares a comparative summary of year-end income and other tax account balances, ascertains that the summary is mathematically accurate, agrees the totals to the general ledger trial balance and the previous year's working papers, and traces significant reconciling items to supporting documentation.

Income Tax Payments and Refunds. Payments of tax should be vouched by inspection of assessment notices, correspondence with the tax authorities, canceled checks, and receipts, if available. The auditor should ascertain whether appropriate amounts of estimated taxes were paid during the year; support for refunds received should also be examined. In addition, the auditor should determine that assessments were reviewed by the client before payment and that payments were made on the due dates. If interest has been charged for late payment of tax, the period of charge should be ascertained and the calculations reviewed. The auditor should also compare taxes payable or refundable as shown on the tax returns filed for the previous year with the amounts recorded for that year and ascertain whether any necessary accounting adjustments have been made. A schedule of carryover items from prior years should be prepared and the current impact of the items considered.

Income Tax Expense, Deferred Taxes, and Related Disclosures. The auditor should obtain or prepare a comparative schedule showing the computation of the tax provision. The tax provision for the current year and changes in deferred tax accounts should be vouched by reference to the tax computation and the deferred tax calculations, respectively. As mentioned earlier, it is normally efficient to gather the information required to prepare or review tax computations during the course of audit work on other accounts. Tax credits (such as investment tax credits) and deductions (such as accelerated depreciation) based on special provisions of the law should be scrutinized and tested for compliance with the Internal Revenue Code. The mathematical accuracy of the schedule should be ascertained, including the computation of income taxes currently payable or refundable. Beginning and ending balances should be traced to the summary of income taxes payable, and significant reconciling items should be traced to supporting documentation.

The schedule supporting the tax calculations should include a reconciliation of accounting income to taxable income. Differences between accounting and taxable income should be individually identified and reconciled to deferred tax balances. In addition, if differences are significant, the auditor may review their nature and amounts for propriety and consistency with the prior year, agree amounts to supporting documentation in the working papers, and determine that the differences are accounted for properly and that the resulting deferred taxes are properly classified on the balance sheet.

The auditor should determine that the client has complied with requirements related to special tax status that may have been claimed. For example, favorable tax treatment may be available to certain entities, such as real estate investment trusts, financial institutions, S Corporations, regulated investment companies, and Foreign Sales Corporations (FSCs). If status as one of those or similar types of enterprises is claimed, the auditor should ascertain that the client has in fact met the relevant eligibility requirements. Similarly, the auditor should test for compliance with federal tax documentation requirements regarding travel and entertainment expenditures, expenditures for charitable purposes, and other similar deductions.

In addition, the auditor should inquire as to the status of all IRS examinations, examine revenue agents' reports for their effect on the prior and current years' tax provisions and financial statements (including necessary disclosures), and review the status of all tax disagreements. Adjustments to tax provisions relating to a previous year determined as a result of examinations by taxing authorities should be vouched to the previous year's computations and any related correspondence. In addition, the auditor should examine prior years' returns not yet examined by taxing authorities for items similar to those adjusted in revenue agents' reports, and determine whether any additional tax provision is required.

The auditor must evaluate the adequacy of financial statement disclosures relating to income taxes as well as the propriety of accounting principles employed in accounting for deferred taxes. Disclosures of accounting changes and significant uncertainties related to tax issues may be particularly sensitive matters. In addition, auditors of public companies must consider SEC disclosure requirements.

Estimated and Contingent Liabilities. As noted above, it is often necessary to provide in the accounts for possible additional liability that might result from revenue agents' examinations of the current year's and prior years' returns. Although such liability may not become payable for a long time, if at all, it should be included in the tax liability and the provision for income taxes in the income statement. Prior-year estimates of tax provisions should be reassessed based on recent IRS or court decisions or interpretations. The amount of any "cushion" should be supported by a detailed listing of possible tax questions and potential liabilities. The auditor should evaluate the propriety of contingent amounts and assess the adequacy of the tax accrual in light of all pending tax matters. The provision for taxes in the income statement is not affected by expected disallowances that produce future tax deductions (e.g., required capitalization of items expensed); except for interest and penalties, a disallowance of that kind affects only deferred taxes and the current liability.

The auditor, through the exercise of judgment and consultation with tax specialists, must reach independent conclusions about each of the issues affecting the tax liability. While the function of a tax specialist who evaluates the tax liability may end with the estimate of the liability, the auditor's responsibility goes further. The auditor must evaluate the adequacy of the evidence supporting the decisions made—whether any data or matters affecting taxes have been overlooked and whether the evidence is adequate in the circumstances. If the treatment and disclosure of taxes in the financial statements depend significantly on the intentions of management, it is generally appropriate to obtain written representation of those intentions in the client representation letter. For example, evidence of management's intentions may be needed to support a decision to provide or not to provide for taxes on the undistributed earnings of subsidiaries. Also, evidence must be present to support the tax basis of assets purchased in an acquisition in which the purchase price must be allocated.

The auditor's need to obtain sufficient competent evidential matter to support the income tax accrual has several implications. First, a mere statement of management's intentions that might affect the tax accrual is insufficient evidence. Management must have specific plans that the auditor can evaluate to determine that they are reasonable and feasible. Second, client restrictions that limit the auditor's access to information necessary to audit the tax accrual, possibly out of concern over IRS access to tax accrual working papers, may constitute a scope limitation and affect the auditor's ability to issue an unqualified opinion. (See an Auditing Interpretation of Section 326, *Evidential Matter*, and the further discussion of IRS access to tax accrual working papers in Chapter 3.) Third, the opinion of the client's outside or in-house legal counsel on the adequacy of the tax accrual is not sufficient competent evidence to support an opinion on the financial statements. According to the Auditing Interpretation of Section 326, *Evidential Matter*, the auditor should not rely on a specialist in another discipline if the auditor possesses the necessary competence to assess the matter.

State and Local Taxes. Accruals for state and local income taxes (including franchise taxes based on income) are reviewed in much the same way as federal income tax accruals. The auditor should obtain or prepare an analysis for the year of deferred and accrued state and local income taxes, showing the computation of the provisions for the current year. The mathematical accuracy of the analysis should be tested and applicable amounts traced to the general ledger, trial balance, and prior year's working papers. Significant reconciling items should be traced to supporting documentation. Support for payments made and refunds received during the year should be examined. The auditor should also compare the liability per the returns filed for the preceding year, the estimated liability recorded for that year, and the payments made to discharge that liability, and should evaluate the reasons for differences, if any, and determine that they have been appropriately accounted for. All state and local tax examinations should be reviewed, and the auditor should determine that appropriate provisions have been made for unresolved assessments.

Although state and local taxes are usually less significant than federal taxes and therefore subject to a much less intensive and detailed analysis, the auditor should not overlook them. For companies operating in many states, the fact that any one individual state or local tax may be insignificant often obscures the total impact of the aggregate state and local tax expense. A 1983 Supreme Court ruling increased the flexibility that state governments have in taxing a share of the total income that United States–based multinational companies earn throughout the world. Under the "unitary tax concept," a state in which the company does business can use a formula to calculate how much of the worldwide income is attributable to that state. The formula is based on how much of a company's total property, payroll, and sales fall within the state. In certain instances, a company may experience an operating loss within a state, but because of the "unitary tax concept," a tax liability will nevertheless result.

In addition to examining individual tax accruals, the auditor should evaluate the company's ability to control and accurately account for all of the taxes to which it may be subject. Analytical review procedures may be particularly appropriate as a means of testing the accuracy of state and local tax accruals if the client is required to file returns in many jurisdictions.

Debt and Equity; Interest and Dividends

The distinctions among debt, equity, and other financing arrangements are blurred in certain businesses, especially large public companies. In those companies, it is more realistic to view various debt, equity, lease, and other contractual arrangements as an array of alternatives that financial managers use to enhance the company's earnings record as well as its financial strength. Common stock is as much a financing instrument as bank loans, and convertible debt may have as many equity characteristics as preferred stock. Financial managers may adjust the legal characteristics of an instrument, whether formally designated as debt or equity, to achieve a desired (or required) balance of protection of principal and income with sharing of the risks and rewards of ownership. Instruments may be designed to reconcile an enterprise's need for financial resources at minimum cost with investors' preferences for safety and rewards. The result is a virtually continuous spectrum of financing instruments, ranging from straight borrowing to borrowing with equity features, borrowing with variable income features, stock with preferences as to income and principal, common stock, and even promises of future stock. The SEC and the IRS have from time to time addressed the distinctions among debt, equity, and other financing arrangements, and the subject continues to be of interest to those agencies, auditors, and users of financial statements. Over the years, a great deal of ingenuity has gone into designing financing that looks like something else, and in particular into disguising what were actually asset acquisitions as lease transactions. The FASB has since addressed many of those transactions, but auditors must constantly be alert to discern the substance of each transaction. If form is allowed to rule over substance, one or more audit objectives are not achieved.

Transactions and accounts related to debt and equity include lessee accounting for capital leases, interest expense, debt discount and premium, early extinguishment of debt (including gain or loss thereon), debt defeasance (and "in substance" defeasance), troubled debt restructuring, product financing arrangements, cash and stock dividends, stock splits, stock warrants, options and purchase plans, and treasury stock transactions. Many of these transactions and accounts involve special accounting measurement, presentation, and disclosure principles that consequently require audit attention. Other matters with audit implications include short-term debt expected to be refinanced, debt covenants and security, compensating balance arrangements, debt conversion features, mandatory stock redemption requirements, and stock conversion features.

Audit Objectives

The auditor's objectives in examining debt and equity transactions and accounts are to obtain reasonable assurance that

- All obligations for notes payable, long-term debt, and capitalized leases and all equity accounts have been properly valued, classified, described, and disclosed.

- All executory or "off-balance sheet" obligations have been identified and considered (e.g., operating leases, product financing arrangements, take-or-pay contracts, and throughput contracts).

- All liability and equity transactions, accounts, and changes therein have been properly authorized and are obligations of the entity or ownership rights in the entity.

- Interest, discounts, premiums, dividends, and other debt-related and equity-related transactions and accounts have been properly valued, classified, described, and disclosed.

- All terms, requirements, instructions, commitments, and other debt-related and equity-related matters have been identified, complied with, and disclosed, as appropriate.

Substantive Tests of Balances

The following discussion applies to all kinds of financing transactions unless clearly inapplicable in the context or specified in the discussion. A convenient vehicle for substantive testing of the various kinds of financing transactions and accounts is an account analysis working paper, that is, a list of the notes, debt issues, or equities outstanding at the beginning of a period, and the additions, reductions, and outstanding amounts at the end of the period. Often the list can be carried forward from year to year if changes are infrequent. It may incorporate all pertinent information about the financing instruments, or that information may be summarized separately. The auditor should compare the list with the accounts and reconcile the total to the general ledger. The list can also be used to document other audit tests performed.

Tests of debt and equity transactions and balances consist primarily of obtaining confirmations from third parties, inspecting items, reperforming computations, and vouching (examining supporting evidence). Although confirmation is the principal test used for debt and equity accounts, all four techniques may be used in certain circumstances. The following are some examples:

Confirmations—debt payable and terms with holder; outstanding stock with holder and registrar; authorized stock with the Secretary of State of the state in which incorporated; and treasury stock with safekeeping agent.

Inspection—unissued debt and stock instruments (as partial substantiation of the completeness of recorded outstanding instruments).

Reperformance of computations—debt discount or premium, interest, gains or losses on debt extinguishment, stock issuances and purchases, and dividends.

Vouching—debt and stock issuances and retirements, and interest and dividend payments to registrar.

Common Substantive Tests of Debt and Equity Accounts. The auditor should trace authorization for all types of financing to a vote of the board of directors. If the directors have delegated authority for the details of financing, individual transactions should be traced to the authorizing officer's signature.

Copies of financing instruments should be carefully read to ascertain that the classification of the financing and its description in the financial statements are proper. The instruments should be examined for commitments, which often accompany financing arrangements, and evidence of rights given or received, which might require accounting recognition or disclosure. Often an instrument is designed to achieve a desired accounting and tax result; it is good practice for clients to seek their auditors' interpretation of accounting and disclosure implications of prospective financing instruments before they are executed. Once the accounting and disclosure implications have been analyzed and understood, it is usually possible to set up a worksheet that can be carried forward from year to year for computing and documenting compliance with pertinent commitments.

If financing is in the form of a lease, the terms must be evaluated to determine whether it should be accounted for as an operating or a capital lease. If leases are capitalized, computations of the carrying amounts of assets and debt should be tested, and the terms should be compared with the underlying lease contract.

The auditor should trace the recording of cash receipts and payments from financing and related activities into the accounts and compare those transactions with the authorization and terms of the instrument for timing and amount. Paid notes should be examined for evidence of proper authorization, documentation, and cancellation; interest expense, accrued interest, and dividends declared should be recomputed to test their mathematical accuracy.

Outstanding balances should be confirmed, usually at year-end, with holders of notes and issuers of lines of credit, trustees under bond and debenture indentures, and registrars and transfer agents for stock issues. Authorized stock often must be recorded with the Secretary of State in the state of incorporation, and confirmation may be requested from that office. Treasury stock should be confirmed with the custodian, or, if there is no custodian, the auditor should examine the certificates in the presence of client personnel.

If several types of financing are outstanding, the auditor should compare transactions in each with restrictions and provisions of the others. Dividend payments may be restricted by bond and note indentures; dividends on common stock may be affected by the rights of preferred stockholders or their rights may change with changes in capital structure or retained earnings accounts; certain transactions may require the consent of holders of senior securities, and so on. It is essential that the client determine and the auditor review the *most restrictive* provisions of the various debt agreements for the required disclosure in the financial statements.

The client's reconciliation of detailed stock ledgers to the control account should be reviewed and tested. Accounting for unissued, issued, and canceled certificates should be similarly tested.

The auditor should reperform computations of shares reserved for issuance on exercise of options and warrants or conversion of convertible securities and of the basis for valuing stock dividends and splits. In reperforming those computations, the auditor should pay close attention to the interrelated effects of one issue on another and on the total amount of each issue authorized and outstanding. The accuracy of accounting for warrants, options, and conversion privileges exercised can often be reviewed by an overall computation based on the terms of the related instruments.

If the interest rate of a financing instrument is not clearly the going market rate for that type of instrument at time of issuance, the auditor should evaluate the reasonableness of the interest rate in terms of the requirements of APB Opinion No. 21, *Interest on Receivables and Payables* (Accounting Standards Section I69), and document the evaluation in the working papers. If the interest rate must be imputed, the documentation for the imputed rate may be carried forward from year to year.

If a financing instrument is issued for property other than cash, the auditor should review the terms of the transaction, basis for recording, and evidence of approval by the board of directors. Usually, a transaction of that kind is significant enough to warrant careful review by the auditor during the client's planning stage. In that event, there is ample opportunity to suggest the appropriate basis for recording the property received and the kind of documentation that should be retained to support it.

Defaults. Examination of financing transactions may reveal that one or more commitments or covenants have not been complied with. The financing instrument usually specifies what constitutes an "event of default" and its consequences. While ultimate legal remedies may be severe, the intent of default provisions is to give the lender or investor adequate protection by restricting the investee's freedom of action in certain circumstances. Therefore, it is common for an event of default to be "waived." The auditor should obtain competent evidential matter that the client has received a waiver extending to the end of the succeeding year (or operating cycle, if longer), usually in the form of a confirmation from the lender.

An exception to the waiver requirement is provided by Statement of Financial Accounting Standards No. 78, *Classification of Obligations That Are Callable by the Creditor* (Accounting Standards Section B05). It provides that long-term obligations may be classified as long-term liabilities if they contain a grace period within which the debtor may cure the violation and it is probable that the violation will be cured within that period. Under this condition, the circumstances must be disclosed. If an event of default is not waived, or cured under this provision, the debt must be classified as a current liability and the facts disclosed in the financial statements, even though immediate payment has not been requested.

Initial Examinations. In an initial examination, the auditor should review the corporation's charter or certificate of incorporation, bylaws, and all pertinent amendments; the extent of review of prior years' minutes of meetings of the board of directors and stockholders and other documents and of capital stock accounts depends on the circumstances and whether the financial statements were previously examined by independent certified public accountants.

The auditor should also analyze the additional paid-in capital and retained earnings accounts from the corporation's inception to determine whether all entries were in conformity with generally accepted accounting principles then prevailing. If, however, previous examinations have been made by independent certified public accountants, the procedures may be limited to a review of analyses made by the previous auditors. Entries in those accounts should also be reviewed for consistency of treatment from year to year. The analyses of additional paid-in capital accounts should segregate the balances by classes of stock outstanding.

Permanent Files. An auditor should include in the permanent working paper files information as to the kinds of stock authorized, the number of shares of each class authorized, par or stated values, provisions concerning dividend rates, redemption values, priority rights to dividends and in liquidation, cumulative or noncumulative rights to dividends, participation or conversion privileges, and other pertinent data. The auditor should also retain the analyses of additional paid-in capital and retained earnings in the permanent files so that changes in the current year may be readily reviewed for consistency with previous years.

Tests Unique to Stockholders' Equity Accounts. Since analyses of stockholders' equity accounts appear in the financial statements and are subject to detailed scrutiny by security analysts and others, the auditor should ordinarily subject changes in those accounts to detailed substantive tests. Some entries, such as appropriations of retained earnings, are simply traced to the authorization by the board of directors. Other entries summarize a large volume of individual transactions and can be tested by means of an overall computation based on the authorizing instrument or vote of the directors. Still other entries—the most common example is the exercise of stock options that were granted in the past at various times and prices—are an aggregation of unique transactions and are best audited by evaluating the internal controls over the transaction system and by reconciling beginning and ending balances with the activity for the year. Each type of entry should be evaluated for compliance with loan agreements or other restrictive commitments.

The auditor should review the terms of outstanding stock subscriptions and make sufficient tests of activity and balances to afford reasonable assurance that they are being complied with. It is preferable to confirm outstanding stock subscriptions receivable even though under SEC rules they do not represent an asset but rather a memorandum entry in the capital section of the balance sheet.

Tests Unique to Dividends. The auditor should determine whether cash dividends, stock dividends and splits, dividends payable in scrip, and dividends payable in assets other than cash have been properly accounted for. One of an auditor's responsibilities is to form an opinion on whether the intentions of the board, as indicated in the resolutions authorizing dividends, are properly reflected in the financial statements.

Covenants of debentures and other debt instruments frequently restrict the payment of cash dividends in some manner (e.g., to earnings subsequent to the date of the instrument). The auditor should ascertain that dividend declarations do not exceed the amount of retained earnings available for dividends, and that the amount of unrestricted retained earnings has been properly calculated in accordance with the debt covenants or other restrictions, and appropriately disclosed.

Holders of noncumulative preferred stock ordinarily have no claim to dividends in a year when the amount of the dividends has not been earned, except possibly when dividends earned in a prior year have been improperly withheld. Dividends paid on common stock may have encroached on the rights of holders of noncumulative preferred stock. An auditor who discovers that situation should bring the matter to the attention of appropriate client personnel and suggest that counsel be consulted about a possible liability to holders of noncumulative preferred stock.

In the event of a stock dividend or split, the auditor must ascertain that the capital stock authorization is not exceeded and that consideration has been given to shares reserved for stock options and conversions of other issues.

Review Questions

Investments

16–1. State the audit objectives for investment accounts.

16–2. What income statement accounts should be considered when auditing investments?

16-3. What are some typical reasons for differences between the count of securities and the list of securities prepared by the client?

16-4. What actions should an auditor take if (a) past-due interest coupons are still attached to bonds, or (b) coupons are missing when the bonds are inspected?

16-5. What procedures should the auditor follow if the entire portfolio of securities is in the custody of a reliable financial institution?

16-6. What procedures should be followed to determine whether securities have been pledged as collateral?

Prepaid expenses, estimated and accrued liabilities, and related expenses

16-7. What characteristics distinguish prepaid expenses from deferred charges?

16-8. How do agency obligations differ from accrued liabilities?

16-9. What are the audit objectives for prepaid expenses? For accrued liabilities?

16-10. With respect to prepaid expenses and accrued liabilities:

> What types of substantive tests of details are performed?
> What types of analytical reviews are applicable?

16-11. What audit procedures are generally applied to prepaid insurance?

16-12. What responsibility does the auditor have with respect to insurance coverage?

16-13. Explain the audit procedures generally followed with respect to

> a. Prepaid and accrued property taxes.
> b. Prepaid and accrued commissions.
> c. Employee advances.

16-14. What audit procedures are generally followed with respect to royalties payable?

16-15. What are suspense accounts and how does the auditor deal with them?

16-16. What audit procedures are generally followed with respect to accrued pension costs?

Income taxes

16-17. What are the audit objectives with respect to income taxes?

16-18. Describe in general terms audit procedures that are typically applied in evaluating the appropriateness of a company's income tax liability.

16-19. Why is it important for an auditor to examine prior years' tax returns examined by taxing authorities (and agents' reports)? Those not yet examined by taxing authorities?

16-20. Briefly describe the audit procedures used with respect to state and local tax accruals.

Debt and equity; interest and dividends

16-21. What are the audit objectives with respect to debt and equity accounts?

16-22. Why are debt covenants significant to accountants and auditors?

16-23. What are the major substantive tests of details used for debt and equity accounts?

16-24. Of what concern to an auditor is the interest rate of a financing instrument?

16-25. What procedures do auditors follow with respect to financing instruments issued for property other than cash?

16-26. When it appears that a debt covenant may not have been complied with, what actions should the auditor take?

16–27. What information related to equity accounts should be included in the permanent working paper files?

16–28. What procedures should an auditor follow with respect to a stock dividend?

Discussion Questions _____

Investments

16–30. Explain how you would obtain evidence that all investment income to which a company is entitled has been recorded. Assume that the company has a sizable portfolio of marketable stocks and bonds (some of which do not have market prices) invested to utilize excess working capital, and a fairly good system of internal control. Explain how you would determine appropriate valuations at year-end, indicating the sources you would use.

16–31. Give substantive procedures for the audit of the transactions in a sinking fund for the redemption of bonds, if the fund is in the custody of an independent trustee.

16–32. A corporation temporarily invested some of its excess funds in stocks of other companies listed on established exchanges. In the course of your preliminary audit work you ascertain that all such stocks were acquired through a brokerage firm at various dates during the year under examination, and that the stock certificates are in the name of the corporation (your client) but are being held in safekeeping by the brokerage firm. The corporation does not maintain an investment ledger.

Required:
Outline the audit procedures for the examination of stocks and income therefrom.

Prepaid expenses, estimated and accrued liabilities, and related expenses

16–33. Explain how an examination of insurance policies might indicate each of the following:

   a. The pledge of inventory as collateral on a loan.
   b. The disposition of fixed assets without entry on the books.

16–34. In an audit of the financial statements of a manufacturing company, what types of information, obtained from an examination of fire insurance policies (in which your client is named as the insured) and the company's insurance register, would you include in your working papers?

   For what purpose or purposes should the auditor examine fire insurance policies?

16–35. Why would an auditor want to examine individual accrued liability accounts even though the account balances were insignificant?

16–36. If a client's accrual for property taxes is based on estimates, what audit steps can be performed to substantiate the amount of the liability?

Income taxes

16–37. The provision for possible additional tax liabilities that might result from revenue agents' examinations is normally included in the current liability account even though it may not be payable for some time.

a. Why is this appropriate?

b. Discuss the appropriate treatment of this "cushion" when the revenue agent's examination of tax returns for all prior years has been completed with no additional assessment required.

16–38. Your client has not provided for deferred taxes on the difference between accelerated depreciation (which is used for tax purposes) and straight-line depreciation (which is used for financial statement purposes). This position is based on the theory that when the same type of timing differences recur in subsequent periods (thus offsetting the reversal of earlier differences), the practical effect is an indefinite postponement of taxes. Hence, the effect is similar to a permanent difference and no interperiod allocation is required.

What is your position regarding this practice? What effect will your position have on your audit of the provision for income taxes?

Debt and equity; interest and dividends

16–39. Outline the auditing procedures for substantiating the issued capital stock of a corporation that does not employ an outside registrar or transfer agent, which you are examining for the first time.

AICPA Multiple Choice Questions ─────────────────

These questions are taken from the Auditing part of Uniform CPA Examinations. Choose the single most appropriate answer.

Investments

16–40. Which of the following is *not* one of the auditor's primary objectives in an examination of marketable securities?

a. To determine whether securities are authentic.

b. To determine whether securities are the property of the client.

c. To determine whether securities actually exist.

d. To determine whether securities are properly classified on the balance sheet.

16–41. Jones was engaged to examine the financial statements of Gamma Corporation for the year ended June 30, 19X0. Having completed an examination of the investment securities, which of the following is the *best* method of verifying the accuracy of recorded dividend income?

a. Tracing recorded dividend income to cash receipts records and validated deposit slips.

b. Utilizing analytical review techniques and statistical sampling.

c. Comparing recorded dividends with amounts appearing on federal information forms 1099.

d. Comparing recorded dividends with a standard financial reporting service's record of dividends.

16–42. The auditor should insist that a representative of the client be present during the physical examination of securities in order to

    a. Lend authority to the auditor's directives.
    b. Detect forged securities.
    c. Coordinate the return of all securities to proper locations.
    d. Acknowledge the receipt of securities returned.

16–43. In a manufacturing company, which one of the following audit procedures would give the *least* assurance of the validity of the general ledger balance of investment in stocks and bonds at the audit date?

    a. Confirmation from the broker.
    b. Inspection and count of stocks and bonds.
    c. Vouching all changes during the year to brokers' advices and statements.
    d. Examination of paid checks issued in payment of securities purchased.

Prepaid expenses, estimated and accrued liabilities, and related expenses

16–44. The audit procedures used to verify accrued liabilities differ from those employed for the verification of accounts payable because

    a. Accrued liabilities usually pertain to services of a continuing nature while accounts payable are the result of completed transactions.
    b. Accrued liability balances are less material than accounts payable balances.
    c. Evidence supporting accrued liabilities is nonexistent while evidence supporting accounts payable is readily available.
    d. Accrued liabilities at year-end will become accounts payable during the following year.

16–45. Which of the following audit procedures is *least* likely to detect an unrecorded liability?

    a. Analysis and recomputation of interest expense.
    b. Analysis and recomputation of depreciation expense.
    c. Mailing of standard bank confirmation form.
    d. Reading of the minutes of meetings of the board of directors.

16–46. The auditor is *most* likely to verify accrued commissions payable in conjunction with the

    a. Sales cutoff review.
    b. Verification of contingent liabilities.
    c. Review of post balance sheet date disbursements.
    d. Examination of trade accounts payable.

Debt and equity; interest and dividends

16–47. Where *no* independent stock transfer agents are employed and the corporation issues its own stocks and maintains stock records, canceled stock certificates should

    a. Be defaced to prevent reissuance and attached to their corresponding stubs.
    b. *Not* be defaced, but segregated from other stock certificates and retained in a canceled certificates file.
    c. Be destroyed to prevent fraudulent reissuance.
    d. Be defaced and sent to the secretary of state.

16–48. When a company has treasury stock certificates on hand, a year-end count of the certificates by the auditor is

    a. Required when the company classifies treasury stock with other assets.
    b. Not required if treasury stock is a deduction from stockholders' equity.
    c. Required when the company had treasury stock transactions during the year.
    d. Always required.

16–49. In connection with the audit of a current issue of long-term bonds payable, the auditor should

    a. Determine whether bondholders are persons other than owners, directors, or officers of the company issuing the bond.
    b. Calculate the effective interest rate to see if it is substantially the same as the rates for similar issues.
    c. Decide whether the bond issue was made without violating state or local law.
    d. Ascertain that the client has obtained the opinion of counsel on the legality of the issue.

16–50. The auditor can *best* verify a client's bond sinking fund transactions and year-end balance by

    a. Confirmation with the bond trustee.
    b. Confirmation with individual holders of retired bonds.
    c. Recomputation of interest expense, interest payable, and amortization of bond discount or premium.
    d. Examination and count of the bonds retired during the year.

16–51. An auditor's client has violated a minor requirement of its bond indenture, which could result in the trustee requiring immediate payment of the principal amount due. The client refuses to seek a waiver from the bond trustee. Request for immediate payment is *not* considered likely. Under these circumstances the auditor must

    a. Require classification of bonds payable as a current liability.
    b. Contact the bond trustee directly.
    c. Disclose the situation in the auditor's report.
    d. Obtain an opinion from the company's attorney as to the likelihood of the trustee's enforcement of the requirement.

Problems and Cases

Investments

16–60. On January 1, 1986 your client owned 1000 shares of Consolidated Textile Co. capital stock, which were purchased April 15, 1984. During 1986 the following purchases and sales were effected:

    Purchases: March 1, 500 shares; June 29, 300 shares.
    Sales: March 23, 150 shares; September 28, 200 shares.

Examination of a dividend service revealed the following dividend record:

Consolidated Textile Co., Cap. (par $0.10)

Amount of Div'd.	Date Declared	Ex-div'd. Date	Stock of Record	Payment Date
$0.20	12/21/85	12/28/85	12/30/85	1/13/86
10%^a stock	2/ 1/86	2/21/86	2/24/86	3/10/86
0.20	3/ 1/86	3/22/86	3/24/86	4/ 7/86
0.25	6/21/86	6/28/86	6/30/86	7/14/86
20%^b stock	9/20/86	9/28/86	10/ 2/86	10/16/86
0.30	9/20/86	9/28/86	10/ 2/86	10/16/86
0.37-1/2	12/20/86	12/28/86	1/ 2/87	1/15/87

^aFractions paid in cash at rate of $0.75 for each 1/10 of a share.
^bFractions paid in cash at rate of $1.75 for each 1/5 of a share.

Required:
Prepare a worksheet to calculate the following:

a. Dividend income for the year 1986, on an accrual basis (use ex–dividend date).
b. Cash dividend receipts that should be traced to the books for the 1986 audit.
c. The number of shares for which stock certificates should be examined on the date of the cash count and cutoff, January 12, 1987.

16–61. The schedule on page 709 was prepared by the controller of World Manufacturing, Inc. for use by the independent auditors during their examination of World's year-end financial statements. All procedures performed by the audit assistant were noted at the bottom "legend" section, and the schedule was properly initialed, dated, and indexed and then submitted to a senior member of the audit staff for review. Internal control was reviewed and is considered to be satisfactory.

Required:
a. What information that is essential to the audit of marketable securities is missing from this schedule?
b. What essential audit procedures were not noted as having been performed by the audit assistant?

(AICPA adapted)

16–62. You are in charge of the audit of the financial statements of Demot Corporation for the year ended December 31. The corporation has had the policy of investing its surplus funds in marketable securities. Its stock and bond certificates are kept in a safe deposit box in a local bank. Only the president and the treasurer of the corporation have access to the box.

You were unable to obtain access to the safe deposit box on December 31 because neither the president nor the treasurer was available. Arrangements were made for your assistant to accompany the treasurer to the bank on January 11 to examine the securities. Your assistant has never examined securities that are kept in a safe deposit box and requires instructions. Your assistant should be able to inspect all securities on hand in an hour.

Required:
a. List the instructions that you would give to your assistant regarding the examination of the stock and bond certificates kept in the safe deposit box. Include in

World Manufacturing, Inc.
Marketable Securities
Year Ended December 31, 1987

Description of Security	%	Yr. Due	Serial No.	Face Value of Bonds	Gen. Ledger 1/1	Purch. in 1987	Sold in 1987	Cost	Gen. Ledger 12/31	12/31 Market	Pay Date(s)	Amt. Rec.	Accruals 12/31
Corp. Bonds													
A	6	97	21-7	10000	9400 a				9400	9100	1/15	300 b,d	275
											7/15	300 b,d	100
D	4	89	73-0	30000	27500 a				27500	26220	12/1	1200 b,d	188
G	9	05	16-4	5000	4000 a				4000	5080	8/1	450 b,d	
R c	5	92	08-2	70000	66000 a		57000 b	66000					
S c	10	06	07-4	100000		100000 e			100000	101250	7/1	5000 b,d	5000
					106900	100000	57000	66000	140900	141650		7250	5563
					a,f	f	f	f	f,g	f		f	f
Stocks													
P 1000 shs. Common			1044		7500 a				7500	7600	3/1	750 b,d	
											6/1	750 b,d	
											9/1	750 b,d	
											12/1	750 b,d	250
U 50 shs. Common			8530		9700 a				9700	9800	2/1	800 b,d	
											8/1	800 b,d	667
					17200				17200	17400		4600	917
					a,f				f,g	f		f	f

Legends and Comments Relative to Above

a = Beginning balances agreed to 1986 working papers
b = Traced to cash receipts
c = Minutes examined (purchase and sale approved by the board of directors)
d = Agreed to 1099
e = Examined broker's advice
f = Totals footed
g = Agreed to general ledger

your instructions the details of the securities to be examined and the reasons for examining those details.

b. When she returned from the bank, your assistant reported that the treasurer had entered the box on January 4. The treasurer stated that she had removed an old photograph of the corporation's original building. The photograph was lent to the local Chamber of Commerce for display purposes. List the additional audit procedures that are required because of the treasurer's action.

(AICPA adapted)

16–63. You were engaged to examine the financial statements of Ronlyn Corporation for the year ended June 30, 1988.

On May 1, the Corporation borrowed $500,000 from Second National Bank to finance plant expansion. Because of unexpected difficulties in acquiring the building site, the plant expansion had not begun at June 30. To make use of the borrowed funds, management decided to invest in stocks and bonds, and on May 16, the $500,000 was invested in securities.

Required:

a. How could you substantiate the security position of Ronlyn at June 30?
b. In your audit of investments, how would you accomplish the following?
   1. Substantiate the dividend or interest income recorded.
   2. Determine market value.
   3. Establish the authority for security purchases.

(AICPA adapted)

16–64. In connection with his examination of the financial statements of Belasco Chemicals, Inc., Kenneth Mack, CPA, is considering the necessity of inspecting marketable securities on the balance sheet date, May 31, 1987, or at some other date. The marketable securities held by Belasco include negotiable bearer bonds, which are kept in a safe in the treasurer's office, and miscellaneous stocks and bonds kept in a safe deposit box at The Merchants Bank. Both the negotiable bearer bonds and the miscellaneous stocks and bonds are material to proper presentation of Belasco's financial position.

Required:

a. What are the factors that Mr. Mack should consider in determining the necessity for inspecting these securities on May 31, 1987, as opposed to other dates?
b. Assume that Mr. Mack plans to send a member of his staff to Belasco's offices and The Merchants Bank on May 31, 1987, to make the security inspection. What instructions should he give to this staff member as to the conduct of the inspection and the evidence to be included in the audit working papers? (*Note:* Do not discuss the valuation of securities, the income from securities, or the examination of information contained in the books and records of the Company.)
c. Assume that Mr. Mack finds it impracticable to send a member of his staff to Belasco's offices and The Merchants Bank on May 31, 1987. What alternative procedures may he employ to assure himself that the Company had physical possession of its marketable securities on May 31, 1987, if the securities are inspected (1) May 27, 1987? (2) June 6, 1987?

(AICPA adapted)

Prepaid expenses, estimated and accrued liabilities, and related expenses

16–65. You are engaged in an audit of the financial statements of the ABC Corporation for the year ended December 31, 1987. You have examined all of the insurance policies (as listed) that were in force during the year.

Scottish Union Insurance Co.:

Policy No.	Kind	Coverage	Term	Premium
N-30393	Fire on contents	4 million	5/25/87–5/25/88	$9,000.00

National Surety Company:

DF1274027	Forgery	300M	6/8/87–6/8/90	1,725.00
LO31487	Forgery	300M	6/8/86–6/8/87	690.00

Zurich Insurance Co.:

206271[a]	Workmen's compensation		6/26/86–6/26/87	1,824.00 (deposit)
228631	Workmen's compensation		6/26/87–6/26/88	2,436.00 (deposit)

American Employers Insurance Co.:

3260945	Auto liability	500M– 1 million	4/22/87–4/22/88	13,524.00
	Property damage	50M	4/22/87–4/22/88	302.00

Providence Washington Insurance Co.:

NY96292	Auto fire, theft, collision	500M	4/25/87–4/25/88	30,000.00[b]

[a]Assessment of $923.00 for year ended 6/26/87 paid 1/8/88.
[b]Return premium of $5,000 received 5/15/87 because of change in rate.

Required:

Prepare a working paper to indicate the audit procedures applied to the prepaid insurance and insurance expense accounts. Compute prepaid balances to the nearest half month. Indicate all audit procedures required to be followed.

16–66. The Moss Company manufactures household appliances that are sold through independent franchised retail dealers. The electric motors in the appliances are guaranteed for five years from the date of sale of the appliances to the consumer. Under the guarantee, defective motors are replaced by the dealers without charge.

Inventories of replacement motors are kept in the dealers' stores and are carried at cost in the Moss Company's records. When a dealer replaces a defective motor, the factory is notified and the defective motor is returned to the factory for reconditioning. After the defective motor is received by the factory, the dealer's account is credited with an agreed fee for the replacement service.

When the appliance is brought to the dealer after the guarantee period has elapsed, the dealer charges the owner for installing the new motor. The dealer notifies the factory of the installation and returns the replaced motor for reconditioning. The motor installed is then charged to the dealer's account at a price in excess of its inventory value. In this instance, to encourage the return of replaced motors, the dealer's account is credited with a nominal value for the returned motor.

Dealers submit quarterly inventory reports of the motors on hand. The reports are later verified by factory salespeople. Dealers are billed for inventory shortages determined by comparison of the dealers' inventory reports with the factory's perpetual records of the dealers' inventories. The dealers order additional motors as they need them. One motor is used for all appliances in a given year, but the motors are changed in basic design each model year.

The Moss Company has established an account, Estimated Liability for Product Guarantees, in connection with the guarantees. An amount representing the estimated guarantee cost prorated per sales unit is credited to the Estimated Liability account for each appliance sold, and the debit is charged to an expense account. The Estimated Liability account is debited for the service fees credited to the dealers' accounts and for the inventory cost of motors installed under the guarantees.

The engineering department keeps statistical records of the number of units of each model sold in each year and the replacements that were made. The effect of improvements in design and construction is under continual study by the engineering department, and the estimated guarantee cost per unit is adjusted annually on the basis of experience and improvements in design. Experience shows that, for a given motor model, the number of guarantees made good varies widely from year to year during the guarantee period, but the total number of guarantees to be made good can be reliably predicted.

Required:
   a. Prepare an audit program to satisfy yourself as to the propriety of transactions recorded in the Estimated Liability for Product Guarantees account for the year ended December 31, 1988.
   b. Prepare the worksheet format that would be used to test the adequacy of the balance in the Estimated Liability for Product Guarantees account. The worksheet column headings should describe clearly the data to be inserted in the columns.

(AICPA adapted)

Income taxes

16–67. ACE Company does business in all 50 states in the United States. However, you discover while speaking with the controller that state tax returns are filed in only 30 states. Discuss the impact of this finding on the audit of ACE Company. Describe additional procedures that you feel may be necessary in the circumstances.

16–68. You happen to come across an article in the *Wall Street Journal* indicating that the Internal Revenue Service has settled a dispute with a large company regarding its tax treatment of certain items. As a result, the company was assessed a substantial additional tax liability. Your client, the XYZ Corporation, currently uses the same disputed treatment for similar items. Discuss how this situation will affect your audit strategy for taxes for your client.

16–69. For each of the following items, describe where in your audit working papers, or elsewhere, this type of information could be found and, once determined, what effect it would have on your review of the provision for federal income taxes.

   a. Difference in basis of depreciable assets as a result of an acquisition.
   b. Charitable contributions in excess of statutory limitation that can be carried forward.

    c. Additions to allowance for doubtful accounts provided for book purposes in excess of direct write-offs deducted for tax purposes.

    d. Differences resulting from the use of percentage-of-completion accounting for long-term contracts for book purposes and completed-contract accounting for tax purposes.

    e. Amortization of goodwill.

    f. Officers' life insurance premiums (client is beneficiary).

    g. A provision for loss on disposal of a segment of a business that is not deductible in the tax return for the current year.

    h. Additions to the allowance for inventory obsolescence in excess of charges for actual losses.

    i. Dividends included in accounting income that are eligible for the 85 percent dividends-received deduction.

    j. Installment sales.

Debt and equity; interest and dividends

16–70. You are assigned to a new client, Dartmouth Industries, whose principal business is the manufacture of custom cutting machines for various commercial applications. On a plant tour of its facilities you observe seven high-cost, new tool-and-die machines, which you learn have been acquired during this year. At year-end, you review the client's fixed asset and debt schedules and become aware that the additions do not appear as assets and related liabilities.

    Required:

    Discuss the client's apparent incorrect treatment of these transactions and the procedures necessary in these circumstances to obtain reasonable assurance that all obligations are properly valued, classified, and disclosed.

16–71. You are engaged in the audit of a corporation whose records have not previously been audited by you. The corporation has both an independent transfer agent and a registrar for its capital stock. The transfer agent maintains the record of stockholders and the registrar is responsible for seeing that there is no overissue of stock. Signatures of both are required to validate stock certificates.

    It has been proposed that confirmations be obtained from both the transfer agent and the registrar as to the stock outstanding at the balance sheet date. If such confirmations agree with the books, no additional work is to be performed as to capital stock.

    Required:

    If you agree that obtaining confirmations would be sufficient in this situation, give the justification for your position. If you do not agree, state specifically all additional steps you would take and explain your reasons for taking them.

16–72. In auditing a corporation that has a bond issue outstanding, the trust indenture is reviewed and a confirmation as to the issue is obtained from the trustee. List the matters of importance to the auditor that might be found either in the indenture or in the confirmation obtained from the trustee. Explain briefly the reason for the auditor's interest in each of the items.

16–73. If a client rents rather than owns its building, it is customary for the auditor to read the lease. List the items that might be found in a lease that would be of interest and significance to the auditor.

16-74. You were engaged to examine the financial statements of Ronlyn Corporation for the year ended June 30, 1987.

On May 1, 1987, the Corporation borrowed $500,000 from Second National Bank to finance plant expansion. The long-term note agreement provided for the annual payment of principal and interest over five years. The existing plant was pledged as security for the loan.

Required:

a. What are the audit objectives in the examination of long-term debt?
b. Prepare an audit program for the examination of the long-term note agreement between Ronlyn and Second National Bank.

(AICPA adapted)

16-75. The following covenants are extracted from the indenture of a bond issue. The indenture provides that failure to comply with its terms in any respect automatically advances the due date of the loan to the date of noncompliance (the maturity date is 20 years hence in the absence of any acts of default).

1. "The debtor company shall endeavor to maintain a working capital ratio of 2 to 1 at all times, and in any fiscal year following a failure to maintain said ratio, the company shall restrict compensation of officers to a total of $100,000. Officers for this purpose shall include chairman of the board of directors, president, all vice presidents, secretary, and treasurer."
2. "The debtor company shall keep all property that is security for this debt insured against loss by fire to the extent of 100 percent of its actual value. Policies of insurance comprising this protection shall be filed with the trustee."
3. "The debtor company shall pay all taxes legally assessed against property that is security for this debt within the time provided by law for payment without penalty and shall deposit receipted tax bills or equally acceptable evidence of payment of same with the trustee."
4. "A sinking fund shall be deposited with the trustee by semiannual payments of $300,000, from which the trustee shall, in his discretion, purchase bonds of this issue."

Required:

Give any audit steps or reporting requirements you believe should be taken or recognized in connection with each one of the covenants.

(AICPA adapted)

Part 4
Completing the Work and Reporting the Results

Chapter 17
Completing the Audit

This chapter deals with auditing procedures and considerations that are part of the completion phase of an audit but are not related to specific transaction cycles or accounts. The completion phase takes place primarily after the balance sheet date. These procedures entail many subjective decisions requiring judgment and experience, and thus are usually performed by the senior members of the engagement team.

The judgments made during this phase of an audit are often crucial to the ultimate outcome of the engagement. Accordingly, the procedures employed should reflect the auditor's (1) overall confidence (or concern) about key aspects of the financial statements; (2) evaluation of the risk factors affecting the financial health of the business; and (3) confidence in representations made by management. The procedures covered in this chapter often bring to light matters that are of major concern in forming an opinion on the financial statements.

First, tests for contingent liabilities are described, followed by a discussion and illustrations of lawyers' letters (dealing with litigation, claims, and assessments) and client representation letters. Then, because questions may arise whose resolution requires the auditor to conduct research, sources frequently used in researching auditing problems are presented. The critical process of summarizing and evaluating the audit findings is described next, and two review functions performed during the completion phase of the audit—the working paper review and the review of the financial statements for appropriate disclosure—are discussed. Finally, the auditor's responsibilities for subsequent events are presented, and the administrative details that remain to be taken care of at the end of an engagement are described.

Tests for Contingent Liabilities

A contingency may be defined as an existing condition, situation, or set of circumstances involving uncertainty as to possible gain (gain contingency) or loss (loss contingency) that will be resolved when one or more future events occur or fail to occur.

Accounting Overview

Contingencies that might result in gains, such as claims against others for patent infringement, usually are not recorded until realized. Adequate disclosure in the notes to the financial statements should be made of contingencies that might result in gains; however, misleading implications as to the likelihood of realization should be avoided.

In many cases, the existence of a loss contingency results in a charge to income and the recording of a liability, for example, a probable loss resulting from the guarantee of the indebtedness of others or an obligation relating to a product warranty or defect. In other cases, such as a probable loss from uncollectible receivables, the existence of a loss contingency results in the write-down of an asset (often by means of an allowance account) and a charge to income. Still other loss contingencies result only in financial statement disclosure, but no recording of a charge to income, an asset write-down, or a liability; an example would be litigation against the company the outcome of which is uncertain. (Loss contingencies arising from litigation, claims, and assessments are discussed in detail in the next section of this chapter.) Last, some loss contingencies need not be either accrued (recorded) or disclosed, for example, the uninsured risk of loss or damage of enterprise property from fire or other hazards. The following tabulation summarizes the proper financial accounting and reporting for material loss contingencies:[1]

	Amount of Loss Can Be Reasonably Estimated	
Likelihood of Occurrence	*Yes*	*No*
Probable	Accrue; consider need to disclose	Disclose
Reasonably possible	Disclose	Disclose
Remote	Not accrued or disclosed	

[1]Departures from unqualified opinions because of potential losses arising from uncertainties are discussed in Chapter 18.

Paragraph 3 of SFAS No. 5, *Accounting for Contingencies* (Accounting Standards Section C59.104), defines the ranges of likelihood of occurrence, as follows:

- Probable—the future event(s) is (are) likely to occur.
- Reasonably possible—the chance of the future event(s) occurring is more than remote but less than likely.
- Remote—the chance of the future event(s) occurring is slight.

When a material loss contingency involves an unasserted claim or assessment, disclosure is not required if there is no evidence that the assertion of a claim is probable. If it is considered probable that the claim will be asserted and there is a reasonable possibility that the outcome will be unfavorable, disclosure is required.

Auditing Procedures

Auditing loss contingencies is one of the most difficult aspects of many examinations, and the variety of conditions encountered makes it impossible to describe the auditor's task definitively. Even in the best and most responsibly managed companies, a loss contingency requiring evaluation can be overlooked. Following is a description of the kinds of procedures usually undertaken to identify material loss contingencies.

The auditor should be cognizant of possible contingent liabilities while performing tests for unrecorded liabilities, described in Chapter 13. For example, when inspecting the minute books, contracts, and other documents, the auditor should be alert for matters indicating contingencies to be investigated. When inquiring of management as to the existence of unrecorded liabilities, the auditor should also review the possibility of loss contingencies. Management's statement as to loss contingencies should be included in the representation letter, discussed later.

Accounts receivable may have been discounted with banks or discount companies and the recourse aspect not recorded in the accounts. An auditor may find a clue to the existence of such receivables if the accounts contain discount transactions such as payments of interest unrelated to recorded debt obligations. Indications of such transactions should be investigated.

A corporation may guarantee payment of the principal amount of indebtedness of another corporation and perhaps also interest and sinking fund payments. If the client guarantor is a parent company and the indebtedness guaranteed is that of an affiliate or a subsidiary, the existence of the guarantee should not be difficult to discern. If there is no apparent relationship between the guarantor and the obligor corporation, and if the guarantor has not been called on to make payments under the guarantee, an auditor must rely on a review of corporate minutes and contractual arrangements, and inquiries of officials of the guarantor corporation for information, including the representation letter from management.

Although it is customary to insure against liability for damages claimed by employees and the public, insurance policies usually do not cover unlimited liabilities and not all companies carry adequate insurance against all potential claims. Furthermore, unusual claims for damages may arise from alleged breach of contract, failure to deliver goods, antitrust violations, existence of foreign substances in a company's product, and other causes. The auditor should inquire about possible liabilities of that general character. Possible sources of information for the auditor include the client's risk manager, risk consultants, and insurance agents or brokers who provide insurance coverage.

Some claims may not be referred to the client's counsel. For example, salespeople may claim commissions in excess of those paid or accrued, or employees who have been dismissed may claim salaries or other compensation for uncompleted terms of service. Often, those claims are handled as purely administrative matters and may not be referred to counsel unless they are substantial in amount. If the auditor learns of a possible material loss contingency from those types of claims, such as from an entire union, the opinion of the client's counsel should be obtained with respect to the possible liability. (See the next section, "Lawyers' Letters.")

Occasionally a company disputes a claim, resorts to litigation, and has a judgment entered against it. If the case is appealed and a bond is given pending final decision, execution of the judgment may be stayed. Such a judgment is seldom entered in the accounts because many business executives consider recording judgments an admission of liability and do not permit recognition of a claim that they propose to fight to be shown as a liability. The auditor should obtain the opinion of the client's counsel in these areas.

Auditors ordinarily must perform additional procedures to obtain sufficient competent evidential matter concerning litigation, claims, and assessments. Those procedures are discussed in the following section.

Lawyers' Letters

With respect to one particular group of loss contingencies—litigation, claims, and assessments—the auditor is required by paragraph 4 of SAS No. 12, *Inquiry of a Client's Lawyer Concerning Litigation, Claims, and Assessments* (AU Section 337.04), to obtain evidential matter related to the following factors:

a. The existence of a condition, situation, or set of circumstances indicating an uncertainty as to the possible loss to an entity arising from litigation, claims, and assessments.

b. The period in which the underlying cause for legal action occurred.

c. The degree of probability of an unfavorable outcome.

d. The amount or range of potential loss.

The term *litigation, claims, and assessments* encompasses both pending and threatened litigation, claims, and assessments and unasserted claims and assessments.

Auditing Procedures

Management is responsible for adopting policies and procedures to identify, evaluate, and account for litigation, claims, and assessments. Accordingly, the auditor's procedures with respect to such matters should include

- Inquiring of management about the policies and procedures adopted for identifying, evaluating, and accounting for litigation, claims, and assessments.
- Near the completion of the field work, obtaining from management a description and evaluation of litigation, claims, and assessments that existed at the date of the balance sheet being reported on, and during the period from the balance sheet date to the date the information is furnished.
- Examining documents related to litigation, claims, and assessments, including correspondence and invoices from lawyers.
- Requesting management to send a letter of audit inquiry to those lawyers with whom they consulted concerning litigation, claims, and assessments.
- Obtaining assurance from management—preferably in the representation letter, discussed later—that all contingencies, including litigation, claims, and assessments, required to be disclosed by SFAS No. 5 have been disclosed.
- Obtaining assurance from management—preferably in the representation letter—that it has disclosed all unasserted claims that counsel has advised it are probable of assertion and must be disclosed in accordance with SFAS No. 5, and, with the client's permission, informing counsel that the client has given this assurance to the auditor.

Other procedures, undertaken for different purposes, may also disclose the existence of litigation, claims, and assessments. Such other procedures include reading minutes, contracts, agreements, leases, and correspondence with taxing authorities.

Inquiry of a Client's Lawyer

The auditor can readily ascertain the existence of litigation, claims, and assessments when provisions for losses are recorded in the accounts. Also, awareness of events that are likely to give or have given rise to litigation, claims, or assessments may be gained in the course of making routine audit inquiries and performing tests for unrecorded and contingent liabilities. Certain events, however, giving rise to litigation, claims, and assessments, such as patent infringement or price fixing, may be less susceptible of detection in an audit. As noted in the report of the Commission on Auditors' Responsibilities, ''Auditors are neither trained nor necessarily able to detect violations of those laws or of the myriad other laws that govern corporate conduct, and they have not traditionally been considered responsible for detecting such violations.''[2]

[2] *Report, Conclusions, and Recommendations*, 1978, p. 43.

During the early 1970s, as the business environment became more litigious, a great deal of attention was given to the need to disclose pending and foreseeable legal claims. As a result, SAS No. 12, *Inquiry of a Client's Lawyer Concerning Litigation, Claims, and Assessments* (AU Section 337), was issued in January 1976. The American Bar Association (ABA) at about the same time issued a "Statement of Policy Regarding Lawyers' Responses to Auditors' Requests for Information," which is reproduced in Appendix C to SAS No. 12. It is now necessary for the auditor, client, and lawyer all to become involved in determining which litigation, claims, and assessments need to be disclosed.

In the past, lawyers' responses to broad requests for information were the primary sources of information concerning litigation, claims, and assessments. As can be seen from the specimen letters of audit inquiry that appear in Appendix A to SAS No. 12 and in a June 1983 Interpretation of that SAS, management is now the primary source for such information; the lawyer is expected to corroborate the completeness of the information supplied by management as to pending or threatened litigation, claims, and assessments.

Specifically, SAS No. 12 requires, among other things, the following to be included in the client's letter of audit inquiry to the lawyer:

- A list prepared by management (or a request by management that the lawyer prepare a list) that describes and evaluates pending or threatened litigation, claims, and assessments with respect to which the lawyer has been engaged. When the list is prepared by the client, the lawyer's response should state that the list is complete (or identify any omissions) and comment on the client's evaluation.

- A list prepared by management (the lawyer will not prepare this list) that describes and evaluates unasserted claims, if any, that management considers to be probable of assertion, and that, if asserted, would have at least a reasonable possibility of an unfavorable outcome, with respect to which the lawyer has been engaged. The lawyer's response will not comment on the completeness of the list, but should comment on the client's descriptions and evaluations.

The lawyer should be informed in the client's letter of audit inquiry, or in a separate letter from the auditor, of management's assurance to the auditor concerning unasserted claims and assessments.

If the lawyer has formed a professional conclusion that the client should consider disclosure of an unasserted possible claim or assessment, the lawyer will, as a matter of professional responsibility to the client, consult with the client concerning the applicable requirements of SFAS No. 5. While the lawyer will not comment on the completeness of the client's list of unasserted claims, the lawyer will, at the client's request, confirm to the auditor this professional responsibility to the client.

Inquiries generally should be sent to all lawyers who have devoted substantive attention to a matter on behalf of the client in the form of legal consultation or representation. The client may not wish, however, to send a letter to a lawyer whose only relationship with the client was representation in a case that was closed during the year or to lawyers handling routine matters such as collection of overdue accounts. If the auditor is satisfied that the case is closed and other auditing procedures do not indicate that the lawyer was involved in other matters, or that lawyers were involved in routine matters only, the auditor may accede to the client's request.

The specimen letters of audit inquiry in Appendix A to SAS No. 12 and in the related Interpretation include a "response date" that, combined with proper timing in mailing letters of audit inquiry, is intended to minimize the need for supplemental letters of audit inquiry. Letters of audit inquiry should be mailed at a date that provides the lawyer sufficient time to meet the response date (two weeks is ordinarily sufficient time). The response date should allow sufficient time prior to the date of the audit report for the auditor to evaluate the response and make supplemental inquiries, if necessary.

Evaluating Lawyers' Responses

In evaluating responses from lawyers, the auditor should consider whether there is any reason to doubt their professional qualifications and reputation. If, as will often be the case, the auditor is familiar with the lawyer's professional reputation, there would be no need to make specific inquiries in this regard. An auditor who is not familiar with a lawyer representing the client in what appears to be a significant case may wish to inquire as to the lawyer's professional background, reputation, and standing in the legal and financial community and to consider information available in such legal publications as the *Martindale-Hubbell Law Directory*. Once satisfied in this regard, the auditor can accept the lawyer's opinion regarding a legal matter, unless it appears to be unreasonable.

The lawyer's response should be read in its totality to ascertain its overall responsiveness to the letter of audit inquiry and to determine whether it conflicts with information otherwise known to the auditor. The language used in responses from lawyers takes many forms, and definitive guidance does not exist on the effect of the language used on the type of opinion the auditor may express. Certain attributes, however, ordinarily lead to an unqualified opinion, while others ordinarily preclude an unqualified opinion.

Responses Permitting an Unqualified Opinion. Responses from lawyers that enable the auditor to render an unqualified opinion usually (1) indicate a high probability of a favorable outcome or that the matters in question are not material, and (2) do not indicate that the lawyer has not made a reasonable investigation of the case. The following examples of actual language from lawyers' letters would permit the auditor to render an unqualified opinion:

- It is our opinion that if the matter is litigated, it will be successfully defended on behalf of the Company.
- We believe plaintiff's assertions to be without merit.

- In connection with your examination of the financial statements of the Company, please be advised that to the best of our knowledge and belief, there were no material pending claims in which the Company was involved as of (date).
- The possibility of an unfavorable outcome is remote (slight).

Responses Leading to a "Subject to" Opinion. If because of inherent uncertainties a lawyer is unable to respond concerning the likelihood of an unfavorable outcome of material litigation, claims, or assessments or concerning the amount or range of potential loss, the auditor ordinarily will conclude that a "subject to" qualification, due to uncertainty, is appropriate (paragraph 14 of SAS No. 12 [AU Section 337.14]). The lawyer may not be able to respond because the factors influencing the likelihood of an unfavorable outcome are not within the competence of lawyers to judge, historical experience of the entity in similar litigation or the experience of other entities may not be relevant or available, or the amount or range of possible loss may vary widely at different stages of litigation. The following examples of actual language from lawyers' letters would, if related to material items that are not remedied, result in qualified "subject to" opinions:

- No demand for monetary damages has been made in the complaint. Consequently, I am unable to give an estimate as to potential loss.
- In the case of nonpersonal injury claims, the Company should be contacted for further information regarding such claims. Our substantive attention to the claims set forth in the exhibits hereto has been limited either to coordinating activities and communication between the Company and its risk managers or to a lesser extent facilitating communications between the Company and the various claimants.

In the latter example, the lawyer did not feel that the factors influencing the likelihood of unfavorable outcomes were within his competence to judge. The company then employed a specialist to determine the likelihood of unfavorable outcomes and amounts or ranges of possible losses. The auditor was able to conclude that the specialist's findings were suitable for corroborating the information related to these claims in the financial statements and a qualified opinion was not required.

Some lawyers may use language that they hope will satisfy the auditor but that actually says very little. Examples of that kind of language are provided in a June 1983 Interpretation of SAS No. 12, as follows:

- This action involves unique characteristics wherein authoritative legal precedents do not seem to exist. We believe that the plaintiff will have serious problems establishing the company's liability under the act; nevertheless, if the plaintiff is successful, the award may be substantial.
- It is our opinion that the company will be able to assert meritorious defenses to the action. (The term *meritorious defenses* indicates that the com-

pany's defenses will not be summarily dismissed by the court; it does not necessarily indicate counsel's opinion that the company will prevail.)

- We believe the action can be settled for less than the damages claimed.

- We are unable to express an opinion as to the merits of the litigation at this time. The company believes there is absolutely no merit to the litigation. (If client's counsel, with the benefit of all relevant information, is unable to conclude that the likelihood of an unfavorable outcome is "remote," it is unlikely that management would be able to form a judgment to that effect.)

- In our opinion, the company has a substantial chance of prevailing in this action. (A "substantial chance," a "reasonable opportunity," and similar terms indicate more uncertainty than an opinion that the company will prevail.)

The Interpretation states that an auditor who is uncertain as to the meaning of a lawyer's evaluation should request clarification either in a follow-up letter or in a conference with the lawyer and client, which should be appropriately documented. If the lawyer is still unable to give, either in writing or orally, an unequivocal evaluation of the likelihood of an unfavorable outcome, the auditor should consider the effect of the resulting uncertainty on the audit opinion.

Responses Resulting in Scope Limitations.   Responses that indicate or imply that the lawyer refuses to furnish or is withholding information ordinarily should, if not remedied, be considered an audit scope limitation (paragraphs 10 and 11 of SAS No. 2, *Reports on Audited Financial Statements* [AU Sections 509.10 and .11]). For example, the lawyer may state that the reply is limited because of the policy of the law firm or the impracticability of reviewing the files, or for reasons not given. Normally, such limitations would be considered significant, since the auditor usually cannot evaluate the effect of withheld information.

A response indicating that the newness of a case precludes evaluating it does not provide sufficient evidence to support an unqualified opinion. The following examples of actual language from lawyers' letters would, if related to material items that are not resolved, constitute limitations on the scope of the engagement requiring modification of the scope paragraph of the audit report and an "except for" opinion:

- The claim has been received by this office only recently, and is being investigated. At this time it is not possible to predict the outcome of the litigation.

- This suit for declaratory judgment by the plaintiff presents some risk for the Bank depending upon the values assigned to parcels of realty transferred to the Bank to reduce a preexisting debt owed by the plaintiff to the Bank. We have not been supplied with sufficient information to determine whether a deficiency existed which warranted the note and mortgage obtained from the plaintiff. At present, we can only assume that the Bank was justified in obtaining this obligation.

Sometimes a response from a lawyer contains the phrase ''not material'' or ''would not have a material effect on the financial condition of the company or the results of its operations.'' Responses containing these or similar phrases are acceptable and do not constitute an audit scope limitation if the response itself provides data sufficient for the auditor to evaluate the lawyer's conclusion. Such responses are also acceptable if materiality guidelines for the lawyer's use on both an individual item and an aggregate basis were included in the letter of audit inquiry from management, as the authors believe should be done. The auditor should be satisfied with the materiality guidelines provided to the client's lawyer. A materiality guideline in the inquiry letter might read as follows: ''This request is limited to contingencies amounting to $XXX individually or items involving lesser amounts that exceed $XXX in the aggregate.''

If the lawyer disclaims responsibility for informing the auditor of any changes in the information reported to the auditor from the date of the response to the date of the auditor's report, it may be necessary to send a supplemental letter of audit inquiry. Factors to be considered in determining the need for a supplemental letter of audit inquiry include: the length of time between the date of the response and the date of the auditor's report, the number and significance of matters included in the lawyer's response, the probability of more current developments related to matters included in the lawyer's response, and the reliability of the client's policies and procedures for identifying, evaluating, and accounting for litigation, claims, and assessments. The auditor may determine that a supplemental letter of inquiry is not required, even though the lawyer's response is dated considerably earlier, for example, 7 to 10 days earlier, than the auditor's report. In those circumstances, the auditor should ordinarily arrange for an oral update and should document it in the working papers.

Inside Counsel. The duties of an inside counsel may vary from handling specialized litigation to acting as general counsel with supervisory authority in all legal matters, including the selection of outside counsel to represent or advise the client on specific matters.

If inside counsel acts as general counsel, evidential matter gathered by and obtained from inside counsel may provide the necessary corroboration for the auditor. Letters of audit inquiry to outside counsel may be appropriate if inside general counsel has retained outside counsel to represent or advise the client on certain matters. Information provided by inside counsel is not a substitute for information that outside counsel refuses to furnish.

Changes or Resignations of Lawyers. Shortly before completing the examination, the auditor should inquire of the client as to whether the client has changed lawyers or whether any lawyer to whom a letter of audit inquiry was sent has resigned or indicated an intention to resign. If the client replies affirmatively, the auditor should inquire as to the reasons. The legal profession's Code of Professional Responsibility requires that, in some circumstances, lawyers must resign if their advice concerning financial accounting for and reporting of litigation, claims, and assessments is disregarded by their clients.

Need for Clarification of Sources of Information on Legal Matters

To correct some of the misunderstandings about the appropriate source of information on legal matters, some groups have suggested that auditors should assume more responsibility for the detection and disclosure of events that are likely to give rise to litigation, claims, and assessments. As a result, the Commission on Auditors' Responsibilities proposed a change in the information presented to users. The Commission suggested that a statement be included in annual reports ''that management believes that all material uncertainties have been appropriately accounted for or disclosed, and that it has consulted with legal counsel with respect to the need for, and the nature of, the accounting for or disclosure of legal matters.''[3] Obviously, this proposal would not satisfy the demands for greater audit assurance in this area. The Commission suggested that such demands might be satisfied by increasing the scope and extent of assurances provided by lawyers. This suggestion makes sense because, in the authors' view, it is not reasonable to expect auditors to undertake responsibilities that would require the knowledge, skills, and experience of members of another profession, namely, law.

Client Representations

The auditor is required by SAS No. 19, *Client Representations* (AU Section 333), to obtain a representation letter from management. The representation letter provides written evidence that the auditor has made certain inquiries of management; ordinarily it documents oral responses given to the auditor, thus reducing the possibility of errors or misunderstandings. A representation letter is one kind of competent evidence, but it is not sufficient in itself to provide the auditor with a reasonable basis for forming an opinion.

Written Representations

The representation letter illustrated in Appendix A to SAS No. 19 and reproduced in Figure 17.1 incorporates the written representations that should ordinarily be obtained by the auditor. The letter should be modified to meet the circumstances of the particular engagement and the nature and basis of presentation of the financial statements being examined. For example, if the auditor

[3]*Ibid.* p. 50.

is reporting on consolidated financial statements, the written representations obtained from the parent company's management should specify that they pertain to the consolidated financial statements. If the auditor is reporting on the parent company's separate financial statements as well, the letter should also extend to them.

Written representations relating to management's knowledge or intent should be obtained when the auditor believes they are necessary to complement other auditing procedures or when corroborating evidential matter is unavailable. For example, after the auditor has performed tests for unrecorded liabilities and has not detected any, written representation should be obtained to document that management has no knowledge of any liabilities that have not been accrued. Any liabilities known to management but not accrued, through oversight, would be brought to the auditor's attention in this manner. Such a written representation, however, does not relieve the auditor of responsibility for planning the audit to identify material unrecorded liabilities. Information may be unintentionally overlooked or intentionally withheld from the auditor. Accordingly, the auditor must still perform all the usual tests to corroborate the accuracy and reliability of representations made by management.

In some cases, evidential matter to corroborate written representations is limited. For example, income taxes may not be provided for undistributed income of a subsidiary because management of the parent company represents that it intends to permanently reinvest that income, but the auditor may not be able to obtain sufficient information through other auditing procedures to corroborate that intent. Unless the auditor obtains evidential matter to the contrary, reliance on the truthfulness of management's representations is reasonable, as discussed in paragraph 10 of SAS No. 16, *The Independent Auditor's Responsibility for the Detection of Errors or Irregularities* (AU Section 327.10).

Materiality. Paragraph 5 of SAS No. 19 (AU Section 333.05) states that "management's representations may be limited to matters that are considered either individually or collectively material to the financial statements, provided management and the auditor have reached an understanding on the limits of materiality for this purpose." The limits of materiality may differ in different circumstances, for example, amounts that affect only the balance sheet versus amounts that affect income. The auditor may wish to request management to specify in the representation letter the materiality limits agreed on.

Definitions. Certain terms used in the specimen representation letter in Figure 17.1 are defined in the authoritative literature, for example, irregularities (SAS No. 16 [AU Section 327]), related party transactions (SFAS No. 57 [Accounting Standards Section R36]), and contingencies (SFAS No. 5 [Accounting Standards Section C59]). The auditor may wish to furnish the applicable literature to the client and request that the client refer to its receipt in the representation letter.

Figure 17.1 Illustrative Client Representation Letter

[Client's Letterhead]

(Date of Auditor's Report)

(To Independent Auditor)

In connection with your examination of the (identification of financial statements) of (name of client) as of (date) and for the (period of examination) for the purpose of expressing an opinion as to whether the (consolidated) financial statements present fairly the financial position, results of operations, and changes in financial position of (name of client) in conformity with generally accepted accounting principles (other comprehensive basis of accounting), we confirm, to the best of our knowledge and belief, the following representations made to you during your examination.

1. We are responsible for the fair presentation in the (consolidated) financial statements of financial position, results of operations, and changes in financial position in conformity with generally accepted accounting principles (other comprehensive basis of accounting).

2. We have made available to you all—

   a. Financial records and related data.

   b. Minutes of the meetings of stockholders, directors, and committees of directors, or summaries of actions of recent meetings for which minutes have not yet been prepared.

3. There have been no—

   a. Irregularities involving management or employees who have significant roles in the system of internal accounting control.

   b. Irregularities involving other employees that could have a material effect on the financial statements.

   c. Communications from regulatory agencies concerning noncompliance with, or deficiencies in, financial reporting practices that could have a material effect on the financial statements.

4. We have no plans or intentions that may materially affect the carrying value or classification of assets and liabilities.

5. The following have been properly recorded or disclosed in the financial statements:

   a. Related party transactions and related amounts receivable or payable, including sales, purchases, loans, transfers, leasing arrangements, and guarantees.

   b. Capital stock repurchase options or agreements or capital stock reserved for options, warrants, conversions, or other requirements.

   c. Arrangements with financial institutions involving compensating

(Continued)

Figure 17.1 *Continued*

---

balances or other arrangements involving restrictions on cash balances and line-of-credit or similar arrangements.

  d. Agreements to repurchase assets previously sold.

6. There are no—

  a. Violations or possible violations of laws or regulations whose effects should be considered for disclosure in the financial statements or as a basis for recording a loss contingency.

  b. Other material liabilities or gain or loss contingencies that are required to be accrued or disclosed by Statement of Financial Accounting Standards No. 5.

7. There are no unasserted claims or assessments that our lawyer has advised us are probable of assertion and must be disclosed in accordance with Statement of Financial Accounting Standards No. 5.

8. There are no material transactions that have not been properly recorded in the accounting records underlying the financial statements.

9. Provision, when material, has been made to reduce excess or obsolete inventories to their estimated net realizable value.

10. The company has satisfactory title to all owned assets, and there are no liens or encumbrances on such assets nor has any asset been pledged.

11. Provision has been made for any material loss to be sustained in the fulfillment of, or from inability to fulfill, any sales commitments.

12. Provision has been made for any material loss to be sustained as a result of purchase commitments for inventory quantities in excess of normal requirements or at prices in excess of the prevailing market prices.

13. We have complied with all aspects of contractual agreements that would have a material effect on the financial statements in the event of noncompliance.

14. No events have occurred subsequent to the balance sheet date that would require adjustment to, or disclosure in, the financial statements.

———————————————

(Name of Chief Executive
Officer and Title)

———————————————

(Name of Chief Financial
Officer and Title)

Dating and Signing. The representation letter should be addressed to the auditor and should be dated as of the date of the auditor's report. Representation letters should ordinarily be signed by both the chief executive and chief financial officers. The signatures of other members of management will suffice, however, in those circumstances in which the auditor is satisfied that they are responsible for and knowledgeable about the matters covered by the representations.

Scope Limitations. In rare instances, management may refuse to furnish a written representation that the auditor believes is essential or may refuse to sign the representation letter. SAS No. 19 (AU Section 333.11) notes that either refusal constitutes a limitation on the scope of the auditor's examination sufficient to preclude an unqualified opinion (paragraphs 10 and 11 of SAS No. 2, *Reports on Audited Financial Statements* [AU Sections 509.10 and .11]). Auditors must consider the effects of a refusal to furnish a written representation on their ability to rely on other management representations. Executives are expected to understand their legal and ethical responsibilities for financial statement representations. Thus, they should also understand that the representation letter only specifies some of those responsibilities but does not increase them. Refusal to sign the letter must be taken as a signal either of withheld evidence or of inadequately understood responsibilities; either destroys the basis for an unqualified opinion.

Representations from Others. In certain circumstances, the auditor may want to obtain representation letters from persons other than management of the client. For example, an auditor who examines the financial statements of a subsidiary but not those of the parent company may want to obtain representations from management or the auditor of the parent company regarding information that might require adjustment or disclosure in the financial statements on which the auditor is to report.

A refusal by the parent company or principal auditor to furnish the written representations believed by the secondary auditor to be essential to the examination of the financial statements of the subsidiary constitutes a scope limitation, as described earlier. It is preferable to obtain the written representations from the parent company, particularly if the principal auditor does not rely on the secondary auditor's report, for example, if the subsidiary on which the secondary auditor is reporting is insignificant to the consolidated statements.

Representations in Other Than Audit Engagements

An accountant is well advised to obtain written representation from clients when engaged to perform services other than audits. Examples of such services would be performing limited reviews of interim financial information, engagements to compile or review annual financial statements, or association with a client's projection or forecast. Generally, the guidance contained in this section relating to written audit representations can be appropriately modified for a particular nonaudit service. As discussed in Chapter 19, AICPA professional standards currently require a CPA to obtain client representations in the course of performing certain specified nonaudit services.

Researching Auditing Problems

When performing an examination of financial statements leading to the expression of an opinion as to whether they are presented fairly in conformity with generally accepted accounting principles (GAAP), the auditor is obligated to conduct the examination in accordance with generally accepted auditing standards (GAAS). GAAS serve a dual purpose: They implicitly require an auditor to be aware of all pertinent literature—the first general standard—and they serve as a first level of research to resolve auditing problems. For example, an auditor may be confronted for the first time with the need to issue a letter for underwriters in connection with an engagement that includes the filing of the auditor's report on financial statements with the SEC under the Securities Act of 1933. The accepted form and content of the letter, as well as important suggestions as to procedures to be followed and cautions to be observed, can be readily researched in SAS No. 49, *Letters for Underwriters* (AU Section 634).

Of course, the auditor should also be familiar with AICPA Auditing Interpretations (AU Section 9000). Interpretations are not as authoritative as pronouncements of the Auditing Standards Board, but they are issued by the staff of the Auditing Standards Division to provide guidance on the application of Statements on Auditing Standards, and CPAs may have to justify departures from Auditing Interpretations. Thus, if an auditor is faced with an auditing problem with respect to, for example, related party transactions (dealt with in AU Section 335), Interpretations in AU Section 9335 should be consulted for additional guidance.

An auditor who does not have prior experience in an industry may be engaged to audit a company in that industry. The auditor should, among other considerations, determine whether an industry audit (or audit and accounting) guide has been issued by the AICPA for that industry. An auditor engaged, for example, to examine a savings and loan association should read the latest edition of the Audit and Accounting Guide for that industry. The guides have authoritative status similar to that of Auditing Interpretations.

Most auditors should be familiar with and have available a copy of the latest edition of *Accounting Trends and Techniques*, published by the AICPA. Issues of disclosure and presentation can be readily researched in this publication. It also contains wording of auditor's reports in unusual situations. While the publication is nonauthoritative, it includes examples from recent practice and can serve to document an auditor's diligence.

An auditor may be faced with a question regarding independence, which is an ethical consideration. In that case, reference should be made to the Code of Professional Ethics of the AICPA (and similar pronouncements of the relevant state society, state board of accountancy, and the SEC).

Thus, there exists a substantial body of authoritative and nonauthoritative literature, which is (or should be) available from libraries to help auditors solve problems concerning auditing standards and procedures. In practice, most auditors are familiar with these sources and refer to them frequently.

Not all problems encountered, however, can be so readily researched. Thus, an auditor seeking to gain assurance of access to all major sources of information on a subject must have other resources. Many state societies and the AICPA offer technical services to assist in research; a local university may also be of help. These organizations often use computer-assisted research sources, such as NAARS, LEXIS, and INFORM. Auditing texts may provide additional guidance. An auditor may also consult relevant trade associations or fellow practitioners with appropriate background and experience.

When a problem is identified, the auditor must document the related issues, develop an approach to obtaining research assistance, evaluate the material uncovered as to relevance and authoritative status, and reach a conclusion. It is important to engagement efficiency and client relations that problems be identified early in the engagement, so that the time spent solving them does not unduly delay completion of the engagement. It is also important that the means by which auditing problems have been resolved be clearly documented in the working papers.

Summarizing and Evaluating the Audit Findings

The discussion of materiality in Chapter 6 noted that auditors frequently maintain a list of unadjusted differences, often referred to as a "score sheet," that summarizes the errors and potential financial statement adjustments found in the course of the various tests and procedures performed throughout the audit. In this context, errors may be factual misstatements, unintentional mistakes, misapplications of GAAP, and unreasonable accounting estimates. Normally the score sheet includes errors arising in the current year, but, as discussed later, may also include waived adjustments from prior years' audits that have an effect on the current year's financial statements. The score sheet serves as the central means of evaluating whether the evidence examined by the auditor supports the conclusion that the financial statements are presented fairly in conformity with generally accepted accounting principles. Neither individual nor aggregated errors should cause the financial statements to be materially misstated. If they do, either the financial statements will have to be revised by the client, or the auditor will have to qualify the opinion or give an adverse opinion because of deficiencies in the application of GAAP. Usually the auditor and the client are able to reach agreement so that a qualified or an adverse opinion is not necessary.

Categories of Errors to Be Evaluated

Authoritative auditing literature addresses the auditor's consideration of errors. SAS No. 39, *Audit Sampling* (AU Section 350), requires the auditor to consider "projected error results for all audit sampling applications and all known errors from nonsampling applications" (para. 30) in the aggregate in evaluating whether the financial statements as a whole may be materially misstated. SAS No. 47, *Audit Risk and Materiality in Conducting an Audit* (AU Section 312), expands on this concept by stating that "the auditor should aggregate errors that the entity has not corrected in a way that enables him to consider whether, in relation to individual amounts, subtotals, or totals in the financial statements, they materially misstate the financial statements taken as a whole" (para. 27).

With regard to the amounts to be aggregated, SAS No. 47 states

> The aggregation of errors should include the auditor's best estimate of the total error in the account balances or classes of transactions that he has examined (hereafter referred to as likely error), not just the amount of errors he specifically identifies (hereafter referred to as known error). . . . Projected error [from audit sampling, if used], along with the results of other substantive tests, contributes to the auditor's assessment of likely error in the balance or class. (para. 28)

As defined in SAS No. 47, likely error includes unreasonable differences between accounting estimates as determined by the client and the amounts supported by audit evidence. SAS No. 47 states

> Since no one accounting estimate can be considered accurate with certainty, the auditor recognizes that a difference between an estimated amount best supported by the audit evidence and the estimated amount included in the financial statements may be reasonable, and such difference would not be considered to be a likely error. However, if the auditor believes the estimated amount included in the financial statements is unreasonable, he should treat the difference between that estimate and the closest reasonable estimate as a likely error and aggregate it with other likely errors. (para. 29)

Preparing and Using the Score Sheet

The exact form of the score sheet used to aggregate errors, and even what it is called, varies in practice. Its complexity depends on the complexity of the engagement (e.g., extensive subsidiary operations may require a more complex format) and circumstances (e.g., if significant errors are expected or many accounts are considered potentially troublesome, a more structured, formal format may be required). Additionally, professional standards may require specific documentation.

In general, the score sheet is a multiple-column worksheet. In the extreme left columns, the auditor records the nature of errors identified, for example, descriptions of known errors from nonsampling procedures and projected errors from sampling procedures in the inventory accounts. The amount in question is then "spread" to show its impact on assets, liabilities and owners' equity, and income, such as a failure to record on a timely basis $10,000 of inventory received before year-end that might result in a $10,000 understatement of assets and a $10,000 understatement of liabilities.

A single document that summarizes and accumulates errors identified in the various accounts, such as receivables and payables, facilitates the auditor's evaluation of the overall audit findings. For example, a review of the score sheet may reveal that individually immaterial errors taken together have a material impact on income or some other financial statement element. The score sheet is helpful in comparing the results of audit procedures with materiality at the account level, for major groups of accounts (such as current assets), and for the financial statements taken as a whole.

Aggregating and Netting

The issue of aggregating and netting error amounts in the final evaluation of audit evidence is complicated and somewhat controversial. The controversy centers around the appropriateness of netting or offsetting certain errors found during the course of the examination.

In aggregating errors affecting the income statement or balance sheet, likely errors relating to each line item on the financial statements are considered together to determine whether the line item is materially correct. The more "cushion" that exists between the total of likely errors and a larger amount that the auditor considers "material" for the line item, the higher the level of assurance the auditor has that the item is materially correct.

One technique used in practice is to aggregate errors within groupings of financial statement components and to assess materiality at that level and at each successively higher logical subdivision of the financial statements. For example, in assessing the fairness of reported assets, the results of the examination of cash and short-term liquid assets might be aggregated to determine whether the sum of those assets, which enters into the computation of the "quick ratio," is reasonable. Other current assets such as accounts receivable might then be added and another assessment made at the current asset level. Finally, these results would be combined with a similar series of aggregations for noncurrent assets to evaluate reported assets in total. The principle here is that neither the line item itself nor subtotals or important ratios of which the line item is a component should cause the financial statements to be materially misstated.

The way items are added together or offset against each other can significantly affect evaluations of materiality. Some items or events are more significant than others, implying that they should be evaluated individually while others may be evaluated in groups. For example, many auditors consider it inappropriate to aggregate or offset an individually immaterial overstatement of cash with a misstatement in an unrelated account. The inherent sensitivity of the cash account as well as the potential for determining its value precisely often precludes an auditor from treating misstatements of cash in the same manner as misstatements in other accounts. Immaterial inventory misstatements and immaterial receivable misstatements, however, are often offset in determining whether the financial statements as a whole may be materially misstated.

Netting separate items to determine the amount to be compared with materiality raises several questions. Is it acceptable, for example, to net the effect of an error against the effect of a change in accounting principle? Clearly, the answer is no. APB Opinion No. 20, paragraph 38 (Accounting Standards Section A06.133) requires that materiality be considered for the separate effects of each accounting change. Also, netting individually material items to obtain an immaterial total would result in inadequate financial statement disclosure. It is acceptable, however, to net immaterial errors in a particular component of financial statements or in related accounts.[4]

Quantitative Aspects of Materiality Judgments

The question of how large a "difference" must be before it is material has never been definitively answered in the accounting and auditing literature. Many auditors have developed rules of thumb for setting materiality thresholds, such as some percentage of one or more financial statement totals. Net income is a commonly cited base for the assessment of materiality, but there are others, such as total assets, equities, or revenues. As long as investors continue to pay attention to net income in their investment assessments, an audit standard of materiality based on net income is likely to be widely used.

A commonly used figure for materiality is 5 percent of the base that is chosen. That is, if the item under scrutiny is within 5 percent of what it might otherwise be, the difference may be immaterial. Obviously, any rule of thumb, such as 5 percent, must be used with a great deal of caution and careful judgment. Qualitative considerations, as discussed later, can render such a range too broad. Most studies of the subject have generally concluded that a single dollar amount or percentage is not appropriate in all situations. Five to ten percent of net income is frequently used, but is affected in individual cases by nonquantitative criteria.[5] Some examples of quantitative criteria for significance or materiality that have been used by professional and regulatory standard-setting bodies are cited in Table 1 in Appendix C of FASB Statement of Financial Accounting Concepts No. 2. In addition, many auditors assign greater significance to differences that change the client's trend of earnings than to those that do not.

Having established that there may be more than one level of materiality— for example, one level for income statement effects and a higher level in absolute terms for balance sheet effects—the auditor should recognize that an error that affects both statements should be compared with the smaller materiality level in determining whether the error requires correction or can be "waived" as immaterial. For example, a misstated accrual may not materially affect the balance sheet, but may materially affect reported expenses and consequently net income. In that situation, the lower income statement threshold would de-

---

[4]For a contrast in perspectives on this issue between preparers and nonpreparers of financial statements, see J. W. Pattillo, *Concept of Materiality in Financial Reporting* (New York: Financial Executives Research Foundation, 1976).

[5]See J. W. Pattillo, *op. cit.*

termine "materiality." Misclassifications that affect only balance sheet accounts would be material if they exceeded the balance sheet materiality threshold.

While materiality is often viewed as a relative concept (i.e., as a percentage of some base), there may be some dollar threshold at which it would be difficult to judge an error to be irrelevant and thus the nature and cause of the error would be carefully evaluated. For example, a possible misstatement of several hundred thousands of dollars might be carefully scrutinized in any circumstances, even for a multibillion dollar client, although the misstatement did not approach the auditor's materiality threshold.

Qualitative Considerations in Assessing Materiality

The types of errors or misstatements found during an examination may influence the auditor's evaluation of the audit results. Known errors in an account discovered by applying either sampling or nonsampling procedures are easiest to deal with. In most cases, such known errors are corrected in the accounts and entail no further score sheet consideration. Errors that arise from projecting the error results of a sample to the population are more difficult to deal with. While projected errors should be included on the score sheet, a practical difficulty is encountered in correcting the financial statements for these errors, since sampling does not help either the auditor or the client to identify all of the specific components, such as the individual accounts receivable, that may be in error. Additionally, according to sampling theory, the projected error is not the "true" error, but only a presumably close approximation of the "true" error. Therefore, correcting the financial statements for nonspecific "projected errors" may create a risk that actual errors will be introduced into the financial statements. Sample results may be used, however, to identify aspects of an account (e.g., inventory) that deserve special management attention, such as repricing, recounting, or further testing. If such procedures are performed, the auditor will need to adjust the projected error amount based on the results of the procedures.

Because of the inherent limitations of audit procedures, including sampling, an auditor may not discover the true amount of error in an account. For example, an auditor may by chance draw an unrepresentative sample, resulting in a lower (or higher) incidence of error than really exists in the population. To maintain the risk of drawing inappropriate conclusions from sampling applications or other procedures at a low level, the auditor must control both sampling and nonsampling risk through proper planning and risk assessment techniques, as discussed in Chapter 6, and the appropriate selection of other audit procedures.

Evaluating some types of errors involves distinguishing between "hard" errors and "soft" errors and properly characterizing the "soft" errors. A mathematical mistake, omission of a segment of inventory from the total inventory, or an accounting principle error, whether discovered by sampling or nonsampling procedures, may be referred to as "hard" errors. In these cases, the auditor knows there is a problem and can calculate the misstatement. If potential misstatements cannot be calculated precisely but must be estimated, they are described as ''soft'' errors.

Accounting and auditing are not exact sciences and much judgment often goes into developing the accounting numbers presented in the financial statements. The auditor must evaluate financial statement accounts, such as the allowance for doubtful accounts and liability for product warranties, that are estimates and not subject to absolute determination. Using methods that are appropriate in the circumstances but are not exactly the same as those used by the client, the auditor may develop an estimate that differs from that of the client. The auditor should exercise care in developing such estimates and comparing them with client estimates to ensure that client estimates considered to be unreasonable are included with other likely errors and evaluated, and that those deemed to be reasonable are excluded from likely error.

Sometimes the auditor may not be able to establish an estimate of a single amount, but may establish a range of ''reasonableness''; if the client's estimate falls within that range, no score sheet item is created. If the client's estimate falls outside that range, a score sheet item representing the difference between the client's estimate and the nearest point in the range is created. For example, if a client established a product warranty liability for $150,000 and the auditor, by analyzing past trends and the experience of other companies in similar circumstances, established a reasonable range of product warranty liability of between $200,000 and $300,000, the auditor might include on the score sheet $50,000 ($200,000 – $150,000) for possible adjustment by the client. This would be a ''soft'' error; only if the auditor knew the liability must exceed $200,000 could the difference in estimates be called a ''hard'' or ''known'' error.

Other qualitative factors may also influence the auditor's reaction to and assessment of likely errors in the financial statements. These factors may warrant consideration that goes beyond the quantitative significance of the errors, and may cause the auditor greater concern and may prompt other reactions than the quantitative amounts might otherwise indicate. Examples of these factors are

- *The sensitivity of the error*. Bribes, illegal transactions, fraud, and related party transactions, if detected, deserve special auditor attention and may require special disclosures.
- *Business conditions*. For example, in a weak economy or in a company with a weak financial condition, special meaning is sometimes given to materiality, since the future of the company may rest on investors' and creditors' evaluations of the current financial position and recent trends.
- *Contractual arrangements*. Debt covenants, buy–sell agreements, and union contracts may be geared to various financial statement elements or relationships (such as the current ratio).

- *Cause of the misstatement.* Errors that arise because of violations of GAAP (e.g., recording a purchase of a business as a pooling of interests or failing to accrue vacation pay or product warranties) may cause the auditor concern beyond the quantitative significance of the misstatement. Possible long-term effects of the misstatement should be assessed, since later correction of the error may erode investors' confidence in the reporting system.

- *Situations in which the "investor based" materiality rule is difficult to apply.* For entities such as privately owned companies, trusts, and others, the auditor may need to assess the likely users of the financial statements and their interests and designate a materiality level appropriate for their needs. Special user needs may tighten customary materiality standards.

- *Susceptibility of an account to misstatement.* Errors in the cash and capital accounts are generally unexpected and may warrant further investigation if discovered. The susceptibility of cash and other liquid assets to misuse or misappropriation should naturally heighten auditor concern about likely errors in these accounts.

- *Trends in financial statement components.* While it may be unrealistic to use a materiality standard as tight as a small fraction of the yearly change in net income or other financial statement components, longer-range trends or averages of balances or components (e.g., "normal income") may serve as useful signals that users react to. Consequently, auditors should be sensitive to departures from trends or normal expectations. Additionally, in a company with a stable earnings history, smaller variations in cash flow, income, or other financial statement components may have more impact than in a less stable business environment in which wider fluctuations are more common.

- *Possible biases on the part of management.* The Commission on Auditors' Responsibilities noted that "the auditor may make many separate evaluations of the appropriateness of accounting principles selected and estimates made by management. On viewing the financial statements as a whole, the auditor may find that most or all of the selections or estimates made by management had the effect of increasing (or decreasing) earnings and that the overall result is a misleading picture of the entity's earning power or liquidity" (page 21). SAS No. 47 addresses that possibility, and suggests that "the auditor should also consider whether the difference between estimates best supported by the audit evidence and the estimates included in the financial statements, which are individually reasonable, indicate a possible bias on the part of the entity's management. For example, if each accounting estimate included in the financial statements was individually reasonable, but the effect of the difference between each estimate and the estimate best supported by the audit evidence was to increase income, the auditor should reconsider the estimates taken as a whole" (para. 29).

Treatment of Prior-Year Waived Adjustments

An issue that often arises in the assessment of materiality is the treatment in the current year of prior-year waived adjustments. For example, the auditor may have waived a known overstatement of $10,000 in ending inventory and income in 1986, caused perhaps by errors in pricing the inventory, on the grounds that the error was not material. The overstatement of the 1986 ending inventory and income will flow through to 1987 income as an overstatement of cost of sales and an understatement of income. The issue in this case is this: Should the auditor, in considering errors affecting income in the audit of the 1987 financial statements, consider the $10,000 understatement of 1987 income caused by the waived adjustment of the 1986 error?

Some auditors believe that prior-year waived adjustments should be ignored in considering likely errors in the current year; in effect, the "correct" beginning 1987 inventory in the example is the 1986 ending inventory with the error in it. Since the error was waived, those auditors treat the error as not existing after 1986 and consider that 1987 starts with a "clean slate." Other auditors believe that the reversal in 1987 of the 1986 error should be considered in assessing likely errors in 1987.

The issue becomes even more complex when unadjusted errors, instead of reversing in the following year as in the example just given, build up. Assume that the auditor determines that the estimated warranty liability at the end of 1986 and warranty expense for 1986 are understated by $15,000 because an unreasonable estimate was made by the client. The auditor waived the adjustment to correct the error because the amount was not material to either the balance sheet or the income statement. In the course of the audit of the 1987 financial statements, the auditor determines that the estimated warranty liability at December 31, 1987 is understated by $35,000—an additional $20,000. In assessing the materiality of the misstatement, the auditor may determine that neither the $35,000 cumulative misstatement on the balance sheet nor the $20,000 impact on current-year income is material and again waive the adjustment. This may continue for several years. At some point, the accumulated error on the balance sheet will become material, and an adjustment will be needed if the financial statements are to be presented fairly in conformity with GAAP. If the accumulated error is corrected at this point, the adjustment may be so large that it will produce a material error on that year's income statement.

Auditors respond to the foregoing situation in several ways. One response is to propose that the client adjust the accounts only for the buildup in the current year—that is, the one in which the balance sheet materiality threshold is crossed. This will prevent the current year's income statement from being severely affected, but it may leave errors in the estimated liability account just below the materiality threshold, which may in turn cause problems if other liability accounts are even immaterially understated. Another response is not to let the buildup occur in the first place, at least not beyond the level of income statement materiality. As a practical matter, clients should be encouraged to correct all errors, even immaterial ones, at the time they are identified, to avoid these kinds of problems. If that is not done, and if adjustments of previously immaterial errors are made through current operations and the amounts are material in the aggregate, separate line item treatment or special disclosure describing the nonrecurring nature of the items may be warranted.

SAS No. 47 provides only the broadest guidance on this topic, stating merely that ''if the auditor believes that there is an unacceptably high risk that the current period's financial statements may be materially misstated when those prior-period likely errors that affect the current period's financial statements are considered along with likely errors arising in the current period, he should include in aggregate likely error the effect on the current period's financial statements of those prior-period likely errors'' (AU Section 312.30). It does not, however, state *how* the auditor should include the effect in likely error, and accordingly does not resolve the issues discussed in this section.

Proper planning is needed to ensure that sufficient audit procedures are performed in the various accounts so that appropriate audit conclusions can be drawn. If there has been a buildup of errors in an account from prior years, the auditor may have to do more work to refine the estimate of the present error in the account. More audit work may also be necessary to prevent a materially misstated balance from going undetected. Of course, assessing at the planning stage whether an immaterially misstated account balance from prior years will become correctly stated, remain similarly misstated, or become misstated in the opposite direction in the current period is difficult. Thus, the auditor's experience with the client, assessment of the possible level of misstatement in the account, and the nature of the account all influence the planning for the current period.

Resolving Material Differences

Occasionally, the auditor will conclude after reviewing the score sheet that one or more financial statement components are materially misstated or cause the aggregate misstatement of the income statement or balance sheet to be material. The auditor then needs to discuss the items in question with the client's management. Management may be able to produce further evidence to justify the initial treatment of some items or may agree to record some of the discovered errors in the accounts and to disclose more about the nature of and assumptions used in creating subjectively developed estimates that may be in dispute. The discussions continue until enough score sheet items are resolved so that the auditor can conclude that the remaining items do not adversely affect the fairness of presentation of the financial statements.

Depending on the size and complexity of an organization, each score sheet item may have to be taken up with several levels of management. The first consultation, of course, is with the individual directly responsible, who must supply all the facts. Additional conferences may include a supervisor and sometimes a plant or division controller. Often the deciding score sheet conference includes top management of the client—the financial vice president and chief executive. If discussions reach that level, two subjects should be probed: how to resolve the current score sheet problems so that an unqualified opinion can be given, and how to prevent similar problems from growing to such magnitude in the future. In these conferences, auditors must be careful not to allow factors such as pressing deadlines, heated arguments, or client dissatisfaction to influence them or to compromise their professional objectivity. Diplomacy and tact and an attitude of constructive assistance are obviously important in such situations. Early and thorough consideration of potential problems is the best way to avoid actual problems. While qualified and adverse opinions are rare, they may be the only appropriate ultimate response to a client's unwillingness to correct material financial statement errors. Departures from unqualified opinions because of GAAP violations are usually a manifestation of an unsatisfactory auditor–client relationship. For that and other reasons, many accounting firms encourage or require the audit partner to consult with other firm members before rendering such opinions.

Working Paper Review

Paragraph 11 of SAS No. 22, *Planning and Supervision* (AU Section 311.11), states that "the work performed by each assistant should be reviewed to determine whether it was adequately performed and to evaluate whether the results are consistent with the conclusions to be presented in the auditor's report."

The review of working papers requires an experienced and fully knowledgeable professional to bring together all of the planning, effort, and documentation necessary to ensure that procedures used are adequate and appropriate, that they have been performed properly, that they generated sufficient evidence to support the auditor's conclusions, that the conclusions reached are objective and logical, and that there is a properly documented basis for an informed opinion. The reviewer must evaluate the completeness of the audit program—including changes made to reflect changes in audit strategy in the course of the audit—in light of the results of the tests, the quality of the work performed by assistants, the quality of the client's judgments and decisions and the assistants' review thereof, and the adequacy of both the work performed and its documentation by the assistants. The exacting but inconclusive nature of most audit tasks makes it imperative that every piece of work be reviewed for completeness and logic by another qualified professional.

Whatever other purposes the review may have, its primary purpose must be to make sure that the logic of the audit is complete and properly documented. The logic calls for evidence in the working papers that: the underlying systems were understood[6] and, if appropriate, tested and evaluated; the under-

---

[6]Current authoritative auditing literature (AU Section 320.55) requires the auditor to document the understanding of the internal accounting control system only if reliance on the system so as to restrict substantive tests is intended. Many auditors, however, including the authors, believe that an understanding of the system is necessary and should be documented even if reliance on specific internal controls is not planned. See the discussion in Chapter 8.

standing and evaluation, if made, were translated explicitly into a program of substantive audit tests; the results of those tests either confirmed the assertions embodied in the financial statement components or led to a rational exploration of differences; and the results support each item disclosed in the financial statements.

Levels of Reviews

Generally, two levels of reviews are performed. The auditor in charge of the field work should review working papers prepared by assistants, to evaluate the results of the examination and ascertain that all appropriate auditing procedures were applied. Additionally, an independent review of audit procedures employed on an engagement should be performed by a competent person or people who did not participate in the field work. This is necessary to obtain the benefit of an independent assessment of the procedures applied during the field work and the results thereof, which forms the basis of the auditor's opinion on the financial statements under audit. This independent review is the responsibility of the engagement partner, who exercises overall supervision but does not usually perform the detailed auditing procedures and is therefore independent for this purpose. When the structure of the audit team allows, the partner may delegate a portion of the independent review to a manager, but the partner is nevertheless responsible for it. The extent of the partner's review would then depend on the circumstances. Primary partner attention is ordinarily directed to those areas in which there is high risk of material error, taking into consideration the dollar amounts involved, the complexity of the problems, and the nature of the system of internal control.

Review by the In-Charge Accountant. The auditor in charge of the field work is responsible for reviewing all completed working papers to

1. Determine that all the appropriate auditing procedures have been completed and that the nature and extent of the work performed has been adequately documented in the working papers.
2. Determine adherence to the requirements of the audit program.
3. Determine that working papers are relevant, clearly presented, orderly, and self-explanatory.
4. Determine that all exceptions have been appropriately cleared and documented.

Independent Review. The independent review requires an inspection of all current working papers, permanent files, and the audit program so that the reviewer may

1. Evaluate the appropriateness of the nature of the auditing procedures employed, the adequacy of the extent of their application, and the care exercised in applying them.

2. Determine adherence to the requirements of the audit program.

3. Evaluate the facts obtained in the course of the audit and the adequacy of their documentation in the working papers as they relate to the consistency and the fairness of presentation of the client's financial statements in conformity with GAAP.

4. Identify and consider matters or information that may call for additional inquiry or other auditing procedures.

The independent reviewer should be satisfied that the working papers have been integrated with the final financial statements. That is, the reviewer should ascertain that each account analysis in the working papers agrees with the corresponding amount shown on the trial balance, and that those amounts are reconcilable with the amounts shown on the financial statements. Amounts or other data appearing in the financial statements that are not reflected on the trial balance (e.g., footnote or supplementary information) must also be agreed to the related working papers.

Key Engagement Matters

It is the responsibility of the auditor in charge of the field work to document significant matters relating to the engagement. Key engagement matters should include, but are not limited to, the following:

1. Significant questions involving accounting principles and auditing procedures employed, or failure to comply with regulatory requirements, even in those instances in which the auditor in charge of the field work is satisfied that the matter has been disposed of properly.

2. Incomplete audit steps or unresolved questions.

3. Matters of significance noted in the previous year's engagement and their disposition.

4. Resolved or unresolved disagreements with the client on accounting and auditing matters.

5. Any information, not otherwise obvious, that should be considered by the independent reviewer in evaluating the results of the examination or in discussing the financial statements with the client.

It is desirable to address significant matters in one section of the working papers. Those matters may be summarized in the lead working paper binder, with cross-references to the related working papers that contain the details.

Review by a Second Partner

Many accounting firms require that all financial statements be reviewed by a second partner before the audit report is released. Other firms limit this requirement to audits of specified entities, for example, entities in specialized industries and publicly owned entities.[7] In this review, the second partner should be particularly concerned that matters of importance have been appropriately dealt with and that the financial statements and the audit report thereon comply with professional and firm standards. The second partner should discuss with the engagement partner questions regarding the consistent application of GAAP, auditing standards, or auditing procedures. The second partner may also consider it advisable to review certain working papers. If a second-partner review is required, the auditor's report should not be signed until all questions raised by the second partner have been disposed of properly.

Aids for the Reviewer

The review process is of such critical importance that accounting firms are constantly seeking ways to help the reviewer by providing aids such as audit engagement control checklists, standardized procedures, and policy bulletins. These aids also help to satisfy the requirements of paragraph 2 of SAS No. 25, *The Relationship of Generally Accepted Auditing Standards to Quality Control Standards* (AU Section 161.02), which states that "a firm should establish quality control policies and procedures to provide it with reasonable assurance of conforming with generally accepted auditing standards in its audit engagements."

In providing such aids to the reviewer, accounting firms must try to guard against routinized performance of a highly judgmental task. The quality of the review, and therefore of the audit, rests on the professional diligence and sense of responsibility of the reviewer. Although guided and supported by aids such as those described above, the reviewer cannot and should not be relieved of the burden of responsibility for understanding all that is needed to be able to form an appropriate opinion on the financial statements.

Timing of the Review Process

It is of great importance in relation to both the efficient conduct of the audit and the maintenance of good client relations that potentially material issues be raised at the earliest possible stage. More time for consideration by the engagement partner and the client is thus available than if the review is postponed until the final stages of the audit when the deadline for the audited financial statements is near.

The real substance of an audit is planning it intelligently and logically, executing it diligently and perceptively, and supervising it so that the review is continuous and active. If an audit is properly planned, executed, and supervised, the working paper review becomes the final control over a result already accomplished—a means of determining that all items of significance have been considered in reaching an audit conclusion.

---

[7]As indicated in Chapter 3, second-partner reviews are required on SEC engagements if the auditor is a member of the SEC practice section of the AICPA Division for CPA Firms.

In practice, the review process rarely works as smoothly as it does in theory. There are delays by client personnel, unexpected auditing or accounting problems, an assistant who falls ill or cannot complete the assignment on time, and innumerable other possible complications. Increasing public pressure for the fastest possible release of significant information causes deadlines to be drawn constantly tighter. The risk of oversight or misjudgment is greatest under the pressure of a deadline. Experienced auditors learn to resist those problems and pressures and make sure they review an integrated set of financial statements supported by coherent working papers before committing themselves, explicitly or implicitly, to an opinion on the financial statements or to approving release of information drawn from them.

Documentation of Significant Review Findings

During the various levels of working paper review, questions usually arise concerning significant unresolved matters. Typically, those questions, commonly referred to as "review notes," involve the appropriateness of accounting principles, auditing procedures employed, or compliance with regulatory requirements, and often call for further investigation. The audit working papers should include a clear and precise record of the resolution of such questions, including, among other things, such matters as the following (if applicable):

- The additional auditing procedures performed.
- The persons with whom the matter was discussed.
- The conclusions arrived at and supporting rationale.

Auditing procedures performed and conclusions reached as a result of review questions should not be documented by mere symbols, such as checks, or cryptic comments, such as "ok." That approach can lead to an obscure record and audit trail. If the resolution of significant review questions is adequately documented in the working papers, as suggested, there is ordinarily no need to also retain the review notes themselves in the working papers.

Review of Financial Statements for Appropriate Disclosure

The third generally accepted auditing standard applicable to reporting is

> Informative disclosures in the financial statements are to be regarded as reasonably adequate unless otherwise stated in the report. (SAS No. 1 [AU Section 150.02])

SAS No. 32, *Adequacy of Disclosure in Financial Statements* (AU Section 431), discusses this standard in very general terms. Essentially, material matters regarding the financial statements are to be disclosed in the financial statements or notes; if they are not, the auditor should express a qualified or an adverse opinion and should, if practicable, provide the information in the auditor's report. The auditor's reporting responsibilities with regard to inadequate disclosures are discussed in Chapter 18.

With the proliferation of accounting standards in recent years, many auditors, including sole practitioners, have adopted checklists as a means of enhancing overall quality control and furthering staff development. Disclosure checklists can deal very adequately with specifically required disclosures; they can, if properly prepared, also assist the auditor in meeting the standard of informative disclosure. Of course, an auditor's level of skill and judgment and the knowledge of the client's affairs obtained during the audit are the ultimate resources available to meet the disclosure standard.

Some auditors have developed separate disclosure checklists for those companies subject to SEC reporting requirements and those that are not. Further, separate checklists may be prepared for certain specialized industries, such as banking, insurance, governmental units, and colleges and universities. A typical arrangement would be to have a series of questions covering all aspects of financial statements in one column; specific references to the relevant authoritative pronouncement or the auditing firm's preferences in another column (by necessity, the requirements can only be generally stated in the checklist but the references can facilitate the preparation and review of the document); and an indication of whether the item is applicable, and, if so, whether it has been complied with in a third column. Room should be allowed for notes or calculations of amounts to demonstrate the extent to which materiality considerations entered into disclosure decisions. A completed checklist for an audit engagement can document in one place all reporting and disclosure considerations. While checklists are often prepared by the in-charge accountant, they should be reviewed by the audit partner responsible for release of the audit report or delegated to the manager on the engagement.

If checklists are used by an auditing firm, it is desirable that a clear statement be appended setting forth the firm's policy as to whether they are mandatory for all engagements, to be prepared for only certain specified engagements, or simply to be used as practice aids. Disclosure checklists should be updated periodically and should also contain the date produced so that authoritative pronouncements after that date will be considered.

Responsibilities for Subsequent Events

SAS No. 1 (AU Section 530) states that the date when the audit field work is completed should be used as the date of the auditor's report. The date of the auditor's report establishes the end of the period for which an auditor takes responsibility for events occurring after the end of the fiscal year. Auditors cannot be held responsible for events occurring after the report date, unless they agree or are required to perform additional procedures, as occurs in connection with "expertised" filings with the SEC under the Securities Act of 1933, discussed later in this chapter. The higher levels of responsibility to which auditors are now being held, the increased demands of users for accurate financial information, and the fact that the report date signifies the end of the period of the auditor's responsibility for the correctness of that information have all imparted greater significance to the date of the auditor's report.

Dating the Report

As indicated earlier, the date of the auditor's report should be the date on which field work is complete. Field work is complete when the auditor has completed substantially all the tests of the accounting records and all other auditing procedures considered necessary in the circumstances of the particular engagement. Matters that may require follow-up with the client, particularly if performed off the client's premises, generally do not affect the date of the auditor's report.

For other reasons as well, the report date is seldom the last day the auditors are on the client's premises. Ancillary matters often require the audit team's presence after the completion of the audit. For example, various regulatory reports, covenant letters, and management letters may have to be prepared or completed. Separate audits may be required for employee benefit plans or related foundations.

A report date of about 25 to 45 days after the end of the fiscal year is common for publicly held commercial and manufacturing companies; 15 to 20 days is usual for commercial banks. It then may take several weeks for the published annual report containing the financial statements to be prepared, printed, and mailed, but the auditor's report carries the date on which agreement on the financial statements was reached (unless new information is incorporated in the statements—see the later discussion under "Dual Dating").

Audit Planning Considerations. If an audit report must be issued within two or three weeks of the end of the fiscal year, the amount of auditing that can take place in that interval is obviously limited. Thus, much of an auditor's examination must be essentially completed by the time the fiscal year ends. This usually requires effective internal control by the client and always requires careful planning by the auditor. As indicated in Chapter 9, there are several strategies under which an auditor can perform substantive tests before the balance sheet date and have a reasonable basis for extending conclusions from those tests to the balance sheet date.

Many companies, however, cannot or do not choose to seek such early publication of their financial statements. Also, the auditor may find it necessary to perform extensive substantive tests after the balance sheet date, or problems may be encountered in making necessary valuations, estimates, and judgments. It may take 8 to 12 weeks, or even longer, for an auditor to complete the examination. During that time, the auditor must "keep current" with client affairs so as to have a basis for an opinion that subsequent events, as described later, are properly reflected or disclosed in the financial statements being reported on.

Dual Dating. Subsequent events that occur after the date of the auditor's report but before the report is issued and that come to the auditor's attention may require adjustment or disclosure in the financial statements. Auditors have no responsibility to perform any procedures for the period after the report date, but they cannot ignore information that comes to their attention. If financial statement disclosure is made of an event occurring after the date of the auditor's report but before its issuance, the auditor can either redate the report as of the date of that event or use "dual dating." In practice, unless the time period is very short, dual dating is more common because of the additional work necessary for the extended period if the report is redated. (That work is discussed later under "Subsequent Events.")

An auditor may be required or requested to reissue a report after it was first issued. If the auditor is aware of subsequent events that occurred after the date of the original report, several alternatives are possible. For those events that require adjustment of the previously issued financial statements, the report should be dual dated. For those events that require disclosure only, the auditor may dual date the report, or the disclosure may be included in an additional (usually the last) note to the financial statements that is labeled "unaudited." When dual dating is used, it usually appears as "January 25, 19X3, except as to Note— for which the date is March 1, 19X3."

Subsequent Events

Subsequent events are referred to in Section 560 of SAS No. 1 (AU Sections 560.01–.09) as events or transactions that "occur subsequent to the balance-sheet date, but prior to the issuance of the financial statements and auditor's report, that have a material effect on the financial statements and therefore require adjustment or disclosure in the statements." The distinction between the discovery of subsequent events before the financial statements are issued (described here) and the later discovery of facts that existed at the date of the auditor's report, discussed in Chapter 18, is significant. Subsequent events that occur after the balance sheet date but before the issuance of the financial statements and the auditor's report fall into two categories: those that require adjustment of account balances (and consequently are reflected on the face of the financial statements) and those that should not be recorded but should be disclosed in the financial statements.

Events Requiring Adjustment. The first category of subsequent event is succinctly described in paragraph 560.03 of SAS No. 1, as follows:

Those events that provide additional evidence with respect to conditions that existed at the date of the balance sheet and affect the estimates inherent in the process of preparing financial statements. All information that becomes available prior to the issuance of the financial statements should be used by management in its evaluation of the conditions on which the estimates were based. The financial statements should be adjusted for any changes in estimates resulting from the use of such evidence.

Events Requiring Disclosure. The second type of subsequent event consists of those events that provide evidence with respect to conditions that did not exist at the balance sheet date but arose afterwards. These events should be reflected in the financial statements of the year in which they occurred, and should not result in adjustment of the statements of the year being reported on. Some of these events, however, may be significant enough to cause the prior-year financial statements to be misleading if they are not disclosed. They include all transactions and other events and circumstances having significant financial impact. Some examples given in SAS No. 1 are issuance of debt or stock, acquisition of a business, and casualty losses.

Occasionally, an event of that type may be so significant that the auditor's report should call attention to it in an explanatory middle paragraph. Sometimes adequate disclosure can be made only by means of pro forma data giving effect to the event as if it had occurred at the balance sheet date; major acquisitions, mergers, and recapitalizations are examples.

Section 560 of SAS No. 1 illustrates the distinction between events that reveal or clarify conditions existing at the balance sheet date and those that represent new conditions. The illustration used is a receivable found to be uncollectible after the end of the fiscal year because of a customer's bankruptcy subsequent to that date. This event is in the first category (requiring adjustment of the gross receivable and possibly recalculation of bad debt expense and the allowance for estimated uncollectibles) because the debtor's poor financial condition existed at the balance sheet date. A similar receivable found to be uncollectible because of a disaster occurring to the debtor after the balance sheet date is a new condition and falls in the second category, requiring disclosure in the notes to the financial statements rather than adjustment of the accounts. The SAS notes that making the distinction requires "the exercise of judgment and knowledge of the facts and circumstances" (AU Section 560.04).

The distinction is often a fine one and the judgment difficult to make. For example, deteriorating market conditions subsequent to year-end could be a new condition that merely requires disclosure, or it could be evidence of a condition that was inherent in the inventory at year-end, which calls for adjusting it to net realizable value. Similarly, a subsequent event that reveals that estimated expenses are insufficient because of conditions occurring after the balance sheet date should be merely disclosed. If the reason for the insufficiency is newly discovered evidence of conditions that existed at the balance sheet date, that evidence should be reflected in the expense and related asset or liability accounts on the face of the statements.

There is a third type of subsequent event—one occurring after year-end that requires neither adjustment nor disclosure in the financial statements. Events that do not affect the interpretation of financial statements should not be disclosed because describing them in notes could cause misleading or confusing inferences. Since every event may have a financial impact, it is often extremely difficult to distinguish between events that should and those that should not be disclosed in the financial statements. Strikes, changes in customers or management, and new contracts and agreements are examples of events that ordinarily should not be disclosed in the financial statements, although management may have a responsibility to make public disclosure apart from the financial statements. If the events occur before the annual report to shareholders is printed, the president's letter is often used as a convenient method of communication.

Auditing Procedures in the Subsequent Period

Paragraphs 10–12 of Section 560 of SAS No. 1 (AU Sections 560.10–.12) define the auditor's responsibility to determine whether relevant subsequent events have occurred and discuss the types of work done in the period between the date of the balance sheet and the date of the auditor's report. The work generally falls into two major categories—completion of auditing procedures that are performed for purposes other than ascertaining the occurrence of subsequent events that require adjustment or disclosure, and procedures performed specifically for the purpose of learning about events occurring in the subsequent period.

The first category consists of substantive tests and other auditing procedures that involve reviewing transactions occurring in the subsequent period as part of the examination of year-end account balances. Illustrations of these procedures, which have been discussed earlier in this book, are tests of the client's cash cutoffs and sales and purchase cutoffs and reviews of collections, payments, and acquisitions after year-end.

The procedures for learning about subsequent events may be summarized as follows:

Read all available information relating to the client's financial affairs: interim financial statements; minutes of meetings of stockholders, directors, and any appropriate committees; pertinent variance and other management reports, and the like. An auditor who understands the client knows which areas are sensitive or volatile and what information about them is likely to be available.

Make inquiries—the more specific the better—about such things as financing activities, unusual entries or adjustments in the accounts, and potential problems discovered during the examination. An auditor who has developed a close working relationship with the client can make those inquiries easily and expeditiously.

Make inquiries of client's legal counsel concerning litigation, claims, and assessments.

Obtain a letter of representation from client officers describing subsequent events or disclaiming knowledge of any.

Although not specifically covered in Section 560 of SAS No. 1, it is sometimes necessary in the subsequent period to perform analytical reviews or other substantive tests in a recognized problem area. Usually, their purpose is to form an opinion on a client's measurement of the impact of a subsequent event. For example, an auditor may perform substantive tests of a client's estimate of the impact of a decision to discontinue a line of business made subsequent to year-end. Sometimes, however, those tests are required to satisfy the auditor that a possible subsequent event did not occur; an example is tests of the net realizable value of inventories due to changed market conditions subsequent to year-end.

The authoritative literature is silent about the auditor's responsibilities in the period (typically a rather short time) between the date of the auditor's report (which is the date when field work is completed) and the date the financial statements are issued by the client. Section 560 clearly applies only through the date of the report. Many auditors believe that from that date until the financial statements are issued, the auditor has no responsibilities to seek any additional evidence, but does have the responsibility to not ignore information that comes to his or her attention.

The Securities Act of 1933

Auditors' SEC practice is dealt with in entire volumes and is beyond the scope of this work. As mentioned in SAS No. 37, *Filings Under Federal Securities Statutes* (AU Section 711.02), "the accountant's responsibility, generally [when reporting on financial statements included in a filing with the SEC], is in substance no different from that involved in other types of reporting." A critical consideration in a 1933 Act filing, however, is that the independent auditor's responsibility with respect to subsequent events extends to the *effective date* of the registration statement and does not terminate at the date of the audit report. This situation results from Section 11(a) of the 1933 Act, which provides for substantial liabilities to those involved in the preparation of a registration statement found to contain untrue statements or material omissions. As pointed out in SAS No. 37 (AU Section 711.10), "To sustain the burden of proof that he has made a 'reasonable investigation,' . . . as required under the Securities Act of 1933, an auditor should extend his procedures with respect to subsequent events from the date of his audit report up to the effective date or as close thereto as is reasonable and practicable in the circumstances."

Subsequent Event Procedures for Keeping Current. The procedures already discussed for keeping current with respect to subsequent events through the date of the auditor's report should be performed at or near the effective date of the registration statement. In addition, the auditor generally should read the entire prospectus and other pertinent sections of the registration statement.

Letters for Underwriters. The procedures for keeping current that were discussed earlier are separate and distinct from any procedures that may be required by underwriters in connection with a 1933 Act filing, even though they may frequently be performed at the same time. Letters for underwriters, commonly called "comfort letters," are the subject of SAS No. 49 (AU Section 634).

Administrative Wrap-Up

After the audit is completed and the working papers reviewed and filed, there are both technical and administrative loose ends to wrap up. Special reports, tax returns, and similar matters are likely to have due dates that act as a professional discipline, but it is easy to let administrative matters slide. Such procrastination is a costly indulgence, but without tight administrative control it can happen.

Time analyses must be completed and budget variances analyzed. Billings must be prepared and processed. The audit program should be revised preliminarily in preparation for the next engagement. Ideally, the next year's engagement should be planned with the client as part of the current wrapping-up process. On many well-organized engagements, the end of one engagement constitutes the beginning of the next.

Review Questions

17-1. Define the term contingency, describe the two general types of contingencies that may arise, and briefly discuss how they are accounted for.

17-2. What authoritative pronouncement governs the treatment of contingencies in financial statements?

17-3. Describe the three ranges of likelihood of a contingency occurrence and the appropriate financial statement treatment in each case.

17-4. With respect to loss contingencies related to litigation, claims, and assessments, list the factors for which the auditor is required to obtain evidence. What auditing procedures are used to obtain this evidence?

17-5. What factors should the auditor bear in mind when evaluating lawyers' responses to audit inquiries?

17-6. What course of action should an auditor take when a lawyer's response is incomplete or equivocal?

17-7. What is a client representation letter and when is it required?

17–8. What matters are usually covered in a representation letter? When, and by whom, is it signed?

17–9. How does the auditor resolve score sheet items?

17–10. What purpose does the review of working papers serve?

17–11. Describe and distinguish between the two levels of working paper reviews.

17–12. Why is a second-partner review necessary? What are the primary concerns in a second-partner review?

17–13. Name and describe the different types of subsequent events auditors must consider.

17–14. How does an auditor's responsibility with respect to subsequent events on a 1933 Act engagement differ from that on other engagements?

Discussion Questions

17–30. During an audit engagement Harper, CPA, has satisfactorily completed an examination of accounts payable and other liabilities and now plans to determine whether there are any loss contingencies arising from litigation, claims, or assessments.

> *Required:*
> What are the audit procedures that Harper should follow with respect to the existence of loss contingencies arising from litigation, claims, and assessments? Do not discuss reporting requirements.

(AICPA adapted)

17–31. Windek, a CPA, is nearing the completion of an examination of the financial statements of Jubilee, Inc. for the year ended December 31, 1988. Windek is currently concerned with ascertaining the occurrence of subsequent events that may require adjustment or disclosure essential to a fair presentation in conformity with generally accepted accounting principles.

> *Required:*
> a. Briefly explain what is meant by the phrase subsequent event.
> b. How do those subsequent events that require financial statement adjustments differ from those that require financial statement disclosure?
> c. What procedures should be performed in order to ascertain the occurrence of subsequent events?

(AICPA adapted)

17–32. During the examination of the annual financial statements of Amis Manufacturing, Inc., the company's president, R. Alderman, and Luddy, the auditor, reviewed matters that were supposed to be included in a written representation letter. On receipt of the following client representation letter, Luddy contacted Alderman to state that it was incomplete.

> To E. K. Luddy, CPA:
>
> In connection with your examination of the balance sheet of Amis Manufacturing, Inc., as of December 31, 1987, and the related statements of income, retained earnings, and changes in financial position for the year then ended,

for the purpose of expressing an opinion as to whether the financial statements present fairly the financial position, results of operations, and changes in financial position of Amis Manufacturing, Inc. in conformity with generally accepted accounting principles, we confirm, to the best of our knowledge and belief, the following representations made to you during your examination. There were no:

- Plans or intentions that may materially affect the carrying value or classification of assets and liabilities.
- Communications from regulatory agencies concerning noncompliance with or deficiencies in financial reporting practices.
- Agreements to repurchase assets previously sold.
- Violations or possible violations of laws or regulations whose effects should be considered for disclosure in the financial statements or as a basis for recording a loss contingency.
- Unasserted claims or assessments that our lawyer has advised are probable of assertion and must be disclosed in accordance with Statement of Financial Accounting Standards No. 5.
- Capital stock repurchase options or agreements or capital stock reserved for options, warrants, conversions, or other requirements.
- Compensating balance or other arrangements involving restrictions on cash balances.

R. Alderman, President
Amis Manufacturing, Inc.

March 14, 1988

Required:
Identify the other matters that Alderman's representation letter should specifically confirm.

(AICPA adapted)

17-33. For items 1 to 6 below, assume that John Jones, CPA, is expressing an opinion on Azalea Company's financial statements for the year ended September 30, 1987, that he completed field work on October 21, 1987, and that he now is preparing his opinion to accompany the financial statements. In each item a "subsequent event" is described. Each event was disclosed to Jones either in connection with his review of subsequent events or after the completion of the field work. You are to indicate in each case the required financial statement adjustment or disclosure of the event. Each of the six cases is independent of the other five and is to be considered separately. *Your answer choice for each item 1 to 6 should be selected from the following responses:*

 a. No financial statement disclosure necessary.
 b. Disclosure in a footnote to the financial statements.
 c. Adjustment of the financial statements for the year ended September 30, 1987.
 d. Disclosure by means of supplemental, pro forma financial data.

 1. A large account receivable from Taylor Industries (material to financial statement presentation) was considered fully collectible at September 30, 1987. Taylor suffered a plant explosion on October 25, 1987. Since Taylor was uninsured, it is unlikely that the account will be paid.

2. A large account receivable from Southern Corporation (material to financial statement presentation) was considered fully collectible at September 30, 1987. Southern filed for bankruptcy on October 17, 1987 as a result of its deteriorating financial condition.

3. Based on a directors' resolution on October 5, 1987, Azalea's common stock was split 3-for-1 on October 10, 1987. Azalea's earnings per share have been computed based on common shares outstanding at September 30, 1987.

4. Azalea's manufacturing division, whose assets constituted 75 percent of Azalea's total assets at September 30, 1987, was sold on November 1, 1987. The new owner assumed the bonded indebtedness associated with this property.

5. On October 15, 1987, a major investment adviser issued a pessimistic report on Azalea's long-term prospects. The market price for Azalea's common stock subsequently declined by 50 percent.

6. At its October 5, 1987, meeting, Azalea's Board of Directors voted to double the advertising budget for the coming year and authorized a change in advertising agencies.

(AICPA adapted)

17–34. What should the reviewer look for during the detailed review of the working papers, and what pitfalls should the reviewer be on guard against?

17–35. What are some of the specific items that should be addressed in preparation for the partner's review?

AICPA Multiple Choice Questions _____

These questions are taken from the Auditing part of Uniform CPA Examinations. Choose the single most appropriate answer.

17–40. Which of the following auditing procedures is ordinarily performed last?

    a. Reading of the minutes of the directors' meetings.
    b. Confirming accounts payable.
    c. Obtaining a management representation letter.
    d. Testing of the purchasing function.

17–41. If management refuses to furnish certain written representations that the auditor believes are essential, which of the following is appropriate?

    a. The auditor can rely on oral evidence relating to the matter as a basis for an unqualified opinion.
    b. The client's refusal does *not* constitute a scope limitation that may lead to a modification of the opinion.
    c. This may have an effect on the auditor's ability to rely on other representations of management.
    d. The auditor should issue an adverse opinion because of management's refusal.

17–42. An auditor must obtain written client representations that normally should be signed by

  a. The president and the chairperson of the board.
  b. The treasurer and the internal auditor.
  c. The chief executive officer and the chief financial officer.
  d. The corporate counsel and the audit committee chairperson.

17-43. An auditor's report on comparative financial statements should be dated as of the date of the

  a. Issuance of the report.
  b. Completion of the auditor's recent field work.
  c. Latest financial statements being reported on.
  d. Last subsequent event disclosed in the statements.

17-44. When financial statements of a prior period are presented on a comparative basis with financial statements of the current period, the continuing auditor is responsible for

  a. Expressing dual dated opinions.
  b. Updating the report on the previous financial statements only if there has *not* been a change in the opinion.
  c. Updating the report on the previous financial statements only if the previous report was qualified and the reasons for the qualification no longer exist.
  d. Updating the report on the previous financial statements regardless of the opinion previously issued.

17-45. The audit step most likely to reveal the existence of contingent liabilities is

  a. A review of vouchers paid during the month following the year-end.
  b. Account-payable confirmations.
  c. An inquiry directed to legal counsel.
  d. Mortgage-note confirmation.

17-46. An attorney is responding to an independent auditor as a result of the audit client's letter of inquiry. The attorney may appropriately limit the response to

  a. Asserted claims and litigation.
  b. Matters to which the attorney has given substantive attention in the form of legal consultation or representation.
  c. Asserted, overtly threatened, or pending claims and litigation.
  d. Items that have an extremely high probability of being resolved to the client's detriment.

17-47. "Subsequent events" for reporting purposes are defined as events that occur subsequent to the

  a. Balance sheet date.
  b. Date of the auditor's report.
  c. Balance sheet date but prior to the date of the auditor's report.
  d. Date of the auditor's report and concern contingencies that are not reflected in the financial statements.

17-48. Harvey, CPA, is preparing an audit program for the purpose of ascertaining the occurrence of subsequent events that may require adjustment or disclosure essential to a fair presentation of the financial statements in conformity with generally accepted accounting principles. Which one of the following procedures would be *least* appropriate for this purpose?

a. Confirm as of the completion of field work accounts receivable that have increased significantly from the year-end date.
b. Read the minutes of the board of directors.
c. Inquire of management concerning events that may have occurred.
d. Obtain a lawyer's letter as of the completion of field work.

17-49. Karr has examined the financial statements of Lurch Corporation for the year ended December 31, 1986. Although Karr's field work was completed on February 27, 1987, Karr's auditor's report was dated February 28, 1987, and was received by the management of Lurch on March 5, 1987. On April 4, 1987, the management of Lurch asked that Karr approve inclusion of this report in their annual report to stockholders, which will include unaudited financial statements for the first quarter ended March 31, 1987. Karr approved of the inclusion of this auditor's report in the annual report to stockholders. Under the circumstances Karr is responsible for inquiring as to subsequent events occurring through

a. February 27, 1987.
b. February 28, 1987.
c. March 31, 1987.
d. April 4, 1987.

17-50. Subsequent events affecting the realization of assets ordinarily will require adjustment of the financial statements under examination because such events typically represent

a. The culmination of conditions that existed at the balance sheet date.
b. The final estimates of losses relating to casualties occurring in the subsequent events period.
c. The discovery of new conditions occurring in the subsequent events period.
d. The preliminary estimate of losses relating to new events that occurred subsequent to the balance sheet date.

17-51. When a contingency is resolved immediately subsequent to the issuance of a report that was qualified with respect to the contingency, the auditor should

a. Insist that the client issue revised financial statements.
b. Inform the audit committee that the report can *not* be relied upon.
c. Take *no* action regarding the event.
d. Inform the appropriate authorities that the report can *not* be relied upon.

17-52. When obtaining evidence regarding litigation against a client, the CPA would be *least* interested in determining

a. An estimate of when the matter will be resolved.
b. The period in which the underlying cause of the litigation occurred.
c. The probability of an unfavorable outcome.
d. An estimate of the potential loss.

Problems and Cases

17-60. In connection with her examination of Flowmeter, Inc. for the year ended December 31, 1987, Jane Hirsch, CPA, is aware that certain events and transactions that took place after December 31, 1987, but before she issued her report dated February 28, 1988, may affect the company's financial statements.

The following material events or transactions have come to her attention:

1. On January 3, 1988, Flowmeter, Inc. received a shipment of raw materials from Canada. The materials had been ordered in October 1987 and shipped FOB shipping point in November 1987.
2. On January 15, 1988, the company settled and paid a personal injury claim of a former employee as the result of an accident that occurred in March 1987. The company had not previously recorded a liability for the claim.
3. On January 25, 1988, the company agreed to purchase for cash the outstanding stock of Porter Electrical Co. The acquisition is likely to double the sales volume of Flowmeter, Inc.
4. On February 1, 1988, a plant owned by Flowmeter, Inc. was damaged by a flood, resulting in an uninsured loss of inventory.
5. On February 5, 1988, Flowmeter, Inc. issued and sold to the public $2 million of convertible bonds.

Required:

For each of these events or transactions, indicate the audit procedures that should have brought the item to the attention of the auditor, and the form of disclosure in the financial statements (including the reasons for such disclosure).

Arrange your answer in the following format.

Item No.	Audit Procedures	Required Disclosures and Reasons

(AICPA adapted)

17-61. The following are unrelated events that occurred after the balance sheet date but before the audit report was prepared:

1. The granting of a retroactive pay increase.
2. Determination by the federal government of additional income tax due for a prior year.
3. Filing of an antitrust suit by the federal government.
4. Declaration of a stock dividend.
5. Sale of a fixed asset at a substantial profit.

Required:

a. Explain how each of the items might have come to the auditor's attention.
b. Discuss the appropriate accounting recognition or disclosure for each of these events.

(AICPA adapted)

17-62. You were in the process of completing your audit of the financial statements of the PEI Company for the year ending December 31, 1988, when on December 1, 1988, the Pentagon announced that it had been investigating the suitability of certain microcircuits made by PEI and suspended the authorization for defense contractors to use these circuits in weapons and military communications devices, pending the results of its investigation.

Several large defense contractors have stated that, in light of this investigation, they will cease purchasing the microcircuits and have instituted proceedings to recover cost overruns due to the additional costs of alternative materials needed to complete their defense contracts, plus damages. The company estimates that these suits could result in awards of not less than $1 million or more than $3 million, exclusive of estimated legal costs of $500,000.

At present, PEI has approximately $800,000 of the microcircuits in question in finished goods inventory and is committed to purchase $200,000 of raw materials used solely for the manufacture of these microcircuits.

Assume that the company has litigation insurance but with a deductible amount of $500,000 and that a disclaimer of opinion is *not* appropriate.

Required:

a. Define the audit problems and cite applicable professional pronouncements.
b. Determine the approach you would propose toward the solution of the problems, including the evidence or other data you would want to review.
c. Indicate the factors you would consider in determining the impact on the audit budget and related timing of year-end field work.

17–63. The in-charge auditor proposed to you, the manager on the engagement, the following adjustments to the December 31, 1986 financial statements of Ace Supply Company as a result of the recently completed audit. Assume that there are no prior-period unadjusted likely errors and that you have reviewed the relevant working papers and agree with the in-charge's conclusions. Assume also that the client will strongly resist making any adjustments that are not absolutely necessary to avoid a qualified audit opinion.

1. Per working paper 55.2, ending inventory is known to be understated by $25,000 as a result of errors in the physical count.
2. Per working paper 55.3, ending inventory is projected to be understated by $49,000 as a result of inventory pricing errors discovered in a sampling application.
3. Per working paper 71.5, known year-end unrecorded expenses and liabilities identified in nonsampling applications amount to $47,500. A projection from sampling procedures indicates that an additional $20,000 should be recorded.
4. Per working paper 53.2, the allowance for doubtful accounts is $79,000 below the lowest reasonable estimate of what the balance should be.
5. Per working paper 23.19, the balance in the pension liability account at December 31, 1983, was discovered to be understated by $95,000. This was not a self-correcting error, and it was not discovered until this year's audit.
6. Per working paper 53.25, a sample of sales transactions revealed that errors in pricing sales invoices are projected to lead to a $164,000 understatement of sales revenue.
7. Per working paper 52.3, $150,000 of cash receipts from collection of accounts receivable was incorrectly included in 1987 cash receipts; another $45,800 of cash receipts from cash sales was incorrectly recorded in 1987 cash receipts. The cost of those sales, also recorded in the wrong period, is $20,000.
8. Per working paper 53.6, year-end cutoff tests of sales indicated that sales on open account in the amount of $865,000 are known to be incorrectly recorded in 1986. They should have been recorded in 1987. The cost of those sales, also recorded in the wrong period, is $415,000.

Financial statement totals (before audit adjustments) are as follows:

Assets	$19,193,000
Liabilities	10,760,000
Owners' equity	8,433,000
Income before taxes	3,793,000

The partner on the engagement has set balance sheet materiality at $400,000 and income statement materiality (pretax) at $150,000. The effective ordinary income tax rate is 45 percent; the capital gains rate is 30 percent.

Required:

a. Prepare a summary of audit differences (i.e., a score sheet) that summarizes proposed audit adjustments. For the balance sheet, consider the impact on assets, liabilities, and owners' equity. For the income statement, distinguish among known errors, projected errors, and errors from unreasonable estimates.

b. What adjustments, if any, would you require the client to make in order that an unqualified opinion could be issued? Explain.

An auditor's report is the formal result of all the effort that goes into an audit. There are many other results—the direct and indirect impact of audits on the control, accountability, and public reporting practices of companies, for example—and some people maintain that these are more significant, but the report is the specific identifiable focal point for the auditor and for all those who rely on the audit. It is also referred to as a "short-form report" or an "opinion." The term *certificate* also still appears occasionally, although auditors have discouraged its use because it implies a degree of precision and certainty that, as a practical matter, cannot be achieved.

This chapter covers the standard report (often called an unqualified or "clean" report or opinion), matters that require explicit attention in issuing a report, and the handling of variations from the standard report. Those variations fall into two categories—modifications in wording of the standard report that do not constitute qualifications of the auditor's opinion, and departures from the standard report to express other than an unqualified opinion. The three types of departures from unqualified opinions—qualified opinions, adverse opinions, and disclaimers of opinion—what each conveys, and the circumstances in which each is appropriate are examined in detail, and illustrations are presented. The reader is advised to review the section on audit reports in Chapter 1 for an overview of the various deviations from the standard report and the reasons for those variations. This chapter elaborates on that discussion. It also includes a discussion of the auditor's responsibilities after the report date.

Standard Reports

The basic form of standard report is as follows:

> [Addressee]
>
> We have examined the balance sheet of X Company as of December 31, 19____, and the related statements of income and retained earnings and changes in financial position for the year then ended. Our examination was made in accordance with generally accepted auditing standards and, accordingly, included such tests of the accounting records and such other auditing procedures as we considered necessary in the circumstances.
>
> In our opinion, the financial statements referred to above present fairly the financial position of X Company at December 31, 19____, and the results of its operations and the changes in its financial position for the year then ended, in conformity with generally accepted accounting principles applied on a basis consistent with that of the preceding year.
>
> January xx, 19____   [Name of Firm]

The first paragraph is called the "scope paragraph" and the second the "opinion paragraph." Some auditors use a one-paragraph report in which the opinion is given first to emphasize its importance.

A standard report asserts that an auditor understands the standards of the profession and has made an examination that measures up to them; that the financial statements being reported on present what they purport to present fairly, in conformity with generally accepted accounting principles (GAAP); and that those principles have been applied on a basis consistent with that of the preceding year. In short, a standard report signifies that no significant problems or deficiencies were found, either in carrying out the work or in the financial statements under examination, of which the auditor believes a reader of the financial statements should be aware.

History of the Standard Report

The wording of the present-day auditor's report was adopted by the accounting profession in 1948; the auditor's report went through various changes before that time. In the early 1920s a typical audit report was worded as follows:

> We have audited the accounts and records of the XYZ Company for the fiscal year ended March 31, 1920, and hereby Certify that, in our opinion, the annexed Balance Sheet correctly reflects the financial condition of the Company at March 31, 1920, subject to the liability for Federal Income and Profits Taxes accrued at that date.

It should be noted that this report refers to an audit of the "accounts and records" as opposed to the financial statements and that the auditors "certified" the balance sheet as being "correct."

By the early 1930s, the accounting profession had come to the realization that it would be unwise to continue to use the word *certify* or similar words in the audit opinion. The word *certify* gives the reader the incorrect impression that the contents of the audited financial statements are subject to precise measurements and that the auditor could guarantee the exactness of the data in those statements. Both of these connotations of the word *certify* are inappropriate for use by an auditor in stating an opinion.

Following is an example of the auditor's report suggested by the American Institute of Certified Public Accountants (AICPA) in 1933:

> We have made an examination of the consolidated balance sheet of ABC Company as at December 31, 1935, and of the statement of consolidated income and surplus for the year 1935. In connection therewith, we examined or tested accounting and other corporate records of the company, its wholly owned subsidiary companies, and companies directly controlled but not consolidated, and obtained information and explanations from officers and employes of the companies; we also made a general review of the accounting methods and of the operating and income accounts for the year but we did not make a detailed audit of the transactions.
>
> In our opinion, based upon such examination, the accompanying consolidated balance sheet and related statement of income and surplus fairly present, in accordance with accepted principles of accounting consistently followed by the companies, the financial position at December 31, 1935, and the results of the operations for the year.

The recommended auditor's report of 1933 clearly omits the word *certify* and introduces two new concepts: consistency of application of accepted accounting principles and fair presentation. Also, the scope paragraph of the report attempts to clarify the extent of the examination.

In 1939, the AICPA issued Statement on Auditing Procedure No. 1, which recommended that the scope paragraph include a specific reference to the review of internal control. This Statement further changed the opinion paragraph to include the application of GAAP "on a basis consistent with the preceding year," and the financial statements were said to "present fairly," as opposed to "fairly present," the financial position and results of operations.

The SEC in 1941 stated that the auditor must indicate whether the examination was made in accordance with "generally accepted auditing standards" and whether all procedures that were deemed necessary were carried out. As a result, the AICPA promptly initiated a change in the wording of the audit report. The 1941 audit report follows:

> We have examined the balance sheet of the XYZ Company as of February 28, 1941, and the statements of income and surplus for the fiscal year then ended, have reviewed the system of internal control and the accounting procedures of

the company and, without making a detailed audit of the transactions, have examined or tested accounting records of the company and other supporting evidence, by methods and to the extent we deemed appropriate. Our examination was made in accordance with generally accepted auditing standards applicable in the circumstances and included all procedures which we considered necessary.

In our opinion, the accompanying balance sheet and related statements of income and surplus present fairly the position of the XYZ Company at February 28, 1941, and the results of its operations for the fiscal year, in conformity with generally accepted accounting principles applied on a basis consistent with that of the preceding year.

In 1944 further modifications were made, such as deleting mention of some of the specific procedures carried out by the auditor. This change was based on the recognition that "generally accepted auditing standards" encompassed the stated audit procedures, therefore making the enumeration redundant. The 1944 report was used until 1948, when minor modifications were made and the current report was adopted.

The Meaning of Fair Presentation in Conformity with GAAP

The first standard of reporting states:

> The report shall state whether the financial statements are presented in accordance with generally accepted accounting principles.

Obviously, an auditor must be thoroughly familiar with generally accepted accounting principles to comply responsibly with this standard. The literature is vast on accounting principles and the meaning of "generally accepted." Nevertheless, the accounting profession has been severely and sometimes cynically criticized from both within and without for failure to be more precise and all-encompassing in promulgating GAAP.

Despite acknowledged deficiencies in generally accepted accounting principles, aggravated by some misunderstanding by nonaccountants, the phrase is generally understood by practitioners. Paragraph 138 of APB Statement No. 4, *Basic Concepts and Accounting Principles Underlying Financial Statements of Business Enterprises*, defines generally accepted accounting principles as "the conventions, rules, and procedures necessary to define accepted accounting practice at a particular time." The Commission on Auditors' Responsibilities noted that generally accepted accounting principles

> Are not limited to the principles in pronouncements of authoritative bodies such as the Financial Accounting Standards Board (FASB). They also include practices that have achieved acceptance through common usage as well as principles in nonauthoritative pronouncements of bodies of recognized stature such as the Accounting Standards Division of the American Institute of Certified Public Accountants. Too narrow a view of the scope of those principles by

auditors and preparers has contributed to the criticism of both generally accepted accounting principles and auditors. (p. 15)

SAS No. 5, *The Meaning of "Present Fairly in Conformity With Generally Accepted Accounting Principles" in the Independent Auditor's Report,* as amended (AU Section 411), also suggests that other possible sources of GAAP include AICPA accounting interpretations, AICPA industry audit guides and accounting guides, industry accounting practices, APB statements, pronouncements of other professional associations and regulatory agencies, and accounting textbooks and articles.

Accountants generally agree that the accounting principles referred to in the first standard of reporting and in the auditor's opinion are not fundamental truths or comprehensive laws, comparable to Newton's laws in physics, from which the details of practice are derived. Fundamental concepts of that nature may yet be discovered in accounting and the search for fundamentals continues. In the meantime, accountants have wrestled over the years with specific situations arising in practice and have developed and adopted numerous rules, conventions, and doctrines, which are now called principles. Some of those principles have been promulgated formally by an authoritative body of the profession (such as the Financial Accounting Standards Board [FASB] or the Accounting Principles Board [APB]) or the SEC, but often they represent a consensus of professional bodies, prominent writers, and eminent practitioners. As suggested earlier, all of those accepted conventions constitute the body of GAAP.

There have been efforts to expand the first reporting standard to require auditors to report on "fairness" separately from GAAP. The reason for these attempts is a belief in some quarters that it is possible to prepare financial statements that conform with GAAP but that nevertheless are not presented fairly and may in fact be misleading. Unfortunately, there has been some basis for that view in the past, principally because some preparers and auditors took a much narrower view of what constitutes GAAP than was explained earlier. SAS No. 5 (AU Section 411) clarified the situation by setting forth what was encompassed by the term "generally accepted accounting principles" (essentially, what was described earlier), and by noting that the auditor's judgment concerning the fairness of financial statement presentation should be applied within that frame of reference. The SAS also enumerated the various judgments that the auditor must make before rendering an unqualified opinion. Clearly, "fairness" is too loose a term to be practical or useful unless it is defined within a specific frame of reference, that is, GAAP. Some auditors believe that the word *fairly* should be removed from the auditor's opinion; that proposal has met widespread resistance.

Routine Variations in the Standard Report

Routine variations in the wording of the standard report include the party or parties to whom it is addressed, the identification of the statements reported

on, the period(s) covered, and the date of the report. An auditor should not alter key words or phrases in the standard report unless there are problems or
unusual conditions to be highlighted—and then the alterations should follow
the carefully drawn rules referred to in the following sections of this chapter—
because any departure from the standard words is usually regarded as some
sort of warning to the reader.

Addressing the Report. The report may be addressed to the client company
itself, to its board of directors, or to its stockholders. Practically speaking, the
address of a published report has little or no significance. The authors believe,
however, that an important point of principle is involved in addressing the report to the stockholders: that an auditor's ultimate responsibility is to the stockholders rather than to the company or its management.

Sometimes an auditor is retained to examine the financial statements of a
nonclient company on behalf of a client. In that case, the report should be addressed to the client and not to the company being examined or its directors or
stockholders (but see the discussion about confidentiality in Chapter 3 concerning the necessity for making sure that all parties to that kind of examination
understand the auditor's responsibility).

Identifying the Statements. The statements should be clearly identified, usually in the scope paragraph. The exact name of the company should be used
and the statements examined should be enumerated. Generally, these are the
balance sheet, the statement of income and retained earnings, and the statement of changes in financial position. If any other statements are covered by
the report, they should also be enumerated; for example, some companies
present a separate statement of changes in stockholders' equity accounts.
Sometimes it is more convenient to refer to an accompanying list or index that
enumerates the statements, in which case the first sentence of the scope paragraph would read as follows: ''We have examined the financial statements of X
Company listed in the accompanying index.'' The enumeration of the statements need not be repeated in the opinion paragraph.

Dating the Report. Inevitably, an auditor's report is issued on a date later
than the end of the period being reported on because it takes time for the books
to be closed, financial statements to be prepared, and final auditing procedures
to be completed. The selection of the appropriate date is discussed in Chapter 17.

Periods Covered. The periods reported on should also be specified. In annual
reports it is common to report on two years for comparative purposes. Companies whose securities are registered with the SEC are, however, required to
present audited comparative income statements and statements of changes in
financial position for three years and balance sheets for two years. In a company's first year of operations, only one year's financial statements can be pre-

sented, and the consistency standard is obviously inapplicable. The standard report is used, but the phrase "applied on a basis consistent with that of the preceding year" is omitted.

Pursuant to SAS No. 15, *Reports on Comparative Financial Statements* (AU Section 505), "a continuing auditor should update his report on the individual financial statements of the one or more prior periods presented on a comparative basis with those of the current period" (para. 2). An example of a report on comparative financial statements that updates, but does not change, the auditor's prior report on the earlier year is as follows:[1]

> We have examined the balance sheets of ABC Company at December 31, 19X2 and 19X1, and the related statements of income, retained earnings, and changes in financial position for the years then ended. Our examinations were made in accordance with generally accepted auditing standards and, accordingly, included such tests of the accounting records and such other auditing procedures as we considered necessary in the circumstances.
>
> In our opinion, the financial statements referred to above present fairly the financial position of ABC Company at December 31, 19X2 and 19X1, and the results of its operations and the changes in its financial position for the years then ended, in conformity with generally accepted accounting principles applied on a consistent basis.

A report on financial statements filed with the SEC covering a balance sheet for two years and the other statements for three years would be identical to the foregoing report except that the phrase "for the years then ended" in both the scope and opinion paragraphs would be replaced by "for each of the three years in the period ended December 31, 19X2." If the auditor is reporting on two or more years and, in addition, the year preceding the earliest year reported on is also presented, SAS No. 1 (AU Section 420.20) provides that the auditor should use language similar to this: "consistently applied during the period and on a basis consistent with that of the preceding year."

Modifications in Wording of the Standard Report

There are several departures from the standard report language that do not constitute qualifications of the auditor's opinion. These departures are merely

---

[1] SAS No. 15 (AU Section 505) states in a footnote to paragraph 2

The term "update" means to re-express a previous opinion or, depending on the circumstances, to express a different opinion from that previously expressed on the financial statements of a prior period. An updated report on prior-period financial statements should be distinguished from a reissuance of a previous report (see section 530.06–.08) since in issuing an updated report the continuing auditor considers information that he has become aware of during his examination of the current-period financial statements (see paragraph .04) and because an updated report is issued in conjunction with the auditor's report on the current-period financial statements.

See also the discussion later in this chapter of "Reports on Comparative Financial Statements with Differing or Updated Opinions."

modifications in wording of the standard report designed to fit particular circumstances and are discussed in the following paragraphs.

Opinion Based in Part on Report of Another Auditor

Chapter 6 discusses audit planning and strategy considerations when part of an examination is made by another auditor. The auditor who serves as the principal auditor may decide not to refer to that circumstance in the report, thus assuming responsibility for the work of the other auditor. If the principal auditor does make reference to the examination of the other auditor, the standard report is expanded. Since reliance on other auditors, however, is a scope limitation that does not result in a qualified opinion, SAS No. 2, *Reports on Audited Financial Statements* (AU Section 509), does not require that a reference or other explanation be set out in a separate paragraph.

If the principal auditor decides to refer to the examination of the other auditor, SAS No. 1 (AU Section 543.07) requires that the ''report should indicate clearly, in both the scope and opinion paragraphs, the division of responsibility'' between auditors. The report should also disclose the magnitude of the portion of the financial statements examined by the other auditor. Normally, this is done by noting the percentage of total assets and total revenues examined by the other auditor. Sometimes, other appropriate criteria, such as the percentage of net income, may be used. The other auditor usually is not named. When other auditors are named, their express permission must be obtained and their reports must be presented together with that of the principal auditor.

If the other auditor's report contains a departure from an unqualified opinion (see the later discussion), the principal auditor should decide whether the cause of the departure is of such a nature and significance in relation to the financial statements on which the principal auditor is reporting that it requires a departure from an unqualified opinion in the principal auditor's report. If the subject of the departure is not material to the overall financial statements, and if the other auditor's report is not presented, the principal auditor need not refer to the departure. If the other auditor's report is presented, the principal auditor may nevertheless wish to make reference to the departure and its disposition.

An example of an unqualified report in which another auditor has been relied on and is referred to follows:

> We have examined the consolidated balance sheets of ABC Company and subsidiaries as of December 31, 19X3, 19X2, and 19X1, and the related consolidated statements of income, changes in shareholders' equity, and changes in financial position for the years then ended. Our examinations were made in accordance with generally accepted auditing standards and, accordingly, included such tests of the accounting records and such other auditing procedures as we considered necessary in the circumstances. We did not examine the financial statements of XYZ Limited, a consolidated subsidiary, which state-

ments reflect (1) total assets constituting 14 percent, 13 percent, and 16 percent of the related consolidated balance sheet amounts at the end of 19X3, 19X2, and 19X1, and (2) net income constituting 20 percent, 22 percent, and 14 percent and total sales constituting 11 percent, 13 percent, and 9 percent of the related amounts in the consolidated statements of income for the years 19X3, 19X2, and 19X1. These statements were examined by other auditors whose report thereon has been furnished to us, and our opinion herein, insofar as it relates to the amounts included for XYZ Limited, is based solely upon the report of the other auditors.

In our opinion, based upon our examinations and the reports of other auditors, the consolidated financial statements referred to above present fairly the consolidated financial position of ABC Company and subsidiaries as of December 31, 19X3, 19X2, and 19X1 and the consolidated results of their operations and changes in their consolidated financial position for the years then ended, in conformity with generally accepted accounting principles applied on a consistent basis.

The disclosure is lengthy and somewhat awkward and much expanded from reporting practice of some years ago when it was customary only to state that part of the examination had been made by other auditors. Employing more than one auditor is an acceptable practice, but inevitably results in divided responsibility and risk of misunderstanding or omission. The practice is sometimes followed, however, to take advantage of specialized expertise or when the principal auditor is not located in areas served by other auditors. Chapter 6 includes a discussion of additional procedures the principal auditor may follow when the work of other auditors is used.

Also as discussed in Chapter 6, an auditor may obtain and use a report by another auditor on internal accounting control at a service organization that is used by the client to execute or record certain transactions or to process certain data. The report on the examination of the financial statements should not refer to the report of the auditor who reported on the service organization's internal control. As stated in AU Section 324.24, "The service [organization's] auditor's report is used in the examination, but the service [organization's] auditor is not responsible for examining a portion of the financial statements. . . . Thus, there cannot be a meaningful indication of a division of responsibility for the financial statements."

Departures from a Promulgated Accounting Principle with Which an Auditor Agrees

Since 1964, members of the AICPA (by action of their governing Council) have been expected to treat departures from accounting principles promulgated in the Opinions of the APB and in the predecessor Accounting Research Bulletins as departures from GAAP, leading to a qualified or an adverse opinion. That expectation is now incorporated in Rule 203 of the AICPA Code of Professional Ethics and the related interpretations; it also applies to the pronouncements of the FASB and the GASB. It is covered as a special case in paragraphs 18 and 19 of SAS No. 2 (AU Sections 509.18 and .19).

In rare and unusual circumstances, a departure from an accounting principle promulgated by the APB or FASB may be required to present a particular transaction or other event or circumstance in a manner that is not misleading. If the auditor and client agree that a certain treatment that departs from an accounting principle promulgated by the APB or FASB is required in order to make the statements not misleading, it is permissible for the financial statements to reflect the departure, provided the departure and its effect are disclosed both in a note to the financial statements and in the auditor's report. The reason for believing that the departure from GAAP is justified should be stated, and the auditor should then express an unqualified opinion.

Although the kind of "unusual circumstances" referred to herein might conceivably exist in which the literal application of a pronouncement covered by Rule 203 would have the effect of making the financial statements misleading, the authors believe instances of this kind would rarely, if ever, arise. Consequently, this type of opinion modification is rare and a recent example of it could not be located. The best-known example of that circumstance dates back to a report on a company's financial statements for the year ended December 31, 1973. A middle paragraph therein read as follows:

> In October, 1973, the Company extinguished a substantial amount of debt through a direct exchange of new equity securities. Application of Opinion No. 26 of the Accounting Principles Board to this exchange requires that the excess of the debt extinguished over the present value of the new securities should be recognized as a gain in the period in which the extinguishment occurred. While it is not practicable to determine the present value of the new equity securities issued, such value is at least $2,000,000 less than the face amount of the debt extinguished. It is the opinion of the Company's Management, an opinion with which we agree, that no realization of a gain occurred in this exchange (Note 1), and therefore, no recognition of the excess of the debt extinguished over the present value of the new securities has been made in these financial statements.

Note 1 read (in part) as follows:

> *Extinguishment of Debt:* In October, 1973, the Company issued 50,000 shares of 6% Prior Preferred Shares, par value $100, in exchange for the outstanding $5,000,000 of 6% senior subordinated notes. It also issued 18,040 shares of convertible $6 Serial Preference Shares, Series A, stated value $100 a share, in exchange for $1,300,000 and $504,000 of outstanding 6% convertible subordinated debentures and 5¾% convertible subordinated debentures, respectively. The Company expensed the unamortized balance (approximately $148,000) of the deferred financing costs associated with the issuance of each of the three classes of subordinated debt to the extent that such unamortized balances were allocable to the debt so extinguished.

> Opinion No. 26 of the Accounting Principles Board of the American Institute of CPA's states that the excess of the carrying amount of the extinguished debt over the present value of the new securities issued should be recognized as a gain in the statement of operations of the period in which the extinguishment occurred. While it is not practicable to determine the present value of the new equity securities issued, such value is at least $2,000,000 less than the face amount of the debt extinguished. However, the terms and provisions of these new equity securities [which included a mandatory redemption provision] are substantially similar to those of the debt securities extinguished, both on the basis of the Company's continuing operations and in the event of liquidation. It is the opinion of the management, therefore, that no gain as a result of this exchange has been realized or should be recognized in the financial statements.

The auditors believed that the financial statements *were* presented fairly in conformity with GAAP, which would not have been the case if APB Opinion No. 26 had been blindly followed. In this instance, the auditors did not, in the opinion paragraph, in any way qualify the opinion as a result of the described departure from a promulgated accounting principle.

Predecessor Auditor's Report Not Presented

When comparative financial statements are presented and the prior year's statements were examined by another auditor, the successor auditor and the client have two options concerning the auditors' reports. Under the first option, the client could make arrangements with the predecessor auditor to reissue the report on the financial statements of the prior period, provided the predecessor auditor performs the procedures described in paragraph 9 of SAS No. 15, *Reports on Comparative Financial Statements* (AU Section 505.09). Paragraph 9 requires that before reissuing a previously issued report, a predecessor auditor should consider whether the previous opinion is still appropriate. To do that:

> A predecessor auditor should (a) read the financial statements of the current period, (b) compare the prior-period financial statements that he reported on with the financial statements to be presented for comparative purposes, and (c) obtain a letter of representations from the successor auditor.

The predecessor auditor should not refer in the reissued report to the report of the successor auditor. The successor auditor should report only on the current year's financial statements.

Under the second option, the predecessor auditor's report is not presented.[2] In this case, pursuant to paragraph 12 of SAS No. 15 (AU Section 505.12):

[2] SEC proxy Rule 14c-3 permits the separate report of the predecessor auditor to be omitted in the annual report to securityholders, provided the registrant has obtained a reissued report from the predecessor auditor. The separate report of the predecessor auditor is, however, required in filings with the Commission.

The successor auditor should indicate in the scope paragraph of his report (a) that the financial statements of the prior period were examined by other auditors, (b) the date of their report, (c) the type of opinion expressed by the predecessor auditor, and (d) the substantive reasons therefor, if it was other than unqualified.

An example of a successor auditor's report when the predecessor auditor's report is not presented follows:

> We have examined. . . . Our examination was made. . . . The balance sheet of ABC Company as of August 31, 1987, and the related statements of earnings, stockholders' equity, and changes in financial position for the two years then ended were examined by other auditors whose report dated November 18, 1987, expressed an unqualified opinion on those statements.
> In our opinion. . . .

If the predecessor auditor's opinion was other than unqualified, the successor auditor should describe the nature of and reasons for the qualification.

Audited and Unaudited Financial Statements Presented in Comparative Form

Another modification in the standard report is required when audited and unaudited financial statements are presented in comparative form. SAS No. 26, *Association With Financial Statements* (AU Sections 504.14–.17) provides guidance for reporting when the unaudited period precedes the audited period and when the unaudited period is the latest period presented. Basically, the SAS provides that the auditor appropriately refer to the audited and the unaudited periods in the auditor's report. There is, however, a specific exemption from this requirement in filings with the SEC, in which case the unaudited financial statements should be clearly marked as unaudited but the auditor should not refer to them in the report.

Report on a Balance Sheet Only

In certain instances, an auditor may be asked to report only on a client's balance sheet, rather than on all of the financial statements. This may occur in filings under debt or credit agreements. The following is an example of a report on a balance sheet only:

> We have examined the balance sheet of X Company as of December 31, 19X1. Our examination was made. . . .
> In our opinion, the financial statement referred to above presents fairly the financial position of X Company at December 31, 19X1, in conformity with generally accepted accounting principles applied on a basis consistent with that of the preceding year.

Emphasis of a Matter

Paragraph 27 of SAS No. 2, *Reports on Audited Financial Statements* (AU Section 509.27), states that

> In some circumstances, the auditor may wish to emphasize a matter regarding the financial statements, but nevertheless intends to express an unqualified opinion. For example, he may wish to point out that the entity is a component of a larger business enterprise or that it has had significant transactions with related parties, or he may wish to call attention to an unusually important subsequent event or to an accounting matter affecting the comparability of the financial statements with those of the preceding period. Such explanatory information may be presented in a separate paragraph of the auditor's report. Phrases such as "with the foregoing explanation" should not be used in the opinion paragraph in situations of this type.

It should be noted that emphasizing a matter in a middle paragraph is rarely done because it can be misconstrued as a qualification.

In the following example, the auditors included a middle paragraph to emphasize that a portion of the consolidated financial statements were prepared on the basis of statutory accounting principles.

> We have examined the consolidated balance sheets of the separate and combined Stock and Mutual Departments of ABC Life Insurance Company and subsidiaries as of December 31, 1986 and 1985, and their related consolidated statements of operations, shareholders' equity and Mutual Department surplus, and changes in financial position for the years then ended. Our examinations were made in accordance with generally accepted auditing standards and, accordingly, included such tests of the accounting records and such other auditing procedures as we considered necessary in the circumstances.
>
> The financial statements of the Stock Department have been prepared on the basis of generally accepted accounting principles for stock life insurance companies. The financial statements of the Mutual Department have been prepared on the basis of statutory accounting practices prescribed or permitted by state regulatory authorities. These statutory accounting practices conform in all material respects with generally accepted accounting principles. The entire company financial statements present the combined financial statements of the Stock and Mutual Departments.
>
> In our opinion, the financial statements referred to above present fairly the consolidated financial position of the separate and combined Stock and Mutual Departments of ABC Life Insurance Company and subsidiaries as of December 31, 1986 and 1985, and the results of their operations and the changes in their financial position for the years then ended, in conformity with generally accepted accounting principles applied on a consistent basis.

Material Inconsistency Between Financial Statements and Other Information Reported by Management

An enterprise may publish a document, such as an annual report, that contains information in addition to audited financial statements and the auditor's report. That information, which is referred to in professional pronouncements (SAS No. 8, *Other Information in Documents Containing Audited Financial Statements* [AU Section 550]) as "other information," encompasses such items as a 10-year financial summary and an analysis of financial data in the president's letter. It also encompasses management's discussion and analysis of operations (for the three most recent years) and of changes in financial position and liquidity (during the two most recent years), as required of enterprises whose securities are registered with the SEC.

The auditor has no responsibility to corroborate "other information," but SAS No. 8 specifies that the auditor does have a responsibility to read it and consider whether it is materially inconsistent with information appearing in the financial statements. If it is, the auditor should request the client to revise the other information. If the other information is not revised to eliminate the inconsistency, the auditor should consider whether to withhold the audit report, withdraw from the engagement, or modify the report to include a middle paragraph explaining the inconsistency. The auditor's opinion would still be unqualified, since the deficiency would not be in the audited financial statements. Such instances are, as might be expected, extremely rare, since even management that is prone to excessive "puffing" of its accomplishments is likely to retreat in the face of the possibility of an explanatory comment in the auditor's report.

A related problem arises when the auditor, on reading the other information, determines that there is a material misstatement of fact that is not inconsistent with information in the audited financial statements. Beyond suggesting that the auditor consult others, including legal counsel, and notify the client, the authoritative literature provides scant guidance; nor does the literature require the auditor to disclose the misstatement. The Commission on Auditors' Responsibilities recommended (page 69) that the auditor be required to read the other information to ensure that it is not inconsistent with *anything* the auditor knows, as a result of the audit, about the company and its operations and that the auditor modify the report to describe the deficiency if management does not correct it. At the date of this writing, no professional standard-setting body has acted on this recommendation.

Departures from Unqualified Opinions

The fourth standard of reporting reads as follows:

> The report shall either contain an expression of opinion regarding the financial statements, taken as a whole, or an assertion to the effect that an opinion cannot be expressed. When an overall opinion cannot be expressed, the reasons therefor should be stated. In all cases where an auditor's name is associated with financial statements, the report should contain a clear-cut indication of the character of the auditor's examination, if any, and the degree of responsibility he is taking.

The standardized language of the conventional report fosters precision in meeting this standard. The professional literature, both at the time of publication of the fourth standard of reporting and since then, has attempted to provide similar precision in describing departures from the standard report. Authoritative pronouncements on the fourth standard of reporting, including SAS No. 2, are set forth in AU Section 500 of *AICPA Professional Standards*.

There are two kinds of problems to overcome in obtaining adequate precision and clarity of communication. First is the problem of trying to find a limited number of precisely defined qualifying or limiting phrases that will cover all possible situations. For professional auditors who have studied and understand the meaning and usage of the common qualifying phrases that have been developed, the effort has been largely successful. New conditions keep appearing, however, and when they do a period of uncertainty ensues while auditors experiment and decide whether the new conditions can be covered by an existing type of qualification or a new phrase is required.

The second problem is communicating to the public the meaning of the qualifying phrases and the distinctions between them. The meaning of a highly stylized phrase can be understood and agreed on by practitioners, but it is useless unless it is equally recognized and understood by most readers. SAS No. 2, paragraph 32 (AU Section 509.32), calls for explaining all departures from an unqualified opinion, other than a consistency exception, in a middle paragraph. Doing so clearly highlights the departures and provides an unmistakable place for full description, improving both disclosure and communication.

SAS No. 2 (AU Section 509) classifies departures from the standard unqualified report, sometimes referred to as a ''clean'' opinion, as qualified opinions, adverse opinions, and disclaimers of opinion. These departures are discussed in the following paragraphs.

Qualified Opinions

Some accountants believe that any modifying phrase in the opinion paragraph qualifies the opinion in one way or another. Others—including the authors of this book—make a distinction between those phrases that point to a diminution in the quality of the financial statements, such as a departure from GAAP, and those that merely modify the language of an unqualified opinion, such as a reference to the report of other auditors. When a qualified opinion is appropriate, an auditor should try to avoid language in the opinion paragraph other than that described here.

There are four basic reasons for qualifying an opinion: departures from GAAP, departures from consistent application of accounting principles, limitations on the scope of the examination, and uncertainties affecting the financial statements that cannot be resolved. The first three give rise to ''exceptions'' (and the qualifying language usually begins with the words *except* or *except for*); the last gives rise to ''subject to'' qualifications.

Departures from GAAP. The standard opinion makes the positive assertion that the financial statements are presented in conformity with generally accepted accounting principles; thus, any departures from GAAP must be noted as "exceptions" to the assertion. Such departures are rare in practice because most companies believe that an auditor's opinion qualified because of a departure from GAAP carries intolerable implications and so they use accounting principles that are generally accepted. Also, only rarely are such qualified opinions acceptable in SEC filings. Nevertheless, instances of departures sometimes occur; the most common ones are described and examples presented in the following paragraphs.

Departures from Measurement Principles. SAS No. 2 (AU Section 509.36) gives the following example of an auditor's report that is qualified because of the use of an accounting principle that is at variance with GAAP:

(Separate paragraph)

The Company has excluded from property and debt in the accompanying balance sheet certain lease obligations, which, in our opinion, should be capitalized in order to conform with generally accepted accounting principles. If these lease obligations were capitalized, property would be increased by $_____, long-term debt by $_____, and retained earnings by $_____, as of December 31, 19XX, and net income and earnings per share would be increased (decreased) by $_____ and $_____ respectively for the year then ended.

(Opinion paragraph)

In our opinion, except for the effects of not capitalizing lease obligations, as discussed in the preceding paragraph, the financial statements present fairly. . . .

Departures from Disclosure Principles. Under the third standard of reporting:

Informative disclosures in the financial statements are to be regarded as reasonably adequate unless otherwise stated in the report.

SAS No. 32, *Adequacy of Disclosure in Financial Statements* (AU Section 431), is general about what constitutes informative disclosures. Some specific disclosures required in financial statements are contained in various pronouncements that constitute GAAP, for example, Statements of Financial Accounting Standards, Opinions of the Accounting Principles Board, and Accounting Research Bulletins. Specific industry disclosures are often called for in AICPA industry audit and accounting guides. Those pronouncements, however, cover only the topics addressed, and not the vast area of financial information on which no pronouncement has been issued. Identifying matters of potential interest to financial statement users, deciding whether and how they should be disclosed, and then demonstrating the appropriateness of the conclusion to the client place great demands on an auditor's skill and judgment.

The intent of the third standard of reporting is that issuers of financial statements and auditors have a responsibility to ensure that disclosures are adequate, regardless of whether a requirement, convention, or precedent covers the matter. Some issuers of financial statements, however, manifest the attitude of ''no rule, no disclosure.'' Court cases and items appearing in the press indicate that a disclosure policy based on this attitude is dangerous, not to mention possibly not being in the public interest. Disclosing more than what is specifically required in authoritative pronouncements, however, presents serious practical problems. For example, SAS No. 32 (AU Section 431) notes the problem of disclosing confidential information or information that could harm a company or its stockholders. The matter is even more difficult than the careful words of the SAS suggest. On the one hand, many managements sincerely believe that almost every additional disclosure requested or required is likely to result in a competitive disadvantage or other detriment to the company or its stockholders. On the other hand, directors, management, auditors, and their legal counsel have to worry about the possibility that a detrimental disclosure not made may be a basis for litigation in the wake of subsequent difficulties, even if the cause of the difficulties is completely unrelated to the undisclosed matter.

Disclosure is never a substitute for proper accounting measurements. In practice, a temptation on the part of issuers and auditors sometimes exists to resolve a difficult problem by presenting information in a footnote rather than by adjusting the financial statements. For example, a contingency that is likely to occur and for which an estimate of loss is known must be accrued in the financial statements according to GAAP; disclosure of such an item is not an acceptable alternative.

An auditor who believes that disclosures in the financial statements are inadequate is required to so state and to make the necessary disclosures in the auditor's report, if it is practicable to do so and unless the omission from the auditor's report is recognized as appropriate in a specific SAS. Since most clients choose to make the necessary disclosures rather than to have them appear in the auditor's report, this type of disclosure in an auditor's report is extremely rare.

There are two exceptions to the requirement that when informative disclosures are omitted from the financial statements, the auditor should make the necessary disclosures in the auditor's report. The two exceptions, specifically sanctioned in the SASs (AU Sections 435.10 and 545.05), pertain to omitted segment information that is required by GAAP and to the statement of changes in financial position. If an entity declines to present the necessary segment information or a statement of changes in financial position, the auditor is not required to provide the omitted information or to prepare the statement of changes in financial position and include it in the report. The auditor should qualify the report if the enterprise does not present a statement of changes in financial position. AU Section 545.05 provides the following example:

We have examined the balance sheet of X Company as of December 31, 19___, and the related statements of income and retained earnings for the year then ended. . . .

The company declined to present a statement of changes in financial position for the year ended December 31, 19___. Presentation of such statement summarizing the company's financing and investing activities and other changes in its financial position is required by Opinion No. 19 of the Accounting Principles Board.

In our opinion, except that the omission of a statement of changes in financial position results in an incomplete presentation as explained in the preceding paragraph, the aforementioned financial statements present fairly. . . .

Departures from Consistency. The second standard of reporting is

The report shall state whether such principles have been consistently observed in the current period in relation to the preceding period.

The consistency standard requires an auditor to state specifically in the report whether GAAP have been applied consistently from period to period; consistency within a period is presumed unless otherwise disclosed. The objective is to ensure that changes in accounting principles do not materially affect the comparability of financial statements between periods or, if they do, that the effect is disclosed.

Of course, factors other than consistent application of accounting principles also affect the comparability of financial statements between periods. For example, changed conditions that necessitate changes in accounting and changed conditions that are unrelated to accounting may exist. The effect of those other factors normally requires disclosure (covered by the third standard of reporting) but not specific comment in the auditor's opinion. In requiring other effects on comparability to be disclosed under the more general third standard, the profession has singled out the consistency of accounting principles for separate attention. The reason for the different treatment lies in the nature of alternative accounting principles—alternatives that are considered generally accepted may be substituted one for another, thus changing accounting results without any change in the underlying economic substance: a sound and sometimes necessary practice that is obviously susceptible to abuse.

In contrast to qualified opinions caused by departures from generally accepted accounting principles, which are rare in practice, consistency exceptions occur fairly often. Companies from time to time change managements, operating philosophies, or judgments about which accounting principles are most appropriate for the company. Any significant change in accounting principle, or method of applying a principle, is a departure from the consistency standard and must be referred to in the auditor's report.

Accounting Principles Board Opinion No. 20, *Accounting Changes* (Accounting Standards Sections A06 and A35), provides standards for accounting for and disclosing accounting changes in financial statements. Section 420, ''Consistency of Application of Generally Accepted Accounting Principles,'' of SAS

No. 1 (AU Section 420) expands the guidelines for applying the consistency standard to accounting changes. Section 546, "Reporting on Inconsistency" (AU Section 546), discusses auditors' reports in cases of inconsistency.

Both the Opinion and SAS No. 1 distinguish changes in accounting principles from changes in accounting estimates or changes in a reporting entity. The three kinds of changes, called collectively "accounting changes," are further distinguished from other factors affecting the comparability of financial statements between periods, including errors in previously issued statements, changes in statement classification, initial adoption of an accounting principle to recognize an event occurring for the first time, and adoption or modification of an accounting principle necessitated by transactions that are clearly different in substance from previous transactions. Of all classes mentioned, only changes in accounting principles and, sometimes, changes in the reporting entity require comment in an auditor's report under the consistency standard of reporting. Of course, the others may have to be either disclosed or commented on under the third standard of reporting.

Changes in Accounting Principle. An accounting change resulting from a choice by management between two or more generally accepted accounting principles affects the comparability of financial statements and requires specific comment by an auditor. Examples of that kind of change include a change from a declining-balance method of computing depreciation to a straight-line method, from the LIFO method to the FIFO method for inventory pricing or vice versa, and from the completed-contract method to the percentage-of-completion method of accounting for long-term contracts.

The methods of accounting for a change in accounting principle are described in APB Opinion No. 20 (Accounting Standards Sections A06 and A35). In a few specified instances, the change should be reflected by retroactively restating the financial statements of prior periods; in other specified instances, the change has only prospective effect and current statements give no reflection of the change, except for footnote disclosure of the future effects. In all other instances, a change in accounting principle is accounted for by calculating the cumulative effect of the change on the amount of retained earnings at the beginning of the period in which the change is made and recording that effect in net income of the period of the change. A company making a change in accounting principle must also disclose the nature of the change, its effect on income, and why the newly adopted principle is preferable.

The words used for the consistency exception depend on the method of accounting for the change. The appropriate auditor's reports in cases of inconsistency are set forth in SAS No. 1 (AU Section 546). If an auditor is reporting only on the year during which a cumulative effect type change is made, the opinion paragraph should read approximately as follows:

> . . . in conformity with generally accepted accounting principles which, except for the change, with which we concur, in the [accounting principle] as described in Note X to the financial statements, have been applied on a basis consistent with that of the preceding year.

If an auditor reports on two or more years, reference to that type of change continues to be made as long as the period of the change is covered by the report. The following wording is used in the opinion paragraph when the period of the change is other than the earliest year being reported on:

> . . . in conformity with generally accepted accounting principles consistently applied during the period except for the change, with which we concur, in the [accounting principle] as described in Note X to the financial statements.

SAS No. 2, paragraph 32 (AU Section 509.32), excludes consistency exceptions from the requirement that the qualification be explained in a separate paragraph of the report.

If the period of the change is the earliest year being reported on, there is no inconsistency during the periods presented, but an auditor should nevertheless make reference to the change in the opinion paragraph with the following words:

> . . . in conformity with generally accepted accounting principles consistently applied during the period subsequent to the change, with which we concur, made as of January 1, 1987, in the [accounting principle] as described in Note X to the financial statements.

If a change in an accounting principle is reported by restating prior periods' financial statements, the opinion must indicate this. The following is an example of an opinion paragraph covering one year:

> . . . applied on a basis consistent with that of the preceding year after giving retroactive effect to the change, with which we concur, in the [accounting principle] as described in Note X to the financial statements.

For a similar change, an opinion paragraph covering two or more years would be as follows:

> . . . applied on a consistent basis after restatement for the change, with which we concur, in the [accounting principle] as described in Note X to the financial statements.

If more than one accounting change has taken place, they all must be referred to in the opinion paragraph. An example of this follows:

> . . . in conformity with generally accepted accounting principles consistently applied during the period except for the changes, with which we concur, in the methods of accounting for investment tax credits and interest costs and after the restatement for the change, with which we concur, in the method of accounting for compensated absences, all of which are described in Note 2 to the financial statements.

Initial Examinations. An auditor's examination of a company for the first time should be extensive enough to permit an opinion on consistency with the prior period. Conditions that would prevent an auditor from forming that opinion would usually also preclude an opinion on the balance sheet at the beginning of the period. In that case, the auditor would have to disclaim an opinion on the income statement and statement of changes in financial position. The most probable cause of that kind of problem would be either inadequate financial records or limitations imposed by the client. The following is an example of the opinion that might result:

> . . . and such other auditing procedures as we considered necessary in the circumstances, except as indicated in the following paragraph.
>
> Because of major inadequacies in the company's accounting records for the previous year, it was not practicable to extend our auditing procedures to enable us to express an opinion on results of operations and changes in financial position for the year ended December 31, 1987, or on the consistency of application of accounting principles with the preceding year.
>
> In our opinion, the accompanying balance sheet presents fairly the financial position of X Company at December 31, 1987, in conformity with generally accepted accounting principles.

In a company's first year of operations, the consistency standard is obviously inapplicable. The standard report is used and the phrase "applied on a basis consistent with that of the preceding year" is omitted.

Auditor's Concurrence in a Change and Its Justification. Although an auditor's concurrence in an accounting change is implicit unless the report states otherwise, SAS No. 1 (AU Section 546.01) requires that concurrence be made explicit with the phrase "with which we concur."

The purpose of a consistency exception is to alert readers to the fact that a change has been made. If the auditor concurs in the change, the exception does not necessarily signal a problem that affects the quality of the financial statements other than the comparability of one period with another. Changes are rarely made that are not in conformity with generally accepted accounting principles, but SAS No. 1 (AU Sections 546.04–.11) covers reporting by means of qualified and adverse opinions in that event. If the auditor does not concur in a change, the reporting described in those paragraphs is appropriate.

An important advance in disclosure standards was the requirement in APB Opinion No. 20 (Accounting Standards Section A06), issued in 1971, that a change in accounting principle be justified by a clear explanation by management of why the newly adopted principle is preferable and that the justification be disclosed in the financial statements. Requiring that changes in accounting principles be justified was a significant step toward expecting issuers of financial statements to explain the "why" of their accounting as well as the "what." It should be noted, however, that while Opinion No. 20 prescribes that a note to the financial statements explain clearly why a newly adopted accounting principle is preferable, the authoritative literature of the profession does not explicitly require the auditor to be satisfied as to that preferability. The authoritative literature requires only that the auditor determine that disclosure of a reasonable justification of preferability was properly made. (That requirement should seldom cause problems because an auditor is certain to have been involved in the consideration of a proposed change, at least in helping to draft the explanatory note and more likely in suggesting the change to a preferable method in the first place.) The SEC, however, requires the auditor to submit a "preferability letter" stating that the auditor is satisfied with the justification provided by the company when an accounting change has been made.

Correction of Errors. There are two types of corrections of errors. Both are accounted for as prior-period adjustments and previous periods' statements are retroactively restated. The first type, which requires recognition in the auditor's opinion as to consistency, involves a change from an accounting principle that is not generally accepted to one that is, including the correction of a mistake in applying a principle. It should be treated in the auditor's report as a change in accounting principle in which the auditor concurs. The appropriate reference to consistency is that the statements are consistent after giving retroactive effect to the change.

The second type of error correction involves errors in previously issued financial statements resulting from mathematical mistakes, oversight, or misuse of facts that existed at the time the financial statements were originally prepared, and does not involve the consistency standard. A correction of an error of this type should be reported in a note to the financial statements; it may, but is not required to, be referred to in the auditor's report.

An example of an auditor's report when there has been a correction of an error resulting from an oversight follows:

> We have examined the consolidated financial statements of ABC Industries, Inc. and subsidiaries as listed in the accompanying index. . . .
>
> As more fully described in note A of notes to statements of consolidated earnings (loss), certain errors resulting in overstatements of previously reported year-end inventories as of April 28, 1987, April 29, 1986 and April 30, 1985 were discovered by management of the Company during the course of determining year-end inventory as of May 3, 1988. Accordingly, the consolidated balance sheet as of April 28, 1987 and the statements of consolidated earnings (loss), consolidated stockholders' equity, and changes in consolidated financial position for each of the three years then ended have been restated to reflect corrections to previously reported year-end inventories and the related tax effect.
>
> In our opinion, the aforementioned consolidated financial statements present fairly the financial position of ABC Industries, Inc. and subsidiaries at May 3, 1988 and April 28, 1987 and the results of their operations and the changes in their financial position for each of the years in the five-year period ended May 3, 1988, in conformity with generally accepted accounting principles applied on a consistent basis.

If significant corrections of the type illustrated are necessary, the auditor should take steps to ensure that users are informed of the corrections. Those steps are discussed in a later section of this chapter, entitled "Discovery of Information After the Report Date."

Change in the Reporting Entity. The consistency standard applies to a change in the reporting entity—a special type of change in accounting principle. No change in reporting entity results from creation, purchase, or disposition of a business or a segment of a business. Those types of economic events, however, may affect comparability and may require disclosure in the notes to the financial statements.

A change in the reporting entity, for example, a change in consolidation policy not resulting from an acquisition or disposition, such as if preexisting subsidiaries or affiliates are added to or excluded from consolidated or combined statements, is an inconsistency. APB Opinion No. 20, paragraphs 12, 34, and 35 (Accounting Standards Sections A35.112 and .113), requires that kind of change to be reflected by restatement of prior periods, and the auditor's report should refer to the statements being consistent after restatement for the change.

An example of the resulting opinion paragraph follows:

In our opinion, the statements mentioned above present fairly the consolidated financial position of ABC Airlines at December 31, 1987 and 1986, and the consolidated results of operations and changes in financial position for each of the three years in the period ended December 31, 1987, in conformity with generally accepted accounting principles applied on a consistent basis during the period after restatement for the change, with which we concur, in the consolidation policy as described in Note 1.

Note 1 read (in part) as follows:

The 1987 consolidated financial statements of ABC Airlines include the accounts of all subsidiaries, including ABC's non-airline subsidiaries. Prior to 1987, these subsidiaries were carried in the consolidated financial statements at cost plus equity in undistributed net earnings. The consolidated financial statements for 1986 and 1985 have been restated to reflect this change in consolidation policy, which results in a more comprehensive financial statement presentation. This change had no effect on net earnings (loss) or the related per share amounts. All significant intercompany transactions have been eliminated.

Change in Classification. SAS No. 1 (AU Section 420.14) discusses changes in classification of financial statements, as follows:

Classifications in the current financial statements may be different from classifications in the prior year's financial statements. . . . These changes . . . ordinarily would not affect the independent auditor's opinion as to consistency and need not be referred to in his report.

An example of a change in classification, provided in paragraph .29 of an Auditing Interpretation of AU Section 420, is that of combining "Cash on hand" with "Cash in bank" to create a new classification, "Cash."

The Interpretation (paragraph .30) goes on to state that "a change in classification that affects significantly the *measurement* of financial position or results of operations . . . would call for a consistency qualification in the auditor's report." For example, the adoption of APB Opinion No. 30 changed the type of items that could be reported as extraordinary. Since this classification materially affects the measurement of the results of operations, it represents a change in accounting principle rather than the routine classification changes covered by Section 420.14. Accordingly, if a change in classification has a material effect on comparability, the auditor's report should comment on the change and the opinion should be qualified as to consistency (paragraph .31 of the Interpretation).

Scope Limitations. An examination can be limited by client-imposed restrictions or by circumstances beyond the client's control that preclude an auditor from employing the auditing procedures that would otherwise be considered necessary.

Client-Imposed Restrictions. The most common client-imposed restrictions are limitations preventing observation of physical inventories, confirmation of accounts receivable, or examination of a significant subsidiary. Usually, if scope is limited by client-imposed restrictions, an auditor should disclaim an opinion (see later discussion) because the client's election to limit the auditor's scope implies also an election to limit the auditor's responsibility.[3]

Occasionally a client-imposed scope limitation may apply to one or a few isolated transactions or accounts, or to an area of lesser significance, so that a qualified opinion is acceptable. In that event, the qualification should be stated so that it clearly relates to the possible effects on the financial statements and not to the scope limitation. That is because relating the qualification to the scope limitation leaves unanswered the question of the possible effects on the financial statements, which is the subject of interest to readers (SAS No. 2, paragraph 40 [AU Section 509.40]). For example:

> . . . and such other auditing procedures as we considered necessary in the circumstances, except as stated in the following paragraph.
>
> In accordance with the terms of our engagement, we did not examine records supporting the company's investment in a foreign company stated at $_____, or its equity in earnings of that company, $_____, which is included in net income as described in Note B to the financial statements.
>
> In our opinion, except for the effect of possible adjustments, if any, to the carrying value or equity in earnings of the above-mentioned investment, the aforementioned financial statements present fairly. . . .

Conditions Precluding Necessary Auditing Procedures. Sometimes an auditor is not able to carry out procedures that customarily are considered neces-

---

[3]See also the discussion in Chapter 19 on the possibility of issuing a "review" type report in accordance with SSARS No. 1 when scope limitations are imposed by the client.

sary in the circumstances as a basis for rendering an unqualified opinion. In most instances, the auditor is able to design and perform alternative procedures that provide sufficient assurance that the relevant audit objectives have been achieved. The most common instances in which alternative procedures might not be able to be performed are when conditions make it impracticable or impossible to confirm accounts receivable or observe inventories. Other examples of such scope limitations involve investments accounted for under the equity method and occur when the auditor is unable to (1) obtain audited financial statements of an investee or apply auditing procedures to unaudited financial statements of an investee, or (2) examine sufficient evidential matter relating to the elimination of unrealized profits and losses resulting from transactions between the investor and the investee.

Before 1970, an auditor was expected to state in the scope paragraph of the report that receivables had not been confirmed or inventory had not been observed even if the auditor had obtained satisfaction as to those accounts by other means and was therefore able to render an unqualified opinion. In 1970, Statement on Auditing Procedure No. 43 concluded that there was no significance to that disclosure and therefore no need to make it. While the auditor is not specifically prohibited from including an explanatory comment in the report that discloses the circumstances of the engagement and describes the alternative procedures, paragraph 27 of SAS No. 2 (AU Section 509.27) makes no provision for emphasizing a matter regarding auditing procedures. It is better for the auditor to decide what auditing procedures are adequate and not to comment on them except as an explanation of a qualified opinion.

If an auditor cannot obtain satisfaction by means of alternative auditing procedures when circumstances preclude the application of conventional procedures to an account, the auditor should describe the problem and modify the standard report. If the auditor decides to express a qualified opinion (rather than disclaim an opinion), the problem should be described in a middle paragraph and referred to in both the scope paragraph and the opinion paragraph. A scope limitation should always be described entirely within the auditor's report, in contrast to the treatment of qualifications related to information presented in the financial statements, which are usually described in a note to the statements and only referred to in the report. That is because a qualification based on a scope limitation arises from the auditor's activities, and limitations on them, rather than from the financial statements themselves. As noted earlier, however, the qualification itself should be stated in terms of its effect on the financial statements rather than in terms of the scope limitation. SAS No. 2, *Reports on Audited Financial Statements* (AU Section 509.40) presents an example regarding inventories (the example assumes that the effects of the scope limitation do not cause the auditor to conclude that a disclaimer of opinion is appropriate).

(Scope paragraph)

Except as explained in the following paragraph, our examination . . . and such other auditing procedures as we considered necessary in the circumstances. . . .

(Separate paragraph)

We did not observe the taking of the physical inventories as of December 31, 19XX (stated at $_____), and December 31, 19X1 (stated at $_____), since those dates were prior to the time we were initially engaged as auditors for the Company. Due to the nature of the Company's records, we were unable to satisfy ourselves as to the inventory quantities by means of other auditing procedures.

(Opinion paragraph)

In our opinion, except for the effects of such adjustments, if any, as might have been determined to be necessary had we been able to observe the physical inventories. . . .

Uncertainties. Management is expected to evaluate and reach a reasoned conclusion on all matters affecting financial position and results of operations, and an auditor is expected to review and form an opinion on those conclusions. Some matters are simply not determinable, however, either by management or by the auditor, and others are determined by management on the basis of evidence too slight or subjective to be accepted by an auditor. Both kinds of matters give rise to "subject to" qualified opinions, or disclaimers when the uncertainties are pervasive (see discussion of disclaimers later in this chapter).

FASB Statement No. 5 (Accounting Standards Section C59) requires that potential losses due to uncertainties be classified as "probable," "reasonably possible," or "remote." If a loss is probable, management must provide for it in the financial statements, either by accruing it if the amount is susceptible of reasonable determination or by disclosing it if the amount cannot be reasonably estimated; no qualification of the auditor's opinion is needed if the auditor agrees that the provision or disclosure is appropriate. Likewise, a "remote" uncertainty would require neither disclosure nor a qualification. If a material loss is "reasonably possible," however, management is required to disclose the uncertainty in the notes to the financial statements, including an estimate of the amount, and the auditor would normally issue a "subject to" qualified opinion if the amount of the potential loss was material.

For instance, if the outcome of a matter having an impact on the financial statements depends on the decisions of others, it may be impossible for management and the auditor to reach a valid conclusion about it. The most common events of that kind are lawsuits and tax disputes. The mere existence of an unresolved question does not relieve management or the auditor of the responsibility of forming a judgment about the outcome, if at all possible; for many disputed tax issues, for example, the outcome is reasonably determinable by an informed analysis. In some cases, however, the best possible efforts result in a judgment that no valid conclusion can be formed. In that event, the uncertainty should be described in a middle paragraph of the report, even though it is also described in a note to the financial statements, and the opinion paragraph should be qualified using the phrase "subject to."

Sometimes the judgments involved in choosing between an ''except for'' and a ''subject to'' qualification can be difficult when the basis for the choice is itself a matter of judgment. For example, disputes over interpretation of income tax regulations that affect the provision for income taxes are common. If the amount involved is material, an auditor is likely to find it difficult to decide whether to issue a ''subject to'' qualification because of an uncertainty that can be resolved only by a future court decision, or whether to evaluate the tax case, reach a judgment on its merits, and express an ''except for'' opinion if the client does not agree.

SAS No. 2, paragraph 39, as amended (AU Section 509.39), gives an example of the wording of a report qualified because of an uncertainty affecting the financial statements, as follows:

(Separate paragraph)

As discussed in Note X to the financial statements, the company is defendant in a lawsuit alleging infringement of certain patent rights and claiming royalties and punitive damages. The company has filed a counter action, and preliminary hearings and discovery proceedings on both actions are in progress. The ultimate outcome of the lawsuits cannot presently be determined, and no provision for any liability that may result has been made in the financial statements.

(Opinion paragraph)

In our opinion, subject to the effects on the financial statements of such adjustments, if any, as might have been required had the outcome of the uncertainty referred to in the preceding paragraph been known, the financial statements referred to above present fairly. . . .

Some important financial statement matters are determined by management based on estimates and judgments for which there is little or no objective evidence for an auditor to review. The most common examples are realizability or recovery of assets such as plant or deferred charges. Long-term investments can be an especially troublesome item because the determination of value may be subjective, judgmental, and highly specialized. When those issues arise, management has a responsibility for making its judgments as objective and rational as possible and for documenting them; an auditor has a responsibility for understanding the client's business well enough to be able to form an opinion on those judgments. Nevertheless, there are occasions when an auditor cannot take a position for or against a client's conclusion reflected in the financial statements, because it is outside the auditor's expertise or because sufficient competent evidential matter simply does not exist. If the uncertainty is the auditor's rather than management's, the opinion must be qualified.

The Materiality of Uncertainties. The auditor must use professional judgment in considering whether the potential effect of an uncertainty is sufficiently material to require a qualified opinion. As with other materiality decisions, official pronouncements do not provide much guidance in this area. (See the discussion of materiality on page 800 in this chapter.) Paragraphs .26–.28 of an Auditing Interpretation of AU Section 509 offer some guidelines for the auditor, as follows:

> Materiality is a relative concept and the basis of comparison is thus an important aspect of the auditor's consideration of whether an uncertainty is material. Some uncertainties relate primarily to financial position while others more closely relate to results of operations. Thus the auditor should consider the potential effect on the financial statement that is most appropriate in the circumstances.
>
> Some uncertainties are unusual in nature or infrequent in occurrence and thus more closely related to financial position than to normal, recurring operations. Examples include the recoverability of start-up costs and litigation relating to alleged violations of antitrust or securities laws. In such instances the auditor should evaluate the materiality of the uncertainty by comparing the potential effect to shareholders' equity and also to other relevant balance sheet components such as total assets, total liabilities, current assets or current liabilities.
>
> In other instances the nature of an uncertainty may be more closely related to normal, recurring operations, for example, litigation with a party to a royalty agreement concerning whether a royalty fee should be paid on certain revenues, and revenues of certain public utilities collected subject to refund. In such circumstances it is appropriate to consider the materiality of the uncertainty in relation to the potential effect on the income statement.

Going Concern. One specific type of uncertainty that the auditor must consider, and that the authoritative auditing literature has addressed, is the client's continued existence as a "going concern." The concept that financial statements are prepared on the basis of a going concern is one of the basic tenets of financial accounting. The going concern assumption is that the carrying value of assets will be realized and liabilities will be liquidated in the ordinary course of continuing business activity. Because the going concern assumption is so basic, the standard auditor's report does not make reference to it.

When a company becomes insolvent, however, or operates for long periods with a net outflow of cash or is unable to meet currently maturing obligations, the going concern assumption must be questioned. That consideration immediately raises a number of questions about realizable value of assets, the order of payment of liabilities, and the proper classification and carrying amounts of both; the unexpired historical carrying amounts may become inappropriate (usually they are in excess of forced liquidation values). Reasonable assurance that the company will not have to suspend operations—a decision that the company is a going concern—must be explicitly considered, and if it cannot be obtained, the auditor's report must be qualified to report that fact.

Two kinds of events create "going concern" problems. One is operational uncertainties—progressive deterioration in a firm's financial health because of operational factors, changing markets, or aging and inefficient plant. That results in, among other things, declining earnings or losses, reduced cash balances, and increasing inability to meet current liabilities on a timely basis. This set of events can occur quite suddenly—within a year—or develop over a long period of time. In its early stages it is likely to appear temporary and not serious; identifying the point at which the going concern question must be recognized is one of the most challenging judgments an auditor is called on to make. Failure to comply with bond indenture provisions—such as maintaining working capital requirements—often results in a technical default that, unless waived, can accelerate maturities and cause a "going concern" problem.

Another type of operational uncertainty results when a newly organized company has not yet achieved success and a solid financial position. In this case, the realizability of its assets (which are usually specialized plant and equipment, inventories, and sometimes deferred charges) can be questionable and the company's continuation not at all ensured.

The other kind of event leading to questions about the ability to continue in business is external—an occurrence beyond the control of an enterprise, and potentially beyond its financial capabilities as well. Governmental actions, mandatory product recalls, or lawsuits of various kinds could all result in that kind of potential catastrophe.

In many situations, a "going concern" qualification is unnecessary because the problems are diagnosed early enough for corrective action, or the enterprise is able to show that it can otherwise overcome its difficulties. When doubts about the ability of a company to continue as a going concern cannot be satisfactorily resolved, they sometimes, but not always, constitute a pervasive uncertainty.

SAS No. 34, *The Auditor's Considerations When a Question Arises About an Entity's Continued Existence* (AU Section 340), provides guidance regarding the auditor's considerations when made aware of information that raises a question about an entity's ability to continue in existence. Paragraph 3 of SAS No. 34 (AU Section 340.03) states that the auditor must, in forming an opinion on the financial statements, consider any information contrary to the going concern assumption, together with any factors tending to mitigate that information and any management plans for dealing with the underlying conditions.

The following examples of contrary information are provided in paragraph 4 of SAS No. 34 (AU Section 340.04):

a. Information that may indicate solvency problems:
- Negative trends (for example, recurring operating losses, working capital deficiencies, negative cash flows from operations, and adverse key financial ratios).
- Other indications (for example, default on loan or similar agreements, arrearages in dividends, denial of usual trade credit from suppliers, noncompliance with statutory capital requirements, and necessity of seeking new sources or methods of financing).

b. Information that may raise a question about continued existence without necessarily indicating potential solvency problems:

- Internal matters (for example, loss of key management or operations personnel, work stoppages or other labor difficulties, substantial dependence on the success of a particular project, and uneconomic long-term commitments).
- External matters (for example, legal proceedings, legislation, or similar matters that might jeopardize an entity's ability to operate; loss of a key franchise, license, or patent; loss of a principal customer or supplier; and uninsured catastrophes such as drought, earthquake, or flood).

SAS No. 34 provides examples of factors tending to mitigate the significance of contrary information concerning solvency (paragraph 5 [AU Section 340.05]), which relate primarily to an entity's alternative means for maintaining adequate cash flows. Such examples follow:

a. Asset factors:
- Disposability of assets not operationally interdependent.
- Capability of delaying the replacement of assets consumed in operations or of leasing rather than purchasing certain assets.
- Possibility of using assets for factoring, sale–leaseback, or similar arrangements.

b. Debt factors:
- Availability of unused lines of credit or similar borrowing capacity.
- Capability of renewing or extending the due dates of existing loans.
- Possibility of entering into debt restructuring agreements.

c. Cost factors:
- Separability of operations producing negative cash flows.
- Capability of postponing expenditures for such matters as maintenance or research and development.
- Possibility of reducing overhead and administrative expenditures.

d. Equity factors:
- Variability of dividend requirements.
- Capability of obtaining additional equity capital.
- Possibility of increasing cash distributions from affiliates or other investees.

Paragraph 6 (AU Section 340.06) suggests that the factors tending to mitigate the significance of contrary information not necessarily concerning solvency relate primarily to the entity's capacity to adopt alternative courses of action with regard to, for example, filling key executive positions, replacing assets seized or destroyed, substituting for lost customers or suppliers, and operating at reduced levels or redeploying resources.

The auditor should also review management's plans that are responsive to the unfavorable conditions, with particular emphasis on plans that might have a significant effect on the entity's solvency within one year following the date of the financial statements being reported on. Paragraph 8 summarizes the auditor's considerations relating to such management plans, as follows:

a. Plans to liquidate assets:
   - Apparent marketability of the assets that management plans to sell.
   - Restrictions on the disposal of assets, such as covenants limiting such transactions in loan or similar agreements or encumbrances against assets.
   - Possible direct and indirect effects of the disposal of assets.

b. Plans to borrow money or restructure debt:
   - Availability of debt financing, including existing or committed credit arrangements, such as lines of credit and arrangements for factoring receivables or sale–leaseback of assets.
   - Existing or committed arrangements to restructure or subordinate debt or to guarantee loans to the entity.
   - Possible effects on management's borrowing plans of existing restrictions on additional borrowing and the sufficiency of available collateral.

c. Plans to reduce or delay expenditures:
   - Apparent feasibility of plans to reduce overhead and administrative expenditures, to postpone maintenance or research and development projects, or to lease rather than purchase assets.
   - Possible direct and indirect effects of reduced or delayed expenditures.

d. Plans to increase ownership equity:
   - Apparent feasibility of plans to increase ownership equity, including existing or committed arrangements to raise additional capital.
   - Existing or committed arrangements to reduce current dividend requirements or to accelerate cash distributions from affiliates or other investees.

After assessing all relevant information, factors, and plans, the auditor must decide whether or not to express a qualified opinion on the financial statements. If a substantial doubt remains about the entity's ability to continue in existence, then the auditor should consider the recoverability and classification of recorded asset amounts, and the amounts and classification of liabilities, in light of that doubt (paragraph 11 [AU Section 340.11]). SAS No. 34, however, provides no specific criteria as to when a qualified opinion should be issued. Paragraph 11 (AU Section 340.11) states:

> Identifying the point at which uncertainties about recoverability, classifications, and amounts require the auditor to modify his report is a complex professional judgment. No single factor or combination of factors is controlling.

Often when a company reaches the point where the auditor decides to qualify the opinion, there are numerous reasons for such qualification. The following example notes several reasons and concludes with a "subject to" qualification:

(Explanatory paragraphs)

As shown in the consolidated financial statements, the Company incurred net losses of $10,000,000, $160,000,000 and $12,000,000 for the three fiscal years ended January 31, 1987, which have significantly weakened the Company's financial position and ability to purchase merchandise and meet operating expenses and, at January 31, 1987, the Company's current liabilities exceeded its current assets by $26,000,000. As discussed in Note 9, at January 31, 1987, the Company is in violation of certain covenants under the Revolving Loan Agreement with banks and is therefore unable to borrow additional funds under this agreement.

As more fully described in Note 9, for the fiscal year ended January 31, 1987, the Company has provided reserves for losses on lease obligations related to retail stores and a warehouse to be closed. The settlement of these lease obligations may ultimately be for amounts materially different from that which has been provided.

The Company is currently negotiating with third parties in an effort to obtain additional sources of funds which, in management's opinion, would provide adequate working capital to finance the Company's operations. The satisfactory completion of these negotiations is essential as the Company has no other immediate plans which will provide sufficient working capital to meet current operating requirements. Because the negotiations are still in progress, there can be no assurance that the Company will have sufficient working capital to finance their operations through the fiscal year ending January 30, 1988.

The matters discussed in the preceding paragraphs indicate that the Company may be unable to continue in existence. The aforementioned consolidated financial statements do not include any adjustments related to the recoverability and classification of recorded asset amounts or the amounts and classification of liabilities that might be necessary should the Company be unable to continue in existence.

(Opinion paragraph)

In our opinion, subject to the effect on the consolidated financial statements and schedules of such adjustments, if any, as might have been required had the outcome of the uncertainties about the recoverability and classification of recorded asset amounts and the amounts and classification of liabilities and other matters referred to in the preceding paragraphs been known, the consolidated financial statements referred to above present fairly the consolidated financial position of ABC Company and Subsidiaries as of January 31, 1987, and the consolidated results of their operations and changes in their financial position for the fiscal year then ended, and the related schedules present fairly the information required to be included therein, all in conformity with generally accepted accounting principles applied on a basis consistent with that of the preceding year.

Reports on Comparative Financial Statements with Differing or Updated Opinions. In accordance with SAS No. 15, *Reports on Comparative Financial Statements* (AU Section 505), an auditor may express a qualified opinion with respect to the financial statements of one of the periods presented and an unqualified opinion on the other financial statements presented. Following are examples of reports on comparative financial statements with differing opinions.

Qualified Opinion on Current Year's Financial Statements with Prior Year Unqualified:

We have examined the consolidated balance sheet of XYZ Company and subsidiaries at December 31, 1987, 1986 and 1985, and the related consolidated statements of income, changes in shareholders' equity, and changes in financial position for the years then ended. Our examinations were made in accordance with generally accepted auditing standards and, accordingly, included such tests of the accounting records and such other auditing procedures as we considered necessary in the circumstances.

As discussed in Note 13, during 1987 the Company became a defendant in a lawsuit relating to the sale in 1987 of a wholly owned subsidiary. The ultimate outcome of the lawsuit cannot be determined, and no provision for any liability that may result has been made in the 1987 financial statements.

In our opinion, subject to the effects in 1987 of such adjustments, if any, as might have been required had the outcome of the uncertainty mentioned in the preceding paragraph been known, the financial statements referred to above present fairly the consolidated financial position of XYZ Company and subsidiaries at December 31, 1987, 1986 and 1985, and the consolidated results of their operations and the consolidated changes in their financial position for the years then ended, in conformity with generally accepted accounting principles applied on a consistent basis.

SAS No. 15 (AU Section 505) also provides guidance when an auditor becomes aware during the current examination of circumstances or events that affect the financial statements of a prior period. The subsequent resolution of an uncertainty, the discovery of an uncertainty in a subsequent period, or the subsequent restatement of prior-period financial statements would cause an auditor to express in an updated report an opinion different from that expressed in an earlier report on the financial statements of the prior period. In these circumstances, SAS No. 15, paragraph 7 (AU Section 505.07), requires that all the substantive reasons for the different opinion be disclosed in a separate explanatory paragraph(s) of the report. According to AU Section 505.07, the explanatory paragraph should include

(a) The date of the auditor's previous report, (b) the type of opinion previously expressed, (c) the circumstances or events that caused the auditor to express a different opinion, and (d) that the auditor's updated opinion on the financial statements of the prior period is different from his previous opinion on those statements.

Adverse Opinions

An adverse opinion expresses a belief that financial statements are not presented fairly in conformity with generally accepted accounting principles or otherwise do not present fairly what they purport to present. It is required when an auditor has sufficient evidence for a belief that one or more departures from GAAP are sufficiently material to make the statements as a whole misleading. The auditor cannot sidestep an adverse opinion simply by disclaiming an opinion.

When an adverse opinion is issued, the opinion paragraph should include a reference to a separate paragraph in the auditor's report that discloses all the reasons for the adverse opinion, including any reservations the auditor may have regarding fair presentation in conformity with GAAP other than those that gave rise to the adverse opinion. The separate paragraph (or paragraphs, if appropriate) should also disclose the effects of the departures from GAAP on the financial statements or state that such a determination is not possible.

Adverse opinions are rare. It is obviously better for all concerned to correct the conditions before such an opinion is issued, and it is usually within the client's power to correct them. In practice, adverse opinions are usually restricted to statements prepared for special and limited purposes, whose users need a particular kind of statement that is at variance with generally accepted accounting principles and are able to understand what is involved thereby. Examples are financial statements showing appraised values of property and statements employing specified accounting principles required and agreed to by parties to a particular transaction, such as a business combination involving unusual terms or agreements among the parties. Even in these cases, however, the auditor may issue a special report (see Chapter 19) rather than an adverse opinion.

Disclaimers of Opinion

If an auditor does not have enough evidence to form an opinion, the appropriate form of report is a disclaimer of opinion. A disclaimer can result because there were major and pervasive uncertainties that could not be resolved, because the scope of the auditor's examination was seriously limited, or because the auditor was not independent. While SAS No. 2 (AU Section 509) indicates that usually a "subject to" opinion is appropriate when there are uncertainties, in some cases an auditor may decide to decline to express an opinion.

Paragraph 45 of SAS No. 2 (AU Section 509.45) states that all substantive reasons for a disclaimer must be given in a separate paragraph of the report. The intention is to make it clear that an auditor should not give only one reason for a disclaimer (such as the inability to conduct an audit) if there is more than one and that the auditor especially should not blanket unfavorable reasons by citing only a relatively innocuous one. That same paragraph also requires the auditor to disclose in a separate paragraph any reservations about fair presentation in conformity with GAAP or the consistent application of GAAP. It would be misleading for an auditor to issue a disclaimer if a basis for an adverse judgment or a qualified ("except for") opinion existed; in that situation, the auditor must make the judgment, issue an adverse or a qualified ("except for") opinion, and describe the reasons therefor. Adverse opinions and disclaimers of opinion are never interchangeable, nor can an auditor's report contain both an adverse opinion and a disclaimer of opinion. A report may, however, contain an opinion that is qualified for more than one reason. For example, an opinion may be qualified because of an uncertainty (''subject to'') *and* because of a departure from GAAP (''except for'').

Uncertainties. The kinds of uncertainties that call for a disclaimer must be distinguished from the necessary estimates of future events, which are a normal management responsibility, and also from those specific uncertainties that can be isolated, defined, explained, and understood—and that therefore result in a qualified ''subject to'' opinion. When the possible effect of one or more uncertainties on the financial statements is so complex or pervasive as to be impossible to assess, a disclaimer may be appropriate. A footnote to paragraph 25 of SAS No. 2 (AU Section 509.25) indicates that issuing a ''subject to'' opinion and explaining the uncertainties should serve adequately to inform financial statement users; however, the auditor is not precluded from disclaiming an opinion in cases involving uncertainties. As a result, disclaimers resulting from uncertainties, while not common, are an accepted feature of financial reporting. A disclaimer because of an uncertainty might be worded as follows:

> Because of the possible material effect on the financial statements referred to above of [describe or refer to a description of the condition], the outcome of which is uncertain, we do not express any opinion on the company's financial statements.

Scope Limitations. Disclaimers because of scope limitations, in contrast, are acceptable only in certain limited circumstances. If evidence exists that could have been examined by an auditor so as to form an opinion, it is considered unacceptable for either the client or the auditor to sidestep that opinion by limiting the scope of the examination, because choosing to do so is deliberately choosing to render the opinion worthless. On the other hand, when evidence is too difficult to obtain or is irrelevant to the purpose for which statements are required, a scope limitation disclaimer can be acceptable because it is not a matter of deliberate choice. After considering the particular circumstances of the engagement, however, an auditor may instead issue a ''review'' type opinion (described in SSARS No. 1 and Chapter 19) in cases of severe scope limitation. The most frequently encountered examples of disclaimers because of scope limitations arise in initial engagements and examinations conducted for certain limited purposes.

Initial Examinations. In an initial engagement for a new client, an auditor is likely to begin work well after the beginning of the year under examination. If the opening inventory has a material effect on income for the year (as it usually does in most manufacturing and commercial enterprises), an auditor either must try to gather evidence on which to base an opinion on the opening inventory or must disclaim an opinion or issue a qualified opinion on the income statement and statement of changes in financial position. When the auditor is able to form an opinion on the opening inventory—which ordinarily happens when another reputable auditor is succeeded—there is no need to cover the point in the report. (Chapter 14 discusses appropriate auditing procedures in this situation.)

Sometimes the client and auditor may agree that it is not worth the time and cost to examine the opening inventory—or that it is not possible. In that event, assuming that the auditor deems it appropriate to disclaim an opinion on the income statement and statement of changes in financial position, the auditor's report, following the form shown in SAS No. 1 (AU Section 542.05), would read

> We have examined the balance sheet of X Company as of December 31, 19X2, and the related statements of income and retained earnings and changes in financial position for the year then ended. Our examination was made in accordance with generally accepted auditing standards and, accordingly, included such tests of the accounting records and such other auditing procedures as we considered necessary in the circumstances, except as stated in the following paragraph.
>
> Because we were not engaged as auditors until after December 31, 19X1, we were not present to observe the physical inventory taken at that date and we have not satisfied ourselves by means of other procedures concerning such inventory quantities. The amount of the inventory at December 31, 19X1, enters materially into the determination of the results of operations and changes in financial position for the year ended December 31, 19X2. Therefore, we do not express an opinion on the accompanying statements of income and retained earnings and changes in financial position for the year ended December 31, 19X2.
>
> In our opinion, the accompanying balance sheet presents fairly the financial position of X Company at December 31, 19X2, in conformity with generally accepted accounting principles applied on a basis consistent with that of the preceding year.

Limited Examinations. Sometimes a client needs an auditor's report for certain limited purposes and does not want a "review" type report, and all parties are willing to accept a disclaimer of opinion. Probably the most common example is when the observation of year-end physical inventories is omitted because it may be relatively expensive and a client (or potential user) may consider it irrelevant for the specific purposes of the report. An explanatory paragraph should describe the limitation, and the opinion paragraph should contain the disclaimer (SAS No. 2, paragraphs 45–47 [AU Sections 509.45–47]). For example:

> . . . and such other auditing procedures as we considered necessary in the circumstances, except as explained in the following paragraph.
>
> In accordance with the terms of our engagement, we did not observe physical inventory taking nor did we employ alternative procedures with respect to inventories at the beginning and end of the year.

Because the inventory at those dates enters materially into the determination of financial position, results of operations, and changes in financial position, the scope of our work was not sufficient to enable us to express, and we do not express, an opinion on the aforementioned financial statements.

An auditor faced with a request for a limited examination should ask the client what the objectives are and should be especially careful to ensure that the reasons for and effects of a disclaimer of opinion are thoroughly understood. A client willing to accept a disclaimer based on omission of inventory observation may have unrealistic assumptions about the purpose of the audit; for example, the client may believe that it provides assurance as to other aspects of the statements or as to the absence of defalcations and similar irregularities.

While an auditor must stand ready to serve a client in any way appropriate, the authors believe that limited engagements likely to lead to a disclaimer should be approached reluctantly because of the high risk that incorrect inferences about the auditor's responsibilities will be drawn by the client and other users. In most cases, a client's needs can be served by a review of financial statements performed in accordance with SSARS No. 1 or by designing a special engagement in which responsibilities can be spelled out explicitly. Various special reports are discussed in Chapter 19.

When an Auditor Is Not Independent. Occasionally, an auditor prepares financial statements for an organization in which the auditor is an officer, director, part owner, or significant creditor or to which the auditor is otherwise related. Since the auditor lacks independence—as called for by the second general standard—a disclaimer of opinion is required. Independence is such an elusive and subjective quality that the profession has deemed it best to permit no exceptions to the rule of absolute disclaimer of opinion in the absence of independence. An auditor should not attempt to mitigate the lack of independence—by describing the reason for it, for example, or by describing auditing procedures that were carried out.

SAS No. 26, *Association With Financial Statements* (AU Section 504), covers that condition and gives, in paragraph 10 (AU Section 504.10), the following example of a disclaimer of opinion:

We are not independent with respect to XYZ Company, and the accompanying balance sheet as of December 31, 19X1, and the related statements of income, retained earnings, and changes in financial position for the year then ended were not audited by us and, accordingly, we do not express an opinion on them.

AU Section 504.11 emphasizes that issuing a disclaimer in this or any other circumstances does not permit an auditor to ignore departures from GAAP; if the auditor knows of them, there are three alternative courses of action: insist on revision of the statements, describe the reservations in the disclaimer, or refuse to be associated with the financial statements.

Piecemeal Opinions

A piecemeal opinion is the complement of a qualified opinion: that is, a qualified opinion gives an opinion on the financial statements as a whole and makes exceptions for certain items, whereas a piecemeal opinion disclaims or is adverse on the financial statements as a whole and gives an opinion on certain items. In the past, piecemeal opinions were not uncommon, but they presented so many problems that they are now prohibited by paragraph 48 of SAS No. 2 (AU Section 509.48).

The SAS states as a reason that "piecemeal opinions tend to overshadow or contradict a disclaimer of opinion or an adverse opinion. . . ." In addition, piecemeal opinions took specific items out of the context of the financial statements as a whole, thus implying a greater degree of precision about those items under conditions that usually entailed a lesser degree of certainty. Also, the defect in the financial statements as a whole that caused the disclaimer or adverse opinion tended to destroy or call into question the interrelated, corroborative nature of accounts on which the audit logic depends. When all of these deficiencies were balanced against the limited usefulness of piecemeal opinions, the profession was well off to abandon them.

Adverse Opinions Versus Disclaimers

There is a fundamental difference between departures from GAAP, which affect the quality of the financial statements, and uncertainties and scope limitations, which affect the sufficiency and competence of audit evidence. If departures from GAAP become so great as to make the financial statements useless, an adverse opinion is called for. On the other hand, if uncertainties or scope limitations are so pervasive that the auditor cannot form an opinion, a disclaimer of opinion may be called for. The following tabulation helps keep in perspective the distinctions among qualified opinions, adverse opinions, and disclaimers of opinion. (See also Figure 1.2 in Chapter 1.)

	Degree of Materiality or Pervasiveness	
Condition	*Less*	*More*
Departures from GAAP	"Except for" qualification	Adverse opinion
Scope limitations	"Except for" qualification	Disclaimer of opinion
Uncertainties	"Subject to" qualification	Disclaimer of opinion permissible

Unresolved uncertainties do not necessarily involve disagreement between client and auditor, but instead affect the degree of assurance of the opinion and call for an opinion "subject to" the uncertainty, or occasionally for a disclaimer because of pervasiveness of the uncertainty. Similarly, scope limitations also affect the degree of assurance contained in the opinion, whether the limitations are client imposed or the result of circumstances, and call for an "except for" opinion or a disclaimer. On the other hand, departures from GAAP are forms of disagreement about the quality of the financial statements and call for an "except for" qualification or, if necessary, an adverse opinion.

The Effect of Materiality on Auditors' Reports

In deciding whether a departure from the standard, unqualified report is appropriate, the auditor considers the materiality of the condition or circumstance in question. A materiality test must be applied in determining not only whether to depart from an unqualified opinion but also whether the appropriate departure is a qualified opinion on the one hand or an adverse opinion or a disclaimer of opinion on the other. As noted earlier, a departure from GAAP that is sufficiently material could lead to an adverse opinion, and scope limitations or uncertainties that are sufficiently material could lead to a disclaimer of opinion.

Authoritative auditing literature provides scant guidance for deciding whether the effects of a particular condition or circumstance are sufficiently material to require a qualified opinion or either an adverse opinion or a disclaimer. Paragraph 16 of SAS No. 2 (AU Section 509.16) suggests several factors to be considered in determining the materiality of the effects of a departure from GAAP, namely, the dollar magnitude of the effects, the significance of an item to a particular enterprise, the pervasiveness of the misstatement, and the impact of the misstatement on the financial statements taken as a whole. Even this type of limited guidance is absent in the authoritative literature concerning scope limitations and uncertainties.

Responsibilities After the Report Date

Discovery of Information After the Report Date

Chapter 17 discusses an auditor's responsibility to obtain knowledge about subsequent events up to certain dates. Clearly, the auditor is not obligated to "keep current" indefinitely; as explained in Chapter 17, the responsibility ends with the issuance of the financial statements and the auditor's report, with the exception of a 1933 Act filing with the SEC. In that situation, the responsibility extends to the effective date of the registration statement.

After the financial statements and audit report have been issued, however, an auditor may become aware of new information regarding the client. If the new information refers to a condition that did not exist at the date of the audit report, or if it refers to final resolutions of contingencies or other matters disclosed in the financial statements or the auditor's report, the auditor has no further obligation. The new information may, however, relate to facts existing at the date of the audit report that might have affected the financial statements or auditor's report had the auditor then been aware of them. For example, the auditor may learn on April 14, 19X2, after the financial statements for 19X1 were issued, that a large receivable on the December 31, 19X1, balance sheet and believed at that date to be collectible was in fact uncollectible because the customer had declared bankruptcy on December 5, 19X1. In those circumstances, the auditor is obligated to pursue the matter.

While the distinction between the two kinds of new information is conceptually clear, in practice it is often difficult to tell, at least initially, whether the new information refers to a new condition or a preexisting one. The new information is often fragmentary, hearsay, or otherwise suspect. If it comes from a source other than the client, the situation is obviously awkward at best and potentially explosive and dangerous at worst, and an auditor in this situation may find it desirable to seek the advice of legal counsel. Subject to that advice, an auditor should ordinarily first discuss the information with the client and request that the client make any necessary investigations. Usually clients comply at once, but occasionally a client may refuse to believe the information, to discuss it with the auditor, or to make any investigation.

SAS No. 1 (AU Section 561) provides guidance to the auditor on subsequent steps to be taken. If the client cooperates and the information is found to be reliable and to have existed at the date of the auditor's report, the client should be advised to disclose the newly discovered facts and their effect on the financial statements by issuing revised financial statements and auditor's report. The reasons for the revisions should be described in a note to the financial statements and referred to in the auditor's report. An auditor's report accompanying revised financial statements would read (in part) as follows: "In our opinion, the aforementioned financial statements, revised as described in Note X, present fairly. . . ." If financial statements for a subsequent period are about to be issued, the revision may be incorporated in those statements, as long as disclosure of the revision is not thereby unduly delayed. The auditor's report on the comparative financial statements need not refer to the revision provided there is appropriate disclosure. The auditor may, however, include an explanatory middle paragraph to emphasize the revision.

Sometimes, determining the effect on the financial statements requires prolonged investigation, or the information is so significant that no delay is tolerable. In those circumstances, the client should notify all persons likely to be relying on the financial statements of the problem under investigation. Usually, that would include stockholders, banks, and, for publicly held companies, the SEC, stock exchanges, regulatory agencies, and the press.

If the client's management refuses to make the appropriate disclosures, the auditor should obtain the advice of legal counsel and should notify each member of the client's board of directors of that refusal and of the subsequent steps the auditor will take to prevent future reliance on the audit report. Unless the auditor's counsel recommends otherwise, the auditor should notify the client that the auditor's report is no longer to be associated with the financial statements. In addition, the auditor should notify the SEC, stock exchanges, and any other regulatory agencies involved of the situation and the withdrawal of the report and request that steps be taken to accomplish the necessary public disclosure (usually this notification is made public at once). The auditor should also notify in writing any others who are known to be currently relying or who are likely to rely on the financial statements and the related auditor's report. The public disclosure following notification to the SEC is intended to take care of all unknown interested parties.

The disclosures made by the auditor to regulatory agencies and other parties should, if possible, describe the information and its effect on the financial statements and the auditor's report. The description should be precise and factual and should avoid references to conduct, motives, and the like. SAS No. 1 (AU Section 561.09) describes the appropriate disclosure if precise and factual information is not available, as follows:

> If the client has not cooperated and as a result the auditor is unable to conduct a satisfactory investigation of the information, his disclosure need not detail the specific information but can merely indicate that information has come to his attention which his client has not cooperated in attempting to substantiate and that, if the information is true, the auditor believes that his report must no longer be relied upon or be associated with the financial statements. No such disclosure should be made unless the auditor believes that the financial statements are likely to be misleading and that his report should not be relied on.

Consideration of Omitted Procedures After the Report Date

The auditor may, subsequent to issuing an audit report, conclude that one or more auditing procedures considered necessary in the circumstances were omitted during the examination. For example, as part of its internal quality review program, a CPA firm may discover that no physical inspection was performed of a significant quantity of a client's inventory stored at a remote location. The actions to be taken by the auditor in this and similar situations vary depending on the circumstances, and the auditor should be guided by the advice of legal counsel. SAS No. 46, *Consideration of Omitted Procedures After the Report Date* (AU Section 390), provides guidance in this area.

The auditor should, as a first step, assess the importance of the omitted procedure in relation to his or her ability to support the previously issued opinion. On further investigation, such as, for example, review of working papers and inquiry of members of the engagement team, the auditor may decide that other procedures that were performed compensated adequately for the omitted procedure. In this instance, the auditor usually does not take any further steps. If, however, the auditor concludes that the omission of the auditing procedure significantly impairs his or her ability to support the previously issued opinion and believes there are persons currently relying or likely to rely on the report, additional procedures necessary to provide an adequate basis for the opinion issued should be performed promptly. Those procedures may be the omitted procedure or appropriate alternatives designed to compensate adequately for it.

The performance of those procedures may disclose facts that existed at the date of the audit report that would have affected the opinion rendered had the auditor been aware of them at the time. In such circumstances, the auditor should follow the steps outlined earlier in this chapter relating to the subsequent discovery of facts that existed at the report date.

Situations may arise, however, when because of the passage of time or other reasons, the auditor is unable to perform the previously omitted or alternative procedures. In such instances, the auditor would be well advised to seek the advice of legal counsel before deciding on the appropriate course of action. In any event, strong consideration should be given to notifying the client regarding the problem and the proposed action.

Review Questions

18-1. What are the four standards of reporting?

18-2. Describe the organization of the standard audit report. What "messages" are intended to be conveyed by the standard report?

18-3. When the principal auditor decides to refer to the examination of a subsidiary by another auditor, how is this indicated in the report? When is this reference necessary?

18-4. When comparative financial statements are presented, and the prior year's statements were examined by another auditor, what are the two alternatives the successor auditor and client have?

18-5. What is the auditor's responsibility concerning additional information published by the client in the same document as the audited financial statements (as, for example, in an annual report to stockholders)?

18-6. What are the four reasons for qualifying an opinion? Indicate the type of qualification that would be appropriate in each case.

18-7. What is the purpose of a consistency exception? Give some examples.

18-8. What are the two types of corrections of errors and how are they handled by the auditor?

18-9. What is a scope limitation? Give an illustration, and indicate when a disclaimer would be necessary.

18-10. For what reasons are "subject to" qualified opinions issued?

18-11. What is the going concern assumption?

18-12. What are some factors that would tend to mitigate the need for a going concern qualification caused by possible insolvency?

18-13. Distinguish between an adverse opinion and a disclaimer of opinion.

18-14. What is a piecemeal opinion? What restrictions are there on piecemeal opinions?

18-15. What are the auditor's responsibilities with regard to new information about a client that becomes available after the report date?

18-16. Why should limited engagements (other than compilations and reviews) that are likely to lead to disclaimers be approached with reluctance by an auditor?

Discussion Questions

18-30. The standard short-form independent auditor's report or opinion includes the following statement:

> Our examination was made in accordance with generally accepted auditing standards and, accordingly, included such tests of the accounting records and such other auditing procedures as we considered necessary in the circumstances.

Analyze and briefly discuss the above-quoted statement.

18-31. What would be the effect of each of the following conditions on the auditor's report?

a. Accounts receivable are significant in amount. The client refused to permit their confirmation by direct correspondence and no other satisfactory means of establishing the substantial correctness of the total were available.

b. The client refused to permit the auditor to examine the minutes of board of directors' meetings.

c. The client has an account receivable, substantial in amount, from a wholly owned subsidiary. The company has expressed its willingness to request the subsidiary to confirm the amount of its indebtedness directly to the auditor. However, the company refused to give the auditor access to the books and records of the subsidiary.

18-32. There are circumstances in which auditors should qualify their opinions in reporting on financial statements and other circumstances in which they should disclaim an opinion on the financial statements. Explain the general nature of the circumstances that would make each course necessary.

18-33. In an annual examination of the accounts of a manufacturing company, the president of the company has requested that you confine your audit work to the balance sheet at the year-end and render an opinion on the balance sheet only. The president contends that if the balance sheet is audited, and you have previously audited the balance sheet at the close of the preceding year, then the net income for the year must be the difference, and thus there is no necessity for spending the time to audit the income statement.

Required:

a. Is it permissible to express an opinion on the balance sheet alone?

b. What reasons would you advance for the desirability of auditing the income and expense accounts in sufficient detail to permit an opinion on the income statement? (Disregard any income tax considerations.)

18-34. You are the in-charge accountant for a new client that has never been audited. Your audit report will cover only the current year. There has been no observation of the opening inventory and you are unable to satisfy yourself as to the opening inventory balance by means of alternative auditing procedures. Inventory represents about 45 percent of the total assets. What effect, if any, would these circumstances have on the audit opinion?

18-35. Assume the same situation as in Question 18-34 but, in addition, the client's records are insufficient to enable you to determine the accounting principles applied in the prior year. What additional effect, if any, would this circumstance have on the audit opinion?

18-36. Your client is issuing comparative financial statements. During the year under audit, the client was named as a defendant in a material lawsuit relating to the sale of a division that occurred during the current period.

The attorney's letter indicates that the client's outside counsel is unable to render any opinion at this time as to the outcome of the litigation. In the absence of an opinion from legal counsel, or of other evidence, what effect, if any, would this have on the audit report?

18-37. Refer to Question 18-36. During the audit of the subsequent year, you learn that the litigation has been resolved in favor of your client. What effect, if any, will this resolution have on your report on comparative financial statements?

18-38. In the current year a client changed its method of valuing inventory from the first-in, first-out (FIFO) to the last-in, first-out (LIFO) method.

    a. What effect, if any, would this have on the audit report for the current year?
    b. How would the change in principle affect the audit report in the next year, assuming the auditor is reporting on comparative financial statements including the year in which the change was made?

18-39. You are newly engaged by the James Company, a New England manufacturer with a sales office and warehouse located in a western state. The James Company audit must be made at the peak of your busy season, when you will not have a senior auditor available for travel to the western outlet. Furthermore, the James Company is reluctant to bear the travel expenses of an out-of-town auditor.

    Required:
    a. Under what conditions would you, the principal auditor, be willing to accept full responsibility for the work of, and not make reference in your report to, another auditor?
    b. What procedures should you follow regardless of whether you accept full or divided responsibility, that is, regardless of whether you decide to make reference to the examination of another auditor?
    c. What reference, if any, would you make to the other auditor in your report if you did not assume full responsibility for the other auditor's work?

(AICPA adapted)

AICPA Multiple Choice Questions

These questions are taken from the Auditing part of Uniform CPA Examinations. Choose the single most appropriate answer.

18–40. In which of the following situations would the auditor appropriately issue a report that contains the standard phrase concerning consistency?

    a. A change in the method of accounting for specific subsidiaries that comprise the group of companies for which consolidated statements are presented.

    b. A change from an accounting principle that is *not* generally accepted to one that is generally accepted.

    c. A change in the percentage used to calculate the provision for warranty expense.

    d. Correction of a mistake in the application of a generally accepted accounting principle.

18–41. When financial statements are presented that are *not* in conformity with generally accepted accounting principles, an auditor may issue a (an)

	"Except for" opinion	*Disclaimer of an opinion*
a.	Yes	No
b.	Yes	Yes
c.	No	Yes
d.	No	No

18–42. In forming his opinion upon the consolidated financial statements of Juno Corp., a CPA relies upon another auditor's examination of the financial statements of Hera, Inc., a wholly owned subsidiary whose operations constitute 30 percent of Juno's consolidated total. Hera's auditor expresses an unqualified opinion on that company's financial statements.

    The CPA examining Juno Corp. may be expected to express an unqualified opinion but refer to the report by the other auditor if

    a. He concludes, based upon a review of the other auditor's professional standing and qualifications, that he is willing to assume the same responsibility as though he had performed the audit of Hera's financial statements himself.

    b. He is satisfied with the audit scope for the subsidiary, based upon his review of the audit program, but his inquiries disclose that the other auditor is not independent or lacks professional standing.

    c. He is satisfied with the other auditor's professional standing but concludes, based upon a review of the audit program, that the audit scope for the examination of Hera's financial statements was inadequate.

    d. He is satisfied with the other auditor's professional reputation and audit scope but is unwilling to assume responsibility for the other auditor's work to the same extent as though he had performed the work himself.

18–43. A CPA has *not* been able to confirm a large account receivable, but he has satisfied himself as to the proper statement of the receivable by means of alternative auditing procedures. The auditor's report on the financial statements should include

    a. A description of the limitation on the scope of his examination and the alternative auditing procedures used, but an opinion qualification is *not* required.

    b. An opinion qualification, but reference to the use of alternative auditing procedures is *not* required.

    c. Both a scope qualification and an opinion qualification.

      d. Neither a comment on the use of alternative auditing procedures nor an opinion qualification.

18-44. Comparative financial statements include the financial statements of a prior period that were examined by a predecessor auditor, whose report is *not* presented. If the predecessor auditor's report was qualified, the successor auditor must

      a. Express an opinion on the current year statements alone and make *no* reference to the prior year statements.

      b. Disclose the reasons for any qualification included in the predecessor auditor's opinion.

      c. Obtain written approval from the predecessor auditor to include the prior year's financial statements.

      d. Issue a standard short-form comparative report indicating the division of responsibility.

18-45. When a client declines to include a statement of changes in financial position in its financial report, the auditor's report will usually

      a. Contain a qualified opinion.

      b. Include a separate paragraph that summarizes the company's financing and investing activities.

      c. Refer to a footnote that contains an auditor prepared statement of changes in financial position.

      d. Refer to the scope limitation.

18-46. When financial statements are prepared on the basis of a going concern and the auditor believes that the client may *not* continue as a going concern, the auditor should issue

      a. A "subject to" opinion.

      b. An unqualified opinion with an explanatory middle paragraph.

      c. An "except for" opinion.

      d. An adverse opinion.

18-47. Approximately 90 percent of Helena Holding Company's assets consist of investments in wholly owned subsidiary companies. The CPA examining Helena's financial statements has satisfied himself that changes in underlying equity in these investments have been properly computed based upon the subsidiaries' unaudited financial statements, but he has not examined the subsidiaries' financial statements. The auditor's report should include

      a. An adverse opinion.

      b. An "except for" opinion.

      c. A "subject to" opinion.

      d. A disclaimer of opinion.

18-48. An auditor includes a middle paragraph in an otherwise unqualified report in order to emphasize that the entity being reported upon is a subsidiary of another business enterprise. The inclusion of this middle paragraph

      a. Is appropriate and would *not* negate the unqualified opinion.

      b. Is considered a qualification of the report.

      c. Is a violation of generally accepted reporting standards if this information is disclosed in footnotes to the financial statements.

    d. Necessitates a revision of the opinion paragraph to include the phrase "with the foregoing explanation."

18–49. With respect to consistency, which of the following should be done by an independent auditor who has *not* examined a company's financial statements for the preceding year but is doing so in the current year?

    a. Report on the financial statements of the current year without referring to consistency.

    b. Consider the consistent application of principles within the year under examination but *not* between the current and preceding year.

    c. Adopt procedures that are practicable and reasonable in the circumstances to obtain assurance that the principles employed are consistent between the current and preceding year.

    d. Rely on the report of the prior year's auditors if such a report does *not* take exception as to consistency.

18–50. When expressing a qualified opinion, the auditor generally should include a separate explanatory paragraph describing the effects of the qualification. The requirement for a separate explanatory paragraph does *not* apply when the opinion paragraph has been modified because of

    a. A change in accounting principles.

    b. Inability to apply necessary auditing procedures.

    c. Reclassification of an expense account.

    d. Uncertainties.

18–51. Which of the following portions of a continuing auditor's opinion paragraph on comparative financial statements is *incorrect*?

    a. In our opinion, the financial statements referred to above present fairly the financial position. . . .

    b. Of XYZ Company as of December 31, 1986 and 1985, and the results of its operations and the changes in its financial position. . . .

    c. For the years then ended, in conformity with generally accepted accounting principles. . . .

    d. Applied on a basis consistent with that of the preceding year.

18–52. Because an expression of opinion as to certain identified items in financial statements tends to overshadow or contradict a disclaimer of opinion or adverse opinion, it is inappropriate for an auditor to issue

    a. A piecemeal opinion.

    b. An unqualified opinion.

    c. An "except for" opinion.

    d. A "subject to" opinion.

Problems and Cases

18–60. Pace Corporation, an audit client of yours, is a manufacturer of consumer products and has several wholly owned subsidiaries in foreign countries that are audited by other independent auditors in those countries. The financial statements of all subsidiaries were properly consolidated in the financial statements of the parent company and the foreign auditors' reports were furnished to your CPA firm.

You are now preparing your auditor's opinion on the consolidated financial statements for the year ended June 30, 1987. These statements were prepared on a comparative basis with those of last year.

Required:

a. How would you evaluate and accept the independence and professional reputation of the foreign auditors?

b. In what circumstances may a principal auditor assume responsibility for the work of another auditor to the same extent as if the principal auditor had performed the work?

c. Assume that both last year and this year you were willing to utilize the reports of the other independent auditors in expressing your opinion on the consolidated financial statements but were unwilling to take full responsibility for performance of the work underlying their opinions. Assuming your examination of the parent company's financial statements would allow you to render an unqualified opinion, prepare (1) the necessary disclosure to be contained in the scope paragraph, and (2) the complete opinion paragraph of your auditor's report.

d. What modification(s), if any, would be necessary in your auditor's opinion if the financial statements for the prior year were unaudited?

(AICPA adapted)

18-61. Items 1 through 4 are based on the following information:

The auditor's report must contain an expression of opinion or a statement to the effect that an opinion cannot be expressed. Four types of opinions or statements that meet these requirements are generally known as

a. An unqualified opinion.
b. A qualified opinion.
c. A disclaimer of opinion.
d. An adverse opinion.

For each of the situations presented in items 1 through 4, indicate the type of opinion or statement that should be rendered, by reference to the appropriate letter from the above list, and give reasons for your answer.

1. Subsequent to the close of Holly Corporation's fiscal year a major debtor was declared a bankrupt due to a rapid series of events. The receivable is significantly material in relation to the financial statements and recovery is doubtful. The debtor had confirmed the full amount due to Holly Corporation at the balance sheet date. Since the account was good at the balance sheet date, Holly Corporation refuses to disclose any information in relation to this subsequent event. The CPA believes that all accounts were stated fairly at the balance sheet date.

2. Kapok Corporation is a substantial user of electronic data processing equipment and has used an outside service bureau to process data in past years. During the current year Kapok adopted the policy of leasing all hardware and expects to continue this arrangement in the future. This change in policy is adequately disclosed in footnotes to Kapok's financial statements, but uncertainty prohibits either Kapok or the CPA from

assessing the impact of this change on future operations.

    3. The president of Lowe, Inc. would not allow the auditor to confirm the receivable balance from one of its major customers. The amount of the receivable is material in relation to the financial statements of Lowe, Inc. The auditor was unable to obtain satisfaction as to the receivable balance by alternative procedures.

    4. Sempier Corporation issued financial statements that purported to present financial position and results of operations but omitted the related statement of changes in financial position (the omission is not sanctioned by APB Opinion No. 19).

(AICPA adapted)

18–62. ABC Company is engaged in the manufacture and wholesale distribution of children's mechanical toys. Its operations have been very successful for a number of years. Because of the increased demand for electronic toys, however, ABC's sales volume declined sharply following a bad Christmas sales period in 1981, and a significant loss was reported for that year. Early in 1982, the Company contracted for the purchase of electronic components and modified its production facilities to provide for the assembly of both mechanical and electronic toys.

    In October 1982, you and the audit manager met with ABC's President to finalize plans for the audit for the year ending December 31, 1982. You were informed that although the Company reduced its loss for the first nine months of the year as compared with the comparable period last year, the amount of the loss was still substantial. The financial condition of ABC Company as of September 30, 1982, is summarized as follows:

		$000's Omitted
Current assets:		
Cash		$ 5
Accounts receivable		800
Inventories		650
		1,455
Fixed assets less depreciation		1,200
		$2,655
Current liabilities:		
Notes payable to bank		$1,000
Accounts payable and current portion of bonds payable		950
		1,950
Long-term bonds (payable over five years)		350
		2,300
Stockholders' equity:		
Common stock		250
Retained earnings at Dec. 31, 1981	$955	
Loss for nine months ended Sept. 30, 1982	(850)	105
		355
		$2,655

The President further informed you that the XYZ Bank had increased the Company's line of credit from $800,000 to $1.2 million on September 1, 1982, based on the Company's forecast of future cash flow. This forecast indicated that this line of credit would be required until September 1, 1983.

You pointed out to the President that the Company already had had to increase its borrowings from the bank to $1 million by September 30 and that she had indicated to you that the customary Christmas season sales increase to retailers during August and September had not improved the cash flow problems of the Company. The President assured you she is confident that the Company's cash flow will improve and that the problems of 1981 have been overcome because the demand for the new electronic toys will increase and justify higher margins than for the mechanical products. She believes that the Company will not have to borrow funds in excess of the present bank limit because cash requirements for the remainder of this year and the first half of 1983 will be relatively small.

Required:

   a. Define the audit problems and cite applicable professional pronouncements, if any.
   b. Determine the approach you would propose to the partner on the engagement for the solution of the problems, including the evidence or other data you would want to review.
   c. Indicate the factors you would consider in determining the impact on the audit budget and timing of field work.

18-63. You have received the following attorney's letter three days before you are to issue the audit opinion. Assume all amounts are material.

A.T. LAW
1000 Capital Bank Square
Houston, Texas 77002

February 8, 1988

Re: Precision Electronics, Inc.

Charles P. Atlantic & Co.
333 Market Street
San Francisco, California 94105

Dear Sir or Madam:

This letter is in response to the audit inquiry letter of Precision Electronics, Inc. ("Company") concerning your examination of the financial statements of the Company as of December 31, 1987.

While this firm represents the Company, our engagement has been limited to specific matters as to which we were consulted by them. On February 1, 1988, the Company was sued by Simplex Electronics Corporation in the United States District Court for the Southern District of California. The complaint alleges that the Company negligently provided defective electronics components to Simplex in 1987 and they subsequently included such components in equipment sold to third parties. Simplex asked for relief, jointly and severally

---

(*Continued*)

(Continued)

in the amount of $5 million. The matter has not been fully investigated at this time; accordingly, we are not able to form an opinion at this time as to the ultimate outcome of this matter.

Referring to the Company's request that we furnish to you a description of any other matters of which we are aware involving a possible actual or contingent liability of the Company at the examination date or subsequent thereto, please be advised that we are not in a position to comment on matters other than claims which to our knowledge have been actually made or threatened against the Company or its subsidiaries and which have been referred to us in a manner so as to require legal advice and, where appropriate, legal representation.

The information contained in this letter is as of the date of this letter, and we assume no obligation to provide you with any changes, whether material or not, which come to our attention after the date of this letter. This response is limited by, and in accordance with, the ABA Statement of Policy Regarding Lawyers' Responses to Auditors' Requests for Information (December 1975); without limiting the generality of the foregoing, the limitations in such Statement on the scope and use of this response (paragraphs 2 and 7) are specifically incorporated herein by reference and any description herein of any "loss contingencies" is qualified in its entirety by paragraph 5 of the Statement and the accompanying Commentary (which is an integral part of the Statement). Consistent with the last sentence of paragraph 6 of the ABA Statement of Policy and pursuant to the Company's request, this will confirm as correct the Company's understanding as set forth in its audit inquiry letter to us that whenever, in the course of performing legal services for the Company with respect to a matter recognized to involve an unasserted possible claim or assessment that may call for financial statement disclosure, we have formed a professional conclusion that the Company must disclose or consider disclosure concerning such possible claim or assessment, we, as a matter of professional responsibility to the Company, will so advise the Company and will consult with the Company concerning the question of such disclosure and the applicable requirements of Statement of Financial Accounting Standards No. 5.

Very truly yours,

A.T. Law

After reading the attorney's letter you contact Precision Electronics' management and it discloses the following:

1. Precision Electronics has filed a counteraction for libel, and preliminary hearings and discovery proceedings are just beginning.
2. Management believes the company has a good chance of prevailing but the outcome cannot presently be determined.
3. No provision for any liability has been made in the financial statements.

Required:

a. Determine what impact, if any, this will have on the financial statements and on the auditor's report.

b. Prepare the middle and opinion paragraphs of the auditor's report and the footnote required to disclose this situation.

c. State any additional audit procedures you may wish to apply.

18-64. Various types of accounting changes can affect the second standard of reporting. This standard reads, "The report shall state whether such principles have been consistently observed in the current period in relation to the preceding period."

Assume that the following list describes changes that have a material effect on a client's financial statements for the current year.

1. A change from the completed-contract method to the percentage-of-completion method of accounting for long-term construction contracts.
2. A change in the estimated useful life of previously recorded fixed assets based on newly acquired information.
3. Correction of a mathematical error in inventory pricing made in a prior period.
4. A change from prime costing to full absorption costing for inventory valuation.
5. A change from presentation of statements of individual companies to presentation of consolidated statements.
6. A change from deferring and amortizing preproduction costs to recording such costs as an expense when incurred because future benefits of the costs have become doubtful. The new accounting method was adopted in recognition of the change in estimated future benefits.
7. A change to including the employer share of FICA taxes as "retirement benefits" on the income statement from including it with "other taxes."
8. A change from the FIFO method of inventory pricing to the LIFO method of inventory pricing.

Required:

Identify the type of change described in each item, state whether any modification is required in the auditor's report as it relates to the second standard of reporting, and state whether the prior year's financial statements should be restated when presented in comparative form with the current year's statements. Organize your answer as shown in the following chart.

For example, a change from the LIFO method of inventory pricing to the FIFO method of inventory pricing would appear as shown:

Item No.	Type of Change	Should Auditor's Report Be Modified?	Should Prior Year's Statements Be Restated?
Example	An accounting change from one generally accepted accounting principle to another generally accepted accounting principle.	Yes	Yes

(AICPA adapted)

18-65. The following auditor's report was drafted by an assistant at the completion of an audit engagement of Cramdon, Inc., and was submitted to the partner with client responsibility for review. The partner has examined matters thoroughly and has properly concluded that the opinion on the 1987 financial report should be modified only for the change in the method for computing sales. Also, because of an uncertainty, a "subject to" opinion was issued on the 1986 financial statements, which are included for comparative purposes. The 1986 auditor's report was dated March 3, 1987. In 1987, the litigation against Cramdon, which was the cause of the 1986 "subject to" opinion, was resolved in favor of Cramdon.

Board of Directors of Cramdon, Inc.

We have examined the financial statements, which are the representations of Cramdon, Inc., incorporated herein by reference, for the years ended December 31, 1987 and 1986. Our examinations were made in accordance with generally accepted auditing standards and, accordingly, included such auditing procedures as we considered necessary in the circumstances.

As discussed in Note 7 to the financial statements, our previous opinion on the 1986 financial statements was other than unqualified pending the outcome of litigation. Because of our attorney's meritorious defense in this litigation, our opinion on these financial statements is different from that expressed in our previous report.

In our opinion, based upon the preceding, the accompanying financial statements referred to above present fairly the financial position, results of operations, and changes in financial position for the period ended December 31, 1987, in conformity with generally accepted accounting principles consistently applied, except for the change in the method of computing sales as described in Note 14 to the financial statements.

CPA
March 5, 1988

Required:

Identify the deficiencies contained in the auditor's report as drafted by the audit assistant in the: (a) scope paragraph, (b) middle paragraph, and (c) opinion paragraph. Rewriting the auditor's report is not an acceptable solution.

(AICPA adapted)

18-66. This is the conclusion of the Quinn Hardware case that began in Chapter 6. Reference should be made to information given in Chapters 6 and 8. This case requires the application of matters discussed in both Chapters 17 and 18 and reflects considerations involved in the conclusion of an audit. You are to apply judgment, particularly as to materiality, in reaching your conclusions.

Quinn Hardware has presented you with a complete set of draft financial statements, additional background information, and related data derived from the audit working papers. Field work was completed on July 10 and the report is to be issued on July 15, 1986.

Required:

a. Review the financial statements in the light of all relevant data and suggest changes needed to provide all necessary disclosures and to ensure conformity with GAAP in other respects as well. It is not necessary to rewrite the statements.

b. Prepare the audit report.

Additional Background Information:

1. The mathematical accuracy of the financial statements and the reasonableness of the amounts need not be reviewed.

2. Various income statement and balance sheet accounts for 1985 have been reclassified by the client to conform to the classifications used in the 1986 financial statements.

3. Included in the May 31, 1986 cash balance of $16,000 are restricted funds of $7,582.

4. Marketable securities are carried at cost; market value was $172,500 at May 31, 1986 and $161,400 at May 31, 1985.

5. Netted against accounts receivable is the allowance for doubtful accounts; activity in the allowance account for the two-year period is summarized as follows:

	Beginning Balance	Additions	Write-Offs	Ending Balance
May 31, 1985	$800,000	$735,000	$635,000	$900,000
May 31, 1986	900,000	775,000	775,000	900,000

6. Included in plant, property, and equipment, at cost, are leasehold improvements, which are not material to the financial statements.

   Included in plant, property, and equipment are idle buildings and improvements with a net book value of $3,450,000 (net of accumulated depreciation of $647,000) at May 31, 1986 and $1,412,000 (net of accumulated depreciation of $227,000) at May 31, 1985. The net book value approximates the estimated net realizable value at both dates.

7. The subordinated debentures mature on December 1, 1990 and require the following sinking fund payments—1986, none; 1987, $2.5 million; 1988, $3 million; 1989, $3 million; and 1990, $1.5 million. The debentures are not registered with the SEC.

8. The Company has issued various stock options for the Quinn Hardware common stock which is not publicly traded. (The preferred stock is also not publicly traded.) Such options, of which 24,000 and 67,000 were exercisable at May 31, 1985 and May 31, 1986, respectively, are summarized as follows:

	Beginning Balance	Granted	Canceled	Ending Balance
May 31, 1985	47,500(1)	48,000(2)	23,500(3)	72,000
May 31, 1986	72,000	25,000(4)	4,600(5)	92,400

	Option Prices		
(1)	4,600	at	$5.00
	15,400	at	$5.25
	17,500	at	$5.75

Option Prices

	10,000	at	$6.00
(2)	24,000	at	$6.50
	10,000	at	$7.00
	10,000	at	$8.00
	4,000	at	$8.50
(3)	17,500	at	$5.75
	6,000	at	$6.00
(4)	25,000	at	$9.75
(5)	4,600	at	$5.00

9. Income taxes comprise the following:

Provision for Income Taxes:	*1986*	*1985*
Currently payable		
Federal	$ 986,000	$1,560,000
State	116,500	180,000
Deferred	147,500	60,500
	$1,250,000	$1,800,000

10. The Company uses the straight-line method of depreciating buildings and improvements for financial statement purposes and principally the ACRS and sum-of-the-years-digits methods for tax purposes.

    Because of more pronounced "wear and tear" during 1986 the Company changed its method of depreciating automotive equipment and furniture and fixtures from the straight-line method to the sum-of-the-years-digits method. The effect of this change, which has the most significant impact in 1986, was to increase the Company's depreciation expense for 1986 by $49,000.

11. Rent expense is net of sublease income of $50,000 in 1986 and $37,000 in 1985. Sublease income under noncancelable leases approximates $47,000 annually from 1986 to 1989, $36,000 in 1990, $22,000 in 1991, and $7,000 annually for 1992 and 1993. Assume all leases are operating leases.

12. Based on prior discussions with the management of the Company and outside counsel, it appears that the litigation (Note 7) is of considerable concern and may have a significant impact in the event of an adverse ruling.

13. The numerical data and related disclosures about the Company's defined contribution pension plan should be assumed to be correct and appropriate.

Draft

Quinn Hardware
Consolidated Balance Sheets
May 31, 1986 and 1985

Assets	1986	1985
Current assets		
Cash	$ 16,000	$ 12,000
Marketable securities	100,000	100,000
Accounts receivable	9,168,000	8,548,000
Merchandise inventory, at lower of cost or market	13,213,000	11,862,000
Prepaid expenses	82,000	96,000
Deferred income tax	30,000	
Other current assets	399,000	296,000
	23,008,000	20,914,000
Property, plant and equipment:		
Buildings and improvements	9,325,000	9,157,000
Furniture and fixtures	3,122,000	2,989,000
Automotive equipment	320,000	226,000
	12,767,000	12,372,000
Less accumulated depreciation	4,197,000	3,720,000
	8,570,000	8,652,000
Land	2,000,000	1,800,000
	10,570,000	10,452,000
	$33,578,000	$31,366,000

Liabilities and Stockholders' Equity	1986	1985
Current liabilities		
Accounts payable and accrued liabilities	$ 6,113,000	$ 5,921,000
Income taxes payable (Note 2)	1,025,000	662,000
Dividends payable	130,000	130,000
	7,268,000	6,713,000
Deferred income taxes (Note 2)	780,000	690,000
Subordinated debentures 10% (Note 4)	10,000,000	10,000,000
Stockholders' equity (Note 4)		
Preferred stock, $1.00 par value; nonparticipating, 9% cumulative preference, 1,000,000 shares authorized, 500,000 shares issued and outstanding	500,000	500,000
Common stock, no par value; 4,000,000 shares authorized, 1,000,000 shares issued and outstanding	2,000,000	2,000,000
Retained earnings	13,030,000	11,463,000
	15,530,000	13,963,000
	$33,578,000	$31,366,000

The accompanying notes are an integral part of the consolidated financial statements.

Draft

**Consolidated Statements of Stockholders' Equity
For the Years Ended May 31, 1986 and 1985**

	Preferred Stock		Common Stock		Retained Earnings	Total Stockholders' Equity
	Number of Shares	*Amount*	*Number of Shares*	*Amount*		
Balances, June 1, 1984			1,000,000	$2,000,000	$10,318,500	$12,318,000
Net income for the year 1985					1,367,000	1,367,000
Issuance of preferred stock	500,000	$500,000				500,000
Cash dividends declared on common stock, $.20 per share					(200,000)	(200,000)
Cash dividends declared on preferred stock					(22,500)	(22,500)
Balances, May 31, 1985	500,000	500,000	1,000,000	2,000,000	11,463,000	13,963,000
Net income for the year 1986					1,862,000	1,862,000
Cash dividends declared on common stock, $.25 per share					(250,000)	(250,000)
Cash dividends declared on preferred stock					(45,000)	(45,000)
Balances, May 31, 1986	500,000	$500,000	1,000,000	$2,000,000	$13,030,000	$15,530,000

The accompanying notes are an integral part of the consolidated financial statements.

Consolidated Statements of Changes in Financial Position
For the Years Ended May 31, 1986 and 1985

Draft

	1986	1985
Net cash flow from operating activities:		
Net income	$1,862,000	$1,367,000
Noncash expenses, revenues, losses, and gains included in income:		
Depreciation	477,000	438,000
Deferred income taxes	60,000	148,000
Net (increase) decrease in accounts receivable, merchandise inventory, and other current assets	(2,060,000)	126,000
Net increase in accounts payable and income taxes payable	555,000	447,500
Net cash flow from operating activities	894,000	2,526,500
Cash flows from investing activities:		
Acquisition of property, plant, and equipment	(395,000)	(4,821,000)
Acquisition of land	(200,000)	
Net cash used by investing activities	(595,000)	(4,821,000)
Cash flows from investing activities:		
Dividends paid	(295,000)	(222,500)
Proceeds from issuance of subordinated debentures		2,000,000
Proceeds from issuance of preferred stock	·	500,000
Net cash provided (used) by financing activities	(295,000)	2,277,500
Net increase (decrease) in cash	$4,000	($17,000)

The accompanying notes are an integral part of the consolidated financial statements.

	Consolidated Statements of Income	*Draft*

Consolidated Statements of Income
For the Years Ended May 31, 1986 and 1985

	1986	*1985*
Sales (Note 1)	$64,219,000	$58,823,000
Cost of goods sold	51,376,000	47,556,000
Gross margin	12,843,000	11,267,000
Other cost and expenses		
Depreciation	477,000	438,000
Interest expense	1,072,500	1,000,000
General and administrative		
expenses (Notes 5 and 6)	7,631,500	7,212,000
	9,181,000	8,650,000
Income before provision		
for income taxes	3,662,000	2,617,000
Provision for income taxes	1,800,000	1,250,000
Net income	$ 1,862,000	$ 1,367,000
Earnings per share	$1.82	$1.34

Draft

NOTES TO CONSOLIDATED FINANCIAL STATEMENTS

1. Significant Accounting Policies

Principles of Consolidation. The consolidated financial statements include the accounts of the Company and its wholly owned subsidiary.

Stock Options. Proceeds from the sale of common stock issued under stock options are credited to common stock. There are no charges to income with respect to these options.

Franchise Fee Revenue. Franchise fee revenue from the sale of individual franchises is recognized when the franchise commences operation. No new franchises were opened during fiscal 1986 and 1985. Continuing franchise fee revenue is a percentage of the net sales of the franchises and is recorded on the accrual basis.

Income Taxes. For income tax purposes, buildings and improvements placed in service prior to January 1, 1981 are depreciated using principally the sum-of-the-years-digits method and such assets placed in service subsequent to December 31, 1980 are depreciated using the accelerated cost recovery system. These methods differ from the straight-line method as reflected in the accompanying consolidated financial statements. Inventory obsolescence expense is accounted for on the accrual basis for financial statement purposes and recognized for tax purposes when the inventory is disposed of. Deferred income taxes have been provided for such differences.

2. Income Taxes

The Internal Revenue Service (IRS) is currently conducting an examination of the Company's Federal income tax returns for the years 1982 to 1984. Although no report has been rendered, informal discussions between management and the IRS have indicated that any adjustments arising from this examination will not have a material effect on the consolidated financial statements.

3. Subordinated Debentures

The Company's subordinated debentures, maturing December 1, 1990, are redeemable at various dates at redemption prices ranging from 107.4 percent to 100 percent of the principal amount thereof.

4. Preferred and Common Stock

The preferred stock may be redeemed by the Company at any time for $1.00 per share, plus accrued and unpaid dividends.

The stock option plan approved by the Company's shareholders provides for the granting of 150,000 options to employees for purchase of the Company's common stock at prices equal to 100 percent of the fair market price at the dates the options are granted. All options are exercisable in full after one year from the date of the grant.

Options to employees under this plan are as follows:

	Shares
Balance at June 1, 1984	47,500
Granted	48,000
Canceled	(23,500)
Balance at May 31, 1985	72,000
Granted	25,000
Canceled	(4,600)
Balance at May 31, 1986	92,400

5. Pension Plan

The Company sponsors a defined contribution pension plan covering substantially all of its full-time employees who meet certain eligibility requirements. Contributions and cost are determined based on a percentage of each covered employee's salary and totaled $79,000 in 1986 and $62,000 in 1985.

6. Lease Commitments

The Company operates certain of its stores and office locations under noncancelable leases which generally are for initial periods of 15 years and contain provisions for renewal options (for up to an additional aggregate period of 20 years). In addition, certain store and delivery equipment is leased over periods ranging from 5 to 10 years.

Rent expense included in general and administrative expenses in the consolidated statements of income for the years 1986 and 1985 is $502,000 and $490,000, respectively.

Minimum rental commitments at May 31, 1986 under long-term noncancelable leases and subleases are as follows (in thousands):

Year Ending May 31	*Minimum Annual Rentals*	
	Buildings	*Equipment*
1986	$ 486	$ 161

Year Ending May 31	Minimum Annual Rentals	
	Buildings	Equipment
1987	489	108
1988	469	119
1989	401	187
1990	347	160
After 1990	1,355	307
Total future minimum rentals	$3,547	$1,042

7. Contingencies

In September 1984, Key Lumber, Alpha Inc., and Syntex Co. filed suit against the Company in the United States District Court. The suit seeks damages which the plaintiffs claim resulted from the Company's nonperformance of certain contractual obligations.

On July 21, 1986, a civil case was filed in the same court by the United States Government charging the Company with a violation of the Sherman Anti-Trust Act. The Government is seeking to enjoin the Company from expanding its interstate sale and shipment of plumbing supplies.

In view of the preliminary nature of these proceedings, it is not possible for the Company to predict the outcome or the range of potential loss, if any, that may result from these proceedings. The Company's present intention is to deny the material allegations of the complaints and to defend the actions vigorously.

8. Subsequent Event

On August 1, 1986, the Company entered into a term loan agreement with an insurance company which provides for the borrowing of $6 million to finance the expansion of its franchise system. The agreement provides for a commitment fee of one-half of 1 percent on the unused amount.

Chapter 19
Special Reporting Situations

The increased sophistication of our society and of the business environment in which we operate, coupled with a better understanding on the part of the public of the skills and experience possessed by auditors, has created a demand for a variety of services much beyond audits of financial statements. The work that accountants in public practice may be asked to perform, the diversity of resulting reports and letters that may be issued, and the reporting problems these create are literally infinite. The profession has tried to keep pace with this explosion in the demand for special services. Today, the professional literature addresses a number of special reporting situations and nonaudit services—among them, compilations, reviews, interim reviews, a variety of special reports, reporting on information accompanying basic financial statements, reporting on prospective financial statements and pro forma statements, reports on internal control, reports on compliance, and letters for underwriters. Both the procedures employed in providing those services and the reports issued are discussed in this chapter.

Special reports, once intended only for management or for a limited and explicitly identified group of outsiders, are now widely circulated to both the public and regulatory agencies. Their increased reliance on special reports has posed problems for the auditor. With more parties relying on them, special reports have taken on greater importance, and the legal and financial responsibility imposed on the auditor has increased correspondingly. The problems center around three professional judgments the auditor must make: The first is a judgment as to the nature and extent of the work required to support the report's conclusions; next is a judgment as to the conclusions reached; and the last is an assessment of how the report will be used, which determines how the auditor communicates those conclusions.

The standards of the profession discussed in Chapter 3 apply with equal rigor to *all* work performed by a CPA—the only exception is the practical irrelevance of some of them in some special reporting situations. SAS No. 43, *Omnibus Statement on Auditing Standards* (AU Section 150.06), states, for example, that the "ten generally accepted standards, to the extent that they are relevant in the circumstances, apply to all other services governed by Statements on Auditing Standards unless the Statement specifies otherwise." Moreover, the AICPA Code of Professional Ethics states that the Rules of Conduct "apply to all services performed in the practice of public accounting . . ." (ET Section 92.02). This applicability of both technical and ethical standards should not be overlooked when an auditor's work and resulting reports reach into areas far removed from audits of conventional financial statements.

As far as the 10 generally accepted auditing standards (GAAS) are concerned, the general standards—adequate training and proficiency, independence of mental attitude, and due care in the performance of the work—are all clearly applicable in every professional effort. Of the standards of field work, the first and third—planning and supervision of field work and sufficiency and competence of evidential matter as a basis for an opinion—are also universal in their applicability. The second standard—a proper study and evaluation of internal control—is generally, though not universally, applicable. Whenever a professional report involves a system of business activity, the auditor must develop an understanding of the system and its controls to make adequate professional judgments. Some reports, however, such as those on the accounting or tax treatment of prospective transactions, do not involve a control system. The standards of reporting are more specific and therefore cannot be as universally applied. The first standard—adherence to generally accepted accounting principles (GAAP)—obviously applies only to financial statements that purport to present financial position and results of operations and to items derived from those statements. The second standard, consistency, applies whenever a report relates to accounting principles in use. The third and fourth standards—adequacy of informative disclosures and the requirement for a clear-cut indication of the degree of responsibility taken by the auditor—although stated in terms of financial statements, can just as well be viewed as generally applicable to every report written by the auditor.

This chapter covers the types of special reports and the attendant special reporting situations most commonly encountered in current practice. The reader should note that some of the special reporting situations addressed in this chapter arise because nonaudit engagements do not require that sufficient competent evidence be obtained to provide the relatively high level of assurance that an opinion based on an audit demands. In those situations, both the professional literature and this chapter refer to a person who undertakes the engagement and issues a report as an *accountant, public accountant,* or *practitioner*. The term *auditor* is reserved for a person who undertakes to perform an audit in accordance with GAAS and expresses an opinion based on the results of that audit.

Nonaudits, Compilations, and Reviews

Association with Financial Data

A public accountant can be either directly or indirectly associated with financial data. In either event, the accountant has a duty to ensure that there is a clear indication of the degree of responsibility being taken. In some circumstances, this professional duty involves making sure that any report the accountant issues contains a clear-cut description of the character of any examination made and the degree of responsibility taken. If an accountant's name is associated with financial data in such a way that readers could reasonably be expected to misinterpret the individual's role and association with the data, the accountant must take other actions to prevent those consequences.

An accountant's direct association with financial data covers the spectrum from a compilation or review of the data to an audit of the data. Similarly, there are different levels of assurance that reflect the different types of association—ranging from zero or little assurance on unaudited or compiled statements, to limited assurance on reviews, to high assurance on audits. For each level of assurance, there is a standard reporting format.

Services Other Than a Compilation or Review of Financial Statements

Indirect association with financial data is present if a certified public accountant is engaged to prepare or assist in preparing financial statements for a client, even if the CPA's name is not attached to the statements. Those services can range from mere typing of financial statements to various types of accounting services such as preparing a trial balance, assisting in adjusting the books of account, consulting on accounting, tax, and similar matters, or preparing financial statements by manual or automated data processing means. If the output of the accountant's work is in the form of financial statements, the accountant is deemed to be associated with them.

Merely Typing or Reproducing Financial Statements as an Accommodation. A client may ask the accountant merely to type or reproduce financial statements that the accountant has not otherwise prepared or assisted in preparing. An accommodation of this nature is not a professional service. Paragraph 7 of Statement on Standards for Accounting and Review Services

(SSARS) No. 1 (AR Section 100.07) prohibits an accountant from rendering such a service for a nonpublic entity.[1]

SAS No. 26, *Association With Financial Statements* (AU Section 504), which discusses unaudited financial statements for a public company, is silent regarding whether that type of service could be rendered. As a practical matter, a public company would rarely look to its public accountant for such a service. Yet there may be occasions when, because of the attendant circumstances, the accountant cannot appropriately refuse the client's request to provide that type of service. In that instance, the accountant is deemed associated and should disclaim an opinion on the unaudited financial statements that have been merely typed or reproduced as an accommodation to the client. The association cannot be avoided by submitting the financial statements on plain paper, to either the client or others. The form of standard report to be issued follows:

> The accompanying balance sheet of X Company as of December 31, 19XX, and the related statements of income, retained earnings, and changes in financial position for the year then ended were not audited by us and, accordingly, we do not express an opinion on them.

The disclaimer may accompany the unaudited financial statements or it may be placed directly on them. If it accompanies the unaudited financial statements, each page of the financial statements should be clearly and conspicuously marked as "unaudited."

Unwarranted Association. An accountant may become aware that his or her name is to be included in a client-prepared written communication containing financial statements that have not been audited, reviewed, or compiled. In that event, the accountant should make sure that either (1) the name is not included in the communication or (2) the financial statements are accompanied by a notation that the accountant has not audited, reviewed, or compiled them and thus does not assume any responsibility or express any opinion on them. If the client does not comply, the accountant should advise the client that consent to use his or her name is not given. Additionally, the accountant should consider what other actions might be appropriate, including consultation with an attorney.

Compilations of Financial Statements

Financial statements are considered unaudited if the accountant has not applied auditing procedures that are sufficient to permit the expression of an opinion concerning them, as described in Chapter 18.

[1]SSARS No. 1 defines "nonpublic entity" in paragraph 4 (AR Section 100.04) as follows: "A nonpublic entity is any entity other than (a) one whose securities trade in a public market either on a stock exchange (domestic or foreign) or in the over-the-counter market, including securities quoted only locally or regionally, (b) one that makes a filing with a regulatory agency in preparation for the sale of any class of its securities in a public market, or (c) a subsidiary, corporate joint venture, or other entity controlled by an entity covered by (a) or (b)."

The Accounting and Review Services Committee of the AICPA has established a level of professional service for nonpublic companies called a compilation, which, if performed in accordance with the Statements on Standards for Accounting and Review Services, results in a different form of reporting than for public companies. This service to compile financial statements involves presenting information that is the representation of management in the form of financial statements, without undertaking to express any assurance on the statements. The accountant is not required to make inquiries or perform other procedures to verify, corroborate, or review the information supplied by the client. The accountant does, however, have certain other duties and responsibilities, specified in SSARS No. 1 (AR Section 100), because of this direct association with the financial statements.

Compilation Procedures. At the outset, the accountant should establish an understanding, preferably in writing, with the client as to the nature and limitations of the service to be performed, together with the type of report to be rendered. Before beginning the work, the accountant should have or acquire a knowledge of the accounting principles and practices of the client's industry and a general understanding of the nature of the client's business transactions, the form of its accounting records, the qualifications of its accounting personnel, the accounting basis used, and the form and content of the financial statements.[2] The accountant should read the financial statements to see if they are free from obvious material errors, such as arithmetical or clerical mistakes, misapplication of accounting principles, and inadequate disclosures.

Any items of concern that arise from performing the foregoing procedures should be discussed with the client. The client should be asked to revise the financial statements, as appropriate; if the client does not comply, the accountant should modify the report. At the extreme, the accountant should withdraw from the engagement if modifying the report is not adequate to communicate the deficiencies.[3]

Form of Reporting. The accountant's report on a compilation engagement explicitly disclaims an opinion and gives no other form of assurance with respect to the financial statements. The standard form of compilation report to be issued for a nonpublic company follows, as suggested in SSARS No. 5, *Reporting on Compiled Financial Statements* (AR Section 500):

> We have compiled the accompanying balance sheet of XYZ Company as of December 31, 19XX, and the related statements of income, retained earn-

[2]SSARS No. 4, *Communications Between Predecessor and Successor Accountants* (AR Section 400), provides guidance on inquiries of a predecessor by a successor accountant regarding acceptance of an engagement and to facilitate the conduct of that engagement.

[3]SSARS No. 6, *Reporting on Personal Financial Statements Included in Written Personal Financial Plans* (AR Section 600), provides an exemption from SSARS No. 1, under specified conditions, for personal financial statements included in written personal financial plans prepared by an accountant. Such financial statements are intended solely to assist in the development of the client's financial plan and frequently omit disclosures required by GAAP and contain other departures from GAAP.

ings, and changes in financial position for the year then ended, in accordance with standards established by the American Institute of Certified Public Accountants.

A compilation is limited to presenting in the form of financial statements information that is the representation of management (owners). We have not audited or reviewed the accompanying financial statements and, accordingly, do not express an opinion or any other form of assurance on them.

The accountant's report should be dated as of the date the compilation was completed. Each page of the financial statements should include a reference such as "See Accountant's Compilation Report." If substantially all disclosures are omitted, the accountant's report should highlight this fact to alert users of the financial statements.[4]

Occasionally an accountant may be engaged to compile financial statements of a public company. Professional standards (AU Section 504.05) do not permit the accountant to describe any procedures that may have been applied or to issue the form of report permitted for a nonpublic company. In this situation, the accountant must simply disclaim an opinion on the unaudited financial statements.

In the opinion of the authors, there is no logical reason why a report on a compilation may be given on financial statements for a nonpublic company but not for a public company. The rules were established by two separate authoritative bodies to meet the needs of the marketplace. From a practical standpoint, however, there should be little demand by public companies for compilation services.

Reviews of Financial Statements

A review of financial statements, as described in SSARS No. 1 (AR Section 100), involves inquiry and analytical procedures intended to provide the accountant with a reasonable basis for expressing limited assurance that there are no material modifications that should be made to the financial statements in order for them to be in conformity with GAAP or with some other comprehensive basis of accounting.[5] Paragraph 4 of SSARS No. 1 (AR Section 100.04) compares a review with a compilation and an audit, as follows:

> The objective of a review differs significantly from the objective of a compilation. The inquiry and analytical procedures performed in a review should provide the accountant with a reasonable basis for expressing limited assurance that there are no material modifications that should be made to the financial statements. No expression of assurance is contemplated in a compilation.

[4]SSARS No. 3, *Compilation Reports on Financial Statements Included in Certain Prescribed Forms* (AR Section 300), provides additional guidance for accountants who are asked to compile financial statements included in a prescribed form that calls for departures from GAAP. Also see footnote 7 on page 831.

[5]Comprehensive bases of accounting other than GAAP are described and discussed later in this chapter. Hereafter, reference to GAAP in this section of the chapter includes, where applicable, another comprehensive basis of accounting.

The objective of a review also differs significantly from the objective of an examination of financial statements in accordance with generally accepted auditing standards. The objective of an audit is to provide a reasonable basis for expressing an opinion regarding the financial statements taken as a whole. A review does not provide a basis for the expression of such an opinion because a review does not contemplate a study and evaluation of internal accounting control, tests of accounting records and of responses to inquiries by obtaining corroborating evidential matter through inspection, observation or confirmation, and certain other procedures ordinarily performed during an audit. A review may bring to the accountant's attention significant matters affecting the financial statements, but it does not provide assurance that the accountant will become aware of all significant matters that would be disclosed in an audit.

As in the case of compilations, reviews may be performed only for nonpublic entities. The one exception is that a review report may be issued for public entities (e.g., some municipalities) that do not have their annual statements audited.

Review Procedures. In a review engagement, either the accountant or the client prepares the financial statements from the entity's books and records. Similar to a compilation engagement, the accountant should have or acquire a knowledge of the client's industry and business. If the client prepares the financial statements, the accountant should ascertain that the financial statements are supported by formalized accounting books and records.

Inquiries ordinarily should be made concerning

- The entity's accounting principles, practices, and methods followed in applying them.
- Procedures for recording, classifying, and summarizing transactions and accumulating information for financial statement disclosures.
- Actions taken at meetings (such as of stockholders or the board of directors) that could affect the financial statements.
- Whether the financial statements have been prepared in conformity with GAAP consistently applied.
- Changes in business activities or accounting principles and practices.
- Subsequent events that would have a material effect on the financial statements.
- Matters as to which questions have arisen during the conduct of the review.

Some accountants may find it helpful in making inquiries to use a checklist covering the general areas to ensure that important questions are not overlooked.

Analytical procedures performed in a review are designed to identify relationships between account balances, and other fluctuations that appear unusual because they do not conform to a predictable pattern (e.g., changes in sales and in accounts receivable and expenses that ordinarily fluctuate with sales). Comparisons also should be made with prior-period financial statements and with budgets and forecasts, if any.

If other accountants have been engaged to audit or review the financial statements of significant components of the reporting entity, its subsidiaries, or other investees, the primary accountant should obtain reports from the other accountants as a basis, in part, for the primary accountant's report on the review of the reporting entity's financial statements. SSARS No. 1 also suggests that the accountant may wish to obtain a representation letter from the client to confirm the oral representations made in the course of the review. Although such a letter from the client is optional, in the opinion of the authors it is highly desirable as a means of reducing possible misunderstandings and of documenting some of the more important inquiries.

Using knowledge based on the results of the review, the accountant should consider whether the financial statements appear to conform with GAAP. Material departures from GAAP should cause the accountant to modify the standard review report, unless the financial statements are revised. If modifying the report is not adequate to indicate the deficiencies in the financial statements taken as a whole, the accountant may have to withdraw from the engagement.

Form of Reporting. The accountant's report on reviewed financial statements expresses limited assurance. The opinion is in the form of "negative assurance" that the accountant is not aware of any material modifications that should be made to the financial statements in order for them to be in conformity with GAAP. The standard form of review report to be issued, as specified in SSARS No. 1 (AR Section 100.35), for either a public[6] or nonpublic entity follows:

> We have reviewed the accompanying balance sheet of XYZ Company as of December 31, 19XX, and the related statements of income, retained earnings, and changes in financial position for the year then ended, in accordance with standards established by the American Institute of Certified Public Accountants. All information included in these financial statements is the representation of the management (owners) of XYZ Company.
>
> A review consists principally of inquiries of company personnel and analytical procedures applied to financial data. It is substantially less in scope than an examination in accordance with generally accepted auditing standards, the objective of which is the expression of an opinion regarding the financial statements taken as a whole. Accordingly, we do not express such an opinion.
>
> Based on our review, we are not aware of any material modifications that should be made to the accompanying financial statements in order for them to be in conformity with generally accepted accounting principles.

---

[6]Reviews of public entities that do not have their annual statements audited are permitted by paragraph 5 of SAS No. 26 (AU Section 504.05). As noted earlier, compilations are not permitted for any public entity.

The accountant's report should be dated as of the date the review was completed. Each page of the financial statements should include a reference such as "See Accountant's Review Report."[7]

Reporting When the Accountant Is Not Independent

Lack of independence precludes an accountant from issuing a review report. The accountant may, however, issue a report on a compilation engagement for a nonpublic company with respect to which the accountant is not independent, provided the report includes language specifically stating the lack of independence. (Similar wording should be included in a disclaimer of opinion issued when an accountant is not independent with respect to a public company, as discussed in Chapter 18.) In either situation, the reason for lack of independence should not be described.

Negative Assurance

Negative assurances in reports issued by accountants (such as appear in a report on a review of financial statements) have traditionally been frowned on by the profession. In fact, AU Section 504.18 specifically prohibits an auditor from including expressions of assurance on the absence of knowledge of departures from GAAP as part of a disclaimer of opinion. A reader of a report containing an expression of negative assurance may attribute a higher level of assurance to the opinion rendered than is warranted by the scope of work that the accountant performed to support the opinion. Furthermore, if, in the absence of authoritative guidance, negative assurances were permitted when an accountant performed procedures not constituting an audit, the amount of work deemed necessary to support the negative assurances could vary widely from one accountant to another. For these reasons, negative assurances are appropriate only in those limited instances, of which a review of financial statements is one, that have been specified in authoritative pronouncements of the AICPA. As noted in Chapter 2, the *Attestation Standards* also permit the practitioner's conclusion in an attest engagement to be expressed in the form of negative assurance when, based generally on only inquiries and analytical procedures, attestation risk (analogous to audit risk) has been reduced only to a moderate level.

Interim Reviews

A public accountant may be requested to perform a preissuance review of interim financial information for a client for a number of reasons. The client may wish to include a representation that the information has been reviewed in a

[7]SSARS No. 2, *Reporting on Comparative Financial Statements* (AR Section 200), provides guidance for reporting on comparative financial statements of a nonpublic entity when financial statements of one or more periods presented have been compiled or reviewed.

document issued to stockholders or third parties or in Form 10-Q, a quarterly report required to be submitted to the SEC pursuant to Section 13 or 15(d) of the Securities Exchange Act of 1934. Such representation may also be included or incorporated by reference in a registration statement.

Certain entities are also required by Item 302(a) of SEC Regulation S-K to include selected quarterly financial data in their annual reports or other documents filed with the SEC that contain audited financial statements. The selected quarterly financial data are required to be reviewed, either on a preissuance or retrospective basis. Other entities may voluntarily include similar information in documents containing audited financial statements. In the latter instance, the interim financial information may or may not have been reviewed. It is unlikely that an entity not required to include that information would do so without having it reviewed, since that would give rise to an expansion of the auditor's report. (See the discussion on pages 834 and 835.)

Most companies that include quarterly financial information with their audited annual financial statements will want their accountants to review those data periodically throughout the year, rather than retrospectively at year-end. There are a number of tangible benefits to this approach. First, a preissuance review facilitates the early recognition of accounting problems and the avoidance of year-end "surprises." Second, there may be some offsetting reductions in the audit fee for the year because, even though the review does not entail audit procedures, it involves steps that, if the work is coordinated, can be utilized in the performance of the audit. Finally, it may prevent the publishing of quarterly financial information with the audited annual financial statements that differs from amounts previously reported during the year.

Objective of Reviews of Interim Financial Information

A review of interim financial information is intended to provide the accountant with a basis for reporting whether material modifications should be made to such information in order for it to conform with GAAP. The accountant forms this opinion by applying a knowledge of financial reporting practices to significant accounting matters that are brought to the accountant's attention through inquiries and analytical procedures.

Nature of Reviews

SAS No. 36, *Review of Interim Financial Information* (AU Section 722), sets forth the procedures established by the profession for a review of interim financial information. With one principal exception, those procedures are similar to the review procedures previously discussed for a review engagement. In an engagement to review interim financial information, as contrasted with an ordinary review engagement, the accountant should normally obtain written representations from management concerning its responsibility for the financial information, completeness of minutes, subsequent events, and other matters for which the accountant believes written representations are appropriate in the circumstances.

Information may come to the accountant's attention that raises questions as to whether the unaudited interim information departs from GAAP insofar as litigation, claims, or assessments are concerned. According to an Auditing Interpretation of AU Section 722, if the accountant believes the client's lawyer may have information concerning that possibility, the accountant should make inquiry of the lawyer, even though a review of interim financial information does not require corroborating evidential matter for responses to inquiries.

Timing of Reviews

The timing of procedures to be performed depends to a large extent on whether the accountant has been engaged to perform a preissuance review of the interim financial information or a review on a retrospective basis.

While adequate planning by the accountant is essential to the timely completion of work done on a preissuance basis, the client's interim reporting system is of paramount importance. It must permit the preparation of reliable interim financial information; otherwise, weaknesses may restrict the scope of the accountant's engagement. In addition, the client's system of interim financial controls should be adequate so that a review on a preissuance basis is not unduly expensive or time consuming.

On the other hand, if a review is done on a retrospective basis, the system must provide sufficient documentation, including the rationale for conclusions reached during the year, for the accountant's purpose. For example, the accountant may review the client's documentation in deciding whether an adjustment arising in a later quarter of the year is a change in estimate or a correction of an error.

Extent of Reviews

The extent to which the accountant makes inquiries and performs analytical reviews concerning significant matters relating to the financial information to be reported on depends on a number of considerations. First, the accountant needs a knowledge of the client's accounting and reporting practices and system of internal accounting control as a practical basis for the inquiry and other review procedures. The accountant ordinarily acquires this knowledge as a result of having audited the client's previous annual financial statements. Knowledge of weaknesses in internal accounting control, accounting changes, and changes in the nature or volume of the client's business activities; the issuance of new pronouncements on financial accounting standards; and questions raised during the review all may prompt the accountant to make more extensive inquiries or to employ other procedures to assess interim financial information.

There are also a number of practical considerations that affect the extent of review procedures. Examples are selecting locations to be visited if the general accounting records are maintained at multiple client locations, and acquiring the necessary "knowledge" if there has been a change in auditors and the current accountant does not have an audit base to work from. These are special matters that the accountant should consider in planning the review strategy.

Reporting Standards

An accountant may address a report on interim financial information to the client company, its board of directors, or its stockholders. The report should be dated as of the date the review was completed and is similar to a review report, as previously discussed. The standard form of interim review report presented in AU Section 722.18 follows:

> We have made a review of (describe the information or statements reviewed) of ABC Company and consolidated subsidiaries as of September 30, 19X1, and for the three-month and nine-month periods then ended, in accordance with standards established by the American Institute of Certified Public Accountants.
>
> A review of interim financial information consists principally of obtaining an understanding of the system for the preparation of interim financial information, applying analytical review procedures to financial data, and making inquiries of persons responsible for financial and accounting matters. It is substantially less in scope than an examination in accordance with generally accepted auditing standards, the objective of which is the expression of an opinion regarding the financial statements taken as a whole. Accordingly, we do not express such an opinion.
>
> Based on our review, we are not aware of any material modifications that should be made to the accompanying financial (information or statements) for them to be in conformity with generally accepted accounting principles.

Each page of the interim financial information should be marked as "unaudited."

When an accountant requires reports from other accountants as a basis, in part, for a report on a review of consolidated interim financial information, the accountant may make reference in the report to the reports of the other accountants to indicate a division of responsibility for performance of the review.

Interim Financial Information Presented in Annual Reports to Shareholders. As previously noted, selected quarterly financial data may be presented in a note to the audited financial statements or as supplementary information outside the audited financial statements. If such information is presented in a note to the audited financial statements, the information should be marked as "unaudited." If quarterly financial data are presented in an annual report to shareholders, either voluntarily or as required by Item 302(a) of SEC Regulation S-K, there is a presumption in the absence of an indication to the contrary that the data have been reviewed in accordance with the established professional standards previously discussed. Because of this presumption, if an accountant has reviewed the data, the audit report on the annual financial statements ordinarily need not be modified nor does the accountant have to report separately on the review.

If the selected quarterly financial data are required by Item 302(a) of Regulation S-K, expansion of the auditor's report on the annual financial statements is called for if such information is omitted, is not appropriately marked as unaudited, has not been reviewed, does not appear to be presented in conformity with GAAP, or includes an indication that a review was made but fails to state that "the review is substantially less in scope than an examination in accordance with generally accepted auditing standards, the objective of which is an expression of opinion regarding the financial statements taken as a whole, and accordingly, no such opinion is expressed" (AU Section 722.30).[8] If selected quarterly financial data that have not been reviewed are voluntarily presented, expansion of the auditor's report on the annual financial statements would be called for if the entity does not indicate that the data have not been reviewed.

Special Reports

An auditor may be asked to audit and report on financial information other than financial statements prepared in conformity with GAAP. This section covers auditors' reports issued in connection with financial statements prepared on a basis of accounting other than GAAP and in connection with parts of a financial statement. It also discusses reports on client compliance with aspects of contracts or regulations and reports involving financial information presented on prescribed forms requiring a prescribed form of auditor's report.

Non-GAAP Financial Statements

Statement of Financial Accounting Concepts No. 1, *Objectives of Financial Reporting by Business Enterprises*, issued by the Financial Accounting Standards Board (FASB) states that "information about enterprise earnings and its components measured by accrual accounting generally provides a better indication of enterprise performance than information about cash receipts and payments" (para. 44). Stated another way, the accrual basis is generally necessary to measure financial position and results of operations properly in conformity with GAAP. Other comprehensive bases of accounting, such as the cash or

---

[8]Under its present standards, it is unlikely that the SEC would accept any expansion of the auditor's report in this regard. A possible exception might be if the auditor could not review the selected quarterly financial data in the annual report because the company's system for preparing interim financial information did not provide an adequate basis for making such a review. In that case, however, there is a possibility that the client might be in violation of the "accounting standards" provisions of the Foreign Corrupt Practices Act. See the discussion of the Act in Chapter 7.

modified accrual basis, the income tax basis, and statutory bases that meet reporting requirements of a government regulatory agency, ordinarily do not accomplish that objective. Nevertheless, there are some organizations that believe they should not prepare or do not need financial statements based on GAAP. Those organizations that do not find the extra effort and cost to prepare accrual basis statements worthwhile believe they are better served by a comprehensive basis of accounting other than GAAP. Typical of these organizations are some not-for-profit entities, certain nonpublic companies, regulated companies that must file financial statements based on accounting principles prescribed by a government regulatory agency, and entities formed for special purposes, such as certain partnerships and joint ventures.

Definition. SAS No. 14, *Special Reports*, paragraph 4 (AU Section 621.04) defines a comprehensive basis of accounting as one of the following:

- A basis of accounting that the reporting entity uses to comply with the requirements or financial reporting provisions of a government regulatory agency to whose jurisdiction the entity is subject. Examples are a basis of accounting prescribed in a uniform system of accounts that the Interstate Commerce Commission requires railroad companies to use and a basis of accounting insurance companies use pursuant to the rules of a state insurance commission.
- A basis of accounting that the reporting entity uses or expects to use to file its income tax return for the period covered by the financial statements.
- The cash receipts and disbursements basis of accounting, and modifications of the cash basis having substantial support, such as recording depreciation on fixed assets or accruing income taxes.
- A definite set of criteria having substantial support that is applied to all material items appearing in financial statements, such as the price-level basis of accounting.

Forms of Reporting. The key element of a special report on a comprehensive basis of accounting other than GAAP is an explanatory paragraph that emphasizes that the financial statements are not intended to be presented in conformity with GAAP and refers to the note to the financial statements that states the basis of the financial statements and how that basis of presentation differs from GAAP. The monetary effect of such differences need not be stated in the auditor's report.

The financial statements should be titled using terms that are not generally associated with financial statements intended to present financial position, results of operations, or changes in financial position in conformity with GAAP. For example, "statement of assets and liabilities arising from cash transactions" should be used instead of "balance sheet." If the financial statements are not suitably titled, the auditor should consider whether the auditor's report should be modified to disclose this; usually the auditor concludes that the matter is not significant enough to affect the report, provided the basis of presentation is disclosed in the financial statements.

The form of reporting prescribed for special reports is appropriate for financial statements prepared in accordance with the requirements or financial reporting provisions of a government regulatory agency only if those statements are intended solely for filing with the regulatory agency. The fact that by law or regulation the auditor's report may be made a matter of public record is not germane.

Illustrations of various reports on financial statements prepared in accordance with a comprehensive basis of accounting other than GAAP can be found in SAS No. 14 (AU Section 621.08). One example, that of a report on financial statements prepared on the entity's income tax basis, follows:

> We have examined the statement of assets, liabilities, and capital—income tax basis of ABC Partnership as of December 31, 19XX, and the related statements of revenue and expenses—income tax basis and of changes in partners' capital accounts—income tax basis for the year then ended. Our examination was made in accordance with generally accepted auditing standards and, accordingly, included such tests of the accounting records and such other auditing procedures as we considered necessary in the circumstances.
>
> As described in Note X, the Partnership's policy is to prepare its financial statements on the accounting basis used for income tax purposes; consequently, certain revenue and the related assets are recognized when received rather than when earned, and certain expenses are recognized when paid rather than when the obligation is incurred. Accordingly, the accompanying financial statements are not intended to present financial position and results of operations in conformity with generally accepted accounting principles.
>
> In our opinion, the financial statements referred to above present fairly the assets, liabilities, and capital of ABC Partnership as of December 31, 19XX, and its revenue and expenses and changes in its partners' capital accounts for the year then ended, on the basis of accounting described in Note X, which basis has been applied in a manner consistent with that of the preceding year.

In some cases, financial statements prepared on a comprehensive basis of accounting other than GAAP are not significantly different from conventional GAAP statements prepared for the same entity. In such circumstances, the auditor should issue the standard two-paragraph report intended for GAAP presentations rather than a special report.

The Board of Directors of the AICPA established a special committee to study accounting standards overload and consider alternative means of providing relief from accounting standards found not to be cost effective, particularly for small, closely held businesses. The special committee issued its tentative conclusions and recommendations for public comment in December 1981. Among them was the recommendation that the income tax basis of accounting be elevated to an acceptable alternative to GAAP and that the Auditing Standards Board and the Accounting and Review Services Committee change their reporting standards to allow a more positive form of reporting on income tax basis financial statements.

The special committee issued its final report in February 1983. It concluded that there is no need at present to change the standards, described previously, for reporting on income tax basis financial statements, but that additional professional guidance is needed on the measurement problems inherent in non-GAAP statements. The authors share this view. In the authors' view, changing reporting standards in any way that would undermine the clear distinction between GAAP statements and non-GAAP statements would contribute toward the probability of user confusion. Furthermore, the alleged negative aspects of the present reporting requirements are not the reason for the limited use of income tax basis financial statements. Rather, the income tax basis of accounting does not satisfy the needs of most users of financial statements of small companies.

Nevertheless, a special report containing an unqualified opinion on financial statements prepared in accordance with a comprehensive basis of accounting other than GAAP is a useful, practical alternative for companies that prepare statements on such a basis and wish an audit.

Reports on Parts of a Financial Statement

An auditor may be engaged to examine and express an opinion on one or more specified elements, accounts, or items of a financial statement. The examination might be performed as a separate engagement or, more commonly, in conjunction with an examination of financial statements taken as a whole. For example, the report might be on the amount of sales for the purpose of computing rentals, royalties, a profit participation, or the adequacy of a provision for income taxes in financial statements. SAS No. 14 (AU Section 621) provides guidance on these kinds of engagements.

Applicability of GAAP. The auditor's report should not address GAAP or the consistent application of GAAP unless the elements, accounts, or items on which the auditor is reporting are prepared in conformity with GAAP. For example, GAAP would normally not be applicable to items prepared in accordance with the provisions of a contract, law, or government regulation.

Materiality. Since the auditor expresses an opinion on each specified element, account, or item of a financial statement covered by the report, the measurement of materiality should be related to each individual element, account, or item rather than to the aggregate thereof or to the financial statements taken as a whole. Thus, an audit of only specified parts of a set of financial statements is usually more extensive than an audit of those same parts if they are included in a full set of audited financial statements. Items that are interrelated with those on which the auditor has been engaged to express an opinion must also be considered. Examples of interrelated financial statement elements are sales and receivables, inventories and payables, and property, plant, and equipment, and depreciation.

Forms of Reporting. As noted in Chapter 18, piecemeal opinions are not permitted, since they are considered to overshadow or contradict a disclaimer of opinion or an adverse opinion. As a consequence, the auditor must be careful to avoid expressing an opinion on specified elements, accounts, or items of a financial statement that is tantamount to a piecemeal opinion, if the audit of the financial statements as a whole resulted in an adverse opinion or a disclaimer. That generally would not be a concern if the special report did not cover a major portion of the financial statement elements, accounts, or items and did not accompany the financial statements of the entity.

The form of report to be rendered depends on the purpose of the examination and the elements, accounts, or items audited. It is not uncommon for a special report of this nature to contain at least three paragraphs. Although the form of report varies, there are characteristics that are common to all reports on specified elements, accounts, or items. An illustration of a report of this type follows. Other examples are presented in SAS No. 14 (AU Section 621.14).

Report Relating to Royalties:

We have examined the schedule of royalties applicable to engine production of the Q Division of XYZ Corporation for the year ended December 31, 19XX, under the terms of a license agreement dated May 14, 19XX, between ABC Company and XYZ Corporation. Our examination was made in accordance with generally accepted auditing standards and, accordingly, included such tests of the accounting records and such other auditing procedures as we considered necessary in the circumstances.

We have been informed that, under XYZ Corporation's interpretation of the agreement referred to above, royalties were based on the number of engines produced after giving effect to a reduction for production retirements that were scrapped, but without a reduction for field returns that were scrapped, even though the field returns were replaced with new engines without charge to customers. This treatment is consistent with that followed in prior years.

In our opinion, the schedule of royalties referred to above presents fairly the number of engines produced by the Q Division of XYZ Corporation during the year ended December 31, 19XX, and the amount of royalties applicable thereto under the license agreement referred to above, on the basis indicated in the preceding paragraph.

Applying Agreed-upon Procedures to Specified Elements, Accounts, or Items of a Financial Statement.
An accountant may be asked to apply agreed-upon procedures to one or more specified elements, accounts, or items of a financial statement that are not sufficient to allow expressing an opinion on the specified elements, accounts, or items. Even though the scope of the en-

gagement is limited, the accountant may accept such an engagement provided the parties involved have a clear understanding of the procedures to be performed and distribution of the accountant's report is restricted to the named parties involved. There are a number of ways the accountant can obtain satisfaction that all parties involved know and agree on what is to be done. They range from meeting with the parties involved to discuss the procedures to be applied, to supplying a draft of the report to such parties with a request for comments before the report is issued. SAS No. 35, *Special Reports—Applying Agreed-Upon Procedures to Specified Elements, Accounts, or Items of a Financial Statement* (AU Section 622), provides for these engagements.

The content of the accountant's report on the results of applying agreed-upon procedures varies with the circumstances. Certain elements, however, are common to all such reports. The report should identify the specified elements, accounts, or items to which the agreed-upon procedures were applied; enumerate the procedures performed; state the accountant's findings; specify the intended distribution of the report; state that the report relates only to the elements, accounts, or items specified and does not extend to the entity's financial statements taken as a whole; and disclaim an opinion with respect to such elements, accounts, or items. Often, the distribution of the report is restricted to interested parties, with a prohibition against further distribution. If the accountant has no adjustments to propose, negative assurance may be expressed to that effect. The nature of the negative assurance and disclaimers is so unique that it is illustrated here:

> Because the above procedures do not constitute an examination made in accordance with generally accepted auditing standards, we do not express an opinion on any of the accounts or items referred to above. In connection with the procedures referred to above, no matters came to our attention that caused us to believe that the specified accounts or items should be adjusted. Had we performed additional procedures or had we made an examination of the financial statements in accordance with generally accepted auditing standards, matters might have come to our attention that would have been reported to you. This report relates only to the accounts and items specified above and does not extend to any financial statements of Y Company, Inc., taken as a whole. (AU Section 622.06)

Reports on Compliance

Compliance audits are performed to determine and report on whether an entity has complied with specified policies, procedures, laws, regulations, or contracts. Companies may be required by a contractual agreement or regulatory agency to furnish a report on compliance with aspects of the agreement or regulatory requirements. For example, a loan agreement may call for assurance from an independent auditor that the borrower has complied with covenants in the agreement relating to accounting or auditing matters, or a contract with a governmental agency may require similar assurance that the enterprise has complied with a specified law or regulation. Although CPAs have performed compliance audits for many years, this type of engagement has grown in recent years and is likely to grow even more in the future. This section considers emerging types of compliance audits that auditors are now performing and the types of reports that are being issued.

Some aspects of compliance audits are integral to an audit of financial statements. If contracts or statutes have an effect on a client's financial statements, the auditor should determine the extent of compliance with them. Two examples will illustrate this. An auditor should determine that the client has conformed with the restrictive covenants in a long-term bond agreement, since a violation of those covenants could make the entire issue due and payable at the lender's option and require the debt to be classified as a current rather than a long-term liability. As a second example, testing compliance with certain statutes and ordinances has always been required in audits of state and local governmental units to enable the auditor to express an opinion on the governmental unit's financial statements. One of the most significant aspects of testing compliance with statutes and ordinances is the legal requirement for compliance with budgetary constraints.

SAS No. 14 (AU Section 621) provides guidance on reports on compliance with aspects of contractual agreements or regulatory requirements related to audited financial statements. Special reports of this type should be issued only if the auditor has examined the financial statements to which the contractual agreement or regulatory requirements relate. The report usually contains negative assurance relative to the applicable covenants of the agreement or the applicable regulatory requirements and a statement that the examination of the financial statements was not directed primarily toward obtaining knowledge regarding compliance. This assurance may be given in a separate report or in one or more paragraphs of the auditor's report accompanying the financial statements.

A practitioner may also be asked to issue a report on compliance with aspects of contractual agreements or regulatory requirements unrelated to financial statements. Because those kinds of reports are not covered by SAS No. 14, the practitioner should seek both performance and reporting guidance from the *Attestation Standards*, which are the applicable authoritative pronouncement in this area.

The practitioner should be careful not to accept an attest engagement to render a compliance report on matters that lie outside the scope of a CPA's professional competence (for example, matters relating to the adequacy of insurance coverage), which would violate the second general attestation standard.

Auditing compliance with the terms and conditions associated with federal or state grants to colleges and universities is a particularly significant application of compliance audits. During the 1960s and 1970s, individual federal agencies such as the National Institutes of Health, the National Science Foundation, the Defense Department, and, most significant, the Office (later Department) of Education became the largest "donors" to many educational institutions. Consistent with the practices of universities' original donors in the early 1900s, these agencies commissioned audits of each of their own separate grants at each grantee institution. The growth of those grants soon outstripped the resources provided by the granting agencies to perform individual project or program audits at colleges and universities. In 1979, the U.S. Office of Management and Budget required educational institutions to engage their auditors to study and evaluate their financial management systems relating to federal projects and to determine that their transactions comply with federal regulations—in effect to perform a "single audit" in which the university, rather than the individual funds, is considered the entity subject to audit. Today, independent auditors of the 4000 educational institutions that receive federal funds are likely to be asked to add federally related procedures to the financial statement audit.

In performing a single audit, the auditor should plan to integrate compliance tests of grant costs with compliance testing of specific internal accounting controls, since both types of tests often require that the auditor obtain and evaluate similar evidence. For example, when determining whether a particular expenditure was properly charged to a specific grant, the auditor should test compliance with the terms of the grant and may also test the controls over those expenditures. The examination should include compliance determinations that costs incurred under federal contracts

- Are necessary and reasonable.
- Conform with any limitation or exclusion in the award.
- Are accounted for consistently and uniformly with other institutional activities.
- Are net of "applicable credits."
- Are approved in advance if required.
- Are incurred in accordance with competitive procurement procedures.
- Absorb indirect costs at the proper rate.

Other examples of compliance audits include

- Determining that a bank or savings and loan association has established operating procedures and compliance guidelines to comply with the Currency and Foreign Transaction Reporting Act, also known as the Bank Secrecy Act. The Act requires those institutions to report to the Internal Revenue Service or the Commissioner of Customs when particular currency transactions (e.g., deposits or withdrawals in excess of $10,000) occur or are attempted. The purpose of the Act is to promote a paper trail of the activities of money launderers serving the interests of drug traffickers and other elements of white-collar and organized crime.
- Determining that another CPA firm's quality control system is appropriate, that its policies and procedures are adequately documented and communi-

cated, that they are being complied with, and that the firm is in compliance with the membership requirements of the AICPA Division for CPA Firms. In other words, the peer review process described in Chapter 3 is a compliance audit.

• Determining that an enterprise has instituted a code of business ethics and conduct, and policies and procedures to ensure adherence to it, and reporting the results of the determination to an external monitoring body and the public.

Reports on Prescribed Forms

Printed forms or schedules designed for filing with various bodies sometimes prescribe the wording of the auditor's report. The prescribed wording may call for assertions by the auditor that do not conform with the applicable professional reporting standards. In those instances, the auditor should either reword the prescribed report language or attach a separate report to the financial information presented in the prescribed forms or schedules.[9]

Reporting on Information Accompanying Basic Financial Statements

Information such as additional details or explanations of items in or related to the basic financial statements, condensed financial statements, consolidating information, historical summaries of items extracted from the basic financial statements, statistical data, and other material, some of which may be from sources outside the accounting system or outside the entity, may be presented in a document, such as an annual report, that also includes basic financial statements. Unless the basic financial statements incorporate such information by reference, the information is not considered necessary for the presentation of financial position, results of operations, or changes in financial position in conformity with GAAP. Such information could be included in either an auditor-submitted document or a client-prepared document. If the information is included in an auditor-submitted document, the auditor has a responsibility to report on all the information contained in the document. If the information is included in a client-prepared document that names the auditor, the auditor is not required to report on the information as long as it is clear what information in the document is covered by the auditor's report.

Additional Details or Commentary in Auditor-Submitted Documents

The auditor may be requested to include a variety of material in addition to the

---

[9]Considerations related to compilation reports issued by an accountant on financial statements included in prescribed forms are discussed in SSARS No. 3, *Compilation Reports on Financial Statements Included in Certain Prescribed Forms* (AR Section 300).

basic financial statements in a document submitted to the client. For example, the document might include details of the subaccounts composing financial statement captions, statistical data, consolidating data, explanatory comments, financial analyses, possibly some operational data, and occasionally a description of the audit procedures applied to specific items in the financial statements. The account details, analytical comment, and audit scope explanations might be combined under appropriate account headings, or these subjects might be separated and presented in different sections of the document.

Reports of this type—commonly called "long-form" reports, although that term has not been used in the authoritative literature since 1980—can be useful historical records of a company's financial activities. With the exception of the additional commentary concerning the audit, however, the information can usually be prepared by the client's internal staff. Consequently, involvement of the auditor in services of this nature is usually restricted to small organizations and acquisition audits.

The purpose of an audit of basic financial statements in accordance with GAAS is to form an opinion on those statements taken as a whole. Although professional standards do not call for applying auditing procedures to information presented outside the basic financial statements, the auditor may choose to modify or redirect certain of the procedures applied in the examination of the basic financial statements so as to be able to express an opinion on the accompanying information rather than disclaiming an opinion on such information. SAS No. 29, *Reporting on Information Accompanying the Basic Financial Statements in Auditor-Submitted Documents* (AU Section 551), contains reporting guidelines for information accompanying the basic financial statements in an auditor-submitted document. The auditor's report on the accompanying information may be either added to the standard report on the basic financial statements or presented separately. In either case, the report should

- State that the examination has been made for the purpose of forming an opinion on the basic financial statements taken as a whole.
- Identify the accompanying information. (Identification may be by descriptive title or page number of the document.)
- State that the accompanying information is presented for purposes of additional analysis and is not a required part of the basic financial statements.
- Include either an opinion on whether the accompanying information is fairly stated in all material respects in relation to the basic financial statements taken as a whole or a disclaimer of opinion, depending on whether the information has been subjected to the auditing procedures applied in the examination of the basic financial statements. The auditor may express an opinion on a portion of the accompanying information and disclaim an opinion on the remainder.

For purposes of reporting in this manner, the measurement of materiality is the same as that used in forming an opinion on the basic financial statements taken as a whole. Accordingly, the auditor need not apply procedures as extensive as would be necessary to express an opinion on a separate presentation of the information, as would be true for a ''special report'' described earlier in this chapter.

If the auditor submits to the client or others a document containing the basic financial statements, other information, and the auditor's report thereon, and the client issues a separate document containing only the basic financial statements and the auditor's standard report, the auditor should be sure that the basic financial statements include all the information considered necessary for presentation in conformity with GAAP. If any of that necessary information accompanied the basic financial statements in an auditor-submitted document, it might later serve to support a contention that those same basic financial statements included in a client-prepared document were not presented in conformity with GAAP because of inadequate disclosure of material information known to the auditor.

Supplementary Information Required by FASB Pronouncements

Supplementary information required by the Financial Accounting Standards Board differs from other types of information outside the basic financial statements. This is because the FASB considers the information an essential part of the financial reporting of certain entities and because the Board establishes guidelines for the measurement and presentation of the information. For this reason, the AICPA has established limited procedures to be applied to this information by the auditor. The limited procedures, found in SAS No. 27, *Supplementary Information Required by the Financial Accounting Standards Board* (AU Section 553), can be summarized as follows:

- Inquire of management as to any significant assumptions or interpretations underlying the measurement or presentation, whether the methods of measurement and presentation are within guidelines prescribed by the FASB and have changed from those used in the prior period, and the reasons for any such changes.
- Compare the information for consistency with the audited financial statements, other knowledge obtained during the examination of the financial statements, and management's responses to the specific inquiries.
- Consider whether specific written representations on the information should be obtained from management.
- Make additional inquiries based on the results of the foregoing if the auditor believes that the measurement or presentation of the information may be inappropriate.

It also may be necessary to apply additional procedures as prescribed by other Statements on Auditing Standards for specific types of supplementary information required by the FASB.

Some examples of supplementary information required by the FASB are data on the effects of changing prices (FASB Statement No. 33, *Financial Reporting and Changing Prices*), oil and gas reserve information (FASB Statements No. 19, 25, and 69 dealing with financial accounting and reporting by oil and gas producing companies), and mineral reserve information (FASB Statement No. 39, *Financial Reporting and Changing Prices: Specialized Assets*).

There is no requirement, however, to report specifically on such data unless the auditor has been engaged to examine and express an opinion thereon. The professional standards do provide for exception reporting; that is, the auditor is required to expand the standard report on the audited financial statements to report deficiencies in, or the omission of, such information or an inability to apply the prescribed limited procedures. The auditor's opinion on the fairness of presentation of the basic financial statements in conformity with GAAP is unaffected by those circumstances. Since the supplementary information is not a required part of the basic financial statements and is not audited, an unqualified opinion, accompanied by an additional explanatory paragraph, could be presented.

When supplementary information required by the FASB is presented outside the basic financial statements in an auditor-submitted document, the auditor has an additional reporting responsibility, namely, to disclaim an opinion on the information. SAS No. 29 (AU Section 551.15) provides an example of a disclaimer an auditor might use in these circumstances.

The guidance in this section also applies to supplementary information required by pronouncements of the Governmental Accounting Standards Board.

Reporting on Prospective Financial Statements and Pro Forma Statements

In the past, accountants have been cautious about their association with reports on prospective financial statements and pro forma statements. That caution may seem inconsistent with their readiness to issue opinions on proposed accounting methods, anticipated tax effects, or control aspects of proposed systems. The reason for the difference in attitude may be that opinions on those kinds of matters are not likely to be of interest to anyone other than specific users presumed to be knowledgeable recipients, and are generally not distributed to anyone else. Prospective financial statements and pro forma statements covered by an accountant's report, on the other hand, are likely to be distributed to people who may not have significant expertise and may make investment decisions in reliance on the accountant's association with the data.

Prospective Financial Statements

The usefulness of prospective financial statements has become widely recognized and they are in demand by the financial community. They are presently used in a wide variety of situations, ranging from public offerings of bonds or other securities and arrangements for bank or other financing, to internal microcomputer ''spread sheet'' software programs designed to facilitate the preparation of various financial analyses, including short-range plans (budgets), long-range plans, cash flow studies, capital improvement decisions, and other plans. Within these areas, one might find the following specific applications:

- Forecasts included in feasibility studies and preliminary feasibility studies. These studies may cover hospitals, sports complexes, homes for the elderly, real estate ventures, and so on. Generally, they involve various types of capital expenditures.
- Forecasts or projections relating to new or expanded projects or operations or existing operations of an entity over specified future periods. The prospective financial information may be, for example, forecasts of target companies in connection with an acquisition, forecasts for the client company itself for purposes of conducting discussions with lenders, forecasts prepared on behalf of creditors (including troubled financial situations, such as bankruptcies), or forecasts for the client company in contemplation of a refinancing or eliminating a line of business.
- Forecasts filed in connection with applications for Mass Transportation Operating Assistance Grants under the Urban Mass Transportation Act.
- Rate studies for municipalities and utilities reported in financial statement format.
- Forecasts, including the actuarial components thereof, of insurance companies. Such forecasts may be filed, for example, with insurance commissions of states in which the insurance company wishes to be licensed to do business.
- Microcomputer projections of sales and operating results.
- Forecasts of future results of a syndicated tax-oriented investment. Syndicated projects could relate to real estate, oil and gas, alternative fuel programs, research and development programs, farming transactions, and equipment leases.
- Housing mortgage revenue bond issues.

The Accountant's Role in the Prospective Presentation Process

The AICPA has issued two related documents containing guidance for accountants who are asked to be associated with prospective financial statements. The first document, a Statement on Standards for Accountants' Services on Prospective Financial Information entitled *Financial Forecasts and Projections*, sets forth standards and provides guidance to accountants on performing and reporting on engagements to examine, compile, or apply agreed-upon procedures to prospective financial statements. The Statement, issued in October 1985, is similar in authority to an SAS. The second document, a *Guide for Pro-*

spective Financial Statements, was issued in January 1986 and is a companion document to the authoritative Statement. The Guide provides more detailed performance and reporting guidance than does the Statement and also establishes preparation and presentation guidelines for forecasts and projections.

The SEC has stated that if companies under its jurisdiction choose to include prospective financial information in prospectuses or reports filed with it, the information should meet certain broad standards and disclosure requirements. The SEC also adopted a rule providing a safe harbor from the liability provisions of the federal securities laws for companies publishing prospective information in good faith and with a reasonable basis, and for third-party reviewers of such information.

The stance of the SEC and prior and current guidance by the AICPA have encouraged registrants to provide forward-looking financial data, but they have not created a rush to include forecasts in SEC filings. There has, however, been extensive use of forecasts in non-SEC filings, such as prospectuses for nonregistered bond offerings, which are usually accompanied by accountant's reports. There has been some cautious use of forecasts with accountant's reports in documents filed with the SEC, but until 1983 no major companies undertook to supply comprehensive forecasts in SEC filings.

In November 1983, in what may well be a milestone, American Telephone and Telegraph Company, in connection with its court-ordered divestiture of the Bell Operating Companies, filed a comprehensive information statement and prospectus for AT&T and each of the seven newly organized regional holding companies into which its 22 Bell Operating Companies were to be spun off. Each entity reported a forecasted income statement for 1984 in lieu of the pro forma statements that would otherwise have been required. Each of these forecasts was reported on by CPAs.

Types of Prospective Financial Information

Prospective financial information can be one of two types defined by the AICPA Statement and Guide. A financial "forecast" is prospective financial information that presents, to the best of the responsible party's knowledge and belief, an entity's expected financial position, results of operations, and changes in financial position. It is based on the responsible party's[10] assumptions reflecting conditions it expects to exist and the *course of action it expects to take*. A financial "projection" is prospective financial information that presents, to the best of the responsible party's knowledge and belief, *given one or more hypothetical assumptions*, an entity's expected financial position, results of operations, and changes in financial position. A financial projection is sometimes prepared to present one or more hypothetical courses of action for evaluation, as in response to a question such as "What would happen if . . .?" It is based on the responsible party's assumptions reflecting conditions it expects would exist and the course of action it expects would be taken, given one or

---

[10]The responsible party, usually management, is the person or persons that are responsible for the assumptions underlying the prospective financial information.

more hypothetical assumptions. Both financial forecasts and projections may be expressed either as a single-point estimate or as a range.

A financial forecast is appropriate for general use, such as inclusion in a bond or equity offering or in an annual report to shareholders of a public company. A financial projection is not appropriate for general use, but it can be used by the entity alone or by the entity and parties with which it is negotiating directly, such as a bank or a regulatory agency.

Scope of Services

Although an accountant may be engaged to perform a wide spectrum of services in assisting management to assemble prospective financial information for internal use, he or she should perform one of three specific types of professional services in connection with prospective financial data intended for either general or limited use by third parties: compilations, examinations, or the application of agreed-upon procedures. The meanings of those terms and the procedures involved in those services are different from the meanings of the terms and the related procedures as applied to historical information because of the differences in the nature of prospective information compared with historical information.

A compilation of a financial forecast or projection involves

- Assembling (involving mathematical or other clerical functions beyond mere reproduction or collation) the prospective data, to the extent necessary, based on the responsible party's assumptions.
- Obtaining satisfaction that the underlying assumptions are not obviously inappropriate.
- Reading the prospective data and considering whether they appear to be presented in conformity with AICPA presentation guidelines.

A compilation is not intended to provide assurance on the prospective data or the underlying assumptions. Consequently, the accountant's procedures are limited, consisting principally of obtaining background knowledge of the industry and the entity, inquiry, reading the data, and confirming with the responsible party the latter's responsibility for the assumptions.

An examination of a financial forecast or projection is the highest level of service offered by an accountant with regard to providing assurance on prospective financial information. An examination involves evaluating the

- Preparation of the forecast or projection.
- Support underlying the assumptions.
- Presentation for conformity with AICPA presentation guidelines.

In examining a projection, the accountant need not obtain support for the hypothetical assumptions but should consider whether they are consistent with the purpose of the presentation.

When an accountant applies agreed-upon procedures to a financial forecast or projection, specified users of the forecast or projection participate in establishing the nature and scope of the engagement and take responsibility for the adequacy of the procedures to be performed by the accountant. Generally, the accountant's procedures may be as limited or extensive as the specified users desire, as long as the users take responsibility for their adequacy. Mere reading of the prospective financial statements, however, is not acceptable as a specified procedure. Distribution of the accountant's report when agreed-upon procedures are applied to a financial forecast or projection is restricted to the specified users noted earlier. The report enumerates the procedures performed and states the accountant's findings; it may not express any form of negative assurance on the financial statements taken as a whole.

An accountant may be associated with a partial presentation, that is, one that excludes one or more of the minimum items required by the AICPA to be included in prospective financial statements. Even though such a presentation may be appropriate in many "limited use" instances, the accountant should consider whether it will adequately present the information for the intended purpose. In any event, since a partial presentation ordinarily has limited use, it is not appropriate for general offerings of debt or equity.

In performing services in connection with financial forecasts and projections for internal use only, the accountant should design the procedures and related reporting to be consistent with the nature and objectives of the engagement.

Reporting

The Ethics Committee of the AICPA, in Interpretation 2 of Rule 201 of the Code of Professional Ethics (ET Section 201.03), makes it clear that a member's name may not be associated with a forecast or projection unless there is full disclosure of the sources of information, the major assumptions made, the character of the work performed by the accountant, and the degree of responsibility being taken. In addition, the AICPA Code of Professional Ethics provides that a member shall not permit his or her name to be used in conjunction with any prediction of future transactions that may lead to the belief that the member vouches for its achievability. These are key elements of all engagements dealing with prospective financial information.

Prospective financial information by its nature calls for a caveat in the accountant's report regarding the ultimate attainment of the prospective results and the responsibility the accountant assumes for updating the report for subsequent events and circumstances. The remainder of the accountant's report pertaining to the degree of responsibility taken depends on the procedures performed to obtain satisfaction as to the reasonableness of the assumptions.

There is a presumption, which is valid, that an accountant who compiles a forecast or projection should be knowledgeable enough about the subject matter to have some basis for believing that the assumptions are not obviously inappropriate, and that, further, the accountant would not be associated with a compilation of a forecast or projection if he or she believed otherwise. The accountant can express a conclusion about whether the underlying assumptions provide a reasonable basis for the presentation, however, only after performing an examination that includes procedures sufficient to determine that the assumptions provide a reasonable basis for the forecast. The AICPA Guide contains standard reporting formats for a variety of situations, as well as examples of reporting when circumstances call for a departure from the accountant's standard reports.

Pro Forma Statements

There is no element of prediction in pro forma financial statements or data. They are intended to show what the significant effects on historical financial information might have been had a consummated or proposed transaction or event occurred at an earlier date.

Pro forma statements giving effect to contemplated transactions are sometimes included in prospectuses, proxy statements, and other public documents and more often in less widely circulated, special-purpose statements. A pro forma statement is frequently the only way to illustrate the effects of contemplated transactions. An important business combination (whether accounted for as a purchase or a pooling of interests), a divestiture, incorporation of a partnership or a propiertorship, a recapitalization, refunding, or reorganization, or an accounting change may be impossible to describe intelligibly without the use of pro forma statements.

Auditors have been issuing opinions on pro forma financial statements in SEC filings for many years, even though the authoritative auditing literature did not provide specific guidance on the procedures the auditor should apply or the wording of the opinion. In an effort to provide that guidance, in June 1984, the Auditing Standards Board issued an exposure draft of a proposed SAS on *Reporting on Pro Forma Financial Information in SEC Filings*. While an SAS on pro forma information has not been issued at the time of this writing, the Board is considering issuing guidance as a Statement on Standards for Attestation Engagements, since an engagement to report on pro forma information would be an attest engagement, as discussed in Chapter 2.

Reports on Internal Control

Interest in the effectiveness of internal accounting controls on the part of financial statement users has increased in the past decade, largely as a result of the Foreign Corrupt Practices Act of 1977 (see Chapter 7) and the events that led to its passage. The SEC stated, for example, that ''information regarding the effectiveness of an issuer's system of internal accounting control may be necessary to enable investors to better evaluate management's performance of its stewardship responsibilities and the reliability of interim financial statements and other unaudited financial information generated from the accounting system . . .'' (Exchange Act Release No. 15772, April 30, 1979). Both the Commission on Auditors' Responsibilities and the Financial Executives Institute have endorsed the publication of a report by enterprise management on, among other matters, the enterprise's system of internal accounting control.

In a related move, the SEC proposed a rule that would have required the management of publicly held companies to include in annual reports to the Commission, proxy material, and reports to shareholders a statement on the adequacy of internal accounting controls. The proposed rule also would have required independent public accountants to review the internal controls and report on them. Although the SEC formally withdrew its proposal, it urged the private sector to develop disclosure practices voluntarily and also urged auditor association with the voluntary management reports.

Industry responded vigorously to these developments. The number of companies including reports of management in their annual reports to shareholders, as reported by the AICPA in their publication *Accounting Trends and Techniques*, rose from 19 in 1977 to 279 in 1985. Management's report is usually presented on the same page as the auditor's report on the financial statements or the two reports appear on adjoining pages. The contents of reports by management vary from company to company, but they generally include at least the following:

- A statement of management's responsibility for the financial statements.
- The role of the audit committee of the board of directors.
- A discussion of corporate conduct policies.
- A discussion of the internal accounting control system.

As an example of the last item, the management report that appeared in the 1985 annual report to shareholders of Aluminum Company of America contained the following paragraph:

> The company maintains a system of internal controls, including accounting controls, and a strong program of internal auditing. The system of controls provides for appropriate division of responsibility and the application of policies and procedures that are consistent with high standards of accounting and administration. The company believes that its system of internal controls provides reasonable assurance that assets are safeguarded against losses from unauthorized use or disposition and that financial records are reliable for use in preparing financial statements.

There has not, however, been an increase in the number of companies engaging their auditors to report publicly on the report of management or on their internal controls. This is attributed to a pervasive view on the part of management that the additional costs of engaging independent auditors to make a study and evaluation for that purpose outweigh the benefits. The line of thinking seems to be that the financial statements are a product of the accounting system, and if an independent auditor expresses an unqualified opinion on the fairness of those statements in conformity with GAAP, a user should be satisfied.

In July 1980, the AICPA issued SAS No. 30, *Reporting on Internal Accounting Control* (AU Section 642), to provide guidance to auditors in connection with various engagements to report on internal accounting control, including engagements to express an opinion on an entity's overall system.

Types of Engagements

Managements (or audit committees) often request their auditors to report to them on the entire internal accounting control system for some assurance of compliance with the FCPA. Such a report need not be restricted as to use since it is usually based on a study and evaluation of internal accounting control beyond that made as part of an audit. Other types of engagements range from those to report on all or part of an entity's system of internal accounting control, based either on a regulatory agency's preestablished criteria or solely on the study and evaluation of the system made as part of an audit, to consultation engagements on improving the system. These types of engagements normally do not provide a sufficient basis for expressing an opinion on the overall system; to prevent misunderstanding, the resulting reports should be restricted to the use of the specific parties concerned.

Reports on internal accounting control are different from management letters (discussed in Chapter 8) and from the required communication of material weaknesses in internal accounting control (also discussed in Chapter 8). Management letters are a routine product of an effective audit. They are informal communications of constructive suggestions, noted during the course of an audit, for improving an entity's internal accounting and administrative controls and business operations, and are intended to assist management in discharging its responsibilities and obligations. Material weaknesses in internal accounting control that come to the auditor's attention during an examination of financial statements made in accordance with GAAS are required to be communicated to senior management and the board of directors. This communication is incidental to the auditor's examination of financial statements, in contrast to an engagement to report specifically on an entity's system of internal accounting control.

Study and Evaluation

The scope of the study and evaluation of internal accounting controls in an engagement to express an opinion on the system of internal accounting control is generally more extensive than that in an audit, although the procedures are similar. SAS No. 30, in paragraphs 13–34 (AU Sections 642.13–.34), contains a lengthy discussion of the various aspects of the study and evaluation. These involve planning the scope of the engagement, reviewing the design of the system, testing compliance with prescribed procedures, and evaluating the results of the review and tests.

Forms of Reporting

AU Section 642 also specifies the forms of reporting on internal accounting control for various types of engagements. A standard form of report expressing an unqualified opinion on an entity's overall system of internal accounting control is presented in AU Section 642.39. The main elements of that report are:

- A description of the scope of the engagement.
- The date to which the opinion relates.
- A statement that the establishment and maintenance of the system is the responsibility of management.
- A brief explanation of the broad objectives and inherent limitations of internal accounting control.
- The accountant's opinion on whether the system taken as a whole was sufficient to meet the broad objectives of internal accounting control insofar as those objectives pertain to the prevention or detection of errors or irregularities in amounts that would be material in relation to financial statements. (Opinions on compliance with the FCPA should be avoided, as this is a legal matter.)

AU Section 642.49 illustrates a report on internal accounting control when the study and evaluation is made as part of the audit and is not sufficient for expressing an opinion on the overall system. The report contains a disclaimer on the system as a whole, with an expression of negative assurance that the study and evaluation disclosed no condition believed to be a material weakness.[11]

Material Weaknesses

If the study and evaluation discloses conditions that, individually or in combination, result in one or more material weaknesses, the accountant's report should be modified to describe the material weaknesses, the general nature of potential errors or irregularities that might occur as a result of the weaknesses, and whether the weaknesses arose from a lack of control procedures or a breakdown in compliance. If the opinion on the internal accounting control system is

[11]AU Section 642 and Auditing Interpretations of AU Section 642 (AU Section 9642) provide further guidance on reports on internal accounting control in several specific circumstances, including reports based on criteria established by regulatory agencies.

issued in conjunction with or as part of an audit of the entity's financial statements, the report should state that the material weaknesses were considered in determining the audit tests to be applied in the examination of the financial statements.

Reports on Internal Control at Service Organizations

Service organizations may record transactions, process related data, or even execute and account for transactions on behalf of others. Companies that provide such services include, for example, trust departments of banks (which invest and hold securities for others), computer service centers (which process data for others), and securities depositories (which hold and account for securities for others). A service organization may seek a special-purpose report from an auditor on the design of its system of internal accounting control, on both the design of the system and compliance tests directed to specific objectives of internal accounting control, or on the system of a segment of the service organization. SAS No. 44, *Special-Purpose Reports on Internal Accounting Control at Service Organizations* (AU Section 324), provides guidance on the responsibilities of the auditor who issues that type of special-purpose report.

Opinions on Accounting Principles

An auditor is often requested to give a formal opinion on an accepted or preferred method of accounting, either for a hypothetical situation or for a specific proposed or completed transaction. It is important to record the facts on which the opinion is based because proposed situations and transactions have a way of changing subsequently, with possible implications for the opinion given. When the auditor's opinion is based on precedent, regulation, or another authoritative source, full and accurate citations should be stated. Any applicable alternatives should be outlined, the auditor's reasoning for selecting among them should be carefully presented, and the opinion should be set forth clearly and unequivocally.

Perhaps the most notable examples of this type of opinion are the reports required by the SEC when a company changes an accounting principle, and by the New York Stock Exchange (NYSE) in connection with the accounting for a business combination as a pooling of interests.

Preferability Letters

Paragraph 20 of APB Opinion No. 20, *Accounting Changes* (Accounting Standards Section A06.112), requires enterprise management to justify the use of an alternative accounting principle on the basis that it is preferable. The SEC requires companies subject to its reporting regulations that make a discretionary accounting change to obtain concurrence from their independent public accountants that the change is to a principle that is preferable in the circumstances. The accountant's concurrence is required to be set forth in a "preferability letter" accompanying the first Form 10-Q filed subsequent to the discretionary accounting change.[12] The requirements are also applicable to Form 10-K if a discretionary accounting change is made in the fourth quarter of a company's fiscal year.

The auditor's evaluation of the justification for a discretionary accounting change depends on the facts and circumstances of the specific situation. Possible justifications for discretionary accounting changes include

- Change to the preferred method where preferability among alternatives is expressed in authoritative pronouncements by organizations such as the AICPA Accounting Standards Executive Committee on specialized accounting principles and practices.
- Change to the method of accounting prevalent in a particular industry.
- Change to reflect new circumstances (such as a change in depreciation methods to reflect the introduction of new types of equipment or new production processes).
- Change where preferability is based solely on elements of business judgment and business planning that do not fit into the aforementioned categories.

The auditor should review carefully the reasonableness of the client's justification for a change. This requires consideration of the client's business as well as industry conditions. If the justification for the change is based on a desire to conform with industry practice, the auditor should corroborate the client's position that the new accounting method is prevalent in the industry. The citing of one or two instances of its use in a large industry would not necessarily indicate that the new method is prevalent in the industry.

Pooling Letters

Since the adoption of APB Opinion No. 16, *Business Combinations* (Accounting Standards Section B50), the NYSE has requested each company listing shares to be issued in a business combination accounted for as a pooling of interests to furnish the Exchange with a letter setting forth the requirements for pooling of interests accounting and indicating that the contemplated transaction meets each of those requirements. The Exchange requires that the other party to the business combination assent to the letter as an indication of its agreement with the specified terms of the transaction. In addition, the Exchange asks that the auditors of the corporation issuing stock in the transaction also furnish a letter

---

[12]Changes necessitated by new authoritative pronouncements do not require preferability letters. The auditor should, of course, evaluate the way in which the client has applied a new pronouncement to meet particular facts and circumstances that face the client.

to the Exchange indicating that they have reviewed the transaction and expressing their opinion that the combination meets the requirements for pooling accounting set forth in Opinion No. 16.

Before furnishing a "pooling letter" to the Exchange, the auditor should obtain copies of the full executed agreements and any other pertinent documents, together with an executed copy of the company's letter to the Exchange pertinent to the transaction. An example of a pooling letter to the NYSE follows:

> We have read the Agreement and Plan of Reorganization between ABC Corporation and XYZ Corporation along with information and representations submitted to us by the companies, and the accompanying Letter of Compliance with Pooling of Interests Criteria. This Agreement is to be consummated through the issuance of (number) shares of ABC Corporation common stock on or about (date).
>
> In our opinion, based upon the information presented to us as of (date), this combination conforms in substance with the principles, guides, rules, and criteria of APB Opinion No. 16, and we concur in the accounting treatment of this combination as a pooling of interests.

Reports on the Application of Accounting Principles

The preceding section of this chapter considered instances in which an auditor is asked by a client to give an opinion on the appropriate accounting for recording a hypothetical, proposed, or consummated transaction. An accountant (the "reporting accountant") may also be asked by a nonaudit client (the "requestor") to give a similar opinion on the application of accounting principles. The requestor may be, among others, an investment banker that has created a new type of financial product and wants to include an opinion from the reporting accountant (sometimes called a "generic letter") in its promotional material, an investment banker representing another auditor's client that is contemplating a specific transaction, or another auditor's (the "continuing accountant") client seeking a "second opinion" on a proposed or consummated transaction. The requestor may have only the purest motives for seeking the advice of a CPA other than its own auditor, perhaps based on a belief that its auditor lacks the expertise to evaluate the appropriate accounting for a new financial product. Or the requestor may be "opinion shopping," seeking an opinion that can be used to intimidate its auditor to accede to its preferences or risk losing the engagement.

The profession has long been concerned with opinion shopping and has tried to prevent it. Chapter 3 pointed out that Ethics Interpretation 201-3 requires the reporting accountant to consult with the continuing accountant before providing advice on an accounting or auditing technical matter. SAS No. 50, *Reports on the Application of Accounting Principles* (AU Section 625), specifies additional standards, for both performance and reporting, that should be fol lowed by the reporting accountant when providing advice (either written or oral) on accounting matters or on the appropriate type of opinion on an entity's financial statements. The performance standards include a requirement that the reporting accountant seek permission from the requestor to consult with the continuing accountant and ask the requestor to authorize the continuing accountant to respond fully to the reporting accountant's inquiries. That requirement serves two purposes. The first, not explicitly stated in the SAS, is to discourage opinion shopping. The second is to provide the reporting accountant with information that the continuing accountant may have and that might not otherwise be available.

Opinions on Tax Consequences, Proposed Systems, and Other Matters

Professional accountants and auditors have traditionally been involved in tax practice and in the role of advisers to taxpayers. The general public probably identifies professional accountants with income taxes as frequently as with the auditing function. Income taxation is a body of statutory and administrative law based in part on accounting theory and practice. Thus, the provinces of the accounting and legal professions overlap in virtually the entire field of taxation; lawyers and accountants usually value the consultation and assistance of each other.

Independent auditors are frequently requested to issue formal opinions on the tax effects of prospective situations and transactions. An opinion may be required for purposes of a client's tax planning or to evaluate the tax effects of a course of action on financial statements. Opinions on tax matters should be prepared following the same principles previously discussed for opinions on accounting principles. The consideration of precedents and regulations and their effects on conclusions reached, however, is likely to be more detailed and specific because of the importance of case law in tax matters.

Public accountants are often asked to evaluate a proposed accounting system or computer program. Most accountants encourage their clients to seek a review of controls to be built into a system. When reporting in this area, accountants should be careful to avoid the possibility of a misunderstanding. The subject matter and the accountant's assignment should be explictly identified, the facts should be stated, alternatives examined, reasoning explained, and conclusions clearly set forth.

The variety of matters on which an accountant may be asked to report is limited only by the breadth of expertise the individual offers to clients. Since conditions and subjects cover such a wide range, standardization in such reports is not possible. Although an auditor may recognize that opinions issued by tax specialists, actuaries, or management consultants are different from audit opinions, users may not. Thus, rigorous logic, clear expression, and appropriate disclaimers are essential to ensure an accurate understanding of the accountant's role and the meaning of reports rendered.

Letters for Underwriters

The requirements of the SEC covering responsibilities for disclosures to be made in prospectuses and registration statements under its jurisdiction are complicated and frequently revised. For that reason, all parties to an SEC filing go to great lengths to make sure that they comply with the requirements. In particular, underwriters have had a long-standing practice of seeking specific assurance from lawyers and accountants that the SEC rules and regulations have been complied with. A common practice for underwriters has long been to seek "comfort" from an auditor on financial information in registration statements that is not covered by the auditor's opinion and on events subsequent to the opinion date.

As public expectations have grown and been reflected in legal and other attacks on those associated with disclosures, underwriters and their counsel have sought to obtain more and more "comfort" from auditors, which is formally expressed in a letter called a comfort letter. (Some lawyers still use the phrase common in earlier, more austere times: "cold comfort" letter.) Although the comfort letter may originally have been an informal or semiformal helpful gesture on the part of an auditor, it is now a significant formal communication. In drafting comfort letters, formally called "letters for underwriters," auditors must therefore be especially careful not to assume unwarranted responsibility, either explicitly or implicitly.

SAS No. 49, *Letters for Underwriters* (AU Section 634), provides guidelines for minimizing misunderstandings in connection with comfort letters. The importance attached to comfort letters is reflected in the length and details of the numerous paragraphs in that statement. It covers the kinds of matters that may properly be commented on by auditors in comfort letters and how the matters should be phrased, suggests forms of letters and how to prepare them, and recommends ways of reducing or avoiding misunderstanding as to responsibility. To avoid the possibility of misunderstanding as to the purpose and intended use of the comfort letter, it is customary to conclude the letter with a paragraph along the following lines:

> This letter is solely for the information of the addressees and to assist the underwriters in conducting and documenting their investigation of the affairs of the company in connection with the offering of the securities covered by the registration statement, and it is not to be used, circulated, quoted, or otherwise referred to within or without the underwriting group for any other purpose, including, but not limited to, the registration, purchase, or sale of securities, nor is it to be filed with or referred to in whole or in part in the registration statement or any other document, except that reference may be made to it in the underwriting agreement or in any list of closing documents pertaining to the offering of the securities covered by the registration statement.

Review Questions

19-1. What are some types of special reporting situations encountered by auditors?

19-2. What professional judgments must an auditor make concerning a special report?

19-3. Explain what is meant by a CPA's association with financial data.

19-4. Why is an auditor ordinarily prohibited from including any expressions of negative assurance?

19-5. What is a compilation and what kind of report is given?

19-6. What is a review and what kind of report is given?

19-7. Would lack of independence preclude the issuance of a review report? A compilation report?

19-8. What are some of the benefits to a company from having the auditor make a pre-issuance review of interim financial information?

19-9. Compare and contrast an ordinary review engagement with an interim review engagement, including procedures followed and report issued.

19-10. In determining the extent of inquiries and analytical reviews to be made for an interim review, what factors does the auditor consider?

19-11. Describe the most significant element in a special report on a comprehensive basis of accounting other than GAAP.

19-12. What should the auditor do if asked to sign a printed prescribed report that does not conform with professional standards?

19-13. How should the auditor report on additional information accompanying the basic financial statements?

19-14. What guidelines should be followed in issuing compliance reports?

19-15. How does supplementary information required by the Financial Accounting Standards Board or the Governmental Accounting Standards Board differ from other types of information accompanying the basic financial statements?

19-16. Distinguish between a financial forecast and a financial projection.

19-17. What are pro forma financial statements? When are they usually presented?

19-18. What key elements must be contained in reports on forecasts or projections?

19-19. What is the SEC safe harbor rule regarding prospective financial information?

19-20. What are the main elements of a special report expressing an unqualified opinion on an entity's overall system of internal accounting control?

19-21. What is a comfort letter and when is it used?

Discussion Questions

19-30. Loman, CPA, who has examined the financial statements of the Broadwall Corporation, a publicly held company, for the year ended December 31, 1986, was asked to perform a limited review of the financial statements of Broadwall Corporation for the period ending March 31, 1987. The engagement letter stated that a limited review does not provide a basis for the expression of an opinion.

Required:

a. Explain why Loman's limited review will *not* provide a basis for the expression of an opinion.

b. What are the review procedures that Loman should perform, and what is the purpose of each procedure? Structure your response as follows:

Procedure	*Purpose of Procedure*

(AICPA adapted)

19–31. In recent years there has been an increasing trend toward the furnishing of compilation or review services for small, growing, nonpublic companies. Discuss the opportunities, desirability, and standards concerning these services from the following standpoints:

a. When would you recommend these services? Can there be a combination of them, such as monthly compilations and annual reviews?

b. What recommendation would you make if a company was growing rapidly and might go public in a few years?

c. What are the differences in reporting between compilations and reviews?

d. What effect does the CPA's independence have on the issuance of these reports?

19–32. The following cases involve auditors' reports issued in connection with financial statements prepared on a comprehensive basis of accounting other than generally accepted accounting principles:

1. The financial statements of a retail grocery store operated as an individual proprietorship are prepared on the basis of cash receipts and disbursements. The statements do not purport to present the financial position and results of operations of the company.

2. The financial statements of a private nonprofit hospital are prepared in accordance with the principles and practices of accounting recommended in an AICPA industry audit and accounting guide for hospitals.

3. The financial statements of an insurance company are prepared in accordance with the principles and practices of uniform accounting prescribed by a state insurance commission. The statements purport to present the financial position and results of operations of the insurance company.

Required:

Discuss the type of opinion the auditor should give in each of these cases.

(AICPA adapted)

AICPA Multiple Choice Questions

These questions are taken from the Auditing part of Uniform CPA Examinations. Choose the single most appropriate answer.

19–40. When an auditor performs a review of interim financial statements, which of the following steps would *not* be part of the review?

a. Review of computer controls.

b. Inquiry of management.

    c. Review of ratios and trends.

    d. Reading the minutes of the stockholders' meetings.

19–41. Which of the following statements with respect to an auditor's report expressing an opinion on a specific item on a financial statement is correct?

    a. Materiality must be related to the specified item rather than to the financial statements taken as a whole.

    b. Such a report can be expressed only if the auditor is also engaged to audit the entire set of financial statements.

    c. The attention devoted to the specified item is usually less than it would be if the financial statements taken as a whole were being audited.

    d. The auditor who has issued an adverse opinion on the financial statements taken as a whole can never express an opinion on a specified item in these financial statements.

19–42. Under which of the following circumstances could an auditor consider rendering an opinion on pro forma statements that give effect to proposed transactions?

    a. When the proposed transactions are subject to a definitive agreement among the parties.

    b. When the time interval between the date of the financial statements and consummation of the transactions is relatively long.

    c. When certain subsequent events have some chance of interfering with the consummation of the transactions.

    d. When the pro forma statements include amounts based on financial projections.

19–43. Whenever special reports, filed on a printed form designed by authorities, call on the independent auditor to make an assertion that the auditor believes is not justified, the auditor should

    a. Submit a short-form report with explanations.

    b. Reword the form or attach a separate report.

    c. Submit the form with questionable items clearly omitted.

    d. Withdraw from the engagement.

19–44. In performing a compilation of financial statements of a nonpublic entity, the accountant decides that modification of the standard report is not adequate to indicate deficiencies in the financial statements taken as a whole, and the client is not willing to correct the deficiencies. The accountant should therefore

    a. Perform a review of the financial statements.

    b. Issue a special report.

    c. Withdraw from the engagement.

    d. Express an adverse audit opinion.

19–45. Basic financial statements that would otherwise receive an unqualified opinion do not contain certain supplementary information that is required to be presented pursuant to an FASB pronouncement. The auditor must identify, in an additional paragraph, the supplementary information that is omitted and express a (an)

    a. "Except for" opinion.

    b. Disclaimer of opinion.

    c. Adverse opinion.

    d. Unqualified opinion.

19–46. The statement that "nothing came to our attention that would indicate that these statements are *not* fairly presented" expresses which of the following?

    a. Disclaimer of an opinion.

    b. Negative assurance.

    c. Negative confirmation.

    d. Piecemeal opinion.

19–47. When an auditor submits a document containing audited financial statements to a client, the auditor has a responsibility to report on

    a. Only the basic financial statements included in the document.

    b. The basic financial statements and only that additional information required to be presented in accordance with provisions of the Financial Accounting Standards Board.

    c. All of the information included in the document.

    d. Only that portion of the document that was audited.

19–48. Inquiry of the entity's personnel and analytical procedures are the primary bases for the issuance of a (an)

    a. Compilation report on financial statements for a nonpublic company in its first year of operations.

    b. Auditor's report on financial statements supplemented with price level information.

    c. Review report on comparative financial statements for a nonpublic company in its second year of operations.

    d. Management advisory report prepared at the request of the client's audit committee.

19–49. In which of the following reports should a CPA *not* express negative or limited assurance?

    a. A standard compilation report on financial statements of a nonpublic entity.

    b. A standard review report on financial statements of a nonpublic entity.

    c. A standard review report on interim financial statements of a public entity.

    d. A standard comfort letter on financial information included in a registration statement of a public entity.

Problems and Cases

19–60. Rose & Co., CPAs, has satisfactorily completed the examination of the financial statements of Bale & Booster, a partnership, for the year ended December 31, 1987. The financial statements that were prepared on the entity's income tax (cash) basis include footnotes that indicate that the partnership was involved in continuing litigation of material amounts related to alleged infringement of a competitor's patent. The amount of damages, if any, resulting from this litigation could not be determined at the time of completion of the engagement. The prior years' financial statements were not presented.

Required:

Based on the information presented, prepare an auditor's report that includes appropriate explanatory disclosure of significant facts.

(AICPA adapted)

19-61. For the year ended December 31, 1986, Novak & Co., CPAs, audited the financial statements of Tillis Ltd., and expressed an unqualified opinion dated February 27, 1987.

For the year ended December 31, 1987, Novak & Co. were engaged by Tillis Ltd. to review Tillis Ltd.'s financial statements, that is, to "look into the company's financial statements and determine whether there are any obvious modifications that should be made to the financial statements in order for them to be in conformity with generally accepted accounting principles."

Novak made the necessary inquiries, performed the necessary analytical procedures, and performed certain additional procedures that were deemed necessary to achieve the requisite limited assurance. Novak's work was completed on March 3, 1988, and the financial statements appeared to be in conformity with GAAP that were consistently applied. The report was prepared on March 5, 1988. It was delivered to Jones, the controller of Tillis Ltd., on March 9, 1988.

Required:

Prepare the properly addressed and dated report on the comparative financial statements of Tillis Ltd. for the years ended December 31, 1986 and 1987.

(AICPA adapted)

19-62. Brown, CPA, received a telephone call from Calhoun, the sole owner and manager of a small corporation. Calhoun asked Brown to prepare the financial statements for the corporation and told Brown that the statements were needed in two weeks for external financing purposes. Calhoun was vague when Brown inquired about the intended use of the statements. Brown was convinced that Calhoun thought Brown's work would constitute an audit. To avoid confusion, Brown decided not to explain to Calhoun that the engagement would only be to prepare the financial statements. Brown, with the understanding that a substantial fee would be paid if the work were completed in two weeks, accepted the engagement and started the work at once.

During the course of the work, Brown discovered an accrued expense account labeled "professional fees" and learned that the balance in the account represented an accrual for the cost of Brown's services. Brown suggested to Calhoun's bookkeeper that the account name be changed to "fees for limited audit engagement." Brown also reviewed several invoices to determine whether accounts were being properly classified. Some of the invoices were missing. Brown listed the missing invoice numbers in the working papers with a note indicating that there should be a follow-up on the next engagement. Brown also discovered that the available records included the fixed asset values at estimated current replacement costs. Based on the records available, Brown prepared a balance sheet, income statement, and statement of stockholders' equity. In addition, Brown drafted the footnotes but decided that any mention of the replacement costs would only mislead the readers. Brown suggested to Calhoun that readers of the financial statements would be better informed if they received a separate letter from Calhoun explaining the meaning and effect of the estimated replacement costs of the fixed assets. Brown mailed the financial statements and footnotes to Calhoun with the following note included on each page:

The accompanying financial statements are submitted to you without complete audit verification.

Required:
Identify Brown's inappropriate actions and indicate what Brown should have done to avoid each one. Organize your answer as follows:

Inappropriate Action	*What Brown Should Have Done to Avoid Inappropriate Action*

(AICPA adapted)

19–63. In order to obtain information that is necessary to make informed decisions, management often calls on the independent auditor for assistance. This may involve a request that the independent auditor apply certain audit procedures to specific accounts of a company that is a candidate for acquisition and report upon the results. In such an engagement, the agreed-upon procedures may constitute a scope limitation.

At the completion of an engagement performed at the request of Sagamore Corporation, which was limited in scope as explained, the following report was prepared by an audit assistant and was submitted to the engagement partner for review:

To the Board of Directors of Ajax Corporation:

We have applied certain agreed-upon procedures, as discussed below, to accounting records of Ajax Corporation as of December 31, 1987, solely to assist Sagamore Corporation in connection with the proposed acquisition of Ajax Corporation.

We have examined the cash in banks and accounts receivable of Ajax Corporation as of December 31, 1987, in accordance with generally accepted auditing standards and, accordingly, included such tests of the accounting records and such other auditing procedures as we considered necessary in the circumstances.

In our opinion, the cash and receivables referred to above are fairly presented as of December 31, 1987, in conformity with generally accepted accounting principles applied on a basis consistent with that of the preceding year. We therefore recommend that Sagamore Corporation acquire Ajax Corporation pursuant to the proposed agreement.

[signature]

Required:
Comment on the proposed report, describing those assertions that are

  a. Incorrect or should otherwise be deleted.
  b. Missing and should be inserted.

19–64. Jiffy Clerical Services, Inc., is a corporation that furnishes temporary office help to its customers. Billings are rendered monthly based on predetermined hourly rates. You have examined the company's financial statements for several years. Following is an abbreviated statement of assets and liabilities on the modified cash basis as of December 31, 1988:

Assets:

Cash	$20,000
Advances to employees	1,000
Equipment and autos, less accumulated depreciation	25,000
Total assets	46,000

Liabilities:

Employees' payroll taxes withheld	8,000
Bank loan payable	10,000
Estimated income taxes on cash basis profits	10,000
Total liabilities	28,000
Net assets	$18,000

Represented by:

Common stock	$ 3,000
Cash profits retained in the business	15,000
	$18,000

Unrecorded receivables were $55,000 and payables were $30,000.

Required:

a. Prepare the report you would issue covering the statement of assets and liabilities as of December 31, 1988, as summarized, and the related statement of revenue collected and expenses paid for the year ended on that date.

b. Briefly discuss and justify your modifications of the conventional report on accrual basis statements.

(AICPA adapted)

Appendix A
Tables for Determining Sample Size: Attributes Sampling
Reliability Levels of 80, 85, 90, and 95 Percent

Appendix A: Table 1 Determination of Sample Size (Reliability = 80%)

Expected Deviation Rate (Percent)	Tolerable Deviation Rate (Percent)														
	1	2	3	4	5	6	7	8	9	10	12	14	16	18	20
0.00	170	80	55	40	35	30	25	20	20	20	15	15	10	10	10
0.50		150	100	75	60	50	45	40	35	30	25	25	20	20	15
1.0		280	100	75	60	50	45	40	35	30	25	25	20	20	15
2.0			340	140	85	50	45	40	35	30	25	25	20	20	15
3.0				400	160	95	60	55	35	30	25	25	20	20	15
4.0					450	150	95	70	50	45	25	25	20	20	15
5.0						500	180	100	60	55	35	30	20	20	15
6.0								190	100	70	45	30	30	20	15
7.0									200	120	55	40	30	25	15
8.0										230	75	50	35	25	25
9.0											130	55	45	30	25
10.0											240	80	50	30	30

Note: These tables are designed for one-sided tests. To determine the relevant table to use for two-sided estimation, double the one-sided test table indicated sampling risk. For example, the 95 percent reliability table implies a 5 percent sampling risk; doubling the sampling risk to 10 percent indicates that this table can also be used for a 90 percent reliability two-sided estimation sample.

Appendix A: Table 2 Determination of Sample Size (Reliability = 85%)

Expected Deviation Rate (Percent)	Tolerable Deviation Rate (Percent)														
	1	2	3	4	5	6	7	8	9	10	12	14	16	18	20
0.00	190	95	65	50	40	35	30	25	25	20	15	15	15	10	10
0.50		170	120	85	70	55	50	45	40	35	30	25	20	20	20
1.0		300	160	85	70	55	50	45	40	35	30	25	20	20	20
2.0			440	150	95	80	50	45	40	35	30	25	20	20	20
3.0					200	100	85	60	55	35	30	25	20	20	20
4.0						200	120	75	70	50	40	25	20	20	20
5.0							220	120	80	60	40	35	20	20	20
6.0								250	140	100	50	35	30	25	20
7.0									280	150	70	45	40	25	25
8.0										300	100	60	40	25	25
9.0											170	80	45	35	30
10.0											330	110	60	40	30

Appendix A: Table 3 Determination of Sample Size (Reliability = 90%)

Expected Deviation Rate (Percent)	Tolerable Deviation Rate (Percent)														
	1	2	3	4	5	6	7	8	9	10	12	14	16	18	20
0.00	230	120	80	60	45	40	35	30	25	25	20	20	15	15	15
0.50		200	130	100	80	65	55	50	45	40	35	30	25	25	20
1.0		400	180	100	80	65	55	50	45	40	35	30	25	25	20
2.0				200	140	90	75	50	45	40	35	30	25	25	20
3.0					240	140	95	65	60	55	35	30	25	25	20
4.0						280	150	100	75	65	45	40	25	25	20
5.0							320	160	120	80	55	40	35	30	20
6.0								350	190	120	65	50	35	30	25
7.0									390	200	100	60	40	30	25
8.0										420	140	75	50	40	25
9.0											230	100	65	45	35
10.0											480	150	80	50	40

Appendix A: Table 4 Determination of Sample Size (Reliability = 95%)

Expected Deviation Rate (Percent)	Tolerable Deviation Rate (Percent)														
	1	2	3	4	5	6	7	8	9	10	12	14	16	18	20
0.00	300	150	100	75	60	50	45	40	35	30	25	20	20	20	15
0.50		320	160	120	95	80	70	60	55	50	40	35	30	25	25
1.0			260	160	95	80	70	60	55	50	40	35	30	25	25
2.0				300	190	130	90	80	70	50	40	35	30	25	25
3.0					370	200	130	95	85	65	55	35	30	25	25
4.0						430	230	150	100	90	65	45	40	25	25
5.0							480	240	160	120	75	55	40	35	30
6.0									270	180	100	65	50	35	30
7.0										300	130	85	55	45	40
8.0											200	100	75	50	40
9.0											350	150	90	65	45
10.0												220	120	70	50

Tables for Evaluating
Sample Results:
Attributes Sampling

Reliability Levels of 80, 85, 90, and 95 Percent

Note: Only upper deviation limits are obtainable using these tables.

Appendix B: Table 1 Evaluation of Results Based on Number of Observed Deviations (Reliability = 80%)

Sample Size	Achieved Upper Deviation Rate Limit (Percent)																
	1	2	3	4	5	6	7	8	9	10	12	14	16	18	20	25	30
5																	0
10														0			1
15											0				1		2
20						0							1			2	3
25					0						1			2		3	5
30					0					1		2	3			4	6
35				0					1		2		3		4	6	7
40			0					1			2	3		4	5	7	9
45			0				1				2	3	4	5	6	8	10
50			0			1				2	3	4	5	6	7	9	11
55			0			1		2			3	4	5	6	7	10	13
60			0		1			2		3	4	5	6	7	8	11	14
65			0		1		2		3		5	6	7	8	9	12	15
70			0		1		2	3		4	5	6	8	9	10	13	17
75			0	1		2		3	4		6	7	8	10	11	15	18
80		0		1		2	3		4	5	6	8	9	10	12	16	20
85		0		1		2	3	4		5	7	8	10	11	13	17	21
90		0		1		2	3	4	5	6	7	9	10	12	14	18	22
95		0		1		2	3	4	5	6	8	9	11	13	15	19	24
100		0	1		2	3	4	5		6	8	10	12	14	16	20	25
110		0	1	2	3		4	5	6	7	9	11	13	15	17	23	28
120		0	1	2	3	4	5	6	7	8	10	13	15	17	19	25	31
130		0	1	2	3	4	6	7	8	9	11	14	16	19	21	27	34
140		0	2	3	4	5	6	8	9	10	13	15	18	20	23	30	36
150		1	2	3	4	6	7	8	10	11	14	16	19	22	25	32	39
160	0	1	2	3	5	6	7	9	10	12	15	18	21	24	27	34	42
170	0	1	2	4	5	7	8	10	11	13	16	19	22	25	29	37	45
180	0	1	3	4	6	7	9	10	12	14	17	20	24	27	30	39	48
190	0	1	3	4	6	8	9	11	13	14	18	22	25	29	32	41	51
200	0	1	3	5	6	8	10	12	14	15	19	23	27	30	34	44	54
210	0	2	3	5	7	9	11	13	15	16	20	24	28	32	36	46	56
220	0	2	4	5	7	9	11	13	15	17	21	25	30	34	38	49	59
230	0	2	4	6	8	10	12	14	16	18	22	27	31	35	40	51	62
240	0	2	4	6	8	10	12	15	17	19	24	28	33	37	42	53	65
250	0	2	4	6	9	11	13	16	18	20	25	29	34	39	44	56	68
260	0	2	5	7	9	11	14	16	19	21	26	31	36	41	46	58	71
270	0	3	5	7	9	12	14	17	20	22	27	32	37	42	47	60	74
280	0	3	5	8	10	12	15	18	20	23	28	33	39	44	49	63	77
290	1	3	5	8	10	13	16	19	21	24	29	35	40	46	51	65	79
300	1	3	6	8	11	14	16	19	22	25	30	36	42	47	53	68	82

Appendix B: Table 2 Evaluation of Results Based on Number of Observed Deviations (Reliability = 85%)

Achieved Upper Deviation Rate Limit (Percent)

Sample Size	1	2	3	4	5	6	7	8	9	10	12	14	16	18	20	25	30
5																	
10														0			1
15											0					1	2
20									0				1			2	3
25								0				1		2		3	4
30							0				1		2		3	4	5
35						0				1		2		3	4	5	7
40					0				1		2		3	4		6	8
45					0			1			2	3	4		5	7	9
50				0			1			2	3		4	5	6	8	11
55				0			1		2		3	4	5	6	7	9	12
60				0		1		2		3	4	5	6	7	8	11	13
65			0			1		2		3	4	5	6	8	9	12	15
70			0		1		2		3		5	6	7	8	10	13	16
75			0		1		2		3	4	5	6	8	9	10	14	17
80			0		1	2		3		4	6	7	8	10	11	15	19
85			0	1		2		3	4	5	6	8	9	11	12	16	20
90			0	1		2	3		4	5	7	8	10	11	13	17	22
95		0		1	2		3	4	5		7	9	11	12	14	18	23
100		0		1	2		3	4	5	6	8	9	11	13	15	20	24
110		0		1	2	3	4	5	6	7	9	11	13	15	17	22	27
120		0	1	2	3	4	5	6	7	8	10	12	14	16	18	24	30
130		0	1	2	3	4	5	6	7	8	11	13	15	18	20	26	33
140		0	1	2	3	5	6	7	8	9	12	14	17	20	22	29	35
150		0	1	3	4	5	6	8	9	10	13	16	18	21	24	31	38
160		0	2	3	4	6	7	8	10	11	14	17	20	23	26	33	41
170		1	2	3	5	6	7	9	11	12	15	18	21	24	28	36	44
180	0	1	2	4	5	7	8	10	11	13	16	19	23	26	29	38	47
190	0	1	2	4	5	7	9	11	12	14	17	21	24	28	31	40	49
200	0	1	3	4	6	8	9	11	13	15	18	22	26	29	33	43	52
210	0	1	3	5	6	8	10	12	14	16	19	23	27	31	35	45	55
220	0	1	3	5	7	9	11	13	15	16	20	24	29	33	37	47	58
230	0	2	3	5	7	9	11	13	15	17	22	26	30	34	39	50	61
240	0	2	4	6	8	10	12	14	16	18	23	27	32	36	41	52	64
250	0	2	4	6	8	10	12	15	17	19	24	28	33	38	42	54	67
260	0	2	4	6	8	11	13	16	18	20	25	30	34	39	44	57	69
270	0	2	4	7	9	11	14	16	19	21	26	31	36	41	46	59	72
280	0	2	5	7	9	12	14	17	20	22	27	32	37	43	48	62	75
290	0	2	5	7	10	12	15	18	20	23	28	33	39	44	50	64	78
300	0	3	5	8	10	13	15	18	21	24	29	35	40	46	52	66	81

Appendix B: Table 3 Evaluation of Results Based on Number of Observed Deviations (Reliability = 90%)

Sample Size							Achieved Upper Deviation Rate Limit (Percent)										
	1	2	3	4	5	6	7	8	9	10	12	14	16	18	20	25	30
5																	
10																0	
15													0			1	
20											0				1	2	
25									0				1		2	3	4
30							0					1		2		4	5
35						0					1		2		3	5	6
40					0					1		2	3		4	6	7
45				0					1		2		3	4	5	7	9
50				0			1				2	3	4	5		8	10
55				0			1			2	3		4	5	6	9	11
60			0				1			2	3	4	5	6	7	10	13
65			0			1			2	3	4	5	6	7	8	11	14
70			0			1			2	3	4	5	6	8	9	12	15
75			0			1	2		3		4	6	7	8	10	13	16
80			0	1		2		3		4	5	6	8	9	10	14	18
85			0	1		2		3		4	5	7	8	10	11	15	19
90			0	1		2		3		4	6	7	9	11	12	16	20
95			0	1		2	3	4		5	6	8	10	11	13	17	22
100			0	1		2	3	4		5	7	9	10	12	14	19	23
110			0	1	2	3	4	5	6		8	10	12	14	16	21	26
120		0		1	2	3	4	5	6	7	9	11	13	15	17	23	29
130		0	1	2	3	4		6	7	8	10	12	15	17	19	25	31
140		0	1	2	3	4	5	6	7	9	11	13	16	18	21	27	34
150		0	1	2	3	4	6	7	8	9	12	15	17	20	23	30	37
160		0	1	2	4	5	6	8	9	10	13	16	19	22	25	32	40
170		0	1	3	4	5	7	8	10	11	14	17	20	23	26	34	42
180		0	2	3	4	6	7	9	11	12	15	18	22	25	28	37	45
190		1	2	3	5	6	8	10	11	13	16	20	23	26	30	39	48
200		1	2	4	5	7	8	10	12	14	17	21	24	28	32	41	51
210		1	2	4	6	7	9	11	13	15	18	22	26	30	34	44	54
220		1	3	4	6	8	10	12	14	15	19	23	27	31	35	46	56
230		1	3	5	6	8	10	12	14	16	20	25	29	33	37	48	59
240		1	3	5	7	9	11	13	15	17	21	26	30	35	39	50	62
250	0	1	3	5	7	9	11	14	16	18	23	27	32	36	41	53	65
260	0	2	4	6	8	10	12	15	17	19	24	28	33	38	43	55	68
270	0	2	4	6	8	10	13	15	18	20	25	30	35	40	45	57	70
280	0	2	4	6	8	11	13	16	18	21	26	31	36	41	47	60	73
290	0	2	4	7	9	11	14	17	19	22	27	32	37	43	48	62	76
300	0	2	4	7	9	12	14	17	20	22	28	33	39	45	50	64	79

Appendix B: Table 4 Evaluation of Results Based on Number of Observed Deviations (Reliability = 95%)

Sample Size	Achieved Upper Deviation Rate Limit (Percent)																
	1	2	3	4	5	6	7	8	9	10	12	14	16	18	20	25	30
5																	
10																	0
15															0		1
20												0				1	2
25											0			1		2	3
30										0			1		2	3	4
35									0			1		2	3	4	5
40								0			1		2	3		5	6
45							0			1		2	3		4	6	8
50						0				1	2		3	4	5	7	9
55						0			1		2	3	4	5	6	8	10
60					0			1		2		3	4	5	6	9	11
65					0			1		2	3	4	5	6	7	10	13
70					0		1		2		3	4	5	7	8	11	14
75				0			1		2	3	4	5	6	7	8	12	15
80				0		1		2		3	4	5	7	8	9	13	16
85				0		1		2	3		5	6	7	9	10	14	18
90				0		1	2		3	4	5	6	8	9	11	15	19
95				0	1		2	3		4	5	7	9	10	12	16	20
100			0		1		2	3		4	6	8	9	11	13	17	22
110			0		1	2	3	4		5	7	9	10	12	14	19	24
120			0	1		2	3	4	5	6	8	10	12	14	16	21	27
130			0	1	2	3	4	5	6	7	9	11	13	15	18	24	30
140			0	1	2	3	4	5	6	7	10	12	14	17	19	26	32
150		0	1	2		4	5	6	7	8	11	13	16	18	21	28	35
160		0	1	2	3	4	5	7	8	9	12	14	17	20	23	30	38
170		0	1	2	3	4	6	7	9	10	13	16	19	22	25	32	40
180		0	1	2	3	5	6	8	9	11	14	17	20	23	26	35	43
190		0	1	3	4	5	7	8	10	11	15	18	21	25	28	37	46
200		0	1	3	4	6	7	9	11	12	16	19	23	26	30	39	48
210		0	2	3	5	6	8	10	12	13	17	20	24	28	32	41	51
220		0	2	3	5	7	8	10	12	14	18	22	25	29	33	44	54
230		1	2	4	5	7	9	11	13	15	19	23	27	31	35	46	57
240		1	2	4	6	8	10	12	14	16	20	24	28	33	37	48	59
250		1	2	4	6	8	10	12	15	16	21	25	30	34	39	50	62
260		1	3	5	7	9	11	13	15	17	22	26	31	36	41	53	65
270		1	3	5	7	9	11	14	16	18	23	28	33	37	42	55	68
280		1	3	5	7	10	12	14	17	19	24	29	34	39	44	57	71
290	0	1	3	6	8	10	12	15	18	20	25	30	35	41	46	60	73
300	0	1	4	6	8	11	13	16	18	21	26	31	37	42	48	62	76

Appendix C
Tables for Two-Stage Sequential Sampling Plans: Attributes Sampling
Reliability Levels of 80, 85, 90, and 95 Percent

Appendix C: Table 1 Two-Stage Sequential Sampling Plan (Reliability = 80%)

Tolerable Deviation Rate (Percent)	Initial Sample Size	Second-Stage Sample Size
10	17	22
9	19	24
8	21	30
7	24	36
6	29	36
5	35	43
4	46	45
3	62	59
2	97	77

Appendix C: Table 2 Two-Stage Sequential Sampling Plan (Reliability = 85%)

Tolerable Deviation Rate (Percent)	Initial Sample Size	Second-Stage Sample Size
10	20	22
9	22	26
8	25	29
7	29	31
6	34	37
5	41	44
4	54	45
3	71	65
2	113	79

Appendix C: Table 3 Two-Stage Sequential Sampling Plan (Reliability = 90%)

Tolerable Deviation Rate (Percent)	Initial Sample Size	Second-Stage Sample Size
10	23	29
9	26	30
8	30	30
7	35	32
6	41	38
5	51	39
4	64	49
3	89	56
2	133	87

Appendix C: Table 4 Two-Stage Sequential Sampling Plan (Reliability = 95%)

Tolerable Deviation Rate (Percent)	Initial Sample Size	Second-Stage Sample Size
10	31	23
9	34	29
8	39	30
7	45	33
6	53	38
5	65	42
4	84	46
3	113	60
2	169	94

Decision Rules for Two-Stage Sequential Sampling Plans

	No Deviations	One Deviation	Two or More Deviations
Initial sample	Stop—achieved goal	Go to next stage	Stop—failed
Second stage	Stop—achieved goal	Stop—failed	Stop—failed

Index

Aaron v. *SEC,* 125
Accept-reject testing, 366–367
Access controls, computer systems, 436
Access to assets, 217, 219
Account analyses, working papers, 169–180
Accountancy, state boards of, 81
Accountancy Law Reporter, 42
Accountants' legal liability, *see* Legal liability
Account balances:
　risk and, 188
　substantive testing, 337–338
Accounting:
　auditing and, 7
　internal control, 218–224
Accounting and Auditing Enforcement Releases, *see* Accounting Series Releases (ASR)
Accounting for Certain Marketable Securities, 678
Accounting Changes, 779–780, 855
Accounting changes, 779–785 (*see also* Consistency)
　auditor's concurrence and justification, 782–783
　classification, 784–785
　departures from, 779–785
　errors correction, 783–784
　initial examination, 782
　principles, 780–781
　reporting entity, 784
　standards of, 18, 60
Accounting for Contingencies, 692
Accounting controls, *see* Controls, internal
Accounting distribution, buying cycle, 552
Accounting firms:
　audit engagement team, 37–38
　audit staffing pyramid, 38
　organization, 34–38
　policies and procedures, 87
　structure, 36–37
Accounting for Income Taxes, 692
Accounting principles (*see also specific cycles and accounts*)
　AICPA Code of Ethics, 64–65

changes, 779–785
opinions, 855–857
　pooling letters, 856–857
　preferability letters, 855–856
　reports on application, 857–858
Accounting Principles Board (APB), 766
departures from, 771
Opinions:
　No. 11, 692
　No. 16, 128
　No. 20, 736, 779–780, 782, 784, 855
　No. 21, 711
　No. 30, 692
　Statement No. 4, 4, 765–766
Accounting procedures, internal control questionnaires, 275–277
Accounting Series Releases (ASRs), 126
　No. 19, 46, 102
　No. 123, 83
　No. 153, 102, 127
　No. 165, 85–86
　No. 173, 126
　No. 176, 126
　No. 191, 126
　No. 196, 126
　No. 209, 126
　No. 210, 126
　No. 241, 126
　No. 248, 127
　No. 288, 127
　No. 292, 102
Accounting services, 38–39
　independence, 72–73
Accounting standards overload, 837–838
Accounting systems:
　documenting, 260–263
　internal controls, 229–230
Accounting Trends and Techniques, 732, 852
Accounts payable:
　buying cycle, 540–542
　substantive tests, 576–578
Accounts receivable, 476
　confirmation, 156–157, 503–511

contingent liabilities, 719–720
revenue cycle, posting, 484–485
Accrued commissions, 688
Accrued liabilities, 684–685
　audit objectives, 685–686
　commissions, 688
　interest payable, 688
　pension costs, 689–690
　prepaid insurance, 687
　professional fees, 688
　property taxes, 687–688
　royalties payable, 689
　substantive tests of balances, 686–691
　suspense debits and credits, 689
　travel and entertainment expenses, 688
　warranty costs, 690–691
Accuracy:
　assertions, 150–151
　confirmation of, revenue cycle, 504
　input controls, 438–439
　internal controls, 220
　　basic controls, 234–235
　substantive testing, 337
Actuarial consulting services, 36
Actuaries, 201
Adams v. *Standard Knitting Mills, Inc.,* 131–132
Adequacy of Disclosure in Financial Statements, 746, 777–779
Administrative controls, 224–225
　legal liability, 125–127
　payments in buying cycle, 548
　production cycle, 598
Administrative reprimand, 80
Administrative wrap-up, 753
Advancement, quality control, 76
Adverse opinions, 794–795
　audit report, 19
　vs. disclaimers, 799–800
Advertising principles, 72
Aged trial balance, 514–515
Agency obligations, 540
Aggregating and netting, 735–736
Agreed-upon procedures, 839–840
　prospective financial statements, 849–850

Alexander Grant & Co. v. *Tiffany Industries,* 110 n.7
Allocated production, 593
Allocation assertion, 150
Allowances, revenue cycle, 484
Alpha risk, 369 nn.3, 5, 377–378
  variables sampling, 385
American Accounting Association (AAA), 41, 102
  Committee on Basic Auditing Concepts, 3–4, 10–11
  materiality, 194
American Assembly of Collegiate Schools of Business (AACSB), 54
American Bar Association, 722
American Institute of Accountants, 9
American Institute of Certified Public Accountants (AICPA), 9
  Accounting and Review Services Committee, 827, 838
  amicus curiae briefs, 131
  attestation standards, 43–45
  Auditing Interpretations, 45, 732
  Auditing Standards Board, 9, 43, 45, 46–47, 732, 838
    pro forma statements, 851
  Board of Examiners, 39
  Code of Professional Ethics, 39, 54–55, 60–73, 127–133, 732, 824
    departures from GAAP, 770–772
    origins, 79–80
  Commission on Auditors' Responsibilities (Cohen Commission), 504, 721–722
  Committee on Auditing Procedure, 9, 43, 225
  compilation and review standards, 35
  Continuing Professional Education Division, 39
  Division for CPA Firms, 39, 76–78, 81–82
  Ethics Committee, 850–851, 857
  Federal Taxation Executive Committee, 48
  Joint Trial Board Division, 79–80
  National Review Board, 80–81

New York Stock Exchange collaboration, 9
  organization, 39
  peer review, 78–79
  professional requirements, 102–105
  Professional Standards, 776
  Quality Control Standards Committee, 77–78
  Senior Technical Committees, 39
  Special Advisory Committee on Internal Accounting Control, 223–224, 228–229
  standard reports, 764
  Tax Division, 48
  Uniform CPA Examination and Advisory Grading Service, 42
  "Verification of Financial Statements", 9
American Law Institute (ALI), 115–117
American Stock Exchange and auditor independence, 83
American Telephone and Telegraph Company, 848
Amortization of prepayments, 226
Analyses of variances, compliance testing of inventory, 611
Analytical Review, 348 n.3
Analytical reviews, 341–349
  assurance, 348–349
  buying cycle, 555
    payroll, 578–579
    substantive tests, 575
  detection risk, 190–192
  evidence and, 156
  financial statements, 344
  industry comparisons, 347–348
  prepayments and accruals, 686–691
  production cycle, 605–606
    substantive testing, 629–630
  revenue cycle, 488
    substantive testing, 513, 516–517
  reviewing subsequent events, 344
  software, 453–454
  state and local taxes, 697
  testing phase, 343–344

  timing and objectives, 342–344
  types, 344–348
    comparison of current and predicted results, 346–347
    industry comparisons, 347–348
    nonfinancial information, 348–349
    prior-period comparisons, 345–346
    relationships between elements, 347
    understanding client's business, 342–344
Analytical tests of working papers, 175–176
Analyzing recent financial information, 253
Ancillary revenues, revenue cycle, 489
Application controls, 437–442
  audit strategy, 445
  computer fraud and abuse, 443
  input, accuracy of, 438–439
  input, completeness of, 437–438
  testing, 446–447
  updating, completeness and accuracy of, 439–440
Approval of transactions, 234
  see also Authorization of transactions
Ashton, Robert H., 510 n.1
Assertions, 149–152
  accuracy, 13
  attest service, 45
  disclosure and valuation, 13
  established criteria, 4–5
  financial audits, 30–31
  financial statements, 4, 149–152
  testing, 332
Assets (*see also specific cycles and accounts*)
  access, internal control and, 217, 219
  accountability compared with, 220
  computerized custody controls, 442
  counting of, 154
  custody controls, 236
  fixed, internal control, 226
  inspection of, 337
  leased, 665
  negotiable, 656

property, plant, and equipment, 661–662
Association With Financial Statements, 133, 773, 798, 826
Assurance:
  analytical reviews, 348–349
  attestation standards, 47
  audit strategy planning, 23
  reliability of evidence, 158–159
  risk and, 192
  sampling methods, 374 n.9
  see also Reliability; Risk
Attestation Standards, 43, 45–47, 831
Attorneys' letters, *see* Lawyers' letters
Attributes sampling, **375**, 375–400
  concepts, 375–378
  results evaluation tables, 870–874
  sample size tables, 867–869
  sequential plans, two-stage tables, 875–876
Audit:
  completion of, 717–753
  summarizing and evaluation, 163, 733–742
Audit and accounting guides, *see specific titles of industry guides*
Audit administration, *see* Audit planning
Audit committees, independence and, 83–84
Audit detection risk, 189, 191–192, 330–331
Audit efficiency and risks, 369
Audit engagement team, 37–38
Audit evidence, *see* Evidence
Audit exposure, 187–188
Auditing, 3–7 (*see also* Assertions, financial statements; Objectives; *specific cycles and accounts; specific types of audits*)
  accounting and, 7
  assertions, 4
  classification, 30–35
  compliance audits, 31
  criteria for, 4–5
  economy and efficiency, 32
  EDP auditing, 35
  evidence, 5–6
  financial audits, 30–31

government auditing, 33–34
independent audits, 10–15, 32–33
internal, 33
limitations, 14–15
operational audits, 31–32
organization, 38–41
origins, 7–9
professional characteristics, 53–55
role in society, 10–11
scientific method, 6
services, 34–35
standards, 43–46 (*see also* Generally accepted auditing standards and Statements on Auditing Standards [SASs])
  attest function, 47–48
  courts, 46–47
  government auditing, 48
  internal auditing, 48
  risk assessment, 254
  Securities and Exchange Commission, 46–47
systematic process, 6
user concerns, 12–14
Auditing: A Journal of Theory and Practice, 41
Auditing: A Practical Manual for Auditors, 9
Auditing Standards Board, 9, 43, 45, 46–47, 732, 838
Auditing Standards Executive Committee, 9
Audit objectives, 149–153
  buying cycle, 554–556
  cash balances, 646
  compliance testing, 266–267
  control objectives, 220–222
  debt and equity, 698
  income taxes, 691–692
  internal control and, 220–222
  investment accounts, 679
  prepaid expenses and accrued liabilities, 685–686
  production cycle, 604–605
  property, plant, and equipment, 657–658
  revenue cycle, 486–487
  risk assessment, 188–192, 329–330
  substantive testing, 329–336

  testing, 336–339
Auditor changes, 84–86
  auditor rotation, 86–87
  client disagreements, 85–86
  opinion shopping, 86
  predecessor auditors, 85
  recurring examinations, 257
Auditor-client relationships, 252–256
Auditors' certificate, 15
Auditor's Considerations When a Question Arises About an Entity's Continued Existence, 790–793
Auditors as insurers, 111–112
Auditors' legal liability, *see* Legal liability
Auditors' opinion, 15
Auditor's responsibilities, 100–109
  detecting misstatements, 101–109
  discovery of irregularities, 106–107
  legal liability, 108–134
  professional requirements, 102–105
Audit planning, 197–204
  analytical review process, 341–349
  auditing standards, 58–59
  controlling engagement, 198
  implementation planning, 197–199
  internal auditors, 199–200
  internal control reports, 203
  materiality and, 195
  rotating audit emphasis, 202
  specialists, 200–202
  subsequent events, 748–749
  work of other auditors, 202–203
Audit procedures, 149–153
Audit process, 149–180
  completion of, 717–753
  flowcharts, 350–353
  overview, 20, 22–24
  risk, 251–252
  steps in audit, 161–168
  summarizing and evaluation, 163, 733–742
  tests of, 338
  working papers, 169–180
Audit programs, 198, 349–350
Audit quality, incentives, 74–81

Audit reports, 6–7, 15–20 (*see also* Accounting changes; Management letters; Special reports; Standard reports)
  adverse opinions, 19, 794–795
  balance sheet only, 773
  communicating weaknesses, 24
  dating, 767
  departures from unqualified opinions, 18–21, 775–776
  disclaimers of opinion, 18–19, 795–796
  dual dating, 749
  emphasis of a matter, 774
  fair presentation, 765–766
  formulating, 169
  GAAP departures, 776–779
  going concern, 789–793
  history, 763–765
  inadequate disclosure, 802
  initial examination, 782
  lawyers' letters, 720–727
  long-form reports, 844
  materiality, 800, 838–839
  modifications in wording, 768–775
  opinion paragraph, 17–18, 763
  other information, 774–775
  piecemeal opinions, 799
  qualified opinions, 19–20, 776–794
    comparative statements, 793–794
    consistency, 779–785
  scope limitations, 725–727, 785–787
  scope paragraph, 16–17, 763, 767
  short-form report, 15–16, 762
  special reporting situations, 823–859
  standard reports, 763–775
    addressing report, 767
    dating, 767
    periods covered, 767–768
    routine variations, 766–767
    statement identification, 767
  subsequent events, 748–750
  subsequent responsibilities, 747–753, 800–803
    discovery of information after report date, 800–802

interim financial information, 831–835
  omitted procedures, 802–803
uncertainties, 787–793
unqualified opinions, evidence, 160–161, 723, 742, 769–770, 775–776
Audit risk, *see* Risk
Audit Risk and Materiality in Conducting an Audit, 194, 734
Audit Sampling, 733
Audit sampling, *see* Sampling
Audit staffing pyramid, 38
Audit strategy, 164–167 (*see also specific cycles and accounts*)
  analytical review procedures, 343
  buying cycle, 554–556
  client's business, 197
    understanding of, 162–164
  compliance tests, 167–168
  coordination, 200
  detection risk, 331–332
  discussing with client, 199
  EDP auditing, 444–445
  internal control evaluation, 166–167, 196
  planning and documenting, 23, 161, 164–165, 196–197
  production cycle, 604–607
  revenue cycle, 486–488
  revision, 24
  timing, 197
  work of other auditors, 197
Audit tests, types of, 159–160
Authorization:
  automated, 236
  check payments, 549
  computer-generated transactions, 440
  employment, 551–552
  recording goods and services, 546
  revenue cycle, 479–480
  of transactions, 234

Balance sheet accounts, 165
Balance sheet audits, 9
Balance sheet date, 607
Bank balances, 645–657
  audit objectives, 646
  client procedures, 646–647
  confirmation, 647–649

counting, 655
  reconciliations, 649–653
  substantive tests, 646–657
Banks:
  audited financial statements, 11
  compliance audits, 842
Bank Secrecy Act, 842
Bank transfer schedule, 653–656
Base Case System Evaluation, 452
Basic Concepts and Accounting Principles Underlying Financial Statements of Business Enterprises, 765–766
Batch totals, 438
Bates v. *State Bar of Arizona,* 72
Bell Operating Companies, 848
Benefits services, 36
Beta risk, 369 n.2, 4, 377–378
Billing, revenue cycle, 480–481
Bonds, as investment, 678
Bonuses, labor, 622
Brown, Richard, 7 n.1
Budget variances, 753
Burton, John C., 123
Business Combinations, 128
Business ethics, compliance audits, 843
Buying cycle, 226, 543–544
  accounts payable, 540–542
    substantive tests, 576–578
  acquisition of goods and services, 541–547
    compliance tests, 556–562
    storing and using, 545
      compliance tests, 564
  agency obligations, 540
  audit strategy, 554–556
  compliance testing, 556–562
  costs and expenses, 579–580
  general and administrative expenses, 541
  internal control, 541–554
  minutes of meetings, 580–581
  payment for goods and services, 547–550
    compliance tests, 565–569
  payrolls, 551–554
    compliance tests, 570–574, 575
    employment authorization, 551–552
    performance of services, 552
  returns, 550–551
    compliance tests, 565, 570

salaries, wages, and payroll taxes, substantive testing, 578–579
selling expenses, 540
substantive tests, 575–581
T-accounts, 542
typical transactions and internal control, 541–554

California, negligent representation, 116 n.18, 117
Canada, auditor's liability, 116
Carrying values, 664–665
tests of, 682–683
Cash balances, 645–657
analytical reviews, 578–579
audit objectives, 646
bank accounts, 646–657
bank transfer schedule, 653–656
buying cycle disbursements, 547, 549–550
compensating balances, 647
confirmation, 646–657
counting of, 656
debt and equity, 699–700
disbursement vouchers, 380
kiting, 653–656
lapping of receipts, 512–513
payrolls, 553–554
proof of cash, 651–652
reconciliation, 648–650
revenue cycle:
receipts, 482–483
sales, 517–518
substantive tests, 646–657
unclaimed, 551
Cathode ray tube (CRT), 429
Cenco, Inc. v. *Seidman & Seidman,* 113 n.8
Certification, 41–50
in standard report, 762
Certified Information Systems Auditor (CISA), 43
Certified Internal Auditor (CIA), 40–41
certification and licensing, 42
qualification, 54
Certified Public Accountants (CPAs):
certification and licensing, 40–42
examination, 41
organization, 34–41

state societies, 39–40
Change orders, systems review, 257–259
Chatfield, Michael, 7 n.1
Checks:
buying cycle:
disbursements, 547–549
wages, 553–554
digit verification, 439
revenue cycle, 483
signing or countersigning, 549
Citizens State Bank v. *Timm Schmidt & Co.,* 116 n.20
Civil liability, 113–123
Claims, revenue cycle, 485–486
Class action lawsuits, 111, 118
Classification of Obligations That Are Callable by the Creditor, 701
Client-auditor relationship:
acceptance and continuance, 76
auditor's responsibility, 67–70
confidentiality, 67–68
conflict of interests, 69–70
contingent fees, 70–71
insider information, 68–69
disagreements with client, 85–86
legal liability, 112–113
Client manuals, 258
Client representations, 720–731, 728
dating and signing, 730–731
illustrative representation letter, 729–730
inquiry of client's lawyer, 721–723
legal counsel, 726–727
materiality, 728
nonaudit services, 731
representations to others, 731
scope limitations, 725–726, 731
written representations, 727–728
Client's business, understanding of:
analytical review procedures, 341–349, 629–630
annual review, 266
aspects of, 164
audit process, 22–24
audit strategy, 197
control environment and, 228–229
detection risk, 338–340

deterrents to irregularities, 105–106
EDP auditing, 258–259, 446–447
illegal acts, 106
industry profile, 164
information about, 162–169
internal controls, 164–167
interviews, 164, 258
inventory conditions, 619–620
costing and summarization, 626–627
lapping, 513
management letter, 12
material differences, 742
plant and office tours, 164
production cycle, analytical review, 629–630
related party transactions, 255–256
revenue cycle, 487–488
risk assessment, 252–254
unrecorded liabilities, 581
Close kin, defined, 65
COBOL language, 432
Code of Professional Ethics, *see* American Institute of Certified Public Accountants (AICPA), Code of Professional Ethics; Ethical principles
Codes of business ethics and conduct, 843
Cohen, Manuel C., 10
Cohen Commission, *see* Commission on Auditors' Responsibilities (Cohen Commission)
Colleagues, auditor's responsibility to, 71
Collectibility, receivable balances, 514–516
Collusion, 105
internal controls and, 223
segregation of duties, 237
Comfort letter, 753, 859
Commission on Auditors' Responsibilities (Cohen Commission), 10, 14
accounting firm policies and procedures, 87
auditor changes, 84–86
auditor's independence, 82–84
client disagreements, 86

Commission on Auditors'
     Responsibilities (Cohen
     Commission) (*Continued*)
   fraud, 102
   prohibition of nonaudit services,
     89
Commissioner of Customs, 842
Commissions:
   ethics of, 73
   prepaid and accrued, 688
Committee on Auditing Procedure,
     see Auditing Standards
     Board
Common stock, 697
Communication of control
     weaknesses, 278–281
*Communications Between Predecessor
     and Successor Accountants,*
     85, 827 n.2
Comparison, periodic, 441
Compensated absences, 578–579
Compensation consulting services,
     36
Competence of evidential matter,
     156–159
Compilation of financial
     statements, 826–828
   form of reporting, 827–828
   procedures, 827
   prospective financial statements,
     849
*Compilation Reports on Financial
     Statements Included in Certain
     Prescribed Forms,* 828
Compilation services, 35
Completeness:
   assertion, 150
   cutoff tests, 503
   input, 437–438
   internal controls, 220, 231–233
   sampling, 373
   tests of, investments, 679–682
   update, 439–440
Compliance audits, 31, 840–843
   control environment and, 229
   government auditing, 33–34
   independent auditing, 33
   internal auditing, 33
Compliance testing, 159–160 (*see
     also specific cycles and
     accounts*)
   attributes sampling, 371–372
   buying cycle, 556–575
   comfort letter, 753, 859

documenting, 270–278
dual-purpose sampling,
     268–269
EDP auditing, 445–447
internal controls, 166–167
management letter, 279–281
nonstatistical sampling, 401
one-sided testing, 378–379
performing, 167–168
production cycle, 607–612
revenue cycle, 489–502
risk assessment, 264–269
   continuous operation of
     controls, 268
   evaluating results, 269
sampling, 365–366
   discovery sampling, 382
   evaluating results, 380–381,
     403
   statistical, 378–379
types, 267
working papers, 175
Computer-assisted audit
     techniques, *see* EDP
     auditing
Computer fraud and abuse,
     442–443
Computer operator, 429
Computer systems, (*see also* EDP
     auditing)
   access controls, 436
   auditing through, auditing
     around, and auditing
     with the computer, 424
   central processing unit (CPU),
     426
   client's, 258–259
   compliance testing for risk
     assessment, 265
   controls, 425
     application, 437–442
     audit objectives and
       techniques, 430–437
     backup and recovery,
       434–435
     data base management
       systems (DBMS), 427
     data file security, 430, 435–436
     data processing, 434
     fraud and abuse, 442–443
     implementation, 430–433
     internal accounting controls,
       226, 230
     matching, 438

operations controls, 430
operations software and
     operating procedures,
     434
parallel running, 431–432
password protection, 436
program security controls,
     430, 433
sequence checks, 431, 438
system software, 430, 436–437
   audit planning, 198
   mean-per-unit estimation,
     397–398
   needs determination, 541,
     543
   sample size, 379
   sequential sampling,
     382–384
   statistical sampling, 380
   valid transactions, 233–234
custom-designed applications,
     428
data generated by, 424
external storage, 426
input-output device, 426–427
internal storage, 426
vs. manual systems, 424–425
operations, 425–428
processing systems, 426–427
   batch, 426
   dispersed or distributed
     processing, 426–427
   on-line, 426
software, 427–428
utilities, 427
Confidence, *see* Assurance;
     Reliability; Risk
Confidentiality:
   conflict of interests and, 69–70
   legal liability and, 113
   maintaining, 68
   vs. privilege, 68
   responsibility to clients, 67–68
Confirmation:
   accounts receivable, 156–157,
     503–511
   bank balances, 646–657
     bank transfer schedule,
       653–656
     compensating balances, 647
     reconciliations, 649–653
     standard form, 647–649
   buying cycle, substantive tests,
     577–578

debt and equity, 699
defined, 154
evidence and, 155–156
exceptions to requests, 511
lapping, 512–513
long-term contracts, 520
negative confirmation, 507–509
positive confirmation, 509–510
procedures in lieu of, 512–513
response rates, 510
revenue cycle, 503–511
securities not on hand, 681–682
substantive tests, 337
Conflict of interests, 69–70, 106
user concerns, 13
*Consideration of Omitted Procedures
        After the Report Date,* 802
Consignment sales, 518
Consistency:
departures from, 779–785
standards of, 18, 60
Construction Contractors, 520
Consultation, quality control, 76
Consumerism, 111
Contingencies:
accounting overview, 718
auditing procedures, 719–720
client representations, 728
income tax liabilities, 695–696
lawyers' letters, 720–727
sales agreements, 515–516
Control environment, 227–229
assessment, 259–260
Control matrices, 266
documentation, 271, 273–274
Control objectives, 220–222
Control risk, 189, 191, 256–257
Controls:
internal, 217–240 (*see also*
        Computer controls)
accounting, 218–224
reports on, 281
systems, 229–230
administrative, 224–225
analytical review procedures,
        341–342
audit objectives, 220–222
audit strategy, 196
service organization
        reporting, 203–204
basic, 230–237
buying cycle, 541–554
cash receipts, revenue cycle,
        482–483

communicating weaknesses
        in, 24, 169
compliance testing, 168
continuous operation, 268
control environment,
        227–229
assessment, 259–260
definitions and objectives,
        218–224
detection risk, 329–353
deterrents to irregularities,
        105
documentation, 270–278
elements, 227–238
engagement, 204
evaluation, 59
financial statements:
compilations, 826–828
disclosures, 746–747
typing or reproducing,
        825–826
Foreign Corrupt Practices Act,
        238–240
inventory, 608–610
invoices, 495–496, 564–565
lapping, 513
legal liability, 132
limits to effectiveness,
        222–223
management reports, 852
management review of reports,
        228–229, 259–260
material weaknesses, 279–281
preliminary phase of
        evaluation of internal
        control, 256–257
production cycle, 594–604,
        607–612
reasonable assurance,
        223–224
revenue cycle, 477–486
payments received,
        496–502
risk assessment, 190–191,
        251–252
minimum requirements,
        256–263
sales orders, 489, 494
segregation of duties, 237
study and evaluation, 166–167
supervision, 230, 238
tests of, 160
service organizations,
        203–204

special reports, 824,
        851–855
supervisory, 230, 238
transaction cycles, 225–227
weaknesses, communicating,
        278–281
quality, 75–79
AICPA standards, 76–81
disciplinary system, 79–81
elements, 75–76
peer review, 78–79
Control totals, 232
Coordination of efforts, audit
        strategy, 200
Corroborating information,
        152–154
Cost-benefit analysis, internal
        controls and, 223
Cost-effective audits:
planning audit strategy and,
        196–197
risks and, 187
Cost of sales, 593
Counting:
assets, 154, 337
bank balances, 655
cash, 656
currency, 656
inventory, 602–603
periodic inventories, 603–604
investment portfolios, 680–681
raw materials on hand, 609–610
Credit:
internal controls, 226–227
returns for, 550–551
revenue cycle:
authorization and
        memoranda, 486
terms of, 479
suspense accounts, 689
Credit Alliance Corp. v. *Arthur Andersen
        & Co.,* 116–117
Credit memoranda:
substantive testing, 513
vendor, 550–551
Creditors, audited
        financial statements, 11
Criminal liability, 123
Currency:
counting, 656
disbursements in buying cycle,
        549
Currency and Foreign Transaction
        Reporting Act, 842

Custody controls, 236
  assets, 442
Customer rights of return,
  515–516
Cutoff:
  assertion, 151
  inventories, 603–604, 623
  periodic inventories, 603–604
  sales, 623–624
  tests:
    buying cycle, 576
    revenue cycle, 502–503
  of transactions, 235
Cycle counts, 618–621

Data base administrator (DBA),
  428
Data base management systems
  (DBMS), 427
  access controls, 436
  software, 427
Data entry operator, 429
Dating auditors' reports, 737
Debit memoranda, revenue cycle,
  485
Debits, suspense accounts,
  689
Debt and equity, 697–702
  audit objectives, 698
  substantive tests of balances,
    698–702
    defaults, 700–701
    dividends, 702
    initial examinations, 701
    permanent files, 701
    stockholders' equity accounts,
      701–702
Declaration of audit, 8
Defalcations (see also Fraud; Kiting;
    Lapping)
  auditor's liability, 112–113
  employee, 104–105
Defaults, 700–701
Deferred charges, 684
Deferred income, 519–520
Departures from disclosure
    principles, 777–778
Departures from measurement
    principles, 777
Departures from unqualified
    opinions, 742,
    775–776
Dependency checks, 439
Deposits, revenue cycle, 483

Depreciation accounts, property,
    plant, and equipment,
    663
  salvage values, 665–666
Desk checking, 431
Detection risk, 189, 191–192,
    330–331
Deviation (error) rates:
  attributes sampling, 375–378
  compliance testing, 269
  expected rate, 372–373,
    405–406
  mean-per-unit estimation,
    391–393
  sample results, 381
  sample size, 370–372
  tolerable rates, 370–372,
    376–377, 379, 383–384
Dicksee, Lawrence R., 9
Difference and ratio estimation,
    398–400
Digest of State Accountancy Laws and
    State Board Regulations, 42
Direct tests, see Substantive testing
Disagreements with clients, 88–89
Disclaimers of opinion, 18–19,
    795–796
  vs. adverse opinions, 799–800
Disclosure:
  assertions, 150–151
  audit reports, subsequent
    responsibilities, 802
  checklists, 747
  comfort letter, 859
  financial statement reviews,
    746–747
  GAAP, 60
    departure from, 777–779
  inadequate disclosures,
    qualified opinions,
    777–778
  income taxes, 694–695
  standard reports, 770
  standards, 60
  subsequent events, 750–751
Discounts, revenue cycle, 484
Discovery sampling, 382
Dividends (see also Debt and equity)
  payments, 700
  substantive tests, 702
Division for CPA Firms, see
    American Institute of
    Certified Public
    Accountants (AICPA)

Division of duties, see Segregation
    of duties
Docket (SEC), 80
Documentation:
  accounting systems, 260–263
  cash balances, 651
  client's understanding, 742 n.6
  compliance testing, 277–278
  controls and compliance testing,
    270–278
  control weaknesses, 278
  evidence and, 154–155
  flowcharts and narratives,
    260–263, 266
    controls and compliance
      testing, 270–273
  internal control questionnaire,
    275–277
  production cycle, 598–599
  property, plant, and equipment,
    662
  sampling, 407–408
  software, 453
  working paper reviews, 746
Dollar value, mean-per-unit
    estimation, 390–391
Dollar-weighted sample selection,
    401–402
Donations in revenue cycle, 519
Dual dating, audit reports, 749
Dual-purpose sample, 268–269
Due care standards, 58, 112
Due diligence standard, 119
Dun & Bradstreet, 348
Duties, segregation of, see
    Segregation of duties

Earle, Victor M., 131 n.44
Economic conditions, risk
    assessment, 253
Edit checks, 439
EDP auditing, 423–452
  application controls, objectives
    and techniques, 437–442
  auditing through, auditing
    around, and auditing
    with the computer, 424
  audit management, 454
  central processing unit (CPU),
    426
  compliance testing:
    financial information,
      445–447
    for risk assessment, 265

computer fraud and abuse, 424–443
computer-generated financial information, 444–454
  compliance testing, 445–447
  substantive testing, 447–453
computer operations, 425–428
  hardware, 425–426
control objectives and techniques, 430–437
custom-designed applications, 428
department organization, 428–429
environment, 425–429
external storage, 426
input-output device, 426–427
internal storage, 426
vs. manual systems, 424–425
operations, 425–428
processing systems, 426–427
  batch, 426
  dispersed or distributed processing, 426–427
  on-line, 426
  real-time, 426
production cycle, raw materials, 599
programmed procedures, testing, 450–453
proposed systems evaluation, 858–859
revenue, aged trial balance, 514–515
software packages, 427–428, 447–450
specialization, 35
telecommunications, 446
utilities, 427
Educational institutions, compliance audits, 842
Education of auditors:
  professionalization, 54–55
  standards, 42
Effect of an Internal Audit Function on the Scope of the Independent Auditor's Examination, 200
Effects of Computer Processing on the Examination of Financial Statements, 198, 424
Efficient market hypothesis, 10
Electronic mail, 454

1136 Tenants' Corp. v. *Max Rothenberg & Co.,* 132–133
Emphasis of matter, 774
Employment authorization, 551–552
Employment Retirement Income Security Act of 1974 (ERISA), 689–690
Engagements:
  assigning personnel, 76
  controlling, 199, 203–204
  letter, 107–109
    legal liability, 134
  planning, 197–204
Engagement team, 37–38
Equity, *see* Debt and equity
Equity Funding case, 123
Ernst & Ernst v. *Hochfelder,* 120–122
Errors:
  aggregating, 406–407
  aggregating and netting, 406–407, 735–736
  computer controls, 441
  control of, 166
  correction, consistency in reports, 783–784
  cutoff, 624
  defined, 103
  evaluating, 733–734
  exception reports, 235
  internal controls, 223
    basic controls, 231–232
  inventory costing, 626
  liability for, 112–113
  materiality:
    qualitative considerations, 737–739
    quantitative, 736–737
  mean-per-unit estimation (MPU), 391–393
  prior-year audits, 254
  prior-year waived adjustments, 740–741
  projected errors, 404–406
  risk of, internal controls, 221
  sampling:
    expected, 372–373
    projection, 404–406
  score sheet, 734–735
  sensitivity, 738
  soft *vs.* hard, 737–739
  standing data, 230
    compliance testing, 570

user concerns, 12–13
variables sampling, 384–385
Error tainting, monetary unit sampling, 386–390
Escott et al. v. *BarChris Construction Corp.,* 119–120, 129, 194
Established criteria, limits of, 14
Estimated lives, depreciation, 666
Estimates:
  difference and ratio, 398–400
  mean-per-unit, 390–398
  true deviation rate, 378–379
Ethical principles (*see also* American Institute of Certified Public Accountants [AICPA], Code of Professional Ethics)
  accounting services, 65
  AICPA code, 60–73
    concepts, 61–73
  general and technical standards, 65–67
  independence, integrity, and objectivity, 62–73
  objectivity, 62–73
  opinion shopping, 66
  practice and name form, 73
  responsibilities and practices, 71–73
    advertising and solicitation, 72
    commissions, 73
    discreditable acts, 71–72
    fees, 72
    incompatible occupations, 73
  responsibilities to clients, 67–70
    confidentiality, 67–68
    conflict of interests, 69
    contingent fees, 70–71
    insider information, 69
  responsibilities to colleagues, 71
Evaluation of internal control, 256–257
Events subsequent to balance sheet date, *see* Subsequent events
Evidence, 152–161 (*see also specific cycles and accounts*)
  analytical, 156
  assertion corroboration, 23–24
  audit standards, 5–6
  competency of, 59, 156–159
  compliance tests, 267
  confirmation of, 155–156, 504–505

Evidence (*Continued*)
  corroborating, 152–154
  cost-benefit trade-offs, 158
  decisions, 160–161
  income taxes, 696
  inquiry, 155
  inspection, 154–155
  inventory substantiation,
    622–623
  objectivity of, 5–6, 158
  observation, 155
  of ownership, 661–662
  persuasive, 160–161
  relevance, 157
  reliability, 157
  reperformance and, 155
  substantive testing, 338–339
  sufficiency of evidential matter,
    169
  types of, 152–154
  underlying accounting data,
    152–154
Evidential Matter, 696
"Except for" opinions, 788
  disclaimers, 796
"Exception reports," 235
  application controls, 437
  employment authorization, 552
  supervisory controls, 238
Exchange Act Release No. 15772,
  852
Existence, assertions about, 150
Existence checks, 439
Expected deviation rate, 372–373,
  405–406
Expenditure cycle, *see* Buying cycle
Expenditures, property, plant,
    and equipment,
    classification of, 664
Expenses, buying cycle,
    579–580
Extensions of Auditing Procedure, 128

Fair presentation, 18
  standard audit report, 765–766
False representation, proof of,
    118 n.26
Family relationships, auditor
    independence and, 65
Federal Securities Acts (*see*
    Securities Act of 1933;
    Securities and Exchange
    Commission [SEC];
    Securities Exchange Act
    of 1934)

FCPA, *see* Foreign Corrupt
    Practices Act
Fees:
  ethical principles, 72
  professional, 688
Fidelity bond insurance, 105–106
Field work:
  auditing standards, 58–59
  special reports, 824
File maintenance, EDP auditing,
    440–441
  file and program access software,
    427
File management software, 435
Financial Accounting Standards
    Board (FASB),
    10, 766, 835
  departures from promulgated
    accounting principle,
    770–771
  Statements of Financial
    Accounting Concepts
    (SFAC):
    No. 1, 10, 835
    No. 2, 193–194
  Statements of Financial
    Accounting Standards
    (SFAS):
    No. 2, 736–737
    No. 5, 692, 719, 721–722,
      728–729, 787
    No. 12, 678
    No. 13, 665
    No. 19, 846
    No. 25, 846
    No. 33, 846
    No. 39, 846
    No. 43, 579
    No. 57, 255
    No. 69, 846
    No. 78, 701
    No. 87, 690
  supplementary information in
    financial statements,
    845–846
Financial audits, 30–31
Financial Executives Institute,
    102
Financial Forecasts and Projections,
    847
*Financial Reporting and Changing
    Prices,* 846
*Financial Reporting and Changing
    Prices: Specialized Assets,*
    846

Financial statements, 4, 149–152
  accompanying information,
    843–846
    details or commentary,
      843–845
    FASB pronouncements,
      845–846
  analytical reviews, 344
  assertions, *see* Assertions,
      financial statements
  audit objectives, 34
  compilations, 826–828
  disclosures, 746–747
  errors, 783–784
  limitations, 14–15
  management responsibility, 88
  non-GAAP, 835–838
  objectives, 11–12
  prospective and pro forma,
    846–851
  reports on parts of, 838–840
  reviews, 828–831
  risk assessment, 253, 338
  trends in components, 739
  typing or reproducing,
    825–826
  user concerns, 12–14
Financing transactions, 677–678
  affiliates, 678
  audit objectives, 679–684
  long-term, 678
  new financial products, 678
  safeguarding, 680
  short-term, 677–678
  substantive tests of balances,
    679–684
    carrying values, 682–683
    classification and presentation,
      683–685
    confirmation of securities not
      on hand, 681–682
    equity method, 682–683
    existence and completeness,
      679–682
    investment income, 683
    portfolio counts, 680–681
  substitutions, 681
Fischer v. *Kletz (Yale Express),*
    128–129
Flowcharts:
  audit planning, 164
  audit process, 350–353
  overview, 260, 263
  software for, 451
  symbols for, 262

systems, 260, 266
controls and compliance
testing, 270–272
Footing, 338
proof of cash, 651, 653
Forecasts, 848
prospective financial statements,
846–847
sales forecasts, 629–630
Foreign Corrupt Practices Act, 106,
835 n.8, 851–852
administrative controls, 223
illegal payments, 238–239
internal accounting controls,
238–240
Foreign Sales Corporations (FSCs),
694
Foreseeable class concept,
115–117
Foreseeable third parties, 114–117
Form 8-K, 85–86
Form 10-K, 129, 856
Form 10-Q, 832, 856
Format checking, 439
Four Seasons case, 123
Fraud (*see also* Collusion; Errors;
Irregularities; Kiting;
Lapping; Misstatements)
auditor's responsibility,
101–102
audits, 105, 553, n.1
collusion, 105, 223, 237
control of, 166
EDP auditing, 442–443
management, 103
Fund drives, auditing procedures,
519
Fund of Funds, Ltd. v. *Arthur Andersen
& Co.,* 70, 113

General Accounting Office (GAO),
34, 48–50
Generally accepted accounting
principles (GAAP):
adherence to, 59–60
adverse opinions, 19, 794–795
applicability, special reports,
838
and auditor liability, 130–131
auditor selection of, 88–89
departures from, 770–771
adverse opinions, 19, 794–795
consistency, 780–781
qualified opinions, 777–779
fair presentation, 18, 765–766

limitations, 14–15
misapplication of, 338
qualified opinions, 19–20
standard reports, 763
departures from, 770–772
tax laws and, 691
assertion criteria, 5
disclosure and valuation, 13
Generally accepted auditing
standards (GAAS), 43–47
attestation standards compared
with, 46–47
and auditor liability, 131
computer fraud and abuse,
442–443
field work standards, 56, 58–59
internal control evaluation, 59
obtaining competent
evidence, 59
planning and supervision,
58–59
financial statements,
accompanying
information, 844
general standards, 56–58
due care, 58
independence, 57–58
training and proficiency, 57
legal liability, 112
origins, 55–56
reporting standards, 56–57, 59
consistency, 60
disclosure, 60
GAAP adherence, 59–60
opinions, 60
special reports, 824
Gerstle v. *Gamble-Skogmo,* 122
Gifts in revenue cycle, 519
Going concern uncertainties,
789–793
Government auditing, 33–34
confirmation procedures, 506,
512–513
special reports, 841–842
standards, 48–50
Governmental Accounting
Standards Board, 67, 846
Grants, compliance audits of, 842
Gross negligence, 112
*Guide for Prospective Financial
Statements,* 847–848

Haig v. *Branford,* 116
Haphazard selection, *see*
Unsystematic selection

Hardware, computer, 425–426
Hash totals, 552
Hedley Byrne & Co. Ltd. v. *Heller &
Partners, Ltd.,* 115
Hiring, quality control, 76
History of auditing, 7–9
Holding file, sales of goods and
services, 480
H. Rosenblum, Inc. v. *Adler,* 116 n.19
Hylas, Robert E., 510 n.1
Hypergeometric formula, 376 n.11

Illegal acts by clients, 106
discovery of, 106–107
Illegal Acts by Clients, 106
Implementation planning, 197–199
Inherent risk, 252–253
Income from investments,
677–684
Income taxes, 691–697
audit objectives, 691–692
estimated and contingent
liabilities, 695–696
expenses, deferrals, and
disclosures, 694–695
payments and refunds, 694
state and local taxes, 696–697
substantive tests of balances,
692–694
working papers, 176–177
Incompatible occupations, 73
Independence of auditors, 32–33
accounting principles, 64–65
advertising, 72
attest service, 47
auditing standards, 10–15
auditor changes, 84–86
disclaimers of opinion, 798
enhancing auditors', 81–89
accounting policies and
procedures, 87
auditor changes, 84–86
nonaudit services, 82, 89
public sector transfer, 88
selecting GAAP for clients,
88–89
ethical principles, 62–74
family relationships, 65
general standards, 57–58
vs. independence of evidence
sources, 157
internal auditors, 33
management influence and,
83–87
past-due fees, 65

Independence of auditors
  (*Continued*)
  quality control, 76
  reconciliations of bank balances,
    651
  of specialists, 201–202
*Independent Auditor's Responsibility for
  the Detection of Errors or
  Irregularities,* 102–104,
  728
Information:
  gathering or updating, 342
  risk, defined, 10
  sources on legal matters, 727
Information for CPA Candidates, 42
Information technology controls,
  226
INFORM data base, 733
Inherent risk, 189–191, 252–253
Initialization as supervisory
  control, 238
Injunctive proceedings, 125
Inquiry, evidence, 155
*Inquiry of a Client's Lawyer Concerning
  Litigation, Claims, and
  Assessments,* 720, 722–723
Insider information, 68–69
Inspection:
  in buying cycle, 545
  debt and equity, 699
  evidence, 154–155
  production cycle, 598–599
  quality control, 76
Institute of Internal Auditors (IIA),
  33, 40–41, 48, 54, 102
  certification and licensing, 42
Insurance:
  contingent liabilities, 720
  irregularities, 105–106
  malpractice, 110–111
  prepaid, 687
  risk analysis, 544
Integrated test facility (ITF),
  451–452
Interest:
  accrued payable, 688
  internal control, 226
  revenue cycle, 518
Interim reviews, 831–835
  annual reports, 834–835
  extent, 833–834
  nature of, 832–833
  objectives, 832
  reporting standards, 834–835

timing, 833
Internal auditing, 33
  audit strategy and planning,
    199–200
  control environment and, 229
  deterrents to irregularities, 105
  organization, 40–41
  standards, 48
Internal Auditor, The, 40
Internal control, *see* Controls,
  internal
Internal control letter, *see*
  Management letter
Internal control questionnaires,
  266, 275–277
Internal Revenue Service (IRS),
  691–692
  compliance audits, 842
International Federation of
  Accountants (IFAC), 44
  International Auditing
    Guideline No. 12, 346 n.1
  International Auditing Practices
    Committee, 4
International Mortgage Co. v. *John P.
  Butler Accountancy Co.,* 117
  n.24
Interviews, 258, 267
Inventories, 592–630
  alternative procedures, 622–623
  analytical review, 344
  assertions, 4
  audit procedures for, 151–152
  buying cycle, 546
  condition of, 619–620
  consignment, 624
  costing and summarization,
    625–628
  difficult, 621–622
  evidence of, 5–6, 153–154
  FIFO and LIFO applications,
    626
  government requirements, 622
  inherent risks in, 190
  internal controls, 226
  obsolete items, 626
  one-time, 602–603
  ownership of, 623–625
  periodic, 603–604
  perpetual records, 609–610
  physical, 601–602
    observation of, 612, 618–623
    vs. recorded, 603
  physical security, 608

pricing and valuation, 610–611
  production cycle, 592–630
  property, plant, and equipment,
    662
  public warehouses, 604
  sampling errors, 371
  scope limitations, 797
  storing finished goods, 601–604,
    612
  substantive testing, 612,
    618–630
  usage records, 626
  work in process, 622
  written program, 602–603
Investments, 677–678
  affiliates, 678
  audit objectives, 679–684
  classification and presentation,
    683–685
  confirmation of securities not on
    hand, 681–682
  counting, 680–681
  income, 683
  interim information, 834–835
  long-term, 678
  new financial products, 678
  safeguarding, 680
  short-term, 677–678
  substantive tests of balances,
    679–684
    carrying values, 682–683
    equity method, 682–683
    existence and completeness,
      679–682
  substitutions, 681
Invoices:
  attributes sampling, 375–378
  buying cycle, 546–547, 564–565
  revenue cycle, 480–481,
    483–484, 495–496
Irregularities, 106–107 (*see also*
  Fraud)
  client deterrents to, 105–106
  defined, 103
  discovery of, 106–107
  insurance, 105–106
  internal control, 105

Jaenicke, Henry R., 128 n.38
Job order system, 594
Job tickets, 599–600
Journal of Accountancy, 39

Key engagement matters, 744

Kiting, bank balances, 653–656

Labor costs:
  direct labor, 593
  production cycle, 599–600
Lapping, 512–513
Lapse schedules, 179–180
Lawyers, 201
Lawyers' letters, 720–727
  auditing procedures, 721–727
  evaluating responses, 723
  information sources, 727
  inside counsel, 726
  lawyer changes, 726–727
  scope limitations, 725–726
  unqualified opinion, 723–724
Lead schedules, 171
Leased property, 665
Leases, operating *vs.* capital, 699
Least squares method, 347
Legal liability:
  administrative proceedings,
    125–127
  auditor's response to, 127–133
  auditor's responsibilities,
    108–134
  authoritative pronouncements,
    127–133
  to clients, 112–113
  criminal liability, 123
  discovery of irregularities,
    106–107
  foreseeable class concept,
    116–117
  injunctive proceedings, 125
  litigation explosion, 109–112
  primary benefit rule, 114–115
  privity of contract doctrine, 114
  protection measures, 133–134
  recklessness, 122–123
  risk, 188
  scienter requirement, 117–118
  Securities Act of 1933, 118–120
  Securities and Exchange Act of
    1934, 118–123
  substantive testing, 580–581
  third parties, 113–123
    foreseen and foreseeable,
      114–117
Letter of minor violation, 80
Letters of representation, 341
Letters for underwriters, 732, 753,
    859
LEXIS data base, 733

Liabilities, *see* Debt and equity
Librarian, EDP systems, 429
Licensing, *see* Certification and
    licensing
Linkediting, 432
Listing, cash receipts, 482–483
Litigation, *see* Legal liability
Load module, 432
Local taxes, 696–697
Lock box system, 483
Loebbecke, James K., 398 n.20
"Long-form" reports, 844
Long-term contracts, 520
Long-term debt, *see* Debt and
    equity
Losses, purchase commitments,
    628
Louis, Arthur M., 110 n.5

Machinery and equipment, *see*
    Property, plant, and
    equipment
McKesson & Robbins fraud case, 83,
    102, 128, 504, 612
MacLean v. *Huddleston,* 123
Mainframe computers, 425–426
Maintenance:
  accounting controls,
    235–236
  compliance tests, 221
  internal control, 220
Malpractice insurance, 110–111
Management:
  auditor-client relationship,
    88–89
  biases, 739
  control environment and,
    228–229, 259–260
  defined, 101 n.2
  EDP auditing, 443
  family relationships, 65
  income tax liabilities, 696
  influence and auditor's
    independence, 83–89
  internal controls and, 223
  responsibility for internal
    controls, 238–240
Management advisory services
    (MAS), 36
  auditor independence, 82
  standards, 48–49
Management consulting services
    (MCS), 36
Management fraud, *see* Fraud

Management information systems
    (MIS):
  designed and implemented by
    auditors, 36
  EDP auditing, 454
Management letter, 12, 278–281
  as auditing-related service,
    34–35
Management reports, internal
    controls, 852
Management representation letter.
    production cycle, 630
Management reviews, 441
  revenue cycle, 481–482
Marketable securities, 678
Marketing plans, production cycle,
    629–630
Martindale-Hubbel Law Directory, 723
Matching techniques, 232, 441
Materiality, 193–196
  aggregating and netting,
    735–736
  auditors' reports, 800
  client representations, 728
  difference and ratio estimation,
    399–400
  prior-year waived adjustments,
    740–741
  qualitative considerations,
    737–738
  qualitative and quantitative
    aspects, 194
  quantitative aspects, 736–737
  resolving differences, 741–742
  sample size, 371–372
  special reports, 838–839
Material weaknesses, internal
    controls, special reports,
    854–855
Mean-per-unit estimation
    (MPU), 390–398
Memo update, 426
Microcomputers, 425–426
Minicomputers, 425–426
Minutes of meetings:
  buying cycle, 580–581
  as evidence, 154
  substantive testing, 340
Misstatements (*see also* Errors;
    Fraud; Irregularities)
  auditor's detection of, 101–109
  causes of, 739
  detection risk, 165, 330–331
  EDP auditing, 446–447

Monetary unit sampling (MUS), 385–390
Montgomery, Robert H., 9, 364 n.1
Moyer, C. A., 8 n.3
Multilocation audits, 198

NAARS data base, 733
Narratives, 266
audit planning, 164
controls and compliance testing, 270
documentation, 260–261
National Commission on Management Fraud, 102
National Student Marketing case, 123
Negative assurance, 47, 831
evidence and, 161
Negative confirmation, 507–509
Negligence:
comparative, 113
contributory, 113
defined, 112–113
foreseen third parties, 114–117
ordinary, 114 n.11
Securities and Exchange Act standard, 122
Negotiable assets, 656
Neter, John, 398 n.20
Net realizable value (ceiling):
inventory, 627
property, plant, and equipment, 662, 665
Netting, 735–736
"New financial products," 678–679
New York Stock Exchange, 855, 857
audited financial statements, 11–12
auditor independence, 83–84
Nonaudits, compilations, and reviews, 825–831
typing or reproducing financial statements, 825–826
unwarranted association, 826
Nonaudit services, prohibition of, 89
Nondependent close relatives, auditor independence, 65
Nonpublic entity defined, 826 n.1
Nonsampling risk, 367–368
Nonstatistical sampling, 370 n.7, 374–375, 400–401

Notes payable, *see* Debt and equity
Notes receivable, 176, 178 (*see also* Revenue cycle)
collectibility, 515

Object code, 432
Objectives of audits, 149–152
Observation, *see also* Inventories
evidence, 155
substantive testing, 337
Ohio Drill & Tool Co. v. *Johnson,* 122
One-for-one checking, 438
"Open to buy" concept, 234
Operating expenses, 594
Operating reports, control environment, 259–260
Operational audits, 31–32
Opinion paragraphs, 17–18, 763 (*see also* Audit reports)
Opinions, 762 (*see also* Qualified opinions; Unqualified opinions)
accounting principles, 855–857
adverse, 19, 794–795
vs. disclaimers, 799–800
disclaimers of, 18–19, 795–796
auditor independence, 798
scope limitations, 796–798
uncertainties, 796
piecemeal, 799
qualified, 19
tax consequences and proposed systems, 858–859
Opinion shopping, 66, 857
auditor changes, 86
Ordering goods and services:
compliance tests, 563–564
control of, 543–544
Organized Crime Control Act of 1970, 110
Other information in annual reports, 774–775
Overall audit risk, 187–192
Overhead, production cycle, 593, 600
Overpayment, 552
Overstatement, compliance testing, 570
Overstocking, production cycle, 597
Overtime, recording, 552

Parallel running, computer systems, 431–432

Password protection, 436
Past-due balances, revenue cycle, 514–515
Past-due fees, 65
Payables, *see* Buying cycle; Debt and equity
Payrolls:
buying cycle, 551–553
compliance tests, 176, 570–575
currency disbursements, 549–550
employment authorization, 551–552
gross pay and deductions, 552–553
production cycle, 599–600
taxes, 578–579
wages, 553–554
unclaimed, 550
Peer review, quality control, 78–79
Pension costs, 689–690
Percentage-of-completion method, long-term contracts, 520
Physical inventory, 601–602 (*see also* Inventories)
Physical security controls:
computer files, 435–436
internal controls, 220, 236–237
inventory, 608
marketable securities, 680
payments for goods and services, 547
Piecemeal opinions, 799
Planning and Supervision, 58–59
Planning audits, *see* Audit planning
Pooling letters, 856–857
Portfolios, 680–681
Positive confirmation, 509–510
Practice, form of, 73
Precision, defined, 374 n.10
Preferability letters, 855–856
Preliminary phase of evaluation of internal control, 256–257
Preliminary judgment, materiality, 194–195
Prepaid expenses, 684–691
audit objectives, 685–686
substantive tests of balances, 686–691
analytical reviews, 686
commissions, 688
interest payable, 688
pension costs, 689–690

prepaid insurance, 687
professional fees, 688
property taxes, 687–688
royalties payable, 689
suspense debits and credits, 689
travel and entertainment expenses, 688
warranty costs, 690–691
Prepaid insurance, 687
Presentation and disclosure assertion, 150–151
"Present fairly concept," 17–18, 765–766
Primary benefit rule, 114–115
Prior years' audit results, 254
Prior year's transactions:
materiality, 740–741
property, plant, and equipment, tests of balances, 660–661
reviews of buying cycle, substantive tests, 575–576
Privilege, confidentiality vs., 68
Privity of contract doctrine, 112–116, 118
Probability-proportional-to-size sampling, 386
Process cost system, 594
Production cycle, 226, 592–630
accounts, 593–596
audit strategy, 604–607
compliance testing, 607–617
goods produced, 596–601
storing finished goods, 601–604
compliance testing, 612
storing raw materials and component parts, 596
compliance testing, 608–610
substantive testing, 612, 618–630
analytical reviews, 629–630
cost of sales, 627–628
inventory costing and summarization, 625–628
inventory ownership, 623–625
purchase commitments, 628
T-accounts, 595
typical transactions and internal control, 594–604
Production library, 432
Production order, 598
Production payments, 518–519

Production requisition, 597–598
Professional ethics, see Ethical principles
Professional fees, 688
Pro forma statements, 851
Program code analysis, 451
Programmed procedures, 425
Program tracing and mapping, 451
Proof of cash, 651–653
Property, plant, and equipment, 657–666
acquisition of assets, 662–663
audit objectives, 657–658
carrying values, 664–665
classification of expenditures, 664
depreciation and salvage values, 665–666
disposition of assets, 663–664
existence and ownership of assets, 661–662
opening balances and prior year's transactions, 660–661
risk evaluation, 658–660
substantive tests of balances, 658–666
Property income in revenue cycle, 518
Property taxes, prepaid and accrued, 687–688
Prospective financial statements, 846–847
Prudent man concept, 112–113
Public sector:
auditor's responsibilities, 55
transfer for auditor independence, 88
Public warehouses, 604
Purchase commitments, 628
Purchase invoices, 338
Purchase orders, 544
Purchases, see Buying cycle

Qualified opinions, 19–20, 776–794
consistency, 779–785
GAAP departures, 777–779
disclosure principles, 777–778
measurement principles, 777
reports with differing or updated opinions, 793–794
scope limitations, 785–787

client-imposed restrictions, 785
uncertainties, 787–793
going concern, 789–793
materiality, 788–789
Qualitative Characteristics of Accounting Information, 193
Quality control, see Control, quality
Quality Control Considerations for a Firm of Independent Auditors, 75
Quantity control, inventory, 618–621
records, 622–623
Questionnaires, audit planning, 164
Quick ratio, 735

Racketeering Influenced and Corrupt Organizations (RICO), 110
Random dollars, 385–390
mean-per-unit estimation, 390–391
Random sample selection, 374, 379–380
Raritan River Steel Co. v. Cherry, Bekaert & Holland, 117
Ratio estimation, 398–400
Ratios:
analytical reviews, 347
production cycle, 629
Raw materials:
physical security, 608–610
storage, 596
Reasonableness checks, 439
Receivables, see Revenue cycle
Receiving reports, 485–486
Recklessness, legal liability and, 122–123
Reconciliations:
bank balances, 483, 649–653
four-column, 651–653
substantive testing, 338–339
Recurring engagements, 166–167
compliance testing, 168
inherent risk assessment, 252–253
management letter, 279
Refunds, income taxes, 694
Regression analysis, 346–347
Related party transactions:
client representations, 728

Related party transactions
 (*Continued*)
 revenue cycle, 516
 risk assessment, 254–256
Relationship of control
  objectives to audit
  objectives, 220–222
*Relationship of Generally Accepted
  Auditing Standards to
  Quality Control Standards,*
  75, 745
Reliability:
 attributes sampling, 377–379
 mean-per-unit estimation
  (MPU), 391–395
 sampling methods, 374, n.9
 sampling risk, 369
 sequential sampling, 383–384
 upper error dollar limit, 389
Rental income, revenue cycle,
  518
Reperformance:
 compliance testing, 267
 evidence and, 155
 sampling, 380
 segregation of duties, 237
 substantive testing, 338, 342
*Report, Conclusions, and
  Recommendations of the
  Commission on Auditors'
  Responsibilities,* 504
*Reporting on Compiled Financial
  Statements,* 827–828, 843
  n.9
*Reporting on Information Accompanying
  the Basic Financial
  Statements in Auditor-
  Submitted Documents,* 844,
  846
*Reporting on Internal Accounting
  Control,* 132, 227–228,
  853–854
*Reporting on Personal Financial
  Statements Included in
  Written Personal Financial
  Plans,* 827 n.3
*Reporting on Pro Forma Financial
  Information in SEC filings,*
  851
Report on internal control at a
  service organization,
  203–204, 770, 855
*Report of the Special Advisory Committee
  on Internal Accounting
  Control,* 225 n.1

*Reports on Audited Financial
  Statements,* 202, 725, 731,
  769, 771, 774, 776,
  781–782, 786–788
*Reports on Comparative Financial
  Statements,* 768, 772,
  793–794
Reports Following a Pooling of Interests,
  128
Reports on the application of
  accounting principles,
  857–858
Reports on compliance, 840–842
Repurchase agreements ("repos"),
  516, 678
*Required Communication of Material
  Weaknesses in Internal
  Accounting Control,* 132,
  279–280
Requisitions, control over, 543
Researching auditing problems,
  732–733
Returns, buying cycle, 550–551
Revenue cycle, 226, 475–520
 accounts receivable, 502–505,
  512–516
  substantive testing, 502–505,
   512–516
 analytical review procedures,
  345–346, 513, 516–517
 audit strategy, 486–488
 cash collections, 482–485,
  496–502
 cash sales, 517–518
 compliance testing, 489–502
 confirmation, 503–511
 consignment sales, 518
 deferred income or unearned
  revenue, 476–477,
  519–520
 gifts and donations, 519
 long-term contracts, 520
 rents, interest and fixed
   payments for property,
   518
 returns and claims, 485–486,
  496, 502
 revenue types, 517–520
 sales of goods and services,
  478–482
 substantive testing, 333, 336,
  502–517
 T-accounts, 476–477
 transactions and internal
   control, 477–486

unearned revenue, 476–477
variable revenues, 518–519
Reviewing prior years' audit
  results, 254
Reviews:
 financial statements, 35,
  828–831
 analytical procedures,
  829–830
 reporting, 830–831
 interim, 831–835
*Rhode Island Hospital Trust National
  Bank* v. *Swartz,* 115
RICO. *see* Racketeering Influenced
  and Corrupt
  Organizations (RICO)
Rights and obligations assertion,
  150
Risk, 186–204
 alpha, 369 n.4, 6, 377–378
  variables sampling, 385
 assessment, 251–252
  buying cycle, 555
  compliance testing, 264–269
   specific controls, 265–269,
    270–278
  detection risk, 330–331
  documentation, 270–278
  flowcharts, 352–353
  minimum requirements,
   256–263
  production cycle, 606
  property, plant, and
   equipment, 658–660
 attributes sampling, 377–378
 beta, 369 n.3, 5, 377–378
 compliance testing, 168,
  264–269, 270–278
 components, 189–193
 control, 189, 191, 265–269
 detection, 189, 191–192,
  329–353
 information risk, 10
 inherent, 189–191
  assessment, 252–256
  characteristics, 190–191
  conditions, 189–190
 insurance analysis, 544
 internal control and, 221,
  223
 materiality and, 193
 nonsampling, 367–368
 overall risk, 187–188
 prior years' audit results, 254
 sampling, 367–370

segregation of duties, 237
summary of model, 192
Robert Morris Associates, 347–348
Roberts, Donald M., 396 n.19
Robertson v. *White,* 117 n.23
Robert Wooler Co. v. *Fidelity Bank,*
    132–133
Rotation of auditors, 86–87
Royalties, 518–519
    payable, 689
    special reports, 839
Run-to-run control totals, 441
Rusch Factors, Inc. v. *Levin,* 115

Salaries, *see* Wages
    buying cycle, 549
    substantive testing, 578–579
Sales, cost of, 627–628
Sales contracts, revenue cycle,
    513
Sales forecasts, inventory and,
    597
Salvage values, 665–666
Sampling, 364–366
    aggregating errors, 406–407
    attributes sampling, 375–400
        concepts, 375–378
        results evaluation tables,
            870–874
        sample size tables, 867–869
        sequential plans, two-stage
            tables, 875–876
    audit procedure as, 154
    compliance testing, 365–366,
        378, 381, 403
    discovery sampling, 382
    documentation, 407–408
    dollar-weighted sample
        selection, 401–402
    dual-purpose, 268–269
    errors, 370–372, 733–734
    evaluating results, 402–407
        average-difference approach,
            403
        projection of average audit
            values, 403–404
        ratio approach, 403
        tables, 380–381, 870–874
    expected deviation rate or error
        amount, 372–373
    materiality, 737–739
    mean-per-unit estimation,
        390–398
    monetary unit sampling
        (MUS), 385–390

nonstatistical, 400–401
one-sided estimate, 378–379
probability-proportional-to-
    size, 386
random number selection, 374
representative selection,
    401–407
risk, 369–370, 405–406
    incorrect acceptance, 369
    incorrect rejection, 369
    overreliance, 369
    underreliance, 369
selection, 379–380
    confirmation procedures,
        505–506
    monetary unit sampling,
        385–390
    random sample technique,
        374
    unsystematic technique, 374
sequential plans, 382–384
size, 370–373
    determinants, 370–373
    table, 379
    mean-per-unit estimation,
        395–398
    monetary unit sampling,
        385–390
    tables for, 867–869
standard deviation, 391–393
statistical, 375–384
    software, 453
    vs. nonstatistical methods,
        374–375
substantive testing, 371, 373
systematic sample selection,
    401
tolerable deviation rate,
    370–372
two-sided estimate, 378–379
two-stage sequential plans:
    tables for, 875–876
underreliance, 369
unsystematic (haphazard)
    technique, 374
variables, 384–400
    application, 385
    difference and ratio
        estimation, 398–400
    mean-per-unit estimation
        (MPU), 390–398
    monetary unit sampling
        (MUS), 385–389
Scienter requirement, 117–118
    injunctive proceedings, 125

Supreme Court definition, 122
Scope limitations, 725–726
    audit reports, 785–787
    client representation, 731
    disclaimers of opinion, 796–798
Scope paragraph, 16–17, 763, 767
Score sheet, 196, 734–735
    aggregating errors, 406–407
    resolving material differences,
        741–742
S Corporations, 694–695
Second Restatement of the Law of
    Torts, 115–117
Second-partner reviews, legal
    liability, 134
Securities, *see* Investments
Securities Act of 1933, 9
    criminal liability, 123
    legal liability, 118–120
    subsequent events, 748, 752
Securities Exchange Act of 1934,
    9, 832
    criminal liability, 123
    legal liability, 118–123
    Section 10(b), 118, 121–122
Securities and Exchange
    Commission (SEC):
    accounting principles,
        855–857
    administrative (Rule 2[e])
        proceedings, 125–127
    audited financial statments, 11
    auditing standards, 46–47
    debt and equity, 697
    Form 8-K, 85–86
    Form 10-K, 856
    Form 10-Q, 832, 856
    fraud detection, 102
    illegal acts by clients, 106
    independence, 33, 82–83
    injunctive proceedings, 125
    internal control reports,
        851–852
    liability sanctions, 131
    management's responsibility for
        internal controls,
        238–240
    peer review, 78–79
    pro forma statements, 851
    prospective financial statements,
        848
    quality control, 77–78
    Regulation S-K, 86, 832
    Regulation S-X, 193–194,
        834–835

Securities and Exchange
    Commission (SEC)
    (*Continued*)
  standard reports, 764–766
  working papers, second-partner
    reviews, 745 n.7
Security administrator, EDP
    systems, 429
  computer files, 435–436
  computer systems, 433
SEC v. *Arthur Young & Co.,* 125–127
SEC v. *Bausch & Lomb, Inc.,* 125
Sedime, S.P.R.L. v. *Imrex Co. Inc.,*
    110
Segregation of duties:
  bank reconciliations, 649–650
  cash control, 548–552
  check preparation, 547–549
  EDP auditing department, 429
  internal controls, 237
  management fraud, 104
  wage payments, 553–554
Selling expenses, 540
Sequential sampling, 382–384
Service organizations:
  internal control reports, 770, 855
  reports on internal controls,
    203–204
Service revenue, *see* Revenue cycle
Shipping documents, 495
"Single audit," 842
Smith, D. G., 348 n.3
Software:
  analytical review, 453–454
  audit documentation, 453
  audit management, 454
  EDP auditing, 447–450
  flowcharting, 451
  label checking, 441
  program code analysis, 451
  program tracing and mapping,
    451
  sampling, 374–375
  statistical sampling, 453
  system, 427–428
    controls, 436–437
  test data and integrated test
    facility, 451–452
  timesharing, 397
Source code, 432
Sources of evidence, 157–158
Specialists:
  audit planning, 198–202

difficult inventory, 621–622
income tax auditing, 693
Special-Purpose Reports on Internal
    Accounting Control at Service
    Organizations, 203, 855
Special reports, 17 n.7, 823–824,
    835–836
  agreed-upon procedures,
    839–840
  auditor independence, 831
  compilations of financial
    statements, 826–828
  compliance audits, 840–843
  GAAP applicability, 838
  information accompanying
    financial statements,
    843–846
    details or commentary,
      843–844
    FASB pronouncements,
      845–846
  interim reviews, 831–835
  internal controls, 851–855
    material weaknesses,
      854–855
    reporting forms, 854
    service organizations, 855
    study and evaluation,
      853–854
    types of engagements, 853
  materiality, 838–839
  negative assurance, 831
  nonaudits, 825–826
  non-GAAP financial statements,
    835–838
  partial reports, 838–840
  prescribed forms, 843
  reporting forms, 836–839
  royalty reports, 839
  wording modification, 768–775
    audited and unaudited
      statements compared,
      773
    other information, 774
    report of another auditor,
      769–770
Spouses, auditor independence, 65
Standard & Poor's, 347
Standard reports, *see* Audit reports
Standard-setting bodies, 43–49
Standards for Audit of Governmental
    Organizations, Programs,
    Activities, and Functions, 48

Standards for the Professional Practice
    of Internal Auditing, 48
Standing data, 230, 440, 553
  compliance tests, 570
  internal controls, 230
State and local taxes, 696–697
Statement of Basic Auditing Concepts,
    A, 3, 5–6
Statement on Quality Control
    Standards (SQCS) No. 1,
    75–76
Statement on Standards for
    Accountants' Services on
    Prospective Financial
    Information, 847
Statement on Standards for
    Attestation Engagements,
    40, 45, 47
Statement on Standards for
    Management Advisory
    Services (SSMAS) No. 1,
    48
Statements on Auditing Procedure
    (SAPs), 9, 43, 56
  No. 1, 128, 764
  No. 6, 128
  No. 7, 128
  No. 27, 128
  No. 33, 129, 225
  No. 37, 128
  No. 41, 128–129
  No. 43, 786
  No. 44, 128
  No. 45, 128
  No. 47, 128–129
  No. 48, 128
Statements on Auditing Standards
    (SASs), 43–45, 56
  No. 1, 9, 11, 18, 56–57
    Section 220, 57–58
    Section 230, 58
    Section 320, 217–225, 239,
      256–257
    Section 331, 503–504,
      507–509, 612, 618, 624
    Section 420, 768, 780,
      784–785
    Section 509, 769
    Section 542, 797
    Section 543, 202–203
    Section 546, 780–782
    Section 560, 747–752
    Section 561, 801

No. 2, 202, 725, 731, 769, 771, 774, 776, 781–782, 786–788, 795–799
No. 3, 423–424
No. 4, 75
No. 5, 131, 766
No. 6, 131
No. 7, 131
No. 8, 775
No. 9, 200
No. 11, 201
No. 12, 720, 722–725
No. 14, 836–839, 841
No. 15, 768, 772, 793–794
No. 16, 102–103, 728
No. 17, 106, 240
No. 19, 134, 727, 728, 731
No. 20, 132, 279–280, 443
No. 22, 58–59, 265, 742–746
No. 23, 341, 344–345
No. 25, 75, 745
No. 26, 133, 773, 798, 826, 830 n.6
No. 29, 844, 846
No. 30, 132, 227–228, 853–854
No. 31, 149–152, 233
No. 32, 746, 777–779
No. 34, 790–793
No. 35, 840
No. 36, 46, 832–833
No. 39, 365–366, 370 n.7, 371–372, 374–375, 385, 391, 393, 401–407, 733
No. 41, 169–170, 407–408
No. 43, 270, 624, 824
No. 44, 203, 855
No. 45, 255, 339–340
No. 46, 802
No. 47, 187–188, 194–195, 256, 734, 739, 741
No. 48, 198, 424
No. 49, 732, 859
No. 50, 857–858
Statements on Responsibilities in Tax Practice, 48
Statements on Standards for Accounting and Review Services (SSARS), 35, 827
No. 1, 785 n.3, 796, 826–830
No. 2, 831 n.7
No. 3, 828 n.4, 843 n.9
No. 4, 827 n.2

No. 5, 827
No. 6, 827 n.3
State societies, certified public accountants, 39–40
State St. Trust Co. v. Ernst, 115
Statistical sampling, *see* Sampling
Statistical techniques:
  analytical reviews, 346–347
  EDP auditing, 454
Stockholders' equity accounts, 701–702
Storing goods, 596
  buying cycle, 545, 564
  raw materials, 601–604, 612
Stratification:
  mean-per-unit estimation, 395–399
  monetary unit sampling, 386 n.12
  projection of results, 404–405
"Subject to" opinions, 724–725, 787–788
  disclaimers, 796
Subsequent Discovery of Facts Existing at the Date of the Auditor's Report, 129
Subsequent events:
  adjustments, 749–750
  auditor's responsibilities, 747–753
  audit planning, 748–749
  dating report, 748
  disclosures, 750–751
  dual dating, 749
  keeping current, 752–753
Substantive testing, 159–160, 333–336
  accounts receivable confirmation, 503–513
  analytical review procedures, 341–349
  audit process flowchart, 353
  audit strategy, 332
  balances:
    debt and equity, 698–702
    income taxes, 692–694
    investments, 679–684
    prepayments and accruals, 686–691
    property, plant, and equipment, 658–666
  buying cycle, 555–556, 575–581

cash balances, 646–657
collectibility, 514–516
details of transactions and balances, 336–341
detection risk, 190–192, 329–333
EDP auditing, 447–448
  programmed accounting procedures, 450–453
exceptions, 340
internal controls, 166–167
objectives, 329–336
performing, 168–169
production cycle, 612, 618–630
restriction of, 166–167
revenue cycle, 333, 336, 487–488, 502–517
risk assessment, 264–265
sample size, 371–373
sampling, 365–366
  discovery sampling, 382
  evaluating results, 403–404
service organizations, 203–204
timing, 339–340, 342–344
trade accounts, 334–335
variables sampling, 384–385
working papers, 175–176
Summary account analysis, 693–694
Supervisory controls:
  bank reconciliations, 650
  EDP auditing department, 429
  quality control, 75–76
Suspense debits and credits, 689
Systematic sample selection, 401
System of Quality Control for CPA Firm, 75
Systems analyst, 428
System software, 431
  controls, 436–437
Systems documentation, 257–259, 266
  control matrices, 271, 273–274
  documenting control weaknesses, 278
  internal control questionnaire, 275–277

Tax Adviser, The, 39
Tax consequences, 858–859
Taxes, *see* Income taxes
Tax practice, standards, 48

Tax returns, compliance audits, 31
Tax services and auditing, 35–36, 82
Telecommunications software, 427
Testing:
  accept-reject, 366–367
  accounting procedures, 333–336
  audit objectives, 336–339
  EDP auditing, 431, 444–445
  library, 432
  materiality and, 195
  one-sided, 378–379
  performance of, 165–166
  supervisory controls, 238
  two-sided, 378–379
  types of, 159–160, 336–339
  working papers, 175–176
Tests of balances, see Substantive testing
Tests of transactions, see Compliance testing; Substantive testing
Third parties, legal liability, 114–123
Tick marks, 171
Time analyses, 753
Time-series analysis, 346–347
To-from technique in working papers, 171–172
Tolerable deviation rates and error amounts, 371 n.8, 389
  attributes sampling, 376–377, 379
  difference and ratio estimation, 399–400
  sample size, 370–372
  sequential sampling, 383–384
Transaction cycles, 644–645 (see also specific cycles)
  control objectives, 225–227
  flowcharts for, 261–263
  substantive testing, types of accounts, 333, 336, 338
Transaction data, 230, 440
Transaction reviews, 167, 264
Transactions:
  approval and authorization of, 234–236
  cutoff, 235

documenting, buying cycle, 576–577
FASB definition, 225 n.2
flow of, 257
numbering for control, 231
recorded, 233
recurring, 235
related parties, 254–256, 516
tests of, 160
unauthorized, 236
unrecorded, 233
validity of, 233–234, 442
Travel and entertainment advances, 688
Trial balance, 172–175
Types of accounts, 333, 336

Ultramares Corp. v. Touche, 114–118, 120
Uncertainties:
  disclaimers of opinion, 796
  financial statements, 787–793
  going concern, 789–793
  materiality, 788–789
Unclaimed wages, 553
Underlying accounting data, 152–154
Underpayments, 552
Underreliance, 369–370
  attributes sampling, 377–378
Understanding client's business, see Client's business, understanding
Underwriters, letters for, 753, 859
Unearned revenue, 519–520
United States, auditing in, 8–9
United States v. Simon (Continental Vending), 123, 130–132
Unqualified opinions, see Audit Reports
Unrecorded liabilities, 581
Unsystematic (haphazard) selection, 374, 401
Updating opinions, 439–440
Upper error dollar limit, 388–389
Upper error rate limit, mean-per-unit estimation, 398
User concerns, financial information, 12–14
"User exits," 428

User IDs, computer security, 436
Using the Work of a Specialist, 201

Validity, internal controls, 220, 233–234
Valuation assertion, 150
Values, carrying, 664–665
  depreciation and salvage, 665–666
  tests of, 682–683
Variables sampling, 384–385
  applications, 385
Variance reports, 686
Volunteer solicitations, auditing procedures, 519
Vouching:
  buying cycle, substantive tests, 576–577
  cash counting, 656
  debt and equity, 699
  substantive testing, 337

Wages:
  buying cycle, 549, 553–554, 575, 578–579
  cash vs. currency, 553–554
  unclaimed, 553
Walkthrough, 167, 264
Warranty costs, 690–691
Working papers, 169–180
  deficiencies, 179–180
  form and content, 170–173
    dating, 170
    heading, 170
    initialing, 170
  inherent risk assessment, 252
  memoranda, 176
  organization, 171–172
  permanent file, 176
  prior year's, 254, 257–258
  reviews, 742–746
  schedules and analyses, 175
  trial balance, 172–175
  typical, 172–175
Wrongful acts, defined, 112

Yellow Book, see Standards for Audit of Governmental Organizations, Programs, Activities, and Functions